# SOCIAL PSYCHOLOGY

## Sixth Edition

PEARSON
**mypsych lab**

### Instant access to interactive learning

With your purchase of a new copy of this textbook, you received a Student Access Kit to **MyPsychLab** for *Social Psychology*, Sixth Edition, by Michael Hogg and Graham Vaughan.

**MyPsychLab** gives you access to an unrivalled suite of online resources. It provides a variety of tools to enable you to assess and progress your own learning, including questions, tests and learning aids for each chapter of the book. You will benefit from a personalised learning experience, where you can:

- Complete a diagnostic 'pre-test' to generate your own Study Plan, which adapts to your strengths and weaknesses and enables you to focus on the topics where your knowledge is weaker.

- Improve your understanding through a variety of resources, including recap and reminder materials, weblinks to sites of interest, and videos

- Measure your progress with a follow-up 'post-test' that ensures you have mastered key learning objectives – and gives you the confidence to move on to the next chapter.

- Study on the go and refer to pages from an e-Text version of this book.

- Check your understanding of each chapter by answering the Revision questions which provide you with instant feedback.

- Learn from the video and audio clips relating to the Focus and Guidance questions used in the book, covering interviews with experts, re-enactments of classic experiments, and extended examples of social psychological concepts in action.

- Check your understanding using a comprehensive glossary of key terms, with flashcards to test your knowledge.

# Advisory editorial board

Sixth Edition

# SOCIAL PSYCHOLOGY

**Michael A. Hogg**
Claremont Graduate University

**Graham M. Vaughan**
University of Auckland

**Prentice Hall**
is an imprint of

PEARSON

Harlow, England • London • New York • Boston • San Francisco • Toronto • Sydney • Singapore • Hong Kong
Tokyo • Seoul • Taipei • New Delhi • Cape Town • Madrid • Mexico City • Amsterdam • Munich • Paris • Milan

Pearson Education Limited
Edinburgh Gate
Harlow
Essex CM20 2JE
England

and Associated Companies throughout the world

*Visit us on the World Wide Web at:*
**www.pearsoned.co.uk**

First published 1995
Second edition published 1998
Third edition published 2002
Fourth edition published 2005
Fifth edition published 2008
**Sixth edition published 2011**

ISBN: 978-0-273-72596-1

**British Library Cataloguing-in-Publication Data**
A catalogue record for this book is available from the British Library

**Library of Congress Cataloging-in-Publication Data**
Hogg, Michael A., 1954–
    Social psychology / Michael A. Hogg, Graham M. Vaughan.—6th ed.
        p. cm.
    Includes bibliographical references and index.
    ISBN 978-0-273-72596-1 (pbk.)
  1. Social psychology.    I. Vaughan, Graham M.    II. Title.
    HM1033.H64 2011
    302—dc22

                                        2010041473

10 9 8 7 6 5 4 3 2
15 14 13 12 11

Typeset in 10/12 Minion by 75
Printed and bound by *Rotolito Lombarda*

# Brief contents

# British Psychological Society
# Standards in Social Psychology

The British Psychological Society (BPS) accredits psychology degree programmes across the UK. It has set guidelines as to which major topics should be covered within social psychology. We have listed these topics below and indicated where in this textbook each is covered most fully.

| BPS guidelines | Coverage in Hogg and Vaughan |
| --- | --- |
| **Social perception including:** | |
| • person perception | Chapter 2 |
| • attitudes | Chapters 5 and 6 |
| • attribution | Chapter 3 |
| **Intergroup processes including:** | |
| • prejudice | Chapter 10 |
| • intergroup conflict | Chapters 11 and 12 |
| • social identification | Chapter 4 |
| **Small group processes including:** | |
| • norms | Chapter 8 |
| • leadership | Chapter 9 |
| • decision making | Chapter 9 |
| • productivity | Chapter 8 |
| **Social influence including:** | |
| • conformity and obedience | Chapter 7 |
| • majority and minority influence | Chapter 7 |
| • the bystander effect | Chapter 13 |
| **Close relationships including:** | |
| • interpersonal attraction | Chapter 14 |
| • relationships | Chapter 14 |

# Contents

## 4  Self and identity                                        111

## 7  Social influence                                                         235

## 8  People in groups                                                         271

## 12 Aggression

## 13 Prosocial behaviour

# 14 Attraction and close relationships                531

## 15    Language and communication                       567

# Preface

This is the sixth edition of our *Social Psychology*. The original idea to write a European social psychology text was born in Oxford in 1992 from meetings with Farrell Burnett, who was then psychology editor at Harvester Wheatsheaf. We decided to write the book because we felt there was a conspicuous need for a comprehensive social psychology text written specifically for university students in Britain and continental Europe. Such a text, we felt, must approach social psychology from a European rather than American perspective not only in terms of topics, orientations and research interests but also in terms of the style and level of presentation of social psychology and the cultural context of the readership. However, a European text certainly cannot ignore or gloss over American social psychology – so, unlike other European texts we located mainstream American social psychology within the framework of the book, covered it in detail and integrated it fully with European work. We intended this to be a self-contained coverage of social psychology. You would not need to switch between American and European texts to ensure a proper understanding of social psychology as a truly international scientific enterprise – an enterprise in which European research has an established and significant profile. The first edition was published in 1995 and was widely adopted throughout Europe.

Subsequent editions followed fast upon earlier editions – no sooner did one edition appear in bookshops than, it seemed, we were hard at work preparing the next. The second edition was prepared while Graham Vaughan was a visiting fellow of Churchill College at Cambridge University and Michael Hogg was a visiting professor at Princeton University. It was published early in 1998 and launched at the 1998 conference of the Social Section of the British Psychological Society at the University of Kent. This edition was a relatively modest revision aimed primarily at improving layout and presentation, though the text and coverage were thoroughly updated, and we raised the profile of some applied topics in social psychology.

The third edition was published in 2002. It represented a major revision to accommodate significant changes in the field since the first edition. The structure and approach remained the same but some chapters were dropped, some entirely rewritten, others amalgamated, and some entirely new chapters written. In addition the text was updated, and the layout and presentation significantly improved. Such a large revision involved substantial input from our Advisory Editorial Board and from lecturers around Britain and Europe, and many meetings in different places (Bristol, Glasgow and Thornbury) with Pearson Education, our publishers.

The fourth edition was published in 2005. We expanded our Editorial Board significantly to include seventeen leading European social psychologists to represent different aspects of social psychology, different levels of seniority and different nations across Europe. However, the key change was that the book was now in glorious full-colour. We also took a rather adventurous step – the sleeve just showed empty chairs, no people at all; quite a departure for a social psychology text. Auckland harbour was the venue for initial planning of the fourth edition, with a series of long meetings in London, capped by a productive few days at the Grand Hotel in Brighton.

The fifth edition, published in 2008, was a very substantive revision with many chapters entirely or almost entirely rewritten. We liked the 'empty chairs' sleeve for the fourth edition so decided to continue that theme but be a bit more jolly – so the sleeve showed those Victorian-style bathing booths that used to be common at British and French beach resorts. Initial planning took place at our favourite writing retreat (Noosa, just North of Brisbane in Australia) and then a string of long meetings with the Pearson team in Bristol, London, Birmingham and even Heathrow. We went back to Noosa to finalise plans and the actual writing was done in Auckland and Los Angeles.

This sixth edition is a relatively modest revision in which we have updated and reconfigured some material to reflect changes in the field, but have not made any dramatic changes. Chapter 13 is now Prosocial behaviour, bringing it closer to Chapter 12 (Aggression), a more natural juxtaposition. We have retained the structure and approach of previous editions, and the book is framed by the same scientific and educational philosophy as before.

To prepare this edition we obtained feedback on the fifth edition from our Editorial Board, and as many of our colleagues and postgraduate and undergraduate students as we could find who had used the text as teacher, tutor or student. We are extremely grateful for this invaluable feedback – we see our text as a genuine partnership between us as authors, and all those who use the book in various different capacities. We are also indebted to our wonderful publishing team at Pearson Education in scenic Harlow – in particular Janey Webb our acquisitions editor, and Tim Parker our desk editor. We were sustained and energised by their enthusiasm, good humour, encouragement and wisdom, and were kept on our toes by their timeline prompts, excellent editing and breathtaking efficiency.

To start the ball rolling Graham spent a week in November 2007 at Mike's new home in the Santa Monica Mountains just outside Los Angeles – for inspiration we were of course compelled to visit the wineries in the nearby Santa Ynez valley. Mike had a number of planning meetings with Janey Webb and her crew at Pearson's swanky London office on The Strand – particularly memorable was one in mid-2008 where we adjourned to a nearby lunch venue and did not resurface until late afternoon, and then another in July 2009 where we ventured to the 'posh' Carluccio's in Covent Garden and Janey almost missed her flight to a meeting in Stockholm. The writing itself was done in late 2009 and early 2010 while Mike was in Los Angeles and Graham was in Auckland.

Writing a big book like this is a courageous undertaking, with a great deal of drama and even more hard slog. We wish to thank John Haller, David Rast and Heather Stopp, members of Mike's social identity laboratory, for undertaking the painstaking task of checking references in the text and references section. As with previous editions, we thank all the people around us, our family, friends and colleagues, for their never-ending patience and understanding. The most special thanks goes of course to our partners, Alison and Jan.

## How to use this book

This sixth edition is a completely up-to-date and comprehensive coverage of social psychology as an international scientific enterprise, written from the perspective of European social psychology and in the cultural and educational context of people living in Britain and Europe.

The book has a range of pedagogical features to facilitate independent study. At the end of Chapter 1 we outline important primary and review sources for finding out more about specific topics in social psychology. Within chapters some material appears in boxes that are labelled to identify the type of material. Many boxes are labelled *research highlight* or *theory and concepts*. Other boxes describe a *research classic*. To capture social psychology's relevance in applied settings such as the study of organisations, health-related behaviour and the criminal justice system, some of our boxes are labelled *applied context*. Our final category of box is labelled *real world* – these boxes illustrate the operation of social psychological principles in everyday life or in wider socio-political or historical contexts.

Each chapter opens with a list of topics covered and some focus questions that help you think about the material, and closes with a detailed summary of the chapter contents, some useful web links, and a fully annotated list of further reading. At the end of each chapter we also have a section called *Literature, film and TV*. Social psychology is part of everyday life – so, not surprisingly, social psychological themes are often creatively and vividly explored in popular media. The *Literature, film and TV* section directs you to some classic and contemporary works we feel have a particular relevance to social psychological themes.

As with the earlier editions, the book has a logical structure, with earlier chapters leading into later ones. A small reordering of chapters brought Prosocial behaviour closer to follow Aggression. As with previous editions, it is not essential to read the book from beginning to end. The chapters are carefully cross-referenced so that, with a few exceptions, chapters or groups of chapters can be read independently in almost any order.

However, some chapters are better read in sequence. For example, it is better to read Chapter 5 before tackling Chapter 6 (both deal with aspects of attitudes), Chapter 8 before Chapter 9 (both deal with group processes), and Chapter 10 before Chapter 11 (both deal with intergroup behaviour). It may also be interesting to reflect back on Chapter 4 (the self) when you read Chapter 16 (culture). Chapter 1 describes the structure of the book, why we decided to write it and how it should be read – it is worthwhile reading the last section of Chapter 1 before starting later chapters. Chapter 1 also defines social psychology, its aims, its methods and its history. Some of this material might benefit from being reread after you have studied some of the other chapters and have become familiar with some of the theories, topics and issues of social psychology.

The primary target of our book is the student, though we intend it to be of use also to teachers and researchers of social psychology. We will be grateful to any among you who might take the time to share your reactions with us.

Michael Hogg, Los Angeles
Graham Vaughan, Auckland
January 2010

## *Social Psychology*, Sixth Edition

### Supporting resources

**MyPsychLab** for students and instructors

### Instant access to interactive learning

**www.mypsychlab.co.uk**

Every new copy of this textbook comes with an access kit for **MyPsychLab**, giving access to an unrivalled suite of online resources that relate directly to the content of *Social Psychology*, Sixth Edition.

#### With a flexible course management platform, instructors can:

- Assess student progress through homework quizzes and tests that are easily set using the extensive pre-prepared question bank.
- Track student activity and performance using detailed reporting capabilities
- Communicate with students and teaching staff using e-mail and announcement tools.
- Access a customisable testbank of question material.
- Assign additional video and audio-based media assignments to students

#### Students will benefit from a personalised learning experience, where they can:

- Complete a diagnostic 'pre-test' to generate a personal self-study plan that enables them to focus on the topics where their knowledge is weaker.
- Improve their understanding through a variety of resources, including: revision flashcards, revision questions, e-text reading assignments, recap and reminder materials, weblinks to sites of interest, videos and audio material
- Measure their progress with a follow-up 'post-test' that ensures they have mastered key learning objectives – and gives them the confidence to move on to the next chapter.

A dedicated team is available to give you all the assistance you need to get online and make the most of **MyPsychLab**. Contact your sales representative for further details.

#### Additional instructor resources

- Complete, downloadable Instructor's Manual, which presents chapter summaries, key terms and teaching ideas including essay questions, discussion topics, class exercises and a list of films that illustrate social psychological concepts.
- Downloadable PowerPoint slides with key figures from the book,

These lecturer resources can be downloaded from the lecturer website at **www.pearsoned.co.uk/hogg** by clicking on the Instructor Resource link next to the cover. All instructor-specific content is password protected.

# About the authors

**Michael Hogg** was educated at Bristol Grammar School and Birmingham University and received his PhD from Bristol University. Currently Professor of Social Psychology at Claremont Graduate University, in Los Angeles, and an Honorary Professor of Social Psychology at the University of Kent, he has held teaching appointments at Bristol University, Princeton University, the University of Melbourne and the University of Queensland. He is a Fellow of the Society for Personality and Social Psychology, the Society for the Psychological Study of Social Issues, the Society of Experimental Social Psychology, the Western Psychological Association, and the Academy of the Social Sciences in Australia. His research interests are group behaviour, intergroup relations and social identity processes; with a specific current interest in uncertainty and extremism, and processes of influence and leadership. In addition to publishing about 280 scientific books, chapters and articles, he is foundation editor with Dominic Abrams of the journal *Group Processes and Intergroup Relations,* senior consulting editor of the *SAGE Social Psychology Program,* and a past associate editor of the *Journal of Experimental Social Psychology.* Two of his books are citation classics, *Rediscovering the Social Group* (1987) with John Turner and others, and *Social Identifications* (1988) with Dominic Abrams. Recent books include *The SAGE handbook of social psychology: Concise student edition* (2007) with Joel Cooper, and a forthcoming book *Extremism and the psychology of uncertainty* with Danielle Blaylock.

**Graham Vaughan** has been a Fulbright Fellow and Visiting Professor at the University of Illinois at Champaign-Urbana, a Visiting Lecturer and a Ford Foundation Fellow at the University of Bristol, a Visiting Professor at Princeton University, a Visiting Directeur d'Etudes at the *Maison des Science de l'Homme,* Paris, a Visiting Senior Fellow at the National University of Singapore, a Visiting Fellow at the University of Queensland and a Visiting Fellow at Churchill College, Cambridge. As Professor of Psychology at the University of Auckland, he served twelve years as Head of Department. He is an Honorary Fellow and past President of the New Zealand Psychological Society, and a past President of the Society of Australasian Social Psychologists. Graham Vaughan's primary areas of interest in social psychology are attitudes and attitude development, group processes and intergroup relations, ethnic relations and identity, culture and the history of social psychology. He has published widely on these topics. His 1972 book, *Racial Issues in New Zealand,* was the first to deal with ethnic relations in that country. Recent books include the new *Essentials of social psychology* (2010) with Michael Hogg.

# Publisher's acknowledgements

The publishers would like to thanks all those who provided feedback and suggestions for this sixth edition of Social Psychology. Their insight and advice has been much appreciated.

Martin Hagger (*University of Nottingham, England*)
Emma Vine (*Sheffield Hallam University, England*)
Helen J. Fawkner (*Leeds Metropolitan University, England*)
Mike Boulton (*University of Chester, England*)
Victoria Gutierrez (*Thames Valley University, England*)
Kerry Greer (*University of Limerick, Ireland*)
Natalie Wyer (*University of Plymouth, England*)
Julian Oldmeadow (*University of York, England*)

We would also like to thank the editorial board and those reviewers who we were unable to contact for permission to print their names.

We are grateful to the following for permission to reproduce copyright material:

## Figures

Figure 8.13 from 'Socialization in small groups: Temporal changes in individual-group relations' in *Advances in Experimental Social Psychology* Vol 15, pp 137–192, published by Elsevier Science Ltd, (Moreland, R. L. & Levine, J. M. 1982); Figure 11.5 from The effect of threat upon interpersonal bargaining, *Journal of Abnormal and Social Psychology*, 61, pp. 181–189, published by American Psychological Association, (Deutsch, M., & Krauss, R. M. 1960); Figure 13.1 from 'Some neo-Darwinian decision rules for altruism: Weighing cues for inclusive fitness as a function of the biological importance of the decision', *Journal of Personality and Social Psychology*, 67, pp. 773–789 (Burnstein, E., Crandall, C., & Kitayama, S. 1994); Figure 13.5 from 'Help in a crisis: Bystander response to an emergency' in J. W. Thibaut & J. T. Spence (Eds.), *Contemporary topics in social psychology*, pp. 309–332, published by General Learning Press (Latané, B., & Darley, J. M. 1976); Figure 14.9 from *The triangle of love*, Basic Books (Sternberg, R. J. 1988); Figure 15.7 from *Nonverbal communication: The unspoken dialogue*. New York: Harper and Row (Burgoon, J. K., Buller, D. B., & Woodall, W. G. 1989).

## Photographs

The publisher would like to thank the following for their kind permission to reproduce their photographs:

(Key: b-bottom; c-centre; l-left; r-right; t-top)

3 Reuters: Luke MacGregor. 7 Alamy Images: Juergen Hasenkopf. 11 Science Photo Library Ltd: STEPHEN AUSMUS / US DEPARTMENT OF AGRICULTURE. 14 Thinkstock: Ryan McVay. 20 Alamy Images: ACE STOCK LIMITED. 27 Getty Images: Phil Walter (l, r). 29 Corbis: Zave Smith. 31 Getty Images: Jonathan Kantor. 41 DK Images: Neil Lukas. 49 Thinkstock: Jupiterimages. 52 Getty Images: Stockbyte Silver. 57 Pearson Education Ltd: Photodisc. Chris Falkenstein (r); Lisa Payne Photography (l). 62 Alamy Images: Niall

McDiarmid. 66 iStockphoto: Laura Hart. 69 Alamy Images: amana images inc.. 79 Pearson Education Ltd: Photodisc. Glen Allison. 81 Reuters: Alessia Pierdomenico. 84 Press Association Images: Lynne Sladky. 89 Press Association Images: Alik Keplicz. 90 Thinkstock: Pixland. 96 Rex Features: LEHTIKUVA OY. 100 Reuters: Livio Anticoli / Italian Prime Minister's Press Office / Handout. 106 Alamy Images: PCL. 111 Andrea Bannuscher. 115 Thinkstock: Creatas Images. 118 Rex Features: Sipa Press. 127 Alamy Images: Don Tonge. 129 Pearson Education Ltd: Imagestate. John Foxx Collection. 132 Linden Lab. 136 Getty Images: Vincent Besnault. 140 Alamy Images: peter jordan. 141 Thinkstock: Hemera. 147 Reuters: Omar Sobhani. 154 Press Association Images: ABACA. 161 Photolibrary.com: Novastock. 165 Press Association Images: Nasser Isstayeh. 170 Pearson Education Ltd: Chris Parker. 172 Department of Health: Leon Steele. 179 Alamy Images: Stock Connection Distribution. 189 Alamy Images: Marina Spironetti. 191 DK Images: Imperial War Museum. 194 Rex Features. 203 Thinkstock: Brand X Pictures. 205 Thinkstock: Hemera. 209 Reuters: Carlos Barria. 212 iStockphoto: Duygu Ozen. 213 Quit Victoria. 218 iStockphoto: Birgitte Magnus. 223 Rex Features: ITV. 235 Rex Features: Sipa Press. 239 Press Association Images: allaction.co.uk. 243 Corbis: Atlantide Phototravel. 247 iStockphoto: Leah Marshall. 251 Action Plus: Neil Tingle. 254 Getty Images: Skip Nall. 256 Reuters: Greenpeace / Pedro Armestre. 260 Pearson Education Ltd: Photodisc. Life File. Emma Lee. 271 Rex Features: Steve Bell. 275 Pearson Education Ltd: Gareth Boden. 279 Photolibrary.com: Superstock. 284 Getty Images: Walter Hodges. 289 Getty Images: Mark Thompson. 292 Thinkstock: Stockbyte. 297 Alamy Images: Cultura RM . 304 Rex Features: Warner Br / Everett. 313 Press Association Images: Bebeto Matthews. 317 Press Association Images: Associated Press / Charles Dharapak. 319 Alamy Images: Radius Images. 322 Alamy Images: UpperCut Images. 326 Lonely Planet Images: Douglas Steakley. 329 Press Association Images: AP / Peter Morrison. 337 Getty Images: GERARD CERLES / AFP. 344 Reuters: Raheb Homavandi. 355 Alamy Images: Les Gibbon. 360 Science Photo Library Ltd: TEK IMAGE . 368 Alamy Images: Janine Wiedel Photolibrary. 375 Pearson Education Ltd: Devon Obugenga Shaw. 380 Thinkstock: Brand X Pictures. 388 Getty Images: DESMOND KWANDE / AFP. 392 Graham Vaughan. 397 Reuters: Yannis Behrakis. 405 Corbis: MM Productions. 410 Reuters: Stringer. 419 Getty Images: Mark Dadswell. 422 Action Plus: Glyn Kirk. 429 Photolibrary.com: www.Britanonview.com. 434 Reuters: Stringer Iran. 436 Press Association Images: Shuji Kajiyama. 439 Corbis. 445 Getty Images: MLADEN ANTONOV / AFP. 451 Press Association Images: Francois Mori. 457 Corbis: Ralph A. Clevenger. 460 Alamy Images: Peter Titmuss. 462 Getty Images: Shannon Fagan. 467 Rex Features: PB / KMLA. 477 Alamy Images: MBI. 481 Thinkstock: iStockphoto. 484 Press Association Images: Khalid Chaudary. 486 Reuters: ACTION IMAGES / Carl Recine. 490 Getty Images: Peter Cade. 495 Mirrorpix. 500 Rex Features: Matt Baron / BEI. 504 Getty Images: PhotoLink. 507 iStockphoto: Laura Eisenberg. 517 Getty Images: Wathiq Khuzaie. 522 Thinkstock: Digital Vision. 523 Thinkstock: Hemera. 531 iStockphoto: Scott Griessel. 536 Photofusion Picture Library: Lisa Woollett. 544 Pearson Education Ltd: Photodisc. 550 Getty Images: Lisa Valder. 551 Pearson Education Ltd: Lisa Payne Photography. 554 Thinkstock: Pixland (l); iStockphoto (r). 558 Photofusion Picture Library: Paul Doyle. 567 iStockphoto: mbbirdy. 574 Graham Vaughan. 578 Alamy Images: The Photolibrary Wales. 584 Thinkstock: Goodshoot (l); Photodisc (r). 585 Godfrey Boehnke. 591 Thinkstock: John Foxx. 592 Thinkstock: iStockphoto. 595 Thinkstock: Christopher Robbins. 602 Corbis: moodboard. 607 Rex Features. 615 Corbis: Charles & Josette Lenars. 621 Alamy Images: Inmagine. 627 Reuters: Adnan Abidi. 630 Alamy Images: david pearson. 633 Alamy Images: Caro. 634 Getty Images: LOUAI BESHARA / AFP. 638 Getty Images: Tim Platt

All other images © Pearson Education

In some instances we have been unable to trace the owners of copyright material, and we would appreciate any information that would enable us to do so.

# Guided tour

## Navigation and setting the scene

Each chapter opens with a short guide to what is covered in the chapter.

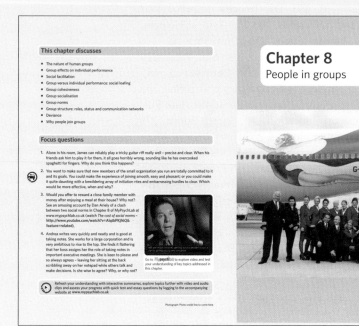

**Focus questions** are a series of thought-provoking questions that raise issues discussed in the chapter. They often ask you to consider how social psychological concepts apply to a real-life scenario. You will find additional resources, including video and audio clips, linked to these questions marked with this symbol.

*Social Psychology* 6th edition is accompanied by **MyPsychLab** which contains a wealth of online resources to support you in your studies. Resources include self test questions, video and audio clips, essay questions with answer guidance, weblinks. For more information please see the website tour on page xxvii. You can log on from **www.mypsychlab.co.uk**

# Aiding your understanding

**Research and applications** sections emphasize the wider relevance of social psychological insights, giving detailed examples of contemporary research and practice.

**Real world** boxes present everyday examples of social psychology in action, applying social psychological principles to familiar, real world scenarios

**Research classic** clips summarise classic research studies, highlighting continuing relevance and discussing any new developments

All chapters are richly illustrated with **diagrams** and **photographs**. Clear and concise definitions of **key terms** can be found in the margins and in the comprehensive glossary at the end of the book.
You can test your knowledge using the flashcards feature available on **MyPsychLab**, accessible from **www.mypsychlab.co.uk**

# Check your progress and deepen your understanding

At the end of each chapter the **summary** pulls together the key points to help you to consolidate your knowledge and understanding

**Literature, film and TV** offers the opportunity to explore key social psychological concepts using popular examples from the media.

**Guided questions** pose typical essay style questions. Video and audio material linked to these questions and guidance on how to answer them can be found on MyPsychLab at **www.mypsychlab.co.uk**

**Learn more** sections provide annotated further reading lists, guiding you towards the right resources to help you to deepen your understanding and prepare for essays and coursework assignments.

# MyPsychLab: resources for students

 Log into www.mypsychlab.co.uk to access all the additional learning materials that accompany *Social Psychology*, Sixth Edition.

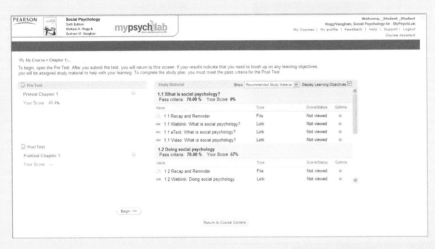

The **Study Plan** section of MyPsychLab is a comprehensive student self-assessment and revision centre, which puts you in control of your learning, helping you to test your knowledge, identify areas for further study, and generate a personalised study plan. When you log into **MyPsychLab** you can select any chapter and take a **'pre-test'**, to check how well you understand the topics in that chapter. This identifies any areas you need to work on and generates a **personal study plan** to help you learn. You can then take a **'post-test'** after revising the study materials in more depth, to check your progress. It includes:

- pre-test and post-test questions;
- self-assessment multiple choice questions;
- recap and reminder materials;
- revision questions.

**Focus Questions** provide video and audio clips that help you explore the focus questions at the start of each chapter in more depth.

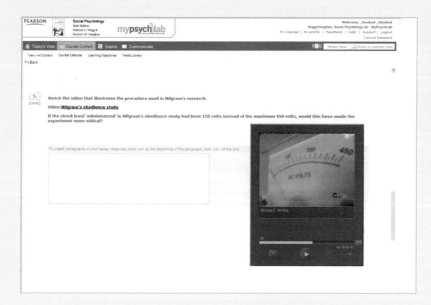

**Guided Questions** provide additional guidance on how to answer the essay-style questions that are found at the end of each book chapter. Additional resources are provided to improve your understanding, including video and audio clips.

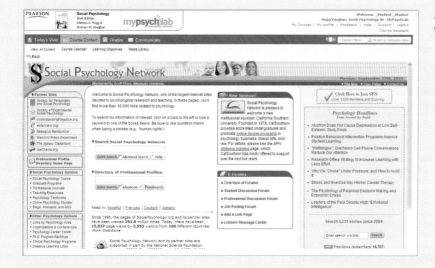

**Annotated links to relevant websites** for further research.

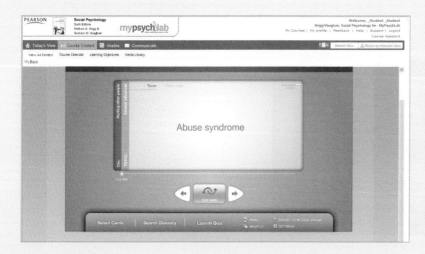

**Flashcards** of all the key terms found in the book, and an online glossary.

The MyPsychLab **Media Library** contains a wealth of video and audio clips to support learning and teaching. You can choose from:

- Key figures in contemporary  social psychology discussing their field of expertise and their research. For example:

    **Robert Cialdini** discussing the 'low-ball technique'

    **Phil Zimbardo** on the Stanford Prison experiment

    **Mahzarin Banaji** on the Implicit Association Test

    **Robert Rosenthal** on the 'Pygmalion effect'

    **Robert Sternberg** on his Triangular Theory of Love.

- Illustrarions or re-enactments of classic social psychology studies, such as:

    **Albert Bandura's** Bobo Doll experiment

    **Stanley Milgram's** studies on obidience to authority.

- Discussions and extended examples exploring key themes  in social psychology, including:

    Evolutionary approaches to selecting a mate

    Cognitive processing and stereotypes

    Children's self knowledge

    Low self esteem

    Justifying our actions

    Group loyalty

    Prejudice against minority groups

    The relation between exposure to TV violence and aggression

    Prosocial behaviour and reactions to bullying

    Attachment styles and insecure attachment

    Bilingualism and cultural identity.

# For lecturers: the teaching and learning package

A full suite of lecturer support material is provided with this textbook, including:

- comprehensive, downloadable Instructor's Manual;
- multiple choice question test bank;
- PowerPoint slides;
- additional video and audio-based 'Media Assignments' and an online Media Library.

Contact your local Pearson Education sales consultant for more details about these resources or to arrange a demonstration. Sales consultant details can be found at **www.pearsoned.co.uk/replocator**.

## This chapter discusses

- Social psychology and its relationship to other disciplines
- Social psychology as an empirical science
- Using statistics and qualitative methods to analyse data
- Ethical considerations for conducting research
- Different theoretical approaches
- Criticisms levelled at social psychology
- The history of social psychology
- European social psychology

## Focus questions

1. Would it ever be ethically acceptable to conceal aspects of the truth from a person volunteering to take part in a psychological experiment?

2. Should we replace a course in social psychology with a course in evolutionary social psychology? Students describe major qualities with some evolutionary significance that they would look for in a mate in Chapter 1 of MyPsychLab at **www.mypsychlab.co.uk** (watch *Choosing a mate*)

3. Many texts in social psychology imply that it is an American rather than an international discipline. Do you have a view on this?

will use which involves getting you to decide to buy a car by giving you a very low price

Go to **mypsychlab** to explore video and test your understanding of key topics addressed in this chapter.

# Chapter 1
## Introducing social psychology

## Key terms

Archival research
Behaviour
Behaviourism
Case study
Cognitive theories
Confounding
Correlation
Data
Demand characteristics
Dependent variables
Double-blind

Evolutionary social psychology
Experimental method
Experimental realism
Experimenter effects
External validity
Hyphotheses
Independent variables
Internal validity
Laboratory
Level of explanation
Metatheory
Mundane realism
Neo-behaviourism
Operational definition

Positivism
Radical behaviourist
Reductionism
Science
Social neuroscience
Social psychology
Statistical significance
Statistics
Subject effects
*t* test
Theory
*Völkerpsychologie*

# What is social psychology?

**Social psychology**
Scientific investigation of how the thoughts, feelings and behaviour of individuals are influenced by the actual, imagined or implied presence of others.

**Social psychology** has been defined as 'the scientific investigation of how the thoughts, feelings and behaviours of individuals are influenced by the actual, imagined or implied presence of others' (G. W. Allport, 1954a, p. 5). But what does this mean? What do social psychologists actually do, how do they do it, and what do they study?

Social psychologists are interested in explaining *human* behaviour and generally do not study animals. Some general principles of social psychology may be applicable to animals, and research on animals may provide evidence for processes that generalise to people (e.g. social facilitation – see Chapter 8). Furthermore, certain principles of social behaviour may be general enough to apply to humans and, for instance, other primates (e.g. Hinde, 1982). As a rule, however, social psychologists believe that the study of animals does not take us very far in explaining human social behaviour, unless we are interested in its evolutionary origins (e.g. Neuberg, Kenrick & Schaller, 2010; Schaller, Simpson & Kenrick, 2006).

**Behaviour**
What people actually do that can be objectively measured.

Social psychologists study **behaviour** because behaviour can be observed and measured. However, behaviour refers not only to very obvious motor activities (such as running, kissing, driving) but also to more subtle actions such as a raised eyebrow, a quizzical smile or how we dress, and, critically important in human behaviour, what we say and what we write. In this sense, behaviour is publicly verifiable. However, the meaning attached to behaviour is a matter of theoretical perspective, cultural background or personal interpretation.

Social psychologists are interested not only in behaviour, but also in feelings, thoughts, beliefs, attitudes, intentions and goals. These are not directly observable but can, with varying degrees of confidence, be inferred from behaviour; and to a varying degree may influence or even determine behaviour. The relationship between these unobservable processes and overt behaviour is in itself a focus of research; for example, in research on attitude–behaviour correspondence (see Chapter 5) and research on prejudice and discrimination (see Chapter 10). Unobservable processes are also the psychological dimension of behaviour, as they occur within the human brain. However, social psychologists almost always go one step beyond relating social behaviour to underlying psychological processes – they almost always relate psychological aspects of behaviour to more fundamental cognitive processes and structures in the human mind and sometimes even to neuro-chemical processes in the brain (see Chapter 2).

What makes social psychology *social* is that it deals with how people are affected by other people who are physically present (e.g. an audience – see Chapter 8) or who are imagined to be present (e.g. anticipating performing in front of an audience), or even whose presence is implied. This last influence is more complex and addresses the fundamentally social nature of our experiences as humans. For instance, we tend to think with words; words derive from language and communication; and language and communication would not exist without social interaction (see Chapter 15). Thought, which is an internalised and private activity that can occur when we are alone, is clearly based on implied presence. As another example of implied presence, consider that most of us do not litter, even if no one is watching and even if there is no possibility of ever being caught. This is because people, through the agency of society, have constructed a powerful social convention or norm that proscribes such behaviour. Such a norm implies the presence of other people and 'determines' behaviour even in their absence (see Chapters 7 and 8).

Social psychology is a **science** because it uses the scientific method to construct and test theories. Just as physics has concepts such as electrons, quarks and spin to explain physical phenomena, social psychology has concepts such as dissonance, attitude, categorisation and identity to explain social psychological phenomena. The scientific method dictates that no **theory** is 'true' simply because it is logical and seems to make sense. On the contrary, the validity of a theory is based on its correspondence with fact. Social psychologists construct theories from **data** and/or previous theories and then conduct empirical research, in which data are collected to test the theory (see below).

**Science**
Method for studying nature that involves the collecting of data to test hypotheses.

**Theory**
Set of interrelated concepts and principles that explain a phenomenon.

**Data**
Publicly verifiable observations.

## Social psychology and its close neighbours

Social psychology is poised at the crossroads of a number of related disciplines and subdisciplines (see Figure 1.1). It is a subdiscipline of general psychology and is therefore

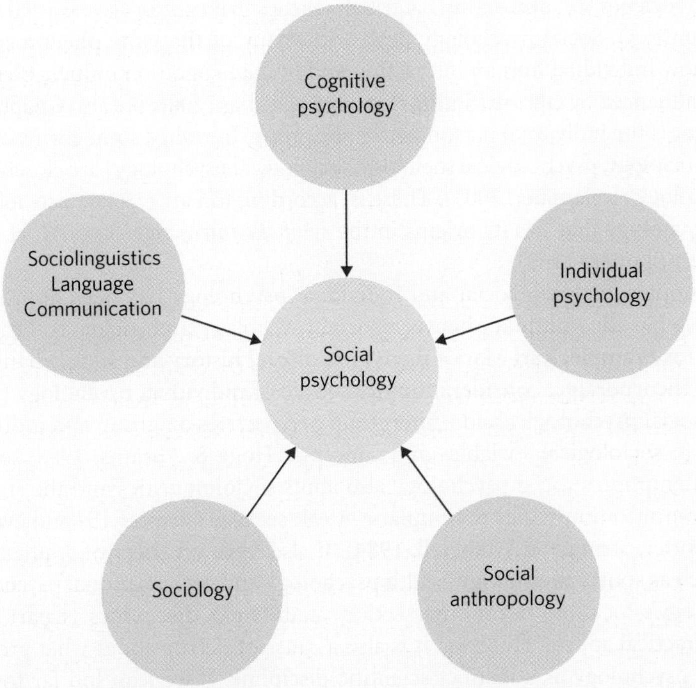

**Figure 1.1** Social psychology and some close scientific neighbours

concerned with explaining human behaviour in terms of processes that occur within the human mind. It differs from individual psychology in that it explains *social* behaviour, as defined in the previous section. For example, a general psychologist might be interested in perceptual processes that are responsible for people overestimating the size of coins. However, a social psychologist might focus on the fact that coins have value (a case of implied presence, because the value of something generally depends on what others think), and that perceived value might influence the judgement of size. A great deal of social psychology is concerned with face-to-face interaction between individuals or among members of groups, whereas general psychology focuses on people's reactions to stimuli that do not have to be social (e.g. shapes, colours, sounds).

The boundary between individual and social psychology is often approached from both sides. For instance, having developed a comprehensive and highly influential theory of the individual human mind, Sigmund Freud set out, in his 1921 essay 'Group psychology and the analysis of the ego', to develop a social psychology. Freudian, or psychodynamic, notions have left an enduring mark on social psychology (Billig, 1976), in particular in the explanation of prejudice (see Chapter 10). Since the late 1970s, social psychology has been influenced by cognitive psychology, in an attempt to employ its methods (e.g. reaction time) and its concepts (e.g. memory) to explain a wide range of social behaviours. In fact, what is now called social cognition (see Chapter 2) is in many ways the dominant approach in contemporary social psychology (Fiske & Taylor, 2008; Moskowitz, 2005; Ross, Lepper & Ward, 2010), and it surfaces in almost all areas of the discipline (Devine, Hamilton & Ostrom, 1994).

In dealing, for example, with groups, social and cultural norms, social representations, and language and intergroup behaviour, social psychology has links with sociology and social anthropology. In general, sociology focuses on how groups, organisations, social categories and societies are organised, how they function and how they change. The unit of analysis (i.e. the focus of research and theory) is the group as a whole rather than the individual people who compose the group. Social anthropology does much the same but historically has focused on 'exotic' societies (i.e. non-industrial tribal societies that exist or have existed largely in developing countries). Social psychology deals with many of the same phenomena but seeks to explain how individual human interaction and human cognition influence 'culture' and, in turn, are influenced by culture (Smith, Bond & Kağitçibaşi, 2006; see also Chapter 16). The unit of analysis is the individual person within the group. In reality, some forms of sociology (e.g. microsociology, psychological sociology, sociological psychology) are closely related to social psychology (Delamater, 2003). There is, according to Farr (1996), a sociological form of social psychology that has its origins in the *symbolic interactionism* of G. H. Mead (1934) and Herbert Blumer (1969).

Just as the boundary between social and individual psychology has been approached from both sides, so has the boundary between social psychology and sociology. From the sociological side, for example, Karl Marx's theory of cultural history and social change has been extended to incorporate a consideration of the role of individual psychology (Billig, 1976). From the social psychological side, intergroup perspectives on group and individual behaviour draw on sociological variables and concepts (Hogg & Abrams, 1988; see also Chapter 11). Contemporary social psychology also abuts sociolinguistics and the study of language and communication (Giles & Coupland, 1991; see also Chapter 15) and even literary criticism (Potter, Stringer & Wetherell, 1984). It also feeds a variety of applied areas of psychology, such as sports psychology, health psychology and organisational psychology.

Social psychology's location at the intersection of different disciplines is part of its intellectual and practical appeal. However, it is also a cause of debate about what precisely constitutes social psychology as a distinct scientific discipline. If we lean too far towards individual cognitive processes, then perhaps we are pursuing individual psychology or cognitive psychology. If we lean too far towards the role of language, then perhaps we are being scholars of language and communication. If we overemphasise the role of social structure in intergroup relations, then perhaps we are being sociologists. The issue of exactly what constitutes social psychology provides an important ongoing metatheoretical debate (i.e. a debate about what sorts of theories are appropriate for social psychology), which forms the background to the business of social psychology (see below).

## Topics of social psychology

One way to define social psychology is in terms of what social psychologists study. This book is a comprehensive coverage of the main phenomena that social psychologists study now and have studied in the past. As such, social psychology can be defined by the contents of this and of other books that present themselves as social psychology texts. A brief look at the contents of this book will give a flavour of the scope of social psychology. Social psychologists study an enormous range of topics, including conformity, persuasion, power, influence, obedience, prejudice, prejudice reduction, discrimination, stereotyping, bargaining, sexism and racism, small groups, social categories, intergroup relations, crowd behaviour, social conflict and harmony, social change, overcrowding, stress, the physical environment, decision making, the jury, leadership, communication, language, speech, attitudes, impression formation, impression management, self-presentation, identity, the self, culture, emotion, attraction, friendship, the family, love, romance, sex, violence, aggression, altruism and prosocial behaviour (acts that are valued positively by society).

One problem with defining social psychology solely in terms of its topics is that this does not properly differentiate it from other disciplines. For example, 'intergroup relations' is a focus not only of social psychologists but also of political scientists and sociologists. The family is studied not only by social psychologists but also by clinical psychologists. What makes social psychology distinct is a combination of *what* it studies, *how* it studies it and what *level of explanation* is sought.

**Conformity**
Norms govern the attitudes and behaviour of group members. These tennis fans not only dress similarly but also share a belief in Roger Federer . . . at least for now.

# Methodological issues

## Scientific method

Social psychology employs the scientific method to study social behaviour (Figure 1.2). Science is a *method* for studying nature, and it is the method – not the people who use it, the things they study, the facts they discover or the explanations they propose – that distinguishes science from other approaches to knowledge. In this respect, the main difference between social psychology and, say, physics, chemistry or biology is that the former studies human social behaviour, while the others study non-organic phenomena and chemical and biological processes.

Science involves the formulation of **hypotheses** (predictions) on the basis of prior knowledge, speculation and casual or systematic observation. Hypotheses are formally stated predictions about what factor or factors may cause something to occur; they are stated in such a way that they can be tested empirically to see if they are true. For example, we might hypothesise that ballet dancers perform better in front of an audience than when dancing alone. This hypothesis can be tested empirically by assessing their performance alone and in front of an audience. Strictly speaking, empirical tests can falsify hypotheses (causing the investigator to reject the hypothesis, revise it or test it in some other way) but not prove them (Popper, 1969). If a hypothesis is supported, confidence in its veracity increases and one may generate more finely tuned hypotheses. For example, if we find that ballet dancers do indeed perform better in front of an audience, we might then go on to hypothesise that this effect occurs only when the dancers are already very well rehearsed. An important feature of the scientific method is replication: it guards against the possibility that a finding is tied to the circumstances in which a test was conducted. It also guards against fraud.

**Hypotheses**
Empirically testable predictions about what goes with what, or what causes what.

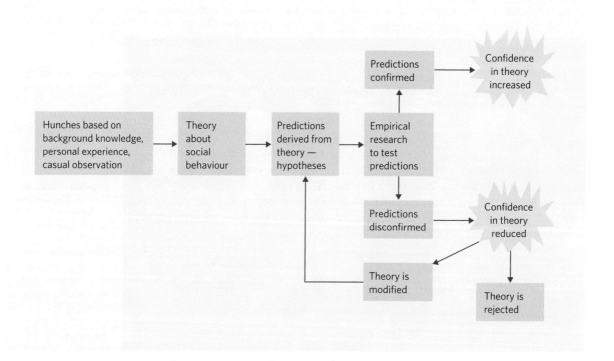

**Figure 1.2** A model of the scientific method employed by social psychologists

METHODOLOGICAL ISSUES    9

The alternative to science is dogma or rationalism, where understanding is based on authority: something is true ultimately because an authority (e.g. the ancient philosophers, religious scriptures, charismatic leaders) says it is so. Valid knowledge is acquired by pure reason: that is, by learning well, and uncritically accepting, the pronouncements of authorities. Even though the scientific revolution, championed by such people as Copernicus, Galileo and Newton, occurred in the sixteenth and seventeenth centuries, dogma and rationalism still exist as influential alternative paths to knowledge.

As a science, social psychology has at its disposal an array of different methods for conducting empirical tests of hypotheses. There are two broad types of method, *experimental* and *non-experimental*: each has its advantages and its limitations. The choice of an appropriate method is determined by the nature of the hypothesis under investigation, the resources available for doing the research (e.g. time, money, research participants) and the ethics of the method. Confidence in the validity of a hypothesis is enhanced if the hypothesis has been confirmed a number of times by different research teams using different methods. Methodological pluralism helps to minimise the possibility that the finding is an artefact of a particular method, and replication by different research teams helps to avoid confirmation bias – a tendency for researchers to become personally involved in their own theories to such an extent that they lose a degree of objectivity in interpreting data (Greenwald & Pratkanis, 1988; Johnson & Eagly, 1989).

## Experiments

An experiment is a hypothesis test in which something is done to see its effect on something else. For example, if I hypothesise that my car greedily guzzles too much petrol because the tyres are under-inflated, then I can conduct an experiment. I can note petrol consumption over an average week, then I can increase the tyre pressure and again note petrol consumption over an average week. If consumption is reduced, then my hypothesis is supported. Casual experimentation is one of the most important and common ways in which people learn about their world. It is an extremely powerful method because it allows us to identify the causes of events and thus gain control over our destiny.

Not surprisingly, systematic experimentation is the most important research method in science. Experimentation involves *intervention* in the form of *manipulation* of one or more **independent variables,** and then measurement of the effect of the treatment (manipulation) on one or more focal **dependent variables**. In the example above, the independent variable is tyre inflation, which was manipulated to create two experimental conditions (lower versus higher pressure), and the dependent variable is petrol consumption, which was measured on refilling the tank at the end of the week. More generally, independent variables are dimensions that the researcher hypothesises will have an effect and that can be varied (e.g. tyre pressure in the present example, and the presence or absence of an audience in the ballet-dancing example). Dependent variables are dimensions that the researcher hypothesises will vary (petrol consumption or quality of the ballet dancer's performance) as a consequence of varying the independent variable. Variation in the dependent variable is *dependent* on variation in the independent variable.

**Independent variables**
Features of a situation that change of their own accord, or can be manipulated by an experimenter to have effects on a dependent variable.

**Dependent variables**
Variables that change as a consequence of changes in the independent variable.

Social psychology is largely experimental, in that most social psychologists would prefer to test hypotheses experimentally if at all possible, and much of what we know about social behaviour is based on experiments. Indeed, one of the most enduring and prestigious scholarly societies for the scientific study of social psychology is the *Society for Experimental Social Psychology*.

A typical social psychology experiment might be designed to test the hypothesis that violent television programmes increase aggression in young children. One way to do this would be to assign twenty children randomly to two conditions in which they individually watch either a violent or a non-violent programme, and then monitor the amount of aggression expressed immediately afterwards by the children while they are at play. Random assignment of participants (in this case, children) reduces the chance of systematic differences between the participants in the two conditions. If there were any systematic differences, say, in age, sex or parental background, then any significant effects on aggression might be due to age, sex or background rather than to the violence of the television programme. That is, age, sex or parental background would be *confounded* with the independent variable. Likewise, the television programme viewed in each condition should be identical in all respects except the degree of violence. For instance, if the violent programme also contained more action, then we would not know whether subsequent differences in aggression were due to the violence, the action, or both. The circumstances surrounding the viewing of the two programmes should also be identical. If the violent programmes were viewed in a bright red room and the non-violent programmes in a blue room, then any effects might be due to room colour, violence, or both. It is critically important in experiments to avoid **confounding**: the conditions must be identical in all respects except for those represented by the manipulated independent variable.

**Confounding**
Where two or more independent variables covary in such a way that it is impossible to know which has caused the effect.

We must also be careful about how we measure effects: that is, the dependent measures that assess the dependent variable. In our example it would probably be inappropriate, because of the children's age, to administer a questionnaire measuring aggression. A better technique would be unobtrusive observation of behaviour, but then what would we code as 'aggression'? The criterion would have to be sensitive to changes: in other words, loud talk or violent assault with a weapon might be insensitive, as all children talk loudly when playing (there is a *ceiling effect*), and virtually no children violently assault one another with a weapon while playing (there is a *floor effect*). In addition, it would be a mistake for whoever records or codes the behaviour to know which experimental condition the child was in: such knowledge might compromise objectivity. The coder(s) should know as little as possible about the experimental conditions and the research hypotheses.

The example used here is of a simple experiment that has only two levels of only one independent variable – called a one-factor design. Most social psychology experiments are more complicated than this. For instance, we might formulate a more textured hypothesis that aggression in young children is increased by television programmes that contain *realistic* violence. To test this hypothesis, a two-factor design would be adopted. The two factors (independent variables) would be (1) the violence of the programme (low versus high) and (2) the realism of the programme (realistic versus fantasy). The participants would be randomly assigned across four experimental conditions in which they watched (1) a non-violent fantasy programme, (2) a non-violent realistic programme, (3) a violent fantasy programme or (4) a violent realistic programme. Finally, independent variables are not restricted to two levels. For instance, we might predict that aggression is increased by moderately violent programmes, whereas extremely violent programmes are so distasteful that aggression is actually suppressed. Our independent variable of programme violence could now have three levels (low versus moderate versus extreme).

### The laboratory experiment

**Laboratory**
A place, usually a room, in which data are collected, usually by experimental methods.

The classic social psychology experiment is conducted in a **laboratory** in order to be able to control as many potentially confounding variables as possible. The aim is to isolate and manipulate a single aspect of a variable, an aspect that may not normally occur in isolation outside the laboratory. Laboratory experiments are *intended* to create artificial conditions. Although a social psychology laboratory may contain computers, wires and flashing lights, quite often it is simply a room containing tables and chairs. For example, our ballet hypothesis could be tested in the laboratory by formalising it to one in which we predict that someone performing any well-learned task performs the task more quickly in front of an audience. We could unobtrusively time individuals for example taking off their clothes and then putting them back on again (a well-learned task) either alone in a room or while being scrutinised by two other people (an audience). We could compare these speeds with those of someone dressing up in unusual and difficult clothing (a poorly learned task). This method was actually used by Markus (1978) when she investigated the effect of an audience on task performance (see Chapter 8 for details).

Laboratory experiments allow us to establish cause–effect relationships between variables. However, laboratory experiments have a number of drawbacks. Because experimental conditions are artificial and highly controlled, laboratory findings cannot be generalised directly to the less 'pure' conditions that exist in the 'real' world outside the laboratory. However, laboratory findings address *theories* about human social behaviour, and on the basis of laboratory experimentation we can generalise these theories to apply to conditions other than those in the laboratory. Laboratory experiments are intentionally low on **external validity** or **mundane realism** (i.e. how similar the conditions are to those usually encountered by participants in the real world) but should always be high on **internal validity** or **experimental realism** (i.e. the manipulations must be full of psychological impact and meaning for the participants) (Aronson, Ellsworth, Carlsmith & Gonzales, 1990).

Laboratory experiments can be prone to a range of biases. There are **subject effects** which can cause participants' behaviour to be an artefact of the experiment rather than a spontaneous and natural response to a manipulation. Artefacts can be minimised by carefully avoiding **demand characteristics** (Orne, 1962), *evaluation apprehension* and *social desirability* (Rosenberg, 1969). Demand characteristics are features of the experiment that seem to 'demand' a particular response: they give information about the hypothesis and thus inform helpful and compliant participants about how to react to confirm the hypothesis. Participants are thus no longer naive or *blind* regarding the experimental hypothesis. Participants in experiments are real people, and experiments are real social situations. Not surprisingly, participants may want to project the best possible image of themselves to the experimenter and other participants present. This can influence spontaneous reactions to manipulations in unpredictable ways. There are also **experimenter effects**. The experimenter is often aware of the hypothesis and may inadvertently give cues that cause participants to behave in a way that confirms the hypothesis. This can be minimised by a **double-blind** procedure, in which the experimenter is unaware of which experimental condition they are running.

**External validity** or **Mundane realism**
Similarity between circumstances surrounding an experiment and circumstances encountered in everyday life.

**Internal validity** or **Experimental realism**
Psychological impact of the manipulations in an experiment.

**Subject effects**
Effects that are not spontaneous, owing to demand characteristics and/or participants wishing to please the experimenter.

**Demand characteristics**
Features of an experiment that seem to 'demand' a certain response.

**Experimenter effects**
Effect that is produced or influenced by clues to the hypotheses under examination, inadvertently given by the experimenter.

**Double-blind**
Procedure to reduce experimenter effects, in which the experimenter is unaware of the experimental conditions.

**Experiments**
Laboratory experiments play a central role in social psychology. Some researchers seeking ways to apply fMRI techniques in studying social behaviour.

Since the 1960s, laboratory experiments have tended to rely on psychology undergraduates as participants (Sears, 1986). The reason is a pragmatic one – psychology undergraduates are readily available in large numbers. In almost all major universities there is a research participation scheme, or 'subject pool', whereby psychology students act as experimental participants in exchange for course credits or as a course requirement. Critics have often complained that this overreliance on a particular type of participant may produce a somewhat distorted view of social behaviour – one that is not easily generalised to other sectors of the population. In their defence, experimental social psychologists point out that theories, not experimental findings, are generalised, and that replication and methodological pluralism ensures that social psychology is about people, not just about psychology students.

### The field experiment

Social psychology experiments can be conducted in more naturalistic settings outside the laboratory. For example, we could investigate the hypothesis that prolonged eye contact is uncomfortable and causes 'flight' by having an experimenter stand at traffic lights and either gaze intensely at the driver of a car stopped at the lights or gaze in the opposite direction. The dependent measure would be the speed at which the car sped away once the lights changed (Ellsworth, Carlsmith & Henson, 1972; see also Chapter 15). Field experiments have high external validity and, as participants are usually completely unaware that an experiment is taking place, are not reactive (i.e. no demand characteristics are present). However, there is less control over extraneous variables, random assignment is sometimes difficult, and it can be difficult to obtain accurate measurements or measurements of subjective feelings (generally, overt behaviour is all that can be measured).

## Non-experimental methods

Systematic experimentation tends to be the preferred method of science, and indeed it is often equated with science. However, there are all sorts of circumstances where it is simply impossible to conduct an experiment to test a hypothesis. For instance, theories about planetary systems and galaxies can pose a real problem: we cannot move planets around to see what happens! Likewise, social psychological theories about the relationship between biological sex and decision making are not amenable to experimentation, because we cannot manipulate biological sex experimentally and see what effects emerge. Social psychology also confronts ethical issues that can proscribe experimentation. For instance, hypotheses about the effects on self-esteem of being a victim of violent crime are not at all easily tested experimentally – we would not be able to assign participants randomly to two conditions and then subject one group to a violent crime and see what happened!

Where experimentation is not possible or not appropriate, social psychologists have a range of non-experimental methods from which to choose. Because these methods do not involve the manipulation of independent variables against a background of random assignment to condition, it is almost impossible to draw reliable causal conclusions. For instance, we could compare the self-esteem of people who have been victims of violent crime with those who have not. Any differences could be attributed to violent crime but could also be due to other uncontrolled differences between the two groups. We can only conclude that there is a **correlation** between self-esteem and being the victim of violent crime. There is no evidence that one causes the other (i.e. being a victim may lower self-esteem or having lower self-esteem may increase the likelihood of becoming a victim). Both could be *correlated* or co-occurring effects of some third variable, such as chronic unemployment, which independently lowers self-esteem *and* increases the probability that one might become a victim. In general, non-experimental methods involve the examination of correlation between naturally occurring variables and as such do not permit us to draw causal conclusions.

**Correlation**
Where changes in one variable reliably map on to changes in another variable, but it cannot be determined which of the two variables *caused* the change.

## Archival research

**Archival research** is a non-experimental method that is useful for investigating large-scale, widely occurring phenomena that may be remote in time. The researcher assembles data collected by others, often for reasons unconnected with those of the researcher. For instance, Janis (1972) used an archival method to show that overly cohesive government decision-making groups may make poor decisions with disastrous consequences because they adopt poor decision-making procedures (called 'groupthink'; see Chapter 9). Janis constructed his theory on the basis of an examination of biographical, autobiographical and media accounts of the decision-making procedures associated with, for example, the 1961 Bay of Pigs fiasco, in which the United States tried to invade Cuba. Archival methods are often used to make comparisons between different cultures or nations regarding things such as suicide, mental health or child-rearing strategies. Archival research is not reactive, but it can be unreliable because the researcher usually has no control over the primary data collection, which might be biased or unreliable in other ways (e.g. missing vital data). The researcher has to make do with whatever is there.

**Archival research**
Non-experimental method involving the assembly of data, or reports of data, collected by others.

## Case studies

The **case study** allows an in-depth analysis of a single case (either a person or a group) or a single event. Case studies often employ an array of data collection and analysis techniques involving structured and open-ended interviews and questionnaires, and the observation of behaviour. Case studies are well suited to the examination of unusual or rare phenomena that could not be created in the laboratory: for instance, bizarre cults, mass murderers or disasters. Case studies are useful as a source of hypotheses, but findings may suffer from researcher or subject bias (the researcher is not blind to the hypothesis, there are demand characteristics and participants suffer evaluation apprehension), and findings may not easily be generalised to other cases or events.

**Case study**
In-depth analysis of a single case (or individual).

## Survey research

Another non-experimental method is data collection by *survey*. Surveys can involve structured interviews, in which the researcher asks the participants a number of carefully chosen questions and notes down the responses, or a questionnaire, in which participants write their own responses to written questions. In either case the questions can be open-ended (i.e. respondents can give as much or as little detail in their answers as they wish) or closed-ended (where there is a limited number of predetermined responses, such as circling a number on a nine-point scale). For instance, to investigate immigrant workers' experiences of prejudice in Germany, one could ask respondents a set of predetermined questions and summarise the gist of their responses or assign a numerical value to their responses. Alternatively, respondents could record their own responses by writing a paragraph, or by circling numbers on scales in a questionnaire.

Surveys can be used to obtain a large amount of data from a large sample of participants; hence generalisation is often not a problem. However, it is a method that, like the case study, is subject to experimenter bias, subject bias and evaluation apprehension. Anonymous and confidential questionnaires may minimise experimenter bias, evaluation apprehension and some subject biases, but demand characteristics may remain. In addition, poorly constructed questionnaires may obtain biased data due to 'response set' – that is, the tendency for some respondents to agree unthinkingly with statements, or to choose mid-range or extreme responses.

## Field studies

The final non-experimental method is the field study. We have already described the field experiment: the field study is essentially the same but without any interventions or manipulations. Field studies involve the observation, recording and coding of behaviour as it occurs. Most often, the observer is non-intrusive by not participating in the behaviour, and 'invisible' by not having an effect on the ongoing behaviour. For instance, one could research the behaviour of students in the student cafeteria by concealing oneself in a corner and observing what goes on. Sometimes 'invisibility' is impossible, so the opposite strategy can be used – the researcher becomes a full participant in the behaviour. For instance, it would be rather difficult to be an invisible observer of gang behaviour. Instead, you could study the behaviour of a street gang by becoming a full member of the gang and surreptitiously taking notes (e.g. Whyte, 1943; see also Chapter 8). Field studies are excellent for investigating spontaneously occurring behaviour in its natural context but are particularly prone to experimenter bias, lack of objectivity, poor generalisability and distortions due to the impact of the researcher on the behaviour under investigation. Also, if you join a gang there is an element of personal danger!

## Data and analysis

Research provides data, which are analysed to draw conclusions about whether hypotheses are supported. The type of analysis undertaken depends on at least:

- *The type of data obtained* – for example, binary responses such as 'yes' versus 'no', continuous variables such as temperature or response latency, defined positions on nine-point scales, rank ordering of choices and open-ended written responses (text).
- *The method used to obtain data* – for example, controlled experiment, open-ended interview, participant observation, archival search.
- *The purposes of the research* – for example, to describe in depth a specific case, to establish differences between two groups of participants exposed to different treatments, to investigate the correlation between two or more naturally occurring variables.

Overwhelmingly, social psychological knowledge is based on statistical analysis of quantitative data. Data are obtained as, or are transformed into, numbers (i.e. quantities), and

**Statistics**
Social psychological data are often quantitative, requiring statistical analysis to find patterns that give meaning to the numbers

these numbers are then compared in various formalised ways (i.e. by **statistics**). For example, to decide whether women are more friendly interviewees than are men, we could compare transcripts of interviews of both men and women. We could then code the transcripts to count how often participants made positive remarks to the interviewer, and compare the mean count for, say, twenty women with the mean for twenty men. In this case, we would be interested in knowing whether the difference between men and women was 'on the whole' greater than the difference among men and among women. To do this, we could use a simple statistic called the **t test**, which computes a single number called the $t$ statistic, which is based on both the difference between the women's and men's mean friendliness scores and the degree of variability of scores within each sex. The larger the value of $t$, the larger the between-sex difference relative to within-sex differences.

The decision about whether the difference between groups is psychologically significant depends on its **statistical significance**. Social psychologists adhere to the arbitrary convention that if the obtained value of $t$ has less than a 1 in 20 (i.e. 0.05) probability of occurring simply by chance (that is, if we randomly selected 100 groups of ten males and ten females, only five times or fewer would we obtain a value of $t$ as great as or greater than that obtained in the study), then the obtained difference is statistically significant and there really is a difference in friendliness between male and female interviewees (see Figure 1.3).

**Statistics**
Formalised numerical procedures performed on data to investigate the magnitude and/or significance of effects.

**t test**
Statistical procedure to test the statistical significance of an effect in which the mean for one condition is greater than the mean for another.

**Statistical significance**
An effect is statistically significant if statistics reveal that it, or a larger effect, is unlikely to occur by chance more often than 1 in 20 times.

**CASE 1.** *A significant difference*: The t statistic is relatively large because the difference between means is large and the variation within sex groups is small.

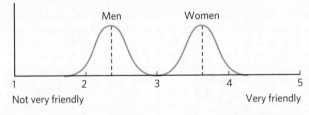

**CASE 2.** *Not a significant difference*: The t statistic is relatively small because, although the difference between means is still large, the variation within sex groups is much larger.

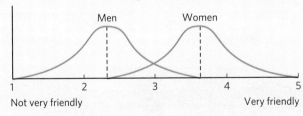

**CASE 3.** *A significant difference*: The t statistic is large because, although the difference between means is smaller, the variation within sex groups is small.

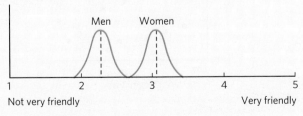

**Figure 1.3**
Distribution of friendliness scores for twenty male and twenty female interviewees: using the t statistic

The *t* test is very simple. However, the principle underlying the *t* test is the same as that underlying more sophisticated and complex statistical techniques used by social psychologists to test whether two or more groups differ significantly. The other major method of data analysis used by social psychologists is correlation, which assesses whether the co-occurrence of two or more variables is significant. Again, although the example below is simple, the underlying principle is the same for an array of correlational techniques.

To investigate the idea that rigid thinkers tend to hold more politically conservative attitudes (Rokeach, 1960; see also Chapter 10), we could have thirty participants answer a questionnaire measuring cognitive rigidity (dogmatism: a rigid and inflexible set of attitudes) and political conservatism (e.g. endorsement and espousal of right-wing political and social policies). If we rank the thirty participants in order of increasing dogmatism and find that conservatism also increases, with the least dogmatic person being the least conservative and the most dogmatic the most conservative, then we can say that the two variables are positively correlated (see Figure 1.4, in which dots represent individual persons, positioned with respect to their scores on both dogmatism and conservatism scales). If we find that conservatism systematically decreases with increasing dogmatism, then we say that the two variables are negatively correlated. If there seems to be no systematic relationship between the two variables, then they are uncorrelated – there is zero correlation. A statistic can be calculated to represent correlation numerically: for instance, Pearson's *r* varies from −1 for a perfect negative to +1 for a perfect positive correlation. Depending on,

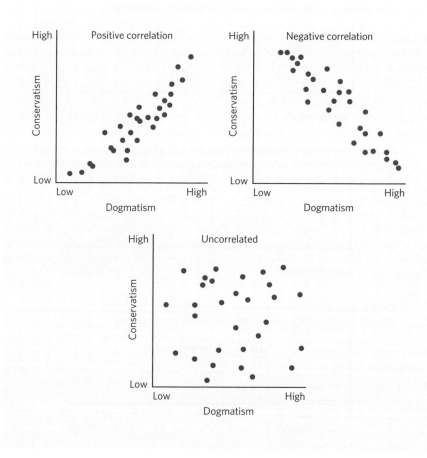

**Figure 1.4** Correlation between dogmatism and conservatism for thirty respondents: using Pearson's correlation coefficient

among other things, the number of persons, we can also know whether the correlation is statistically significant at the conventional 5 per cent level.

Although statistical analysis of quantitative data is the bread and butter of social psychology, some social psychologists find that this method is unsuited to their purposes and prefer a more *qualitative* analysis. For example, analysis of people's explanations for unemployment or prejudice may sometimes benefit from a more discursive, non-quantitative analysis in which the researcher tries to unravel what is said in order to go beyond surface explanations and get to the heart of the underlying beliefs and reasons. One form of qualitative analysis is *discourse analysis* (e.g. Potter & Wetherell, 1987; Tuffin, 2005; Wetherell, Taylor & Yates, 2001). Discourse analysis treats all 'data' as 'text' – that is, as a communicative event that is replete with multiple layers of meaning but that can be interpreted only by considering the text in its wider social context. For example, discourse analysts believe that we should not take people's responses to attitude statements in questionnaires at face value and subject them to statistical analysis. They believe, instead, that we should interpret what is being communicated. This is made possible only by considering the response as a complex conjunction of social-communicative factors deriving from the immediate context and the wider sociohistorical context. However, discourse analysis is more than a research method: it is also a systematic critique of 'conventional' social psychological methods and theories (see below).

# Research ethics

As researchers, social psychologists confront important ethical issues. For instance, is it ethical to expose experimental participants to a treatment that is embarrassing or has potentially harmful effects on their self-concept? If such research is important, what are the rights of the person, what are the ethical obligations of the researcher, and what guidelines are there for deciding? Although ethical considerations surface most often in experiments (e.g. Milgram's 1974 obedience studies; see Chapter 7) they can also confront non-experimental researchers. For example, is it ethical for a non-participant observer investigating crowd behaviour to refrain from interceding in a violent assault?

To guide researchers, the American Psychological Association established, in 1972, a set of principles for ethical conduct in research involving humans, which was completely revised and updated in 2002 (American Psychological Association, 2002). These principles are reflected in the ethics codes of national societies of psychology in Europe. Researchers design their studies with these guidelines in mind and then obtain official approval from a university or departmental research ethics committee. There are five ethical principles that have received most attention: protection from harm, right to privacy, deception, informed consent and debriefing.

## Physical welfare of participants

Clearly it is unethical to expose people to physical *harm*. For example, the use of electric shocks that cause visible burning would be difficult to justify. However, in most cases it is also difficult to establish whether non-trivial harm is involved and, if so, what its magnitude is, and whether debriefing (see below) deals with it. For instance, telling experimental participants that they have done badly on a word-association task may have long-term effects on self-esteem and could therefore be considered harmful. On the other hand, the effects may be so minor and transitory as to be insignificant.

## Respect for privacy

Social psychological research often involves invasion of *privacy*. Participants can be asked intimate questions, can be observed without their knowledge and can have their moods, perceptions and behaviour manipulated. It is sometimes difficult to decide whether the research topic justifies invasion of privacy. At other times it is more straightforward – for example, intimate questions about sexual practices are essential for research into behaviour that may put people at risk of contracting HIV and developing AIDS. Concern about privacy is usually satisfied by ensuring that data obtained from individuals are entirely *confidential*: that is, only the researcher knows who said or did what. Personal identification is removed from data (rendering them anonymous), research findings are reported as means for large groups of people, and data no longer useful are usually destroyed.

## Use of deception

Laboratory experiments, as we have seen, involve the manipulation of people's cognition, feelings or behaviour in order to investigate the spontaneous, natural and non-reactive effect of independent variables. Because participants need to be naive regarding hypotheses, experimenters commonly conceal the true purpose of the experiment. A degree of *deception* is often necessary. Between 50 and 75 per cent of published experiments involve some degree of deception (Adair, Dushenko & Lindsay, 1985; Gross & Fleming, 1982). Because the use of deception seems to imply 'trickery', 'deceit' and 'lying', it has attracted a frenzy of criticism – for example, Baumrind's (1964) attack on Milgram's (1963, 1974) obedience studies (see Chapter 7). Social psychologists have been challenged to abandon controlled experimental research in favour of role playing or simulations (e.g. Kelman, 1967) if they cannot do experiments without deception. This is probably too extreme a request, as social psychological knowledge has been enriched enormously by classic experiments that have used deception (many such experiments are described in this book). Although some experiments have used an amount of deception that seems excessive, in practice the deception used in the overwhelming majority of social psychology experiments is trivial. For example, an experiment may be introduced as a study of group decision making when in fact it is part of a programme of research into prejudice and stereotyping. In addition, no one has yet shown any long-term negative consequences of the use of deception in social psychology experiments (Elms, 1982), and experimental participants themselves tend to be impressed, rather than upset or angered, by cleverly executed deceptions, and they view deception as a necessary withholding of information or a necessary ruse (Christensen, 1988; Sharpe, Adair & Roese, 1992; Smith, 1983). How would you address the first focus question at the beginning of this chapter?

## Informed consent

A way to safeguard participants' rights in experiments is to obtain their *informed consent* to participate. In principle, people should give their consent freely (preferably in writing) to participate on the basis of full information about what they are consenting to take part in, and they must be entirely free to withdraw without penalty from the research whenever they wish. Researchers cannot lie or withhold information in order to induce people to participate; nor can they make it 'difficult' to say 'no' or to withdraw (i.e. via social pressure or by exercise of personal or institutionalised power). In practice, however, terms such as 'full information' are difficult to define, and, as we have just seen, experiments often require some deception in order that participants remain naive.

## Debriefing

Participants should be fully *debriefed* after taking part in an experiment. Debriefing is designed to make sure that people leave the laboratory with an increased respect for and understanding of social psychology. More specifically, debriefing involves a detailed explanation of the experiment and its broader theoretical and applied context. Any deceptions are explained and justified to the satisfaction of all participants, and care is taken to make sure that the effects of manipulations have been undone. However, strong critics of deception (e.g. Baumrind, 1985) believe that no amount of debriefing puts right what they consider to be the fundamental wrong of deception that undermines basic human trust.

Social psychologists often conduct and report research into socially sensitive phenomena, or research that has implications for socially sensitive issues: for example, prejudice, discrimination, racism, sexism and ageism (see Chapters 10, 11 and 15). In these sorts of areas the researcher has to be especially careful that both the conducting and reporting of research are done in such a way that they are not biased by personal prejudices and are not open to public misinterpretation, distortion or misuse. For example, early research into sex differences in conformity found that women conformed more than men. This finding is, of course, fuel to the view that women are more dependent than men. Later research discovered that men and women conform equally, and that whether one conforms or not depends largely on how much familiarity and confidence one has with the conformity task. Early research used tasks that were more familiar to men than to women, and many researchers looked no further because the findings confirmed their assumptions (Chapters 7 and 10).

# Theoretical issues

Social psychologists construct and test theories of human social behaviour. A social psychological theory is an integrated set of propositions that explains the causes of social behaviour, generally in terms of one or more social psychological processes. Theories rest on explicit assumptions about social behaviour and contain a number of defined concepts and formal statements about the relationship between concepts. Ideally, these relationships are causal ones that are attributed to the operation of social and/or psychological processes. Theories are framed in such a way that they generate hypotheses that can be tested empirically. Social psychological theories vary greatly in terms of their rigour, testability and generality (Van Lange, Kruglanski & Higgins, 2010). Some theories are short-range mini-theories tied to specific phenomena, whereas others are broader general theories that explain whole classes of behaviour. Some even approach the status of 'grand theory' (such as evolutionary theory, Marxism, general relativity theory and psychodynamic theory) in that they furnish a general perspective on social psychology.

Social identity theory (e.g. Tajfel & Turner, 1979; see Chapters 4 and 11) is a good example of a relatively general mid-range social psychological theory. It is an analysis of the behaviour of people in groups and how this relates to their self-conception as group members. The theory integrates a number of compatible (sub)theories that deal with and emphasise (see Hogg, 2006):

- intergroup relations and social change;
- motivational processes associated with group membership and group behaviour;
- social influence and conformity processes within groups;
- cognitive processes associated with self-conception and social perception.

These, and other associated processes, operate together to produce group behaviour, as distinct from interpersonal behaviour. This theory generates testable predictions about a range of group phenomena, including stereotyping, intergroup discrimination, social influence in groups, group cohesiveness, social change and even language and ethnicity.

## Theories in social psychology

Theories in social psychology can generally be clustered into types of theory, with different types of theory reflecting different *metatheories*. Just as a theory is a set of interrelated concepts and principles that explain a phenomenon, a **metatheory** is a set of interrelated concepts and principles about which theories or types of theory are appropriate. Some theories can be extended by their adherents to account for almost the whole of human behaviour – the 'grand theories' mentioned above. In this section, we discuss several major types of theory that have had an impact on social psychology.

### Behaviourism

Behaviourist or learning perspectives derive originally from Ivan Pavlov's early work on conditioned reflexes and B. F. Skinner's work on operant conditioning. **Radical behaviourists** believe that behaviour can be explained and predicted in terms of reinforcement schedules – behaviour associated with positive outcomes or circumstances grows in strength and frequency. However, more popular with social psychologists is **neo-behaviourism,** which maintains that one needs to invoke unobservable intervening constructs (e.g. beliefs, feelings, motives) to make sense of behaviour.

The behaviourist perspective in social psychology produces theories that emphasise the role of situational factors and reinforcement/learning in social behaviour. One example is the *reinforcement–affect model of interpersonal attraction* (e.g. Lott, 1961; Chapter 14): people grow to like those people with whom they associate positive experiences (e.g. we like people who praise us). Another more general example is *social exchange theory* (e.g. Kelley & Thibaut, 1978; Chapter 14): the course of social interactions depends on subjective evaluation of the rewards and costs involved. *Social modelling* is another broadly behaviourist

**Metatheory**
Set of interrelated concepts and principles concerning which theories or types of theory are appropriate.

**Radical behaviourist**
One who explains observable behaviour in terms of reinforcement schedules, without recourse to any intervening unobservable (e.g. cognitive) constructs.

**Neo-behaviourism**
One who attempts to explain observable behaviour in terms of contextual factors and unobservable intervening constructs such as beliefs, feelings and motives.

**Social identity**
Hoodies belong to groups too. They dress to emphasize group membership and social identity

perspective: we imitate behaviour that is reinforced in others, and thus our behaviour is shaped by vicarious learning (e.g. Bandura, 1977; Chapter 12). Finally, *drive theory* (Zajonc, 1965; Chapter 8) explains improvement and deterioration of task performance in front of an audience in terms of the strength of a learned response.

## Cognitive psychology

Critics have argued that behaviourist theories exaggerate the extent to which people are passive recipients of external influences. **Cognitive theories** redress the balance by focusing on how people actively interpret and change their environment through the agency of cognitive processes and cognitive representations. Cognitive theories have their origins in Kurt Koffka and Wolfgang Köhler's *Gestalt* psychology of the 1930s, and in many ways social psychology has always been very cognitive in its perspective (Landman & Manis, 1983; Markus & Zajonc, 1985). One of social psychology's earliest cognitive theories was Kurt Lewin's (1951) field theory, which dealt, in a somewhat complicated manner, with the way in which people's cognitive representations of features of the social environment produce motivational forces to behave in specific ways. Lewin is generally considered the father of experimental social psychology.

In the 1950s and 1960s, cognitive consistency theories dominated social psychology (Abelson et al., 1968). These theories assumed that cognitions about ourselves, our behaviour and the world, which were contradictory or incompatible in other ways, produced an uncomfortable state of cognitive arousal that motivated people to resolve the cognitive conflict. This perspective has been used to explain attitude change (e.g. Aronson, 1984; Chapter 6). In the 1970s, attribution theories dominated social psychology. Attribution theories focus on the way in which people explain the causes of their own and other people's behaviour, and on the consequences of causal explanations (e.g. Hewstone, 1989; Chapter 3). Finally, since the late 1970s, social cognition has been the dominant perspective in social psychology. This is a perspective that subsumes a number of theories dealing with the way in which cognitive processes (e.g. categorisation) and cognitive representations (e.g. schemas) are constructed and influence behaviour (e.g. Fiske & Taylor, 2008; Chapter 2).

**Cognitive theories**
These attempt to explain behaviour in terms of the way people actively interpret and represent their experiences and then plan action.

## Neuroscience and biochemistry

A recent development or offshoot of social cognition is a focus in social psychology on neurological and biochemical correlates of social behaviour. Called **social neuroscience,** or social cognitive neuroscience, this approach is predicated on the view that because psychology happens in the brain, cognition must be associated with electro-chemical brain activity (e.g. Harmon-Jones & Winkielman, 2007; Lieberman, 2010; Ochsner, 2007; Ochsner & Lieberman, 2001, see Chapter 2). Social neuroscience uses brain imaging methodologies, for example fMRI (functional magnetic resonance imaging), to detect and locate brain activity associated with social thinking and social behaviour. This general idea that we are biological entities and that therefore social behaviour has neuro- and biochemical correlates surfaces in other theorising that focuses more on biochemical markers of social behaviour – for example, measures of the hormone cortisol in people's blood as a marker of stress (see Blascovich & Seery, 2007).

**Social neuroscience**
The exploration of the neurological underpinnings of the processes traditionally examined by social psychology.

**Evolutionary social psychology**
An extension of evolutionary psychology that views complex social behaviour as adaptive, helping the individual, kin and the species as a whole to survive.

## Evolutionary social psychology

Another theoretical development is **evolutionary social psychology** (Caporael, 2007; Kenrick, Maner & Li, 2005; Neuberg, Kenrick & Schaller, 2010; Schaller, Simpson & Kenrick, 2006; Simpson & Kenrick, 1997). Drawing on nineteenth-century Darwinian theory, modern **evolutionary psychology** and sociobiology (e.g. Wilson, 1975, 1978), evolutionary social psychologists argue that much of human behaviour is grounded in the

**Evolutionary psychology**
A theoretical approach that explains 'useful' psychological traits, such as memory, perception or language, as adaptations through natural selection.

ancestral past of our species. Buss and Reeve (2003, p. 849) suggest that evolutionary processes have shaped 'cooperation and conflict within families, the emergence of cooperative alliances, human aggression, acts of altruism . . .'. These behaviours had survival value for the species and so, over time, became a part of our genetic make-up.

A biological perspective can be pushed to an extreme and used as a sovereign explanation for most, even all, behaviour. However, it should be noted that when the human genome had finally been charted in 2003, researchers felt that the 20,000–25,000 genes and 3 billion chemical base pairs making up human DNA were insufficient to account for the massive diversity of human behaviour – context and environment play a significant role (e.g. Lander et al., 2001).

This is where social psychology steps in – social psychology can account for the role of learning, subtle effects of social context on behaviour, and for cultural variation in behaviour. Nevertheless, evolutionary social psychology has relevance for several topics covered in this book – for example, leadership (Chapter 9), aggression (Chapter 12), prosocial behaviour (Chapter 13), interpersonal attraction (Chapter 14), and non-verbal and human spatial behaviour (Chapter 15).

### Personality

Social psychologists have often tried to explain social behaviour in terms of enduring (sometimes innate) personality attributes. For instance, good leaders have charismatic personalities (Chapter 9), people with prejudiced personalities express prejudice (Chapter 10), and people who conform too much have conformist personalities (Chapter 7). In general, social psychologists now consider personality to be at best a partial explanation, at worst an inadequate explanation, of social phenomena. There are at least two reasons for this:

1 There is actually very little evidence for stable personality traits. People behave in different ways at different times and in different contexts – they are influenced by situation and context.
2 If personality is defined as behavioural consistency across contexts, then rather than being an explanation of behaviour, personality is something to be explained. Why do some people resist social and contextual influences on behaviour? What is it about their interpretation of the context that causes them to behave in this way?

Overall most contemporary treatments of personality see personality as interacting with many other factors to impact behaviour (e.g. Funder & Fast, 2010; Snyder & Cantor, 1998).

Personality theories can be contrasted with collectivist theories. Collectivist theories focus on the way in which people are socially constituted by their unique location in society. People behave as they do, not because of personality or individual predispositions, but because they internally represent socially constructed group norms that influence behaviour in specific contexts. An early collectivist viewpoint was McDougall's (1920) theory of the 'group mind' (Chapter 11). In groups, people change the way they think, process information and act, so that group behaviour is quite different from interpersonal behaviour – a group mind emerges.

More recently, this idea has been significantly elaborated and developed by European social psychologists seeking a perspective on social behaviour that emphasises the part played by the wider social context of intergroup relations in shaping behaviour (e.g. Tajfel, 1984). Of these, social identity theory is perhaps the most developed (Tajfel & Turner, 1979; Chapter 11). Its explanation of the behaviour of people in groups is strongly influenced by an analysis of the social relations between groups. Collectivist theories adopt a 'top-down' approach, in which individual social behaviour can be properly explained only with reference to groups, intergroup relations and social forces. Individualistic theories, in contrast, are 'bottom-up': individual social behaviour is constructed from individual cognition or personality.

It is important to recognise that many social psychological theories contain elements of two or more different perspectives, and also that these and other perspectives often merely lend emphasis to different theories. Metatheory does not usually intentionally reveal itself with a great fanfare (but see Abrams & Hogg, 2004).

## Social psychology in crisis

Social psychology occurs against a background of, often latent, metatheoretical differences. In many respects this is an intellectually engaging feature of the discipline. From time to time these differences come to the fore and become the focus of intense public debate. The most recent occurrence was in the late 1960s and early 1970s, when social psychology appeared to many to have reached a crisis of confidence (e.g. Elms, 1975; Israel & Tajfel, 1972; Rosnow, 1981; Strickland, Aboud & Gergen, 1976). There were two principal worries about social psychology:

1  It was overly *reductionist* (i.e. by explaining social behaviour mainly in terms of individual psychology it failed to address the essentially social nature of the human experience).
2  It was overly *positivistic* (i.e. it adhered to a model of science that was distorted, inappropriate and misleading).

## Reductionism and levels of explanation

**Reductionism** is the practice of explaining a phenomenon in terms of the language and concepts of a lower level of analysis. Society is explained in terms of groups, groups in terms of interpersonal processes, interpersonal processes in terms of intrapersonal cognitive mechanisms, cognition in terms of neuropsychology, neuropsychology in terms of biology, and so on. A problem of reductionist theorising is that it can leave the original scientific question unanswered. For example, the act of putting one's arm out of the car window to indicate an intention to turn can be explained in terms of muscle contraction, or nerve impulses, or understanding of and adherence to social conventions, and so on. If the **level of explanation** does not match the level of the question, then the question remains, in effect, unanswered. In researching interpersonal relations, to what extent does an explanation in terms of social neuroscience really address interpersonal relations?

Although a degree of reductionism is possibly necessary for theorising, too great a degree is undesirable. Social psychology has been criticised for being inherently reductionist because it tries to explain social behaviour in terms of asocial intrapsychic cognitive and motivational processes (e.g. Moscovici, 1972; Pepitone, 1981; Sampson, 1977; Taylor & Brown, 1979). The recent trends towards social cognitive neuroscience and evolutionary social psychology, explaining behaviour in terms of neural activity and genetic predisposition, can be criticised on the same grounds (cf. Dovidio, Pearson & Orr, 2008). Reflect now on the second focus question.

The problem is most acute when social psychologists try to explain group processes and intergroup relations. By tackling these phenomena exclusively in terms of personality, interpersonal relations or intrapsychic processes, social psychology may leave some of its most important phenomena inadequately explained – for example, prejudice, discrimination, stereotyping, conformity and group solidarity (Billig, 1976; Hogg & Abrams, 1988; Turner & Oakes, 1986).

Doise (1986; Lorenzi-Cioldi & Doise, 1990) has suggested that one way around this problem is to accept the existence of different levels of explanation but to make a special effort to construct theories that formally integrate (Doise uses the French term 'articulate') concepts from different levels (see Box 1.1). This idea has been adopted, to varying degrees,

**Reductionism**
A phenomenon in terms of the language and concepts of a lower level of analysis, usually with a loss of explanatory power.

**Level of analysis (or explanation)**
The types of concepts, mechanisms and language used to explain a phenomenon.

by many social psychologists (see Tajfel, 1984). One of the most successful attempts is social identity theory (e.g. Tajfel & Turner, 1979), as we have noted (see Chapter 11), in which individual cognitive processes are articulated with large-scale social forces to explain group behaviour. Doise's ideas have also been employed to reinterpret group cohesiveness (Hogg, 1992, 1993), attribution theories (Hewstone, 1989) and social representations (e.g. Doise, Clémence & Lorenzi-Cioldi, 1993; Lorenzi-Cioldi and Clémence, 2001). Organisational psychologists have also advocated articulation of levels of analysis – although here the debate is less developed than in social psychology; the issue is one of cross-level research, and very little has actually been done (Wilpert, 1995; but see Haslam, 2004).

## Positivism

**Positivism**
Non-critical acceptance of science as the only way to arrive at true knowledge: science as religion.

**Positivism** is the non-critical acceptance of scientific method as the only way to arrive at true knowledge. Positivism was introduced in the early nineteenth century by the French mathematician and philosopher Auguste Comte and was enormously popular until the end of that century. The character Mr Gradgrind in Charles Dickens's 1854 novel *Hard Times* epitomises positivism: science as a religion.

Social psychology has been criticised for being positivistic (e.g. Gergen, 1973; Henriques et al., 1984; Potter, Stringer & Wetherell, 1984; Shotter, 1984). It is argued that because social psychologists are ultimately studying themselves they cannot achieve the level of objectivity of, say, a chemist studying a compound or a geographer studying a landform. Since complete objectivity is unattainable, scientific methods, particularly experimental ones, are simply not appropriate for social psychology. Social psychology can only masquerade as a science – it cannot be a true science. Critics argue that what social psychologists propose as fundamental causal mechanisms (e.g. categorisation, attribution, cognitive balance, self-concept) are only 'best-guess' concepts that explain some historically and culturally restricted data – data that are subject to unavoidable and intrinsic bias. Critics also feel that by treating humans as objects or clusters of variables that can be manipulated experimentally we are not only cutting ourselves off from a rich reservoir of subjective or introspective data, we are also dehumanising people.

These criticisms have produced some quite radical alternatives to traditional social psychology. Examples include social constructionism (Gergen, 1973), humanistic psychology (Shotter, 1984), ethogenics (Harré, 1979), discourse analysis or discursive psychology (Edwards, 1997; Potter & Wetherell, 1987) and poststructuralist perspectives (Henriques et al., 1984). There are marked differences between these alternatives, but they share a broad emphasis on understanding people as whole human beings who are constructed historically and who try to make sense of themselves and their world. Research methods tend to emphasise in-depth subjective analysis (often called *deconstruction*) of the relatively spontaneous accounts that people give of their thoughts, feelings and actions. Subjectivity is considered a virtue of, rather than an impediment to, good research. More recently, some authors who have noted that discursive psychology is fundamentally incommensurate with 'mainstream' social psychology have taken a position of relative tolerance (e.g. Tuffin, 2005), and have sought avenues of cooperative research (e.g. Rogers, 2003).

However, most mainstream social psychologists respond to the problem of positivism in a less dramatic manner, which does not involve abandoning the scientific method. Instead, they deal with the pitfalls of positivism by being rigorous in the use of appropriate scientific methods of research and theorising (e.g. Campbell, 1957; Jost & Kruglanski, 2002; Kruglanski, 1975; Turner, 1981a). Included in this is an awareness of the need for **operational definitions** of social processes such as aggression, altruism and leadership. Operationalism is a product of positivism and refers to a plea that theoretical terms in science be defined in a manner that renders them susceptible to measurement. As scientists, we should be mindful of our own subjectivity, and should acknowledge and make explicit our biases. Our theories should be sensitive to the pitfalls of reductionism and, where appropriate, articulate different levels of

**Operational definition**
Defines a theoretical term in a way that allows it to be manipulated or measured.

## Research and applications 1.1
Levels of explanation in social psychology

### I Intrapersonal

Analysis of psychological processes to do with individuals' organisation of their experience of the social environment (e.g. research on cognitive balance).

### II Interpersonal and situational

Analysis of interindividual interaction within circumscribed situations. Social positional factors emanating from outside the situation are not considered. The object of study is the dynamics of relations established at a given moment by given individuals in a given situation (e.g. some attribution research, research using game matrices).

### III Positional

Analysis of interindividual interaction in specific situations, but with the role of social position (e.g. status, identity) outside the situation taken into consideration (e.g. some research into power and social identity).

### IV Ideological

Analysis of interindividual interaction that considers the role of general social beliefs, and of social relations between groups (e.g. some research into social identity, social representations and minority influence; studies considering the role of cultural norms and values).

Source: taken from material in Hogg (1992, p. 62) and based on Lorenzi-Cioldi & Doise (1990, p. 73) and Doise (1986, pp. 10–16)

analysis. We should also recognise that experimental participants are real people who do not throw off their past history and become unidimensional 'variables' when they enter the laboratory. On the contrary, culture, history, socialisation and personal motives are all present in the laboratory – experiments are social situations (Tajfel, 1972). Finally, attention should be paid to language, as that is perhaps the most important way in which people represent the world, think, plan action and manipulate the world around them (Chapter 15). Language is also the epitome of a social variable: it is socially constructed and internalised to govern individual social cognition and behaviour.

# Historical context

Social psychology, as we have described it, is not a static science. It has a history, and it is invaluable to consider a science in its proper historical context in order to understand its true nature. Here we give an overview of the history of social psychology. Although ancient forms of social and political philosophy considered such questions as the nature–nurture controversy, the origins of society and the function of the state, it was mostly a speculative exercise and devoid of fact gathering (Hollander, 1967). An empirical approach to the study of social life did not appear until the latter part of the nineteenth century.

## Social psychology in the nineteenth century

### Anglo-European influences

An important precursor to the development of social psychology as an independent discipline was the work of a number of scholars in Germany known as the *folk psychologists*. In 1860, a journal devoted to **Völkerpsychologie** was founded by Steinthal and Lazarus. It

*Völkerpsychologie*
Early precursor of social psychology, as the study of the collective mind, in Germany in the mid- to late nineteenth century.

contained both theoretical and factual articles. In contrast to general psychology (elaborated later by Wundt) which dealt with the study of the individual mind, folk psychology, which was influenced by the philosopher Hegel, dealt with the study of the *collective* mind. This concept of collective mind was interpreted in conflicting ways by Steinthal and Lazarus, meaning on the one hand a societal way of thinking within the individual and on the other a form of super-mentality that could enfold a whole group of people.

This concept, of a *group mind*, became, in the 1890s and early 1900s, a dominant account of social behaviour. An extreme example of it can be found in the work of the French writer Gustav LeBon (1896/1908). LeBon argued that crowds often behave badly because the behaviour of the individual becomes subject to the control of the *group mind*. Likewise, the English psychologist William McDougall (1920) subscribed to the group mind explanation when he dealt with collective behaviour, devoting an entire book to the topic. Much later, Asch (1951) observed that the basic issue that such writers wanted to deal with has not gone away: that to understand the complexities of an individual's behaviour requires us to view the person in the context of group relations.

### Early texts

At the turn of the century there were two texts dealing with social psychology, by Bunge (1903) and Orano (1901). Because they were not in English, they received little attention in Britain and the United States. Even earlier, an American, Baldwin (1897), touched on social psychology in a work that dealt mainly with the social and moral development of the child. A book by the French sociologist Gabriel Tarde (1898) had clear implications for the kind of data and the level of explanation that social psychology should adopt. He adopted a bottom-up approach, which was offered in debate with Emile Durkheim. Whereas Durkheim argued that the way people behave is determined by social laws that are fashioned by society, Tarde proposed that a science of social behaviour must derive from laws that deal with the individual case. His conception of social psychology is closer in flavour to most current American thinking than any of the other early texts (Clark, 1969).

The two early texts that caught the attention of the English-speaking world were written by McDougall (1908) and the American sociologist Ross (1908). Neither looks much like a modern social psychology text, but we need to remember that living scientific disciplines continue to be redefined. The central topics of McDougall's book, for example, were the principal instincts, the primary emotions, the nature of sentiments, moral conduct, volition, religious conceptions and the structure of character. Compare these with the chapter topics of the present textbook.

## The rise of experimentation

An influential textbook by Floyd Allport (1924) provided an agenda for social psychology that was quickly and enduringly followed by many teachers in psychology departments for years to come. Following the manifesto for psychology as a whole laid out by the behaviourist John Watson (1913), Allport argued strongly that social psychology would flourish only if it became an experimental science. A little later, Murphy and Murphy (1931/1937) felt justified in producing a book actually entitled *Experimental social psychology*. Not all of the studies reviewed were true experiments, but the authors' intentions for the discipline were clear.

Although the earlier texts had not shown it, the closing decade of the nineteenth century had set a scene in which social psychology would be inextricably entwined with the broader discipline of general psychology. As such, social psychology's subsequent development reflects the way in which psychology was defined and taught in university departments of psychology, particularly in the United States, which rapidly replaced Germany as the leading country for psychological research. Just as the psychological laboratory at Leipzig founded by Wilhelm Wundt in 1879 had provided an experimental basis for psychology in Germany, the laboratories set up at American universities did likewise in the United States. In the period 1890–1910, the growth of laboratories devoted to psychological research was rapid (Ruckmick, 1912). Thirty-one American universities established experimental facilities in those twenty years. The subject taught in these departments was clearly defined as an experimental science. In the United States, therefore, it is not surprising that social psychology should quite early on view the **experimental method** as a touchstone. By the time Allport produced his 1924 text, this trend was well established.

**Experimental method**
Intentional manipulation of independent variables in order to investigate effects on one or more dependent variables.

## When was social psychology's first experiment?

This is a natural question to ask, but the answer is clouded. One of the oldest psychological laboratories was at Indiana University. It was here that Norman Triplett (1898) conducted a study that some modern textbooks have cited as the first experiment in social psychology (e.g. Lippa, 1990; Penrod, 1983; Sears, Peplau & Taylor, 1991) and have listed as an experiment on social facilitation (e.g. Baron & Byrne, 1994; Brigham, 1991; Deaux & Wrightsman, 1988; see also Chapter 8). Gordon Allport (1954a) implied that what Wundt did in Leipzig for experimental psychology Triplett did in Indiana for a scientific social psychology. A different picture emerges in the literature of that time.

Norman Triplett was a mature teacher who returned to postgraduate study to work on his master's thesis, published in 1898. His supervisors were two experimental psychologists

**Social facilitation**
These pictures represent an idea that caught Triplett's (1898) attention. At the Athens Olympics, Sarah Ulmer won a gold medal in the Women's Pursuit event. Would Sarah ride faster when competing alone or with others? Why?

and the research was conducted in a laboratory that was one of the very best in the world. His interest had been stimulated by popular wisdom that racing cyclists go faster when racing or being paced, than when riding alone. Cycling as an activity had increased dramatically in popularity in the 1890s and had spectacular press coverage. Triplett listed possible explanations for superior performance by cyclists who were racing or being paced:

- The pacer in front provided suction that pulled the following rider along, helping to conserve energy; or else the front rider provided shelter from the wind.
- A popular 'brain worry' theory predicted that solitary cyclists did poorly because they worried about whether they were going fast enough. This exhausted their brain and muscles, numbing them and inhibiting motor performance.
- Friends usually rode as pacers and no doubt encouraged the cyclists to keep up their spirits.
- In a race, a follower might be hypnotised by the wheels in front and so rode automatically, leaving more energy for a later, controlled burst.
- A dynamogenic theory – Triplett's favourite – proposed that the presence of another person racing aroused a 'competitive instinct' that released 'nervous energy', similar to the modern idea of arousal. The sight of movement in another suggested more speed, inspired greater effort, and released a level of nervous energy that an isolated rider cannot achieve alone. The energy of the cyclist's movement was in proportion to the idea of that movement.

In the most famous of Triplett's experiments, schoolchildren worked in two conditions, alone and in pairs. They worked with two fishing reels that turned silk bands around a drum. Each reel was connected by a loop of cord to a pulley two metres away, and a small flag was attached to each cord. To complete one trial, the flag had to travel four times around the pulley. Some children were slower and others faster in competition, while others were little affected. The faster ones showed the effects of both 'the arousal of their competitive instincts and the idea of a faster movement' (Triplett, 1898, p. 526). The slower ones were overstimulated and 'going to pieces' – a rather modern turn of phrase!

In drawing on the *dynamogenic theory* of his day, Triplett focused on ideo-motor responses – that is, one competitor's bodily movements acted as a stimulus for the other competitor. Essentially, Triplett highlighted *non-social* cues to illustrate the idea of movement being used as a cue by his participants.

The leading journals in the decade after Triplett's study scarcely referred to it. It was catalogued in general sources, but not under any headings with a 'social' connotation. Clearly, Triplett was neither a social psychologist nor considered to be one. If we adopt a revisionist view of history, then the spirit of his experiment emerges as a precursor to the theme of social facilitation research. The search for a founding figure, or a first idea, is not a new phenomenon in the history of science or, indeed, in the history of civilisation. The Triplett study has the trappings of an origin myth. There were other, even earlier, studies that might just as easily be called the 'first' in social psychology (Burnham, 1910; Haines & Vaughan, 1979). Vaughan and Guerin (1997) point out that sports psychologists have claimed Triplett as one of their own.

## Later influences

**Behaviourism**
An emphasis on explaining observable behaviour in terms of reinforcement schedules.

Social psychology's development after the early impact of **behaviourism** was redirected by a number of other important developments, some of which came from beyond mainstream psychology.

## Attitude scaling

One of these developments was the refinement of several methods for constructing scales to measure attitudes (Bogardus, 1925; Likert, 1932; Thurstone, 1928; see Chapter 5), two of which were published in sociology journals. Sociology has often championed approaches to social psychology that have been critical of an individual-behaviour level of analysis. Thomas and Znaniecki (1918), for example, defined social psychology as the scientific study of attitudes rather than of social behaviour.

## Studies of the social group

Central to social psychology is an abiding interest in the structure and function of the social group (see Chapters 8, 9 and 11). Kurt Lewin, considered the 'father' of experimental social psychology, put much of his energy into the study of group processes (Marrow, 1969). For example, one of Lewin's imaginative studies was an experiment on the effect of leadership style on small-group behaviour (Lewin, Lippitt & White, 1939; see also Chapter 9), and by 1945 he had founded a research centre devoted to the study of group dynamics (which still exists, in a different guise and now at the University of Michigan).

Another important thread in research on the social group came from industrial psychology. A key study carried out in a factory setting showed that work productivity can be more heavily influenced by the psychological properties of the work group and the degree of interest that management shows in its workers (Roethlisberger & Dickson, 1939) than by mere physical working conditions. A significant outcome of research of this kind was consolidation of an approach to social psychology in which theory and application can develop together. Indeed, Lewin is often quoted as saying 'there is nothing so practical as a good theory'. He was a passionate advocate of what he called 'full cycle' research, where symbiosis exists between basic and applied research.

## Popular textbooks

The 1930s marked several quite different themes that had a striking impact on the continuing development of the discipline. Murchison (1935) produced the first handbook,

**Role transition**
Birthdays are landmarks that can mark important changes in your role in society as you move into an older group. They can also be great fun!

a weighty tome that proclaimed that here was a field to be taken seriously. A later, expanded edition of the Murphy and Murphy text (1931/1937) appeared that summarised the findings of more than 1,000 studies, although it was used mainly as a reference work. Perhaps the most widely used textbook of this period was written by LaPiere and Farnsworth (1936). Another by Klineberg (1940) was also popular; it featured contributions from cultural anthropology and emphasised the crucial role played by culture in the development of a person's personality. Just after the Second World War, Krech and Crutchfield (1948) published an important text that emphasised a *phenomenological approach* to social psychology: that is, an approach focusing on the way in which people actually experience the world and account for their experiences.

In the 1950s and thereafter, the number of textbooks appearing on the bookshelves increased exponentially. Most have been published in the United States, with a heavy reliance on both American data and American theory.

### Famous experiments

For different reasons, several experiments stand out over the years that have fascinated teachers and students alike. The following have had an impact beyond the immediate discipline, reaching out to the wider perspective of general psychology, and some out further, to other disciplines. We will not go into detail about these studies here, as they are described in later chapters.

Muzafer Sherif (1935) conducted an experiment on *norm formation,* which caught the attention of psychologists eager to pinpoint what could be 'social' about social psychology (Chapter 7). Solomon Asch (1951) demonstrated the dramatic effect that *group pressure* can have in persuading an individual to conform (Chapter 7). Muzafer and Carolyn Sherif (Sherif & Sherif, 1953) examined the role that competition for resources can have on intergroup conflict (Chapter 11). Leon Festinger (1957) used his theory of *cognitive dissonance* to show that a smaller reward can change attitudes more than can a larger reward (Festinger & Carlsmith, 1959), a finding that annoyed the orthodox reinforcement theorists of the time (Chapters 5 and 6). Stanley Milgram's (1963) study of *destructive obedience* highlighted the dilemma facing a person ordered by an authority figure to perform an immoral act, a study that unwittingly became one focus of critics who questioned the future of the experimental method in social psychology (Chapter 7). Henri Tajfel (1970; Tajfel, Billig, Bundy & Flament, 1971) conducted a watershed experiment to show that merely being categorised into groups was sufficient to generate *intergroup discrimination* (Chapter 11).

Finally, Zimbardo (1971) set up a simulated prison in the basement of the Stanford University psychology department to study *deindividuation* and the reality of and extremity of *roles* (Chapter 8). This study has caught the imagination of a reality-TV oriented society; to the extent that two prominent British social psychologists, Alex Haslam and Stephen Reicher, were commissioned as consultants on a 2002 BBC TV programme re-running the experiment (Reicher & Haslam, 2006).

### Famous programmes

One way of viewing the network within which a discipline develops is to ask the question 'Who's who?' and then 'Who influenced whom?' Looked at in this way, the group-centred research of the charismatic Lewin (Marrow, 1969) had a remarkable impact on other social psychologists in the United States. One of his students was Leon Festinger, and one of Festinger's students was Stanley Schachter. The latter's work on the cognitive labelling of emotion is a derivative of Festinger's notion of social comparison (i.e. the way in which individuals use other people as a basis for assessing their own thoughts, feelings and behaviour).

There have been other groups of researchers whose impact is more obvious by the nature of the concepts emerging from their programmes. There were two influential groups whose research concerned questions raised and made urgent by events during and surrounding the Second World War. One group studied the *authoritarian personality* (Adorno, Frenkel-Brunswik, Levinson & Sanford, 1950). Inspired by the possibility that an explanation for the rise of German autocracy resided in the personality and child-rearing practices of a nation, the researchers embarked on an ambitious cross-cultural study of authoritarianism in the United States (Chapter 10). Another group studied how to change people's attitudes. The Yale *attitude change* programme, led by Carl Hovland, was designed to uncover the theory and techniques of propaganda (Hovland, Janis & Kelley, 1953; see also Chapter 6).

## Later developments

Thibaut and Kelley (1959) developed an influential approach to the study of interpersonal relationships, based on an economic model of *social exchange* (Chapter 14), which continued to stimulate theories into the 1980s. Likewise, Deutsch's (Deutsch & Krauss, 1960) application of exchange theory to interpersonal bargaining subsequently attracted enormous research interest and activity form psychologists. Once again, the long arm of Lewin is clearly evident – all of these innovators (Thibaut, Kelley, Deutsch) were his students.

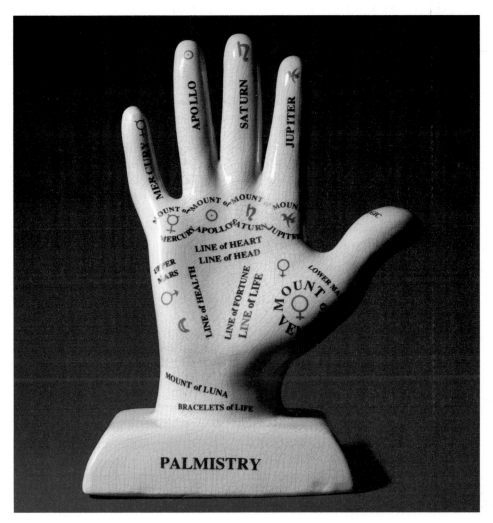

**Attribution**

People try to make sense of their lives in many different ways. We can try palmistry, or more mundanely examine the immediate causes of our experiences

The modern period has been dominated by cognitive approaches. *Attribution theory* was set on its path by Ned Jones (Jones & Davis, 1965), who focused attention on the ordinary person's ideas about causality (Chapter 3). Darley and Latané (1968) employed an innovative cognitive model to research *prosocial behaviour* by throwing light on the way in which people interpret an emergency and sometimes fail to help a victim (Chapter 13).

Following earlier work by Heider (1946) and Asch (1946) in a field loosely described as social perception, a major restructuring reconfigured this field into modern *social cognition* (see Chapter 2). Several researchers made major contributions to this development, including Mischel (Cantor & Mischel, 1977), who explored the way that perceived behaviour traits can function as prototypes, and Nisbett and Ross (1980), who explored the role of cognitive heuristics (mental short-cuts) in social thinking.

## The journals

Traditional journals that were important up to the 1950s were the *Journal of Abnormal and Social Psychology* and the *Journal of Personality*. A sociological journal, *Sociometry,* also catered for social psychological work.

From the 1960s there was increased demand for outlets. This reflected not only the increase in the number of actively researching social psychologists around the world but also the demand for some regional representation. The *Journal of Abnormal and Social Psychology* divided into two, one part devoted to abnormal psychology and the other titled the *Journal of Personality and Social Psychology* (founded in 1965). *Sociometry* was re-titled *Social Psychology Quarterly* (1979) to reflect more accurately its heavy social psychological content. Anglo-European interests were represented by the *British Journal of Social and Clinical Psychology* (1963) (which split in about 1980 to spin off the *British Journal of Social Psychology*), and the *European Journal of Social Psychology* (1971). Scope for a second, American, journal dedicated to experimental research was realised by the *Journal of Experimental Social Psychology* (1965), and then in 1975 a third major American social psychology journal was launched, *Personality and Social Psychology Bulletin.* Other journals devoted to the area include *Journal of Applied Social Psychology* (1971), *Social Cognition* (1982) and *Journal of Social and Personal Relationships* (1984). In the last fifteen years there has been an explosion of other key journals, including *Personality and Social Psychology Review, Group Processes and Intergroup Relations, Group Dynamics, Social Cognition* and *Self and Identity.*

From the point of view of articles published, therefore, there was huge growth of interest in the subject during the decade bridging the 1960s and the 1970s.

# Social psychology in Europe

Although, as our historical overview has shown, the beginnings of social psychology, and indeed psychology as a whole, were in Europe, America quickly assumed leadership in terms not only of concepts but also of journals, books and organisations. One important reason for this shift in hegemony was the rise of fascism in Europe in the late 1930s. For instance, in Germany in 1933 Jewish professors were dismissed from the universities, and from then until the end of the Second World War the names of Jewish authors were expunged from university textbooks in the name of National Socialism and to promulgate Aryan doctrine (Baumgarten-Tramer, 1948). This led, during the immediate prewar period, to a massive exodus of European social psychologists and other scholars to the United States. By 1945, social psychology in Europe had been significantly weakened, particularly when compared with the rapid development of the field in the United States. By 1945, very little European social psychology remained.

From 1945 into the 1950s the United States provided resources (e.g. money and academic links) to (re-)establish centres of European social psychology. Although partly a scientific gesture, this was also part of a wider Cold War strategy to provide an intellectual environment in Western Europe to combat the potential encroachment of communism. These centres were linked to the United States rather than to one another. In fact, there were very few links among European social psychologists, who were often unaware of one another and who tended instead to have lines of communication with American universities. Europe, including Britain, was largely an outpost of American social psychology. In the period from 1950 to the end of the 1960s, social psychology in Britain was largely based on American ideas. Likewise in the Netherlands, Germany, France and Belgium, most work was influenced by American thinking (Argyle, 1980).

Gradually, however, European social psychologists became more conscious of the hegemony of American ideas and of the intellectual, cultural and historical differences between Europe and America. For instance, at that time the recent European experience was of war and conflict, while America's last major conflict within its own borders was its Civil War in the 1860s. Not surprisingly, Europeans considered themselves to be more concerned with intergroup relations and groups, while Americans were perhaps more interested in interpersonal relations and individuals. Europeans pushed for a more *social* social psychology. There was a clear need for better communication channels among European scholars and some degree of intellectual and organisational independence from the United States.

The first step along this road was initiated in the early 1950s by Eric Rinde in Norway, who, in collaboration with the American David Krech, brought together several American and more than thirty European social psychologists to collaborate on a cross-national study of threat and rejection. The wider goal was to encourage international collaboration and to increase training facilities for social scientists in Europe. Building on this project, the next step was a *European conference on experimental social psychology* organised by John Lanzetta and Luigi Petrullo, both from the United States, held in Sorrento in 1963. Among the twenty-eight participants were five Americans and twenty-one Europeans from eight countries. The organising committee (Mulder, Pages, Tajfel, Rommetveit and Thibaut) was also charged with preparing a proposal for the development of experimental social psychology in Europe.

It was decided to hold a second European conference and a summer school (held later in Leuven in 1967). The conference was held in Frascati in 1964, and it elected a 'European planning committee' (G. Jahoda, Moscovici, Mulder, Nuttin and Tajfel) to explore further a formal structure for European social psychology. A structure was approved at the third European conference, held in 1966 at Royaumont near Paris: thus was formally born the *European Association of Experimental Social Psychology* (EAESP). Moscovici was the foundation president, and there were approximately forty-four members. EAESP, which was renamed the *European Association of Social Psychology* (EASP) in 2008 has been the enormously successful focus for the development of European social psychology for almost fifty years, and by January 2010 had over 1,140 members. It is a dynamic and integrative force for social psychology that for many years now has reached outside Europe with strong links with the leading international social psychology organisations (*Society for Personality and Social Psychology, Society for Experimental Social Psychology, Society for the Psychological Study of Social Issues*) – its last triennial conference, held in Opatija in June 2008 (the previous five conferences were held in Lisbon, Gmunden, Oxford, San Sebastián, and Würzburg), had almost 1000 delegates from Europe, North America and the rest of the world.

European journals and textbooks have provided additional focus for European social psychology. The *European Journal of Social Psychology* was launched in 1971 and is now generally considered one of the most prestigious social psychology journals in the world. In 1990, another European periodical was launched: the *European Review of Social Psychology*. Textbooks used in Europe have largely been American or, more recently, European adaptations of American books. But there have been notable European texts, probably beginning with Moscovici's *Introduction à la psychologie sociale* (1973), followed by Tajfel and Fraser's *Introducing social psychology* (1978) and then Moscovici's *Psychologie sociale* (1984). Aside of course from our own, the most recent other European text is Hewstone, Stroebe and Jonas's *Introduction to social psychology*, which is now in its fourth edition (2008).

Since the early 1970s, then, European social psychology has undergone a powerful renaissance (Doise, 1982; Jaspars, 1980, 1986). Initially, it self-consciously set itself up in opposition to American social psychology and adopted an explicitly critical stance. However, since the late 1980s European social psychology, although not discarding its critical orientation, has attained substantial self-confidence and international recognition. Its impact on American social psychology, and thus on international perspectives, is significant and acknowledged (e.g. Hogg & Abrams, 1999). Moreland, Hogg and Hains (1994) document how a recent upsurge in research into group processes (as evidenced from publication trends over the past twenty years in the three major American social psychology journals) was almost exclusively due to European research and perspectives. It is, perhaps, through work on social representations (Chapter 3), social identity and intergroup behaviour (Chapter 11) and minority influence (Chapter 7) that Europe has had its most visible and significant international impact. Now revisit the third focus question.

Europe is a continent of many languages and a historical diversity of national emphases on different aspects of social psychology: for example, social representations in France, political psychology and small-group processes in Germany, social justice research and social cognition in the Netherlands, social development of cognition in French-speaking Switzerland, goal-oriented action in German-speaking Switzerland, applied and social constructionist approaches in Scandinavia, and intergroup processes and discourse analysis in Britain. A great deal of research is published in national social psychology journals. However, in recognition of the fact that English is now the global language of science, European social psychologists publish in English so that their ideas might have the greatest impact both internationally and within Europe: most major European journals, series and texts publish in English.

Historically, there are two figures that have particularly shaped European social psychology: Henri Tajfel and Serge Moscovici. Tajfel (1974), at the University of Bristol, revolutionised how we think about intergroup relations. His *social identity theory* focused on how a person's identity is grounded in belonging to a group, and how such *social* identity shapes intergroup behaviour. It questioned Sherif's argument that an objective clash of interests was the necessary ingredient for intergroup conflict (Chapter 11). Moscovici (1961), at the Maison des Sciences de l'Homme in Paris, resuscitated an interest in the work of the nineteenth-century sociologist Durkheim with his idea of social representations (Chapter 3). In addition, he initiated a radical new interpretation of conformity processes – developing an entirely new focus on how minorities can influence majorities and thus bring about social change (Chapter 7).

## About this book

We have written this introductory text, now in its sixth edition, to reflect contemporary European social psychology: a social psychology that smoothly integrates American and European research but with a distinct emphasis that is framed by European, not American, intellectual and sociohistorical priorities. Students of social psychology in Britain and Europe tend to use a mixture of American and European texts. American texts are comprehensive, detailed and well produced, but are pitched too low for British and European universities, do not cover European topics well or at all, and quite naturally are grounded in the day-to-day cultural experiences of Americans. European texts, which are generally edited collections of chapters by different authors, address European priorities but tend to be idiosyncratic, uneven and less well produced, and incomplete in their coverage of social psychology. Our text satisfies the need for a single comprehensive introduction to social psychology for British and European students of social psychology.

Our aim has been to write an introduction to social psychology for undergraduate university students of psychology. Its language caters to intelligent adults. However, since it is an *introduction* we pay careful attention to accessibility of specialist language (i.e. scientific or social psychological jargon). It is intended to be a comprehensive introduction to mainstream social psychology, with no intentional omissions. We cover classic and contemporary theories and research, generally adopting a historical perspective that most accurately reflects the unfolding of scientific inquiry. The degree of detail and scope of coverage are determined by the scope and intensity of undergraduate social psychology courses in Britain and Europe. We have tried to write a text that combines the most important and enduring features of European and American social psychology. As such, this can be considered an international text, but one that specifically caters for the British and European intellectual, cultural and educational context.

Many social psychology texts separate basic theory and research from applied theory and research, generally by exiling to the end of the book 'applied' chapters that largely address health, organisations, justice or gender. Much like Kurt Lewin's view that there is nothing so practical as a good theory, our philosophy is that basic and applied research and theory are intertwined or best treated as intertwined: they are naturally interdependent. Thus, applied topics are interwoven with basic theory and research. Currently, some significant areas of application of social psychology include human development (e.g. Bennett & Sani, 2004; Durkin, 1995), health (e.g. Rothman & Salovey, 2007; Taylor, 2003), gender (e.g. Eagly, Beall & Sternberg, 2005), organisations (e.g. Haslam, 2004; Thompson & Pozner, 2007), law and criminal justice (e.g. Kovera & Borgida, 2010; Tyler & Jost, 2007), political behaviour (e.g. Krosnick, Visser & Harder, 2010; Tetlock, 2007) and culture (e.g. Heine, 2010; Smith, Bond & Kağitçibaşi, 2006). The latter, culture, is now an integral part of contemporary social psychology (see Chapter 16); and language and communication (e.g., Holtgraves, 2010), which is central to social psychology but is often treated as an application, has its own chapter (Chapter 15).

The book is structured so that Chapters 2 to 5 deal with what goes on in people's head – cognitive processes and cognitive representations, including how we conceive of ourselves and how our attitudes are structured. Chapter 6 continues the attitude theme but focuses on how attitudes change and how people are persuaded. This leads directly into Chapter 7, which discusses more broadly how people influence one another. Because groups play a key role in social influence, Chapter 7 flows logically into Chapters 8 and 9, which deal with group processes. Chapters 10 and 11 broaden the discussion of groups to consider what happens between groups – prejudice, discrimination, conflict and intergroup behaviour. The sad fact that intergroup behaviour so often involves conflict invites a discussion of human aggression, which is dealt with in Chapter 12.

Lest we become disillusioned with our species, Chapter 13 discusses how people can be altruistic and can engage in selfless prosocial acts of kindness and support. Continuing the general emphasis on more positive aspects of human behaviour, Chapter 14 deals with interpersonal relations, including attraction, friendship and love, but also with breakdowns in relationships. At the core of interpersonal interaction lies communication, of which spoken language is the richest form: Chapter 15 explores language and communication. Chapter 16 discusses the cultural context of social behaviour – an exploration of cultural differences, cross-cultural universals, and the significance of culture in contemporary multicultural society.

Each chapter is self-contained, although integrated into the general logic of the entire text. There are plentiful cross-references to other chapters, and at the end of each chapter are references to further, more detailed coverage of topics covered by the chapter. We also suggest classic and contemporary literature, films and TV programmes that deal with subject matter that is relevant to the chapter topic.

Many of the studies referred to in this book can be found in the social psychology journals that we have already noted in the historical section – check new issues of these journals to learn about up-to-date research. In addition, there are three social psychology journals that are dedicated to scholarly state-of-the-art summaries and reviews of topics in social psychology: *Advances in Experimental Social Psychology, Personality and Social Psychology Review* and *European Review of Social Psychology*. Topics in social psychology are also covered in general psychology theory and review journals such as *Annual Review of Psychology, Psychological Bulletin,* and *Psychological Review*.

For a short general introduction to social psychology, see Hogg's (2000a) chapter in Pawlik and Rosenzweig's (2000) *International Handbook of Psychology*. For a stripped-down simple introductory European social psychology text that focuses in on only the very essentials of the subject see Hogg and Vaughan's (2010) *Essentials of Social Psychology*. In contrast, the most authoritative and detailed sources of information about social psychology are undoubtably the current handbooks of social psychology, of which there are four: (1) Fiske, Gilbert and Lindzey's (2010) *Handbook of Social Psychology,* which is currently in its fifth edition; (2) Hogg and Cooper's (2007) *The SAGE Handbook of Social Psychology: Concise Student Edition*; (3) Kruglanski and Higgins's (2007) *Social Psychology: Handbook of Basic Principles,* which is in its second edition; and (4) Hewstone and Brewer's four-volume *Blackwell Handbook of Social Psychology,* each volume of which is a stand-alone book with a different pair of editors: *Intraindividual Processes* by Tesser and Schwartz (2001), *Interpersonal Processes* by Fletcher and Clark (2001), *Group Processes* by Hogg and Tindale (2001) and *Intergroup Processes* by Brown and Gaertner (2001).

A wonderful source of shorter overview pieces is Baumeister and Vohs's (2007) two-volume 1020-page *Encyclopedia of Social Psychology* – there are more than 550 entries written by an equal number of the leading social psychologists from around the world. Two other similar but topic-specific encyclopedias are Reis and Sprecher's (2009) *Encyclopedia of Human Relationships,* and Levine and Hogg's (2010) *Encyclopedia of Group Processes and Intergroup Relations*. Finally, Hogg's (2003b) *SAGE Benchmarks in Psychology: Social Psychology* is a four-volume edited and annotated collection of almost 80 benchmark research articles in social psychology – it contains many of the discipline's most impactful classic and recent works. The volumes are divided into sections with short introductions.

## Summary

- Social psychology can be defined as the scientific investigation of how the thoughts, feelings and behaviour of individuals are influenced by the actual, imagined or implied presence of others. Although social psychology can also be described in terms of what it studies, it is more useful to describe it as a way of looking at human behaviour.

- Social psychology is a science. It employs the scientific method to study social behaviour. Although this involves a whole range of empirical methods to collect data to test hypotheses and construct theories, experimentation is usually the preferred method as it is the best way to reveal causal processes. Nevertheless, methods are matched to research questions, and methodological pluralism is highly valued.

- Social psychological data are usually transformed into numbers, which are analysed by a range of formal numerical procedures – that is, statistics. Statistics allow conclusions to be drawn about whether a research observation is a true effect or some chance event.

- Social psychology is enlivened by fierce and invigorating debates about the ethics of research methods, the appropriate research methods for an understanding of social behaviour, the validity and power of social psychology theories, and the type of theories that are properly social psychological.

- Although having origins in nineteenth-century German folk psychology and French crowd psychology, modern social psychology really began in the United States in the 1920s with the adoption of the experimental method. In the 1940s, Kurt Lewin provided significant impetus to social psychology, and the discipline has grown exponentially ever since.

- Despite its European origins, social psychology quickly became dominated by the United States – a process greatly accelerated by the rise of fascism in Europe during the 1930s. However, since the late 1960s there has been a rapid and sustained renaissance of European social psychology, driven by distinctively European intellectual and sociohistorical priorities to develop a more *social* social psychology with a greater emphasis on collective phenomena and group levels of analysis. European social psychology is now a dynamic and rapidly growing discipline that is an equal but complementary partner to the United States in social psychological research.

## Literature, film and TV

### Das Experiment

This 2001 Oliver Hirschbiegel film, in German with English subtitles, starts with a fairly accurate treatment of Zimbardo's Stanford prison experiment. It engages with ethical issues associated with the research, but deteriorates rapidly into a dramatisation that would do Hollywood proud. This is a good example of how the popular media can distort science and scientific issues and debates. A more recent 2008 film, again German, that builds on Zimbardo and shows how science can go wrong, is *Die Welle* (*The Wave*). A schoolteacher's attempt to demonstrate to his class what life is like under a dictatorship spins horribly out of control as the class takes on a life of its own.

### The Double Helix

1968 book by James Watson. It is an account of how Francis Crick and James Watson identified the structure of DNA, for which they won the Nobel Prize. The book is readable, engrossing and even thrilling. It shows how science is conducted – the rivalries, the squabbles, the competition, set against the backdrop of great minds and great discoveries. It captures the excitement of doing science.

### Bad Science

A weekly column in *The Guardian* in which Ben Goldacre skewers those who distort and misrepresent science for the sake of spin, promotion or a headline. There is also a 2009 book by Ben Goldacre entitled *Bad Science,* published by Fourth Estate.

### Lord of the Flies

William Golding's (1954) classic novel about the disintegration of civilised social norms among a group of boys marooned on an island. A powerful portrayal of a whole range of social psychological phenomena, including leadership, intergroup conflict, norms and cultures, conformity, deviance, aggression and so forth. A very social psychological book.

### War and Peace

Leo Tolstoy's (1869) masterpiece on the impact of society and social history on people's lives. It does a wonderful job of showing how macro- and micro-levels of analysis influence one another, but cannot be resolved into one another. A wonderful literary work of social psychology – how people's day-to-day lives are located at the intersection of powerful interpersonal, group and intergroup processes. Other classic novels of Leo Tolstoy, Emile Zola, Charles Dickens and George Eliot accomplish much the same social psychological analysis.

### Reality TV

At the opposite end of the spectrum from *War and Peace,* is reality TV (e.g. *Big Brother, I'm a Celebrity, Get Me Out of Here*), which is also, ultimately, all about social psychology – human interaction in groups, interpersonal relations and so forth.

## Guided questions

**1**  What do social psychologists study? Can you give some examples of interdisciplinary research?

**2**  Sometimes experiments are used in social psychological research. Why?

**3**  What do you understand by levels of explanation in social psychology? What is meant by reductionism?

**4**  If you or your lecturer were to undertake research in social psychology you would need to gain ethical approval. Why is this, and what criteria would be required?

5  If the shock level 'administered' in Milgram's obedience study had been 150 volts instead of the maximum 450 volts, would this have made the experiment more ethical? Watch the video illustrating this pivotal research in Chapter 1 of MyPsychLab at **www.mypsychlab.co.uk** (watch *Milgram's obedience study*).

## Learn more

Allport, G. W. (1954). The historical background of modern social psychology. In G. Lindzey (ed.), *Handbook of social psychology* (Vol. 1, pp. 3–56). Reading, MA: Addison-Wesley. Classic and often-cited account of the history of social psychology, covering the period up to the 1950s.

Aronson, E., Ellsworth, P. C., Carlsmith, J. M., & Gonzales, M. H. (1990). *Methods of research in social psychology* (2nd ed.). New York: McGraw-Hill. Detailed, well-written and now classic coverage of research methods in social psychology.

Crano, W. D., & Brewer, M. B. (2002). *Principles and methods of social research* (2nd ed.). Mahwah, NJ: Erlbaum. A detailed but very readable overview of research methods in social psychology.

Denzin, N. K., & Lincoln, Y. S. (eds) (2005). *The SAGE handbook of qualitative research* (3rd ed.). Thousand Oaks, CA: SAGE. This academic bestseller is considered the gold standard for qualitative research methods.

Ellsworth, P. C., & Gonzales, R. (2007). Questions and comparisons: Methods of research in social psychology. In M. A. Hogg & J. Cooper (eds), *The SAGE handbook of social psychology: Concise student edition* (pp. 24–42). London: SAGE. A concise and readable overview of how one moves from research question to research itself in social psychology, and how one makes choices about methods.

Farr, R. M. (1996). *The roots of modern social psychology: 1872-1954*. Oxford, UK: Blackwell. A very scholarly and provocative discussion of the intellectual roots of modern social psychology. Farr is a renowned historical commentator on social psychology.

Goethals, G. R. (2007). A century of social psychology: Individuals, ideas, and investigations. In M. A. Hogg & J. Cooper (eds), *The SAGE handbook of social psychology* (pp. 3–23). London: SAGE. A very readable, comprehensive and inclusive coverage of the history of social psychology.

Howell, D. C. (2007). *Statistical methods for psychology* (6th ed.). Belmont, CA: Duxbury. Highly respected and often-used basic introduction to psychological statistics. With the usual equations and formulae that we all love so much – it is also easy to read.

Jones, E. E. (1998). Major developments in five decades of social psychology. In D. T. Gilbert, S. T. Fiske, & G. Lindzey (eds), *The handbook of social psychology* (4th ed., Vol. 1, pp. 3–57). Boston, MA: McGraw-Hill. This treatment overlaps with and moves on from Allport's (1954a) treatment, covering the period from 1935 to 1985. In addition to classical developments, it also covers the growth of research on social comparison, cognitive dissonance, attitude change, conformity, person perception and attribution.

Rosnow, R. L., & Rosenthal, R. (1997). *People studying people: Artifacts and ethics in behavioral research*. New York: Freeman. An introduction to the major biases that can distort research on human behaviour. There is also coverage of ethical issues.

Ross, L., Lepper, M., & Ward, A. (2010). History of social psychology: Insights, challenges, and contributions to theory and application. In S. T. Fiske, D. T. Gilbert, & G. Lindzey (eds), *Handbook of social psychology* (5th ed., Vol. 1, pp. 3–50). New York: Wiley. The most recent overview and account of the history of social psychology.

Sansone, C., Morf, C. C., & Panter, A. T. (eds) (2004). *The SAGE handbook of methods in social psychology*. Thousand Oaks, CA: SAGE. At over 500 pages and 22 chapters this is a comprehensive coverage of quantitative and qualitative research methods in social psychology, including discussion of research ethics, programme development, cultural sensitivities, and doing interdisciplinary and applied research.

Tabachnik, B. G., & Fidell, L. S. (1989). *Using multivariate statistics* (2nd ed.). New York: HarperCollins. The acknowledged 'bible' for doing, interpreting and reporting multivariate statistics in psychology.

Van Lange, P. A. M., Kruglanski, A. W., & Higgins, E. T. (eds) (2010). *Handbook of theories of social psychology*. Thousand Oaks, CA: SAGE. All the major theories in social psychology are here, described clearly and concisely, in a completely up-to-date form by experts in the theory or by the theorists themselves.

 Refresh your understanding, assess your progress and go further with interactive summaries, questions, podcasts and much more at **www.mypsychlab.co.uk**

## This chapter discusses

- How we cognitively process social information
- How we form impressions of other people
- The role of categorisation and social schemas
- Storing and recalling information about people
- How social inference is affected by biases and errors
- Cognitive short-cuts or heuristics
- Feelings and emotions

## Focus questions

1. You have just been interviewed for a job. Ms Jones in the human resources department has decided that you are intelligent, sincere and helpful. However, you did not laugh readily at one of her jokes – she may suspect you don't have a sense of humour! How would she form an overall impression of you?

2. John's hair is multi-coloured and the colours change every couple of weeks. Would others spot him immediately at a student–staff meeting in your psychology department? What about at a board meeting of your capital city's largest accountancy firm?

3. Aaron comes to mind rather differently for Julie and Rosa. Julie remembers him mostly when she thinks of the various lawyers whom she knows. Rosa thinks about his quirky smile and his knowledge of best-selling novels. Why might their memories differ in these ways?

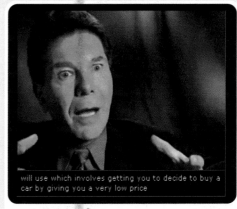

will use which involves getting you to decide to buy a car by giving you a very low price

4.  During her candidacy for the United States presidency, Hillary Clinton once claimed she ran with her head down to escape sniper fire at a Bosnian airport, when in fact she was greeted very peacefully. 'I misremembered,' she later explained. Was she lying or was her memory unreliable? What factors intrude on people's capacity as eyewitnesses to recall events accurately? Memory researcher Elizabeth Loftus refers to the Clinton episode in Chapter 2 of MyPsychLab at **www.mypsychlab.co.uk** (watch *Rich false memories*; see **http://www.youtube.com/watch?v=hER-5mdIoNO**).

Go to **mypsych lab** to explore video and test your understanding of key topics addressed in this chapter.

Refresh your understanding with interactive summaries, explore topics further with video and audio clips and assess your progress with quick test and essay questions by logging to the accompanying website at **www.mypsychlab.co.uk**

# Chapter 2
## Social cognition and social thinking

## Key terms

Accentuation principle
Accessibility
Affect–infusion model
Anchoring and adjustment
Associative meaning
Associative network
Attribution
Availability heuristic
Averaging
Base-rate information
Behavioural decision theory
Behaviourism
Bookkeeping
Central traits
Cognitive algebra
Cognitive consistency

Cognitive miser
Configural model
Conversion
Exemplars
Family resemblance
Fuzzy sets
Gestalt psychology
Heuristics
Illusory correlation
Implicit personality theories
Motivated tactician
Naive psychologist (or scientist)
Normative models
Paired distinctiveness
Peripheral traits
Personal constructs
Primacy
Priming
Prototype

Recency
Reductionism
Regression
Representativeness heuristic
Roles
Salience
Schema
Script
Self-categorisation theory
Social cognition
Social identity theory
Social judgeability
Social neuroscience
Stereotype
Subtyping
Summation
Vividness
Weighted averaging

# Social psychology and cognition

Social psychology is the science of human thought, feeling and behaviour as they are influenced by and have influence on other people. Within this broad definition (see Chapter 1), *thought* has always occupied a pivotal position: people think about their social world, and on the basis of thought they act in certain ways. Thought is very much the internal language and symbols we use; it is often conscious, or at least something we are or could be aware of. In contrast, cognition is largely automatic; we are unaware of it and only with difficulty notice it, let alone characterise it in language or shared symbols. A useful way to think about cognition is as a computer program: it operates in the background, running all the functions of the computer that we are aware of.

Cognition and thought occur within the human mind. They are the mental activities that mediate between the world out there and what people subsequently do. Their operation can be inferred from what people do and say – from people's actions, expressions, sayings and writings. If we can understand cognition, we may gain some understanding of how and why people behave the way they do. **Social cognition** is an approach in social psychology that focuses on how cognition is affected by wider and more immediate social contexts and on how cognition affects our social behaviour.

During the 1980s there was an explosion in social cognition research. According to Taylor (1998), during social cognition's heyday 85 per cent of submissions to the *Journal of Personality and Social Psychology,* social psychology's flagship journal, were social cognition articles. Social cognition remains healthy and vibrant as perhaps the dominant perspective on the explanation of social behaviour (e.g. Fiske & Taylor, 2008; Hamilton & Stroessner, in press; Moskowitz, 2005). It has taught us much about how we process and store information about people, and how this information affects the way we perceive and interact with people. It has also taught us new methods and techniques for conducting social psychological research – methods and techniques borrowed from cognitive psychology and then refined for social psychology. Social cognition has had, and continues to have, an enormous impact on social psychology (Devine, Hamilton & Ostrom, 1994).

**Social cognition**
Cognitive processes and structures that influence and are influenced by social behaviour.

# A short history of cognition in social psychology

Wundt (1897) was one of the founders of modern empirical psychology. He used self-observation and introspection to gain an understanding of cognition (people's subjective experience), which he believed to be the main purpose of psychology. This methodology became unpopular because it was not scientific. Data and theories were idiosyncratic, and because they were effectively autobiographical they were almost impossible to refute or generalise.

Because psychologists felt that theories should be based on publicly observable and replicable data, there was a shift away from studying internal (cognitive) events towards external, publicly observable events. The ultimate expression of this change in emphasis was American **behaviourism** of the early twentieth century (e.g. Skinner, 1963; Thorndike, 1940; Watson, 1930) – cognition became a dirty word in psychology for almost half a century. Behaviourists focused on overt behaviour (e.g. a hand wave) as a response to observable stimuli in the environment (e.g. an approaching bus), based on past punishments and rewards for the behaviour (e.g. being picked up by the bus).

**Behaviourism**
An emphasis on explaining observable behaviour in terms of reinforcement schedules.

By the 1960s, psychologists had begun to take a fresh interest in cognition. This was partly because behaviourism seemed terribly cumbersome and inadequate as an explanation of human language and communication (see Chomsky, 1959); some consideration of how people represent the world symbolically and how they manipulate such symbols was needed. Moreover, the world was becoming dominated by the manipulation and transfer of information: information processing became an increasingly important focus for psychology (Broadbent, 1985; Wyer & Gruenfeld, 1995). This development continued with the computer revolution, which has encouraged and enabled psychologists to model or simulate highly complex human cognitive processes. The computer has also become a metaphor for the human mind, with computer software/programs standing in for cognition. Cognitive psychology, sometimes called cognitive science, re-emerged as a legitimate scientific pursuit (e.g. Anderson, 1990; Neisser, 1967).

In contrast to general psychology, social psychology has almost always been strongly cognitive (Manis, 1977; Zajonc, 1980). This emphasis can be traced at least as far back as Lewin, who is often referred to as the father of experimental social psychology. Drawing on **gestalt psychology,** Lewin (1951) believed that social behaviour is most usefully understood as a function of people's perceptions of their world and of their manipulation of such perceptions. As such, cognition and thought are placed centre stage in social psychology. The cognitive emphasis in social psychology has had at least four guises (Jones, 1998; Taylor, 1998): cognitive consistency, naive scientist, cognitive miser and motivated tactician.

**Gestalt psychology**
Perspective in which the whole influences constituent parts rather than vice versa.

After the Second World War, in the 1940s and 1950s, there was an enormous amount of research on attitude change. This produced a number of theories sharing an assumption that people strive for **cognitive consistency**: that is, people are motivated to reduce perceived discrepancies between their various cognitions because such discrepancies are aversive (e.g. Abelson et al., 1968; Festinger, 1957; Heider, 1958; see also Chapters 5 and 6). Consistency theories gradually lost popularity in the 1960s as evidence accumulated that people are in fact remarkably tolerant of cognitive inconsistency.

**Cognitive consistency**
A model of social cognition in which people try to reduce inconsistency among their cognitions, because they find inconsistency unpleasant.

In its place there arose in the early 1970s a **naive scientist** model, which characterised people as having a need to attribute causes to behaviour and events in order to render the world a meaningful place in which to act. This model underpins the **attribution** theories of human behaviour that dominated social psychology in the 1970s (see Chapter 3). The naive scientist model assumes that people are basically rational in making scientific-like cause–effect analyses. Any errors or biases that creep in are departures from normality that can be traced to limited or inaccurate information and to motivational considerations such as self-interest.

**Naive psychologist (or scientist)**
Model of social cognition that characterises people as using rational, scientific-like, cause–effect analyses to understand their world.

**Attribution**
The process of assigning a cause to our own behaviour, and that of others.

**Cognitive miser**
A model of social cognition that characterises people as using the least complex and demanding cognitions that are able to produce generally adaptive behaviours.

**Motivated tactician**
A model of social cognition that characterises people as having multiple cognitive strategies available, which they choose among on the basis of personal goals, motives and needs.

**Social neuroscience**
The exploration of the neurological underpinnings of the processes traditionally examined by social psychology.

**Configural model**
Asch's gestalt-based model of impression formation, in which central traits play a disproportionate role in configuring the final impression.

**Central traits**
Traits that have a disproportionate influence on the configuration of final impressions, in Asch's configural model of impression formation.

**Peripheral traits**
Traits that have an insignificant influence on the configuration of final impressions, in Asch's configural model of impression formation.

In the late 1970s, however, it became clear that even in ideal circumstances people are not very careful scientists at all. The 'normal' state of affairs is that people are limited in their capacity to process information, and take numerous cognitive short-cuts: they are **cognitive misers** (Nisbett & Ross, 1980; Taylor, 1981). The various errors and biases associated with social thinking are not motivated departures from some ideal form of information processing but are intrinsic to social thinking. Motivation is almost completely absent from the cognitive miser perspective. However, as this perspective has matured, the importance of motivation has again become evident (Gollwitzer & Bargh, 1996; Showers & Cantor, 1985) – the social thinker has become characterised as a **motivated tactician:**

> a fully engaged thinker who has multiple cognitive strategies available and chooses among them based on goals, motives, and needs. Sometimes the motivated tactician chooses wisely, in the interests of adaptability and accuracy, and sometimes . . . defensively, in the interests of speed or self-esteem. (*Fiske & Taylor, 1991, p. 13*)

The most recent development in social cognition is **social neuroscience,** sometimes called cognitive neuroscience or social cognitive neuroscience (Harmon-Jones & Winkielman, 2007; Lieberman, 2010). Social neuroscience is largely a methodology in which cognitive activity can be monitored by the use of functional magnetic resonance imaging (fMRI), which detects and localises electrical activity in the brain associated with cognitive activities or functions. In this way, different parts of the brain 'light up' when people are, for example, thinking positively or negatively about friends or strangers or social categories, or when they are attributing causality to different behaviours. Social neuroscience is now widely applied to social psychological phenomena – for example, interpersonal processes (Gardner, Gabriel & Diekman, 2000), attributional inference (Lieberman, Gaunt, Gilbert & Trope, 2002), the experience of being socially excluded (Eisenberger, Lieberman & Williams, 2003) and even religious conviction (Inzlicht, McGregor, Hirsh & Nash, 2009).

# Forming impressions of other people

People spend an enormous amount of time thinking about other people. We form impressions of the people we meet, have described to us or encounter in the media. We communicate these impressions to others, and we use them as bases for deciding how we will feel and act. Impression formation and person perception are important aspects of social cognition (Schneider, Hastorf & Ellsworth, 1979).

## Asch's configural model

According to Asch's (1946) **configural model,** in forming first impressions we latch on to certain pieces of information, called **central traits,** which have a disproportionate influence over the final impression. Other pieces of information, called **peripheral traits,** have much less influence. Central and peripheral traits are ones that are more or less intrinsically correlated with other traits, and therefore more or less useful in constructing an integrated impression of a person. Central traits influence the meanings of other traits and the perceived relationship among traits: that is, they are responsible for the integrated configuration of the impression.

To investigate this idea, Asch had students read one of two lists of seven adjectives describing a hypothetical person (see Figure 2.1). The lists differed only slightly – one contained the word *warm* and the other the word *cold*. Participants then evaluated the target

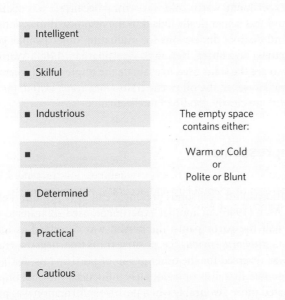

■ Intelligent

■ Skilful

■ Industrious

The empty space
contains either:

■

Warm or Cold
or
Polite or Blunt

■ Determined

■ Practical

■ Cautious

% assigning additional traits as function of focal trait inserted:

| Additional traits | Focal traits inserted in the list | | | |
| --- | --- | --- | --- | --- |
| | Warm | Cold | Polite | Blunt |
| Generous | 91 | 8 | 56 | 58 |
| Wise | 65 | 25 | 30 | 50 |
| Happy | 90 | 34 | 75 | 65 |
| Good-natured | 94 | 17 | 87 | 56 |
| Reliable | 94 | 99 | 95 | 100 |

**Figure 2.1** Impressions of a hypothetical person, based on central and peripheral traits

Asch (1946) presented participants with a seven-trait description of a hypothetical person in which either the word *warm* or *cold*, or *polite* or *blunt* appeared. The percentage of participants assigning other traits to the target was markedly affected when *warm* was replaced by *cold*, but not when *polite* was replaced by *blunt*

*Source*: based on Asch (1946)

person on a number of other bipolar evaluative dimensions, such as generous/ungenerous, happy/unhappy, reliable/unreliable. Asch found that participants exposed to the list containing *warm* generated a much more favourable impression of the target than did those exposed to the list containing the trait *cold*. When the words *warm* and *cold* were replaced by *polite* and *blunt*, the difference in impression was far less marked. Asch argued that warm/cold is a central trait dimension that has more influence on impression formation than polite/blunt, which is a peripheral trait dimension.

Asch's experiment was replicated in a naturalistic setting by Kelley (1950), who ended his introduction of a guest lecturer to students with: 'People who know him consider him to be a rather *cold* [or very *warm*] person, *industrious, critical, practical* and *determined*.' The lecturer gave identical lectures to a number of classes, half of which received the *cold* and half the *warm* description. After the lecture, the students rated the lecturer on a number of dimensions. Those who received the *cold* trait rated the lecturer as more *unsociable, self-centred, unpopular, formal, irritable, humourless* and *ruthless*. They were also less likely to ask questions and to interact with the lecturer. This seems to support the gestalt view that impressions are formed as integrated wholes based on central cues.

However, critics have wondered how people decide that a trait is central. Gestalt theorists believe that the centrality of a trait rests on its intrinsic degree of correlation with other traits. Others have argued that centrality is a function of context (e.g. Wishner, 1960; Zanna & Hamilton, 1972). In Asch's experiment, warm/cold was central because it was distinct from the other trait dimensions and was semantically linked to the response dimensions. People tend to employ two main and distinct dimensions for evaluating other people: good/bad social, and good/bad intellectual (Rosenberg, Nelson & Vivekanathan, 1968). Warm/cold is clearly good/bad social, and so are the traits used to evaluate the impression (*generous, wise, happy, good-natured, reliable*). However, the other cue traits (*intelligent, skilful, industrious, determined, practical, cautious*) are clearly good/bad intellectual.

## Biases in forming impressions

### Primacy and recency

The order in which information about a person is presented can have profound effects on the subsequent impression. Asch (1946), in another experiment, used six traits to describe a hypothetical person. For half the participants, the person was described as *intelligent, industrious, impulsive, critical, stubborn, envious* (i.e. positive traits first, negative traits last). The order of presentation was reversed for the other group of participants. Asch found a **primacy** effect: the traits presented first disproportionately influenced the final impression, so that the person was evaluated more favourably when positive information was presented first than when negative information was presented first. Perhaps early information acts much like central cues, or perhaps people simply pay more attention to earlier information.

A **recency** effect can emerge where later information has more impact than earlier information. This might happen when you are distracted (e.g. overworked, bombarded with stimuli, tired) or when you have little motivation to attend to someone. Later, when you learn, for example, that you may have to work with this person, you may attend more carefully to cues. All other things being equal, however, primacy effects are more common (Jones & Goethals, 1972), with the clear implication that first impressions do indeed matter.

### Positivity and negativity

Research indicates that, in the absence of information to the contrary, people tend to assume the best of others and form a positive impression (Sears, 1983). However, if there is any negative information, this tends to attract our attention and assume disproportionate significance in the subsequent impression – we are biased towards negativity (Fiske, 1980). Furthermore, once formed, a negative impression is much more difficult to change in the light of subsequent positive information than is a positive impression likely to change in the light of subsequent negative information (e.g. Hamilton & Zanna, 1974). We may be sensitive in this way to negative information for two reasons:

1   The information is unusual and distinctive – unusual, distinctive or extreme information attracts attention (Skowronski & Carlston, 1989).

2   The information indirectly signifies potential danger, so its detection has survival value for the individual and ultimately the species.

### Personal constructs and implicit personality theories

Kelly (1955) has suggested that even within a culture, individuals can develop their own idiosyncratic ways of characterising people. These **personal constructs** can, for simplicity, be treated as sets of bipolar dimensions. For example, I might consider *humour* the single most important organising principle for forming impressions of people, while you might prefer *intelligence*. We have different personal construct systems and would be likely to form different impressions of the same person. Personal constructs develop over time as adaptive forms of person perception and so are resistant to change. We also tend to develop

**Primacy**
An order of presentation effect in which earlier presented information has a disproportionate influence on social cognition.

**Recency**
An order of presentation effect in which later presented information has a disproportionate influence on social cognition.

**Personal constructs**
Idiosyncratic and personal ways of characterising other people.

our own **implicit personality theories** (Bruner & Tagiuri, 1954; Schneider, 1973; Sedikides & Anderson, 1994) or *philosophies of human nature* (Wrightsman, 1964). These are general principles concerning what sorts of characteristics go together to form certain types of personality. For instance, Rosenberg and Sedlak (1972) found that people assumed that intelligent people are also friendly but not self-centred. Implicit personality theories are widely shared within cultures but differ between cultures (Markus, Kitayama & Heiman, 1996). But, like personal constructs, they are resistant to change, and can be idiosyncratically based on personal experiences (Smith & Zárate, 1992).

**Implicit personality theories**
Idiosyncratic and personal ways of characterising other people and explaining their behaviour.

## Physical appearance

Although we would probably like to believe that we are way too sophisticated to be swayed in our impressions by mere physical appearance, research suggests this is not so. Because appearance is often the first information we have about people, it is very influential in first impressions; and, as we have seen above, primacy effects are influential in enduring impressions (Park, 1986). This is not necessarily always a bad thing – according to Zebrowitz and Collins (1997), appearance-based impressions can be surprisingly accurate. One of the most immediate appearance-based judgements we make is whether we find someone physically attractive or not. Research confirms that we tend to assume that physically attractive people are 'good' (Dion, Berscheid & Walster, 1972) – they are interesting, warm, outgoing, socially skilled and have what the German poet Schiller (1882) called an 'interior beauty, a spiritual and moral beauty'.

Physical attractiveness has a marked impact on affiliation, attraction and love (see Chapter 13), but can also have problematic effects on people's careers. For example in the United States where being taller, for men, is generally considered attractive, Knapp (1978) found that professional men taller than 1.88 m received 10 per cent higher starting salaries than men under 1.83 m. In another study Heilman and Stopeck (1985) found that attractive male executives were considered more able than less attractive male executives. Interestingly, attractive female executives were considered less able than less attractive female executives; participants suspected that attractive females had been promoted because of their appearance, not their ability (see Chapter 10).

## Stereotypes

Impressions of people are also strongly influenced by widely shared assumptions about the personalities, attitudes and behaviours of people based on group membership: for example, ethnicity, nationality, sex, race and class. These are **stereotypes** (discussed below, and in detail in Chapters 3, 10 and 11). One of the salient characteristics of people we first meet is their category membership (e.g. ethnicity), and this tends to engage a stereotype-consistent impression. Haire and Grune (1950) found that people had little difficulty composing a paragraph describing a 'working man' from stereotype-consistent information, but enormous difficulty incorporating one piece of stereotype-inconsistent information – that the man was *intelligent*. Participants ignored the information, distorted it, took a very long time or even promoted the man from worker to supervisor.

**Stereotype**
Widely shared and simplified evaluative image of a social group and its members.

## Social judgeability

People form impressions largely to make judgements about other people: whether they are mean, friendly, intelligent and helpful. Research by Leyens and Yzerbyt and their colleagues suggests that people are unlikely to form impressions and make judgements if the target is deemed not to be **socially judgeable** in the specific context: that is, if there are social rules (norms, conventions, laws) that proscribe making judgements (Leyens, Yzerbyt & Schadron, 1992; Yzerbyt, Leyens & Schadron, 1997; Yzerbyt, Schadron, Leyens & Rocher, 1994). However, if the target is deemed to be socially judgeable, then judgements are more

**Social judgeability**
Perception of whether it is socially acceptable to judge a specific target.

polarised and are made with greater confidence the more socially judgeable the target is considered to be. One implication is that people will not make stereotype-based judgements if conventions or legislation proscribe such behaviour as 'politically incorrect', but will readily do so if conventions encourage and legitimise such behaviour.

## Cognitive algebra

Impression formation involves the integration of sequential pieces of information about a person (i.e. traits presented over time) into a complete image. The image is generally evaluative, and so are the pieces of information themselves. Imagine being asked your impression of a person you met at a party. You might answer: 'He seemed very friendly and entertaining – all in all a nice person.' The main thing we learn from this is that you formed a positive/favourable impression. Impression formation is very much a matter of evaluation, not description. **Cognitive algebra** refers to an approach to the study of impression formation that focuses on how we assign positive and negative valence to attributes and how we then combine these pluses and minuses into a general evaluation (Anderson, 1965, 1978, 1981). There are three principal models of cognitive algebra: summation, averaging and weighted averaging (see Table 2.1).

### Summation

**Summation** refers to a process where the overall impression is simply the cumulative sum of each piece of information. Say that we have a mental rating scale that goes from −3 (very negative) to +3 (very positive), and that we can assign values to specific traits such as *intelligent* (+2), *sincere* (+3) and *boring* (−1). If we met someone who had these characteristics, our overall impression would be the sum of the constituents: (+2 + 3 − 1) = +4 (see Table 2.1). If we now learned that the person was *humorous* (+1), our impression would

**Cognitive algebra**
Approach to the study of impression formation that focuses on how people combine attributes that have valence into an overall positive or negative impression.

**Summation**
A method of forming positive or negative impressions by summing the valence of all the constituent person attributes.

**Table 2.1** Forming an impression by summation, averaging or weighted averaging

|  | Summation All traits weighted 1 | Averaging All traits weighted 1 | Weighted averaging | |
|---|---|---|---|---|
|  |  |  | Potential 'friend' weighting | Potential 'politician' weighting |
| Initial traits |  |  |  |  |
| *Intelligent* (+2) |  |  | 2 | 3 |
| *Sincere* (+3) |  |  | 3 | 2 |
| *Boring* (−1) |  |  | 3 | 0 |
| Initial impression | +4.0 | +1.33 | +3.33 | +4.00 |
| Revised impression on learning that the person is also *humorous* (+1) | +5.0 | +1.25 | (weight = 1) +2.75 | (weight = 0) +3.00 |
| Final impression on learning that the person is also *generous* (+1) | +6.0 | +1.20 | (weight = 2) +2.60 | (weight = 1) +2.60 |

improve to +5. It would improve to +6 if we then learned that the person was also *generous* (+1). Every bit of information counts, and to project a favourable impression you would be advised to present every facet of yourself that was positive, even marginally positive. In this example, you would be wise to conceal the fact that you were *boring*; your impression on others would now be $(2 + 3 + 1 + 1) = +7$.

## Averaging

**Averaging** refers to a process where the overall impression is the cumulative average of each piece of information. So, from the example above, our initial impression would be $(+2 + 3 - 1)/3 = +1.33$ (see Table 2.1). The additional information that the person was *humorous* (+1) would actually worsen the impression to +1.25: $(+2 + 3 - 1 + 1)/4 = +1.25$. It would worsen still further to +1.20 with the information that the person was *generous* (+1): $(+2 + 3 - 1 + 1 + 1)/5 = +1.20$. The implication is that, to project a favourable impression, you would be advised to present only your single very best facet. In this example, you would be wise to present yourself as sincere, and nothing else; your impression on others would now be +3.

**Averaging**
A method of forming positive or negative impressions by averaging the valence of all the constituent attributes.

## Weighted averaging

Although research tends to favour the averaging model, it has some limitations. The valence of separate pieces of information may not be fixed but may depend on the context of the impression-formation task. Context may also influence the relative importance of pieces of information and thus weight them in different ways in the impression. These considerations led to the development of a **weighted averaging** model. For example (see Table 2.1), if the target person was being assessed as a potential friend, we might assign relative weights to *intelligent, sincere* and *boring* of 2, 3 and 3. The weighted average would be +3.33: $((+2 \times 2) + (+3 \times 3) + (-1 \times 3))/3 = +3.33$. If the person was being assessed as a potential politician, we might assign weights of 3, 2 and 0, to arrive at a weighted average of +4: $((+2 \times 3) + (+3 \times 2) + (-1 \times 0))/3 = +4.00$. Table 2.1 shows how additional information with different weighting might affect the overall impression. (Refer back to the first focus question at the beginning of this chapter. Suggest different ways that Ms Jones might form her overall impression of you.)

**Weighted averaging**
Method of forming positive or negative impressions by first weighting and then averaging the valence of all the constituent person attributes.

Weights reflect the subjective importance of pieces of information in a particular impression-formation context. They may be determined in a number of ways. For instance, we have already seen that negative information may be weighted more heavily (e.g. Kanouse & Hanson, 1972). Earlier information may also be weighted more heavily (the primacy effect

**Making an impression**
He really wants this job and has been short-listed for interview. Should he highlight ALL of his positive qualities or just the very best?

discussed above). Paradoxically, we may now have come full circle to Asch's central traits. The weighted averaging model seems to allow for something like central traits, which are weighted more heavily in impression formation than are other traits. With respect to central traits, the difference between Asch and the weighted averaging perspective is that for the latter central traits are simply more salient and heavily weighted information, while for Asch central traits actually influence the meaning of surrounding traits and reorganise the entire way we view the person. Asch's perspective retains the descriptive or qualitative aspect of traits and impressions, whereas cognitive algebra focuses only on quantitative aspects and suffers accordingly. More recent developments in social cognition have tended to supplant central traits with the more general concept of cognitive schema (Fiske & Taylor, 2008).

# Social schemas and categories

**Schema**
Cognitive structure that represents knowledge about a concept or type of stimulus, including its attributes and the relations among those attributes.

A **schema** is a 'cognitive structure that represents knowledge about a concept or type of stimulus, including its attributes and the relations among those attributes' (Fiske & Taylor, 1991, p. 98). It is a set of interrelated cognitions (e.g. thoughts, beliefs, attitudes) that allows us quickly to make sense of a person, situation, event or place on the basis of limited information. Certain cues activate a schema. The schema then 'fills in' missing details.

For example, imagine you are visiting Paris. Most of us have a place schema about Paris, a rich repertoire of prior knowledge about what one does when in Paris – sauntering along boulevards, sitting in parks, sipping coffee at pavement cafés, browsing through bookshops, or eating at restaurants. The reality of life in Paris is more diverse, yet this schema helps to interpret events and guide choices about how to behave. While in Paris you might visit a restaurant. Arrival at a restaurant might invoke a 'restaurant schema', which is a set of assumptions about what ought to take place (e.g. someone ushers you to a table, you study the menu, someone takes your order, you eat, talk and drink, you pay the bill, you leave). An event schema such as this is called a **script** (see below). While at the restaurant, your waiter may have a rather unusual accent that identifies him as English – this would engage a whole set of assumptions about his attitudes and behaviour. A schema about a social group, particularly if it is widely shared, is a stereotype (Chapters 10, 11 and 15).

**Script**
A schema about an event.

Once invoked, schemas facilitate top-down, concept-driven or theory-driven processing, as opposed to bottom-up or data-driven processing (Rumelhart & Ortony, 1977). We tend to fill in gaps with prior knowledge and preconceptions, rather than seek information gleaned directly from the immediate context. The concept of cognitive schema first emerged in research by Bartlett (1932) on non-social memory, which focused on how memories are actively constructed and organised to facilitate understanding and behaviour. It also has a precedent in Asch's (1946) *configural model* of impression formation (discussed above), Heider's (1958) *balance theory* of person perception (see Chapters 3 and 5) and, more generally, in gestalt psychology (Brunswik, 1956; Koffka, 1935). These are all approaches in which simplified and holistic cognitive representations of the social world act as relatively enduring templates for the interpretation of stimuli and the planning of action.

The alternative to a schema approach is one in which perception is treated as an unfiltered, veridical representation of reality (e.g. Mill, 1869); impression formation is, as discussed above, the cognitive algebra of trait combination (e.g. Anderson, 1981); and memory is laid down passively through the repetitive association of stimuli (e.g. Ebbinghaus, 1885).

## Types of schema

There are many types of schema; however, they all influence the encoding (internalisation and interpretation) of new information, memory of old information and inferences about missing information. The most common schemas, some of which have been used as examples above, are person schemas, role schemas, event schemas or scripts, content-free schemas and self-schemas.

## Person schemas

Person schemas are individualised knowledge structures about specific people. For example, you may have a person schema about your best friend (e.g. that she is kind and intelligent but is silent in company and would rather frequent cafés than go mountain climbing), or about a specific politician, a well-known author or a next-door neighbour.

## Role schemas

Role schemas are knowledge structures about role occupants: for example, airline pilots (they fly the plane and should not be seen swigging whisky in the cabin) and doctors (although often complete strangers, they are allowed to ask personal questions and get you to undress). Although role schemas can quite properly apply to **roles** (i.e. types of function or behaviour in a group; see Chapter 8), they can sometimes be better understood as schemas about social groups, in which case if such schemas are shared, they are, in effect, social stereotypes (Chapters 10 and 11).

**Roles**
Patterns of behaviour that distinguish between different activities within the group, and that interrelate to one another for the greater good of the group.

## Scripts

Schemas about events are generally called scripts (Abelson, 1981; Schank & Abelson, 1977). We have scripts for attending a lecture, going to the cinema, having a party, giving a presentation or eating out in a restaurant. For example, people who often go to football matches might have a very clear script for what happens both on and off the pitch. This makes the entire event meaningful. Imagine how you would fare if you had never been to a football match and had never heard of football (see Box 3.2 in Chapter 3, which describes one such scenario). The lack of relevant scripts can often be a significant contributor to feelings of disorientation, frustration and lack of efficacy encountered by sojourners in foreign cultures (e.g. new immigrants; see Chapter 16).

## Content-free schemas

Content-free schemas do not contain rich information about a specific category but rather a limited number of rules for processing information. Content-free schemas might specify that if you like John and John likes Tom, then in order to maintain balance you should also like Tom (see balance theory, Heider, 1958; discussed in Chapter 6), or they might specify how to attribute a cause to someone's behaviour (e.g. Kelley's 1972a idea of causal schemata, discussed in Chapter 3).

## Self-schemas

Finally, people have schemas about themselves. They represent and store information about themselves in a similar but more complex and varied way than information about others. Self-schemas form part of people's concept of who they are, the self-concept; they are discussed in Chapter 4, which deals with self and identity.

# Categories and prototypes

To apply schematic knowledge, you first need to categorise a person, event or situation as fitting a particular schema. Building on early work by the philosopher Wittgenstein (1953), cognitive psychologists believe that categories are collections of instances that have a **family resemblance** (e.g. Cantor & Mischel, 1977, 1979; Mervis & Rosch, 1981; Rosch, 1978). There is rarely a specific combination of attributes that all instances must have as a necessary

**Family resemblance**
Defining property of category membership.

**Are prototypes accurate?**
Is this young man a typical student? People have fuzzy prototypes of social categories that they use as the basis of more general impressions

criterion for category membership. Instead, instances vary in terms of a range of attributes, with some instances seeming to have an overall better fit to the category than others – they are more *prototypical* of the category. Because prototypes are cognitively abstracted and constructed from instances, no specific instance or member of the category may exactly fit the **prototype** – instances vary in prototypicality.

Prototypes are cognitive representations of the category – standards against which family resemblance is assessed and category membership decided. As instances within a category are not identical but differ from one another to varying degrees, categories can be considered **fuzzy sets** centring on a prototype (see Box 2.1).

**Prototype**
Cognitive representation of the typical/ideal defining features of a category.

**Fuzzy sets**
Categories are considered to be fuzzy sets of features organised around a prototype.

Although prototypes can represent the average/typical category member, this may not always be the case (Chaplin, John & Goldberg, 1988). Under some circumstances, the prototype may be the typical member (e.g. the typical conservationist), while under other circumstances the prototype may be an extreme member (the most radical conservationist). Extreme prototypes may prevail when social categories are in competition (e.g. conservationists versus developers): this analysis is used in Chapter 7 to explain how people conform to more extreme or polarised group norms (e.g. Wetherell, 1987).

The relationship between categories is hierarchical, with less inclusive categories nested beneath more inclusive categories (i.e. categories that include fewer members and fewer attributes are nested under categories that include more members and more attributes; see Figure 2.2). In general, people are more likely to rely on intermediate-level categories than on those that are very inclusive or very exclusive: these basic-level categories are neither too broad nor too narrow. For instance, most of us are more likely to identify something as a car than as a vehicle (too inclusive) or a Saab (too exclusive).

## Real world 2.1
### Categories are fuzzy sets organised around prototypes

Here is a short exercise to illustrate the nature of categories as fuzzy sets:

1 Consider the category 'university lecturer'. Whatever comes immediately to mind is your prototype of a university lecturer – most likely it will be a set of characteristics and images.

2 Keep this in mind, or write it down. You may find this more difficult than you anticipated – prototypes can become frustratingly nebulous and imprecise when you try to document them.

3 Now picture all the university lecturers you can think of. These will be lecturers who have taught you in large lecture halls or small classes, lecturers you have met after classes, in their offices, or lecturers just seen lurking around your psychology department.

Also include lecturers whom you have read about in books and newspapers, or seen in movies or on television. These are all instances of the category 'university lecturer'.

4 Which of these instances is most prototypical? Do any fit the prototype perfectly, or are they all more or less prototypical? Which of these instances is least prototypical? Is any so non-prototypical that it has hardly any family resemblance to the rest? You should discover that there is an enormous range of prototypicality (the category is relatively diverse, a fuzzy set containing instances that have family resemblance) and that no instance fits the prototype exactly (the prototype is a cognitive construction).

5 Finally, compare your prototype with those of your classmates. You may discover a great deal of similarity; your prototype is shared among students. Prototypes of social groups (e.g. lecturers) that are shared by members of a social group (e.g. students) can be considered social stereotypes.

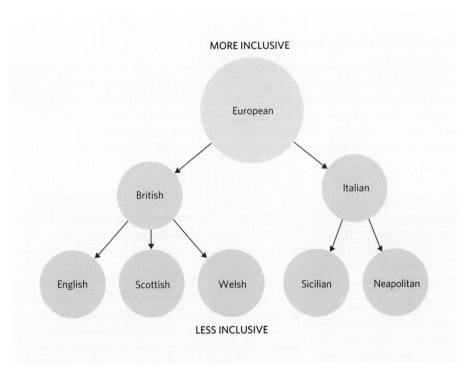

**Figure 2.2**  Categories organised by level of inclusiveness

Categories are organised hierarchically so that less inclusive categories are nested beneath more inclusive categories

Basic-level categories are the default option, but they may not actually be that common in social perception, where contextual and motivational factors dominate the choice of level of categorisation (Cantor & Kihlstrom, 1987; Hampson, John & Goldberg, 1986; Turner, 1985).

In addition to representing categories as abstractions from many instances (i.e. proto-types), people may represent categories in terms of specific concrete instances they have encountered (i.e. **exemplars**; Smith & Zárate, 1992). For example, Europeans may represent the category 'American' in terms of Barack Obama, or perhaps still George W. Bush.

**Exemplars**
Specific instances of a member of a category.

To categorise new instances, people sometimes use exemplars rather than prototypes as the standard. For instance, Brewer (1988) suggests that as people become more familiar with a category, they shift from prototypical to exemplar representation, and Judd and Park (1988; Klein, Loftus, Trafton & Fuhrman, 1992) suggest that people use both prototypes and exemplars to represent groups to which they belong, but only exemplars to represent outgroups. Social psychologists are still not certain about the conditions of use of proto-types versus exemplars (Fiske & Neuberg, 1990; Linville, Fischer & Salovey, 1989; Park & Hastie, 1987), or about the advisability of blurring the distinction between abstraction-based prototypes and instance-based exemplars in so-called 'blended' models of category representation (Hamilton & Sherman, 1994; Hilton & von Hippel, 1996). A third way in which we can represent categories is as **associative networks** of affectively, causally or merely associatively linked attributes such as traits, beliefs or behaviour (e.g. Wyer & Carlston, 1994; see below).

**Associative network**
Model of memory in which nodes or ideas are connected by associative links along which cognitive activation can spread.

Once a person, event or situation is categorised, a schema is invoked. Schemas and pro-totypes are similar and indeed are often used interchangeably. One way to distinguish them is in terms of their organisation. Prototypes, as just described, are relatively nebulous, unorganised fuzzy representations of a category; schemas are highly organised specifica-tions of features and their interrelationships (Wyer & Gordon, 1984).

## Categorisation and stereotyping

Stereotypes are widely shared generalisations about members of a social group (Hilton & von Hippel, 1996; Leyens, Yzerbyt & Schadron, 1994; Macrae, Stangor & Hewstone, 1996). They are usually simplified images, they are often derogatory when applied to outgroups, and they are often based on, or create, clearly visible differences between groups (e.g. in terms of physical appearance; Zebrowitz, 1996). Box 2.2 describes a study by Linssen and Hagendoorn (1994) of Europeans' stereotypes of northern and southern European nations.

### Research highlight 2.2
#### Students' stereotypes of northern and southern European nations

During December 1989 and January 1990, Linssen and Hagendoorn (1994) distributed a questionnaire to 277 16- and 18-year-old school pupils in Denmark, England, the Netherlands, Belgium, Germany, France and Italy. The respondents indicated the percentage of each national group whom they thought had each of twenty-two characteristics. These clustered into four general dimensions:

1  *dominant* – e.g. proud, assertive, aggressive;

2  *efficient* – e.g. industrious, scientific, rich;

3  *empathic* – e.g. helpful, friendly;

4  *emotional* – e.g. enjoying life, religious.

In general, there was a clear north/south polarisation, with southern European nations being considered distinctly more emotional and less efficient than northern European nations. These stereotypes were independent of other differences between northern and southern European nations (e.g. size, political power, social organisation).

*Source*: based on Linssen & Hagendoorn (1994)

In another study, of central and eastern European nations, Poppe & Linssen (1999) showed that geographical features become attached in an evaluative way to national stereotypes.

Stereotypes and stereotyping are central aspects of prejudice and discrimination (see Chapter 10) and of intergroup behaviour as a whole (see Chapter 11).

First described scientifically by Lippman (1922), stereotypes were treated as simplified mental images that act as templates to help to interpret the bewildering diversity of the social world. Decades of research aimed at describing the content and form of stereotypes have produced a number of clear findings (Brigham, 1971; Katz & Braly, 1933; Oakes, Haslam & Turner, 1993; Tajfel, 1978):

- People show an easy readiness to characterise large human groups in terms of a few fairly crude common attributes.

- Stereotypes are slow to change.

- Stereotype change is generally in response to wider social, political or economic changes.

- Stereotypes are acquired at an early age, often before the child has any knowledge about the groups that are being stereotyped (but other research suggests that some stereotypes crystallise later in childhood, after age 10 – Rutland, 1999).

- Stereotypes become more pronounced and hostile when social tensions and conflict exist between groups, and then they are extremely difficult to modify.

- Stereotypes are not inaccurate or wrong; rather, they serve to make sense of particular intergroup relations.

Although stereotypes have usually been thought to be associated in some way with social categories (e.g. Allport, 1954b; Ehrlich, 1973), it was Tajfel (1957, 1959) who specified exactly how the process of categorisation might be responsible for stereotyping. Tajfel reasoned that in making judgements on some focal dimension, people recruit any other peripheral dimension that might be of some assistance (see also Bruner & Goodman, 1947). So, for example, if you had to judge the length of a series of lines (focal dimension), and you knew that all lines labelled *A* were bigger than all lines labelled *B* (peripheral dimension), then you might use these labels to help your judgement.

Tajfel and Wilkes (1963) tested this idea. They had participants judge the length of a series of lines presented one at a time, a number of times and in varying order. There were three conditions: (1) the lines were randomly labelled *A* or *B*; (2) all the shorter lines were labelled *A*, and all the longer ones *B*; and (3) there were no labels. Participants appeared to use the information in the second condition to aid judgement and tended to underestimate the average length of *A*-type lines and overestimate the average length of *B*-type lines.

The relevance of this experiment to social stereotyping becomes clear if, for example, you substitute singing ability for line length and Welsh/English for the *A/B* labels. Because people might believe that the Welsh sing particularly beautifully (i.e. a social stereotype exists), the categorisation of people as Welsh or English produces a perceptual distortion on the focal dimension of singing ability: that is, categorisation produces stereotyping.

This, and a number of other experiments with physical and social stimuli (see Doise, 1978; Eiser, 1986; Eiser & Stroebe, 1972; McGarty & Penny, 1988; McGarty & Turner, 1992; Taylor, Fiske, Etcoff & Ruderman, 1978; Tajfel, 1981a), confirms Tajfel's (1957, 1959) **accentuation principle**:

- The categorisation of stimuli produces a perceptual accentuation of intra-category similarities and inter-category differences on dimensions believed to be correlated with the categorisation.

- The accentuation effect is enhanced where the categorisation has importance, relevance or value to the participant.

**Accentuation principle**
Categorisation accentuates perceived similarities within and differences between groups on dimensions that people believe are correlated with the categorisation. The effect is amplified where the categorisation and/or dimension has subjective importance, relevance or value.

A third condition could be added. Research by Corneille, Klein, Lambert and Judd (2002) has shown that the accentuation effect is most pronounced when people are uncertain about the dimension of judgement. Accentuation was greater for Belgians making length judgements in inches and Americans making length judgements in centimetres (unfamiliar units), than Belgians using centimetres and Americans using inches (familiar units).

The accentuation principle lies at the core of Tajfel's work on intergroup relations and group membership, which has fed into the subsequent development by Turner and his associates of **social identity theory** and **self-categorisation theory** (e.g. Hogg, 2006; Hogg & Abrams, 1988; Tajfel & Turner, 1979; Turner, 1982; Turner, Hogg, Oakes, Reicher & Wetherell, 1987); these theories are described in Chapter 11. However, Tajfel (1981a) felt that while categorisation might explain the process of stereotyping as a context-dependent perceptual distortion of varying strength, it could not explain, for example, the origins of specific stereotypes about specific groups.

Stereotypes are not only consensual beliefs held by members of one group about members of another group, they are also more general *theories* (von Hippel, Sekaquaptewa & Vargas, 1995) or social representations (Farr & Moscovici, 1984; Lorenzi-Cioldi & Clémence, 2001; see also Chapters 3 and 5) of the attributes of other groups. To flesh out our understanding of stereotypes, we may need to go beyond cognitive processes and once again incorporate an analysis of the content of specific stereotypes (Hamilton, Stroessner & Driscoll, 1994) and an analysis of how stereotypes are formed, represented and used in language and communication (Maass, 1999; Maass & Arcuri, 1996). Tajfel believed that to do this both the social functions of stereotypes and the wider sociohistorical context of relations between groups would need to be considered (Tajfel, 1981a; see also Hogg & Abrams, 1988; Leyens, Yzerbyt & Schadron, 1994; Oakes, Haslam & Turner, 1994) – this idea is pursued in Chapters 3 and 11.

Although stereotypes have inertia, they are not static. They respond to features of the social context and to people's motives. The idea that immediate or more enduring changes in social context (e.g. whom one compares oneself with, and for what purpose) affect the content and expression of stereotypes has been explored by Oakes and her associates (Oakes, Haslam & Turner, 1994). Generally speaking, stereotypes will persist if they are readily accessible to us in memory (probably because we use them a great deal and they are self-conceptually important) and they seem to make good sense of people's attitudes and behaviour (i.e. they neatly fit 'reality'). Changes in accessibility or fit will change the stereotype.

Motivation also plays an important role, because stereotypical thinking serves multiple purposes (Hilton & von Hippel, 1996). In addition to helping with cognitive parsimony and the reduction of social uncertainty (Hogg, 2007b, in press), stereotypes can clarify social roles (Eagly, 1995), power differentials (Fiske, 1993b) and intergroup conflicts (Robinson, Keltner, Ward & Ross, 1995), and they can justify the status quo (Jost & Banaji, 1994; Jost & Kramer, 2002) or contribute to a positive sense of ingroup identity (Hogg & Abrams, 1988).

# Schema use and development

## Schema use

People, situations and events possess so many features that it may not be immediately obvious which features will be used as a basis of categorisation, and consequently which schemas will apply (see Figure 2.3). For instance, someone may be a British female Catholic from Aberdeen who is witty, well read, not very sporty and works as an engineer. What determines which of these cues will be used as a basis for categorisation and schema use?

Because people tend to use basic-level categories that are neither too inclusive nor too exclusive (Mervis & Rosch, 1981; Rosch, 1978; see above), they initially access subtypes

**Social identity theory**
Theory of group membership and intergroup relations based on self-categorisation, social comparison and the construction of a shared self-definition in terms of ingroup-defining properties.

**Self-categorisation theory**
Turner and associates' theory of how the process of categorising oneself as a group member produces social identity and group and intergroup behaviours.

**Commonly used schemas** Social settings can invoke many schemas. Is a mother someone who is in the home, playing with a child, and perhaps thinking about cooking dinner? Or maybe she is doing something rather dangerous — like climbing a big rock!

rather than superordinate or subordinate categories (e.g. career woman, not woman or female lawyer; Ashmore, 1981; Pettigrew, 1981), and they access social stereotypes and role schemas rather than trait schemas (e.g. politician, not intelligent). People are also more likely to use schemas that are cued by easily detected features, such as skin colour, dress or physical appearance (Brewer & Lui, 1989; Zebrowitz, 1996), or features that are contextually distinctive, such as a single man in a group of women. Accessible schemas, ones that are habitually used or are salient in memory (Bargh, Lombardi & Higgins, 1988; Bargh & Pratto, 1986; Wyer & Srull, 1981), and schemas that have a bearing on features that are important to oneself in that context, have a high probability of being invoked. So, for example, a racist (someone for whom race is important, salient in memory and habitually used to process person information) would tend to use racial schemas more than someone who was not racist. Finally, people tend to cue mood-congruent schemas (Erber, 1991) and schemas that are based on earlier rather than later information (i.e. a primacy effect; see above).

These fairly automatic schema-cueing processes are typically functional and accurate enough for immediate interactive purposes. They have *circumscribed accuracy* (Swann, 1984). Sometimes, however, people need to use more accurate schemas that correspond more closely to the data at hand, in which case there is a shift from theory-driven cognition towards data-driven cognition (Fiske, 1993a; see Figure 2.3). If the costs of being wrong are increased, people are more attentive to data and may use more accurate schemas.

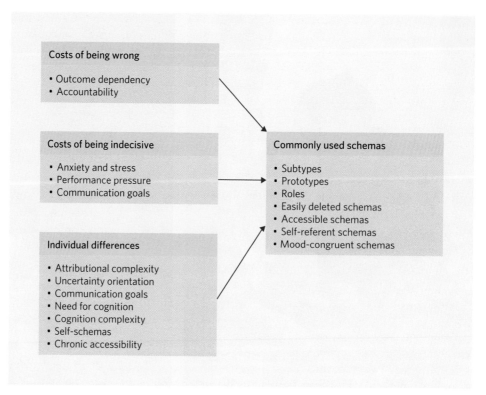

**Figure 2.3** Some major influences on commonly used schemas

Some schemas are more commonly used than others, and their use is influenced by a range of individual and information-processing factors

The costs of being wrong can become important where people's outcomes (i.e. rewards and punishments) depend on the actions or attitudes of others (Erber & Fiske, 1984; Neuberg & Fiske, 1987). Under these circumstances, people probe for more information, attend more closely to data, particularly to schema-inconsistent information, and generally attend more carefully to other people. The costs of being wrong can also be important where people need to be more accountable: that is, to explain or justify their decisions or actions. Under these circumstances, there is greater vigilance and attention to data and generally more complex cognition, which may improve accuracy (Tetlock & Boettger, 1989; Tetlock & Kim, 1987).

If the costs of being indecisive are high, people tend to make a quick decision or form a quick impression; indeed, any decision or impression, however inaccurate, may be preferable to no decision or impression, so people rely heavily on schemas. Performance pressure (i.e. making a judgement or performing a task with insufficient time) can increase schema use. For example, in one study, time pressure caused men and women with conservative sex-role attitudes to discriminate against female job applicants and women with more progressive sex-role attitudes to discriminate against male applicants (Jamieson & Zanna, 1989).

Distraction and anxiety can also increase the subjective cost of indecisiveness and cause people to become more reliant on schematic processing (Wilder & Shapiro, 1989). When one has the task of communicating information to others (e.g. formal presentations), it often becomes more important to be well organised, decisive and clear, and thus it is more important to rely on schemas (Higgins, 1981). This may particularly be the case when the communication is in a scientific mode rather than a narrative mode: that is, when one is communicating about something technical rather than telling a story that requires rich description and characterisation (Zukier, 1986).

SCHEMA USE AND DEVELOPMENT

People can be aware that schematic processing is inaccurate, and in the case of schemas of social groups undesirable, because it involves stereotyping and prejudice. Consequently, people can actively try not to be over-reliant on schemas. Although this can have some success, it is often rather insignificant against the background of the processes described above (Ellis, Olson, & Zanna, 1983). However, there are some general *individual differences* that may influence the degree and type of schema use:

- *Attributional complexity* – people vary in the complexity and number of their explanations of other people (Fletcher, Danilovics, Fernandez, Peterson & Reeder, 1986).

- *Uncertainty orientation* – people vary in their interest in gaining information versus remaining uninformed but certain (Sorrentino & Roney, 1999).

- *Need for cognition* – people differ in how much they like to think deeply about things (Cacioppo & Petty, 1982).

- *Cognitive complexity* – people differ in the complexity of their cognitive processes and representations (Crockett, 1965).

People also differ in the sorts of schema they have about themselves (Markus, 1977; see above). In general, components that are important in our self-schema are also important in the schematic perception of others (Markus, Smith & Moreland, 1985). Individual differences in the chronic **accessibility** (i.e. frequent use, ease of remembering) of schemas can also quite obviously impact on schema use for perceiving others. For instance, Battisch, Assor, Messé and Aronoff (1985) conducted a programme of research showing that people differ in terms of their habitual orientations to others in social interaction (some being more dominant and controlling, some more dependent and reliant) and that this influences schematic processing.

**Accessibility**
Ease of recall of categories or schemas that we already have in mind.

Two types of schema that have been relatively extensively researched, and on which people differ, are gender and political schemas. People tend to differ in terms of the traditional or conservative nature of their gender or sex-role schemas (Bem, 1981), and, among other things, this influences the extent to which they perceive others as being more or less masculine or feminine (see Chapter 10). Political schemas appear to rest on political expertise and knowledge, and their use predicts rapid encoding, focused thought and relevant recall (Fiske, Lau & Smith, 1990; Krosnick, 1990).

## Acquisition, development and change

We can acquire schemas second-hand: for example, you might have a lecturer schema based only on what you have been told about lecturers. In general, however, schemas are constructed, or at least modified, from encounters with category instances (e.g. exposure to individual lecturers in literature, the media or face-to-face). *Schema acquisition* and *development* involve a number of processes:

- Schemas become more abstract, less tied to concrete instances, as more instances are encountered (Park, 1986).

- Schemas become richer and more complex as more instances are encountered: greater experience with a particular person or event produces a more complex schema of that person or event (Linville, 1982).

- With increasing complexity, schemas also become more tightly organised: there are more and more complex links between schematic elements (McKiethen, Reitman, Rueter & Hirtle, 1981).

- Increased organisation produces a more compact schema, one that resembles a single mental construct that can be activated in an all-or-nothing manner (Schul, 1983).

- Schemas become more resilient – they are better able to incorporate exceptions, rather than disregard them because they might threaten the validity of the schema (Fiske & Neuberg, 1990).
- All other things being equal, this entire process should make schemas generally more accurate, in the sense of accurately mapping social reality.

Schemas lend a sense of order, structure and coherence to a social world that would otherwise be highly complex and unpredictable. For this reason, there are strong pressures to maintain schemas (Crocker, Fiske & Taylor, 1984). People are enormously resistant to schema-disconfirming information, which they generally disregard or reinterpret. For example, Ross, Lepper and Hubbard (1975) allowed participants to form impressions of a target individual on the basis of the information that the target made good decisions or poor decisions (getting 24 or 10 items correct out of a total of 25). Although participants were then told that the information was false, they maintained their impressions – predicting that, on average on a subsequent task, the target would get 19 or 14.5 items correct.

The perseverance of schemas has implications for courtroom practice, especially in the United States, where lawyers introduce inadmissible evidence. The judge demands that the evidence be withdrawn and struck from the official trial record, and instructs the jury to disregard the evidence. But we know full well that an impression formed from inadmissible evidence will not vanish just because the judge has instructed jurors to disregard it (Thompson, Fong, & Rosenhan 1981).

Schemas are also maintained by thought: people think a great deal about schemas, which effectively involves a process of cognitively mustering schema-consistent evidence (Millar & Tesser, 1986). People also protect their schemas by relying uncritically on their own earlier judgements – they construct justifications and rationalisations based on prior judgements, which are in turn based on even earlier judgements. The original basis of the schema is lost in the mists of time and is rarely unearthed, let alone critically re-examined (Schul & Burnstein, 1985).

The possession of relatively stable and unchanging schemas, even slightly inaccurate ones, provides us with significant information-processing advantages. However, gross inaccuracy will lead to schema change. For example, a schema that characterised wild lions as cuddly, good-natured and playful pets might, if you encountered one on foot in the wild, change rather dramatically – assuming that you survived the encounter!

Rothbart (1981) has suggested three processes of schema change:

**Bookkeeping**
Gradual schema change through the accumulation of bits of schema-inconsistent information.

**Conversion**
Sudden schema change as a consequence of gradual accumulation of schema-inconsistent information.

**Subtyping**
Schema change as a consequence of schema-inconsistent information, causing the formation of subcategories.

1 **Bookkeeping** – a slow process of gradual change in response to new evidence.
2 **Conversion** – disconfirming information gradually accrues until something like a critical mass has been attained, at which point there is a sudden and massive change.
3 **Subtyping** – schemas change their configuration, in response to disconfirming instances, by the formation of subcategories.

Research tends to favour the subtyping model (Weber & Crocker, 1983; see Chapter 11 for a discussion of stereotype change). For example, a woman who believes that men are violent might, through encountering many who are not, form a subtype of non-violent men to contrast with violent men.

Schema change may also depend on the extent to which schemas are *logically disconfirmable* or *practically disconfirmable* (Reeder & Brewer, 1979). Logically disconfirmable schemas are more easily changed by disconfirming evidence: if my schema of Paul is that he is *honest*, then evidence that he has cheated is very likely to change my schema (honest people do not cheat). Practically disconfirmable schemas are also more easily changed: they are ones for which the likelihood of encountering discrepant instances is relatively high – for example, *friendliness*, because it is often displayed in daily life (Rothbart & Park, 1986). There is less opportunity to display *cowardice*, for example, so a *cowardly* schema is less practically disconfirmable.

# Social encoding

Social encoding refers to the process whereby external social stimuli are represented in the mind of the individual. There are several stages to this process (Bargh, 1984):

1 *Pre-attentive analysis* – a general, automatic and non-conscious scanning of the environment.

2 *Focal attention* – once noticed, stimuli are consciously identified and categorised.

3 *Comprehension* – stimuli are given semantic meaning.

4 *Elaborative reasoning* – the semantically represented stimulus is linked to other knowledge to allow for complex inferences.

Clearly, the process of social encoding depends heavily on what captures our attention.

## Salience

Attention-capturing stimuli are salient stimuli. In social cognition, **salience** refers to the property of a stimulus that makes it stand out relative to other stimuli. Consider the second focus question. For example, a single male is salient in an all-female group but not salient in a sex-balanced group; a woman in the late stages of pregnancy is salient in most contexts except at the obstetrician's clinic; and someone wearing a bright T-shirt is salient at a funeral but not on the beach. Salience is 'out there' – a property of the stimulus domain. People can be salient because:

● they are novel (single man, pregnant woman) or figural (bright T-shirt) in the immediate context (McArthur & Post, 1977);

● they are behaving in ways that do not fit prior expectations of them as individuals, as members of a particular social category or as people in general (Jones & McGillis, 1976); or

● they are important to your specific or more general goals, they dominate your visual field, or you have been told to pay attention to them (Erber & Fiske, 1984; Taylor & Fiske, 1975; see Figure 2.4).

**Salience**
Property of a stimulus that makes it stand out in relation to other stimuli and attract attention.

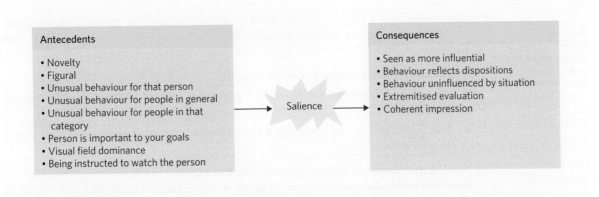

**Figure 2.4**  Some antecedents and consequences of social salience

For social cognition, salience is mainly a property of the stimulus in relation to other stimuli in the social context. It has predictable consequences for perception, thought and behaviour

**Standing out**
Salient stimuli capture our attention. The man on the left stands out against a Hari Krishna group — a case of salience in reverse!

Salient people attract attention and, relative to non-salient people, tend to be considered more influential in a group. They are also more personally responsible for their behaviour and less influenced by the situation, and they are generally evaluated more extremely (McArthur, 1981; Taylor & Fiske, 1978; see Figure 2.4). Because we attend more to salient people, they dominate our thoughts and, consequently, increase the coherence (i.e. organisation and consistency) of our impressions. People do not necessarily recall more about salient people; rather, they find it easier to access a coherent impression of the person. For example, imagine you generally do not like very tall men. If you now go to a party where one particularly tall man stands out, you may feel very negative about him and feel that he dominated conversation and was relatively uninfluenced by others. Although you will not necessarily recall much accurate information about his behaviour, you will have formed a fairly coherent impression of him as a person.

## Vividness

**Vividness**
An intrinsic property of a stimulus on its own that makes it stand out and attract attention.

While salience is a property of the stimulus in relation to other stimuli in a particular context, **vividness** is an intrinsic property of the stimulus itself. Vivid stimuli are ones that are:

- emotionally interesting (e.g. a violent crime);
- concrete and image-provoking (e.g. a gory and detailed description of a violent crime); or
- close to you in time and place (e.g. a violent crime committed yesterday in your street) (Nisbett & Ross, 1980).

Vivid stimuli ought to attract attention just like salient stimuli, and ought therefore to have similar social cognitive effects. However, research has not confirmed this (Taylor & Thompson, 1982). Vividly presented information (e.g. through direct experience or colour-ful language accompanied by pictures or videos) may be more entertaining than pallidly presented information, but it is not more persuasive than pallidly presented information.

Apparent effects of vividness can often be attributed to other factors that co-occur with vividness. For example, vivid stimuli may convey more information, and thus it may be the information and not the vividness that influences social cognition.

## Accessibility

Attention is often directed not so much by stimulus properties 'out there' but by the accessibility, or ease of recall, of categories or schemas that we already have in our heads (Higgins, 1996). Accessible categories are readily and automatically **primed** by features of the stimulus domain to make sense of the intrinsically ambiguous nature of social information. They are categories that we often use, have recently used and are consistent with current goals, needs and expectations (Bruner, 1957, 1958). For example, people who are very concerned about sex discrimination (i.e. it is an accessible category) may find that they see sexism almost everywhere: it is readily primed and used to interpret the social world. Some categories are chronically accessible; they are habitually primed in many contexts (Bargh, Lombardi & Higgins, 1988), and this can have pervasive effects. Bargh and Tota (1988) suggest that depression may be attributed in part to chronic accessibility of negative self-schemas.

**Priming**
Activation of accessible categories or schemas in memory that influence how we process new information.

Research on accessibility exposes people to cues that prime particular categories. This is done in such a way that people do not consciously detect the cue/category link. Participants then interpret ambiguous behaviour (Higgins, Bargh & Lombardi, 1985). Participants could be exposed to words such as *adventurous* or *reckless* and then be asked to interpret behaviour such as 'shooting rapids in a canoe'. The interpretation of the behaviour would be different depending on the category primed by the cue word. For example, studies in the United States have shown that racial categories can be primed by words relating to African Americans. White participants so primed interpreted ambiguous behaviour as being more hostile and aggressive, which is consistent with racial stereotypes (Devine, 1989).

Once primed, a category tends to encode stimuli by assimilating them into the primed category: that is, interpreting them in a *category-consistent* manner. This is particularly true of ambiguous stimuli. However, when people become aware that a category has been primed, they often contrast stimuli with the category: that is, they interpret them in a *category-incongruent* manner (Herr, Sherman & Fazio, 1983; Martin, 1986). For example, gender is often an accessible category that is readily primed and used to interpret behaviour (Stangor, 1988); but if you knew that gender had been primed, you might make a special effort to interpret behaviour in a non-sexist way.

# Person memory

Social behaviour depends very much on how we store information about other people: that is, on what we remember about other people (Fiske & Taylor, 1991; Martin & Clark, 1990; Ostrom, 1989b). Social psychological approaches to person memory draw on cognitive psychological theories of memory and mainly adopt what is called an **associative network** or *propositional* model of memory (e.g. Anderson, 1990). The general idea is that we store *propositions* (e.g. 'The student reads the book', 'The book is a social psychology text', 'The student has a ponytail') that consist of nodes or ideas (e.g. book, ponytail, student, reads) that are linked by relationships between ideas. The links are *associative* in so far as nodes are associated with other nodes (e.g. *student* and *ponytail*), but some associative links are stronger than others. Links become strengthened the more they are activated by cognitive rehearsal (e.g. recalling or thinking about the propositions), and the more different links there are to a specific idea (i.e. alternative retrieval routes) the more likely it is to be recalled.

**Associative network**
Model of memory in which nodes of ideas are connected by associative links along which cognitive activation can spread.

Recall is a process in which nodes become activated and the activation spreads to other nodes along established associative links: for example, the node *student* activates the node *ponytail* because there is a strong associative link. Finally, a distinction is made between *long-term memory*, which is the vast store of information that can potentially be brought to mind, and *short-term memory* (or working memory), which is the much smaller amount of information that you actually have in consciousness, and is the focus of your attention, at a specific time.

This sort of memory model has been applied to person memory (Hastie, 1988; Srull & Wyer, 1989; Wyer & Carlston, 1994), with the important feature that information that is inconsistent with our general impression of someone is generally better recalled than impression-consistent information. This is because impression-inconsistent information attracts attention and generates more cognition and thought, thus strengthening linkages and retrieval routes. However, inconsistent information is not recalled better in the following circumstances:

- if we already have a well-established impression (Fiske & Neuberg, 1990);
- if the inconsistency is purely descriptive and not evaluative (Wyer & Gordon, 1982);
- if we are making a complex judgement (Bodenhausen & Lichtenstein, 1987);
- if we have time afterwards to think about our impression (Wyer & Martin, 1986).

## Contents of person memory

Consider your best friend for a moment. No doubt, an enormous amount of detail comes to mind – her likes and dislikes, her attitudes, beliefs and values, her personality traits, the things she does, what she looks like, what she wears, or where she usually goes. This array of information varies in terms of how concrete and directly observable it is: it ranges from appearance, which is concrete and directly observable, through behaviour, to traits that are not directly observable but are based on inference (Park, 1986). Cutting across this continuum is a general tendency for people to cluster together features that are positive and desirable and, separately, those that are negative and undesirable.

Most person-memory research concerns *traits*. Traits are stored in the usual propositional form ('Mary is mean and nasty') but are based on elaborate inferences from behaviour and situations. The inference process rests heavily on making causal attributions for people's behaviour (the subject matter of Chapter 3). The storage of trait information appears to be organised with respect to two continua: social desirability (e.g. *warm, pleasant, friendly*) and competence (e.g. *intelligent, industrious, efficient*; see Schneider, Hastorf & Ellsworth, 1979). Trait memories can be quite abstract and can colour more concrete memories of behaviour and appearance.

*Behaviour* is usually perceived as purposeful action, so memory for behaviour may be organised with respect to people's goals: the behaviour 'Michael runs to catch the bus' is stored in terms of Michael's goal to catch the bus. In this respect, behaviour, although more concrete and observable than traits, also involves some inference – inference of purpose (Hoffman, Mischel & Mazze, 1981).

Memory for *appearance* is usually based on directly observable concrete information ('Winston has long blond hair and an aquiline nose') and is stored as an analogue rather than a proposition. In other words, appearance is stored directly, like a picture in the mind, which retains all the original spatial information, rather than as a deconstructed set of propositions that have symbolic meaning. Laboratory studies reveal that we are phenomenally accurate at remembering faces: we can often recall faces with 100 per cent accuracy over very long periods of time (Freides, 1974). However, we tend to be less accurate at recognising the faces of people who are of a different race from our own (Malpass &

## Research and applications 2.3
### Eyewitness testimony is often highly unreliable

On 22 July 2005, two weeks after the 7 July London bombings and the day after the 21 July failed bombing, a Brazilian electrician who had been under surveillance by the police entered Stockwell tube station in London dressed in a bulky winter coat. It was a hot midsummer's day. Plain-clothes police followed him into the station and ordered him to stop. Instead, he ran – vaulting barriers and jumping on to a tube. The police brought him to the ground and shot him five times in the head. There were many witnesses – they gave very different accounts of what had happened. According to the *Guardian* (23 July 2005, p. 3) one eyewitness reported that the man had been pursued by 3 plain-clothes police, and that there were 5 shots; another reported 10 policemen armed with machine guns and that there were 6 to 8 shots; another reported shots from a 'silencer gun'; another reported 20 cops carrying big black guns; another reported that the man had a bomb belt with wires, and that there were 2 shots.

Different people witnessing the same event can see very different things, especially when the situation is fast-moving, confusing and frightening. Eyewitness testimony can be highly unreliable. (Reflect on the fourth focus question at the beginning of this chapter. Perhaps Hillary Clinton was not actually lying).

Kravitz, 1969). One explanation of this effect is that we simply pay less attention to, or process more superficially, outgroup faces (Devine & Malpass, 1985). Indeed, superficial encoding undermines memory for faces in general, and one remedy for poor memory for faces is simply to pay more attention (Wells & Turtle, 1988).

We are also remarkably inaccurate at remembering appearances in natural contexts where eyewitness testimony is required: for example, identifying or describing a stranger we saw commit a crime (Kassin, Ellsworth & Smith, 1989; Loftus, 1979). This is probably because witnesses or victims often do not get a good, clear look at the offender: the offence may be frightening, unexpected, confusing and over quickly, and the offender may only be glimpsed through a dirty car window or may wear a mask or some other disguise. More broadly, eyewitness testimony, even if confidently given, should be treated with caution (see Box 2.3). However, eyewitness testimony is more accurate if certain conditions are met (Shapiro & Penrod, 1986; see Box 2.4).

## Organisation of person memory

In general, we remember people as a cluster of information about their traits, behaviour and appearance. However, we can also store information about people in a very different way: we can cluster people under attributes or groups. Social memory, therefore, can be

## Research and applications 2.4
### Factors that improve the accuracy of eyewitness testimony

Although eyewitness testimony is often unreliable, there are various ways in which its accuracy can be improved.

#### The witness
- mentally goes back over the scene of the crime to reinstate additional cues;
- has already associated the person's face with other symbolic information;
- was exposed to the person's face for a long time;
- gave testimony a very short time after the crime;
- is habitually attentive to the external environment;
- generally forms vivid mental images.

#### The person
- had a face that was not altered by disguise;
- looked dishonest.

*Source:* based on Shapiro & Penrod, 1986

**Person memory**
How accurately do you think you might
describe a person who stole your bag?
Check Box 2.3

organised by *person* or by *group* (Pryor & Ostrom, 1981; see Figure 2.5). In most settings, the preferred mode of organisation is by person, probably because it produces richer and more accurate person memories that are more easily recalled (Sedikides & Ostrom, 1988). (Recall that Julie and Rosa have different memories of Aaron in the third focus question.) Organisation by person is particularly likely when people are significant to us because they are familiar, real people with whom we expect to interact across many specific situations (Srull, 1983).

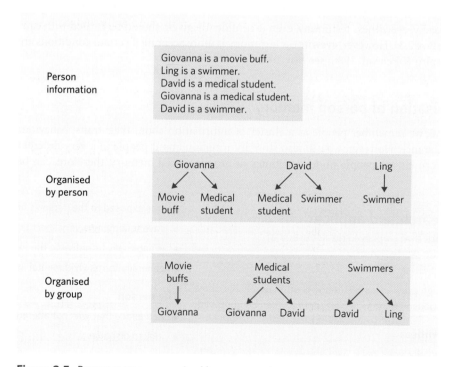

**Figure 2.5** Person memory organised by person or by group

We can organise information about people in two quite different ways. We can cluster attributes under individual people, or we can cluster people under attributes or groups

*Source*: based on Fiske & Taylor (1991)

Organisation by group membership is likely in first encounters with strangers: the person is pigeonholed, described and stored in terms of stereotypical attributes of a salient social category (e.g. age, ethnicity, sex; see Chapter 10). Over time, the organisation may change to one based on the person. For example, your memory of a lecturer you have encountered only a few times lecturing on a topic you are not very interested in will most likely be organised in terms of the stereotypical properties of the social group 'lecturers'. If you should happen to get to know this person a little better, you might find that your memory gradually or suddenly becomes reorganised in terms of the lecturer as a distinct individual person.

There is an alternative perspective on the relationship between person-based and group-based person memory, and that is that they can coexist as essentially distinct forms of representation (Srull & Wyer, 1989; Wyer & Martin, 1986). These distinct forms of representation may be associated with different sorts of identity that people may have, based on either interpersonal relationships or group memberships. This idea is consistent with *social identity theory*, which is a theory of group behaviour as something quite distinct from interpersonal behaviour (e.g. Hogg & Abrams, 1988; Tajfel & Turner, 1979; see Chapter 11).

## Using person memory

Presumably, in making social judgements we draw upon person memory. In fact, it appears that sometimes we do, but sometimes we do not. Hastie and Park (1986) have integrated the findings from a large number of studies to conclude that, by default, people tend to form impressions of people *on-line*: that is, they rely disproportionately on incoming data, which are assimilated by schemas to produce an impression. There is little correlation between memory and judgement. It is more unusual for people to draw on memory and make *memory-based* judgements, but when they do there is a stronger correlation between memory and judgement. Whether people make on-line or memory-based judgements or

### Research and applications 2.5
Goals and their effects on person memory

People's information processing and social interactive goals affect their memory for people.

| Goal | Effect |
| --- | --- |
| Comprehension | Limited memory |
| Memorising | Variable memory, organised in an ad hoc manner, often by psychologically irrelevant categories |
| Forming impressions | Good memory, organised by traits |
| Empathising | Good memory, organised by goals |
| Comparing with oneself | Excellent memory, organised by psychological categories (traits or goals) |
| Anticipated interaction | Excellent, well-organised memory, type of organisation not yet clear |
| Actual interaction | Variable memory, depending on concurrent goal |

*Source:* based on Fiske & Taylor (1991)

impressions is influenced by the goals and purposes they bring to the interaction or to the judgement task.

The general principle is that recall of information about other people improves as the purpose of the interaction becomes more psychologically engaging and less superficial (Srull & Wyer, 1986, 1989; Wyer & Srull, 1986). Psychologically engaging interactions entail information processing at a deeper level that involves the elaboration of more complex and more varied links between elements, and consequently a more integrated memory (Greenwald & Pratkanis, 1984). Paradoxically, then, instructing someone to memorise another person (psychologically not very engaging) will be less effective than asking someone to form an impression, which in turn will be less effective than asking someone to empathise. Box 2.5 shows a number of goals and how they affect person memory.

# Social inference

Social inference is, in many respects, the core of social cognition. It addresses the inferential processes (which can be quite formal and abstract, or intuitive and concrete) that we use to identify, sample and combine information to form impressions and make judgements. There are two distinct ways in which we process social information: (a) we can rely automatically on general schemas or stereotypes in a top-down deductive fashion; or (b) we can deliberatively rely on specific instances in a bottom-up inductive fashion. This distinction is a theme that runs through social cognition, and it surfaces in different guises.

We have already discussed the distinction between Asch's configural model (impressions are based on holistic images) and Anderson's cognitive algebra model (impressions are based on integration of pieces of information) earlier in this chapter. More recently, Brewer (1988, 1994) has proposed a dual-process model that contrasts relatively automatic category-based processing of social information with more deliberate and personalised attribute-based processing. Closely related is Fiske and Neuberg's (1990; Fiske & Dépret, 1996) continuum model, which makes a similar distinction between schema-based and data-based inferences. From research into attitudes come two other related distinctions (Eagly & Chaiken, 1993; see Chapter 6 for details). Petty and Cacioppo's (1986b) elaboration-likelihood model distinguishes between *central route processing*, where people carefully and deliberately consider information, and *peripheral route processing*, where people make rapid top-of-the-head decisions based on stereotypes, schemas and other cognitive short-cuts. Almost identical is Chaiken's (Bohner, Moskowitz & Chaiken, 1995; Chaiken, Liberman & Eagly, 1989) heuristic–systematic model: people process information carefully and systematically, or they rather automatically rely on cognitive heuristics.

Generally, social cognition researchers have studied inferential processes in comparison with ideal processes, called **normative models,** which produce the best possible inferences. Collectively, these normative models are known as **behavioural decision theory** (Einhorn & Hogarth, 1981). The intuitive strategies of social inference involve a range of biases and errors, which produce suboptimal inferences – inferences that fall short of those dictated by the principles of behavioural decision theory (e.g. Fiske & Taylor, 2008; Nisbett & Ross, 1980).

**Normative models**
Ideal processes for making accurate social inferences.

**Behavioural decision theory**
Set of normative models (ideal processes) for making accurate social inferences.

## Departures from normality

### Gathering and sampling social information

The first stage in making an inference involves the gathering of data and the sampling of information from those data. In doing this, people tend to rely too heavily on schemas. This can cause them to overlook information that is potentially useful, or to exaggerate the importance of information that is misleading. For example, members of selection committees

**Departures from normality**
If we rely too heavily on schemas, we may ignore interesting details, attend too closely to misleading information, or even worse!

believe they are assessing candidates objectively on the basis of information provided by the candidate. However, what often seems to happen is that person schemas are quickly, and often unconsciously, activated and used as the basis for candidate assessment. This reliance on person schemas is referred to as 'clinical judgement' and, although by no means all bad, it can produce suboptimal inferences and judgements (Dawes, Faust & Meehl, 1989).

People can also be unduly influenced by extreme examples and small samples (small samples are rarely representative of larger populations: this is called the *law of large numbers*); and they can be inattentive to biases in samples and to how typical a sample is of its population. For example, in Europe there is substantial media coverage of hate-speech by radical 'Islamists' who promote anti-western violence and terrorism. From this, people may infer that Muslims in general behave like this. However, this inference is based on unrepresentative information (most mass media present extreme, not ordinary, cases) that portrays a small sample of atypical Muslims behaving in an extreme manner.

## Regression

Individual cases or instances are often more extreme than the average of the population from which they are drawn: over a number of cases or instances, there is a **regression** to the population mean. For example, a restaurant you have just visited for the first time may have been truly excellent, causing you to extol its virtues to all your friends. However, the next time you go it turns out to be mediocre. On the next visit, it is moderately good, and on the next fairly average. This is an example of regression. The restaurant is probably actually moderately good, but this would not become apparent from one visit: a number of visits would have to be made. The way to control for regression effects in forming impressions is to be conservative and cautious in making inferences from limited information (one or a few cases or instances). However, people tend not to do this: they are generally ignorant of regression, and do not control for it in forming impressions and making judgements (Kahneman & Tversky, 1973).

People can, however, be induced to make more conservative inferences if the initial information is made to seem less diagnostic by the presence of other information. For example, knowing that Hans shoots cats may generate an extreme and negative impression

**Regression**
Tendency for initial observations of instances from a category to be more extreme than subsequent observations.

of him: shooting cats is relatively diagnostic of being a nasty person. However, if this piece of information is *diluted* (Nisbett, Zukier & Lemley, 1981) by other information that he is a committed conservationist who writes poetry, collects antiques, drives a hybrid and cares for his infirm mother, the impression is likely to become less extreme, because the tendency to use the diagnosis 'he shoots cats' is weakened.

## Base-rate information

**Base-rate information**
Pallid, factual, statistical information about an entire class of events.

**Base-rate information** is general information, usually factual and statistical, about an entire class of events. For instance, if we knew that only 5 per cent of university lecturers gave truly awful lectures, or that only 7 per cent of social security recipients preferred being on the dole to working, this would be base-rate information. Research shows that people chronically under-use this information in making inferences, particularly when more concrete anecdotal case studies exist (Bar-Hillel, 1980; Taylor and Thompson, 1982). So, on the basis of vivid and colourful media exposés of dull lecturers or social security cheats, people would tend to infer that these are stereotypical properties of the parent categories, even if they have the relevant base-rate information to hand.

The main reason that base-rate information is ignored is not so much that it is pallid and uninteresting in comparison with vivid individual instances, but rather that people often fail to see the relevance of base-rate information, relative to other information, to the inference task (Bar-Hillel, 1980). People increase their use of base-rate information when it is made clear that it is more relevant than other information (e.g. case studies) to the inferential task.

## Covariation and illusory correlation

Judgements of covariation are judgements of how strongly two things are related. They are essential to social inference and form the very basis of schemas (schemas, as we saw above, are beliefs about the covariation of behaviour, attitudes or traits). To judge covariation accurately – for example, the relationship between hair colour and how much fun one has – we should consider the number of blondes having fun and not having fun, and the number of brunettes having fun and not having fun. The scientific method provides formal statistical procedures that we could use to assess covariation (Chapter 1). However, in making covariation judgements, people fall far short of normative prescriptions (Alloy & Tabachnik, 1984; Crocker, 1981). In general, this is because they are influenced by prior assumptions (i.e. schemas) and tend to search for or recognise only schema-consistent information: people are generally not interested in disconfirming their cherished schemas. So, in assessing the relationship between hair colour and fun, people may have available the social schema that 'blondes have more fun', and instances of blondes who have fun will come to mind much more readily than blondes who are having a miserable time or brunettes who are having a ball.

**Illusory correlation**
Cognitive exaggeration of the degree of co-occurrence of two stimuli or events, or the perception of a co-occurrence where none exists.

When people assume that a relationship exists between two variables, they tend to over-estimate the degree of correlation or see a correlation where none actually exists. This phenomenon, called **illusory correlation,** was demonstrated by Chapman (1967), who presented students with lists of paired words such as *lion/tiger, lion/eggs, bacon/eggs, blossoms/notebook* and *notebook/tiger*. The students then had to recall how often each word was paired with each other word. Although every word was paired an equal number of times with every other word, participants overestimated meaningful pairings (e.g. *bacon/eggs*) and distinctive pairings (e.g. *blossoms/notebook* – words that were much longer than all the other words in the list).

**Associative meaning**
Illusory correlation in which items are seen as belonging together because they 'ought' to, on the basis of prior expectations.

Chapman reasoned that there are two bases for illusory correlation: **associative meaning** (items are seen as belonging together because they 'ought' to, on the basis of prior expectations) and **paired distinctiveness** (items are thought to go together because they share some unusual feature).

**Paired distinctiveness**
Illusory correlation in which items are seen as belonging together because they share some unusual feature.

Distinctiveness-based illusory correlation may help to explain stereotyping, particularly negative stereotypes of minority groups (Hamilton, 1979; Hamilton & Sherman, 1989; Mullen & Johnson, 1990; see also Chapter 11). Hamilton and Gifford (1976) had participants recall statements describing two groups, A and B. There were twice as many statements about group A as there were about group B, and there were twice as many positive as negative statements about each group. Participants erroneously recalled that more negative statements (the less common statements) were paired with group B (the less common group). When the experiment was replicated but with more negative than positive statements, participants now overestimated the number of positive statements paired with group B.

In real life, negative events are distinctive, as they are perceived to be more rare than positive events (Parducci, 1968), and minority groups are distinctive, as people have relatively few contacts with them. Thus, the conditions for distinctiveness-based illusory correlation are met. There is also evidence for an associative-meaning basis to negative stereotyping of minority groups: people have preconceptions that negative attributes go with minority groups (McArthur & Friedman, 1980).

Although illusory correlation may be involved in the formation and use of stereotypes, its role may be limited to conditions where people make memory-based rather than on-line judgements (McConnell, Sherman & Hamilton, 1994) – after all, they have to remember distinctiveness or associative information in order to make illusory correlations.

More radically, it can be argued that stereotypes are not 'illusory' at all. Rather, they are rational, even deliberate, constructs that differentiate ingroups from outgroups in ways that evaluatively favour the ingroup (Leyens, Yzerbyt & Schadron, 1994; McGarty, Haslam, Turner & Oakes, 1993; Oakes, Haslam & Turner, 1994). In this sense stereotypical differences are functionally adaptive to the stereotyper – they are 'real', and the process of stereotyping is one in which these differences are automatically (and strategically; for example, through rhetoric) accentuated as a consequence of categorising oneself as a member of one of the groups.

## Heuristics

We have now seen how bad we are, in comparison with standards from behavioural decision theory, at making inferences. Perhaps the reason for this is that we have limited short-term memory available for on-line processing but enormous capacity for long-term memory – using the analogy of a computer the former is RAM, random access memory, and the latter hard-drive capacity. It pays, then, to store information schematically in long-term memory and call up schemas to aid inference. Social inference is thus likely to be heavily theory/schema-driven, with the consequence that it is biased towards conservative, schema-supportive inferential practices. Despite doing this, and being so poor at social inference, human beings seem to muddle through. Perhaps the process is adequate for most of our inferential needs most of the time, and we should study these 'adequate' rather than optimal processes in their own right.

With just this idea in mind, Tversky and Kahneman (1974; Kahneman & Tversky, 1973) detail the sorts of cognitive short-cut, called **heuristics,** that people use to reduce complex problem solving to simpler judgemental operations. Three principal heuristics have been researched: (1) representativeness, (2) availability and (3) anchoring and adjustment.

**Heuristics**
Cognitive short-cuts that provide adequately accurate inferences for most of us most of the time.

### Representativeness heuristic

In deciding how likely it is that a person or an event is an instance of one category or another, people often simply estimate the extent to which the instance superficially represents or is similar to a typical or average member of the category. The **representativeness heuristic** is basically a relevance judgement that disregards base-rate

**Representativeness heuristic**
A cognitive short-cut in which instances are assigned to categories or types on the basis of overall similarity or resemblance to the category.

information, sample size, quality of information and other normative principles. Nevertheless, it is fast and efficient and produces inferences that are accurate enough for our purposes most of the time. For example, consider the following information: 'Steve is very shy and withdrawn, invariably helpful, but with little interest in people, or in the world of reality. A meek and tidy soul, he has a need for order and structure, and a passion for detail' (Tversky & Kahneman, 1974). The representativeness heuristic would very quickly lead to the inference that Steve is a librarian rather than, say, a farmer, surgeon or trapeze artist, and in general that would probably be correct.

## Availability heuristic

**Availability heuristic**
A cognitive short-cut in which the frequency or likelihood of an event is based on how quickly instances or associations come to mind.

The **availability heuristic** is used to infer the frequency or likelihood of an event on the basis of how quickly instances or associations come to mind. Where instances are readily available, we tend to inflate frequencies. For example, exposure to many media reports of violent Muslim extremists will make that information available and will tend to inflate our estimate of the overall frequency of violent Muslims. Similarly, in forming an impression of Paul, who has short hair, wears big boots and carries a cane, you might overestimate the likelihood that he will be violent because you have just seen the film *A Clockwork Orange*.

Under many circumstances, availability is adequate as a basis for making inferences – after all, things that come to mind easily are probably fairly plentiful. However, availability is subject to bias, as it does not control for such factors as idiosyncratic exposure to unusual samples.

## Anchoring and adjustment

**Anchoring and adjustment**
A cognitive short-cut in which inferences are tied to initial standards or schemas.

In making inferences we often need a starting point – an anchor – from which, and with which, we can adjust subsequent inferences (e.g. Wyer, 1976). **Anchoring and adjustment** is a heuristic that ties inferences to initial standards. So, for example, inferences about other people are often anchored in beliefs about ourselves: we decide how intelligent, artistic or kind someone else is with reference to our own self-schema. Anchors can also come from the immediate context. For example, Greenberg, Williams and O'Brien (1986) found that participants in a mock jury study who were instructed to contemplate the harshest verdict first used this as an anchor from which only small adjustments were made. A relatively harsh verdict was rendered. Participants instructed to consider the most lenient verdict first likewise used this as an anchor, subsequently rendering a relatively lenient verdict.

## Improving social inference

Social inference is not optimal. We are biased, we misrepresent people and events, and we make mistakes. However, many of these shortcomings may be more apparent than real (Funder, 1987). Social cognition experiments may provide unnatural contexts, for which our inference processes are not well suited. Intuitive inference processes may actually be well suited to everyday life. For example, on encountering a pit bull terrier in the street, it might be very adaptive to rely on availability (media coverage of attacks by pit bull terriers) and to flee automatically rather than adopt more time-consuming normative procedures: what is an error in the laboratory may not be so in the field.

Nevertheless, inferential errors can sometimes have serious consequences. For example, negative stereotyping of minority groups and suboptimal group decisions may be partly caused by inferential errors. In this case, there may be something to be gained by considering ways in which we can improve social inference. The basic principle is that social inference will improve to the extent that we become less reliant on intuitive inferential strategies. This may be achieved through formal education in scientific and rational thinking as well as in statistical techniques (Fong, Krantz & Nisbett, 1986; Nisbett, Krantz, Jepson & Fong, 1982).

# Affect and emotion

Traditionally, social cognition has focused on thinking rather than feeling, but in recent years there has been an 'affective revolution' (e.g. Forgas, 2006; Forgas & Smith, 2007; Haddock & Zanna, 1999; Keltner & Lerner, 2010). Research has focused on how feelings (affect, emotion, mood) influence and are influenced by social cognition. Different situations (funeral, party) evoke different emotions (sad, happy), but also the same situation (examination) can evoke different emotions (anxiety, challenge) in different people (weak student, competent student).

## Antecedents of affect

Research suggests that people process information about the situation and their hopes, desires and abilities, and on the basis of these cognitive *appraisals* different affective reactions and physiological responses follow. Because affective response (emotion) is, fundamentally, a mode of action readiness tied to appraisals of harm and benefit, the appraisal process is continuous and largely automatic (see Box 2.6). Blascovich and his colleagues have proposed a model of challenge and threat. When people feel there is a demand on them they appraise their resources for dealing with the demand – if perceived resources equal or exceed the demand people experience a feeling of challenge that motivates approach behaviours (fight), if perceived resources are inadequate to meet the demand people experience a feeling of threat that motivates avoidance behaviours (flight) (Blascovich, 2008; Blascovich & Tomaka, 1996).

## Consequences of affect

Emotion and mood influence thought and action. Affect infuses and therefore affects thinking, judgement and behaviour. The **affect-infusion model** describes the effects of mood on social cognition (Forgas, 1994, 1995, 2002). The core prediction is that affect

**Affect-infusion model**
Cognition is infused with affect such that social judgements reflect current mood.

---

### Research highlight 2.6
#### How we decide when to respond affectively

According to Smith and Lazarus (1990), affective response rests on seven appraisals, which can be framed as questions that people ask themselves in particular situations. There are two sets of appraisal dimensions, primary and secondary, that are relevant to all emotions.

#### Primary appraisals

1 How relevant (important) is what is happening in this situation to my needs and goals?

2 Is this congruent (good) or incongruent (bad) with my needs or goals?

#### Secondary appraisals

These appraisals relate to accountability and coping.

1 How responsible am I for what is happening in this situation?

2 How responsible is someone or something else?

3 Can I act on this situation to make or keep it more like what I want?

4 Can I handle and adjust to this situation however it might turn out?

5 Do I expect this situation to improve or to get worse?

Together, these seven appraisal dimensions produce a wide array of affective responses and emotions. For example, if something were important and bad and caused by someone else, we would feel anger and be motivated to act towards the other person in a way that would fix the situation. If something were important and bad, but caused by ourselves, then we would feel shame or guilt and be motivated to make amends for the situation.

infusion occurs only where people process information in an open and constructive manner that involves active elaboration of stimulus details and information from memory.

According to Forgas, there are four distinct ways in which people can process information about one another:

- Direct access – they can directly access schemas or judgements stored in memory.
- Motivated processing – they can form a judgement on the basis of specific motivations to achieve a goal or to 'repair' an existing mood.
- Heuristic processing – they can rely on various cognitive short-cuts or heuristics.
- Substantive processing – they can deliberately and carefully construct a judgement from a variety of informational sources.

Current mood states do not influence judgements involving direct access or motivated processing, but they do affect judgements involving heuristic processing or substantive processing. In the latter cases, cognition is infused with affect such that social judgements reflect current mood, either indirectly (affect primes target judgement) or directly (affect acts as information about the target). For example, under heuristic processing mood may itself be a heuristic that determines response – being in a bad mood would produce a negative reaction to another person (i.e. mood-congruence). Under substantive processing, the more we deliberate, the greater the mood-congruence effect. This model fares well in predicting the effects of affect on social cognition.

Affect influences social memory and social judgement – for example, people tend to recall current mood-congruent information more readily than current mood-incongruent information, and judge others and themselves more positively when they themselves are in a positive mood. In line with the affect–infusion model, the effect of mood on self-perception is greater for peripheral than central aspects of self – peripheral aspects are less firmly ensconced and therefore require more elaboration and construction than central aspects (e.g. Sedikides, 1995). Stereotyping is also affected by mood. Being in a good mood can increase reliance on stereotypes when group membership is not very relevant (Forgas & Fiedler, 1996), but negative affect can encourage people to correct hastily made negative evaluations of outgroups (Monteith, 1993).

## Where is the 'social' in social cognition?

Social psychology has always described the cognitive processes and structures that influence and are influenced by social behaviour, and there is no doubt that modern social cognition, which really only emerged in the late 1970s, has made enormous advances in this direction. However, some critics have wondered if social cognition has been *too* successful. It may have taken social psychology too far in the direction of cognitive psychology, and more recently neuroscience, while it has diverted attention from many of social psychology's traditional topics. There has been a worry that there may not be any 'social' in social cognition (Kraut & Higgins, 1984; Markus & Zajonc, 1985; Moscovici, 1982; Zajonc, 1989).

Many of the social cognitive processes and structures that are described seem to be little affected by social context and seem more accurately to represent *asocial* cognition operating on social stimuli (i.e. people). In this respect, critics have characterised social cognition as **reductionist** (see Chapter 1) and have focused on three main areas of concern – a failure to deal properly with language and communication, which are two fundamentally social variables, a failure to deal with processes of human interaction, and a failure properly to articulate cognitive processes with wider interpersonal, group and societal processes. However, there are exceptions; for example, Maass and Arcuri's (1996) research on language

**Reductionism**
A phenomenon in terms of the language and concepts of a lower level of analysis, usually with a loss of explanatory power.

and stereotyping (see Chapter 15), and self-categorisation research on collective self and group behaviour (Turner, Hogg, Oakes, Reicher & Wetherell, 1987; see Chapter 11). It is also the case that in recent years there has been a more systematic attempt to (re)-socialise social cognition (e.g., Abrams & Hogg, 1999; Hamilton & Stroessner, in press; Levine, Resnick & Higgins, 1993; Moskowitz, 2005; Nye & Bower, 1996; Wyer & Gruenfeld, 1995).

One strand of social cognition has, however, moved in the opposite direction towards greater reductionism – in the guise of social neuroscience (e.g., Harmon-Jones & Winkielman, 2007; Lieberman, 2010; Ochsner, 2007; Ochsner & Lieberman, 2001). Social neuroscience, which focuses on brain correlates of behaviour, would seem to suffer all the problems of traditional social cognition, but even more so – mapping complex social behaviour on to localised electrical activity in the brain. Although advocates for social neuroscience see much of value and a central contribution to social psychology in this particular form of reductionism, many other social psychologists are wary, wondering how knowledge of what part of the brain 'lights up' can help us understand complex social behaviours such as negotiation, social dilemmas and conformity – for a discussion of pros and cons of social neuroscience in explaining group processes and intergroup relations, see Prentice and Eberhardt (2008).

## Summary

- Social cognition refers to cognitive processes and structures that affect and are affected by social context. It is assumed that people have a limited capacity to process information and are cognitive misers who take all sorts of cognitive short-cuts; or they are motivated tacticians who choose, on the basis of their goals, motives and needs, among an array of cognitive strategies.

- The overall impressions we form of other people are dominated by stereotypes, unfavourable information, first impressions and idiosyncratic personal constructs. Research suggests that in forming impressions of other people we weight components and then average them in complex ways; or certain components may influence the interpretation and meaning of all other components and dominate the resulting impression.

- Schemas are cognitive structures that represent knowledge about people, events, roles, the self and the general processing of information. Once invoked, schemas bias all aspects of information processing and inference in such a way that the schema remains unassailed.

- Categories are fuzzy sets of features organised around a prototype. They are hierarchically structured in terms of inclusiveness in such a way that less inclusive categories are subsets of broader, more inclusive categories. The process of categorisation accentuates perceived intracategory similarities and intercategory differences on dimensions that a person believes are correlated with the categorisation. This accentuation effect is the basis for stereotyping, but it requires articulation with a consideration of intergroup relations to provide a full explanation.

- In processing information about other people, we tend to rely on schemas relating to subtypes, stereotypes, current moods, easily detected features, accessible categories and self-relevant information. However, people are less dependent on schemas when the cost of making a wrong inference is increased, when the cost of being indecisive is low, and when people are aware that schematic processing may be inaccurate.

- Schemas become more abstract, complex, organised, compact, resilient and accurate over time. They are hard to change but can be modified by schema-inconsistent information, mainly through the formation of subtypes.

- The encoding of information is heavily influenced by the salience of stimuli and by the cognitive accessibility of existing schemas.

- We tend to remember people mainly in terms of their traits but also in terms of their behaviour and appearance. They can be stored as individual people, or as category members.

- The processes we use to make inferences fall far short of ideal. Our schemas dominate us, we disregard regression effects and base-rate information, and we perceive illusory correlations. We rely on cognitive short-cuts (heuristics) such as representativeness, availability, and anchoring and adjustment, rather than on more optimal information-processing techniques.

- Affect and emotion are cognitively underpinned by appraisals of accountability, and our needs, goals and capacity to deal with a demand in a particular situation. In turn, affect influences social cognition – it infuses social cognition only where people process information in an open and constructive manner that involves active elaboration of stimulus details and information from memory.

- Social cognition has been criticised for being too cognitive and for not properly relating cognitive processes and structures to language, social interaction and social structure, consequently failing to address many topics of central concern to social psychology. This situation has improved in recent years; however, social neuroscience may fall prey to these limitations in an even bigger way.

## Literature, film and TV

### *Calendar Girls*

2003 film directed by Nigel Cole, written by Tim Firth and Juliette Towhidi, and starring Helen Mirren and Julie Walters. A Women's Institute fundraising effort for a local hospital by posing nude for a calendar becomes a media sensation. A comedy with serious undertones – it focuses on stereotypical expectations and scripted behaviour, and how society and institutions react when people act out of role or against expectations.

### *The Reader*

2008 film directed by Stephen Daldry and starring Ralph Fiennes, Jeanette Hain and David Kross. A teenage boy, Michael, in post-Second World War Germany develops a passionate relationship with an older woman, Hanna, which profoundly affects him. Hanna suddenly disappears, but reappears 8 years later in Michael's life when she is on trial for War Crimes. The impression of Hanna that Michael has cherished for so long is dramatically and upsettingly turned upside down. One way in which Michael deals with this is by focusing on a positive aspect of his former impression of her – her vulnerability in one aspect of her life.

### *Billy Elliot*

2000 film by Stephen Daldry, and with Julie Walters. Set in a north of England mining town against the backdrop of the very bitter 1984 miners' strike. Billy Elliot is an 11-year-old boy who rejects the traditional male activity of boxing – preferring to become a ballet dancer. Shows what happens when people violate social scripts and behave out of role in counter-stereotypical ways.

### Reality TV

In shows such as *I'm a Celebrity, Get Me Out of Here,* minor celebrities attempt to gain publicity by projecting particular images of themselves to the public. These programmes show how people construct, manage and project impressions about themselves, and form impressions of other people. Also relevant to Chapter 4 (self), Chapter 13 (relationships) and to social psychology in general.

### *About a Boy*

2002 feel-good comedy by Chris and Paul Weitz, starring Hugh Grant. One of the themes in this light-hearted film is the embarrassment felt by the young boy, Marcus (Nicholas Hoult), because of the weirdness of his mother Fiona (Toni Collette), an ex-hippie depressive who tries to commit suicide and dresses Marcus strangely for school. Marcus is made to stand out and be salient at an age where one simply wants to fit in and be ordinary and part of the crowd.

## Guided questions

1   You have heard the saying that people sometimes 'judge a book by its cover'. Use this idea as a springboard to outline how we form our first impressions of another person.
2   How are *schemas* related to *stereotypes*? Give an example. See an experimental demonstration of how rapid cognitive processing might lead people to fire a weapon at someone based on their race in Chapter 2 of MyPsychLab at **www.mypsychlab.co.uk** (watch *Social cognition*).
3   Why are stereotypes slow to change?
4   How reliable is witness testimony? Apply what you know about *person memory* to this issue.
5   Can thinking be affected by our moods?

## Learn more

Devine, P. G., Hamilton, D. L., & Ostrom, T. M. (eds) (1994). *Social cognition: Impact on social psychology*. San Diego: Academic Press. Leading experts discuss the impact that social cognition has had on a wide range of topics in social psychology.

Dijksterhuis, A. (2010). Automaticity and the unconscious. In S. T. Fiske, D. T. Gilbert, & G. Lindzey (eds), *Handbook of social psychology* (5th ed., Vol. 1, pp. 228–267). New York: Wiley. Detailed and comprehensive coverage of perhaps the core of social cognition – automatic cognitive processes.

Fiske, S. T., & Taylor, S. E. (2008). *Social cognition: From brains to culture*. New York: McGraw-Hill. This is essentially the third edition of Fiske and Taylor's classic social cognition text – it is comprehensive, detailed and well written, and covers the recent development of social neuroscience.

Forgas, J. P., & Smith, C. A. (2007). Affect and emotion. In M. A. Hogg & J. Cooper (eds), *The SAGE handbook of social psychology: Concise student edition* (pp. 146–175). London: SAGE. Comprehensive and readable overview of what we know about the social cognitive antecedents and consequences of people's feelings.

Hamilton, D. L. (ed.) (2004). *Social cognition: Essential readings*. New York: Psychology Press. An edited collection of classic publications in social cognition. The book has an introductory overview chapter and shorter introductory chapters for each section.

Hamilton, D., & Stroessner, S. J. (in press). *Social cognition*. London: SAGE. Completely up-to-date and readable coverage of social cognition from one of social cognition's founding fathers, David Hamilton.

Keltner, D., & Lerner, J. S. (2010). Emotion. In S. T. Fiske, D. T. Gilbert, & G. Lindzey (eds), *Handbook of social psychology* (5th ed., Vol. 1, pp. 317–352). New York: Wiley. Completely up-to-date and very detailed overview of what we know about affect and emotion.

Lieberman, M. D. (2010). Social cognitive neuroscience. In S. T. Fiske, D. T. Gilbert, & G. Lindzey (eds), *Handbook of social psychology* (5th ed., Vol. 1, pp. 143–193). New York: Wiley. Up-to-date and very detailed overview of social neuroscience from one of its leading researchers.

Macrae, C. N., & Quadflieg, S. (2010). Perceiving people. In S. T. Fiske, D. T. Gilbert, & G. Lindzey (eds), *Handbook of social psychology* (5th ed., Vol. 1, pp. 428–463). New York: Wiley. Comprehensive coverage of what we know about person perception – how we form and use our cognitive representations of people.

Moskowitz, G. B. (2005). *Social cognition: Understanding self and others*. New York: Guilford. A relatively recent comprehensive social cognition text that is written in a relatively accessible style as an introduction to the topic.

 Refresh your understanding, assess your progress and go further with interactive summaries, questions, podcasts and much more at **www.mypsychlab.co.uk**

## This chapter discusses

- How people explain their own and others' behaviour
- Major theories of causal attribution
- Biases and errors in attribution
- Intergroup attributions
- Social knowledge, social representations and societal attributions

## Focus questions

1. Helen is angry with her husband Lewis who avoids approaching his boss for a pay rise. Lewis argues that the timing is not right. Helen says he simply fails to face up to people. How are these attributions different in kind? Watch Helen and Lewis debate this issue in Chapter 3 of MyPsychLab at **www.mypsychlab.co.uk** (watch *Social perception*).

2. You read a newspaper report about a rape case in which the defence lawyer pointed out that a young woman was actually dressed provocatively. What attributional error is involved here?

3. The job market was tight and Rajna began to worry that she might be made redundant. Then she heard a rumour that the worst had come – several staff were about to be fired. She was itching to pass this on to the next colleague that she saw. Why would Rajna want to spread the rumour further?

will use which involves getting you to decide to buy a car by giving you a very low price

Go to **mypsychlab** to explore video and test your understanding of key topics addressed in this chapter.

Refresh your understanding with interactive summaries, explore topics further with video and audio clips and assess your progress with quick test and essay questions by logging to the accompanying website at **www.mypsychlab.co.uk**

# Chapter 3
## Attribution and social explanation

## Key terms

Actor–observer effect
Attribution
Attributional style
Belief in a just world
Causal schemata
Cognitive miser
Consensus information
Consistency information
Conspiracy theory
Correspondence bias

Correspondent inference
Covariation model
Discount
Distinctiveness information
Essentialism
Ethnocentrism
External (or situational) attribution
False consensus effect
Fundamental attribution error
Hedonic relevance
Illusion of control
Intergroup attributions
Internal (or dispositional) attribution

Level of analysis (or explanation)
Motivated tactician
Naive psychologist (or scientist)
Non-common effects
Outcome bias
Personalism
Self-handicapping
Self-perception theory
Self-serving bias
Social representations
Societal identity theory
Stereotype
Ultimate attribution error

# Social explanation

Human thought is preoccupied with seeking, constructing and testing explanations of our experiences. We try to understand our world in order to render it orderly and meaningful enough for adaptive action, and we tend to feel uncomfortable if we do not have such an understanding. In particular we need to understand people. Through life most of us gradually construct adequate explanations (i.e. theories) of why people behave in certain ways; in this respect, we are all 'naive' or lay psychologists. This is enormously useful, because it allows us (with varying accuracy) to predict when someone will behave in a certain way; it also allows us to influence whether someone will behave in that way or not. Thus, we gain some control over our destiny.

People construct explanations for both physical phenomena (e.g. earthquakes, the seasons) and human behaviour (e.g. anger, a particular attitude), and in general such explanations are *causal* explanations, in which specific conditions are attributed a causal role. Causal explanations are particularly powerful bases for prediction and control (Forsterling & Rudolph, 1988).

In this chapter, we discuss how people make inferences about the causes of their own and other people's behaviour, and the antecedents and consequences of such inferences. Social psychological theories of causal inference are called *attribution theories* (Harvey & Weary, 1981; Hewstone, 1989; Kelley & Michela, 1980; Ross & Fletcher, 1985). There are seven main theoretical emphases that make up the general body of **attribution** theory:

**Attribution**
The process of assigning a cause to our own behaviour, and that of others.

1  Heider's (1958) theory of naive psychology;

2  Jones and Davis's (1965) theory of correspondent inference;

3  Kelley's (1967) covariation model;

4  Schachter's (1964) theory of emotional lability;

5  Bem's (1967, 1972) theory of self-perception;

6  Weiner's (1979, 1985) attributional theory; and

7  Deschamps's (1983), Hewstone's (1989) and Jaspars' (Hewstone & Jaspars, 1982, 1984) intergroup perspective.

We discuss the first six of these below and then deal with intergroup attribution by itself in greater detail later in the chapter.

**In search of the meaning of life**
Religions are one expression of our most basic need to understand the world we live in

# Basic attribution processes

## Heider's theory of naive psychology

Fritz Heider (1958) believed it was crucially important for social psychologists to study people's naive, or common sense, psychological theories, because such theories influenced ordinary people's everyday perceptions and behaviour. For example, people who believe in astrology are likely to have different expectations and are likely to act in different ways from those who do not. Heider believed that people are intuitive psychologists who construct causal theories of human behaviour, and because such theories have the same form as systematic scientific social psychological theories, people are actually intuitive or **naive psychologists.**

Heider based his ideas on three principles:

1  Because we feel that our own behaviour is motivated rather than random, we tend to look for the causes and reasons for other people's behaviour in order to discover their motives. The search for causes does seem to pervade human thought, and indeed it can be difficult to explain or comment on something without using causal language. Heider and Simmel (1944) demonstrated this in an ingenious experiment in which people who

**Naive psychologist (or scientist)**
Model of social cognition that characterises people as using rational, scientific-like, cause-effect analyses to understand their world.

**Internal (or disposi-**
**tional) attribution**
Process of assigning the
cause of our own or
others' behaviour to
internal or dispositional
factors.

were asked to describe the movement of abstract geometric figures described them as if they were humans with intentions to act in certain ways. Nowadays, we can witness the same phenomenon in people's often highly emotional ascription of human motives to inanimate figures in video and computer games. The pervasive need that people have for causal explanation reveals itself most powerfully in the way that almost all societies construct an origin myth, an elaborate causal explanation for the origin and meaning of life that is often a centrepiece of a religion.

2   Because we construct causal theories in order to be able to predict and control the environment, we tend to look for stable and enduring properties of the world around us. We try to discover personality traits and enduring abilities in people, or stable properties of situations, that cause behaviour.

3   In attributing causality for behaviour, we distinguish between personal factors (e.g. personality, ability) and environmental factors (e.g. situations, social pressure). The former are examples of an **internal (or dispositional) attribution** and the latter of an **external (or situational) attribution**. So, for example, it might be useful to know whether someone you meet at a party who seems aloof and distant is an aloof and distant person or is acting in that way because she is not enjoying that particular party. Heider believed that because internal causes, or intentions, are hidden from us, we can only infer their presence if there are no clear external causes. However, as we see below, people tend to be biased in preferring internal to external attributions even in the face of evidence for external causality. It seems that we readily attribute behaviour to stable properties of people. Scherer (1978), for example, found that people made assumptions about the stable personality traits of complete strangers simply on the basis of hearing their voices on the telephone.

**External (or situational)**
**attribution**
Assigning the cause of our
own or others' behaviour
to external or
environmental factors.

Heider identified the major themes and provided the insight that forms the blueprint for all subsequent, more formalised, theories of attribution.

## Jones and Davis's theory of correspondent inference

**Correspondent inference**
Causal attribution of
behaviour to underlying
dispositions.

Jones and Davis's (1965; Jones & McGillis, 1976) theory of **correspondent inference** explains how people infer that a person's behaviour corresponds to an underlying disposition or personality trait – how we infer, for example, that a friendly action is due to an underlying disposition to be friendly. People like to make correspondent inferences (attribute behaviour to underlying disposition) because a dispositional cause is a stable cause that renders people's behaviour predictable and thus increases our own sense of control over our world.

To make a correspondent inference, we draw on five sources of information, or cues (see Figure 3.1):

1   *Freely chosen* behaviour is more indicative of a disposition than is behaviour that is clearly under the control of external threats, inducements or constraints.

**Non-common effects**
Effects of behaviour that
are relatively exclusive to
that behaviour rather than
other behaviours.

**Outcome bias**
Belief that the outcomes
of a behaviour were
intended by the person
who chose the behaviour.

2   Behaviour with effects that are relatively exclusive to that behaviour rather than common to a range of other behaviour (i.e. behaviour with **non-common effects**) tells us more about dispositions. People assume that others are aware of non-common effects and that the specific behaviour was performed intentionally to produce the non-common effect – this tendency has been called **outcome bias** (Allison, Mackie & Messick, 1996). So, for example, if a person has to choose between behaviour A and behaviour B, and both produce roughly the same effects (i.e. no non-common effects) or a very large number of different effects (i.e. many non-common effects), the choice tells us little about the person's disposition. However, if the behaviours produce a small number of different effects (i.e. few non-common effects – e.g. behaviour A produces

only terror and behaviour B produces only joy), then the choice does tell us something about that person's disposition.

3   *Socially desirable* behaviour tells us little about a person's disposition, because it is likely to be controlled by societal norms. However, socially undesirable behaviour is generally counter-normative and is thus a better basis for making a correspondent inference.

4   We make more confident correspondent inferences about others' behaviour that has important consequences for ourselves: that is, behaviour that has **hedonic relevance.**

5   We make more confident correspondent inferences about others' behaviour that seems to be directly intended to benefit or harm us: that is, behaviour that is high in **personalism.**

**Hedonic relevance**
Refers to behaviour that has important direct consequences for self.

**Personalism**
Behaviour that appears to be directly intended to benefit or harm oneself rather than others.

Experiments testing correspondent inference theory provide some support. Jones and Harris (1967) found that American students making attributions for speeches made by other students tended to make more correspondent inferences for freely chosen socially unpopular positions, such as freely choosing to make a speech in support of Fidel Castro.

In another experiment, Jones, Davis and Gergen (1961) found that participants made more correspondent inferences for out-of-role behaviour, such as friendly, outer-directed behaviour by someone who was applying for an astronaut job, in which the required attributes favour a quiet, reserved, inner-directed person.

Correspondent inference theory has some limitations and has declined in importance as an attribution theory (Hewstone, 1989; Howard, 1985). For instance, the theory holds that correspondent inferences depend to a great extent on the attribution of intentionality, yet unintentional behaviour (e.g. careless behaviour) can be a strong basis for a correspondent inference (e.g. that the person is a careless person).

There is also a problem with the notion of non-common effects. While correspondent inference theory maintains that people assess the commonality of effects by comparing chosen and non-chosen actions, other research indicates that people simply do not attend to non-occurring behaviours and so would not be able to compute the commonality of effects

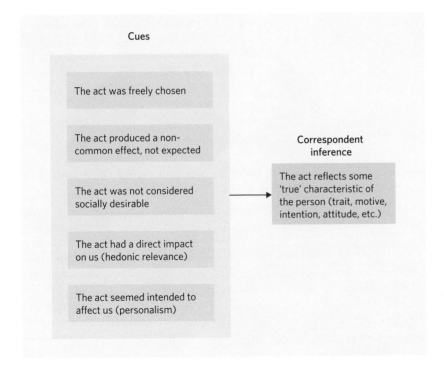

**Figure 3.1** How we make a correspondent inference

To make an inference that a person's behaviour corresponds to an underlying disposition, we draw on five sources of information

**Covariation model**
Kelley's theory of causal attribution – people assign the cause of behaviour to the factor that covaries most closely with the behaviour.

**Consistency information**
Information about the extent to which a behaviour Y always co-occurs with a stimulus X.

**Distinctiveness information**
Information about whether a person's reaction occurs only with one stimulus, or is a common reaction to many stimuli.

**Consensus information**
Information about the extent to which other people react in the same way to a stimulus X.

accurately (Nisbett & Ross, 1980; Ross, 1977). More generally, although we may correct dispositional attributions in the light of situational factors, this is a rather deliberate process, whereas correspondent inferences themselves are relatively automatic (Gilbert, 1995).

## Kelley's covariation model

The best-known attribution theory is Kelley's (1967, 1973) **covariation model**. Kelley believed that in trying to discover the causes of behaviour people act much like scientists. They identify what factor covaries most closely with the behaviour and then assign that factor a causal role. The procedure is similar to that embodied by the statistical technique of analysis of variance (ANOVA), and for this reason Kelley's model is often referred to as an ANOVA model. People use this covariation principle to decide whether to attribute a behaviour to internal dispositions (e.g. personality) or external environmental factors (e.g. social pressure).

In order to make this decision, people assess three classes of information associated with the co-occurrence of a certain action (e.g. laughter) by a specific person (e.g. Tom) with a potential cause (e.g. a comedian):

1 **Consistency information** – whether Tom always laughs at this comedian (high consistency) or only sometimes laughs at this comedian (low consistency).

2 **Distinctiveness information** – whether Tom laughs at everything (low distinctiveness) or only at the comedian (high distinctiveness).

3 **Consensus information** – whether everyone laughs at the comedian (high consensus) or only Tom laughs (low consensus).

**Freely chosen behaviour?**
Information based on a confession under duress contravenes the Third Geneva Convention of 1949 for the treatment of prisoners. It is also unreliable

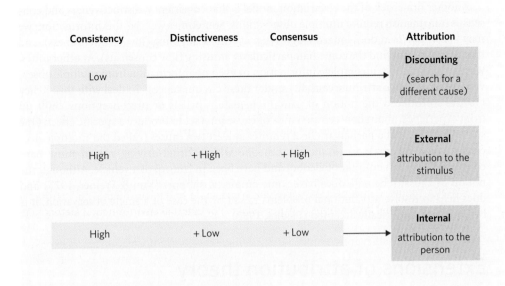

**Figure 3.2** Kelley's attribution theory

Kelley's covariation model states that people decide what attributions to make after considering the consistency, distinctiveness and consensus of a person's behaviour

Where consistency is low, people **discount** the potential cause and search for an alternative (see Figure 3.2). If Tom sometimes laughs and sometimes does not laugh at the comedian, then presumably the cause of the laughter is neither the comedian nor Tom but some other covarying factor: for example, whether or not Tom inhaled laughing gas before listening to the comedian or whether or not the comedian told a funny joke or not (see McClure, 1998, for a review of the conditions under which discounting is most likely to occur). Where consistency is high, and distinctiveness and consensus are also high, one can make an external attribution to the comedian (the cause of Tom's laughter was the comedian), but where distinctiveness and consensus are low, one can make an internal attribution to Tom's personality (Tom laughed at the comedian because Tom is simply the sort of person who tends to laugh a lot).

**Discount**
If there is no consistent relationship between a specific cause and a specific behaviour, that cause is discounted in favour of some other cause.

McArthur (1972) tested Kelley's theory by having participants make internal or external attributions for a range of behaviours, each accompanied by one of the eight possible configurations of high or low consistency, distinctiveness and consensus information. Although the theory was generally supported (see review by Kassin, 1979), there was a tendency for people to under-use consensus information. There are also some general issues worth considering:

- Just because people can use pre-packaged consistency, distinctiveness and consensus information to attribute causality (the case in experimental tests of Kelley's model), this does not mean that in the normal course of events they do.

- There is evidence that people are actually poor at assessing the covariation of different events (Alloy & Tabachnik, 1984).

- There is no guarantee that people are using the covariation principle – they may attribute causality to the most salient feature or to whatever causal agent appears to be similar to the effect (Nisbett & Ross, 1980).

- If people do attribute causality on the basis of covariance or correlation, then they certainly are *naive* scientists (Hilton, 1988) – covariation is not causation.

**Causal schemata**
Experience-based beliefs about how certain types of cause interact to produce an effect.

Another drawback of the covariation model is that consistency, distinctiveness and consensus information require multiple observations. Sometimes we have this information: we may know that Tom does indeed laugh often at almost anything (low distinctiveness), and that others do not find the comedian particularly amusing (low consensus). At other times, we may have, at best, incomplete information or even no information from multiple observations. How do we attribute causality under these circumstances? To deal with this, Kelley (1972a) introduced the notion of **causal schemata** – beliefs or preconceptions, built up from experience, about how certain kinds of cause interact to produce a specific effect. One such schema is that a particular effect requires at least two causes (called the 'multiple necessary cause' schema): for example, someone with a drink-driving record must have consumed a certain amount of alcohol and have been in control of a vehicle. Although the notion of causal schemata does have some empirical support (Kun & Weiner, 1973) and does help to resolve attributional problems raised by the case of a single observation, it is by no means uncritically accepted (Fiedler, 1982).

# Extensions of attribution theory

## Emotional lability

Schachter (1964, 1971; Schachter & Singer, 1962) has suggested the intriguing idea that emotions have two distinct components: a state of physiological *arousal* that does not differentiate among emotions, and *cognitions* that label the arousal and determine which emotion is experienced. Sometimes cognitions precede arousal (e.g. identifying a dog as a Rottweiler may produce arousal that is experienced as fear), but at other times arousal may occur that prompts a search of the immediate environment for possible causes.

To test this idea that emotions may indeed be labile, Schachter and Singer (1962) conducted a classic experiment. Students were given an injection of either adrenalin (the drug epinephrine), or a placebo (salt water) that provided a control condition. Students who had been administered the drug were then allocated to one of three conditions: (1) they were correctly informed that this would cause symptoms of arousal (e.g. rapid breathing, increased heart rate); (2) they were given no explanation; or (3) they were misinformed that they might experience a slight headache and some dizziness. All participants then waited in a room with a confederate to complete some paperwork. For half the participants, the confederate behaved euphorically (engaging in silly antics and making paper aeroplanes), and for the other half angrily (ripping up the papers and stomping around).

Schachter and Singer predicted that the 'drug-misinformed' participants would experience arousal and would search for a cause in their immediate environment (see Figure 3.3). The behaviour of the confederate would act as a salient cue, encouraging participants in the 'euphoric' condition to feel euphoric and those in the 'angry' condition to feel angry. The emotions of the other two drug groups and the control group would be unaffected by the behaviour of the confederate: the control participants had experienced no arousal from the drug, and the 'informed participants' already had an explanation for their arousal. The results of the experiment largely supported these predictions.

Perhaps the most significant implication of Schachter's work is its therapeutic application (Valins & Nisbett, 1972). If emotions depend on what cognitive label is assigned, through causal attribution to undifferentiated arousal, then it might, for example, be possible to transform depression into cheerfulness simply by reattributing arousal. A paradigm has been devised to test this idea – called the misattribution paradigm (Valins, 1966). People who feel anxious and bad about themselves because they attribute arousal internally are encouraged to attribute arousal to external factors. For example, someone who is shy can be encouraged to attribute the arousal associated with meeting new people to ordinary

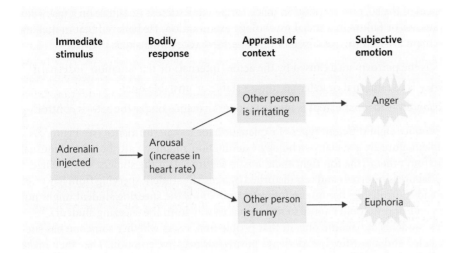

**Figure 3.3**  Attributing a likely cause to an experimentally induced emotion

environmental causes rather than to personality deficiencies and thus no longer feel shy. A number of experiments have employed this type of intervention with some success (e.g. Olson, 1988; Storms & Nisbett, 1970; for critical reviews of clinical applications of attribution theory, see Buchanan & Seligman, 1995; Forsterling, 1988).

However, initial enthusiasm for emotional lability and the clinical application of mis-attribution has waned in the light of subsequent criticisms (Reisenzein, 1983):

- Emotions may be significantly less labile than was originally thought (Maslach, 1979). Environmental cues are not readily accepted as bases for inferring emotions from unexplained arousal, and because unexplained arousal is intrinsically unpleasant, people have a propensity to assign it a negative label.

- The misattribution effect seems to be limited (Parkinson, 1985). It is largely restricted to laboratory investigations and is unreliable and short-lived. It is not clear that the effect is mediated by an attribution process, and in any case it is restricted to a limited range of emotion-inducing stimuli.

The more general idea that cognition, in particular appraisals of the surrounding situation, plays a role in the experience of emotion has, however, fed into the contemporary revival of research on affect and emotion (e.g., Blascovich, 2008; Forgas, 2006; Keltner & Lerner, 2010; see Chapter 2).

## Self-perception theory

One far-reaching implication of treating emotion as cognitively labelled arousal is that people may make more general attributions for their *own* behaviour. This idea has been elaborated by Bem (1967, 1972) in his **self-perception theory**. Because this is an account of how people construct their self-concept, we describe it in Chapter 4 which explores the nature of self and identity.

**Self-perception theory**
Bem's idea that we gain knowledge of ourselves only by making self-attributions: for example, we infer our own attitudes from our own behaviour.

## Weiner's attributional theory

Attributional dimensions of task achievement are the focus of another extension of attribution theory, by Weiner (1979, 1985, 1986). Weiner was interested in the causes and consequences of the sorts of attribution made for people's success or failure on a task – for example, success or failure in a social psychology examination. He believed that in making an achievement attribution, we consider three performance dimensions:

1  *Locus* – is the performance caused by the actor (internal) or the situation (external)?

2  *Stability* – is the internal or external cause a stable or unstable one?

3  *Controllability* – to what extent is future task performance under the actor's control?

These produce eight different types of explanation for task performance (see Figure 3.4). For example, failure in a social psychology examination might be attributed to 'unusual hindrance from others' (the top right-hand box in Figure 3.4) if the student was intelligent (therefore, failure is external) and was disturbed by a nearby student sneezing from hay fever (unstable and controllable, because in future examinations the sneezing student might not be present, and/or one could choose to sit in a place away from the sneezing student).

Weiner's model is a dynamic one, in that people first assess whether someone has succeeded or failed and accordingly experience positive or negative emotion. They then make a causal attribution for the performance, which produces more specific emotions (e.g. pride for doing well due to ability) and expectations that influence future performance.

Weiner's model is relatively well supported by experiments that provide participants with performance outcomes and locus, stability and controllability information, often under role-playing conditions (e.g. de Jong, Koomen & Mellenbergh, 1988; Frieze & Weiner, 1971). However, critics have suggested that the controllability dimension may be less important than was first thought. They have also wondered to what extent people outside controlled laboratory conditions really analyse achievement in this way. More recently, Weiner (1995) has extended his model to place an emphasis on judgements of responsibility. On the basis of causal attributions people make judgements of responsibility, and it is these latter judgements, not the causal attributions themselves, that influence affective experience and behavioural reactions.

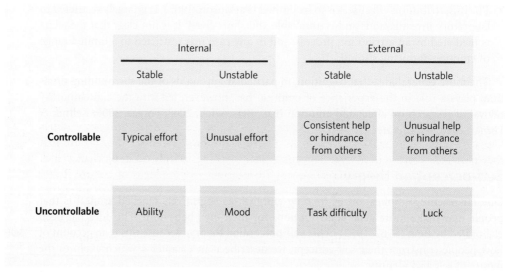

**Figure 3.4** Achievement attributions as a function of locus, stability and controllability

How we attribute someone's task achievement depends on:

- *Locus*–is the performance caused by the actor (internal) or the situation (external)?
- *Stability*–is the internal or external cause a stable or unstable one?
- *Controllability*–to what extent is future task performance under the actor's control?

**Achievement attribution**
Isn't she lovely? Will Miss World attribute her new crown to her hard work, her physical beauty, biased judges — or perhaps to luck?

# Applications of attribution theory

Application of the idea that people need to discover the cause of their own and others' behaviour in order to plan their own actions has had a significant impact on social psychology. We have already seen two examples – achievement attributions and the reattribution of arousal as a therapeutic technique. In this section, we explore two further applications: attributional styles and interpersonal relationships.

## Individual differences and attributional styles

Research suggests there are enduring individual differences in the sorts of attribution that people make: their **attributional style**. Rotter (1966) believes that people differ in the amount of control they feel they have over the reinforcements and punishments they receive. *Internals* believe they have significant personal control over their destiny – things happen because they make them happen. *Externals* are more fatalistic: they believe that they have little control over what happens to them – things simply occur by chance, luck or the actions of powerful external agents. To measure people's locus of control Rotter devised a 29-item scale. This scale has been used to relate locus of control to a range of behaviours, including political beliefs, achievement behaviour and reactions to illness. One problem with the scale is that it may not measure a unitary construct (i.e. a single personality dimension) but, rather, a number of relatively independent beliefs to do with control (Collins, 1974).

A number of other questionnaires have been devised to measure attributional styles – a tendency for individuals to make particular kinds of causal inference, rather than others, over time and across different situations (Metalsky & Abramson, 1981). Of these, the attributional style questionnaire or ASQ (Peterson et al., 1982; Seligman, Abramson, Semmel & von Baeyer, 1979) is perhaps the most widely known. It measures the sorts of explanation that people give for aversive (i.e. unpleasant) events on three dimensions: internal/external,

**Attributional style**
An individual (personality) predisposition to make a certain type of causal attribution for behaviour.

stable/unstable, global/specific. The global/specific dimension refers to the extent to which a cause has a wide or narrow range of effects – 'the economy' is a global explanation for someone being made redundant, whereas the closing of a specific company is a specific explanation. People who view aversive events as being caused by internal, stable, global factors have a 'depressive attributional style' (i.e. the glass is half empty), which may promote helplessness and depression and may have adverse health consequences (Abramson, Seligman & Teasdale, 1978; Crocker, Alloy & Kayne, 1988).

Another slightly different scale, called the attributional complexity scale (ACS), has been devised by Fletcher et al. (1986) to measure individual differences in the complexity of the attributions that people make for events.

The notion of attributional style as a personality trait is not without problems: for instance, the ASQ and the ACS provide only limited evidence of cross-situational individual consistency in causal attribution (e.g. Cutrona, Russell & Jones, 1985). Also not without problems is the important link between attributional style, learned helplessness and clinical depression. Although more than 100 studies involving about 15,000 participants confirm an average correlation of 0.30 between attributional style and depression (Sweeney, Anderson & Bailey, 1986), this does not prove causation – it is a correlation in which one factor explains 9 per cent of variance in the other.

More useful are diachronic studies, which show that attributional style measured at one time predicts depressive symptoms at a later date (Nolen-Hoeksma, Girgus & Seligman, 1992), but again causality is not established. Causality is difficult to establish because it is unethical to induce clinical depression in experimental settings. We are largely left with experimental evidence from studies of transitory mood, which is a rather pale analogue of depression. Is it justified to generalise from feelings about doing well or poorly on a trivial laboratory task to full-blown clinical depression?

## Interpersonal relationships

Attributions play an important role in interpersonal relationships (see Chapter 13), particularly close interpersonal relationships (e.g. friendship and marriage) where attributions are *communicated* to fulfil a variety of functions: for instance, to explain, justify or excuse behaviour, as well as to attribute blame and instil guilt (Hilton, 1990).

Harvey (1987) suggests that interpersonal relationships go through three basic phases: formation, maintenance and dissolution (see also Moreland & Levine's (1982, 1984) model

**Attributing blame**
Couples sometimes cannot agree on what is cause and what is effect. For example, does nagging cause withdrawal or vice versa?

of group socialisation in Chapter 8). Fincham (1985) explains that during the formation stage, attributions reduce ambiguity and facilitate communication and an understanding of the relationship. In the maintenance phase, the need to make attributions wanes because stable personalities and relationships have been established. The dissolution phase is characterised by an increase in attributions in order to regain an understanding of the relationship.

A notable feature of many interpersonal relationships is attributional conflict (Horai, 1977), in which partners proffer divergent causal interpretations of behaviour and disagree over what attributions to adopt. Often partners cannot even agree on a cause–effect sequence, one exclaiming, 'I withdraw because you nag', the other, 'I nag because you withdraw'. From research mainly on heterosexual couples, attributional conflict has been shown to be correlated strongly with relationship dissatisfaction (Kelley, 1979; Orvis, Kelley & Butler, 1976; Sillars, 1981).

However, the main thrust of research has focused on the role of attributions in heterosexual marital satisfaction (e.g. Fincham & Bradbury, 1991; Fletcher & Thomas, 2000; Noller & Ruzzene, 1991). An important aim has been to distinguish between distressed and non-distressed spouses in order to provide therapy for dysfunctional marital relationships. Correlational studies (e.g. Fincham & O'Leary, 1983; Holtzworth-Munroe & Jacobson, 1985) reveal that happily married (or non-distressed) spouses tend to credit their partners for positive behaviour by citing internal, stable, global and controllable factors to explain them. Negative behaviour is explained away by ascribing it to causes viewed as external, unstable, specific and uncontrollable. Distressed couples behave in exactly the opposite way.

It also appears that, while women tend fairly regularly to engage in attributional thought about the relationship, men do so only when the relationship becomes dysfunctional. In this respect, and contrary to popular opinion, men may be the more diagnostic barometers of marital dysfunction.

Do attributional dynamics produce dysfunctional marital relationships, or do dysfunctional relationships distort the attributional dynamic? This important causal question has been addressed by Fincham and Bradbury (1987; see overview by Hewstone, 1989), who obtained responsibility attributions, causal attributions and marital satisfaction measures from 39 married couples on two occasions 10–12 months apart. Attributions made on the first occasion were found reliably to predict marital satisfaction 10–12 months later, but only for wives.

Another longitudinal study (although over only a two-month period) confirmed that attributions do have a causal impact on subsequent relationship satisfaction (Fletcher, Fincham, Cramer & Heron, 1987). Subsequent, more extensive and better-controlled longitudinal studies have replicated these findings for both husbands and wives (Fincham & Bradbury, 1993; Senchak & Leonard, 1993).

# Biases in attribution

The attribution process, then, is clearly subject to bias: for example, it can be biased by personality, biased by interpersonal dynamics or biased to meet communication needs. We do not approach the task of attributing causes for behaviour in an entirely dispassionate, disinterested and objective manner, and the cognitive mechanisms that are responsible for attribution may themselves be subject to imperfections that render them suboptimal.

Accumulating evidence for attributional biases and 'errors' has occasioned a shift of perspective. Instead of viewing people as naive scientists or even statisticians (in which case biases were largely considered a theoretical nuisance), we now think of people as **cognitive misers** or **motivated tacticians** (Moscowitz, 2005; Fiske & Taylor, 2008; see also Chapter 2). People use cognitive short-cuts (called heuristics) to make attributions that, although not

**Cognitive miser**
A model of social cognition that characterises people as using the least complex and demanding cognitions that are able to produce generally adaptive behaviours.

**Motivated tactician**
A model of social cognition that characterises people as having multiple cognitive strategies available, which they choose among on the basis of personal goals, motives and needs.

**Correspondence bias**
A general attribution bias in which people have an inflated tendency to see behaviour as reflecting (corresponding to) stable underlying personality attributes.

**Fundamental attribution error**
Bias in attributing another's behaviour more to internal than to situational causes.

objectively correct all the time, are quite satisfactory and adaptive. Sometimes the choice of short-cut and choice of attribution can also be influenced by personal motives.

Biases are entirely adaptive characteristics of ordinary, everyday social perception (Fiske & Taylor, 2008; Nisbett & Ross, 1980; Ross, 1977). In this section, we discuss some of the most important attributional biases.

## Correspondence bias and the fundamental attribution error

One of the best known attribution biases is **correspondence bias** – a general tendency for people to overly attribute behaviour to stable underlying personality dispositions (Gilbert & Malone, 1995). This bias was originally called the **fundamental attribution error,** and the terms are often used interchangeably – the change in label reflects accumulating evidence that this bias or error may not be quite as 'fundamental' as originally thought (see below).

The fundamental attribution error, originally identified by Ross (1977), refers to a tendency for people to make dispositional attributions for others' behaviour, even when there are clear external/environmental causes. For example, in the Jones and Harris (1967) study mentioned earlier, American participants read speeches about Fidel Castro ostensibly written by fellow students. The speeches were either pro-Castro or anti-Castro, and the writers had ostensibly either freely chosen to write the speech or been instructed to do so. Where there was a choice, participants not surprisingly reasoned that those who had written a pro-Castro speech were in favour of Castro, and those who had written an anti-Castro speech were against Castro – an internal, dispositional attribution was made (see Figure 3.5).

However, a dispositional attribution was also made even when the speech writers had been *instructed* to write the speech. Although there was overwhelming evidence for an exclusively external cause, participants seemed largely to overlook this information and to still prefer a dispositional explanation – the fundamental attribution error. (Bearing these points in mind, how would you account for the different views held by Helen and Lewis? See the first focus question.)

Other studies furnish additional empirical evidence for the fundamental attribution error (Jones, 1979; Nisbett & Ross, 1980). Indeed, the fundamental attribution error, or correspondence bias, has been demonstrated repeatedly both inside and outside the social

**Figure 3.5** The fundamental attribution error: attributing speech writers' attitudes on the basis of their freedom of choice in writing the speech

- Students who freely chose to write a pro- or an anti-Castro speech were attributed with a pro- or anti-Castro attitude respectively.

- Although less strong, this same tendency to attribute the speech to an underlying disposition (the fundamental attribution error) prevailed when the writers had no choice and were simply instructed to write the speech

*Source*: based on data from Jones and Harris (1967)

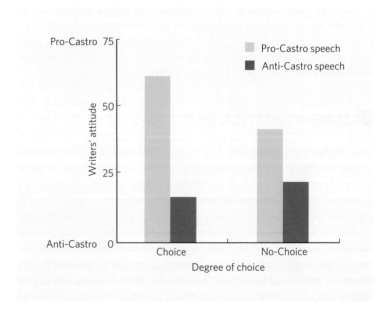

psychology laboratory (Gilbert, 1998; Jones, 1990). Correspondence bias may also be responsible for a number of more general explanatory tendencies: for example, the tendency to attribute road accidents unduly to the driver rather than to the vehicle or the road conditions (Barjonet, 1980); and the tendency among some people to attribute poverty and unemployment to the person rather than to social conditions (see below).

Pettigrew (1979) has suggested that the fundamental attribution error may emerge in a slightly different form in intergroup contexts where groups are making attributions about ingroup and outgroup behaviour – he calls this the *ultimate attribution error* (see below). Correspondence bias and the fundamental attribution error are closely related to two other biases: the *outcome bias* (e.g. Allison, Mackie & Messick, 1996) in which people assume that a person behaving in some particular way intended all the outcomes of that behaviour; and **essentialism** (Haslam, Rothschild & Ernst, 1998; Medin & Ortony, 1989), in which behaviour is considered to reflect underlying and immutable, often innate, properties of people or the groups they belong to.

**Essentialism**
Pervasive tendency to consider behaviour to reflect underlying and immutable, often innate, properties of people or the groups they belong to.

Essentialism can be particularly troublesome when it causes people to attribute stereotypically negative attributes of outgroups to essential and immutable personality attributes of members of that group (e.g. Bain, Kashima & Haslam, 2006; Haslam, Bastian, Bain & Kashima, 2006; Haslam, Bastian & Bissett, 2004). For example, the stereotype of an outgroup as being laid-back, liberal and poorly educated becomes more pernicious if these attributes are considered immutable, perhaps genetically induced, properties of the group's members – the people themselves are considered to have personalities that are immutably lazy, immoral and stupid.

Different explanations of the fundamental attribution error have been proposed:

## Focus of attention

The actor's behaviour attracts more attention than the background: it is disproportionately salient in cognition, stands out as the figure against the situational background, and is therefore overrepresented causally (Taylor & Fiske, 1978). Thus the actor and the actor's behaviour form what Heider (1958) called a 'causal unit'. This explanation makes quite a lot of sense. Procedures designed to focus attention away from the actor and on to the situation have been shown to increase the tendency to make a situational rather than dispositional attribution (e.g. Rholes & Pryor, 1982). When people really want to find out about a situation from a person's behaviour, they focus on the situation and are less likely to leap to a dispositional attribution – the fundamental attribution error is muted or reversed (e.g. Krull, 1993).

## Differential forgetting

Attribution requires the representation of causal information in memory. There is some evidence that people tend to forget situational causes more readily than dispositional causes, thus producing a dispositional shift over time (e.g. Moore, Sherrod, Liu & Underwood, 1979; Peterson, 1980). Other studies show the opposite effect (e.g. Miller & Porter, 1980), and Funder (1982) has argued that the direction of shift depends on the focus of information processing and occurs immediately after the behaviour being attributed.

## Cultural and developmental factors

The correspondence bias was originally called the fundamental attribution error because it was considered to be an automatic and universal outcome of perceptual experience and cognitive activity (e.g. McArthur & Baron, 1983). However, there is evidence that both developmental factors and culture may affect the correspondence bias. For example, in Western cultures, young children explain action in concrete situational terms and learn to make dispositional attributions only in late childhood (Kassin & Pryor, 1985; White, 1988).

Furthermore, this developmental sequence itself may not be universal. Miller (1984; see Figure 3.7) reports data showing that Hindu Indian children do not drift towards dispositional explanations at all, but rather towards increasingly situational explanations.

These differences quite probably reflect different cultural norms for social explanation, or more basic differences between Western and non-Western conceptions of self – the autonomous and independent Western self and the interdependent non-Western self (Chiu & Hong, 2007; see Chapters 4 and 16). The fundamental attribution error is a relatively ubiquitous and socially valued feature of Western cultures (Beauvois & Dubois, 1988; Jellison & Green, 1981), but, although present, it is less dominant in non-Western cultures (Fletcher & Ward, 1988; Morris & Peng, 1994).

The fundamental attribution error may not be quite as fundamental as was first thought. It may, to some extent, be a normative way of thinking (see discussion of norms in Chapters 7 and 8). This is one reason why Gilbert and colleagues (e.g. Gilbert & Malone, 1995) recommend that the term 'correspondence bias' be used in preference to the term 'fundamental attribution error'.

### Linguistic factors

One final, rather interesting, observation by Nisbett and Ross (1980) is that the English language is so constructed that it is usually relatively easy to describe an action and the actor in the same terms, and much more difficult to describe the situation in the same way. For example, we can talk about a kind or honest person, and a kind or honest action, but not a kind or honest situation. The English language may facilitate dispositional explanations (Brown & Fish, 1983; Semin & Fiedler, 1991).

## The actor–observer effect

Imagine the last time a shop assistant was rude to you. You probably thought, 'What a rude person!' though perhaps put less politely – in other words, you made an internal attribution to the shop assistant's enduring personality. In contrast, how did you explain the last time *you* snapped at someone? Probably not in terms of your personality, more likely in terms of external factors such as time pressure or stress. The **actor–observer effect** (or the self–other effect) is really an extension of the correspondence bias. It refers to the tendency for people to attribute others' behaviour internally to dispositional factors and their own behaviour externally to environmental factors (Jones & Nisbett, 1972). Twenty years of research has provided substantial evidence for this effect (Watson, 1982), and some extensions and qualifications. For example, not only do we tend to attribute others' behaviour more dispositionally than our own, but we also tend to consider their behaviour to be more stable and predictable than our own (Baxter & Goldberg, 1988).

**Actor–observer effect**
Tendency to attribute our own behaviours externally and others' behaviours internally.

A number of factors can influence the actor–observer effect. People tend to make more dispositional attributions for socially desirable than socially undesirable behaviour, irrespective of who the actor is (e.g. Taylor & Koivumaki, 1976), and there is a tendency for actors to be more dispositional in attributing positive behaviour and more situational in attributing negative behaviour than are observers (e.g. Chen, Yates & McGinnies, 1988).

The actor–observer effect can be inverted if the actor knows that his or her behaviour is dispositionally caused. For example, you may 'adopt' an injured hedgehog in the full knowledge that you are a sucker for injured animals and you have often done this sort of thing in the past (Monson & Hesley, 1982). Finally, the actor–observer effect can be abolished or reversed if the actor is encouraged to take the role of the observer regarding the behaviour to be attributed, and the observer the role of the actor. Under these circumstances, the actor becomes more dispositional and the observer more situational (e.g. Frank & Gilovich, 1989).

There are two main explanations for the actor–observer effect:

1 *Perceptual focus.* This explanation is almost identical to the 'focus of attention' explanation for the correspondence bias (see above). For the observer, the actor and the actor's behaviour are figural against the background of the situation. However, an actor cannot 'see' him/herself behaving, so the background situation assumes the role of figure against the background of self. The actor and the observer quite literally have different perspectives on the behaviour and thus explain it in different ways (Storms, 1973). Perceptual salience does indeed seem to have an important role in causal explanation. For example, McArthur and Post (1977) found that observers tended to make more dispositional attributions for an actor's behaviour when the actor was strongly illuminated than when dimly illuminated.

2 *Informational differences.* Another reason why actors tend to make external attributions and observers internal ones is that actors have a wealth of information to draw on about how they have behaved in other circumstances. They may actually know that they behave differently in different contexts and thus quite accurately consider their behaviour to be under situational control. Observers are not privy to this autobiographical information. They tend simply to see the actor behaving in a certain way in one context, or a limited range of contexts, and have no information about how the actor behaves in other contexts. It is therefore not an unreasonable assumption to make a dispositional attribution. This explanation, first suggested by Jones and Nisbett (1972), does have some empirical support (Eisen, 1979; White & Younger, 1988).

## The false consensus effect

Kelley (1972b) identified consensus information as being one of the three types of information that people used to make attributions about others' behaviour (see above). One of the first cracks in the naive scientist model of attribution was McArthur's (1972) discovery that attributors in fact underused or even ignored consensus information (Kassin, 1979).

Subsequently, it became apparent that people do not ignore consensus information but rather provide their own consensus information. People see their own behaviour as typical and assume that under similar circumstances others would behave in the same way. Ross, Greene and House (1977) first demonstrated this **false consensus effect**. They asked students if they would agree to walk around campus for 30 minutes wearing a sandwich board carrying the slogan 'Eat at Joe's'. Those who agreed estimated that 62 per cent of their peers would also have agreed, while those who refused estimated that 67 per cent of their peers would also have refused.

**False consensus effect**
Seeing our own behaviour as being more typical than it really is.

There are well over 100 studies that bear testimony to the robust nature of the false consensus effect (Marks & Miller, 1987; Mullen, Atkins, Champion, Edwards, Hardy, Story & Vanderklok, 1985; Wetzel & Walton, 1985). The effect may have a number of causes. As people tend to seek out the company of similar others, they may simply encounter more people who are similar to than different from themselves – thus experiencing inflated consensus. Another possibility is that our own opinions tend to be so salient that they displace consideration of alternatives and thus any comparison that provides a more accurate estimate of consensus. A third possibility is that we subjectively justify the correctness of our opinions and actions by grounding them in an exaggerated consensus. This suggests the possibility that false consensus is a mechanism for maintaining a stable perception of reality – reality grounded in consensus.

Research into factors influencing the false consensus effect suggests that the effect is stronger for important beliefs that we care a great deal about (e.g. Granberg, 1987) and for beliefs about which we are very certain (e.g. Marks & Miller, 1985). External threat, positive

**The false consensus effect**
This mid-winter Arctic dipper discovers a major attributional bias. Who else would swim here before breakfast?

qualities, the perceived similarity of others and minority group status all also inflate perceptions of consensus (e.g. Sanders & Mullen, 1983; Sherman, Presson & Chassin, 1984; van der Pligt, 1984).

## Self-serving biases

There is a range of attributional biases that are clearly self-serving, because they appear to protect or enhance self-evaluation (see Chapter 4). People tend to attribute internally and take credit for their successes (a self-enhancing bias), or attribute externally and deny responsibility for their failures (a self-protecting bias). This is a robust effect that has been found in many different cultures (Fletcher & Ward, 1988). Although initial explanations for success and failure may be relatively modest, dispositional attributions for success and situational attributions for failure become more pronounced with time (Burger, 1986). In general, self-enhancing biases are more common than self-protecting biases (Miller & Ross, 1975), but this may partly be because people with low self-esteem tend not to protect themselves by attributing their failures externally; rather, they attribute them internally (Campbell & Fairey, 1985).

**Self-serving biases**
Attributional distortions that protect or enhance self-esteem or the self-concept.

**Self-serving biases** are clearly ego-serving (Snyder, Stephan & Rosenfield, 1978). However, Miller and Ross (1975) suggest that there may also be a cognitive component, particularly for the self-enhancing aspect. People generally expect to succeed and therefore accept responsibility for success. If they try hard to succeed, they correlate success with their own effort, and they generally exaggerate the amount of control they have over successful performances. Together, these cognitive factors might encourage internal attribution of success. In general, however, it seems likely that both cognitive and motivational factors have a role (Anderson & Slusher, 1986; Tetlock & Levi, 1982) and that they are difficult to disentangle from one another (Tetlock & Manstead, 1985; Zuckerman, 1979).

Self-serving biases have a number of other ramifications. Self-presentational considerations may influence the degree to which people publicly take credit for success (modesty can often preclude self-enhancement), or deny responsibility for failure (the facts may make attempts at self-protection embarrassingly transparent) (e.g. Schlenker, Weingold & Hallam,

## Research highlight 3.1
### Self-handicapping: Explaining away your failure

Imagine that you are waiting to take an examination in a subject you find difficult and that you fully anticipate failing. You might well make sure that as many people as possible know that you have done no revision, are not really interested in the subject and have a mind-numbing hangover to boot. Your subsequent failure is thus externally attributed without it seeming that you are making excuses to explain away your failure. Berglas (1987) has called this self-handicapping.

To investigate this idea, Berglas and Jones (1978) had introductory psychology students try to solve some problems where the problems were either solvable or not solvable. They were told that they had done very well, and before continuing with a second problem-solving task they were given the choice of taking either a drug called 'Actavil', which would ostensibly improve intellectual functioning and performance, or 'Pandocrin', which would have the opposite effect. As predicted, those students who had succeeded on the solvable puzzles felt confident about their ability and so chose Actavil in order to improve further (see Figure 3.6). Those who had succeeded on the not-solvable puzzles attributed their performance externally to luck and chose Pandocrin in order to be able to explain away more easily the anticipated failure on the second task.

*Source*: based on data from Berglas & Jones (1978)

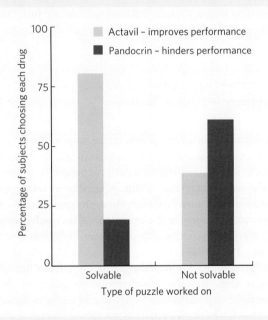

**Figure 3.6** Self-handicapping: choosing a drug depends on a puzzle's solvability

- Students who had done well on a solvable puzzle could attribute their performance internally (e.g. to ability): anticipating an equally good performance on a second similar task, they chose a performance-enhancing drug, Actavil, rather than a performance-impairing drug, Pandocrin

- Students who had done well on a not-solvable puzzle could only attribute their performance externally (e.g. to luck): with the prospect of an equivalent performance on the second task they chose the performance-impairing drug, as the self-handicapping option

*Source*: based on data from Berglas & Jones (1978)

1990). Riess, Rosenfield, Melburg and Tedeschi (1981) investigated this idea and found that self-presentational considerations weakened but did not abolish self-serving biases.

There is also evidence for an anticipatory self-serving bias, in which people who anticipate failure, intentionally and publicly make external attributions before the event. Berglas (1987) has called this **self-handicapping** (see Box 3.1 and Figure 3.6).

Another self-serving attributional phenomenon is the attribution of responsibility (Weiner, 1995), which is influenced by an outcome bias (Allison, Mackie & Messick, 1996). People tend to attribute greater responsibility to someone who is involved in an accident with large rather than small consequences (Burger, 1981; Walster, 1966). For example, we would attribute greater responsibility to the captain of a tanker that spills millions of litres of oil than to the captain of a small boat that spills only a few litres, although the degree of responsibility may actually be the same.

**Self-handicapping**
Publicly making advance external attributions for our anticipated failure or poor performance in a forthcoming event.

**Illusion of control**
Belief that we have more control over our world than we really do.

This effect may be part of a general tendency to cling to an **illusion of control** (Langer, 1975) by believing in a *just world* (Furnham, 2003; Lerner, 1977). People like to believe that bad things happen to 'bad people' and good things to 'good people' (i.e. people get what they deserve), and that people have control over their outcomes. This pattern of attributions makes the world seem a controllable and secure place in which we can determine our own destiny.

**Belief in a just world**
Belief that the world is a just and predictable place where good things happen to 'good people' and bad things to 'bad people'.

The **belief in a just world** can result in a general pattern of attribution in which victims are deemed responsible for their misfortune – poverty, oppression, tragedy and injustice all happen because victims deserve it. Examples of the just world hypothesis in action are such views as the unemployed are responsible for being out of work, and rape victims are responsible for the violence against them. Another example is the belief, held by some people, that the six million Jewish victims of the Holocaust were responsible for their own fate – that they deserved it (Davidowicz, 1975). Refer back to the second focus question. Just world beliefs are also an important component of many religious ideologies (Hogg, Adelman & Blagg, in press).

The belief in a just world may also be responsible for self-blame. Victims of traumatic events such as incest, debilitating illness, rape and other forms of violence can experience a strong sense that the world is no longer stable, meaningful, controllable and just. One way to reinstate an illusion of control is, ironically, to take some responsibility for the event (Miller & Porter, 1983).

# Intergroup attribution

Attribution theories are concerned mainly with how people make dispositional or situational attributions for their own and others' behaviour, and the sorts of bias that distort this process. The perspective is very much tied to interpersonal relations: people as unique individuals make attributions for their own behaviour or the behaviour of other unique individuals. However, there is another attributional context – intergroup relations – where individuals as group members make attributions for the behaviour of themselves as group members and others as either ingroup or outgroup members (Deschamps, 1983; Hewstone, 1989; Hewstone & Jaspars, 1982, 1984).

**Intergroup attributions**
Process of assigning the cause of one's own or others' behaviour to group membership.

Examples of **intergroup attributions** abound. One example is the attribution of economic ills to minority outgroups (e.g. Eastern European immigrants in Britain, *Gastarbeiter* in Germany). Another is the explanation of behaviour in terms of stereotypical properties of group membership – for example, attributions for performance that are consistent with sex-stereotypes (Deaux, 1984), or racial stereotypes (Steele, Spencer & Aronson, 2002).

**Ethnocentrism**
Evaluative preference for all aspects of our own group relative to other groups.

**Ultimate attribution error**
Tendency to attribute bad outgroup and good ingroup behaviour internally, and to attribute good outgroup and bad ingroup behaviour externally.

The first point that can be made about intergroup attributions is an extension of the self-serving bias described above. Intergroup attributions are characterised by **ethnocentrism,** or an ingroup-serving bias, in which socially desirable (positive) behaviour by ingroup members and socially undesirable (negative) behaviour by outgroup members are internally attributed to dispositions, and negative ingroup and positive outgroup behaviour are externally attributed to situational factors (Hewstone & Jaspars, 1982; Hewstone, 1989, 1990). This effect is more prevalent in Western than in non-Western cultures (Fletcher & Ward, 1988). It is common in team sports contexts, where the success of one's own team is attributed to internal stable abilities rather than effort, luck or task difficulty; this group-enhancing bias is stronger and more consistent than the corresponding group-protective bias (Mullen & Riordan, 1988; Miller & Ross, 1975).

Pettigrew (1979) has described a related bias, called the **ultimate attribution error** – an extension of Ross's (1977) fundamental attribution error into the domain of attributions for outgroup behaviour. Pettigrew argued that negative outgroup behaviour is disposition-ally attributed, and positive outgroup behaviour is externally attributed or explained away in other ways that preserve our unfavourable outgroup image. The ultimate attribution error refers to attributions made for outgroup behaviour only, whereas broader intergroup perspectives focus on ingroup attributions as well.

An early study of intergroup attributions was conducted by Taylor and Jaggi (1974) in southern India, against a background of intergroup conflict between Hindus and Muslims. Hindu participants read vignettes describing Hindus or Muslims acting in a socially desir-able way (e.g. offering shelter from the rain) or socially undesirable way (e.g. refusing shelter) towards them, and then chose one of a number of explanations for the behaviour. The results were as predicted. Hindu participants made more internal attributions for socially desirable than socially undesirable acts by Hindus (ingroup). This difference dis-appeared when Hindus made attributions for Muslims (outgroup).

Hewstone and Ward (1985) conducted a more complete and systematic follow-up, with Malays and Chinese in Malaysia and Singapore. Participants made internal or external attributions for desirable or undesirable behaviour described in vignettes as being per-formed by Malays or by Chinese. In Malaysia, Malays showed a clear ethnocentric attribution bias – they attributed a positive act by a Malay more to internal factors than a similar act by a Chinese, and a negative act by a Malay less to internal factors than a simi-lar act by a Chinese (see Figure 3.7). The ingroup enhancement effect was much stronger

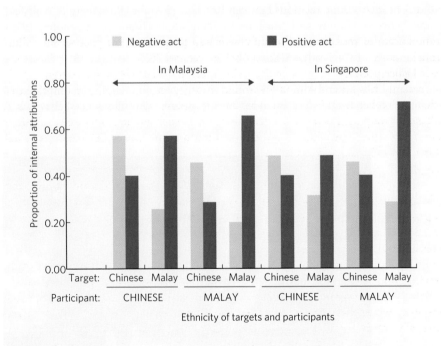

**Figure 3.7** Internal attribution of positive and negative acts by Malays or Chinese as a function of attributor ethnicity

Malays showed an ethnocentric attributional bias in which a positive act was more internally attributed to a Malay than a Chinese, and a negative act less internally attributed to a Malay than a Chinese: the effect was more pronounced in Malaysia, where Malays are the dominant group and Chinese the ethnic minority, than in Singapore. Chinese did not show an ethnocentric attribution bias

*Source*: based on data from Hewstone & Ward (1985)

than the outgroup derogation effect. The Chinese participants showed no ethnocentric bias – instead, they showed a tendency to make similar attributions to those made by Malays. In Singapore, the only significant effect was that Malays made internal attributions for positive acts by Malays.

Hewstone and Ward explain these findings in terms of the nature of intergroup relations in Malaysia and Singapore. In Malaysia, Malays are the clear majority group and Chinese an ethnic minority. Furthermore, relations between the two groups were tense and relatively conflictual at the time, with Malaysia pursuing a policy of ethnic assimilation. Both Malays and Chinese generally shared an unfavourable **stereotype** of Chinese and a favourable stereotype of Malays. In contrast, Singapore is ethnically more tolerant. The Chinese are in the majority, and ethnic stereotypes are markedly less pronounced.

The important implication of this analysis is that ethnocentric attribution is not a universal tendency that reflects asocial cognition; rather, it depends on intergroup dynamics in a sociohistorical context. The sorts of attribution that group members make about ingroup and outgroup behaviour are influenced by the nature of the relations between the groups.

This is consistent with Hewstone's (1989) argument that a proper analysis of attribution, more accurately described as social explanation, requires a careful articulation (i.e. theoretical integration or connection) of different **levels of analysis (or explanation)** (see Doise, 1986; see also Chapter 1). In other words, we need to know how individual cognitive processes, interpersonal interactions, group membership dynamics and intergroup relations all affect, are affected by and are interrelated with one another.

Further evidence for ethnocentric intergroup attributions comes from studies of interracial attitudes in educational settings in the United States (Duncan, 1976; Stephan, 1977); from studies of inter-ethnic relations between Israelis and Arabs (Rosenberg & Wolfsfeld, 1977) and between Hindus and Muslims in Bangladesh (Islam & Hewstone, 1993); and from studies of race, sex and social class-based attributions for success and failure (Deaux & Emswiller, 1974; Feather & Simon, 1975; Greenberg & Rosenfield, 1979; Hewstone, Jaspars & Lalljee, 1982).

More recently, Mackie and Ahn (1998) found that the *outcome bias,* the assumption that the outcomes of behaviour were intended by the person who chose the behaviour, is

**Stereotype**
Widely shared and simplified evaluative image of a social group and its members.

**Level of analysis (or explanation)**
The types of concepts, mechanisms and language used to explain a phenomenon.

**Counter-stereotypical behaviour**
What next, Silvio? President Berlusconi has made an art of failing to behave — or sometimes even to look — like a national leader

affected by whether the actor is a member of your group or not and whether the outcome was desirable or not. Mackie and Ahn found that there was an outcome bias in the case of an ingroup member and a desirable outcome but not when the outcome was undesirable.

There are at least two processes that may be responsible for ethnocentric intergroup attributions. The first is a cognitive one. Social categorisation generates category-congruent expectations in the form of expectancies (Deaux, 1976), schemas (e.g. Fiske & Taylor, 1991), or group prototypes or stereotypes (e.g. Hogg & Abrams, 1988; Turner, Hogg, Oakes, Reicher & Wetherell, 1987; see Chapter 11).

Research shows that stereotype-consistent or expectancy-consistent behaviour is attributed to stable internal factors, whereas expectancy-inconsistent behaviour is attributed to unstable or situational factors (e.g. Bell, Wicklund, Manko & Larkin, 1976; Rosenfield & Stephan, 1977). When people explain expectancy-confirming behaviour, they may simply rely on dispositions implied by a stereotype without bothering to put cognitive effort into the consideration of additional factors (Kulik, 1983; Pyszczynski & Greenberg, 1981).

The second process involved in intergroup attributions is people's need to secure group membership-based self-esteem from intergroup comparisons. This process is described by **social identity theory** (e.g., Tajfel & Turner, 1979; also Hogg & Abrams, 1988; see Chapter 11). Because people derive their social identity from the groups to which they belong (a description and evaluation of themselves in terms of the defining features of the group), they have a vested interest in maintaining or obtaining an ingroup profile that is more positive than that of relevant outgroups. The ethnocentric attributional bias quite clearly satisfies this aim: it internally attributes good things about the ingroup and bad things about the outgroup, and it externally attributes bad things about the ingroup and good things about the outgroup.

**Social identity theory**
Theory of group membership and intergroup relations based on self-categorisation, social comparison and the construction of a shared self-definition in terms of ingroup-defining properties.

## Attribution and stereotyping

Attribution processes operating at the societal level in an intergroup context may play an important role in shaping the profile and dominance of specific stereotypes. Stereotyping is not only an individual cognitive activity (see Chapter 2); it can also serve ego-defensive functions (making one feel good in contrast to others) and social functions (allowing one to fit in with other people's world views) (Snyder & Miene, 1994).

According to Tajfel (1981a) social groups may activate or accentuate existing stereotypes in order to attribute large-scale distressing events to the actions of specific outgroups – that is, scapegoats. For instance, during the 1930s in Germany the Jews were blamed for the economic crisis of the time. It was convenient to activate the 'miserly Jew' stereotype to explain in simplistic terms the lack of money: there is no money because the Jews are hoarding it. Stereotypes may also be elaborated to justify actions committed or planned against an outgroup. For instance, a group might develop a stereotype of an outgroup as dull-witted, simple, lazy and incompetent in order to explain or justify the economic and social exploitation of that group.

# Social knowledge and societal attributions

People do not wake up every morning and causally reconstruct their world anew. In general, we rely on well-learned causal scripts (Abelson, 1981) and general causal schemata attached to situational, personality and group membership labels. We stop, think and make causal attributions only when events are unexpected or inconsistent with expectations (e.g. Hastie, 1984; Langer, 1978; Pyszczynski & Greenberg, 1981), when we are in a bad mood (Bohner, Bless, Schwarz & Strack, 1988), when we feel a lack of control (Liu & Steele, 1986), or when

## Real world 3.2
### A very strange custom: The cultural context of causal attribution

Gün Semin tells a fictitious story about a Brazilian aborigine who visits Rio de Janeiro and then returns home to his tribe deep in the Amazonian rainforest to give an account of the visit (Semin, 1980, p. 292).

On particular days more people than all those you have seen in your whole lifetime roam to this huge place of worship, an open hut the size of which you will never imagine. They come, chanting, singing, with symbols of their gods and once everybody is gathered the chanting drives away all alien spirits. Then, at the appointed time the priests arrive wearing colourful garments, and the chanting rises to war cries until three high priests, wearing black, arrive. All priests who were running around with sacred round objects leave them and at the order of the high priests begin the religious ceremony. Then, when the chief high priest gives a shrill sound from himself they all run after the single sacred round object that is left, only to kick it away when they get hold of it. Whenever the sacred object goes through one of the two doors and hits the sacred net the religious followers start to chant, piercing the heavens, and most of the priests embark on a most ecstatic orgy until the chief priest blows the whistle on them.

This is, of course, a description of a football match by someone who does not know the purpose or rules of the game. It illustrates an important point. For causal explanations to be meaningful they need to be part of a highly complex general interpretative framework that constitutes our socially acquired cultural knowledge.

attributions are occasioned by conversational goals: for example, when we want to offer a particular explanation or justification of behaviour to someone with whom we are conversing (Hewstone & Antaki, 1988; Lalljee, 1981; Tetlock, 1983). Usually, we rely on a wealth of acquired and richly textured cultural knowledge that automatically explains what is going on around us. This knowledge resides in cultural beliefs, social stereotypes, collective ideologies and social representations (see Box 3.2).

## Social representations

**Social representations**
Collectively elaborated explanations of unfamiliar and complex phenomena that transform them into a familiar and simple form.

One way in which cultural knowledge about the causes of things may be constructed and transmitted is described by Moscovici's theory of **social representations** (e.g. Farr & Moscovici, 1984; Lorenzi-Cioldi & Clémence, 2001; Moscovici, 1961, 1981, 1988; Purkhardt, 1995). (See Chapter 5 for a discussion of the relationship between social representations and attitudes.) Social representations are consensual understandings shared among group members. They emerge through informal everyday communication. They transform the unfamiliar and complex into the familiar and straightforward, and thus provide a common sense framework for interpreting our experiences.

An individual or a specialist interest group derives a sophisticated, non-obvious, technical explanation of a commonplace phenomenon (e.g explaining mental illness in terms of biological or social factors rather than spiritual forces). This attracts public attention and becomes widely shared and popularised (i.e. simplified, distorted and ritualised) through informal discussion among non-specialists. It is now a social representation – an accepted, unquestioned common sense explanation that tends to oust alternatives to become the orthodox explanation.

Moscovici's original formulation focused on the development of the theory of psychoanalysis, but it is just as applicable to other formal theories and phenomena that have been transformed to become part of popular consciousness: for example, evolutionary theory, relativity theory, dietary and health theories, Marxist economics and AIDS. The theory of social representations has come under some criticism, often for the rather imprecise way in which it is formulated (e.g. Augoustinos & Innes, 1990). Nonetheless, it does suggest a way in which ordinary social interaction in society constructs commonsense or 'naive' causal theories that are widely used to explain events (Heider, 1958).

One source of criticism is that it has always been difficult to analyse social representations quantitatively. Some steps have, however, been taken towards the development of appropriate quantitative techniques (Doise, Clémence & Lorenzi-Cioldi, 1993). In addition, Breakwell and Canter (1993) have assembled a collection of chapters describing in concrete terms the variety of ways that different researchers have approached the measurement of social representations. These methods include qualitative and quantitative analyses of interviews, questionnaires, observational data and archival material. A good example of this methodological pluralism is Jodelet's (1991) classic description of social representations of mental illness in the small French community of Ainay-le-Chateau, in which questionnaires, interviews and ethnographic observation were all used.

Social representations, like norms (see Chapters 7 and 8), tend to be grounded in groups and differ from group to group, such that intergroup behaviour can often revolve around a clash of social representations (Lorenzi-Cioldi & Clémence, 2001). For example, in Western countries attitudes and behaviour that promote healthy lifestyles are positively associated with social status, and health promotion messages tend to emanate from middle-class professional groups (Salovey, Rothman & Rodin, 1998). A social representations analysis suggests that these messages are relatively ineffective in promoting healthy lifestyles for non-middle-class people because they are inconsistent with the wider representational framework of a good life for such people.

The development of the European Union (EU) has provided fertile ground for social representation research (e.g. Chryssochoou, 2000) that links to the study of European identity dynamics (e.g. Cinnirella, 1997; Huici, Ros, Cano, Hopkins, Emler & Carmona, 1997). In many respects the EU can be considered a prototypical social representation – a relatively new and quite technical idea that has its roots in complex economic matters to do with free trade, subsidies, and so forth. But the EU is now an accepted and commonplace part of European discourse which often emphasises more emotive issues of national and European identity rather than economic and trade matters.

## Rumour

The process through which social representations are constructed has more than a passing resemblance to the way in which rumours develop and are communicated (Allport & Postman, 1947; DiFonzo & Bordia, 2007). One of the earliest studies of rumour was conducted by Allport and Postman (1945), who found that if experimental participants described a photograph to someone who had not seen the photo, and then this person described it to another person, and so on, only 30 per cent of the original detail remained after five retellings. Allport and Postman identified three processes associated with rumour transmission:

1 *Levelling* – the rumour quickly becomes shorter, less detailed and less complex.

2 *Sharpening* – certain features of the rumour are selectively emphasised and exaggerated.

3 *Assimilation* – the rumour is distorted in line with people's pre-existing prejudices, partialities, interests and agendas.

More naturalistic studies have found rather less distortion as a consequence of rumour transmission (e.g. Caplow, 1947; Schachter & Burdeck, 1955).

Whether or not rumours are distorted, and even whether rumours are transmitted at all, seems to depend on the anxiety level of those who hear the rumour (Buckner, 1965; Rosnow, 1980). Uncertainty and ambiguity increase anxiety and stress, which leads people to seek out information with which to rationalise anxiety, which in turn enhances rumour transmission. (Check the third focus question. Here is one reason why Rajna wanted to pass a rumour on.) Whether the ensuing rumour is distorted or becomes more precise depends on whether people approach the rumour with a critical or uncritical orientation. In the former case the rumour becomes refined, while in the latter (which often accompanies a crisis) the rumour becomes distorted.

Rumours always have a source, and often this source purposely elaborates the rumour for a specific reason. The stock market is a perfect context for rumour elaboration. At the end of the 1990s, rumour played a clear role in inflating the value of 'dot-com' companies, which then crashed in the NASDAQ meltdown early in 2000 – a concrete example was the rapid hype and then crash of 'boo.com'. Exactly the same process played a significant role in the global stockmarket crash at the end of 2008 and beginning of 2009.

Another reason why rumours are purposely elaborated is to discredit individuals or groups. An organisation can spread a rumour about a competitor in order to undermine the competitor's market share (Shibutani, 1966), or a group can spread a rumour to blame another group for a widespread crisis. A good example of this is the fabrication and promulgation of conspiracy theories (Graumann & Moscovici, 1987).

## Conspiracy theories

**Conspiracy theory**

Explanation of widespread, complex and worrying events in terms of the premeditated actions of small groups of highly organised conspirators.

**Conspiracy theories** are elementary and exhaustive causal theories that attribute widespread natural and social calamities to the intentional and organised activities of certain social groups that are seen to form conspiratorial bodies set on ruining and then dominating the rest of humanity. One of the best-known conspiracy theories is the myth of the Jewish world conspiracy (Cohn, 1966), which surfaces periodically and often results in massive systematic persecution. Other conspiracy theories include the belief that immigrants are intentionally plotting to undermine the economy, that homosexuals are intentionally spreading HIV, and that witches (in the Middle Ages) and Al-Qaida (most recently) are behind virtually every world disaster you care to mention (e.g. Cohn, 1975).

Conspiracy theories wax and wane in popularity. They were particularly popular from the mid-seventeenth to the mid-eighteenth century:

> Everywhere people sensed designs within designs, cabals within cabals; there were court conspiracies, backstairs conspiracies, ministerial conspiracies, factional conspiracies, aristocratic conspiracies, and by the last half of the eighteenth century even conspiracies of gigantic secret societies that cut across national boundaries and spanned the Atlantic.
> (*Wood, 1982, p. 407*)

The accomplished conspiracy theorist can, with consummate skill and breathtaking versatility, explain even the most arcane and puzzling events in terms of the devious schemes and inscrutable machinations of hidden conspirators. Billig (1978) believes it is precisely this that can make conspiracy theories so attractive – they are incredibly effective at reducing uncertainty (Hogg, 2007b, in press). They provide a causal explanation in terms of enduring dispositions that can explain a wide range of events, rather than complex situational factors that are less widely applicable. Furthermore, worrying events become controllable and easily remedied because they are caused by small groups of highly visible people rather than being due to complex sociohistorical circumstances (Bains, 1983).

Not surprisingly, conspiracy theories are almost immune to disconfirming evidence. For example, in December 2006 the outcome of a three-year, 3.5 million pound enquiry into the death in 1997 of Princess Diana was reported – although there was absolutely no evidence that the British Royal family conspired with the British Government to have her killed to prevent her marrying an Egyptian Muslim, this conspiracy theory still persists. There are also conspiracy theories revolving around the 9/11 terrorist attacks in the United States in 2001 – some Americans are absolutely convinced it was the doing of the US government, and in parts of the Muslim world many people believe it was perpetrated by Israel (Lewis, 2004).

## Societal attributions

The emphasis on attributions as social knowledge finds expression in research into the explanations that people give for large-scale social phenomena. In general, this research supports the view that causal attributions for specific phenomena are located within and shaped by wider, socially constructed belief systems.

For example, research into explanations for poverty reveals that both the rich and the poor tend to explain poverty in terms of the behaviour of poor people rather than the situation that those people find themselves in (e.g. Feagin, 1972; Feather, 1974). This individualistic tendency is not so strong for people with a more left-wing or socialist ideology, or for people living in developing countries, where poverty is widespread (Pandey, Sinha, Prakash & Tripathi, 1982).

Explanations for wealth tend to depend on political affiliation. In Britain, Conservatives often ascribe it to positive individual qualities of thrift and hard work, while Labour supporters attribute it to the unsavoury individual quality of ruthless determination (Furnham, 1983). Not surprisingly, there are also cross-cultural differences: for example, individualistic explanations are very common in Hong Kong (Forgas, Morris & Furnham, 1982; Furnham & Bond, 1986).

Similarly, the sorts of explanation given for unemployment are influenced by people's wider belief and value systems (Chapter 5). Feather (1985) had Australian students give their explanations of unemployment on a number of dimensions. They preferred societal over individualistic explanations: for example, defective government, social change and economic recession were seen as more valid causes of unemployment than lack of motivation and personal handicap (see also Feather & Barber, 1983; Feather & Davenport, 1981). However, students who were politically more conservative tended to place less emphasis on societal explanations. Studies conducted in Britain also reveal that societal explanations are more prominent than individualistic explanations, and that there is a fair amount of agreement between employed and unemployed respondents (Furnham, 1982; Gaskell & Smith, 1985; Lewis, Snell & Furnham, 1987).

Other research has focused on the sorts of explanation that people give for riots (social unrest, collective behaviour and riots are discussed in detail in Chapter 11). Riots are enormously complicated social phenomena in that there are both proximal and distal causes – a specific event or action might trigger the riot, but only because of the complex conjunction of wider conditions. For instance, the proximal cause of the 1992 Los Angeles riot may have been the acquittal of white police officers charged with the beating of a black motorist, Rodney King (see Box 11.1); however, this alone would have been unlikely to promote a riot without the background of racial unrest and socio-economic distress in the United States at the time.

As with explanations of poverty, wealth and unemployment, the sorts of explanation that people give for a specific riot seem to be influenced by the person's sociopolitical perspective (e.g. Litton & Potter, 1985; Reicher, 1984, 2001; Reicher & Potter, 1985; Schmidt, 1972). More conservative members of the establishment tend to identify deviance, or personal or social pathology, while people with more liberal social attitudes tend to identify social circumstances.

For example, Schmidt (1972) analysed printed media explanations of the spate of riots that occurred in American cities during 1967. The explanations could be classified with respect to the three dimensions of:

1 legitimate–illegitimate
2 internal–external cause
3 institutional–environmental cause.

The first two dimensions were strongly correlated, with legitimate external causes (e.g. urban renewal mistakes, slum conditions) going together and illegitimate internal causes (e.g. criminal intent, belief that violence works) going together. Media sources on the political right tended to identify illegitimate internal causes, whereas those classified as 'left–centre' (i.e. liberal) emphasised legitimate external causes.

Finally, Sniderman, Hagen, Tetlock and Brady (1986) investigated the way in which people give explanations for racial inequality and have preferences for different government policies. They used a national sample of Whites in the United States (in 1972) and were interested in investigating the influence of level of education. They found that less-educated Whites employed an 'affect-driven' reasoning process. They started with their (mainly negative) feelings about Blacks, then proceeded directly to advocate minimal government assistance. Having done this, they 'doubled back' to fill in the intervening link to justify their advocacy – namely that Blacks were personally responsible for their own disadvantage. In contrast, better-educated Whites adopted a 'cognition-driven' reasoning process, in which they reasoned both forwards and backwards. Their policy recommendations were based on causal attributions for inequality, and in turn their causal attributions were influenced by their policy preference.

## Culture's contribution

The casual attributions and explanations that people proffer for events and behaviours are influenced not only by the nature of the information available, but also by people's wider belief and value systems. We have already seen, for example, the influence of sociopolitical values, educational status, group membership and ethnicity; and some evidence for the impact of culture.

People from different cultures often make very different attributions, make attributions in different ways or approach the entire task of social explanation in different ways (Chiu & Hong, 2007; Heine, 2010; Smith, Bond & Kağıtçıbaşi, 2006). Consequently, the potential for cross-cultural interpersonal misunderstanding is enormous. For example, the Zande people of West Africa have a dual theory of causality, where common sense proximal causes

**Culture and attribution**
Is the puppet responsible for its own actions? Easterners are less likely than Westerners to make dispositional attributions about people — let alone puppets!

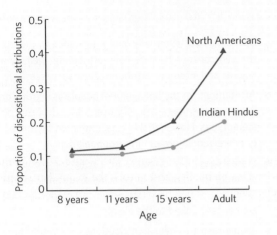

**Figure 3.8** Dispositional attributions as a function of age and cultural background

North Americans and Indian Hindus initially do not differ in the proportion of dispositional attributions made for behaviour. However, by the age of 15 there is a clear difference that strengthens in adulthood, with Americans being significantly more dispositional than Indians in their attributions

*Source:* based on data from Miller (1984)

operate within the context of witchcraft as the distal cause (Evans-Pritchard, 1937; see also Jahoda, 1979). For the Zande, an internal–external distinction would make little sense.

Another example: Lévy-Bruhl (1925) reported that the natives of Motumotu in New Guinea attributed a pleurisy epidemic to the presence of a specific missionary, his sheep, two goats and, finally, a portrait of Queen Victoria. Although initially quite bizarre, these sorts of attribution are easily explained as social representations: how much more bizarre are they than, for example, the 'string theories' that became popular in physics in the mid-1980s to construct a unified theory of the universe (see Hawking, 1988)?

One area of cross-cultural attribution research is the correspondence bias (see above). We have seen that in Western cultures people have a tendency to make dispositional attributions for others' behaviour (Gilbert & Malone, 1995; Ross, 1977). There is also evidence that such dispositional attributions become more evident over ontogeny (e.g. Pevers & Secord, 1973). In non-Western cultures, however, people are less inclined to make dispositional attributions (Carrithers, Collins & Lukes, 1986; Morris & Peng, 1994). This is probably partly a reflection of the more pervasive and all-enveloping influence of social roles in more collectivist non-Western cultures (Fletcher & Ward, 1988; Jahoda, 1982) and partly a reflection of a more holistic worldview that promotes context-dependent, occasion-bound thinking (Shweder & Bourne, 1982).

To investigate further the role of culture in dispositional attributions, Miller (1984) compared middle-class North Americans and Indian Hindus from each of four age groups (adults, and 15-, 11- and 8-year-olds). Participants narrated prosocial and antisocial behaviour and gave their own spontaneous explanations of the causes of this behaviour. Miller was able to code responses to identify the proportion of dispositional and contextual attributions that participants made. Among the youngest children there was little cross-cultural difference (see Figure 3.8). As age increased, however, the two groups diverged, mainly because the Americans increasingly came to adopt dispositional attributions. For context attributions the results were reversed.

The important lesson this study teaches us is that cultural factors have a significant impact on attribution and social explanation. We return to the role of culture in social behaviour in Chapter 16.

## Summary

- People are naive psychologists seeking to understand the causes of their own and other people's behaviour.

- Much like scientists, people take account of consensus, consistency and distinctiveness information in deciding whether to attribute behaviour internally to personality traits and dispositions, or externally to situational factors.

- The attributions that we make can have a profound impact on our emotions, self-concept and relationships with others. There may be individual differences in propensities to make internal or external attributions.

- People are actually poor scientists when it comes to making attributions. They are biased in many different ways, the most significant of which are a tendency to attribute others' behaviour dispositionally and their own behaviour externally, and a tendency to protect the self-concept by externally attributing their own failures and internally attributing their successes.

- Attributions for the behaviour of people as ingroup or outgroup members are ethnocentric and based on stereotypes. However, this bias is affected by the real or perceived nature of intergroup relations.

- Stereotypes may originate in a need for groups to attribute the cause of large-scale distressing events to outgroups that have (stereotypical) properties that are causally linked to the events.

- People resort to causal attributions only when there is no readily available social knowledge (e.g. scripts, causal schemata, social representations, cultural beliefs) to explain things automatically.

## Literature, film and TV

### The Third Policeman

1967 Flan O'Brien book. A wacky and bizarre/magical book about the absurd. It has a very funny section that is relevant to social representations. There is a hilarious account of how bizarre social representations (in this case about atomic theory) can be formed and sustained.

### JFK

1991 film by Oliver Stone. It stars Kevin Costner as a New Orleans district attorney who reopens the case to find out who really assassinated JFK on 22 November 1963, in Dallas, and what the process/plot behind it was. This is a wonderful encounter with conspiracy theories and people's need to construct a causal explanation, however bizarre, of a disturbing event. The film also stars Tommy Lee Jones and Sissy Spacek.

### The Devils

Very harrowing 1971 Ken Russell cult classic about the inquisition and political intrigue in the church/state. The scenes are grotesque, evocative of the paintings of Hieronymus Bosch. The film is based on an Aldous Huxley novel and stars Vanessa Redgrave and Oliver Reed. It shows the awful lengths to which a group can go to protect its ultimate causal explanation – any divergence is seen as heresy or blasphemy, and is severely punished in order to make sure that everyone believes in its explanation of the nature of things.

### Macbeth

Shakespeare's 1606/07 tragedy in which three witches prophesise a string of evil deeds committed by Macbeth during his bloody rise to power, including the murder of the Scottish king Duncan. The causal question is whether the prophecy caused the events – or was there some other complex of causes.

## Guided questions

1   What is meant by *locus of control*? Compare the contributions that are made by people's efforts to their chances of success in life with those made by fate or by circumstances. See what other students think about these issues in Chapter 6 of MyPsychLab at **www.mypsychlab.co.uk** (watch *IT video: Where is your locus of control?*).

2   Do attributional dynamics lead to problems in close relationships, or vice versa?

3   Sometimes our mental short-cuts lead us into error. One of these is *correspondence bias*. Describe and illustrate this concept.

4   What is meant by self-handicapping? Provide a real-world setting in which it can be applied.

5   The term *conspiracy theory* has entered everyday language. Can social psychology help us understand what purpose these theories serve?

### Learn more

Fiske, S. T., & Taylor, S. E. (2008). *Social cognition: From brains to culture*. New York: McGraw-Hill. This is essentially the third edition of Fiske and Taylor's classic social cognition text – it is comprehensive, detailed and well written, and covers the recent development of social neuroscience.

Fletcher, G., & Fincham, F. D. (eds) (1991). *Cognition in close relationships*. Hillsdale, NJ: Erlbaum. A collection of leading scholars provide detailed chapters on attribution and other sociocognitive approaches to close relationships.

Hewstone, M. (1989). *Causal attribution: From cognitive processes to collective beliefs*. Oxford: Blackwell. A comprehensive and detailed coverage of attribution theory and research, which also includes coverage of European perspectives that locate attribution processes in the context of society and intergroup relations.

Hilton, D. J. (2007). Causal explanation: From social perception to knowledge-based causal attribution. In A. W. Kruglanski & E. T. Higgins (eds), *Social psychology: Handbook of basic principles* (2nd ed., pp. 232–253). New York: Guilford. Comprehensive and up-to-date coverage of research on causal attribution processes and social explanation.

Macrae, C. N., & Quadflieg, S. (2010). Perceiving people. In S. T. Fiske, D. T. Gilbert, & G. Lindzey (eds), *Handbook of social psychology* (5th ed., Vol. 1, pp. 428–463). New York: Wiley. Comprehensive coverage of what we know about person perception – how we form and use our cognitive representations of people.

McClure, J. (1991). *Explanations, accounts, and illusions: A critical analysis*. Cambridge, UK: Cambridge University Press. A critical, wide-ranging and eclectic discussion of attribution as social explanation.

Moskowitz, G. B. (2005). *Social cognition: Understanding self and others*. New York: Guilford. A relatively recent comprehensive social cognition text that is written in a relatively accessible style as an introduction to the topic.

Smith, E. R. (1994). Social cognition contributions to attribution theory and research. In P. G. Devine, D. L. Hamilton & T. M. Ostrom (eds), *Social cognition: Impact on social psychology* (pp. 77–108). San Diego, CA: Academic Press. A focused coverage of social cognitive dimensions of attribution processes.

Trope, Y., & Gaunt, R. (2007). Attribution and person perception. In M. A. Hogg & J. Cooper (eds), *The SAGE handbook of social psychology: Concise student edition* (pp. 176–194). London: SAGE. A relatively recent, comprehensive and readable overview of attribution research.

Weary, G., Stanley, M. A., & Harvey, J. H. (1989). *Attribution*. New York: Springer-Verlag. A discussion of applications of attribution theory and the operation of attribution processes in clinical settings and everyday life outside the laboratory.

 Refresh your understanding, assess your progress and go further with interactive summaries, questions, podcasts and much more at **www.mypsychlab.co.uk**

## This chapter discusses

- Theories of the self
- Awareness of and knowledge about ourselves
- Types of selves and identities
- The search for self-conceptual coherence
- Social identity and personal identity
- Motives influencing the pursuit of self-knowledge
- Why we need self-esteem
- How we present ourselves
- Self, identity and culture

## Focus questions

1. To what extent is your identity unique, distinguishing you from all other human beings?

2. Would you accept that you are overwhelmingly driven to look good in other people's eyes?

3. Manfred asks: if people generally want to feel good about themselves, have those with low self-esteem failed in their quest? Clarify this apparent anomaly for Manfred. You can get some help by listening to an account based on the work of Diane Tice in Chapter 4 of MyPsychLab at www.mypsychlab.co.uk (listen to *selfesteem.mp3*).

4. Andrea has found out that you are studying social psychology. She asks your advice for presenting herself in the best possible light to others. Can you give her some tips?

will use which involves getting you to decide to buy a car by giving you a very low price

Go to **mypsychlab** to explore video and test your understanding of key topics addressed in this chapter.

Refresh your understanding with interactive summaries, explore topics further with video and audio clips and assess your progress with quick test and essay questions by logging to the accompanying website at www.mypsychlab.co.uk

# Chapter 4
## Self and identity

# Who are you?

Take a look in your wallet. You will probably find numerous cards and pieces of paper that have your name on them, and probably a rather gruesome photograph of yourself. What happens when you meet someone socially? Very early in the piece you discover each other's name, and soon after that you establish such things as their occupation, their attitudes and what they like to do. You also try to identify mutual acquaintances. In more formal contexts, people sometimes display their identity through uniforms, name/role badges and business cards.

Social interaction, and social existence itself, depends on people knowing who they are and who others are. Identity and self-conception underpin everyday life – knowing who you are allows you to know what you should think and do, and knowing who others are allows you to predict what they think and what they do. Knowledge of identity regulates and structures human interaction; and in turn, interactive and societal structures provide identities for us.

Many scholars have argued that it is reflexive thought – that is, the ability to think about ourselves thinking – that separates us from almost all other animals. Reflexive thought means that we can think about ourselves, about who we are, how we would like to be and how we would like others to see us. Humans have a highly developed sense of self and identity, and self and identity are fundamental parts of being human. We should not be surprised that psychologists, particularly social psychologists, have always been intrigued by the self.

In this chapter, we explore the self – where it comes from, what it looks like and how it influences thought and behaviour. Because self and identity are cognitive constructs that influence social interaction and perception, and are themselves influenced by society, the material in this chapter connects to virtually all other chapters in the book. The self is an enormously popular focus of research (e.g. Leary & Tangney, 2003; Sedikides & Brewer, 2001; Swann & Bosson, 2010). A 1997 review by Ashmore and Jussim reported 31,000 social psychological publications on the self over a two-decade period to the mid-1990s, and there is now even a scholarly journal entitled *Self and Identity*.

# Self and identity in historical context

The self is, historically, a relatively new idea. Baumeister (1987) paints a picture of medieval society in which social relations were fixed and stable and legitimised in religious terms. People's lives and identities were tightly mapped out according to their position in the social order – by visible ascribed attributes such as family membership, social rank, birth order and place of birth. In many ways, what you saw was what you got, so the idea of a complex individual self lurking underneath it all was difficult to entertain and probably superfluous.

All this started to change in the sixteenth century, and the change has gathered momentum ever since. The forces for change included the following:

- *Secularisation* – the idea that fulfilment occurs in the afterlife was replaced by the idea that you should actively pursue personal fulfilment in this life.
- *Industrialisation* – people were increasingly seen as units of production that would move from place to place to work, and thus would have a portable personal identity that was not locked into static social structures such as the extended family.
- *Enlightenment* – people felt that they could organise and construct different, better, identities and lives for themselves by overthrowing orthodox value systems and oppressive regimes (e.g. the French and American revolutions of the late eighteenth century).
- *Psychoanalysis* – Freud's (e.g. 1921) theory of the human mind crystallised the notion that the self was unfathomable because it lurked in the gloomy depths of the unconscious.

Psychoanalysis has probably done most to problematise self and identity, because it attributes behaviour to complex dynamics that are hidden deep within the person's sense of who they are. In Chapter 3 (see also Chapter 5), we explored the theory of social representations – a theory that invoked psychoanalysis as an example of how a novel idea or analysis can entirely change the way that people think about their world (e.g. Moscovici, 1961; see Lorenzi-Cioldi & Clémence, 2001).

Together, these and other social, political and cultural changes caused people to think about self and identity as highly complex and problematic. Theories of self and identity propagated and flourished in this fertile soil.

## Psychodynamic self

Freud (e.g. 1921) believed that unsocialised and selfish libidinal impulses (the id) are repressed and kept in check by internalised societal norms (the superego), but that, from time to time and in strange and peculiar ways, repressed impulses surface. Freud's view of the self is one in which you can only truly know yourself, or indeed others, when special procedures, such as hypnosis or psychotherapy, are employed to reveal repressed thoughts. Freud's ideas about self, identity and personality are far-reaching in social psychology: for example, Adorno, Frenkel-Brunswik, Levinson and Sanford's (1950) influential authoritarian personality theory of prejudice is a psychodynamic theory (see Chapter 10).

## Individual versus collective self

Freud, like many other psychologists, viewed the self as very personal and private – the apotheosis of individuality: something that uniquely describes an individual human being. When someone says 'I am . . .' they are describing what makes them different from all other human beings. But think about this for a moment. 'I am British', 'I come from Bristol', 'I am a social psychologist' – these are all descriptions of my*self*, but they are also descriptions of many other people's selves (there are 60 million Britons, 400,000 people currently living in Bristol, and many thousands of social psychologists). So the self can also be a shared or collective self – a 'we' or 'us'.

Social psychologists have argued long and hard for more than a century about whether the self is an individual or a collective phenomenon. The debate has created polarised camps with advocates of the individual self and advocates of the collective self slogging it out in the literature. It is fair to say that the advocates of the individual self have tended to prevail. This is largely because social psychologists have considered groups to be made up of individuals who interact with one another rather than individuals who have a collective sense of shared identity. Individuals interacting in aggregates make up the province of social psychology, whereas groups as collectives are the province of several other social sciences, such as sociology and political science (see Chapters 1 and 11).

This perspective on groups, summed up by Floyd Allport's legendary proclamation that 'There is no psychology of groups which is not essentially and entirely a psychology of individuals' (1924, p. 4), has made it difficult for the collective self to thrive as a research topic.

## Collective self

It was not always like this. In the early days of social psychology, things were very different (see Farr, 1996; Hogg & Williams, 2000). Wundt was the founder of psychology as an experimental science, and he proposed that social psychology was the study of:

> those mental products which are created by a community of human life and are, therefore, inexplicable in terms merely of individual consciousness since they presuppose the reciprocal action of many. *(Wundt, 1916, p. 3)*

Wundt's social psychology dealt with collective phenomena, such as language, religion, customs and myth, that, according to Wundt, could not be understood in terms of the psychology of the isolated individual. Durkheim (1898), one of the founding fathers of sociology, was influenced by Wundt's interest in collective life and also maintained that collective phenomena could not be explained in terms of individual psychology.

The view that the self draws its properties from groups is shared by many other early social psychologists: for example, early theorists of collective behaviour and the crowd (e.g. LeBon, 1908; Tarde, 1901; Trotter, 1919; see also Chapter 11). Notably, McDougall, in his book *The Group Mind* (1920), argued that out of the interaction of individuals there arose a 'group mind', which had a reality and existence that was qualitatively distinct from the isolated individuals making up the group. There was a collective self that was grounded in group life. Although phrased in rather quaint old-fashioned language, this idea has a direct line of descent to subsequent experimental social psychological research which confirms that human interaction has emergent properties that endure and influence other people: for example, Sherif's (1936) research on how norms emerge from interaction and are internalised to influence behaviour, and some of Asch's (1952) research on conformity to norms.

Since the early 1980s there has been a revival of interest in the notion of a collective self; largely initiated by European research on the emergence of social representations out of social interaction (e.g. Farr & Moscovici, 1984; Lorenzi-Cioldi & Clémence, 2001; see Chapters 3, 5, 7 and 8), and on the role of social identity in group processes and intergroup behaviour (e.g. Tajfel & Turner, 1979; also see Hogg, 2006; Hogg & Abrams, 1988; discussed later in this chapter but covered fully in Chapter 11).

## Symbolic interactionist self

Another twist to the idea of the collective self is recognition that the self emerges and is shaped by social interaction. Early psychologists such as William James (1890) distinguished between self as stream of consciousness, 'I', and self as object of perception, 'me'. In this way, reflexive knowledge is possible because 'I' can be aware of 'me', and people can thus know themselves. However, this is not to say that people's self-knowledge is particularly accurate. People tend to reconstruct who they are without being aware of having done

**The looking-glass self**
According to G. H. Mead, our self-concept derives from seeing ourselves as others see us

it (Greenwald, 1980), and, in general, although people may be aware of who they are in terms of their attitudes and preferences, they are rather bad at knowing how they arrived at that knowledge (Nisbett & Wilson, 1977).

Nevertheless, people do have a sense of 'me', and according to **symbolic interactionism** the self arises out of human interaction (Mead, 1934; see also Blumer, 1969). Mead believed that human interaction is largely symbolic. When we interact with people it is mainly in terms of words and non-verbal cues that are rich with meaning because they are symbolise much more than is superficially available in the behaviour itself (see Chapter 15). Mead believed that society influences individuals through self-conception, and that self-conception arises and is continually modified through interaction between people. This interaction involves symbols that must have shared meaning if they are to be communicated effectively.

Effective interaction also rests on being able to take the role of the other person; which of course entails 'looking in from outside' and seeing oneself as others do – as a social object, 'me', rather than social subject, 'I'. Because others often see us as category representatives, the 'me' is often viewed as a collective 'me' – we might even think of it as an 'us'. The way that society views the world is negotiated and traded through symbolic interaction. In order to do this effectively, we need to take the role of the other, and thus we see ourselves as others (ultimately society) do. In this way, we construct a self-concept that reflects the society we live in; we are socially constituted.

Symbolic interactionism offers quite a sophisticated and complex model of self-conception. Nevertheless, it generates a very straightforward prediction. Because self-conception comes from seeing ourselves as others see us (the idea of the **looking-glass self**), there should be a strong correlation between how we rate ourselves and how others rate us. Shrauger and Schoeneman (1979) reviewed sixty-two relevant empirical studies to see whether this was true. What they found was that people did *not* tend to see themselves as others saw them but instead saw themselves as they *thought* others saw them.

So, for example, Tice (1992) had participants provide information that indicated that they were emotionally stable or emotionally responsive to different situations – in other words, this is how they thought others would see them. They provided this information under private conditions in which they believed no one was watching them or under public conditions in which they believed a graduate student was closely monitoring their behaviour – the latter condition would engage the looking-glass self. As predicted, subsequent descriptions of self were more radically altered under public conditions than private conditions (see Figure 4.1).

**Symbolic interactionism**
Theory of how the self emerges from human interaction, which involves people trading symbols (through language and gesture) that are usually consensual, and represent abstract properties rather than concrete objects.

**Looking-glass self**
The self derived from seeing ourselves as others see us.

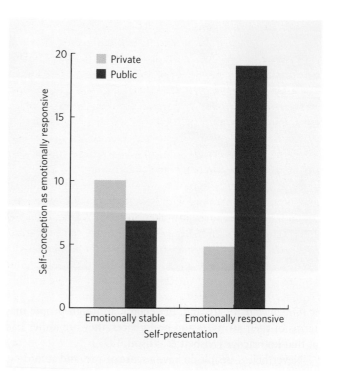

**Figure 4.1** Self-conception as emotionally stable or responsive, as a function of public or private self-presentation

People who were instructed to present themselves as either less emotionally responsive (i.e. move stable) or more emotionally responsive.

- Next, they rated themselves for their 'true' level of emotionally on a 25-point scale, ranging from a low score (less emotionally responsive) to a high score (more emotionally responsive).

- When they believed that their earlier behaviour had been public, their self-conception moved in the direction of their action: closer to a score of 1 for those who had been less emotionally responsive, or closer to a score of 25 for those who had been more emotionally responsive.

*Source*: based on data from Tice (1992), Study 1

One implication of the idea that people do not see themselves as others see them, but instead see themselves as they think others see them, is that we do not actually take the role of the other in constructing a sense of self. An alternative reading is that the communication process in social interaction is noisy and inaccurate. It is influenced by a range of self-construal motivations (motives to view others, and be viewed by them, in particular ways) that conspire to construct an inaccurate image of others and what they think about us. People are generally unaware of what other people really think of them (Kenny & DePaulo, 1993).

As we discover below, self-conception is tightly associated with self-enhancement motives. For example, Taylor and Brown (1988) found that people normally overestimate their good points, overestimate their control over events and are unrealistically optimistic – Sedikides and Gregg (2007) call this the *self-enhancing triad*.

## Self-awareness

People do not spend all their time thinking about the self. Self-awareness comes and goes for different reasons and has an array of consequences.

Duval and Wicklund (1972) believe that self-awareness is a state in which you are aware of yourself as an object, much as you might be aware of a tree or another person. Thus they speak of objective self-awareness. When you are objectively self-aware you make comparisons between how you actually are and how you would like to be – an ideal, a goal or some other standard. The outcome of this comparison is often a sense that you have shortcomings – and negative emotions associated with this recognition. People then try to overcome their shortcomings by bringing the self closer into line with ideal standards. This can sometimes be very difficult, and people can give up trying, experience reduced motivation and feel even worse about themselves.

Objective self-awareness is generated by any circumstances that focus your attention on yourself as an object: for example, being in front of an audience (Chapter 8) or catching your image in a mirror or window. Indeed, a very popular method for raising self-awareness in laboratory studies is precisely to place participants in front of a mirror.

Carver and Scheier (1981; Scheier & Carver, 1981) introduce a qualification to self-awareness theory. They distinguish between two types of self that one can be aware of: (1) the *private self* – your private thoughts, feelings and attitudes; (2) the *public self* – how other people see you, your public image. Private self-awareness produces behaviour aimed at matching your internalised standards, whereas public self-awareness is oriented towards presenting yourself to others in a positive light.

Being self-aware can be very uncomfortable. We all feel self-conscious from time to time and are only too familiar with how it affects our behaviour – we feel anxious, we become tongue-tied, or we make mistakes on tasks. We can even feel slightly paranoid (Fenigstein, 1984). However, sometimes being self-aware can be a terrific thing, particularly on those occasions when we have accomplished a great feat. In early December 2003, having won the rugby world cup, the England team paraded through London and ended up in Trafalgar Square in front of three-quarters of a million people – standing in an open-topped bus, the team looked freezing, but certainly did not seem to be suffering any aversive consequences from the adulation they were receiving.

Self-awareness can also make us feel good when the standards against which we compare ourselves are not too exacting: for example, if we compare ourselves against standards derived from 'most other people' or from people who are less fortunate than ourselves (Taylor & Brown, 1988; Wills, 1981). Self-awareness can also improve introspection, intensify emotions and improve performance of controlled effort-sensitive tasks that do not require undue skill (e.g. proof-reading an essay you have written).

The reverse side of being objectively self-aware is being in a state of reduced objective self-awareness. Because elevated self-awareness can be stressful or aversive, people may try to avoid this state by drinking alcohol, or by more extreme measures such as suicide (Baumeister, 1991). Reduced self-awareness has also been identified as a key component of deindividuation – 'deindividuated persons are blocked from awareness of themselves as separate individuals and from monitoring their own behaviour' (Diener, 1980, p. 210), and therefore are able to behave in uninhibited, impulsive and anti-normative ways. Thus reduced self-awareness may be implicated in crowd behaviour and other forms of social unrest (see Chapter 11 for a full discussion of crowd behaviour).

# Self-knowledge

When people are self-aware, what are they aware of? What do we know about ourselves and how do we construct a sense of who we are? Self-knowledge is constructed in much the same way and through many of the same processes as we construct representations of other people. Chapter 2, on social cognition and social thinking, and Chapter 3, on attribution and social explanation, have already described some of these general processes.

## Self-schemas

In Chapter 2, we saw how information about other people is stored in the form of a **schema**. Research suggests that we store information about the self in a similar but more complex and varied way. Information about the self is stored as separate context-specific nodes such that different contexts activate different nodes and thus, effectively, different aspects of self (Breckler, Pratkanis & McCann, 1991; Higgins, van Hook & Dorfman, 1988).

**Schema**
Cognitive structure that represents knowledge about a concept or type of stimulus, including its attributes and the relations among those attributes.

**An ideal self**
This wealthy socialite with an interest in exotic cats underwent extreme plastic surgery to achieve that leonine look

People tend to have clear conceptions of themselves (i.e. self-schemas) on some dimensions but not others – they are schematic on some but aschematic on others. People are self-schematic on dimensions that are important to them, on which they think they are extreme and on which they are certain the opposite does not hold (Markus, 1977). For example, if you think you are sophisticated, definitely not unsophisticated, and being sophisticated is important to you, then you are self-schematic on that dimension – it is part of your self-concept. If you do not consider yourself sophisticated, and you do not really care much about being sophisticated or about the attribute *sophisticated,* then you are aschematic on that dimension.

Most people have a complex self-concept with a relatively large number of discrete self-schemas. Linville (1985, 1987; see below) has suggested that this variety helps to buffer people from the negative impact of life events by making sure that there are always self-schemas from which they can derive a sense of satisfaction.

Showers (1992) suggested that self-schemas that are too highly compartmentalised may have some disadvantages. Specifically, if some self-schemas are very negative and some are very positive, events may cause extreme mood swings according to whether a positive or negative self-schema is primed. Evaluatively, more integrated self-schemas may be preferable. For example, if James believes that he is a wonderful cook but an awful musician, he has evaluatively compartmentalised self-schemas – contexts that prime one or the other self-schema will produce very positive or very negative moods. Contrast this with Sally, who believes that she is a reasonably good cook and a fairly poor musician. She has self-schemas that are evaluatively more integrated – context effects on mood will be much less extreme.

Self-schemas influence information processing and behaviour in much the same way as schemas about other people (Markus & Sentis, 1982): self-schematic information is more readily noticed, is overrepresented in cognition and is associated with longer processing time. Self-schemas do not only describe how we are. Markus and Nurius (1986) have suggested that we have an array of possible selves – future-oriented schemas of what we would like to become, or what we fear we might become. For example, a postgraduate student may have future selves as a university lecturer or a rock musician.

Another perspective is offered by Higgins's (1987) **self-discrepancy theory**. Higgins suggests that we have three types of self-schema:

**Self-discrepancy theory**
Higgins' theory about the consequences of making actual–ideal and actual–'ought' self comparisons that reveal self-discrepancies.

1   *actual self* – how we currently are;

2   *ideal self* – how we would like to be;

3   *'ought' self* – how we think we should be.

The latter two are 'self-guides' that mobilise different types of self-related behaviours. The same goal – for example, prosperity – can be constructed as an ideal (strive to be prosperous) or an 'ought' (strive to avoid not being prosperous). Discrepancies between actual, and ideal or 'ought' can motivate change to reduce the discrepancy – in this way we engage in **self-regulation**. (In Chapter 13 we discuss self-regulation in the context of close relationships.) Failure to resolve the actual–ideal discrepancy produces dejection-related emotions (e.g. disappointment, dissatisfaction, sadness), whereas failure to resolve the actual–ought discrepancy produces agitation-related emotions (e.g. anxiety, threat, fear).

One test of self-discrepancy theory, by Higgins, Bond, Klein and Strauman (1986), identified students who either had a low discrepancy between their actual and ideal and actual and 'ought' selves, or had a high discrepancy. Four to six weeks later, these students participated in an experiment in which a range of dejection and agitation emotions were measured both before and after a procedure in which their ideal or their 'ought' self was primed. The priming procedure involved focusing on and describing the relevant self and its discrepancy with their actual self. Figure 4.2 shows the priming-induced change in emotion for high-discrepancy participants – low-discrepancy participants experienced insignificant change in either emotion.

**Self-regulation**
Strategies that we use to match our behaviour to an ideal or 'ought' standard.

## Regulatory focus theory

Self-discrepancy theory and the general notion of self-regulation have been elaborated into **regulatory focus theory** (Higgins, 1997, 1998). Higgins proposes that people have two separate self-regulatory systems, termed promotion and prevention, which are concerned with the pursuit of different types of goals.

The *promotion system* is concerned with the attainment of one's hopes and aspirations – one's *ideals*. It generates sensitivity to the presence or absence of positive events. People in a promotion focus adopt *approach strategic means* to attain their goals. For example, promotion-focused students would seek ways to improve their grades, find new challenges and

**Regulatory focus theory**
A promotion focus causes people to be approach-oriented in constructing a sense of self; a prevention focus causes people to be more cautious and avoidant in constructing a sense of self.

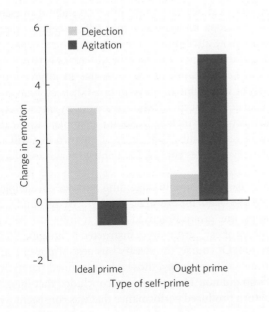

**Figure 4.2** Priming the ideal self can lead to dejection, whereas priming the 'ought' self can lead to agitation

People with a high actual–ideal and actual–ought self-discrepancy experienced:

- an increase in dejection but not agitation emotions after being primed to focus on their *ideal self*, and

- an increase in agitation but not dejection emotions after being primed to focus on their *'ought' self*.

*Source*: based on Higgins, Bond, Klein & Strauman (1986), Experiment 2

treat problems as interesting obstacles to overcome. The *prevention system* is concerned with the fulfilment of one's duties and obligations – one's *oughts*. It generates sensitivity to the presence or absence of negative events. People in a prevention focus use *avoidance strategic means* to attain their goals. For example, prevention-focused students would avoid new situations or new people, and concentrate more on avoiding failure than achieving the highest possible grade.

Research shows that people who are promotion-focused are especially likely to recall information relating to the pursuit of success by others (Higgins & Tykocinski, 1992), are most inspired by positive role models who emphasise strategies for achieving success (Lockwood, Jordan & Kunda, 2002), and show elevated motivation and persistence on tasks that are framed in terms of gains and non-gains (Shah, Higgins & Friedman, 1998). People who are prevention-focused behave quite differently – they recall information relating to the avoidance of failure by others, are most inspired by negative role models who highlight strategies for avoiding failure, and exhibit motivation and persistence on tasks that are framed in terms of losses and non-losses.

Some people are habitually more approach-focused and others more prevention-focused – it is an individual difference that can arise during childhood (Higgins & Silberman, 1998). A promotion-focus can arise if children are habitually hugged and kissed for behaving in a desired manner (a positive event) and love is withdrawn as a form of discipline (absence of a positive event). A prevention-focus can arise if children are encouraged to be alert to potential dangers (absence of a negative event) and punished and shouted at when they behave undesirably (a negative event). Against the background of individual differences, regulatory focus can also be influenced by the immediate context, for example by structuring the situation so that people focus on prevention or on promotion (Higgins, Roney, Crowe & Hymes, 1994).

## Inferences from our behaviour

One of the most obvious ways to learn about who you are is to examine your private thoughts and feelings about the world – knowing what you think and feel about the world is a very good clue to the sort of person you are.

**Self-perception theory**
Bem's idea that we gain knowledge of ourselves only by making self-attributions: for example, we infer our own attitudes from our own behaviour.

However, when these internal cues are weak we may make inferences about ourselves from what we do – our behaviour. This idea underpins Bem's **self-perception theory** (Bem, 1967, 1972). Bem argues that we make attributions not only for others' behaviour (see Chapter 3) but also for our own, and that there is no essential difference between self-attributions and other-attributions. Furthermore, just as we construct an impression of someone else's personality on the basis of being able to make internal dispositional attributions for their behaviour, so we construct a concept of who we are not by introspection but by being able to attribute our own behaviour internally. So, for example, I know that I enjoy eating curry because, if given the opportunity, I eat curry of my own free will and in preference to other foods, and not everyone likes curry – I am able to make an internal attribution for my behaviour.

Self-perception processes can also be based on simply imagining ourselves behaving in a particular way (Anderson & Godfrey, 1987). So, for example, van Gyn, Wenger and Gaul (1990) divided runners into two groups; one group practised power training on exercise bikes, the other did not. Half the members of each group were instructed to imagine themselves sprint training, the others were not. Of course, the sweaty business of power training improved subsequent performance, but, remarkably, those who imagined themselves sprint training did better than those who did not. The researchers concluded that imagery had affected self-conception, which in turn produced performance that was consistent with that self-conception.

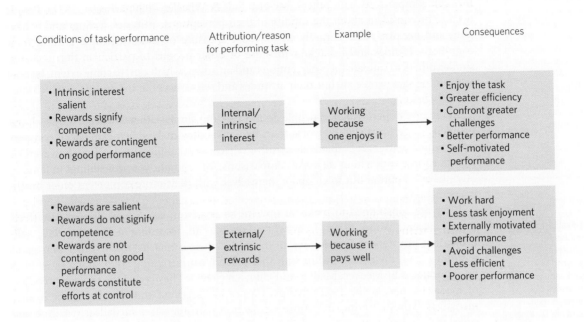

| Conditions of task performance | Attribution/reason for performing task | Example | Consequences |
|---|---|---|---|
| • Intrinsic interest salient<br>• Rewards signify competence<br>• Rewards are contingent on good performance | Internal/intrinsic interest | Working because one enjoys it | • Enjoy the task<br>• Greater efficiency<br>• Confront greater challenges<br>• Better performance<br>• Self-motivated performance |
| • Rewards are salient<br>• Rewards do not signify competence<br>• Rewards are not contingent on good performance<br>• Rewards constitute efforts at control | External/extrinsic rewards | Working because it pays well | • Work hard<br>• Less task enjoyment<br>• Externally motivated performance<br>• Avoid challenges<br>• Less efficient<br>• Poorer performance |

**Figure 4.3**  The overjustification effect

One's motivation to perform a task can be reduced, and performance of the task impaired, if there are obvious external causes for task performances – an overjustification effect that is reversed if performance can be internally attributed

Self-attributions have important implications for motivation. The theory predicts that if someone is induced to perform a task by either enormous rewards or fearsome penalties, task performance is attributed externally and thus motivation to perform is reduced. If there are minimal or no external factors to which performance can be attributed, we cannot easily avoid attributing performance internally to enjoyment or commitment, so motivation increases. This has been called the **overjustification effect** (see Figure 4.3), for which there is now substantial evidence (Deci & Ryan, 1985).

For example, Lepper, Greene and Nisbett (1973) had nursery-school children draw pictures. Some of the children simply drew of their own free will, while the rest were induced to draw with the promise of a reward, which they were subsequently given. A few days later, the children were unobtrusively observed playing; the children who had previously been rewarded for drawing spent half as much time drawing as did the other group. Those who had received no extrinsic reward seemed to have greater intrinsic interest in drawing.

In fact, there is evidence that the provision of external rewards for a previously intrinsically motivated task can actually reduce motivation and enjoyment and worsen performance of that task (e.g. Condry, 1977). An interesting paradox follows from this: antisocial behaviour might be controlled by *rewarding* people, rather than punishing them, for behaving antisocially!

**Overjustification effect**
In the absence of obvious external determinants of our behaviour, we assume that we freely choose the behaviour because we enjoy it.

## Social comparison and self-knowledge

Although we can learn about ourselves through introspection and self-perception, we can also learn about ourselves by comparing ourselves with other people. Indeed, Festinger (1954) developed **social comparison theory** to describe how people learn about themselves

**Social comparison (theory)**
Comparing our behaviours and opinions with those of others in order to establish the correct or socially approved way of thinking and behaving.

through comparisons with others (see also Suls & Wheeler, 2000; Wheeler, 1991). People need to be confident about the validity of their perceptions, attitudes, feelings and behaviour, and because there is rarely an objective measure of validity, people ground their cognitions, feelings and behaviour in those of other people. In particular, they seek out similar others to validate their perceptions and attitudes, which can, to some extent, be read as meaning that people anchor their attitudes and self-concept in the groups to which they feel they belong.

In the case of performance, people do not seek out similar others. Instead, they seek out people who perform slightly worse than they do – they make downward social comparisons, which deliver an evaluatively positive self-concept (Wills, 1981). Often, however, we cannot choose with whom we make comparisons: for example, younger siblings in families often have no option but to compare themselves with their more competent older brothers and sisters.

**Self-evaluation mainte-nance model**

People who are constrained to make esteem-damaging upward comparisons can underplay or deny similarity to the target, or they can withdraw from their relationship with the target.

If we are constrained to make an upward comparison, it can have deleterious effects on self-esteem (Wood, 1989). To avoid this, people can, according to Tesser's (1988) **self-evaluation maintenance model,** try to downplay their similarity to the other person or withdraw from their relationship with that person. An intriguing study along these lines was conducted by Medvec, Madley and Gilovich (1995). They coded the facial expressions of medal winners at the 1992 Olympic Games in Barcelona and found that the bronze medallists expressed noticeably more satisfaction than the silver medallists! Medvec and colleagues argued that silver medallists were constrained to make unfavourable upward comparisons with gold medallists, whereas bronze medallists could make self-enhancing downward comparisons with the rest of the field, who received no medal at all.

Downward comparisons also occur between groups. Groups try to compare themselves with inferior groups in order to feel that 'we' are better than 'them'. Indeed, intergroup relations are largely a struggle for evaluative superiority of one's own group over relevant outgroups (see Hogg, 2000c; Turner, 1975). This in turn influences self-conception as a group member – social identity (Tajfel & Turner, 1979). According to **self-categorisation theory** (Turner et al., 1987), an extension of social identity theory, the underlying process is one in which people who feel they belong to a group categorise themselves as group members and automatically internalise as a self-evaluation the attributes that describe the group – if the group is positive, the attributes are positive, and thus the self is positive (see also Chapter 11).

**Self-categorisation theory**

Turner and associates' theory of how the process of categorising oneself as a group member produces social identity and group and intergroup behaviours.

**BIRGing**

Basking in Reflected Glory – that is, name-dropping to link yourself with desirable people or groups and thus improve other people's impression of you.

Sport provides an ideal context in which the outcome of this process can be seen. Few Italians will not have felt enormously positive when their team beat Germany in the finals of the 2006 World Cup. Cialdini and his associates have referred to this phenomenon as 'basking in reflected glory', or **BIRGing** (Cialdini et al., 1976). To illustrate the effect, they conducted experiments in which they raised or lowered self-esteem via feedback on a general knowledge test; and student participants were then, seemingly incidentally, asked about the outcome of a recent football game. Cialdini and associates found that participants who had had their self-esteem lowered tended to associate themselves with winning and not with losing teams – they tended to refer to the teams as 'we' in the former case and as 'they' in the latter.

## Selves and identities

Most researchers now believe that it is probably inaccurate to characterise the self as a single undifferentiated entity. It is more accurate to think of the self-concept as containing a repertoire of relatively discrete and often quite varied identities, each with its own circumscribed body of self-knowledge (e.g. Gergen, 1971). These identities probably have their origins in the vast array of different social relationships that form, or have formed, the anchoring points for our lives, ranging from close personal relationships with friends and family, through relationships and roles defined by work groups and professions, to relationships defined by ethnicity, race and nationality.

Research suggests that people differ in self-complexity (Linville, 1985; see above), with some people having a much more diverse and extensive set of selves than do others – people with many independent aspects of self have higher self-complexity than people with only a few, relatively similar, aspects of self. The notion of self-complexity is given a slightly different emphasis by Brewer and colleagues (Brewer & Pierce, 2005; Roccas & Brewer, 2002) who focus on self defined in group terms, social identity, and the relationship among identities rather than the number of identities people have. They argue that people have a complex social identity if they have discrete social identities that do not share many attributes; and a simple social identity if they have overlapping social identities that share many attributes.

## Types of self and identity

Social identity theorists (Tajfel & Turner, 1979; see below) have argued that there are two broad classes of identity that define different types of self:

1 **social identity,** which defines self in terms of group memberships;

2 **personal identity,** which defines self in terms of idiosyncratic traits and close personal relationships.

Now check the first focus question.

Brewer and Gardner (1996) have argued that there are three types of self: (1) the *individual self,* defined by personal traits that differentiate the self from all others; (2) the *relational self,* defined by dyadic relationships that assimilate the self to significant other persons; and (3) the *collective self,* defined by group membership that differentiates 'us' from 'them'.

More recently it has been proposed that there are four types of identity (Brewer, 2001; also Chen, Boucher & Tapias, 2006): (1) *person-based social identities* emphasise the way that group properties are internalised by individual group members as part of their self-concept; (2) *relational social identities* define the self in relation to specific other people with whom one interacts in a group context – this corresponds to Brewer and Gardner's (1996) relational identity and to Markus and Kitayama's (1991) 'interdependent self'; (3) *group-based social identities* are equivalent to social identity as defined above; and (4) *collective identities* refer to a process whereby group members not only share self-defining attributes but also engage in social action to forge an image of what the group stands for and how it is represented and viewed by others.

The relational self is interesting. Although in one sense it is an interpersonal form of self, it can also be considered a particular type of collective self – some groups and some cultures, notably collectivist cultures, define groups in terms of networks of relationships or place greater importance on relationships as a defining feature of group membership (Yuki, 2003). Not surprisingly, there is evidence that women, who tend to be more collectivist than men, place greater importance on the relational self in their group memberships (Baumeister & Sommer, 1997; Cross & Madson, 1997; Seeley, Gardner, Pennington & Gabriel, 2003).

Table 4.1 shows one way in which different types of self and self-attributes could be classified according to level of identity (social versus personal) and type of attributes (identity defining versus relationship defining).

**Social identity**
That part of the self-concept that derives from our membership of social groups.

**Personal identity**
The self defined in terms of unique personal attributes or unique interpersonal relationships.

**Table 4.1**    Self and self-attributes as a function of social versus personal level of identity, and identity versus relationship types of attribute

|  | Identity attributes | Relationship attributes |
|---|---|---|
| Social identity | *Collective self*<br>Set of attributes shared with others and contrasted with a specific outgroup or with outgroups in general. | *Collective relational self*<br>Set of attributes specifying the relationship between self as an ingroup member and specific others as ingroup or outgroup members. |
| Personal identity | *Individual self*<br>Set of attributes unique to self and contrasted with specific other individuals or with other individuals in general. | *Individual relational self*<br>Set of attributes specifying the relationship between self as a unique individual and others as individuals. |

## Contextual sensitivity of self and identity

Evidence for the existence of multiple selves comes from research where contextual features are varied to discover that people describe themselves differently, and may even behave differently, in different contexts. For example, Fazio, Effrein and Falender (1981) were able to get participants to describe themselves in very different ways by asking them loaded questions that made them search through their stock of self-knowledge for information that presented the self in a different light.

Other researchers have found, time and time again, that experimental procedures that focus on group membership produce very different behaviour from procedures that focus on individuality and interpersonal relationships. For example, minimal group studies, in which participants are identified as individuals or explicitly categorised, randomly or by some trivial criterion as group members, find that categorisation leads people to discriminate against an outgroup, conform to ingroup norms, express attitudes and feelings that favour the ingroup, and evince a sense of belonging and loyalty to the ingroup (e.g. Tajfel, 1970; see Diehl, 1990, and Chapter 11).

The idea that we may have many selves, and that contextual factors can bring different selves into play, has a number of ramifications. Social constructionists have suggested that the self is entirely situation-dependent. An extreme form of this position argues that we do not carry self-knowledge around in our heads as cognitive representations at all, but rather that we construct disposable selves through talk (e.g. Potter & Wetherell, 1987; see the discussion of discourse analysis in Chapter 15). A less extreme version has been proposed by Oakes (e.g. Oakes, Haslam & Reynolds, 1999), who does not emphasise the role of talk but still maintains that self-conception is highly context-dependent. A middle way is to argue that people do have cognitive representations of the self that they carry in their heads as organising principles for perception, categorisation and action, but that these representations are temporarily or more enduringly modified by situational factors (e.g. Abrams & Hogg, 2001; Turner, Reynolds, Haslam & Veenstra, 2006).

## In search of self-conceptual coherence

The fact that we may have many selves needs to be placed in perspective. Although we may have a diversity of relatively discrete selves, there needs to be a degree of self-conceptual integration and coherence to provide a continuing theme for our lives – an 'autobiography' that weaves our various identities and selves together into a whole person. People who have highly fragmented selves (e.g. some people with schizophrenia, amnesia or Alzheimer's disease) find it extraordinarily difficult to function effectively.

People use many strategies to construct a coherent sense of self (Baumeister, 1998). One strategy is to restrict your life to a limited set of contexts, in which case, since selves are cued by context, you will protect yourself from self-conceptual clashes. Another strategy is to keep revising your integrative autobiography to accommodate new identities – like the societal practice of rewriting history to demonise or revere past leaders (Greenwald, 1980). A third strategy is to attribute changes in the self to changing circumstances rather than to fundamental changes in who we are. This reflects the actor–observer attribution effect, in which people are more inclined to attribute their own behaviour externally to situations and others' behaviour internally to their personality (Jones & Nisbett, 1972; see also Chapter 3).

Finally, people can develop a self-schema (Markus, 1977; see above) that embodies a core set of attributes that they feel distinguishes them from all other people. People then tend to recognise these attributes disproportionately in all their other selves, and this provides a linkage that delivers a sense of a stable and unitary self (Cantor & Kihlstrom, 1987).

# Social identity theory

Over the past thirty-five years, **social identity theory** has grown to be a major influence on how social psychologists conceptualise the relationship between social categories and the self-concept (see Abrams & Hogg, in press; Hogg, 2006; Hogg & Abrams, 1988, 2003). Because this theory addresses a wide range of social psychological phenomena, aspects of social identity theory surface in almost every chapter of this book; however, it is discussed fully in Chapter 11.

Social identity theory has its origins in the work of Henri Tajfel on social categorisation, intergroup relations, social comparison, and prejudice and stereotyping (e.g. Tajfel, 1969, 1974; Tajfel & Turner, 1979) – often called the *social identity theory of intergroup relations* – and in later theorising by John Turner and his associates on the role of self-categorisation in generating group behaviour associated with collective self-conception (Turner, Hogg, Oakes, Reicher, & Wetherell, 1987) – called the *social identity theory of the group*, or self-categorisation theory.

**Social identity theory**
Theory of group membership and intergroup relations based on self-categorisation, social comparison and the construction of a shared self-definition in terms of ingroup-defining properties.

## Social identity and personal identity

As mentioned above, social identity theorists have suggested that there are two broad classes of identity that define different types of self: (1) *social identity*, which defines the self in terms of group memberships, and (2) *personal identity*, which defines the self in terms of idiosyncratic personal relationships and traits. Social identity is associated with group and intergroup behaviours such as ethnocentrism, ingroup bias, group solidarity, intergroup discrimination, conformity, normative behaviour, stereotyping and prejudice. Personal identity is associated with positive and negative close interpersonal relationships and with idiosyncratic personal behaviour. We have as many social identities as there are groups that we feel we belong to, and as many personal identities as there are interpersonal relationships we are involved in and clusters of idiosyncratic attributes that we believe we possess. Social identity can be a very important aspect of our self-concept. For example, Citrin, Wong and Duff (2001) describe a study in which 46 per cent of Americans reported that they felt being an American, a social identity, was the most important thing in their life.

## Processes of social identity salience

In any given situation, our sense of self and associated perceptions, feelings, attitudes and behaviour rests on whether social or personal identity, and which specific social or personal identity, is the psychologically salient basis of self-conception. The principle that governs social identity salience hinges on the process of social categorisation and on people's motivation to make sense of and reduce uncertainty about themselves and others, and to feel relatively positive about themselves (e.g. Hogg, 2001a; Oakes, 1987; see Figure 4.4).

People use limited perceptual cues (what someone looks like, how they speak, what attitudes they express, how they behave) to categorise other people. Generally, we first 'try out' categorisations that are readily accessible to us because we often use them, they are important to us, or perhaps they are glaringly obvious in the situation. The categorisation brings into play all the additional schematic information we have about the category. This information is cognitively stored as a **prototype,** which describes and prescribes the attributes of the category in the form of a fuzzy set of more or less related attributes, rather than a precise checklist of attributes.

Category prototypes not only accentuate similarities within groups but also accentuate differences between groups – they obey what is called the **metacontrast principle**. As such, group prototypes usually do not identify average or typical members or attributes, but ideal

**Prototype**
Cognitive representation of the typical/ideal defining features of a category.

**Metacontrast principle**
The prototype of a group is that position within the group that has the largest ratio of 'differences to ingroup positions' to 'differences to outgroup positions'.

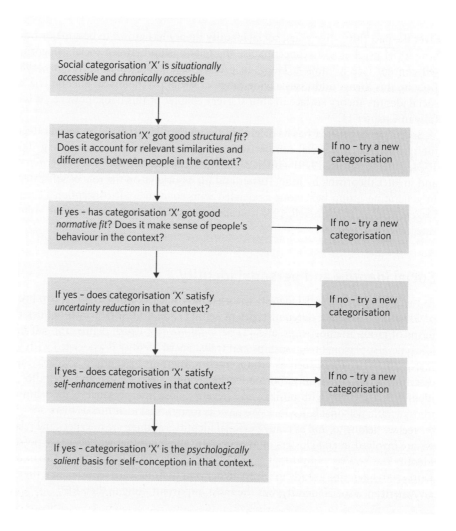

**Figure 4.4** A social identity model of the sequence through which a particular self-conception becomes psychologically salient in a specific context

**Social identity salience**

The wearing of the kilt is a mark of nationalism, commitment to the cause, and a resolve to act in unison in times of stress

members or attributes. If the categorisation fits, in the sense that it accounts for similarities and differences between people satisfactorily (called *structural fit*), and it makes good sense of why people are behaving in particular ways (called *normative fit*), then the categorisation becomes psychologically salient.

## Some consequences of social identity salience

When a categorisation becomes psychologically salient, people's perception of themselves and others becomes *depersonalised*. What this means is that people no longer consider themselves or others as unique multidimensional persons but as simple embodiments of the category prototype – they are viewed through the relatively narrow lens of a group membership that is defined by the specific ingroup or outgroup prototype.

In addition to the transformation of self-conception into social identity, people also think, feel, believe and behave in terms of the relevant prototype. The process produces the range of general behaviour we characteristically associate with people in groups and with the way groups treat each other, a theme that recurs throughout this book.

The actual nature of the behaviour (what people think and do) depends on the specific content of the relevant prototype, and on people's beliefs about the status of their group in society and about the nature of the relations between groups (Tajfel & Turner, 1979; see Ellemers, 1993; Hogg & Abrams, 1988). Group status is important because groups define social identity and social identity defines our self-concept; thus the evaluative implications of a specific group (the status, prestige and regard in which it is held) reflect the esteem in which others hold us, and influence the esteem in which we hold ourselves, our self-esteem (Crocker & Major, 1994; see the discussion of social stigma in Chapter 10).

Thus people strive for membership in prestigious groups, or strive to protect or enhance the prestige and esteem of their existing group. How they go about this is influenced by their understanding of the nature of the status relations between their group and a specific outgroup – is it permeable, is it stable, is it legitimate? If the group's evaluation in society is generally unfavourable and you feel you can pass into a more prestigious group, you might try to leave the group entirely; however, this can often be very difficult, because in reality the psychological boundaries between groups can be impermeable or impassable. For example, various immigrant groups in Germany may find it difficult to 'pass' as German because they simply do not look German or they are readily 'given away' by subtle clues in their accent. If 'passing' is not possible, people can try to make sure that the attributes that do define their group are positive ones, or they can focus attention on less prestigious groups, in comparison with which they will look rather good.

Groups can sometimes recognise that the entire basis on which their group is considered low status is illegitimate, unfair and unstable. If this recognition is tied to feasible strategies for change, then groups will compete directly with one another to gain the upper hand in the status stakes – a competition that can range from rhetoric and democratic process to terrorism and war.

# Self-motives

Because selves and identities are such critical reference points for adaptive life, people are enthusiastically motivated to secure self-knowledge. Entire industries are based on this search for knowledge, ranging from relatively scientific personality tests to scientifically more dubious practices such as astrology and palmistry. However, people do not go about this search in a dispassionate manner; they have preferences about the sort of information they want, and they can be dismayed when the quest unearths information that they did not expect or did not want to find.

Social psychologists have identified three classes of motive that may interact to influence self-construction and the search for self-knowledge: self-assessment in pursuit of validity, self-verification in pursuit of consistency, and self-enhancement in pursuit of favourability.

## Self-assessment and self-verification

The first motive is a simple desire to have accurate and valid information about oneself – there is a **self-assessment** motive (e.g. Trope, 1986). People strive to find out the truth about themselves, regardless of how unfavourable or disappointing the truth may be. But people also like to engage in a quest for confirmation – to confirm what they already know about themselves they seek out self-consistent information through a **self-verification** process (e.g. Swann, 1987). So, for example, people who have a negative self-image will actually seek out negative information to confirm the worst.

## Self-enhancement

Above all else, people like to learn things about themselves that cast the self in a favourable light. People seek new favourable knowledge about themselves as well as ways to revise pre-existing but unfavourable views of themselves. People are guided by a **self-enhancement** motive (e.g. Kunda, 1990). One manifestation of this motive is described by **self-affirmation theory** (Sherman & Cohen, 2006; Steele, 1988). People strive publicly to affirm positive aspects of who they are; this can be done blatantly by boasting or more subtly through rationalisation or dropping hints. The urge to self-affirm is particularly strong when an aspect of one's self-esteem has been damaged. So, for example, if someone draws attention to the fact that you are a lousy artist, you might retort that while that might be true, you are an excellent dancer. Self-affirmation rests on people's need to maintain a global image of themselves as being competent, good, coherent, unitary, stable, capable of free choice, capable of controlling important outcomes, and so on.

Steele (1975) reports a study in which Mormon women in Salt Lake City who were at home during the day were telephoned by a female researcher posing as a community

**Self-assessment**
The motivation to seek out new information about ourselves in order to find out what sort of person we really are.

**Self-verification**
Seeking out information that verifies and confirms what we already know about ourselves.

**Self-enhancement**
The motivation to develop and promote a favourable image of self.

**Self-affirmation theory**
The theory that people reduce the impact of threat to their self-concept by focusing on and affirming their competence in some other area.

**Self-affirmation theory**
Publicly affirming a positive aspect of oneself sometimes conceals other aspects that are less positive. Perhaps this young man's biceps are more impressive than his grades!
*Source:* Pearson Online Database (POD)

member. She asked them if they would be willing to list everything in their kitchen to assist the development of a community food cooperative; those who agreed would be called back the following week. Because community cooperation is a very strong ethic among Mormons, about 50 per cent of women agreed to this large request.

In addition to this baseline condition, there were three other conditions in the study, which involved a previous call, two days earlier, by an entirely unrelated researcher posing as a pollster. In the course of the call, the pollster mentioned in passing that it was common knowledge that as members of their community, they were (1) uncooperative with community projects (a direct threat to a core component of their self-concept), or (2) unconcerned about driver safety and care (a threat to a relatively irrelevant component of their self-concept), or (3) cooperative with community projects (positive reinforcement of their self-concept). Consistent with self-affirmation theory, *both* threats greatly increased the probability that women would subsequently agree to help the food cooperative – about 95 per cent of women agreed to help. Among women who had been given positive reinforcement of their self-concept, 65 per cent agreed to help the cooperative.

Which of these motives (self-assessment, self-verification, self-enhancement) is more fundamental and more likely to prevail in the pursuit of self-knowledge? Sedikides (1993) conducted a series of six experiments that pitted the three motives against one another. He used a self-reflection task where participants can ask themselves more or less diagnostic questions about different aspects of self – the asking of more diagnostic questions indicates greater self-reflection. Self-reflection differs depending on what self-motive is operating:

- *Self-assessment* – greater self-reflection on peripheral than core aspects of self, irrespective of whether the aspect is desirable or undesirable, indicates a drive to find out more about self (people already have knowledge about their more central attributes).

## Research highlight 4.1
### Strategies and techniques that people use to enhance or protect the positivity of their self-concepts

You may have noticed how people (perhaps you!) are sometimes inclined to boost themselves in the following ways:

- They take credit for their successes but deny blame for their failures (e.g. Zuckerman, 1979) – in the terminology of attribution theory, this is called the self-serving attribution bias (see Chapter 3).
- They forget failure feedback more readily than success or praise (e.g. Mischel, Ebbesen & Zeiss, 1976).
- They accept praise uncritically but receive criticism sceptically (e.g. Kunda, 1990).
- They try to dismiss interpersonal criticism as being motivated by prejudice (e.g. Crocker & Major, 1989).
- They perform a biased search of self-knowledge to support a favourable self-image (e.g. Kunda & Sanitoso, 1989).
- They place a favourable spin on the meaning of ambiguous traits that define self (e.g. Dunning, Meyerowitz & Holzberg, 1989).
- They persuade themselves that their flaws are widely shared human attributes but that their qualities are rare and distinctive (e.g. Campbell, 1986).

- *Self-verification* – greater self-reflection on core than on peripheral aspects of self, irrespective of attribute valence, indicates a drive to confirm what one already knows about oneself.
- *Self-enhancement* – greater self-reflection on positive than on negative aspects of self, irrespective of attribute centrality, indicates a drive to learn positive things about self.

From the six experiments, Sedikides found that self-enhancement was strongest, with consistency (self-verification) a distant second and validity an even more distant third. The desire to think well of ourselves reigns supreme; it dominates both the pursuit of accurate self-knowledge and the pursuit of information that confirms self-knowledge. (Does this apply to you? See the second focus question.)

Because self-enhancement is so important, people have developed a formidable repertoire of strategies and techniques to pursue it. People engage in elaborate self-deceptions to enhance or protect the positivity of their self-concepts (Baumeister, 1998). See Box 4.1 for examples of esteem-enhancing and esteem-protecting behaviours; and Box 4.2 and Figure 4.5 for an applied example of self-enhancement among young drivers.

## Self-esteem

Why are people so strongly motivated to think well of themselves – to self-enhance? That people do like to think well of themselves has enormous empirical support. Research suggests that people generally have a rosy sense of self – they see, or try to see, themselves through 'rose-tinted spectacles'. For example, people who are threatened or distracted have been shown to display what Paulhus and Levitt (1987) have called *automatic egotism* – a wildly favourable self-image. Taylor and Brown (1988) conclude, from a review of research, that people normally overestimate their good points, overestimate their control over events and are unrealistically optimistic.

Sedikides and Gregg (2007) call these the self-enhancing triad. For example, Kruger and Dunning (1999) found, in an American setting, that very low achievers (in the bottom 12

## Research and applications 4.2
### Self-enhancement in young drivers

How able and cautious young drivers think they are predicts their level of crash-risk optimism, along with one other measure — perceived luck in avoiding crashes!

Can people accurately judge how good they are as drivers? Harré and her colleagues addressed this question in a study of self-enhancement bias and crash optimism in young drivers. More than three hundred male and female technical institute students (aged 16–29 years) compared their driving attributes to their peers on a series of ten items.

Each item was responded to on a seven-point scale that ranged from 1 *much less* to 7 *much more* with the mid-point 4 labelled *about the same*. Factor analysis showed that the ten items reflected two underlying dimensions, perceived driving ability (e.g. 'Do you think you are more or less *skilled* as a driver than other people your age?') and perceived driving caution (e.g. 'Do you think you are more or less *safe* as a driver than other people your age?')

A self-enhancement bias was found on both scales and all items. The results for the *skilled* and *safe* items are shown in Figure 4.5. Most rated themselves as above average or well above average, both on skill and safety. Although there was no age difference, the genders did differ: in comparison to their peers, men gave themselves slightly higher skill ratings while women gave themselves slightly higher safety ratings.

Crash-risk optimism was also measured. These young drivers estimated the likelihood of being involved in a crash, again relative to their peers. Perceived ability and perceived caution were significant predictors of crash-risk optimism, in combination with another measure – believing that luck would help them avoid crashes!

Harré and her colleagues noted that their study was not designed to identify which young drivers are biased, since to do so would require measuring a person's actual skill and actual safety when driving. Nevertheless, these drivers had an overly optimistic view of themselves. Other research suggests that optimistic drivers may, for example, ignore safety messages because they do not believe they are relevant (Walton & McKeown, 1991). This is a concern, given that safe-driving campaigns are a major strategy for reducing the road toll.

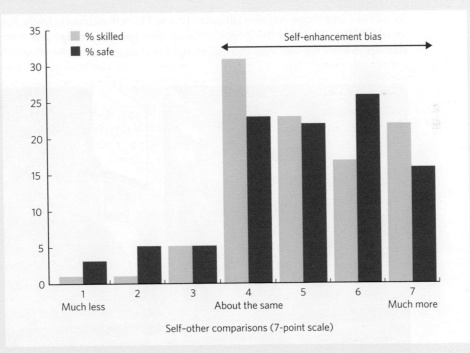

**Figure 4.5** Self-enhancement bias: rating one's driving as above average
- Young drivers compared attributes of their individual driving behaviour (skilled, safe) with their peers
- Most showed a self-enhancement bias, using above-average ratings of 5, 6 or 7

*Source:* based on data from Harré, Foster & O'Neill (2005)

per cent of grades) considered themselves to be relatively high achievers (in the top 38 per cent of grades). You might also be interested to learn that your lecturers may be equally prone to positivity bias. Cross (1977) found that 94 per cent of lecturers regarded their teaching ability to be above average.

People who fail to exhibit these biases tend towards depression and some other forms of mental illness (e.g. Tennen & Affleck, 1993). Thus a self-conceptual positivity bias, based on positive illusions, is psychologically adaptive. Box 4.3 describes some health aspects of self-esteem and self-conception.

However, a breathlessly inflated sense of how wonderful one is is not only nauseatingly gushy but also maladaptive, as it does not match reality. Having an accurate sense of self is also important (Colvin & Block, 1994), but, as we have seen, less important than feeling good about oneself. Generally, it seems that the self-conceptual positivity bias is small enough not to be a serious threat to self-conceptual accuracy (Baumeister, 1989), and that people suspend their self-illusions when important decisions need to be made (Gollwitzer & Kinney, 1989). Nevertheless, a positive self-image and associated self-esteem is a significant goal for most people most of the time.

**Self-esteem**
Feelings about and evaluations of oneself.

The pursuit of **self-esteem** can be found in different cultures. For example, although Japanese society stresses communality and interconnectedness and engages in self-criticism, researchers argue that this is simply a different way of satisfying self-esteem – in Western countries self-esteem is more directly addressed by overt self-enhancement (Kitayama, Markus, Matsumoto & Norasakkunkit, 1997). According to Leary, Tambor, Terdal and Downs (1995), self-esteem is a reflection of successful social connectedness, as we see below.

## Self-esteem and social identity

As we have seen above (see also Chapters 10 and 11), self-esteem is closely associated with social identity – by identifying with a group, that group's prestige and status in society attaches to one's self-concept. Thus, all things being equal, being identified as belonging to

**Self-esteem**
Living one's dream as an avatar can prop up a seemingly wonderful, but actually maladaptive, sense of self

## Research and applications 4.3
### Threats to your self-concept can damage your health: Ways of coping

There are three major sources of threat to our self-concept and all can affect our sense of self-worth:

1  *Failures* – these can range from failing a test, through failing a job interview, to a marriage ending in divorce.

2  *Inconsistencies* – these can be unusual and unexpected positive or negative events that make us question the sort of person we are.

3  *Stressors* – these are sudden or enduring events that seem to exceed our capacity to cope; they can include bereavement, a sick child and over-commitment to work.

Self-conceptual threats not only arouse negative emotions that can lead to self-harm and suicide, they also contribute to physical illness (Salovey, Rothman & Rodin, 1998) – they affect our immune responses, nervous system activity and blood pressure. For example, Strauman, Lemieux and Coe (1993) found that when people were reminded of significant self-discrepancies, the level of natural killer cell activity in their bloodstream decreased. These cells are important in defending the body against cancers and viral infections.

There are several ways in which people try to cope with self-conceptual threats.

- *Escape* – people may remove themselves physically from the threat situation. Duval and Wicklund (1972) found that people who had done poorly on an intelligence and creativity task and were then asked to wait in another room that was equipped with a mirror and video camera (to heighten self-awareness) fled the scene much more quickly than participants who had done well on the task.

- *Denial* – people may take alcohol or other drugs, or engage in risky 'just for kicks' behaviour. This is not a particularly constructive coping mechanism, since it can create additional health problems.

- *Downplay the threat* – this is a more constructive strategy, either by re-evaluating the aspect of self that has been threatened or by reaffirming other positive aspects of the self (Steele, 1988). For example, Taylor (1983) found that breast cancer patients who were facing the possibility of death often expressed and reaffirmed what they felt were their most basic self-aspects – some quit dead-end jobs, others turned to writing and painting, and others reaffirmed important relationships.

- *Self-expression* – this is a very effective response to threat. Writing or talking about one's emotional and physical reactions to self-conceptual threats can be an extraordinarily useful coping mechanism. It reduces emotional heat, reduces headaches, muscle tension and pounding heart, and improves immune system functioning (Pennebaker, 1997). Most benefits come from communication that enhances understanding and self-insight.

- *Attack the threat* – people can directly confront threat by discrediting its basis ('This is an invalid test of my ability'), by denying personal responsibility for the threat ('The dog ate my essay'), by setting up excuses for failure before the event (on the way into an exam, announcing that you have a terrible hangover – **self-handicapping** [Berglas, 1987; see Chapter 3]) or by taking control of the problem directly, such as seeking professional help or addressing any valid causes of threat.

---

the group of obese people is less likely to generate positive self-esteem than being identified as belonging to the group of Olympic athletes (Crandall, 1994). However, there is a general caveat – members of stigmatised social groups can generally be extremely creative in avoiding the self-esteem consequences of stigmatised group membership (Crocker & Major, 1989; Crocker, Major & Steele, 1998; see also Chapter 10).

In practice, and according to social comparison theory (see above and also Chapter 11), there can be several outcomes when self-esteem interfaces with social identity. These depend on the perceived relative status of the outgroups with which our various ingroups are usually compared.

Take the example of Jesse Owens: he was the star athlete at the 1936 Berlin Olympics, the winner of four gold medals. As a member of the United States team he was triumphant in demonstrating the athletic superiority of the United States over Germany against the

**Self-handicapping**
Publicly making advance external attributions for our anticipated failure or poor performance in a forthcoming event.

backdrop of Hitler's White supremacist notion of the Master Race. Ironically, Jesse Owens was less happy on his return home, where he was just another member of an underprivileged Black minority.

Ethnic and racial identity are significant sources of self-esteem mediated by social identity. For example, studies have shown that members of ethnic minorities often report perceptions of lowered self-esteem when making inter-ethnic comparisons. However, these findings need to be treated with caution, since the conditions under which they occur are restricted in at least two ways (see Chapter 10):

**Level of analysis (or explanation)**
The types of concepts, mechanisms and language used to explain a phenomenon.

1 The **level of analysis** for self-esteem should be *intergroup* (e.g. question: 'As an African American I feel good/bad'; answer: 'very often, often, occasionally, seldom') rather than *personal* (e.g. question: 'I often feel good/bad'; answer: 'very often, often, occasionally, seldom') – see Cross (1987).

2 The status relationship between the ethnic minority and the majority must be distinctly unequal (Tajfel & Turner, 1979).

The seminal research dealing with ethnic identity was carried out in the United States in the 1930s and 1940s and was restricted to studies of African American and White American children (see Box 4.4). Later work has extended the samples to include other non-White minorities, such as Native Americans, 'Chicanos', Chinese and French Canadians (see review by Aboud, 1987), New Zealand Maoris (e.g. Vaughan, 1978a), and Australian Aborigines (Pedersen, Walker & Glass, 1999). Consistently, children from non-White minorities showed clear outgroup preference and wished they were White themselves.

Although pre-adolescent children from an ethnic minority might prefer to be members of the ethnic majority, this effect gradually declines with age (see Box 11.3 for an example). It is probable that young, disadvantaged children experience a conflict between their actual and ideal selves (discussed above). As they grow older, they are able to pursue various options to resolve this problem:

- They can avoid making self-damaging intergroup comparisons (see Chapter 11).
- They can join with other ingroup members in a quest to establish more equal status relative to the majority group (again see Chapter 11).
- They can identify or develop ingroup characteristics that provide a sense of uniqueness and positivity, such as their language and culture (see Chapter 15).

## Individual differences

We all know people who seem to hold themselves in very low regard and others who seem to have a staggeringly positive impression of themselves. Do these differences reflect enduring and deep-seated differences in self-esteem? The main thrust of research on self-esteem as a trait is concerned with establishing individual differences in self-esteem and investigating the causes and consequences of these differences.

One view that has become somewhat entrenched, particularly in the United States, is that low self-esteem is responsible for a range of personal and social problems such as crime, delinquency, drug abuse, unwanted pregnancy and underachievement in school. This view has spawned a huge industry, with accompanying mantras, to boost individual self-esteem, particularly in child-rearing and school contexts. However, critics have argued that low self-esteem may be a product of the stressful and alienating conditions of modern industrial society, and that the self-esteem 'movement' is an exercise in rearranging deck chairs on the *Titanic* that merely produces selfish and narcissistic individuals.

So, what is the truth? First, research suggests that individual self-esteem tends to vary between moderate and very high, not between low and high – most people, as we discussed

## Research classic 4.4
### Depressed self-esteem and ethnic minority status

Studies of children's ethnic identity have a long history in social psychology. Among the earliest were those carried out by two African Americans, Kenneth and Mamie Clark (1939a, 1939b, 1940). The Clarks showed young African American children pairs of Black and White dolls, probing for the children's ethnic identity and ethnic preference. Independently, Horowitz (1936, 1939) used a different method – sketches of Black and White people to test White children's awareness of differences between ethnic groups and attitudes towards Blacks. Mary Goodman (1946, 1952), who worked with the social psychologist Gordon Allport at Harvard University, studied ethnic awareness and attitudes among White and African American nursery-school children in more detail. She extended the Clarks' method by including a doll play technique to allow the children to project attitudes towards their ethnic ingroup and outgroup.

These investigations used different samples in various American states, at slightly different periods and with an extensive range of tests. Their results consistently showed that, when making ethnic comparisons:

- White children preferred White children;
- African American children preferred white children;
- African American children had lower self-esteem.

Goodman referred to the main effect as 'White over Brown'. A wider recognition of the impact of these studies led to Kenneth Clark appearing as a witness in a landmark case in the United States Supreme Court – *Brown* versus the *Topeka Board of Education* (1954) – in which he testified that Black children's self-esteem was extensively damaged over time. Flowing from this case, the legal decision to outlaw school segregation was instrumental in helping to legitimise the civil rights movement in the United States (Goodman, 1964).

Despite later claims that the 'doll studies' were methodologically flawed (Hraba, 1972; Banks, 1976), an analysis of the trends in ethnic identity studies carried out in other countries pointed to at least two stable patterns (Vaughan, 1986):

1 Ethnic minorities that are disadvantaged (educationally, economically, politically) are typified by lowered self-esteem when intergroup comparisons are made.

2 Social change in the status relationship between ethnic groups leads to a significant improvement in minority pride and individuals' feelings of self-worth.

With respect to the second pattern, Hraba and Grant (1970) documented a phenomenon in African American children called 'Black is Beautiful', following the success of the American Black Power movement in the late 1960s. (There is a detailed discussion of the processes underlying social change in Chapter 11, and a discussion of social stigma and self-esteem in Chapter 10.)

above, feel relatively positive about themselves, at least university students in the United States do (Baumeister, Tice & Hutton, 1989). However, lower self-esteem scores have been obtained from Japanese students studying in Japan or the United States (Kitayama, Markus, Matsumoto, & Norasakkunkit, 1997; see also Chapter 16).

Even if we focus on those people who have low self-esteem, there is little evidence that low self-esteem causes the social ills that it is purported to cause. For example, Baumeister, Smart and Boden (1996) searched the literature for evidence for the popular belief that low self-esteem causes violence (see also Chapter 12). They found quite the opposite. Violence was associated with high self-esteem; more specifically, violence seems to erupt when individuals with high self-esteem have their rosy self-images threatened.

However, we should not lump together everyone with high self-esteem. Consistent with common sense, some people with high self-esteem are quietly self-confident and non-hostile, whereas others are arrogant, conceited and overly assertive (Kernis, Granneman & Barclay, 1989). These latter individuals also feel 'special' and superior to others, and they actually have relatively volatile self-esteem – they are narcissistic (Rhodewalt, Madrian & Cheney, 1998). Colvin, Block and Funder (1995) found that it was this latter type of high self-esteem individual that was likely to be maladjusted in terms of interpersonal problems. Narcissistic individuals may also be more prone to aggression in response to an ego threat.

**Self-esteem**
Positive self-esteem seems to
have won out

Indeed, this does seem to be true. Bushman and Baumeister (1998) conducted laboratory experiments to test Baumeister, Smart and Boden's (1996) threatened egotism model of the relationship between self-esteem and aggression. Participants were provoked by being given a bad evaluation (or not, in a control condition) of an essay they had written, and they were then given the opportunity to be aggressive against the person who had offended them. Self-esteem did not predict aggression, but narcissism did – narcissistic individuals were more aggressive towards people who had provoked and offended them. An interesting extension to this idea has focused on group level narcissism, collective narcissism, and shown how narcissistic groups (e.g., narcissistic ethnic groups, religions or nations) that experience a status threat are more likely than non-narcissistic groups to resort to collective violence (Golec de Zavala, Cichocka, Eidelson, & Jayawickreme, in press).

Overall, research into self-esteem as an enduring trait provides quite a clear picture of what people with high and low self-esteem are like (Baumeister, 1998; see Table 4.2). There are two main underlying differences associated with trait self-esteem (Baumeister, Tice & Hutton, 1989; Campbell, 1990): (1) self-concept confusion – high self-esteem people have a more thorough, consistent and stable stock of self-knowledge than do low self-esteem people; (2) motivational orientation – high self-esteem people have a self-enhancing orientation in which they capitalise on their positive features and pursue success, whereas low self-esteem people have a self-protective orientation in which they try to remedy their

**Table 4.2**   Characteristics of people with high and low self-esteem

| High self-esteem | Low self-esteem |
| --- | --- |
| Persistent and resilient in the face of failure | Vulnerable to impact of everyday events |
| Emotionally and affectively stable | Wide swings in mood and affect |
| Less flexible and malleable | Flexible and malleable |
| Less easily persuaded and influenced | Easily persuaded and influenced |
| No conflict between wanting and obtaining success and approval | Want success and approval but are sceptical of it |
| React positively to a happy and successful life | React negatively to a happy and successful life |
| Thorough, consistent and stable self-concept | Sketchy, inconsistent and unstable self-concept |
| Self-enhancement motivational orientation | Self-protective motivational orientation |

shortcomings and avoid failures and setbacks. (Knowing this, you might want to learn a bit more about Manfred. See the third focus question.)

## In pursuit of self-esteem

Why do people pursue self-esteem? This may initially seem a silly question – the obvious answer is that having self-esteem makes you feel good. There is probably a grain of truth here, but on the other hand there are causality issues to be addressed – being in a good mood, however caused, may provide a rosy glow that distorts the esteem in which people hold themselves. So, rather than self-esteem producing happiness, feeling happy may inflate self-esteem.

One intriguing, and somewhat gloomy, reason given for why people pursue self-esteem is that they do so in order to overcome their fear of death. Greenberg, Pyszczynski and Solomon (1986; Greenberg, Solomon & Pyszczynski, 1997; Pyszczynski, Greenberg & Solomon, 1999, 2004; Solomon, Greenberg & Pyszczynski, 1991) developed this idea in their **terror management theory**. They argue that knowledge of the inevitability of death is the most fundamental threat that people face, and therefore it is the most powerful motivating factor in human existence. Self-esteem is part of a defence against that threat. Through high self-esteem, people can escape from the anxiety that would otherwise arise from continual contemplation of the inevitability of their death – the drive for self-esteem is grounded in terror of death. High self-esteem makes people feel good about themselves – they feel immortal, and positive and excited about life.

In support of this analysis, Greenberg and his colleagues conducted three experiments in which participants did or did not receive success and positive personality feedback (manipulation of self-esteem) and then either watched a video about death or anticipated painful electric shocks (Greenberg et al., 1992). They found that participants who had had their self-esteem raised had lower physiological arousal and reported less anxiety (see Figure 4.6).

Another reason why people pursue self-esteem is that self-esteem is a very good index, or internal monitor, of social acceptance and belonging. In this respect, self-esteem has been referred to as a 'sociometer'. Leary and his colleagues have shown that self-esteem is quite strongly correlated (at about 0.50) with reduced anxiety over social rejection and exclusion (e.g. Leary & Kowalski, 1995), and there is strong evidence that people are

**Terror management theory**
The notion that the most fundamental human motivation is to reduce the terror of the inevitability of death. Self-esteem may be centrally implicated in effective terror management.

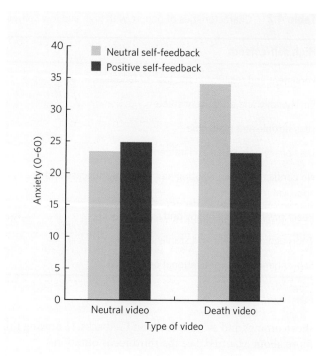

**Figure 4.6** Anxiety as a function of positive or neutral self-esteem feedback and of having viewed a death video

People felt more anxious (on a 0–60 scale) after having watched an explicit video about death if their self-esteem had not previously been elevated through positive feedback, than if their self-esteem had previously been elevated

*Source:* based on data from Greenberg et al. (1992), Experiment 1

pervasively driven by a need to form relationships and to belong (e.g. Baumeister & Leary, 1995; the consequences of social ostracism are also discussed in Chapter 8, and social isolation in Chapter 14). Leary feels that having high self-esteem does not mean that we have conquered the fear of death but rather that we have conquered the threat of loneliness and social rejection. Other critics of terror management theory suggest that high self-esteem may be a response to overcoming existential uncertainty or uncertainty about who we are and our place in the world, rather than overcoming fear associated with dying (Hogg, 2007b, in press; Van den Bos, in press).

Leary and colleagues conducted a series of five experiments to support their view (Leary, Tambor, Terdal & Downs, 1995). They found that high self-esteem participants reported greater inclusion in general and in specific real social situations. They also found that social exclusion from a group for personal reasons depressed participants' self-esteem.

## Self-presentation and impression management

**Impression management**
People's use of various strategies to get other people to view them in a positive light.

**Self-monitoring**
Carefully controlling how we present ourselves. There are situational differences and individual differences in self-monitoring.

Selves are constructed, modified and played out in interaction with other people. Since the self that we project has consequences for how others react, we try to control the self that we present. Goffman (1959) likens this process of **impression management** to theatre, where people play different roles for different audiences. There is evidence from hundreds of studies that people behave differently in public than in private (Leary, 1995). There are two general classes of motive for self-presentation: strategic and expressive. Research by Snyder (1974) into individual differences in **self-monitoring** suggests that high self-monitors adopt strategic self-presentation strategies because they typically shape their behaviour to project the impression they feel their audience or the situation demands, whereas low self-monitors adopt expressive self-presentation strategies because their behaviour is less responsive to changing contextual demands.

## Strategic self-presentation

Building on classic work by Jones (1964), Jones and Pittman (1982) identified five strategic motives:

1  *self-promotion* – an attempt to persuade others that you are competent;

2  *ingratiation* – an attempt to get others to like you;

3  *intimidation* – an attempt to get others to think you are dangerous;

4  *exemplification* – an attempt to get others to regard you as a morally respectable individual; and

5  *supplication* – an attempt to get others to take pity on you as helpless and needy.

The behaviour that represents the operation of these motives is fairly obvious (see Chapter 6 on persuasion tactics). In fact, ingratiation and self-promotion service two of the most common goals of social interaction: to get people to like you and to get people to think you are competent (Leary, 1995). Research into ingratiation tends to show that ingratiation has little effect on an observer's liking for you but a big effect on the target – flattery can be hard to resist (Gordon, 1996). (Use Box 4.5 to help advise Andrea. See the fourth focus question.)

## Expressive self-presentation

While strategic **self-presentation** focuses on manipulating others' perceptions of you, expressive self-presentation is a process in which people try to demonstrate and gain validation for their self-concept through their actions – the focus is more on self than on others (Schlenker, 1980). The expressive motive for self-presentation is a strong one. People do tend to seek out and interact or form relationships with others who are likely to validate who they are. This is because a particular identity or self-concept is worthless unless it is recognised and validated by others – it is of little use to me if I think I am a genius but no one else does. Identity requires validation for it to persist and serve a useful function.

For example, research by Emler and Reicher (1995) shows that delinquent behaviour among boys is almost always performed publicly, or in forms that can be publicly verified,

**Self-presentation**
A deliberate effort to act in ways that create a particular impression, usually favourable, of ourselves.

---

### Real world 4.5
#### Some tips on how to present yourself so that others like you

The key to getting people to like you through strategic self-presentation is to be relatively subtle so that it does not look too obviously like ingratiation. According to Jones (1990), there are four principal strategies you should adopt:

1  Try to agree with people's opinions (similarity enhances attraction - see Chapter 13), but make it credible (a) by balancing agreement on important issues with disagreement on trivial issues and (b) by balancing forceful agreement with weak disagreement.

2  Be selectively modest (a) by making fun of your standing on unimportant issues and (b) by putting yourself down in areas that do not matter very much.

3  Try to avoid appearing too desperate for others' approval. Try to get others to do the strategic self-presentation for you and, if it is left up to you, use the strategy sparingly and do not use it under conditions where it would be expected.

4  Basking in reflected glory really does work. Make casual references to your connections with winners, and only make links with losers when such links cannot be turned against you.

*Source:* based on Jones (1990)

**Identity on display**
Punks will argue that they are fierce individualists who share anti-establishment views. They like to be out and about, and to have it known that they are 'not to be messed with'

because its primary function is identity validation – validation of possession of a delinquent reputation. There is little point in being a closet delinquent. Other research confirms that people prefer social situations that allow them to act in ways that are consistent with their self-concept (e.g. Snyder & Gangestad, 1982), and they prefer partners who agree with their own self-images (Swann, Hixon & de la Ronde, 1992).

Social validation of expressed behaviour also seems to be implicated in self-concept change. For example, Tice (1992) conducted a series of experiments in which she asked participants to act as if they were emotionally stable or emotionally volatile. Half the participants performed the behaviour very publicly and half very privately. They all then completed ratings of what they believed their 'true self' was like. Tice found that only publicly performed behaviour was internalised as a descriptor of the self-concept. It appears that what is important in self-concept change is that other people perceive you in a particular way – it is not enough for you to perceive the self in a particular way internally (Schlenker, Dlugolecki & Doherty, 1994).

The self-conceptual consequences of public behaviour have additional support from a programme of research by Snyder (1984; see Figure 10.10). Observers were led to believe that a target stranger they were about to meet was an extrovert. Snyder then monitored what happened. The expectation constrained the target's behaviour to be extrovert, which confirmed the expectation and strengthened the constraint and subsequently led the target to believe that he or she really was an extrovert.

## Cultural differences in self and identity

We discuss culture and cultural differences fully in Chapter 16. As far as self and identity are concerned, however, there is one pervasive finding. Western cultures such as Western Europe, North America and Australia tend to be individualistic, whereas most other cultures, such as those found in Asia, South America and Africa, are collectivist (Triandis,

**Interdependent self**
Women from traditional collectivist cultures have strong family connections, are non-confrontational, and often dress demurely in public settings

1989; also see Chiu & Hong, 2007; Heine, 2010; Oyserman, Coon & Kemmelmeier, 2002). The anthropologist Geertz puts it beautifully:

> The Western conception of the person as a bounded, unique, more or less integrated, motivational and cognitive universe, a dynamic centre of awareness, emotion, judgement, and action organized into a distinctive whole and set contrastively both against other such wholes and against a social and natural background is, however incorrigible it may seem to us, a rather peculiar idea within the context of the world's cultures. *(Geertz, 1975, p. 48)*

Markus and Kityama (1991) describe how people in individualistic cultures tend to have an independent self, whereas people in collectivist cultures have an interdependent self. Although, in both cases, people seek a coherent sense of who they are, the independent self is grounded in a view of the self as autonomous, separate from other people and revealed through one's inner thoughts and feelings. The interdependent self is grounded in one's connection to and relationships with other people. It is expressed through one's roles and relationships. 'Self . . . is defined by a person's surrounding relations, which often are derived from kinship networks and supported by cultural values such as filial piety, loyalty, dignity, and integrity' (Gao, 1996, p. 83). Table 4.3 shows the ways in which independent and interdependent selves differ. We return to this cultural difference in the self in Chapter 16.

**Table 4.3**    Differences between independent and interdependent selves

|  | Independent self | Interdependent self |
|---|---|---|
| Self-definition | Unique, autonomous individual, separate from context, represented in terms of internal traits, feelings, thoughts and abilities. | Connected with others, embedded in social context, represented in terms of roles and relationships. |
| Self-structure | Unitary and stable, constant across situations and relationships. | Fluid and variable, changing across situations and relationships. |
| Self-activities | Being unique and self-expressive, acting true to your internal beliefs and feelings, being direct and self-assertive, promoting your own goals and your difference from others. | Belonging, fitting in, acting appropriately to roles and group norms, being indirect and non-confrontational, promoting group goals and group harmony. |

*Source:* based on Markus & Kitayama (1991)

From a conceptual review of the cultural context of self-conception, Vignoles, Chryssochoou and Breakwell (2000) conclude that the need to have a distinctive and integrated sense of self is probably universal. However, self-distinctiveness means something quite different in individualist and collectivist cultures. In one it is the isolated and bounded self that gains meaning from separateness, whereas in the other it is the relational self that gains meaning from its relations with others.

Consistent with our historical analysis of conceptions of the self at the beginning of this chapter, the most plausible account of the origins of individualist and collectivist cultures, and the associated independent and interdependent self-conceptions, is probably in terms of economic activity. Western cultures have, over the past two or three hundred years, developed an economic system based on labour mobility. People are units of production that are expected to move from places of low labour demand to places of high labour demand – they are expected to organise their lives, their relationships and their self-concepts around mobility and transient relationships.

Independence, separateness and uniqueness have become more important than connectedness and the long-term maintenance of enduring relationships – these values have become enshrined as key features of Western culture. Self-conceptions reflect cultural norms that codify economic activity.

# Summary

- The modern Western idea of the self has gradually crystallised over the past two hundred years as a consequence of a number of social and ideological forces, including secularisation, industrialisation, enlightenment and psychoanalysis. As a recent science, social psychology has tended to view the self as the essence of individuality.

- In reality, there are many different forms of self and identity. The three most important are probably the collective self (defined in terms of attributes shared with ingroup members and distinct from outgroup members), the individual self (defined in terms of attributes that make one unique relative to other people) and the relational self (defined in terms of relationships that one has with specific other people).

- People experience different selves in different contexts, yet they also feel that they have a coherent self-concept that integrates or interrelates all these selves.

- People are not continuously consciously aware of themselves. Self-awareness can sometimes be very uncomfortable and at other times very uplifting – it depends on what aspect of self we are aware of and on the relative favourability of that aspect.

- Self-knowledge is stored as schemas. We have many self-schemas, and they vary in terms of how clear they are. In particular, we have schemas about our actual self, our ideal self and our 'ought' self. We often compare our actual self with our ideal and 'ought' selves – an actual–ideal self-discrepancy makes us feel dejected, whereas an actual–ought self-discrepancy makes us feel anxious. The way in which we construct and regulate our sense of self is influenced by the extent to which we are prevention- or promotion-focused.

- People construct a concept of self in a number of ways in addition to introspection. They can observe what they say and what they do, and if there are no external reasons for behaving in that way, they assume that the behaviour reflects their true self.

- People can compare themselves with others to get a sense of who they are – they ground their attitudes in comparisons with similar others but their behaviour in comparison with slightly less well-off others. The collective self is also based on downward comparisons, but with outgroup others.

- The collective self is associated with group memberships, intergroup relations and the range of specific and general behaviour that we associate with people in groups.

- Self-conception is underpinned by three major motives: self-assessment (to discover what sort of person you really are), self-verification (to confirm what sort of person you are) and self-enhancement (to discover what a wonderful person you are). People are overwhelmingly motivated by self-enhancement, with self-verification a distant second and self-assessment bringing up the rear. This is probably because self-enhancement services self-esteem, and self-esteem is a key feature of self-conception.

- Some people have generally higher self-esteem than others. High self-esteem people have a clear and stable sense of self and a self-enhancement orientation; low self-esteem people have a less clear self-concept and a self-protective orientation.

- People pursue self-esteem for many reasons – probably mainly because it is a good internal index of social integration, acceptance and belonging. It may indicate that one has successfully overcome loneliness and social rejection. To protect or enhance self-esteem, people carefully manage the impression they project – they can do this strategically (manipulating others' images of the self) or expressively (behaving in ways that project a positive image of the self).

- Individualist Western cultures emphasise the independent self, whereas other (collectivist) cultures emphasise the interdependent self (the self defined in terms of one's relations and roles relative to other people).

## Literature, film and TV

### Invisible Man

Ralph Ellison's (1947) novel about how black people in the United States are 'invisible' to white people. It shows the consequences of ostracism or denial of identity and existence.

### The Handmaid's Tale

1986 Margaret Atwood novel, made into a film in 1990 starring Natasha Richardson. In a dystopian future where most of the human race is sterile, a young woman is kept in reproductive servitude because of her fertility. This story explores the destruction of individual identity and the creation of a group self that demands conformity. In the service of the state, the protagonist's identity is submerged as she is demoted to a faceless child-bearing machine while the rest of the women, all sterile, are forced to become passive housewives.

### The Beach

1997 Alex Garland novel (also the 2000 eponymous film starring Leonardo DiCaprio). Backpackers in Thailand drop out to join a group that has set up its own normatively regimented society on a remote island. They are expected to submerge their own identity in favour of the group's identity. This is a dramatic book which engages with many social psychological themes to do with self and identity – the tension between individual and relational self and collective self/social identity. The book could be characterised as *Apocalypse Now* meets *Lord of the Flies*.

### Samuel Beckett's classic trilogy

*Molloy* (1951), *Malone Dies* (1951) and *The Unnameable* (1953) is ultimately about a person's frenzied and purgatorial quest throughout life for a sense of identity and an understanding of self – a quest for the true self among the many selves of one's life.

### Witness

1985 film by Peter Weir, with Harrison Ford. This is an exciting thriller in which Ford hides out in an Amish community to protect a young Amish boy who witnessed a brutal crime in New York. From a self and identity point of view the rugged individualist, Ford, has to fit into the ultra-collectivist Amish society in which self is deeply integrated with and subservient to the group, and expression of individuality is not valued – is even punished.

### The Departed

Starring Leonardo DiCaprio, Matt Damon and Jack Nicholson, this is a dramatic and violent 2006 film about Irish-American organised crime in Boston. But it is also a study of the strain of nourishing multiple identities and living an all-consuming double life – Billy Costigan is an undercover cop who has infiltrated the mob, and Colin Sullivan is a hardened criminal who has infiltrated the police.

### Waco: The Rules of Engagement

1997 documentary by William Gazechi. In February 1993 the US Bureau of Alcohol and Tobacco raided and lay siege for 51 days to the compound, in Waco, Texas, of the Branch Davidian sect, led by David Koresh. All 80 sect members were killed. This documentary is a chilling account of just how far a cult can go in controlling one's self and identity.

## Guided questions

1 Do you have a looking-glass self? How and why might you present yourself differently in public and in private?

2 If the way you actually are is different from the way you would like to be, or how you think you should be, how might this be revealed?

3 What are the usual ways that people try to enhance their sense of self-worth?

4 How could threats to your sense of self-worth damage your health?

5 What does it mean to say that you are objectively aware of yourself? See how this has been demonstrated in children in Chapter 3 of MyPsychLab at **www.mypsychlab.co.uk** (watch *Self awareness*).

### Learn more

Abrams, D., & Hogg, M. A. (2001). Collective identity: group membership and self-conception. In M. A. Hogg & R. S. Tindale (eds), *Blackwell handbook of social psychology: Group processes* (pp. 425–460). Oxford, UK: Blackwell. Detailed discussion and overview of the relationship between the self-concept and group membership, with an emphasis on the collective self and social identity.

Baumeister, R. F. (ed.) (1993). *Self-esteem: The puzzle of low self-regard*. New York: Plenum. An edited collection of chapters from most of the leading researchers of self-esteem, each describing and overviewing their research programme and general conclusions.

Baumeister, R. F. (ed.) (1999). *The self in social psychology*. Philadelphia, PA: Psychology Press. A detailed overview of theory and research on self and identity, organised around reprints of a set of twenty-three key and classic publications on the self. There is an integrative introductory chapter and short introductory pieces to each set of readings. This is an excellent resource for the study of self and identity.

Leary, M. R., & Tangney, J. P. (eds) (2003). *Handbook of self and identity*. New York: Guilford. A wide-ranging selection of scholarly chapters from leading scholars of self and identity.

Oyserman, D. (2007). Social identity and self-regulation. In A. W. Kruglanski & E. T. Higgins (eds), *Social psychology: Handbook of basic principles* (2nd ed., pp. 432–53). New York: Guilford. Detailed and up-to-date coverage of research on self and identity, with a particular emphasis on collective identity.

Sedikides, C., & Gregg, A. P. (2007). Portraits of the self. In M. A. Hogg & J. Cooper (eds), *The SAGE handbook of social psychology: Concise student edition* (pp. 93–122). London: SAGE. A detailed but accessible overview of research and theory on self and identity. Sedikides is one of the world's leading self researchers.

Swann, W. B. Jr., & Bosson, J. K. (2010) Self and identity. In S. T. Fiske, D. T. Gilbert, & G. Lindzey (eds), *Handbook of social psychology* (5th ed., Vol. 1, pp. 589–628). New York: Wiley. Comprehensive and up-to-date coverage of the literature on self and identity – in the most recent edition of the authoritative handbook of social psychology.

Refresh your understanding, assess your progress and go further with interactive summaries, questions, podcasts and much more at **www.mypsychlab.co.uk**

## This chapter discusses

- Historical and contemporary views of 'attitude'
- How attitudes are structured
- Functions of attitudes
- Cognitive theories of attitudes and their relationship to behaviour
- Theories of reasoned action and planned behaviour
- Cognitive and behavioural approaches to attitude formation
- Values, ideology and social representations
- Explicit and implicit measures of attitudes

## Focus questions

1.  What meanings do you give to the term *attitude*? An animal lover says that an attitude is the body posture a hunting dog assumes when indicating the presence of a prey. A sports coach says that a certain team player has an 'attitude problem', which presumably is something to do with the player's state of mind. Is the term worth keeping in our psychological dictionary if it has several quite different everyday meanings?

2.  Citizens sometimes say that paying research companies to ask people about their political attitudes is a waste of money. One poll may contradict another carried out around the same time, and poll predictions of who will be voted into power have not always been very good. Is there any use, therefore, in trying to link people's attitudes to people's behaviour?

3.  Rita polls people's attitudes and believes she knows what makes them tick. Her advice to psychologists is: if you want to find out what people's attitudes are, ask them! Is she right?

4.  Are there ways in which attitudes that are beyond awareness may be uncovered? Mahzarin Banaji outlines the nature of implicit attitudes and introduces the Implicit Association Test (IAT), a technique that has been used to reveal them, in Chapter 5 of MyPsychLab at www.mypsychlab.co.uk (watch *Attitudes and attitude change*).

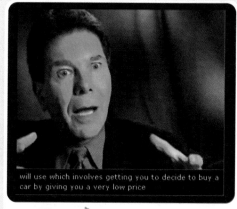

will use which involves getting you to decide to buy a car by giving you a very low price

Go to **mypsychlab** to explore video and test your understanding of key topics addressed in this chapter.

Refresh your understanding with interactive summaries, explore topics further with video and audio clips and assess your progress with quick test and essay questions by logging to the accompanying website at www.mypsychlab.co.uk

# Chapter 5
## Attitudes

## Key terms

Acquiescent response set
Attitude
Attitude formation
Automatic activation
Balance theory
Bogus pipeline technique
Cognition
Cognitive algebra
Cognitive consistency theories
Expectancy–value model
Guttman scale

Ideology
Implicit association test
Information integration theory
Information processing
Likert scale
Mere exposure effect
Meta-analysis
Modelling
Moderator variable
Multiple act criterion
One-component attitude model
Priming
Protection motivation theory
Relative homogeneity effect

Self-efficacy
Self-perception theory
Social neuroscience
Social representations
Sociocognitive model
Spreading attitude effect
Terror management theory
Theory of planned behaviour
Theory of reasoned action
Three-component attitude model
Two-component attitude model
Unidimensionality
Unobtrusive measures
Values

# Structure and function of attitudes

## Background

**Attitude**
(a) A relatively enduring organisation of beliefs, feelings and behavioural tendencies towards socially significant objects, groups, events or symbols. (b) A general feeling or evaluation – positive or negative – about some person, object or issue.

The term 'attitude' is part of our common sense language. Many years ago, the social psychologist Gordon Allport referred to **attitude** as social psychology's most indispensable concept. In the 1935 *Handbook of Social Psychology,* an influential treatise on the discipline at that time, he wrote:

> The concept of attitudes is probably the most distinctive and indispensable concept in contemporary American social psychology. No other term appears more frequently in the experimental and theoretical literature. (*Allport, 1935, p. 798*)

In the historical context in which Allport was writing, his view is not surprising. Others, such as Thomas and Znaniecki (1918) and Watson (1930), had previously equated social psychology and attitude research – actually defining social psychology as the scientific study of attitudes! The early 1930s also witnessed the first generation of questionnaire-based scales to measure attitudes. According to Allport, an attitude is:

> a mental and neural state of readiness, organised through experience, exerting a directive or dynamic influence upon the individual's response to all objects and situations with which it is related. (*Allport, 1935, p. 810*)

Allport was not to know that such a fashionable concept would become the centre of much controversy in the decades ahead. For example, a radical behavioural view would emerge to argue that an attitude is merely a figment of the imagination – people invent attitudes to explain behaviour that has already occurred.

In charting the history of attitude research in social psychology, McGuire (1986) identified three main phases separated by periods of waning interest:

1 A concentration on attitude measurement and how these measurements related to behaviour (1920s and 1930s).

2 A focus on the dynamics of change in an individual's attitudes (1950s and 1960s).

3 A focus on the cognitive and social structure and function of attitudes and attitude systems (1980s and 1990s).

The word 'attitude' is derived from the Latin *aptus,* which means 'fit and ready for action'. This ancient meaning refers to something that is directly observable, such as a boxer in a boxing ring. Today, however, attitude researchers view 'attitude' as a construct that, although not directly observable, precedes behaviour and guides our choices and decisions for action.

Attitude research in psychology and the social sciences has generated enormous interest and many hundreds, probably thousands, of studies covering almost every conceivable topic about which attitudes might be expressed. During the 1960s and 1970s attitude research entered a period of pessimism and decline. To some extent, this was a reaction to concern about the apparent lack of relationship between expressed attitudes and overt behaviour.

However, during the 1980s attitudes again became a centre of attention for social psychologists, stimulated by modern cognitive psychology (see reviews by Olson & Zanna, 1993; Tesser & Shaffer, 1990). This resurgence included a focus on applications from research on how information is processed and how memory works, and the effects of these, and of affect and feelings, on attitude formation and change (Haddock & Zanna, 1999; Lieberman, 2000; Murphy, Monahan & Zajonc, 1995). There has also been extensive research on attitude strength and accessibility, on how attitudes relate to behaviour (Ajzen, 2001), and on implicit measures of attitude (Crano & Prislin, 2006; Fazio & Olson, 2003b).

In Chapters 5 and 6, we take the view that attitudes are basic to and pervasive in human life. In doing this, we will not take McGuire's evolutionary sequence too literally, as the three foci he refers to have always been, and continue to be, of interest to social psychologists. Without having attitudes, people would have difficulty in construing and reacting to events, in trying to make decisions and in making sense of their relationships with other people in everyday life. Attitudes continue to fascinate researchers and remain a key, if sometimes controversial, part of social psychology.

## How many components?

One of the most fundamental questions that can be asked about attitudes is whether they are a unitary construct or whether they have a number of different components.

### One component

Thurstone preferred a **one-component attitude model**, defining an attitude as 'the affect for or against a psychological object' (1931, p. 261). An influential later text focusing on how one constructs scales to measure attitudes reiterated this view: an attitude is 'the degree of positive or negative affect associated with some psychological object' (Edwards, 1957, p. 2). How simple can you get – do you like the object or not? With hindsight, it can be argued that the dominant feature of affect became the basis of a more sophisticated sociocognitive model proposed by Pratkanis and Greenwald (1989) (see below).

**One-component attitude model**
An attitude consists of affect towards or evaluation of the object.

### Two components

Another approach, with its origins in Allport's (1935) theory, favoured a **two-component attitude model**. To Thurstone's affect, being for or against a psychological object, Allport added a second component – a state of mental readiness. It is an implicit predisposition that has a generalising and consistent influence on how we decide what is good or bad, desirable or undesirable, and so on. An attitude is therefore a private event that is unobservable externally and whose existence we can only infer. We might do this by examining our own mental processes introspectively. As we see later, we might also make inferences by examining the ways in which we behave, speak or act. You cannot see, touch or physically examine an attitude; it is a hypothetical construct.

**Two-component attitude model**
An attitude consists of a mental readiness to act. It also guides evaluative (judgemental) responses.

**Three-component attitude model**
An attitude consists of cognitive, affective and behavioural components. This threefold division has an ancient heritage, stressing thought, feeling and action as basic to human experience.

### Three components

A third view is the **three-component attitude model**, which is an approach to the definition of attitude that has its root in ancient philosophy:

> The trichotomy of human experience into thought, feeling, and action, although not logically compelling, is so pervasive in Indo-European thought (being found in Hellenic,

> Zoroastrian and Hindu philosophy) as to suggest that it corresponds to something basic in our way of conceptualisation, perhaps . . . reflecting the three evolutionary layers of the brain, cerebral cortex, limbic system, and old brain. (*McGuire, 1989, p. 40*)

The three-component model of attitude was particularly popular in the 1960s (e.g., Krech, Crutchfield & Ballachey, 1962; Rosenberg & Hovland, 1960). It was also represented in the later work of Himmelfarb and Eagly (1974), who described an attitude as a relatively enduring organisation of beliefs, feelings and behavioural tendencies towards socially significant objects, groups, events or symbols. Note that this definition not only included the three components but also emphasised that:

- Attitudes are relatively permanent: that is, they persist across time and situations. A momentary feeling is not an attitude.
- Attitudes are limited to socially significant events or objects.
- Attitudes are generalisable and involve at least some degree of abstraction. If you drop a book on your toe and find that it hurts, this is not sufficient basis for forming an attitude, because it is a single event in one place and at one time. But if the experience makes you dislike books or libraries, or clumsiness in general, then that dislike is an attitude.

Each attitude, then, is made up of a cluster of feelings, likes and dislikes, behavioural intentions, thoughts and ideas. Other theorists who have favoured the three-component model include Ostrom (1968) and Breckler (1984).

Despite the appeal of the 'trinity', this model presents a problem by prejudging a link between attitude and behaviour (Zanna & Rempel, 1988), itself a thorny issue and of sufficient complexity to be dealt with in detail in Chapter 6. Suffice to say that most modern definitions of attitude involve both belief and feeling structures and are much concerned with how, if each can indeed be measured, the resulting data may help predict people's actions. (Based on what you have read so far, try to answer the first focus question.)

## Function of attitudes

Presumably attitudes exist because they are useful – they serve a purpose, they have a function. The approaches we have considered so far make at least an implicit assumption of purpose. Some writers have been more explicit. Katz (1960), for example, proposed that there are various kinds of attitude, each serving a different function, such as:

- knowledge;
- instrumentality (means to an end or goal);
- ego defence (protecting one's self-esteem);
- value expressiveness (allowing people to display those values that uniquely identify and define them).

An attitude saves cognitive energy, as we do not have to figure out 'from scratch' how we should relate to the object or situation in question (Smith, Bruner & White, 1956), a function that parallels the utility of schemas and fits the cognitive miser or motivated tactician models of contemporary social cognition (e.g. Fiske & Taylor, 2008; see Chapter 2).

Fazio (1989) later argued that the main function of any kind of attitude is a utilitarian one: that of object appraisal. This should hold regardless of whether the attitude has a positive or negative valence (i.e. whether our feelings about the object are good or bad). Merely possessing an attitude is useful because of the orientation towards the object that it provides for the person. For example, having a negative attitude towards snakes (believing they are dangerous) is useful if we cannot differentiate between safe and deadly varieties. However, for an attitude truly to fulfil this function it must be accessible. We develop this aspect of Fazio's thinking about attitude function when we deal below with the link between attitude and behaviour.

## Cognitive consistency

In the late 1950s and 1960s **cognitive consistency theories** came to dominate social psychology, and their emphasis on **cognition** dealt a fatal blow to simplistic reinforcement explanations (e.g. by learning theorists such as Thorndike, Hull and Skinner) in social psychology (Greenwald, Banaji, Rudman, Farnham, Nosek & Mellott, 2002). The best known of these cognitive consistency theories was cognitive dissonance theory (Cooper, 2007; Festinger, 1957), which, because of its importance in explaining attitude change we deal with in detail in Chapter 6. Another early example was balance theory (see below).

As well as specifying that beliefs are the building blocks of attitude structure, this family of theories focused on inconsistencies among people's beliefs. Consistency theories differ in how they define consistency and inconsistency, but they all assume that it is aversive to have inconsistent beliefs. Two thoughts are inconsistent if one seems to contradict the other, and such a state of mind is bothersome. This disharmony is known as *dissonance*. Consistency theories argue that people are motivated to change one or more contradictory beliefs so that the belief system as a whole is in harmony. The outcome is restoration of consistency.

### Balance theory

The consistency theory with the clearest implications for attitude structure is **balance theory,** derived from Heider (1946) and extended by Cartwright and Harary (1956). Heider's ideas were grounded in *Gestalt* psychology, an approach to perception popular in Germany in the early twentieth century and applied by Heider to interpersonal relations. In *Gestalt* psychology, psychological phenomena are made up of interacting forces. The content of the mind is a person's cognitive field, a field that is both dynamic and subjective, containing the person's perceptions of people, objects and events.

Balance theory focuses on the P–O–X unit of the individual's cognitive field. Imagine a triad consisting of three elements: a person (P), another person (O), and an attitude, object or topic (X). A triad is consistent if it is balanced, and balance is assessed by counting the number and types of relationships between the elements. For instance, P liking X is a positive (+) relationship, O disliking X is negative (–), and P disliking O is negative (–).

There are eight possible combinations of relationships between two people and an attitude object, four of which are balanced and four unbalanced (Figure 5.1). A triad is balanced if there are an odd number of positive relationships and can occur in a variety of ways. If P likes O, O likes X and P likes X, then the triad is balanced. From P's point of view, balance theory acts as a divining rod in predicting interpersonal relationships: if P likes the object X, then any compatible other, O, should feel the same way. Likewise, if P already likes O, then O will be expected to evaluate object X in a fashion similar to P. By contrast, if P likes O, O likes X and P dislikes X, then the relationship is unbalanced. The principle of consistency that underlies balance theory means that in unbalanced triads people may feel tense and motivated to restore balance. Balance is generally restored in a manner requiring the least effort. So, in the last example, P could decide not to like O or to change his/her opinion about X, depending on which is the easier option.

Unbalanced structures are usually less stable and more unpleasant than balanced structures. However, in the absence of contradictory information, people assume that others will like what they like. Further, we often prefer to agree with someone else – or in balance-theory language, P and O seek structures where they agree rather than disagree about how they evaluate X (Zajonc, 1968). Again, people do not always seek to resolve inconsistency.

**Cognitive consistency theories**
A group of attitude theories stressing that people try to maintain internal consistency, order and agreement among their various cognitions.

**Cognition**
The knowledge, beliefs, thoughts and ideas that people have about themselves and their environment. May also refer to mental processes through which knowledge is acquired, including perception, memory and thinking.

**Balance theory**
According to Heider, people prefer attitudes that are consistent with each other, over those that are inconsistent. A person (P) tries to maintain consistency in attitudes to, and relationships with, other people (O) and elements of the environment (X).

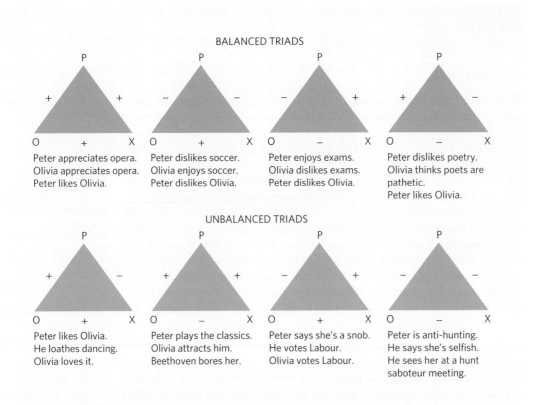

**Figure 5.1** Examples of balanced and unbalanced triads from Heider's theory of attitude change

In the balanced triads the relationships are consistent, in the unbalanced triads they are not

Sometimes they organise their beliefs so that elements are kept isolated and are resistant to change (Abelson, 1968). For example, if P likes opera and O does not, and if P and O like each other, P may decide to isolate the element of opera from the triad by listening to opera when O is not present.

Overall, research on balance theory has been extensive and mostly supportive.

## Cognition and evaluation

We noted above the existence of a one-component view of attitudes – initially one in which affect reigns supreme (Thurstone, 1931), but subsequently focusing on evaluation as the core component (e.g., Osgood, Suci & Tannenbaum, 1957). This simple idea resurfaces in a more complicated guise in Pratkanis and Greenwald's **sociocognitive model**, where an attitude is defined as 'a person's evaluation of an object of thought' (1989, p. 247). An atti-tude object (see Figure 5.2) is represented in memory by:

**Sociocognitive model**
Attitude theory highlighting an evaluative component. Knowledge of an object is represented in memory along with a summary of how to appraise it.

- an object label and the rules for applying that label;
- an evaluative summary of that object; and
- a knowledge structure supporting that evaluation.

For example, the attitude object we know as a 'shark' may be represented in memory as a really big fish with very sharp teeth (*label*); that lives in the sea and eats other fish and sometimes people (*rules*); is scary and best avoided while swimming (*evaluative summary*);

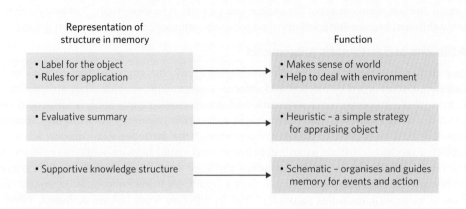

| Representation of structure in memory | Function |
|---|---|
| • Label for the object<br>• Rules for application | • Makes sense of world<br>• Help to deal with environment |
| • Evaluative summary | • Heuristic – a simple strategy for appraising object |
| • Supportive knowledge structure | • Schematic – organises and guides memory for events and action |

**Figure 5.2**  The sociocognitive model of attitude structure and function

This theory draws on research in social cognition and studies of memory. Just as physical objects or even people can be represented in memory, so too can an attitude object

*Source*: based on Pratkanis & Greenwald (1989)

and is a scientifically and fictionally well-documented threat to our physical well-being (*knowledge structure*). However, despite the cognitive emphasis, it was the evaluative component that Pratkanis and Greenwald highlighted.

The evaluative dimension of attitudes is of course a key focus of research on prejudice where the key problem is that members of one group hold evaluatively negative attitudes towards members of another group (Dovidio, Glick & Rudman, 2005; Jones, 1996; see Chapter 10). In the attitude literature, various terms have been used almost interchangeably in denoting this evaluative component, such as 'affect', 'evaluation', 'emotion' and 'feeling', suggesting an urgent need for the terminology to be tidied up and standardised. Breckler and Wiggins (1989a, 1989b), for example, distinguished between affect (an emotional reaction to an attitude object) and evaluation (particular kinds of thought, belief and judgement about the object).

## Decision making and attitudes

### Do we perform cognitive algebra?

**Information processing** approaches emphasise how complex it is to acquire knowledge and to form and change our attitudes. According to **information integration theory** (Anderson, 1971, 1981; see Chapter 2), we use **cognitive algebra** to construct our attitudes from information we receive about attitude objects. People are sophisticated problem solvers and vigilant evaluators of new information. How we receive and combine this information provides the basis for attitude structure. For example, the salience of some items and the order in which they are received become important determinants of the way in which they are processed. As new information arrives, people evaluate it and combine it with existing information stored in memory. For example, a warning from health authorities that a certain brand of food may cause serious illness may lead people to re-evaluate their attitude, change their behaviour and not eat that brand again.

In Anderson's approach, we acquire and re-evaluate attitudes by using cognitive algebra. We 'mentally' average out the values attached to discrete bits of information that are collated and stored in memory about an attitude object. Ordinary people habitually use such

**Information processing**
The evaluation of information; in relation to attitudes, the means by which people acquire knowledge and form and change attitudes.

**Information integration theory**
The idea that a person's attitude can be estimated by averaging across the positive and negative ratings of the object.

**Cognitive algebra**
Approach to the study of impression formation that focuses on how people combine attributes that have valence into an overall positive or negative impression.

mathematics: for example, if you think a friend is shy, energetic and compassionate, your overall attitude is an average of the evaluations you attach to those traits. You would calculate a different average for another friend who was outgoing, energetic and charismatic.

### Attitudes and automatic judgements

As a challenge to classical attitude theory, Devine (1989) has suggested that people's attitudes are underpinned by implicit and automatic judgements of which they are unaware. Because these judgements are automatic and unconscious, people are less influenced by *social desirability bias* (i.e. how others might judge their response). As such, they should therefore be a more reliable measure of a person's 'true' attitudes. According to Schwarz (2000), a model of attitude as an implicit construct could help us better to understand the relationship between people's attitudes and their behaviour (see below). Others are more cautious. For example, implicit measures (again, see below) may be as dependent on context as explicit measures (attitudes), but in different ways (Glaser & Banaji, 1999). Implicit measures correlate only weakly with both explicit self-reports and overt behaviour (Hilton & Karpinski, 2000), and correlations between implicit and explicit measures of intergroup attitudes are generally low (Dovidio, Kawakami & Beach, 2001). In considering recent developments in attitude theory, van der Pligt and de Vries (2000) proposed a decision-making strategy continuum, which ranges from intuition at one end to controlled information processing (e.g. Anderson, 1971) at the other.

Dispute over the best way to characterise attitudes continues and shows little sign of abating. Is an attitude a directive and organised state of readiness (Allport), an outcome of algebraic calculation (Anderson) or an automatic judgement (Devine)?

# Can attitudes predict behaviour?

Why study attitudes if scientists disagree about how best to define them? One answer is that attitudes may be useful for predicting what people will do – maybe if we change people's attitudes, we might be able to change their behaviour. Perhaps with tongue in cheek, Crano and Prislin have written in a recent review: 'Because attitudes predict behavior, they are

**Attitudes and behaviour**
This voter is under surveillance. Will her selection reflect her own view, or might it be constrained by a prevailing norm?

considered the crown jewel of social psychology' (2006, p. 360). As we shall see, a number of social scientists have questioned this assumption.

For instance, Gregson and Stacey (1981) found only a small positive correlation between attitudes and self-reported alcohol consumption. Furthermore, there was no evidence of any benefits in focusing on attitude change rather than on economic incentives to control alcohol use (e.g. avoiding fines, increasing taxes). This sort of finding has caused some critics to question the utility of the concept of attitude: if attitude measures bear no relation to what people actually do, then what is the use of the concept? It is interesting that an early study of ethnic attitudes by LaPiere (1934) revealed a glaring inconsistency between what people do and what they say (see Box 5.1; see also Chapter 10).

Following LaPiere's provocative study, which effectively called into question the predictive validity of questionnaires, researchers have used more sophisticated methods to study the attitude–behaviour relationship. Many obtained relatively low correspondence between questionnaire measures of attitudes and measures of overt behaviour. After reviewing this research, Wicker (1969) concluded that the correlation between attitudes and behaviour is seldom as high as 0.30 (which, when squared, indicates that only 9 per cent of the variability in a behaviour is accounted for by an attitude). In fact, Wicker found that the average correlation between attitudes and behaviour was only 0.15. This view was seized upon during the 1970s as telling evidence that the attitude concept is not worth a fig, since it has little predictive power. A sense of despair settled on the field (Abelson, 1972). Nevertheless, attitudes are still being researched (see Fazio & Olson, 2003a), and the topic commands two chapters of this book.

What emerged later was that attitudes and overt behaviour are not related in a one-to-one fashion. There are conditions that promote or disrupt the correspondence between having an attitude and behaving (Doll & Ajzen, 1992; Smith & Stasson, 2000). For example, attitude–behaviour consistency can vary according to whether:

- an attitude is more rather than less accessible (see below);
- an attitude is expressed publicly, say in a group, or privately, such as when responding to a questionnaire;
- an individual identifies strongly or weakly with a group for which the attitude is normative.

## Research classic 5.1
### Do attitudes really predict behaviour?

The sociologist LaPiere (1934) was interested in the difference between prejudiced attitudes towards Chinese in general and discriminatory behaviours towards a Chinese couple in particular. In the early 1930s, anti-Asian prejudice was quite strong among Americans. LaPiere embarked on a 10,000-mile sightseeing tour of the United States, accompanied by two young Chinese friends. They visited 66 hotels, caravan parks and tourist homes and were served in 184 restaurants. As they went from place to place, LaPiere was concerned that his friends might not be accepted but, as it turned out, they were refused service only once.

Six months after their trip, LaPiere sent a questionnaire to all the places they had visited, asking, 'Will you accept members of the Chinese race as guests in your establishment?' Of the 81 restaurants and 47 hotels that replied, 92 per cent said that they would *not* accept Chinese customers! Only 1 per cent said they would accept them, and the remainder checked 'Uncertain, depends on circumstances'. These written replies from the erstwhile hosts directly contradicted the way they had actually behaved.

This study was not, of course, scientifically designed – perhaps the people who responded to the letters were not those who dealt face-to-face with the Chinese couple; they might have responded differently in writing if they had been told that the couple was educated and well dressed; attitudes may have changed in the six months between the two measures. Nevertheless, the problem that LaPiere had unearthed provided an early challenge to the validity of the concept of attitude.

Not all classes of social behaviour can be predicted accurately from verbally expressed attitudes. We look now at research that has explored in detail why attitude–behaviour correspondence is often weak, and what factors may strengthen the correspondence.

## Beliefs, intentions and behaviour

According to Fishbein (1967a, 1967b, 1971), the basic ingredient of an attitude is affect, a position that reflects Thurstone's (1931) early definition. However, an attitude measure based entirely on a unidimensional, bipolar evaluative scale (such as good/bad) does not predict reliably how a person will later behave. Better prediction depends on accounting for the interaction between attitudes, beliefs and behavioural intentions, and the connections of all of these with subsequent actions.

In this equation, we need to establish both how strong and how valuable a person's beliefs are: some beliefs will carry more weight than others in relation to the final act. For example, the strength or weakness of a person's religious convictions may be pivotal in their decision-making processes regarding moral behaviour – moral norms may play a very important role in attitude–behaviour relations (Manstead, 2000). Without this information, trying to predict an outcome for a given individual must inevitably be a hit-or-miss affair.

Consider the example in Table 5.1. A young, heterosexually active man might believe, strongly or not, that certain things are true about two forms of contraception, the pill and the condom. *Belief strength* (or expectancy) has a probability estimate, ranging from 0 to 1, regarding the truth; for example, he may hold a very strong belief (0.90) that the pill is a highly reliable method of birth control. Reliability of a contraceptive is a 'good' thing, so his *evaluation* (or value) of the pill is +2, say, on a five-point scale ranging from –2 to +2. Belief strength and evaluation interact, producing a final rating of +1.80. (Like Anderson, Fishbein's view incorporates the idea that people are able to perform cognitive algebra.)

Next, the young man might be fairly sure (0.70) that the condom is less reliable (–1), a rating of –0.70. Likewise, he thinks that using a condom is potentially embarrassing in a sexual encounter. His further belief that using a condom has no known side effects is not sufficient to offset the effects of the other two beliefs. Check the hypothetical algebra in Table 5.1. Consequently, the young man's intention to use a condom, should he possess one, may be quite low (perhaps he hopes that the women who cross his path use the pill!). Only by having all of this information could we be fairly confident about predicting his future behaviour.

This approach to prediction also offers a method of measurement, the expectancy–value technique. In subsequent work with his colleague Ajzen, Fishbein developed the *theory of*

**Table 5.1** A young man's hypothetical attitude towards contraceptive use: the strength and value of his beliefs

| Attribute | Man's belief about woman using pill | | | | | | | Man's belief about man using condom | | | | | | |
|---|---|---|---|---|---|---|---|---|---|---|---|---|---|---|
| | Strength of belief | | Value of belief | | Result | | | Strength of belief | | Value of belief | | Result | | |
| Reliability | 0.90 | × | +2 | = | +1.80 | | | 0.70 | × | −1 | = | −0.70 | | |
| Embarrassment | 1.00 | × | +2 | = | +2.00 | | | 0.80 | × | −2 | = | −1.60 | | |
| Side effects | 0.10 | × | −1 | = | −0.10 | | | 1.00 | × | +2 | = | +2.00 | | |
| Outcome | | | | | +3.70 | | | | | | | −0.30 | | |

The strength of a belief, in this example, is the probability (from 0 to 1) that a person thinks that the belief is true. The value of a belief is an evaluation on a bipolar scale (in this case, ranging from +2 to −2).

*reasoned action* to link beliefs to intentions to behaviour (we return to this model later). Fishbein and Ajzen's work was a significant advance in understanding issues that had previously complicated the overall relationship between attitudes and behaviour. Predictions can be clarified when the inherent links are brought to the surface. Furthermore, behavioural predictions can be much improved if the measures of attitudes are specific rather than general.

## Specific attitudes

Ajzen and Fishbein believed that success in predicting the way we behave is determined by asking whether we would perform a given act or series of acts. The key lies in asking questions that are quite specific rather than ones that deal with generalities.

Ajzen and Fishbein argued that much previous attitude research had suffered from either trying to predict specific behaviours from general attitudes or vice versa, so that low correlations were to be expected. This is, in essence, what LaPiere did. An example of a specific attitude predicting specific behaviour would be a student's attitude towards a psychology exam predicting how diligently he or she studies for that exam. In contrast, an example of a general attitude predicting a general class of behaviour would be attitudes towards psychology as a whole, predicting the behaviour generally relevant to learning more about psychology, such as reading magazine articles or talking with your tutor. How interested you are in psychology generally is not likely to be predictive of how well you prepare for a specific psychology exam.

In a two-year longitudinal study by Davidson and Jacard (1979), women's attitudes towards birth control were measured at different levels of specificity and used as predictors of their actual use of the contraceptive pill. The measures, ranging from very general to very specific, were correlated as follows with actual pill use (correlations in parentheses): 'Attitude towards birth control' (0.08); 'Attitude towards birth control pills' (0.32); 'Attitude towards using birth control pills' (0.53); and 'Attitude towards using birth control pills during the next two years' (0.57). Thus, this last measure was the variable most highly correlated with actual use of the contraceptive pill. It indicates quite clearly that the closer the question was to the actual behaviour, the more accurately the behaviour was predicted. (See Kraus, 1995, for a **meta-analysis** of attitudes as predictors of behaviour.)

## General attitudes

Fishbein and Ajzen (1975) also argued that we can predict behaviour from more general attitudes, but only if we adopt a **multiple-act criterion**. This criterion is a general behavioural index based on an average or combination of various specific behaviours. General attitudes usually predict multiple-act criteria much better than they predict single acts, because single acts are usually affected by many factors. For example, the specific behaviour of participating in a paper-recycling programme on a given day is a function of many factors, even the weather. Yet a person engaging in such behaviour may claim to be 'environmentally conscious', a general attitude. Environmental attitudes are no doubt one determinant of this behaviour, but they are not the only, or even perhaps the major, one.

## Reasoned action

The ideas outlined so far were integrated into a general model of the links between attitude and behaviour – the **theory of reasoned action** (Ajzen & Fishbein, 1980; Fishbein & Ajzen, 1974). The model comprised three broad processes of beliefs, intention and action and included the following components:

- *Subjective norm* – a product of what the individual perceives others to believe. Significant others provide direct or indirect information about 'what is the proper thing to do'.

**Meta-analysis**
Statistical procedure that combines data from different studies to measure the overall reliability and strength of specific effects.

**Multiple-act criterion**
Term for a general behavioural index based on an average or combination of several specific behaviours.

**Theory of reasoned action**
Fishbein and Ajzen's model of the links between attitude and behaviour. A major feature is the proposition that the best way to predict a behaviour is to ask whether the person intends to do it.

- *Attitude towards the behaviour* – a product of the individual's beliefs about the target behaviour and of how these beliefs are evaluated (refer back to the cognitive algebra in Table 5.1). Note that this is an attitude towards behaviour (such as taking a birth control pill in Davidson and Jacard's study), not towards the object (such as the pill itself).
- *Behavioural intention* – an internal declaration to act.
- *Behaviour* – the action performed.

Usually, an action will be performed if (1) the person's attitude is favourable; and (2) the social norm is also favourable. In early tests of the theory, Fishbein and Feldman (1963) and Fishbein and Coombs (1974) gave participants a series of statements about the attributes of various attitude objects: for example, political candidates. The participants estimated *expectancies* – that is, how likely it was that the object (candidate) possessed the various attributes – and gave the attributes a *value*. These expectancies and values were then used to predict the participants' feelings towards the attitude object, assessed by asking the participants how much they liked or disliked that object. The correlation between the scores and the participants' feelings was high, pointing to some promise for the model.

Other research reported that when people's voting intentions were later compared with how they actually voted, the correlations were:

- 0.80 in the 1976 American presidential election (Fishbein, Ajzen & Hinkle, 1980); and
- 0.89 in a referendum on nuclear power (Fishbein et al., 1980).

### Planned behaviour: the role of volition

The theory of reasoned action (TRA) emphasises not only the rationality of human behaviour but also the belief that the behaviour is under the person's conscious control: for example, 'I know I can stop smoking if I really want to'. However, some actions are less under people's control than others.

Consequently, the basic model was extended by Ajzen (1989) to emphasise the role of volition. Perceived behavioural control is the extent to which the person believes it is easy or difficult to perform an act. The process of coming to such a decision includes consideration of past experiences, as well as present obstacles that the person may envisage. For example, Ajzen and Madden (1986) found that students, not surprisingly, want to achieve A-grades in their courses: A-grades are highly valued by the students (attitude), and they are the grades that their family and friends want them to achieve (subjective norm). However, prediction of actually getting an A will be unreliable unless the students' perceptions of their own abilities are taken into account.

Ajzen has argued that perceived behavioural control can act on either the behavioural intention or directly on the behaviour itself. He referred to this modified model as the **theory of planned behaviour** (TPB), and it is still actively researched (Ajzen & Fishbein, 2005). In a recent meta-analysis, Cooke and Sheeran (2004) have referred to TPB as 'probably the dominant account of the relationship between cognitions and behaviour in social psychology' (2004, p. 159). The two theories, TRA and TPB, are not in conflict. The concepts and the way in which they are linked in each theory are shown in Figure 5.3.

In one study, Beck and Ajzen (1991) started with students' self-reports of the extent to which they had been dishonest in the past. The behaviour sampled included exam cheating, shoplifting and telling lies to avoid completing written assignments, actions that were quite often reported. They found that measuring the perception of control that students thought they had over these actions improved the accuracy of prediction of future actions, and, to some extent, the actual performance of the act. This was most successful in the case of cheating, which may well be planned in a more deliberate way than shoplifting or lying.

In another study, Madden, Ellen and Ajzen (1992) measured students' perceptions of control in relation to nine behaviours. These ranged from 'getting a good night's sleep' (quite hard to control) to 'taking vitamin supplements' (quite easy to control). The results

**Theory of planned behaviour**
Modification by Ajzen of the *theory of reasoned action*. It suggests that predicting a behaviour from an attitude measure is improved if people believe they have control over that behaviour.

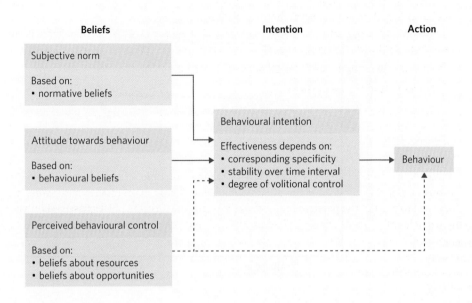

**Figure 5.3** A comparison of the theory of reasoned action (TRA) and the theory of planned behaviour (TPB)

The solid lines show the concepts and links in the original theory of reasoned action; the dotted lines show an addition introduced in the theory of planned behaviour

*Source:* based on Ajzen & Fishbein (1980); Madden, Ellen & Ajzen (1992)

were calculated to compare predictive power by squaring the correlation coefficient between each of the two predictors (sleep and vitamins) and each of the outcomes (intentions and actions). Perceived control improved the prediction accuracy for both intentions and actions, and this improvement was substantially effective in predicting the action itself. These effects are evident in the steep gradient of the two lower lines in Figure 5.4, an outcome that has been confirmed in an independent study using a wide range of thirty behaviours (Sheeran, Trafimow, Finlay & Norman, 2002).

Features of both models have been used to understand people's attitudes towards their health. Terry and her colleagues (Terry, Gallois & McCamish, 1993) have shown how Fishbein and Ajzen's concepts can be applied to the study of safe sex behaviour as a response to the threat of contracting HIV (see Box 5.2). Specifically, the target behaviour included monogamous relationships, non-penetrative sex and the use of condoms. All of the variables shown in Figure 5.3 can be applied in this setting. In the context of practising safe sex, the particular variable of perceived behavioural control needs to be accounted for, particularly where neither of the sex partners may be fully confident of controlling the wishes of the other person. A practical question that may need to be examined is the degree of control that a woman might perceive she has about whether a condom will be used in her next sexual encounter.

Parker, Manstead and Stradling (1995) applied TPB to the study of driver behaviour in Britain. Parker and colleagues' concern was the predictability of intention to commit driving offences. Nearly 600 British drivers were interviewed and questioned about their attitudes and intentions regarding three driving scenarios: cutting in, reckless weaving and illegal overtaking on the inside lanes of a motorway. Questionnaires assessed what drivers believed would be their reaction in each situation (belief-based measure). Results showed that adding the belief-based measure to TRA, to become TPB, significantly enhanced the predictive value of the former. Significant correlations were found between participants'

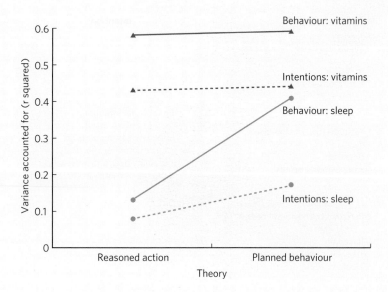

**Figure 5.4**  Theories of reasoned action and planned behaviour compared: the effect of including perceived behavioural control as a variable

*Source:* based on data from Madden, Ellen & Ajzen (1992)

## Research and applications 5.2
### Reasoned action, planned behaviour and safe sex

**TRA and TPB have proved useful in understanding and promoting responsible sex behaviour**

Social psychologists have increasingly turned their attention to promoting health practices such as avoiding the abuse of alcohol, tobacco and other substances; promoting dental hygiene; vaccinating against infectious diseases; participating in cervical smear tests; and using sun-screen products (see also Chapter 6).

Another sphere of application has been the promotion of contraceptive practices to avoid unwanted pregnancies. Health professionals have also been concerned about the spread of HIV and contraction of AIDS. (We noted in Chapter 2 that some people tend to underestimate the riskiness of their sexual practices.)

In this context, social psychologists have mounted a concerted campaign of research promoting condom use, safe sex and monogamous relationships. Several researchers have explicitly recognised Fishbein and Ajzen's (Fishbein & Ajzen, 1974; Ajzen & Fishbein, 1980) theory of reasoned action as a model that helps to account for variability in people's willingness to practise safe sex (see Terry, Gallois & McCamish, 1993). One feature of this work has been to focus on establishing

how much people feel they can actually exert control over their health. A woman with this sense of control is more likely to wear a seat belt, examine her breasts, use a contraceptive, have sex in an exclusive relationship, and discuss her partner's sexual and intravenous drug-use history.

Apart from a sense of control, other factors such as perceptions of condom proposers (those who initiate condom use), as well as the expectations and experience of safe sex, are implicated in initiating safe sex (Hodges, Klaaren & Wheatley, 2000). Coupled with these factors, cultural background also plays a role in the gender and sexuality equation. For example, Conley, Collins and Garcia (2000) found that Chinese Americans reacted more negatively than European Americans to the female condom proposer. Furthermore, Japanese Americans perceived the female condom proposer to be less sexually attractive than did the Chinese or European Americans (see also Chapter 16).

A problem with practising safe sex with one's partner is that it is not a behaviour that comes completely under one individual's *volitional control,* whereas going for a run usually is. The theory of reasoned action, together with its extension, the theory of planned behaviour (see Figure 5.3), provides a framework for psychologists and other health professionals to target particular variables that have the potential to encourage safe sex, as well as other health behaviour.

**Planned behaviour**
The promotion of a health practice, such as breast self-examination, requires that a woman believes that she knows what to do and what to look for

perceived control over their driving behaviour and their attitudes to committing each of the three driving offences.

In critically evaluating both TRA and TPB, Manstead and Parker (1995) argued that the inclusion of 'perceived behavioural control' in TPB is an improvement on the original theory. In a meta-analysis by Armitage and Conner (2001), perceived behavioural control emerged as a significant variable and could account for up to 20 per cent of prospective actual behaviour.

In contrast to both the TRA and TPB models, some researchers have suggested that other variables play a role in determining action, such as people's moral values (Gorsuch & Ortbergh, 1983; Manstead, 2000; Pagel & Davidson, 1984; Schwartz, 1977). For example, if someone wanted to find out whether we would donate money to charity, they would do well to find out whether acting charitably is a priority in our lives. In this specific context, Maio and Olson (1995) found that general altruistic values predicted charitable behaviour (donating to cancer research), but only where the context emphasised the *expression* of one's values. Where the context emphasised rewards and punishments (i.e. a utilitarian emphasis) values did not predict donating.

*Habit* is also a predictor of future behaviour in that an action can become relatively automatic (discussed in a later section in this chapter), and can operate independently of processes underlying TPB. Trafimow (2000) found that male and female students who were in the habit of using condoms reported that they would continue to do so on the next occasion. In effect, habitual condom users do not 'need' to use reasoned decisions, such as thinking about what their attitudes are or about what norms are appropriate. In a recent TPB study of binge drinking (Norman & Conner, 2006), the way that students viewed their drinking history could predict their future behaviour. For example, if Bill believes he is a binge drinker, he will attend less to his attitude towards alcohol abuse and will also feel that he has less control over how much he drinks.

Both the TRA and TPB models have implications for how we can strive for a healthy lifestyle. Likewise, in health psychology, **protection motivation theory** focuses on how people can make a start to protect their health, maintain better practices and avoid risky behaviour (see Box 5.3 and Figure 5.5).

**Protection motivation theory**
Adopting a healthy behaviour requires cognitive balancing between the perceived threat of illness and one's capacity to cope with the health regimen.

## Research and applications 5.3
### Can we protect ourselves against major diseases?

Cardiovascular disease and cancer were the leading causes of death in the early 1990s, according to American health statistics; a trend that continues in most Western nations. It is well known that preventive behaviour for both diseases includes routine medical examinations, regular blood pressure readings, exercising aerobically for at least twenty minutes three times per week, eating a well-balanced diet that is low in salt and fat, maintaining a healthy weight and not smoking. It is a major challenge for health psychologists to find a model of health promotion that is robust enough to encourage people to engage in these preventative behaviours.

According to Floyd, Prentice-Dunn and Rogers (2000), protection motivation theory has emerged as just such a model. The model was developed initially to explain the effects of fear-arousing appeals on maladaptive health attitudes and behaviour, and was derived from Fishbein's theories of expectancy-value and reasoned action. Other components built into protection motivation theory included the effects of intrinsic and extrinsic reward (related to social learning theory) and Bandura's (1986, 1992) concept of **self-efficacy**, which in turn is closely related to that of *perceived behavioural control* in TPB (Ajzen, 1998).

From their meta-analysis of research based on sixty-five studies and more than twenty health issues, Floyd,

Prentice-Dunn and Rogers argue that adaptive intentions and behaviour are facilitated by:

- an increase in the perceived severity of a health threat;
- the vulnerability of the individual to that threat;
- the perceived effectiveness of taking protective action; and
- self-efficacy.

In considering why Joe, for example, might either continue to smoke or decide to quit, protection motivation theory specifies two mediating cognitive processes:

1  *Threat appraisal* – smoking has intrinsic rewards (e.g. taste in mouth, nicotine effect) and extrinsic rewards (e.g. his friends think it's cool). These are weighed up against the extent to which Joe thinks there is a severe risk to his health (e.g. after reading the latest brochure in his doctor's waiting room) and that he is vulnerable (e.g. because a close relative who smoked died of lung cancer).

2  *Coping appraisal* – Joe takes into account response efficacy (whether nicotine replacement therapy might work) and self-efficacy (whether he thinks he can adhere to the regime).

The trade-off when Joe compares his appraisals of threat and coping determines his level of protection motivation and whether he decides to quit smoking (see Figure 5.5).

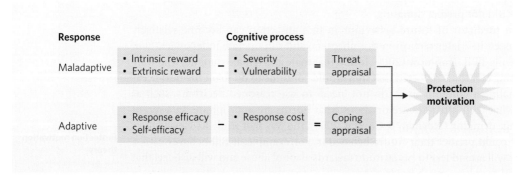

**Figure 5.5**   Mediating cognitive processes in protection motivation theory

This theory grew from psychological research into health promotion. Adopting a healthy practice will depend on several cognitive processes that lead to a balancing up of perceived threat versus the capacity to cope with a health regime

*Source:* based on Floyd, Prentice-Dunn & Rogers (2000)

Various issues to which these models have been applied include HIV prevention (Smith & Stasson, 2000), condom use and safer sex behaviour (Sheeran & Taylor, 1999), alcohol consumption (Conner, Warren, Close & Sparks, 1999) and smoking (Godin, Valois, Lepage & Desharnais, 1992). However, the models are not restricted to the health domain. For example, Fox-Cardamone, Hinkle and Hogue (2000) used TPB to examine antinuclear behaviour. Antinuclear attitudes emerged as significant predictors of either antinuclear intentions or behaviour. All three theories share the idea that motivation towards protection results from a perceived threat and the desire to avoid potential negative outcomes (Floyd, Prentice-Dunn & Rogers, 2000).

There is a reservation about TRA and TPB – it is assumed that attitudes are rational and socially significant behaviour is intentional, reasoned and planned. This may not always be true. How would you apply these theories to answer the second focus question?

**Self-efficacy**
Expectations that we have about our capacity to succeed in particular tasks.

## Attitude accessibility

Many models of attitude feature a cognitive component, in that beliefs are the building blocks of the more general concept of attitude, and even approaches that emphasise an evaluative component agree on one matter: attitudes are represented in memory (Olson & Zanna, 1993).

Accessible attitudes are those that can be recalled from memory more easily and can therefore be expressed more quickly (Eagly & Chaiken, 1998). They can exert a strong influence on behaviour (Fazio, 1986) and are associated with greater attitude–behaviour consistency (Doll & Ajzen, 1992). They are also more stable, more selective in judging relevant information and more resistant to change (Fazio, 1995). There is some evidence that affective evaluations are faster than cognitive evaluations, suggesting more evaluative attitudes are more accessible in memory (Verplanken & Aarts, 1999; Verplanken, Hofstee & Janssen, 1998).

Most studies of attitude accessibility have focused on highly accessible attitudes, drawing on Fazio's (1995) model of attitudes as an association in memory between an object and an evaluation. The rationale behind Fazio's model is that the extent to which an attitude is 'handy' or functional and useful for the individual depends on the extent to which the attitude can be automatically activated in memory. The likelihood of automatic activation depends on the strength of the association between the object and the evaluation (Bargh, Chaiken, Govender & Pratto, 1992). Strong object–evaluation associations should therefore be highly functional because they help us make decisions.

Although the ideas behind attitude accessibility are intuitively appealing and supported by some research (e.g. Fazio, Ledbetter & Towles-Schwen, 2000), there is also some evidence that implicit measures (as object–evaluation associations) correlate only weakly with explicit self-reports, what people actually say (Hilton & Karpinski, 2000). We return to this topic later in this chapter when we examine how attitudes are measured.

As well as facilitating decision making, accessible attitudes orient visual attention and categorisation processes (Roskos-Ewoldsen & Fazio, 1992; Smith, Fazio & Cejka, 1996), and free up resources for coping with stress (Fazio & Powell, 1997). How might accessible attitudes affect the way we categorise? Smith, Fazio and Cejka (1996) showed that, when choosing from a number of possible categories to describe an object, we are more likely to select an accessible one. For example, when participants rehearsed their attitudes towards dairy products, yoghurt was more likely to cue as a *dairy product*. On the other hand, if attitudes towards health food were experimentally enhanced, and therefore made more accessible in memory, yoghurt was more likely to cue as a *health food* (Eagly & Chaiken, 1998).

Fazio's studies confirmed earlier findings that perceptions of stimuli will probably be biased in the direction of an individual's attitude (Lambert, Solomon & Watson, 1949;

## Research and applications 5.4
### Accessible attitudes can be costly

There may be costs associated with highly accessible attitudes. Fazio, Ledbetter and Towles-Schwen (2000) tested this idea in several experiments using computer-based morphing. Twenty-four same-sex digital facial photographs were paired so that one image in each pair was relatively attractive and one was not, based on earlier data. Five morphs (composites) of the images of each pair were created that varied in attractiveness determined by the percentage (e.g. 67/37, 50/50, 13/87) that each image contributed to a morph.

In part 1 of an experimental sequence, participants 'formed' attitudes that were either highly accessible (HA) or less accessible (LA). HA participants verbally rated how attractive each morph was, whereas LA participants verbally estimated the morph's probable physical height. Part 2 involved the detection of change in an image. Participants were told that they would see more faces, some of which were different photographs of people they had already seen, and they were to choose both quickly and accurately whether each image was the same or different from those seen earlier. HA participants were slower to respond than LA participants and also made more errors than LA participants. In an experimental variation, they also noticed less change in a morphed image.

All attitudes are functional and accessible attitudes even more so, since they usually deal with objects, events and people that are stable. However, if the attitude object changes over time then a highly accessible attitude may become dysfunctional – it is stuck in time.

Zanna, 1993). However, he also demonstrated that costs are associated with highly accessible attitudes. Recall that accessible attitudes remain stable over time. If the object of an attitude changes, then accessible attitudes toward that object may begin to function less adequately (Fazio, Ledbetter & Towles-Schwen, 2000). Accessibility can actually produce insensitivity to change – we have become set in our ways. Consequently, an individual who feels negatively about a particular attitude object may not be able to detect if it has changed for the better, or perhaps for the worse (see Box 5.4).

Another way to conceptualise accessibility is in the language of *connectionism*. An accessible attitude is a cognitive node in the mind that is well connected to other cognitive nodes (thorough learning and perhaps conditioning), and so the focal attitude can be activated in many different ways and along many different cognitive paths. According to Van Overwalle and Siebler:

> This allows a view of the mind as an adaptive learning mechanism that develops accurate mental representations of the world. Learning is modeled as a process of online adaptation of existing knowledge to novel information . . . the network changes the weights of the connections with the attitude object so as to better represent the accumulated history of co-occurrences between objects and their attributes and evaluations. (*Van Overwalle & Siebler, 2005, p. 232*)

Van Overwalle and Siebler suggest that a connectionist approach is consistent with: (1) dual-process models of attitude change (see Chapter 6), and (2) the notion of algebraic weights placed on beliefs, introduced by Fishbein (see the example in Table 5.1).

## Attitude strength

Do strong attitudes guide behaviour? The results of a study of attitudes towards Greenpeace suggest so (Holland, Verplanken & Van Knippenberg, 2002). People with very positive attitudes towards Greenpeace were much more likely to make a donation to the cause than those with weak positive attitudes.

Almost by definition, strong attitudes must be highly accessible. They come to mind more readily and exert more influence over behaviour than weak attitudes. Fazio argued that attitudes are evaluative associations with objects, which makes his approach a one-component

**Attitude strength**
If your home had been bulldozed how do you think you would feel?

model. Associations can vary in strength from 'no link' (i.e. a non-attitude), to a weak link, to a strong link. Only an association that is strong allows the **automatic activation** of an attitude (Fazio, 1995; Fazio, Blascovich & Driscoll, 1992; Fazio & Powell, 1997; Fazio, Sanbonmatsu, Powell & Kardes, 1986; see Figure 5.6).

**Automatic activation**
According to Fazio, attitudes that have a strong evaluative link to situational cues are more likely to come automatically to mind from memory.

Direct experience of an object and having a vested interest in it (i.e. something with a strong effect on your life) make the attitude more accessible and increase its effect on behaviour. For example, people who have had a nuclear reactor built in their neighbourhood will have stronger and more clearly defined attitudes regarding the safety of nuclear reactors. These people will be more motivated by their attitudes – they may be more involved in protests or more likely to move house.

As another example, consider attitudes towards doctor-assisted suicide (Haddock, Rothman, Reber & Schwarz, 1999). As subjective experience with this form of dying increased – its certainty, intensity and importance – the corresponding attitude about doctor-assisted suicide became stronger. It became more certain, intense and important.

The more often you *think* about an attitude, the more likely it is to resurface and influence your behaviour through easier decision making (Fazio, Blascovich & Driscoll, 1992). Powell and Fazio (1984) were able to make an attitude more accessible simply by asking on six different occasions what people's attitudes were as opposed to asking them only once. Accessing general attitudes can affect behaviour in specific situations. If the general attitude is never accessed, it cannot affect behaviour. Therefore, the activation step of Fazio's model is critical, since only activated attitudes can guide subsequent information processing and behaviour. Think of a sports coach priming a team by asking the question 'Which is the greatest team?' demanding a shouted response of 'We are!' and repeating this scenario a number of times before the match begins.

## Direct experience

In addition to the role of strength, an attitude becomes more accessible as direct experience with the attitude object increases. Attitudes formed through actual experience are more consistently related to behaviour (Regan & Fazio, 1977; Doll & Ajzen, 1992). Suppose Mary

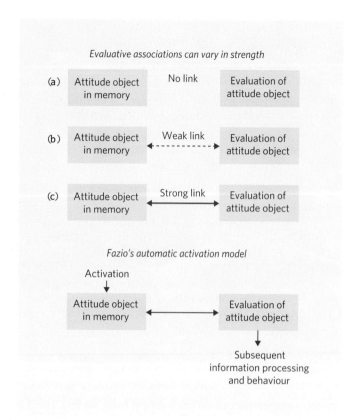

**Figure 5.6**    When is an attitude accessible?

A stronger attitude is more accessible than a weaker
attitude. It can be automatically activated and will exert
more influence over behaviour

has participated in several psychology experiments but William has only read about them.
We can predict Mary's willingness to participate in the future more accurately than
William's (Fazio & Zanna, 1978). Another example: your attitude to UFOs is far less likely
to predict how you will act should you encounter one (!) than your attitude to lecturers is
likely to predict your lecture room behaviour. Likewise, it would be reassuring to think that
those people who had been caught driving with excessive blood alcohol levels would be less
likely to drink and drive in the future. Unfortunately, this is not always the case.

Therefore, although direct experience seems appealing as an influence on attitude
accessibility, establishing its actual effectiveness is a difficult task. We consider the role
of direct experience again in the context of attitude formation in a later section in this
chapter.

Apart from attitude accessibility and direct experience with the attitude object, issues such
as attitude salience, ambivalence, consistency between affect and cognition, attitude extremity, affective intensity, certainty, importance, latitudes of rejection and non-commitment
are common themes in attitude research that fall under the general rubric of 'attitude
strength'. Not surprisingly, attitude strength may consist of many related constructs rather
than just one (Krosnick et al., 1993). Although some dimensions of attitude strength are
strongly related, most are not.

### Reflecting on the attitude–behaviour link

Let us take stock of what research tell us (Glassman & Albarracín, 2006). As attitudes are
being *formed,* they correlate more strongly with a future behaviour when:

- the attitudes are *accessible* (easy to recall);
- the attitudes are *stable over time*;

- people have had *direct experience* with the attitude object;
- people *frequently report* their attitudes.

The attitude–behaviour link is stronger when relevant information – such as persuasive arguments – is relevant to the actual behaviour, one-sided and supportive of the attitude object, rather than two-sided. We deal with the topic of attitude formation below, and the role of persuasive arguments is part of our treatment of attitude change (Chapter 6).

## Moderator variables

Although it is difficult to predict single acts from general attitudes, prediction can be improved by the addition of a **moderator variable** that specifies conditions under which the attitude–behaviour relationship is stronger or weaker. Moderators include the situation, personality, habit, sense of control and direct experience. The attitude itself can also act as a moderator – for example an attitude that functions to emphasise a person's self-concept and central values has stronger attitude–behaviour correspondence than one that simply maximises rewards and minimises punishments (Verplanken & Holland, 2002; Maio & Olson, 1994). Ironically, moderator variables may turn out to be more powerful predictors of an action than the more general, underlying attitude. We consider two cases.

**Moderator variable**
A variable that qualifies an otherwise simple hypothesis with a view to improving its predictive power (e.g. A causes B, but only when C (the moderator) is present).

### Situational variables

Aspects of the situation, or context, can cause people to act in a way that is inconsistent with their attitudes (Calder & Ross, 1973). Weak attitudes are particularly susceptible to context (Lavine, Huff, Wagner & Sweeney, 1998), and in many cases what tends to happen is that social norms that are contextually salient overwhelm people's underlying attitudes. For instance, if university students expect each other to dress in jeans and casual clothes, these expectations represent a powerful norm for how students dress on campus.

Norms have always been considered important in attitude–behaviour relations, but they have generally been separated from attitudes: attitudes are 'in here' (private, internalised cognitive constructs), while norms are 'out there' (public, external pressures representing the cumulative expectations of others). This view of norms has been challenged by social identity theory (see Chapter 11), which sees no such distinction – attitudes can be personal and idiosyncratic but much more typically they are a normative property of a social group and group identification causes one to internalise the groups normative properties, including its attitudes, as an aspect of self (e.g. Abrams & Hogg, 1990a; Turner, 1991; see Chapter 7).

This idea has been applied to attitude–behaviour relations to argue that attitudes are more likely to express themselves as behaviour if the attitudes and associated behaviour are normative properties of a contextually salient social group with which people identify (Hogg & Smith, 2007; Terry & Hogg, 1996; Terry, Hogg & White, 2000). To test this, Terry and Hogg (1996) conducted two longitudinal questionnaire studies of students' intentions to take regular exercise and to protect themselves from the sun. These intentions were stronger when participants identified strongly with a self-relevant student peer group whom participants believed took regular exercise or habitually protected themselves from the sun (Figure 5.7).

### Individual differences

Social psychologists tend to be divided into two camps – those who prefer situational explanations of social behaviour and those who prefer personality and individual difference explanations (Ross & Nisbett, 1991). Although this distinction has become less stark in recent years (Funder & Fast, 2010) it nevertheless has impacted attitude research. For

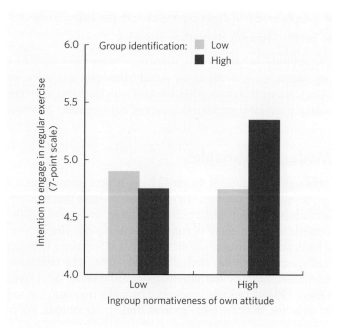

**Figure 5.7** The role of norms and group identification in attitude–behaviour consistency

Students expressed a stronger intention to engage in regular exercise when they felt their attitudes towards exercise were normative of a student peer group with which they identified strongly

*Source*: based on data by Terry & Hogg (1996)

example, Mischel (1968) argued that situational characteristics were more reliable predictors of behaviour than were personality traits (see also the weak correlations reported between personality measures and leadership in Chapter 9). Whereas Bem and Allen (1974) and Vaughan (1977) have shown that people who were consistent in their *answers* on a personality scale were more likely to be consistent in their *behaviour* across a variety of relevant situations than people who gave variable answers. For example, a high scorer on an extraversion–introversion scale would be more likely to behave in an extroverted manner and a low scorer in an introverted manner, across different social settings. On the other hand, those who were variable (mid-range scorers) in their answers on the scale would not behave consistently.

It is therefore useful to know how people's behavioural *habits* are related to their *degree of control* over the behaviour (Langer, 1975; Petty & Cacioppo, 1981; Triandis, 1980; Verplanken, Aarts, van Knippenberg & Moonen, 1998). Triandis (1977) proposed a model similar to Fishbein and Ajzen's, which included a habit factor to reflect the number of times a person had performed a particular action in the past. Smoking, for instance, is habitual for many people and is often partly due to a physiological and/or psychological dependency. Thus, the behaviour of smokers may bear little relationship to their attitudes towards cigarettes. Oskamp (1984) reported that about 70 per cent of smokers agreed that 'smoking is one of the causes of lung cancer', and that 'cigarette smoking causes disease and death'.

In a review of research on 'habit', Verplanken and Aarts (1999) concluded that the relationship between attitudes and behaviour and between intentions and behaviour were near zero when habits were strong but sizeable when habits were weak. However, psychologists are fiercely vigilant in protecting their theories! In this instance, Ajzen (2002) does not see an inconsistency between habitual behaviour and planned behaviour:

The theory of planned behavior [and of reasoned action] does not propose that individuals review their behavioral, normative, and control beliefs prior to every enactment of a frequently performed behavior. Instead, attitudes and intentions – once formed and well-established – are assumed to be activated automatically and to guide behavior without the necessity of conscious supervision. (*Ajzen, 2002, p. 108*)

*Mood* as a moderator variable may be considered both a situational and a personality variable. Semmler and Brewer (2002) examined the effects of trial-induced mood on how jurors processed information and made decisions. They found that being sad did not affect a juror's judgement, despite an increase in irrelevant thought. However, angry jurors actually reported more irrelevant thoughts, detected fewer inconsistencies in the witness's testimony and judged the defendant more harshly.

If we replace 'mood' with terms like 'affect' and 'emotion', we invoke part of the three-component model of attitude structure discussed earlier. In this wider context, there has been considerable research into affect-based evaluations of an attitude object (e.g. 'I hate broccoli, but I love ice cream'), especially in the context of persuasion and advertising (see Chapter 6).

*Cognitive biases,* one of which is self–other discrepancy (see Chapter 4), are also moderators that can affect attitude–behaviour correspondence. Paglia and Room (1999) studied what more than 800 people expected to happen when they drank alcohol and also how readily available they thought alcohol should be. They found that support for tighter control over alcohol availability stems partly from what people expect to happen, both from their own drinking and from the drinking of others. There was a distinct self–other discrepancy: people expect alcohol to affect others more adversely than themselves! Furthermore, the greater the bias the greater the support for alcohol restriction.

Finally, some people are more focused than others on what has been called their *self-identity* – their sense of who they are as defined by the roles they occupy in society; although similar to social identity (See Chapter 11) self-identity is more focused on roles than group membership (Terry, Hogg & White, 1999; also see Chapter 4). Self-identity has been viewed as an influence on people's intentions to act, which is a component of the theory of planned behaviour, discussed above (Hagger & Chatzisarantis, 2006). In one study, people were more likely to express an intention to donate blood if being a blood donor was an important part of their self-identity (Charng, Piliavin & Callero, 1988).

# Forming attitudes

Attitudes are learned as part of the socialisation process (Fishbein & Ajzen, 1975; McGuire, 1969; Oskamp, 1977). They may develop through direct experiences or vicariously through interactions with others, or be a product of cognitive processes and thought. Generally, social psychologists have confined their work to understanding the basic psychological processes that underlie **attitude formation** rather than exploring how particular classes of attitude develop. The study of these processes usually involves laboratory experiments rather than survey or public opinion research.

**Attitude formation**
The process of forming our attitudes, mainly from our own experiences, the influences of others and our emotional reactions.

## Behavioural approaches

### Effects of direct experience

Many of the attitudes that people hold are the products of direct experience with attitude objects. There are several explanations for this process: mere exposure, classical conditioning, operant conditioning, social learning theory and self-perception theory.

Direct experience provides us with information about the attributes of an object, and helps to shape beliefs that influence how much we like or dislike the object (Fishbein & Ajzen, 1975). Even a mildly traumatic experience can trigger a negative attitude (Oskamp, 1977; Sargant, 1957), and make certain beliefs more salient than others. If your first visit to the dentist is painful, you may conclude that dentists hurt rather than help you, despite their friendly smile.

Mere exposure to an object on several occasions is likely to affect how we evaluate it – the **mere exposure effect** (Zajonc, 1968). The first time you hear a new song on the radio, you may find you neither strongly like nor dislike it, but with repetition your response in one direction or the other is likely to strengthen. However, the effect of continued repeated exposure diminishes. For example, increased liking for photos of people levelled off after about ten exposures (Bornstein, 1989). Mere exposure has most impact when we lack information about an issue. Sitting MPs, for example, usually have an advantage over other candidates in an election, simply because their names are more familiar.

**Mere exposure effect**
Repeated exposure to an object results in greater attraction to that object.

### Classical conditioning

Repeated association may cause a formerly neutral stimulus to elicit a reaction that was previously elicited only by another stimulus. In the more specific case of *evaluative conditioning,* a stimulus will probably become more liked or less liked when it is consistently paired with stimuli that are either positive or negative (De Houwer, Thomas & Baeyens, 2001). For example, children may initially be indifferent to politics but later vote as young adults for a party after years of exposure to a parent who has been an enthusiastic supporter – a classically conditioned response has become the basis of a subsequent political attitude. Classical conditioning may underlie the formation of a wide variety of attitudes (Zanna, Kiesler & Pilkonis, 1970).

Classical conditioning can be a powerful, even insidious, form of attitude learning. One study demonstrated the power of contextual stimuli by reinforcing some participants with soft drinks while they were reading a persuasive message (Janis, Kaye & Kirschner, 1965). Those given soft drinks were more persuaded by what they read than those who were not. In another study, participants listened to pleasant guitar music as an accompaniment to persuasive messages presented as folk songs. The songs proved more persuasive when accompanied by guitar music than without (Galizio & Hendrick, 1972). We may reasonably conclude that the positive feelings associated with the soft drinks or with guitar music became associated, via classical conditioning, with the persuasive messages. An interesting corollary is the **spreading attitude effect**. Walther (2002) gives this example: Mary is at a conference where she notices Peter and

**Spreading attitude effect**
A liked or disliked person (or attitude object) may affect not only the evaluation of a second person directly associated but also others merely associated with the second person.

**Classical conditioning**
A memorable holiday puts us in a good mood which we associate with the people present, increasing our liking for them. When liking turns to love, our memories of contexts enrich our schema of a partner

Paul talking. She barely knows either one – they are affectively neutral. Then she sees Peter talking with Marc, someone she dislikes. First, Peter is now less likeable (evaluative conditioning); second, Paul is also less likeable (the spreading attitude effect). Peter's bad company has had a ripple effect on someone merely associated with him (in this case, Paul).

## Instrumental conditioning

Behaviour that is followed by positive consequences is reinforced and is more likely to be repeated, whereas behaviour that is followed by negative consequences is not. For example, parents use verbal reinforcers to encourage acceptable behaviour in their children – quiet, cooperative play wins praise. However, when they fight a reward is withheld or a punishment such as scolding is introduced. Instrumental learning can be accelerated or slowed by the frequency, temporal spacing and magnitude of the reinforcement (Kimble, 1961). When parents reward or punish their children they are shaping their attitudes on many issues, including religious or political beliefs and practices.

Adults' attitudes can also be shaped by verbal reinforcers. Insko (1965) showed that students' responses to an attitude survey had been influenced by an apparently unrelated telephone conversation, which took place a week earlier, in which particular opinions were 'rewarded' by the interviewer responding with the reinforcer 'good'.

Both classical and instrumental conditioning emphasise the role of direct reinforcers in how behaviour is acquired and maintained. This is relevant to attitudes when we define an attitude as a class of behaviour. This becomes fairly straightforward if an attitude is further operationalised as an *evaluative response* (Fishbein, 1967a; Osgood, Suci & Tannenbaum, 1957).

## Observational learning

Other psychologists view attitude formation as a *social* learning process, one that does not depend on direct reinforcers. Bandura (1973) and others have concentrated on a process of **modelling** (see also Chapters 12 and 14), where one person's behaviour is a template for another's. Modelling requires observation: individuals learn new responses, not by directly experiencing positive or negative outcomes but by observing the outcomes of others' responses. Having a successful working mother, for instance, is likely to influence the future career and lifestyle choices of a daughter. Likewise, ethnic attitudes can be instilled in otherwise naive children if the models are significant adults in their lives. This can be seen in the case of children who use ethnic slurs and insults, and claim to hate a certain ethnic group, but who are unable correctly to define the group or to show any factual knowledge regarding its members (Allport, 1954b; see also Chapter 11).

**Modelling**
Tendency for a person to reproduce the actions, attitudes and emotional responses exhibited by a real-life or symbolic model. Also called *observational learning*.

## Cognitive development

Other social psychologists prefer to think of attitude formation in terms of cognitive development. Cognitive consistency theories (such as balance; and cognitive dissonance, treated in Chapter 6) allow us to view attitude acquisition as an elaborative exercise of building connections (balanced or consonant) between more and more elements (e.g. beliefs). As the number of related elements increases, it is more likely that a generalised concept – an attitude – is being formed. Similarly, information integration theory can handle attitude learning as a case in which more and more items of information about an attitude object have been processed (say, by averaging their weights).

A difference between cognitive and behavioural approaches is the relative weight that each gives to internal events versus external reinforcement. Although since the 1970s there has been a shift in social psychology towards cognitive perspectives (Chapters 2 and 3), we should not ignore some advantages of behavioural approaches. These are linked to the

**If you smoke, your children are more likely to smoke.**

Call the NHS Smoking Helpline on 0800 169 0 169

*NHS*

*Crayon*

Smoking. Don't keep it in the family.    **SMOKEFREE**

**Observational learning**
Young children model their behaviour on significant adults. The remnants in an ashtray symbolises what is 'okay'

study of learning and often deal directly with developmental data (generated from studies of animals or children). Thus, learning theories continue to appeal to social psychologists who study attitude acquisition.

One interesting approach with both a behavioural and a perceptual flavour is Bem's (1972) **self-perception theory** (see Chapter 4 for details). Bem proposed that people acquire knowledge about what kind of person they are, and thus their attitudes, by examining their own behaviour and asking: 'Why did I do that?' A person may act for reasons that are not obvious and then determine their attitude from the most readily available cause. For example, if you often go for long walks, you may conclude that 'I must like them, as I'm always doing that'. Bem's theory suggests that people act, and form attitudes, without much deliberate thinking.

**Self-perception theory**
Bem's idea that we gain knowledge of ourselves only by making self-attributions: for example, we infer our own attitudes from our own behaviour.

## Sources of learning

### Parents

An important source of your attitudes is the actions of other people around you. For children their parents are a powerful influence, involving all the kinds of learning mentioned above (classical conditioning, instrumental conditioning and observational learning).

According to Connell (1972), however, although the correlation between the *specific* attitudes of parents and their children is generally positive, it is also surprisingly weak; the correlation is stronger for *broad* attitudes.

Jennings and Niemi (1968) found a 0.60 correlation between high-school children's preferences for a particular political party and their parents' choices, and a correlation of 0.88 between parents' and children's choices of religion. Of course, such correlations may be constrained by parental opposition, a common experience of adolescents. Many high-school pupils deliberately adopt, or appear to adopt, attitudes that are inconsistent with their parents' merely to be contrary. In a longitudinal study of values, Kasser, Koestner and Lekes (2002) found strong links between childhood environmental factors, such as parenting behaviour, and later adult values. Restrictive parenting, for example, experienced at age five was reflected in higher conformity values and lower self-directed values in adulthood. Values are discussed later in this chapter.

### Mass media

The mass media have a major influence on attitudes, and there is little question that television in particular plays an important part in attitude formation in children, particularly when attitudes are not strongly held (Goldberg & Gorn, 1974). A study by Chaffee, Jackson-Beeck, Durall & Wilson (1977) showed that, before age seven, American children get most of their political information from television and that this affected their views on politics and political institutions (Atkin, 1977; Rubin, 1978).

Among adults, MacKay and Covell (1997) reported a relationship between viewing sexual images of women in advertisements and holding attitudes sympathetic to sexual aggression (see also Chapter 12). While the impact of television on adults is generally less clear-cut (Oskamp, 1984), some discernible trends occur on a larger scale. Kellstedt (2003) conducted an extensive statistical analysis of changes in Americans' racial attitudes over the last half-century. He found that media coverage does more than reflect public opinion – it has helped shape it. Long periods of liberalism have been followed by periods of conservatism, and these eras have responded to cues in the American media.

The impact of commercials on children's attitudes has also been investigated. Atkin (1980) found that children who watched a lot of television were twice as likely as those who watched a little to believe that sugar-coated sweets and cereals were good for them. In the same study, two-thirds of a group of children who saw a circus strong man eat a breakfast cereal believed it would make them strong too! These findings are of particular concern in the light of murders committed by young children (e.g the murder in Liverpool in 1993 of 2-year-old James Bulger by two 10-year-old boys), and carried out in ways similar to those portrayed in certain films. Media effects on aggression are discussed in Chapter 12.

# Concepts related to attitudes

## Values

We have treated attitudes as a relatively high-level concept involving affect as a central dimension, with many theorists arguing that beliefs constitute an additional dimension. If we accept both views, an attitude is a set of integrated beliefs with an affective loading. From such an approach springs a further level of analysis, and another term, **values** (e.g., Bernard, Maio & Olson, 2003; Rohan, 2000).

Values and attitudes are usually measured differently. Attitudes are measured to reflect varying degrees of favourability towards an object, whereas values are rated for their importance as guiding principles in life. An early emphasis on the global concept of values

**Values**
A higher-order concept thought to provide a structure for organising attitudes.

was the basis for a psychological test (Allport & Vernon, 1931) designed to measure the relative importance to a person of six broad classes of value orientation:

1 *theoretical* – an interest in problem solving, the basis of how things work;

2 *economic* – an interest in economic matters, finance and money affairs;

3 *aesthetic* – an interest in the arts, theatre, music, etc;

4 *social* – a concern for one's fellows, a social welfare orientation;

5 *political* – an interest in political structures and power arrangements;

6 *religious* – a concern with theology, the afterlife and morals.

Rokeach (1973) later suggested that values should be conceived less in terms of interests or activities and more as preferred goals (end-states). He distinguished between *terminal values* (e.g. equality and freedom) and *instrumental values* (e.g. honesty and ambition). A terminal value, such as equality, could have significant effects on the way someone might feel about racial issues, which is just what Rokeach found. From this viewpoint, a value is a higher-order concept having broad control over an individual's more specific attitudes. For example, measuring values can help to predict people's attitudes to the unemployed (Heaven, 1990) and to beliefs in a just world (Feather, 1991). When values are primed, we are more likely to make choices consistent with our values. For example, if information enhances our thoughts about the environment, we are more likely to behave in an environmentally friendly way (Verplanken & Holland, 2002).

Himmelweit, Humphreys and Jaeger (1985) conducted a longitudinal study, spanning almost a quarter of a century, of social psychological influences on voting in Britain. They found that specific attitudes were usually poor predictors, while broader sociopolitical values and party identifications were much better predictors. In another large-scale study by Hewstone (1986), this time of attitudes of French, Italian, German and British students towards European integration, general value orientation changes were seen to have some influence on changed attitudes towards integration.

According to Feather (1994), values are general beliefs about desirable behaviour and goals, with an 'oughtness' quality about them. They both transcend attitudes and influence the form that attitudes take. Values offer standards for evaluating actions, justifying opinions and conduct, planning behaviour, deciding between different alternatives, engaging in social influence and presenting the self to others. Within the person, they are organised into hierarchies, and their relative importance may alter during a lifetime. Value systems vary across individuals, groups and cultures.

Feather (2002) tested some of these principles among a group of third-party participants in a study of an ongoing, major industrial dispute. Judgements about the quality of the behaviour (e.g. procedural fairness) of both the employer and the union were based on values such as authority, wealth, power, equality and being prosocial. Hofstede (1980) and S. H. Schwartz (1992), among others, have also explored the way that entire cultures can be characterised and differentiated by their underlying value systems (see Chapter 16).

Can values predict behaviour? If the target behaviour is a specific act, it is very unlikely, given that a value is an even more general concept than an attitude. Although Bardi and Schwartz (2003) found correlations between some values and self-reported congruent behaviour (e.g. traditionalism and observing traditional holiday customs), they did not collect actual behavioural data.

## Ideology

**Ideology**
A systematically interrelated set of beliefs whose primary function is explanation. It circumscribes thinking, making it difficult for the holder to escape from its mould.

**Ideology** overlaps to some extent with the term 'value'. It connotes an integrated and widely shared system of beliefs, usually with a social or political reference, that serves an explanatory function (Thompson, 1990). Most familiar to us are the religious and sociopolitical ideologies that serve as rallying points for many of the world's most intransigent intergroup conflicts (see Chapters 10 and 11). Ideologies have a tendency to make the state of things as they are seem quite natural (the naturalistic fallacy), to justify or legitimise the status quo (Jost & Hunyadi, 2002; Major, Quinton & McCoy, 2002), and to enhance hierarchical social relations (e.g. Sidanius, Levin, Federico & Pratto, 2001; Sidanius & Pratto, 1999). Ideologies also frame more specific values, attitudes and behavioural intentions (e.g. Crandall, 1994).

Tetlock (1989) has proposed that terminal values, such as those described by Rokeach (1973), underlie many *political ideologies*. For example, Machiavellianism as an ideology, named after Machiavelli (a sixteenth-century Florentine diplomat considered by some to have been the first social scientist), is the notion that craft and deceit are justified in pursuing and maintaining power in the political world (Saucier, 2000). Ideologies can vary as a function of two characteristics:

1 They may assign different priorities to particular values: traditionally, we might expect liberals and conservatives to rank 'individual freedom' and 'national security' in opposite ways.

2 Some ideologies are pluralistic and others monistic. A pluralistic ideology can tolerate a conflict of values: for example, neoliberalism as a pluralistic ideology emphasises economic growth and also a concern with social justice. A monistic ideology will be quite intolerant of conflict, seeing issues in starkly simplistic terms (see the discussion of authoritarianism in Chapter 10). An example of a monistic ideology is Manicheism – the notion that the world is divided between good and evil principles.

Billig (1991) has suggested that much of our everyday thinking arises from what he calls ideological dilemmas. Teachers, for example, face the dilemma of being an authority and yet encouraging equality between teacher and student. When conflict between values arises, it can trigger a clash of attitudes between groups. For example, Katz and Hass (1988) reported a polarisation of ethnic attitudes in a community when values such as communalism and individualism clashed.

Ideology, in the guise of ideological orthodoxy, has also been implicated in societal extremism. Ideology, because of its all-embracing explanatory function, provides an immensely comforting buffer against uncertainty; uncertainty about what to think, what to do, who one is, and ultimately the nature of existence (Hogg, 2007b, in press; Solomon, Greenberg, Pyszczynski & Pryzbylinski, 1995; Van den Bos, in press). It is only a short step to recognise that people will go to great lengths to protect their ideology and the group that defines it. One reason why religious ideologies are so powerful and enduring, and why religious fundamentalism arises, is precisely because organised religions are uncertainty-reducing groups that have sophisticated ideologies that define one's self and identity and normatively regulate both secular and existential aspects of life (Hogg, Adelman & Blagg, in press).

According to **terror management theory** (e.g. Greenberg, Solomon, & Pyszczynski, 1997; Pyszczynski, Greenberg, & Solomon, 1999; Solomon, Greenberg, & Pyszczynski, 1991) people may also subscribe to an ideology and defend their worldview as a way to buffer themselves against paralysing terror over the inevitability of their own death. Numerous studies have shown that making a person's own death salient leads to worldview defence.

## Social representations

Researchers who work in a **social representations** tradition have a somewhat different perspective on attitudes. In Chapter 3 we described social representations in detail. First introduced by Moscovici (1961) and based on earlier work by the French sociologist Emile Durkheim (1912/1995) on 'collective representations', social representations refer to the

**Terror management theory**
The notion that the most fundamental human motivation is to reduce the terror of the inevitability of death. Self-esteem may be centrally implicated in effective terror management.

**Social representations**
Collectively elaborated explanations of unfamiliar and complex phenomena that transform them into a familiar and simple form.

**Likert scale**
Scale that evaluates how strongly people agree/disagree with favourable/unfavourable statements about an attitude object. Initially, many items are tested. After item analysis, only those items that correlate with each other are retained.

**Acquiescent response set**
Tendency to agree with items in an attitude questionnaire. This leads to an ambiguity in interpretation if a high score on an attitude questionnaire can be obtained only by agreeing with all or most items.

**Unidimensionality**
A Guttman scale is cumulative: that is, agreement with the highest-scoring item implies agreement with all lower-scoring items.

**Guttman scale**
A scale that contains either favourable or unfavourable statements arranged hierarchically. Agreement with a strong statement implies agreement with weaker ones; disagreement with a weak one implies disagreement with stonger ones.

way that people elaborate simplified and shared understandings of their world through social interaction (Deaux & Philogene, 2001; Farr & Moscovici, 1984; Lorenzi-Cioldi & Clémence, 2001; Moscovici, 1981, 1988, 2000; Purkhardt, 1995).

Moscovici has maintained that people's beliefs are socially constructed; they are shaped by what other people believe and say and they are shared with other members of one's community:

> Our reactions to events, our responses to stimuli, are related to a given definition, common to all the members of the community to which we belong. (*Moscovici, 1983, p. 5*)

From an attitudinal perspective, the important point is that specific attitudes are framed by, and embedded within, wider representational structures, which are in turn grounded in social groups. In this sense, attitudes tend to reflect the society or groups in which people live their lives.

This type of perspective on attitudes reflects a broader 'top-down' perspective on social behaviour, which is a hallmark of European social psychology (see Chapter 1). It prompted the American social psychologist William McGuire (1986) to observe that 'the two movements serve mutually supplementary uses' in that the European concept of collective representations highlights how *alike* group members are, while the American individualist tradition shows how *different* they are (see also Tajfel, 1972).

Social representations may influence the evaluative tone of attitudes 'nested' within them. For example, Moliner and Tafani (1997) have argued that attitudes towards objects are based on the evaluative components of the representation of those objects, and that a change in attitudes towards an object may be accompanied by changes in the evaluative dimension of its representation.

Rafiq, Jobanuptra and Muncer (2006) studied how Muslim and Christian students in the UK represented the second Iraq war. Rafiq and colleagues focused on causal networks used by each group as explanations of the conflict. Muslims and Christians agreed that there were causal links (sometimes bi-directional) between racism, religious prejudice and the history of conflict in the Middle East; however, Christians were more likely than Muslims to believe that the war was connected with a hunt for terrorist cells in Iraq – a reason consistently emphasised by then-US President G. W. Bush. Ironically, God's Will did not feature in either the Muslim or the Christian causal network!

# Measuring attitudes

## Attitude scales

How should we measure attitudes; explicitly or implicitly? Some forms of attitude measurement can be completely explicit: people are simply asked to agree or disagree with various statements about their beliefs. Particularly in the early days of attitude research, in the 1930s, it was assumed that explicit measures would get at people's real beliefs and opinions. There was intense US media interest in predicting election results based on opinion polling (in particular, the Gallup Poll), and in establishing what election candidates believed and how they might act. The result was frenzied development of attitude questionnaires targeting a host of social issues. Several scales that were technically sophisticated for their time were developed by Thurstone, Likert, Guttman and Osgood, and are briefly described in Box 5.5.

**Expectancy-value model**
Direct experience with an attitude object informs a person how much that object should be liked or disliked in the future.

In addition to scales based on summing scores across items, other researchers tried to get a better fit between a single item and a specific behaviour. We might ask, can this fit be improved if an attitude measure includes both an evaluative and a belief component? To this end, Fishbein and Ajzen (1974) developed the **expectancy-value model**, in which each contributing belief underlying an attitude domain is weighted by the strength of its relationship to the attitude object. The main elements of this model were described earlier

## Research classic 5.5
### Attitude scales

An enormous volume of research that measured people's attitudes towards social and political issues was stimulated by four early attitude scales.

### Thurstone scale

When Thurstone (1928) published his landmark paper 'Attitudes can be measured', his approach was based on methods of psychophysical scaling in experimental psychology. In an innovative study of attitudes towards religion, more than 100 statements of opinion ranging from extremely favourable to extremely hostile were collected, statistically analysed and refined as a scale (Thurstone & Chave, 1929). Participants then classified the statements into eleven categories on a favourable–unfavourable continuum. Their responses were used to select a final scale of twenty-two items, two for each of the eleven points on the continuum, using items with the strongest of inter-judge agreement. Such a scale is then ready to measure other people's attitudes towards the issue. On a **Thurstone scale** a person's attitude score is calculated by averaging the scale values of the items endorsed.

### Likert scale

A Thurstone scale is tedious to construct, and Likert (1932) developed a technique that produces a reasonably reliable attitude measure with relative ease. Respondents use a five-point response scale to indicate how much they agree or disagree with each of a series of statements. The points use labels such as 'strongly agree', 'agree', 'undecided', 'disagree', 'strongly disagree', ranging numerically from 5 to 1.

A person's score is summed across the statements and the total used as an index of the person's attitude. When developing a **Likert scale**, researchers find that responses to questions will not correlate equally with the total score. Those that do not correlate well are considered unreliable and dropped. Any ambiguous items – those that do not differentiate between people with differing attitudes – are dropped. The remainder constitute the final scale and, when the responses are summed, measure a person's attitude.

Where possible, items are selected so that for half of the items 'agree' represents a positive attitude and for the other half it represents a negative attitude. The scoring of the latter set of items is reversed (i.e. 5 becomes 1, 4 becomes 2, etc.) before the item scores are summed. This procedure controls **acquiescent response set**, a bias that otherwise could affect a variety of psychometric (such as personality) scales.

### Guttman scale

A score on Thurstone and Likert scales does not have a unique meaning because two persons could receive the same score (averaged or summated) yet endorse quite different items. Guttman (1944) tried a different approach – a single, unidimensional trait can be measured by a set of statements that are ordered along a continuum ranging from least extreme to most extreme. Such a scale possesses **unidimensionality**. The statements vary from those that are easy to endorse to those that few people might endorse. Items on a **Guttman scale** are cumulative: acceptance of one item implies that the person accepts all other items that are less extreme. We could then predict a person's response to less extreme statements by knowing the most extreme item they will accept. Consider these items relating to the topic of inter-ethnic social contact – *I would accept people who are members of the immigrant ethnic group 'X':* . . . (1) *into my country;* . . . (2) *into my neighbourhood;* . . . (3) *into my house.* Agreement with (3) implies agreement with (1) and (2). Agreement with (2) implies agreement with (1), but not necessarily with (3). In practice, it is very difficult to develop a perfect unidimensional scale, which suggests that people respond on multiple dimensions rather than a single dimension.

### Osgood's semantic differential

Osgood (Osgood, Suci & Tannenbaum, 1957) avoided using opinion statements altogether by focusing on the connotative meaning that people give to a word or concept. Studies of connotative meanings of words show that one of the major underlying dimensions is evaluation – the goodness or badness implied by the word. The word 'friend' tends to be thought of as *good* and the word 'enemy' as *bad*. According to Osgood, this evaluative dimension corresponds to our definition of an attitude. We should therefore be able to measure attitudes by having people rate a particular concept on a set of evaluative semantic scales. The concept of 'nuclear power' could be measured by responses on several evaluative (seven-point) scales (e.g *good/bad, nice/awful, pleasant/unpleasant, fair/unfair, valuable/worthless*). An attitude score is averaged across the scales used. Osgood scales do not require writing attitude-relevant questions, and their reliability increases as more semantic scales are used. A disadvantage is that the measure can be too simple: it deals with evaluative meanings of a concept but not with opinions, which of course are the meat of the other classic scales.

in this chapter (see also Table 5.1). Despite some criticisms (see Eagly & Chaiken, 1993), this technique has had some predictive success in a variety of settings – in marketing and consumer research (Assael, 1981), politics (Bowman & Fishbein, 1978), family planning (Vinokur-Kaplan, 1978), classroom attendance (Fredericks & Dossett, 1983), seat-belt wearing (Budd, North & Spencer, 1984), preventing HIV infection (Terry, Gallois & McCamish, 1993), and how mothers feed their infants (Manstead, Proffitt & Smart, 1983).

## Using attitude scales today

Combinations of the Likert scale and the semantic differential have been used successfully to measure quite complex evaluations. For example, voters can be asked to evaluate various issues using a semantic differential scale. Then, using a Likert scale, they can be asked how they think each candidate stands on particular issues. Combining the two measures enables us to predict for whom they will vote (Ajzen & Fishbein, 1980).

The Likert scale has also contributed significantly to many modern questionnaires that start from the premise that the attitude being measured may be complex in having many underlying dimensions. The availability of powerful computer programs means that researchers are likely to choose from a variety of multivariate statistical methods such as factor analysis to analyse the underlying structure of questionnaire data.

Whereas Likert tested for unidimensionality in a fairly simple way by calculating item–total score correlations, factor analysis starts from a matrix based on correlations between all pairs of items making up the questionnaire scale. One can then estimate whether a single general factor (or dimension), or more than one factor, is required to explain the variance in the respondents' pattern of responses to the questionnaire. For example, your attitudes towards your country's possession of nuclear weapons might depend on your reactions to war, nuclear contamination and relationships with other countries. Each of these might be measured on a different dimension and so the questionnaire could consist of several sub-scales (see Oppenheim, 1992).

Sometimes, factor analysis unearths substructures underlying a set of items that can be both interesting and subtle. In the development of a scale designed to measure 'sexism towards women', Glick and Fiske (1996) found evidence for two underlying subscales – 'hostile sexism' and 'benevolent sexism' – pointing to a covert ambivalence in their participants (see Chapter 10).

In this treatment of attitude scales we have not dealt with issues relating to developing an effective questionnaire. For example, the order in which questions are put can have subtle effects upon the way that people respond (Schwarz & Strack, 1991; for an overview of developing a sound questionnaire, see Oppenheim, 1992).

## Physiological measures

Attitudes, particularly ones that have a strong evaluative or affective component, can also be measured indirectly by monitoring various physiological indices such as skin resistance (Rankin & Campbell, 1955), heart rate (Westie & DeFleur, 1959) and pupil dilation (Hess, 1965). Does your heart beat faster each time a certain person comes close? If so, we might surmise you have an attitude of some intensity!

Physiological measures have one big advantage over self-report measures: people may not realise that their attitudes are being assessed and, even if they do, they may not be able to alter their responses. This is why a polygraph or 'lie detector' is sometimes used in criminal investigations. However, physiological measures also have drawbacks since most are sensitive to variables other than attitudes (Cacioppo & Petty, 1981). Skin resistance can change in the presence of novel or incongruous stimuli that may have nothing to do with the attitude in question. Similarly, heart rate is sensitive to task requirements – problem-solving tasks raise heart rate, while vigilance tasks (such as watching a VDU

**The lie detector**
A suspect takes a polygraph test in a Texas police station

screen) usually lower it. Further, these measures provide limited information: they can indicate intensity of feeling but not direction. Two, totally opposed people who feel equally strongly about an issue cannot be distinguished.

One measure that can distinguish between positive and negative attitudes is facial expression. Building on Darwin's suggestion that different facial expressions are used to convey different emotions (see Chapter 15), Cacioppo and his colleagues (Cacioppo & Petty, 1979; Cacioppo & Tassinary, 1990) have linked facial muscle movements to underlying attitudes. They reasoned that people who agreed with a speech that they were listening to would display facial movements different from those of people who disagreed with the speech. To test this, they recorded the movements of specific facial muscles (associated with smiling or frowning) before and during a speech that advocated a conservative or a liberal view – either stricter or more lenient university regulations regarding alcohol or visiting hours. Before the speech, different patterns of muscle movement were associated with agreement compared with disagreement. These differences became more pronounced when people actually listened to the speeches. Thus, facial muscle movements provide a useful way of distinguishing people with favourable attitudes on a topic from those with unfavourable attitudes.

If attitudes, as internal states, can be inferred from external physiological indices such as heart rate and facial expression, why not take this one stage further and measure electrical activity in the brain. This idea underpins **social neuroscience** (e.g. Harmon-Jones & Winkielman, 2007; Lieberman, 2010; Ochsner, 2007; see Chapter 2), and in the context of attitude measurement the intensity and form of electrical activity and where it occurs in the brain should give an indication of what the attitude is.

**Social neuroscience**
The exploration of the neurological underpinnings of the processes traditionally examined by social psychology.

For example, Levin (2000) investigated racial attitudes by measuring event-related brain potentials (ERPs) that indicate electrical activity when we respond to different stimuli. An ERP waveform includes several components, each providing evidence of different types of processing. In Levin's study, where white participants viewed a series of white and black faces, an ERP component indicated that white faces received more attention – suggesting that participants were processing their racial ingroup more deeply and the racial outgroup

**Relative homogeneity effect**
Tendency to see outgroup members as all the same, and ingroup members as more differentiated.

more superficially. This is consistent with other experimental evidence that people tend to perceptually differentiate ingroup members more than outgroup members – called the **relative homogeneity effect** (see Chapter 11). In addition, there was greater ingroup evaluative bias shown by participants who were more prejudiced, assessed on an explicit attitude measure (Ito, Thompson & Cacioppo, 2004).

## Measures of overt behaviour

We may also measure and infer attitudes by recording what people do. Sometimes, what they really do does not accord with what they *say* they do. For example, people's verbal reports of behaviours such as smoking, calories consumed and dental hygiene practices may not correspond very well to their actual physical condition. However, if we do not take what is said at face value, but instead consider the entire discursive event (what is said, how it is said, what non-verbal cues accompany the words, and the context in which it all happens), we can do a better job of inferring behaviour from what people say (see Chapter 15).

### Unobtrusive measures

**Unobtrusive measures**
Observational approaches that neither intrude on the processes being studied nor cause people to behave unnaturally.

Counts of empty beer and whisky bottles in dustbins are examples of **unobtrusive measures** of attitudes towards alcohol in your neighbourhood, while chemists' records show which doctors prescribe new drugs. Bodily traces and archival records can furnish evidence of people's attitudes (Webb, Campbell, Schwartz & Sechrest, 1969). In a museum, the number of prints made by noses or fingers on a display case might show how popular the display was – and the height of the prints might indicate the viewers' ages! Public records and archival information can yield evidence about past and present community attitudes – for example the ebb and flow of authoritarianism and changes in prejudice (Simonton, 2003).

Changes in sex-role attitudes might be reflected in the roles of male and female characters in children's books. Library book withdrawals of fiction, not non-fiction, declined when television was introduced – suggesting one effect of television on people's behaviour. Will a book or play be more popular if it receives a favourable review? DVD rental stores' records of rental statistics also give an indication of trends in viewing preferences.

Non-verbal behaviour, which we discuss in Chapter 15, can also be used as an unobtrusive measure of people's attitudes. For example, people who like each other tend to sit closer together – so physical distance can be measured as an index of 'social distance' and tolerance of intimacy (Bogardus, 1925). Strangers in a waiting room who sit far apart from members of particular other groups are perhaps indicating intergroup antipathy, or maybe they are simply anxious about how to interact with a specific outgroup (Stephan & Stephan, 2000). Interpersonal distance can also measure fear. In one study (Webb, Campbell, Schwartz & Sechrest, 1969), adults told ghost stories to young children seated in a circle. The size of the circle of children grew smaller with each successive scary story!

Overall, however, unobtrusive measures are probably not as reliable as self-reported attitudes. Their value is that their limitations are different from those of standard measures. A researcher who wanted to be more confident of valid results would use both types and then correlate the data.

**Bogus pipeline technique**
A measurement technique that leads people to believe that a 'lie detector' can monitor their emotional responses, thus measuring their true attitudes.

We have discussed unobtrusive measures of behaviour in this section. Is it possible to have an obtrusive measure that will work? One instance is the **bogus pipeline technique** (Jones & Sigall, 1971), which is designed to convince participants that they cannot hide their true attitudes. People are connected to a machine said to be a lie detector and are told that it measures both the strength and direction of emotional responses, thus revealing their true attitudes and implying that there is no point in lying. Participants usually find this deception convincing and are less likely to conceal socially unacceptable attitudes such as racial prejudice (Allen, 1975; Quigley-Fernandez & Tedeschi, 1978), and socially undesirable or potentially embarrassing behaviours such as drinking in excess, snorting cocaine and having frequent oral sex (Tourangeau, Smith & Rasinski, 1997). So take care when you trial psychological equipment at the next university open day!

## Measuring covert attitudes

Two terms have been used in this and related literature, 'implicit' and 'unobtrusive'. Although both methods are designed to measure attitudes, Kihlstrom (2004) has made a conceptual distinction. Although it does not have a major impact on the discussion that follows, Kihlstrom argues that an unobtrusive method assesses an attitude that people are aware of but may be unwilling to reveal, whereas an implicit method assesses an attitude that people are not actually aware of.

Social psychologists have trialled a variety of implicit (or unobtrusive) measures to min-imise the tendency for people to conceal their underlying attitudes by responding in socially desirable ways (Crosby, Bromley & Saxe, 1980; Devine, 1989; Gregg, Seibt & Banaji, 2006). We discuss three methods: detecting bias in language use, the priming of attitudes, and the implicit association test (IAT).

### Bias in language use

Maass and her colleagues (Franco & Maass, 1996; Maass, 1999; Maass, Salvi, Arcuri & Semin, 1989) have found that there are positive ingroup and negative outgroup biases in the way that language is used. People are more likely to talk in abstract than concrete terms about undesirable characteristics of an outgroup, and vice versa for desirable characteristics. Consequently, the ratio of abstract to concrete language usage, in relation to desirable versus undesirable characteristics, could be used as an index of prejudiced attitudes towards a particular group. Other techniques have involved the detailed analysis of discourse to reveal hidden attitudes (van Dijk, 1987, 1993; see Chapter 15) and likewise of non-verbal commu-nication (Burgoon, Buller & Woodall, 1989; see Chapter 15). (What do you think of Rita's view of measuring attitudes in the third focus question?)

### Attitude priming

Fazio and his colleagues (Fazio, Jackson, Dunton & Williams, 1995) used **priming** to explore how we make a judgement more quickly when an underlying attitude is congruent with a 'correct' response. While looking at a series of photos of Black and White people, participants decided by pressing a button whether an adjective (from a series of positive and negative adjec-tives) that followed very quickly after a particular image was 'good' or 'bad'. White participants were slower in rating a positive adjective as good when it followed a Black image, and Black participants were slower in rating a positive adjective as good when it followed a white image.

Kawakami, Young and Dovidio (2002) used a similar rationale to explore how stereo-typic judgements follow when a social category is invoked. Students participated and were either in a primed group or a control (non-primed) group. There were two phases:

1  *Priming the category 'elderly'.* A series of photographs of two different age sets, elderly people and college-age people, were shown to the primed group in random order on a computer screen, one at a time for 250 milliseconds. Each photograph was followed by the word *old* ? and participants responded yes/no on either of two buttons.

2  *Activation of stereotypes.* Both groups were shown a list of strings of words (anagrams) and non-words and asked to respond yes/no if the word string was a real word or not. The real words were either age-stereotypic (e.g. serious, distrustful, elderly, pensioner) or not age-stereotypic (e.g. practical, jealous, teacher, florist).

There are two significant effects in the response latencies (time taken to respond) shown in Figure 5.8. First, the primed group took longer overall to respond than the control group. It is likely that the concept *elderly* activates a behavioural representation in memory of people who are mentally and physically slower than the young. The participants

**Priming**
Activation of accessible categories or schemas in memory that influence how we process new information.

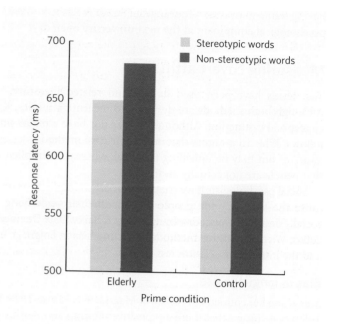

**Figure 5.8**  Priming the category 'elderly' can activate stereotypes

- The category 'elderly' was primed when participants chose whether persons in a series of photographs were *old* or not
- The primed participants then decided whether word strings were real words or non-words. Half of the real words were age-stereotypic

*Source:* based on data from Kawakami, Young & Dovidio (2002)

unwittingly slowed down when they responded. Second, the primed group (but not the control group) were a little quicker in responding to age-stereotypic words.

## Implicit association test

**Implicit association test**
Reaction-time test to measure attitudes – particularly unpopular attitudes that people might conceal.

In a generally similar way to attitude priming, Greenwald and his colleagues (Greenwald et al., 2002; Greenwald, McGhee & Schwartz, 1998; also see Kihlstrom, 2004) developed the **implicit association test** (IAT) (see Box 5.6) using a computer display coupled with responding on a keyboard. Greenwald, McGhee and Schwartz aimed to reveal underlying negative interethnic attitudes, for example, by comparing the response latencies of American Japanese with American Koreans. The Japanese responded more quickly when a Japanese name was paired with a pleasant word, and the Koreans did the same when a Korean name

## Research and applications 5.6
### The implicit association test

Cognitive research methods used in social cognition have produced an ingenious solution to the problem of measuring underlying attitudes in contexts where people may want to conceal what they really think – the implicit association test (IAT) (Greenwald, McGhee & Schwartz, 1998).

Based on the ideas that attitudes are associative mental networks and that associations are stronger if the attitude exists than if it doesn't, it follows that people will more quickly link concepts that are related than those that are not. So, if you dislike property developers, you will more quickly respond 'yes' to the word 'nasty' and

'no' to the word 'nice' than if you do not have a negative attitude towards developers. The IAT has participants press different keys on a keyboard or button box to match concepts (e.g. Algerian, lazy). What happens is that, where an attitude exists, the reaction is much faster when the concepts share a response key than when they do not.

The IAT has become remarkably popular in recent years as a technique for measuring prejudice in liberal Western societies such as the United States (see Chapter 10). It appears to be internally consistent and well correlated with, and often superior to, other measures of prejudice and implicit attitudes (Cunningham, Preacher & Banaji, 2001; Greenwald et al., 2002). It seems that the test can even measure newly emergent negative attitudes towards very minimally defined laboratory groups (Ashburn-Nardo, Voils & Monteith, 2001).

was paired with a pleasant word. (Reflect on the fourth focus question at the beginning of this chapter). In their review of implicit measures used in social cognition research, Fazio and Olson (2003b) noted that much of the data relating to the IAT is based on 'known-groups' – people who differ in an expected way. For example, when East Germans and West Germans responded more positively towards their respected ingroup (Kuhnen, Schiessl, Bauer, Paulig, Poehlmann et al., 2001). Fazio and Olson have asked for more convincing evidence that the IAT has predictive validity (i.e from IAT responses to actual behaviour). Fiedler, Messner and Bluemke (2006) have added methodological concerns about the IAT as well, so the test's progress report at this stage is mixed.

## Concluding thoughts

Attitudes have been treated as comprising three components: cognitive, affective and behavioural. Traditional research using questionnaires uses items about beliefs to measure the degree of affect (like or dislike) towards an attitude object. A well-researched questionnaire is usually based on a quantitative scale involving statistical analysis. Older questionnaire data were often not checked against real behavioural outcomes (such as the result of an election). More recently, some researchers versed in experimental methods in social cognition have shifted their focus towards using implicit measures, being less concerned with scaling individuals. They are much more interested in uncovering what people may try to conceal and in enlightening our understanding of how attitudes are structured and how they function. In Fazio and Olson's (2003b) review, implicit measures have some way to go to yield consistently valid and reliable results, but they hold promise for the future.

We should also remember that the failure to detect an attitude does not imply that it does not exist; the way we have chosen to measure it may limit our capacity to unearth it. Furthermore, an attitude may 're-emerge' after a period of time. Consider the very public expressions of racism in recent years by national figures in a number of countries. In the case of race, has an attitude re-emerged that was more prevalent in years gone by, or is it an overt expression of a commonly held attitude that runs counter to the usually expressed norm of equality? Chapter 10 confronts some of these issues.

# Summary

- Attitudes have been a major interest of social psychologists for many years. They have been described as the most important concept in social psychology.

- Theories of attitude structure generally agree that attitudes are lasting, general evaluations of socially significant objects (including people and issues). Some emphasise that attitudes are relatively enduring organisations of beliefs and behavioural tendencies towards social objects.

- Attitude structure has been studied mostly from a cognitive viewpoint. Balance theory and the theory of cognitive dissonance (see Chapter 6) suggested that people strive to be internally consistent in their attitudes and beliefs.

- The link between attitudes and behaviour has been a source of controversy. The apparently poor predictive power of attitude measures led to a loss of confidence in the concept of attitude itself. Fishbein argued that attitudes can indeed predict behaviour. However, if the prediction concerns a specific act, the measure of attitude must also be specific.

- The interrelated theories of reasoned action and planned behaviour included the need to relate a specific act to a measure of the intention to perform that act. Other variables that affect the predicted behaviour are norms provided by other people and the extent to which the individual has control over the act.

- A strong attitude has a powerful evaluative association with the attitude object. It is more accessible in memory and more likely to be activated and the related behaviour performed. A more accessible attitude can involve a cost; high accessibility can lead to insensitivity to change in the attitude object.

- Attitudes that are accessible are more likely to be acted on.

- The prediction of behaviour from an attitude can be improved partly by accounting for moderator variables (situational and personality factors).

- Attitudes are learned. They can be formed by direct experience, by conditioning, by observational learning and by drawing inferences from our own behaviour (self-perception).

- Parents and the mass media are powerful sources of attitude learning in children.

- A value is a higher-order concept that can play a guiding and organising role in relation to attitudes. Ideology and social representations are other related concepts.

- Measuring attitudes is both important and difficult. Traditional attitude scales of the 1930s are less frequently used today. While the response format of many modern measures is still based on the old Likert scale, the data are analysed by sophisticated statistical programs.

- A variety of physiological and behavioural indexes, both explicit and implicit, have been used to measure attitudes. The implicit association test has proved particularly popular. Brain imaging technology is also being used to record neural processes correlated with implicit attitudes.

## Literature, film and TV

### 1984

George Orwell's 1949 novel about life in a fictional totalitarian regime, based on Stalin's Soviet Union. The book shows how such a regime controls all aspects of human existence, and has a particular emphasis on the crucial role of ideology. Through the creation of a new language, 'Newspeak', the regime is able to control thought and the way that people view the world. The book touches on the relationship between language and thought (see Chapter 15), and how language constrains and reflects what we can easily think about.

### The Office

TV series in which David Brent (played by Ricky Gervais) and Gareth Keenan (played by Mackenzie Crook) are both prejudiced in old-fashioned and modern ways. Their antics are acutely embarrassing, and a wonderful illustration of how prejudiced attitudes reveal themselves in behaviour – all played out in a suburban British office environment.

### A Few Good Men

1992 film directed by Rob Reiner, with Tom Cruise, Jack Nicholson, Demi Moore, Kevin Bacon and Kiefer Sutherland. Cruise and Moore are defence attorneys who have to find out what really happened in a murder at the Guantanamo Bay military base in Cuba. Different tactics are used to try to see through behaviour, and normative responses, to what people really know. The entire genre of courtroom dramas is often about the problem of discovering underlying attitudes and beliefs from what people say and do.

### The Wicker Man

This 1973 cult shocker follows a devout Christian police sergeant played by Edward Woodward as he investigates the disappearance of a little girl on a remote Scottish Island. His Christian attitudes are challenged during a series of clashes with the inhabitants who have pagan beliefs and practice ancient rituals but his strength of conviction is demonstrated by his resistance to their way of life, despite temptation. In his final moments, as he is burnt in sacrifice within their 'wicker man' he recites the Lord's Prayer, a poignant demonstration that his behaviour is informed by his attitudes and beliefs.

### Pride and Prejudice

Jane Austen's classic 1813 novel about life and love in the genteel rural society of the day. The focal characters are Elizabeth and Darcy. One of the key features of this society is the possibility of misunderstanding based on the fact that there are strong normative pressures that inhibit the expression of one's true attitudes.

## Guided questions

1 What we do does not always follow from what we think. Why not?

2 What is the theory of *planned behaviour*? How can it be used to improve the predictive power of an attitude measure? Give an example from research.

3 Discuss the meaning of attitude accessibility and attitude strength. Illustrate your answer.

4 How are attitudes learned?

5 Outline the connections between attitudes, values and ideology. Give an example of each. You can get a brief outline of the recent Hamas ideology in Chapter 5 of MyPsychLab at **www.mypsychlab.co.uk** (watch *Israel Gaza Hamas recent history explained and Hamas ideology,* see **http://www.youtube.com/watch?v=MdvN9s-YTic**).

## Learn more

Banaji, M. R., & Heiphetz, L. (2010). Attitudes. In S. T. Fiske, D. T. Gilbert, & G. Lindzey (eds), *Handbook of social psychology* (5th ed., Vol. 1, pp. 353–93). New York: Wiley. A completely up-to-date, comprehensive and detailed discussion of attitude research.

Eagly, A. H. & Chaiken, S. (2005). Attitude research in the 21st century: The current state of knowledge. In D. Albarracin, B. T. Johnson & M. P. Zanna (eds), *The handbook of attitudes* (pp. 742–67). Mahwah, NJ: Erlbaum.

Fazio, R. H., & Olson, M. A. (2007). Attitudes: Foundations, functions, and consequences. In M. A. Hogg & J. Cooper (eds), *The SAGE handbook of social psychology: Concise student edition* (pp. 123–45). London: SAGE. A readable yet detailed overview of attitude theory and research.

Kihlstrom, J. F. (2004). Implicit methods in social psychology. In C. Sansone, C. C. E. Morf & A. T. Panter (eds), *The SAGE handbook of methods in social psychology* (pp. 195–212). Thousand Oaks, CA: SAGE. A survey of methods used to assess people's unconscious (or implicit) attitudes, beliefs, and other mental states.

Maio, G., & Haddock, G. (2010). *The science of attitudes*. London: SAGE. A mid- to upper-level text dedicated to the science of attitudes – written by two leading attitude researchers.

Oppenheim, A. N. (1992). *Questionnaire design, interviewing and attitude measurement* (2nd ed.). London: Pinter. A well-illustrated and comprehensive guide with easy-to-follow examples.

Robinson, J. P., Shaver, P. R., & Wrightsman, L. S. (eds) (1991). *Measures of personality and social psychological attitudes*. New York: Academic Press. A source-book of scales that have been used in social psychology and the study of personality.

Schwarz, N. (1996). Survey research: Collecting data by asking questions. In G. R. Semin & K. Fiedler (eds), *Applied social psychology* (pp. 65–90). London: SAGE. A brief bird's-eye view of questionnaire design; with examples.

Terry, D. J., & Hogg, M. A. (eds) (2000). *Attitudes, behavior, and social context: The role of norms and group membership*. Mahwah, NJ: Erlbaum. A collection of chapters discussing attitudes and attitude phenomena form the perspective of group norms, group membership and social identity.

Refresh your understanding, assess your progress and go further with interactive summaries, questions, podcasts and much more at **www.mypsychlab.co.uk**

## This chapter discusses

- The persuasion process
- Communicator, message and audience
- Dual-process models of persuasion
- Tactics for enhancing compliance
- Cognitive dissonance and attitude change
- Resistance to persuasion

## Focus questions

1. Someone offers you what you believe is a fair price to buy your prized racing bike. After they have checked their bank balance, the would-be purchaser reduces the offer by 15 per cent, saying that's all they can afford. Could such a tactic work? This is the low-ball technique and is discussed by Robert Cialdini in Chapter 6 of MyPsychLab at www.mypsychlab.co.uk (watch the car salesman example: Robert Cialdini).

2. You have just joined the army. Along with other cadets you listen to an amazing talk by an officer skilled in the use of survival techniques in difficult combat conditions. Among other things, he asks you to eat some fried grasshoppers. 'Try to imagine this is the real thing! You know, you might have to do this to save your life one day,' he says. Despite your first reaction, you go ahead and eat them. Would you end up liking the delicacy more if the officer's style of presentation was warm and friendly or cold and distant?

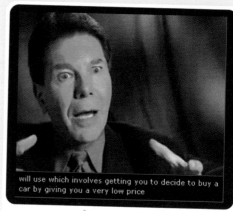

will use which involves getting you to decide to buy a car by giving you a very low price

Go to **mypsychlab** to explore video and test your understanding of key topics addressed in this chapter.

---

Refresh your understanding with interactive summaries, explore topics further with video and audio clips and assess your progress with quick test and essay questions by logging to the accompanying website at **www.mypsychlab.co.uk**

# Chapter 6
## Persuasion and attitude change

# Attitudes, arguments and behaviour

In Chapter 5 we saw that attitudes do not readily predict behaviour, and that the attitude–behaviour relationship can be so weak that some researchers have, in frustration, even suggested abandoning the attitude concept entirely.

In this chapter we focus on how attitudes can change over time, concentrating our attention on what kinds of intervention might bring about such change, and on the nature of the processes involved. By the time we have finished, we trust you will conclude that much of the reservation about the usefulness of the concept of attitude is misguided. In particular, we hope to show that discrepancies between attitudes and behaviour, rather than being an embarrassment to attitude theory, actually engage the very processes through which **attitude change** can occur.

The persuasion and attitude change literature is enormous (Albarracín & Vargas, 2010; Maio & Haddock, 2010; Visser & Cooper, 2007) – there are thousands of studies and a daunting variety of theories and perspectives. In our coverage we have focused on two general orientations. The first concentrates on people's use of arguments to convince others that a change of mind, and perhaps of behaviour, is needed. Research in this area has focused on the nature of the message – that is, the persuasive communication that will be effective – and considers a large number of variables that may determine what will do the trick in changing another person's point of view. Obvious areas of application relate to political propaganda and advertising.

The second orientation focuses on the active participation of the person. By getting people to carry out certain activities, we may actually be trying to change their underlying attitudes. This path to attitude change is the focus of **cognitive dissonance**, one of the consistency theories of attitude referred to in Chapter 5. Whereas the first orientation starts from the premise that you reason with people to change how they think and act, the second orientation eliminates reasoning. Simply persuade others to act differently, even if you have to use trickery; later they may come to *think* differently (i.e. change their attitude) and should then continue acting the way you want.

## Persuasive communications

The receptive powers of the masses are very restricted, and their understanding is feeble. On the other hand, they quickly forget. Such being the case, all effective propaganda must be confined to a few bare essentials and those must be expressed as far as possible in

**Attitude change**
Any significant modification of an individual's attitude. In the persuasion process this involves the communicator, the communication, the medium used, and the characteristics of the audience. Attitude change can also occur by inducing someone to perform an act that runs counter to an existing attitude.

**Cognitive dissonance**
State of psychological tension, produced by simultaneously having two opposing cognitions. People are motivated to reduce the tension, often by changing or rejecting one of the cognitions. Festinger proposed that we seek harmony in our attitudes, beliefs and behaviours, and try to reduce tension from inconsistency among these elements.

**Persuading the masses**
Hitler felt that the content of an effective public message needed to be simple. Slogans were a key ingredient of Nazi propaganda

stereotyped formulas. These slogans should be persistently repeated until the very last individual has come to grasp the idea that has been put forward. If this principle be forgotten and if an attempt be made to be abstract and general, the propaganda will turn out ineffective; for the public will not be able to digest or retain what is offered to them in this way. Therefore, the greater the scope of the message that has to be presented, the more necessary it is for the propaganda to discover that plan of action which is psychologically the most efficient. (*Hitler,* Mein Kampf, *1933*)

Has there ever been a more dramatic, mesmerising and chilling communicator than Adolf Hitler? His massive audiences at the Nazi rallies of the 1930s and 1940s might not have been so impressed had they known what he thought of them. The extreme case of Hitler, but also of other demagogues, allows us to connect the study of persuasive communication to leadership (see Chapter 9), rhetoric (e.g. Billig, 1991, 1996), and social mobilisation and crowd behaviour (see Chapter 11).

At a more day-to-day level, research on the relationship between **persuasive communication** and attitude change is more narrowly focused, and has been most thoroughly applied to advertising and marketing (Johnson, Pham, & Johar, 2007). According to Schwerin and Newell (1981, p. 7), behavioural change 'obviously cannot occur without [attitude change] having taken place'. For a long time, social psychologists have been interested in the nature of successful versus unsuccessful persuasion. Yet, despite the large part that persuasive messages play in influencing behaviour, only in the past forty or so years have social scientists studied what makes persuasive messages effective.

**Persuasive communication**
Message intended to change an attitude and related behaviours of an audience.

Systematic investigation began towards the end of the Second World War, at a time when President Roosevelt was concerned that Americans, after being victorious in Europe, would lose the will to fight on against Japan. Carl Hovland was contracted by the US War Department to investigate how propaganda could be used to rally support for the American war effort – as it already had for the German cause by Hitler and the Nazi party. After the war, Hovland continued this work at Yale University in what was the first coordinated research programme dealing with the social psychology of persuasion. Research funding was again politically motivated, this time by Cold War considerations – the United States' perception of threat from the Soviet Union, and its 'wish to justify its ways to the classes and win the hearts and minds of the masses' (McGuire, 1986, p. 99). The main features of this pioneering work were outlined in the research team's book, *Communication and persuasion* (Hovland, Janis & Kelley, 1953). They suggested that the key to understanding why people attend to, understand, remember and accept a persuasive message is to study the characteristics of the person presenting the message, the contents of the message, and the characteristics of the receiver of the message.

The general model of the Yale approach, shown in Figure 6.1, is still employed as the basis of contemporary *communications theory* in marketing and advertising (see Belch & Belch, 2007). Hovland, Janis and Kelley asked, 'Who says what to whom and with what effect?' and studied three general variables involved in persuasion:

1  the communicator, or the source (who);

2  the communication, or message (what);

3  the audience (to whom).

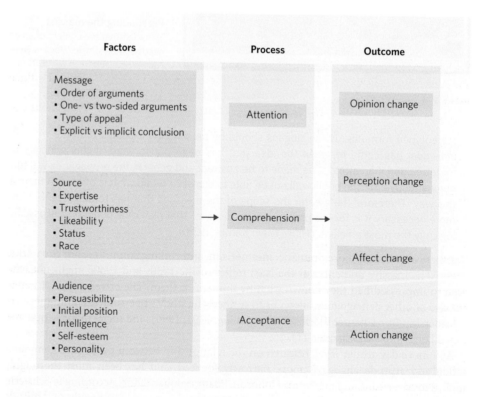

**Figure 6.1** The Yale approach to communication and persuasion

In this classic research, various message, source and audience factors were found to affect the extent that people can be persuaded. See Box 6.1 for details of such message factors

*Source:* based on Janis & Hovland (1959)

## Real world 6.1
### Persuasive communications that can lead to attitude change

#### WHO: source factors

- Experts are more persuasive than non-experts. The same arguments carry more weight when delivered by someone who seems to know all the facts (Hovland & Weiss, 1952).

- Popular and attractive communicators are more effective than unpopular or unattractive ones (Kiesler & Kiesler, 1969).

- People who speak rapidly are more persuasive than people who speak slowly. Rapid speech gives an impression of 'I know what I'm talking about' (Miller, Maruyama, Beaber & Valone, 1976).

#### WHAT: message factors

- We are more easily persuaded if we think the message is not deliberately intended to manipulate us (Walster & Festinger, 1962).

- A message in a powerless linguistic style (frequent hedges, tag questions, hesitations) is less persuasive than one in a powerful linguistic style. A powerless style gives a negative impression of both the arguments and the speaker (Blankenship & Holtgraves, 2005).

- Messages that arouse fear can be very effective. For example, to stop people smoking we might show them pictures of cancerous lungs (Leventhal, Singer & Jones, 1965).

#### TO WHOM: audience factors

- People with low self-esteem are persuaded more easily than people with high self-esteem (Janis, 1954).

- People are sometimes more susceptible to persuasion when they are distracted than when paying full attention, at least when the message is simple (Allyn & Festinger, 1961).

- People in the 'impressionable years' are more susceptible to persuasion than those who are older (Krosnick & Alwin, 1989).

Hovland and his colleagues identified four distinct steps in the persuasion process: attention, comprehension, acceptance and retention. This research programme spanned nearly three decades and produced a vast amount of data. Box 6.1 is a summary of the main findings.

A taste of research over many years that has a real life flavour is shown in Box 6.1. If you were planning to make a public campaign as persuasive as possible, there are points to bear in mind: some communicators, message strategies and speech styles are more effective than others; and the nature of the audience needs to be accounted for.

Not all findings from the early Yale research programme have lasted. Baumeister and Covington (1985) found that people with high self-esteem are just as easily persuaded as those with low self-esteem, but they do not want to admit it. When persuasion does occur, people may even deny it. Bem and McConnell (1970) reported that when people do succumb to persuasion they conveniently fail to recall their original opinion.

Most contemporary social psychologists view the persuasion process as a series of steps. They do not always agree about what the important steps are, but they do agree that the audience has at least to pay attention to the communicator's message, understand the content and think about what was said (Eagly & Chaiken, 1984). The audience's thoughts are critical in this process (Petty & Cacioppo, 1981); the message will ultimately be accepted if it arouses favourable thoughts, whereas it will be rejected if the recipients argue strongly against it in their minds.

People are not oblivious to persuasion attempts. We can hardly avoid commercial advertising, public education programmes and political propaganda. Interestingly, most people consider that they are less likely to be influenced than others by advertisements. This has been called the **third-person effect** ('You and I are not influenced, but they are'). For example, if we see a mundane product being advertised by using attractive models in an exotic setting, we assume that we (and those like us) are wiser than others to the tricks of the advertising industry. In reality, we are just as susceptible.

**Third-person effect**
Most people think that they are less influenced than others by advertisements.

Duck and her associates have conducted a series of studies of the third-person effect, demonstrating its application to political advertising and AIDS prevention (see Duck, Hogg & Terry, 2000).

In the next three sections, we look at each of the three links in the persuasion chain: the communicator, the message and the audience. However, in any given context all three are of course operative. Some of the studies noted below do indeed analyse more than one of these three variables at a time, and they often interact: for example, whether an argument should present a one-sided or a two-sided case can depend on how intelligent the audience is.

## The communicator

The Yale communication programme showed early on that there is a group of variables relating to characteristics of the source (communicator) that can have significant effects on the acceptability of a message to an audience. A high level of expertise, good physical looks and extensive interpersonal and verbal skills make a communicator more effective. Triandis (1971) has argued that a communicator who is an expert, with knowledge, ability and skill, demands more of our respect. Furthermore, people we feel familiar, close and attracted to, are able to exert more influence over us than others. There are other people who have power and can therefore exert some control over the kinds of reinforcement we might receive. In all of these cases, such sources of influence are likely to have the best chance of persuading us to change our attitudes and behaviour.

### Source credibility

The communicator variable affects the acceptability of persuasive messages. Other source characteristics playing a part in whether recipients will accept or reject a persuasive message include attractiveness, likeability and similarity. Source *attractiveness* is exploited mercilessly by the advertising industry. In the 1980s the American actor Bill Cosby was used extensively in television commercials advertising everything from home computers to frozen ice-cream, while rock stars Michael Jackson and Tina Turner advertised soft drinks. The assumption of these advertising campaigns is that attractive, popular and likeable spokespersons are persuasive, and thus are instrumental in enhancing consumer demand for a product. Attitude research generally supports this logic (Chaiken, 1979, 1983).

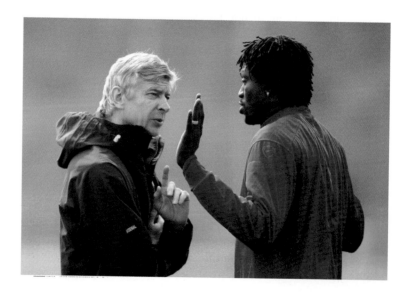

**Source credibility**
This is not a job for you! It takes a top manager to advise Alex Song about team tactics

With regard to *similarity*, because we tend to like people who are similar to us we are more persuaded by similar than dissimilar sources: for example, a member of your peer group should be more persuasive than a stranger. However, it is not quite this simple (Petty & Cacioppo, 1981). When the issue concerns a matter of taste or judgement (e.g. who was Italy's greatest football player of all time?), similar sources are accepted more readily than dissimilar sources. But when the issue concerns a matter of fact (e.g. at which Olympic Games did your country win its greatest number of gold medals?), dissimilar sources do better (Goethals & Nelson, 1973).

We have already noted that no single communication variable can be treated in isolation, and that what works best in the persuasion process is an interaction of three categories of variables ('communication language' terms are given in parentheses):

1  The **source** (sender) – from whom does the communication come?

2  The **message** (signal) – what medium is used, and what kinds of argument are involved?

3  The **audience** (receiver) – who is the target?

**Source**
The point of origin of a persuasive communication.

**Message**
Communication from a source directed to an audience.

**Audience**
Intended target of a persuasive communication.

Many experiments have focused on a single variable; others on two variables, one from each of two categories. An example of the latter kind was a study by Bochner and Insko (1966), which dealt with source *credibility* in combination with the discrepancy between the opinion of the target and that of the source. With respect to credibility, Bochner and Insko expected that an audience would pay more attention to the opinion of the communicator who was thought to be more believable. They predicted that there is more room for attitude change when the target's opinion is more discrepant from that of the source.

Bochner and Insko's participants were students who were initially asked how much sleep was required to maintain one's health. Most said eight hours. They were then exposed to two sources of opinion that varied in expertise and therefore credibility. One was a Nobel Prize-winning physiologist with expertise in sleep research (higher credibility) and the other a YMCA instructor (lower credibility). Discrepancy was manipulated in terms of the amount of variation between student opinion and that of the source. If the source said that five hours was enough, the discrepancy was three hours with respect to the typical view of eight hours: the pressure to shift should be higher than if the discrepancy was only one hour. However, what would happen if the source said that two hours was sufficient? Look at the results in Figure 6.2.

In terms of the discrepancy variable, more opinion change occurred at moderate levels of difference between the students and the source. It seems that extreme discrepancy is not a good tactic in influencing a target. The audience will resist if the difference is too great and may look for ways of discrediting the communicator ('They don't know what they are talking about!'). However, this effect interacted with the variable of credibility. It was the expert who could induce the greatest amount of change, and this took place when discrepancy was marked. In Bochner and Insko's study, the change was maximal when the highly credible source advocated one hour of sleep and students had suggested eight hours, a discrepancy of seven hours.

## The message

> An important idea not communicated persuasively is like having no idea at all. (*Bernbach, 2002*)

Several message variables have been intensively investigated for their relative power to induce attitude change. When, for example, should we present both sides of an argument rather than just our own? This variable seems to interact quite strongly with characteristics of the audience. If the audience is against the argument but is also fairly intelligent, it is more effective to present both sides. However, it is better to present only one side if a less

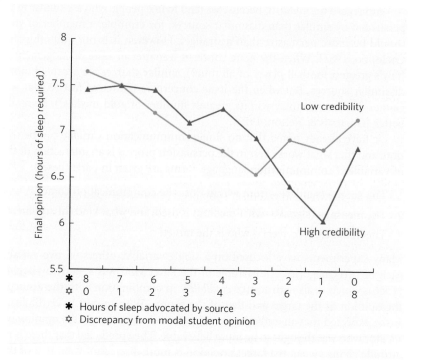

**Figure 6.2** The effect of communicator credibility and position discrepancy on opinion change

As a position adopted in a message becomes increasingly discrepant from what most people would accept, a more credible communicator becomes very effective in inducing opinion change

*Source*: based on data from Bochner & Insko (1966)

intelligent audience is already favourably disposed towards the argument (Lumsdaine & Janis, 1953; McGinnies, 1966).

Comparative advertising, in which a rival product is presented as inferior to a target product, is a common instance of using two-sided messages. When a consumer is not very motivated to buy the target product, comparative advertising can work (Pechmann & Esteban, 1994). An attentive and interested consumer is likely to process message information quite carefully, whereas comparative advertising is simply geared to making a product appear better. Explanations of how messages are handled in terms of dual-processing models of attitude change are dealt with below. Other examples of message variables that have been studied are shown in Box 6.1.

### Effects of repetition

In the advertising industry, it is a maxim that a message needs repeating often in order to be both understood and recalled. A sceptic might conclude that this maxim is self-interested – it justifies more advertising and thus increased profit for advertising agencies. If we believe the advertising industry, however, this is not a major motive. According to Ray (1988), the main goal is to strive for repetition minimisation: that is, to have the maximum impact with the minimum exposure and therefore the most cost-effective expenditure. It seems that television advertising exposure reinforces preferences more than it motivates brand choices; and that the optimum rate is two to three times per week (Tellis, 1987).

In general, the issue of message repetition invites, as we shall see below, examination of the way in which information is processed and of how memory works. Somewhat more startling is a finding by Arkes, Boehm and Xu (1991) that simple repetition of a statement makes it appear more true! Repeated exposure to an object clearly increases familiarity with that object. Repetition of a name can make that name seem famous (Jacoby, Kelly, Brown & Jasechko, 1989). (Note also that an increase in familiarity between people can increase interpersonal liking: see Chapter 13.) There is a catch to the use of repetition, identified in a study of TV and internet advertising: it may not work very well with a totally new product, and may even become decreasingly effective. Even a little brand familiarity helps (Campbell & Keller, 2003).

Another variable that has received substantial attention, because of the way in which it has been used by the media to induce people to obey the law or to care for their health, is the use of fear.

## Does fear work?

Fear-arousing messages may enhance persuasion – but how fearful can a message become and still be effective? Many agencies in our community persist with forms of advertising that are intended to frighten us into complying with their advice or admonitions. Health workers may visit the local school to lecture children on how 'smoking is dangerous to your health'. To drive the point home, they might show pictures of a diseased lung. Television advertising may remind you that 'if you drink, don't drive', and perhaps try to reinforce this message with graphic scenes of carnage on the roads. In the late 1980s an advertising campaign associated the Grim Reaper with unsafe sexual practices and the likelihood of contracting HIV. Does this work? The answer is a mixed one.

In an early study by Janis and Feshbach (1953), there were three different experimental conditions under which participants were encouraged to take better care of their teeth. In a low-fear condition, they were told of the painful outcomes of diseased teeth and gums, and suggestions were made about how to maintain good oral health. In a moderate-fear condition, the warning about oral disease was more explicit. In a high-fear condition, they were told that the disease could spread to other parts of their body, and very unpleasant visual slides were used showing decayed teeth and diseased gums. The participants reported on their current dental habits and were followed up one week later. Janis and Feshbach found an inverse relationship between degree of (presumed) fear arousal and change in dental hygiene practices. The low-fear participants were taking the best care of their teeth after one week, followed by the moderate-fear group and then the high-fear group.

Leventhal, Watts and Pagano (1967) reported a conflicting result from a study of how a fearful communication might aid in persuading people to stop smoking. The participants were volunteers who wished to give up smoking. In a moderate-fear condition, the participants listened to a talk with charts illustrating the link between death from lung cancer and the rate at which cigarettes were used. In a high-fear condition, they also saw a graphic film about an operation on a patient with lung cancer. Their results showed a greater willingness to stop smoking among people in the high-fear condition.

How do we explain the discrepancy between these results? Both Janis (1967) and McGuire (1969) suggested that an inverted U-curve hypothesis might be applied to the conflicting results (see Figure 6.3). McGuire's analysis distinguishes two parameters that could control the way we respond to a persuasive message, one involving comprehension and the other involving the degree to which we yield to change. The more we can understand what is being presented to us and can conceive of ways to put this into effect, the more likely we are to go along with a particular message.

According to Keller and Block (1995) and in line with dual-process models of information processing (see Chapters 2 and 5) when fear is at a very low level an audience may be little motivated to attend to the message because the message does not spell out sufficiently the harmful consequences of an act. As fear increases, so does arousal, interest and attention to what is going on. However, a very frightening presentation of an idea may arouse so much anxiety, even a state of panic, that we become distracted, miss some of the factual content of the message and are unable to process the information properly or know what to do.

What we do not know is whether the high-fear condition in the Janis and Feshbach study aroused more fear than the one in the Leventhal, Watts and Pagano study. If it did, then a curvilinear fit might be appropriate for the data. Therefore, there may be a limit to the effectiveness of fear-arousing messages. Disturbing TV images, for example, may

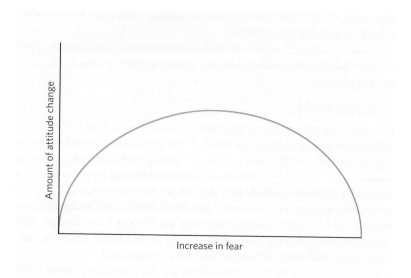

**Figure 6.3** The inverted U-curve relationship between fear and attitude change

The amount of attitude change increases as a function of fear up to a medium level of arousal. At high levels of fear, however, there is a fall-off in attitude change. This could be due to lack of attention to the stimulus, or to the disruptive effects of intense emotion, or both

distract people from the intended message or, even if the message is attended to, may so upset people that the entire episode is avoided.

According to *protection motivation theory* (see Chapter 5) fear appeals should work to eliminate dangerous health practices if they include an effective presentation of how to cope with the danger (see Wood, 2000, for a review). Witte, Berkowitz, Cameron and McKeon (1998), for example, combined a fear appeal with the promotion of self-protective behaviours in a campaign to reduce the spread of genital warts.

These approaches to the study of the differential effects of scary messages do not directly address the inverted U-curve hypothesis. Whether a message achieves its goals is probably determined by a trade-off between the perception of danger (*threat appraisal*) and whether people believe they can carry out the corrective behaviour (*coping appraisal*; see Figure 5.5 in Chapter 5). The underlying idea here is consistent with Blascovich's biopsychosocial model of challenge and threat (Blascovich 2008, Blascovich & Tomaka, 1996; see Chapter 2) – a demand can be perceived as a threat if one feels one does not have the resources to cope, and a challenge if one feels one does have the resources to cope.

The nature of threat appraisal was carefully examined in a German study of stress-related illness. Das, de Wit and Stroebe (2003) reason that ordinary people in a health-risk setting ask themselves two questions:

1　How vulnerable am I?
2　How severe is the risk?

In this study, risk following long-term stress could range from fairly mild (e.g. fever or cold hands and feet) to very severe (e.g. stomach ulcers or heart disease). Once it was accepted there was even a mild risk (the second question), people were more likely to follow a health recommendation provided they believed they were very vulnerable to a threat (the first question). This therefore suggests that impactful messages about risky health practices should pinpoint the matter of *vulnerability* to a greater degree than simply severity.

### Facts versus feelings

We noted in Chapter 5 that a distinction is commonly drawn between belief and affect as components of an attitude (e.g. Haddock & Zanna, 1999). In the advertising industry, a related distinction is sometimes made between *factual* and *evaluative* advertising. The former deals with claims of fact and is thought to be objective, whereas the latter reflects opinion and is subjective. A factually oriented advertisement is high on information and is likely to emphasise one or more attributes among the following: price, quality, performance, components or contents, availability, special offer, taste, packaging, guarantees or warranties, safety, nutrition, independent research, company-sponsored research or new ideas. However, the simple recall of facts from an advertisement does not guarantee a change in the brand purchased. Furthermore, if there is factual content in a message, it is important for people to be able to assimilate and understand the general conclusion of the message (Albion & Faris, 1979; Beattie & Mitchell, 1985).

Even if a distinction is made between beliefs and feelings, evaluating an object (say, judging whether it is good or bad) is not identical to experiencing affect or an emotion (see Chapter 5). From this point of view, we can repeat the argument that attitudes are fundamentally evaluations, which is where Thurstone (1928) started out. Applying this to an advertising context, evaluation means that instead of conveying facts or objective claims, the message is couched in such a way that it makes the consumer feel generally 'good' about the product. A common method in evaluative advertising is to capitalise on the *transfer of affect*, which itself is based on learning by association.

The distinction between facts and feelings does not imply that a given advertisement contains only factual or only evaluative material. On the contrary, modern marketing strategy favours using both approaches in any advertisement. A consumer can be led to *feel* that one product is superior to another by subtle associations with music or colour, or through the use of attractive models. The same consumer can be led to *believe* that the product is a better buy because it is better value for money.

Social psychologists debate whether the kind of appeal should fit the basis on which an attitude is held (Petty & Wegener, 1998). According to Edwards (1990), if the underlying attitude is emotional (affect-based) then the appeal should be as well, but if the attitude is centred on beliefs (cognition-based) then a factual appeal should work better. Millar and Millar (1990) argue for a mismatch: for example, using a factual appeal when the attitude is emotional. However, the attitude objects used by Edwards (e.g. photographs of strangers, a fictitious insecticide) were unknown to the participants, whereas Millar and Millar tapped established attitudes (a list of drinks actually generated by the participants), so participants could counter with effective arguments.

## The medium and the message

Chaiken and Eagly (1983) compared the relative effects on an audience of presenting messages in video, audio and written forms. This has obvious implications for advertising. Which has more impact on the consumer: television, radio or printed media? It depends. If the message is simple, as much advertising is, the probable answer is: video > audio > written. A moderating variable in this context is the relative ease or difficulty of comprehension required of the audience. If the points of a message require considerable processing by the target, a written medium is likely to be best. Readers have the chance to go back at will, mull over what is being said and then read on. If the material is quite complex, then newspapers and magazines can come into their own. However, there is an interesting interaction with the difficulty of the message. Look at the difference in effectiveness between various media in Figure 6.4. When the message was easy to comprehend, Chaiken and Eagly found that a videotaped presentation brought about most opinion change. When the message was difficult, however, opinion change was greatest when the material was written. Only recently has research included a focus on computer-mediated attitude change (e.g. Sassenberg & Boos, 2003 – see Chapter 15).

## Framing a message

The way in which a message is framed or slanted can have subtle effects on its meaning, and therefore on whether it is accepted. For example, if the issue of 'affirmative action' is presented as 'equal opportunity' rather than 'reverse discrimination', people will view it

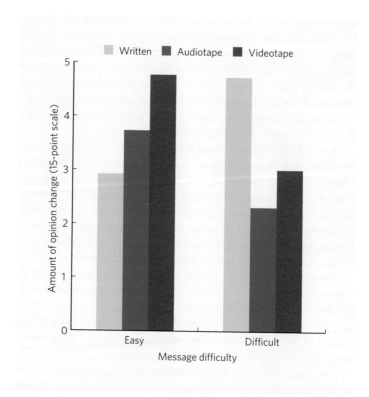

**Figure 6.4** The effects of source modality and message difficulty on opinion change

Using sound or a visual image rather than the printed word makes an easily understood message more acceptable. However, a difficult message profits from using a verbal document

*Source:* based on Chaiken & Eagly (1983)

more favourably (Bosveld, Koomen & Vogelaar, 1997). In their review of how to promote health-related behaviour, Rothman and Salovey (1997) found that message framing plays an important role. If the behaviour relates to detecting an illness, such as breast self-examination, the message should be framed in terms of preventing loss; but if the behaviour leads to a positive outcome, such as taking regular exercise, the message should be framed in terms of gain.

### The sleeper effect

**Sleeper effect**

The impact of a persuasive message can increase over time when a discounting cue, such as an invalid source, can no longer be recalled.

A persuasive message should have its greatest impact just after it is presented. It is counter-intuitive to think that its power might increase with the passage of time, and yet this is precisely what the **sleeper effect** suggests (Kelman & Hovland, 1953). An early finding in the Yale attitude change programme (Hovland, Lumsdaine & Sheffield, 1949) was that films promoting more positive attitudes among American soldiers towards their British allies in the Second World War became more effective well after they had been viewed. Kelman and Hovland reasoned that we initially associate the conclusion of a message with: (1) the quality of its argument, and (2) other cues, such as the credibility of its source. Of these, memory of the argument becomes more enduring as time goes by. Take the part played by source credibility as it interacts with our views on how much sleep we need each night, discussed earlier (see Figure 6.2). Were we to take a measure of the impact of an extreme message about a month later, the sleeper effect predicts that the less credible source would probably be as persuasive as the more credible source: the message survives but the source does not.

Crano and Prislin (2006) have described the sleeper effect, usually associated with studies in mass communication, as an 'old chestnut'. Its reliability has long been questioned (e.g. Gillig & Greenwald, 1974), but it has been replicated under quite strict conditions (e.g. Pratkanis, Greenwald, Leippe & Baumgardner, 1988). More recently, a meta-analysis by

### Research and applications 6.2
Delayed impact of a negative political attack

**The curious case of the exploding lie detector**

A context ripe for the operation of the sleeper effect is a political campaign. Parties quite frequently resort to messages that attack an opponent. These are built around specific, easily remembered content, such as Joe Black 'has been caught lying', 'is corrupt' or 'yet again has been cheating on his wife'. Public statements or advertising of this nature are often disliked by the public and are capable of alienating potential voters. The real-world response to an attack is to mount a defence. A direct, defensive message – typical in a political context – becomes the 'discounting cue' found in many laboratory sleeper-effect studies. A discounting cue is intended to undermine either the credibility of the source or the content of the attack message, or both, and to suppress the impact of the attack.

Lariscy and Tinkham (1999) tested for a sleeper effect among registered voters in the American state of Georgia. A political advertisement was professionally produced in a real-world political form, including subtle humour. It featured two fictitious candidates running for the US Congress in Kentucky, with 'Pat Michaels' as the sponsor of the advertisement and 'John Boorman' as his opponent.

A voice-over lists Boorman's claims about his military record in Vietnam, his tax policy and his heart-felt concern for Kentuckians. With each claim, a lie detector that is visually central in the sequences shows wild swings on a graph – lie, lie, lie! At the mention of Boorman's care for Kentucky the detector finally explodes.

Following the attack advertisement were Boorman's direct and defensive advertisements, arriving almost immediately or else after a delay. These were designed to suppress the impact of the original message by refuting Michaels' attacks and discounting his credibility. Michaels' credibility was designed to be at its lowest when the defensive messages were immediate.

To reduce confusion with real-world candidates in their own state, the voters in Georgia were asked to assume that they were voting in Kentucky. During a telephone call-back made one week after the attack advertisement and repeated six weeks later, they were asked which candidate they would endorse. When Michaels' credibility was lowest, only 19.6% of participants were prepared to vote for him. After a delay of six weeks, however, support for Michaels had risen to an astonishing 50%. Behold the sleeper effect – the exploding lie detector had done its job: 'negative advertising is not only damaging, it can wreak havoc that lasts until election day' (Lariscy & Tinkham, 1999, p. 26).

*Source*: Lariscy & Tinkham (1999)

Kumkale and Albarracín (2004) has detailed the particular circumstances where it is robust and points to a reawakened interest in the literature. See Box 6.2 for an experimental example that applies to the world of politics.

## The audience

### Self-esteem

In their 1950s studies, Hovland and his colleagues had noted that a distracted audience is more easily persuaded than one that is paying full attention, provided that the message is simple; and that those who have low self-esteem are more susceptible than those who have high self-esteem (see Box 6.1). McGuire (1968) suggested that the relationship between persuasibility and self-esteem is actually curvilinear: that is, it follows an inverted U-curve of the kind shown in Figure 6.3 (substituting 'self-esteem' for 'fear'). This curve suggests that people with either low or high self-esteem are less persuasible than those with moderate self-esteem. He reasoned that those with low self-esteem would be either less attentive or else more anxious when processing a message, whereas those with high self-esteem would be less susceptible to influence, presumably because they are generally more self-assured. According to a review by Rhodes and Wood (1992), research generally confirms this curvilinear relationship. As an aside, McGuire has also proposed a similar curvilinear relationship between intelligence and persuasibility.

## Men and women

Another consistent, but more controversial, finding is that women are more easily persuaded than men (Cooper, 1979; Eagly, 1978). Crutchfield (1955) was the first to report this effect when he found that women were more conforming and susceptible to social influence than men. Some researchers have proposed that this difference exists because women are socialised to be cooperative and non-assertive and are therefore less resistant than men to attempts to influence them (Eagly, Wood & Fishbaugh, 1981). Sistrunk and McDavid (1971) favoured another explanation – women are more easily influenced than men, but only when the subject discussed is one with which men are more familiar. When the topic is female-oriented, men are more influenced than women (see also Chapters 7 and 10).

This finding led to the proposition that the consistent difference found in persuasibility had been due to a methodological bias. The persuasive messages used in attitude research had typically dealt with male-oriented topics, and the researchers were usually male. If the topics had not been gender-biased, the male–female differences would not have been found. Because more recent studies are more sophisticated in both design and execution (e.g. Eagly & Carli, 1981), the conclusion they support is now widely accepted.

Carli (1990) investigated male–female differences in both the audience and the source. Participants heard a recorded message read by either a man or a woman, who spoke either tentatively or assertively. When the reader was female and tentative rather than assertive, male listeners were more easily persuaded than female listeners. In contrast, male readers were equally influential in each condition. This suggests that gender-related persuasiveness is a complex interaction of who is speaking, who is listening and whether the message is delivered in a sex-stereotyped way.

Covell, Dion and Dion (1994) investigated the effectiveness of tobacco and alcohol advertising as a function of gender and generation. The participants were male and female adolescents and their mothers and fathers. They rated the image and the quality of the advertised products and showed a preference for image-oriented over quality-oriented advertising. A gender difference was restricted to the adolescents, among whom female adolescents showed an even higher preference for image-oriented advertising. Covell, Dion and Dion suggested that when advertisements target adolescents and feature alcohol and tobacco, young women might be particularly attentive to image-oriented messages and judge drinking and smoking to be more desirable.

## Individual differences

Research into individual differences in persuasibility has focused on individual differences in *need for cognition* (Haugtvedt & Petty, 1992), *need for closure* (Kruglanski, Webster & Klem, 1993), *need to evaluate* (Jarvis & Petty, 1995) and *preference for consistency* (Cialdini, Trost & Newsom, 1995). Individual differences have also been found in *attitude importance* (Zuwerink & Devine, 1996). In these studies, people who scored high on these various needs were less likely to be persuaded than those who scored low. However, the relationship between personality variables and persuasion is not simple. The role of the **moderator variable** is important. For instance, in almost all cases, social contextual factors influence the personality–persuasibility relationship.

**Moderator variable**
A variable that qualifies an otherwise simple hypothesis with a view to improving its predictive power (e.g. A causes B, but only when C (the moderator) is present).

## Age

Visser and Krosnick (1998) and Tyler and Schuller (1991) have suggested five hypotheses about a relationship between age and susceptibility to attitude change:

1 *Increasing persistence* – susceptibility to attitude change is high in early adulthood but decreases gradually across the lifespan; attitudes reflect the accumulation of relevant experiences (a negative linear line).

2   *Impressionable years* – core attitudes, values and beliefs are crystallised during a period of great plasticity in early adulthood (an S-curve).

3   *Life stages* – there is a high susceptibility during early adulthood and later life, but a lower susceptibility throughout middle adulthood (a U-curve).

4   *Lifelong openness* – individuals are to some extent susceptible to attitude change throughout their lives.

5   *Persistence* – most of an individual's fundamental orientations are established firmly during pre-adult socialisation; susceptibility to attitude change thereafter is low.

These hypotheses are derived as much from developmental psychology as from social psychology. Which has the greatest explanatory power remains an open question. Tyler and Schuller's (1991) field study of attitudes towards the government supports the *lifelong openness* hypothesis: that is, age is generally irrelevant to attitude change. On the other hand, Visser and Krosnick's (1998) laboratory experiments support the *life stages* hypothesis. Rutland's (1999) research on the development of prejudice shows that negative attitudes towards ethnic and national outgroups only crystallise in later childhood (around age 10).

## Other variables

There are at least two other audience variables that relate to the persuasion process.

1   *Prior beliefs* affect persuasibility. There is evidence for a **disconfirmation bias** in argument evaluation. Arguments that are incompatible with prior beliefs are scrutinised longer, subjected to more extensive refutational analyses and are judged weaker than arguments compatible with prior beliefs. Furthermore, the magnitude and form of a disconfirmation bias is higher if prior beliefs are accompanied by emotional conviction (Edwards & Smith, 1996). Even if arguments contain only facts, prior beliefs affect whether factual information is considered at all. In a political discussion of the controversy over the causes for the stranding of a Soviet submarine near a Swedish naval base in 1981, the contending sides were most unwilling to accept facts introduced by each other into the debate, querying whether they were relevant and reliable (Lindstrom,

**Disconfirmation bias**
The tendency to notice, refute and regard as weak, arguments that contradict our prior beliefs.

**The impressionable years**
Respected adults, such as this teacher, are enormously influential in the development of young children's attitudes

1997). The disconfirmation bias is evident daily in media political discussions. For example, the disaster of the *Kursk,* a Russian submarine that sank in the Barents Sea in 2000, and the refusal of Western help in the rescue mission, sparked a similar debate to that in 1981.

2   *Cognitive biases* are important in both attitude formation and change (see Chapter 3 for an overview). For example, Duck, Hogg and Terry (1999) demonstrated the *third-person effect* in media persuasion (discussed earlier). According to this bias, people believe that they are less influenced than others by persuasion attempts. Students' perceptions of the impact of AIDS advertisements on themselves, students (ingroup), non-students (outgroup) and people in general were examined. Results showed that perceived self–other differences varied with how strongly students identified with being students. Those who did not identify strongly as students (low identifiers) exhibited the third-person effect, while those who did identify strongly as students (high identifiers) were more willing to acknowledge impact on themselves and the student ingroup.

In closing, we stress that the three major categories of variables dealt with – source, message and audience – interact in practice. For example, whether one would choose to employ an expert source to deliver a message can depend on the target group:

> A guiding principle in both marketing research and in persuasion theory is to 'know your audience' . . . marketers realize that a key to capturing a significant portion of the market share is to target one's product to those who are most likely to want or need it. *(Jacks & Cameron, 2003, p. 145)*

In the next section we examine how the persuasion process works.

## Dual-process models of persuasion

Recent attitude research has focused on how we respond to the content of a message. Although different approaches have been taken by Petty and Cacioppo (e.g. Petty & Cacioppo, 1986a, 1986b) and by Chaiken (e.g. Chaiken, 1987; Chaiken, Liberman & Eagly, 1989), there are elements in common. Each approach postulates two processes and draws on developments in research on memory from cognitive psychology (see Chapter 2). Both theories deal with persuasion cues. Sometimes it may not be the quality and type of the persuasion cues that matter but rather the quantity of message processing that underlies attitude change (Mackie, Worth & Asuncion, 1990). After more than twenty years of exposition and testing, are these theories still relevant?

> Without question, the dual-process models remain today's most influential persuasion paradigms, as they have been since their inception. In these models, source and message may play distinct roles that, in concert with motivation and ability to process information, determine the outcomes of persuasive interactions. *(Crano & Prislin, 2006, p. 348)*

### Elaboration–likelihood model

**Elaboration–likelihood model**

Petty and Cacioppo's model of attitude change: when people attend to a message carefully, they use a central route to process it; otherwise they use a peripheral route. This model competes with the heuristic–systematic model.

According to Petty and Cacioppo's **elaboration–likelihood model** (ELM), when people receive a persuasive message they think about the arguments it makes. However, they do not necessarily think deeply or carefully, because to do so requires considerable cognitive effort. People are cognitive misers who are motivated to expend cognitive effort only on issues that are important to them (see Chapter 2). Persuasion follows two routes, depending on whether people expend a great deal or very little cognitive effort on the message.

If the arguments of the message are followed closely, a *central route* is used. We digest the arguments in a message, extract a point that meets our needs and even indulge mentally in counter-arguments if we disagree with some of them. If the central route to persuasion is

**Peripheral cues in advertising**
Feeling hot and thirsty? Fancy buying a glass of cold mineral water?

to be used, the points in the message need to be put convincingly, as we will be required to expend considerable cognitive effort – that is, to work hard – on them. For example, suppose that your doctor told you that you needed major surgery. The chances are that you would take a considerable amount of convincing, that you would listen carefully to what the doctor says, read what you could about the matter and even seek a second medical opinion. On the other hand, when arguments are not well attended to a *peripheral route* is followed. By using peripheral cues we act in a less diligent fashion, preferring a consumer product on a superficial whim, such as an advertisement in which the product is used by an attractive model. The alternative routes available according to the elaboration–likelihood model are shown in Figure 6.5.

## Heuristic–systematic model

Chaiken's **heuristic–systematic model** (HSM) deals with the same phenomena using slightly different concepts, distinguishing between *systematic* processing and heuristic processing. Systematic processing occurs when people scan and consider available arguments. In the case of heuristic processing, we do not indulge in careful reasoning but instead use cognitive heuristics, such as thinking that longer arguments are stronger. Persuasive messages are not always processed systematically. Chaiken has suggested that people will sometimes employ cognitive heuristics to simplify the task of handling information.

You will recall that heuristics are a variety of simple decision rules or 'mental short-cuts', the tools that cognitive misers use. So, when we are judging the reliability of a message, we may resort to such truisms as 'statistics don't lie' or 'you can't trust a politician' as an easy way of making up our minds. As previously discussed, this feature of judgement is actively exploited by advertising companies when they seek to influence consumers by portraying their products as supported by scientific research or expert opinion. For instance, washing detergents are often advertised in laboratory settings, showing technical equipment and authoritative-looking people in white coats.

At what point would we switch from heuristic to systematic processing? According to Petty (Petty & Wegener, 1998), people have a *sufficiency threshold*: heuristics will be used as

**Heuristic–systematic model**
Chaiken's model of attitude change: when people attend to a message carefully, they use systematic processing; otherwise they process information by using heuristics, or 'mental short-cuts'. This model competes with the elaboration–likelihood model.

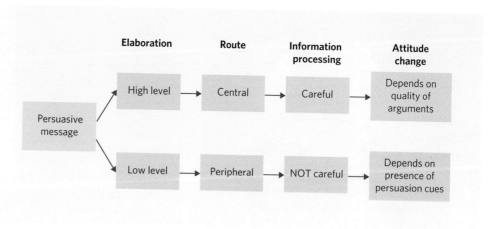

**Figure 6.5** The elaboration–likelihood model of persuasion
*Source*: based on Petty & Cacioppo (1986b)

long as they satisfy our need to be confident in the attitude that we adopt. When we lack sufficient confidence, we resort to the more effortful systematic mode of processing.

The role of cognition is fundamental in handling a persuasive message. Other work features the influence of our transient states, such as mood (e.g. Mackie & Worth, 1989; Petty, Schuman, Richman & Stratham, 1993; Wegener, Petty & Smith, 1995). Mackie and Worth (1989), for example, have shown that merely being in a good mood changes the way we attend to information.

Gorn (1982) reported that people were more likely to choose a product featured in an advertisement when the background music appealed to them. According to principles widely accepted in the fields of marketing and advertising (Belch & Belch, 2007), two factors underlie the use of background music: (1) music that appeals induces a good mood; and (2) through classical conditioning, a product repeatedly associated with a good mood will come to be evaluated positively.

In addition, feeling 'good' makes it difficult to process a message systematically. When time is limited, such as when we watch a TV advertisement, feeling really good can make us more susceptible to peripheral heuristic processing. Bohner, Chaiken and Hunyadi (1994) induced either a happy or a sad mood in students and then read an argument to them that was either strong, weak or ambiguous. All arguments were attributed to a highly credible source. When the message was unambiguous, sad participants were more easily influenced when they used heuristic processing. The effects of a sad mood have been studied experimentally in a mock court setting (Semmler & Brewer, 2002). When jurors feel sad, their accuracy (i.e. systematic processing) in detecting witness inconsistencies and their perceptions of witness reliability and a defendant's culpability is improved.

How emotional the content of a message is can influence our 'choice' between processing methods. Hale, Lemieux and Mongeau (1995) investigated the type of processing when a message varies in its level of fear. Information tended to be processed centrally for low-fear messages and peripherally for high-fear messages.

Wegener, Petty and Smith (1995) demonstrated that, contrary to the common view that happy people scrutinise messages superficially, sometimes being happy leads to more extensive processing. Happy people may actually be more attentive because the message seems more relevant to their happy mood (the *hedonic contingency* hypothesis).

Again, when people are focused on the impression they might make on another person, and want to have pleasant interaction, rather than being accurate in reflecting their opin-

## Research and applications 6.3
### Systematic processing can be undermined

This study dealt with complex interactions between source and message variables, as well as task importance, in relation to whether people use heuristic or systematic processing. In New York, students were asked to rate a new telephone-answering machine in an experiment with three independent variables:

1 *Task importance*. Some students believed that their opinion would weigh heavily, since sample size was small, in whether the machine would be distributed throughout New York; other students thought that their opinion would merely contribute to a much larger sample of New Yorkers and would not alter the outcome very much.

2 *Source credibility*. The product description was supposedly written by either a high-credibility source (Consumer Reports) or a low-credibility source (the sales staff of K-mart).

3 *Message type*. A pretest established eight product features, four of which were important (e.g. could

take different cassette types, screening of incoming calls) and four unimportant (e.g. colour range, special bolts for a wall). The important-to-unimportant ratio of these features was varied to create messages that were strong (4:2), ambiguous (3:3) or weak (2:4).

The findings for the students showed that:

- For the unimportant task (their opinion did not count for much), the machine was rated in terms of the credibility of the source – heuristic processing was used – regardless of whether the message was strong, ambiguous or weak.

- For the important task (their opinion really counted), the machine was rated in terms of message content – systematic processing was used – provided the message was clearly strong or clearly weak. Source credibility did not affect these ratings.

- However, source credibility did play a role when the task was important but the message was ambiguous. Both systematic and heuristic processing were used.

*Source*: Chaiken & Maheswaran (1994)

ions, they express an attitude that they believe will be more acceptable. They use a low-effort, 'go along to get along' heuristic rather than systematic and accurate processing (Chen, Shechter & Chaiken, 1996).

As a reminder that social processes can be complex, consider a study by Chaiken and Maheswaran (1994), who argued that systematic processing can be eroded when certain variables interact (see Box 6.3).

In summary, when people are motivated to attend to a message and to deal with it *thoughtfully*, they use a central route to process it according to the ELM (Petty & Cacioppo) or process it systematically according to the HSM (Chaiken). When attention is reduced so that people become cognitively *lazy*, they use a peripheral route (Petty & Cacioppo) or resort to heuristics – simple decision rules (Chaiken).

# Compliance

The literature on social influence sometimes uses the term **compliance** interchangeably with conformity. This can happen when 'conformity' is broadly defined to include a change in behaviour, as well as beliefs, as a consequence of group pressure. In this chapter, compliance refers to a surface *behavioural* response to a *request by another individual*; whereas conformity, which is dealt with in Chapter 7, refers to the influence of a group upon an individual that usually produces more enduring internalised changes in one's attitudes and beliefs (see Hogg, 2010). Because compliance is more closely associated with behaviour, and conformity with attitudes the compliance–conformity distinction engages with the attitude–behaviour relationship we discussed in Chapter 5 (see Sheeran, 2002).

**Compliance**
Superficial, public and transitory change in behaviour and expressed attitudes in response to requests, coercion or group pressure.

Compliance is also more closely associated with individuals having some form of power over you (French & Raven, 1959 – see Fiske & Berdahl, 2007).

We are confronted daily with demands and requests. Often they are put to us in a straightforward and clear manner, such as when a friend asks you to dinner, and nothing more is requested. At other times, requests have a 'hidden agenda': for example, an acquaintance invites you to dinner to get you into the right mood to ask you to finance a new business venture. The result is often the same – we comply.

What are the factors and situations that make us more compliant, and why is it that we are more influenced on some occasions than others? Generally, people influence us when they use effective tactics or have powerful attributes.

## Tactics for enhancing compliance

To persuade people to comply with requests to buy certain products has been the cornerstone of many economies. It is not surprising, therefore, that over the years many different tactics have been devised to enhance compliance. Salespeople, especially, have designed and refined many indirect procedures for inducing compliance, as their livelihood depends on it. We have all come across these tactics.

These tactics typically involve strategic self-presentation designed to elicit different emotions to compel others to comply (also see Chapter 4). Jones and Pittman (1982) describe five such strategies and emotions: *intimidation* is an attempt to elicit fear by getting others to think you are dangerous; *exemplification* is an attempt to elicit guilt by getting others to regard you as a morally respectable individual; *supplication* is an attempt to elicit pity by getting others to believe you are helpless and needy; *self-promotion* is an attempt to elicit respect and confidence by persuading others that you are competent; and *ingratiation* is simply an attempt to get others to like you in order to secure compliance with a subsequent request. These last two, self-promotion and ingratiation, service two of the most common goals of social interaction: to get people to think you are competent and to get people to like you (Leary, 1995).

**Ingratiation**
Strategic attempt to get someone to like you in order to obtain compliance with a request.

**Ingratiation** (Jones, 1964) is a particularly common tactic. A person attempts to influence others by first agreeing with them and getting them to like him/her. Next, various requests are made. You would be using ingratiation if you agreed with other people to appear similar to them or to make them feel good, made yourself look attractive, paid compliments, dropped names of those held in high esteem or physically touched them. However, ingratiation that is transparent can backfire, leading to the 'ingratiator's dilemma': the more obvious it is that an ingratiator will profit by impressing the target person, the less likely it is that the tactic will succeed (see Gordon, 1996, for a meta-analysis).

**Reciprocity principle**
The law of 'doing unto others as they do to you'. It can refer to an attempt to gain compliance by first doing someone a favour, or to mutual aggression or mutual attraction.

Using the **reciprocity principle** is another tactic, based on the social norm that 'we should treat others the way they treat us'. If we do others a favour, they feel obliged to reciprocate. Regan (1971) showed that greater compliance was obtained from people who had previously received a favour than from those who had received none. Similarly, *guilt arousal* produces more compliance. People who are induced to feel guilty are more likely to comply with a later request: for example, to make a phone call to save native trees, to agree to donate blood, or at a university to participate in an experiment (Carlsmith & Gross, 1969; Darlington & Macker, 1966; Freedman, Wallington & Bless, 1967).

Have you had your car windscreen washed while waiting at traffic lights? If the cleaner washes it before you can refuse, there is subtle pressure on you to pay for the service. In some cities (e.g. in Portugal), people might guide you into parking spaces that one could have easily located and then ask for money. These are real-life examples of persuasion to give money that involves activation of the reciprocity principle.

**Ingratiation**
Would you agree with Sarah
Palin that posing with babies
will capture votes?

## Multiple requests

A very effective tactic is the use of **multiple requests**. Instead of a single request, a two-step procedure is used, with the first request functioning as a set-up or softener for the second, real request. Three classic variations are the foot-in-the-door, the door-in-the-face and low-balling tactics (see Figure 6.6; for a recent review, see Cialdini & Goldstein, 2004).

According to the **foot-in-the-door tactic**) if someone agrees to a small request, they will be more willing to comply with a later, large request. Some salespeople use this approach. At first they might telephone you to ask just a few questions 'for a small survey that we are doing' and then entice you to join 'the hundreds of others in your area' who subscribe to their product.

In a study by Freedman and Fraser (1966), people were first contacted in their home to answer a few simple questions about the kind of soap they used at home. Later, they were more willing to comply with the larger request of allowing six people to make a thorough inventory of all the household items present. Only 22 per cent complied when they received the larger request 'cold', but 53 per cent complied when they had been softened up by the initial questions about soap.

The foot-in-the-door tactic may not always work. If the initial request appears too small or the second too large, the link between the multiple requests breaks down (Foss & Dempsey, 1979; Zuckerman, Lazzaro & Waldgeir, 1979). Nevertheless, a review by Saks (1978) suggested that if the technique is tuned carefully, people can even be induced to act as donors for organ and tissue transplants.

In a refinement of the tactic, people agreed to a series of graded requests rather than jumping from a small to a large request. They were presented with two preliminary requests, increasingly demanding, prior to an ultimate request (Goldman, Creason & McCall, 1981;

**Multiple requests**
Tactics for gaining
compliance using a
two-step procedure:
the first request functions
as a set-up for the second,
real request.

**Foot-in-the-door tactic**
Multiple-request
technique to gain
compliance, in which the
focal request is preceded
by a smaller request that
is bound to be accepted.

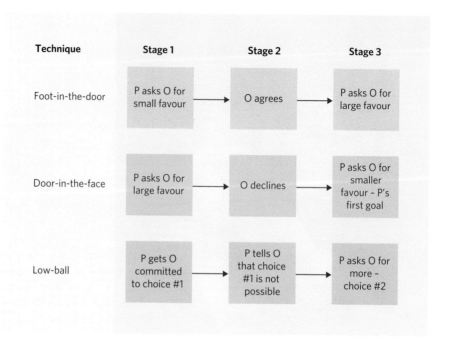

| Technique | Stage 1 | Stage 2 | Stage 3 |
|-----------|---------|---------|---------|
| Foot-in-the-door | P asks O for small favour | O agrees | P asks O for large favour |
| Door-in-the-face | P asks O for large favour | O declines | P asks O for smaller favour – P's first goal |
| Low-ball | P gets O committed to choice #1 | P tells O that choice #1 is not possible | P asks O for more – choice #2 |

**Figure 6.6**  Three classic techniques for inducing compliance

Dolinski, 2000). This has proved more effective than the classic foot-in-the-door technique. Think of this, perhaps, as the 'two-feet-in-the-door technique'! Graded requests occur often when someone asks someone out on a 'date'. At first, a prospective partner might not agree to go out with you, but might well agree to go with you to study in the library. Your next tactic is to request another meeting, and eventually a proper date.

In a Polish field experiment, Dolinski (2000) arranged for a young man to ask people in the city of Wroclaw for directions to Zubrzyckiego Street. There is no such street. Most said they did not know, although a few gave precise directions! Further down the street, the same people were then asked by a young woman to look after a huge bag for five minutes while she went up to the fifth floor in an apartment building to see a friend. A control group was asked to look after the bag, but not for the street directions. Compliance with the second, more demanding request was higher in the experimental group (see Figure 6.7; see also Chapter 14 for discussion of altruism).

Since there is reasonable evidence across a variety of studies that the foot-in-the-door technique actually works, what psychological process could account for it? A likely candidate for an explanation is Bem's (1967) self-perception theory (DeJong (1979; also see Chapter 4). By complying with a small request, people become committed to their behaviour and develop a picture of themselves as 'giving'. The subsequent large request compels them to appear consistent. Dolinski explained his results in the same way. In trying to help a stranger, although unsuccessfully, his participants would have inferred that they were altruistic. They were therefore more susceptible to a later influence – even if that request was more demanding.

Similarly, Cialdini and Trost (1998) explain the effect in terms of the principle of *self-consistency*. We try to manage our self-concept in such a way that if we are charitable on one occasion then we should be charitable again on the second occasion. Gorassini and Olson (1995), however, are sceptical that something as dramatic as self-conceptual change mediates the effect. Instead, they proposed an explanation with fewer assumptions. The

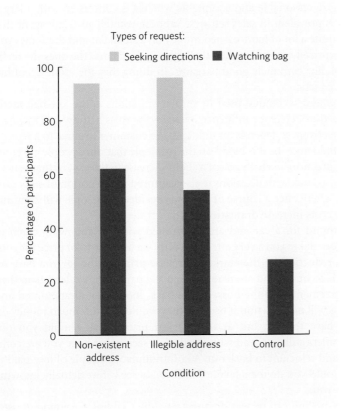

Types of request:
Seeking directions ■ Watching bag

**Figure 6.7** The foot-in-the-door technique: compliance with an impossible request followed by a possible request

Percentage of participants who answered 'I do not know' when asked about a non-existent or illegible address and of those who then complied with the request to keep an eye on the confederate's bag

*Source:* based on data from Dolinski (2000), Experiment 2

foot-in-the-door tactic alters people's interpretation of situations that activate attitudes enhancing compliance. The self is left out of the loop.

What happens if an attempt to get a foot in the door fails? Common sense suggests that this should reduce the likelihood of future compliance. Surprisingly, the opposite strategy, the **door-in-the-face tactic**, can prove successful (Cialdini et al., 1975; Patch, 1986). Here a person is asked a large favour first and a small request second. Politicians especially are masters of this art. To illustrate, say that the government warns the media that student fees will need go up 30 per cent. Are you angry? Later, however, it announces officially that the increase will 'only' be 10 per cent – the actual figure planned. You probably feel relieved and think 'that's not so bad', and consequently are more accepting.

Cialdini et al. (1975) tested this tactic by approaching students with a huge request: 'Would you serve as a voluntary counsellor at a youth offenders' centre two hours a week for the next two years?' Virtually no one agreed. However, when the researchers then asked for a considerably smaller request, 'Would you chaperone a group of these offenders on a two-hour trip to the zoo?' 50 per cent agreed. When the second request was presented alone, less than 17 per cent complied. For the tactic to be effective, the researchers noted that the final request should come from the same person who made the initial request. According to them, participants perceive the scaled-down request as a concession by the influencer, and consequently they feel pressure to reciprocate. If some other person were to make the second request, reciprocation would not be necessary.

According to Cialdini, the door-in-the-face technique may well capitalise on a contrast effect: just as lukewarm water feels cool when you have just had your hand in hot water, a

**Door-in-the-face tactic**
Multiple-request technique to gain compliance, in which the focal request is preceded by a larger request that is bound to be refused.

second request seems more reasonable and acceptable when it is contrasted with a larger request. This procedure is prevalent in sales settings. Suppose you tell an estate agent that you would like to spend quite a lot of hard-earned money on a small flat and she shows you a few run-down and overpriced examples. Then the higher-priced flats (the ones she really wants to show you!) look like extremely good bargains. In doing this, the estate agent has used the door-in-the-face tactic.

The other multiple-request technique used in similar situations is the **low-ball tactic** (check the first focus question). Here the influencer changes the rules halfway and manages to get away with it. Its effectiveness depends on inducing the customer to agree to a request before revealing certain hidden costs. It is based on the principle that once people are committed to an action, they are more likely to accept a slight increase in the cost of that action. This tendency for people to stick with decisions is also captured in the notion of *sunk costs* (Fox & Hoffman, 2002), where once a course of action is decided on, people will continue to invest in it even if the costs increase dramatically.

Suppose you shop around for a car and are confronted with the following chain of events. The car salesperson makes you a very attractive offer – a high trade-in price for your old car – and suggests a reduction on the marked purchase price for the car you have set your heart on. You decide to buy it and are ready to sign the papers. The salesperson then goes off to check the agreement with the boss, comes back, looks very disappointed and informs you that the boss will not sanction it because they would lose too much money on the deal. You can still have the car, but at the marked price. What should you do? Surprisingly, many customers still go ahead with the deal. It seems that once you are committed, you are hooked and reluctant to back out. A commonplace example of low-balling is when someone asks 'Could you do me a favour?' and you agree before actually knowing what will be expected of you.

Just how effective low-balling can be was demonstrated by Cialdini, Cacioppo, Bassett and Miller (1978). They asked half their participants to be in an experiment that began at 7 a.m. The other half were asked first to commit to participating in an experiment and then

**Low-ball tactic**
Technique for inducing compliance in which a person who agrees to a request still feels committed after finding that there are hidden costs.

**Low ball**
After consulting with his boss a salesman will tell a keen buyer that the quoted price for a new car no longer includes certain attractive 'extras'

were informed that it would start at 7 a.m. The latter group had been low-balled and complied more often (56 per cent) than the control group (31 per cent) and also tended to keep their appointments.

These studies show us the circumstances in which compliance is likely to occur. Sometimes our decision to comply may be rational: we weigh the pros and cons of our action. However, often we act before we think. According to Langer, Blank and Chanowitz (1978), much compliance is due to **mindlessness**: we agree without giving it a thought. Langer and her colleagues conducted experiments in which people were asked to comply with requests with little or no justification. In one, a person about to use a photocopier was interrupted by an experimenter, who requested first use for: (1) no reason, (2) a non-informative reason ('I have to make copies'), or (3) a justified reason ('I'm in a rush'). They found that as long as the request was small, people were likely to agree, even for a spurious reason. There was lower compliance when there was no reason.

Though being mindless may be a deciding factor in compliant behaviour, studies of power strategies indicate that this compliance often depends on the sources of power used.

**Mindlessness**
The act of agreeing to a request without giving it a thought. A small request is likely to be agreed to, even if a spurious reason is provided.

## Action research

At about the time that Hovland and his associates were studying attitude change in the US Army, the expatriate German psychologist Kurt Lewin was undertaking another piece of practical wartime research on the home front for a civilian government agency. With the

**Action research**
A set of stickers offering positive anti-smoking slogans for use around children and babies

aim of conserving supplies at a time of food shortages and rationing, he tried to convince American housewives to feed their families unusual but highly nutritious foods, such as beef hearts and kidneys, rather than steak or roast beef.

Lewin considered that attitude change could best be achieved if the recipients were somehow actively engaged in the change process rather than just being passive recipients. He referred to this involvement of the participants in the actual research process, and its outcome, as **action research**. Lewin demonstrated that an active discussion among 'housewives' about how best to present beef hearts and other similar foods to their families was much more effective than merely giving them a persuasive lecture presentation. His data showed that 32 per cent of the women in the discussion group went on to serve the new food, compared with only 3 per cent in the lecture group (Lewin, 1943).

The emphasis on action by participants fitted in with parts of the attitude change programme of Hovland and his associates. For instance, Janis and King (1954) investigated the effects of role playing by their participants. They found that those who gave a speech arguing against something that they believed in (i.e. acted out a role) experienced more attitude change than when they listened passively to a speech arguing against their position.

This early study of counter-attitudinal behaviour foreshadowed research into cognitive dissonance (discussed in the next section). One of Lewin's students was Festinger, who believed that humans are active processors and organisers of the information they receive from the world around them and of the cognitions (attitudes, beliefs, ideas, opinions) they have about the world. He accepted the consistency principle and argued that people will even change their ideas to make them consistent with what they are feeling or with how they are acting (Festinger, 1980). This would be the basis of the theory of cognitive dissonance.

In recent years, action research has been used increasingly by social psychologists to address community health issues relating to smoking, sun exposure and risky sexual practices. For example, prompted by the fact that Australia has one of the highest rates of melanoma in the world, Hill and his colleagues (Hill, White, Marks & Borland, 1993) conducted a three-year study dedicated to changing attitudes and behaviour related to sun exposure, called the SunSmart health promotion programme. This campaign was called SLIP! SLOP! SLAP! ('slip on a shirt, slop on some sunscreen, slap on a hat'), and was conducted via an array of media over three successive summers throughout the state of Victoria in southern Australia. Hill and associates found a significant change among 4,500 participants in sun-related behaviour over this period. There was:

- a drop in those reporting sunburn – 11 to 7 per cent;
- an increase in hat wearing – 19 to 29 per cent;
- an increase in sunscreen use – 12 to 21 per cent;
- an increase in body area covered by clothing – 67 to 71 per cent.

An important correlate of these behavioural changes was attitude change. Agreement declined with items such as 'A suntanned person is more healthy' and 'There is little chance I'll get skin cancer'.

Action research methods have also been used to reduce smoking (see Box 6.4).

More recently, there have been media campaigns focusing on nearly 1,400 patients living with HIV or AIDS in France (Peretti-Watel, Obadia, Dray-Spira, Lert, & Moatti, 2005). The respondents reported that information provided in the mass media helped them to manage their sexual life by using condoms and avoiding secondary infection.

**Action research**

The simultaneous activities of undertaking social science research, involving participants in the process, and addressing a social problem.

## Real world 6.4
### Quit smoking: anti-smoking campaigns

**Anti-smoking campaigns have reported some success in changing a habit that is very resistant to change**

Smoking has become deeply unfashionable in most Western countries over the past 20 years or so, yet its incidence remains stubbornly high. Even legislation against smoking in shared public spaces (e.g., work, restaurants, pubs, public transport) has had limited success when measured by a decline in the percentage of people who still smoke. In these countries, the highest rates of smoking tend to be found among people in the 20–29 age group, teenage women and working-class ('lower blue-collar') groups.

Smokers are usually well informed about illnesses related to smoking, such as lung cancer, emphysema and heart disease. Despite this knowledge, current smokers tend to underestimate the risk of dying from smoking when compared with former smokers and those who have never smoked. This bias in risk perception has also been reported for those who engage in risky sexual practices.

Anti-smoking campaigns have used a wide variety of media and techniques to discourage smoking (Hill, White, Marks & Borland, 1993). For example, one campaign adopted a television commercial and poster, while another used a direct-mail approach, along with radio advertisements. Various celebrities have helped by performing at places of work and by recording verbal messages. A classic, two-sided argument technique has been tried by providing counter-arguments for several commonly held self-exempting beliefs: that is, notions applied to exonerate oneself from the habit.

Target groups have varied. One campaign aimed to reach women, who outnumber men in the under-18 smokers' group, stressing the benefits of not smoking with respect to health, beauty and fitness. Another used baby stickers. Another campaign highlighted the benefits of a smoke-free workplace in major clothing chain stores, supplemented by radio and television advertisements. Nowadays, there is a socially supportive context to quit, and the recognition that passive smoking is dangerous may help some in the future to quit permanently.

How can smoking cessation be connected to the smoker's *intention to quit*? Giving up the habit can be traced through several stages. According to Biener and Abrams (1991), the 'contemplation ladder' suggests that a person moves from thought to action thus:

1 *I'm taking action to quit – for example, cutting down (top of ladder).*

2 *I'm starting to think about how to change my smoking patterns.*

3 *I think I should quit, but I'm not quite ready.*

4 *I think I should consider quitting some day.*

5 *I have no thought of quitting (bottom of ladder).*

Clearly, quitting is not an overnight decision. We can relate this analysis to the work of Ajzen and Fishbein (1980), which dealt with the relationship between attitude and intention, to Ajzen's (1989) theory of planned behaviour, and to protection motivation theory (Floyd, Prentice-Dunn & Rogers, 2000) (see Chapter 5).

# Attitude–behaviour discrepancy and cognitive dissonance

One of the most influential theories of attitude and behaviour change is the theory of cognitive dissonance (Festinger, 1957), which became the most studied topic in social psychology during the 1960s (see Cooper, 2007). Its major premise is that cognitive dissonance is an unpleasant state of psychological tension generated when a person has two or more cognitions (bits of information) that are inconsistent or do not fit together. Cognitions are thoughts, attitudes, beliefs or states of awareness of behaviour. For example, if a woman believes that monogamy is an important feature of her marriage and yet is having an extramarital affair, she may experience a measure of guilt and discomfort (dissonance).

Festinger proposed that we seek harmony in our attitudes, beliefs and behaviour, and try to reduce tension from inconsistency between these elements. The theory holds that people will try to reduce dissonance by changing one or more of the inconsistent cognitions (e.g. in the case of the unfaithful wife, 'what's wrong with a little fun if no one finds out?'), by looking for additional evidence to bolster one side or the other ('my husband doesn't understand me'), or by derogating the source of one of the cognitions ('fidelity is an outcome of religious indoctrination'). The maxim appears to be: *The greater the dissonance, the stronger the attempts to reduce it.* Experiencing dissonance leads people to feel physiologically 'on edge' – as evidenced by changes in the electrical conductivity of the skin that can be detected by a polygraph.

**Selective exposure hypothesis**
People tend to avoid potentially dissonant information.

For dissonance to lead to attitude change, it is necessary that two sets of attitudes are in contradiction (see Box 6.5). Because dissonance is unpleasant, people will tend to avoid exposure to ideas that bring it about. According to the **selective exposure hypothesis**, people are remarkably choosy when potentially dissonant information is on the horizon. Exceptions are when their attitude is either: (1) very strong, and they can integrate or argue against contrary information, or (2) very weak, and it seems better to discover the truth now and then make appropriate attitudinal and behavioural changes (Frey, 1986; Frey & Rosch, 1984).

For example, Frey and Rosch (1984) gave participants written profiles on the basis of which they had to form an attitude about whether to terminate or continue a 'manager'. Half the participants were told that their attitude was reversible (they could change their mind later on) and half that their attitude was irreversible. Then they selected as many bits of additional information as they wished from a pool containing five items of consonant information (in support of their attitude) and five items of dissonant information (in opposition to their attitude). Participants chose more consonant than dissonant information, and the effect was greatly magnified in the irreversible condition (see Figure 6.8).

A virtue of cognitive dissonance theory is that it is stated in a broad and general way. It is applicable in many situations, particularly ones involving attitude or behaviour change. For instance, it has been applied to understanding:

- people's feelings of regret and changes of attitude after making a decision;
- their patterns of exposing themselves to and searching for new information;
- reasons why people seek social support for their beliefs;

## Research and applications 6.5
### The impact of student exchange on national stereotypes

Student exchanges provide a wonderful opportunity for sojourners to confront stereotypic attitudes about other nations with new information gleaned from personal experience in a foreign country. From a cognitive dissonance perspective, one would expect (or hope) that pleasant personal experiences would conflict with ingrained negative attitudes towards a foreign nation, and would arouse cognitive dissonance which, under the circumstances, could only be resolved by changing the initial attitude.

This idea is illustrated in a study by Stroebe, Lenkert and Jonas (1988) of American students on one-year exchanges in Germany and France. They found that in the case of sojourners in Germany, reality matched existing attitudes and consequently there was no dissonance and no attitude change. Sojourners in France, however, found that realities were less pleasant than pre-existing attitudes led them to believe. There was dissonance, and consequently they departed from France with changed attitudes – unfortunately changed for the worse. These findings are consistent with other research into sojourners' attitudes (e.g. Klineberg & Hull, 1979), and they foreshadow the complexity of studying the way that stereotypes may change after direct contact with an outgroup (see Chapter 11).

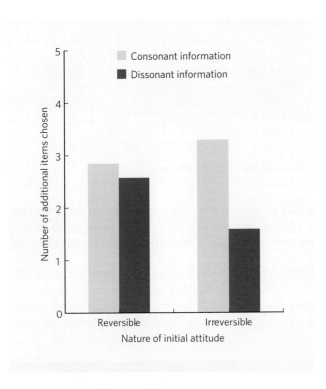

**Figure 6.8** Selection of consonant and dissonant information as a function of attitude irreversibility

*Source*: based on data from Frey & Rosch (1984)

- attitude change in situations where lack of support from fellow ingroup members acted as a dissonant cognition;
- attitude change in situations where a person has said or done something contrary to their customary beliefs or practice; and
- attitude change to rationalise hypocritical behaviour (Stone, Wiegand, Cooper & Aronson, 1997).

Dissonance theory is often grouped with balance theory as one of a family of models assuming that people try to be consistent in thought and action (see Chapter 5). A particularly appealing feature of dissonance theory is that it can generate non-obvious predictions about how people make choices when faced with conflicting attitudes and behaviours (Insko, 1967). Dissonance research falls largely into one of three research paradigms (Worchel, Cooper & Goethals, 1988): effort justification, induced compliance and free choice. Let us see how these differ.

## Effort justification

Now here is a surprise. The moment you choose between alternatives, you invite a state of dissonance. Suppose you need some takeaway food tonight. You make the momentous decision to go to the hamburger bar rather than to the stir-fry outlet. You keep mulling over the alternatives even after making your choice. Tonight's the night for a hamburger – you can taste it in your mouth already! The hamburger will be evaluated more favourably, or perhaps the stir-fry becomes less attractive, or maybe both – and tomorrow is another day. The way the **effort justification** paradigm works is shown in Figure 6.9.

Aronson and Mills (1959) explored what effort justification means in an early study. Female students volunteered to take part in a group discussion about sex, but were told that before they could join a group they must first pass a screening test for their capacity to

**Effort justification**
A special case of cognitive dissonance: inconsistency is experienced when a person makes a considerable effort to achieve a modest goal.

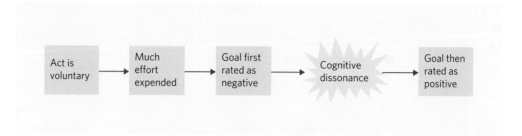

**Figure 6.9**  The general model of the effort justification paradigm

speak frankly. Those who agreed were assigned to one of two conditions. In the severe condition, they were given a list of obscene words and explicit sexual descriptions to read aloud; in the mild condition, they were to read words that included some such as 'petting' and 'prostitution'.

After being initiated, they listened over headphones to a discussion held by a group with a view to joining in during the following week. What they heard was tame – far short of embarrassing. The discussion was in fact a recording in which the participants had been primed to mumble, be incoherent and plain boring. As well as the severe and mild

**Effort justification**
Winning makes it all
worthwhile

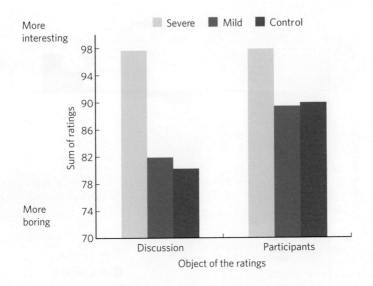

**Figure 6.10** Interest in a group discussion in relation to the severity of the initiation procedure

Some degree of 'suffering' makes a voluntary activity seem more attractive

*Source:* based on data from Aronson & Mills (1959)

initiation conditions, there was a control condition in which the participants did not undergo the screening experience.

The hypothesis was that the severe condition would cause some suffering to the participants, but yet they had volunteered to participate. The act of volunteering for embarrassment should cause dissonance. The predicted outcome would be increased liking for the chosen option (to participate in the discussion group), because the choice had entailed suffering. To make this sequence consonant would require the participant to rate the group discussion as more interesting than it really was. The hypothesis was confirmed. Those who went through the severe initiation thought that both the group discussion and the other group members were much more interesting than did those in the mild or control conditions (see Figure 6.10).

Later studies have shown that effort justification is a useful device to induce important behavioural changes relating to phobias and alcohol abuse. An interesting example is a study by Cooper and Axsom (1982). The participants were women who felt they needed help to lose weight and were willing to try a 'new experimental procedure'. They were required to come to a laboratory, where they were weighed and the procedure was explained to them.

In a high-effort condition, some were told that they needed to participate in a variety of time-consuming and effortful tasks, including reading tongue twisters aloud for a session lasting forty minutes. These tasks required psychological effort rather than physical exercise. When the effort was low, the tasks were shorter and easier; and in a control condition, the volunteers did not participate in any tasks at all but were simply weighed and asked to report again at a later date. The high-effort and low-effort groups came to the laboratory for five sessions over a period of three weeks, at which point they were weighed again. The results are shown in Figure 6.11.

Cooper and Axsom were encouraged to find that the weight loss in the high-effort group was not just an artefact of the interest shown in the women during the time of the five-week study. The participants were contacted again after six months and after one year and agreed to be weighed again. The weight loss was much more marked after time had elapsed. After six months, a remarkable 94 per cent of the high-effort group had lost some weight, while only 39 per cent of the low-effort group had managed to do so.

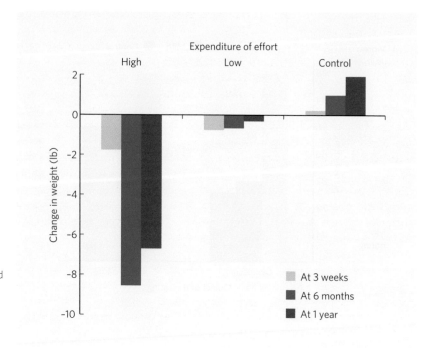

**Figure 6.11** Change in weight among overweight women after expending psychological effort

You may think that physical effort should reduce weight. This study suggests that mental effort is an important ingredient in a programme's effectiveness

*Source:* based on data from Cooper & Axsom (1982)

## Induced compliance

**Induced compliance**

A special case of cognitive dissonance: inconsistency is experienced when a person is persuaded to behave in a way that is contrary to an attitude.

Sometimes people are induced to act in a way that is inconsistent with their attitudes. An important aspect of the **induced compliance** paradigm is that the inducement should not be so strong that people feel they have been forced against their will. Festinger and Carlsmith (1959) carried out an often-quoted experiment in which students who had volunteered to participate in a psychology experiment were asked to perform an extremely boring task for an hour, believing that they were contributing to research on 'measures of performance'.

Imagine that you are the volunteer and that in front of you is a board, on which there are several rows of square pegs, each one sitting in a square hole. You are asked to turn each peg a quarter of a turn to the left and then a quarter of a turn back to the right. When you have finished turning all the pegs, you are instructed to start all over again, repeating the sequence over and over for twenty minutes. (This was not designed to be fun!) When the twenty minutes are up, the experimenter tells you that you have finished the first part, and you can now start on the second part, this time taking spools of thread off another peg board and placing them all back on again, and again, and again. Finally, the mind-numbing jobs are over.

At this point, the experimenter lets you in on a secret: you were a control participant, but you can now be of 'real' help. It seems that a confederate of the experimenter has failed to show up. Could you fill in? All you have to do is tell the next person that the tasks are really very interesting. The experimenter explains that he was interested in the effects of preconceptions on people's work on a task. Later, the experimenter offers a monetary incentive if you would be willing to be on call to help again at some time in the future. Luckily, you are never called.

In the Festinger and Carlsmith study, participants in one condition were paid the princely sum of $1 for agreeing to cooperate in this way, while others in a second condition were paid $20 for agreeing to help. The experimental design also included a control group of participants who were not asked to tell anyone how interesting the truly boring experience had been, and they were paid no incentive. On a later occasion, all were asked to rate how interesting or otherwise this task had been.

According to the induced compliance paradigm, dissonance follows from the fact that you have agreed to say things about what you have experienced when you know that the opposite is true. You have been induced to behave in a *counter-attitudinal* way.

The variation in levels of incentive adds an interesting twist. Participants who had been paid $20 could explain their lie to themselves with the thought, 'I did it for the $20. It must have been a lousy task, indeed.' In other words, dissonance would probably not exist in this condition. (We should point out that $20 was a sum of money not to be sneezed at by a student in the late 1950s.) On the other hand, those who told the lie and had been paid only $1 were confronted with a dilemma: 'I have done a really boring task, then told someone else that it is interesting, and finally even agreed to come back and do this again for a measly $1!' Herein lies the dissonance. One way of reducing the continuing arousal is to convince yourself that the experiment was really quite interesting after all. The results of this now classic study are shown in Figure 6.12.

The interest ratings of the two reward groups confirmed the main predictions. The $1 group rated the task as fairly interesting, whereas the $20 group found it slightly boring (while control participants found it even more so). The $1 participants were also more willing to take part in similar experiments in the future. The main thrust of this experiment, which is to use a smaller reward to bring about a larger attitude change, has been replicated several times. To modify an old saying: 'If you are going to lead a donkey on, use a carrot, but make it a small one if you want the donkey to enjoy the trip.'

Talking of carrots brings us to consider eating fried grasshoppers. An intriguing experiment carried out in a military setting by Zimbardo and his colleagues (Zimbardo, Weisenberg, Firestone & Levy, 1965) tackled this culinary question. The participants were asked to comply with the aversive request to eat grasshoppers by an authority figure whose interpersonal style was either positive (warm) or negative (cold). According to the induced compliance variation of cognitive dissonance, **post-decisional conflict** (and consequent

**Post-decisional conflict**
The dissonance associated with behaving in a counter-attitudinal way. Dissonance can be reduced by bringing the attitude into line with the behaviour.

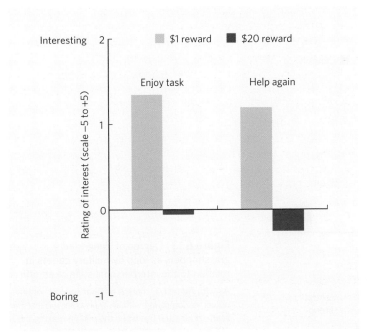

**Figure 6.12** The effect of incentives on evaluating a boring task in an induced-compliance context

One of social psychology's counter-intuitive findings: commitment to return to repeat a boring task is maximised, as is dissonance, by offering a minimal reward

*Source:* based on data from Festinger & Carlsmith (1959)

## Research classic 6.6
### To know grasshoppers is to love them

#### Attitude change following induced compliance

Let us consider the second focus question at the beginning of the chapter. This scenario, involving young military cadets, was actually researched by Zimbardo and his colleagues (Zimbardo, Ebbesen & Maslach, 1977). They arranged for an officer in command to suggest to the cadets that they might eat a few fried grasshoppers, and mild social pressure was put on them to comply. By administering a questionnaire about food habits earlier, they had ascertained that all the cadets thought there were limits to what they should be expected to eat, and that a meal of fried grasshoppers was one such limit. However, the officer gave them a talk indicating that modern soldiers in combat conditions should be mobile and, among other things, be ready literally to eat off the land. After his talk, the cadets were each given a plate with five fried grasshoppers and invited to try them out.

A critical feature of the experiment was the way in which the request was made. For half the cadets the officer was cheerful, informal and permissive. For the other half, he was cool, official and stiff. There was also a control group who gave two sets of food ratings but were never induced, or had the chance to eat grasshoppers. The social pressure on the experimental participants had to be subtle enough for them to feel they had freely chosen whether or not to eat the grasshoppers. Indeed, an order to eat would not arouse dissonance, because a cadet could then justify his compliance by saying 'He made me do it'. Furthermore, the cadets who listened to the positive officer might justify complying by thinking 'I did it as a favour for this nice guy'. However, those who might eat the grasshoppers for the negative officer could not justify their behaviour in this way. The resulting experience should be dissonance, and the easy way of reducing this would be to change their feelings about grasshoppers as a source of food.

As it turned out, about 50 per cent of the cadets actually ate some grasshoppers. Those who complied ate, on average, two of the five hoppers sitting on their plate. The results in Figure 6.13 show the percentage of participants who changed their ratings of liking or disliking grasshoppers as food. It is interesting to note that in both the negative and positive officer conditions, eaters were more favourable and non-eaters less favourable. This suggests that a degree of self-justification was required to account for an act that was voluntary but aversive. However, the most interesting result concerned the negative officer condition. This is the case in which dissonance should be maximal and, in line with the theory, it was here that the biggest change towards liking the little beasties was recorded.

*Source*: based on Zimbardo, Ebbesen & Maslach (1977); Zimbardo, Weisenberg, Firestone & Levy (1965)

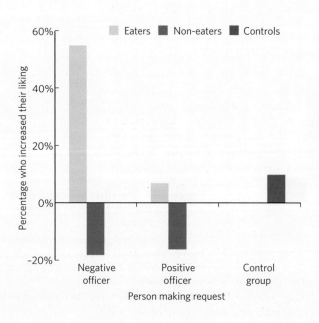

**Figure 6.13** Degree of liking fried grasshoppers as food by military cadets in relation to the interpersonal style of an officer

As with Figure 6.12, here is another counter-intuitive outcome: complying with an unpleasant request can seem more attractive when the person making the request is less attractive (see also Box 6.6)

*Source*: based on data from Zimbardo, Weisenberg, Firestone & Levy (1965)

**Induced compliance**
Let me out of here! Will this close encounter with spiders lead to an increased liking for these creepy wonders of nature?

attitude change) should be greater when the communicator is negative – how else could one justify behaving voluntarily in a counter-attitudinal way? Read what happened in this study in Box 6.6, and check the results in Figure 6.13.

Inducing people to act inconsistently with their attitudes is not an easy task and often requires a subtle approach. Counter-attitudinal actions with foreseeable negative consequences, such as being quoted in a newspaper saying that smoking is not harmful, requires an intricate inducement, whereas actions with less serious or less negative consequences, such as voting anonymously that smoking is harmless, may be less difficult to bring about. However, once people have been induced to act counter-attitudinally, the theory predicts that dissonance will be strong and that they will seek to justify their action (Riess, Kalle & Tedeschi, 1981).

## Free choice

Suppose that your choices between alternative courses of action are fairly evenly balanced, and that you are committed to making some kind of decision. This applies to numerous situations in our everyday lives: whether to buy this product or that; go to this tourist spot or another for a holiday; take this job offer or some other one. Based on Festinger's (1964) blueprint of the process of conflict in decision making, the pre-decision period is marked by uncertainty and dissonance, and the post-decision period by relative calm and confidence.

Free-choice dissonance reduction is likely to be a feature of bets laid on the outcome of sporting events, horse racing, gambling and so on. Once a person has made a choice between decision alternatives, dissonance theory predicts that the person making a bet will become more confident about a successful outcome. Younger, Walker and Arrowood (1977) interviewed people at a Canadian national exposition who were either about to bet or had just placed their bets, on games such as bingo and wheel of fortune, and asked them to rate their confidence in winning. They found that people who had already made their bet were more confident of winning (see Figure 6.14).

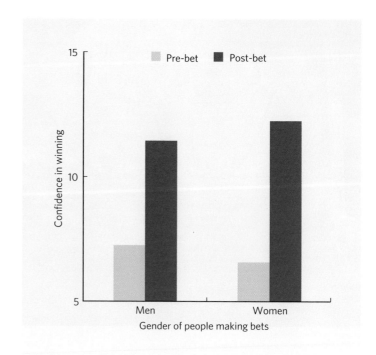

**Figure 6.14** Degree of confidence in winning before and after making a bet

Making a commitment reduces dissonance. When we make a bet we 'had better believe' we have just increased our chances of winning!

*Source:* based on data from Younger, Walker & Arrowood (1977)

## The role of self

According to Aronson (e.g. 1999) *self-consistency* is central to dissonance. People strive for a view of themselves as moral and competent human beings. Counter-attitudinal behaviour is inconsistent with this view, and is thus distressing and motivates change, particularly among people who think relatively highly of themselves (i.e. they have higher self-esteem).

This idea that self-consistency is crucial for dissonance is taken up in a slightly different guise by **self-affirmation theory** (Steele, 1988; Steele, Spencer & Lynch, 1993; also see Sherman & Cohen, 2006). The key idea is that if your self-concept is evaluatively challenged in one domain then you can rectify the problem by publicly making positive statements about yourself in another domain. For example, if my competence as a scholar is challenged, I might emphasise (affirm) that I am a wonderful cook and a great athlete. From a dissonance point of view, negative behaviours are particularly threatening to one's sense of self. People who have high self-esteem can respond via self-affirmation – they experience no dissonance. However, people who have low self-esteem and are therefore less able to self-affirm, do experience dissonance. Here, there is a conflict: Aronson (self-consistency) predicts greater dissonance under high self-esteem, whereas Steele (self-affirmation) predicts greater dissonance under low self-esteem (see Tesser, 2000).

Stone (2003) has suggested that these contradictions involving self-esteem can be accounted for by recasting an explanation in terms of *self-standards*. When we evaluate our actions to judge if they are good or sensible rather than bad or foolish, we use our personal (individualised) standards or normative (group, or cultural) standards as yardsticks. The standards operating at a point in time are those that are readily or chronically accessible in memory. If we believe we have acted foolishly, dissonance will probably occur; but self-esteem will not enter the equation unless a personal standard has been brought to mind.

**Self-affirmation theory**
The theory that people reduce the impact of threat to their self-concept by focusing on and affirming their competence in some other area.

Overall, dissonance research involving the self, self-concept and self-esteem remains fluid, though this much seems agreed:

> contemporary views of the self in dissonance have at least one common bond – they all make important assumptions about how people assess the meaning and significance of their behavior. *(Stone & Cooper, 2001, p. 241)*

## Vicarious dissonance

There is some intriguing evidence that people can experience dissonance vicariously (Cooper & Hogg, 2007; Norton, Monin, Cooper & Hogg, 2003). When two people share a strong bond, such as identifying strongly with the same group, dissonance experienced by one person may be felt by the other. This implies that a community advertisement could induce dissonance in viewers who watch someone 'like them' engaging in counter-attitudinal behaviour. The viewer does not actually have to behave counter-attitudinally. If the viewer also engages in counter-attitudinal behaviour, there may be a rebound effect because the common category member being observed provides social support for the viewer's dissonance. Research by McKimmie and his colleagues has found that ingroup social support for counter-attitudinal behaviour reduces dissonance (McKimmie, Terry, Hogg, Manstead, Spears & Doosje, 2003).

## Alternative views to dissonance

Cognitive dissonance theory has had a chequered history in social psychology (see Visser & Cooper, 2003). Festinger's original ideas have been refined and sharpened. Dissonance was not as easy to create as Festinger originally believed, and in some cases other theories (e.g. self-perception theory, discussed next) may provide a better explanation of attitude change than cognitive dissonance. Despite this, cognitive dissonance theory remains one of the most widely accepted explanations of attitude change and much other social behaviour. It has generated well over 1,000 empirical studies and will probably continue to be an integral part of social psychological theory for many years (Beauvois & Joule, 1996; Cooper, 2007; Cooper & Croyle, 1984; Joule & Beauvois, 1998).

### Self-perception theory

Some of the results of the dissonance experiments can be explained by **self-perception theory** (Bem, 1972; see Chapter 4). Some have suggested that attitude change does not occur according to the basic mechanisms proposed by dissonance theory and there have been several experimental attempts to compare the two. Both theories have been shown to be helpful in understanding behaviour (Fazio, Zanna & Cooper, 1977).

To understand the uses of each theory, imagine that attitudes fall on a continuum, spread over a range of acceptable choices. The idea that there are latitudes of acceptance and rejection around attitudes forms the basis of social judgement theory (Sherif & Sherif, 1967). If you are in favour of keeping the drinking age at 18, you might also agree to 17 or 19. There is a latitude of acceptance around your position. Alternatively, there is also a latitude of rejection: you might definitely be against a legal drinking age of either 15 or 21. Mostly we act within our own latitudes of acceptance. Sometimes we may go outside them: for instance, when we pay twice the amount for a dinner at a restaurant than we planned. If you feel you chose freely, you will experience dissonance.

A view that integrates self-perception and dissonance theories suggests that when your actions fall within your range of acceptance, self-perception theory best accounts for your response. So, if you had been willing to pay up to 25 per cent more than your original budget, there is no real conflict: 'I suppose I was willing to pay that little bit more.' However, when you

**Self-perception theory**
Bem's idea that we gain knowledge of ourselves only by making self-attributions: for example, we infer our own attitudes from our own behaviour.

find yourself acting outside your previous range of acceptance, dissonance theory gives a better account of your response. We reduce our dissonance only by changing our attitude: 'I paid twice what I had budgeted, but that's okay because I thought the food was fantastic' (Fazio, Zanna & Cooper, 1977). Thus attitudes may be changed either through a self-attributional process such as self-perception or through attempts to reduce the feeling of cognitive dissonance.

## A new look at cognitive dissonance

Cooper and Fazio (1984), in their *new look* model, countered some of the objections to cognitive dissonance theory. One controversy was how to retain and defend the concept of attitude when a person's observed behaviour and beliefs are in contradiction. According to Cooper and Fazio, when behaviour is counter-attitudinal we try to figure out what the consequences might be. If these are thought to be negative and fairly serious, we must then check to see if our action was voluntary. If it was, we then accept responsibility, experience arousal from the state of dissonance that follows and bring the relevant attitude into line, so reducing dissonance. This revision, shown in Figure 6.15, also includes attributional

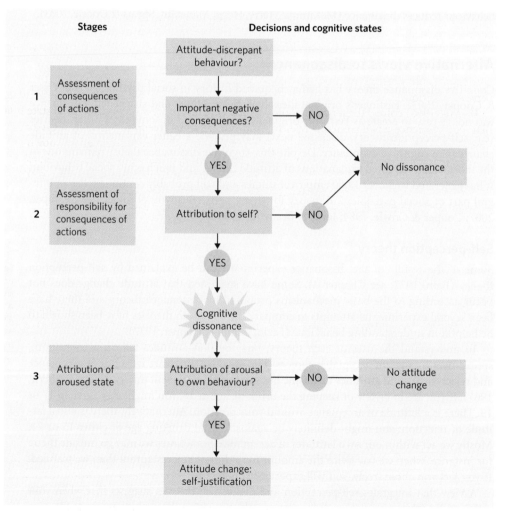

**Figure 6.15**   A revised cognitive dissonance model of attitude-discrepant behaviour
*Source:* based on Cooper & Fazio (1984)

processes, in terms both of whether we acted according to our free will and of whether external influences were more or less important.

The new look model is supported by considerable evidence (Cooper, 1999), but so is the traditional cognitive dissonance theory that focuses on inconsistency rather than behavioural consequences (e.g. Harmon-Jones, 2000).

# Resistance to persuasion

When we feel strongly about an issue we can be quite stubborn in resisting attempts to change our position (Zuwerink & Devine, 1996). However, much of the material presented in this chapter highlights factors that are conducive to our altering our attitudes, very often beyond a level of direct awareness. Yet far more attempts at persuasion fail than ever succeed. Researchers have identified three major reasons: reactance, forewarning and inoculation.

## Reactance

We noted in Box 6.1 that we are more easily persuaded if we think the message is not deliberately intended to be persuasive. Where a deliberate persuasion attempt is suspected, a process of **reactance** can be triggered. Think back to an occasion when someone obviously tried to change your attitudes. You might recall having an unpleasant reaction, and even hardening your existing attitude – perhaps becoming even more opposed to the other person's position.

Brehm (1966) coined the term 'reactance' to describe this process – a psychological state that we experience when someone tries to limit our personal freedom. Research suggests that when we feel this way, we often tend to shift in the opposite direction, an effect known as *negative attitude change*. The treatment a doctor recommends to a patient is sometimes responded to in this way (Rhodewalt & Strube, 1985). What happened the last time you were told to ease up, maybe go to bed and miss a wild party you had really been looking forward to? Brehm felt that the underlying cause of reactance is a sense of having our personal freedom infringed.

**Reactance**
Brehm's theory that people try to protect their freedom to act. When they perceive that this freedom has been curtailed, they will act to regain it.

## Forewarning

**Forewarning** is prior knowledge of persuasive intent – telling someone that you are going to influence them. When we know this in advance, persuasion is less effective (Cialdini & Petty, 1979; Johnson, 1994), especially with respect to attitudes and issues that we consider important (Petty & Cacioppo, 1979). When people are forewarned, they have time to rehearse counter-arguments that can be used as a defence. From this point of view, forewarning can be thought of as a special case of inoculation.

**Forewarning**
Advance knowledge that one is to be the target of a persuasion attempt. Forewarning often produces resistance to persuasion.

## The inoculation effect

The Chinese Communists have developed a peculiar brand of soul surgery which they practice with impressive skill – the process of 'thought reform'. They first demonstrated this to the American public during the Korean conflict . . . And more recently we have seen . . . Western civilians released from Chinese prisons, repeating their false confessions, insisting upon their guilt, praising the 'justice' and 'leniency' which they have received, and expounding the 'truth' and 'righteousness' of all Communist doctrine. *(R. J. Lifton, 1956; cited in Bernard, Maio & Olson, 2003, p. 63)*

**Inoculation**
A way of making people resistant to persuasion. By providing them with a diluted counter-argument, they can build up effective refutations to a later, stronger argument.

As the term suggests, **inoculation** is a form of protection. In biology, we can inject a weakened or inert form of disease-producing germs into the patient to build up resistance to a more powerful form. In social psychology, we might seek an analogous method of providing a defence against persuasive ideas (McGuire, 1964). The technique of inoculation, described as 'the grandparent theory of resistance of attitude change' (Eagly & Chaiken, 1993, p. 561), is initiated by exposing a person to a weakened counter-attitudinal argument.

McGuire and his associates (e.g. McGuire & Papageorgis, 1961; Anderson & McGuire, 1965) became interested in the technique following reports of 'brainwashing' of American soldiers imprisoned by Chinese forces during the Korean War of the early 1950s. Some of these made public statements denouncing the American government and saying they wanted to remain in China when the war ended. McGuire reasoned that these soldiers were mostly inexperienced young men who had not previously been exposed to attacks on the American way of life and were not forearmed with a defence against the Marxist logic.

The biological analogy implies that a weak attack is mounted on the body's system, which in turn mobilises its defences, effects a recovery and is reinforced by antibodies against a subsequent stronger attack. McGuire continued the metaphor by observing that there is another major way of heading off illness, namely by strengthening our bodies against disease through diet, exercise and so on. In the case of persuasive communications, this led him to distinguish between two kinds of defence:

1 *The supportive defence* – a person's resistance could be strengthened by providing additional arguments that support the original beliefs.

2 *The inoculation defence* – perhaps more effectively, the person might learn what the counter-attitudinal arguments are and then hear them demolished.

Inoculation at the outset poses some degree of threat, since a counter-argument is an attack on one's attitude (Insko, 1967). Note that the inoculation defence picks up on the advantage of a two-sided presentation, discussed earlier in relation to characteristics of a persuasive message. In general terms, this defence starts with a weak attack on the person's position, as a strong one might be fatal! The person can then be told that the weak argument is not too strong and should be easy to rebut, or else an argument is to be provided that deals directly with the weak attack. Increased resistance to persuasion may come about because we become motivated to defend our beliefs, and we acquire some skill in doing this.

In a study by McGuire and Papageorgis (1961), both forms of defence were put to the test. Students were asked to indicate their agreement on a fifteen-point scale with a series of truisms relating to health beliefs, such as:

- It's a good idea to brush your teeth after every meal if at all possible.
- The effects of penicillin have been, almost without exception, of great benefit to mankind.
- Everyone should get a yearly chest X-ray to detect any signs of TB at an early stage.
- Mental illness is not contagious.

Before the experiment began, many of the students thoroughly endorsed these propositions by checking 15, at one extreme on the response scale. The main variables of interest were the effects of introducing defences and attacks on these health beliefs in the form of essays offering arguments for or against the truisms. Students who were in the defence groups were allocated to one of two conditions, the first was a *supportive* defence group (the students received support for their position) and the second an *inoculation* defence group (their position was subjected to a weak attack, which was then refuted). There were also two control groups, one in which the students were neither attacked nor

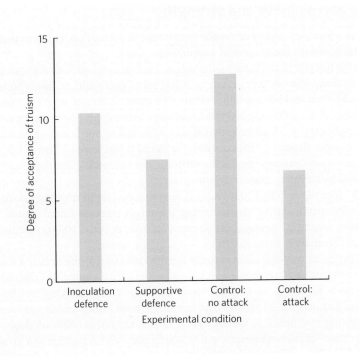

**Figure 6.16** Degree of acceptance of health truisms in modes of reading and writing as a function of supportive and inoculation defences

One of the best forms of defence against counter-arguments is to be exposed to small doses of these arguments

*Source:* based on data from McGuire & Papageorgis (1961)

defended, and another that read essays that strongly attacked the truisms but none defending them.

Not surprisingly, control participants who had been neither attacked nor defended continued to show the highest level of acceptance of the truisms. In dealing with their central hypotheses, McGuire and Papageorgis found that providing a supportive defence helped just a little when compared with the controls, who had been attacked without any defence. However, participants in the inoculation condition were substantially strengthened in their defence against a strong attack compared with the same control group. The results are shown in Figure 6.16.

McGuire (1964) went on to argue that the supportive defence is not to be ignored but that it is most effective when attacks upon one's position are well understood, so that established and rehearsed supportive arguments can be called up. For example, try persuading committed visitors to your door that they are in error when they are intent on telling you about the wonders of their religion. The chances are that they have heard your counter-arguments before. McGuire favoured the inoculation defence when the audience is to be exposed to a new argument. By having to deal with a mild earlier attack on their position, they will be better equipped to innovate when a stronger one is mounted.

The inoculation phenomenon has been further applied to advertising practices with the introduction of 'issue/advocacy advertising campaigns'. Issue/advocacy refers to the instance of a company protecting consumer loyalty from 'attitude slippage' by issuing media releases on controversial issues (Burgoon, Pfau & Birk, 1995). For example, a chemical company may issue a statement about environmental pollution in order to inoculate its consumers against allegations of environmental misconduct from competing companies, or from other 'enemies' such as a local green party. This practice is now widespread: an alcohol company may fund alcohol research and alcohol-moderation campaigns, and a fashion company may support the protection of wildlife.

## Role of attitude accessibility and strength

Several other variables affect the viability of people's resistance to persuasion, either in their own right or in interaction with the process of inoculation.

There is considerable interest in the roles of *attitude accessibility* and *attitude strength* in relation to persuasion. Accessible attitudes come to mind more easily and are likely to be stronger (see Chapter 5). Pfau and his colleagues (Pfau, Compton, Parker, et al., 2004; Pfau, Roskos-Ewoldsen, Wood, et al., 2003) applied this knowledge to the study of resistance and confirmed what we might expect. An attitude that is accessible and strong is more resistant to persuasion. If we consider the case of inoculation, the initial threat to one's attitude that might be posed by a persuasive message makes the attitude more accessible. Further, accessibility can be increased by forming counter-arguments.

On a different tack, Tormala & Petty (2002) have shown that success in resisting persuasion can rebound on the persuader by strengthening the target person's initial attitude. This effect held up even when the message was strong (Tormala & Petty, 2004a) or came from an expert source (Tormala & Petty, 2004b).

To be effective, a persuasive message must account for the kinds of real-life decision that people later make – their *post-message behaviour*. Consider the varied campaigns directed at risky behaviour, such as trying to dissuade young people from drinking alcohol. Albarracín, Cohen and Kumkale (2003) found that warnings about health and injury were not effective in promoting abstinence. A message such as 'just say no' to offers of alcohol may not stand much chance at the next teenage party. Young people who indulge in a 'trial' drink will immediately be in conflict – experience dissonance – between their behaviour and the content of the message. One outcome could be a weakening of the very attitude that the message was designed to support.

Research on resistance to persuasion has expanded during the last decade and been applied to a wide range of persuasion domains (see Knowles & Linn, 2004). However, let us close this section with an irony. McGuire's seminal work was triggered by the dramatic events surrounding wartime brainwashing in the 1950s. Those real-world events were actually deep-reaching attempts to induce value conversion rather than more surface-level attitude change, and resonate today with the strategies of religious cults that are determined to undermine people's cherished values (Bernard, Maio & Olson, 2003). For this reason, more research attention to strategies for defending values against psychological attacks would be timely.

## Summary

- The Yale research programme was a major approach to the study of communication and persuasion. It focussed on three kinds of factors: the source of a message (*who* factors), the message itself (*what* factors) and the audience (*to whom* factors).

- A communicator variable that has been studied in some depth is source credibility. A well-researched message variable is an appeal based on fear. There has been renewed interest in the sleeper effect, according to which some messages gain impact after the passage of time.

- Two important areas of our lives that employ relevant principles from social-psychological research are advertising and political propaganda.

- Two models, each dealing with how a persuasive message is learned, draw heavily on social cognition. Petty and Cacioppo's elaboration–likelihood model proposes that when people attend to a message carefully, they use a central route to process it; otherwise they use a peripheral route. Chaiken's heuristic-systematic model suggests that people use systematic processing when they attend to a message carefully;

otherwise they use heuristic processing. The models are not in conflict.

- A variety of techniques that deal with ways of inducing another person to comply with our requests have been intensively studied: these include ingratiation, reciprocity and guilt arousal. There are also multiple-request techniques (foot-in-the-door, door-in-the-face and low-balling), in which a first request functions as a set-up for the second, real, request.

- Festinger's cognitive dissonance theory is a major approach to the topic of attitude change. It addresses not only conflict between a person's beliefs but also discrepancy between behaviour and underlying attitudes, and behaviour and self-conception. It includes three variations on the way in which dissonance is brought about: effort justification, induced compliance and free choice.

- Reactance is an increase in resistance to persuasion when the communicator's efforts to persuade are obvious. Techniques for building up resistance include forewarning and the inoculation defence. In recent years, manufacturing companies have used inoculating media releases to shore up consumer loyalty.

## Literature, film and TV

### Tin Men

1987 comedy written and directed by Barry Levinson, starring Richard Dreyfuss and Danny Devito. Two aluminium salesmen are in competition. They use all their skills to outsell each other by persuading customers.

### Devil's Advocate

In this 1997 film Keanu Reeves, a small-town lawyer in the southern United States, is headhunted by Al Pacino who is head of a rich New York law firm. Soon we realise that Pacino is actually the Devil and their relationship becomes an exercise in persuasion and attitude change as Reeves is slowly sucked into an amoral world of infidelity, greed and power; losing his scruples and his wife along the way.

### Glengarry Glen Ross

1992 film directed by James Foley, written by David Mamet, and starring Jack Lemmon, Al Pacino, Ed Harris, Kevin Spacey, Alec Baldwin and others. The film is about a real estate office and the different ways in which salesmen under pressure try to sell, and to persuade others.

### Holy Smoke

This 1999 film by Jane Campion follows Kate Winslet's Ruth, a young girl who is obsessed with a charismatic Indian guru and is subsequently captured by P. J. Waters (played by Harvey Keitel), an 'anti-programmer', hired by her family to bring her back to 'normality'. They spend four days in the desert together locked in a battle of wills but despite trying every tactic in the book, P. J. realises that Ruth is just as persuasive as him in changing his views and attitudes to life. An intense demonstration of the power of persuasion and the different methods used to change attitudes.

### Frost/Nixon

In the summer of 1977 ex-president Richard Nixon, three years after being forced from office in disgrace for the Watergate scandal, decides to put the record straight and repair his legacy through a televised interview. He chooses the breezy young jet-setting British interviewer David Frost. What follows, in this 2009 film, is an exercise in persuasion and attitude change as Nixon cleverly seems to prevail over Frost for most of the interview and surrounding events.

### The Godfather trilogy: 1901–80

All three *Godfather* movies together (1992). Directed by Francis Ford Coppola, and with stars such as Marlon Brando, Al Pacino, Robert Duvall, James Caan, Robert de Niro, Diane Keaton, Andy Garcia and even the young Sofia Coppola. A trilogy about the persuasive power exerted by the Mafia through fear, and the actual, implied or imagined presence of the Godfather.

## Guided questions

1  The university doctor wants your classmate Joseph to stop smoking. She thinks she might ask him to look at a large jar containing a chemical solution and a diseased lung. Why might this not work very well? Watch real-life clips of people justifying why they smoke, or do not smoke, in Chapter 6 of MyPsychLab at **www.mypsychlab.co.uk** (watch *The need to justify our actions*).

2  How effective is it to use fear as the basis of a persuasive message?

3  The sleeper effect has been described as an 'old chestnut'. Do you think it still has some merit?

4  Describe any one *multiple-request tactic* for gaining compliance. Can you think of an everyday example where it has been used?

5  If your aim was to 'inoculate' someone against an upcoming propaganda campaign how would you go about it?

## Learn more

Albarracín, D., & Vargas, P. (2010). Attitudes and persuasion: From biology to social responses to persuasive intent. In S. T. Fiske, D. T. Gilbert, & G. Lindzey (eds), *Handbook of social psychology* (5th ed., Vol. 1, pp. 394–427). New York: Wiley. Detailed and authoritative discussion of the social psychology of persuasion.

Banaji, M. R., & Heiphetz, L. (2010). Attitudes. In S. T. Fiske, D. T. Gilbert, & G. Lindzey (eds), *Handbook of social psychology* (5th ed., Vol. 1, pp. 353–93). New York: Wiley. A completely up-to-date, comprehensive and detailed discussion of attitude research, which also covers processes of attitude change.

Belch, G. E., & Belch, M. A. (2007). *Advertising and promotion: An integrated marketing communications perspective* (7th ed.). New York: McGraw-Hill/Irwin. A well-known textbook that uses a communications theory approach (source, message, receiver) to explore how consumer attitudes and behaviour can be changed. It is rich with examples and illustrations of advertisements.

Bohner, G., Moskowitz, G. B., & Chaiken, S. (1995). The interplay of heuristic and systematic processing of social information. *European Review of Social Psychology, 6*, 33–68. An in-depth overview of the heuristic–systematic model of social information processing, which links attitude change more broadly to social influence.

Johnson, E. J., Pham, M. T., & Johar, G. V. (2007). Consumer behavior and marketing. In A. W. Kruglanski &

E. T. Higgins (eds), *Social psychology: A handbook of basic principles* (2nd ed., pp. 869–87). New York: Guilford Press. This up-to-date and detailed chapter also discusses persuasion and attitude change in the realm of consumer behaviour.

Knowles, E. S., & Linn, J. A. (eds) (2004). *Resistance and persuasion*. Mahwah, NJ: Erlbaum. A discussion of persuasion with a particular emphasis on resistance to persuasion.

Maio, G. R., & Haddock, G. (2007). Attitude change. In A. W. Kruglanski & E. T. Higgins (eds), *Social psychology: Handbook of basic principles* (2nd ed., pp. 565–86). New York: Guilford. Comprehensive and up-to-date coverage of what we know about processes of attitude change.

Maio, G., & Haddock, G. (2010). *The science of attitudes*. London: SAGE. A mid- to upper-level text dedicated to the science of attitudes – written by two leading attitude researchers.

Rothman, A. J., & Salovey, P (2007). The reciprocal relation between principles and practice: Social psychology and health behaviour. In A. W. Kruglanski & E. T. Higgins (eds), *Social psychology: A handbook of basic principles* (2nd ed., pp. 826–49). New York: Guilford Press. Detailed overview of social psychological processes in the context of health; including coverage of heath attitudes and behaviour.

Visser, P. S., & Cooper, J. (2007). Attitude change. In M. A. Hogg & J. Cooper (eds), *The SAGE handbook of social psychology: Concise student edition* (pp. 197–218). London:

SAGE. A comprehensive and accessible overview of theory and research on attitude change.

Zimbardo, P. G., & Leippe, M. R. (1991). *The psychology of attitude change and social influence*. New York: McGraw-Hill. A detailed look at attitudes and social influences in society, with particular attention to persuasion, influence and change. Well illustrated with relevant examples.

 Refresh your understanding, assess your progress and go further with interactive summaries, questions, podcasts and much more at **www.mypsychlab.co.uk**

## This chapter discusses

- Types of social influence
- Power and influence
- Obedience to authority
- Ethical issues in social psychology experiments
- Classic studies of conformity
- Theories of conformity
- Minority influence and social change

## Focus questions

1. While serving in the army on combat duty, Private Jones is ordered to set booby traps in a neighbourhood that is also used as a playground by small children. Although he feels very distressed about doing this, he sees that other members of his unit are already obeying the order. What is Private Jones likely to do and how will he feel about it? What factors might make it easier for him to disobey this order?

2. Tom entered an elevator with several people already in it. Like them, he positioned himself to face the door. At the next floor, a few more people entered, and stood immediately in front of him. As the elevator moved off, they all turned to face the rear. Tom thought this was strange, even stupid. Why did they do this? Should he do the same? (Watch *What is social proof?* – http://www.youtube.com/watch?v=sicoCkUZ-dk.)

3. While playing Trivial Pursuit®, Sarah simply agrees with Paul and John when they decide which plane first broke the sound barrier. They say she is a typical conformist female. What do you say?

4. Peter and Dave work for a large multinational corporation. They agree that many conditions of their employment are highly exploitative. Peter wants to take the corporation on, but Dave exclaims, 'How can we possibly succeed? There are only two of us up against the system!' What tips would you give Peter and Dave to improve their chance of success?

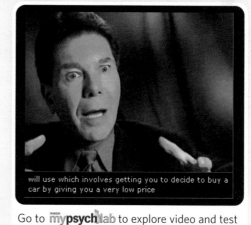

will use which involves getting you to decide to buy a car by giving you a very low price

Go to **mypsychlab** to explore video and test your understanding of key topics addressed in this chapter.

Refresh your understanding with interactive summaries, explore topics further with video and audio clips and assess your progress with quick test and essay questions by logging to the accompanying website at www.mypsychlab.co.uk

# Chapter 7
## Social influence

# Types of social influence

Social psychology has been defined as 'an attempt to understand and explain how the thoughts, feelings, and behaviours of individuals are influenced by the actual, imagined, or implied presence of others' (G. Allport, 1954a, p. 5). This widely accepted and often quoted definition of social psychology (see Chapter 1) identifies a potential problem for the study of **social influence** – how does the study of social influence differ from the study of social psychology as a whole? There is no straightforward answer. Instead, social influence research can be circumscribed by the sorts of issue addressed by social psychologists who claim to be studying social influence.

Social life is characterised by argument, conflict and controversy in which individuals or groups try to change the thoughts, feelings and behaviour of others by persuasion, argument, example, command, propaganda or force. People can be quite aware of influence attempts and can form impressions of how affected they and other people are by different types of influence (see Chapter 6).

Social life is also characterised by **norms**: that is, by attitudinal and behavioural uniformities among people, or what Turner has called 'normative social similarities and differences between people' (1991, p. 2). One of the most interesting sets of issues in social influence, perhaps even in social psychology, is how people construct norms, how they conform to or are regulated by those norms, and how those norms change. Since norms are very much group phenomena, we discuss their structure, their origins and some of their effects in Chapter 8, reserving for this chapter, Chapter 7, discussion of the processes of conformity and resistance to norms.

## Compliance, obedience, conformity

We are all familiar with the difference between yielding to direct or indirect pressure from a group or an individual, and being genuinely persuaded. For example, you may simply agree publicly with other people's attitudes, comply with their requests or go along with their behaviour, yet privately not feel persuaded at all. On other occasions, you may privately change your innermost beliefs in line with their views or their behaviour. This has not gone unnoticed by social psychologists, who find it useful to distinguish between coercive **compliance** on the one hand and persuasive influence on the other.

Some forms of social influence produce public compliance – an outward change in behaviour and expressed attitudes in response to a request from another person, or as a consequence of persuasion or coercion. As compliance does not reflect internal change, it usually persists only while behaviour is under surveillance. For example, children may obey parental directives to keep their room tidy, but only if they know that their parents are watching! An important prerequisite for coercive compulsion and compliance is that the source of social influence is perceived by the target of influence to have power; power is the basis of compliance (Moscovici, 1976).

**Social influence**
Process whereby attitudes and behaviour are influenced by the real or implied presence of other people.

**Norms**
Attitudinal and behavioural uniformities that define group membership and differentiate between groups.

**Compliance**
Superficial, public and transitory change in behaviour and expressed attitudes in response to requests, coercion or group pressure.

However, because evidence for internal mental states is gleaned from observed behaviour it can be difficult to know whether compliant behaviour does or does not reflect internalisation (Allen, 1965). People's strategic control over their behaviour for self-presentation and communication purposes can amplify this difficulty. Because research into compliance with direct requests has generally been conducted within an attitude-change and persuasion framework, we cover this topic in detail in Chapter 6.

In contrast to compliance, other forms of social influence produce private acceptance and internalisation. There is subjective acceptance and conversion (Moscovici, 1976), which produces true internal change that persists in the absence of surveillance. Conformity is not based on power but rather on the subjective validity of social norms (Festinger, 1950): that is, a feeling of confidence and certainty that the beliefs and actions described by the norm are correct, appropriate, valid and socially desirable. Under these circumstances, the norm becomes an internalised standard for behaviour, and thus surveillance is unnecessary.

Kelley (1952) has made a valuable distinction between reference group and membership group. **Reference groups** are groups that are psychologically significant for people's attitudes and behaviour, either in the positive sense that we seek to behave in accordance with their norms, or in the negative sense that we seek to behave in opposition to their norms. **Membership groups** are groups to which we belong (which we are *in*) by some objective criterion, external designation or social consensus. A positive reference group is a source of conformity (which will be socially validated if that group also happens to be our membership group), while a negative reference group that is also our membership group has enormous coercive power to produce compliance. For example, if I am a student but I despise all the attributes of being a student, and if I would much rather be a lecturer because I value lecturer norms so much more, then 'student' is my membership group and is also a negative reference group, while 'lecturer' is a positive reference group but not my membership group. I will comply with student norms but conform to lecturer norms.

The general distinction between coercive compliance and persuasive influence is a theme that surfaces repeatedly in different guises in social influence research. The distinction maps on to a general view in social psychology that two quite separate processes are responsible for social influence phenomena. Thus Turner and colleagues refer to traditional perspectives on social influence as representing a **dual-process dependency model** (e.g. Turner, 1991). This dual-process approach is currently perhaps most obvious in Petty and Cacioppo's (1986b) elaboration–likelihood model and Chaiken's (Bohner, Moskowitz & Chaiken, 1995) heuristic–systematic model of attitude change (see Chapter 6; Eagly & Chaiken, 1993).

## Power and influence

As mentioned above, compliance tends to be associated with power relations, whereas conformity is not. Compliance is influenced not only by the persuasive tactics that people use to make requests but also by how much power they are perceived to have. **Power** can be interpreted as the capacity or ability to exert influence; and influence is power in action. For example, French and Raven (1959) identified five bases of social power, and later Raven (1965, 1993) expanded this to six: reward power, coercive power, informational power, expert power, legitimate power and referent power (see Figure 7.1). Because it is almost a truism in psychology that the power to administer reinforcements or punishments should influence behaviour, there have been virtually no attempts to demonstrate reward and coercive power (Collins & Raven, 1969).

One general problem is that reinforcement formulations, particularly of complex social behaviour, tend to strike enormous difficulty in specifying in advance what are rewards and what are punishments, yet find it very easy to do so after the event. Thus reinforcement formulations tend to be unfalsifiable, and it may be more useful to focus on the cognitive and social processes that cause specific individuals in certain contexts to treat some things as reinforcement and others as punishment.

**Reference group**
Kelley's term for a group that is psychologically significant for our behaviour and attitudes.

**Membership group**
Kelley's term for a group to which we belong by some objective external criterion.

**Dual-process dependency model**
General model of social influence in which two separate processes operate – dependency on others for social approval and for information about reality.

**Power**
Capacity to influence others while resisting their attempts to influence.

| 1 Reward power | The ability to give or promise rewards for compliance |
| 2 Coercive power | The ability to give or threaten punishment for non-compliance |
| 3 Informational power | The target's belief that the influencer has more information than oneself |
| 4 Expert power | The target's belief that the influencer has generally greater expertise and knowledge than oneself |
| 5 Legitimate power | The target's belief that the influencer is authorised by a recognised power structure to command and make decisions |
| 6 Referent power | Identification with, attraction to or respect for the source of influence |

**Figure 7.1**  There are many different sources of power that people can access to persuade others
*Source:* based on Raven (1965)

While information may have the power to influence, it is clearly not true that all information has such power. If I were earnestly to tell you that I had knowledge that pigs really do fly, it is very unlikely that you would be persuaded. For you to be persuaded, other influence processes would also have to be operating: for instance, the information might have to be perceived to be consistent with normative expectations, or coercive or reward power might have to operate.

However, information can be influential when it originates from an expert source. Bochner and Insko (1966) provided a nice illustration of expert power. They found that participants more readily accepted information that people did not need much sleep when the information was attributed to a Nobel Prize-winning physiologist than to a less prestigious source. The information lost the power to influence only when it became intrinsically implausible – stating that almost no sleep was needed (see Figure 6.2 in Chapter 6).

Legitimate power is based in authority and is probably best illustrated by a consideration of obedience (see below). Referent power may operate through a range of processes (see also Collins & Raven, 1969), including consensual validation, social approval and group identification (all of which are discussed below in the section on conformity).

In addition to power as the ability to influence, there are other perspectives on social power (Fiske & Berdahl, 2007; Keltner, Gruenfeld & Anderson, 2003; Ng, 1996). For example, Fiske (1993b; Fiske & Dépret, 1996; Goodwin, Gubin, Fiske & Yzerbyt, 2000) presents a social cognitive and attributional analysis of power imbalance within a group (see Chapter 9). Moscovici (1976) actually contrasts power with influence, treating them as two different

**Legitimate power**
You may want the world's most powerful national leader to have expertise, charisma and be greeted by respect. You would not want this leader to act like a turkey

processes. Power is the control of behaviour through domination that produces compliance and submission: if people have power, in this sense, they do not need influence; and if they can influence effectively, they need not resort to power. There is also a whole literature on intergroup power relations (e.g. Hornsey, Spears, Cremers & Hogg, 2003; Jost & Major, 2001; see Chapter 11).

Power can also be considered as a role within a group that is defined by effective influence over followers: that is, as a leadership position. However, as we shall see in Chapter 9, the relationship between power and leadership is not clear-cut. Some leaders certainly do influence by the exercise of power through coercion, but most influence by persuasion and by instilling their vision in the rest of the group. Groups tend to permit leaders to be idiosyncratic and innovative (Hollander, 1985), and they see their leaders as being charismatic (Avolio & Yammarino, 2003) and, in many cases, as having legitimate authority (Tyler, 1997).

Generally, leadership researchers distinguish leadership from power (e.g. Chemers, 2001; Lord, Brown & Harvey, 2001). Leadership is a process of influence that enlists and mobilises others in the attainment of collective goals; it imbues people with the group's attitudes and goals, and inspires them to work towards achieving them. Leadership is not a process that requires people to exercise power over others in order to gain compliance or, more extremely, in order to coerce or force people. Leadership may actually be more closely associated with conformity processes than power processes (Hogg, 2010; Hogg, 2001b; Hogg & Reid, 2001; Hogg & van Knippenberg, 2003; Reid & Ng, 1999).

# Obedience to authority

In 1951 Asch published the results of a now classic experiment on conformity, in which student participants conformed to erroneous judgements of line lengths made by a numerical majority (see later in this chapter for details). Some critics were simply unimpressed by this study: the task, judging line length, was trivial, and there were no significant consequences for self and others of conforming or resisting.

Milgram (1974, 1992) was one of these critics; he tried to replicate Asch's study, but with a task that had important consequences attached to the decision to conform or remain independent. He decided to have experimental confederates apparently administer electric shocks to another person to see whether the true participant, who was not a confederate, would conform. Before being able to start the study, Milgram needed to run a control group to obtain a base rate for people's willingness to shock someone *without* social pressure from confederates. For Milgram, this almost immediately became a crucial question in its own right. In fact, he never actually went ahead with his original conformity study, and the control group became the basis of one of social psychology's most dramatic research programmes.

Milgram was also influenced by a wider social issue. Adolf Eichmann was the Nazi official most directly responsible for the logistics of Hitler's 'Final Solution', in which six million Jews were systematically slaughtered. A book entitled *Eichmann in Jerusalem* (Arendt, 1963) was published reporting his trial. The subtitle of this book, *A report on the banality of evil*, captures one of the most disturbing findings that emerged from Eichmann's trial, and indeed from the trials of other war criminals. These 'monsters' did not appear to be monsters at all. They were often mild-mannered, softly spoken, courteous people who repeatedly and politely explained that they did what they did not because they hated Jews but because they were ordered to do it – they were simply obeying orders. Looks can, of course, be deceiving. Peter Malkin, the Israeli agent who captured Adolf Eichmann in 1960, discovered that Eichmann knew some Hebrew words, and he asked:

> 'Perhaps you're familiar with some other words,' I said. '*Aba. Ima.* Do those ring a bell?'
>
> '*Aba, Ima,*' he mused, trying hard to recall. 'I don't really remember. What do they mean?'
>
> 'Daddy, Mommy. It's what Jewish children scream when they're torn from their parents' arms.' I paused, almost unable to contain myself. 'My sister's boy, my favorite playmate, he was just your son's age. Also blond and blue-eyed, just like your son. And you killed him.'
>
> Genuinely perplexed by the observation, he actually waited a moment to see if I would clarify it. 'Yes,' he said finally, 'but he was Jewish, wasn't he?' *(Malkin & Stein, 1990, p. 110)*

## Milgram's obedience studies

Milgram brought these strands together in a series of experiments with the underlying feature that people are socialised to respect the authority of the state (Milgram, 1963, 1974; see Blass, 2004). If we enter an **agentic state**, we can absolve ourselves of responsibility for what happens next. Participants in his experiments were recruited from the community by advertisement and reported to a laboratory at Yale University to participate in a study of the effect of punishment on human learning. They arrived in pairs and drew lots to determine their roles in the study (one was the 'learner', the other the 'teacher'). See Box 7.1 for a description of what happened next, and check how the shock generator looked in Figure 7.2.

### Factors influencing obedience

Milgram (1974) conducted a total of eighteen experiments, in which he varied different parameters to investigate factors influencing obedience. In all but one experiment the participants were 20–50-year-old males, not attending university, from a range of occupations and socioeconomic levels. In one study in which women were the participants, exactly the same level of obedience was obtained as with male participants. Milgram's experiment

**Agentic state**
A frame of mind thought by Milgram to characterise unquestioning obedience, in which people as agents transfer personal responsibility to the person giving orders.

## Research classic 7. 1
### Milgram's procedure in an early study of obedience to authority

Together with the experimenter in the Yale laboratory, there was a teacher (the real participant) and a learner (actually, a confederate).

The learner's role was to learn a list of paired associates, and the teacher's role was to administer an electric shock to the learner every time the learner gave a wrong associate to the cue word. The teacher saw the learner being strapped to a chair and having electrode paste and electrodes attached to his arm. The teacher overheard the experimenter explain that the paste was to prevent blistering and burning, and overheard the learner telling the experimenter that he had a slight heart condition. The experimenter also explained that although the shocks might be painful, they would cause no permanent tissue damage.

The teacher was now taken into a separate room housing a shock generator (see Figure 7.2). He was told to administer progressively larger shocks to the learner every time the learner made a mistake – 15 V for the first mistake, 30 V for the next mistake, 45 V for the next, and so on. An important feature of the shock generator was the descriptive labels attached to the scale of increasing voltage. The teacher was given a sample shock of 45 V, and then the experiment commenced.

The learner got some pairs correct but also made some errors, and very soon the teacher had reached 75 V, at which point the learner grunted in pain. At 120 V the learner shouted out to the experimenter that the shocks were becoming painful. At 150 V the learner, or now more accurately the 'victim', demanded to be released from the experiment, and at 180 V he cried out that he could stand it no longer. The victim continued to cry out in pain at each shock, rising to an 'agonised scream' at 250 V. At 300 V the victim ceased responding to the cue words; the teacher was told to treat this as a 'wrong answer'.

Throughout the experiment, the teacher was agitated and tense, and often asked to break off. To such requests, the experimenter responded with an ordered sequence of replies proceeding from a mild 'please continue', through 'the experiment requires that you continue' and 'it is absolutely essential that you continue', to the ultimate 'you have no other choice, you must go on'.

A panel of 110 experts on human behaviour, including 39 psychiatrists, were asked to predict how far a normal, psychologically balanced human being would go in this experiment. These experts believed that only about 10 per cent would exceed 180 V, and no one would obey to the end. These predictions, together with the actual and the remarkably different behaviour of the participants are shown schematically in Figure 7.3). Compare these with the actual behaviour of the participants (Figure 7.3).

In a slight variant of the procedure described above, in which the victim could not be seen or heard but pounded on the wall at 300 V and 315 V and then went silent, almost everyone continued to 255 V, and 65 per cent continued to the very end – administering massive electric shocks to someone who was not responding and who had previously reported having a heart complaint!

The participants in this experiment were quite normal people – forty 20–50-year-old men from a range of

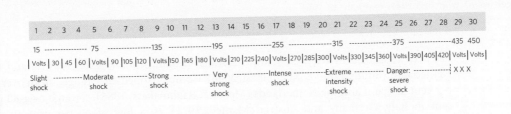

**Figure 7.2**  Milgram's shock generator

Participants in Milgram's obedience studies were confronted with a 15–450 Volt shock generator that had different descriptive labels, including the frighteningly evocative 'XXX', attached to the more impersonal voltage values

*Source*: Milgram (1974)

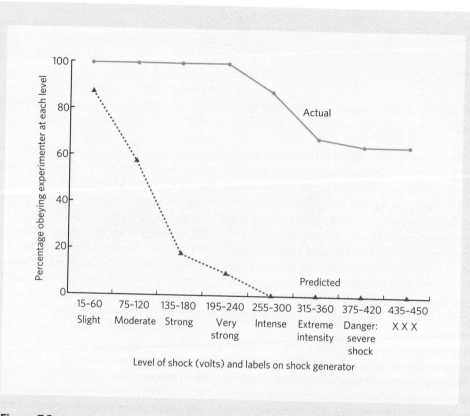

**Figure 7.3** Predicted versus actual levels of shock given to a victim in Milgram's obedience-to-authority experiment

'Experts' on human behaviour predicted that very few normal, psychologically balanced people would obey orders to administer more than a 'strong' electric shock to the 'incompetent' learner in Milgram's experiment – in actual fact 65 per cent of people were obedient right to the very end, going beyond 'danger: severe shock', into a zone labelled 'XXX'

*Source:* based on data from Milgram (1974)

occupations. Unknown to them, however, the entire experiment involved an elaborate deception in which they were always the teacher, and the learner/victim was actually an experimental stooge (an avuncular-looking middle-aged man) who had been carefully briefed on how to react. No electric shocks were actually administered apart from the 45 V sample shock to the teacher.

*Note:* See extracts from Milgram's work at http://www.panarchy.org/milgram/obedience.html.

has been replicated in Italy, Germany, Australia, Britain, Jordan, Spain, Austria and the Netherlands (Smith, Bond & Kağitçibaşi, 2006). Complete obedience ranged from over 90 per cent in Spain and the Netherlands (Meeus & Raaijmakers, 1986), through over 80 per cent in Italy, Germany and Austria (Mantell, 1971), to a low of 40 per cent among Australian men and only 16 per cent among Australian women (Kilham & Mann, 1974). Some studies have also used slightly different settings: for example, Meeus and Raaijmakers (1986) used an administrative obedience setting.

One reason why people continue to administer electric shocks may be that the experiment starts very innocuously with quite trivial shocks. Once people have committed themselves to a course of action (i.e. to give shocks), it can be difficult subsequently to change their mind. The process, which reflects the psychology of sunk costs in which once

**Obedience to authority**

This guard's uniform symbolises complete unquestioning obedience to the British monarch as a legitimate authority

committed to a course of action people will continue their commitment even if the costs increase dramatically (Fox & Hoffman, 2002), may be similar to that involved in the foot-in-the-door technique of persuasion (Freedman & Fraser, 1966; see Chapter 6).

An important factor in obedience is *immediacy* – social proximity of the victim to the participant. Milgram (1974) varied the level of immediacy across a number of experiments. We have seen above that 65 per cent of people 'shocked to the limit' of 450 V when the victim was unseen and unheard except for pounding on the wall. In an even less immediate condition in which the victim was neither seen nor heard at all, 100 per cent of people went to the end. The baseline condition (the one described in detail above) yielded 62.5 per cent obedience. As immediacy increased from this baseline, obedience decreased: when the victim was visible in the same room, 40 per cent obeyed to the limit; and when the teacher actually had to hold the victim's hand down on to the electrode to receive the shock, obedience dropped to a still frighteningly high 30 per cent.

Immediacy may prevent dehumanisation of the victim (cf. Haslam, 2006; Haslam, Loughnan, & Kashima, 2008), making it easier to view a victim as a living and breathing person like oneself and thus to empathise with their thoughts and feelings. Hence, pregnant women express greater commitment to their pregnancy after having seen an ultrasound scan that clearly reveals body parts (Lydon & Dunkel-Schetter, 1994); and it is easier to press a button to wipe out an entire village from 12,000 metres or from deep under the ocean in a submarine than it is to shoot an individual enemy from close range.

Another important factor is proximity/immediacy of the authority figure. Obedience was reduced to 20.5 per cent when the experimenter was absent from the room and relayed directions by telephone. When the experimenter gave no orders at all, and the participant was entirely free to choose when to stop, 2.5 per cent still persisted to the end. Perhaps the most dramatic influence on obedience is group pressure. The presence of two disobedient peers (i.e. others who appeared to revolt and refused to continue after giving shocks in the 150–210 V range) reduced complete obedience to 10 per cent, while two obedient peers raised complete obedience to 92.5 per cent.

Group pressure probably has its effects because the actions of others help to confirm that it is either legitimate or illegitimate to continue administering the shocks. Another important factor is the legitimacy of the authority figure, which allows people to abdicate personal responsibility for their actions. For example, Bushman (1984, 1988) had confederates, dressed in uniform, neat attire or a shabby outfit stand next to someone fumbling for change for a parking meter. The confederate stopped passers-by and 'ordered' them to give the person change for the meter. Over 70 per cent obeyed the uniformed confederate (giving 'because they had been told to' as the reason) and about 50 per cent obeyed a confederate who was either neatly attired or shabbily dressed (generally giving altruism as a reason). These studies suggest that mere emblems of authority can create unquestioning obedience.

Milgram's original experiments were conducted by lab-coated scientists at prestigious Yale University, and the purpose of the research was quite clearly the pursuit of scientific knowledge. What would happen if these trappings of legitimate authority were removed? Milgram ran one experiment in a run-down inner-city office building. The research was ostensibly sponsored by a private commercial research firm. Obedience dropped, but to a still remarkably high 48 per cent.

Milgram's research addresses one of humanity's great failings – the tendency for people to obey orders without first thinking about (1) what they are being asked to do and (2) the consequences of their obedience for other living beings. However, obedience can sometimes be beneficial: for example, many organisations would grind to a halt or would be catastrophically dysfunctional if their members continually painstakingly negotiated orders (think about an emergency surgery team, a flight crew, a commando unit). (Now consider the first focus question.) However, the pitfalls of blind obedience, contingent on immediacy, group pressure, group norms and legitimacy, are also many. For example, American research has shown that medication errors in hospitals can be attributed to the fact that nurses overwhelmingly defer to doctors' orders, even when metaphorical alarm bells are ringing (Lesar, Briceland & Stein, 1977).

In another study focusing on organisational obedience, 77 per cent of participants who were playing the role of board members of a pharmaceutical company advocated continued marketing of a hazardous drug merely because they felt that the chair of the board favoured this decision (Brief, Dukerich & Doran, 1991).

## Some ethical considerations

One enduring legacy of Milgram's experiments is the heated debate that it stirred up over research ethics (Baumrind, 1964; Rosnow, 1981). Recall that Milgram's participants really believed they were administering severe electric shocks that were causing extreme pain to another human being. Milgram was careful to interview and, with the assistance of a psychiatrist, to follow up the more than 1,000 participants in his experiments. There was no evidence of psychopathology, and 83.7 per cent of those who had taken part indicated that they were glad, or very glad, to have been in the experiment (Milgram, 1992, p. 186). Only 1.3 per cent were sorry or very sorry to have participated.

The ethical issues really revolve around three questions concerning the ethics of subjecting experimental participants to short-term stress:

1  Is the research important? If not, then such stress is unjustifiable. However, it can be difficult to assess the 'importance' of research objectively.

2  Is the participant free to terminate the experiment at any time? How free were Milgram's participants? In one sense they were free to do whatever they wanted, but it was never made explicit to them that they could terminate whenever they wished – in fact, the very purpose of the study was to persuade them to remain!

3  Does the participant freely consent to being in the experiment in the first place? In Milgram's experiments the participants did not give fully informed consent: they volunteered to take part, but the true nature of the experiment was not fully explained to them.

This raises the issue of deception in social psychology research. Kelman (1967) distinguishes two reasons for deceiving people: the first is to induce them to take part in an otherwise unpleasant experiment. This is, ethically, a highly dubious practice. The second reason is that in order to study the automatic operation of psychological processes, participants need to be naive regarding the hypotheses, and this often involves some deception concerning the true purpose of the study and the procedures used. The fallout from this debate has been a code of ethics to guide psychologists in conducting research. The principal components of the code are:

- participation must be based on fully informed consent;
- participants must be explicitly informed that they can withdraw, without penalty, at any stage of the study;
- participants must be fully and honestly debriefed at the end of the study.

It is unlikely that a modern university ethics committee would approve the impressively brazen deceptions that produced many of social psychology's classic research programmes of the 1950s, 1960s and early 1970s. What is more likely to be endorsed is the use of minor and harmless procedural deceptions enshrined in clever cover stories that are considered essential to preserve the scientific rigour of much experimental social psychology. The main ethical requirements in all modern research involving human participants are also discussed in Chapter 1, and see the American Psychological Association's Code of Ethics (2002) at http://www.apa.org/ethics/code2002.html.

# Conformity

## The formation and influence of norms

Although much social influence is reflected in compliance with direct requests and obedience to authority, social influence can also operate in a less direct manner, through **conformity** to social or group norms. For example, Allport (1924) observed that people in groups gave less extreme and more conservative judgements of odours and weights than when they were alone. It seemed as if, in the absence of direct pressure, the group could cause members to converge and thus become more similar to one another.

Sherif (1936) made a major step forward by explicitly linking this convergence effect to the development of *group norms*. Proceeding from the premise that people need to be certain and confident that what they are doing, thinking or feeling is correct and appropriate, Sherif argued that people use the behaviour of others to establish the range of possible behaviour: we can call this the **frame of reference**, or relevant *social comparative context*. Average, central or middle positions in such frames of reference are typically perceived to be more correct than fringe positions, thus people tend to adopt them. Sherif believed that this explained the origins of social norms and the concomitant convergence that accentuates consensus within groups.

To test this idea, he conducted his classic studies using **autokinesis** (see Box 7.2 and Figure 7.4 for details), in which two- or three-person groups making estimates of physical movement quickly converged over a series of trials on the mean of the group's estimates and remained influenced by this norm even when subsequently making their estimates alone.

The origins, structure, function and effects of norms are discussed fully in Chapter 8. However, it is worth emphasising that normative pressure is one of the most effective ways to change people's behaviour. For example, we noted in Chapter 6 that Lewin (1947) tried to encourage American housewives to change the eating habits of their families – specifically to eat more offal (beef hearts and kidneys). Three groups of thirteen to seventeen housewives attended an interesting factual lecture that, among other things, stressed how valuable

**Conformity**
Deep-seated, private and enduring change in behaviour and attitudes due to group pressure.

**Frame of reference**
Complete range of subjectively conceivable positions that relevant people can occupy in that context on some attitudinal or behavioural dimension.

**Autokinesis**
Optical illusion in which a pinpoint of light shining in complete darkness appears to move about.

### Research Classic 7. 2
#### Sherif's autokinetic study: the creation of arbitrary norms

Muzafer Sherif (1936) believed that social norms emerge in order to guide behaviour under conditions of uncertainty. To investigate this idea, he took advantage of a perceptual illusion – the autokinetic effect. Autokinesis is an optical illusion where a fixed pinpoint of light in a completely dark room appears to move: the movement is actually caused by eye movement in the absence of a physical frame of reference (i.e. objects). People asked to estimate how much the light moves find the task very difficult and generally feel uncertain about their estimates. Sherif presented the point of light a large number of times (i.e. trials) and had participants, who were unaware that the movement was an illusion, estimate the amount the light moved on each trial. He discovered that they used their own estimates as a frame of reference:

over a series of 100 trials they gradually focused on a narrow range of estimates, with different people adopting their own personal range, or norm (see session 1 in Figure 7.4a, when participants responded alone).

Sherif continued the experiment in further sessions of 100 trials on subsequent days, during which participants in groups of two or three took turns in a random sequence to call out their estimates. Now the participants used each other's estimates as a frame of reference, and quickly converged on a group mean, so that they all gave very similar estimates (see sessions 2–4 in Figure 7.4a).

This norm seems to be internalised. When participants start and then continue as a group (sessions 1–3 in Figure 7.4b), the group norm is what they use when they finally make autokinetic estimates on their own (session 4 in Figure 7.4b).

*Note:* The results shown in Figure 7.4 are based on two sets of three participants who made 100 judgements on each of four sessions, spread over four different days.

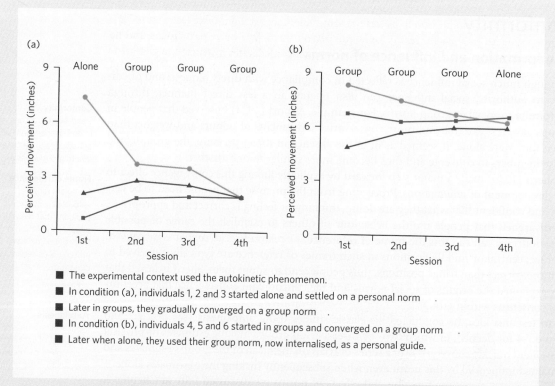

- ■ The experimental context used the autokinetic phenomenon.
- ■ In condition (a), individuals 1, 2 and 3 started alone and settled on a personal norm  .
- ■ Later in groups, they gradually converged on a group norm  .
- ■ In condition (b), individuals 4, 5 and 6 started in groups and converged on a group norm  .
- ■ Later when alone, they used their group norm, now internalised, as a personal guide.

**Figure 7.4** Experimental induction of a group norm
*Source:* based on data from Sherif (1936)

such a change in eating habits would be to the war effort (it was 1943). Another three groups were given information but were also encouraged to talk among themselves and arrive at some kind of consensus (i.e. establish a norm) about buying the food.

A follow-up survey revealed that the norm was far more effective than the abstract information in causing some change in behaviour: only 3 per cent of the information group had changed their behaviour, compared with 32 per cent of the norm group. Subsequent research confirmed that it was the norm not the attendant discussion that was the crucial factor (Bennett, 1955).

## Yielding to majority group pressure

Like Sherif, Asch (1952) believed that conformity reflects a relatively rational process in which people construct a norm from other people's behaviour in order to determine correct and appropriate behaviour for themselves. Clearly, if you are already confident and certain about what is appropriate and correct, then others' behaviour will be largely irrelevant and thus not influential. In Sherif's study, the object of judgement was ambiguous: participants were uncertain, so a norm arose rapidly and was highly effective in guiding behaviour. Asch argued that if the object of judgement was entirely unambiguous (i.e. one would expect no disagreement between judges), then disagreement, or alternative perceptions, would have no effect on behaviour: people would remain entirely independent of group influence.

To test this idea, Asch (1951, 1956) created a classic experimental paradigm. Male students, participating in what they thought was a visual discrimination task, seated themselves around a table in groups of seven to nine. They took turns in a fixed order to call out publicly which of three comparison lines was the same length as a standard line (see Figure 7.5). There were eighteen trials. In reality, only one person was a true naive participant, and he answered second to last. The others were experimental confederates instructed to give erroneous responses on twelve focal trials: on six trials they picked a line that was too long and on six a line that was too short. There was a control condition in which participants performed the task privately with no group influence; as less than 1 per cent of the control participants' responses were errors, it can be assumed that the task was unambiguous.

The experimental results were intriguing. There were large individual differences, with about 25 per cent of participants remaining steadfastly independent throughout, about 50 per cent conforming to the erroneous majority on six or more focal trials, and 5 per cent

**Conformity and group acceptance**
All groups have norms. These young women know how to dress for a 'girls night out'

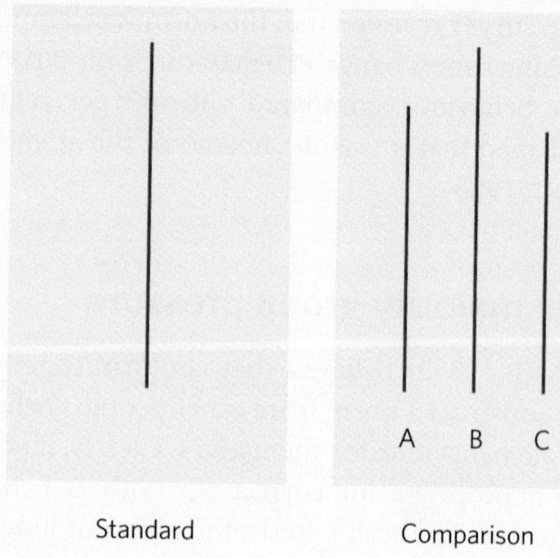

**Figure 7.5** Sample lines used in conformity experiment

Participants in Asch's conformity studies had simply to say which one of the three comparison lines was the same length as the standard line

*Source:* based on Asch (1951)

conforming on all twelve focal trials. The average conformity rate was 33 per cent: computed as the total number of instances of conformity across the experiment, divided by the product of the number of participants in the experiment and the number of focal trials in the sequence.

After the experiment, Asch asked his participants why they conformed. They all reported initially experiencing uncertainty and self-doubt as a consequence of the disagreement between themselves and the group, which gradually evolved into self-consciousness, fear of disapproval, and feelings of anxiety and even loneliness. Different reasons were given for yielding. Most participants knew they saw things differently from the group but felt that their perceptions may have been inaccurate and that the group was actually correct. Others did not believe that the group was correct but simply went along with the group in order not to stand out. (Consider how this might apply to Tom's self-doubts in the second focus question). A small minority reported that they actually saw the lines as the group did. Independents were either entirely confident in the accuracy of their own judgements or were emotionally affected but guided by a belief in individualism or in doing the task as directed (i.e. being accurate and correct).

These subjective accounts suggest that one reason why people conform, even when the stimulus is completely unambiguous, may be to avoid censure, ridicule and social disapproval. This is a real fear. In another version of his experiment, Asch (1951) had sixteen naive participants confronting one confederate who gave incorrect answers. The participants found the confederate's behaviour ludicrous and openly ridiculed and laughed at him. Even the experimenter found the situation so bizarre that he could not contain his mirth and also ended up laughing at the poor confederate!

Perhaps, then, if participants were not worried about social disapproval, there would be no subjective pressure to conform? To test this idea, Asch conducted another variation of the experiment, in which the incorrect majority called out their judgements publicly but the single naive participant wrote his down privately. Conformity dropped to 12.5 per cent.

This modification was taken further by Deutsch and Gerard (1955) who believed that they could entirely eradicate pressure to conform if the task was unambiguous and the participant was anonymous, responded privately and was not under any sort of surveillance by the group. Why should you conform to an erroneous majority when there is an obvious, unambiguous and objectively correct answer, and the group has no way of knowing what you are doing?

To test this idea, Deutsch and Gerard confronted a naive participant face-to-face with three confederates, who made unanimously incorrect judgements of lines on focal trials, exactly as in Asch's original experiment. In another condition, the naive participant was anonymous, isolated in a cubicle and allowed to respond privately – no group pressure existed. There was a third condition in which participants responded face-to-face, but with an explicit group goal to be as accurate as possible – group pressure was maximised. Deutsch and Gerard also manipulated subjective uncertainty by having half the participants respond while the stimuli were present (the procedure used by Asch) and half respond after the stimuli had been removed (there would be scope for feeling uncertain).

As predicted, the results showed that decreasing uncertainty and decreasing group pressure (i.e. the motivation and ability of the group to censure lack of conformity) reduced conformity (Figure 7.6). Perhaps the most interesting finding was that people still conformed at a rate of about 23 per cent even when uncertainty was low (stimulus present) and responses were private and anonymous.

The discovery that participants still conformed when isolated in cubicles greatly facilitated the systematic investigation of factors influencing conformity. Crutchfield (1955) devised an apparatus in which participants in cubicles believed they were communicating with one another by pressing buttons on a console that illuminated responses, when in reality the cubicles were not interconnected and the experimenter was the source of all communication. In this way, many participants could be run simultaneously and yet all would believe they were being exposed to a unanimous group. The time-consuming, costly and risky practice of using confederates was no longer necessary, and data could now be collected much more quickly under more controlled and varied experimental conditions (Allen, 1965, 1975). Nowadays, one can, of course, use a much more efficient computerised variant of Crutchfield's methodology.

## Who conforms? Individual and group characteristics

The existence of significant individual differences in conformity has led some social psychologists to search for personality attributes that predispose some people to conform

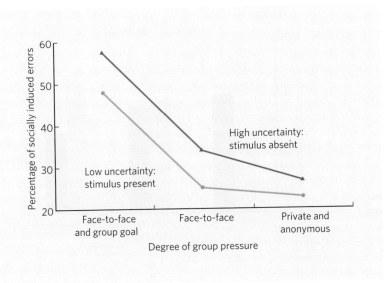

**Figure 7.6** Conformity as a function of uncertainty and perceived group pressure

- The length of lines was estimated either (a) when they were present (low uncertainty) or (b) after they had been removed (high uncertainty).
- Participants were confronted with the judgements of an incorrect and unanimous majority.
- Influence (percentage of errors) was stronger in the high uncertainty condition.
- Influence was weaker when accuracy was stressed as an important group goal.
- Influence was further weakened when judgements were private and anonymous.

*Source*: based on data from Deutsch & Gerard (1955)

more than others. Those who conform tend to have low self-esteem, a high need for social support or approval, a need for self-control, low IQ, high anxiety, feelings of self-blame and insecurity in the group, feelings of inferiority, feelings of relatively low status in the group, and a generally authoritarian personality (Costanzo, 1970; Crutchfield, 1955; Elms & Milgram, 1966; Raven & French, 1958; Stang, 1972). However, contradictory findings, and evidence that people who conform in one situation do not conform in another, suggest that situational factors may be more important than personality in conformity (Barocas & Gorlow, 1967; Barron, 1953; McGuire, 1968; Vaughan, 1964).

A similar conclusion can be drawn from research into sex differences in conformity. Women have typically been found to conform slightly more than men in conformity studies. However, this can generally be explained in terms of the conformity tasks employed – ones with which women have less familiarity and expertise, experience greater subjective uncertainty, and thus are influenced more than men (Eagly, 1978, 1983; Eagly & Carli, 1981; Eagly & Chrvala, 1986; Eagly & Wood, 1991).

For example, Sistrunk and McDavid (1971) exposed male and female participants to group pressure in identifying various stimuli. For some participants the stimuli were traditionally masculine items (e.g. identifying a special type of wrench), for some, traditionally feminine items (e.g. identifying types of needlework), and for others the stimuli were neutral (e.g. identifying popular rock stars). As expected, women conformed more on masculine items, men more on feminine items, and both groups equally on neutral (non-sex-stereotypical) items (see Figure 7.7). (Is Sarah really a conformist female? See the third focus question.)

Women do, however, tend to conform a little more than men in public interactive settings like that involved in the Asch paradigm. One explanation is that it reflects women's greater concern with maintaining group harmony (Eagly, 1978). However, a later study put the emphasis on men's behaviour; women conformed equally in public and private contexts whereas it was men who were particularly resistant to influence in public settings (Eagly, Wood, & Fishbaugh, 1981).

## Cultural norms

Do cultural norms affect conformity? Smith, Bond and Kağitçibaşi (2006) surveyed conformity studies that used Asch's paradigm or a variant thereof. They found significant

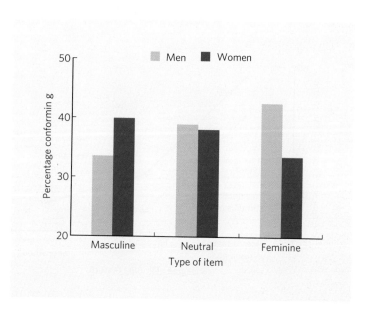

**Figure 7.7** Conformity as a function of sex of participant and sex-stereotypicality of task

When a task is male-stereotypical, more women conform. When the task is female-stereotypical, more men conform

*Source:* based on data from Sistrunk & McDavid (1971)

intercultural variation. The level of conformity (i.e. percentage of incorrect responses) ranged from a low of 14 per cent among Belgian students (Doms, 1983) to a high of 58 per cent among Indian teachers in Fiji (Chandra, 1973), with an overall average of 31.2 per cent. Conformity was lower among participants from individualist cultures in North America and north-western Europe (25.3 per cent) than among participants from collectivist or interdependent cultures in Africa, Asia, Oceania and South America (37.1 per cent).

A meta-analysis of 133 replications of the Asch paradigm in seventeen countries (R. Bond & Smith, 1996) confirmed that people who score high on Hofstede's (1980) collectivism scale conform more than people who score low (see also Figure 16.1 in Chapter 16, which shows summary data for non-Western versus various Western samples). For example, Norwegians, who have a reputation for social unity and responsibility, were more conformist than the French, who value critical judgement, diverse opinions and dissent (Milgram, 1961); and the Bantu of Zimbabwe, who have strong sanctions against nonconformity, were highly conformist (Whittaker & Meade, 1967).

The higher level of conformity in collectivist or interdependent cultures arises because conformity is viewed favourably, as a form of social glue (Markus & Kitayama, 1991). What is perhaps more surprising is that although conformity is lower in individualist Western societies, it is still remarkably high; even when conformity has negative overtones people find it difficult to resist conforming to group norms.

## Situational factors in conformity

The two situational factors in conformity that have been most exhaustively researched are group size and group unanimity (Allen, 1965, 1975). Asch (1952) found that as the unanimous group increased from one person to two, to three, to four, to eight, to ten, to fifteen, the conformity rate increased and then decreased slightly: 3, 13, 33, 35, 32, 31 per cent. Although some research reports a linear relationship between size and conformity (e.g. Mann, 1977), the most robust finding is that conformity reaches its full strength with a three- to five-person majority, and additional members have little effect (e.g. Stang, 1976).

Campbell and Fairey (1989) suggest that group size may have a different effect depending on the type of judgement being made and the motivation of the individual. With

**Group size and conformity**
Could an individual in this throng resist joining in?

matters of taste, where there is no objectively correct answer (e.g. musical preferences), and where you are concerned about 'fitting in', group size will have a relatively linear effect: the larger the majority, the more you will be swayed. When there is a correct response and you are concerned about being correct, then the views of one or two others will usually be sufficient: the views of additional others will be largely redundant.

Finally, Wilder (1977) observed that size may not refer to the actual number of physically separate people in the group but to the number of seemingly *independent* sources of influence in the group. For instance, a majority of three individuals who are perceived to be independent will be more influential than a majority of, say, five who are perceived to be in collusion and thus represent a single information source. In fact, people may actually find it difficult to represent more than four or five discriminable or independent pieces of information and thus tend to assimilate additional group members into one or other of these initial sources of information – hence the relative lack of effect of group size above three to five members.

Asch's original experiment employed a unanimous erroneous majority to obtain a conformity rate of 33 per cent. Subsequent experiments have shown that conformity is significantly reduced if the majority is not unanimous (Allen, 1975). Asch found that a correct supporter (i.e. a member of the majority who always gave the correct answer, and thus agreed with and supported the true participant) reduced conformity from 33 to 5.5 per cent. The effectiveness of a supporter in reducing conformity is marginally greater if the supporter responds before rather than after the majority (Morris & Miller, 1975).

Support itself may not be the crucial factor in reducing conformity. Any sort of lack of unanimity among the majority seems to be effective. For example, Asch found that a dissenter who was even more wildly incorrect than the majority was equally effective, and Shaw, Rothschild and Strickland (1957) found that a dithering and undecided deviate was also effective. Allen and Levine (1971) conducted an experiment in which participants, who were asked to make visual judgements, were provided with a supporter who had normal vision or a supporter who wore such thick glasses as to raise serious doubts about his ability to see anything at all, let alone judge lines accurately. In the absence of any support, participants conformed 97 per cent of the time. The 'competent' supporter reduced conformity to 36 per cent, but most surprising was the fact that the 'incompetent' supporter reduced conformity as well, to 64 per cent (see Figure 7.8).

Supporters, dissenters and deviates may be effective in reducing conformity because they shatter the unanimity of the majority and thus raise or legitimise the possibility of alternative ways of responding or behaving. For example, Nemeth and Chiles (1988) confronted participants with four confederates who either all correctly identified blue slides as blue, or among whom one consistently called the blue slide 'green'. Participants were then exposed to another group that unanimously called red slides 'orange'. The participants who had previously been exposed to the consistent dissenter were more likely to correctly call the red slides 'red'.

## Processes of conformity

Social psychologists have proposed three main processes of social influence to account for conformity (Nail, 1986): informational influence, normative influence, and referent informational influence.

### Informational and normative influence

**Informational influence**
An influence to accept information from another as evidence about reality.

The most enduring distinction is between informational influence and normative influence (Deutsch & Gerard, 1955; Kelley, 1952). **Informational influence** is an influence to accept information from another as *evidence* about reality. People have a need to feel confident that

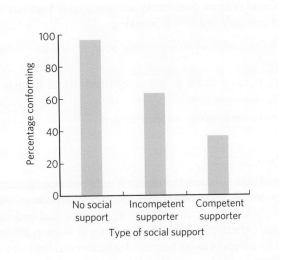

**Figure 7.8** Conformity as a function of presence or absence of support, and of competence of supporter

Social support on a line judgement task reduced conformity, even when the supporter was patently unable to make accurate judgements because he was visually impaired

*Source:* based on data from Allen & Levine (1971)

their perceptions, beliefs and feelings are correct. Informational influence comes into play when people are uncertain, either because stimuli are intrinsically ambiguous or because there is social disagreement. Under these circumstances, people initially make objective tests against reality, but if this is not possible they make social comparisons (Festinger, 1950, 1954; Suls & Wheeler, 2000). Effective informational influence causes true cognitive change.

Informational influence was probably partially responsible for the effects found by Sherif (1936) in his autokinetic studies. Reality was ambiguous, and participants used other people's estimates as information to remove the ambiguity and resolve subjective uncertainty. When participants were told that the apparent movement was in fact an illusion, they did not conform (e.g. Alexander, Zucker & Brody, 1970); presumably, since reality itself was uncertain, their own subjective uncertainty was interpreted as a correct and valid representation of reality, and thus informational influence did not operate. Asch's stimuli were designed to be unambiguous in order to exclude informational influence. However, Asch (1952) found that conformity increased as the comparison lines were made more similar to one another and the judgement task thus became more difficult.

**Normative influence** is an influence to conform to the positive expectations of others. People have a need for social approval and acceptance, which causes them to 'go along with' the group for instrumental reasons – to cultivate approval and acceptance, avoid censure or disapproval, or achieve specific goals. Normative influence comes into play when the group is perceived to have the power and ability to mediate rewards and punishment contingent on our behaviour. An important precondition is that one believes one is under surveillance by the group. Effective normative influence creates surface compliance in public settings rather than true enduring cognitive change. There is considerable evidence that people often conform to a majority in public but do not necessarily internalise this as it does not carry over to private settings or endure over time (Nail, 1986).

Normative influence was, no doubt, the principal cause of conformity in the Asch paradigm – the stimuli were unambiguous (informational influence would not be operating), but participants' behaviour was under direct surveillance by the group. We saw above how privacy, anonymity and lack of surveillance reduced conformity in the Asch paradigm, presumably because normative influence was weakened.

Deutsch and Gerard (1955) tried to remove normative influence entirely but, as we saw above, even under conditions in which neither informational nor normative influence

**Normative influence**
An influence to conform with the positive expectation of others, to gain social approval or to avoid social disapproval.

would be expected to operate, they found residual conformity at a remarkably high rate of about 23 per cent. From this, we can conclude one of the following:

- The conditions of the experiment were such that informational and/or normative influence were not completely eradicated.
- They were inoperative, but there is some third, as yet unspecified, social influence process.
- Social influence in groups needs to be explained in a different way.

## Referent informational influence

The distinction between informational and normative influence is only one among many different terminologies that have been used in social psychology to distinguish between two types of social influence. It represents what Turner and his colleagues call a dual-process dependency model of social influence (Abrams & Hogg, 1990a; Hogg & Turner, 1987a; Turner, 1991). People are influenced by others because they are dependent on them either for information that removes ambiguity and thus establishes subjective validity, or for reasons of social approval and acceptance.

This dual-process perspective has been challenged on the grounds that as an explanation of conformity it underemphasises the role of group belongingness. After all, an important feature of conformity is that we are influenced because we feel we belong, psychologically, to the group, and therefore the norms of the group are relevant standards for our own behaviour. The dual-process model has drifted away from group norms and group belongingness and focused on *interpersonal* dependency, which could just as well occur between individuals as among group members.

**Marching to a different drum**
An independent freespirit? No. This young man is conforming to a sub-group norm

This challenge has come from **social identity theory** (Tajfel & Turner, 1979; also Hogg, 2006; Hogg & Abrams, 1988; see Chapter 11), which proposes a separate social influence process responsible for conformity to group norms, called **referent informational influence** (Hogg & Turner, 1987a; Turner, 1981b).

In situations where group membership is psychologically salient – that is, we feel a sense of belonging and we define ourselves in terms of the group – we recruit from memory and we use information available in the social context to determine the relevant normative attributes of our group. Although this latter contextual information can be gleaned from the behaviour of outgroup members or unrelated individuals, the most immediate source is the behaviour of fellow ingroup members, particularly those we consider to be generally reliable sources of ingroup normative information. The context-relevant ingroup norm that is constructed captures and accentuates not only similarities among ingroup members but also differences between our group and relevant outgroups – it obeys the **metacontrast principle**. The process of self-categorisation associated with social identity processes, group belongingness and group behaviour (Turner et al., 1987; see Chapter 11) causes us to see ourselves in group terms and assimilate our thoughts, feelings and behaviour to the group norm – thus we behave in normative terms. To the extent that all members of the group construct a very similar group norm, self-categorisation produces intragroup convergence on that norm and increases intragroup uniformity – the typical conformity effect.

Referent informational influence differs from normative and informational influence in a number of important ways. For example, people conform because they are group members, not to validate physical reality or to avoid social disapproval. People do not conform to other people but to a norm: other people act as a source of information about the appropriate ingroup norm. Because the norm is an internalised representation, people can conform to it in the absence of surveillance by group members, or for that matter anybody else.

Referent informational influence has direct support from a series of four conformity experiments by Hogg and Turner (1987a). For example, under conditions of private responding (i.e. no normative influence), participants conformed to a non-unanimous majority containing a correct supporter (i.e. no informational influence) only if it was the participant's explicit or implicit ingroup (see also Abrams et al., 1990). Other support for referent informational influence comes from research into group polarisation (e.g. Turner, Wetherell, & Hogg, 1989; see Chapter 9), crowd behaviour (e.g. Reicher, 1984; see Chapter 11), and social identity and stereotyping (e.g. Oakes, Haslam, & Turner, 1994; see Chapter 11).

**Social identity theory**
Theory of group membership and intergroup relations based on self-categorisation, social comparison and the construction of a shared self-definition in terms of ingroup-defining properties.

**Referent informational influence**
Pressure to conform with a group norm that defines oneself as a group member.

**Metacontrast principle**
The prototype of a group is that position within the group that has the largest ratio of 'differences to ingroup positions' to 'differences to outgroup positions'.

# Minority influence and social change

Our discussion of social influence, particularly conformity, has thus far been concerned with how individuals yield to direct or indirect social influence from a numerical majority – the usual Asch-type arrangement. Dissenters, deviates or independents have mainly been of interest indirectly, either as a means of investigating the effects of different types of majority or to investigate conformist personality attributes. However, we are all familiar with a very different, and very common, type of influence that can occur in a group: an individual or a numerical minority can sometimes change the views of the majority. Often such influence is based (in the case of individuals) on leadership or (in the case of subgroups) legitimate power (leadership is discussed in Chapter 9).

However, minorities are typically at an influence disadvantage relative to majorities. Often, they are less numerous, and in the eyes of the majority, they have less legitimate power and are less worthy of serious consideration. Asch (1952), as we have already seen, found that a single deviate (who was a confederate) from a correct majority (true participants) was ridiculed and laughed at. Sometimes, however, a minority that has little or no legitimate power can be influential and ultimately sway the majority to its own viewpoint. For example, in a variant of the single deviate study, Asch (1952) found a quite different response. When a correct majority of eleven true participants was confronted by a deviant/incorrect minority of nine confederates, the majority remained independent (i.e. continued responding correctly) but took the minority's responses far more seriously – no one laughed. Clearly, the minority had some influence over the majority, albeit not enough in this experiment to produce manifest conformity.

History illustrates the power of minorities. It could be argued that if the only form of social influence was majority influence, then complete social homogeneity would have been reached tens of thousands of years ago, individuals and groups always being swayed to adopt the views and practices of the growing numerical majority. Minorities, particularly those that are active and organised, introduce innovations that ultimately produce social change: without **minority influence**, social change would be very difficult to explain. For example, the anti-war rallies during the 1960s in the United States had an effect on majority attitudes that hastened withdrawal from Vietnam. Similarly, the suffragettes of the 1920s gradually changed public opinion so that women were granted the vote, and the CND (Campaign for Nuclear Disarmament) rallies in Western Europe in the early 1980s gradually shifted public opinion away from the 'benefits' of nuclear proliferation. An excellent example of an active minority is Greenpeace: the group is numerically small (in terms of 'activist' members) but has important influence on public opinion through the high profile of some of its members and the wide publicity of its views.

The sorts of question that are important here are whether minorities and majorities gain influence via different social practices, and, more fundamentally, whether the underlying psychology is different. For recent overviews of minority influence research and theory see Hogg (2010), Martin and Hewstone (2003, 2008) and Martin, Hewstone, Martin, and Gardikiotis (2008), and for a meta-analysis of research findings, see Wood, Lundgren, Ouellette, Busceme, and Blackstone (1994).

**Minority influence**
Social influence processes whereby numerical or power minorities change the attitudes of the majority.

**An active minority with style**
Supporters in Madrid show solidarity for Spanish Greenpeace activists arrested during a climate change conference in Copenhagen

## Conformity bias

Social influence research has generally adopted a perspective in which people conform to majorities because they are dependent on them for normative and informational reasons. Moscovici and his colleagues mounted a systematic critique of this perspective (Moscovici, 1976; Moscovici & Faucheux, 1972). They argued that there had been a **conformity bias** underpinned by a functionalist assumption in the literature on social influence. Nearly all research focused on how individuals or minorities yield to majority influence and conform to the majority, and assumed that social influence satisfies an adaptive requirement of human life, to align with the status quo and thus produce uniformity, perpetuate stability and sustain the status quo. In this sense, social influence *is* conformity. Clearly conformity is an important need for individuals, groups and society. However, innovation and normative *change* are sometimes required to adapt to altered circumstances. Such change is difficult to understand from a conformity perspective, because it requires an understanding of the dynamics of active minorities.

**Conformity bias**
Tendency for social psychology to treat group influence as a one-way process in which individuals or minorities always conform to majorities.

Moscovici and Faucheux (1972) also famously 'turned Asch on his head'. They cleverly suggested that Asch's studies had actually been studies of minority influence, not majority influence. The Asch paradigm appears to pit a lone individual (true participant) against an erroneous majority (confederates) on an unambiguous physical perception task. Clearly a case of majority influence in the absence of subjective uncertainty? Perhaps not.

The certainty with which we hold views lies in the amount of agreement we encounter for those views: ambiguity and uncertainty are not properties of objects 'out there' but of other people's disagreement with us. This point is just as valid for matters of taste (if everyone disagrees with your taste in music, your taste is likely to change) as for matters of physical perception (if everyone disagrees with your perception of length, your perception is likely to change) (Moscovici, 1976, 1985a; Tajfel, 1969; Turner, 1985).

This sense of uncertainty would be particularly acute when an obviously correct perception is challenged. Asch's lines were *not* 'unambiguous'; there was disagreement between confederates and participants over the length of the lines. In reality, Asch's lone participant was a member of a large majority (those people outside the experiment who would call the lines 'correctly': that is, the rest of humanity) confronted by a small minority (the confederates who called the lines 'incorrectly'). Asch's participants were influenced by a minority: participants who remained 'independent' can be considered to be the conformists! 'Independence' in this sense is nicely described by Henry Thoreau in his famous quote from *Walden* (1854): 'If a man does not keep pace with his companions, perhaps it is because he hears a different drummer.'

In contrast to traditional conformity research, Moscovici (1976, 1985a) believed that there is disagreement and conflict within groups, and that there are three *social influence modalities* that define how people respond to such social conflict:

1 *Conformity* – majority influence in which the majority persuades the minority or deviates to adopt the majority viewpoint.

2 *Normalisation* – mutual compromise leading to convergence.

3 *Innovation* – a minority creates and accentuates conflict in order to persuade the majority to adopt the minority viewpoint.

## Behavioural style and the genetic model

Building on this critique, Moscovici (1976) proposed a genetic model of social influence. He called it a 'genetic' model because it focused on the way in which the dynamics of social conflict can generate (are genetic of) social change. He believed that in order to create change active minorities actually go out of their way to create, draw attention to and accentuate conflict. The core premise was that all attempts at influence create disagreement-based conflict between the source and the target of influence. Because people generally do not like conflict, they try to avoid or resolve it. In the case of disagreement with a minority, an easy and common resolution is to simply dismiss, discredit or pathologise the minority (Papastamou, 1986).

However, it is difficult to dismiss a minority if it 'stands up to' the majority and adopts a behavioural style that conveys uncompromising certainty about and commitment to its position, and a genuine belief that the majority ought to change to adopt its position. Under these circumstances, the majority takes the minority seriously, reconsidering its own beliefs and considering the minority's position as a viable alternative. The most effective behavioural style a minority can adopt to prevail over the majority is one in which, among other things, the minority behaves consistently across time and context, shows *investment* in its position by making significant personal and material sacrifices, and evinces *autonomy* by acting out of principle rather than from ulterior or instrumental motives.

Consistency is the most important behavioural style for effective minority influence, as it speaks directly to the existence of an alternative norm and identity rather than merely an alternative opinion. When a number of people repeatedly agree on an alternative view-point, this draws attention to them as a distinct entity (e.g. Hamilton & Sherman, 1996) with a coherent and unshakable commitment to an alternative reality. From an attribution theory perspective (e.g. Kelley, 1967; see Chapter 3) this form of consistent and distinctive behaviour cries out for explanation as it cannot be discounted. Furthermore, the behaviour is likely to be internally attributed to invariant and perhaps essentialist (e.g. Haslam, Rothschild, & Ernst, 1998) properties of the minority rather than to transient situational factors, which makes the minority even more of a force to be reckoned with and a focus of cogitation by the majority. Overall, minority consistency raises uncertainty in such a way that espousal of the minority viewpoint is the obvious and most viable resolution. (Considering these points, might Peter and Dave have a chance against the system in the fourth focus question?)

The role of consistency has been demonstrated by Moscovici and his colleagues in a series of ingenious experiments, referred to as the 'blue–green' studies (Maass & Clark, 1984). In a modified version of the Asch paradigm, Moscovici, Lage, and Naffrechoux (1969) had four participants confront two confederates for a colour perception task involving blue slides that varied only in intensity. The confederates were either consistent, always calling the slides 'green', or inconsistent, calling the slides 'green' two-thirds of the time and 'blue' one-third of the time. There was also a control condition with no confederates, just six true partici-pants. Figure 7.9 shows that the consistent minority had significantly more influence (9 per cent conformity) than the inconsistent minority (less than 2 per cent conformity). Although the conformity rate is much lower than with a consistent majority (recall that Asch reported an average conformity rate of 33 per cent), it is, nevertheless, remarkable that four people (a numerical majority) were influenced by two people (a minority).

There are two other notable results from an extension of this experiment, in which par-ticipants' real colour thresholds were tested privately after the social influence stage: (1) both experimental groups showed a lower threshold for 'green' than the control group – that is, they erred towards seeing ambiguous green–blue slides as 'green'; and (2) this effect was greater among experimental participants who were resistant to the minority – that is, participants who did not publicly call the blue slides 'green'.

Moscovici and Lage (1976) employed the same colour perception task to compare con-sistent and inconsistent minorities with consistent and inconsistent majorities. There was also a control condition. As before, the only minority to produce conformity was the con-sistent minority (10 per cent conformity). Although this does not compare well with the

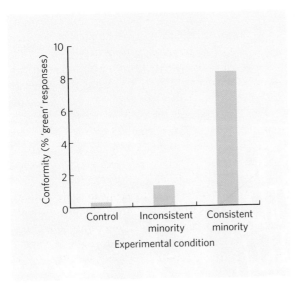

**Figure 7.9** Conformity to a minority as a function of minority consistency

Although not as effective as a consistent majority, a consistent two-person minority in a six-person group was more influential than an inconsistent minority; that four people were influenced by two is quite remarkable

*Source:* based on data from Moscovici, Lage & Naffrechoux (1969)

rate of conformity to the consistent majority (40 per cent), it is comparable with the rate of conformity to the inconsistent majority (12 per cent). However, the most important finding was that the *only* participants in the entire experiment who actually changed their blue–green thresholds were those in the consistent minority condition. Other studies have shown that the most important aspects of consistency are synchronic consistency (i.e., consensus) among members of the minority (Nemeth, Wachtler, & Endicott, 1977) and perceived consistency, not merely objective repetition (Nemeth, Swedlund, & Kanki, 1974).

Moscovici's (1976) focus on the importance of behavioural style was extended by Mugny (1982) who focused on the strategic use of behavioural styles by real, active minorities struggling to change societal practices. Mugny argued that because minorities are typically in powerless positions relative to majorities, they have to negotiate their influence with the majority rather than unilaterally adopt a behavioural style. Mugny distinguished between rigid and flexible negotiating styles, arguing that a rigid minority that refuses to compromise on any issues risks being rejected as dogmatic, and a minority that is too prepared to flexibly shift its ground and compromise risks being rejected as inconsistent (the classic case of 'flip-flopping'). There is a fine line to tread, but a degree of flexibility is more effective than rigidity. A minority should be absolutely consistent with regard to its core position but should adopt a relatively open-minded and reasonable negotiating style on less core issues (e.g. Mugny & Papastamou, 1981).

## Conversion theory

In 1980 Moscovici supplemented his earlier genetic model of social influence with his conversion theory (Moscovici, 1980, 1985a). Conversion theory remains the dominant explanation of minority influence. The genetic model focused largely on how a minority's behavioural style (in particular, attributions based on the minority's consistent behaviour) could enhance its influence over a majority, whereas conversion theory is a more cognitive account of how a member of the majority processes the minority's message.

Moscovici argued that majorities and minorities exert influence through different processes. Majority influence produces direct public compliance for reasons of normative

**Conversion**
If you and your friends repeatedly and consistently told your friend Pierre that this was the Eiffel Tower, would he eventually believe you?

or informational dependence. People engage in a *comparison process* in which they concentrate attention on what others say to know how to fit in with them. Majority views are accepted passively without much thought. The outcome is public compliance with majority views with little or no private attitude change.

In contrast, minority influence produces indirect, often latent, private change in opinion due to the cognitive conflict and restructuring that deviant ideas produce. People engage in a *validation process* in which they carefully examine and cogitate over the validity of their beliefs. The outcome is little or no overt public agreement with the minority, for fear of being viewed as a member of the minority, but a degree of private internal attitude change that may only surface later on. Minorities produce a **conversion effect** as a consequence of active consideration of the minority point of view.

**Conversion effect**
When minority influence brings about a sudden and dramatic internal and private change in the attitudes of a majority.

Moscovici's dual-process model of influence embodies a distinction that is very similar to that discussed earlier between normative and informational influence, and is related to Petty and Cacioppo's (1986a) distinction between peripheral and central processing, and Chaiken's (Bohner, Moskowitz & Chaiken, 1995) distinction between heuristic and systematic processing (see Chapter 6; Eagly & Chaiken, 1993).

Empirical evidence for conversion theory can be organised around three testable hypotheses (Martin & Hewstone, 2003): direction-of-attention, content-of-thinking, differential-influence. There is support for the *direction-of-attention hypothesis* – majority influence causes people to focus on their relationship to the majority (interpersonal focus) whereas minority influence causes people to focus on the minority message itself (message focus) (e.g. Campbell, Tesser, & Fairey, 1986). There is also support for the *content-of-thinking hypothesis* – majority influence leads to superficial examination of arguments whereas minority influence leads to detailed evaluation of arguments (e.g. Maass & Clark, 1983; Martin, 1996; Mucchi-Faina, Maass, & Volpato, 1991).

The *differential-influence hypothesis,* that majority influence produces more public/direct influence than private/indirect influence whereas minority influence produces the opposite has received most research attention and support (see Wood, Lundgren, Ouellette, Busceme, & Blackstone, 1994). For example, the studies described above by Moscovici, Lage, and Naffrechoux (1969) and Moscovici and Lage (1976) found, as would be expected from conversion theory, that conversion through minority influence took longer to manifest itself than compliance through majority influence; there was evidence for private change in colour thresholds (i.e., conversion) among participants exposed to a consistent minority, although they did not behave (or had not yet behaved) publicly in line with this change.

Another series of studies, by Maass and Clark (1983, 1986), report three experiments investigating people's public and private reactions to majority and minority influence regarding the issue of gay rights. In one of these experiments Maass & Clark (1983) found that publicly expressed attitudes conformed to the expressed views of the majority (i.e. if the majority was pro-gay, then so were the participants), while privately expressed attitudes shifted towards the position espoused by the minority (see Figure 7.10).

Perhaps the most intriguing support for the *differential-influence hypothesis* comes from an intriguing series of experiments by Moscovici and Personnaz (1980, 1986), who employed the blue–green paradigm described above. Individual participants, judging the

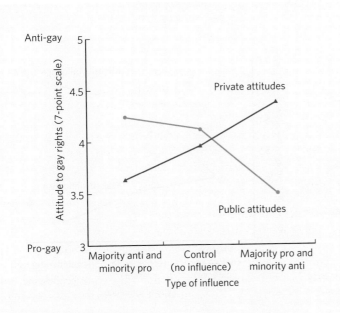

**Figure 7.10** Public and private attitude change in response to majority and minority influence

Relative to a no-influence control condition, heterosexual *public* attitudes towards gay rights closely reflected the pro- or anti-gay attitudes of the majority. However, *private* attitudes reflected the pro- or anti-gay attitudes of the minority

*Source*: based on data from Maass & Clark (1983)

colour of obviously blue slides that varied only in intensity, were exposed to a single confederate who always called the blue slides 'green'. They were led to believe that most people (82 per cent) would respond as the confederate did, or that only very few people (18 per cent) would. In this way, the confederate was a source of majority or minority influence. Participants publicly called out the colour of the slide and then (and this is the ingenious twist introduced by Moscovici and Personnaz) the slide was removed and participants wrote down privately the colour of the after-image. Unknown to most people, including the participants, the after-image is always the complementary colour. So, for blue slides the after-image would be yellow, and for green slides it would be purple.

There were three phases to the experiment: an influence phase, where participants were exposed to the confederate, preceded and followed by phases where the confederate was absent and there was thus no influence. The results were remarkable (see Figure 7.11). Majority influence hardly affected the chromatic after-image: it remained yellow, indicating that participants had seen a blue slide. Minority influence, however, shifted the after-image towards purple, indicating that participants had actually 'seen' a green slide! The effect persisted even when the minority confederate was absent.

This remarkable finding clearly supports the idea that minority influence produces indirect, latent internal change, while majority influence produces direct, immediate behavioural compliance. Moscovici and Personnaz have been able to replicate it, but others have been less successful. For example, in a direct replication Doms and van Avermaet (1980) found after-image changes after both minority and majority influence, and Sorrentino, King and Leo (1980) found no after-image shift after minority influence, except among participants who were suspicious of the experiment.

To try to resolve the contradictory findings, Martin conducted a series of five careful replications of Moscovici and Personnaz's paradigm (Martin, 1998). His pattern of findings revealed that participants tended to show a degree of after-image shift only if they paid close attention to the blue slides – this occurred among participants who were either suspicious of the experiment or who were exposed to many, rather than a few, slides.

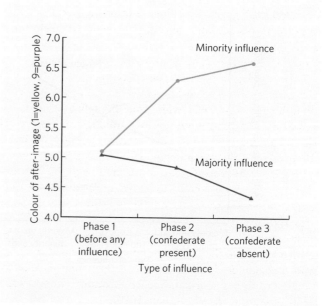

**Figure 7.11** Reported colour of chromatic after-image as a result of majority and minority influence

Participants exposed to a majority member who wrongly identified blue slides as green did not change their perception: their after-images did not alter. However, participants exposed to a minority member who called the blue slides green did change their perception: their after-images changed and continued to change even after influence had ceased

*Source:* based on data from Moscovici & Personnaz (1980)

The key point is that circumstances that made people attend more closely to the blue slides caused them actually to see more green in the slides and thus to report an after-image that was shifted towards the after-image of green. These findings suggest that Moscovici and his colleagues' intriguing after-image findings may not reflect distinct minority/majority influence processes but may be a methodological artefact. This does not mean that conversion theory is wrong, but it does question the status of the blue–green studies as evidence for conversion theory. Martin (1998) comes to the relatively cautious conclusion that the findings may at least partially be an artefact of the amount of attention participants were paying to the slides: the greater the attention, the greater the after-image shift.

## Convergent–divergent theory

A slightly different account of majority/minority differences in influence has been proposed by Nemeth (1986, 1995). Because people expect to share attitudes with the majority, the discovery through majority influence that their attitudes are in fact in disagreement with those of the majority is surprising and stressful. It leads to a self-protective narrowing of focus of attention. This produces convergent thinking that inhibits consideration of alternative views. In contrast, because people do not expect to share attitudes with a minority, the discovery of disagreement associated with minority influence is unsurprising and not stressful and does not narrow focus of attention. It allows divergent thinking that involves consideration of a range of alternative views, even ones not proposed by the minority.

In this way, Nemeth believes that exposure to minority views can stimulate innovation and creativity, generate more and better ideas, and lead to superior decision making in groups. The key difference between Nemeth's (1986) convergent–divergent theory and Moscovici's (1980) conversion theory hinges on the relationship between 'stress' and message processing: for Nemeth, majority-induced stress restricts message processing; for Moscovici, minority-induced stress elaborates message processing.

Convergent–divergent theory is supported by research using relatively straightforward cognitive tasks. Minority influence improves performance relative to majority influence on tasks that benefit from divergent thinking (e.g. Martin & Hewstone, 1999; Nemeth & Wachtler, 1983); majority influence improves performance relative to minority influence on tasks that benefit from convergent thinking (e.g. Peterson & Nemeth, 1996); and minority influence leads to the generation of more creative and novel judgements than does majority influence (e.g. Mucchi-Faina, Maass, & Volpato, 1991; Nemeth & Wachtler, 1983).

For example, the Nemeth studies (Nemeth, 1986; Nemeth & Wachtler, 1983) employed Asch-type and blue–green paradigms in which participants exposed to majority or minority influence converged, with little thought, on majority responses; but minorities stimulated divergent, novel, creative thinking, and more active information processing, which increased the probability of correct answers. Mucchi-Faina, Maass and Volpato (1991) used a different paradigm to find that students at the University of Perugia generated more original and creative ideas for promoting the international image of the city of Perugia when they had been exposed to a conventional majority and a creative minority than vice versa, or where the majority and the minority were both original or both conventional.

Research on convergent–divergent theory also shows that minority influence leads people to explore different strategies for problem solving whereas majority influence restricts people to the majority-endorsed strategy (e.g. Butera, Mugny, Legrenzi, & Pérez, 1996; Peterson & Nemeth, 1996) and that minority influence encourages issue-relevant thinking whereas majority influence encourages message-relevant thinking (e.g. De Dreu, De Vries, Gordijn, & Schuurman, 1999).

## Social identity and self-categorisation

We already saw above that the social identity theory of influence in groups, referent informational influence theory (e.g., Abrams & Hogg, 1990a; Hogg & Turner, 1987a; Turner & Oakes, 1989), views prototypical ingroup members as the most reliable source of information about what is normative for the group – the attitudes and behaviours that define and characterise the group. Through the process of self-categorisation group members perceive themselves and behave in line with the norm.

From this perspective, minorities should be extremely ineffective sources of influence. Groups in society that promulgate minority viewpoints are generally widely stigmatised by the majority as social outgroups, or are 'psychologised' as deviant individuals. Their views are, at best, rejected as irrelevant, but they are often ridiculed and trivialised in an attempt to discredit the minority (e.g. the treatment of gays, environmentalists, intellectuals; see Chapter 10 for a discussion of discrimination against outgroups). All this resistance on the part of the majority makes it very difficult for minorities to have effective influence.

So, from a social identity perspective, how can a minority within one's group be influential? According to David and Turner (2001), the problem for ingroup minorities is that the majority group makes intragroup social comparisons that highlight and accentuate the minority's otherness, essentially concretising a majority-versus-minority intergroup contrast within the group.

The key to effective minority influence is for the minority to somehow make the majority shift its level of social comparison to focus on intergroup comparisons with a genuine shared outgroup. This process automatically transcends intragroup divisions and focuses attention on the minority's ingroup credentials. The minority is now viewed as part of the ingroup, and there is indirect attitude change that may not be manifested overtly. For example, a radical faction within Islam will have more influence within Islam if Muslims make intergroup comparisons between Islam and the West than if they dwell on intra-Islam comparisons between majority and minority factions.

Research confirms that minorities do indeed exert more influence if they are perceived by the majority as an ingroup (Maass, Clark & Haberkorn, 1982; Martin, 1988; Mugny & Papastamou, 1982); and studies by David and Turner (1996, 1999) show that ingroup minorities produced more indirect attitude change (i.e., conversion) than did outgroup minorities, and majorities produced surface compliance. However, other research has found that an outgroup minority has just as much indirect influence as an ingroup minority (see review by Pérez & Mugny, 1998) and, according to Martin and Hewstone (2003), more research is needed to confirm that conversion is generated by the process of self-categorisation.

## Vested interest and the leniency contract

Overall minorities are more influential if they can avoid being categorised by the majority as a despised outgroup and can be considered by the majority as part of the ingroup. The challenge for a minority is to be able to achieve this at the same time as promulgating an unwaveringly consistent alternative viewpoint that differs from the majority position. How can minorities successfully have it both ways – be thought of as an ingroup *and* hold an unwavering outgroup position?

The trick is psychologically to establish one's legitimate ingroup credentials before drawing undue critical attention to one's distinct minority viewpoint. Crano's context-comparison model of minority influence describes how this may happen (e.g. Crano, 2001; Crano & Alvaro, 1998; Crano & Chen, 1998; Crano & Seyranian, 2009). When a minority's message involves weak or unvested attitudes (i.e. attitudes that are relatively flexible, not fixed or absolute), an ingroup minority can be quite persuasive — the message is distinctive and attracts attention and elaboration, and, by virtue of the message being unvested and the minority a clear ingroup, there is little threat that might invite derogation or rejection of the minority. An outgroup minority is likely to be derogated and not influential.

When the message involves strong or vested (i.e. fixed, inflexible and absolute) attitudes, it is more difficult for the minority to prevail. The message is not only highly distinctive but speaks to core group attributes. The inclination is to reject the message and the minority outright. However, the fact that the minority is actually part of the ingroup makes members reluctant to do so – to derogate people who are, after all, ingroup members. One way out of this dilemma is to establish with the minority what Crano calls a leniency contract. Essentially, the majority assumes that because the minority is an ingroup minority it is unlikely to want to destroy the majority's core attributes, and in turn the majority is lenient towards the minority and its views. This enables the majority to elaborate open-mindedly on the ingroup minority's message, without defensiveness or hostility and without derogating the minority. This leniency toward an ingroup minority leads to indirect attitude change. An outgroup minority does not invite leniency and is therefore likely to be strongly derogated as a threat to core group attitudes.

The logic behind this analysis is that disagreement between people who define themselves as members of the same group is both unexpected and unnerving – it raises subjective uncertainty about themselves and their attributes, and motivates uncertainty reduction (Hogg, 2007b, in press). Where common ingroup membership is important and 'inescapable', there will be a degree of redefinition of group attributes in line with the minority: that is, the minority has been effective. Where common ingroup membership is unimportant and easily denied, there will be no redefinition of ingroup attributes in line with the minority: that is, the minority will be ineffective.

## Attribution and social impact

Many aspects of minority influence suggest an underlying **attribution** process (Hewstone, 1989; Kelley, 1967; see also Chapter 3). Effective minorities are consistent and consensual, distinct from the majority, unmotivated by self-interest or external pressures, and flexible in style. This combination of factors encourages a perception that the minority has chosen its position freely. It is therefore difficult to explain away its position in terms of idiosyncrasies of individuals (although this is, as we saw above, a strategy that is attempted), or in terms of external inducements or threats. Perhaps, then, there is actually some intrinsic merit to its position. This encourages people to take the minority seriously (although again social forces work against this) and at least consider its position; such cognitive work is an important precondition for subsequent attitude change.

Although majorities and minorities can be defined in terms of power, they also of course refer to numbers of people. Although 'minorities' are often both less powerful and less numerous (e.g. West Indians in Britain), they can be less powerful but more numerous (e.g. Tibetans versus Chinese in Tibet). Perhaps not surprisingly, an attempt has been made to explain minority influence purely in terms of social influence consequences of relative numerosity.

Latané and Wolf (1981) draw on **social impact** theory (e.g. Latané, 1981) to argue that as a source of influence increases in size (number), it has more influence. However, as the cumulative source of influence gets larger, the impact of each additional source is reduced – a single source has enormous impact, the addition of a second source increases impact but not by as much as the first, a third even less, and so on. A good analogy is switching on a single light in a dark room – the impact is enormous. A second light improves things, but only a little. If you have ten lights on, the impact of an eleventh is negligible. Evidence does support this idea: the more numerous the source of influence, the more impact it has, with

**Attribution**
The process of assigning a cause to our own behaviour, and that of others.

**Social impact**
The effect that other people have on our attitudes and behaviour, usually as a consequence of factors such as group size, and temporal and physical immediacy.

incremental changes due to additional sources decreasing with increasing size (e.g. Mullen, 1983; Tanford & Penrod, 1984).

But how does this account for the fact that minorities can actually have influence? One explanation is that the effect of a large majority on an individual majority member has reached a plateau: additional members or 'bits' of majority influence have relatively little impact. Although a minority viewpoint has relatively little impact, it has not yet attained a plateau: additional members or 'bits' of minority influence have a relatively large impact. In this way, exposure to minority positions can, paradoxically, have greater impact than exposure to majority viewpoints.

## Two processes or one?

Although the social impact perspective can account for some quantitative differences between majority and minority influence at the level of overt public behaviour, even Latané and Wolf (1981) concede that it cannot explain the qualitative differences that seem to exist, particularly at the private level of covert cognitive changes. These qualitative differences, and particularly the process differences proposed by Moscovici's (1980) conversion theory, are themselves the focus of some debate, however.

For instance, there is some concern (e.g. Abrams & Hogg, 1990a; Turner, 1991) that the postulation of separate processes to explain minority and majority influence has revived the opposition of informational and normative influence. As we saw earlier in this chapter, this opposition has problems in explaining other social influence phenomena. Instead, whether minorities or majorities are influential or not may be a matter of social identity dynamics that determine whether people are able to define themselves as members of the minority (majority) group or not (e.g. Crano & Seyranian, 2009; David & Turner, 2001).

In addition, theoretical analyses by Kruglanski and Mackie (1990) and a meta-analysis by Wood and colleagues (Wood, Lundgren, Ouellette, Busceme, & Blackstone, 1994) together suggest that people who are confronted with a minority position, particularly face-to-face with real social minorities and majorities, tend not only to resist an overt appearance of alignment with the minority, but also privately and cognitively to avoid alignment with the minority. This conflicts with Moscovici's dual-process conversion theory.

# Summary

- Social influence can produce surface behavioural compliance with requests, obedience of commands, internalised conformity to group norms, and deep-seated attitude change.

- People tend to be more readily influenced by reference groups, because they are psychologically significant for our attitudes and behaviour, than by membership groups, as they are simply groups to which we belong by some external criterion.

- Given the right circumstances, we all have the potential to obey commands blindly, even if the consequences of such obedience include harm to others.

- Obedience is affected by the proximity and legitimacy of authority, by the proximity of the victim, and by the degree of social support for obedience or disobedience.

- Group norms are enormously powerful sources of conformity: we all tend to yield to the majority.

- Conformity can be reduced if the task is unambiguous and we are not under surveillance, although even under these circumstances there is often residual conformity. Lack of unanimity among the majority is particularly effective in reducing conformity.

- People may conform in order to feel sure about the objective validity of their perceptions and opinions, to obtain social approval and avoid social disapproval, or to express or validate their social identity as members of a specific group.

- Active minorities can sometimes influence majorities: this may be the very essence of social change.

- To be effective, minorities should be consistent but not rigid, should be seen to be making personal sacrifices and acting out of principle, and should be perceived as being part of the ingroup.

- Minorities may be effective because, unlike majority influence which is based on 'mindless' compliance, minority influence causes latent cognitive change as a consequence of thought produced by the cognitive challenge posed by the novel minority position.

- Minorities can be more effective if they are treated by the majority group as ingroup minorities rather than outgroup minorities.

## Literature, film and TV

### *American Beauty* and *Revolutionary Road*

Two powerful films by Sam Mendes that explore conformity and independence. Set in American suburbia the 1999 film *American Beauty,* starring Kevin Spacey, is a true classic about suffocating conformity to social roles, and what can happen when people desperately try to break free. *Revolutionary Road* is a 2008 film, starring Leonardo DiCaprio and Kate Winslet, which explores the same theme with a focus on the drudgery and routine of adult life and the lost dreams of youth, and again on the challenge and consequences of change.

### *Little Miss Sunshine*

Hilarious 2006 film, directed by Jonathan Dayton and Valerie Faris. A breathtakingly dysfunctional family sets out in their decrepit VW van to drive from Arizona to Los Angeles for their daughter Olive (Abigail Breslin) to appear in an absolutely grotesque children's beauty pageant. Featuring Toni Collette, Steve Carell, Greg Kinnear and Alan Arkin, this is a film about interpersonal relations and families (relevant to Chapter 13) but also about non-conformity and violation of social conventions.

### *Eichmann in Jerusalem: A report on the banality of evil*

1963 book by H. Arendt on the Nuremberg war trials of the Nazis. It shows how these people came across as very ordinary people who were only following orders.

### *Rebel Without a Cause*

1955 film directed by Nicholas Ray, and with James Dean and Natalie Wood. An all-time classic film about non-conformity, counter-conformity and independence. James Dean stands out against social and group roles and expectations, and sets the mould for teenage 'rebellion' in future decades.

### *Che*

2008 two-part biopic of Che Guevara's role in Fidel Castro's toppling of the Cuban Dictator Fulgencia Batista in 1959. The films, directed by Stephen Soderbergh and starring Benicio del Toro as the now legendary Che Guevara, bring to life the nature of social change through revolution.

### *Town Bloody Hall*

1979 documentary by D. A. Pennebaker and Chris Hegedus. Pennebaker and Hegedus simply filmed a 1971 public debate between grizzly Norman Mailer (representing conservative male attitudes of the early 1970s) and a group of radical feminists including Germaine Greer, Susan Sontag and Jill Johnston. The film illustrates the clash of attitudes and how dominant groups often do not hear or simply ridicule the position taken by active minorities who are trying to change the status quo. What characterises this film is that the speakers are, for the most part, highly intelligent and articulate advocates for their positions.

## Guided questions

1  Is it true that women conform more than men to group pressure?

2  Why did Stanley Milgram undertake his controversial studies of *obedience to authority*? Watch the video illustrating Milgram's research in Chapter 7 of MyPsychLab at **www. mypsychlab.co.uk** (watch *Milgram's obedience study*).

3  How does the social context impact on people when they need to state their opinions in public?

4  What are the two major social influence processes associated with conformity?

5  Can a *minority group* really bring about social change by confronting a majority?

## Learn more

Baron, R. S., & Kerr, N. (2003). *Group process, group decision, group action* (2nd ed.). Buckingham, UK: Open University Press. A general overview of some major topics in the study of group processes; includes discussion of social influence phenomena.

Brown, R. J. (2000). *Group processes* (2nd ed.). Oxford, UK: Blackwell. A very readable introduction to group processes, which also places an emphasis on social influence processes within groups, especially conformity, norms and minority influence.

Cialdini, R. B., & Trost, M. R. (1998). Social influence: Social norms, conformity, and compliance. In D. Gilbert, S. T. Fiske & G. Lindzey (eds), *The handbook of social psychology* (4th ed., Vol. 2, pp. 151–92). New York: McGraw-Hill. A thorough overview of social influence research with a particular emphasis on norms and persuasion.

Fiske, S. T. (2007). Social power. In A. W. Kruglanski & E. T. Higgins (eds), *Social psychology: Handbook of basic principles* (2nd ed., pp. 678–92). New York: Guilford Press. A complete, detailed and up-to-date overview of the social psychology of power.

Hogg, M. A. (2010). Influence and leadership. In S. T. Fiske, D. T. Gilbert, & G. Lindzey (eds), *Handbook of social psychology* (5th ed., Vol. 2, pp. 1166–207). New York: Wiley. Up-to-date and detailed coverage of research on social influence processes, with a major section on minority influence.

Martin, R., & Hewstone, M. (2007). Social influence processes of control and change: Conformity, obedience to authority, and innovation. In M. A. Hogg & J. Cooper (eds), *The SAGE handbook of social psychology: Concise student edition* (pp. 312–32). London: SAGE. An up-to-date and comprehensive review of social influence research, including conformity, obedience and minority influence.

Mugny, G., & Pérez, J. A. (1991). *The social psychology of minority influence*. Cambridge, UK: Cambridge University Press. An overview of research on minority influence by two leading scholars of this notably European topic; also coverage of Mugny and Moscovici's own theories of minority influence.

Turner, J. C. (1991). *Social influence*. Buckingham, UK: Open University Press. Scholarly discussion of social influence which takes a critical stance from a European perspective and places particular emphasis on social identity, minority influence and the role of group membership and group norms.

Refresh your understanding, assess your progress and go further with interactive summaries, questions, podcasts and much more at **www.mypsychlab.co.uk**

## This chapter discusses

- The nature of human groups
- Group effects on individual performance
- Social facilitation
- Group versus individual performance: social loafing
- Group cohesiveness
- Group socialisation
- Group norms
- Group structure: roles, status and communication networks
- Deviance
- Why people join groups

## Focus questions

1. Alone in his room, James can reliably play a tricky guitar riff really well – precise and clear. When his friends ask him to play it for them, it all goes horribly wrong, sounding like he has overcooked spaghetti for fingers. Why do you think this happens?

2. You want to make sure that new members of the small organisation you run are totally committed to it and its goals. You could make the experience of joining smooth, easy and pleasant; or you could make it quite daunting with a bewildering array of initiation rites and embarrassing hurdles to clear. Which would be more effective, when and why?

3. Would you offer to reward a close family member with money after enjoying a meal at their house? Why not? See an amusing account by Dan Ariely of a clash between two social norms in Chapter 8 of MyPsychLab at **www.mypsychlab.co.uk** (watch *The cost of social norms* – **http://www.youtube.com/watch?v=AlqtbPKjf6Q& feature=related**).

4. Andrea writes very quickly and neatly and is good at taking notes. She works for a large corporation and is very ambitious to rise to the top. She finds it flattering that her boss assigns her the role of taking notes in important executive meetings. She is keen to please and so always agrees – leaving her sitting at the back scribbling away on her notepad while others talk and make decisions. Is she wise to agree? Why, or why not?

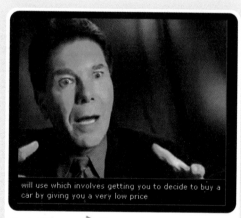

will use which involves getting you to decide to buy a car by giving you a very low price

Go to **mypsychlab** to explore video and test your understanding of key topics addressed in this chapter.

Refresh your understanding with interactive summaries, explore topics further with video and audio clips and assess your progress with quick test and essay questions by logging to the accompanying website at **www.mypsychlab.co.uk**

# Chapter 8
## People in groups

**Key terms**

Audience effects
Cognitive dissonance
Cohesiveness
Communication network
Coordination loss
Correspondence bias
Diffuse status characteristics
Distraction–conflict theory
Drive theory
Entitativity
Ethnomethodology

Evaluation apprehension model
Expectation states theory
Frame of reference
Free-rider effect
Group
Group socialisation
Group structure
Initiation rites
Mere presence
Meta-analysis
Norms
Personal attraction
Process loss
Ringelmann effect

Roles
Schism
Social attraction
Social compensation
Social facilitation
Social impact
Social loafing
Social ostracism
Specific status characteristics
Status
Stereotype
Task taxonomy
Terror management theory

# What is a group?

**Group**
Two or more people who share a common definition and evaluation of themselves and behave in accordance with such a definition.

The social **group** occupies much of our day-to-day life. We work in groups, we socialise in groups, we play in groups, and we represent our views and attitudes through groups. Groups also largely determine the people we are and the sorts of lives we live. Selection panels, juries, committees and government bodies influence what we do, where we live and how we live. The groups to which we belong determine what language we speak, what accent we have, what attitudes we hold, what cultural practices we adopt, what education we receive, what level of prosperity we enjoy and ultimately who we are. Even those groups to which we do not belong, either by choice or by exclusion, have a profound impact on our lives. In this tight matrix of group influences, the domain of the autonomous, independent, unique self may indeed be limited.

Groups differ in all sorts of respects (Deaux, Reid, Mizrahi & Ethier, 1995). Some have a large number of members (e.g. a nation, a sex), and others are small (a committee, a family); some are relatively short-lived (a group of friends, a jury), and some endure for thousands of years (an ethnic group, a religion); some are concentrated (a flight crew, a selection committee), others dispersed (academics, computer-mediated communication groups); some are highly structured and organised (an army, an ambulance team), and others are more informally organised (a supporters' club, a community action group); some have highly specific purposes (an assembly line, an environmental protest group), and others are more general (a tribal group, a teenage 'gang'); some are relatively autocratic (an army, a police force), others relatively democratic (a university department, a commune); and so on.

Any social group can thus be described by an array of features that highlight similarities to, and differences from, other groups. These can be very general features, such as membership size (e.g. a religion versus a committee), but they can also be very specific features, such as group practices and beliefs (e.g. Catholics versus Muslims, liberals versus conservatives, Masai versus Kikuyu). This enormous variety of groups could be reduced by limiting the number of significant dimensions to produce a restricted taxonomy of groups. Social psychologists have tended to focus more on group size, group 'atmosphere', task structure and leadership structure than other dimensions.

## Categories and group entitativity

Human groups are quite clearly categories – some people share characteristics and are in the group and people who do not share the characteristics are not in the group. As such, human groups should differ in ways that categories in general differ. One of the key ways in which categories differ is in terms of entitativity (Campbell, 1958). **Entitativity** is the property of a group that makes it appear to be a distinct, coherent and bounded entity. High-entitativity groups have clear boundaries, and are internally well-structured and relatively homogeneous; low entitativity groups have fuzzy boundaries and structure and are relatively heterogenous.

**Entitativity**
The property of a group that makes it seem like a coherent, distinct and unitary entity.

Groups certainly differ in terms of entitativity (Hamilton & Sherman, 1996; Lickel, Hamilton, Wieczorkowska, Lewis, & Sherman, 2000). Hamilton and Lickel and colleagues claim there are qualitative differences in the nature of groups as they decrease in entitativity, and that groups can be classified into four different general types with decreasing entitativity: intimacy groups, task groups, social categories, loose associations.

## Common-bond and common-identity groups

One classic and important distinction in the social sciences between types of human groups was originally made in 1887 by Tönnies (1955) between *Gemeinschaft* (i.e. community) and *Gesellschaft* (i.e. association): that is, social organisation based on close interpersonal bonds and social organisation based on more formalised and impersonal associations. This distinction has resurfaced in contemporary social psychology in a slightly different form that focuses on a general distinction between similarity-based or categorical groups, and interaction-based or dynamic groups (Arrow, McGrath & Berdahl, 2000; Wilder & Simon, 1998).

For example, Prentice, Miller and Lightdale (1994) distinguish between *common-bond* groups (groups based upon attachment among members) and *common-identity* groups (groups based on direct attachment to the group). Resarch by Utz and Sassenberg has found that members of common-bond groups operate according to an egocentric principle of maximising their rewards and minimising their costs with respect to their own contributions – in common-bond groups, personal goals are more salient than group goals. In contrast members of common-identity groups operate according to an altruistic principle of maximising the group's rewards and minimising its costs through their own contributions – in common-identity groups, group goals are more salient than personal goals because the group provides an important source of identity (Sassenberg, 2002; Utz & Sassenberg, 2002).

Other research, by Seeley and colleagues (Seeley, Gardner, Pennington, & Gabriel, 2003) has found sex differences in preferences for group type that may have consequences for the longevity of the group. Women were attached to groups in which they felt close to the other members (common bonds were more important), whereas men rated groups as important when they were attached to individual members and the group as a whole (common identity was more important). If the common bonds in a group disappear, the group may no longer be valuable for women, whereas the common identity of the group would allow men to remain attracted to it. Thus some men's groups may last longer than women's groups because of the greater importance they place on group identity.

## Groups and aggregates

Not all collections of people can be considered groups in a psychological sense. For example, people with green eyes, strangers in a dentist's waiting room, people on a beach, children waiting for a bus – are these groups? Perhaps not. More likely these are merely social aggregates, collections of unrelated individuals – not groups at all. The important social psychological question is what distinguishes groups from aggregates; it is by no means an easy question to answer. Social psychologists differ in their views on this issue. These differences are, to some extent, influenced by whether the researcher favours an individualistic or a collectivistic perspective on groups (Hogg & Abrams, 1988; Turner & Oakes, 1989).

*Individualists* believe that people in groups behave in much the same way as they do in pairs or by themselves, and that group processes are really nothing more than interpersonal processes between a number of people (e.g. Allport, 1924; Latané, 1981). *Collectivists* believe that the behaviour of people in groups is influenced by unique social processes and cognitive representations that can only occur in and emerge from groups (Abrams & Hogg, 2004; McDougall, 1920; Sherif, 1936; Tajfel & Turner, 1979).

## Definitions

Although there are almost as many definitions of the social group as there are social psychologists who research social groups, Johnson and Johnson (1987) have identified seven major emphases. The group is:

1  a collection of individuals who are interacting with one another;
2  a social unit consisting of two or more individuals who perceive themselves as belonging to a group;
3  a collection of individuals who are interdependent;
4  a collection of individuals who join together to achieve a goal;
5  a collection of individuals who are trying to satisfy a need through their joint association;
6  a collection of individuals whose interactions are structured by a set of roles and norms;
7  a collection of individuals who influence each other.

Their definition incorporates all these emphases:

> A group is two or more individuals in face-to-face interaction, each aware of his or her membership in the group, each aware of the others who belong to the group, and each aware of their positive interdependence as they strive to achieve mutual goals. (*Johnson & Johnson, 1987, p. 8*)

You will notice that this definition, and many of the emphases in the previous paragraph, cannot encompass large groups and/or do not distinguish between interpersonal and group relationships. This is a relatively accurate portrayal of much of the classic social psychology of group processes, which is generally restricted, explicitly or implicitly, to small, face-to-face, short-lived, interactive, task-oriented groups. In addition, 'group processes' generally do not mean *group* processes but interpersonal processes between more than two people. However, in more recent years the study of group processes has been increasingly strongly influenced by perspectives that consider the roles of identity and relations between large-scale social categories (e.g. Brown, 2000; Hogg & Tindale, 2001; Stangor, 2004).

# The effect of the group on individual performance

## Mere presence and audience effects: social facilitation

Perhaps the most elementary *social* psychological question concerns the effect of the presence of other people on someone's behaviour: 'What changes in an individual's normal solitary performance occur when other people are present?' (Allport, 1954a, p. 46). You are playing a musical instrument, fixing the car, reciting a poem or exercising in the gym, and someone comes to watch; what happens to your performance? Does it improve or deteriorate?

This question intrigued Norman Triplett (1898), credited by some as having conducted the first social psychology experiment, although there has been controversy about this (see Chapter 1). From observing that people cycled faster when paced than when alone, and faster when in competition than when paced, Triplett hypothesised that competition between people energised and improved performance on motor tasks. To test this idea, he had young children reeling a continuous loop of line on a 'competition machine'. He confirmed his hypothesis: more children reeled the line more quickly when racing against each other in pairs than when performing alone.

Floyd Allport (1920) termed this phenomenon **social facilitation** but felt that Triplett confined it too narrowly to a context of competition, and it could be widened to allow for a more general principle: that an improvement in performance could be due to the **mere presence** of conspecifics (i.e. members of the same species) as coactors (doing the same thing but not interacting) or as a passive audience (passively watching).

Until the late 1930s, there was an enormous amount of research on social facilitation, much of it conducted on an exotic array of animals. For example, we now know that cockroaches run faster, chickens, fish and rats eat more, and pairs of rats copulate more, when being 'watched' by conspecifics or when conspecifics are also running, eating or copulating! However, research has also revealed that social presence can produce quite the opposite effect – social inhibition, or a decrease in task performance.

Contradictory findings such as these, in conjunction with imprecision in defining the degree of social presence (early research focused on coaction, whereas later research focused on passive **audience effects**), led to the near demise of social facilitation research by about 1940.

## Drive theory

In 1965, Zajonc published a classic theoretical statement, called **drive theory** (see Figure 8.1), which revived social facilitation research and kept it alive for many decades (see Geen, 1989; Guerin, 1986, 1993). Zajonc set himself the task of explaining what determines whether social presence (mainly in the form of a passive audience) facilitates or inhibits performance.

**Social facilitation**
An improvement in the performance of well-learned/easy tasks and a deterioration in the performance of poorly learned/difficult tasks in the mere presence of members of the same species.

**Mere presence**
Refers to an entirely passive and unresponsive audience that is only physically present.

**Audience effects**
Impact on individual task performance of the presence of others.

**Drive theory**
Zajonc's theory that the physical presence of members of the same species instinctively causes arousal that motivates performance of habitual behaviour patterns.

**Social facilitation**
He has been practicing hard at home. What will determine whether he will soar or crash in front of an audience?

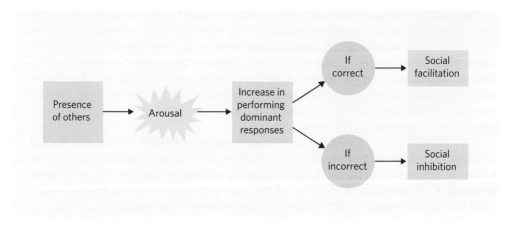

**Figure 8.1** Zajonc's drive theory of social facilitation
- The presence of others automatically produces arousal, which 'drives' dominant responses.
- Performance is improved by a 'correct' dominant response, but is impaired by an 'incorrect' dominant response

*Source*: based on Zajonc (1965)

Drive theory argues that because people are relatively unpredictable (you can rarely know with any certainty exactly what they are going to do), there is a clear advantage to the species for people's presence to cause us to be in a state of alertness and readiness. Increased arousal or motivation is thus an instinctive reaction to social presence. Such arousal functions as a 'drive' that energises (i.e. causes us to enact) that behaviour which is our dominant response (i.e. best learned, most habitual) in that situation. If the dominant response is correct (we feel the task is easy), then social presence produces an improved performance; if it is incorrect (we feel the task is difficult), then social presence produces an impaired performance.

Let us illustrate this with an example. You are a novice violinist with a small repertoire of pieces to play. There is one piece that, when playing alone, you find extremely easy because it is very well learned – you almost never make mistakes. If you were to play this piece in front of an audience (say, your friends), drive theory would predict that, because your dominant response is to make no mistakes, your performance would be greatly improved. In contrast, there is another piece that, when playing alone, you find extremely difficult because it is not very well learned – you almost never get it right. It would be a rash decision indeed to play this in front of an audience – drive theory would predict that, because the dominant response contains all sorts of errors, your performance would be truly awful, much worse than when you play alone.

### Evaluation apprehension

Although early research tends on the whole to support drive theory (Geen & Gange, 1977; Guerin & Innes, 1982), some social psychologists have questioned whether mere presence instinctively produces drive. Cottrell (1972) has proposed an **evaluation apprehension model**, in which he argues that we quickly learn that the social rewards and punishments (e.g. approval and disapproval) we receive are based on others' evaluations of us. Social presence thus produces an acquired arousal (drive) based on evaluation apprehension.

In support of this interpretation, Cottrell, Wack, Sekerak and Rittle (1968) found no social facilitation effect on three well-learned tasks when the two-person audience was inattentive (i.e. blindfolded) and merely present (i.e. only incidentally present while ostensibly waiting to take part in a different experiment). This audience would be unlikely to produce much evaluation apprehension. However, a non-blindfolded audience that

**Evaluation apprehension model**
The argument that the physical presence of members of the same species causes drive because people have learned to be apprehensive about being evaluated.

attended carefully to the participant's performance and had expressed an interest in watching would be expected to produce a great deal of evaluation apprehension. Indeed, this audience did produce a social facilitation effect.

Other research is less supportive. For example, Markus (1978) had male participants undress, dress in unfamiliar clothing (laboratory coat, special shoes), and then in their own clothing again. To minimise apprehension about evaluation by the experimenter, the task was presented as an incidental activity that the experimenter was not really interested in. The task was performed under one of three conditions: (1) alone; (2) in the presence of an incidental audience (low evaluation apprehension) – a confederate who faced away and was engrossed in some other task; (3) in the presence of an attentive audience (high evaluation apprehension) – a confederate who carefully and closely watched the participant dressing and undressing.

The results (see Figure 8.2) confirmed evaluation apprehension theory on the relatively easy task of dressing in familiar clothing; only an attentive audience decreased the time taken to perform this task. However, on the more difficult task of dressing in unfamiliar clothing, mere presence was sufficient to slow performance down and an attentive audience had no additional effect; this supports drive theory rather than evaluation apprehension.

Schmitt, Gilovich, Goore and Joseph (1986) conducted a similarly conceived experiment. Participants were given what they thought was an incidental task that involved typing their name into a computer (a simple task), and then entering a code name by typing their name backwards interspersed with ascending digits (a difficult task). These tasks were performed (1) *alone* after the experimenter had left the room; (2) in the *mere presence* of only a confederate who was blindfolded, wore a headset and was allegedly participating in a separate experiment on sensory deprivation; or (3) under the close *observation of the experimenter*, who remained in the room carefully scrutinising the participant's performance.

The results of the study (see Figure 8.3) show that mere presence accelerated performance of the easy task and slowed performance of the difficult task, and that evaluation apprehension had little additional impact. Mere presence appears to be a sufficient cause of, and evaluation apprehension not necessary for, social facilitation effects. (Can you reassure James about his guitar practice problem? See the first focus question.)

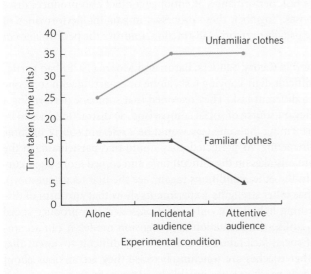

**Figure 8.2** Time taken to dress in familiar and unfamiliar clothes as a function of social presence

- Participants dressed in their own clothing (easy task) or in unfamiliar clothing (difficult task),
- They dressed either alone, with an incidental audience present or with an attentive audience present.
- Evaluation apprehension occurred on the easy task: only the attentive audience reduced the time taken to dress up.
- There was a drive effect on the difficult task: both incidental and attentive audiences increased the time taken to dress

*Source*: based on data from Markus (1978)

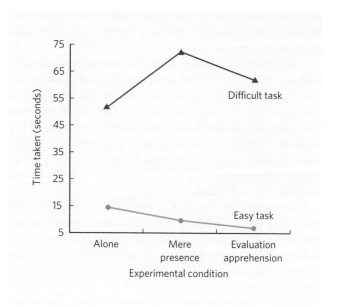

**Figure 8.3** Time taken for an easy and a difficult typing task as a function of social presence

- Participants typed their name on a computer (easy task) or typed it backwards interspersed with digits (difficult task), alone, with an incidental audience present or with an attentive audience present.
- There was a drive effect on both the easy and the difficult task.
- The incidental audience improved performance on the easy task and impaired it on the difficult task. The attentive audience had no additional effect

*Source*: based on data from Schmitt, Gilovich, Goore & Joseph (1986)

Guerin and Innes (1982) have suggested that social facilitation effects may occur only when people are unable to monitor the audience and are therefore uncertain about the audience's evaluative reactions to their performance. In support of this idea, Guerin (1989) found a social facilitation effect on a simple letter-copying task only among participants who were being watched by a confederate whom they could *not* see. When the confederate could be clearly seen, there was no social facilitation effect.

### Distraction–conflict theory

**Distraction–conflict theory**
The physical presence of members of the same species causes drive because people are distracting and produce conflict between attending to the task and attending to the audience.

The link between social presence and drive has been explained in another way by Baron and others (Baron, 1986; Sanders, 1983; Sanders, Baron & Moore, 1978) – **distraction–conflict theory** (see Figure 8.4). They argue that people are a source of distraction, which produces cognitive conflict between attending to the task and attending to the audience or co-actors. While distraction alone impairs task performance, attentional conflict also produces drive that facilitates dominant responses. Together, these processes impair the performance of difficult tasks and, because drive usually overcomes distraction, improve the performance of easy tasks.

In support of distraction–conflict theory, Sanders, Baron and Moore (1978) had participants perform an easy and a difficult digit-copying task, alone or co-acting with someone performing either the same or a different task. They reasoned that someone performing a different task would not be a relevant source of social comparison, so distraction should be minimal, whereas someone performing the same task would be a relevant source of comparison and therefore highly distracting. As predicted, they found that participants in the distraction condition made more mistakes on the difficult task, and copied more digits correctly on the simple task, than in the other conditions (again, see the first focus question).

Distraction–conflict theory has other strengths. Experiments show that any form of distraction (noise, movement, flashing lights), not only social presence, can produce social facilitation effects. In addition, unlike the evaluation apprehension model, it can accommodate results from studies of social facilitation in animals. It is difficult to accept that cockroaches eat more while other roaches are watching because they are anxious about evaluation; however, even the lowly roach can presumably be distracted.

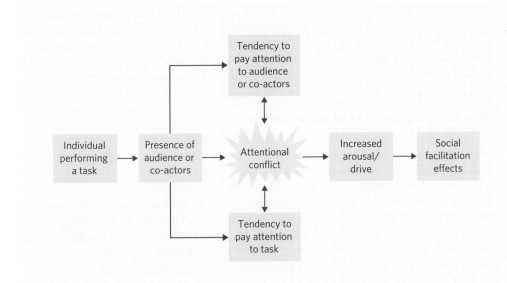

**Figure 8.4**  Distraction–conflict theory of social facilitation

The presence of an audience creates conflict between attending to the task and attending to the audience: attentional conflict produces drive that has social facilitation effects

*Source*: based on Baron & Byrne (1987)

Distraction–conflict theory also had the edge on evaluation apprehension in an experiment by Groff, Baron and Moore (1983). Whenever a tone sounded, participants had to rate the facial expressions of a person appearing on a TV monitor. At the same time, but as an ostensibly incidental activity, they had to squeeze as firmly as possible a bottle held in the hand (latency and strength of squeeze were measures of arousal/drive). Participants

**Distraction–conflict theory**

Even an audience who cannot see what you are doing can be distracting, and can impair your performance

undertook the experiment (1) alone; (2) closely scrutinised by a confederate sitting to one side – this would be highly distracting, as the participant would need to look away from the screen to look at the observer; or (3) closely scrutinised by a confederate who was actually the person on the screen – no attentional conflict. As predicted by distraction–conflict theory, participants squeezed the bottle more strongly in the second condition.

## Non-drive explanations of social facilitation

So far, we have discussed explanations of social facilitation that retain the notion of drive and differ only over whether drive is an innate response to mere presence, a learned response based on evaluation apprehension or a product of attentional conflict. Although to date these are the better established and most researched explanations of social facilitation, there are other approaches that do not retain the notion of drive. After all, it is difficult to confirm or refute the existence of drive as a mediating mechanism. There are no unambiguous and direct ways to measure it: although physiological measures of arousal (e.g. sweating palms) presumably may access drive, the absence of physiological arousal is no guarantee that drive is not operating, as drive is defined in psychological, not physiological terms.

One non-drive explanation of social facilitation is based on *self-awareness theory* (Carver & Scheier, 1981; Duval & Wicklund, 1972; Wicklund, 1975). When people focus their attention on themselves as an object, they make comparisons between their actual self (their actual task performance) and their ideal self (how they would like to perform) – see Higgins' self-discrepancy theory (Higgins, 1987, 1998) described in Chapter 4. The discrepancy between actual and ideal self increases motivation and effort to bring actual into line with ideal, so on easy tasks performance improves. On difficult tasks the discrepancy is too great, so people give up trying, and performance deteriorates. Self-awareness can be produced by a range of circumstances, such as looking at oneself in a mirror, but also by the presence of co-actors or an audience.

Still focusing on the role of 'self' in social facilitation, Bond (1982) believes that people are concerned with presenting to others the best possible impression of themselves. As this is achievable on easy tasks, social presence produces an improved performance. On more difficult tasks, people make, or anticipate making, errors: this creates embarrassment, and embarrassment impairs task performance.

Another way to explain social facilitation, without invoking self or drive, is in terms of the purely attentional consequences of social presence. This analysis is based on the general idea that people narrow the focus of their attention when they experience attentional overload (Easterbrook, 1959). Baron (1986) believes that people have a finite attention capacity, which can be overloaded by the presence of an audience. Attention overload makes people narrow their attention, give priority to attentional demands and focus on a small number of central cues. Difficult tasks are those that require attention to a large number of cues, so attentional narrowing is likely to divert attention from cues that we really ought to attend to: thus social presence impairs performance. Simple tasks are ones that require attention to only a small number of cues, so attentional narrowing actually eliminates distraction caused by attending to extraneous cues and focuses attention on to central cues: thus social presence improves performance.

This general idea has been nicely supported in an experiment by Monteil and Huguet (1999). The task was a *Stroop* task, in which participants simply have to name the colour of ink that different words are written in. Some words are neutral or consistent with the colour of ink (e.g. 'red' written in red ink) – this is an easy task with low response latencies (people respond quickly); whereas others clash (e.g. 'red' written in blue) – this is a difficult task with high latencies (people respond slowly). The participants performed the Stroop task alone or in the presence of another person. They found that latencies on the difficult task were significantly lower in the social presence condition. Social presence had narrowed attention on to the colour of ink, so that semantic interference from the word itself was reduced.

Manstead and Semin (1980) have proposed a similar attention-based model, but with the emphasis on automatic versus controlled task performance. They argue that difficult tasks require a great deal of attention because they are highly controlled. An audience distracts vital attention from task performance, which thus suffers. Easy tasks require little attention because they are fairly automatic. An audience causes more attention to be paid to the task, which thus becomes more controlled and better performed.

## Social facilitation revisited

Social psychologists have suggested and investigated many different explanations of what initially may have appeared to be a basic and straightforward social phenomenon. Some explanations fare better than others, some have not yet been properly tested, and after more than 100 years of research a number of questions remain unanswered. Nevertheless, the study of audience effects remains an important topic for social psychology, as much of our behaviour occurs in the physical presence of others as an audience. A survey administered by Borden (1980) revealed that people feared speaking in front of an audience more than heights, darkness, loneliness and even death!

However, we should keep in perspective the actual magnitude of impact that mere presence has on behaviour. From a review of 241 social facilitation experiments involving 24,000 participants, using a **meta-analysis**, Bond and Titus (1983) concluded that mere presence accounted for only a tiny 0.3 to 3.0 per cent of variation in behaviour

Social presence may have significantly greater impact if we focus on more than *mere* presence. For example, a comprehensive review of the effects of social presence on how much people eat reveals that the nature of one's relationship to those who are socially present has an influence (Herman, Roth & Polivy, 2003). When the others are friends or family and they are also eating, people tend to eat more simply because they spend more time at the table. In the presence of strangers who are eating, people follow the norm set by the others – if others eat more, they do also. In the presence of others who are not eating, people eat less because they are apprehensive about being evaluated negatively for eating too much.

In order to explain additional variation in social facilitation, we now move from non-interactive contexts to more interactive contexts and true group processes.

**Meta-analysis**
Statistical procedure that combines data from different studies to measure the overall reliability and strength of specific effects.

## Classification of group tasks

Traditional social facilitation research distinguishes between easy and difficult tasks but restricts itself to tasks that do not of necessity involve interaction, inter-individual coordination, division of labour and so forth. While many tasks fall into this category (e.g. dressing, washing the car, cycling), many others do not (e.g. building a house, playing football, running a business). It is not unreasonable to assume that social presence will have different effects on task performance, not only as a function of the degree of social presence (passive audience, co-actor, interdependent interaction on a group task) but also as a function of the specific task being performed. What is needed is a taxonomy of types of task based on a limited number of psychologically meaningful parameters.

The pragmatic question of whether groups perform better than individuals has produced such a taxonomy (Steiner, 1972, 1976). Steiner's **task taxonomy** has three dimensions, which are best captured by asking three questions:

**Task taxonomy**
Group tasks can be classified according to whether a division of labour is possible; whether there is a predetermined standard to be met; and how an individual's inputs can contribute.

1   Is the task divisible or unitary?

- A *divisible* task is one that benefits from a division of labour, where different people perform different subtasks.

- A *unitary* task cannot sensibly be broken into subtasks. Building a house is a divisible task and pulling a rope a unitary task.

2  Is it a maximising or an optimising task?

- A *maximising* task is an open-ended task that stresses quantity: the objective is to do as much as possible.

- An *optimising* task is one that has a predetermined standard: the objective is to meet the standard, neither to exceed nor fall short of it. Pulling on a rope would be a maximising task, but maintaining a specified fixed force on the rope would be an optimising task.

3  How are individual inputs related to the group's product?

- An *additive* task is one where the group's product is the sum of all the individual inputs (e.g. a group of people planting trees).

- A *compensatory* task is one where the group's product is the average of the individuals' inputs (e.g. a group of people estimating the number of bars in Amsterdam).

- A *disjunctive* task is one where the group selects as its adopted product one individual's input (e.g. a group of people proposing different things to do over the weekend will adopt one person's suggestion).

- A *conjunctive* task is one where the group's product is determined by the rate or level of performance of the slowest or least able member (e.g. a group working on an assembly line).

- A *discretionary* task is one where the relationship between individual inputs and the group's product is not directly dictated by task features or social conventions; instead, the group is free to decide on its preferred course of action (e.g. a group that *decides* to shovel snow together).

These parameters allow us to classify tasks. For example, a tug-of-war is unitary, maximising and additive; assembling a car is divisible, optimising and conjunctive; and many group decision-making tasks are divisible, optimising and disjunctive (or compensatory). As to whether groups are better than individuals, Steiner believes that in general the actual group performance is always inferior to the group's potential (based on the potential of its human resources). This shortfall is due mainly to a **process loss** (e.g. losses due to the coordination of individual members' activities, disproportionate influence on the part of specific powerful group members and various social distractors). However, against this background, Steiner's taxonomy allows us to predict what sort of tasks favour group performance.

For additive tasks, the group's performance is better than the best individual's performance. For compensatory tasks, the group's performance is better than that of most individuals, because the average is most likely to be correct. For disjunctive tasks, the group's performance is equal to or worse than the best individual – the group cannot do better than the best idea proposed. And for conjunctive tasks, the group's performance is equal to the worst individual's performance – unless the task is divisible, in which case a division of labour can redirect the weakest member to an easier task and so improve the group's performance.

Although Steiner emphasised the role of **coordination loss** in preventing a group performing optimally in terms of the potential of its members, he also raised the possibility of an entirely different, and more fundamentally psychological, type of loss – motivation loss.

**Process loss**

Deterioration in group performance in comparison to individual performance due to the whole range of possible interferences among members.

**Coordination loss**

Deterioration in group performance compared with individual performance, due to problems in coordinating behaviour.

## Social loafing and social impact

Ringelmann (1913), a French professor of agricultural engineering, conducted a number of experiments to investigate the efficiency of various numbers of people, animals and machines performing agricultural tasks (Kravitz & Martin, 1986). In one study, he had

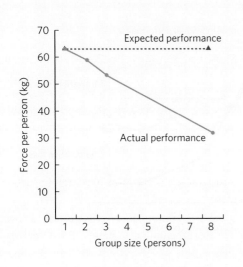

**Figure 8.5** The Ringelmann effect: force per person as a function of group size

As the number of people pulling horizontally on a rope increased, each person's exertion was reduced: people pulling in eight-person groups each exerted half the effort of a person pulling alone

*Source*: based on data from Ringelmann (1913)

young men, alone or in groups of two, three or eight, pull horizontally on a rope attached to a dynamometer (an instrument that measures the amount of force exerted). He found that the force exerted per person decreased as a function of group size: the larger the group, the less hard each person pulled (see Figure 8.5). This is called the **Ringelmann effect**.

Our previous discussion suggests two possible explanations for this:

1  *Coordination loss* – owing to jostling, distraction, and the tendency for people to pull slightly against one another, participants were prevented from attaining their full potential.

2  *Motivation loss* – participants were less motivated; they simply did not try so hard.

To investigate these explanations, Ingham, Levinger, Graves and Peckham (1974) replicated Ringelmann's study, but with two experimental conditions: one in which real groups of varying size pulled on a rope, and the other involving pseudo-groups with only one true participant and a number of confederates. The confederates were instructed only to pretend to pull on the rope while making realistic grunts to indicate exertion. The true participant was in the first position and so did not know that the confederates behind him were not actually pulling.

The results (see Figure 8.6) indicate a decrease in individual performance in pseudo-groups. Because there was no coordination, there can be no loss due to poor coordination; the decrease can be attributed only to a loss of motivation. In real groups, there was an additional decrease in individual performance that can be attributed to coordination loss.

This motivation loss has been termed **social loafing** by Latané, Williams and Harkins (1979), who replicated the effect with shouting, cheering and clapping tasks. For instance, they had participants cheer and clap as loudly as possible alone or in groups of two, four or six. The amount of noise produced per person was reduced by 29 per cent in two-person groups, 49 per cent in four-person groups and 60 per cent in six-person groups. For the shouting task, participants shouted alone or in two- or six-person real groups or pseudo-groups (they wore blindfolds, and headsets transmitting continuous 'white noise'). As in Ingham and colleagues' experiment, there was a clear reduction in effort for participants in pseudo-groups, with additional coordination loss for participants in real groups (see Figure 8.7).

**Ringelmann effect**
Individual effort on a task diminishes as group size increases.

**Social loafing**
A reduction in individual effort when working on a collective task (one in which our outputs are pooled with those of other group members) compared with working either alone or co-actively (our outputs are not pooled).

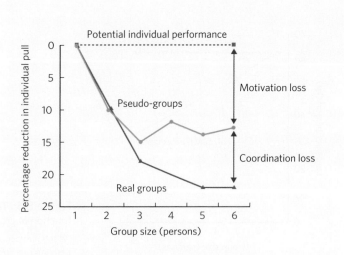

**Figure 8.6** Coordination and motivation losses in group rope-pulling

- As group size increased from 1 to 6, there was a decrease in each person's output.
- In pesudo-groups, this is due to reduced effort, i.e. motivation loss.
- In real groups, this is more marked as a result of coordination loss.

*Source*: based on data from Ingham, Levinger, Graves & Peckham (1974)

Social loafing, then, is a tendency for individuals to work less hard (i.e. loaf) on a task when they believe that others are also working on the task. More formally, it refers to 'a reduction in individual effort when working on a collective task (in which one's outputs are pooled with those of other group members) compared to when working either alone or coactively' (Williams, Karau & Bourgeois, 1993, p. 131).

A notable feature of loafing is that as group size increases, the addition of new members to the group has a decreasingly significant impact on effort: the reduction of effort conforms to a negatively accelerating power function (see Figure 8.8). So, for example, the reduction in individual effort as the consequence of a third person joining a two-person group is relatively large, while the impact of an additional member on a twenty-person group is minimal. The range within which group size seems to have a significant impact is about one to eight members.

**Social loafing**
Modern offices can make people feel like clones working on mindless tasks in boring settings – not a great recipe for thrilling personal engagement in hard work.

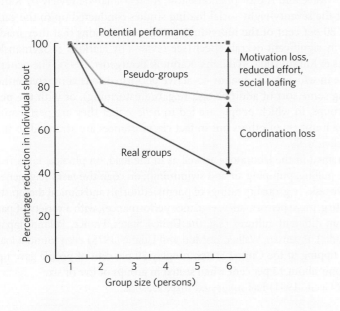

**Figure 8.7** Reduction in volume of individual shout in two-person and six-person real and pseudo-groups

- Social loafing: individual students shouted less loudly as group size increased.
- AS in Figure 8.6, this demonstrates a loss of motivation in pseudo-groups and an additional loss due to a lack of coordination in real groups.

*Source*: Latané, Williams & Harkins, 1979 Experiment 2

Social loafing is related to the **free-rider effect** (Frohlich & Oppenheimer, 1970; Kerr, 1983) in research into social dilemmas and public goods (Chapter 11). A free rider is someone who takes advantage of a shared public resource without contributing to its maintenance. For example, a tax evader who uses the road system, visits national parks and benefits from public medical provision is a free rider. The main difference between loafing and free riding is that although loafers reduce effort on co-active tasks, they nevertheless do contribute to the group product (there is a *loss* of motivation); in contrast, free riders exploit the group product while contributing nothing to it (there is a *different* motivation; see Williams, Karau & Bourgeois, 1993).

**Free-rider effect**
Gaining the benefits of group membership by avoiding costly obligations of membership and by allowing other members to incur those costs.

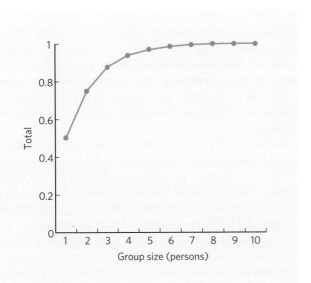

**Figure 8.8** Total group output as a negatively accelerating power function of group size

As the group gets larger, each new member has less and less impact on group behaviour: the reduction in effort due to new members gets smaller

Social loafing is a pervasive and robust phenomenon. A meta-analytic review by Karau and Williams (1993) of the seventy-eight social loafing studies conducted up to the early 1990s found loafing in 80 per cent of the individual–group comparisons that they made. This is an extraordinarily significant overall effect (see reviews by Harkins & Szymanski, 1987; Williams, Harkins & Karau, 2003; Williams, Karau & Bourgeois, 1993). The general loafing paradigm is one in which individual or co-active performance is compared either with groups performing some sort of additive task (e.g. brainstorming), or with the performance of pseudo-groups, in which people are led to *believe* that they are performing collectively with varying numbers of others but in fact circumstances are arranged so that they are performing individually.

Loafing has been obtained in the laboratory as well as in the field, on physical tasks (e.g. shouting, clapping, rope pulling, pumping air and swimming), on cognitive tasks (e.g. generating ideas), on evaluative tasks (e.g. quality ratings of poems, editorials and clinical therapists) and on perceptual tasks (e.g. maze performance, vigilance performance), with a variety of participant populations from different cultures (e.g. the United States, France, Poland, Japan, Taiwan, Thailand and India). Freeman, Walker, Bordon and Latané (1975) even found a loafing effect on restaurant tipping in the United States: roughly 20 per cent of people gave tips when seated alone, but only about 13 per cent when seated in groups of five or six.

Why do people loaf? Geen (1991) has suggested three reasons:

1  *Output equity* – people may loaf on collective tasks because they believe that people loaf in groups; thus they expect their partners to loaf and therefore loaf themselves in order to maintain equity (Jackson & Harkins, 1985), or avoid appearing to be a 'sucker' (Kerr & Bruun, 1983).

2  *Evaluation apprehension* – the presence of group members provides a sense of being anonymous and unidentifiable for people who are not motivated on a task (e.g. an uninteresting, boring or tiring task; Kerr & Bruun, 1981). When performing individually or co-actively rather than collectively, people are identifiable and thus apprehensive about performance evaluation by others, and they therefore overcome their unmotivated state (Harkins, 1987; Harkins & Szymanski, 1987).

3  *Matching to standard* – people loaf because they have no clear performance standard to match. The presence of a clear personal, social or group performance standard should reduce loafing (Goethals & Darley, 1987; Harkins & Szymanski, 1987; Szymanski & Harkins, 1987).

**Social impact**
The effect that other people have on our attitudes and behaviour, usually as a consequence of factors such as group size, and temporal and physical immediacy.

Group size may have the effect it does due to **social impact** (Latané, 1981; see also Chapter 14). The experimenter's instructions to clap, shout, brainstorm or whatever (i.e. the social obligation to work as hard as possible) have a social impact on the participants. To the extent that there is one participant and one experimenter, the experimenter's instructions have maximal impact. If there are two participants, the impact on each participant is halved; if three it is one-third, and so on. There is a diffusion of individual responsibility that grows with group size (see Chapter 14).

Loafing is not an inevitable consequence of group performance. Research has identified certain factors, apart from group size, that influence the tendency to loaf (see Geen, 1991; Williams, Karau & Bourgeois, 1993). For example, personal identifiability by the experimenter (Williams, Harkins & Latané, 1981), personal involvement in the task (Brickner, Harkins & Ostrom, 1986), partner effort (Jackson & Harkins, 1985), intergroup comparison (Harkins and Szymanski, 1989) and a highly meaningful task in association with expectation of poor performance by co-workers (Williams & Karau, 1991) have all been shown to reduce loafing.

In some circumstances, people may even work harder collectively than co-actively, in order to compensate for anticipated loafing by others on important tasks or in important groups (Williams & Karau, 1991; Williams, Karau & Bourgeois, 1993; Zaccaro, 1984). This **social compensation** effect may be responsible for the results of an intriguing study by Zaccaro (1984). Male and female participants constructed 'moon tents' out of sheets of paper in co-active two- or four-person groups – the usual loafing effect emerged (see Figure 8.9). However, other participants who believed they were competing against an out-group and for whom the attractiveness and social relevance of the task were accentuated, behaved quite differently. The loafing effect was actually reversed: individuals constructed more 'moon tents' in the larger group. This was an unusual finding. In contrast to the rather pessimistic view of some social psychologists that groups inevitably inhibit individuals from attaining their true potential (Steiner, 1972), this study indicates that group life may, under certain circumstances, cause people to exceed their individual potential. There may be process gains in groups (Shaw, 1976).

There are other circumstances when people may work harder in groups than when alone (e.g. Guzzo & Dickson, 1996). One is when people place greater value on groups than individuals: that is, they have a collectivist rather than individualist social orientation (Hofstede, 1980). Western and Eastern cultures are significantly different in social orientation (Smith, Bond & Kağıtçıbaşı, 2006; see Chapter 16), so it comes as no surprise to discover that people can work harder in groups than alone in, for example, China (Earley, 1989, 1994) and Japan (Matsui, Kakuyama & Onglatco, 1987). Another circumstance where people may be motivated to work harder in groups is when groups and their members believe and expect that the group will be effective in achieving important goals (Guzzo, Jost, Campbell & Shea, 1993; Sheppard, 1993).

Recent years have witnessed a revival of interest in the possibility of process gains in groups and in the ability of groups to increase task motivation (Brown, 2000; Kerr & Park, 2001). From their meta-analysis of seventy-eight loafing studies, Karau and Williams (1993) identified task importance and the significance of the group to the individual as the two key factors that promote increased effort in groups. These factors may be related. People may be particularly motivated to work hard on tasks that are important precisely because they define membership of a group that is vital to one's self-concept or social identity (see Fielding & Hogg, 2000).

For example, Worchel and his colleagues (Worchel, Rothgerber, Day, Hart, & Butemeyer, 1998) had participants make paper chains alone and then as a group. In the

**Social compensation**
Increased effort on a collective task to compensate for other group members' actual, perceived or anticipated lack of effort or ability.

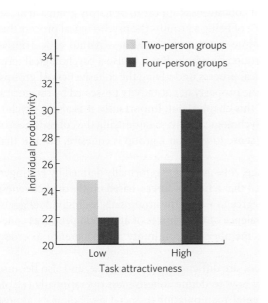

**Figure 8.9** Individual effort as a function of task attractiveness and group size

- Social compensation. Participants performing a relatively unattractive paper-folding task loafed.
- Individual productivity was lower in four- than two-person groups.
- For an attractive task, the loafing effect was reversed: individual productivity was higher in four- than two-person groups

*Source*: based on data from Zaccaro (1984)

group phase of the experiment, participants simply worked in their groups, or they were also in competition against an outgroup, and they either had individual name tags and different-coloured coats, or everyone in the group had identical group name tags and wore identical coloured coats. Worchel and his associates found clear evidence that people worked significantly harder in groups than alone when the group was highly salient – group name tags, identical coloured coats and intergroup competition. The productivity increase was five paper chains. In the least salient condition, there was loafing (productivity dropped by four paper chains), and in the intermediate salience conditions there was no significant departure from base rate (productivity changes of 11). Karau and Hart (1998) found a similar process gain in groups that were highly cohesive because they contained people who liked one another.

Generally, research on group performance has assumed that groups perform worse than individuals, and that process and motivation gains are more the exception than the rule. This premise that groups are generally worse than individuals also underpins much classic research on collective behaviours such as crowds (e.g. Zimbardo, 1970; see Chapter 11). However, other research emphasises that although people in groups may behave differently to people alone, there is a *change* rather than a deterioration of behaviour (Hogg & Abrams, 1988; Klein, Spears, & Reicher, 2007; Reicher, Spears & Postmes, 1995), and that people, in organisational settings, actually like to work in groups and find them satisfying and motivating (Allen & Hecht, 2004). Surowiecki (2004) assembled a huge list of instances where the group performs better than the individual. For example, in the TV game show *Who wants to be a millionaire?* – where contestants can call an expert or poll the studio audience to decide which of four answers to the question is correct, Surowiecki found that the expert was correct 65% of the time but the audience (a collection of random people) yielded the right answer 91% of the time.

## Group cohesiveness

**Cohesiveness**
The property of a group that affectively binds people, as group members, to one another and to the group as a whole, giving the group a sense of solidarity and oneness.

One of the most basic properties of a group is its **cohesiveness** (solidarity, *esprit de corps*, team spirit, morale) – the way it 'hangs together' as a tightly knit, self-contained entity characterised by uniformity of conduct and mutual support between members. Cohesiveness is a variable property: it differs between groups, between contexts and across time. Groups with extremely low levels of cohesiveness appear to be hardly groups at all, so the term may also capture the very essence of being a group – the psychological process that transforms an aggregate of individuals into a group. Cohesiveness is thus a descriptive term, used to define a property of the group as a whole. But it is also a psychological term to characterise the individual psychological process underlying the cohesiveness of groups. In this sense it is quite closely related to the property of entitativity possessed by categories, which we discussed at the beginning of this chapter. But, importantly, it is also a psychological term to describe the individual psychological process underlying the cohesiveness of groups. Herein lies a problem: it makes sense to say that a group is cohesive, but not that an individual is cohesive.

After almost a decade of informal usage, cohesiveness was formally defined by Festinger, Schachter and Back (1950). They believed that a field of forces, based on the attractiveness of the group and its members and the degree to which the group satisfies individual goals, acts upon the individual. The resultant valence of these forces of attraction produces cohesiveness, which is responsible for group membership continuity and adherence to group standards (see Figure 8.10).

Because concepts such as 'field of forces' are difficult to operationalise, and also because the theory was not precise about exactly how to define cohesiveness operationally (i.e. in terms of specific measures or experimental manipulations), social psychologists almost

**Group cohesiveness**
Is this team cohesive –
or what! Accuracy and
timing in a pit stop is
essential. Any Grand
Prix driver expects
nothing less than the
ultimate effort

immediately simplified their conception of cohesiveness. For instance, in their own research into the cohesiveness of student housing projects at the Massachusetts Institute of Technology, Festinger, Schachter and Back simply asked students: 'What three people ... do you see most of socially?' (1950, p. 37; see Chapter 13 for details of this study).

Major reviews (Cartwright, 1968; Dion, 2000; Hogg, 1992; Lott & Lott, 1965) indicate that the bulk of research conceptualises cohesiveness as attraction to the group or interpersonal attraction, derives the cohesiveness of the group as a whole from summing (or some other arithmetical procedure), and operationalises cohesiveness accordingly. Not surprisingly, this

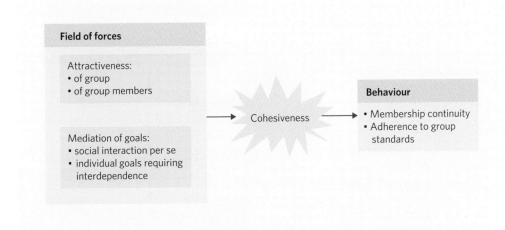

**Figure 8.10** Festinger, Schachter and Back's (1950) theory of group cohesiveness

Festinger, Schachter and Back (1950) believed that a field of forces, based on attraction and goal mediation, acts on individual group members to render the group more or less cohesive, and that cohesiveness influences membership continuity and adherence to group norms

*Source:* Hogg (1992)

research reveals that factors that increase interpersonal attraction (e.g. similarity, cooperation, interpersonal acceptance, shared threat; see Chapter 13) generally elevate cohesiveness, and elevated cohesiveness produces, for example, conformity to group standards, accentuated similarity, improved intragroup communication and enhanced liking.

It has been suggested (Hogg, 1992, 1993; Turner, 1982, 1984) that this perspective on group cohesiveness represents a much wider *social cohesion* or *interpersonal interdependence* model of the social group (see Figure 8.11), where researchers tend to differ only in which components of the model they emphasise. Because social psychologists have not really resolved the problem of knowing unambiguously how to operationalise cohesiveness (Evans & Jarvis, 1980; Mudrack, 1989), more recent research has tended to be in applied areas (Levine & Moreland, 1990). In sports psychology, in particular, some quite rigorous scales have been devised: for example, Widmeyer, Brawley and Carron's (1985) eighteen-item *group environment questionnaire* to measure the cohesiveness of sports teams.

A fundamental question that has been raised by social identity researchers (Hogg, 1992, 1993; Turner, 1984, 1985; see also Chapter 11) asks to what extent an analysis of group cohesiveness in terms of aggregation (or some other arithmetic integration) of interpersonal attraction really captures a group process at all. To all intents and purposes, the group has disappeared entirely from the analysis and we are left simply with interpersonal attraction, about which we already know a great deal (Berscheid & Reis, 1998; see Chapter 13). Hogg (1993) suggests that a distinction should be made between **personal attraction** (true interpersonal attraction based on close relationships and idiosyncratic preferences) and **social attraction** (inter-individual liking based on perceptions of self and others in terms not of individuality but of group norms or prototypicality). Personal attraction is nothing to do with groups, while social attraction is the 'liking' component of group membership. Social attraction is merely one of a constellation of effects (ethnocentrism, conformity, intergroup differentiation, stereotyping, ingroup solidarity) produced by the process of

**Personal attraction**
Liking for someone based on idiosyncratic preferences and interpersonal relationships.

**Social attraction**
Liking for someone based on common group membership and determined by the person's prototypicality of the group.

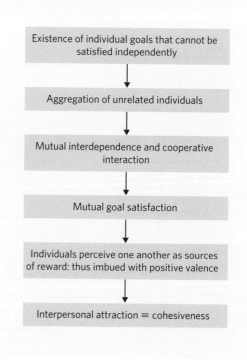

**Figure 8.11** General framework of the social cohesion/ interpersonal interdependence model

*Source:* based on Hogg (1992)

self-categorisation specified in self-categorisation theory (Turner, Hogg, Oakes, Reicher, & Wetherell, 1987; see Chapter 11).

This analysis has at least two major advantages over the traditional model:

1 It does not reduce group solidarity and cohesiveness to interpersonal attraction.

2 It is as applicable to small interactive groups (the only valid focus of traditional models) as to large-scale social categories, such as an ethnic group or a nation (people can feel attracted to one another on the basis of common ethnic or national group membership).

This perspective is quite promising. For example, Hogg and Turner (1985) aggregated people with others whom they ostensibly would like or dislike (the fact that the others were people they would like or dislike was irrelevant to the existence of the group), or explicitly categorised them as a group on the basis of the criterion that they would like, or dislike, one another. They found that interpersonal attraction was not automatically associated with greater solidarity (see Figure 8.12). Rather, where interpersonal liking was neither the implicit nor explicit basis for the group (i.e. in the random categorisation condition), group solidarity was unaffected by interpersonal attraction.

In another study, Hogg and Hardie (1991) gave a questionnaire to a football team in Australia. Perceptions of team prototypicality and of norms were significantly related to measures of group-based social attraction but were not related to measures of interpersonal attraction. This differential effect was strongest among members who themselves identified most strongly with the team. Similar findings have been obtained from studies of women's netball teams playing in an amateur league (Hogg & Hains, 1996), and of organisational subgroups and quasi-naturalistic discussion groups (Hogg, Cooper-Shaw & Holzworth, 1993).

This broader view of cohesion as linked to group solidarity and social identity may explain why loyalty is so important in group life. For example, in their social glue hypothesis, Van Vugt and Hart (2004) argue that group cooperation can be sustained only if members show ingroup loyalty and willingness to sacrifice self-gain or advantage for the good of the group; thus, disloyalty is reacted to very strongly (also see Levine & Moreland, 2002).

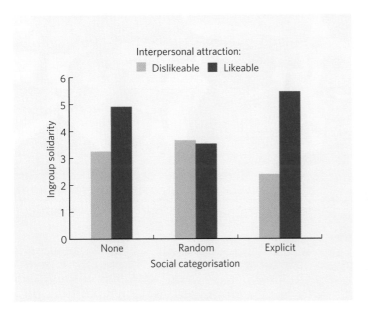

**Figure 8.12** Ingroup solidarity as a function of interpersonal attraction and social categorisation

Students who were explicitly categorised as a group on the basis of interpersonal liking or who were merely aggregated showed greater solidarity with likeable groups, while participants who were randomly categorised showed equal solidarity, irrespective of how likeable the group was

Source: Hogg & Turner (1985)

# Group socialisation

An obvious feature of many of the groups with which we are familiar is that new members join, old members leave, members are socialised by the group, and the group in turn is imprinted with the contribution of individuals. Groups are dynamic structures that change continuously over time; however, this dynamic aspect of groups is often neglected in social psychology: social psychologists have tended towards a rather static analysis that excludes the passage of time. Many social psychologists feel that this considerably weakens the explanatory power of social psychological theories of group processes and intergroup behaviour (Condor, 1996; Levine & Moreland, 1994; Tuckman, 1965; Worchel, 1996).

The effects of time are taken more seriously in organisational psychology, where longitudinal analyses are relatively common and quite sophisticated (Wilpert, 1995). For example, Cordery, Mueller and Smith (1991) studied job satisfaction, absenteeism and employee turnover for a twenty-month period in two mineral-processing plants to discover that although autonomous work groups improved work attitudes, they also increased absenteeism and employee turnover.

Within social psychology, Tuckman (1965) described a now famous five-stage developmental sequence that small groups go through:

1 *forming* – an orientation and familiarisation stage;

2 *storming* – a conflict stage, where members know each other well enough to start working through disagreements about goals and practices;

3 *norming* – having survived the storming stage, consensus, cohesion and a sense of common identity and purpose emerge;

4 *performing* – a period in which the group works smoothly as a unit that has shared norms and goals, and good morale and atmosphere;

5 *adjourning* – the group dissolves because it has accomplished its goals, or because members lose interest and motivation and move on.

**Role transition**
Graduation is a ritualised public ceremony that marks an important role transition in a student's life

More recently, Moreland and Levine (1982, 1984; Levine & Moreland, 1994; Moreland, Levine & Cini, 1993) have presented a model of **group socialisation** to describe and explain the passage of individuals through groups over time. They focus on the dynamic interrelationship of group and individual members across the lifespan of the group. A novel feature of this analysis is that it focuses not only on how individuals change in order to fit into the group but also on how new members can, intentionally or unintentionally, be a potent source of innovation and change within the group (Levine, Moreland & Choi, 2001). Three basic processes are involved in group socialisation:

**Group socialisation**
Dynamic relationship between the group and its members that describes the passage of members through a group in terms of commitment and of changing roles.

1 Evaluation refers to an ongoing comparison by individuals of the past, present and future rewards of the group with the rewards of potential alternative relationships (Thibaut & Kelley, 1959; see discussion of social exchange theory in Chapter 13). Simultaneously, the group evaluates individuals in terms of their contribution to the life of the group. Behind this idea lies an assumption that people have goals and needs, which create expectations. To the extent that expectations are, or are likely to be, met, social approval is expressed. Actual or anticipated failure to fulfil expectations invites social disapproval and actions to modify behaviour or to reject individuals or the group.

2 Evaluation affects commitment of the individual to the group and vice versa in a relatively straightforward manner. However, at any given time, commitment disequilibrium may exist, such that the individual is more committed to the group or the group to the individual. This endows the least committed party with greater power and so is unstable. There is pressure towards commitment equilibrium. Commitment produces agreement on group goals and values, positive ties between individual and group, willingness to exert effort on the part of the group or the individual, and a desire for continuance of membership.

3 Role transition refers to discontinuities in the role relationship between individual and group. These discontinuities overlay a continuum of temporal variation in commitment and are governed by groups' and individuals' decision criteria for the occurrence of a transition. There are three general types of role: (1) non-member, including prospective members who have not joined the group and ex-members who have left the group; (2) quasi-member, including new members who have not yet attained full member status and marginal members who have lost that status; and (3) full member. Full members are those who are most closely identified with the group and who have all the privileges and responsibilities associated with group membership. Role transitions can be smooth and easy where individual and group are equally committed and share the same decision criteria. However, commitment disequilibrium and unshared decision criteria can introduce conflict over whether a role transition should or did occur. For this reason, transition criteria often become formalised and public, and rites of passage become a central part of the life of the group.

Equipped with these processes, Moreland and Levine (1982, 1984) provide a detailed account of the passage of individual members through the group (see Figure 8.13). There are five distinct phases of group socialisation, involving reciprocal evaluation and influence by group and individual, each heralded and/or concluded by a clear role transition (see Box 8.1).

The occurrence of role transitions is considered an important aspect of group life. Indeed, Moreland and colleagues have conducted research on specific transitions, particularly those associated with becoming a member (Brinthaupt, Moreland & Levine, 1991; Moreland, 1985; Moreland & Levine, 1989; Pavelchak, Moreland & Levine, 1986). Generally, role transitions are ritualised public events – rites of passage: that is, **initiation rites**. They can be pleasant events marked by celebration and the giving of gifts (e.g. graduation, a

**Initiation rites**
Often painful or embarrassing public procedure to mark group members' movements from one role to another.

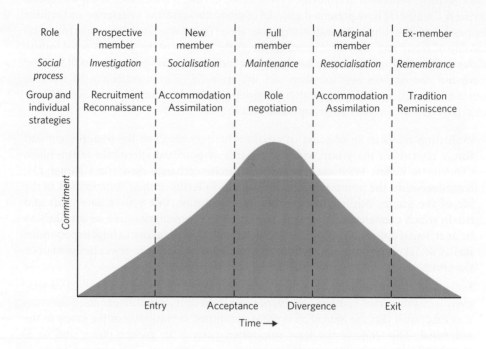

**Figure 8.13** A model of the process of group socialisation

Group socialisation. The passage of an individual member through a group is accompanied by variation in commitment and is marked by role discontinuities

*Source:* Moreland & Levine (1982)

## Research and applications 8.1
### Phases of group socialisation

Moreland and Levine (1982, 1984; Moreland, Levine & Cini, 1993) distinguished five phases of group socialisation (see Figure 8.13):

1  *Investigation*. The group recruits prospective members, who in turn reconnoitre the group. This can be more formal, involving interviews and questionnaires (e.g. joining an organisation), or less formal (e.g. associating yourself with a student political society). A successful outcome leads to a *role transition*: entry to the group.

2  *Socialisation*. The group assimilates new members, educating them in its ways. In turn, new members try to get the group to accommodate their views. Socialisation can be unstructured and informal, but also quite formal (e.g. an organisation's induction programme). Successful socialisation is marked by *acceptance*.

3  *Maintenance*. Role negotiation takes place between full members. Role dissatisfaction can lead to a role transition called *divergence,* which can be unexpected and unplanned. It can also be expected – a typical group feature (e.g. university students who diverge by graduating and leaving university).

4  *Resocialisation*. When divergence is expected, resocialisation is unlikely; when it is unexpected, the member is marginalised into a deviant role and tries to become resocialised. If successful, full membership is reinstated – if unsuccessful, the individual leaves. Exit can be marked by elaborate retirement ceremonies (e.g. the ritualistic stripping of insignia in a court martial).

5  *Remembrance*. After the individual leaves the group both parties reminisce. This may be a fond recall of the 'remember when . . .' type or the more extreme exercise of a totalitarian regime in rewriting history.

*Source:* Moreland & Levine (1982).

wedding), but more often than not they involve a degree of pain, suffering or humiliation (e.g. circumcision, a wake). These rites may serve a number of functions:

- *symbolic* – to allow a consensual and public recognition of identity discontinuity;
- *apprenticeship* – some rites help individuals to become accustomed to new roles and normative standards;
- *loyalty elicitation* – pleasant initiations involving gifts and special dispensations may elicit gratitude, which should enhance commitment to the group.

In the light of this last function, the prevalence and apparent effectiveness of disagreeable initiation rites is puzzling. Surely people would avoid joining groups with severe initiations, and if unfortunate enough not to be able to do this, then at the very least they should subsequently hate the group and feel no sense of commitment.

One way to explain this paradox is in terms of **cognitive dissonance** theory (Festinger, 1957) which is described in Chapter 6. An aversive initiation creates subsequent dissonance between the two cognitions 'I knowingly underwent a painful experience to join this group' and 'Some aspects of this group are not that good' (group life is usually a mixture of positive and negative aspects). As the initiation cannot be denied (after all, it is usually a public event), dissonance can be reduced by revising one's opinion of the group (downplaying negative aspects and focusing on more positive aspects). The consequence is a more favourable evaluation of the group and thus greater commitment.

This analysis clearly predicts that the more unpleasant the initiation is, the more positive the subsequent evaluation of the group will be. The Aronson and Mills (1959) experiment described in Chapter 6 is an investigation of this idea. You will recall that Aronson and Mills recruited female students to participate in a group discussion of the psychology of sex. Before joining the group, they listened to and rated a short extract of the discussion – an extremely tedious and stilted discussion of the secondary sexual characteristics of lower animals. It was quite rightly rated as such by control participants, and also by a second group of participants who had gone through a mild initiation where they read aloud five words with vague sexual connotations. However, a third group, who underwent an extreme initiation where they read out loud explicit and obscene passages, rated the discussion as very interesting.

Gerard and Mathewson (1966) were concerned that the effect may have arisen because the severe-initiation participants were either sexually aroused by the obscene passage and/or relieved at discovering that the discussion was not as extreme as the passage. To discount these alternative explanations, they replicated Aronson and Mills's study. Participants, who audited and rated a boring discussion they were about to join, were given mild or severe electric shocks either explicitly as an initiation or under some other pretext completely unrelated to the ensuing discussion. As predicted from cognitive dissonance theory, the painful experience enhanced evaluation of the group only when it was perceived to be an initiation (see Figure 8.14). (Now answer the second focus question.)

**Cognitive dissonance**
State of psychological tension, produced by simultaneously having two opposing cognitions. People are motivated to reduce the tension, often by changing or rejecting one of the cognitions. Festinger proposed that we seek harmony in our attitudes, beliefs and behaviours, and try to reduce tension from inconsistency among these elements.

# Norms

Many years ago Sumner (1906) talked about **norms** as 'folkways', meaning habitual customs displayed by a group because they had originally been adaptive in meeting basic needs. Later Sherif (1936) described norms as 'customs, traditions, standards, rules, values, fashions, and all other criteria of conduct which are standardized as a consequence of the contact of individuals' (p. 3). Although norms can take the form of explicit rules that are enforced by legislation and sanctions (e.g. societal norms to do with private property, pollution and aggression), most social psychologists agree with Cialdini and Trost (1998) that norms are

**Norms**
Attitudinal and behavioural uniformities that define group membership and differentiate between groups.

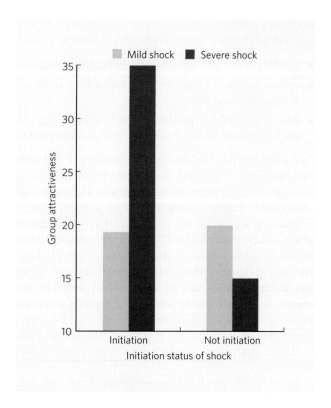

**Figure 8.14** Group attractiveness as a function of severity of electric shock and initiation status of the shock

- Cognitive dissonance and the effectiveness of initiation rites.
- Participants about to join a boring group discussion were given a mild or severe electric shock.
- When the shock was billed as an initiation, participants given the severe shock rated the group as more attractive than participants given the mild shock

*Source:* based on data from Gerard & Mathewson (1966)

rules and standards that are understood by members of a group and that guide and/or constrain social behaviour without the force of laws. These norms emerge out of interaction with others; they may or may not be stated explicitly, and any sanctions for deviating from them come from social networks, not the legal system. (p. 152)

Garfinkel (1967) focused very much on norms as the implicit, unobserved, taken-for-granted background to everyday life. People typically assume a practice is 'natural' or simply 'human nature' until the practice is disrupted by norm violation and people suddenly realise the practice is 'merely' normative. Indeed, Piaget's influential theory of cognitive development describes how children only slowly begin to realise that norms are not objective facts, and suggests that even adults find it difficult to come to this realisation (Piaget, 1928, 1955).

Garfinkel devised a methodology, called **ethnomethodology**, to detect these background norms. One method involved the violation of norms in order to attract people's attention to them. For example, Garfinkel had students act at home for fifteen minutes as if they were boarders: that is, be polite, speak formally and only speak when spoken to. Their families reacted with astonishment, bewilderment, shock, embarrassment and anger, backed up with charges of selfishness, nastiness, rudeness and lack of consideration! An implicit norm for familial interaction was revealed, and its violation provoked a strong reaction.

Social identity theorists place a particular emphasis on the group-defining dimension of norms (e.g., Abrams & Hogg, 1990a; Abrams, Wetherell, Cochrane, Hogg, & Turner, 1990; Hogg, 2010; Hogg & Smith, 2007; Turner, 1991). Norms are attitudinal and behavioural regularities that map the contours of social groups (small groups or large social categories) such that normative discontinuities mark group boundaries. Norms capture attributes that describe one group and distinguish it from other groups, and because groups define who we are, group norms are also prescriptive, telling us how we should behave as group members. Thus the behaviour of students and lecturers at a university is governed by very

**Ethnomethodology**
Method devised by Garfinkel, involving the violation of hidden norms to reveal their presence.

**Ethnomethodology**
Non-normative
behaviour (being
dressed rather too
casually) draws
attention to the
implicit norm of being
formal when meeting
an important client.

different norms: knowing whether someone is a student or a lecturer establishes clear expectations of appropriate normative behaviour. (Reflect on the third focus question: what norms are in conflict?)

This perspective on norms transcends (see Hogg & Reid, 2006) the traditional distinction drawn in social psychology between descriptive norms ('is' norms) that describe behavioural regularities and injunctive norms ('ought' norms) that convey approval or disapproval of the behaviour (e.g., Cialdini, Kallgren, & Reno, 1991). Instead, by tying norms to group membership the descriptive and injunctive aspects of norms become tightly integrated.

As an aside, norms and **stereotypes** are closely related – the terms 'normative behaviour' and 'stereotypical behaviour' mean virtually the same thing. However, research traditions have generally separated the two areas: norms referring to behaviour that is shared in a group, and stereotypes (see Chapters 2, 10 and 11) to shared generalisations made by individuals about members of other groups.

**Stereotype**
Widely shared and
simplified evaluative
image of a social group
and its members.

Group norms can have a powerful effect on people. For example, Newcomb (1965) conducted a classic study of norms in the 1930s at a small American college called Bennington. The college had progressive and liberal norms but drew its students from conservative, upper-middle-class families. The 1936 American presidential election allowed Newcomb to conduct a confidential ballot. First-year students strongly favoured the conservative candidate, while third- and fourth-year students had shifted their voting preference towards the liberal and communist/socialist candidates (see Figure 8.15). Presumably, prolonged exposure to liberal norms had produced the change in political preference.

Siegel and Siegel's (1957) study was slightly better controlled. New students at a private American college were randomly assigned to different types of student accommodation – sororities and dormitories. At this particular college, sororities had a conservative ethos

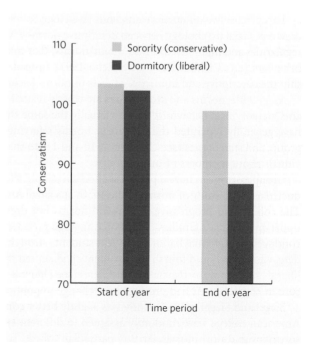

**Figure 8.15** Newcomb's 1965 Bennington study: voting preference for 1936 presidential candidates as a function of exposure to liberal norms

First-year students at Bennington college in the USA showed a traditionally conservative voting pattern during the 1936 presidential election, while third- and fourth-year students, who had been exposed for longer to the college's liberal norms, showed a significantly more liberal voting pattern

*Source:* based on data from Newcomb (1965)

**Frame of reference**
Complete range of subjectively conceivable positions that relevant people can occupy in that context on some attitudinal or behavioural dimension.

and the dormitories had more progressive liberal norms. Siegel and Siegel measured the students' degree of conservatism at the beginning and end of the year. Figure 8.16 clearly shows how exposure to liberal norms reduced conservatism.

Norms serve a function for the individual. They specify a limited range of behaviour that is acceptable in a certain context and thus they reduce uncertainty and facilitate confident choice of the 'correct' course of action. Norms provide a **frame of reference** within

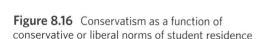

**Figure 8.16** Conservatism as a function of conservative or liberal norms of student residence

Students at a private American college were randomly assigned to more conservative sorority-type accommodation or more liberal dormitory-style accommodation. After a year of exposure to these different norms the dormitory group became significantly less conservative in its attitudes

*Source:* based on data from Siegel & Siegel (1957)

which to locate our own behaviour. You will recall that this idea was explored by Sherif (1936) in his classic experiments dealing with norm formation (see Box 7.1 in Chapter 7 for details). Sherif showed that when people made perceptual judgements alone, they relied on their own estimates as a reference frame; however, when they were in a group, they used the group's range of judgements to converge quickly on the group mean.

Sherif believed that people were using other members' estimates as a social frame of reference to guide them: he felt that he had produced a primitive group norm experimentally. The norm was an emergent property of interaction between group members, but once created it acquired a life of its own. Members were later tested alone and still conformed to the norm. In one study people who were retested individually as much as a year later were, quite remarkably, still influenced by the group norm (Rohrer, Baron, Hoffman, & Swander, 1954).

This same point was strikingly demonstrated in a couple of related autokinetic studies (Jacobs & Campbell, 1961; MacNeil & Sherif, 1976). In a group comprising three confederates, who gave extreme estimates, and one true participant, a relatively extreme norm emerged. The group went through a number of 'generations', in which a confederate would leave and another true participant would join, until the membership of the group contained none of the original members. The original extreme norm still powerfully influenced the participants' estimates. This is a very elegant demonstration that a norm is a true group phenomenon: it can emerge only from a group, yet it can influence the behaviour of the individual in the physical absence of the group (Turner, 1991). It is as if the group is carried in the head of the individual in the form of a norm.

Norms also serve functions for the group in so far as they coordinate the actions of members towards the fulfilment of group goals. In an early study of factory production norms, Coch and French (1948) describe a group that set itself a standard of fifty units per hour as the minimum level to secure job tenure. New members quickly adopted this norm. Those who did not were strongly sanctioned by ostracism and in some cases had their work sabotaged. Generally speaking, there is good evidence from the study of goal setting in organisational work teams that, where group norms embody clear group goals for performance and production, group members work harder and are more satisfied (Guzzo & Dickson, 1996; Weldon & Weingart, 1993).

Norms are inherently resistant to change – after all, their function is to provide stability and predictability. However, norms initially arise to deal with specific circumstances. They endure as long as those circumstances prevail but ultimately change with changing circumstances. Norms vary in their 'latitude of acceptable behaviour': some are narrow and restrictive (e.g. military dress codes) and others wider and less restrictive (e.g. dress codes for university lecturers). In general, norms that relate to group loyalty and to central aspects of group life have a narrow latitude of acceptable behaviour, while norms relating to more peripheral features of the group are less restrictive. Finally, certain group members are allowed a greater latitude of acceptable behaviour than others: higher-status members (e.g. leaders) can get away with more than lower-status members and followers (this phenomenon is discussed in Chapter 9 when we talk about leadership).

There is evidence for the patterning and structure of different types of norm from Sherif and Sherif's (1964) pioneering study of adolescent gangs in American cities. Participant observers infiltrated these gangs and studied them over several months. The gangs had given themselves names, had adopted various insignia and had strict codes about how gang members should dress. Dress codes were important, as it was largely through dress that the gangs differentiated themselves from one another. The gangs also had strict norms concerning sexual mores and how to deal with outsiders (e.g. parents, police); however, leaders were allowed some latitude in their adherence to these and other norms.

Norms are the yardstick of group conduct, and it is through norms that groups influence the behaviour of their members. The exact processes responsible are the subject of much of Chapter 7, which deals with social influence.

# Group structure

**Group structure**
Division of a group into different roles that often differ with respect to status and prestige.

Cohesiveness, socialisation and norms refer mainly to uniformities in groups. However, we have just seen how there can also be a degree of patterning and differentiation of norms within groups. Here we develop this theme. In few groups indeed does it happen that all members are equal, perform identical activities or communicate freely with one another. **Group structure** is clearly reflected in roles, status relations and communication networks. Groups are also structured in terms of subgroups and in terms of the central or marginal group membership credentials of specific members.

## Roles

**Roles**
Patterns of behaviour that distinguish between different activities within the group, and that interrelate to one another for the greater good of the group.

**Roles** are much like norms in so far as they describe and prescribe behaviour. However, while norms apply to the group as a whole, roles apply to a subgroup of people within the group. Furthermore, while norms may distinguish between groups, they are generally not intentionally derived to benefit the framework of groups in a society. In contrast, roles are specifically designed to differentiate between people in the group for the greater good of the group as a whole.

Roles are not people but behavioural prescriptions that are assigned to people. They can be informal and implicit (e.g. in groups of friends) or formal and explicit (e.g. in aircraft flight crews). One quite general role differentiation in small groups is between task specialists (the 'ideas' people, who get things done) and socioemotional specialists (the people everyone likes because they address relationships in the group) (e.g. Slater, 1955). Roles may emerge in a group for a number of reasons:

- They represent a division of labour; only in the simplest groups is there no division of labour.
- They furnish clear-cut social expectations within the group and provide information about how members relate to one another.
- They furnish members with a self-definition and a place within the group.

Clearly, roles emerge to facilitate group functioning. However, there is evidence that inflexible role differentiation can sometimes be detrimental to the group. Gersick and Hackman (1990) found that rigid role differentiation relating to pre-flight checks by the flight crew of a passenger airliner caused the crew to fail to engage a de-icing device, with the tragic consequence that the plane crashed shortly after take-off.

Roles can sometimes also be associated with larger category memberships (e.g. professional groups) outside the specific task-oriented groups, in which case the task-oriented group can become a context for role conflict that is actually a manifestation of wider intergroup conflict. A good example of this might be intergroup conflict in a hospital between doctors and nurses.

Although we tend to adopt a dramaturgical perspective when we speak of people 'acting' or 'assuming' roles, we are probably only partly correct. We may assume roles much like actors taking different parts, but many people see us only in particular roles and so infer that that is how we really are. Professional actors are easily typecast in exactly the same way – one reason why Paul Greengrass's 2006 film, *United 93*, about the 11 September 2001 terrorist attacks on the United States, is so incredibly powerful is that the actors are not high-profile individuals who have already been typecast. This tendency to attribute roles internally to dispositions of the role player may be an example of **correspondence bias** (Gilbert & Malone, 1995; see Chapter 3).

**Correspondence bias**
A general attribution bias in which people have an inflated tendency to see behaviour as reflecting (corresponding to) stable underlying personality attributes.

One practical implication of this is that you should avoid low-status roles in groups, or you will subsequently find it difficult to escape their legacy. Perhaps the most powerful and

## Research classic 8.2
### Guards versus prisoners: role behaviour in a simulated prison

Philip Zimbardo was interested in investigating the way in which people can adopt and internalise roles to guide behaviour. He was also interested to establish that it is largely the prescription of the role rather than the personality of the role occupant that governs in-role behaviour. In a famous role-playing exercise, twenty-four psychologically stable male Stanford University student volunteers were randomly assigned the roles of prisoners or guards. The prisoners were arrested at their homes and initially processed by the police, then handed over to the guards in a simulated prison constructed in the basement of the Psychology Department at Stanford University.

Zimbardo had planned to observe the role-playing exercise over a period of two weeks. However, he had to stop the study after six days. Although the students were psychologically stable and those assigned to the guard or prisoner roles had no prior dispositional differences, things got completely out of hand. The guards continually harassed, humiliated and intimidated the prisoners,

and they used psychological techniques to undermine solidarity and sow the seeds of distrust among them. Some guards increasingly behaved in a brutal and sadistic manner.

The prisoners initially revolted but gradually became passive and docile as they showed symptoms of individual and group disintegration and an acute loss of contact with reality. Some prisoners had to be released from the study because they showed symptoms of severe emotional disturbance (disorganised thinking, uncontrollable crying and screaming); and in one case, a prisoner developed a psychosomatic rash all over his body.

Zimbardo's role compliance explanation of what happened in the simulated prison (Haney, Banks & Zimbardo, 1973) has recently been challenged. Reicher and Haslam (2006) argue that the participants were confronted by a situation that raised their feelings of uncertainty about themselves and that in order to reduce this uncertainty they internalised the identities available (prisoners or guards), and adopted the appropriate behaviours to define themselves. The process was one of group identification and conformity to group norms motivated by self-conceptual uncertainty (see Hogg, 2007b).

well-known social psychological illustration of the power of roles to modify behaviour is Zimbardo's (1971; Banuazizi & Movahedi, 1975) simulated prison experiment (see Box 8.2).

Ultimately, roles can actually influence who we are – our identity and concept of self (Haslam & Reicher, 2005). This idea has been extensively elaborated by sociologists to explain how social interaction and wider societal expectations about behaviour can create enduring and real identities for people – role identity theory (McCall & Simmons, 1978; Stryker & Statham, 1986; see Hogg, Terry & White, 1995).

## Status

All roles are not equal: some are consensually more valued and respected and thus confer greater **status** on the role occupant. The highest-status role in most groups is the role of leader (see Chapter 9). In general, higher-status roles or their occupants tend to have two properties:

**Status**
Consensual evaluation of the prestige of a role or role occupant in a group, or of the prestige of a group and its members as a whole.

1 consensual prestige;
2 a tendency to initiate ideas and activities that are adopted by the group.

For example, from his participant observation study of gangs in an Italian American immigrant community, Whyte (1943) reported that even the relatively inarticulate 'Doc', who described his assumption of leadership of the thirteen-member Norton gang in terms of who he had 'walloped', found that the consensual prestige that such wallopings earned him was insufficient alone to ensure his high-status position. He admitted that his status also derived from the fact that he was the one who always thought of things for the group to do.

Status hierarchies in groups are not fixed: they can vary over time, and also from situation to situation. Take an orchestra: the lead violinist may have the highest-status role at a concert, while the union representative has the highest-status role in negotiations with management. One explanation of why status hierarchies emerge so readily in groups is in terms of social comparison theory (Festinger, 1954; Suls & Miller, 1977) – status hierarchies are the expression and reflection of intragroup social comparisons. Groups furnish a pool of relevant others with whom we can make social comparisons in order to assess the validity of our opinions and abilities.

Certain roles in the group have more power and influence and, because they are therefore more attractive and desirable, have many more 'applicants' than can be accommodated. Fierce social comparisons on behavioural dimensions relevant to these roles inevitably mean that the majority of group members, who are unsuccessful in securing the role, must conclude that they are less able than those who are successful. Thus there arises a shared view that those occupying the attractive role are superior to the rest – consensual prestige and high status. (Do you have any advice for Andrea? See the fourth focus question.)

Status hierarchies often become institutionalised, so that individual members do not engage in ongoing systematic social comparisons. Rather, they simply assume that particular roles or role occupants are of higher status than their own role or themselves. Research into the formation of status hierarchies in newly created groups tends to support this view. Strodtbeck, James and Hawkins (1957) assembled mock juries to consider and render a verdict on transcripts of actual trials. They found that the high-status role of jury foreman almost always went to people who had higher occupational status outside the context of the jury (e.g. teachers or psychologists rather than janitors or mechanics).

One explanation of this phenomenon is proposed by **expectation states theory** (Berger, Fisek, Norman & Zelditch, 1977; Berger, Wagner & Zelditch, 1985; de Gilder & Wilke, 1994; Ridgeway, 2001). Status derives from two distinct sources:

1 **Specific status characteristics** – a person's attributes that relate directly to ability on the group task (e.g. being a good athlete in a sports team, a good musician in a band).

2 **Diffuse status characteristics** – a person's attributes that do not relate directly to ability on the group task but are generally positively or negatively valued in society (e.g. being wealthy, having a white-collar occupation, being white).

Diffuse status characteristics generate favourable expectations that are generalised to all sorts of situations, even those that may not have any relevance to what the group does. Group members simply assume that someone who rates highly on diffuse status (e.g. a medical doctor) will be more able than others to promote the group's goals (e.g. analysing trial transcripts in order to render a verdict) and therefore has higher specific status.

Specific and diffuse status are independent and additive sources of status in a newly formed group, according to a study by Knottnerus and Greenstein (1981). Female participants worked with a female confederate on two supposedly related tasks. Specific status was manipulated by informing participants that they had performed better or worse than the confederate on the first task – a perceptual task. Diffuse status was manipulated by leading participants to believe that they were either younger or older than the confederate. The second task, a word construction task, allowed measures of yielding to the confederate's suggestions to be used as an index of effective status. The results (see Figure 8.17) showed that participants yielded more if they believed that they were of lower specific or lower diffuse status than the confederate. Other factors shown to contribute to high status in a group include seniority, assertiveness, past task success and high group orientation.

**Expectation states theory**

Theory of the emergence of roles as a consequence of people's status-based expectations about others' performance.

**Specific status characteristics**

Information about those abilities of a person that are directly relevant to the group's task.

**Diffuse status characteristics**

Information about a person's abilities that are only obliquely relevant to the group's task, and derive mainly from large-scale category memberships outside the group.

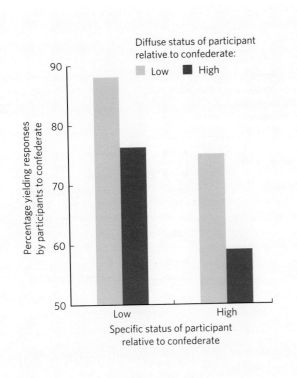

**Figure 8.17** Yielding as a function of specific and diffuse status of participants relative to a confederate

Female participants yielded more often to a female confederate's suggestions in a word-construction task if the confederate had higher specific status (had performed well on a similar task) and had higher diffuse status (was older)

*Source:* based on data from Knottnerus & Greenstein (1981).

## Communication networks

People occupying different roles in a group need to coordinate their actions through communication, although not all roles need to communicate with one another. Thus the structuring of a group with respect to roles entails an internal **communication network** that regulates who can communicate with whom. Although such networks can be informal, we are probably more familiar with the rigidly formalised ones in large organisations and bureaucracies (e.g. a university or government office). What are the effects on group functioning of different types of communication network, and what factors affect the sort of network that evolves?

Bavelas (1968) suggested that an important factor was the number of communication links to be crossed for one person to communicate with another. For example, if I can communicate with the dean of my faculty directly, there is one link; but if I have to go through the head of department, there are two. In Franz Kafka's (1925) classic novel *The Trial,* the central character 'K' was confronted by a bewildering and ever-increasing number of communication links in order to communicate with senior people in the organisation. Figure 8.18 shows some of the communication networks that have been researched experimentally; those on the left are more highly centralised than those on the right.

For relatively simple tasks, greater centralisation improves group performance (Leavitt, 1951): the hub person is able to receive, integrate and pass on information efficiently while allowing peripheral members to concentrate on their allotted roles. For more complex tasks, a less centralised structure is superior (Shaw, 1964), because the quantity and complexity of information communicated would overwhelm a hub person, who would be unable to integrate, assimilate and pass it on efficiently. Peripheral members would thus experience delays and miscommunication. For complex tasks, there are potentially serious coordination losses (Steiner, 1972; see above) associated with overly centralised communication networks.

**Communication network**
Set of rules governing the possibility or ease of communication between different roles in a group.

**Three-person**

Wheel
(or chain)

Circle
(or completely
connected)

**Figure 8.18** Communication
networks that have been studied
experimentally

The most studied communication
networks are those involving three,
four or five members (dots represent
positions or roles or people, and lines
represent communication channels).
The networks on the left are highly
centralised, and become increasingly
less centralised as you move to the
right of the figure

**Four-person**

Wheel          Chain                    Circle          Completely connected

**Five-person**

Wheel          Chain                    Circle          Completely connected

However, centralisation for complex tasks may pay off in the long run once appropriate procedures have been well established and well learned.

Another important consideration is the degree of autonomy felt by group members.
Because they are dependent on the hub for regulation and flow of information, peripheral
members have less power in the group, and they can feel restricted and dependent.

**Communication networks**

A multifaceted activity like making a film
requires a division of labour, and a
centralised communication network focused
on the team leader – something Clint
Eastwood knows well

According to Mulder (1960), having more power leads to a greater sense of autonomy and satisfaction, so peripheral members can become dissatisfied, while hub members, who are often perceived to be group leaders, feel a sense of satisfaction. Centralised communication networks can thus reduce group satisfaction, harmony and solidarity, and instead produce internal conflict. Research on organisations confirms that job satisfaction and organisational commitment are influenced by the amount of control that employees feel they have, and that control is related to communication networks, in particular to employees' perceived participation in decision making (Evans & Fischer, 1992).

In almost all groups, particularly organisational groups, the formal communication network is complemented by an informal communication 'grapevine'. You might be surprised to learn that, contrary to popular opinion and according to a study by Simmonds (1985), 80 per cent of grapevine information is work-related, and 70–90 per cent of that information is accurate.

Finally, the rules for studying communication networks in organisations now need to be rewritten with the explosion of computer-mediated communication (CMC) in the past fifteen years (Hollingshead, 2001). Organisations now have virtual groups and teams that rarely need to meet; they use electronic communication channels instead, and are often highly distributed without a centralised communication hub (Hackman, 2002). One positive effect of CMC is that it can de-emphasise status differences and can thus promote more equal participation among all members (see Chapter 15).

## Subgroups and crosscutting categories

Almost all groups are structurally differentiated into subgroups. These subgroups can be nested within the larger group (e.g. different departments in a university, different divisions in a company). However, many subgroups represent larger categories that have members outside the larger group (e.g. social psychologists in a psychology department are also members of the larger group of social psychologists). In this case the subgroups are not nested but are crosscutting categories (Crisp & Hewstone, 2007; Crisp, Ensari, Hewstone & Miller, 2003).

Group processes are significantly affected by subgroup structure. The main problem is that subgroups can engage in intergroup competition that can sometimes be harmful to the group as a whole. For example, divisions in a company can take healthy competition one step too far and slip into outright conflict. Research shows that when one company takes over another company and therefore contains within it two subgroups, the original company and the new company, conflict between these two subgroups can be extreme (e.g. Terry, Carey & Callan, 2001). When groups contain subgroups that differ ideologically or in their core values and attitudes, a schism can occur in which one group feels that the larger group no longer represents its values. The smaller group may then decide to split off and try to convert the larger group. This can create extreme conflict that can tear the larger group apart – this often happens in political, religious and scientific contexts (Sani & Reicher, 1998, 2000).

The problem of subgroup conflict is often most evident, and indeed harmful, when larger groups contain sociodemographic subgroups that have destructive intergroup relations in society as a whole, such as Protestants and Catholics who work together in a Northern Irish business (Hewstone et al., 2005). See Chapter 11 for a full treatment of intergroup relations, including intergroup relations among crosscutting and nested subgroups.

## Deviants and marginal members

Many, if not most, groups are also structured in terms of two kinds of member:

1  Those who best embody the group's attributes – core members who are highly prototypical of the group.

2  Those who do not – marginal or non-prototypical members.

Highly prototypical members often have significant influence over the group and may occupy leadership roles – we discuss them in Chapter 9. Marginal members are an entirely different story.

Research by Marques and his colleagues shows that marginal members are often disliked by the group, and treated as 'black sheep' (Marques & Páez, 1994) or deviants. People whose attributes place them on the boundary between ingroup and outgroup are actually disliked more if they are ingroup members than outgroup members – they are treated as deviants or even traitors. According to subjective group dynamics theory, one reason for this is that marginal members threaten the integrity of group norms by undermining normative consensus within the group (Marques, Abrams, Páez & Hogg, 2001; Marques, Abrams & Serodio, 2001). Paradoxically, for this very reason, marginal members serve an important function for groups – groups, particularly their leaders, can engage in a rhetoric of vilification and exclusion of marginal members precisely to throw into stark relief what the group is and what the group is not.

Marginal members may play another important role in groups – they can be the agents of social change within the group. Under the right conditions, marginal members may be uniquely placed to act as critics of group norms, precisely because they are normatively marginal. Studies by Hornsey and his colleagues show that groups are more accepting of criticism from ingroup than outgroup members (Hornsey, 2005; Hornsey & Imani, 2004; Hornsey, Oppes & Svensson, 2002). Of course, ingroup critics have an uphill struggle to be heard if they are labelled and treated as deviants. The task may be made easier if a number of dissenters unite as a subgroup – we then, effectively, have a **schism** or an active minority within the group. Indeed the analysis of how marginal members, deviants and dissenters may influence the larger group is the analysis of minority influence, which we discussed at length in Chapter 7.

**Schism**
Division of a group into subgroups that differ in their attitudes, values or ideology.

# Why do people join groups?

This is not an easy question to answer. It depends on how we define a group, and of course 'why' people join groups is not the same thing as 'how' people join groups. We also need to recognise that the groups to which we belong vary in the degree of free choice we had in joining. There is little choice in what sex, ethnic, national or social class groups we 'join': membership is largely designated externally. There is a degree of choice, although possibly less than we might think, in what occupational or political group we join; and there is a great deal of freedom in what clubs, societies and recreational groups we join. Even the most strongly externally designated social-category memberships, such as sex and ethnicity, can permit a degree of choice in what the implications of membership in that group may be (e.g. the group's norms and practices), and this may reflect the same sorts of motives and goals for choosing freely to join less externally designated groups.

## Reasons for joining groups

However, we can identify a range of circumstances, motives, goals and purposes that tend to cause, in more or less immediate ways, people to join or form groups (e.g. aggregate, coordinate their actions, declare themselves members of a group). For example, physical proximity can promote group formation. We tend to get to like, or at least learn to put up with, people we are in close proximity with (Tyler & Sears, 1977). This appears to promote group formation: we form groups with those around us. Festinger, Schachter and Back's (1950) classic study of a student housing programme, which we discussed earlier (see also Chapter 13), concerned just this – the role of proximity in group formation, group cohesiveness and subsequent adherence to group standards. The recognition of similar interests, attitudes and beliefs can also cause people to become or join a group.

If people share goals that require behavioural interdependence for their achievement, this is another strong and reliable reason for joining groups. This idea lies at the heart of Sherif's (1966) realistic conflict theory of intergroup behaviour (discussed in Chapter 11). For example, if we are concerned about degradation of the environment, we are likely ultimately to join an environmental conservation group, because division of labour and interdependent action among like-minded people will achieve a great deal more than the actions of a lone protester. People join groups to get things done that they cannot do on their own.

We can join groups for mutual positive support and the mere pleasure of affiliation: for example, to avoid loneliness (Peplau & Perlman, 1982). We can join groups for self-protection and personal safety: for example, adolescents join gangs (Ahlstrom & Havighurst, 1971) and mountaineers climb in groups for this reason. We can join groups for emotional support in times of stress: for example, support groups for AIDS sufferers and their relatives and friends fulfil this function.

Oscar Lewis's (1969) account of a Catholic wake in Mexico in his novel *A Death in the Sanchez Family* describes the way in which people come together in stressful circumstances. Schachter (1959) has explored the same idea in controlled experimental circumstances. However, a word of qualification is needed. Extreme stress and deprivation (e.g. in concentration camps, or after natural disasters) sometimes produces social disintegration and individual isolation rather than group formation (Middlebrook, 1980). This is probably because the link between stress and affiliation is not mechanical: if affiliation is not the effective solution to the stress, then it may not occur. Thomas Keneally's (1982) account, in his powerful biographical novel *Schindler's Ark,* of atrocities committed by the Nazis against Jews in the Polish city of Kraków, supports this. Despite extreme stress, remarkably little affiliation occurred, for the reason that affiliation was difficult to sustain and would probably only exacerbate the situation.

## Motivations for affiliation and group formation

The question of why people join groups can be reframed in terms of what basic motivations cause people to affiliate (see also Chapter 13). According to Baumeister and Leary (1995), human beings simply have a basic and overwhelming need to belong, and this causes them to affiliate and to join and be members of groups. Furthermore, the sense of belonging and being successfully connected to other human beings, interpersonally or in groups, produces a powerful and highly rewarding sense of self-esteem and self-worth (Leary, Tambor, Terdal & Downs, 1995).

According to **terror management theory** (Greenberg, Pyszczynski & Solomon, 1986; Greenberg, Solomon & Pyszczynski, 1997; Pyszczynski, Greenberg & Solomon, 2004; Solomon, Greenberg & Pyszczynski, 1991; see Chapter 4) the most fundamental threat that people face is the inevitability of death, and therefore people live in perpetual terror of death. Fear of death is the most powerful motivating factor in human existence. People affiliate and join groups in order to reduce fear of death. Affiliation and group formation are highly effective terror management strategies because they raise self-esteem and make people feel good about themselves – they feel immortal, and positive and excited about life.

One final and important motive for joining a group is to obtain a social identity (Hogg, 2006; Hogg & Abrams, 1988; Tajfel & Turner, 1979). Groups provide us with a consensually recognised definition and evaluation of who we are, how we should behave and how we will be treated by others. There is thus a highly sought-after and satisfying reduction in subjective uncertainty. Hogg and his associates (see Hogg, 2007b) conducted a series of experiments to show that people who are randomly categorised as members of a group

**Terror management theory**
The notion that the most fundamental human motivation is to reduce the terror of the inevitability of death. Self-esteem may be centrally implicated in effective terror management.

under abstract laboratory conditions (minimal group paradigm; see Chapter 11) actually identify with the group only if (1) they are in a state of uncertainty, and (2) the group is able to reduce uncertainty. In addition to uncertainty considerations, because we and others evaluate us in terms of the relative attractiveness, desirability and prestige of the groups to which we belong, we are motivated to join groups that are consensually positively evaluated (e.g. high status). We are motivated to join groups that will furnish a positive social identity (Hogg & Abrams, 1990; Long & Spears, 1997; Tajfel & Turner, 1979; see also Chapter 11).

## Why not join groups?

**Social ostracism**
Exclusion from a group by common consent.

Perhaps the question 'Why do people join groups?' should be stood on its head: 'Why do people not join groups?' Not being a member of a group is a lonely existence, depriving us of social interaction, social and physical protection, the ability to achieve complex goals, a stable sense of who we are, and confidence in how we should behave (see Chapter 13). Williams has devised an intriguing and powerful paradigm to study the consequences of being excluded from a group – **social ostracism** (Williams, 2002; Williams, Shore & Grahe, 1998; Williams & Sommer, 1997). Three-person groups of students waiting for an experiment begin to throw a ball to one another across the room. After a while two of the students (actually confederates) exclude the third student (true participant) by not throwing him or her the ball. It is very uncomfortable even to watch the video of this study (imagine how the participant felt!). True participants appear self-conscious and embarrassed, and many try to occupy themselves with other activities such as playing with keys, staring out of the window or meticulously scrutinising their wallets.

## Summary

- Although there are many definitions of the group, social psychologists generally agree that at the very least a group is a collection of people who define themselves as a group and whose attitudes and behaviour are governed by the norms of the group. Group membership often also entails shared goals, interdependence, mutual influence and face-to-face interaction.

- People tend to perform easy, well-learned tasks better, and difficult, poorly learned tasks worse, in the presence of other people than on their own.

- We may be affected in this way for a number of reasons. Social presence may instinctively drive habitual behaviour, we may learn to worry about performance evaluation by others, we may be distracted by others, or others may make us self-conscious or concerned about self-presentation.

- Tasks differ not only in difficulty but also in their structure and objectives. Whether a task benefits from division of labour, and how individual task performances are interrelated, have important implications for the relationship between individual and group performance.

- People tend to put less effort into task performance in groups than when alone, unless the task is involving and interesting, their individual contribution is clearly identifiable, or the group is important to their self-definition, in which case they can sometimes exert more effort in a group than alone.

- Members of cohesive groups tend to feel more favourably inclined towards one another as group members and are more likely to identify with the group and conform to its norms.

- Group membership is a dynamic process in which our sense of commitment varies, we occupy different roles at different times, we endure sharp transitions between roles, and we are socialised by the group in many different ways.

- Groups develop norms in order to regulate the behaviour of members, to define the group and to distinguish the group from other groups.

- Groups are structured internally into different roles that regulate interaction and best serve the collective interest of the group. Roles prescribe behaviour. They also vary in their desirability and thus influence status within the group. Groups are also internally structured in terms of subgroups and central and marginal group members.

- People may join or form groups to get things done that cannot be done alone, to gain a sense of identity, to obtain social support or simply for the pleasure of social interaction.

## Literature, film and TV

### A League of Their Own

1992 film directed by Penny Marshall, and starring Madonna, Tom Hanks and Geena Davis. About a women's baseball team during the Second World War, the film shows how a rabble of very different people is forged into a cohesive team. The film also confronts issues of non-stereotypical role behaviours – in America, women don't play baseball.

### Brassed Off

1996 Mark Herman film with Ewan McGregor. The local Grimley Colliery Brass Band is central to life in a small northern English coal-mining town. The mine is closing down and the conflict between strikers and non-strikers spills over into the band and almost all other aspects of life. A wonderful illustration of the impact of intergroup relations on intragroup dynamics.

### Castaway

2000 film directed by Robert Zemeckis, starring Tom Hanks. The film is about the consequences of exclusion, and loneliness. Tom Hanks is abandoned on an island. He uses pictures, and decorates a volleyball to look like a person whom he calls 'Wilson' – Wilson allows him to remain socially connected.

### The Full Monty

1997 film directed by Peter Cattaneo. Set in Sheffield, the film is about a group of chronically out-of-work people who decide to become a group of male strippers. This is totally out-of-role behaviour for working-class males in the north of England. The film documents the sorts of reaction they get from their friends, family and the community.

### Lost

J. J. Abrams's incredibly popular TV show that follows the survivors of a plane crash who have to work together to survive on an island. This series explores almost all aspects of group dynamics. A small community is formed with the common goal of survival and each character is encouraged to assume a role. Problems always arise when people are unwilling to cooperate for the good of the group.

## Guided questions

1. What makes a group a group?
2. How and why does the presence of other people affect an individual's performance?
3. Use your knowledge of *social loafing* to explain why workers are sometimes less productive than expected.
4. *Roles* have an important function in groups – but can role-play be dangerous? Phil Zimbardo sets the scene for his famous guards vs. prisoners experiment in Chapter 8 of MyPsychLab at **www.mypsychlab.co.uk** (watch *The Stanford Prison experiment*).
5. Why do people join groups?

## Learn more

Cialdini, R. B., & Trost, M. R. (1998). Social influence: Social norms, conformity, and compliance. In D. Gilbert, S. T. Fiske & G. Lindzey (eds), *The handbook of social psychology* (4th ed., Vol. 2, pp. 151–92). New York: McGraw-Hill. A thorough overview of social influence research, with an excellent section on norms.

Baron, R. S., & Kerr, N. (2003). *Group process, group decision, group action* (2nd ed.). Buckingham, UK: Open University Press. A general overview of topics in the study of group processes.

Brown, R. J. (2000). *Group processes* (2nd ed.). Oxford, UK: Blackwell. A very readable introduction to group processes, which also places an emphasis on social influence processes within groups, especially conformity, norms and minority influence.

Gruenfeld, D. H., & Tiedens, L. Z. (2010). Organizational preferences and their consequences. In S. T. Fiske, D. T. Gilbert, & G. Lindzey (eds), *Handbook of social psychology* (5th ed., Vol. 2, pp. 1252–87). New York: Wiley. Up-to-date and detailed overview of social psychological theory and research on organisational processes, including group processes in organisations.

Hackman, J. R., & Katz, N. (2010). Group behavior and performance. In S. T. Fiske, D. T. Gilbert, & G. Lindzey (eds), *Handbook of social psychology* (5th ed., Vol. 2, pp. 1208–51). New York: Wiley. Comprehensive, detailed and up-to-date coverage of group behaviour.

Hogg, M. A., & Smith, J. R. (2007). Attitudes in social context: A social identity perspective. *European Review of Social Psychology, 18,* 89–131. A theory oriented review article that hinges on a discussion of how norms are tied to groups, group membership and social identity.

Hogg, M. A., & Tindale, R. S. (eds) (2001). *Blackwell handbook of social psychology: Group processes.* Oxford, UK: Blackwell. A collection of twenty-six chapters from leading experts covering the entire field of group processes.

Leary, M. R. (2010). Affiliation, acceptance, and belonging: The pursuit of interpersonal connection. In S. T. Fiske, D. T. Gilbert, & G. Lindzey (eds), *Handbook of social psychology* (5th ed., Vol. 2, pp. 864–97). New York: Wiley. This chapter includes detailed discussion of why people might be motivated to affiliate with others and thus form groups.

Levine, J., & Moreland, R. L. (1998). Small groups. In D. Gilbert, S. T. Fiske, & G. Lindzey (eds), *The handbook of social psychology* (4th ed., Vol. 2, pp. 415–69). New York: McGraw-Hill. A comprehensive overview of the field of small groups – the most recent fifth edition of the handbook does not have a chapter dedicated to small interactive groups.

Stangor, C. (2004). *Social groups in action and interaction.* New York: Psychology Press. Comprehensive and accessible coverage of the social psychology of processes within and between groups.

Williams, K. D., Harkins, S. G., & Karau, S. J. (2007). Social performance. In M. A. Hogg & J. Cooper (eds), *The SAGE handbook of social psychology: Concise student edition* (pp. 291–311). London: SAGE. A comprehensive overview of theory and research focusing on how people's performance is affected by being in a group.

 Refresh your understanding, assess your progress and go further with interactive summaries, questions, podcasts and much more at **www.mypsychlab.co.uk**

## This chapter discusses

- Defining leadership
- Theories of leadership: personality traits, situational influences, leadership style, contingency theories, transactional and transformational leadership, leader perceptions and schemas, social identity theory
- Gender and leadership

- Group decision making
- Brainstorming
- Transactive memory
- Groupthink
- Group polarisation
- Decision making in juries

## Focus questions

1. Jane is a fearsome and energetic office manager who bustles around issuing orders. She expects and gets prompt action from her employees when she is around. How hard do you think her employees work when she is out of the office?

2. Your organisation is faced by a crisis that has united you all into a tight and cohesive unit. You need a new boss who is able to be innovative and to have the group's full support. Should you appoint Steve, who has all the leadership skills but comes from outside the organisation? Or should you appoint Martin, who has compliantly worked his way up through the organisation for over ten years? Michael Hogg discusses the nature of intergroup leadership in Chapter 9 of MyPsychLab at www.mypsychlab.co.uk (also watch *Intergroup leadership: a unifying force* – http://knowledge.insead.edu/Intergroup Leadership080807.cfm?vid=78?).

3. The design group at Acme Aerospace meets to design a rocket for a Mars landing. There are eight of you. Because decisions have to be made quickly and smoothly, your charismatic and powerful group leader has selected members so that you are all very much of one mind. This is a very difficult task and there is a great deal of competitive pressure from other space agencies. Will this arrangement deliver a good design?

will use which involves getting you to decide to buy a car by giving you a very low price

Go to **mypsych**lab to explore video and test your understanding of key topics addressed in this chapter.

Refresh your understanding with interactive summaries, explore topics further with video and audio clips and assess your progress with quick test and essay questions by logging to the accompanying website at www.mypsychlab.co.uk

# Chapter 9
## Leadership and decision making

| **Key terms** | Groupthink | Relational model of authority in |
|---|---|---|
| | Idiosyncrasy credit | groups |
| Autocratic leaders | Illusion of group effectivity | Risky shift |
| Big Five | Laissez-faire leaders | Role congruity theory |
| Brainstorming | Leader behaviour description | Self-categorisation theory |
| Charismatic leadership | questionnaire | Situational control |
| Contingency theories | Leader categorisation theory | Social comparison (theory) |
| Cultural values theory | Leader–member exchange theory | Social decisions schemes |
| Democratic leaders | Leadership | Social dilemmas |
| Distributive justice | Least-preferred co-worker scale | Social identity theory |
| Glass ceiling | Multifactor leadership questionnaire | Social transition scheme |
| Great person theory | Normative decision theory | Status characteristics theory |
| Group mind | Path–goal theory | Transactional leadership |
| Group polarisation | Persuasive arguments theory | Transactive memory |
| Group value model | Procedural justice | Transformational leadership |
| | Production blocking | Vertical dyad linkage model |

# Leaders and group decisions

We saw in Chapter 8 that groups vary in their size, composition, longevity and purpose. They also vary in cohesiveness, have different norms and are internally structured into roles in different ways. However, almost all groups have some form of unequal distribution of power and influence whereby some people lead and others follow. Indeed, even in the case of ostensibly egalitarian or leaderless groups, one rarely needs to scratch far beneath the surface to stumble upon a tacit leadership structure (e.g. Counselman, 1991). Although leadership can take a variety of forms (e.g. democratic, autocratic, informal, formal, laissez-faire), it is a fundamental aspect of almost all social groups.

We know (see end of Chapter 8) that people can assemble as a group for many different reasons and to perform many different tasks. One of the most common reasons is to make decisions through some form of group discussion. In fact, many of the most important decisions that affect our lives are made by groups, often groups of which we are not members. Indeed, one could argue that most decisions that people make are actually group decisions – not only do we frequently make decisions as a group, but even those decisions that we seem to make on our own are made in reference to what groups of people may think or do.

This chapter continues the discussion of group processes begun in Chapter 8. It focuses on two of the most significant group phenomena – leadership and group decision making.

# Leadership

In the many groups to which we may belong – teams, committees, organisations, friendship cliques, clubs – we encounter leaders: people who have the 'good' ideas that everyone else agrees on; people whom everyone follows; people who have the ability to make things happen. Leaders enable groups to function as productive and coordinated wholes. Leadership is so integral to the human condition that it may even serve an evolutionary function for the survival of our species (Van Vugt, Hogan, & Kaiser, 2008).

Effective leadership has a enormous impact. For example, one US study showed that highly performing executives added US$25 million more than average performers to the value of their company (Barrick, Day, Lord & Alexander, 1991), and another study showed that effective CEOs (chief executive officers) improved company performance by 14 per cent (Joyce, Nohria & Roberson, 2003). In the sports context, Jacobs and Singell (1993) studied the performance of American baseball teams over a twenty-year period and found that successful teams had managers who exercised superior tactical skills or who were skilled in improving the performance of individual team members.

On a larger canvas, history and political news often comprise stories of the deeds of leaders and tales of leadership struggles – for an enthralling and beautifully written insight into the life of one of the twentieth century's greatest leaders, read Nelson Mandela's (1994) autobiography *The Long Walk to Freedom*. Margaret Thatcher's (1993) autobiography *The Downing Street Years* also makes fascinating reading. There are also (auto)biographies of Richard Branson, Bob Geldof and Bono that provide insight into effective leadership in the business and public spheres.

Biography is frequently about leadership, and most classic accounts of history are mainly accounts of the actions of leaders. Our day-to-day life is pervaded by the impact of leadership – for example, leadership in the political, governmental, corporate, work, educational, scientific and artistic spheres – and we all, to varying degrees, occupy leadership roles ourselves. Not surprisingly, people take a keen interest in leadership and we all have our own views on leaders and leadership.

Incompetent leadership and leadership in the service of evil, in particular, are of great concern to us all (e.g. Kellerman, 2004). Whereas good leaders tend to have the attributes of integrity, decisiveness, competence and vision (Hogan & Kaiser, 2006), extremely bad or dangerous leaders tend to devalue others and be indifferent to their suffering, are intolerant of criticism and suppress dissent, and have a grandiose sense of entitlement (Mayer, 1993). The four most prominent patterns of bad leadership are: failure to build an effective team, poor interpersonal skills to manage the team, insensitivity and lack of care about others, and inability to adjust to being promoted above one's skills or qualifications (Leslie & Van Velsor, 1996).

To understand how leaders lead, what factors influence the person who is likely to be a leader in a particular context and what the social consequences of **leadership** may be, social psychology has embraced a variety of theoretical perspectives and emphases. However, after the end of the 1970s, social psychology paid diminishing attention to leadership. The 1985 third edition of the *Handbook of social psychology* dedicated a full chapter to leadership (Hollander, 1985), whereas the 1998 fourth edition had no chapter on leadership. Instead, there has been a corresponding frenzy of research on leadership in organisational psychology (e.g. Northhouse, 2004; Yukl, 2010) – it is here, in the management and organisational sciences, where most leadership research is to be found. However, leadership is quite definitely a topic that transcends disciplinary boundaries – although organisational leadership is important, so is political/public leadership and team leadership.

**Leadership**
Getting group members to achieve the group's goals.

Recently, there has been a revival of interest in leadership among social psychologists – for instance, there are two chapters on leadership in Hogg and Tindale's (2001) *Blackwell handbook of social psychology: Group processes* (Chemers, 2001; Lord, Brown & Harvey, 2001), one in Kruglanski and Higgins's (2007) second edition of *Social psychology: A handbook of basic principles* (Hogg, 2007a), and one in the fifth edition of the *Handbook of social psychology* (Hogg, 2010).

## Defining leadership

It is difficult to find a consensual definition of leadership – definitions depend on what aspect of leadership is being investigated, from what disciplinary or theoretical perspective, and for what practical purpose. From a social psychological perspective, Chemers defined leadership as 'a process of social influence through which an individual enlists and mobilizes the aid of others in the attainment of a collective goal' (Chemers, 2001, p. 376). Leadership requires there to be an individual, or clique, who influences the behaviour of another individual or group of individuals – where there are leaders there must be followers.

Another way to look at leadership is to ask: what is *not* leadership? If a friend cajoled you to spend the weekend cleaning her flat and you agreed, either because you liked her or because you were afraid of her, it would be influence but not leadership – a classic case of compliance (e.g. Cialdini & Trost, 1998; see Chapter 6). Related to this, the exercise of power is generally not considered to be leadership (e.g. Chemers, 2001; Lord, Brown & Harvey, 2001; Raven, 1993). If you agreed because you knew that there was a community norm to clean at the weekend, that would be conformity to a norm (e.g. Turner, 1991), not an example of leadership. If, on the other hand, your friend had first convinced you that a community cleaning norm should be developed, and you subsequently adhered to that norm, then that most definitely would be leadership. Leaders play a critical role in defining collective goals. In this respect, leadership is more typically a group process than an interpersonal process. It is an influence process that plays out more noticeably in group contexts than in interpersonal contexts.

Another question about leadership is: what is 'good' leadership? This question is poorly put; it needs to be unpacked into two different questions relating to effective/ineffective leaders and good/bad leaders. An *effective* leader is someone who is successful in setting new goals and influencing others to achieve them. Here, the evaluation of leadership is largely an objective matter of fact – how much influence did the leader have in setting new goals and were the goals achieved?

In contrast, evaluating whether the leader is good or bad is largely a subjective judgement based on one's preferences, perspectives and goals, and on whether the leader belongs to one's own group or another group. We evaluate leaders in terms of their character (e.g. nice, nasty, charismatic), the ethics and morality of the means they use to influence others and achieve goals (e.g. persuasion, coercion, oppression, democratic decision making), and the nature of the goals that they lead their followers towards (e.g. saving the environment, reducing starvation and disease, producing a commodity, combating oppression, engaging in genocide). Here *good* leaders are those who have attributes we applaud, use means we approve of, and set and achieve goals we value.

Thus, secular Westerners and supporters of al-Qaeda might disagree on whether Osama bin Laden is a *good* leader (they disagree on the value of his goals and the morality of his means) but may agree that he has been a relatively *effective* leader (agreeing that he has mobilised fundamentalist Muslims around his cause).

## Personality traits and individual differences

Great, or notorious, leaders such as Churchill, Gandhi, Hitler, Mandela, Stalin and Thatcher seem to have special and distinctive capabilities that mark them off from the rest of us. Unsurprisingly, we tend to seek an explanation in terms of unique properties of these people (i.e. personality characteristics that predispose certain people to lead) rather than the context or process of leadership. For example, we tend to personify history in terms of the actions of great people: the French occupation of Moscow in 1812 was Napoleon's doing; the 1917 Russian Revolution was 'caused' by Lenin; and the 1980s in Britain were 'the Thatcher years'. Folk wisdom also tends to attribute great leaps forward in science – what Kuhn (1962) calls *paradigm shifts* – to the independent actions of great people such as Einstein, Freud, Darwin and Copernicus.

**Great person theory**
Perspective on leadership that attributes effective leadership to innate or acquired individual characteristics.

This preference for a **great person theory** that attributes leadership to personality may be explained in terms of how people construct an understanding of their world. In Chapter 3 we saw that people have a tendency to attribute others' behaviour to stable underlying traits (e.g. Gilbert & Malone, 1995; Haslam, Rothschild & Ernst, 1998) and that this is

**Perhaps greatness beckons**
Barack Obama, the first black president of the United States.

accentuated where the other person is the focus of our attention. Leaders certainly do stand out against the background of the group, and are therefore the focus of our attention, which strengthens the perception of a correspondence between traits and behaviour (e.g. Fiske & Dépret, 1996; Meindl, 1995; Meindl, Ehrlich & Dukerich, 1985).

Social psychologists are little different from people in everyday life. They have, therefore, tried to explain leadership in terms of personality traits that equip some people for effective leadership better than others. The great person theory of leadership has a long and illustrious pedigree, going back to Plato and ancient Greece. Although some scholars, for example Francis Galton (1892) in the nineteenth century, have maintained that leaders are born not made, most scholars do not believe that effective leadership is an innate attribute. Instead they believe leadership ability is a constellation of personality attributes acquired very early in life that imbues people with charisma and a predisposition to lead (e.g. Carlyle, 1841; House, 1977).

A prodigious quantity of research has been conducted to identify these correlates of effective leadership. For example, leaders apparently tend to be above average with respect to size, health, physical attractiveness, self-confidence, sociability, need for dominance and, most reliably, intelligence and talkativeness. Intelligence is important probably because leaders are expected to think and respond quickly and have more ready access to information than others, and talkativeness because it attracts attention and makes the person perceptually salient. But we can all identify effective 'leaders' who do not possess these attributes – for example, Gandhi and Napoleon certainly were not large, the Dalai Lama is not 'talkative', and we'll let you generate your own examples of leaders who do not appear to be very intelligent!

Early on Stogdill reviewed the leadership literature and concluded that leadership is not the 'mere possession of some combination of traits' (Stogdill, 1948, p. 66), and more recently others have exclaimed that the search for a leadership personality is simplistic and futile (e.g. Conger & Kanungo, 1998). In general, correlations among traits, and between traits and effective leadership, are low (Stogdill, 1974, reports an average correlation of 0.30).

Nevertheless, the belief that some people are better leaders than others because they have enduring traits that predispose them to effective leadership persists. This view has re-emerged in a different guise in modern theories of transformational leadership (see below) that emphasise the role of charisma in leadership (e.g. Avolio & Yammarino, 2003; Bass, 1985; Conger & Kanungo, 1998). Rather than focusing on specific traits, this tradition focuses on what are called the **Big Five** personality dimensions: extraversion/surgency, agreeableness, conscientiousness, emotional stability, and intellect/openness to experience. A definitive meta-analysis by Judge, Bono, Ilies and Gerhardt (2002) has found that these attributes have an overall correlation of 0.58 with leadership, with extraversion/surgency, intellect/openness to experience, and conscientiousness as the best predictors of effective leadership.

**Big Five**

The five major personality dimensions of extraversion/surgency, agreeableness, conscientiousness, emotional stability, and intellect/openness to experience.

## Situational perspectives

In contrast to personality and individual differences approaches that attribute effective leadership to having particular enduring trait constellations is the view that anyone can lead effectively if the situation is right. The most extreme form of this perspective is to deny any influence at all to the leader. For example, much of Tolstoy's epic novel *War and Peace* is a vehicle for his critique of the great person account of history: 'To elicit the laws of history we must leave aside kings, ministers and generals, and select for study the homogeneous, infinitesimal elements which influence the masses' (Tolstoy, 1869, p. 977). Likewise, Karl Marx's theory of history places explanatory emphasis on the actions of groups, not individuals.

This perspective may be too extreme. For example, Simonton (1980) analysed the outcome of 300 military battles for which there were reliable archival data on the generals and their armies. Although situational factors, such as the size of the army and diversification of command structure, were correlated with casualties inflicted on the enemy, some personal attributes of the leader, to do with experience and previous battle record, were also associated with victory. In other words, although situational factors influenced outcome, so did the attributes of the leader.

From time to time, then, we may find ourselves in situations in which we are leaders. An often-cited illustration of this is the case of Winston Churchill. Although he was considered by many to be argumentative, opinionated and eminently unsuited to government, these were precisely the characteristics needed in a great wartime leader. However, as soon as the Second World War was over he was voted out of government, as these were not considered to be the qualities most needed in a peacetime leader.

Social psychologists have found the same thing under more controlled conditions. For example, in their classic studies of intergroup relations at boys' summer camps in the United States (see Chapter 11 for details), Sherif and his colleagues (Sherif, 1966; Sherif, Harvey, White, Hood, & Sherif, 1961) divided the boys into groups and found that in one group there was a leadership change under conditions of intergroup competition. The former leader was displaced by someone with greater physical prowess, who was better equipped to lead the group successfully in the changed circumstances. In an experimental study, Carter and Nixon (1949) demonstrated the same point by having pairs of school pupils perform three different tasks – an intellectual task, a clerical task and a mechanical assembly task. Those who took the lead in the first two tasks rarely led in the mechanical assembly task.

Overall, leadership reflects task or situational demands and is not purely a property of individual personality, although personal qualities may play a role. Balancing the Churchill example above, leaders can sometimes change to accommodate changed circumstances. When Nelson Mandela was released in 1990 from twenty-six years of imprisonment, most of it in isolation on Robben Island off Cape Town, the political terrain had altered dramatically. Yet he was able to read the changes and go on to lead the African National Congress to political victory in South Africa. Effective leadership is a matter of the right combination of personal characteristics and situational requirements.

## What leaders do

If effective leadership is an interaction between leader attributes and situational require-ments, then we need to know about leader attributes. We have seen that personality may not be as reliable a leadership attribute as one might think. Perhaps what leaders actually do, their actual behaviour, is more reliable? This idea spawned some of social psychology's classic leadership research.

In a classic study, Lippitt and White (1943) used after-school activities clubs for young boys as an opportunity to study the effects of different styles of leadership on group atmos-phere, morale and effectiveness. The leaders of the clubs were actually confederates of the researchers, and they were trained in each of three distinct leadership styles:

1 **Autocratic leaders** organised the club's activities, gave orders, were aloof and focused exclusively on the task at hand.

2 **Democratic leaders** called for suggestions, discussed plans and behaved like ordinary club members.

3 **Laissez-faire leaders** left the group to its own devices and generally intervened minimally.

Each club was assigned to a particular leadership style. One confederate was the leader for seven weeks and then the confederates were swapped around; this happened twice, so that each confederate adopted each leadership style, but each group was exposed to only one leadership style (although enacted by three different confederates). This clever control allowed Lippitt and White to distinguish leadership behaviour per se from the specific leader who was behaving in that way. In this way they could rule out personality explanations.

Lippitt and White's findings are described in Figure 9.1. Democratic leaders were liked significantly more than autocratic or laissez-faire leaders. They created a friendly, group-centred, task-oriented atmosphere that was associated with relatively high group productivity, which was unaffected by the physical absence or presence of the leader. In con-trast, autocratic leaders created an aggressive, dependent and self-oriented group atmosphere, which was associated with high productivity only when the leader was present.

**Autocratic leaders**
Leaders who use a style based on giving orders to followers.

**Democratic leaders**
Leaders who use a style based on consultation and obtaining agreement and consent from followers.

**Laissez-faire leaders**
Leaders who use a style based on disinterest in followers.

**An autocratic leader**
'I like to do all the talking myself. It saves time and prevents arguments' (Oscar Wilde)

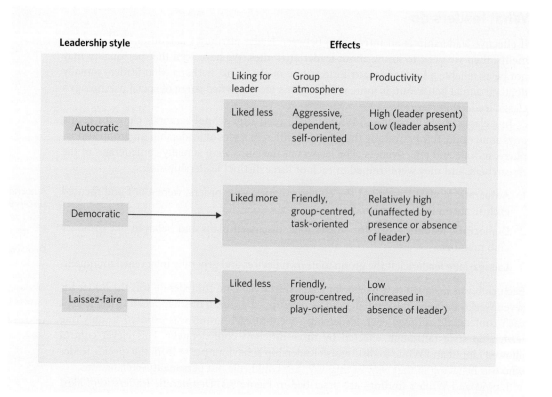

**Figure 9.1** Leadership styles and their effects

Autocratic, democratic and laissez-faire leadership styles have different combinations of effects on group atmosphere and productivity, and on liking for the leader

*Source:* based on Lippitt & White (1943)

(How would you rate bustling Jane in the first focus question?) Laissez-faire leaders created a friendly, group-centred but play-oriented atmosphere that was associated with low productivity, which increased only if the leader was absent. Lippitt and White used these findings to promote their view that democratic leadership was more effective than other leadership behaviour.

Lippitt and White's distinction between autocratic and democratic leadership styles re-emerges in a slightly different guise in later work. From his studies of interaction styles in groups, Bales (1950) identified two key leadership roles – *task specialist* and *socio-emotional specialist* (Slater, 1955). No one person could occupy both roles simultaneously. Rather, the roles tended to devolve on to separate individuals, and the person occupying the task-specialist role was more likely to be the dominant leader. Task specialists tend to be centrally involved, often by offering opinions and giving directions, in the task-oriented aspects of group life, whereas socio-emotional specialists tend to respond and pay attention to the feelings of other group members.

Casual observation of groups and organisations supports this dual-leadership idea. For example, one theme that punctuated election struggles between the Labour Party and the Conservative Party during the 1980s in Britain was to do with what sort of leader the country should have. The Labour leader at the time, Neil Kinnock, was, among other things, heralded as a friendly and approachable leader concerned with people's feelings, and the Conservative leader, Margaret Thatcher, as the hard-headed, task-oriented economic rationalist.

The Ohio State leadership studies constitute a third major leadership programme (e.g. Fleishman, 1973; Stogdill, 1974). In this research a scale for measuring leadership behaviour was devised, the **leader behaviour description questionnaire** (LBDQ) (Shartle, 1951), and a distinction was drawn between *initiating structure* and *consideration*. Leaders high on initiating structure define the group's objectives and organise members' work towards the attainment of these goals: they are task-oriented. Leaders high on consideration are concerned with the welfare of subordinates and seek to promote harmonious relationships in the group: they are relationship-oriented. Unlike Bales (1950), who believed that task-oriented and socio-emotional attributes were inversely related, the Ohio State researchers believed their dimensions to be independent – a single person could be high on both initiating structure (task-oriented) and consideration (socio-emotional), and such a person would be a particularly effective leader.

Research tends to support this latter view – the most effective leaders are precisely those who score above average on both initiating structure and consideration (Stogdill, 1974). For example, Sorrentino and Field (1986) conducted detailed observations of twelve problem-solving groups over a five-week period. Those group members who were rated as being high on both the task and socio-emotional dimensions of Bales's (1950) system were subsequently elected by groups to be their leaders.

The general distinction between a leadership style that pays more attention to the group task and getting things done, and one that pays attention to relationships among group members, is quite pervasive. For example, as we shall see below, it appears in Fiedler's (1964) influential contingency theory of leadership, and in a slightly different guise in leader–member exchange (LMX) theory's emphasis upon the quality of the leader's relationship with his or her followers (e.g. Graen & Uhl-Bien, 1995).

Furthermore, it is a distinction that may hold across cultures, but with the caveat that what counts as task-oriented or socio-emotional leadership behaviour may vary from culture to culture. For example, from their leadership research in Japan, Misumi and Peterson (1985) identify a similar distinction – in this case between task performance and group maintenance. They go on to note that whether a behaviour counts as one or the other differs from culture to culture – for example, the leader eating lunch with his or her workmates is associated with high group maintenance in some cultures but not others.

The same conclusion was drawn by Smith and colleagues (Smith. Misumi, Tayeb, Peterson, & Bond, 1989) from research in the United States, Britain, Hong Kong and Japan. They found that performance and maintenance behaviour were universally valued in leaders, but that what counted as each type of behaviour varied from culture to culture. For example, leaders need to assess workers' task performance; in Britain and America, the considerate way to do this is by speaking directly with workers, whereas in Asia this is viewed as inconsiderate, and the considerate way is to speak with the individual's co-workers.

Having learned something about what effective leaders do, we now need to turn our attention to what situational factors invite or benefit from which leadership behaviours. How do behaviour and situation interact to produce effective leadership?

## Contingency theories

**Contingency theories** of leadership recognise that the leadership effectiveness of particular leadership behaviours or styles is *contingent* on the properties of the leadership situation – some styles are better suited to some situations or tasks than are others. For example, different behavioural styles are suited to an aircrew in combat, an organisational decision-making group, a ballet company, or a nation in economic crisis.

### Fiedler's contingency theory

The best-known contingency theory in social psychology is that proposed by Fiedler (1964). Fiedler, like Bales (1950), distinguished between task-oriented leaders who are authoritarian,

**Leader behaviour description questionnaire**
Scale devised by the Ohio State leadership researchers to measure leadership behaviour and distinguish between 'initiating structure' and 'consideration' dimensions.

**Contingency theories**
Theories of leadership that consider the leadership effectiveness of particular behaviours or behavioural styles to be contingent on the nature of the leadership situation.

**Least preferred co-worker**
A first step in measuring your leadership style is to nominate the person with whom you find it most difficult to work

**Least-preferred co-worker scale**
Fiedler's scale for measuring leadership style in terms of favourability of attitude towards one's least-preferred co-worker.

**Situational control**
Fiedler's classification of task characteristics in terms of how much control effective task performance requires.

value group success and derive self-esteem from task accomplishment rather than being liked by the group; and relationship-oriented leaders who are relaxed, friendly, non-directive and sociable, and gain self-esteem from happy and harmonious group relations.

Fiedler measured leadership style in a rather unusual way; with his **least preferred co-worker (LPC) scale** in which respondents rated the person they least preferred as a co-worker on a number of dimensions (e.g. pleasant–unpleasant, boring–interesting, friendly–unfriendly). High LPC scores meant that the respondent felt favourably inclined towards a fellow member even if he or she was not performing well (indicating a relationship-oriented style), and low LPC scores indicated a task-oriented style because the respondent was harsh on a poorly performing co-worker.

Fiedler classified situations in terms of three dimensions in descending order of importance:

- the quality of leader–member relations;
- the clarity of the structure of the task; and
- the intrinsic power and authority the leader had by virtue of his or her position as leader.

Good leader–member relations in conjunction with a clear task and substantial position power furnished maximal 'situational control' (making leadership easy), whereas poor leader–member relations, a fuzzy task and low position power furnished minimal 'situational control' (making leadership difficult). **Situational control** can be classified quite precisely from I 'very high' to VIII 'very low', by dichotomising conditions under each of the three factors as good or bad (high or low) (see Figure 9.2).

Fiedler's prediction was that low LPC, task-oriented leaders would be most effective when situational control was low (the group needs a directive leader to focus on getting things done) *and* when it was high (the group is doing just fine, so there is little need to worry about morale and relationships within the group). High LPC, relationship-oriented leaders are more effective when situational control lies between these extremes. This prediction is illustrated in Figure 9.3, which also shows a composite of LPC–performance correlations reported by Fiedler (1965) from published studies. The results match the prediction rather well.

Meta-analyses confirm this. Strube and Garcia (1981) conducted a meta-analysis of 178 empirical tests of the theory, and Schriesheim, Tepper and Tetrault (1994) conducted a further meta-analysis of a subset of these studies. Overall, Fiedler's predictions based on contingency

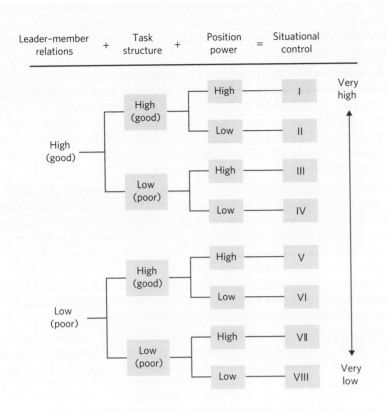

**Figure 9.2** Fiedler's eight-category situational control scale as a function of leader–member relations, task structure and position power

- An eight-category scale of situational control (I, very high, to VIII, very low) can be constructed by classifying situations as having good/bad leader–member relations, good/bad task structure, and high/low position power.

- The a priori assumption, that leader–member relations are more important than task structure, which is more important than position power, means that a situation is first classified by leader–member relations, then within that by task structure, and then within that by position power

*Source:* based on Fiedler (1965)

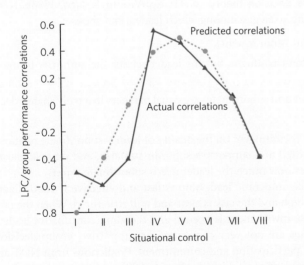

**Figure 9.3** Predicted and obtained correlations between LPC scores and group performance as a function of situational control

- When situational control is very high or very low, contingency theory predicts a negative correlation between LPC scores and quality of group performance.

- A group performs poorly for a relationship-oriented leader (high LPC score), but well for a task-oriented leader (low LPC score).

- When control is intermediate a positive correlation is predicted: relationship-oriented leaders are more effective. The obtained correlations came from a series of supportive studies.

*Source:* based on data from Fiedler (1965)

theory have generally been supported. However, let's not be too hasty – there is some controversy and there are some criticisms (e.g. Peters, Hartke & Pohlmann, 1985):

- Fiedler's view that leadership style is a characteristic of the individual that is invariant across time and situation is inconsistent with: (1) contemporary conceptualisations of personality that view personality as having substantial temporal and situational variability (e.g. Snyder & Cantor, 1998); (2) evidence of relatively low test–retest reliability (correlations range from 0.01 to 0.93 with a median of 0.67) for LPC scores (Rice, 1978); and (3) the ease with which Lippitt and White (1943) trained their confederates to adopt different leadership styles in the study described earlier.

- Fiedler may be wrong to make the a priori assumption that leader–member relations are more important than task structure, which is more important than position power in the assessment of overall situational control. It would not be surprising if the relative order of importance were itself a function of situational factors. Indeed, Singh, Bohra and Dalal (1979) obtained a better fit between prediction and results under conditions where the situational favourability of the eight octants was based on subjective ratings by participants rather than Fiedler's a priori classification.

- Contingency theory distinguishes between the leadership effectiveness of high- and low-LPC leaders, generally classifying 'highs' as those with an LPC score greater than 64 and 'lows' as those with an LPC score of less than 57. So, how do people in the 57–64 range behave? This is a valid question, since about 20 per cent of people fall in this range. Kennedy (1982) conducted a study to answer this question. He found that high and low scorers behaved as predicted by contingency theory, but that middle scorers performed best of all and that their effectiveness was uninfluenced by situational favourability. This certainly limits contingency theory – it does not seem to be able to explain the leadership effectiveness of approximately 20 per cent of people or instances.

- Although contingency theory explores the interaction between properties of the person and properties of the situation in the assessment of leadership effectiveness, it neglects the group processes that are responsible for the rise and fall of leaders, and the situational complexion of leadership.

### Normative decision theory

**Normative decision theory**
A contingency theory of leadership that focuses on the effectiveness of different leadership styles in group decision-making contexts.

Another contingency theory, which is focused specifically on leadership in group decision-making contexts, is **normative decision theory** (NDT; e.g. Vroom & Jago, 1988). NDT identifies three decision-making strategies among which leaders can choose:

- *autocratic* (subordinate input is not sought);

- *consultative* (subordinate input is sought, but the leader retains the authority to make the final decision); and

- *group decision making* (leader and subordinates are equal partners in a truly shared decision-making process).

The efficacy of these strategies is contingent on the quality of leader–subordinate relations (which influences how committed and supportive subordinates are), and on task clarity and structure (which influences how much the leader needs subordinate input).

In decision-making contexts, autocratic leadership is fast and effective if subordinate commitment and support are high and the task is clear and well structured. When the task is less clear, greater subordinate involvement is needed and therefore consultative leadership is best. When subordinates are not very committed or supportive, group decision making is required to increase participation and commitment. Predictions from NDT are reasonably well supported empirically (e.g. Field & House, 1990) – leaders and managers report better decisions and better subordinate ratings when they follow the prescriptions of the theory. However, there is a tendency for subordinates to prefer fully participative group decision making, even when it is not the most effective strategy.

### Path-goal theory

**Path-goal theory**
A contingency theory of leadership that can also be classified as a transactional theory – it focuses on how 'structuring' and 'consideration' behaviours motivate followers.

**Path-goal theory** (PGT; e.g. House, 1996) is another well-known contingency theory, although it can also be classified as a transactional leadership theory (see below). PGT rests on the assumption that a leader's main function is to motivate followers by clarifying the paths (i.e. behaviours and actions) that will help them reach their goals. It distinguishes between the two classes of leader behaviour identified by the leader behaviour description questionnaire (LBDQ), described above: *structuring* where the leader directs task-related activities, and *consideration* where the leader addresses followers' personal and emotional needs.

PGT predicts that structuring will be most effective when followers are unclear about their goals and how to reach them – for example, when the task is new, difficult or ambiguous. When tasks are well understood, structuring is less effective, or can even backfire because it is viewed as undue meddling and micro-management. Consideration is most effective when the task is boring or uncomfortable, but it can backfire when followers are already engaged and motivated because it is considered distracting and unnecessary.

Empirical support for PGT is mixed, with most scholars agreeing that tests of the theory suffer from flawed methodology and from being incomplete and simplistic (Schriesheim & Neider, 1996). The theory also has an interpersonal focus that underplays the ways in which a leader can motivate an entire work group rather than just individual followers.

## Transactional leadership

A significant limitation of contingency theories is that they are somewhat static – failing to capture the dance of leadership in which leaders and followers provide support and gratification to one another, which allows leaders to lead and encourages followers to follow (Messick, 2005). This limitation is addressed by theories of **transactional leadership**.

The key assumption here is that leadership is a 'process of exchange that is analogous to contractual relations in economic life [and] contingent on the good faith of the participants' (Downton, 1973, p. 75). Leaders transact with followers to get things done – creating expectations and setting goals, and providing recognition and rewards for task completion (Burns, 1978). Mutual benefits are exchanged (transacted) between leaders and followers against a background of contingent rewards and punishments that shape up cooperation and trust (Bass, 1985). Leader–member transactions may also have an equity dimension (Walster, Walster & Berscheid, 1978; also see Chapter 13). Because effective leaders play a greater role in steering groups to their goals than do followers, followers may reinstate equity by rewarding the leader with social approval, praise, prestige, status and power – in other words, with the trappings of effective leadership.

**Transactional leadership**
Approach to leadership that focuses on the transaction of resources between leader and followers. Also a style of leadership.

### Idiosyncrasy credit

A well-known early approach to leadership that focused on leader–follower transactions is Hollander's (1958) analysis of **idiosyncrasy credit**. Hollander believed that in order to be effective, leaders needed their followers to allow them to be innovative, to be able to experiment with new ideas and new directions – to be idiosyncratic. Drawing on the equity argument, above, Hollander wondered what circumstances would encourage such a transaction between leader and followers – one in which followers would provide their leader with the resources to be able to be idiosyncratic.

**Idiosyncrasy credit**
Hollander's transactional theory, that followers reward leaders for achieving group goals by allowing them to be relatively idiosyncratic.

He believed that certain behaviours build up idiosyncrasy credit with the group – a resource that the leader can ultimately 'cash in'. A good 'credit rating' can be established by:

- initially conforming closely to established group norms;
- ensuring that the group feels that it has democratically elected you as the leader;
- making sure that you are seen to have the competence to fulfil the group's objectives; and
- being seen to identify with the group, its ideals and its aspirations.

A good credit rating gives the leader legitimacy in the eyes of the followers to exert influence over the group and to deviate from existing norms – in other words, to be idiosyncratic, creative and innovative.

**Transactional leadership**
In many cultures, the trappings of status and power are associated with an ornate dress style

Research provides some support for this analysis. Merei (1949) introduced older children who had shown leadership potential into small groups of younger children in a Hungarian nursery. The most successful leaders were those who initially complied with existing group practices and who only gradually and later introduced minor variations. In another study, Hollander and Julian (1970) found that leaders of decision-making groups who were ostensibly democratically elected enjoyed more support from the group, felt more competent at the task and were more likely to suggest solutions that diverged from those of the group as a whole.

An alternative explanation, not grounded in notions of interpersonal equity and transaction, and idiosyncrasy credit, for why the conditions described above may allow a leader to be innovative is provided by the social identity theory of leadership (Hogg, 2001b; Hogg & Van Knippenberg, 2003; see below). The argument is that group normative behaviour on the part of a leader communicates that the leader is 'one of us' – a central group member who identifies strongly with the group, and who embodies the norms and aspirations of the group, and who is therefore unlikely to do the group any harm (e.g. Platow & Van Knippenberg, 2001). If one identifies strongly with the group oneself, then one trusts such a leader (e.g. Yamagishi & Kiyonari, 2000) and is prepared to follow his or her lead largely irrespective of how innovative and counter-normative his or her behaviour may be – whatever he or she does is likely to be in the best interest of the group.

## Leader–member exchange theory

Leader–member transactions play a central role in **leader–member exchange (LMX) theory** (e.g. Graen & Uhl-Bien, 1995; Sparrowe & Liden, 1997), which describes how the quality of exchange relationships (i.e. relationships in which resources such as respect and trust, liking are exchanged) between leaders and followers can vary. Originally, LMX theory was called the **vertical dyad linkage (VDL) model** (Danserau, Graen & Haga, 1975). According to VDL researchers, leaders develop dyadic exchange relationships with different specific subordinates. In these dyadic relationships, the subordinate can be treated either as a close and valued 'ingroup' member with the leader or in a more remote manner as an 'outgroup' member who is separate from the leader.

As the VDL model evolved into LMX theory, this dichotomous, ingroup versus outgroup, treatment of leader–member exchange relationships was replaced by a continuum of quality of exchange relationships ranging from ones that are based on mutual trust, respect and obligation (high-quality LMX relationships), to ones that are rather mechanically based on the terms of the formal employment contract between leader and subordinate (low-quality LMX relationships).

In high-quality LMX relationships, subordinates are favoured by the leader and receive many valued resources, which can include material (e.g. money, privileges) as well as psychological (e.g. trust, confidences) benefits. Leader–member exchanges go beyond the formal employment contract, with managers showing influence and support, and giving the subordinate greater autonomy and responsibility. High-quality relationships should motivate subordinates to internalise the group's and the leader's goals. In low-quality LMX relationships, subordinates are disfavoured by the leader and receive fewer valued resources. Leader–member exchanges simply adhere to the terms of the employment contract, with little attempt by the leader to develop or motivate the subordinate. Subordinates will simply comply with the leader's goals, without necessarily internalising them as their own.

LMX theory predicts that effective leadership hinges on the development of high-quality LMX relationships. These relationships enhance subordinates' well-being and work performance, and bind them to the group more tightly through loyalty, gratitude and a sense of inclusion. Because leaders usually have to relate to a large number of subordinates, they cannot develop high-quality LMX relationships with everyone – it is more efficient to select some subordinates in whom to invest a great deal of interpersonal energy, and to treat the others in a less personalised manner. The selection process takes time because it goes through a number of stages: *role taking* in which the leader has expectations and tries out different roles on the subordinate, *role making* in which mutual leader–member exchanges (e.g. of information, support) establish the subordinate's role, and *role routinisation* in which the leader–member relationship has become stable, smooth-running and automatic.

Research confirms that differentiated LMX relationships do exist in most organisations; that high-quality LMX relationships are more likely to develop when the leader and the subordinate have similar attitudes, like one another, belong to the same sociodemographic groups and both perform at a high level; and that high-quality LMX relationships are associated with (most studies are correlational, not causal) better-performing and more satisfied workers who are more committed to the organisation and less likely to leave (see Schriesheim, Castro & Cogliser, 1999). The stages of LMX relationship development are consistent with more general models of group development (e.g. Levine & Moreland, 1994; Tuckman, 1965; see Chapter 8).

The main limitation of LMX theory is that it focuses on dyadic leader–member relations. The problem here is that leadership is, as discussed earlier in this chapter, a group process – even if a leader appears to be interacting with an individual group member, that interaction is framed by and located in the wider context of shared group membership, in which followers interact with one another as group members and are influenced by their

**Leader–member exchange theory**
Theory of leadership in which effective leadership rests on the ability of the leader to develop good-quality personalised exchange relationships with individual members.

**Vertical dyad linkage model**
An early form of leader-member exchange (LMX) theory in which a sharp distinction is drawn between dyadic leader-member relations in which the member is treated effectively as ingroup or as outgroup.

perceptions of the leader's relations with other group members (e.g. Hogg, Martin & Weeden, 2004; Scandura, 1999).

So, from the perspective of the social identity theory of leadership (e.g. Hogg & Van Knippenberg, 2003; see below), we would expect that when members identify strongly with a group, they might find differentiated LMX relationships that favour some members over others to be uncomfortably personalised and fragmentary of the group, and would not endorse such leaders. Instead, members might prefer a somewhat more depersonalised leadership style that treated all members relatively equally as group members – endorsing such leaders more strongly. This hypothesis has been tested and supported in two field surveys of leadership perceptions in organisations in Wales and India (Hogg, Martin, Epitropaki, Mankad, Svensson, & Weeden, 2005).

## Transformational leadership

**Transformational leadership**

Approach to leadership that focuses on the way that leaders transform group goals and actions – mainly through the exercise of charisma. Also a style of leadership based on charisma.

Transactional theories of leadership represent a particular focus on leadership. However, transactional leadership is itself a particular leadership *style* that can be contrasted to other leadership styles. In defining transactional leadership, Burns (1978) contrasted it with **transformational leadership**: transactional leaders appeal to followers' self-interest, whereas transformational leaders inspire followers to adopt a vision that involves more than individual self-interest (Judge & Bono, 2000).

There are three key components of transformational leadership:

1 *individualised consideration* (attention to followers' needs, abilities and aspirations, in order to help raise aspirations, improve abilities and satisfy needs);

2 *intellectual stimulation* (challenging followers' basic thinking, assumptions and practices to help them develop newer and better mindsets and practices); and

3 *charismatic/inspiring leadership,* which provides the energy, reasoning and sense of urgency that transforms followers (Avolio & Bass, 1987; Bass, 1985).

Transformational leadership theorists were mortified that the charisma/inspiration component inadvertently admitted notorious dictators such as Hitler, Stalin and Pol Pot into the hallowed club of transformational leaders – all were effective leaders in so far as they mobilised groups around their goals. So, a distinction was drawn between good charismatic leaders with socialised charisma that they use in a 'morally uplifting' manner to improve society, and bad charismatic leaders who use personalised charisma to tear down groups and society – the former are transformational, the latter are not (e.g. O'Connor et al., 1995; also see the earlier section of this chapter on defining leadership).

**Laissez-faire leaders**

Leaders who use a style based on disinterest in followers.

The distinction between transactional and transformational leadership has been joined by a third type of leadership – laissez-faire (non-interfering) leadership, which involves not making choices or taking decisions, and not rewarding others or shaping their behaviour. Avolio (1999) uses **laissez-faire leadership** as a baseline anchor-point in what he calls his 'full-range leadership model', which has transformational leadership sitting at the apex (Antonakis & House, 2003).

**Multifactor leadership questionnaire**

The most popular and widely used scale for measuring transactional and transformational leadership.

First published by Bass and Avolio in 1990, the **multifactor leadership questionnaire** (MLQ) was designed to measure transactional and transformational leadership. It is now in its fifth version, and has been used in every conceivable organisation, at every conceivable level, and on almost every continent. It has become the de facto leadership questionnaire of choice of the organisational and management research communities – producing numerous large-scale meta-analyses of findings (e.g. Lowe, Kroeck & Sivasubramaniam, 1996; also see Avolio & Yammarino, 2003).

A contemporary challenge for transformational leadership theory is to fill in the 'black box' of transformation – to specify exactly what happens psychologically in the head of

**Transformational leadership**
A nation yearns for a leader who inspires,
who exudes energy and a sense of urgency

individual followers, which transforms their thoughts and behaviour to conform to the
leader's vision. Shamir, House and Arthur (1993) suggest that followers personally identify
with the leader and in this way make the leader's vision their own. Dvir, Eden, Avolio and
Shamir (2002) suggest that the behaviour of transformational leaders causes followers to
identify more strongly with the organisation's core values.

Both these ideas resonate with the social identity theory of leadership (e.g. Hogg & Van
Knippenberg, 2002; see below). Where group members identify strongly with a group, leaders who are considered central/prototypical group members are able to be innovative in
defining a group's goals and practices. Strong identification is associated with internalisation
of group norms as one's own beliefs and actions. In this way, leaders can transform groups.

## Charisma and charismatic leadership

The notion of charisma is so central to transformational leadership theory that, as we saw
above, a distinction was drawn between good and bad charisma in order to distinguish
between non-transformational villains (e.g. Hitler) and transformational heroes (e.g.
Gandhi). This distinction is, of course, problematic – one person's transformational leader
can be another's war criminal or vice versa (much as one person's freedom fighter is
another's terrorist). For example, whether Osama bin Laden is considered a transformational leader or not may rest more on one's political persuasion and ideological leanings
than on transformational leadership theory's notion of good versus bad charisma (see the
earlier discussion of effective/ineffective versus good/bad dimensions of leadership).

There is a more general issue concerning the role of charisma in transformational leadership. Scholars talk of **charismatic leadership** as a product of (a) the leader's personal
charisma and (b) followers' reactions to the leader's charisma in a particular situation –
personal charisma alone may not guarantee charismatic leadership (e.g. Bryman, 1992).
However, it is difficult to escape the inference that personal charisma is an enduring personality trait – in which case some of the problems of past personality theories of
leadership have been reintroduced (Haslam & Platow, 2001; Mowday & Sutton, 1993).
Indeed, charismatic/transformational leadership has explicitly been linked to the Big Five
personality dimensions of extraversion/surgency, agreeableness and intellect/openness to
experience (e.g. Judge, Bono, Ilies & Gerhardt, 2002). Charismatic leadership is also linked
to the related construct of visionary leadership (e.g. Conger & Kanungo, 1998) and the

**Charismatic leadership**
Leadership style based
upon the leader's
(perceived) possession of
charisma.

view that people differ in terms of how visionary they are as leaders. Visionary leaders are special people who can identify attractive future goals and objectives for a group and mobilise followers to internalise these as their own.

There is no doubt that charisma facilitates effective leadership, probably because charismatic people are emotionally expressive, enthusiastic, driven, eloquent, visionary, self-confident and responsive to others (e.g. House, Spangler, & Woycke, 1991; Riggio & Carney, 2003). These attributes allow a person to be influential and persuasive, and therefore able to make others buy their vision for the group and sacrifice personal goals for collective goals. Meindl and Lerner (1983; Meindl, Ehrlich & Dukerich, 1985) talk about visionary leaders heightening followers' sense of shared identity, and how this shared identity produces a collective 'heroic motive' that puts group goals ahead of personal goals.

An alternative perspective on the role of charisma in leadership is that a charismatic personality is constructed for the leader by followers; charisma is a consequence or correlate, not a cause, of effective leadership. For example, Meindl (1995; Meindl, Ehrlich, & Dukerich, 1985) talks of the *romance of leadership*; people have a strong tendency to attribute effective leadership to the leader's behavior and to overlook the leader's shortcomings (e.g. Fiske & Dépret, 1996). The social identity theory of leadership (e.g., Hogg, 2001b; Hogg & Van Knippenberg, 2003; see below) provides a similar analysis, but with an emphasis on the role of shared identity in charismatic leadership. Social identity processes in groups that members identify strongly with make group prototypical (central) leaders influential, attractive and trustworthy, and allow them to be innovative. Followers attribute these qualities internally to the leader's personality, thus constructing a charismatic leadership personality (Haslam & Platow, 2001; Platow & Van Knippenberg, 2001).

## Leader perceptions and leadership schemas

### Leader categorisation theory

**Leader categorisation theory**
We have a variety of schemas about how different types of leader behave in different leadership situations. When a leader is categorised as a particular type of leader, the schema fills in details about how that leader will behave.

Social cognition (see Chapter 2) has framed an approach to leadership that focuses on the schemas we have of leaders and on the causes and consequences of categorising someone as a leader. Called **leader categorisation theory** (LCT) or implicit leadership theory (e.g. Lord, Brown, Harvey & Hall, 2001; Lord & Brown, 2004; Lord & Hall, 2003), it is assumed that our perceptions of leadership play a key role in decisions we make about selecting and endorsing leaders. This influences leaders' power bases, and thus their ability to influence others and to lead effectively.

People have implicit theories of leadership that shape their perceptions of leaders. In assessing a specific leader, leadership schemas (called 'prototypes' by Lord and his colleagues) based on these implicit theories of leadership are activated, and characteristics of the specific leader are matched against the relevant schema of effective leadership. These schemas of leadership can describe general context-independent properties of effective leaders, or very specific properties of leadership in a very specific situation.

LCT predicts that the better the match is between the leader's characteristics and the perceiver's leadership schema, the more favourable are leadership perceptions. For example, if your leadership schema favours 'intelligent', 'organised' and 'dedicated' as core leadership attributes, you are more likely to endorse a leader the more you perceive that leader actually to be intelligent, organised and dedicated.

LCT focuses on categories and associated schemas of leadership and leaders (e.g. military generals, prime ministers, CEOs), not on schemas of social groups as categories (e.g. a psychology department, a corporation, a sports team). LCT's leader categories are tied to specific tasks and functions that span a variety of different groups: for example, a CEO schema applies similarly to companies such as Apple, Dell, Virgin, Toyota, Starbucks and Google, whereas each company may have very different group norms and prototypes. LCT largely leaves unanswered the question of how schemas of group membership influence leadership, a question which is addressed by the social identity theory of leadership (e.g. Hogg & Van Knippenberg, 2003, described below).

## Expectation states and status characteristics

Another theory that focuses on leader categorisation processes, but is more sociological and does not go into social cognitive details as extensively as leader categorisation theory, is expectation states theory or **status characteristics theory** (e.g. Berger, Fisek, Norman & Zelditch, 1977; Berger, Wagner & Zelditch, 1985; Ridgeway, 2003). Influence (and thus leadership) within groups is attributed to possession of *specific status characteristics* (characteristics that match what the group actually does) and *diffuse status characteristics* (stereotypical characteristics of high-status groups in society). To be effective, leaders need to have characteristics that equip them for effective task performance (i.e. specific status characteristics) and characteristics that categorise them as members of high-status sociodemographic categories (i.e. diffuse status characteristics). Effective leadership is an additive function of perceived group task competence and perceived societal status.

**Status characteristics theory**
Theory of influence in groups that attributes greater influence to those who possess both task-relevant characteristics (specific status characteristics) and characteristics of high-status groups in society (diffuse status characteristics). Also called *expectation states theory*.

## Social identity and leadership

Leadership is a relationship in which some members of a group (usually one member) are able to influence the rest of the group to embrace, as their own, new values, attitudes and goals, and to exert effort on behalf of and in pursuit of those values, attitudes and goals. Effective leadership inspires others to adopt group membership defining values, attitudes and goals, and to behave in ways that serve the group as a collective. Effective leaders are able to transform individual action into group action. Thus, leadership has an important identity function. People look to their leaders to express and epitomise their identity, to clarify and focus their identity, to forge and transform their identity, and to consolidate, stabilise and anchor their identity.

This identity perspective on leadership has been placed centre-stage by the **social identity theory of leadership** (Hogg, 2001b; Hogg & Van Knippenberg, 2003). As people identify more strongly with a group, they pay closer attention to the group prototype and to what and who is more prototypical of the group – this is because the prototype defines the group and one's identity as a group member. Under these circumstances, being prototypical makes one more influential and thus more effective as a leader. Although leadership schemas generally do govern leader effectiveness, when a social group becomes a salient and important basis for self-conception and identity, group prototypicality becomes important, perhaps more important than leader schemas.

**Social identity theory of leadership**
Development of social identity theory to explain leadership as an identity process in which in salient groups prototypical leaders are more effective than less prototypical leaders.

This idea was supported in a laboratory experiment by Hains, Hogg and Duck (1997). Participants were explicitly categorised or merely aggregated as a group (the manipulation of group salience). Before participating in an interactive task, they rated the leadership effectiveness of a randomly appointed leader, who was described as being a prototypical or non-prototypical group member and as possessing or not possessing leader schema-consistent characteristics. As predicted, schema-consistent leaders were generally considered more effective than schema-inconsistent leaders; however, when group membership was salient, group prototypicality became an important influence on perceived leadership effectiveness (see Figure 9.4).

These findings were replicated in a longitudinal field study of Outward Bound groups (Fielding & Hogg, 1997), and in further experiments (Hogg, Hains & Mason, 1998), and correlational studies (Platow & Van Knippenberg, 2001). Other studies show that in salient groups, ingroup leaders (i.e. more prototypical leaders) are more effective than outgroup leaders (i.e. less prototypical leaders) (Duck & Fielding, 1999; Van Vugt & De Cremer, 1999).

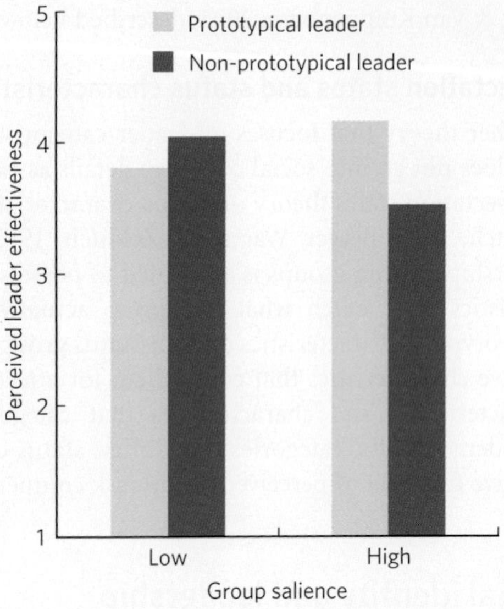

**Figure 9.4** Leader effectiveness as a function of group prototypicality of the leader and salience of the group

- When group salience was high, features of the leader that were prototypical for the group became important in determining how effective the leader was perceived as being.
- When group salience was low, being prototypical did not have this impact.

*Source*: based on data from Hains, Hogg & Duck (1997)

A number of social identity-related processes (see Hogg, 2006, for overview) make prototypical leaders more influential in salient groups:

- Because prototypical members best embody the group's attributes, they are viewed as the source rather than target of conformity processes – they are the ones with whom other members seem to align their behaviour (cf. Turner, 1991).

- Prototypical members are liked as group members (a process of depersonalised social attraction), and, because group members usually agree on the prototype, the group as a whole likes the leader – he or she is popular (Hogg, 1993). This process facilitates influence (we are more likely to comply with requests from people we like – Berscheid & Reis, 1998), and accentuates perceived evaluative (status) differential between leader and followers.

- Prototypical leaders find the group more central and important to self-definition, and therefore identify more strongly with it. They have significant investment in the group and thus are more likely to behave in group-serving ways. They closely embody group norms and are more likely to favour the ingroup over outgroups, to treat ingroup members fairly, and to act in ways that promote the ingroup. These behaviours confirm their prototypicality and membership credentials, and encourage group members to trust them to be acting in the best interest of the group even when it may not appear that they are – they are furnished with legitimacy (Tyler, 1997; Tyler & Lind, 1992; see Platow, Reid & Andrew, 1998). One consequence of this is that prototypical leaders can be innovative and transformational – they can, paradoxically, diverge from group norms and be less conformist than less prototypical leaders (cf. discussion above of Hollander's, 1958, notion of idiosyncrasy credit).

- Because the prototype is central to group life, information related to the prototype attracts attention. A prototypical leader is the most direct source of prototype information, and so stands out against the background of the group. Members pay close attention to the leader and, as in other areas of social perception and inference, attribute his or her behaviour to invariant or essential properties of the leader's personality – they engage in the correspondence bias (Gilbert & Malone, 1995; see Chapter 3). This process can construct a charismatic personality for the leader (the behaviours being attributed include being the source of influence, being able to gain compliance from others, being popular, having higher status, being innovative, and being trusted) which further strengthens his or her position of leadership (Haslam & Platow, 2001).

Prototypical leaders have considerable ability to maintain their leadership position by acting as prototype managers. Through communication and talk they can construct, reconstruct or change the group prototype in ways that protect or promote their central position in the group – a process of 'norm talk' (Hogg & Tindale, 2005; also see Fiol, 2002; Gardner, Paulsen, Gallois, Callan, & Monaghan, 2001; Reid & Ng, 2000). Indeed, one of the key attributes of an effective leader is precisely this visionary and transformational activity. Effective leaders can change what the group sees itself as being – they are 'entrepreneurs of identity' (Reicher & Hopkins, 2003). Generally, leaders who feel they are not, or are no longer, prototypical strategically engage in a range of group-oriented behaviours to strengthen their membership credentials (e.g. Platow & Van Knippenberg, 2001). Research has identified many ways in which leaders can engage in norm talk and act as entrepreneurs of identity (Reicher & Hopkins, 1996a, 1996b, 2001, 2003) – see Box 9.1.

The social identity theory of leadership has empirical support from laboratory experiments and more naturalistic studies and surveys, and has re-energised leadership research in social and organisational psychology that focuses on the role of group membership and social identity (Ellemers, De Gilder & Haslam, 2004; Van Knippenberg & Hogg, 2003; Van Knippenberg, Van Knippenberg, De Cremer & Hogg, 2004; also see Hogg, 2007a). It also, along with leader categorisation theory (Lord & Brown, 2004; see above), connects with a trend in leadership research to focus upon the role of followers in leadership – for leaders to lead followers must follow. One aspect of this trend focuses on what is rather awkwardly dubbed 'followership' and research also explores how followers can be empowered to create great and effective leaders (e.g., Kelley, 1992; Riggio, Chaleff, & Lipman-Blumen, 2008; Shamir, Pillai, Bligh, & Uhl-Bien, 2006).

## Trust and leadership

Trust plays an important role in leadership (e.g. Dirks & Ferrin, 2002) – we all get very concerned about corporate corruption and untrustworthy business and government

### Real world 9.1
#### Norm talk and identity entrepreneurship

**Five ways in which you as a leader can protect and enhance how group prototypically you are perceived by your followers**

1  Talk up your prototypicality and/or talk down aspects of your own behaviour that are non-prototypical.

2  Identify deviants or marginal members to highlight your own prototypicality or to construct a particular prototype for the group that enhances your prototypicality.

3  Secure your own leadership position by vilifying contenders for leadership and casting them as non-prototypical.

4  Identify as relevant comparison outgroups groups that cast the most favourable light on your own prototypicality.

5  Engage in a discourse that raises or lowers salience. If you are highly prototypical then raising salience will provide you with the leadership benefits of high prototypicality; if you are not very prototypical then lowering salience will protect you from the leadership pitfalls of not being very prototypical.

**Group value model**
View that procedural justice within groups makes members feel valued, and thus leads to enhanced commitment to and identification with the group.

**Relational model of authority in groups**
Tyler's account of how effective authority in groups rests upon fairness- and justice-based relations between leader and followers.

**Distributive justice**
The fairness of the outcome of a decision.

**Procedural justice**
The fairness of the procedures used to make a decision.

leaders (e.g. Kellerman, 2004). If we are to follow our leaders, we need to be able to trust them to be acting in the best interest of us all as a group, rather than in their own self-interest. Leaders also need their followers, as we have seen above, to trust them in order to be able to be innovative and transformational.

## Justice and fairness

An important basis for trusting one's leaders is the perception that they have acted in a fair and just manner. According to Tyler's **group value model** (Lind & Tyler, 1988) and his **relational model of authority in groups** (Tyler, 1997; Tyler & Lind, 1992), perceptions of fairness and justice are critical to group life. Because leaders make decisions with important consequences for followers (e.g. promotions, performance appraisals, allocation of duties), followers are concerned about how fair the leader is in making these decisions. In judging fairness, followers evaluate a leader in terms of both **distributive justice** and **procedural justice**. Justice and fairness judgements influence reactions to decisions and to the authorities making these decisions, and thus influence leadership effectiveness (De Cremer, 2003; De Cremer & Tyler, 2005).

Procedural justice is particularly important in leadership contexts, probably because fair procedures convey respect for group members and thus build member identification that sponsors cooperative and compliant behaviour (Tyler, 2003). Research shows that, as members identify more strongly with the group, they care more strongly that the leader is procedurally fair (e.g. Brockner et al., 2000), and care less strongly that the leader is distributively fair. This asymmetry arises because with increasing identification, instrumental outcome-oriented considerations (distributive justice) become less important relative to intragroup relational and membership considerations (procedural justice) (e.g. Vermunt, Van Knippenberg, Van Knippenberg & Blaauw, 2001).

## Social dilemmas

**Social dilemmas**
Situations in which short-term personal gain is at odds with the long-term good of the group.

The fact that justice, particularly procedural justice, facilitates effective leadership because it builds trust and strengthens group identification, raises the possibility that leadership may be a way to resolve social dilemmas. **Social dilemmas** are essentially a crisis of trust – people behave selfishly because they do not trust others to sacrifice their immediate self-interest for the longer-term greater good of the collective (e.g. Dawes & Messick, 2000; Liebrand, Messick & Wilke, 1992; see Chapter 11).

Social dilemmas are notoriously difficult to resolve (Kerr & Park, 2001). However, they are not impossible to resolve if one can address the trust issue. One way to do this is to build mutual trust among people by causing them to identify strongly as a group – people tend to trust ingroup members (e.g. Brewer, 1981; Yamagishi & Kiyonari, 2000) and therefore are more likely to sacrifice self-interest for the greater good (e.g. Brewer & Schneider, 1990; De Cremer & Van Vugt, 1999). Leadership plays a critical role in this process because a leader can transform selfish individual goals into shared group goals by building a sense of common identity, shared fate, interindividual trust and custodianship of the collective good (e.g. De Cremer & Van Knippenberg, 2003; Van Vugt & De Cremer, 1999).

## Gender gaps and glass ceilings

**Glass ceiling**
An invisible barrier that prevents women, and minorities, from attaining top leadership positions.

Throughout the world, leadership roles are dominated by men. If one restricts oneself to liberal democracies like those in western Europe, where more progressive gender attitudes have developed over the past forty years, it is still the case that although women are now relatively well represented in middle management, they are still underrepresented in senior management and 'elite' leadership positions – there is a **glass ceiling** (Eagly & Karau, 1991; Eagly, Karau & Makhijani, 1995; Eagly, Makhijani & Klonsky, 1992).

Is this because men really are better suited than women to leadership? Research suggests not. Although women and men tend to adopt different leadership styles, which implies that different leadership contexts may suit different genders, women are usually rated as just as effective leaders as men – and in general they are perceived to be marginally more transformational and participative, and more praising of followers for good performance (Eagly, Johannesen-Schmidt, Van Engen & Vinkenburg, 2002).

If women and men are equally capable of being effective leaders, why is there a gender gap in leadership? One explanation is in terms of **role congruity theory** (Eagly, 2003; Eagly & Karau, 2002; Heilman, 1983), which argues that because there is greater overlap between general leader schemas and agentic male stereotypes than between leader schemas and communal female stereotypes, people tend to have more favourable perceptions of male leaders than of female leaders. These leadership perceptions facilitate or impede effective leadership. Research provides some support for role congruity theory (Martell, Parker, Emrich & Crawford, 1998; Shore, 1992). One implication of role incongruity theory is that the evaluation of male and female leaders will change if the leadership schema changes or if people's gender stereotypes change. For example, research has shown that men leaders are evaluated more favourably than women leaders when the role is defined in more masculine terms, and vice versa when the role is defined in less masculine terms (Eagly, Karau & Makhijani, 1995).

Another related explanation is in terms of the social identity theory of leadership (discussed above). In high-salience groups that members identify with, male or female leaders are perceived to be and actually are effective if the group's norms are consistent with the members' gender stereotypes. So, people with traditional gender stereotypes will endorse a male not a female leader of a group with instrumental norms (e.g. a trucking company) and a female not a male leader of a group with more expressive norms (e.g. a childcare group), whereas among people with less traditional gender stereotypes this effect may not be so pronounced and may be reversed (Hogg, Fielding, Johnson, Masser, Russell, & Svensson, 2006).

Another reason for the gender gap in leadership is that women claim authority less effectively than men – men claim and hold many more leadership positions than women (Bowles & McGinn, 2005). Once they claim authority, there is no gender difference in leadership effectiveness. Bowles and McGinn propose four main barriers to women claiming authority. The first is role incongruity, as discussed above. The second is lack of critical management experience. The third is family responsibility, which compromises a woman's ability to find the time commitment required of leadership positions.

The fourth obstacle is lack of motivation – women are not as 'hungry' for leadership as are men. They shy away from self-promotion and take on less visible background roles with informal titles like 'facilitator' or 'coordinator'. Although the link has not been made explicit, the underlying reason for women's alleged reticence to claim authority may be stereotype-threat (Steele & Aronson, 1995; Steele, Spencer & Aronson, 2002; see Chapter 10). Women fear that negative stereotypes about women and leadership will be confirmed, and so they feel less motivated to lead. In addition, self-promotion and leadership-claiming go against a stereotype for women – behaving in these ways could be seen as 'pushy' and can attract negative reactions from both male and female group members (Rudman, 1998; Rudman & Glick, 1999).

## Intergroup leadership

An under-explored aspect of leadership is its intergroup context – leaders not only lead the members of their group, but in different ways they lead their group *against* other groups. The political and military leaders who are often invoked in discussions of leadership are leaders in a truly intergroup context – they lead their political parties, their nations or their armies *against* other political parties, nations or armies.

**Role congruity theory**
Mainly applied to the gender gap in leadership – because social stereotypes of women are inconsistent with people's schemas of effective leadership, women are evaluated as poor leaders.

Leadership rhetoric is often about *us* versus *them,* about defining the ingroup in contrast to specific outgroups or deviant ingroup factions (Reicher & Hopkins, 1996a, 1996b, 2003). The nature of intergroup relations can also influence leadership by changing group goals or altering intragroup relations. Earlier, we described how a leadership change in one of Sherif's groups of boys at a summer camp was produced by intergroup competition (Sherif, Harvey, White, Hood, & Sherif, 1961). In another study, Rabbie and Bekkers (1978) simulated union–management bargaining so that relatively insecure leaders (who were likely to be deposed by their group) actively sought to bargain by competing in order to secure their leadership. Perhaps this captures the familiar tactic where political leaders pursue an aggressive foreign policy (where they believe they can win) in order to combat unpopularity experienced at home: for example, the 1982 Falklands War between Argentina and Britain, which arose in the context of political unpopularity at home for both governments, certainly boosted Margaret Thatcher's leadership; and the two Gulf Wars of 1991 and 2003 may initially have consolidated leadership for US Presidents Bush senior and Bush junior respectively.

But there is another side to intergroup leadership – the building of a unified group identity, vision and purpose across deep subgroup divisions within the group. Although social identity theory is a theory of intergroup relations (e.g. Tajfel & Turner, 1979), the social identity theory of leadership actually has an intragroup focus – for example, on within-group prototypicality, shared group membership and ingroup trust. The great challenge of effective leadership, however, often is not merely to transcend *differences among individuals,* but to bridge profound *divisions between groups* to build an integrative vision and identity. For example: effective leadership of Iraq must bridge historic differences between Sunnis, Shi'ites and Kurds; effective leadership of the US must bridge a profound gulf between Democrats and Republicans; effective leadership of the EU must bridge vast differences among its 27 member states. Leadership is often better characterised as intergroup leadership (Hogg, 2009; Pittinsky, 2009; Pittinsky & Simon, 2007). (Reflect on focus question 2. Should Steve or Martin take the role of new boss?)

Effective intergroup leadership faces the daunting task of building social harmony and a common purpose and identity out of conflict among groups. One problem is that intergroup leaders are often viewed as representing one group more than the other; they are outgroup leaders to one subgroup and, thus, suffer compromised effectiveness (Duck & Fielding, 1999, 2003). This problem has been well researched in the context of organisational mergers and acquisitions. Acquisitions often fail precisely because the leader of the acquiring organisation is viewed with suspicion as a member of the former outgroup organisation (e.g., Terry, Carey, & Callan, 2001). These problems can be accentuated by ingroup projection – a phenomenon where groups nested within a larger superordinate group overestimate how well their own characteristics are represented in the superordinate group (Wenzel, Mummendey & Waldzus, 2007). In this case, a leader of the superordinate group who belongs to one subgroup will be viewed by the other subgroup as very un-prototypical of the superordinate group.

One interesting wrinkle to this is that lower/minority status subgroups often do not engage in ingroup projection; both subgroups agree that the dominant subgroup's attributes are best represented in the superordinate group (Sindic & Reicher, 2008). In this situation the minority subgroup *will* view a superordinate leader who comes from the majority subgroup as prototypical; but such a leader will not gain a prototypicality-based advantage because the minority group feels underrepresented and, thus, is unlikely to identify sufficiently strongly with the superordinate group (Hohman, Hogg, & Bligh, 2010).

Effective intergroup leaders need to build a common ingroup identity (Gaertner & Dovidio, 2000; Gaertner, Dovidio, Anastasio, Bachman, & Rust, 1993; see Chapter 11). But this can threaten the subgroup identity of subgroups, so another strategy is to balance the superordinate identity and associated vision with recognition of the integrity and valued contribution of subgroup identities (e.g., Hornsey & Hogg, 2000a).

# Group decision making

Groups perform many tasks, of which making decisions is one of the most important. The course of our lives is largely determined by decisions made by groups: for example, selection committees, juries, parliaments, committees of examiners and groups of friends. In addition, many of us spend a significant portion of our working lives making decisions in groups. Social psychologists have long been interested in the social processes involved in group decision making, and in whether groups make better or different decisions than do individuals. Another dimension of group decision making comes into play when members of the decision-making group are formally acting as *representatives* of different groups. This is more properly called intergroup decision making and is dealt with in Chapter 11.

A variety of models have been developed to relate the distribution of initial opinions in a decision-making group to the group's final decision (Stasser, Kerr & Davis, 1989; Stasser & Dietz-Uhler, 2001). Some of these are complex computer-simulation models (Hastie, Penrod & Pennington, 1983; Penrod & Hastie, 1980; Stasser & Davis, 1981), while others, although expressed in a formalised mathematical style, are more immediately related to real groups.

Davis's **social decisions schemes** model identifies a small number of explicit or implicit decision making rules that groups can adopt (Davis, 1973; Stasser, Kerr & Davis, 1989). Knowledge of the initial distribution of individual opinions in the group, and what rule the group is operating under, allows prediction, with a high degree of certainty, of the final group decision. These rules include the following:

**Social decisions schemes**
Explicit or implicit decision-making rules that relate individual opinions to a final group decision.

- *Unanimity* – discussion serves to pressurise deviants to conform.
- *Majority wins* – discussion simply confirms the majority position, which is then adopted as the group position.

**Social decisions schemes**
In a high-level international political forum, like this one, would a decision be reached by a 'truth wins' rule?

- *Truth wins* – discussion reveals the position that is demonstrably correct.
- *Two-thirds majority* – unless there is a two-thirds majority, the group is unable to reach a decision.
- *First shift* – the group ultimately adopts a decision consistent with the direction of the first shift in opinion shown by any member of the group.

For intellective tasks (those where there is a demonstrably correct solution, such as a mathematical puzzle), groups tend to adopt the truth-wins rule, and for judgemental tasks (no demonstrably correct solution, such as aesthetic preference) the majority-wins rule (Laughlin, 1980; Laughlin & Ellis, 1986). Rules differ in:

- *strictness* – that is, the degree of agreement required by the rule (unanimity is extremely strict and majority less strict);
- the *distribution of power* among members – that is, authoritarian rules concentrate power in one member, while egalitarian rules spread power among all members (Hastie, Penrod & Pennington, 1983).

In general, the stricter the rule, the less the power concentration – unanimity is very strict but very low in power concentration, while two-thirds majority is less strict but has greater power concentration. The type of rule adopted can have an effect, largely as a function of its strictness, not only on the group's decision itself but also on members' preferences, their satisfaction with the group decision, the perception and nature of group discussion, and members' feelings for one another (Miller, 1989). For example, stricter decision rules can make final agreement in the group slower, more exhaustive and difficult to attain, but it can enhance liking for fellow members and satisfaction with the quality of the decision.

**Social transition scheme**

Method for charting incremental changes in member opinions as a group moves towards a final decision.

Kerr's **social transition scheme** model focuses attention on the actual pattern of member positions moved through by a group operating under a particular decision, en route to its final decision (Kerr, 1981; Stasser, Kerr & Davis, 1989). In order to do this, members' opinions are monitored during the process of discussion (Kerr & MacCoun, 1985), either by periodically asking the participants or by having them note any and every change in their opinion. These procedures can be intrusive, so an issue is how much they affect the natural ongoing process of discussion.

## Brainstorming

An important part of the group decision-making process can be the generation of novel ideas. Indeed, some groups come together almost exclusively for this purpose, the goal being to be as creative as possible in generating ideas. The technique of **brainstorming**, initially popularised by Osborn (1957), is now commonly used for this purpose. Group members are asked to generate as many ideas as possible as quickly as possible. They are told not to be inhibited or concerned about quality (simply to say whatever comes to mind), to be non-critical, and to build on others' ideas when possible. Brainstorming is a group performance technique designed to facilitate creative thinking and thus make the group more creative. Popular opinion is so convinced that brainstorming works that it is widely used in business organisations and advertising agencies.

**Brainstorming**

Uninhibited generation of as many ideas as possible in a group, in order to enhance group creativity.

However, although research reveals that groups that have been given brainstorming instructions do generate more ideas than groups that have not been so instructed, there is no evidence that individuals are more creative in brainstorming groups than on their own (Diehl & Stroebe, 1987; Mullen, Johnson & Salas, 1991; Stroebe & Diehl, 1994). On the contrary, *nominal* groups (i.e. brainstorming groups in which individuals create ideas on their own and do not interact) are twice as creative as true interactive groups.

The inferior performance of brainstorming groups can be attributed to at least four factors (Paulus, Dzindolet, Poletes & Camacho, 1993):

1 *Evaluation apprehension* – despite explicit instructions to encourage the uninhibited generation of as many ideas as possible, members may still be concerned about making a good impression. This introduces self-censorship and a consequent reduction in productivity.

2 *Social loafing and free riding* – there is motivation loss because of the collective nature of the task (see Chapter 8).

3 *Production matching* – because brainstorming is novel, members use average group performance to construct a performance norm to guide their own generation of ideas. This produces regression to the mean.

4 **Production blocking** – individual creativity and productivity are reduced owing to interference effects from contending with others who are generating ideas at the same time as one is trying to generate one's own ideas.

**Production blocking**
Reduction in individual creativity and productivity in brainstorming groups due to interruptions and turn taking.

Stroebe and Diehl (1994) review evidence for these processes and conclude that production blocking is probably the main obstacle to unlocking the creative potential of brainstorming groups. They discuss a number of remedies, two of which have promise:

1 *Electronic brainstorming* reduces the extent to which the production of new ideas is blocked by such things as listening to others or waiting for a turn to speak (Hollingshead & McGrath, 1995): groups that brainstorm electronically via computer can produce more ideas than non-electronic groups (Gallupe, Cooper, Grise & Bastianutti, 1994) and more ideas than nominal electronic groups (Dennis & Valacich, 1993).

2 *Heterogeneous groups* in which members have diverse types of knowledge about the brainstorming topic may create a particularly stimulating environment that alleviates the effects of production blocking; Stroebe and Diehl (1994) suggest that if production blocking is also reduced by other means, heterogeneous brainstorming groups might outperform heterogeneous nominal groups.

Given convincing evidence that face-to-face brainstorming does not actually improve individual creativity, why do people so firmly believe that it does and continue to use it as a technique for generating new ideas in groups? Diehl and Stroebe suggest that this paradox stems from the existence of an **illusion of group effectivity** (Diehl & Stroebe, 1991; Stroebe, Diehl & Abakoumkin, 1992; see also Paulus, Dzindolet, Poletes & Camacho, 1993). We all take part in group discussions from time to time, and thus we all have some degree of personal experience with generating ideas in groups. The illusion of group effectivity is an experience-based belief that we actually produce more and better ideas in groups than when alone.

**Illusion of group effectivity**
Experience-based belief that we produce more and better ideas in groups than alone.

This illusion may be generated by at least three processes:

1 Although groups have fewer non-redundant original ideas than the sum of individuals working alone, they produce more ideas than any single member would produce alone. People in groups are exposed to more ideas than when alone. They find it difficult to remember whether the ideas produced were their own or those of other people and so tend to exaggerate their own contribution. They feel that they have been individually more productive and were facilitated by the group when in fact they were less productive. Stroebe, Diehl and Abakoumkin (1992) had participants brainstorm in four-person nominal or real groups and asked them to estimate the percentage of ideas they had suggested, the percentage that others had suggested but they had also thought of, and the percentage that others had suggested but they had not thought of. The results (see Figure 9.5) show that participants in real groups overestimate the percentage of ideas that they thought they had but did not suggest, relative to participants in nominal groups.

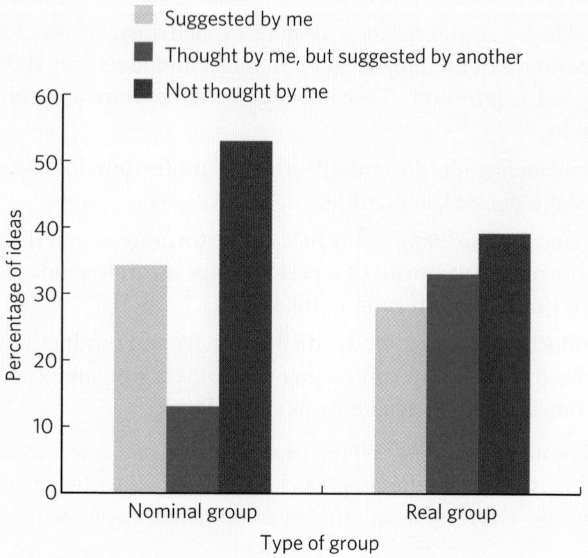

**Figure 9.5** Percentage of ideas assigned to self and to others in nominal and real brainstorming groups

Relative to participants in nominal brainstorming groups, participants in real brainstorming groups underestimated the number of ideas they had not thought of and overestimated the number of ideas they had thought of but actually had been suggested by others

*Source:* based on data from Stroebe, Diehl & Abakoumkin (1992)

2 Brainstorming is generally great fun. People enjoy brainstorming in groups more than alone and so feel more satisfied with their performance.

3 People in groups know they only call out some of the ideas they have, because other ideas have already been called by other group members. Although all group members are in the same position, the subject is of course not privy to others' undisclosed ideas – and so attributes the relatively low overt productivity of others to their own relatively high latent productivity. The group is seen to have enhanced or confirmed their own high level of performance.

## Group memory

Another important dimension of group decision making is the ability to recall information. For instance, juries need to recall testimony in order to be able to arrive at a verdict, and personnel selection panels need to recall data that differentiate candidates in order to make an appointment. Group remembering can even be the principal reason for certain groups to come together: for example, groups of old friends often meet mainly to reminisce. On a larger scale, organisations need to acquire, distribute, interpret and store enormous amounts of information. The analysis of exactly how this complex task of *organisational learning* is accomplished is still in its infancy (Wilpert, 1995).

### Group remembering

Do groups remember more material than individuals? In summarising research on group remembering, Clark and Stephenson (1989, 1995) concluded that groups remember more material than individuals and more material than the best individual in the group. Groups recall more than individuals because members communicate unshared information and because the group recognises true information when it hears it (Lorge & Solomon, 1995).

However, the superiority of groups over individuals varies depending on the memory task. On simplistic and artificial tasks (e.g. nonsense words), group superiority is more marked than on complex and realistic tasks (e.g. a story). One explanation is 'process loss' (Steiner, 1976; see Chapter 8). In trying to recall complex information, groups fail to adopt appropriate recall and decision strategies, and so do not fully utilise all of the group's human resources.

However, group remembering is more than a collective regurgitation of facts. It is often a constructive process by which an agreed joint account is worked out. Some individuals' memories will contribute to the developing consensus, while others' will not. In this way, the group shapes its own version of the truth. This version then guides individual members about what to store as a true memory and what to discard as an incorrect memory. The process of reaching consensus is subject to the range of social influence processes discussed in Chapter 7, and to the group decision-making biases discussed in this chapter. Most research into group remembering focuses on how much is remembered by individuals and by groups. Recently, however, other approaches have emerged: Clark and Stephenson and their associates have looked at the content and structure of what is remembered (see Box 9.2 and Figure 9.6), and Middleton and Edwards (1990) have adopted a discourse analysis approach (discussed in Chapter 15).

## Transactive memory

A different perspective on group remembering has been proposed by Wegner (1987, 1995; Wegner, Erber & Raymond, 1991; also see Moreland, Argote & Krishnan, 1996). Individuals in couples and groups have a **transactive memory**, which is greater than their individual memories. This idea refers to the way in which couples and groups can share memory load so that each individual is responsible for remembering only part of what the group needs to know, but all members know who is responsible for each memory domain. Transactive memory is a shared system for encoding, storing and retrieving information. It allows a group to remember significantly more information than if no transactive memory system was present (Hollingshead, 1998).

For example, the psychology departments in our universities need to remember an enormous amount of practical information to do with research, postgraduate supervision, undergraduate teaching, equipment and administrative matters. There is far too much for a single individual to remember. Instead, certain individuals are formally responsible for particular domains (e.g. research), but all of us have a transactive memory that allows us to remember who is responsible for each domain. Transactive memory is also very common in close relationships such as marriage: for example, both partners know that one of them remembers financial matters and the other remembers directions.

Transactive memory is a group-level representation: although it is represented in the mind of the individual, it can emerge only through psychological involvement in a group and otherwise has no value or use. For example, who else beyond her team-mates cares if it is Mary's turn to bring orange juice to the sports team's practice this month? There can be no such thing as individual transactive memory. In this respect, the concept of transactive memory is related to McDougall's (1920) notion of a **group mind** (Chapters 1 and 11) – a state of mind and mode of cognition found in groups that is qualitatively different from that found in individuals.

Wegner, Erber and Raymond (1991) describe the development of transactive memory. When groups or couples first form, the basis of transactive memory is usually social categorisation. People stereotypically assign memory domains to individuals on the basis of their category memberships. For example, members of heterosexual couples might initially develop a transactive memory in which there is sex-role stereotypical allocation of memory (the woman remembers things to do with cooking and believes that information to do with the car can be obtained from the man, and vice versa). Category-based transactive memory

**Transactive memory**
Group members have a shared memory for who within the group remembers what and is the expert on what.

**Group mind**
McDougall's idea that people adopt a qualitatively different mode of thinking when in a group.

## Research and applications 9.2
### Can two heads remember better than one?

There are differences between individual and group remembering

Noel Clark and Geoffrey Stephenson and their associates have conducted a series of experiments on group remembering (e.g. Clark, Stephenson & Rutter, 1986; Stephenson, Abrams, Wagner & Wade, 1986; Stephenson, Clark & Wade, 1986). Clark and Stephenson (1989, 1995) give an integrated overview of this research. Generally, students or police officers individually or collectively (in four-person groups) recalled information from a five-minute police interrogation of a woman who had allegedly been raped. The interrogation was real, or it was staged and presented as an audio recording or a visual transcript. The participants had to recall freely the interrogation and answer specific factual questions (cued recall). The way in which they recalled the information was analysed for content to investigate:

- the amount of correct information recalled;
- the number of reconstructive errors made – that is, inclusion of material that was consistent with but did not appear in the original stimulus;
- the number of confusional errors made – that is, inclusion of material that was inconsistent with the original stimulus;
- the number of metastatements made – that is, inclusion of information that attributed motives to characters or went beyond the original stimulus in other ways.

Figure 9.6 (adapted from Clark & Stephenson, 1989) shows that groups recalled significantly more correct information and made fewer metastatements than individuals, but they did not differ in the number of reconstructions or confusional errors.

*Source*: based on Clark & Stephenson (1989)

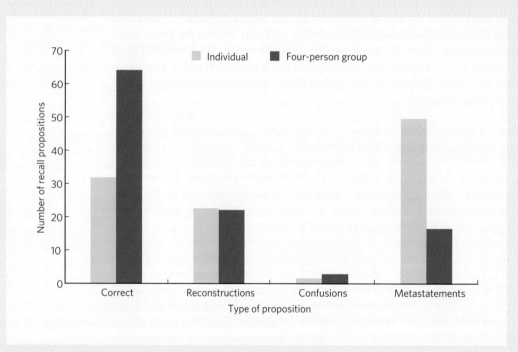

**Figure 9.6** Differences between individual and collective remembering

There are qualitative and quantitative differences between individual and collective remembering. Isolated individuals or four-person groups recalled police testimony from the interrogation of an alleged rape victim. In comparison to individuals, groups recalled more information that was correct and made fewer metastatements (statements making motivational inferences and going beyond the information in other related ways)

*Source*: based on data from Clark & Stephenson (1989)

is the default mode. In most cases, however, groups go on to develop more sophisticated memory-assignment systems.

- *Groups can negotiate responsibility for different memory domains* – for instance, couples can decide through discussion who will be responsible for bills, who for groceries, who for cars, and so forth.
- *Groups can assign memory domains on the basis of relative expertise* – for instance, a conference-organising committee might assign responsibility for the social programme to someone who has successfully discharged that duty before.
- *Groups can assign memory domains on the basis of access to information* – for instance, the conference-organising committee might assign responsibility for publicity to someone who has a good graphics package and a list of potential registrants, and who has close contacts with advertising people.

There is a potential pitfall to transactive memory – the uneven distribution of memory in a couple or a group. This means that when an individual leaves, there is a temporary loss of, or reduction in, group memory (see Box 9.3). This can be very disruptive: for example, if the person in my department who is responsible for remembering undergraduate teaching matters should suddenly leave, a dire crisis would arise. Groups often recover quickly, as there may be other people (often already with some expertise and access to information) who can immediately shoulder the responsibility. In couples, however, partners are usually irreplaceable. Once one person leaves the couple, perhaps through death or separation, a whole section of group memory vanishes. It is possible that the depression usually associated with bereavement is, at least in part, due to the loss of memory. Happy memories are lost, our sense of who we are is undermined by lack of information, and we have to take responsibility for remembering a variety of things we did not have to remember before.

---

### Research and applications 9.3
#### The group that learns together stays together

**Transactive memory: combating its loss and facilitating its development**

Transactive memory means that when an individual leaves a group there is a temporary loss of, or reduction in, group memory, which can be very disruptive for group functioning. Argote, Insko, Yovetich and Romero (1995) performed an experiment in which laboratory groups met over a number of consecutive weeks to produce complex origami objects. Member turnover did indeed disrupt group learning and performance, and its impact grew worse over time, presumably because more established groups had more established transactive memories. Attempts to reduce the problem by providing newcomers with individual origami training were unsuccessful.

The productivity implications for work groups and organisations are very serious, given that staff turnover is a fact of organisational life and that new members are almost always trained individually. Moreland, Argote and Krishnan (1996) argue that transactive memory systems develop more rapidly and operate more efficiently if group members learn together rather than individually. Thus new members of organisations or work groups should be trained together rather than apart. Moreland and associates report a series of laboratory experiments in which group training is indeed superior to individual training for the development and operation of transactive memory.

A natural example of a pitfall of transactive memory comes from the 2000 Davis Cup tennis tournament. The British doubles team comprised Tim Henman and Greg Rusedski, who had trained together as a smoothly operating team for which Britain had very high hopes. Immediately before the doubles match against the Ecuadorian team, Rusedski had to drop out and was replaced by Arvind Parmar. Henman and Parmar had not teamed up before and so had not developed a transactive memory system. They went down to a wholly unexpected straight-sets defeat by Ecuador.

### Group culture

The analysis of group memory in terms of group remembering and transactive memory can be viewed as part of a broader analysis of socially shared cognition and group culture (Tindale, Meisenhelder, Dykema-Engblade & Hogg, 2001). We tend to think of culture as something that exists at the societal level – the customs (routines, rituals, symbols and jargon) that describe large-scale social categories such as ethnic or national groups (see Chapter 16). However, there is no reason to restrict culture to such groups. Moreland, Argote and Krishnan (1996) argue that culture is an instance of group memory and therefore can exist in smaller groups such as organisations, sports teams, work groups and even families. The analysis of group culture is most developed in the study of work groups (Levine & Moreland, 1991): such groups develop detailed knowledge about norms, allies and enemies, cliques, working conditions, motivation to work, performance and performance appraisal, who fits in, and who is good at what.

## Groupthink

Groups sometimes employ deficient decision-making procedures that produce poor decisions. The consequences of such decisions can be disastrous. Janis (1972) used an archival method, relying on retrospective accounts and content analysis, to compare a number of American foreign policy decisions that had unfavourable outcomes (e.g. the 1961 Bay of Pigs fiasco, the 1941 defence of Pearl Harbor) with others that had favourable outcomes (e.g. the 1962 Cuban missile crisis). Janis coined the term **groupthink** to describe the group decision-making process that produced the poor decisions. Groupthink was defined as a mode of thinking in which the desire to reach unanimous agreement overrides the motivation to adopt proper rational decision-making procedures (Janis, 1982; Janis & Mann, 1977).

The antecedents, symptoms and consequences of groupthink are displayed in Figure 9.7. The principal cause of groupthink is excessive group cohesiveness (see Chapter 8 for discussion of cohesiveness), but there are other antecedents that relate to basic structural faults in the group and to the immediate decision-making context. Together, these factors generate a range of symptoms that are associated with defective decision-making procedures: for example, there is inadequate and biased discussion and consideration of objectives and alternative solutions, and a failure to seek the advice of experts outside the group (see the third and fourth focus questions).

**Groupthink**
A mode of thinking in highly cohesive groups in which the desire to reach unanimous agreement overrides the motivation to adopt proper rational decision-making procedures.

**Groupthink**
With one voice those present decide what action should be followed: 'Death to America!'. Was discussion encouraged? Was it adequate and unbiased?

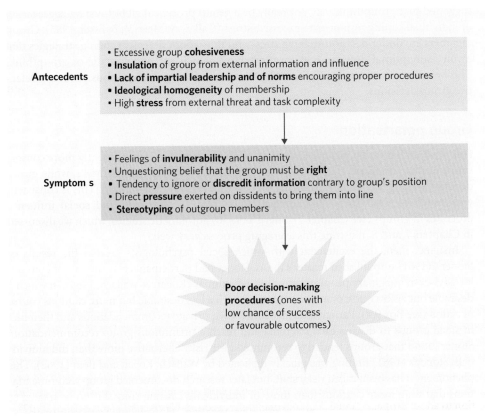

**Figure 9.7** Antecedents, symptoms and consequences of groupthink
*Source:* Janis & Mann (1977)

Descriptive studies of groupthink (e.g. Hart, 1990; Hensley & Griffin, 1986; Tetlock, 1979) largely support the general model (but see Tetlock, Peterson, McGuire, Chang, & Feld, 1992), whereas experimental studies tend to find mixed or little support for the role of cohesiveness. Experiments establish background conditions for groupthink in four-person laboratory or quasi-naturalistic groups, and then manipulate cohesiveness (usually as friends versus strangers), and either a leadership variable (directiveness or need-for-power) or procedural directions for effective decision making.

Some have found no relationship between cohesiveness and groupthink (Flowers, 1977; Fodor & Smith, 1982), some have found a positive relationship only under certain conditions (Callaway & Esser, 1984; Courtright, 1978; Turner, Pratkanis, Probasco & Leve, 1992), and some a negative relationship (Leana, 1985).

These problems have led people to suggest other ways to approach the explanation of groupthink (Aldag & Fuller, 1993; Hogg, 1993). For example, group cohesiveness may need to be more precisely defined before its relationship to groupthink can be specified (Longley & Pruitt, 1980; McCauley, 1989); at present, it ranges from close friendship to group-based liking. Hogg and Hains (1998) conducted a laboratory study of four-person discussion groups involving 472 participants to find that symptoms of groupthink were associated with cohesiveness, but only where cohesion represented group-based liking, not friendship or interpersonal attraction.

It has also been suggested that groupthink is merely a specific instance of 'risky shift', in which a group that already tends towards making a risky decision polarises through discussion to an even more risky decision (Myers & Lamm, 1975; see below). Others have suggested that groupthink may not really be a group process at all but just an aggregation of individual coping responses to excessive stress (Callaway, Marriott & Esser, 1985). Group members are under decision-making stress and thus adopt defensive coping strategies that involve suboptimal decision-making procedures, which are symptomatic of groupthink. This behaviour is mutually reinforced by members of the group and thus produces defective group decisions.

## Group polarisation

**Risky shift**
Tendency for group discussion to produce group decisions that are more risky than the mean of members' pre-discussion opinions, but only if the pre-discussion mean already favoured risk.

**Group polarisation**
Tendency for group discussion to produce more extreme group decisions than the mean of members' pre-discussion opinions, in the direction favoured by the mean.

Folk wisdom has it that groups, committees and organisations are inherently more conservative in their decisions than individuals. Individuals are likely to take risks, while group decision making is a tedious averaging process that errs towards caution. This is consistent with much of what social psychologists know about conformity and social influence processes in groups (see Chapter 7). Sherif's (1936) autokinetic studies, which we discussed in Chapters 7 and 8, illustrate this averaging process very well.

Imagine, then, the excitement with which social psychologists greeted the results of Stoner's (1961) unpublished master's thesis. Stoner had participants play the role of counsellor/adviser to imaginary people facing choice dilemmas (Kogan & Wallach, 1964), in which a desirable but risky course of action contrasted with a less desirable but more cautious course of action (see Box 9.4). Participants made their own private recommendations and then met in small groups to discuss each dilemma and reach a unanimous group recommendation. Stoner found that groups tended to recommend the risky alternative more than did individuals. Stoner's (1961) finding was quickly replicated by Wallach, Kogan and Bem (1962). This phenomenon has been called **risky shift**, but later research documented group recommendations that were more cautious than those of individuals, causing risky shift to be treated as part of a much wider phenomenon of **group polarisation** (Moscovici & Zavalloni, 1969).

Group polarisation (Isenberg, 1986; Myers & Lamm, 1976; Wetherell, 1987) is defined as a tendency for groups to make decisions that are more extreme than the mean of individual

---

### Research classic 9.4
Giving advice on risk-taking

#### An example of a choice dilemma

Suppose that the participant's task was to advise someone else on a course of action that could vary between two extremes – risky and cautious. The following is an example of such a choice dilemma (Kogan & Wallach, 1964).

> Mr L, a married 30-year-old research physicist, has been given a five-year appointment by a major university laboratory. As he contemplates the next five years, he realises that he might work on a difficult long-term problem which, if a solution can be found, would resolve basic scientific issues in the field and bring him scientific honours. If no solution were found, however, Mr L would have little to show for his five years in the laboratory and this

would make it hard for him to get a good job afterwards. On the other hand, he could, as most of his professional associates are doing, work on a series of short-term problems where solutions would be easier to find but where the problems are of lesser scientific importance.

Imagine that you (the participant) are advising Mr L. Listed below are several probabilities or odds that a solution would be found to the difficult, long-term problem that Mr L has in mind. Please put a cross beside the *lowest* probability that you would consider acceptable to make it worthwhile for Mr L to work on the more difficult, long-term problem.

The participant then responds on a ten-point scale, indicating the odds that Mr L would solve the long-term problem.

*Source*: based on Kogan & Wallach (1964)

members' initial positions, in the direction already favoured by that mean. So, for example, group discussion among a collection of people who already slightly favour capital punishment is likely to produce a group decision that strongly favours capital punishment.

Although forty years of research have produced many different theories to explain polarisation, they can perhaps be simplified to three major perspectives: persuasive arguments, social comparison/cultural values and self-categorisation theories.

## Persuasive arguments

**Persuasive arguments theory** focuses on the persuasive impact of novel arguments in changing people's opinions (Burnstein & Vinokur, 1977; Vinokur & Burnstein, 1974). People tend to rest their opinions on a body of supportive arguments that they express publicly in a group. So people in a group that leans in a particular direction will hear not only familiar arguments they have heard before, but also some novel ones not heard before, but supportive of their own position (Gigone & Hastie, 1993; Larson, Foster-Fishman & Keys, 1994). As a result, their opinions will become more entrenched and extreme, and thus the view of the group as a whole will become polarised.

For example, someone who already favours capital punishment is likely, through discussion with like-minded others, to hear new arguments in favour of capital punishment and come to favour its introduction more strongly. The process of thinking about an issue strengthens our opinions (Tesser, Martin & Mendolia, 1995), as does the public repetition of our own and others' arguments (Brauer, Judd & Gliner, 1995).

> **Persuasive arguments theory**
> View that people in groups are persuaded by novel information that supports their initial position, and thus become more extreme in their endorsement of their initial position.

## Social comparison/cultural values

According to this view, referred to as either **social comparison theory** or **cultural values theory** (Jellison & Arkin, 1977; Sanders & Baron, 1977), people seek social approval and try to avoid social censure. Group discussion reveals which views are socially desirable or culturally valued, so group members shift in the direction of the group in order to gain approval and avoid disapproval. For example, favouring capital punishment and finding yourself surrounded by others with similar views might lead you to assume that this is a socially valued attitude – even if it is not. In this example, seeking social approval could lead you to become more extreme in supporting capital punishment. There are two variants of the social comparison perspective:

> **Social comparison (theory)**
> Comparing our behaviours and opinions with those of others in order to establish the correct or socially approved way of thinking and behaving.
>
> **Cultural values theory**
> The view that people in groups use members' opinions about the position valued in the wider culture, and then adjust their views in that direction for social approval reasons.

- *The bandwagon effect* – on learning which attitude pole (i.e extreme position) is socially desirable, people in an interactive discussion may compete to appear to be stronger advocates of that pole. Codol (1975) called this the *primus inter pares* (first among equals) effect.

- *Pluralistic ignorance* – because people often behave publicly in ways that do not reflect their internal beliefs (see Chapters 5 and 6), they are often quite ignorant of what others really think. This is called pluralistic ignorance (Miller & McFarland, 1987; Prentice & Miller, 1993).

One thing that group discussion can do is to dispel pluralistic ignorance. Where people have relatively extreme attitudes but believe that others are mostly moderate, group discussion can reveal how extreme others' attitudes really are. This liberates people to be true to their underlying beliefs. Polarisation is not so much a shift in attitude as an expression of true attitudes.

## Social identity theory

The persuasive arguments and social comparison approaches are supported by some studies but not by others (Mackie, 1986; Turner, 1991; Wetherell, 1987). For example, polarisation has been obtained under circumstances (e.g. perceptual tasks) where arguments and persuasion

**Social identity theory**
Theory of group
membership and
intergroup relations based
on self-categorisation,
social comparison and the
construction of a shared
self-definition in terms of
ingroup-defining
properties.

**Self-categorisation
theory**
Turner and associates'
theory of how the process
of categorising oneself as
a group member produces
social identity and group
and intergroup
behaviours.

are unlikely to play a role (Baron & Roper, 1976) and under circumstances where lack of surveillance by the group should minimise the role of social desirability (Goethals & Zanna, 1979; Teger & Pruitt, 1967). In general, it is not possible to argue that one perspective has a clear empirical advantage over the other. Isenberg (1986) has suggested that both are correct (they explain polarisation under different circumstances) and that we should seek to specify the range of applicability of each.

There is a third perspective, advanced by Turner and his colleagues (Turner, 1985; Turner et al., 1987; see also Chapter 11). Unlike persuasive arguments and social comparison/cultural values theories, **social identity theory**, specifically its focus on the social categorisation process (**self-categorisation theory**), treats polarisation as a regular conformity phenomenon (Turner & Oakes, 1989). People in discussion groups actively construct a representation of the group norm from the positions held by group members in relation to those positions assumed to be held by people not in the group, or known to be held by people explicitly in an outgroup.

Because such norms not only minimise variability within the group (i.e. among ingroup members) but also distinguish the ingroup from outgroups, they are not necessarily the mean ingroup position: they can be polarised away from an explicit or implicit outgroup (see Figure 9.8). Self-categorisation, the process responsible for identification with a group, produces conformity to the ingroup norm – and thus, if the norm is polarised, group polarisation. If the norm is not polarised, self-categorisation produces convergence on the mean group position.

Research supports this perspective in (1) confirming how a norm can be polarised (Hogg, Turner & Davidson, 1990); (2) showing that people are more persuaded by ingroup members than outgroup members or individuals; and (3) showing that group polarisation occurs only if an initial group tendency is perceived to represent a norm rather than an aggregate of individual opinions (Mackie, 1986; Mackie & Cooper, 1984; Turner, Wetherell & Hogg, 1989).

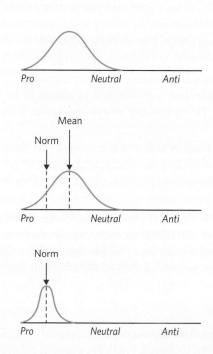

**Figure 9.8** Group
polarisation as self-
categorisation induced
conformity to a polarised
group

Group polarisation can occur
because people categorise
themselves in terms of, and
conform to, an ingroup defined
by a norm that is polarised
away from positions not held
by ingroup members

**Stage 1:**
Actual distribution of ingroup
positions on an attitudinal
dimension. Scale positions not
under the bell curve are positions
held by people not in the group.

**Stage 2:**
Perceptual polarisation of the
ingroup norm away from positions
not held by ingroup members.

**Stage 3:**
Ingroup members conform to
the polarised ingroup norm, causing
the distribution of ingroup positions
to be both homogenised and polarised.

# Jury decision making

People are fascinated by juries. They are the focus of a disproportionate number of novels and movies – John Grisham's novel *The Runaway Jury* and the 2003 movie adaptation dramatically highlight many of the important social psychological points made below about jury decision making. Returning to reality, the 1995 murder trial of the American sports star O. J. Simpson and the 2004 child 'abuse' trial of Michael Jackson virtually brought the United States to a standstill because people could not miss the exciting televised instalments. Juries represent one of the most significant decision-making groups, not only because they are brandished as a symbol of all that is democratic, fair and just in a society, but also because of the consequences of their decisions for defendants, victims and the community.

A case in point is the 1992 Los Angeles riots, which were sparked by an unexpected 'not guilty' verdict delivered by an all-white jury in the case of the police beating of a black suspect (see Box 11.1 in Chapter 11). Juries are groups and thus are potentially prey to the deficiencies of group decision making discussed in this chapter (e.g. decision schemes, leadership, groupthink and group polarisation) (Hastie, 1993; Hastie, Penrod & Pennington, 1983; Tindale, Nadler, Krebel & Davis, 2001).

In addition to these problems, research has identified a number of issues specifically related to the task confronted by juries. Characteristics of the defendant and the victim can affect the jury. Physically attractive defendants are more likely to be acquitted (Michelini & Snodgrass, 1980) or to receive a lighter sentence (Stewart, 1980), although biases can be reduced by furnishing sufficient factual evidence (Baumeister & Darley, 1982), by presenting the jury with written rather than spoken, face-to-face testimony (Kaplan, 1977; Kaplan & Miller, 1978), or by explicitly directing the jury to consider the evidence alone (Weiten, 1980).

Race can also affect the jury. In the United States, for example, Blacks are more likely to receive prison sentences (Stewart, 1980), and people who murder a White are more likely than those who murder a Black to receive the death penalty (11.1 per cent versus 4.5 per cent; Henderson & Taylor, 1985).

Another issue is the influence of laws and penalties on the jury. Harsh laws with stiff penalties (e.g. the death penalty) tend to discourage juries from convicting (Kerr, 1978) – quite the reverse of the intention of legislators who introduce such laws. For instance, consider some of the pressures on a jury deliberating on a case in which the defendant vandalised a car, if conviction carried a mandatory death penalty. Research in the United States has tended to show that whether jurors do or do not support the death penalty has a reliable but small impact on the verdict – one to three verdicts out of one hundred would be affected (Allen, Mabry & McKelton, 1998).

Juries have to deal with enormous amounts of information presented in court. Research suggests that there is a recency effect, in which information delivered later in the trial is more heavily weighted in decision making (Horowitz & Bordens, 1990), and that inadmissible evidence (evidence that is given by witnesses or interjected by counsel but is subsequently ruled to be inadmissible for procedural reasons by the judge) still has an effect on jury deliberation (Thompson & Fuqua, 1998). Juries also deal with complex evidence, enormous amounts of evidence, and complex laws and legal jargon – all three of which make the jury deliberation process extremely complex and prey to suboptimal decision making (Heuer & Penrod, 1994).

The jury 'foreman' is important in guiding the jury to its verdict, as he/she occupies the role of leader (see earlier in this chapter). Research suggests that the foreman is most likely to be someone of higher socioeconomic status, someone who has had previous experience as a juror, or someone who simply occupies the seat at the head of the table at the first sitting of the jury (Strodtbeck & Lipinski, 1985). This is of some concern, as diffuse status characteristics (Berger, Fisek, Norman & Zelditch, 1977; Ridgeway, 2001), discussed in Chapter 8, are influencing the jury process.

Jurors who are older, less well educated or of lower socioeconomic status are more likely to vote to convict. However, men and women do not differ, except that women are more likely to convict defendants in rape trials (Nemeth, 1981). Jurors who score high on authoritarianism favour conviction when the victim is an authority figure (e.g. a police officer), while jurors who are more egalitarian have the opposite bias of favouring conviction when the defendant is an authority figure (Mitchell, 1979).

In general, if two-thirds or more of the jurors initially favour one alternative, then that is likely to be the jury's final verdict (Stasser, Kerr & Bray, 1982). Without such a majority, a hung jury is the likely outcome. The two-thirds majority rule is modified by a tendency for jurors to favour acquittal, particularly where evidence is not highly incriminating; under these circumstances, a minority favouring acquittal may prevail (Tindale et al., 1990).

Jury size itself may matter (Saks & Marti, 1997). Larger juries, of say twelve rather than six members, are more likely to empanel representatives of minority groups. If a particular minority is 10 per cent of the jury pool, random selection means that a minority member will be included in each twelve-person jury but in only 50 per cent of six-person juries. Furthermore, if minority or dissident viewpoints matter, they have more impact in larger than in smaller juries. If one-sixth of a jury favours acquittal, then in a six-person jury the 'deviate' has no social support, whereas in a twelve-person jury he/she does. Research on conformity and independence, and on minority influence (see Chapter 7), suggests that the dissident viewpoint is more likely to prevail in the twelve- than in the six-person jury.

## Summary

- Leadership is a process of influence that does not require coercion – coercion may undermine true leadership and produce mere compliance and obedience.

- Although some broad personality attributes are associated with effective leadership (e.g. extraversion/surgency, intellect/openness to experience, and conscientiousness), personality alone is rarely sufficient.

- Leadership is a group process in which one person transforms other members of the group so that they adopt a vision and are galvanised into pursuing the vision on behalf of the group – leadership is not simply managing a group's activities. Transformational leadership is facilitated by charisma, consideration and inspiring followers.

- Leadership involves transactions between leader and followers – leaders do something for the group and the group in return does something for the leader to allow the leader to lead effectively.

- Leadership has an identity dimension – followers look to their leaders to mould, transform and express who they are, their identity. Being perceived to be 'one of us' can often facilitate leadership.

- Trust plays an important role in leadership – leaders have greater scope to be innovative if the group trusts them.

- Effective and good leadership are not the same thing – effective leaders successfully influence the group to adopt and achieve (new) goals, whereas good leaders pursue goals that we value, use means that we approve of, and have qualities that we applaud.

- There is a general distinction between task-focused (structuring) and person/relationship-focused (consideration) leadership style – their relative effectiveness and the effectiveness of other leadership styles depends on context (e.g. the nature of the group, the nature of the task).

- Leadership effectiveness can be improved if the leaders' attributes and behaviour are perceived to fit general or task-specific schemas that we have of effective leadership, or the norms/prototype of a group membership/identity that we share with the leader.

- Group decisions can sometimes be predicted accurately from the pre-discussion distribution of opinions in the group, and from the decision-making rule that prevails in the group at that time.

- People believe that group brainstorming enhances individual creativity, despite evidence that groups do not do better than non-interactive individuals and that individuals do not perform better in groups than alone. This illusion of group effectivity may be due to distorted perceptions during group brainstorming and the enjoyment that people derive from group brainstorming.

- Groups, particularly established groups that have a transactive memory structure, are often more effective than individuals at remembering information.

- Highly cohesive groups with directive leaders are prone to groupthink – poor decision making based on an overzealous desire to reach consensus.

- Groups that already tend towards an extreme position on a decision-making dimension often make even more extreme decisions than the average of the members' initial positions would suggest.

- Juries are not free from the usual range of group decision-making biases and errors.

## Literature, film and TV

### Triumph of the Will and Downfall

A pair of films portraying one of the most evil leaders of the twentieth century in two different ways. *Triumph of the Will* is Leni Reifenstahl's classic 1934 film about Adolf Hitler – a film that largely idolises him as a great leader come to resurrect Germany. The film 'stars' the likes of Adolph Hitler, Hermann Goering and others. This film is also relevant to Chapter 6 (persuasion). *Downfall* is a controversial 2004 film by Oliver Hirschbiegel based on a book by the historian Joachim Fest. It portrays Hitler's last days in his bunker beneath Berlin up to his suicide on 30 April 1945. The film is controversial because it portrays Hitler largely as a sad dysfunctional human being rather than a grotesque monster responsible for immeasurable human suffering.

### Twelve Angry Men and The Runaway Jury

Two films based on books that highlight jury decision making. *Twelve Angry Men* is a classic 1957 film directed by Sidney Lumet and starring Henry Fonda – set entirely in the jury room it is an incredibly powerful portrayal of social influence and decision-making processes within a jury. *The Runaway Jury* is a 2003 film by Gary Fleder, with John Cusack, Dustin Hoffman and Gene Hackman, that dramatises the way that juries can be unscrupulously manipulated.

### Thirteen Days

2000 film by Roger Donaldson. It is about the Cuban missile crisis which lasted for two weeks in October 1962 and was about as close as we got to all-out nuclear war between the West and the Soviet Union. The focus is on Kennedy's decision-making group. Is there groupthink or not? Wonderful dramatisation of presidential/high-level decision making under crisis. Also relevant to Chapter 11 (intergroup behaviour).

### The Last King of Scotland

This 2006 film by Kevin MacDonald, based on the eponymous novel by Giles Foden, is a complex portrayal of the 1970s Ugandan dictator Idi Amin (played by Forest Whitaker) – an all-powerful and charismatic leader who can be charming interpersonally but will go to any lengths to protect himself from his paranoia about forces trying to undermine him. Amin was responsible for great brutality – 500,000 deaths and the expulsion of all Asians from the country.

### Autobiographies

Autobiographies by Margaret Thatcher (*The Downing Street Years,* 1993), Nelson Mandela (*The Long Walk to Freedom,* 1994), Richard Branson (*Richard Branson,* 1998) and Barack Obama (*Dreams from my Father,* 1995) – all great leaders but in quite different ways and domains.

## Guided questions

1 What is the *great person* theory of leadership and how effective a theory is it?

2 How is a transformational leader different from a transactional leader?

3 Is it possible for a highly cohesive group to become oblivious to the views and expectations of the wider community? Watch the video in Chapter 9 of MyPsychLab at **www.mypsychlab.co.uk** for some of the symptoms of *groupthink* that contributed to the Challenger space shuttle launch in 1986 (watch *Groupthink*; see **http://www.youtube.com/watch?v=qYpbStMyz_I**).

4 What factors inhibit the productivity of group brainstorming?

5 Sometimes a group makes a decision that is even more extreme than any of its individual members might have made. How so?

## Learn More

Baron, R. S., & Kerr, N. (2003). *Group process, group decision, group action* (2nd ed.). Buckingham, UK: Open University Press. A general overview of topics in the study of group processes, with excellent coverage of group decision making.

Brown, R. J. (2000). *Group processes* (2nd ed.). Oxford, UK: Blackwell. A very readable introduction to group processes, which takes a European perspective and also covers intergroup relations. It has a section on leadership.

Gilovich, T. D., & Griffin, D. W. (2010). Judgment and decision making. In S. T. Fiske, D. T. Gilbert, & G. Lindzey (eds), *Handbook of social psychology* (5th ed., Vol. 1, pp. 542–88). New York: Wiley. Although primarily about individual decision making, this detailed and up-to-date chapter is also relevant to group decision making.

Goethals, G. R., & Sorenson, G. (eds) (2004). *Encyclopedia of leadership*. Thousand Oaks, CA: Sage. This is a true monster resource – four volumes, around 2,000 pages, 1.2 million words, 373 short essay-style entries written by 311 scholars including virtually everyone who is anyone in leadership research. All you ever wanted to know about leadership is somewhere in this book.

Gruenfeld, D. H., & Tiedens, L. Z. (2010). Organizational preferences and their consequences. In S. T. Fiske, D. T. Gilbert, & G. Lindzey (eds), *Handbook of social psychology* (5th ed., Vol. 2, pp. 1252–87). New York: Wiley. Up-to-date and detailed overview of social psychological theory and research on organisational processes, including decision making and leadership in organisations.

Hackman, J. R., & Katz, N. (2010). Group behavior and performance. In S. T. Fiske, D. T. Gilbert, & G. Lindzey (eds), *Handbook of social psychology* (5th ed., Vol. 2, pp. 1208–51). New York: Wiley. Comprehensive, detailed and up-to-date coverage of group behaviour.

Hogg, M. A. (2007). Social psychology of leadership. In A. W. Kruglanski & E. T. Higgins (eds), *Social psychology: Handbook of basic principles* (2nd ed., pp. 716–33). New York: Guilford. An up-to-date and comprehensive overview of leadership research, from the perspective of social psychology rather than organisational and management science; although the latter are also covered.

Hogg, M. A. (2010). Influence and leadership. In S. T. Fiske, D. T. Gilbert, & G. Lindzey (eds), *Handbook of social psychology* (5th ed., Vol. 2, pp. 1166–207). New York: Wiley. Detailed and up-to-date overview of leadership theory and research, which treats leadership as a process of social influence in groups.

Hollander, E. P. (1985). Leadership and power. In G. Lindzey & E. Aronson (eds), *Handbook of social psychology* (3rd ed., Vol. 2, pp. 485–537). New York: Random House. A classic review of leadership research in social psychology.

Levine, J., & Moreland, R. L. (1998). Small groups. In D. Gilbert, S. T. Fiske, & G. Lindzey (eds), *The handbook of social psychology* (4th ed., Vol. 2, pp. 415–69). New York: McGraw-Hill. A comprehensive overview of the field of small groups in which most group decision-making research is done – the most recent fifth edition of the handbook does not have a chapter dedicated to small interactive groups.

Stangor, C. (2004). *Social groups in action and interaction*. New York: Psychology Press. Comprehensive and accessible coverage of the social psychology of processes within and between groups.

Tindale, R. S., Kameda, T., & Hinsz, V. B. (2003). Group decision making. In M. A. Hogg & J. Cooper (eds), *The SAGE handbook of social psychology* (pp. 381–403). London: SAGE. Comprehensive coverage of research on group decision making, with a particular emphasis on the shared nature of group decisions.

Yukl, G. (2010). *Leadership in organizations* (7th ed.). Upper Saddle River, NJ: Prentice Hall. Straightforward, comprehensive, completely up-to-date and very readable coverage of leadership from the perspective of organisations, where most leadership research tends to be done.

 Refresh your understanding, assess your progress and go further with interactive summaries, questions, podcasts and much more at **www.mypsychlab.co.uk**

## This chapter discusses

- The nature and dimensions of prejudice
- Prejudiced attitudes and discriminatory behaviour
- Targets of prejudice: sex, race, age, sexual preference, physical and mental health
- Forms of discrimination: reluctance to help, tokenism, reverse discrimination
- Stigma and other effects of prejudice on victims
- Personality and individual-level explanations of prejudice and discrimination

## Focus questions

1. Tom is convinced that he is not homophobic – he just doesn't much want to talk to gays or about homosexuality. As proof of his 'goodwill' he donates five dollars each year to AIDS charity collectors. Are you convinced that Tom is not prejudiced?

2. How would you feel if someone less qualified than you was given a job in preference to you because that person belonged to a historically disadvantaged social group?

3. A neighbourhood group in an English city proposes to send the children of new immigrants into a special school, where first they can learn to speak English and later continue the rest of their education. The group says that this is for the good of the children. Would you have any concerns about this? See some real-life footage of negative comments about minority groups in Chapter 10 of MyPsychLab at www.mypsychlab.co.uk (watch *Prejudice*).

will use which involves getting you to decide to buy a car by giving you a very low price

Go to **mypsychlab** to explore video and test your understanding of key topics addressed in this chapter.

4. Armand is a native of Israel now living in Sweden, and is very traditional in his politics and religion. He does not like local immigrants from Palestine, as he believes the Palestinians occupy land belonging to Israel. But actually, he doesn't like any immigrants. How might you explain his views?

Refresh your understanding with interactive summaries, explore topics further with video and audio clips and assess your progress with quick test and essay questions by logging to the accompanying website at www.mypsychlab.co.uk

# Chapter 10
## Prejudice and discrimination

**Key terms**

Acquiescent response set
Ageism
Attribution
Authoritarian personality
Belief congruence theory
Closed-mindedness
Collective behaviour
Dehumanisation
Discrimination
Displacement

Dogmatism
Ethnocentrism
Face-ism
Frustration–aggression hypothesis
Gender
Genocide
Glass ceiling
Implicit association test
Mere exposure effect
Meta-analysis
Minimal group paradigm
Prejudice
Racism

Relative deprivation
Reverse discrimination
Scapegoat
Self-esteem
Self-fulfilling prophecy
Sex role
Sexism
Social dominance theory
Stereotype
Stereotype threat
Stigma
System justification theory
Tokenism

# Nature and dimensions of prejudice

**Prejudice**
Unfavourable attitude towards a social group and its members.

**Prejudice** and discrimination are two of the greatest problems faced by humanity. When one group of people hates another group of people so profoundly that they can intentionally torture and murder innocent non-combatants, we have a serious problem on our hands. Because prejudice and discrimination stand squarely in the path of enlightenment, an understanding of the causes and consequences of prejudice is one of humanity's great challenges. We can put people on the moon, we can genetically modify living organisms, we can replace dysfunctional organs, we can whizz around the world at an altitude of 10,000 metres, and we can communicate with almost anyone anywhere via the Internet. But, in recent history, we have seemed helpless in preventing the Palestinians and the Israelis from fighting over Jerusalem, the Catholics and Protestants from tearing Northern Ireland apart, and various groups in Africa from hacking each other to death with machetes.

**Dehumanisation**
Stripping people of their dignity and humanity.

One of the awful aspects of prejudice is that it involves the **dehumanisation** of an outgroup. If people can be viewed as less than human, then atrocities against them become essentially no different to squishing an insect. Dehumanisation is commonplace. Europeans, who had extensive commerce with China by the sixteenth century, apparently thought that the Oriental was a 'strange and wondrous creature'. After meeting some Jesuit priests, a Confucian scholar in China offered a more damning contrary view in a letter to his son:

> These 'Ocean Men' are tall beasts with deep sunken eyes and beak-like noses . . . Although undoubtedly men, they seem to possess none of the mental faculties of men. The most bestial of peasants is far more human . . . It is quite possible that they are susceptible to training, and could with patience be taught the modes of conduct proper to a human being. (*cited by LaPiere & Farnsworth, 1949, p. 228*)

**Genocide**
The ultimate expression of prejudice by exterminating an entire social group.

Prejudice is responsible for or associated with much of the pain and human suffering in the world, ranging from restricted opportunities and narrowed horizons to physical violence and **genocide**. It has always been with us, and it is a depressing thought that it may remain with us as a fundamental part of the human condition.

Most people in liberal democratic societies consider prejudice a particularly unpalatable aspect of human behaviour, with terms such as 'racist' and 'bigot' being reserved as profound insults. Yet almost all of us experience prejudice in one form or another, ranging from relatively minor assumptions that people make about us to crude and offensive bigotry, or violence. People make and behave in accordance with assumptions about our abilities and aspirations on the basis of, for example, our age, ethnicity, race or sex, and we often find ourselves automatically making the same sorts of assumption about others.

Herein lies a paradox: prejudice is socially undesirable, yet it pervades social life. Even in societies where prejudice is institutionalised, sophisticated justifications are used to deny that it is actually prejudice that is being practised. The system of apartheid in South Africa was a classic case of institutionalised prejudice, yet it was packaged publicly as recognition of and respect for cultural differences (see Nelson Mandela's fascinating autobiography, 1994).

Prejudice is a topic of research in its own right, but it is also a topic that draws upon a range of other aspects of social psychology. In this chapter, we discuss the nature of prejudice, what forms it takes and what its consequences are, and we also discuss some theories of prejudice. In Chapter 11, we continue our treatment but focus more widely on intergroup relations – prejudice and discrimination are intergroup phenomena, and thus Chapters 10 and 11 go together. However, prejudice rests on negative stereotypes of groups (see Chapter 2), it often translates into aggression towards an outgroup (see Chapter 12), and it pivots on the sort of people we think we are (see Chapter 4) and the sorts of people we think others are (see Chapters 2 and 3). The relationship between prejudice and discrimination can also be viewed as the attitude–behaviour relationship in the context of attitudes towards a group (see Chapters 5 and 6).

In many respects, social psychology is uniquely placed to rise to the challenge of understanding prejudice. Prejudice is a social psychological phenomenon. In fact, prejudice is doubly social – it involves people's feelings about and actions towards other people, and it is guided and given a context by the groups to which we belong and the historical circumstances of specific intergroup relations in which these groups find themselves.

# Prejudiced attitudes and discriminatory behaviour

As the term 'prejudice' literally means 'prejudgement' (from the Latin *prae* and *judicium*), it is usual to consider prejudice as an attitude (see Chapter 5) where the attitude object is a social group (e.g. Americans, West Indians, politicians, musicians). A traditional view (e.g. Allport, 1954b) of prejudice is that it has three components:

1 *cognitive* – beliefs about the attitude object;

2 *affective* – strong feelings (usually negative) about the attitude object and the qualities it is believed to possess;

3 *conative* – intentions to behave in certain ways towards the attitude object (the conative component is an *intention* to act in certain ways, not the action itself).

However, not all attitude theorists are comfortable with the *tripartite model* of attitude (see Chapter 5), and there are other definitions of prejudice that do include discriminatory behaviour. For example, Brown defines prejudice as:

the holding of derogatory social attitudes or cognitive beliefs, the expression of negative affect, or the display of hostile or discriminatory behaviour towards members of a group on account of their membership of that group. (*Brown, 1995, p. 8*)

Box 10.1 provides a fanciful account of how prejudice may arise and become the basis for discrimination. Although a fictional example, it does capture many of the principal features

## Real world 10.1
### Prejudice and discrimination on campus

#### The emergence of a fictional 'stigmatised group'

A study by Forgas (1983) showed that students can have clear beliefs about different campus groups. One such target group was 'engineering students', who were described in terms of their drinking habits (beer, and lots of it), their cultural preferences (sports and little else) and their style of dress (practical and conservative). This is a prejudgement, in so far as it is assumed that all engineering students are like this. If these beliefs (the *cognitive* component) are not associated with any strong feelings (*affect*) or any particular intention to act (*conation*), then no real problem exists and we would probably not call this a prejudice – simply a harmless generalisation (see Chapter 5 for a discussion of the tripartite model of attitude).

However, if these beliefs were associated with strong negative feelings about engineering students and their characteristics, then a pattern of conations would almost inevitably arise. If you hated and despised engineering students and their characteristics, you would probably intend to avoid them, perhaps humiliate them whenever possible, and even dream of a brave new world without them.

This is now quite clearly prejudice, but it may still not be much of a social problem. Strong pressures would exist to inhibit expression of such views or the realisation of conation in action, so people with such prejudices would probably be unaware that others shared their views. However, if people became aware that their prejudices were widely shared, they might engage in discussion and form organisations to represent their views. Under these circumstances, more extreme conations might arise, such as suggestions to isolate engineering students in one part of the campus and deny them access to certain resources on campus (e.g. the bar, the refectory). Individuals or small groups might now feel strong enough to discriminate against individual engineering students, although wider social pressures would probably prevent widespread discrimination.

However, if the students gained legitimate overall power in the university, they would be free to put their plans into action. They could indulge in dehumanising engineering students: deny them their human rights, degrade and humiliate them, herd them into ghettos behind barbed wire, and systematically exterminate them. Prejudice would have become enshrined in, and legitimated by, the norms and practices of the community.

---

of prejudice that need to be explained. The first issue, which is essentially the attitude–behaviour relationship (see Chapter 5), is the relationship between prejudiced beliefs and the practice of discrimination. You will recall from Chapter 5 that LaPiere (1934), a social scientist, spent two years travelling around the United States with a young Chinese American couple. They visited 250 hotels, caravan parks, tourist homes and restaurants, and were refused service in only one (i.e. 0.4 per cent); it would appear that there was little anti-Chinese prejudice. After returning home, LaPiere contacted 128 of these establishments with the question, 'Will you accept members of the Chinese race as guests in your establishment?' The responses included 92 per cent 'No', 7 per cent 'Uncertain, depends on circumstances' and 1 per cent 'Yes'. It would appear there was overwhelming prejudice!

A controlled experiment was conducted later by Gaertner and Dovidio (1977). White female undergraduates waiting to participate in an experiment overheard a supposed 'emergency' in an adjoining room in which several chairs seemed to fall on a female confederate, who was either White or Black. The participants were led to believe that they were alone with the confederate or that there were two other potential helpers. Ordinarily, we would expect the usual bystander effect (see Chapter 14 for details), in which participants would be less willing to go to the aid of the 'victim' when other potential helpers were available. Figure 10.1 shows that there was only a weak bystander effect when the victim was White, but that the effect was greatly amplified when the victim was Black (compare columns 3 and 4). The White participants discriminated overtly against the Black victim

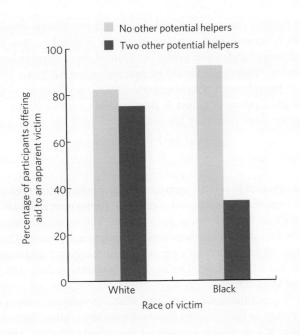

**Figure 10.1** Bystander apathy as a function of race of victim

When there were no other potential helpers available, White females were slightly likely to go to the aid of a Black or a White confederate who had suffered an emergency. However, when other helpers were available they were not inclined to assist the Black confederate: weak bystander apathy in the presence of a White victim was amplified many times over when the victim was Black

*Source:* based on data from Gaertner & Dovidio (1977)

only when other potential helpers were present. There is an important lesson here: under certain circumstances, prejudice may go undetected. If the 'two potential helpers' condition had not been included, this experiment would have revealed that White women were more willing to aid a Black victim than a White victim. It was only with the inclusion of the 'two potential helpers' condition that underlying prejudice was revealed. The absence of overt discrimination should always be treated with caution, as prejudice can be expressed in many indirect and subtle ways (see below).

# Targets of prejudice and discrimination

Prejudice knows no cultural or historical boundaries – it is certainly not the exclusive province of people who are middle-aged, White, heterosexual or male. Human beings are remarkably versatile in being able to make almost any social group a target of prejudice. However, certain groups are the enduring victims of prejudice because they are formed by social categorisations that are vivid, omnipresent and socially functional, and the target groups themselves occupy low power positions in society. These groups are those based on race, ethnicity, sex, age, sexual orientation, and physical and mental health. Research shows that of these, sex, race and age are the most prevalent bases for stereotyping (Mackie, Hamilton, Susskind & Rosselli, 1996).

Not surprisingly, most research on prejudice has focused on these three dimensions, particularly on sex and race/ethnicity. For example, in his 1995 book on the social psychology of prejudice, Brown has a great deal to say about sexism and racism but only touches on ageism and on handicap and disability, and he says nothing about homophobia or discrimination based on sexual orientation.

## Sexism

**Sexism**
Prejudice and
discrimination against
people based on their
gender.

Almost all research on **sexism** focuses on prejudice and discrimination against women (Deaux & LaFrance, 1998). This is because women have historically suffered most as the victims of sexism – primarily because of their lower power position relative to men in business, government and employment. However, it should be noted that sex roles may have persisted because, although they provide men with structural power, they have provided women with dyadic or interpersonal power (e.g. Jost & Banaji, 1994). And of course, to the extent that women have power over men they are just as capable of discriminating against men.

### Sex stereotypes

Research on sex stereotypes has revealed that both men and women believe that men are competent and independent, and women are warm and expressive (Broverman et al., 1972; Spence, Helmreich & Stapp, 1974). As Fiske (1998, p. 377) puts it: 'The typical woman is seen as nice but incompetent, the typical man as competent but maybe not so nice.' These beliefs have substantial cross-cultural generality: they prevail in Europe, North and South America, Australia and parts of the Middle East (Deaux, 1985; Williams & Best, 1982). These are really consensual social **stereotypes**.

**Stereotype**
Widely shared and
simplified evaluative
image of a social group
and its members.

Knowledge of such stereotypes is not inevitably associated with a stereotype-consistent personal belief about the target group. In fact, it seems that such a correspondence between knowledge and belief occurs only among highly prejudiced individuals (Devine, 1989).

**Sex stereotypes can be
challenged**
This young scientist refined a
method of DNA matching that
helps in solving crime

There is some evidence that, all things being equal, men and women do not describe themselves in such strongly sex-stereotypical terms (e.g. Martin, 1987) and that women deny feeling that they have been personally discriminated against: sex discrimination is something experienced by *other* women (Crosby, Cordova & Jaskar, 1993; Crosby et al., 1989; see below).

Although there are generic stereotypes of men and women, people tend to represent the sexes in terms of subtypes (Deaux & LaFrance, 1998; Fiske, 1998). Western research identifies four main female subtypes (housewife, sexy woman, career woman and feminist/athlete/lesbian), which emphasise interpersonal versus competence dimensions. The typical woman is closest to the housewife or sexy woman subtype. Male subtypes are less clear-cut, but the two main ones are businessman and macho man. Here the emphasis is very much on the competence dimension. The typical man falls between the two poles. Generally speaking, research shows that both men and women see women as a more homogeneous group than men (Lorenzi-Cioldi, Eagly & Stewart, 1995).

Presumably, competence, independence, warmth and expressiveness are all highly desirable and valued human attributes. If this were true, there would be no differential evaluative connotation of the stereotype. However, earlier research suggested that female-stereotypical traits are significantly less valued than male-stereotypical traits. Broverman and colleagues (Broverman et al., 1970) asked seventy-nine practising mental health clinicians (clinical psychologists, psychiatrists, social workers) to describe a healthy, mature, socially competent individual, who was either (1) 'a male', (2) 'a female' or (3) 'a person'. Both male and female clinicians described a healthy adult man and a healthy adult person in almost exactly the same terms (reflecting competence). The healthy adult woman was seen to be significantly more submissive, excitable and appearance-oriented, characteristics not attached to either the healthy adult or the healthy man. It is ominous that women were not considered to be normal, healthy adult people!

## Behaviour and roles

Might sex stereotypes accurately reflect sex differences in personality and behaviour? Perhaps men and women really do have different personalities? Bakan (1966), for example, has argued that men are more agentic (i.e. action-oriented) than women, and women are more communal than men (see also Williams, 1984). This is a complicated issue. Traditionally, men and women have occupied different **sex roles** in society (men pursue full-time out-of-home jobs, while females are 'homemakers'), and, as we saw in Chapter 8, roles constrain behaviour in line with role requirements. Sex differences, if they do exist, may simply reflect roles not sex, and role assignment may be determined and perpetuated by the social group that has more power (in most cases, men). An alternative argument might be that there are intrinsic personality differences between men and women that suit the sexes to different roles: that is, there is a biological imperative behind role assignments. This is a debate that can be, and is, highly politicised.

**Sex role**
Behaviour deemed sex-stereotypically appropriate.

Social psychological research indicates that there are a small number of systematic differences between the sexes, but that they are not very diagnostic: in other words, knowing someone's position on one of these dimensions is not a reliable predictor of that person's sex (Parsons, Adler & Meece, 1984). For example, research on male and female military cadets (Rice, Instone & Adams, 1984) and male and female managers (Steinberg & Shapiro, 1982) indicated that perceived stereotypical differences were an exaggeration of minor differences. In general, sex stereotypes are more myth than a reflection of reality (Eagly & Carli, 1981; Swim, 1994).

One reason why sex stereotypes persist is that role assignment according to **gender** persists. In general, women make up the overwhelming majority of restaurant servers, telephone operators, secretaries, nurses, babysitters, dental hygienists, librarians and elementary/kindergarten teachers, while most lawyers, dentists, truck drivers, accountants, top executives

**Gender**
Sex-stereotypical attributes of a person.

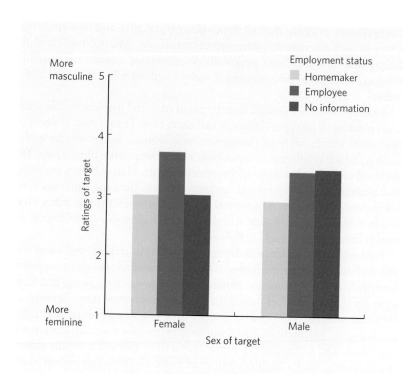

**Figure 10.2** Trait ratings as a function of sex and employment status of target

Male and female students rated a 'homemaker' as significantly more feminine than someone described as a full-time employee, irrespective of the target's sex

*Source:* based on data from Eagly & Steffen (1984)

and engineers are male (Greenglass, 1982). Certain occupations become labelled as 'women's work' and are accordingly valued less.

To investigate this idea, Eagly and Steffen (1984) asked male and female students to rate, on sex-stereotypical dimensions, an imaginary man or woman who was described as being either a 'homemaker' or employed full-time outside the home. In a third condition, no employment information was given. Figure 10.2 shows that, irrespective of sex, homemakers were perceived to be significantly more feminine (in their traits) than full-time employees. This indicates that certain roles may be sex-typed, and it suggests the possibility that as women increasingly take on masculine roles there will be substantial change in sex stereotypes. However, the converse may also occur: as a traditionally male role becomes increasingly occupied by women, that role may become less valued.

Any analysis of intergroup relations between the sexes should not lose sight of the fact that in general men still have more sociopolitical power than women to define the relative status of different roles in society. Not surprisingly, women can find it difficult to gain access to higher-status masculine roles/occupations. Older research found that in some American universities women applicants for postdoctoral positions could be discouraged by condescending reactions from male peers and academic staff (e.g. 'You're so cute, I can't see you as a professor of anything'; Harris, 1970), and that there was a bias against hiring women for academic positions (e.g. Fidell, 1970; Lewin & Duchan, 1971). Things have changed a great deal in the last thirty-five years, so it would be most alarming to find this form of blatant discrimination in modern Western universities (see below).

However, these changes have been slower and less extensive outside the more progressive environment of universities, and women can still find it difficult to attain top leadership positions in large organisations – a phenomenon called the **glass ceiling** (e.g. Eagly, 2003; Eagly, Karau & Makhijani, 1995). Women are well represented in middle management, but on the way up, and just within sight of the top, they hit an invisible ceiling, a glass ceiling. One explanation is that male prejudice against women with power generates a *backlash* that constructs the glass ceiling (e.g. Rudman & Glick, 1999, 2001) – see Box 10.2. Again, either

**Glass ceiling**
An invisible barrier that prevents women, and minorities, from attaining top leadership positions.

## Research and applications 10.2
### Backlash

Violation of gender stereotypes can result in social and economic reprisal – called *backlash* (Rudman, 1998). For example, women who are perceived to be assertive or highly competent violate stereotypical expectations that women possess *communal* traits and ought therefore to be social- and service-oriented (e.g. kind, sympathetic and concerned about others), and it is men who should be *agentic* (e.g. forceful, decisive and independent) (Rudman & Glick, 1999, 2001). As a consequence, competent women can be disliked and viewed as interpersonally unskilled, and therefore less likely to be hired than identically qualified men. Penalising agentic women is especially pronounced if a job inherently requires feminine skills. Men do not suffer comparable consequences (i.e. a decrease in perceived competence) when they are seen as highly communal. According to Rudman and Glick, this asymmetry rests on the fact that gender stereotypes are more prescriptive of how women should behave than of how men should behave.

Research provides evidence for this analysis of backlash. For example, Heilman and colleagues (Heilman, Wallen, Fuchs & Tamkins, 2004) had students take part in a personnel decision-making task. They were given information about a male-stereotypical job (Assistant Vice President for Sales in an aircraft company) and about fictitious employees who were holding the job. These employees were described as either male or female, and as having a record of either clear previous success or ambiguous previous success. Participants rated the employees on competence-related measures and on interpersonal liking and hostility. There were two findings:

- If previous success was clear, male and female employees were rated as equally competent; but if previous success was ambiguous, the male employee was rated as significantly more competent than the female.

- If previous success was clear, male employees were liked significantly more than female; but if previous success was ambiguous, males and females were equally liked.

These findings indicate that in ambiguous situations, women are denied competence in a male-stereotypical arena, and in situations where their competence cannot be doubted, they are less liked and personally derogated. (For a review of how gender stereotypes affect women in the workplace, see Heilman & Parks-Stamm, 2007).

---

sex can hit a glass ceiling if gender stereotypes are inconsistent with the organisation's norms. For example, Young and James (2001) found that male flight attendants hit a glass ceiling because, to put it simply, stereotypes about men prevent people from expecting men to make 'good' flight attendants – male stereotypes block promotion.

## Maintenance of sex stereotypes and roles

One of the most powerful forces in the transmission and maintenance of traditional sex stereotypes is the media. We are all familiar with the unsubtle forms that this may take: semi-clad women draped over boats, cars, motorcycles and other consumer products; the purely decorative role of women in some TV game shows; the way that women can be extraneous to the central plot of a drama and are presented only as sexual/romantic entertainment. Although the cumulative power of these images should not be underestimated, there are more subtle forms that may be equally or even more powerful, as they are more difficult to detect and thus combat.

For example, Archer, Iritani, Kimes and Barrios (1983) coined the term **face-ism** to describe the way in which depictions of men often give greater prominence to the head, while depictions of women give greater prominence to the body. Archer and colleagues analysed 1,750 visual images of men and women (newspaper and magazine pictures, as well as drawings made by students) and discovered that in almost all instances this was the case. Next time you watch a TV interview or documentary, for example, note how the camera tends to focus on the face of men but on the face and upper body of women. Face-ism conveys the view that, relative to men, women are more important for their physical

**Face-ism**
Media depiction that gives greater prominence to the head and less prominence to the body for men, but vice versa for women.

appearance than for their intellectual capacity: facial prominence in photos has been shown to signify ambition and intelligence (Schwartz & Kurz, 1989).

Ng has noted another subtle form of sexism in the use of the generic masculine (Ng, 1990; see also Wetherell, 1986) – people's use of the masculine pronouns (he, him, his, etc.) and terms such as 'mankind' when they are talking about people in general. This practice can convey the impression that women are an aberration from the basic masculine mould of humanity. The sex-typing of occupations and roles was also maintained by terms such as 'housewife' and 'chairman'. Because it is largely through language that we represent our world (see Chapter 15), it is important, in order to change sex stereotypes, that the implicit meanings of words and phrases be considered and that those expressions that are clearly sexist (or prejudiced in other ways) be changed. For example, language codes such as the publication manual for the American Psychological Association (adhered to by psychologists around the world) have clear guidelines for non-sexist use of language enshrined within them.

There is now substantial evidence that success or failure is explained in different ways depending on the sex of the actor (see intergroup attribution in Chapter 3). In general, a successful performance by a man tends to be attributed to ability, while an identical performance by a woman is attributed to luck or the ease of the task (see Figure 10.3). For example, Deaux and Emswiller (1974) had students watch fellow students perform well on perceptual tasks that were male-stereotypical (e.g. identifying a wheel jack) or female-stereotypical (e.g. identifying types of needlework). On the masculine tasks, male success was attributed to ability more than was female success (see Figure 10.4). On feminine tasks, there was no differential **attribution**.

**Attribution**
The process of assigning a cause to our own behaviour, and that of others.

There are some circumstances when this bias may be overturned. For example, sex-stereotypical attributions disappear when the attention of the person who is evaluating the behaviour is firmly directed on to the behaviour and away from the actor (Izraeli, Izraeli & Eden, 1985). There is also evidence that women who succeed in traditionally masculine activities (e.g. becoming a top manager) are seen as more deserving than a similarly successful man (Taynor & Deaux, 1973).

In general, however, sex-stereotypical attributions (made by both men and women) tend to create different evaluations of our own worth as a man or a woman. That is, for the same level of achievement, women may consider themselves less deserving than men. Indeed, Major and Konar (1984) found this among male and female management students in the early 1980s. The women's estimates of their realistic starting salaries were approximately 14 per cent lower than the men's estimates of their starting salaries, and 31 per cent lower with regard to estimated peak salaries.

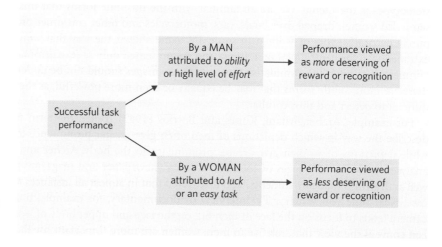

**Figure 10.3** Attribution of successful performance of an identical task performed by a man or a woman

Different attributions are made for a successful performance by a man (ability, effort) or a woman (luck, easy task), and this leads to different assessments of deservingness and recognition

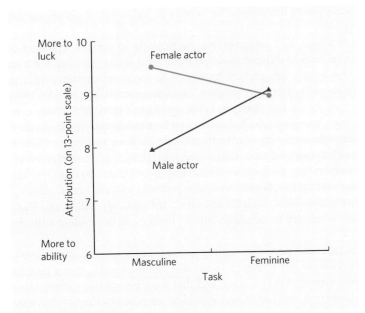

**Figure 10.4** Ability versus luck attribution for male or female success on masculine and feminine tasks

Students who watched fellow students perform well on male-stereotypical or female-stereotypical perceptual tasks over-attributed male success on male tasks to ability relative to luck

*Source:* based on data from Deaux & Emswiller (1974)

## Changes in sexism

While these forms of discrimination are difficult, and thus slow, to change, there is evidence that in Western democratic societies some forms of blatant sex discrimination are on the wane – although sexual harassment in various forms persists (Gutek, 1985). Western nations vary considerably in when women were granted the right to vote. For example, this occurred in Britain in 1928 and in New Zealand in 1893. Switzerland delayed until 1971, and in one Swiss canton (Appenzell Inner-Rhoden), women were excluded from the cantonal vote until as recently as 1990. Societies are also increasingly passing anti-discrimination legislation and (particularly in the United States) legislation for affirmative action. Affirmative action (see below) involves systematically appointing properly qualified minorities to positions in which they are historically underrepresented (e.g. senior management in organisations, senior government positions), with the aim of making such positions appear more attainable for minorities. One of the features of the 1997 British general election was an affirmative action push to increase the representation of women in Parliament – when the Blair government took office in May 1997, the number of women MPs almost doubled, from 62 to 120 out of 659 seats.

Social psychological research has detected some effects of these changes. For example, in the early 1970s, Bartol and Butterfield (1976) found that female leaders in organisations were valued less relative to male leaders. By the early 1980s, this effect had vanished (Izraeli & Izraeli, 1985), though Eagly (2003) cites a Gallup Poll conducted in 1995 that found that across twenty-two nations both sexes still preferred to have a male boss.

In the mid-1960s, Goldberg (1968; see also Pheterson, Kiesler & Goldberg, 1971) had women students evaluate identical pieces of written work attributed to a man (John T. McKay) or a woman (Joan T. McKay) and found that those pieces ostensibly authored by a woman were downgraded relative to those ostensibly authored by a man. A replication of this study in the late 1980s found no such effect, and indeed a survey of 104 studies involving 20,000 people showed that the most common finding was no gender bias (Swim, Borgida, Maruyama & Myers, 1989). Finally, no sex discrimination was found in a study of performance evaluations of more than 600 male and female store managers (Peters et al., 1984), nor in a study of the compensation worth of predominantly male or predominantly female occupations determined by experts in employment compensation (Schwab & Grams, 1985).

Because sexism is now illegal, and unacceptable, particularly in certain segments of Western society, it can sometimes be difficult to detect traditional sexism (see below for an extensive discussion of this issue). Researchers have tried to measure sex stereotypes in more subtle and complex ways to reflect more modern forms of sexism (Glick & Fiske, 1996; Swim, Aikin, Hall & Hunter, 1995). For example, Glick and Fiske (1996, 1997) have constructed an *ambivalent sexism inventory,* which differentiates between hostile and benevolent attitudes to women on dimensions relating to attractiveness, dependence and identity. Sexists have benevolent attitudes (heterosexual attraction, protection, gender role complementarity) towards traditional women (e.g. pink-collar job holders, 'sexy chicks', housewives) and hostile attitudes (heterosexual hostility, domination, competition) towards non-traditional women (e.g. career women, feminists, athletes, lesbians). Interestingly, Glick and Fiske (1997) have extended their inventory to measure women's hostile and benevolent attitudes towards men.

In their review of research into prejudice against women, Eagly and Mladinic (1994) concluded that there is no longer any tendency to devalue women's work, that a positive stereotype of women relative to men is emerging, and that most people like women more than men. Although no doubt true, this conclusion should be tempered by the fact that most research is conducted in democratic Western societies; elsewhere, the plight of women is not so rosy. For example, under the rule of the Taliban in Afghanistan women were denied the right to an education, in Nigeria women have been sentenced to death by stoning for infidelity, and in many cultures there are restrictions placed on women's choices about their bodies and reproduction. The list is long. One particularly sobering statistic comes from Klasen (1994): sex-selective abortions and infanticide have led to 76,000,000 (that's right, seventy-six *million*) 'missing women'.

## Racism

Discrimination on the basis of race or ethnicity is responsible historically for some of the most appalling acts of mass inhumanity. While sexism is responsible for the continuing practice of selective infanticide, in which female babies (and foetuses) are killed, this is largely restricted to a handful of developing countries (Freed & Freed, 1989). Genocide is universal: in recent times it has been carried out in, for example, Germany, Iraq, Bosnia and Rwanda.

**Racism**
Prejudice and discrimination against people based on their ethnicity or race.

Most research on **racism** has focused on anti-Black attitudes and behaviour in the United States. Historically, White people's stereotypes of Blacks in the United States are negative and reflect a general perception of rural, enslaved, manual labourers (LeVine & Campbell, 1972; Mackie, Hamilton, Susskind & Rosselli, 1996; Plous & Williams, 1995). In this respect, the stereotype is similar to that of Latino Americans but quite different from that of Asians and Jews.

Research into anti-Black attitudes in the United States documents a dramatic reduction in unfavourable attitudes since the 1930s (e.g. Devine & Elliot, 1995; Dovidio, Brigham, Johnson & Gaertner, 1996; Smedley & Bayton, 1978; see Figure 10.5). Much the same has occurred with respect to ethnic minorities in Britain and western Europe.

### New racism

From this, should we conclude that racial prejudice has disappeared in Western industrial nations? Possibly not. Figure 10.5 shows a decline over sixty years in the characterisation of African Americans as superstitious, lazy and ignorant. What the figure does not show are data from a study by Devine and Elliot (1995), in which 45 per cent of respondents felt that African Americans were lazy. In addition, Devine and Elliot found that more than 25 per cent of

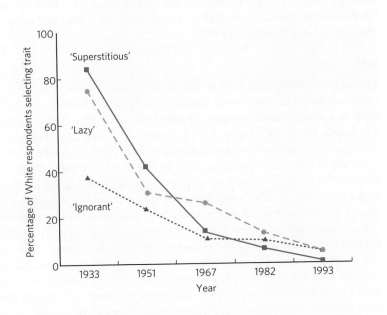

**Figure 10.5** Decline over time of White derogation of African Americans

The percentage of White participants selecting the derogatory stereotypic traits 'superstitious', 'lazy' and 'ignorant' to describe African Americans has diminished dramatically since 1933

*Source*: based on data from Dovidio, Brigham, Johnson & Gaertner (1996)

their respondents characterised African Americans as athletic, rhythmic, low in intelligence, criminal, hostile and loud. The stereotype has changed but not gone away. Furthermore, when a group of covert racists get together, wider social mores of respect and tolerance hold little sway and the public expression of racist attitudes is common.

Because explicit and blatant racism (derogatory stereotypes, name calling or ethnophaulisms, abuse, persecution, assault and discrimination) is illegal and thus socially censured, it is now more difficult to find. Most people in most contexts do not behave in this way. However, racism may not only or merely have gone 'underground'; it may actually have changed its form. This idea lies at the heart of a number of theories of new or modern racism. People may still be racist at heart, but in a different way – they may represent and express racism differently, perhaps more subtly (Crosby, Bromley & Saxe, 1980).

This new form of racism has been called *aversive racism* (Gaertner & Dovidio, 1986), *modern racism* (McConahay, 1986), *symbolic racism* (Kinder & Sears, 1981; Sears, 1988), *regressive racism* (Rogers & Prentice-Dunn, 1981) and *ambivalent racism* (Hass et al., 1991). Although there are differences between these theories, they all share the view that people experience a conflict between deep-seated emotional antipathy towards racial outgroups and modern egalitarian values that exert pressure to behave in a non-prejudiced manner (see overviews by Brewer & Miller, 1996; Brown, 1995; Hilton & von Hippel, 1996). For example, according to Gaertner and Dovidio's (1986) notion of aversive racism, deep-seated racial antipathy expresses itself as overt racism when the situation is one in which egalitarian values are weak. According to Sears's (1988) notion of symbolic racism, negative feelings about Blacks (based on early learned racial fears and stereotypes) blend with moral values embodied in the Protestant ethic to justify some anti-Black attitudes and therefore legitimise their expression.

Generally, modern or subtle forms of racism reflect how people resolve an underlying antipathy based on race with their belief in equality between groups. This is achieved by avoidance and denial of racism – separate lives, avoidance of the topic of race, denial of being prejudiced, denial of racial disadvantage, and thus opposition to affirmative action or other measures to address racial disadvantage.

These ideas, although focused on race relations in the United States, have been applied to gender (Glick & Fiske, 1996; Swim, Aikin, Hall & Hunter, 1995; see above) and to racial attitudes in Europe (Pettigrew & Meertens, 1995).

## Detecting racism

The challenge to social psychology, then, is to be able to detect new racism. A number of scales have been devised; however unobtrusive measures are generally needed, otherwise people may respond in a socially desirable way (Crosby, Bromley & Saxe, 1980; Devine, 1989; Greenwald & Banaji, 1995); see Chapter 5 for a discussion of unobtrusive measures of attitudes (physiological indices, behavioural measures, the bogus pipeline and the implicit association test). One way to measure prejudice unobtrusively is in terms of social distance – how close, psychologically or physically, people are willing to get to one another. For example, racist attitudes persist in contexts of close social distance (such as marriage), although they may have disappeared in less close social relations (such as attending the same school) (Schofield, 1986). In India, people who subscribe to the caste system will typically accept a lower-caste person into their home but will not consider marrying one (Sharma, 1981).

Another context in which underlying prejudice can emerge is when prejudiced behaviour does not obviously look like prejudice. Rogers and Prentice-Dunn (1981) had White or Black confederates insult White participants (in Alabama), who then had an opportunity to administer a shock to the confederate. Angered Whites gave larger shocks to the Black confederate. In another condition where no insults were forthcoming, participants gave smaller shocks to the Black confederate than to the White confederate.

Prejudice can also surface inadvertently in people's relatively automatic cognition (see Chapter 2). For example, Duncan (1976) had White students in California observe on TV what they thought was a live conversation between a Black man and a White man. The conversation degenerated into an argument in which one lightly shoved the other. When the White did the shoving, the behaviour was interpreted as playful: only 13 per cent of participants interpreted it as violent. When the Black did the shoving, 73 per cent interpreted the action as violent.

**Inadvertent racism**
Members of visible minorities often report that they are 'first cabs off the rank' as suspects of crime

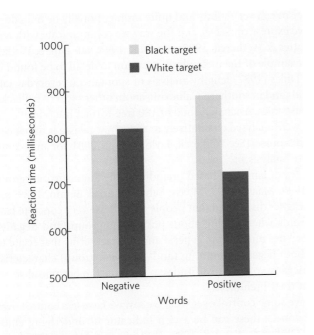

**Figure 10.6** Reaction time for deciding whether positive or negative words are meaningfully paired with the social categories Black or White

White participants did not differentially associate negative words with racial labels. However, positive words were more quickly associated with 'White' than 'Black'

*Source*: based on data from Gaertner & McLaughlin (1983)

Other evidence for well-concealed prejudice comes from an experiment by Gaertner and McLaughlin (1983). Participants were given pairings of the social categories White or Black with various positive or negative descriptive adjectives, and they had to decide whether the pairings were meaningful or not and then communicate their decision by pressing a button labelled 'yes' or 'no'. The latency of response is an index of how well the pairing represents an existing attitude in the mind of the participant – faster responses indicate an existing attitude. The results (see Figure 10.6) show no tendency among participants to pair negative words more strongly with Black or White. However, participants were much quicker at deciding whether positive words were meaningfully paired with White than with Black.

The general principle underlying this procedure for detecting prejudice is automaticity (Bargh, 1989). Stereotypes can be automatically generated by categorisation, and categorisation can automatically arise from category primes (e.g. an accent, a face, a costume). If the primes or the categories are outside consciousness, then people can have little control over the stereotype.

Devine (1989) discovered that African American primes (e.g. lazy, slavery, Blacks, Negroes, niggers, athletic) that were presented too quickly for people to be aware of them caused people to interpret a subsequent neutral act by someone called 'Donald' in stereotypically negative ways. This showed that people had deep-seated negative stereotypes of African Americans. High- and low-prejudice people did not differ in their susceptibility to preconscious priming, a provocative result that was conceptually replicated by Fazio, Jackson, Dunton and Williams (1995). However, other research shows that the automatic effect is more marked for people who score high on prejudice as measured by various modern racism scales (Lepore & Brown, 1997; Wittenbrink, Judd & Park, 1997).

The notion of automaticity is related to the idea that categories and their stereotypical attributes are implicitly linked in memory. Thus, concealed prejudice can be detected by unobtrusive methods that reveal underlying stereotypical associations. This idea is the basis of the popular **implicit association test** (IAT) described in detail in Chapter 5 (Greenwald, McGhee & Schwartz, 1998 – also see Ashburn-Nardo, Voils & Monteith, 2001; Cunningham, Preacher & Banaji, 2001; Greenwald et al., 2002).

**Implicit association test**
Reaction-time test to measure attitudes – particularly unpopular attitudes that people might conceal.

Research has shown how racism can very subtly and quite unintentionally be imbedded in the words we use, the way we express ourselves and the way we communicate with and about racial outgroups (e.g. Potter & Wetherell, 1987; van Dijk, 1993; van Dijk & Wodak, 1988; see also Chapter 15). An example of the meticulous attention to detail to be found in some of this work is Teun van Dijk's (1987) lengthy analysis of spontaneous everyday talk among Whites in the Netherlands and in southern California about other races (e.g. Blacks, East Indians, North Africans, Hispanics, Asians). A total of 180 free-format interviews conducted between 1980 and 1985 were analysed qualitatively to show how racism is imbedded in and reproduced by everyday discourse. (See Wetherell, Taylor & Yates, 2001, for an account of the methodology of discourse analysis.)

A slightly more cognitive index of language-based prejudice is the linguistic intergroup bias effect (Franco & Maass, 1996; Maass, 1999; Maass, Salvi, Arcuri & Semin, 1989; see Chapter 5). Maass and her colleagues discovered that people tend to use very concrete language that simply describes events when talking about positive outgroup (and negative ingroup) characteristics, but they use much more general and abstract terms that relate to enduring traits when talking about negative outgroup (and positive ingroup) characteristics. In this way, we can detect negative outgroup attitudes: people start to become abstract and general when talking about their prejudices.

Finally, although we often have some control over what we say, we have less control over non-verbal communication channels; these can be a rich indicator of underlying emotions and prejudices (Burgoon, Buller & Woodall, 1989; DePaulo & Friedman, 1998; see also Chapter 15).

Racial and ethnic prejudices are extremely pervasive if, as is almost always the case, we have been brought up in societies in which such prejudices have prevailed. Most of us are aware of the relevant stereotypes, and the task at hand is consciously to resist automatic stereotypical reactions – it would seem that less prejudiced people are more adept at this (Devine, 1989). Pettigrew noted:

> Many Southerners have confessed to me . . . that even though in their minds they no longer feel prejudice toward Blacks, they still feel squeamish when they shake hands with a Black. These feelings are left over from what they learned in their families as children. (*Pettigrew, 1987, p. 20*)

In summary, although overt racism and ethnic prejudice are both illegal and morally condemned, and most people think and act accordingly, a long history of such prejudices cannot be shrugged off so easily. The germs of racism still exist, and racism can be detected in various subtle forms. Racial and cultural resentment and partiality lurk beneath the surface – relatively dormant but ready to be activated by a social environment (political regime) that might legitimise the expression of prejudice. The violence in Bosnia that began in 1992 and the horrors in Rwanda in 1994 have been chilling reminders of this. Also worrying is the increased media prominence over the past decade of the far right in, for example, France and Germany, which at least partially provides a supportive and legitimising environment for the public expression of old-fashioned racist attitudes.

A final important point to bear in mind is that, although research suggests that overt discrimination may be on the wane in many Western democracies, this does not mean that the social consequences of decades or even centuries of racism will change so quickly. For example, although attitudes towards Blacks have improved dramatically over the past twenty-five years, the physical, material and spiritual plight of Blacks in much of Europe has not.

## Ageism

The existence of age related, or generational, stereotypes is undeniable. We all have them, and they can generate expectancies and misunderstandings that are felt particularly strongly in work contexts. Mitchell (2002) identifies four distinct generational stereotypes that may be partly attributable to real changes in behaviour due to ageing, but are also highly influenced by value differences in the social environment you are born into and go through early adult development in:

- *Traditionalists,* born between 1925 and 1945, are practical; patient, loyal and hard-working; respectful of authority; and rule followers.
- *Baby boomers,* born between 1946 and 1960, are optimistic; value teamwork and cooperation; are ambitious; and are workaholic.
- *Generation X,* born between 1961 and 1980, are sceptical, self-reliant risk-takers who balance work and personal life.
- *Millennials,* born between 1981 and the present, are hopeful; they value meaningful work, diversity and change; and are technologically savvy.

The main issue, however, of ageism is how the elderly are treated. In many cultures, particularly those in which the extended family thrives, older members of the community are revered – they are considered to be wise and knowledgeable teachers and leaders. In other societies, largely those in which the nuclear family has displaced the extended family, this is often not the case. Countries such as Britain, the Netherlands, Australia and the United States fall into this latter category. In these societies, the qualities of youth are highly valued, and elderly people (a group that is rapidly increasing in relative number) attract unfavourable stereotypes. However, there is a range of subtypes, including the John Wayne conservative (patriotic, religious, nostalgic), the small-town neighbour (frugal, quiet, conservative), the perfect grandparent (wise, kind, happy), the golden-ager (adventurous, sociable, successful), the despondent (depressed, neglected), the severely impaired (incompetent, feeble) and the shrew/curmudgeon (bitter, complaining, prejudiced) (Brewer, Dull & Lui, 1981).

Elderly people are generally treated as relatively worthless and powerless members of the community. They are denied many basic human rights, and their special needs go untended. Social psychologists have only recently begun systematically to investigate **ageism**, and much of the research has been done in the area of intergenerational communication (e.g. Fox & Giles, 1993; Harwood, Giles & Ryan, 1995; Hummert, 1990; Kite & Johnson, 1988; Williams, 1996; see Chapter 15).

**Ageism**
Prejudice and discrimination against people based on their age.

Young adults may consider people over 65 to be grouchy, unhealthy, unattractive, unhappy, miserly, less efficient, less socially skilled, overly self-disclosing, overly controlling, feeble, egocentric, incompetent, abrasive, frail and vulnerable (see Noels, Giles & Le Poire, 2003). Furthermore, the young generally have little to do with the elderly, so intergenerational encounters tend to activate intergroup rather than interpersonal perceptions, which reinforce negative stereotypes that lead to avoidance and minimisation of intergenerational contact. The cycle continues and the elderly remain socially isolated and societally marginalised.

An interesting observation is that the extremely old seem to pass through the ageism lens and are once again accorded respect – however, perhaps more in the media than in the street. For example, witness the media coverage of the British Queen Mother's 100th birthday in 2000.

## Discrimination against homosexuals

Two millennia ago, the Romans were relatively tolerant of all forms of sexual orientation, and even today there is still substantial cross-cultural variability in attitudes towards sexual orientation (Gosselin & Wilson, 1980). It was with the advent of Christianity that social norms regarding sexual behaviour became more restrictive. Homosexuality was considered deviant and immoral, and the persecution of homosexuals became legitimate and acceptable. Prejudice against homosexuals is widespread: for example, an older survey in the United States showed that the majority of people believed that homosexuality was 'sick' and should be outlawed (Levitt & Klassen, 1974), and more recently it was found that only 39 per cent of people 'would see a homosexual doctor' (Henry, 1994). It was only in 1973 that the American Psychiatric Association formally removed homosexuality from its list of mental disorders.

In general, since the late 1960s there has been a progressive liberalisation of attitudes towards homosexuals. However, the AIDS epidemic has, since the mid-1980s, whipped up negative attitudes in some sections of society towards homosexuals (Altman, 1986; Herek & Glunt, 1988; see Box 10.3). Against this background, continued liberalisation often reveals deeply entrenched homophobia in certain sectors of the community.

For example, the Sydney Gay and Lesbian Mardi Gras, the world's largest public celebration of homosexuality, repeatedly provokes fierce public reaction from a number of religious groups – there is solid evidence for a correlation between prejudice and traditional or fundamentalist Christian attitudes (Batson, Schoenrade & Ventis, 1993). Similarly, President Clinton met strong opposition to his proposal in 1993 that homosexuals should be able to enlist in the American armed forces, and in the United States whenever the proposal to grant same-sex couples the right to marry is put forward or is on a state ballot there is a quite grotesque storm of outrage from religious groups across the nation. In California the existing right for same-sex couples to marry was actually overturned in 2008 – an

## Research and applications 10.3
### AIDS and anti-gay prejudice

**Fear surrounding AIDS has been used to justify discrimination against homosexuals**

AIDS is a serious and, as far as is known, fatal illness that develops in people infected with HIV. The virus is transmitted through exchange of certain bodily fluids: for example, through blood transfusions, by needle sharing among intravenous drug users and by some sexual practices among gay men. Although AIDS is by no means a gay disease, the majority of people infected in Western countries have tended to be gay (63 per cent of AIDS cases in the United States up to 1988 were gay – Herek & Glunt, 1988), so people assume a link between AIDS and homosexuality.

Fear and ignorance of AIDS, in conjunction with knowledge of its association with gays, has activated latent prejudices against gays. In many ways, AIDS has provided moral justification (grounded in fear for self and society) for overt discrimination against gay people: homophobics have felt free to come out of the closet. The promotion of gay rights can be seen by such people as tantamount to the promotion of AIDS itself.

Herek and Glunt's (1988, p. 888) discussion of public reaction in the United States to AIDS produced telling evidence for the way AIDS has been linked to homosexuality and used to justify anti-gay attitudes. The epidemic was virtually ignored by the US media in the early 1980s because it was merely a 'story of dead and dying homosexuals', and it was sometimes referred to as the 'gay plague'. Patrick Buchanan, a Republican columnist, wrote (1987, p. 23): 'There is one, only one, cause of the AIDS crisis – the wilful refusal of homosexuals to cease indulging in the immoral, unnatural, unsanitary, unhealthy, and suicidal practice of anal intercourse, which is the primary means by which the AIDS virus is being spread'. He felt (Buchanan, 1987: p. 23) that the 'Democratic Party should be dragged into the court of public opinion as an un-indicted co-conspirator in America's AIDS epidemic [for] seeking to amend state and federal civil rights laws to make sodomy a protected civil right, to put homosexual behaviour, the sexual practice by which AIDS is spread, on the same moral plane with being female or being black.'

The Catholic Church used the apparent link between AIDS and homosexuality to argue against civil rights protection for gay people. Others were more extreme: a mayoral candidate for the city of Houston was heard to joke publicly that his solution to the city's AIDS problem would be to 'shoot the queers' (quoted in Herek & Glunt, 1988, p. 888).

extraordinary situation in which 52 per cent of Californians voted 'yes' on 'Proposition 8', actively denying homosexuals the same rights as heterosexuals.

## Discrimination on the basis of physical or mental handicap

Prejudice and discrimination against the physically handicapped has a long past, in which such people have been considered repugnant and subhuman (Jodelet, 1991). For example, most circuses had a side-show alley in which various 'freaks' would be displayed (powerfully portrayed in Kevin Brownlow's movie *Freaks*), and many dramas hinge on the curiosity value of the physically handicapped (e.g. David Lynch's movie *Elephant Man*, Fellini's *Satyricon* and Victor Hugo's *Notre-Dame de Paris*).

Overt discrimination against people on the basis of physical handicap is now illegal and socially unacceptable in most Western societies. Many countries go out of their way to be sensitive to the special requirements of people with various physical disabilities: for example, the provision of ramps for people in wheelchairs, and audible signals at pedestrian crossings. The staging of the Paralympics every four years is another step in the normalisation of physical handicap. People generally no longer derogate the physically handicapped, but often they are uneasy in their presence and uncertain about how to interact with them (Heinemann, 1990) – an instance of intergroup anxiety (e.g. Stephan & Stephan, 1985; see Chapter 11). This can unintentionally produce patronising attitudes, speech and behaviour that serve to emphasise and perpetuate handicap (Fox & Giles, 1996a, 1996b; see also Chapter 15).

The improvement of attitudes over the past twenty-five years towards physical handicap has not extended to mental/psychological handicap. In medieval times, women with schizophrenia were labelled witches and burned at the stake; Hitler's 'Final Solution' applied not only to the Jews but also to the insane; and in Stalin's Soviet Union, dissidents were labelled 'insane' in order to justify their incarceration. Although the Hospital of St Mary of Bethlehem (popularly corrupted to Bedlam) in London has long been closed, similar conditions may prevail in asylums around the world: instances have been exposed in, for example, Greece and Romania. These are extreme cases, but ignorance and fear fuel strong prejudices, and both institutionalised and face-to-face discrimination still prevail.

Western societies prefer to overlook the existence of mental illness and to abdicate responsibility for the mentally ill. This is reflected in remarkably low funding for research into most mental illnesses and poor resourcing for the care and therapy of psychiatric patients. Since the early 1980s there has been a policy in, for example, Britain and the United States to 'deinstitutionalise' chronic psychiatric patients and simply to release them on to the streets: that is, to release them from hospital without providing adequate alternative community resources for their support.

Another facet of prejudice against the mentally ill is the use of the 'mad' label to dehumanise and justify discrimination against minority-status groups as a whole. 'Different' becomes 'mad' (Szasz, 1970). This is the serious side of what we regularly do in jest – 'You must be mad!' is a frequent exclamation on hearing someone outline a novel (read 'different') scheme. Research from the 1960s and 1970s indicates that the stereotypical behaviour of women did not conform to what people considered to be the behaviour of a typical, well-adjusted, adult human being (Broverman et al., 1970) – in this sense, women were 'maladjusted' (Chesler, 1972; Eichler, 1980). A similar process, in which cultural difference is pathologised by the dominant White middle-class group, occurs with respect to Blacks and other racial/ethnic minorities (Nahem, 1980; Waxman, 1977).

There is a further twist to the story. Prejudice often creates brutal conditions of existence (poverty, poor health, low self-esteem, violence, etc.), which may produce certain types of psychiatric disorder in minority groups. In this way, fear and ignorance about psychiatric illness dovetails with and may amplify ethnic or racial prejudices.

# Forms of discrimination

The preceding discussion deals with some general targets of prejudice, and in so doing it inevitably speaks about different forms that discrimination may take. One important point to emerge is that a great deal of prejudice is expressed in subtle and often hidden ways – crude overt discrimination is now less common. We have already described modern forms of prejudice. Here we say a bit more about three types of behaviour that do not look obviously like discrimination but nevertheless may conceal underlying prejudices: reluctance to help, tokenism and reverse discrimination.

## Reluctance to help

Reluctance to help other groups to improve their position in society, by passively or actively failing to assist their efforts, is one way to make sure they remain disadvantaged. This strategy can be adopted by individuals (landlords may be reluctant to rent accommodation to ethnic minorities), organisations (organisations are reluctant to provide new mothers with flexible working hours or opportunities for job sharing), or society as a whole (until recently, government resistance to legislate in favour of adequate maternity leave provisions).

Reluctance to help can also be a hallmark of aversive racism (see above) – the combination of racial anxiety and antipathy, coupled with a belief that the magnitude of disadvantage is overstated, encourages people not to offer help. Studies show that reluctance to help is manifested only in certain conditions: specifically, when such reluctance can be attributed to some factor other than prejudice. Gaertner and Dovidio's (1977) experiment, described earlier in this chapter, is an illustration of reluctance to help. White participants were more reluctant to help a Black than a White confederate faced with an emergency, but only when they believed that other potential helpers were present.

## Tokenism

**Tokenism**
Practice of publicly making small concessions to a minority group in order to deflect accusations of prejudice and discrimination.

**Tokenism** refers to a relatively small or trivial positive act, a token, towards members of a minority group. The action is then invoked to deflect accusations of prejudice and as a justification for declining to engage in larger and more meaningful positive acts or for subsequently engaging in discrimination ('Don't bother me, haven't I already done enough?'). For example, studies by Dutton and Lake (1973) and Rosenfield and colleagues (Rosenfield, Greenberg, Folger & Borys, 1982) found that White participants who had performed a small favour for a Black stranger were subsequently less willing to engage in more effortful forms of helping than were those who had not performed the small favour. This effect was accentuated when the token action (the small favour) activated negative stereotypes about Blacks: for example, when the favour involved giving money to a Black panhandler (beggar). (Do you think Tom has a problem? See the first focus question.)

Tokenism can be employed by organisations and society in general. In the United States, there has been criticism of the token employment of minorities (e.g. African Americans, Latinos) by organisations that then fail to take more fundamental and important steps towards equal opportunities. Such organisations may employ minorities as tokens to help deflect accusations of prejudice. Tokenism at this level can have damaging consequences for the self-esteem of those who are employed as token minorities (Chacko, 1982; see below).

Tokenism can also be considered in a very straightforward numerical sense. For example, Kanter (1977) considered a minority to be a token when its numerical representation in a group was very small. Wright has built on this to focus on the nature of the barriers a minority may confront to enter a majority group, defining tokenism as 'any intergroup context in which the boundaries between the advantaged and disadvantaged groups are not

**Tokenism**
She is content for now, but she may be less so if she learned that she was hired merely to fill a gender quota

entirely closed, but where there exists severe restrictions on access to advantaged positions on the basis of group membership' (Wright, 2001, p. 224).

## Reverse discrimination

A more extreme form of tokenism is **reverse discrimination**. People with residual prejudiced attitudes may sometimes go out of their way to favour members of a group against which they are prejudiced more than members of other groups. For example, Chidester (1986) had White students engage in a 'get acquainted' conversation through audio equipment with another student, who was ostensibly either Black or White. The White students systematically evaluated Black strangers more favourably than White strangers. Similar findings emerged from the Dutton and Lake (1973) study cited above. (Relate these results to the first focus question.)

Because reverse discrimination favours a minority group member, it can have beneficial effects in the short term. In the long run, however, it may have some harmful consequences for its recipients (Fajardo, 1985; see below), and there is no evidence that reverse discrimination reduces the deep-seated prejudices of the discriminator. Reverse discrimination is an effective way to conceal prejudices, but it can also reflect ambivalence, the desire to appear egalitarian, or genuine feelings of admiration and respect (Carver, Glass & Katz, 1977; Gaertner & Dovidio, 1986).

For the researcher, the challenge is to know when behaviour that goes out of its way to favour a minority is reverse discrimination or is actually a genuine attempt to rectify disadvantage (e.g. affirmative action – see the second focus question).

**Reverse discrimination**
The practice of publicly being prejudiced in favour of a minority group in order to deflect accusations of prejudice and discrimination against that group.

## Stigma and other effects of prejudice

The effects of prejudice on the victims of prejudice are diverse, ranging from relatively minor inconvenience to enormous suffering. In general, prejudice is harmful because it stigmatises groups and the people who belong to those groups (Crocker, Major & Steele,

1998; Goffman, 1963; Swim & Stangor, 1998). Allport (1954b) identified more than fifteen possible consequences of being a victim of prejudice. Let us examine some of these.

## Social stigma

**Stigma**
Group attributes that mediate a negative social evaluation of people belonging to the group.

Crocker and her associates define **stigma** as follows: 'Stigmatised individuals possess (or are believed to possess) some attribute, or characteristic, that conveys a social identity that is devalued in a particular social context' (Crocker, Major & Steele, 1998, p. 505). The targets of prejudice and discrimination are members of stigmatised groups; thus they are stigmatised individuals. The subjective experience of stigma hinges on two factors: visibility/concealability and controllability.

Visible stigmas, such as race, gender and obesity, mean that people cannot easily avoid being the target of stereotypes and discrimination – being a member of a visibly stigmatised group makes the experience of prejudice inescapable (Steele & Aronson, 1995). Visibly stigmatised people cannot use concealment of the stigma to cope with the stereotypes, prejudice and harassment that the stigma may trigger. Concealable stigmas, such as homosexuality, some illnesses, and some ideologies and religious affiliations, allow people to avoid the experience of prejudice. However, the cost of concealment can be high (Goffman, 1963). People have to be untrue to themselves, and super-vigilant to ensure their stigma does not surface inadvertently.

Controllable stigmas are those that people believe are chosen rather than assigned: for example, obesity, smoking and homosexuality are thought to be controllable – people are responsible for having chosen to be these things. Uncontrollable stigmas are those that people have little choice in possessing: for example, race, sex and some illnesses. Controllable stigmas invite much harsher reactions and more extreme discrimination than uncontrollable stigmas. For example, Crandall (1994) has shown that the reason why 'fat' people attract such negative reactions in contemporary Western cultures is not only that obesity is highly stigmatised but also that people believe it is controllable.

People who believe they have a controllable stigma tend to try hard to escape the stigma. As with concealability, this can have a high cost. Many stigmas that people believe are controllable are actually not controllable or are extremely difficult to control (in some cases, obesity falls into this category). Attempts to control the stigma are largely futile, and people can experience profound feelings of failure and inadequacy in addition to the negativity of the stigma itself. However, some people do focus their energy on re-evaluating the stigma and on fighting prejudice and discrimination against their group (Crocker & Major, 1994).

Stigma persists for a number of obvious reasons (see Crocker, Major & Steele, 1998). Individuals and groups gain a relatively positive sense of self and social identity if they compare themselves or their group with other individuals or groups that are stigmatised – there is a self-evaluative advantage in having stigmatised outgroups as downward comparison targets (Hogg, 2000b). Stigma can legitimise inequalities of status and resource distribution that favour a dominant group; such groups are certainly going to ensure that the stigma remains in place, because it serves a system justification function – it justifies the status quo (Jost & Banaji, 1994; Jost & Kramer, 2002). People may need to stigmatise groups that have different world views from their own, because if they did not degrade and discredit outgroups in this way then the frail sense of certainty in, and controllability over, life that they gain from their own world view would be shattered (Solomon, Greenberg & Pyszczynski, 1991).

Finally, Kurzban and Leary (2001) provide an evolutionary account of stigma. They argue that the stigmatisation is the outcome of an adaptive cognitive process designed to help us avoid poor social exchange partners who may threaten our access to resource or who, by virtue of being different, may carry communicable pathogens.

## Self-worth, self-esteem and psychological well-being

Stigmatised groups are, by definition, devalued in and by society. They are groups that have relatively low status and little power in society, and they find it difficult to avoid society's consensual negative image of them. For example, African Americans over the age of 14 are aware that others have negative images of them (Rosenberg, 1979), as are Mexican Americans (Casas, Ponterotto & Sweeney, 1987), homosexuals (D'Emilio, 1983) and many women (Crosby, 1982). Members of stigmatised groups tend to internalise these evaluations and can form an unfavourable self-image that can be manifested in relevant contexts as low **self-esteem**. For example, research reveals that women generally share men's negative stereotypes of women, often evaluate themselves in terms of such stereotypes and, under circumstances where sex is the salient basis of self-perception, actually report a reduction in self-esteem (e.g. Hogg, 1985; Hogg & Turner, 1987b; Smith, 1985).

**Self-esteem**
Feelings about and evaluations of oneself.

However, groups and their members are ingenious in finding ways to combat low status and consensual low regard, so depressed self-esteem is by no means an inevitable consequence of prejudice (e.g. Dion & Earn, 1975; Dion, Earn & Yee, 1978; Tajfel & Turner, 1979; see also Chapter 11). Although some stigmatised individuals are vulnerable to low self-esteem, diminished life satisfaction and in some cases depression, most members of stigmatised groups are able to weather the assaults and maintain a positive self-image (Crocker & Major, 1989, 1994; Crocker, Major & Steele, 1998).

On a day-to-day basis, self-esteem can be assailed by prejudice. The experience can range from crude racial epithets and blatant physical attack to slights such as being ignored by a salesperson in a store or being served last in a bar. Cose (1993) describes the case of an African American partner in a law firm being denied access to his office because a young White lawyer who did not know him assumed that because he was Black he was engaged in criminal activity.

There is, however, evidence that more subtle forms of prejudice can also damage self-esteem. For example, Chacko (1982) asked women managers to rate the extent to which a number of factors (their ability, experience, education or sex) had influenced their being hired for the job. They also indicated their commitment to the organisation and their satisfaction with various aspects of the job. Those who felt that they had been hired only as token women reported less organisational commitment and job satisfaction than those who felt that they had been hired on the basis of their ability (see Figure 10.7). This is one way in which tokenism can have negative consequences.

Reverse discrimination can also affect self-esteem. Fajardo (1985) had White teachers grade essays that were designed to be poor, average or excellent in quality and were attributed to either a Black or a White student. The teachers evaluated identical essays more favourably when they were attributed to Black students than to White students (see Figure 10.8). Moreover, the reverse discrimination effect was more marked for average-quality essays. In the short run, this practice may furnish minority students with self-confidence. In the long run, however, some students will develop unrealistic opinions of their abilities and future prospects, resulting in severe damage to self-esteem when such hopes collide with reality.

Reverse discrimination may also prevent students seeking the help they sometimes need early in their academic careers, with the consequence perhaps of contributing to educational disadvantage. Relatedly, the policy of affirmative action can have the unintended effect of provoking negative reaction from members of traditionally advantaged groups. They may experience a sense of injustice and relative deprivation (see Chapter 11), which provokes behaviour designed to re-establish equity (see Chapter 12) or reassert the superior status of their group. This can impact on minorities in ways that eventually affect their self-esteem.

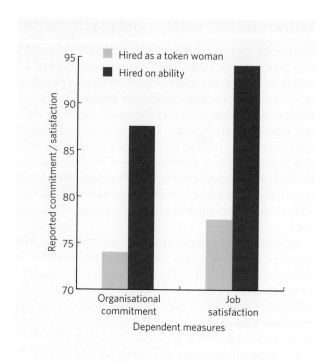

**Figure 10.7** Organisational commitment and job satisfaction as a function of perceived basis of being hired

A pitfall of tokenism. Women managers who felt they had been hired as a token woman reported less organisational commitment and less job satisfaction than women who felt they had been hired because of their ability

*Source:* based on data from Chacko (1982)

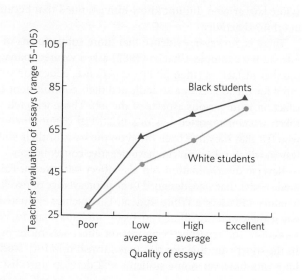

**Figure 10.8** White teachers' evaluations of student essays of varying quality as a function of student race

White teachers evaluated Black students' essays more favourably than White students' essays, particularly where the essays were of average, rather than poor or excellent, quality. An unintended consequence of reverse discrimination such as this is that Black students would be less likely to seek or be given guidance to improve their actually very average performance

*Source:* based on data from Fajardo (1985)

**Stereotype threat**

Feeling that we will be judged and treated in terms of negative stereotypes of our group, and that we will inadvertently confirm these stereotypes through our behaviour.

## Stereotype threat

Because stigmatised groups know exactly the negative stereotypes that others have of them, they experience what Steele and Aronson (1995; Steele, Spencer & Aronson, 2002) have called **stereotype threat**. Stigmatised individuals are aware that others may judge and treat them stereotypically, and thus, on tasks that really matter to them, they worry that through their behaviour they may confirm the stereotypes – that their behaviour will become a self-fulfilling prophecy (see below). These concerns not only increase anxiety but can also impair task performance. For example, an academically ambitious West Indian Briton, aware of stereotypes of intellectual inferiority, may be extremely anxious when answering a question in class – she would be worried that the slightest mistake would be interpreted stereotypically. This anxiety may actually impact adversely on behaviour. According to Steele, Spencer and Aronson (2002), stereotype threat is greatest when there are cues that the context is dominated by a cultural world view that differs from that of our own group.

To test the stereotype threat hypothesis, Steele and Aronson had Black and White students anticipate taking a 'very difficult' test that was defined as being 'diagnostic of intellectual ability' or as 'just a laboratory exercise'. They then completed a number of measures designed to assess awareness of racial stereotypes: for example, they completed ambiguous sentence fragments such as _____CE or _____ERIOR. As predicted, Black students who were anticipating a difficult test that was diagnostic of intellectual ability were more likely than other participants to complete the fragments with race-related words (e.g. race, inferior). Steele and Aronson also found that Black students actually performed worse on these tests than White students of equivalent scholastic aptitude.

Stereotype threat has now been found in many different contexts (see the summary by Wright & Taylor, 2003): for example, women and mathematics, low socioeconomic status and intelligence, the elderly and memory, women and negotiation skills, and Black and White men and athletic performance. On intriguing study by Goff, Steele and Davies (2008) found that stereotype threat even caused people in interracial encounters to position themselves further apart from one another.

There is also some evidence for the opposite of stereotype threat, called *stereotype lift*, among members of groups that attract favourable societal stereotypes (Walton & Cohen, 2003). One way of coping with stereotype threat is *domain disidentification* – that is, reducing the degree to which our identity is tied to the performance that may attract negative feedback (e.g. Major & Schmader, 1998).

## Failure and disadvantage

The victims of prejudice belong to groups that are denied access to those resources that society makes available for people to thrive and succeed, such as good education, health, housing and employment. Discrimination thus creates clearly visible evidence of real disadvantage and of manifest failure to achieve society's high standards. This sense of failure can be internalised by victims of prejudice so that they become chronically apathetic and un-motivated: they simply give up trying because of the obvious impossibility of succeeding.

There is some evidence that in certain circumstances women tend to anticipate failure more than men and thus tend to lose motivation (e.g. Smith, 1985). As we saw earlier, when they do succeed they may attribute their success externally to factors such as luck or the ease of the task.

In Chapter 11, we discuss deprivation and disadvantage more fully. One observation that needs to be made is that, although stigmatised groups are clearly disadvantaged, members of those groups often deny any personal experience of discrimination. For example, Crosby (1982) found that employed women who were discriminated against with respect to pay rarely indicated that they had personally experienced any sex discrimination. The denial of personal discrimination was remarkably high (e.g. Crosby, 1984; Crosby, Cordova & Jaskar, 1993; Crosby et al., 1989) and has been found among members of other stigmatised groups (Guimond & Dubé-Simard, 1983; Major, 1994; Taylor, Wright & Porter, 1994).

## Attributional ambiguity

Attribution processes can impact on stigmatised people in a rather unusual way, via attributional ambiguity. Stigmatised individuals are very sensitive to the causes of others' treatment of them (Crocker & Major, 1989). Did she fail to serve me at the bar because I am Black, or simply because someone else shouted louder? Did she serve me ahead of all others because I am Black and she is trying to conceal her racism? Was I promoted quickly to comply with an affirmative action policy or because of my intrinsic ability? Attributional ambiguity can quite obviously lead to suspicion and mistrust in relationships.

Attributional ambiguity also does no favours to stigmatised individuals' self-esteem. Stigmatised people often fail to take personal credit for positive outcomes – they attribute them to affirmative action, tokenism or reverse discrimination. Stigmatised individuals may also under-attribute negative reactions from others to prejudice. For example, Ruggiero and Taylor (1995) had women receive negative evaluations from a male evaluator. The likelihood that the evaluator was prejudiced was varied experimentally. The women attributed the negative evaluation to prejudice only when the evaluator was almost 100 per cent likely to be prejudiced. Otherwise, they attributed all of the more ambiguous evaluations to the inadequacy of their own work.

## Self-fulfilling prophecies

**Self-fulfilling prophecy**
Expectations and assumptions about a person that influence our interaction with that person and eventually change their behaviour in line with our expectations.

Prejudiced attitudes covertly or overtly produce discriminatory behaviour, which cumulatively, across time and individuals, creates disadvantage. In this way, a stereotypical belief can create a material reality that confirms the belief: it is a **self-fulfilling prophecy** (see reviews by Jussim & Fleming, 1996; Jussim, Eccles & Madon, 1996). For example, Eden (1990) primed platoon leaders in the Israeli Defence Force with high-performance expectations for their platoon. After an eleven-week training programme, platoons with high-expectation leaders outperformed platoons with 'no-expectation' leaders.

The most famous study of self-fulfilling prophecy is Rosenthal and Jacobson's (1968) classic experiment on teachers' expectations in the classroom. Rosenthal and Jacobson

**Self-fulfilling prophecy**
These children differ in personality, race and gender — all factors that can create in their teacher scholastic expectations that may become a reality

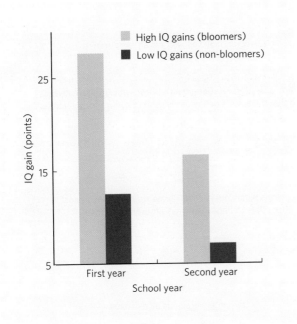

**Figure 10.9**  IQ gain among elementary schoolchildren as a function of teachers' stereotypical expectations

Pygmalion in the classroom. Elementary schoolchildren showed IQ gains over their first and second years at school; however, the gains were much greater for the 'bloomers' – a randomly selected group that the teacher was led to believe had greater IQ potential

*Source*: based on data from Rosenthal & Jacobson (1968)

administered an IQ test to elementary school children and told their teachers that the results of the test would be a reliable predictor of which children would 'bloom' (show rapid intellectual development in the near future). The teachers were given the names of the twenty 'bloomers'; in fact, the twenty names were chosen randomly by the researchers, and there were no IQ differences between bloomers and non-bloomers. Very quickly, the teachers rated the non-bloomers as being less curious, less interested and less happy than the bloomers: that is, the teachers developed stereotypical expectations about the two groups. Grades for work were consistent with these expectations.

Rosenthal and Jacobson measured the children's IQ at the end of the first year, and at the start and end of the second year. They found that in both years the bloomers showed a significantly greater IQ gain than the non-bloomers (see Figure 10.9). Sceptics simply did not believe this, so Rosenthal and Rubin (1978) conducted a **meta-analysis** of 345 follow-up studies to prove that the phenomenon really exists.

Another classic study of self-fulfilling prophecy was conducted by Word, Zanna and Cooper (1974). In a first experiment, White participants, acting as job interviewers, interviewed Black and White applicants. They were found to treat the Black and White applicants very differently – more speech errors (e.g. poor grammar, imprecision, disrupted fluency), shorter interviews and less non-verbal engagement with the Blacks than with the Whites. In a second experiment, another set of White participants was trained to use either the Black or the White interview style obtained in the first experiment to interview a White job applicant. Interviewers who used the Black interview style subsequently considered that the White applicant had performed less well and was more nervous than did those interviewers who used the White interview style.

The process whereby beliefs create reality has been researched systematically by Snyder and his colleagues (Snyder, 1981, 1984). One paradigm they have used involves creating an expectation in the observer that someone he is going to meet ('the actor') has an extrovert personality. The consequences for both the observer's and the actor's beliefs and behaviour are carefully tracked through the entire interaction process to an end point, where the actor's behaviour and self-perception conform to the initial expectation (see Figure 10.10).

**Meta-analysis**
Statistical procedure that combines data from different studies to measure the overall reliability and strength of specific effects.

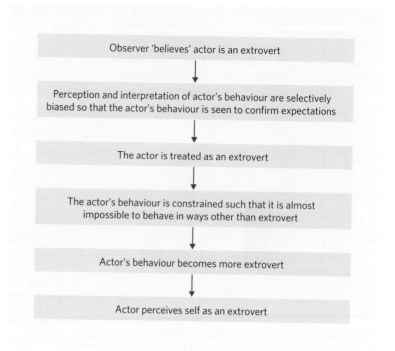

**Figure 10.10** A sequence of steps through which beliefs may ultimately create reality

*Source:* based on data in Snyder (1981, 1984)

According to Jussim and Fleming's (1996) review, there is good evidence for the creation of behavioural confirmation of stereotypical expectations based on gender, limited evidence in the case of race and ethnicity, and no evidence for socioeconomic status.

Social psychological research on self-fulfilling prophecy has focused almost exclusively on dyadic influence. Under these circumstances, expectations do create reality, but the overall effect is small: only about 4 per cent of someone's behaviour is affected by another's expectations. Jussim and associates reviewed the relevant literature (Jussim & Fleming, 1996; Jussim, Eccles, & Madon, 1996) and concluded that, although 4 per cent may appear small, it is quite significant if you consider self-fulfilling prophecy effects in the real world of intergroup relations. In natural dyadic interactions, people may be more inclined to perceive others in terms of personality rather than social stereotypes. In intergroup contexts, however, stereotypes and group perceptions come into play, the stereotypes match reality to some degree (stereotypes are not entirely arbitrary), and the actor encounters stereotypical expectations over and over again from many different outgroup members in a variety of social contexts. The 4 per cent will probably be greatly magnified.

Stereotype threat (Steele, Spencer & Aronson, 2002; see above) may also contribute to a self-fulfilling prophecy. Indeed, research into race-related academic underachievement in the United States invokes stereotype threat as a contributing factor. Black students are continually anxious about stereotypical interpretation of their academic failures. Cumulatively, this produces enormous anxiety and can encourage Black students to reduce their efforts, to have lower academic ambitions and ultimately to drop out of school altogether. A similar stereotype threat analysis has been used in the United States for women's underachievement and underrepresentation in mathematics and science.

## Dehumanisation, violence and genocide

Much of the emphasis of this chapter has been on indirect or subtle forms of prejudice and their effects. This reflects relatively accurately the state of affairs in most Western democracies, where anti-discrimination legislation is in place. For example, there is a lively campaign to purge language of racist and sexist terminology. However, it is important not to lose sight of the extremes of prejudiced behaviour. Prejudiced attitudes tend to have common themes: the targets of prejudice are, for example, considered to be dirty, stupid, insensitive, repulsive, aggressive and psychologically unstable (Brigham, 1971; Katz & Braly, 1933). This is a constellation that evaluates others as relatively worthless human beings who do not need or deserve to be treated with consideration, courtesy and respect. Together with fear and hatred, this is a potent mix. It dehumanises other people (Haslam, 2006), and given certain social circumstances it can permit individual violence, mass aggression or even systematic extermination.

Dehumanisation, first explored scientifically by Kelman (1976), is a process through which people are denied membership in a community of interconnected individuals and are thus cast outside the 'moral circle', to a place where the rights and considerations attached to being human no longer apply (Opotow, 1990). Dehumanisation denies people *human uniqueness* and *human nature* (Haslam, 2006; Haslam, Loughnan, & Kashima, 2008).

Human uniqueness refers to attributes that distinguish humans from other animals, such as refinement, civility, morality and higher cognition. When people are denied human uniqueness they are implicitly likened to animals, and seen as childlike, immature, coarse, irrational or backward. Human nature refers to attributes that are seen as shared and fundamental features of humanity, such as emotionality, agency, warmth and cognitive flexibility. When people are denied human nature attributes they are explicitly or implicitly likened to objects or machines and seen as cold, rigid, inert, and lacking emotion and agency.

Overall dehumanisation is associated with infrahumanisation – a tendency to internally attribute sophisticated, uniquely human, secondary and higher emotions more to ingroup members than outgroup members, and thus view outgroups as less human and more infrahuman (animal-like) than ingroups (e.g. Cortes, Demoulin, Rodriguez, Rodriguez, & Leyens, 2005; Leyens, Demoulin, Vaes, Gaunt, & Paladino, 2007; Leyens, Rodriguez-Perez, Rodriguez-Torres, Gaunt, Paladino, Vaes, et al., 2001).

In the absence of explicit institutional or legislative support, dehumanisation usually sponsors individual acts of violence. For example, in Britain there are attacks on Asian immigrants, in the United States the Ku Klux Klan was notorious for its lynchings of Blacks (see the powerful movie *Mississippi Burning*), in Germany there are Nazi-style attacks on Turkish immigrants, and in India female infanticide is still practised – albeit covertly (Freed & Freed, 1989). The Abu Ghraib prisoner abuse scandal which broke in 2004 is a good example of dehumanisation – some American guards at Abu Ghraib prison just outside Baghdad engaged in appalling acts of degradation of Iraqi prisoners of war, all caught on video.

When prejudice is morally accepted and legally endorsed in a society, then systematic acts of mass discrimination can be perpetrated. This can take the form of systems of apartheid, in which target groups are isolated from the rest of the community. South Africa from 1948 to 1994 is probably the best known recent example of this, but a similar system of segregation was practised in educational contexts in the United States until the mid-1950s, and the existence of reservations for native peoples in 'new world' countries, such as Australia and the United States, may also attest to a form of segregation. Apartheid and segregation often come equipped with a formidable array of social justifications in terms of benefits for the segregated group (see the third focus question).

The most extreme form of legitimised prejudice is genocide (Staub, 1989), where the target group is systematically exterminated. The dehumanisation process makes it relatively easy for people to perpetrate the most appalling acts of degradation and violence on others (see Thomas Keneally's biographical novel *Schindler's Ark* (1982), or the movie *The Killing Fields*). For example, Stalin targeted anyone he felt was plotting against him and, until his death in 1953, exiled 40 million people to brutal and dehumanising labour camps in Siberia (the Gulags); 15 million people died. The most chilling and best-documented instance of highly targeted genocide is the Holocaust of the early 1940s, in which six million Jews were systematically exterminated by the Nazis in death camps in central Europe. At the massive Auschwitz–Birkenau complex in Poland, two million Jews were gassed between January 1942 and the summer of 1944 (a rate of 2,220 men, women and children each day).

There are more recent examples of genocide: Pol Pot's 'killing fields' in Cambodia in the 1970s; Saddam Hussein's extermination of Kurds in northern Iraq and Shi'ites in southern Iraq; the Bosnian Serbs' campaign of 'ethnic cleansing' in Bosnia; the mutual genocide practised by the Hutu and Tutsi in Rwanda in 1994; and the recent systematic slaughter of non-Arabs in the western Sudanese region of Darfur.

Genocide can also be practised more indirectly, by creating conditions of massive material disadvantage in which a group effectively exterminates itself through disease, and through suicide and murder based on alcoholism, drug abuse and acute despair. The plight of the Australian Aborigines, Canadian 'Eskimos' and Brazilian Indians falls squarely into this camp. Another form of genocide (although 'ethnic death' is a more appropriate term to distinguish it from the brutality of the Holocaust) is cultural assimilation, in which entire cultural groups may disappear as discrete entities through widespread intermarriage and systematic suppression of their culture and language (e.g. Taft, 1973; see Chapter 15). This may be particularly prevalent if societies do not practise some form of multiculturalism (e.g. England's past treatment of the Welsh and the Scottish, China's treatment of the people of Tibet, and Japan's stance towards Filipinos living in Japan). Another form of ethnic death occurs when a group is excluded from the official history of a nation. Pilger (1989) notes that this was the case for Australian Aborigines.

# Explanations of prejudice and discrimination

Why are people prejudiced? Not surprisingly, theories of prejudice have tended to focus on more extreme forms of prejudice, in particular the aggression and violence discussed above. At the beginning of the twentieth century, it was popular to consider prejudice to be an innate and instinctive reaction to certain categories of person (e.g. certain races), much as animals would react in instinctive ways to one another (Klineberg, 1940). This sort of approach is no longer popular, as it does not stand up well to scientific scrutiny. However, there may be an innate *component* to prejudice. There is some evidence that higher animals, including humans, have an inherent fear of the unfamiliar and unusual (Hebb & Thompson, 1968), which might set the mould for negative attitudes towards groups that are considered different in certain ways.

**Mere exposure effect**
Repeated exposure to an object results in greater attraction to that object.

There is also evidence for a **mere exposure effect** (Zajonc, 1968), in which people's attitudes towards various stimuli (e.g. other people) improve as a direct function of repeated exposure or familiarity with the stimulus, provided that initial reactions to the stimuli are not negative (Perlman & Oskamp, 1971).

Another perspective rests on the belief that prejudices are learned. Indeed, Tajfel (1981b) argues that hatred and suspicion of certain groups is learned early in life, before the child even knows anything about the target group, and that this provides an emotional framework that colours all subsequent information about, and experience with, the group (see Brown, 1995; Durkin, 1995; Milner, 1996). For example, Barrett and Short (1992) found that 5- to 10-year-old English children had little factual knowledge about other European countries, yet they expressed clear preferences; French and Spanish were liked most, followed by Italians, and Germans were liked least. Generally speaking, ethnic biases are very marked among 4- to 5-year-olds because at that age the sociocognitive system is reliant on obvious perceptual features that are unambiguous bases for categorisation and social comparison (Aboud, 1988). However, Rutland (1999) found that national and ethnic stereotypes did not crystallise until a little later, after the age of 10. In any case, these emotional preferences provide a potent framework for acquisition of parental attitudes and behaviour (Goodman, 1964; Katz, 1976; see Chapter 5).

The transmission of parental prejudices can occur through parental modelling (e.g. the child witnesses parental expressions of racial hatred), instrumental/operant conditioning (e.g. parental approval for racist behaviour and disapproval for non-racist behaviour) and classical conditioning (e.g. a White child receives a severe parental scolding for playing with an Asian child).

Below we discuss some major theories of prejudice. These approaches focus largely on prejudice as the mass expression of aggression against certain groups. In Chapter 11, we continue with the theme of prejudice, but in a different guise – one that considers prejudice to be a form of intergroup behaviour based on social psychological processes associated with the categorisation of people into social categories.

## Frustration–aggression

The rise of anti-Semitism in Europe, particularly Germany, during the 1930s placed the explanation of prejudice high on social psychology's agenda. In 1939, Dollard and colleagues published their **frustration–aggression hypothesis**, in which they argued that 'the occurrence of aggressive behaviour always presupposes the existence of frustration, and contrariwise, the existence of frustration always leads to some form of aggression' (Dollard, Doob, Miller, Mowrer, & Sears, 1939, p. 1). The theory was grounded in the psychodynamic assumption that a fixed amount of psychic energy is available for the human mind to perform psychological activities, and that the completion of a psychological activity is *cathartic*: that is, it dissipates aroused energy and returns the system to psychological equilibrium.

Dollard and associates argued that personal goals entail arousal of psychic energy for their achievement, and that goal achievement is cathartic. However, if goal achievement is impeded (i.e. frustrated), psychic energy remains activated, and the system is in a state of psychological disequilibrium that can be corrected only by aggression. In other words, frustration produces an 'instigation to aggress', and the only way to achieve catharsis is through aggression.

The target of aggression is usually the perceived agent of frustration, but in many cases the agent of frustration is amorphous (e.g. a bureaucracy), indeterminate (the economy), too powerful (someone very big and strong wielding a weapon), unavailable (a specific individual bureaucrat), or someone you love (a parent). These, and many other circumstances, prevent or inhibit aggression against the perceived source of frustration and cause the entire amount of frustration-induced aggression to be *displaced* on to an alternative target (a person or an inanimate object) that can be legitimately aggressed against without fear. In other words, a **scapegoat** is found.

Although this theory has been applied extensively, and relatively successfully, to the study of interpersonal aggression (see Chapter 12), Dollard and associates' principal aim was to explain intergroup aggression – specifically, the violence and aggression associated with prejudice. If a large number of people (a group) is frustrated in its goals by another group that is too powerful or too remote to be aggressed against, the aggression is displaced on to a weaker group, which functions as a scapegoat. Figure 10.11 shows how the frustration–aggression hypothesis could be used to explain the rise of anti-Semitism in Germany in the 1920s and 1930s.

An archival study by Hovland and Sears (1940) provides some support for this sort of analysis. They correlated an economic index of frustrated ambitions (the price of cotton)

**Frustration–aggression hypothesis**
Theory that all frustration leads to aggression, and all aggression comes from frustration. Used to explain prejudice and intergroup aggression.

**Scapegoat**
Individual or group that becomes the target for anger and frustration caused by a different individual or group or some other set of circumstances.

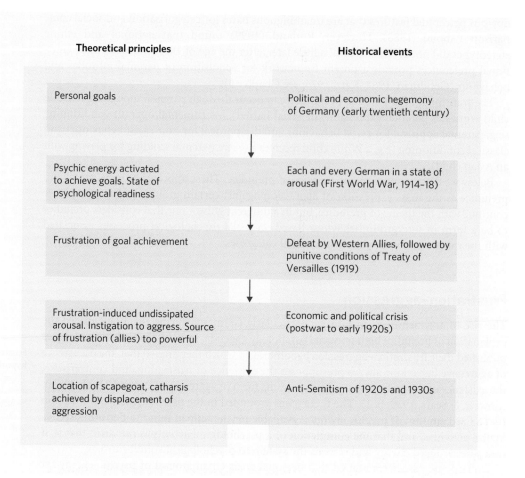

| Theoretical principles | Historical events |
|---|---|
| Personal goals | Political and economic hegemony of Germany (early twentieth century) |
| Psychic energy activated to achieve goals. State of psychological readiness | Each and every German in a state of arousal (First World War, 1914–18) |
| Frustration of goal achievement | Defeat by Western Allies, followed by punitive conditions of Treaty of Versailles (1919) |
| Frustration-induced undissipated arousal. Instigation to aggress. Source of frustration (allies) too powerful | Economic and political crisis (postwar to early 1920s) |
| Location of scapegoat, catharsis achieved by displacement of aggression | Anti-Semitism of 1920s and 1930s |

**Figure 10.11** The frustration–aggression hypothesis account of the rise of anti-Semitism in Germany in the 1920s and 1930s

The sequence of principles in the frustration–aggression hypothesis is mirrored in the way events unfolded in Germany, before and after the First World War, that led to blatant anti-Semitism

---

with an index of racial aggression (number of lynchings of Blacks) in the southern United States over a fifty-year period. The two indices were negatively correlated: as the price of cotton fell (frustration), the number of lynchings increased (displaced aggression).

**Displacement**
Psychodynamic concept referring to the transfer of negative feelings on to an individual or group other than that which originally caused the negative feelings.

Much research on intergroup aggression has focused on the notion of **displacement**, which lies at the heart of Dollard and associates' account of scapegoating and thus prejudice and intergroup aggression. In one study (Miller & Bugelski, 1948), young men at a summer camp eagerly anticipated a night on the town but had their goals frustrated by the camp authorities, which announced that they would have to stay behind to perform some boring and difficult tests. Relative to a control group that was not frustrated in this way, the young men's stereotypical attitudes towards two minority groups were found to deteriorate as a consequence of the frustration.

Other research is inconclusive (see Baumeister, Dale & Sommer, 1998). For example, the frustration of doing badly on a test or experimental task has been shown to increase racial prejudice (Cowen, Landes & Schaet, 1958), reduce prejudice (Burnstein & McRae, 1962) or leave prejudice unaffected (Stagner & Congdon, 1955), and there is no systematic evidence for an inverse correlation between international and intranational aggression (i.e. aggression displaced on to another nation is not available to be vented intranationally) (Tanter, 1966, 1969).

In some of this research, it is difficult to know whether aggression is displaced (i.e. the entire quantity of aggression is vented on a specific scapegoat) or generalised (i.e. anger towards the agent of frustration spills over on to irrelevant other stimuli). For example, in the Miller and Bugelski (1948) study, the participants also felt angry towards the camp authorities. If both displacement and generalisation are operating, it becomes difficult to predict the target of aggression.

To address this problem, Miller (1948) suggested that displacement and generalisation might work against one another. Thus scapegoats are likely to be not too similar to the real source of frustration (displacement is based on inhibition of aggression against the real source of frustration, and such inhibition will be stronger for targets that are more similar to the real source), but not too dissimilar either (generalisation implies that the magnitude of aggression will decrease as the potential target is less and less similar to the real source). Although it is often possible with the advantage of hindsight to use this principle to account for the scapegoat, it is difficult to predict it with any certainty (e.g. Horowitz, 1973).

The frustration–aggression hypothesis confronts another, major, obstacle from research showing that frustration is neither necessary nor sufficient for aggression. Aggression can occur in the absence of frustration, and frustration does not necessarily result in aggression (Bandura, 1973; Berkowitz, 1962). The consequence is that the frustration–aggression hypothesis can explain only a limited subset of intergroup aggression. Other constructs are needed to explain either other forms of intergroup aggression or prejudice and intergroup aggression as a whole.

In an attempt to rescue the hypothesis, Berkowitz (1962) proposed three major changes:

1   The probability of frustration-induced aggression actually being vented is increased by the presence of situational cues to aggression, including past or present associations of a specific group (scapegoat) with conflict or dislike.

2   It is not objective frustration that instigates aggression but the subjective (cognitive) feeling of being frustrated.

3   Frustration is only one of a large number of aversive events (e.g. pain, extreme temperatures and other noxious stimuli) that can instigate aggression.

This revamped frustration–aggression theory has attracted empirical support for the role of environmental cues and cognitive mediators in controlling the amount and direction of aggression (Berkowitz, 1974; Konečni, 1979). However, its main application has been in the explanation of **collective behaviour** (riots) and **relative deprivation** (both discussed in Chapter 11).

Despite these modifications, the frustration–aggression hypothesis has other limitations as an explanation of mass intergroup aggression and prejudice. The phenomenon to be explained is one in which the attitudes and behaviour of a large number of people are regulated and directed so that there is a great deal of uniformity as well as a clear logic to it. Critics have argued that the frustration–aggression hypothesis does not adequately explain this core feature of prejudice, and that the reason for this is that it is a reductionist approach that arrives at group behaviour by aggregating individual psychological/emotional states in a communication vacuum (Billig, 1976; Brown, 2000; Hogg & Abrams, 1988).

For instance, the group members in this model do not speak to one another and are not exposed to mass communication or history. They are passive victims of individual frustration and anger, rather than active participants in a social process involving construction, internalisation and the enacting of group norms (see Chapter 7). Aggression is only widespread and directed at the same target because a large number of people individually express aggression simultaneously, and coincidentally select the same target.

**Collective behaviour**
The behaviour of people en masse – such as in a crowd, protest or riot.

**Relative deprivation**
A sense of having less than we feel entitled to.

# The authoritarian personality

In their work *The Authoritarian Personality* published in 1950, Theodor Adorno, Else Frenkel-Brunswik (along with Levinson and Sanford) described what they believed to be a personality syndrome that predisposed certain people to be authoritarian. The historical context for the concept of the **authoritarian personality** theory was the role of fascism, an extreme form of right-wing ideology, in the Holocaust – Adorno and Frenkel-Brunswik, who were both Jewish, had fled Hitler's regime in Germany and Austria respectively. The theory proposed that autocratic and punitive child-rearing practices were responsible for the emergence in adulthood of various clusters of beliefs. These included: **ethnocentrism**; an intolerance of Jews, African Americans, and other ethnic and religious minorities; a pessimistic and cynical view of human nature; conservative political and economic attitudes; and a suspicion of democracy. (Apply these ideas to the case of Erasmus in the fourth focus question – and check out photos of the De Punt train hijacking at the Dutch site: http://gaf.zeelandnet.nl/yp408/de_punt.html.)

With the publication of their major work, Adorno reported that he and his group had constructed a questionnaire known as the California F-scale, intended at first to assess tendencies towards fascism, but which turned out to be a purported measure of general authoritarianism.

The results of this early research were encouraging, although Brown (1965) raised several methodological criticisms. Among the most damning were the following:

- The various scales used were scored in such a way that people's tendency to agree with items (**acquiescent response set**) would artificially inflate the correlation between the scales.

**Authoritarian personality**
A syndrome of personality characteristics originating in childhood that predispose individuals to be prejudiced.

**Ethnocentrism**
Evaluative preference for all aspects of our group relative to other groups.

**Acquiescent response set**
Tendency to agree with items in an attitude questionnaire. This leads to an ambiguity in interpretation if a high score on an attitude questionnaire can be obtained only by agreeing with all or most items.

**Power and authority**
Respect for authority figures, deference to authority, and obsession with rank and status

- Because the interviewers knew both the hypotheses and the authoritarianism scores of the interviewees, there was a danger of confirmatory bias (Rosenthal, 1966).

Nevertheless, the authoritarian personality has, over half a century, attracted an enormous amount of interest (e.g. Bray & Noble, 1978; Christie & Jahoda, 1954; Titus & Hollander, 1957; for an overview, see Duckitt, 2000).

However, there are a number of limitations to a personality explanation of prejudice (Billig, 1976; Brown, 1995, 2000; Hogg & Abrams, 1988; Reynolds, Turner, Haslam & Ryan, 2001). Powerful situational and sociocultural factors are underemphasised. For instance, Pettigrew (1958) tested the authoritarian personality theory in a cross-cultural comparison between South Africa and the southern and the northern United States. He found that although Whites from South Africa and the southern United States were significantly more racist than those from the northern United States, they did not differ in terms of how authoritarian their personalities were. Pettigrew concluded from this and other findings that, while personality may predispose some people to be prejudiced in some contexts, a culture of prejudice that embodies societal norms legitimising prejudice is both necessary and sufficient.

This conclusion is supported by other findings. For example, Minard (1952) found that the majority (60 per cent) of White miners in a West Virginian coal-mining community readily shifted from racist to non-racist attitudes and behaviour as a function of situational norms encouraging or inhibiting prejudice, and Stephan and Rosenfield (1978) found that interracial contact was a more important determinant of change in racial attitudes among children than parental background.

Adorno and associates believed that prejudice is laid down in childhood as an enduring personality style. This perspective is particularly troublesome in the light of evidence for sudden and dramatic changes in people's attitudes and behaviour regarding social groups. For example, the extreme anti-Semitism in Germany between the wars arose in a short period of only ten years – far too short a time for a whole generation of German families to adopt new child-rearing practices giving rise to authoritarian and prejudiced children.

Even more dramatic are sudden changes in attitudes and behaviour contingent on single events. There are numerous examples: the Japanese bombing of Pearl Harbor in 1941, the Argentinian occupation of the Falkland Islands in 1982, and of course the 9/11 terrorist attacks in New York and Washington in 2001. Personalities did not have time to change, yet attitudes and behaviour did.

## Dogmatism and closed-mindedness

Another personality theory of prejudice has been proposed by Rokeach (1948, 1960). It is closely related to the authoritarian personality theory, but in the light of evidence that authoritarianism is not restricted to people who are politically and economically right wing (e.g. Tetlock, 1984), it focuses on cognitive style. Rokeach argues for the existence of a more generalised syndrome of intolerance, called **dogmatism** or closed-mindedness. It is characterised by isolation of contradictory belief systems from one another, resistance to belief change in the light of new information, and appeals to authority to justify the correctness of existing beliefs. Scales devised by Rokeach (1960) to measure these personality styles have good reliability, correlate well with measures of authoritarianism and have been used extensively.

**Dogmatism**
Cognitive style that is rigid and intolerant and predisposes people to be prejudiced.

However, the concept of dogmatism as an explanation of prejudice has the same limitations as the authoritarian personality theory. It is a concept that reduces a group phenomenon to an aggregation of individual personality predispositions and largely overlooks the wider sociocultural context of prejudice and the role of group norms (Billig, 1976; Billig & Cochrane, 1979).

## Right-wing authoritarianism

Recently, the idea of authoritarianism has been revived but without the psychodynamic and personality aspect. Altemeyer (e.g. 1988, 1994, 1998; see also Duckitt, 1989; Duckitt, Wagner, du Plessis & Birum, 2002) has approached authoritarianism as a collection of attitudes, with three components:

1 *conventionalism* – adherence to societal conventions that are endorsed by established authorities;

2 *authoritarian aggression* – support for aggression towards social deviants; and

3 *authoritarian submission* – submission to society's established authorities.

Altemeyer (1981) devised the Right-Wing Authoritarianism (RWA) scale to measure this constellation of attitudinal factors. From this perspective, authoritarianism is an ideology that varies from person to person. It is an ideology that suggests positions of power within a social hierarchy come from correct and moral behaviour (i.e. following social conventions). Questioning authority and tradition is a transgression that ought to invite the wrath of legitimate authorities. Authoritarianism thus legitimises and maintains the status quo.

## Social dominance theory

**Social dominance theory**
Theory that attributes prejudice to an individual's acceptance of an ideology that legitimises ingroup-serving hierarchy and domination, and rejects egalitarian ideologies.

The role of ideology in prejudice is also important in work by Sidanius, Pratto and associates. They have described a relatively sophisticated, but nonetheless mainly 'individual differences', analysis of exploitative power-based intergroup relations – called **social dominance theory** (e.g. Pratto, 1999; Pratto, Sidanius, Stallworth & Malle, 1994; Sidanius & Pratto, 1999).

Social dominance theory explains the extent to which people accept or reject societal ideologies or myths that legitimise hierarchy and discrimination or equality and fairness. People who desire their own group to be dominant and superior to outgroups have a high social dominance orientation, which encourages them to reject egalitarian ideologies and to accept myths that legitimise hierarchy and discrimination. These kinds of people are more inclined to be prejudiced than people with a low social dominance orientation.

Social dominance theory was originally about the desire for ingroup domination over outgroups. More recently, it has offered a view of a more general desire for unequal relations between groups, irrespective of whether one's own group is at the top or the bottom of the status hierarchy (e.g. Sidanius, Levin, Federico & Pratto, 2001; Duckitt, 2006). This development makes social dominance theory look more like **system justification theory** (e.g. Jost & Hunyadi, 2002; see Chapter 11 for details). System justification theory argues that certain social conditions cause people to resist social change and instead justify and protect the existing social system, even if it maintains one's own group's position of disadvantage.

**System justification theory**
Theory that attributes social stasis to people's adherence to an ideology that justifies and protects the status quo.

## Belief congruence

**Belief congruence theory**
The theory that similar beliefs promote liking and social harmony among people while dissimilar beliefs produce dislike and prejudice.

At the same time as his personality theory of prejudice (above), Rokeach (1960) proposed a separate **belief congruence theory**. Belief systems are important anchoring points for individuals, and thus inter-individual similarity or congruence of belief systems confirms the validity of our own beliefs. Congruence is therefore rewarding and produces attraction and positive attitudes (Byrne, 1971; Festinger, 1954). The converse is that incongruence produces negative attitudes. For Rokeach, 'belief is more important than ethnic or racial membership as a determinant of social discrimination' (1960, p. 135) – prejudice is not an attitude based on group memberships but an individual's reaction to a perceived lack of congruence of belief systems.

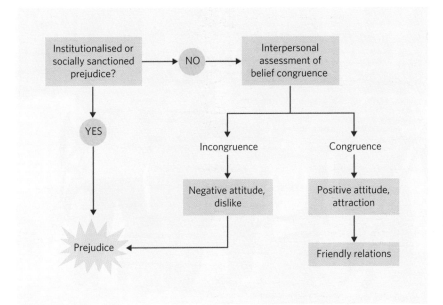

**Figure 10.12** Belief congruence theory

In the absence of socially sanctioned prejudice, prejudice is a matter of interpersonal assessment of belief congruence

*Source*: based on Rokeach (1960)

Some research has used a paradigm in which participants report their attitudes towards others (presented photographically or as verbal descriptions) who are either of the same or a different race, and have either similar or different beliefs to the participant. The findings show that belief does seem to be a more important determinant of attitude than race (e.g. Byrne & Wong, 1962; Hendrick, Bixenstine & Hawkins, 1971; Rokeach & Mezei, 1966). However, when it comes to more intimate behaviour such as friendship, race is more important than belief (e.g. Insko, Nacoste & Moe, 1983; Triandis & Davis, 1965).

There are at least two problems with belief congruence as an explanation of prejudice. The first is that Rokeach (1960) hedges his theory with an important qualification. Under circumstances where prejudice is institutionalised or socially sanctioned, belief congruence plays no part – prejudice is a matter of ethnic group membership (see Figure 10.12). This is a restrictive exemption clause that excludes what we would consider to be the most obvious and distressing manifestations of prejudice: for example, ethnic prejudice in Rwanda and religious prejudice in Northern Ireland would be excluded.

A second problem arises with the relatively small amount of prejudice that Rokeach has left himself to explain. His explanation of how belief congruence may influence prejudice in these circumstances may actually be an explanation of how belief similarity produces interpersonal attraction (Brown, 2000; Brown & Turner, 1981). The research paradigm used to test belief congruence theory has people rate their attitude towards a number of stimulus individuals presented one after the other (a repeated measures design). Some stimuli are of the same race and others of a different race (the race variable), and they all have different beliefs from one another (the belief variable). The absence of clear belief homogeneity within each group and belief discontinuity between groups may muddy intergroup boundaries and focus attention on differences between stimulus individuals rather than on their racial or ethnic group memberships. The research paradigm may inadvertently have diminished the contextual salience of race or ethnicity, such that participants react to the stimulus individuals as individuals, not as members of racial or ethnic groups.

This interpretation has some support from experiments where group membership is clearly differentiated from belief similarity. For example, Billig and Tajfel (1973) had children allocate rewards to anonymous other children, who either were defined as having similar attitudes to them (on the basis of a bogus picture-preference task) or for whom no information on similarity was provided, and who were either explicitly categorised as being

**Belief congruence**
Similar clothes, similar behaviour, and similar beliefs make a potent recipe for liking and social harmony. Now – let's ski!

**Minimal group paradigm**
Experimental methodology to investigate the effect of social categorisation alone on behaviour.

**Discrimination**
The behavioural expression of prejudice.

members of the same group (simply labelled X group) or for whom no categorisation information was provided. This research adopted the **minimal group paradigm**, which is described in detail in Chapter 11. The focal outcome measure was **discrimination** in favour of some target individuals over others.

Figure 10.13 shows that, although belief similarity increased favouritism (as would be predicted from belief congruence theory), the effect of categorisation on favouritism was much stronger, and it was only in the two categorisation conditions that the amount of discrimination was statistically significant (i.e. discrimination scores were significantly greater than zero). Belief congruence theory would not predict these last two effects; similar findings emerged from an experiment by Allen and Wilder (1975). Perhaps most conclusively, Diehl (1988) found that, although attitudinally similar individuals were liked more than dissimilar individuals (though there was little difference in discrimination), attitudinally similar outgroups were liked less than (and discriminated against more than) dissimilar outgroups.

## Other explanations

There are two other major perspectives on the explanation of prejudice. The first concerns how people construct and use stereotypes. This is dealt with mainly in Chapter 2 as part of our discussion of social cognition and social thinking, but it also surfaces in Chapter 11. The second approaches prejudice and discrimination as an aspect of intergroup behaviour as a whole. This is dealt with in Chapter 11.

Because it can be treated as an extension and continuation of this chapter, we have reserved our discussion of prejudice reduction for the end of Chapter 11. The main practical reason for studying the social psychology of prejudice is to gain sufficient understanding of the phenomenon to try to reduce its incidence and to alleviate conflict. Arguments about ways in which prejudice may be reduced rest on the particular perspectives on, and theories of, prejudice to which one subscribes. The intergroup perspectives and theories dealt with in Chapter 11 suggest strategies that are different from those that derive from the person-centred explanations in this chapter.

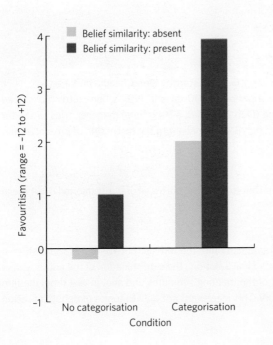

**Figure 10.13** Favouritism as a function of belief similarity and common group membership

Although participants in a minimal group study favoured similar others over those for whom no similarity information was provided, there was much stronger favouritism for others who were simply explicitly categorised as being ingroup members: in fact, statistically significant favouritism was expressed only towards ingroup members

*Source*: based on data from Billig & Tajfel (1973)

## Summary

- Prejudice can be considered to be an attitude about a social group, which may or may not be expressed in behaviour as overt discrimination.

- The most pervasive prejudices are based on sex, race, ethnicity, age, sexual orientation, and physical and mental handicap. In most Western nations, legislation and social attitudes have significantly reduced these prejudices in recent years (with the exception perhaps of the last two), but there is still a long way to go.

- Legislation and social disapproval have inhibited the more extreme expressions of prejudice. Prejudice is more difficult to detect when it is expressed covertly or in restricted contexts, and it may go almost unnoticed as it is embedded in ordinary everyday assumptions, language and discourse.

- The victims of prejudice can suffer material and psychological disadvantage, low self-esteem, stigma, depressed aspirations, and physical and verbal abuse.

In its most extreme form prejudice can express itself as dehumanisation and genocide.

- Prejudice may be a relatively ordinary reaction to frustrated goals, in which people vent their aggression on weaker groups, which serve as scapegoats for the original source of frustration. By no means can all prejudices be explained in this way.

- Prejudice may be abnormal behaviour expressed by people who have developed generally prejudiced personalities, perhaps as a consequence of being raised in harsh and restrictive families. This may explain why some individuals are prejudiced, but the presence of a social environment that encourages prejudice seems to be a much stronger and more diagnostic determinant.

- These sorts of explanation of prejudice do not deal well with the widespread collective nature of the phenomenon. They overlook the fact that people communicate with one another and are influenced by propaganda and mass communication.

## Literature, film and TV

### Hotel Rwanda

Chilling 2004 biographical and historical drama directed by Terry George, starring Don Cheadle and also with Nick Nolte. Set against the backdrop of the Rwandan genocide – a period of 100 days in 1994 when Hutus massacred between 500,000 and one million Tutsis – Paul Rusesabagina (Don Cheadle), a Hutu hotel manager, tries to shelter Tutsi refugees in his Belgian-owned luxury hotel in Kigali. This film is also relevant to the discussion of pro-social and altruistic behaviour in Chapter 14.

### Mississippi Burning

1988 film by Alan Parker, starring Gene Hackman and Willem Dafoe. A classic portrayal of old-fashioned overt racial prejudice in the American south – Ku Klux Klan and all.

### Conspiracy

2001 film with Kenneth Branagh and Colin Firth. A chilling dramatisation of the top-secret two-hour Nazi meeting in which fifteen men debated and ultimately agreed upon Hitler's 'Final Solution', the extermination of the entire Jewish population of Europe. Based on the lone surviving transcript of the meeting's minutes and shot in real time, the film recreates one of the most infamous gatherings in world history. This is relevant not only to topics of dehumanisation and genocide but also group decision making in general.

### Far from Heaven

2002 film by Todd Haynes, with Dennis Quaid and Julianne Moore. Set in 1950s middle-America, this is a powerful and brilliantly filmed and acted portrayal of intolerance and prejudice (racism and homophobia) against a backdrop of ultraconservative attitudes.

### The Boy in the Striped Pyjamas

2008 film by Mark Herman. A young boy, Bruno, befriends another boy, Shmuel, who wears strange striped pyjamas and lives behind an electrified fence. Bruno discovers that he is not permitted to be friends with Shmuel. Bruno is German and his father runs a World War Two prison camp for Jews awaiting extermination; and Shmuel who is Jewish is awaiting extermination. A very powerful film that engages with issues of intergroup contact and friendship across group boundaries.

### Cry the Beloved Country

1948, pre-apartheid Alan Patton novel about race in South Africa. A small-town Zulu priest encounters a range of prejudice and discrimination as he goes to Johannesburg to try to find his delinquent son.

## Guided questions

1  Which groups are the most common targets of prejudice? Give an account of why any one group has traditionally been such a target.

2  Blatant racism may be publicly censured yet still lurk in the background. How might you detect it? One method is the Implicit Association Test, a technique discussed by Mahzarin Banaji in Chapter 10 of MyPsychLab at **www.mypsychlab.co.uk** (watch *Attitudes and attitude change*).

3  What does the frustration–aggression hypothesis really tell us about prejudice?

**4** What is the background to the study of the *authoritarian personality*?

**5** Is it possible for a teacher's expectations of a pupil's educational capacity – for better or for worse – to influence the intellectual development of that pupil? Robert Rosenthal discusses research dealing with the 'Pygmalion effect', or the self-fulfilling prophecy, in Chapter 10 of MyPsychLab at **www.mypsychlab.co.uk** (watch *Self-fulfilling.flv*).

## Learn more

Brewer, M. B. (2003). *Intergroup relations* (2nd ed.). Philadelphia, PA: Open University Press. A readable overview of research on intergroup relations, which includes coverage of issues directly relating to prejudice.

Brewer, M. B. (2007). The social psychology of inter-group relations: Social categorization, ingroup bias, and outgroup prejudice. In A. W. Kruglanski & E. T. Higgins (eds), *Social psychology: Handbook of basic principles* (2nd ed., pp. 785–804). New York: Guilford Press. Comprehensive coverage of research on prejudice, discrimination and intergroup behaviour.

Brown, R. J. (1995). *Prejudice: Its social psychology*. Oxford, UK: Blackwell. Styled as the sequel to Allport's classic 1954 book, *The nature of prejudice*, this is an accessible, detailed and comprehensive coverage of what social psychology has learned about prejudice.

Crocker, J., Major, B., & Steele, C. (1998). Social stigma. In D. T. Gilbert, S. T. Fiske & G. Lindzey (eds), *The hand-book of social psychology* (4th ed., Vol. 2, pp. 504–53). New York: McGraw-Hill. A thorough overview of research into the experience of being the target of preju-dice and a member of a stigmatised group.

Dovidio, J. F., & Gaertner, S. L. (2010). Intergroup bias. In S. T. Fiske, D. T. Gilbert, & G. Lindzey (eds), *Handbook of social psychology* (5th ed., Vol. 2, pp. 1084–121). New York: Wiley. Up-to-date and detailed coverage of research on intergroup discrimination.

Dovidio, J., Glick. P. Hewstone, M., & Esses, V. (eds) (2010). *Handbook of prejudice, stereotyping and discrimi-nation*. London: SAGE. A collection of chapters by leading researchers on stereotyping, prejudice and intergroup behaviour.

Dovidio, J. F., Glick, P. G., & Rudman, L. (eds) (2005). *On the nature of prejudice: Fifty years after Allport*. Malden, MA: Blackwell. Collection of chapters on prejudice by leading scholars to mark the 50th anniversary of Allport's classic, *The nature of prejudice*.

Duckitt, J. (1992). *The social psychology of prejudice*. New York: Praeger. A comprehensive review of the literature on the nature and causes of prejudice and ethnocentrism.

Jones, J. M. (1996). *The psychology of racism and preju-dice*. New York: McGraw-Hill. An authoritative discussion of the causes and consequences of stereotyping and prejudice.

Stangor, C. (ed.) (2000). *Stereotypes and prejudice: Essential readings*. Philadelphia, PA: Psychology Press. Annotated collection of key publications on stereotyping and prejudice. There is an introductory overview chapter and commentary chapters introducing each reading.

Wright, S. C., & Taylor, D. M. (2007). The social psychology of cultural diversity: Social stereotyping, prejudice, and discrimination. In M. A. Hogg & J. Cooper (eds), *The SAGE handbook of social psychology: Concise student edition* (pp. 361–87). London: SAGE. A compre-hensive overview of research on prejudice and discrimination, which deals with stereotyping and also tackles issues to do with social diversity.

Yzerbyt, V., & Demoulin, S. (2010). Intergroup relations. In S. T. Fiske, D. T. Gilbert, & G. Lindzey (eds), *Handbook of social psychology* (5th ed., Vol. 2, pp. 1024–83). New York: Wiley. A thorough overview of the field of inter-group relations, which includes discussion of prejudice and discrimination. This most recent edition of the classic handbook is a primary source for theory and research.

**Refresh your understanding, assess your progress and go further with interactive summaries, questions, podcasts and much more at www.mypsychlab.co.uk**

## This chapter discusses

- The definition and context of intergroup behaviour
- Relevance to an explanation of prejudice and discrimination
- Relative deprivation, intergroup aggression, social protest and collective action
- Realistic conflict theory
- Cooperation, conflict and social dilemmas
- Social identity theory and social identity processes
- Social cognition and intergroup emotions
- Collective behaviour and the crowd
- Improving intergroup relations and reducing prejudice

## Focus questions

1. Richard, an old-fashioned conservative, agrees with the newspaper editorial: 'Nurses should stop complaining about their pay. After all, the hospital orderlies, with even lower pay, keep their mouths shut and just get on with their job.' What can you say?

2. Jean and Alison are close schoolfriends. When they first get to university they are assigned to different halls of residence that are right next door to one another but that have very different cultures and are in fierce competition with each other. What will happen to their friendship?

3. 'There is no other way. The rainforest has to go. We need the timber now – and if we don't take it, they will.' The news bulletin gets you thinking about the way people abuse scarce resources. Is there a way forward?

4. Have you watched a crowd demonstrating in a TV news item and wondered how it actually started? Is it possible that a fundamental aspect of their belief system has somehow been transformed? See Martin Luther King share his 1963 dream that African Americans might achieve equality in Chapter 11 of MyPsychLab at **www.mypsychlab.co.uk** (watch *I have a dream* speech; see **http://www.youtube.com/watch?v=Y4AltMg7Okg&feature=related**).

will use which involves getting you to decide to buy a car by giving you a very low price

Go to **mypsychlab** to explore video and test your understanding of key topics addressed in this chapter.

5. When football supporters get together in a crowd they seem to regress into some sort of super-beast – emotional, fickle, antisocial and dangerous. You've probably heard this kind of description before, but is it psychologically correct?

Refresh your understanding with interactive summaries, explore topics further with video and audio clips and assess your progress with quick test and essay questions by logging to the accompanying website at **www.mypsychlab.co.uk**

# Chapter 11
## Intergroup behaviour

## Key terms

Accentuation effect
Arbitration
Authoritarian personality
Bargaining
Cognitive alternatives
Collective behaviour
Commons dilemma
Conciliation
Contact hypothesis
Deindividuation
Depersonalisation
Egoistic relative deprivation
Emergent norm theory
Entitativity

Ethnocentrism
Extended contact effect
Fraternalistic relative deprivation
Free-rider effect
Frustration–aggression hypothesis
Illusory correlation
Ingroup favouritism
Intergroup behaviour
Intergroup differentiation
Intergroup emotions theory
J-curve
Mediation
Metacontrast principle
Metatheory
Minimal group paradigm
Optimal distinctiveness
Prisoner's dilemma

Prototype
Realistic conflict theory
Reductionism
Relative deprivation
Relative homogeneity effect
Self-categorisation theory
Social categorisation
Social change belief system
Social competition
Social creativity
Social identity
Social identity theory
Social mobility belief system
Stereotype
Superordinate goals
System justification theory
Weapons effect

# What is intergroup behaviour?

**Intergroup behaviour**

Behaviour among
individuals that is
regulated by those
individuals' awareness
of and identification with
different social groups.

Conflicts between nations, political confrontations, revolutions, inter-ethnic relations, negotiations between corporations, and competitive team sports are all examples of **intergroup behaviour**. An initial definition of intergroup behaviour might therefore be 'any behaviour that involves interaction between one or more representatives of two or more separate social groups'. This sort of definition fairly accurately characterises much of the intergroup behaviour that social psychologists study; however, by focusing on face-to-face *interaction,* it might be a little restrictive.

A broader, and perhaps more accurate, definition would be that any perception, cognition or behaviour that is influenced by people's recognition that they and others are members of distinct social groups is intergroup behaviour. This broader definition has an interesting implication: it acknowledges that the real or perceived relations between social groups (e.g. between ethnic groups, between nations) can have far-reaching and pervasive effects on the behaviour of members of those groups – effects that go well beyond situations of face-to-face encounters. This type of definition stems from a particular perspective in social psychology: an intergroup perspective which maintains that a great deal of social behaviour is fundamentally influenced by the social categories to which we belong, and the power and status relations existing between those categories. A broad perspective such as this on the appropriate type of theory to develop is called a **metatheory** (see Chapter 1).

**Metatheory**

Set of interrelated
concepts and principles
concerning which theories
or types of theory are
appropriate.

In many ways, this chapter on intergroup behaviour brings together under one umbrella the preceding discussions of social influence (Chapter 7), group processes (Chapters 8 and 9), and prejudice and discrimination (Chapter 10). Social influence and group processes are generally treated as occurring within groups, but wherever there is a group to which people belong (i.e. an ingroup), there are other groups to which those people do not belong (outgroups). Thus there is almost always an intergroup, or ingroup–outgroup, context for whatever happens in groups. It is unlikely that processes in groups will be unaffected by relations between groups. As we saw in Chapter 10, prejudice and discrimination are clear instances of intergroup behaviour (e.g. between different races, between different age groups, between the sexes). One of the recurring themes of Chapter 10 is that personality or interpersonal explanations of prejudice and discrimination (e.g. authoritarian personality, dogmatism, frustration–aggression) may have limitations precisely because they do not adequately consider the intergroup aspect of the phenomena.

In dealing with intergroup behaviour, this chapter confronts important questions about the difference between individuals (and interpersonal behaviour) and groups (and intergroup behaviour), and the way in which harmonious intergroup relations can be transformed into conflict, and vice versa. Social psychological theories of intergroup behaviour ought therefore to have immediate relevance to applied contexts: for example, in the explanation of intergroup relations in employment contexts (Hartley & Stephenson, 1992).

# Relative deprivation and social unrest

Our discussion in Chapter 10 of the frustration–aggression hypothesis (Dollard, Doob, Miller, Mowrer, & Sewars, 1939) as an explanation of intergroup prejudice, discrimination and aggression concluded with Berkowitz's (1962) modification of the original theory. Berkowitz argued that subjective (not objective) frustration is one of an array of aversive events (e.g. heat, cold) that produce an instigation to aggress, and that the actual expression of aggression is strengthened by aggressive associations (e.g. situational cues, past associations).

Berkowitz (1972a) used this analysis to explain collective intergroup aggression – specifically riots. The best-known application is to riots that occurred during long periods of hot weather in the United States: for example, the Watts riots in Los Angeles in August 1965 and the Detroit riots in August 1967 (see Figure 11.1). Heat can be an 'aversive event' that facilitates individual and collective aggression (e.g. Anderson & Anderson, 1984; Baron & Ransberger, 1978; Carlsmith & Anderson, 1979; see also Chapter 12).

Berkowitz (1972a) argues that under conditions of perceived relative deprivation (e.g. Blacks in the United States in the late 1960s) people feel frustrated. The heat of a long, hot summer amplifies the frustration (especially in poor, overcrowded neighbourhoods with little air conditioning or cooling vegetation) and increases the prevalence of individual acts of aggression, which are in turn exacerbated by the presence of aggressive stimuli (e.g. armed police). Individual aggression becomes widespread and is transformed into true collective violence by a process of social facilitation (Zajonc, 1965; see Chapter 8), whereby the physical presence of other people facilitates dominant behaviour patterns (in this case, aggression).

## Relative deprivation

A crucial precondition for intergroup aggression is **relative deprivation** (Walker & Smith, 2002). Deprivation is not an absolute condition but is always relative to other conditions: one person's new-found prosperity may be someone else's terrible deprivation. George Orwell captures this point beautifully in *The Road to Wigan Pier*, his essay on the plight of the British working class in the 1930s: 'Talking once with a miner I asked him when the housing shortage first became acute in his district; he answered, "When we were told about it", meaning that " 'til recently people's standards were so low that they took almost any degree of overcrowding for granted" ' (Orwell, 1962, p. 57).

The concept of relative deprivation was introduced by Stouffer, Suchman, DeVinney, Star, and Williams (1949) in their classic wartime study of the American soldier. Its role in intergroup conflict and aggression was developed more formally by Davis (1959). Relative deprivation refers to a perceived discrepancy between attainments or actualities ('what is') and expectations or entitlements ('what ought to be'). In its simplest form, relative

**Relative deprivation**
A sense of having less than we feel entitled to.

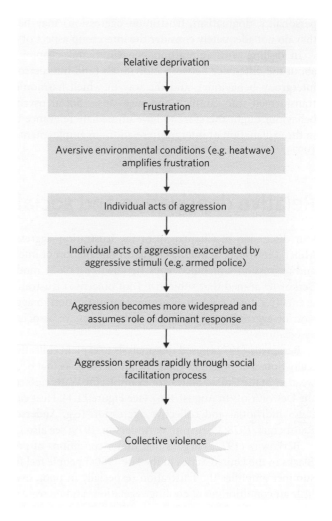

**Figure 11.1** A 'long, hot summer' explanation of collective violence

Frustration induced by relative deprivation is expressed as individual aggression due to the presence of aversive and aggressive environmental stimuli, and this becomes collective aggression through a process of social facilitation

*Source*: based on Berkowitz (1972a)

**J-curve**
A graphical figure that captures the way in which relative deprivation arises when attainments suddenly fall short of rising expectations.

**Egoistic relative deprivation**
A feeling of personally having less than we feel we are entitled to, relative to our aspirations or to other individuals.

deprivation arises from comparisons between our experiences and our expectations (Gurr, 1970). (Can you respond to Richard in the first focus question?)

In his **J-curve** hypothesis (see Figure 11.2), Davies (1969) suggested that people construct their future expectations from past and current attainments, and that under certain circumstances attainments may suddenly fall short of rising expectations. When this happens, relative deprivation is particularly acute, with the consequence of collective unrest – revolutions of rising expectations (see Box 11.1). The J-curve gets its name from the solid line in Figure 11.2.

Some historical events do seem to fit this model. For example, the Depression of the early 1930s caused a sudden fall in farm prices, which was associated with increased anti-Semitism in Poland (Keneally, 1982, p. 95). Davies (1969) himself cites the French and Russian Revolutions, the American Civil War, the rise of Nazism in Germany and the growth of Black Power in the United States in the 1960s. In all these cases, a long period (twenty to thirty years) of increasing prosperity was followed by a steep and sudden recession. Systematic tests of predictions from Davies's theory are less encouraging. For example, from a longitudinal survey of American political and social attitudes, Taylor (1982) found little evidence that people's expectations were constructed from their immediate past experience, or that satisfaction was based on the degree of match between actualities and these expectations.

## Real world 11.1
### Rising expectations and collective protest

**The 1992 Los Angeles riots provided a riveting, real-life example of relative deprivation perceived by a large group of people**

The Los Angeles riots that erupted on 29 April 1992 resulted in more than 50 dead and 2,300 injured. The proximal cause was the acquittal by an all-White suburban jury of four Los Angeles police officers accused of beating a Black motorist, Rodney King. The assault with which the police officers were charged had been captured on video and played on national TV. Against a background of rising unemployment and deepening disadvantage, this acquittal was seen by Blacks as a particularly poignant symbol of the low value placed by White America on American Blacks.

The flashpoint for the riot was the intersection of Florence and Normandie Avenues in South Central Los Angeles. Initially, there was some stealing of liquor from a local liquor store, breaking of car windows and pelting of police. The police moved in en masse but then withdrew to try to de-escalate the tension. This left the intersection largely in the hands of the rioters, who attacked Whites and Hispanics. Reginald Denny, a White truck driver who happened to be driving through, was dragged from his cab and brutally beaten; the incident was watched live on TV by millions and has largely come to symbolise the riots.

South Central Los Angeles was relatively typical of Black ghettos in the United States at that time. However, the junction of Florence and Normandie was not in the worst part of the ghetto by any means. It was a relatively well-off Black neighbourhood in which the poverty rate dropped during the 1980s from 33 to only 21 per cent. That the initial outbreak of rioting would occur here, rather than in a more impoverished neighbourhood, is consistent with relative deprivation theories of social unrest.

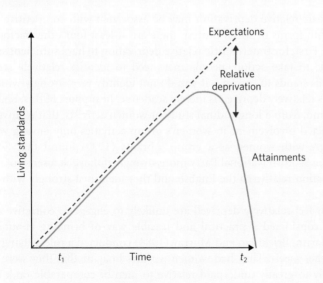

**Figure 11.2** The J-curve hypothesis of relative deprivation

Relative deprivation is particularly acute when attainments suffer a sudden setback in the context of expectations which continue to rise

*Source:* based on Davies (1969)

Runciman (1966) has made an important distinction between two forms of relative deprivation:

1 **egoistic relative deprivation**, which derives from the individual's sense of deprivation relative to other similar individuals; and

2 **fraternalistic relative deprivation**, which derives from comparisons with dissimilar others, or members of other groups.

**Fraternalistic relative deprivation**
Sense that our group has less than it is entitled to, relative to its aspirations or to other groups.

Studies that include measures of both types of relative deprivation furnish some evidence that they are independent (e.g. Crosby, 1982). Research indicates that it is fraternalistic, particularly intergroup, relative deprivation, not egoistic relative deprivation, that is associated with social unrest. Vanneman and Pettigrew (1972) conducted surveys in large cities in the United States to discover that Whites who expressed the most negative attitudes towards Blacks were those who felt most strongly that Whites as a group were poorly off relative to Blacks as a group. The deprivation is cleary fraternalistic and, as Whites were in reality *better off* than Blacks, illustrates the subjective nature of relative deprivation.

Abeles (1976) found that Black militancy in the United States was more closely associated with measures of fraternalistic than egoistic relative deprivation, and Guimond and Dubé-Simard (1983) found that militant Francophones in Montreal felt more acute dissatisfaction and frustration when making intergroup salary comparisons between Francophones and Anglophones, rather than egoistic comparisons. In India, where there had been a rapid decline in the status of Muslims relative to Hindus, Tripathi and Srivasta (1981) found that those Muslims who felt most fraternalistically deprived (e.g. in terms of job opportunities, political freedom) expressed the greatest hostility towards Hindus.

Finally, in a study of unemployed workers, Walker and Mann (1987) found that it was principally those who reported most fraternalistic deprivation who were prepared to contemplate militant protest, such as demonstrations, law breaking and destruction of private property. Those who felt egoistically deprived reported symptoms of personal stress (e.g. headaches, indigestion, sleeplessness). This study is particularly revealing in showing how egoistic and fraternalistic deprivation produce different outcomes, and that it is the latter that is associated with social unrest as intergroup or collective protest (see below) or aggression.

Although fraternalistic relative deprivation may be associated with competitive intergroup behaviour or with forms of social protest, there are at least four other factors that need to be considered. First, for fraternalistic relative deprivation to have sufficient subjective impact for people to take action, people may need to identify relatively strongly with their ingroup. This stands to reason – if you do not identify very strongly with your group, the fact that it is relatively deprived is merely academic. In support of this, Kelly and Breinlinger (1996) found, from a longitudinal study of women activists, that relative deprivation reliably predicted involvement in women's group activities only among women who identified strongly with women as a group. Abrams (1990) found that Scottish teenagers supported the Scottish National Party more strongly if they felt a sense of fraternalistic relative deprivation relative to the English and they identified strongly with being Scottish.

Second, groups that feel relatively deprived are unlikely to engage in collective action unless such action is considered a practical and feasible way of bringing about social change (see below). Martin, Brickman and Murray (1984) conducted a role-playing study that illustrates this rather nicely. They had women workers imagine that they were managers who were slightly to greatly underpaid relative to men of comparable rank in the company. They were also given information that portrayed the women managers as well placed or poorly placed to mobilise resources to change their situation. Martin and his associates found that relative deprivation was closely tied to the magnitude of pay inequality, but that protest was tied much more closely to the perceived probability that protest would be successful.

Third, relative deprivation rests on perceptions of injustice. Generally, the injustice we have had in mind is distributive injustice – feeling that you have less than you are entitled to relative to expectations, other groups and so forth. However, there is another form of injustice – procedural injustice, in which you feel that you have been the victim of unfair procedures. Tyler and his colleagues have explored this distinction between distributive and procedural justice (Tyler & Lind, 1992; Tyler & Smith, 1998; see De Cremer & Tyler, 2005).

They suggest that the perception of procedural injustice may be a particularly potent motivation for intergroup protest. Procedural justice seems to be especially important within groups – if people experience unfair procedures within a group, they tend to dis-identify and lose commitment to group goals (see discussion of leadership in Chapter 9). In intergroup contexts, however, it may be very difficult to untangle unjust procedures from unjust distributions: for example, status differences (distributive injustice) between groups may rest on unfair procedures (procedural injustice) (Brockner & Wiesenfeld, 1996).

Finally, as fraternalistic relative deprivation depends on the particular ingroup–outgroup comparison that is made, it is important to be able to predict whom we compare ourselves with (Martin & Murray, 1983; Walker & Pettigrew, 1984). From social comparison theory (Festinger, 1954; see Suls & Wheeler, 2000), we would expect comparisons to be made with similar others, and some of the work cited above certainly supports this (e.g. Abeles, 1976; Runciman, 1966). For instance, Crosby's (1982) 'paradox of the contented female worker' may arise because women workers compare their salaries and working conditions with those of other women, which narrows the potential for recognising much larger gender-based inequalities in pay and conditions (Major, 1994). However, many intergroup comparisons, particularly those that lead to the most pronounced conflict, are made between markedly different groups (e.g. Black and White South Africans). One way to approach this issue is to consider the extent to which groups are involved in real conflict over scarce resources (see below).

## Social protest and collective action

Social unrest associated with relative deprivation often represents sustained social protest to achieve social change. However, the study of protest is complex, requiring a sophisticated articulation of constructs from social psychology, sociology and political science (Klandermans, 1997, 2003; Reicher, 1996, 2001; Stürmer & Simon, 2004). As the study of how individual discontents or grievances are transformed into collective action, the study of protest has as its key question: how and why do sympathisers become mobilised as activists or participants?

Klandermans (1997) argues that this involves the relationship between individual attitudes and behaviour (see Chapter 5). Sympathisers, by definition, hold sympathetic attitudes towards an issue, yet these attitudes do not automatically translate into behaviour. Participation also resembles a social dilemma (see below). Protest is generally *for* a social good (e.g. equality) or *against* a social ill (e.g. pollution), and as success benefits everyone irrespective of participation, but failure harms participants more, it is tempting to 'free ride' (see Chapter 8) – to remain a sympathiser rather than become a participant. Finally, Klandermans notes that protest can only be understood as intergroup behaviour that occurs in what he calls 'multiorganisational fields': that is, protest movements involve the clash of ideas and ideologies between groups, and politicised and strategic articulation with other more or less sympathetic organisations.

Klandermans (1997; for an overview, see Stürmer & Simon, 2004) described four steps in social movement participation:

1 Becoming part of the mobilisation potential. First, you must be a sympathiser. The most important determinants of mobilisation potential are fraternalistic relative deprivation (feeling relatively deprived as a group), an us-versus-them orientation that targets an outgroup as being responsible for your plight, and a belief that social change through collective action is possible.

2 Becoming a target of mobilisation attempts. Being a sympathiser is not enough – you must also be informed about what you can do and what is being done (e.g. sit-ins, demonstrations, lobbying). Media access and informal communication networks are critical here.

3  Developing motivation to participate. Being a sympathiser and knowing what is going on is not sufficient – you must also be motivated to participate. Motivation arises from the value that you place on the outcome of protest and the extent to which you believe that the protest will actually deliver the goods (an expectancy–value analysis; Ajzen & Fishbein, 1980). Motivation is strongest if the collective benefit of the outcome of protest is highly valued (collective motive), if important others value your participation (normative motive), and if valued personal outcomes are anticipated (reward motive). The normative and reward motives are important to prevent sympathisers from free-riding on others' participation. This analysis of motivation is strikingly similar to Ajzen and Fishbein's (1980) theory of reasoned action account of the attitude–behaviour relationship (see Chapter 5).

4  Overcoming barriers to participation. Finally, even substantial motivation may not translate into action if there are insurmountable obstacles, such as no transport to the demonstration, or ill health. However, these obstacles are more likely to be overcome if motivation is very high.

Simon (2003; Stürmer & Simon, 2004) argues that the cost–benefit aspect of Klanderman's model places too much emphasis on individual decision making. Simon proposes a social identity analysis. Drawing on social identity theory (e.g. Hogg, 2006 – see below for details), Simon argues further that when people identify very strongly with a group they have a powerfully shared perception of collective injustice, needs and goals. They also share attitudes and behavioural intentions, trust and like one another, and are collectively influenced by group norms and legitimate group leaders. Furthermore, group motivation eclipses personal motivation – it overcomes the dilemma of social action (Klandermans, 2002). Provided that members believe that protest is an effective way forward, these processes increase the probability of participation in collective protest (Bluic, McGarty, Reynolds, & Muntele, 2007).

# Realistic conflict

A key feature of intergroup behaviour is ethnocentrism (Brewer & Campbell, 1976; LeVine & Campbell, 1972), described by Sumner as:

> a view of things in which one's own group is the centre of everything, and all others are scaled and rated with reference to it . . . Each group nourishes its own pride and vanity, boasts itself superior, exalts its own divinities, and looks with contempt on outsiders. Each group thinks its own folkways the only right one . . . Ethnocentrism leads a people to exaggerate and intensify everything in their own folkways which is peculiar and which differentiates them from others. (*Sumner, 1906, p. 13*)

In contrast to other perspectives on prejudice, discrimination and intergroup behaviour that explain the origins of ethnocentrism in terms of individual or interpersonal processes (e.g. frustration–aggression, relative deprivation, authoritarianism, dogmatism), Sherif believed that 'we cannot extrapolate from the properties of individuals to the characteristics of group situations' (1962, p. 8) and that the origins of ethnocentrism lie in the nature of intergroup relations. For Sherif:

> *Intergroup relations* refer to relations between two or more groups and their respective members. Whenever individuals belonging to one group interact, collectively or individually, with another group or its *members in terms of their group identifications* we have an instance of intergroup behaviour. (*Sherif, 1962, p. 5*)

Sherif believed that where groups compete over scarce resources, intergroup relations become marked by conflict, and ethnocentrism arises. To investigate this idea, Sherif and

**Realistic conflict**
Sherif showed that intergroup competition led to conflict and then discrimination. This is heightened when the people compete for a goal that only one group can win

his colleagues conducted three famous field experiments in 1949, 1953 and 1954 at summer camps for young boys in the United States (Sherif, 1966). The general procedure involved three phases:

1  *Phase 1* – The children arrived at the camp, which, unknown to them, was run by the experimenters. They engaged in various camp-wide activities, through which they formed friendships.

2  *Phase 2* – The camp was divided into two separate groups that split up friendships. The groups were entirely isolated from each other: they had separate living quarters, engaged in separate activities, and developed their own norms and status differentials. Although little reference was made to the outgroup, there was some embryonic ethnocentrism.

3  *Phase 3* – The two groups were brought together to engage in organised intergroup competitions embracing sports contests and other activities. This produced fierce competition and intergroup hostility, which rapidly generalised to situations outside the organised competitions. Ethnocentric attitudes and behaviour were amplified and coupled with intergroup aggression and ingroup solidarity. Almost all intergroup encounters degenerated into intergroup hostility: for example, when the two groups ate together, the meal became an opportunity for the groups to throw food at each other. Intergroup relations deteriorated so dramatically that two of the experiments were hastily concluded at this stage.

In one experiment, however, it was possible to proceed to a fourth stage:

4  *Phase 4* – The two groups were provided with **superordinate goals**, goals they both desired but were unable to achieve on their own. The groups had to work together in cooperation.

**Superordinate goals**
Goals that both groups desire but that can be achieved only by both groups cooperating.

As an example of a superordinate goal (also dealt with later in this chapter), the groups were told that the truck delivering a movie that both groups wanted to watch had become bogged down and would need to be pulled out, but that everyone would be needed to help as the truck was very heavy. Sherif had a wonderful sense of symbolism – the rope used cooperatively by the boys to pull the truck was the same rope that had previously been used in an aggressive tug-of-war between the warring groups. Sherif and colleagues found a gradual improvement in intergroup relations as a consequence of a number of cooperative intergroup interactions in order to achieve superordinate goals.

There are some notable points about these experiments:

- There was a degree of latent ethnocentrism even in the absence of intergroup competition (more of this below).
- Prejudice, discrimination and ethnocentrism arose as a consequence of real intergroup conflict.
- The boys did not have authoritarian or dogmatic personalities.
- The less frustrated group (the winning group) was usually the one that expressed the greater intergroup aggression.
- Ingroups formed despite the fact that friends were actually outgroup members (see Chapter 8).
- Simple contact between members of opposing groups did not improve intergroup relations (see below).

## Realistic conflict theory

**Realistic conflict theory**
Sherif's theory of intergroup conflict that explains intergroup behaviour in terms of the nature of goal relations between groups.

To explain this, Sherif (1966) proposed a **realistic conflict theory** of intergroup behaviour, in which the nature of the goal relations among individuals and groups determines the nature of interindividual and intergroup relations. He argued that individuals who share goals requiring interdependence for their achievement tend to cooperate and form a group (see Figure 11.3), while individuals who have mutually exclusive goals (i.e. a scarce resource that only one can obtain, such as winning a chess game) engage in interindividual competition,

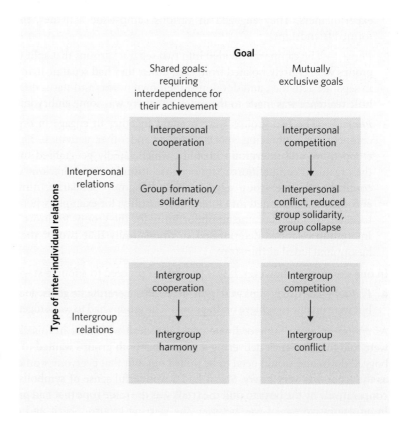

**Figure 11.3** Realistic group conflict theory

Goal relations between individuals and groups determine cooperative or competitive interdependence, and thus the nature of interpersonal and intergroup behaviour

*Source*: based on Sherif (1966)

which prevents group formation or contributes to the collapse of an existing group. At the intergroup level, mutually exclusive goals produce realistic intergroup conflict and ethnocentrism, while shared goals requiring intergroup interdependence for their achievement (i.e. superordinate goals) reduce conflict and encourage intergroup harmony. For a summary of Sherif's range of contributions to social psychology, see Vaughan (2010a).

Sherif's model is generally supported by other naturalistic experiments (Fisher, 1990). For example, Blake and Mouton (1961) employed similar procedures in a series of thirty studies, each run for two weeks, involving more than 1,000 business people on management training programmes in the United States. Zimbardo's simulated prison experiment (Haney, Banks & Zimbardo, 1973; see Chapter 8) also illustrates the way in which mutually exclusive intergroup goals produce conflict and hostile intergroup relations. Sherif's studies have been successfully replicated in Lebanon (Diab, 1970) and the former Soviet Union (Andreeva, 1984), but in Britain, Tyerman and Spencer (1983) were not so successful. Tyerman and Spencer used an established Scout group as participants and found that the different 'patrols' did not express anywhere near as much hostility as expected. Furthermore, it was easy to increase inter-patrol cooperation even in the absence of a superordinate goal. Tyerman and Spencer attribute this to the fact that a well-established superordinate group already existed.

Realistic conflict theory makes good sense and is generally useful for understanding intergroup conflict, particularly in applied settings (Fisher, 1990). For example, Brewer and Campbell (1976; see also Chapter 13) conducted an ethnographic survey of thirty tribal groups in Africa and found, among other things, greater derogation of tribal outgroups that lived close by and were thus likely to be direct competitors for scarce resources such as water and land. (This study casts some light on the predicament facing Jean and Alison. See the second focus question.)

Realistic conflict theory suffers from a problem. Because so many variables are operating together in the various studies, how can we know that it is the nature of goal relations that ultimately determines intergroup behaviour rather than, for example, the cooperative or competitive nature of interaction, or perhaps merely the existence of two separate groups (e.g. Dion, 1979; Turner, 1981b)? These causal agents are confounded – an observation that we pursue later in this chapter.

## Cooperation, competition and social dilemmas

Realistic conflict theory focuses attention on the relationship between people's goals, the competitive or cooperative nature of their behaviour and the conflicting or harmonious nature of their relations. We can study these relationships in abstract settings by designing 'games' with different goal relations for two or more people to play. Von Neumann and Morgenstern (1944) introduced a model for analysing situations where people are in conflict over some non-trivial outcome (e.g. money, power). Variously called *decision theory, game theory* or *utility theory,* this initiated a prodigious amount of research in the 1960s and 1970s. (This topic is also dealt with in the context of interpersonal relations in Chapter 13.) The highly abstract nature of the research raised questions about its relevance (generalisability) to real-world conflict and led to its decline in the 1980s (Apfelbaum & Lubek, 1976; Nemeth, 1970). Much of this research is concerned with interpersonal conflict; however, much of it also has important implications for intergroup conflict: for example, the prisoner's dilemma, the trucking game and the commons dilemma (e.g. Liebrand, Messick & Wilke, 1992).

### The prisoner's dilemma

Introduced by Luce and Raiffa (1957; Rapoport, 1976), the **prisoner's dilemma** is the most widely researched game. It is based on an anecdote. Detectives question two obviously

**Prisoner's dilemma**
Two-person game in which both parties are torn between competition and cooperation and, depending on mutual choices, both can win or both can lose.

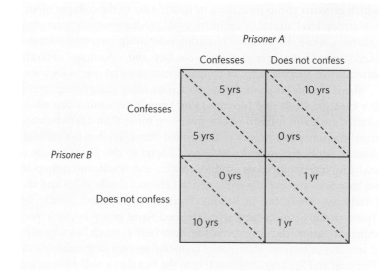

**Figure 11.4** The prisoner's dilemma

Each quadrant displays the prison sentence that Prisoner A receives (above the diagonal) and Prisoner B receives (below in diagonal) if both, one or neither confesses

guilty suspects separately, with only enough evidence to convict them of a lesser offence. The suspects are separately offered a chance to confess, knowing that if one confesses but the other does not, the confessor will be granted immunity and the confession will be used to convict the other of the more serious offence. If both confess, each will receive a moderate sentence. If neither confesses, each will receive a very light sentence. The dilemma faced by the prisoners can be summarised by a *pay-off matrix* (see Figure 11.4).

Although mutual non-confession produces the best joint outcome, mutual suspicion and lack of trust almost always encourage both to confess. This finding has been replicated in literally hundreds of prisoner's dilemma experiments, using a variety of experimental conditions and pay-off matrices (Dawes, 1991). The prisoner's dilemma is described as a 'two-person, mixed motive, non-zero-sum game'. This is quite a mouthful, but it means that two people are involved, they each experience a conflict between being motivated to cooperate and motivated to compete, and the outcome can be that both parties gain or both lose. In contrast, a zero-sum game is one in which one party's gain is always the other's loss.

### The trucking game

In this game, there are two trucking companies, Acme and Bolt, which have to transport goods from one place to another (Deutsch & Krauss, 1960). Each company has its own private route, but there is a much faster shared route, which has a major drawback – a one-lane section (see Figure 11.5). Clearly, the mutually beneficial solution is for the two companies to agree to take it in turns to use the one-lane section. Instead, research reveals again and again that participants prefer to fight for use of the one-lane section. Typically, both enter and meet head-on in the middle and then waste time arguing until one backs up. Again, mutual mistrust has produced a suboptimal joint outcome.

These games highlight the detrimental consequences of lack of trust that have clear real-world analogues. For example, mutual distrust between Iran and Iraq fuelled their terrible conflict in the 1980s over which of them rightfully owned the Shatt-al-Arab waterway. When they laid down their arms in 1988 after horrific atrocities, over a million civilian and military casualties, and the devastation of their economies, the borders remained precisely where they were when the war began eight years earlier.

Game theory rests on a rationalistic characterisation of humankind as *homo œconomicus* – a Western model of human psychological functioning that derives from Western thinking

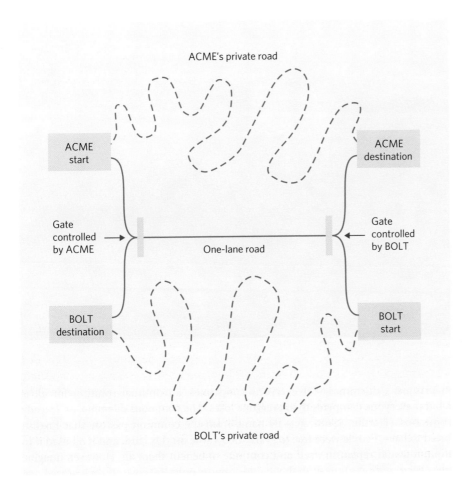

ACME's private road

ACME start

ACME destination

Gate controlled by ACME →

One-lane road

← Gate controlled by BOLT

BOLT destination

BOLT start

BOLT's private road

**Figure 11.5** The trucking game

Two participants play a game where they work for separate trucking companies that transport goods from one place to another. They can use their own private roads, but there is also a much shorter shared route which has the drawback of having a one-lane section

*Source*: Deutsch & Krauss (1960)

about work and industry (Stroebe & Frey, 1982; see also the discussions of normative models and behavioural decision theory in Chapter 2). Possibly due to this perspective, a problem with research based on game theory is that it is relatively asocial. For example, it often overlooks the role of direct communication, although communication in two- and *n*-person prisoner's dilemma games actually reliably reduces conflict and increases cooperation (Liebrand, 1984). Interactants' responses also tend to fulfil a communicative function, such that flexible and responsive partners tend to raise the level of cooperation (Apfelbaum, 1974).

Similarly, subjective perceptions of the game are often overlooked. For example, the allocation or exchange of goods or resources always raises questions of perceived fairness and justice, and it would appear that interactants are more confident of fair solutions, behave more cooperatively and are more satisfied with outcomes if rules of fairness are explicitly invoked (McClintock & van Avermaet, 1982; Mikula, 1980). There is also some evidence that experimental games are spontaneously construed by participants as competitive contexts. When the game is introduced in different terms – for example, as an investigation of human interaction or international conflict resolution – people behave in a more cooperative manner (Abric & Vacherot, 1976; Eiser & Bhavnani, 1974).

## The commons dilemma

Many other social dilemmas involve a number of individuals or groups exploiting a limited resource (Foddy, Smithson, Schneider & Hogg, 1999; Kerr & Park, 2001). These are essentially

**Commons dilemma**

A climatic tragedy in which a failure to cooperate by all leads to harm for all

**Commons dilemma**

Social dilemma in which cooperation by all benefits all, but competition by all harms all.

**Free-rider effect**

Gaining the benefits of group membership by avoiding costly obligations of membership and by allowing other members to incur those costs.

*n*-person prisoner's dilemmas – if everyone cooperates, an optimal solution for all is reached, but if everyone competes then everyone loses. The **commons dilemma**, or 'tragedy of the commons' (Hardin, 1968), gets its name from the common pasture that English villages used to have. People were free to graze their cattle on this land, and if all used it in moderation, it would replenish itself and continue to benefit them all. However, imagine 100 farmers surrounding a common that could support only 100 cows. If each grazed one cow, the common would be maximally utilised and minimally taxed. However, one farmer might reason that if he or she grazed an additional cow, his or her output would be doubled, minus a very small cost due to overgrazing – a cost borne equally by all 100 farmers. So this farmer adds a second cow. If all 100 farmers reasoned in this way, they would rapidly destroy the common, thus producing the tragedy of the commons.

The commons dilemma is an example of a replenishable resource dilemma – the commons is a renewable resource that will continually support many people provided that all people show restraint in 'harvesting' the resource. Many of the world's most pressing environmental and conservation problems are replenishable resource dilemmas: for example, rain forests and the world's population of ocean fish are renewable resources if harvested appropriately (Clover, 2004) (see the third focus question).

Another type of social dilemma is called a *public goods dilemma*. Public goods are provided for everyone: for example, public health, national parks, the national road network, public radio and TV. Because public goods are available to all, people are tempted to use them without contributing to their maintenance. There is a **free-rider effect** (Kerr, 1983; Kerr & Bruun, 1983; see also Chapter 8), in which people self-interestedly exploit a resource without caring for it. For example, if you alone avoid paying your taxes it only minimally impacts the provision of a police force, an ambulance service, or a functioning road system, but if everyone reasoned similarly there would be no emergency service to race to your rescue on the now effectively non-existent road system. Likewise, if I fail to fix my car exhaust or fail to plant trees in my garden, it contributes minimally to noise, atmospheric and visual pollution; if everyone living in my neighbourhood did likewise, then it would become a horrible place to live.

Reflecting on the commons dilemma, Hardin observed:

Ruin is the destination to which all men rush, each pursuing his own best interest in a society that believes in the freedom of the commons. Freedom in a commons brings ruin to all. (*Hardin, 1968 p. 162*)

Experimental research on social dilemmas finds that when self-interest is pitted against the collective good, the usual outcome is competition and resource destruction (Edney, 1979; Sato, 1987). However, laboratory and field studies also obtain high levels of voluntary social cooperation (Caporael, Dawes, Orbell & van de Kragt, 1989). A series of studies by Brewer and her colleagues (Brewer & Kramer, 1986; Brewer & Schneider, 1990; Kramer & Brewer, 1984, 1986) identifies one condition under which this can occur. When people identify with the common good – in other words, they derive their social identity (see below) from the entire group that has access to the resource – self-interest is subordinate to the common good.

However, the same research indicates that when different *groups,* rather than individuals, have access to a public good, the ensuing intergroup competition ensures ethnocentric actions that are far more destructive than mere self-interest. International competition over limited resources such as rain forests, whales and wetlands tragically accelerates their disappearance.

## Resolving social dilemmas

Generally, people find it difficult to escape the trap of a social dilemma. Even appeals to altruistic norms are surprisingly ineffective (Kerr, 1995) – if you know that others are free riding, you certainly do not want to be taken for a sucker (Kerr & Bruun, 1983). Because selfish behaviour is so prevalent in social dilemmas, structural solutions often have to be imposed to cause the dilemma to disappear (Kerr, 1995). Structural solutions include a range of measures such as limiting the number of people accessing the resource (e.g. via permits), limiting the amount of the resource that people can take (e.g. via quotas), handing over management of the resource to an individual (a leader) or a single group, facilitating free communication among those accessing the resource, and shifting the pay-off to favour cooperation over competition.

The problem with structural solutions is that they require an enlightened and powerful authority to implement measures, manage the bureaucracy and police violations. This can be hard to bring about. A case in point is the inability, in the face of global catastrophe, for the world's nations to put a structural solution in place to limit carbon emissions and try to reduce global warming. We have had global summit meetings and accords a-plenty, Rio, Kyoto, The Hague, Paris, and in 2009 Copenhagen, and still some nations will not sacrifice personal gain for the greater good of humanity – leading, in complete frustration and desperation, to an alliance in 2007 between Richard Branson and Al Gore to provide a 25 million dollar carrot to try to get something positive to happen.

A structural solution that has been well researched is the appointment of a leader to manage the resource (e.g. de Cremer & Van Vugt, 2002; Rutte & Wilke, 1984; Van Vugt & De Cremer, 1999). Leaders are very effective at resolving social dilemmas under certain circumstances. People with a generally prosocial orientation are relatively open to leadership when their group is faced with a social dilemma, particularly if they identify strongly with the group (De Cremer, 2000; De Cremer & Van Vugt, 1999). Leader charisma is typically not critical, but it is important that the leader can be viewed as 'one of us', as a representative member of the group (De Cremer, 2002). People with a pro-self orientation are less open to leadership unless they identify strongly with the group and the leader's behaviours and qualities are group serving and representative of the group. Charismatic leaders are particularly good at helping pro-self members behave in prosocial and group-serving ways.

If structural solutions are so difficult, what other options do we have? One factor that seems particularly effective in resolving social dilemmas is group identification (Foddy, Smithson, Schneider & Hogg, 1999; Van Vugt & De Cremer, 1999). Where people identify very strongly with a group that accesses a shared resource, those people act in ways that benefit the group as a whole rather than themselves as separate from the group (e.g. Brewer & Kramer, 1986; Brewer & Schneider, 1990). It is as if a large number of individuals competing for access have been transformed into a single person who carefully tends the resource. Indeed, this is a good analogy. As we see shortly, identification with a group actually does transform people psychologically in this way. Identification seems to facilitate communication that develops conserving norms (e.g. Bouas & Komorita, 1996); it encourages adherence to those norms (e.g. Sattler & Kerr, 1991); it inspires perceptions of distributive and procedural justice (Tyler & Smith, 1998); and it makes people feel that their conserving actions really do have an effect (Kerr, 1995). Indeed, privatisation of a public good can increase selfish non-conserving behaviour precisely because it inhibits these social identity processes (Van Vugt, 1997).

# Social identity

## Minimal groups

We have seen that realistic conflict theory (Sherif, 1966) traces the origins and form of intergroup behaviour to goal interdependence, and that research tends to confound a number of possible causal agents. Research also suggests that ethnocentric attitudes and competitive intergroup relations are easy to trigger and difficult to suppress. For example, embryonic ethnocentrism was found in phase 2 of Sherif's summer camp studies, when groups had just been formed but there was no realistic conflict between them (see also Blake & Mouton, 1961; Kahn & Ryen, 1972). Other researchers have found that competitive intergroup behaviour spontaneously emerges:

- even when goal relations between groups are not interdependent (Rabbie & Horwitz, 1969);
- under conditions of explicitly non-competitive intergroup relations (Ferguson & Kelley, 1964; Rabbie & Wilkens, 1971);
- under conditions of explicitly cooperative intergroup relations (Rabbie & DeBrey, 1971).

What, then, are the minimal conditions for intergroup behaviour: that is, conditions that are both necessary and sufficient for a collection of individuals to be ethnocentric and to engage in intergroup competition? (Jean and Alison's problem can be approached in the context of the minimal intergroup paradigm. See the second focus question.)

**Minimal group paradigm**
Experimental methodology to investigate the effect of social categorisation alone on behaviour.

Tajfel and his colleagues devised an intriguing way to answer this question – the **minimal group paradigm** (Tajfel, Billig, Bundy & Flament, 1971). British schoolboys, participating in what they believed was a study of decision making, were assigned to one of two groups completely randomly, but allegedly on the basis of their expressed preference for paintings by the artists Vassily Kandinsky or Paul Klee. The children knew only which group they themselves were in (Kandinsky group or Klee group), with the identity of outgroup and fellow ingroup members concealed by the use of code numbers. The children then individually distributed money between pairs of recipients identified only by code number and group membership.

This pencil-and-paper task was repeated for a number of different pairs of ingroup and outgroup members, excluding self, on a series of distribution matrices carefully designed

## Research classic 11.2
### The minimal group paradigm

**Distribution strategies and sample distribution matrices (participants circled pairs of numbers to indicate how they wished to distribute the points)**

A. *Two sample distribution matrices.* Within each matrix, participants circle the column of numbers that represents how they would like to distribute the points (representing real money) in the matrix between ingroup and outgroup members.

| 1 | Ingroup member: | 7 | 8 | 9 | 10 | 11 | 12 | 13 | 14 | 15 | 16 | 17 | 18 | 19 |
|---|---|---|---|---|---|---|---|---|---|---|---|---|---|---|
|   | Outgroup member: | 1 | 3 | 5 | 7 | 9 | 11 | 13 | 15 | 17 | 19 | 21 | 23 | 25 |
| 2 | Ingroup member: | 18 | 17 | 16 | 15 | 14 | 13 | 12 | 11 | 10 | 9 | 8 | 7 | 6 |
|   | Outgroup member: | 5 | 6 | 7 | 8 | 9 | 10 | 11 | 12 | 13 | 14 | 15 | 16 | 17 |

B. *Distribution strategies.* From an analysis of responses on a large number of matrices it is possible to determine the extent to which the participants' distribution of points is influenced by each of the following strategies.

- Fairness　　　　　　　　　F　　Equal distribution of points between groups
- Maximum joint profit　　　MJP　Maximise total number of points obtained by both recipients together, irrespective of which group receives most
- Maximum ingroup profit　　MIP　Maximise number of points for the ingroup
- Maximum difference　　　　MD　Maximise the difference in favour of the ingroup in the number of points awarded
- Favouritism　　　　　　　FAV　Composite employment of MIP and MD

*Source:* Tajfel (1970); based on Hogg & Abrams (1988).

to tease out the sort of strategies that were being used. The results showed that against a background of some fairness, the children strongly favoured their own group: they adopted the ingroup favouritism strategy (FAV) described in Box 11.2. This is a rather startling finding, as the groups were indeed minimal. They were created on the basis of a flimsy criterion, had no past history or possible future, the children did not even know the identity of other members of each group, and no self-interest was involved in the money distribution task as self was not a recipient.

Subsequent experiments were even more minimal in character. For example, Billig and Tajfel (1973) explicitly randomly categorised their participants as X- or Y-group members, thereby eliminating any possibility that they might infer that people in the same group were interpersonally similar to one another because they ostensibly preferred the same artist. Turner (1978) abolished the link between points and money. The task was simply to distribute points. Other studies have included, in addition to the points distribution task, measures of attitudinal, affective and conative aspects of ethnocentrism. Another study used actual coins as rewards (Vaughan, Tajfel & Williams, 1981). Children who were either seven or twelve years old simply distributed coins to unidentified ingroup and outgroup members. Marked ingroup bias was reported in both age groups.

The robust finding from hundreds of minimal group experiments conducted with a wide range of participants is that the mere fact of being categorised as a group member seems to be necessary and sufficient to produce ethnocentrism and competitive intergroup behaviour (Bourhis, Sachdev & Gagnon, 1994; Diehl, 1990; Tajfel, 1982).

More accurately, **social categorisation** is necessary but may not be sufficient for intergroup behaviour. For example, Hogg and his colleagues conducted a number of minimal

**Social categorisation**
Classification of people as members of different social groups.

group experiments to show that if participants are made more certain and confident about how to use the complex and unusual minimal group matrices, categorisation does not produce group identification and intergroup discrimination (e.g. Grieve & Hogg, 1999; see Hogg, 2000c, 2007b, in press). It seems that one reason why people identify with groups, even minimal groups, is to reduce feelings of uncertainty (see below). Thus categorisation will produce identification and discrimination only if people identify with the category, and they will identify with the category only if the categorisation reduces subjective uncertainty in the situation.

The minimal group paradigm has not gone unchallenged. For example, there has been a lively debate over the measures, procedures and statistics used (Aschenbrenner & Schaefer, 1980; Bornstein et al., 1983; Branthwaite, Doyle & Lightbown, 1979; Turner, 1980, 1983), and over the extent to which favouritism reflects rational economic self-interest rather than social identity-based intergroup differentiation (Rabbie, Schot & Visser, 1989; Turner & Bourhis, 1996).

Another objection is that the conditions of the experiments create a demand characteristic whereby participants conform to the transparent expectations of the experimenters or simply to general norms of intergroup competitiveness (Gerard & Hoyt, 1974). This interpretation seems unlikely in the light of evidence that discrimination is not associated with awareness of being under surveillance (Grieve & Hogg, 1999) and that discrimination can be reduced when adherence to and awareness of discriminatory norms is increased (Billig, 1973; Tajfel & Billig, 1974). In fact, participants who are not actually categorised but only have the experiment described to them predict significantly less discrimination (i.e. there is no norm of discrimination) than is actually expressed by participants who are categorised (St Claire & Turner, 1982). Also, it can be almost impossible to encourage participants to follow an explicitly cooperative norm in a minimal intergroup situation (Hogg, Turner, Nascimento-Schulze, & Spriggs, 1986).

Although it is not a criticism of the minimal group paradigm, Mummendey and her associates have identified a positive–negative asymmetry in the minimal group effect (Mummendey & Otten, 1998; Otten, Mummendey & Blanz, 1996; see also Peeters & Czapinski, 1990). In the usual paradigm, participants give positively valued resources (points); the effect is much weaker or can disappear when they give negatively valued resources (e.g. punishment), or when instead of giving resources they subtract resources.

Finally, the minimal group effect really does reflect what happens in maximal or real-life groups. Groups really do strive to favour themselves over relevant outgroups. For example, Brown (1978), capitalising on competitive wage negotiations in Britain in the 1970s, found that shop stewards from one department in an aircraft engineering factory sacrificed as much as £2 a week in absolute terms in order to increase their relative advantage over a competing outgroup to £1. Furthermore, studies of nurses revealed that although nurses are supposed to be caring and self-sacrificing, ingroup identification was associated with just as much ingroup favouritism as among other less self-sacrificing groups (Oaker & Brown, 1986; Skevington, 1981; Van Knippenberg & Van Oers, 1984).

## Social identity theory

**Social identity theory**
Theory of group membership and intergroup relations based on self-categorisation, social comparison and the construction of a shared self-definition in terms of ingroup-defining properties.

The pivotal role of social categorisation in intergroup behaviour, as demonstrated by minimal group studies, led to the development by Tajfel and Turner of the concept of social identity (Tajfel, 1974; Tajfel & Turner, 1979). This simple idea has developed and evolved over the years to become perhaps the pre-eminent contemporary social psychological analysis of group processes, intergroup relations and the collective self – **social identity theory**. Social identity theory has a number of theoretically compatible and integrated subtheories and emphases – for example, Tajfel and Turner's (1979) original analysis focused on intergroup relations and can be referred to as the *social identity theory of intergroup relations,* and

Turner and colleagues' later focus on self-categorisation and group processes as a whole, **self-categorisation theory** (Turner, Hogg, Oakes, Reicher, & Wetherell, 1987), can be referred to as the *social identity theory of the group* (see Abrams & Hogg, 2001, in press; Hogg, 2006; Hogg & Abrams, 1988, 2003; Turner, 1999; see also Chapter 4). For a summary of Tajfel's range of contributions to social psychology, see Vaughan (2010b).

## Social identity and group membership

Based on the assumption that society is structured into distinct social groups that stand in power and status relations to one another (e.g. Blacks and Whites in the United States, Catholics and Protestants in Northern Ireland, Sunnis and Shi'ites in Iraq), a core premise of the social identity approach is that social categories (large groups such as a nation or church, but also intermediate groups such as an organisation, or small groups such as a club) provide members with a **social identity** – a definition and evaluation of who one is and a description and evaluation of what this entails. Social identities not only *describe* attributes but, very importantly, also *prescribe* what one should think and how one should behave as a member. For example, being a member of the social category 'student' means not only defining and evaluating yourself and being defined and evaluated by others as a student, but also thinking and behaving in characteristically student ways.

Social identity is that part of the self-concept that derives from group membership. It is associated with group and intergroup behaviours, which have some general characteristics: **ethnocentrism, ingroup favouritism, intergroup differentiation**; conformity to ingroup norms; ingroup solidarity and cohesion; and perception of self, outgroupers and fellow ingroupers in terms of relevant group **stereotypes**.

Social identity is quite separate from personal identity, which is that part of the self-concept that derives from personality traits and the idiosyncratic personal relationships we have with other people (Turner, 1982). Personal identity is not associated with group and intergroup behaviours – it is associated with interpersonal and individual behaviour. People have a repertoire of as many social and personal identities as they have groups they identify with, or close relationships and idiosyncratic attributes in terms of which they define themselves. However, although we have many discrete social and personal identities, we subjectively experience the self as an integrated whole person with a continuous and unbroken biography – the subjective experience of self as fragmented discontinuous selves would be problematic and associated with various psychopathologies.

Social identity theory distinguishes social from personal identity as a deliberate attempt to avoid explaining group and intergroup processes in terms of personality attributes or interpersonal relations. Social identity theorists believe that many social psychological theories of group processes and intergroup relations are limited because they explain the phenomena by aggregating effects of personality predispositions or interpersonal relations.

The **authoritarian personality** theory and the **frustration–aggression hypothesis** are examples of this latter type of explanation of prejudice and discrimination (Billig, 1976; see Chapter 10). To illustrate: if a social psychologist asks why people stick their arms out of car windows to indicate a turn, the question would remain unanswered by an explanation in terms of the biochemistry of muscle action. An explanation in terms of adherence to social norms would be more appropriate (though inappropriate to a biochemist asking the same question). It is the problem of **reductionism** (see Chapter 1 for details) that prompts social identity theorists to distinguish between social and personal identity (Doise, 1986; Israel & Tajfel, 1972; Moscovici, 1972; Taylor & Brown, 1979; Turner & Oakes, 1986).

## Social categorisation, prototypes and depersonalisation

Self-categorisation theory (Turner, Hogg, Oakes, Reicher, & Wetherell, 1987), the social identity theory of the group, specifies how categorisation is the social cognitive underpinning

**Self-categorisation theory**
Turner and associates' theory of how the process of categorising oneself as a group member produces social identity and group and intergroup behaviours.

**Social identity**
That part of the self-concept that derives from our membership of social groups.

**Ethnocentrism**
Evaluative preference for all aspects of our own group relative to other groups.

**Ingroup favouritism**
Behaviour that favours one's own group over other groups.

**Intergroup differentiation**
Behaviour that emphasises differences between our own group and other groups.

**Stereotype**
Widely shared and simplified evaluative image of a social group and its members.

**Authoritarian personality**
A syndrome of personality characteristics originating in childhood that predispose individuals to be prejudiced.

**Frustration–aggression hypothesis**
Theory that all frustration leads to aggression, and all aggression comes from frustration. Used to explain prejudice and intergroup aggression.

**Reductionism**
A phenomenon in terms of the language and concepts of a lower level of analysis, usually with a loss of explanatory power.

**Prototype**
Cognitive representation of the typical/ideal defining features of a category.

**Metacontrast principle**
The prototype of a group is that position within the group that has the largest ratio of 'differences to ingroup positions' to 'differences to outgroup positions'.

**Entitativity**
The property of a group that makes it seem like a coherent, distinct and unitary entity.

**Depersonalisation**
The perception and treatment of self and others not as unique individual persons but as prototypical embodiments of a social group.

of social identity phenomena. People cognitively represent social categories/groups as prototypes. A **prototype** is a fuzzy set of attributes (perceptions, beliefs, attitudes, feelings, behaviours) that describes one group and distinguishes it from relevant other groups. Prototypes obey the **metacontrast principle** – they maximise the ratio of intergroup differences to intragroup differences, and in so doing they accentuate group entitativity. **Entitativity** (Campbell, 1958; Hamilton & Sherman, 1996) is the property of a group that makes it seem like a coherent, distinct and unitary entity (see Chapter 8).

Metacontrast and entitativity imply that group prototypes are not simply the average of ingroup attributes, and the most prototypical person in a group is not the average group member. Because of the important intergroup distinctiveness function, prototypes are typically displaced from the group average in a direction that is further away from the relevant comparison outgroup. Prototypes are thus ideal rather than average types. It is quite conceivable that a group prototype may be so ideal that not a single member actually embodies it.

Prototypes are cognitive representations of groups. As such they are closely related to stereotypes (see Chapter 2). However, from a social identity perspective a prototype is a stereotype only if it is *shared* by group members (Tajfel, 1981a). Finally, prototypes are context dependent. What this means is that the content of a specific prototype changes as a function of the comparison outgroup and the relevant ingroup members present. This context dependence can be quite extreme in newly forming groups (a task group), but is probably less extreme in better established groups (e.g. ethnic groups) that are more firmly anchored in enduring global intergroup stereotypes. Good examples of context effects on prototypes can be found in international perceptions (e.g. Rutland & Cinnirella, 2000). For example, Hopkins and Moore (2001) found that Scots perceived themselves to be different from the English, but that this perceptual difference was diminished when they made comparisons between Scots and Germans.

The process of categorising someone leads to **depersonalisation**. When we categorise others, we see them through the lens of the relevant ingroup or outgroup prototype – we view them as members of a group, not as idiosyncratic individuals. We perceptually accentuate their similarity to (i.e. assimilate them to) the relevant prototype, thus perceiving them stereotypically and ethnocentrically. When we categorise ourselves, exactly the same happens – we define, perceive and evaluate ourselves in terms of our ingroup prototype, and behave in line with that prototype. Self-categorisation produces ingroup normative behaviour (conformity to group norms; see Chapter 7) and self-stereotyping (see Chapter 2), and is thus the process that causes us to behave like group members. Depersonalisation is not the same thing as dehumanisation – though it can produce dehumanisation (see Chapter 10) if the outgroup is deeply hated and is stereotyped in terms that deny its members any respect or human dignity.

## Psychological salience

What determines the point at which one social identity or another becomes the psychologically salient basis for social categorisation of self and others? Without an answer to this question, social identity researchers would have a serious scientific problem – they would be unable to predict or manipulate social identity-contingent behaviours. Oakes and her associates have drawn on work by Campbell (1958) to answer this critical question (Oakes, 1987; Oakes, Haslam & Turner, 1994; Oakes & Turner, 1990; see Chapter 2). Social categories that are (a) chronically accessible to us (e.g. in memory), and/or (b) accessible in the situation (e.g. there are obvious cues to the category), come into operation as the basis of self-categorisation if they make good sense of the situation (a) by accounting for similarities and differences between people (i.e. they fit the way the situation is structured) and (b) by accounting for why people behave as they do (i.e. they fit the norms that people seem to adhere to). This can be put technically: salience is an interactive function of *chronic accessibility* and *situational accessibility* on the one hand, and *structural fit* and *normative fit* on the other.

## Positive distinctiveness and self-enhancement

Social identity phenomena are motivated by two underlying processes: self-enhancement and uncertainty reduction. One of the key premises of social identity theory is that groups stand in status and prestige relations to one another – some groups are simply more prestigious and higher status than others, and most people in a given social context know this. Intergroup relations are characterised by a struggle over prestige and status (Tajfel & Turner, 1979; also see Hogg & Abrams, 1988). From a social identity point of view, groups compete to be different from one another in favourable ways because positive intergroup distinctiveness provides group members with a favourable (positive) social identity. Unlike interpersonal comparisons, which generally strive for similarity (e.g. Festinger, 1954; Suls & Wheeler, 2000), intergroup comparisons strive to maximise differences in ways that evaluatively favour the ingroup.

Researchers have found these positive distinctiveness and positive social identity ideas helpful in understanding a range of phenomena (Ellemers, Spears & Doosje, 1999): for example, delinquency. Emler and his colleagues have suggested that delinquency, particularly among boys, is strategic behaviour designed to establish and manage a favourable reputation among groups of peers (Emler & Hopkins, 1990; Emler & Reicher, 1995). Consistent with this view is the fact that delinquent behaviour is usually a group activity that occurs in public, thus maximising its identity-confirming function (Emler, Ohana & Moscovici, 1987). Furthermore, delinquent behaviour is particularly appealing to children who come from backgrounds that are unlikely to facilitate good academic performance at school: delinquency therefore offers an alternative source of positive identity (it is so attractive that most children toy with it to some extent at one time or another). Reicher and Emler (1985) have suggested that one reason that boys are much more likely than girls to become delinquent is that there is greater pressure on boys to perform well at school and therefore underachievement is more poignantly felt: the motivation to establish an alternative positive social identity is so much stronger.

Positive distinctiveness as a group-level process is believed to map on to a very basic human motivation for self-enhancement (Sedikides & Strube, 1997, see Chapter 4). Drawing on this analysis, social identity researchers have suggested that self-esteem is a key motive in social identity contexts. Research (Abrams & Hogg, 1988; Crocker & Luhtanen, 1990; Crocker & Major, 1989; Hogg & Abrams, 1990; Long & Spears, 1997; Rubin & Hewstone, 1998) on self-esteem motivation has shown that:

- intergroup differentiation tends to elevate self-esteem;
- depressed self-esteem does not motivate intergroup differentiation;
- it is collective self-esteem, not personal self-esteem, that is related to group processes;
- people in groups are highly creative and competent at protecting themselves from the low self-esteem consequences of low status group membership.

## Uncertainty reduction

Social identity processes are, according to *uncertainty–identity theory,* also motivated by uncertainty reduction (Hogg, 2000c, 2007b, in press). In life, people are fundamentally motivated to know who they are and how they relate to other people – they need to feel relatively certain about what to think, feel and do, and about what others will think, feel and do. We need to know what to expect from other people in order to make life predictable and allow us to plan effective action.

Group identification is a highly effective way of reducing uncertainty. Identification with a group, through relevant prototypes, immediately and automatically defines our relationships with ingroup and outgroup others and sets out how we and others will act. Experimental research, largely using variants of the minimal group paradigm, has shown that people identify with groups and identify more strongly with groups when they are uncertain (e.g. Grieve & Hogg, 1999).

However, when people feel uncertain about themselves they prefer to identify with highly entitative groups as they provide a better structured and clearer sense of self (Hogg, Sherman, Dierselhuis, Maitner, & Moffitt, 2007); people can also perceptually accentuate the entitativity of existing groups they belong to (Sherman, Hogg, & Maitner, 2009). One implication of this preference for high entitativity groups is that when uncertainty is acute, enduring and highly self relevant people may strive to identify with groups that are not merely entitative but extreme, in so far as they are normatively homogenous, inward looking, intolerant of dissent, highly ethnocentric, and governed by a powerful, all-embracing, orthodox ideological system. This may explain why extremism, orthodoxy and group intolerance often arise in times of societal uncertainty associated with war, revolution, economic collapse, natural disaster and so forth. It also explains the enduring attraction of religious identities (they provide a distinctive sense of self, a repertoire of customs and rituals, a well-established ideology, a powerful moral compass, and even deal with existential uncertainty), and the tendency for religiosity to drift into religious zealotry (Hogg, Adelman, & Blagg, in press).

## Social identity and intergroup relations

Social identity theory was originally founded on an attempt to explain intergroup conflict and social change – this was Tajfel's original social identity theory (Tajfel, 1974; Tajfel & Turner, 1979).

In pursuit of positive social identity, groups and individuals can adopt an array of different behavioural strategies, the choice of which is determined by people's beliefs about the nature of relations between their own and other groups (Ellemers, 1993; Hogg & Abrams, 1988; Tajfel & Turner, 1979; Taylor & McKirnan, 1984) – see Figure 11.6. These beliefs, which may or may not accord with the reality of intergroup relations (they are ideological constructs), hinge first on whether it is possible, as an individual, to 'pass' from a lower-status group and gain acceptance in a higher-status group. A **social mobility belief system** inhibits group action on the part of subordinate groups, and instead encourages individuals to dissociate themselves from the group and try to gain acceptance for themselves and their immediate family in the dominant group. The belief in social mobility is enshrined in Western democratic political systems.

Where individuals believe that intergroup boundaries are impermeable to 'passing', a **social change belief system** exists (e.g. the Hindu caste system in India). In these circumstances, positive social identity can be achieved only by forms of group action, and the sort of action taken is influenced by whether the status quo (the existing status and power hierarchy) is perceived to be secure or insecure. If the status quo is considered stable, legitimate and thus secure, it is difficult to conceive of an alternative social structure (i.e. no **cognitive alternatives** exist), let alone a path to real social change. Groups tend to adopt **social creativity** strategies:

- They can engage in intergroup comparisons on novel or unorthodox dimensions that tend to favour the subordinate group. For example, Lemaine (1966, 1974) had children engage in an intergroup competition to build the best hut, and found that groups that were provided with poor building materials, and thus had no possibility of winning, went on to emphasise how good a garden they had made.

- They can attempt to change the consensual value attached to ingroup characteristics (e.g. the slogan 'Black is beautiful').

- They can compare themselves with other low- or lower-status groups (e.g. 'poor-White racism').

**Social mobility belief system**
Belief that intergroup boundaries are permeable. Thus, it is possible for someone to pass from a lower-status into a higher-status group to improve social identity.

**Social change belief system**
Belief that intergroup boundaries are impermeable. Therefore, a lower-status individual can improve social identity only by challenging the legitimacy of the higher-status group's position.

**Cognitive alternatives**
Belief that the status quo is unstable and illegitimate, and that social competition with the dominant group is the appropriate strategy to improve social identity.

**Social creativity**
Group-based behavioural strategies that improve social identity but do not directly attack the dominant group's position.

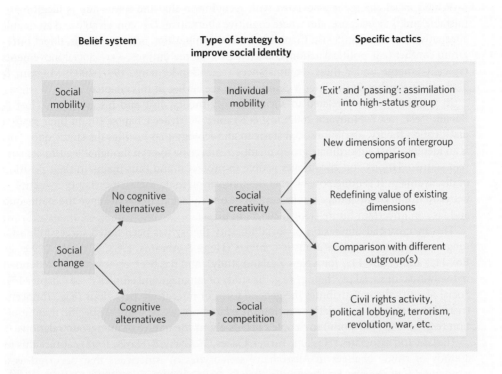

**Figure 11.6**  Social identity theory: belief structures and strategies for improving social identity

Beliefs about the nature of intergroup relations influence the general strategies and specific tactics that group members can adopt to try to maintain or achieve positive social identity

**Social action**
Even a peaceful demonstration can challenge the status quo and a state's power base

**Social competition**
Group-based behavioural strategies that improve social identity by directly confronting the dominant group's position in society.

**System justification theory**
Theory that attributes social stasis to people's adherence to an ideology that justifies and protects the status quo.

Where social change is associated with recognition that the status quo is illegitimate, unstable and thus insecure, and where cognitive alternatives (i.e. conceivable and attainable alternative social orders) exist, then direct **social competition** occurs – that is, direct intergroup conflict (e.g. political action, collective protest, revolutions, war). Social movements typically emerge under these circumstances (e.g. Klandermans, 1997, 2003; Milgram & Toch, 1969; Reicher, 2001; Tyler & Smith, 1998; see earlier in this chapter).

In a manner closely related to social identity theory, Jost and his associates (Jost & Banaji, 1994; Jost & Hunyadi, 2002; Jost & Kramer, 2002; see Chapter 10), in their **system justification theory**, attribute social stasis to an ideology that justifies the status quo. This is an ideology that subordinate group members subscribe to even though it legitimises current status relations and encourages people to protect it and thus maintain their position of disadvantage. It is quite possible that the motivation to do this is uncertainty reduction – better to live in disadvantage but be certain of one's place than to challenge the status quo and face an uncertain future (Hogg, 2007b, in press).

This macrosocial dimension of social identity theory has been tested successfully in a range of laboratory and naturalistic contexts (Hogg & Abrams, 1988; Ellemers, 1993; see Box 11.3 and Figure 11.7 for a New Zealand study), and has been elaborated and extended in many areas of social psychology (e.g. the study of language and ethnicity; see Chapter 15). Social identity theory attributes the general form of intergroup behaviour (e.g. ethnocentrism, stereotyping) to social categorisation related processes, and the specific manifestation (e.g. conflict, harmony) to people's beliefs about the nature of intergroup relations.

Haslam and associates (Haslam, Turner, Oakes, McGarty, & Hayes, 1992) capture this in a study of subtle changes in Australians' stereotypes of Americans that occurred as a consequence of changes in intergroup attitudes caused by the first (1991) Gulf War. They discovered that Australians who were making comparisons between Australia, Britain and the United States had a relatively unfavourable stereotype of Americans that deteriorated further during the course of the Gulf conflict, particularly on dimensions reflecting arrogance, argumentativeness and traditionalism. The authors argue that the reason why attitudes deteriorated on these particular dimensions rather than others was that these dimensions related directly to the perceived actions of Americans in relation to other nations during the war.

## Other aspects

Social identity theory has a number of other important components, most of which are discussed elsewhere in this book. These include the following:

- Referent informational influence theory (Abrams & Hogg, 1990a; Turner, 1991; Turner & Oakes, 1989), which deals with conformity (Chapter 7) and group polarisation (Chapter 9).
- The social attraction hypothesis (Hogg, 1993), which deals with cohesion and attraction phenomena in groups (Chapter 8).
- The theory of subjective group dynamics (Marques, Abrams & Serodio, 2001), which deals with deviance processes in groups (Chapter 8).
- The social identity theory of leadership (Hogg, 2001b; Hogg & van Knippenberg, 2003; Chapter 9).
- The social identity theory of attitude–behaviour relations (Terry & Hogg, 1996; Hogg & Smith, 2007; Chapter 5).
- The social identity theory of deindividuation phenomena (Klein, Spears, & Reicher, 2007; Reicher, Spears & Postmes, 1995; see below).
- Collective guilt – where you feel guilty, as a group member, about past transgressions committed by your group (Doosje, Branscombe, Spears & Manstead, 1998).

## Research and applications 11.3
### Social change: growth of pride in an indigenous people

Maori people are New Zealand's indigenous people and make up about 10 per cent of the population. The remainder of the population is predominantly Pakeha (i.e. European). Graham Vaughan has collected data on ingroup (ethnic) preferences of younger (6–8 years) and older (10–12 years) Maori and Pakeha children from urban and rural backgrounds (Vaughan, 1978a, 1978b). The data were collected at various times during the 1960s, which was a period of considerable social change in New Zealand, and these data are displayed in Figure 11.7. The arrows represent an age trend from younger to older children within each ethnic group at each time and at each location. Choices above 50 per cent represent ingroup preference and those below 50 per cent outgroup preference.

Against an overall reduction in ethnocentrism for older children (presumably a developmental trend), the data show that urban Pakeha preferred their own group but were less ethnocentric than rural Pakeha, and rural Maori showed more marked outgroup preference than urban Maori. The most interesting finding was that, between 1961 and 1971 urban Maori actually changed from making outgroup to making ingroup preferences – a change that reflected the rise in the late 1960s and early 1970s of an assertive Brown (Maori) Power movement modelled on the American Black Power movement of the 1960s.

Intergroup perceptions may be less ethnocentric in the city for a number of reasons, including perhaps inter-ethnic contact. Maori who moved to the city were often cut off from the traditional Polynesian extended family (and from other aspects of Maori culture) and found that they had to compete with Pakeha for work. There was a gradual realignment of ethnic power relations and greater possibility of less unequal-status inter-ethnic contact. Perhaps this contributed to some extent to reduced prejudice on the part of Pakeha and elevated ethnic pride on the part of Maori.

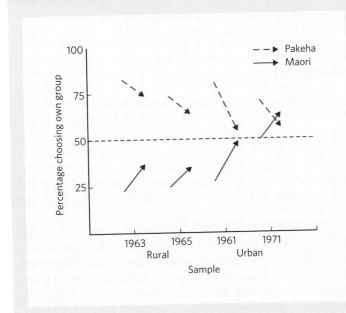

**Figure 11.7**  Ingroup bias among Maori and Pakeha children as a function of social change (time, nature of intergroup contact)

The direction of the arrows emphasises an age trend from younger to older children in each group. By 1971, older urban Maori were exhibiting more ingroup bias than older urban Pakeha. Between 1961 and 1971 there was a systematic decrease in Pakeha ingroup bias and Maori outgroup bias, which was more pronounced for older than younger children

Source: Vaughan (1978b); in Tajfel (1978)

# Social cognition

Although self-categorisation theory has a social cognitive emphasis on the role of cognitive processes and cognitive representations in intergroup behaviour (Farr, 1996), it is a theory that explicitly articulates with a more broadly social analysis (Doise, 1986; see Chapter 1). This is because, as we have seen, it is part of the broader social identity theory.

**Social change**
For this Paralympics athlete victory brings glory to her country. She also promotes a positive image of disabled people

Social cognition (see Chapter 2 for full coverage), however, provides a number of other more purely cognitive explanations, which focus on certain cognitive and perceptual effects that have important implications for intergroup behaviour.

## Categorisation and relative homogeneity

**Accentuation effect**
Overestimation of similarities among people within a category and dissimilarities between people from different categories.

The most obvious effect is stereotyping. The categorisation of people (or objects) has been shown to cause an **accentuation effect** (Tajfel, 1959): the perceptual accentuation of similarities among people in a category and of differences between people from different categories on those dimensions believed to be associated with the categorisation: that is, stereotypical dimensions (Doise, 1978; Eiser & Stroebe, 1972; Tajfel & Wilkes, 1963). There is some evidence that people perceptually homogenise outgroup members more than ingroup members: '*they* all look alike, but *we* are diverse' (Brigham & Malpass, 1985; Quattrone, 1986).

For example, Brigham and Barkowitz (1978) had Black and White college students indicate for seventy-two photographs of Black and White faces how certain they were that they had seen each photograph in a previously presented series of twenty-four photographs (twelve of Blacks and twelve of Whites). Figure 11.8 shows that participants found it more difficult to recognise outgroup than ingroup faces. This effect is quite robust. It has emerged from other studies comparing 'Anglos' with Blacks (Bothwell, Brigham & Malpass, 1989), with Hispanics (Platz & Hosch, 1988) and with Japanese (Chance, 1985), and from studies of student eating clubs (Jones, Wood & Quattrone, 1981), college sororities (Park & Rothbart, 1982) and artificial laboratory groups (Wilder, 1984).

**Relative homogeneity effect**
Tendency to see outgroup members as all the same, and ingroup members as more differentiated.

The **relative homogeneity effect** is enhanced on group-defining dimensions (Lee & Ottati, 1993) and when groups are in competition (Judd & Park, 1988) – see Ostrom and Sedikides (1992). The principal explanation for this effect is that, because we are generally more familiar with ingroup than outgroup members, we have more detailed knowledge about the former and thus are better able to differentiate them (Linville, Fischer & Salovey, 1989; Wilder, 1986). Although quite sensible, this may not be the complete story. For

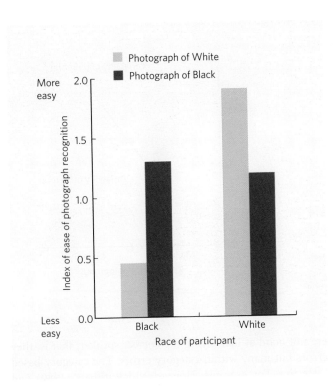

**Figure 11.8** Ease of recognition of faces as a function of race of participant and race of person in photograph

Black and White participants had more difficulty identifying faces they had seen before if the faces were of racial outgroup rather than racial ingroup members

*Source:* based on data from Brigham & Barkowitz (1978)

example, the outgroup homogeneity effect occurs when participants report no greater familiarity with the ingroup than the outgroup (Jones, Wood & Quattrone, 1981) and when there is equally minimal information about both groups (Wilder, 1984). Stephan (1977) found that children in both segregated and integrated schools (i.e. with lower or higher intergroup familiarity) actually rated their own group as more homogeneous than two outgroups. If outgroup homogeneity is not inevitable, what factors influence the relative homogeneity effect?

One clue is that, while most research has used majority or equal-sized groups, Stephan's (1977) groups were minority groups (Chicanos and Blacks). Also, the relative outgroup homogeneity effect is enhanced when the outgroup is perceived to be relatively small – a minority (Bartsch & Judd, 1993; Mullen & Hu, 1989). To test the idea that relative homogeneity is influenced by the majority–minority status of the ingroup, Simon and Brown (1987) conducted a minimal group study. Relative group size was varied, and participants were asked to rate the variability of both ingroup and outgroup and to indicate how much they identified with the ingroup. Figure 11.9 shows that while majorities rated the outgroup as less variable than the ingroup (the usual outgroup homogeneity effect), minorities did the opposite. In addition, this latter ingroup homogeneity effect was accompanied by greater group identification. This is consistent with social identity theory: minorities categorise themselves more strongly as a group and are thus more strongly depersonalised (see above) in their perceptions, attitudes and behaviour.

## Memory

Social categorisation is associated with category-based person memory effects (Fiske & Taylor, 1991). For example, Taylor, Fiske, Etcoff and Ruderman (1978) had participants listen to taped mixed-sex or mixed-race discussion groups and later attribute various statements to the correct speaker. They rarely attributed the statements to the wrong category,

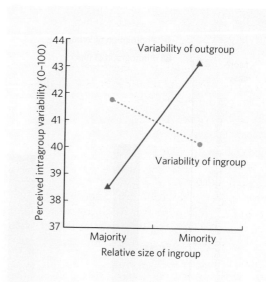

**Figure 11.9** Perceived intragroup variability of ingroup and outgroup as a function of relative majority or minority status of ingroup

Majorities rated the outgroup as less variable than the ingroup (the usual relative homogeneity effect). However, minorities did the opposite – they rated the outgroup as more variable than the ingroup

*Source*: based on data from Simon & Brown (1987)

but within categories they were not good at identifying the correct speaker: that is, they made few between-category errors but many within-category errors. The category-based memory effect can be quite selective. For example, Howard and Rothbart (1980) had participants read statements describing ingroup or outgroup members behaving in different ways – some of the behaviour reflected favourably and some unfavourably on the actor. Later, for each behaviour, they had to recall whether it was an ingroup or an outgroup member who performed each behaviour. The participants were equally accurate at recalling whether it was an ingroup or outgroup member who performed the favourable behaviour, but they were more accurate at recalling outgroup than ingroup actors who performed unfavourable behaviour (see Figure 11.10).

These two experiments illustrate the way in which information about individuals can be represented cognitively and organised as category attributes that submerge individual differences between people in the same category. Furthermore, evaluative biases may influence what information is associated with a particular category.

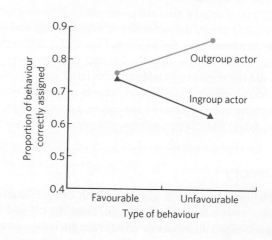

**Figure 11.10** Assignment of behaviours to actors as a function of item favourability and ingroup/outgroup status of actor

Participants were equally good at recalling whether it was an ingroup or outgroup member who performed favourable behaviours, but they were better at recalling outgroup than ingroup actors who performed unfavourable behaviours

*Source*: based on Howard & Rothbart (1980)

## Distinctive stimuli and illusory correlation

A particularly important influence on what information is associated with which categories is the distinctiveness of the information. Anything that is out of the ordinary (objects, events and people who are statistically infrequent, rare, unusual, relatively vivid or conspicuous) tends to attract our attention and engage a disproportionate amount of cognitive activity (Taylor & Fiske, 1978). So, for example, we tend to attend more to a single man in a group of women, a single Black in a group of Whites, or to a person we understand to be a genius, a homosexual or a movie star. Distinctive individuals can also disproportionately influence the generalised images we construct of groups. There is a tendency to generalise from distinctive individuals to the group as a whole, particularly when we have few prior expectations and/or are unfamiliar with the category (Quattrone & Jones, 1980). For instance, on the basis of meeting one extremely stupid (i.e. distinctive individual) Martian (i.e. unfamiliar group), we are apt to stereotype the group as stupid.

Another effect of distinctiveness is that people tend to perceive an **illusory correlation**, based on *paired distinctiveness* or *associative meaning*, between distinctive events that occur at the same time (Chapman, 1967; illusory correlation is discussed fully in Chapter 2). Distinctiveness-based illusory correlation may help to explain stereotyping, particularly negative stereotypes of minority groups (Hamilton 1979; Hamilton & Sherman, 1989; Mullen & Johnson, 1990): negative events are distinctive because they are subjectively less frequent than positive events; and minority groups are distinctive because people have relatively few contacts with them. Illusory correlation based on associative meaning may also be involved in negative stereotyping of minority groups: people have preconceptions that negative attributes go with minority groups (McArthur & Friedman, 1980).

Distinctiveness-based illusory correlation is a robust empirical effect, which is stronger for negative behaviour, under conditions of high memory load (McConnell, Sherman & Hamilton, 1994; Mullen & Johnson, 1990), and when people are aroused (Kim & Baron, 1988). Once an illusory correlation between a group and a negative attribute in one domain (e.g. intellectual) has been established, there is a tendency to generalise the negative impression to other domains (e.g. social; Acorn, Hamilton & Sherman, 1988).

A limitation of viewing illusory correlation as an explanation of stereotyping is that it does not consider the emotional and self-conceptual investment that people have in stereotyping, or the material bases of power and status differentials between groups that stereotype one another. As we have seen in this chapter and in Chapter 10, the construction and use of stereotypes is framed by intergroup relations and governed by cognitive, affective and rhetorical motives (Leyens, Yzerbyt & Schadron, 1994; McGarty, Haslam, Turner & Oakes, 1993; Oakes, Haslam & Turner, 1994).

**Illusory correlation**
Cognitive exaggeration of the degree of co-occurrence of two stimuli or events, or the perception of a co-occurrence where none exists.

## Optimal distinctiveness

Distinctiveness enters into intergroup behaviour in rather a different way in Brewer's (1991, 1993) theory of **optimal distinctiveness**. Building on her dual-process model of information processing (Brewer, 1988, 1994; see Chapter 2), she argues that the default mode for processing information about others is in terms of their category membership (satisfying a need to recognise similarities among people). However, if one feels ego-involved in the task, or related to or interdependent with the stimulus person, then information processing is based on very specific and personalised information about the stimulus person (this satisfies a need to recognise differences between people). In most contexts, people strive to achieve a satisfactory level of distinctiveness for others and for themselves in order to resolve the tension between the needs for similarity and difference. In intergroup behaviour, this manifests itself as a degree of differentiation between group members, including self, against a background of homogenisation. A related phenomenon was earlier identified by Codol

**Optimal distinctiveness**
People strive to achieve a balance between conflicting motives for inclusiveness and separateness, expressed in groups as a balance between intragroup differentiation and intragroup homogenisation.

(1975), called the *primus inter pares* effect, in which individuals in a group seemed to differentiate themselves from one another in competition to be the most representative or best group member.

From Brewer's perspective, people are driven by conflicting motives for inclusion/sameness (satisfied by group membership) and for distinctiveness/uniqueness (satisfied by individuality), so they try to strike a balance between these two motives in order to achieve optimal distinctiveness. Smaller groups more than satisfy the need for distinctiveness, so people strive for greater inclusiveness, while large groups more than satisfy the need for inclusiveness, so people strive for distinctiveness. One implication of this idea is that people should be more satisfied with membership of mid-size groups than groups that are very large or very small. This idea is usually tested in the laboratory with a restricted range of relative group sizes. To investigate groups that varied enormously in relative size, Abrams (1994) analysed survey data on political identity from over 4,000 18–21-year-olds in England and Scotland. He found that small parties (Green, Social Democrat, Scottish Nationalist) did indeed provide members with a more solid and distinct identity than did the large parties (Labour, Conservative).

## Intergroup emotions

**Intergroup emotions theory**
Theory that, in group contexts, appraisals of personal harm or benefit in a situation operate at the level of social identity and thus produce mainly positive ingroup and negative outgroup emotions.

People in groups that are important to them tend to feel strong emotions about outgroups and fellow members of their own groups. Mackie and Smith and their associates have recently proposed **intergroup emotions theory** (IET) to address emotions in group contexts (Mackie, Devos & Smith, 1999; Mackie & Smith, 2002a; also see Mackie, Maitner & Smith, 2009; Mackie & Smith, 2002b).

IET argues that individual emotions are based on appraisals of whether a situation is going to harm or benefit oneself personally. Drawing on social identity theory, IET goes on to argue that in group contexts the self is a collective self and so appraisals operate at the level of whether a situation is going to harm or benefit 'us'. When people identify with a group, intergroup emotions come into play. Harm to the ingroup, which often emanates from the actions of outgroups, is appraised as self-harming and generates negative emotions about the outgroup. Behaviour that promotes the ingroup, often emanating from fellow ingroup members, generates positive emotions about the ingroup and its members. Emotions have an action tendency and so outgroup emotions may translate into discrimination and ingroup emotions into solidarity and cohesion. From IET it can also be predicted that emotions felt by fellow ingroup members will quickly be felt by self – owing to the common identity bond that exists.

## Collective behaviour and the crowd

**Collective behaviour**
The behaviour of people en masse – such as in a crowd, protest or riot.

**Collective behaviour** usually refers to large numbers of people who are in the same place at the same time, and who behave in a uniform manner that is volatile, highly emotional and in violation of social norms (Graumann & Moscovici, 1986; Milgram & Toch, 1969; Moscovici, 1985b). Some social psychologists interpret this to include the study of rumours (see Chapter 3), fads and fashions, social movements and cults, and contagions of expression, enthusiasm, anxiety, fear and hostility.

Contagions include some of the most bizarre behaviour imaginable (Klapp, 1972). In the 1630s, tulip mania swept north-western Europe, with people trading small fortunes for a single, ultimately worthless, bulb; in the fifteenth century, there was an epidemic in Europe in which nuns bit each other; in the eighteenth century, there was an epidemic of nuns meowing like cats; between the tenth and the fourteenth centuries in Europe there were frequent episodes of dancing mania, with people continually dancing from town to town until they dropped and even died; and in the mid- and late 1980s, there were epidemics in China of men complaining hysterically about shrinkage of the penis and an overwhelming fear of impending death!

Usually, however, the study of collective behaviour is a more sober business. It is the study of crowd behaviour. The crowd is a vivid social phenomenon both for those who are involved and for those who witness the events first-hand or through literature and the media. Consider the Tiananmen Square protest in 1989, the Los Angeles riots of 1992, Nazi rallies of the 1930s, celebrations at the fall of the Berlin Wall in 1990, political demonstrations in the streets of Tehran in 2009, street marches in Madrid in 2004 over the terrorist bombing of commuter trains, anti-war demonstrations over Vietnam in the late 1960s and Iraq in the mid-2000s, rock festivals since the late 1960s, and the crowd scenes in Richard Attenborough's movie *Gandhi*. Crowd events are nothing if not varied.

Crowd behaviour, in its full manifestation, can be difficult to research in the laboratory, although attempts have been made. For example, French (1944) locked his participants in a room and then wafted smoke under the door while sounding the fire alarm. Ethics aside, the study was not successful as an attempt to create panic in the laboratory. One group kicked open the door and knocked over the smoke generator, and another group calmly discussed the possibility that its reactions were being observed by the experimenters!

## Early theories

One of the earliest theories of collective behaviour was proposed by LeBon (1896/1908), who lived through a period of profound social turmoil in France. He observed and read accounts of the great revolutionary crowds of the revolution of 1848 and the Paris Commune of 1871 – accounts such as those to be found in Zola's novels *Germinal* and *La Débâcle*, and Hugo's *Les Misérables*. He was appalled by the 'primitive, base and ghastly' behaviour of the crowd, and the way in which people's civilised conscious personality seemed to vanish and be replaced by savage animal instincts. LeBon believed that:

> by the mere fact that he forms part of an organised crowd, a man descends several rungs in the ladder of civilisation. Isolated, he may be a cultivated individual; in a crowd he is a barbarian – that is, a creature acting by instinct. (*LeBon, 1908, p. 12*)

According to LeBon, crowds produce primitive and homogeneous behaviour because (see Figure 11.11):

- members are anonymous and thus lose personal responsibility for their actions;
- ideas and sentiments spread rapidly and unpredictably through a process of contagion;
- unconscious antisocial motives ('ancestral savagery') are released through suggestion (a process akin to hypnosis).

LeBon is still important nowadays (see Apfelbaum & McGuire, 1986; Hogg & Abrams, 1988; Reicher, 1987, 1996, 2001), owing mainly to the influence of his perspective, in which crowd behaviour is considered to be pathological/abnormal, on later theories of collective behaviour (e.g. Freud, 1921; McDougall, 1920; Zimbardo, 1970). Freud, for example, argued that the crowd 'unlocks' the unconscious. Society's moral standards maintain civilised behaviour because they are installed in the human psyche as the super-ego. However, in crowds, the super-ego is supplanted by the leader of the crowd, who now acts as the hypnotist controlling unconscious and uncivilised id impulses. Crowd leaders have this effect because of a deep and primitive instinct in all of us to regress, in crowds, to the 'primal horde' – the original brutal human group at the dawn of existence. Civilisation is

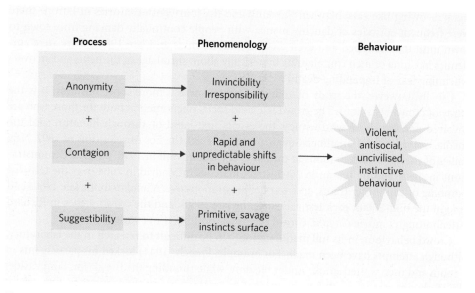

**Figure 11.11** LeBon's model of the crowd

Anonymity, contagion and suggestibility operate together to produce antisocial, violent crowd behaviour

*Source:* based on Hogg (1992)

able to evolve and thrive only to the extent that the leader of the primal horde, the 'primal father', is overthrown. This analysis has been used to explain how the 'Reverend' Jim Jones had such enormous power over his cult followers that more than 900 of them collectively committed suicide at Jonestown in Guyana in 1978 (Ulman and Abse, 1983). (Reflect on the fourth focus question at the beginning of this chapter).

Another important early theorist is McDougall, who characterised the crowd as:

> excessively emotional, impulsive, violent, fickle, inconsistent, irresolute and extreme in action, displaying only the coarser emotions and the less refined sentiments; extremely suggestible, careless in deliberation, hasty in judgment, incapable of any but the simpler and imperfect forms of reasoning, easily swayed and led, lacking in self-consciousness, devoid of self-respect and of a sense of responsibility, and apt to be carried away by the consciousness of its own force, so that it tends to produce all the manifestations we have learnt to expect of any irresponsible and absolute power. (*McDougall, 1920, p. 45*)

McDougall believed that the most widespread instinctive emotions are the simple primitive ones (e.g. fear, anger), and that these would therefore be the most common and widely shared emotions in any human aggregate. More complex emotions would be rare and less widely shared. Stimuli eliciting the primitive simple emotions would therefore cause a strong consensual reaction, while those eliciting more complex emotions would not. Primary emotions spread and strengthen rapidly in a crowd, as each member's expression of the emotion acts as a further stimulus to others – a snowball effect dubbed 'primitive sympathy'. This effect is not easily modulated, as individuals feel depersonalised and have a lowered sense of personal responsibility.

## Deindividuation and self-awareness

More recent explanations of collective behaviour discard some of the specifics of earlier approaches (e.g. the emphasis on instinctive emotions, the psychodynamic framework) but retain the overall perspective. People usually refrain from exercising their basically impulsive, aggressive and selfish nature because of their identifiability as unique individuals in

**Deindividuation**
People in uniforms, and in a large group, have a cloak of anonymity

societies that have strong norms against 'uncivilised' conduct. In crowds, these restraints are relaxed and we can revert to type and embark on an orgy of aggressive, selfish, antisocial behaviour. The mediating mechanism is **deindividuation**.

The term 'deindividuation', coined by Festinger, Pepitone and Newcomb (1952), originates in Jung's definition of 'individuation' as 'a process of differentiation, having for its goal the development of the individual personality' (Jung, 1946, p. 561). It was Zimbardo (1970) who developed the concept most fully. He believed that being in a large group provides people with a cloak of anonymity that diffuses personal responsibility for the consequences of their actions. This leads to a loss of identity and a reduced concern for social evaluation: that is, to a state of deindividuation, which causes behaviour to become impulsive, irrational, regressive and disinhibited because it is not under the usual social and personal controls.

Research into deindividuation has tended to focus on the effects of anonymity on behaviour in groups. Festinger, Pepitone and Newcomb (1952) found that participants dressed in grey laboratory coats and seated in a poorly lit room for a group discussion of their parents made more negative comments about their parents than did participants in a control condition (see also Cannavale, Scarr & Pepitone, 1970). Similarly, participants dressed in laboratory coats used more obscene language when discussing erotic literature than did more easily identifiable individuals (Singer, Brush & Lublin, 1965).

Zimbardo (1970) conducted a series of experiments in which participants were deindividuated by wearing cloaks and hoods (reminiscent of the Ku Klux Klan). In one such experiment, deindividuated female students gave electric shocks to a female confederate in a paired-associate learning task that were twice the duration of those given by conventionally dressed participants. In another classic study, in which a simulated prison was constructed in the basement of the Psychology Department of Stanford University, Zimbardo (Zimbardo, Haney, Banks & Jaffe, 1982; see Chapter 8) found that students who were deindividuated by being dressed as guards were extremely brutal to other students who were deindividuated as prisoners. There is also evidence that people are more willing to lynch someone (Mullen, 1986) or bait a disturbed person to jump from a building if it is dark and if they are in a larger group (Mann, 1981; see Chapter 12).

**Deindividuation**
Process whereby people lose their sense of socialised individual identity and engage in unsocialised, often antisocial, behaviours.

Finally, Diener and colleagues (Diener, Fraser, Beaman & Kelem, 1976) conducted a clever study that took advantage of Hallowe'en – when the streets were filled with children, disguised and thus anonymous, who were trick-or-treating. The researchers observed the behaviour of 1,352 children, alone or in groups, who approached twenty-seven focal homes in Seattle where they were warmly invited in and told to 'take *one* of the candies' on a table. Half the children were first asked their names and where they lived, to reduce deindividuation. Groups and deindividuated children were more than twice as likely to take extra candy. The transgression rate varied from 8 per cent of individuated individuals to 80 per cent of deindividuated groups.

Although, in general, anonymity seems to increase aggressive antisocial behaviour (Dipboye, 1977), there are problematic findings. Zimbardo (1970) employed his deindividuation paradigm with Belgian soldiers and found that they gave electric shocks of shorter duration when dressed in cloaks and hoods. Zimbardo suggests that this might be because the soldiers were an intact group (i.e. already deindividuated), and the 'cloak and hood' procedure had the paradoxical effect of reducing deindividuation.

However, other studies reported reduced aggression when a person is anonymous or when a member of a group (Diener, 1976). In one study, Johnson and Downing (1979) had female participants administer shocks to confederate 'learners' in a paired-associate learning task. The women were deindividuated when clothed to resemble either a Ku Klux Klan member or a nurse. The experimenter highlighted the impact of the clothing by explicitly commenting on the resemblance. Half of each group also wore a large badge displaying their name in order to individuate them (i.e. deindividuation was reduced). Deindividuation failed to increase aggression, even among those dressed as Ku Klux Klan members (see Figure 11.12). However, those dressed as nurses were significantly less aggressive than those dressed as Ku Klux Klan members, and deindividuated nurses were the least aggressive of all. These studies tell us two important things:

1   Anonymity does not automatically lead people to be more aggressive and antisocial.

2   Normative expectations surrounding situations of deindividuation may influence behaviour. In the Johnson and Downing study, when women were dressed like a nurse they became more caring.

Regarding this second point, Jahoda (1982) has noted the similarity between Zimbardo's method of deindividuation (i.e. hood and robe), and the wearing of the *chadoor* (full-length

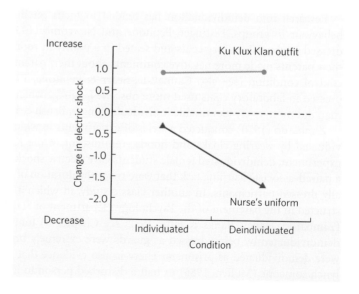

**Figure 11.12**  Administration of electric shocks as a function of deindividuation and type of uniform

- In a paired-associate learning task, women participants dressed in either of two uniforms believed that they gave shocks of various levels to a confederate learner.

- Those dressed ad Ku Klux Klan members gave increased levels of shock to the learner, whereas those dressed as nurses gave reduced levels.

- Further, deindividuated participants (i.e. those not wearing large personal name badges) were not more aggressive, and in fact those deindividuated as nurses were the least aggressive of all.

*Source*: based on data from Johnson & Downing (1979)

veil) by women in some Islamic countries. Far from setting free antisocial impulses, the *chador* very precisely specifies one's social obligations.

More recently, Diener has assigned Duval and Wicklund's (1972) notion of objective self-awareness (awareness of oneself as an object of attention) a central role in the deindividuation process:

> A deindividuated person is prevented by situational factors present in a group from becoming self-aware. Deindividuated persons are blocked from awareness of themselves as separate individuals and from monitoring their own behaviour. (*Diener, 1980, p. 210*)

Factors present in crowds reduce self-awareness and create a psychological state of deindividuation that has specific consequences for behaviour (see Figure 11.13). Although these consequences do not inevitably include aggression, they do tend to facilitate the emergence of antisocial behaviour. In support of Diener's model, Prentice-Dunn and Rogers (1982) found that participants who were prevented from becoming self-aware, by being subjected to loud rock music in a darkened room while working on a collective task, subsequently administered more intense electric shocks to a 'learner' than did participants who had been working individually in a quiet, well-illuminated room under instructions to concentrate on their own thoughts and feelings.

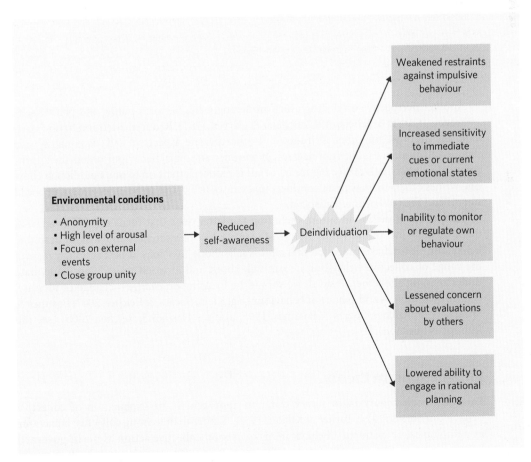

**Figure 11.13**  Self-awareness and deindividuation

Environmental factors present in crowd situations reduce self-awareness and create a state of deindividuation that produces typical crowd behaviours

*Source:* based on Diener (1980)

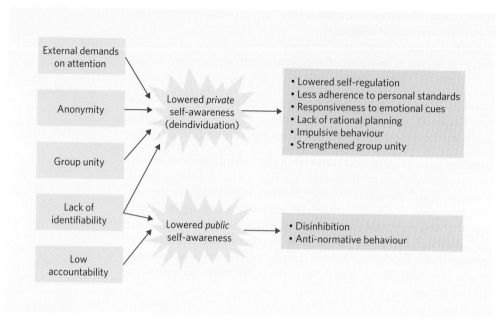

**Figure 11.14** Private and public self-awareness and deindividuation

Environmental factors present in crowd situations reduce public and/or private self-awareness, but it is the reduction of public self-awareness that is associated with disinhibited and anti-normative crowd behaviours

*Source*: based on Hogg & Abrams (1988)

Another perspective on deindividuation distinguishes between public and private self-awareness (Carver & Scheier, 1981; Scheier & Carver, 1981). Reduced attention to one's private self (feelings, thoughts, attitudes and other private aspects of self) is equated with deindividuation, but it does not necessarily produce antisocial behaviour unless the appropriate norms are in place (see Figure 11.14). It is reduced attention to one's public self (how one wishes others to view one's conduct) that causes behaviour to be independent of social norms and thus to become antisocial.

All models of deindividuation, including the latter ones that focus on self-awareness, dwell on *loss* – loss of individuality, loss of identity, loss of awareness and 'loss' of desirable behaviour. Critics have suggested that all this talk about 'loss' may at best seriously restrict the range of collective behaviour we can talk about and at worst provide an inadequate understanding altogether. Instead, we should be focusing on *change* – change of identity, change of awareness and change of behaviour (e.g. Klein, Spears, & Reicher, 2007; Postmes & Spears, 1998; Reicher, Spears & Postmes, 1995; also see Haslam & Reicher, 2005) (see the fifth focus question).

## Emergent norm theory

**Emergent norm theory**
Collective behaviour is regulated by norms based on distinctive behaviour that arises in the initially normless crowd.

**Emergent norm theory** takes a very different approach to the explanation of collective behaviour (Turner, 1974; Turner & Killian, 1957). Rather than treating collective behaviour as pathological or instinctual behaviour, it focuses on collective action as norm-governed behaviour, much like any other group behaviour. Turner (the sociologist R. H. Turner, not the social psychologist J. C. Turner) believes that what is distinct about the crowd is that it has no formal organisation or tradition of established norms to regulate behaviour, so the problem of explaining crowd behaviour is to explain how a norm emerges from within the crowd (hence, 'emergent norm theory'; see Figure 11.15). People in a crowd find themselves

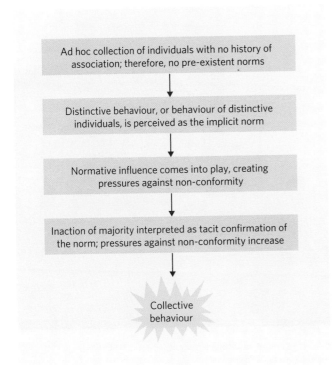

**Figure 11.15** Emergent norm theory

In initially normless crowds, distinctive behaviours are the basis for a relevant norm to emerge to regulate behaviour

*Source:* based on Turner & Killian (1957)

together under circumstances in which there are no clear norms to indicate how to behave. Their attention is attracted by distinctive behaviour (or the behaviour of distinctive individuals). This behaviour implies a norm and consequently there is pressure against non-conformity. Inaction on the part of the majority is interpreted as tacit confirmation of the norm, which consequently amplifies pressures against non-conformity.

By focusing on norms, emergent norm theory acknowledges that members of a crowd may communicate with one another in the elaboration of appropriate norms of action. However, the general nature of crowd behaviour is influenced by the role of distinctive behaviour, which is presumably behaviour that is relatively rare in most people's daily lives: for instance, antisocial behaviour. Two other critical observations have been made. Diener (1980) correctly observes that a norm-regulated crowd would have to be a self-aware crowd (there is no need for people to comply with norms unless they are identifiable and thus individuated and self-aware), yet evidence indicates that self-awareness is very low in crowds. Indeed, an experiment by Mann and his associates (Mann, Newton & Innes, 1982) supports Diener's view: irrespective of whether a norm of leniency or aggressiveness had been established by a confederate, participants were more aggressive when anonymous than when identifiable. However, anonymous participants were also more aggressive when the aggressive norm was in place.

The second critical observation comes from Reicher (1982, 1987), who reminds us that crowds rarely come together in a normative vacuum. More often than not, members of a crowd congregate for a specific purpose and thus bring with them a clear set of shared norms to regulate their behaviour as members of a specific group (e.g. a crowd of people welcoming the Queen, watching the Olympics, demonstrating outside Parliament or protesting on campus). The lack of tradition of established norms that Turner refers to may be more myth than reality. There is a logic to the crowd, Reicher argues, that is not adequately captured by emergent norm theory.

**Emergent norms theory**
Is urban disorder a response to primitive aggressive instincts – or is it an extreme example of normatively regulated goal-oriented action?

## Social identity theory

An important aspect of crowd behaviour that is usually ignored is that it is actually an *intergroup* phenomenon (Reicher & Potter, 1985). Many crowd events involve a direct collective confrontation between, for instance, police and rioters or rival gangs or team supporters, and even where no direct confrontation occurs, there is symbolic confrontation in that the crowd event symbolises a confrontation between, for instance, the crowd (or the wider group it represents) and the state. For example, Stott and his colleagues' analysis of riots at football matches shows quite clearly how these events are intergroup confrontations between supporters and police, and that how the rioting supporters behave is impacted quite significantly by how the police behave, and vice versa (Stott & Adang, 2004; Stott, Hutchison & Drury, 2001).

A second point is that, far from losing identity, people in the crowd actually assume the identity provided by the crowd: there is a change from idiosyncratic personal identity to shared social identity as a crowd member. These points are made by Reicher (1982, 1987, 1996, 2001), who applies social identity theory (this chapter) to collective behaviour. This analysis has been extended and called the SIDE model, or social identity model of deindividuation phenomena (Klein, Spears, & Reicher, 2007; Postmes & Spears, 1998; Reicher, Spears & Postmes, 1995).

Individuals come together, or find themselves together, as members of a specific social group for a specific purpose (e.g. conservationists protesting against environmental destruction). There is a high degree of shared social identity, which promotes social categorisation of self and others in terms of that group membership. It is this wider social identity that provides the limits for crowd behaviour. For example, for certain groups violence may be legitimate (e.g. neo-Nazi groups in Germany), while for others it may not (e.g. supporters at a cricket match).

While these general group norms provide the limits for acceptable crowd behaviour, there are often few norms to indicate how to behave in the specific context of the crowd event. Crowd members look to the identity-consistent behaviour of others, usually core group members, for guidance. Self-categorisation produces conformity to these context-specific norms of conduct. This explains why different groups in a crowd event often behave differently. For example, the police act in one way, while the protesters act in a different way because, despite being exposed to the same environmental stimuli, their behaviour is being controlled by different group memberships.

This analysis seems to be consistent with what actually goes on in a crowd. For example, Fogelson's (1970) analysis of American race riots of the 1960s showed one noteworthy feature: that the violence was not arbitrary and without direction; and Milgram and Toch (1969) report accounts from participants in the Watts riot in which a sense of positive social identity is strongly emphasised. Reicher (1984; Reicher & Potter, 1985) uses his analysis to account for a specific riot, which occurred in the spring of 1980 in the St Paul's district of Bristol (this was a forerunner of subsequent widespread rioting in other cities in Britain during the early 1980s). Three important points that emerged from this analysis were:

1  The violence, burning and looting were not unconstrained: the crowd was 'orderly' and the rioters were selective. Aggression was directed only at symbols of the state – the banks, the police and entrepreneurial merchants in the community.

2  The crowd remained within the bounds of its own community – St Paul's.

3  During and as a consequence of the riot, rioters felt a strong sense of positive social identity as members of the St Paul's community.

All this makes sense when it is recognised that the riot was an anti-government protest on the part of the St Paul's community, an economically disadvantaged area of Bristol with very high unemployment during a time of severe national unemployment.

# Improving intergroup relations

Different theories of prejudice and intergroup behaviour spawn different emphases in the explanation of prejudice and conflict reduction. From the perspective of personality theories (e.g. authoritarian personality, dogmatism; see Chapter 10), prejudice reduction entails changing the personality of the prejudiced person. More precisely, it would involve ensuring that particular parental strategies of child rearing were avoided in order to prevent the creation of bigoted people. From the perspective of frustration–aggression theory (Chapter 10) or relative deprivation theory (this chapter), prejudice and intergroup conflict can be minimised by preventing frustration, lowering people's expectations, distracting people from realising that they are frustrated, providing people with harmless (non-social) activities through which to vent their frustration, or ensuring that aggressive associations are minimised among frustrated people.

Minimisation of aggressive cues and increasing non-aggressive cues seem to be important. For example, there is substantial research showing that if weapons are made less available, aggression is reduced. When Jamaica implemented strict gun control and censorship of gun scenes on TV and in films in 1974, robbery and shooting rates dropped dramatically (Diener & Crandall, 1979). When Washington, DC, introduced handgun control laws there was a similar reduction in violent crime (Loftin, McDowall, Wiersema & Cottey, 1991). The mere sight of a gun, either real or an image of one, can actually induce the **weapons effect** (see Chapter 12). On the other hand, the presence of non-aggressive cues such as infants and laughter can reduce aggression (Berkowitz, 1984; see also an account in Chapter 12 of how the depiction of violence in the media can increase the incidence of later antisocial acts).

**Weapons effect**
The mere presence of a weapon increases the probability that it will be used aggressively.

For realistic conflict theory (this chapter), it is the existence of superordinate goals and cooperation for their achievement that gradually reduces intergroup hostility and conflict.

The avoidance of mutually exclusive goals would also help. Finally, from a social identity perspective (this chapter), prejudice and overt conflict will wane to the extent that intergroup stereotypes become less derogatory and polarised, and mutually legitimised non-violent forms of intergroup competition exist.

## Propaganda and education

Propaganda messages, such as official exhortations that people should not be prejudiced, are usually formulated with reference to an absolute standard of morality (e.g. humanism). This may be effective for those people who subscribe to the standard of morality that is being invoked. It may also suppress more extreme forms of discrimination because it communicates social disapproval of discrimination.

Since prejudice is at least partly based in ignorance (Stephan & Stephan, 1984), education – particularly the formal education of children – that promotes tolerance of diversity may reduce bigotry (Stephan & Stephan, 2001). This can involve teaching children about the moral implications of discrimination or teaching them facts about different groups. One problem with this strategy is that formal education has only a marginal impact if children are systematically exposed to prejudice outside the classroom (e.g. bigoted parents, chauvinistic advertising and the material consequences of discrimination).

Another educational strategy that may be more effective is to allow children to experience being a victim of prejudice. Jane Elliot, an Iowa schoolteacher, made a short movie called *The Eye of the Storm* of a classroom demonstration in which she divided her class of very young children into those with blue and those with brown eyes. For one day the 'brown eyes', and then for one day the 'blue eyes', were assigned inferior status: they were ridiculed, denied privileges, accused of being dull, lazy and sloppy, and made to wear a special collar. It was hoped that the experience of being stigmatised would be unpleasant enough to make the children think twice about being prejudiced against others.

**Traditional sex roles**
Stereotypes are difficult to change, and perhaps more so in the face of subtle advertising

One problem about prejudice is that it is *mindless* – a knee-jerk reaction to others as stereotypes. Perhaps if people, particularly when they are children, were taught to be mindful of others – to think about others not as stereotypes but as complex, whole individuals – then stereotypical reactions would be reduced. Langer, Bashner and Chanowitz (1985) explored this idea in the context of young children's attitudes towards the handicapped. They found a definite improvement in attitudes towards and treatment of handicapped children by children who had been trained to be *mindful* of others. Generally, the development of an ability to empathise with others significantly reduces one's capacity to harm those others physically, verbally, or indirectly via decisions and institutions (Miller & Eisenberg, 1988).

## Intergroup contact

A core feature of prejudice and conflict is the existence of unfavourable outgroup attitudes. Such attitudes are enshrined in widespread social ideologies and are maintained by lack of access to information that may disconfirm or improve negative attitudes. In most cases, such isolation is reinforced by real social and physical isolation of different groups from one another – the Protestant–Catholic situation in Northern Ireland is a case in point (Hewstone, Cairns, Voci, Paolini, McLernon, Crisp, et al., 2005). In other words, there is simply a chronic lack of intergroup contact, and little opportunity to meet real members of the outgroup. The groups are kept apart by educational, occupational, cultural and material differences, as well as by anxiety about negative consequences of contact for oneself (Stephan & Stephan, 1985).

In their integrated threat model Stephan and Stephan (2000) outline four sources of a feeling of threat and anxiety that people can experience about and in anticipation of intergroup contact:

1 *realistic threat* – a sense of threat to the very existence of one's group, well-being, political power and so forth;

2 *symbolic threat* – a threat posed by the outgroup to one's values, beliefs, morals and norms;

3 *intergroup anxiety* – a threat to self (e.g. embarrassment, fear of rejection) which is experienced during intergroup interactions; and

4 *negative stereotypes* – fear of intergroup anxiety (not actually experienced intergroup anxiety but imagined or anticipated) based on negative stereotypes of an outgroup.

These feelings of anxiety and threat can cause people to avoid face-to-face intergroup contact and prefer some form of segregated existence. In some cases a more extreme response to perceived intergroup threat may be *collective narcissism* (Golec de Zavala, Cichocka, Eidelson, & Jayawickreme, in press) – in which a group develops a strong sense of ethnocentrism, entitlement, superiority, omnipotence, egocentrism, need for recognition and acknowledgement, coupled with high but unstable self-esteem and a fragile sense of self.

One situation in which contact or anticipated contact always whips up a storm of discontent is immigration – we have seen coverage of the migrant camp near Calais, called 'the jungle', and conflict between immigrants and Calabrian locals in Rosarno in southern Italy in early 2010. Immigration raises all sorts of fears ranging from competition for employment to erosion of cultural values.

Although the ideas outlined in Box 11.4 make good sense, more than half a century of research on the contact hypothesis yields a complex picture (e.g. Amir, 1976; Cook, 1985; Fox & Giles, 1993; Schofield, 1991), at least partly due to the predominance of uncontrolled field studies and partly because Allport's list of conditions has been extended to become

## Research and applications 11.4
### Can intergroup contact improve intergroup relations?

One interesting line of research suggests that host nations construe the threat posed by immigration in different ways and thus respond to immigration differently depending on whether they define their national cultural identity in terms of heritage, history, blood ties and ties to the land (e.g. Germany, Italy and France), or in terms of common identity, shared civic values, and the social contract (e.g. Canada, Australia and the United States) (e.g. Citrin, Green, Muste, & Wong, 1997; Esses, Dovidio, Semenya, & Jackson, 2005; Esses, Jackson, Dovidio, & Hodson, 2005). The former is largely an ethnic national identity that prioritises community and common bonds (*Gemeinschaft*) – immigration is viewed as a cultural threat; the latter is largely a civic national identity that prioritises instrumental association and common identity (*Gesellschaft*) – immigration is viewed as a threat to civil society and access to employment. This distinction closely maps on to Prentice, Miller, and Lightdale's (1994) distinction between common bond and common identity groups discussed in Chapter 8.

Under the right circumstances, however, contact can reduce anxiety and improve intergroup relations

(Brown & Hewstone, 2005; Pettigrew, 1998; Pettigrew & Tropp, 2006). This is the **contact hypothesis** and was first proposed scientifically by Gordon Allport (1954b) in the very year that the United States Supreme Court paved the way for the racial desegregation of the American education system. Here are Allport's conditions for contact:

- It should be prolonged and involve cooperative activity rather than casual and purposeless interaction. It was precisely this sort of contact that improved relations in Sherif's (1966) summer camp studies.
- It should occur within the framework of official and institutional support for integration. Although legislation against discrimination, or for equal opportunities, will not in itself abolish prejudice, it provides a social climate that is conducive to the emergence of more tolerant social practices.
- It should bring together people or groups of equal social status. Unequal status contact is more likely to confirm stereotypes and thus entrench prejudices.

For the role that the Internet can play in intergroup contact, together with a review of the contact hypothesis by the Israeli social psychologists Amichai-Hamburger and McKenna (2006), go to **http://jcmc.indiana.edu/ vol11/issue3/amichai-hamburger.html**.

---

**Contact hypothesis**
The view that bringing members of opposing social groups together will improve intergroup relations and reduce prejudice and discrimination.

overly specific. Nevertheless, Pettigrew and Tropp (2006) report an authoritative meta-analysis of 515 contact studies conducted between 1949 and 2000 with 713 samples across 38 participating nations that reveals a robust effect – there is good evidence for Allport's core contention that cooperation, shared goals, equal status and the support of local authorities and norms are the most important and beneficial preconditions for intergroup contact to produce positive intergroup attitude change.

There are, however, some critical issues concerning precisely how contact may have effects (see overviews by Brewer & Miller, 1996; Brown, 1995, 1996; Hewstone, 1994, 1996; Pettigrew, 1998). These issues include the role of similarity and the process of generalisation of favourable interindividual attitudes to favourable intergroup attitudes.

### Similarity

It has long been believed that prejudice is based in ignorance and the perception of irreconcilable intergroup differences (Pettigrew, 1971; Stephan & Stephan, 1984). Contact causes people to recognise that they are in fact a great deal more similar than they had thought and hence to get to like one another (Byrne, 1971; also see Chapter 13). There are some problems with this perspective:

- Because groups are often very different, contact is likely to bring to light more profound or more widespread differences, and hence to reduce liking further and produce a deterioration in intergroup attitudes (e.g. Bochner, 1982).
- As groups are actually so different, it may be misleading to promulgate the view that they are similar; this will establish false-positive expectations that are disconfirmed by contact.

**The contact hypothesis**
Ethnically mixed classrooms are now common in many countries. Under what conditions can contact between cultures improve intergroup relations?

- Research indicates that intergroup attitudes are not merely a matter of ignorance or unfamiliarity; rather, they reflect real conflict of interest between groups and are often maintained by the very existence of social categories. New knowledge made available by contact is unlikely to change attitudes.

## Generalisation

Contact between representatives of different groups is supposed to improve attitudes towards the group as a whole – not just the specific outgroup members involved in the encounter. Weber and Crocker (1983) suggested three models of how this might happen:

1  *Bookkeeping* – the accumulation of favourable information about an outgroup gradually improves the stereotype. If outgroup information is stored in terms of exemplars, dramatic attitude changes can occur as new exemplars are added or retrieved (Smith & Zárate, 1992).

2  *Conversion* – dramatically counter-stereotypical information about an outgroup causes a sudden change in attitudes.

3  *Subtyping* – stereotype-inconsistent information produces a subtype, so the outgroup stereotype becomes more complex but the superordinate category remains unchanged.

In general, research indicates that contact improves attitudes towards the participants but does not generalise to the group as a whole (Amir, 1976; Cook, 1978). One explanation is that most intergroup contact is actually *interpersonal* contact: that is, contact between individuals as individuals, not group members. There is no good reason why an attitude towards one person should generalise to other people who are not categorically related to that person. For example, if you like Miguel as a friend, and the fact that he happens to be Spanish is irrelevant, then your liking for Miguel will not generalise to anyone else who just happens to be Spanish, or to the category 'Spanish' as a whole.

This raises an interesting paradox: perhaps intergroup contact is more likely to generalise if people's group affiliations are made *more*, not less, salient during contact – the *mutual differentiation model* (Hewstone & Brown, 1986; Johnston & Hewstone, 1990). There is some support for this idea. Wilder (1984) had participants from rival colleges come into contact over a cooperative task in which the outgroup person, who was either highly typical or highly atypical of that college, behaved in a pleasant or unpleasant manner. Those taking part evaluated the other college as a whole after the contact. Figure 11.16 shows that, relative to a no-contact control, it was only where contact was both pleasant and with a typical outgroup member that there was generalised improvement of attitude (see also Rothbart & John, 1985; Weber & Crocker, 1983).

Miller and Brewer (1984; Miller, Brewer & Edwards, 1985) have a different perspective. They argue that contact that draws attention to people's group affiliations will rapidly degenerate into conflict and thus to a deterioration of generalised attitudes. Instead, they recommend interpersonal encounters that stress socio-emotional aspects and avoid group or task-related aspects of the encounter: that is, 'decategorisation' or personalisation. This seems to work (Hamburger, 1994), but as yet the idea has been tested only in abstract experimental settings, where intergroup relations lack the powerful emotions and personal investments associated with 'real' intergroup relations. Where real intergroup conflict exists (e.g. between Catholics and Protestants in Northern Ireland), it may be almost impossible to distract people from their group affiliations.

A more promising variant of the interpersonal contact idea, called the **extended contact effect**, has been proposed by Wright, Aron, McLaughlin-Volpe and Ropp (1997). Wright and his colleagues suggest, and provide some evidence, that intergroup attitudes can improve if people witness or have knowledge of rewarding intergroup friendships between others – if my friend John has close outgroup friends then maybe the outgroup isn't quite

**Extended contact effect**
Knowing about an ingroup member who shares a close relationship with an outgroup member can improve one's own attitudes towards the outgroup.

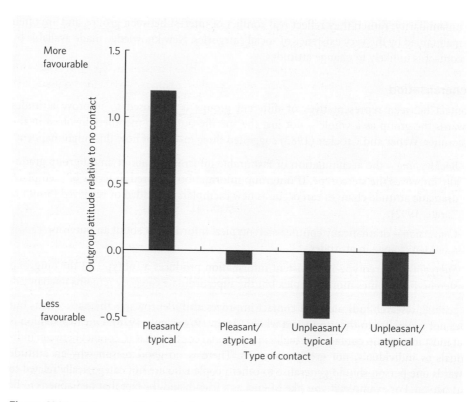

**Figure 11.16** Outgroup attitude as a function of pleasantness of contact and outgroup typicality of target

Relative to no contact, attitudes towards a rival college improved only when contact was both pleasant and with a typical member of the other college

*Source:* based on data from Wilder (1984)

as bad as I thought. This is able to happen because members of the same group have a common identity that links them and allows them, in the words of Wright, Aron and Tropp (2002), to *include the other in the self* – that is, to develop a degree of intersubjectivity that allows them to experience others as themselves. Intersubjectivity may also be implicated in vicarious dissonance (Cooper & Hogg, 2007; see Chapter 6) and intergroup emotions (Mackie, Maitner & Smith, 2009; see above).

Related to the extended contact idea is the notion that perspective taking plays a role in improving intergroup attitudes. If we are able to take the perspective of another person and experience the world as they do, we are less likely to harbour harmful negative attitudes about that person and perhaps more likely to behave prosocially towards them (see Chapter 14). There is now some evidence that perspective taking can improve intergroup attitudes (Galinsky, 2002; Galinsky & Moskowitz, 2000; Vescio, Sechrist & Paolucci, 2003).

Another process that does not involve drawing attention to the original intergroup context is 'recategorisation'. Gaertner's *common ingroup identity model* (Gaertner & Dovidio, 2000; Gaertner et al., 1993; Gaertner, Mann, Murrell & Dovidio, 1989; Gaertner et al., 1996) suggests that if members of opposing groups can be encouraged to recategorise themselves as members of the same group, intergroup attitudes will, by definition, not only improve but actually disappear (see below for some limitations of this process).

## Contact policy in multicultural contexts

Initially, it might seem that the most non-discriminatory and unprejudiced way to approach inter-ethnic relations is to be 'colour-blind': that is, to ignore group differences completely (Berry, 1984; Schofield, 1986). This is a 'melting-pot' policy, where all groups are ostensibly treated as equal (see also the concept of *assimilation* discussed in Chapter 16). There are at least three problems with this approach:

1  It ignores the fact that discrimination has disadvantaged certain groups (e.g. regarding education or health), and that unless positive steps are taken to rectify the problem, the disadvantage will simply persist.

2  It ignores the reality of ethnic/cultural differences (e.g. the Muslim dress code for women).

3  The melting pot is not really a melting pot at all, but rather a 'dissolving' pot, where ethnic minorities are dissolved and assimilated by the dominant social group: minority groups are stripped of their cultural heritage and cease to exist.

The extensive riots in France in November 2005 have been attributed to that country's adoption of cultural monism and ethnic assimilation – an approach that does not formally recognise cultural/ethnic differences within France despite the presence of huge numbers of North African Muslims. This assimilationist policy of being blind to cultural/ethnic/racial differences has, ironically, created ghettos of cultural disadvantage and associated discrimination and prejudice. A quite remarkable side effect of this denial of culture difference is that there are virtually no statistics on cultural/ethnic issues in France.

The alternative to assimilationism is pluralism or multiculturalism (Verkuyten, 2006) – an approach that draws attention to and responds to the reality of cultural diversity in an attempt to improve negative attitudes and redress disadvantage, at the same time as the cultural integrity of different groups is preserved (see Chapter 16). This approach aims to achieve a multicultural society in which intergroup relations between the constituent groups are harmonious. Empirical research suggests that intergroup arrangements that resemble multiculturalism may be quite effective in reducing intergroup conflict (Hornsey & Hogg, 2000a; see below). However, recent events indicate that pluralism may need to be implemented carefully in order for it not to sustain hidden conflicts and nourish separatism. Cases in point are Britain and Australia, two countries that in different ways provide strong political support for pluralism – for example, it was disaffiliated Muslim youths who bombed public transport in London in July 2005, and in Australia there were large anti-Lebanese riots in Sydney in December 2005.

## Superordinate goals

In his summer camp studies, Sherif (1966) managed to improve intergroup relations between warring factions by allowing them to cooperate to achieve a number of superordinate goals (shared goals that were unachievable by either group alone). The effectiveness of providing a superordinate goal has been confirmed by other studies (Brown & Abrams, 1986; Ryen & Kahn, 1975; Turner, 1981b; Worchel, 1979). The European Union provides a wonderful natural laboratory to study the effect of a superordinate identity (European) on inter-subgroup relations (between nations within Europe) (e.g. Chryssochoou, 2000; Cinnirella, 1997; Huici et al., 1997). One particularly effective superordinate goal is resistance to a shared threat from a common enemy (Dion, 1979; Wilder & Shapiro, 1984). This is the basis of alliances that can temporarily improve relations between erstwhile opponents (e.g the existence of the former Soviet Union provided a common foe to unite Western nations for almost forty-five years).

There is an important qualification. Superordinate goals do not reduce intergroup conflict if the groups fail to achieve the goal. For example, Worchel, Andreoli and Folger (1977) created competitive, cooperative or independent relations between two groups and then provided a superordinate goal that the groups either achieved or failed to achieve. The superordinate goal improved intergroup relations in all cases except where previously competitive groups failed to achieve the goal. In this condition, relations actually deteriorated. Unsuccessful intergroup cooperation to achieve a superordinate goal appears to worsen intergroup relations only when the failure can be attributed, rightly or wrongly, to the actions of the outgroup (Worchel & Novell, 1980). Where there is sufficient external justification, and the outgroup is not blamed, there is the more usual improvement in intergroup relations.

For example, the 1982 Falklands conflict between Britain and Argentina provided a superordinate goal to reduce factional conflict within Argentina. The cooperative exercise failed (Argentina lost the war), and, because the actions of the junta could easily be blamed, there was renewed factional conflict, which led almost immediately to the junta being overthrown (Latin American Bureau, 1982).

## Pluralism and diversity

One of the main problems of intergroup relations is that, in most contexts, groups are actually subgroups wholly nested within larger groups or cross-cut with them (Crisp, Ensari, Hewstone & Miller, 2003; see Chapter 8). For example, the psychology department at your university is a group nested with the larger university, whereas the group of social psychologists is a cross-cutting category because its membership stretches across many universities around the world. In these situations it is rare for all subgroups to have an equal representation in the defining features of the overarching identity – more often than not, one group is much better represented, with the consequence that other groups feel subordinate (Mummendey & Wenzel, 1999; Wenzel, Mummendey, & Waldzus, 2007). A similar problem exists when one organisation merges with or acquires another organisation – the post-merger entity contains within it both pre-merger entities and usually one pre-merger entity has lower status and poor representation in the post-merger entity (e.g. Terry, Carey & Callan, 2001).

Even where relations among subgroups are reasonably good, another problem, associated with superordinate goals, emerges. Intense or prolonged cooperation to achieve a shared goal can gradually blur intergroup boundaries (Gaertner & Dovidio, 2000; see discussion above of the common ingroup identity model). Although this may seem an ideal solution to intergroup conflict, it can backfire. Even though the groups may have superordinate goals, they may also wish to maintain their individual identities and so resist the perceived threat of becoming a single entity. New conflicts can thus arise to maintain intergroup distinctiveness. This effect has been observed in a chemical plant (Blake, Shepard & Mouton, 1964), an engineering factory (Brown, 1978) and the laboratory (Brown & Wade, 1987; Deschamps and Brown, 1983). It will be interesting to see if the current pressures in Europe for international cooperation in the service of superordinate economic goals (the European Union) increase international conflict on other dimensions in order to maintain national distinctiveness.

Hornsey and Hogg (2000a, 2000b, 2000c) have conducted a programme of research suggesting that a careful balancing of superordinate identity and positive subgroup distinctiveness may provide a promising blueprint for social harmony. This mimics the sociopolitical strategy of multiculturalism or cultural pluralism that is pursued by countries such as Australia and Canada. This arrangement works because by retaining distinct cultural identities there is no threat that would provoke intergroup hostility. At the same time, the existence of a superordinate identity can cause subgroups to see themselves as distinct groups, with complementary roles, all working on the same team towards integrative goals. More broadly, this idea suggests that the answer to intergroup conflict may be to build groups that not only are based on tolerance for diversity but actually celebrate diversity as a defining feature of their social identity (Niedenthal & Beike, 1997; Roccas & Brewer, 2002; Wright, Aron & Tropp, 2002; see also Hogg & Hornsey, 2006).

A final point about goal relations and social harmony picks up on our earlier discussion of zero-sum and non-zero-sum goals. Where two groups see their goal relations as zero-sum, they are characterising their relationship as competitive – if they get a lot, we get a little. There is a fixed pie to divide up, and therefore their actions are frustrating our goals. Where two groups see their goal relations as non-zero-sum, they are characterising their relationship as cooperative – if they get a lot, we get a lot. The pie can get bigger if we work together, and therefore their actions are helping us to achieve our goals. Goal relations do not have to be accurate perceptions – they are subject to ideology and rhetoric. Take the immigration debates in Britain, France, Germany and virtually any country around the world. One side argues that immigration is bad because immigrants come along and take people's jobs and soak up public money – a zero-sum rhetoric that is associated with xenophobia, prejudice and intolerance towards immigrants. The other side argues that immigration is good because immigrants bring skills, energy and enthusiasm, which create new jobs and additional wealth – a non-zero-sum rhetoric that is associated with internationalism and positive attitudes towards immigrants and immigration.

## Communication and negotiation

Groups in conflict can try to improve intergroup relations by communicating directly about the conflict and negotiating to resolve it. This can be done through bargaining, mediation or arbitration. These are very complex procedures that are prey to all sorts of psychological barriers to dispute resolution (e.g. self-esteem, emotion, misattribution; Ross & Ward, 1995; Thompson & Loewenstein, 2003; Thompson, 2009; Thompson, Medvec, Seiden & Kopelman, 2001). One real problem is that it can be difficult for negotiators to take the perspective of the other – a failure that is amplified by the intergroup nature of the negotiation and which makes compromise almost impossible (Carroll, Bazerman & Maury, 1988; Galinsky & Mussweiler, 2001). In addition, many crucial negotiations are between cultures, and thus a host of cross-cultural communication issues can arise to complicate things (e.g. Carnevale & Leung, 2001; Kimmel, 1994; see also R. Bond & Smith, 1996; Smith & Bond, 1998).

## Bargaining

Intergroup negotiations are generally between representatives of the opposing groups: for example, trade union and management may try to resolve disputes by direct negotiation between representatives. One of the most significant intergroup negotiations of the twentieth century was the February 1945 meeting in Yalta in the Crimea between Stalin, Churchill and Roosevelt, as representatives of the soon-to-be victorious Allies of the Second World War: the Soviet Union, Britain and the United States. The negotiation of international differences at that meeting has determined the nature of the world to the present day. Social psychological research indicates that when people are **bargaining** on behalf of social groups to which they belong, they tend to bargain much more fiercely and less compromisingly than if they were simply bargaining for themselves (Benton & Druckman, 1974; Breaugh & Klimoski, 1981). The effect is enhanced when negotiators are aware that they are being observed by their constituents, either directly or through the media (Carnevale, Pruitt & Britton, 1979).

**Bargaining**
Process of intergroup conflict resolution where representatives reach agreement through direct negotiation.

This 'bullish' strategy of relative intransigence is less likely to secure a satisfactory compromise than a more interpersonal orientation in which both parties make reciprocal concessions (Esser & Komorita, 1975; Komorita & Esser, 1975). Direct negotiation between group representatives is therefore quite likely to reach an impasse, in which neither group feels it can compromise without losing face. A case in point is George Bush senior and Saddam Hussein's media-orchestrated bargaining over the plight of Kuwait in 1990, which seemed mainly to involve Bush threatening to 'kick Saddam's ass' and Hussein threatening to make 'infidel' Americans 'swim in their own blood' – not a good start. More recently, in 2006, the Iranian president Mahmoud Ahmadinejad and the US president George Bush Jr traded insults in which Ahmadinejad accused Bush of being an infidel, and the latter accused the former of being a member of the 'axis of evil' – again, not a promising start.

Morley and Stephenson (1977) have explored the interplay of intergroup and interpersonal factors in bargaining. They demonstrate that bargaining often follows a sequence of stages. The first stage is an intergroup one, in which representatives act very much in terms of group memberships and assess each group's power and the strength of each group's case. The second stage is more interpersonal, with individuals trying to establish harmonious interpersonal relations with one another in order to be able to solve problems more easily. The final stage is again more intergroup, with negotiators making sure that the final decision is consistent with the historical aims of their own group. Close interpersonal relations, which are encouraged by more informal bargaining procedures and contexts, can facilitate negotiation. However, close interpersonal relations also have a drawback – the group as a whole can become fearful of a 'sell-out' and can resort or return to more confrontational intergroup behaviour, which hinders the negotiation process.

There is a potentially important limitation of much social psychological research on bargaining – the wider intergroup context is often neglected as researchers focus only on the specific bargaining event as a form of social change (Morley, Webb & Stephenson, 1988). In reality, bargaining is often a way to maintain the status quo. Groups in conflict isolate from the wider context of intergroup relations a specific and circumscribed point of disagreement – one that can be solved. The solution of the specific problem then allows broader intergroup issues to remain unchanged.

## Mediation

**Mediation**
Process of intergroup conflict resolution where a neutral third party intervenes in the negotiation process to facilitate a settlement.

To break the deadlock, a third party can be brought in for **mediation** between the groups (Pruitt, 1981). To be effective, mediators should have power and must be seen by both groups to be impartial (Lim & Carnevale, 1990), and the groups should already be fairly close in their positions (Rubin, 1980). Biased mediators are ineffective because they are not trusted, and weak mediators are ineffective because they exert little pressure on intransigent groups to be reasonable.

**Mediation**
An effective mediator needs to have power and to be seen as impartial. In this respect, a football World Cup context is no different from a legal setting

Although mediators have no power to impose a settlement, they can help in several important ways:

1 They are able to *reduce the emotional heat* associated with deadlock (Tetlock, 1988).

2 They can help to *reduce misperceptions,* encourage understanding and establish trust.

3 They can propose *novel compromises* that allow both groups to appear to win: that is, to change a zero-sum conflict (one in which one group's gains are precisely the other group's losses; the more one gains, the more the other loses) into a non-zero-sum conflict (where both groups can gain).

4 They can help both parties to make a *graceful retreat*, without losing face, from untenable positions.

5 They can *inhibit unreasonable claims* and behaviour by threatening to expose the group publicly as being unreasonable.

6 They can *reduce intragroup conflict* and thus help a group to clarify its consensual position.

History provides instances of effective mediation. For example, Henry Kissinger's shuttle diplomacy of the mid-1970s, which involved meeting each side separately over a period of two years after the 1973 Arab–Israeli conflict, produced a number of significant agreements between Israel and its Arab neighbours (Pruitt, 1981). In the late 1970s, using a slightly different strategy, Jimmy Carter secluded Egypt's president Anwar Sadat and Israel's prime minister Menachem Begin at Camp David near Washington in the United States. After thirteen days, an agreement was reached that ended a state of war that had existed between Israel and Egypt since 1948.

## Arbitration

Many intergroup conflicts are so intractable, the underlying interests so divergent, that mediation is ineffective. The last resort is **arbitration**, in which the mediator or some other third party is invited to impose a mutually binding settlement. Research shows that arbitration really is the last resort for conflict resolution (McGillicuddy, Welton & Pruitt, 1987). The prospect of arbitration can backfire, because both groups adopt outrageous final

**Arbitration**
Process of intergroup conflict resolution in which a neutral third party is invited to impose a mutually binding settlement.

positions in the hope that arbitration will produce a more favourable compromise (Pruitt, 1986). A way to combat this is through *final-offer arbitration,* where the third party chooses one of the final offers. This tends to encourage more reasonable final positions.

### Conciliation

Although direct communication may help to improve intergroup relations, tensions and suspicions often run so high that direct communication is all but impossible. Instead, conflicting groups threaten, coerce or retaliate against one another, and if this behaviour is reciprocated, there is an escalation of the conflict. For example, during the Second World War Germany believed it could move Britain to surrender by bombing its cities, and the Allies believed that they could break Germany's will by bombing *its* cities. Similarly, Japan believed it could dissuade the United States from interfering in its imperial expansion in Asia by bombing Pearl Harbor, and the United States believed it could bring North Vietnam to the negotiating table by sustained bombing of cities and villages.

There are uncountable examples of the terrible consequences of threat, coercion and retaliation. Can this cycle be broken by one side adopting an unconditionally cooperative strategy in the hope that the other side will reciprocate? Laboratory research suggests that this does not work: unilateral unconditional cooperation simply invites retaliation and exploitation (Shure, Meeker & Hansford, 1965).

Osgood (1962) suggested a more effective alternative that involves **conciliation** (i.e. not retaliation), but with enough strength to discourage exploitation. Called 'graduated and reciprocated initiatives in tension reduction' (with the acronym GRIT), it invokes social psychological principles to do with the norm of reciprocity and the attribution of motives. GRIT involves at least two stages:

**Conciliation**
Process whereby groups make cooperative gestures to one another in the hope of avoiding an escalation of conflict.

1 One party announces its conciliatory intent (allowing a clear attribution of non-devious motive), clearly specifies a small concession it is about to make (activates reciprocity norm) and invites its opponent to do likewise.

2 The initiator makes the concession exactly as announced and in a publicly verifiable manner. There is now strong pressure on the other group to reciprocate.

Laboratory research provides evidence for the effectiveness of this procedure. For example, a *tit-for-tat* strategy that begins with one cooperative act and proceeds by matching the other party's last response is both conciliatory and strong, and can improve interparty relations (Axelrod & Dion, 1988; Komorita, Parks & Hulbert, 1992). Direct laboratory tests of GRIT by Linskold and his colleagues (e.g. Linskold, 1978; Linskold & Han, 1988) confirm that the announcement of cooperative intent boosts cooperation, repeated conciliatory acts breed trust, and maintenance of power equality protects against exploitation. GRIT-type strategies have been used effectively from time to time in international relations: for example, between the Soviet Union and the United States during the Berlin crisis of the early 1960s, and between Israel and Egypt on a number of occasions.

## Summary

- Intergroup behaviour can be defined as any behaviour that is influenced by group members' perceptions of an outgroup.

- Group members may engage in collective protest to the extent that subjectively they feel deprived as a

group relative to their aspirations or relative to other groups.

- Competition for scarce resources tends to produce intergroup conflict. Cooperation to achieve a shared goal reduces conflict.

- Social categorisation may be the only necessary precondition for being a group and engaging in intergroup behaviour, provided that people identify with the category.

- Self-categorisation is the process responsible for psychologically identifying with a group and behaving as a group member (e.g. conformity, stereotyping, ethnocentrism, ingroup solidarity). Social comparison and the need for self-esteem motivate groups to compete in different ways (depending on the nature of intergroup relations) for relatively positive social identity.

- Crowd behaviour may not represent a loss of identity and regression to primitive antisocial instincts. Instead, it may be group behaviour that is governed by local contextual norms that are framed by a wider social identity.

- Prejudice, discrimination and intergroup conflict are difficult to reduce. Together, education, propaganda and shared goals may help, but simply bringing groups into contact with one another is unlikely to be effective. Other strategies include bargaining, mediation, arbitration and conciliation.

## Literature, film and TV

### Gandhi

1982 classic film by Richard Attenborough, starring Ben Kingsley as Gandhi. A film about social mobilisation, social action and collective protest. It shows how Gandhi was able to mobilise India to oust the British. The film touches on prejudice and group decision making.

### Germinal

Emile Zola's 1885 novel drawing attention to the misery experienced by poor French people during France's Second Empire. The descriptions of crowd behaviour are incredibly powerful, and were drawn upon by later social scientists, such as Gustave Le Bon, to develop their theories of collective behaviour.

### The Road to Wigan Pier

George Orwell's 1937 novel capturing the plight of the English working class. A powerful, and strikingly contemporary, portrayal of relative deprivation.

### Gran Torino

Clint Eastwood's 2008 film in which he also stars. Set in contemporary Detroit, Eastwood's character, Walt Kowalski, is a proud and grizzled Korean War veteran whose floridly bigoted attitudes are out of step with changing times. Walt refuses to abandon the neighbourhood he has lived in all his life, despite its changing demographics. The film is about his developing friendship with a Hmong teenage boy and his immigrant family – a poignant, and subtly uplifting, commentary on intergroup friendship and the development of intergroup tolerance and respect.

### Gulliver's Travels

Jonathan Swift's 1726 satirical commentary on the nature of human beings. This book is relevant to virtually all the themes in our text; however, the section on Big-Endians and Little-Endians is particularly relevant to this chapter on intergroup behaviour. Swift provides a hilarious and incredibly full and insightful description of a society that is split on the basis of whether people open their boiled eggs at the big or the little end – highly relevant to the minimal group studies in this chapter.

## Guided questions

1 How does the experience of relative deprivation impact on the tendency to aggress?
2 According to Sherif, prejudice arises when intergroup goals are incompatible. What does this mean? Did he offer a solution?
3 What is social identity? Can a person have multiple social identities? Watch *Social identity* in Chapter 11 of MyPsychLab at **www.mypsychlab.co.uk** (see also **http://www. youtube.com/watch?v=USxOoPu5a_g&feature=PlayList&p=CF9BEB353C1ABF85 &playnext_from=PL&playnext=1&index=2**).
4 How are minority group members' beliefs about intergroup relations important in planning for social change?
5 Trying to reduce prejudice by simply providing intergroup contact between people from different groups may not work very well. Why?

### Learn more

Brewer, M. B. (2003). *Intergroup relations* (2nd ed.). Philadelphia, PA: Open University Press. A very readable and complete overview of research on intergroup relations.

Brewer, M. B. (2007). The social psychology of intergroup relations: Social categorization, ingroup bias, and outgroup prejudice. In A. W. Kruglanski & E. T. Higgins (eds), *Social psychology: Handbook of basic principles* (2nd ed., pp. 785–804). New York: Guilford Press. Comprehensive coverage of research on intergroup behaviour, and prejudice and discrimination.

Brown, R. J., & Gaertner, S. (eds) (2001). *Blackwell handbook of social psychology: Intergroup processes.* Oxford, UK: Blackwell. A collection of twenty-five chapters from leading social psychologists, covering the entire field of intergroup processes.

De Dreu, C. K. W. (2010). Social conflict: The emergence and consequences of struggle and negotiation. In S. T. Fiske, D. T. Gilbert, & G. Lindzey (eds), *Handbook of social psychology* (5th ed., Vol. 2, pp. 983–1023). New York: Wiley. Up-to-date and comprehensive discussion of intergrop conflict and the role of negotiation in resolving such conflicts.

Dovidio, J. F., & aertner, S. L. (2010). Intergroup bias. In S. T. Fiske, D. T. Gilbert, & G. Lindzey (eds), *Handbook of social psychology* (5th ed., Vol. 2, pp. 1084–1121). New York: Wiley. Up-to-date and detailed coverage of research on intergroup bias as a feature of intergroup behaviour.

Dovidio, J., Glick. P. Hewstone, M., & Esses, V. (eds) (2010). *Handbook of prejudice, stereotyping and discrimination.* London: SAGE. A collection of chapters by leading researchers on intergroup behaviour in the context of stereotyping and prejudice.

Fiske, S. T. (2010). Interpersonal stratification: Status, power, and subordination. In S. T. Fiske, D. T. Gilbert, & G. Lindzey (eds), *Handbook of social psychology* (5th ed., Vol. 2, pp. 941–82). New York: Wiley. Up-to-date and detailed overview of research on the power and status aspects of intergroup relations.

Hogg, M. A. (2003). Intergroup relations. In J. Delamater (ed.), *Handbook of social psychology* (pp. 479–501). New York: Kluwer Academic/Plenum. Very accessible overview and review of social psychology research on intergroup relations, prejudice and discrimination.

Hogg, M. A. (2006). Social identity theory. In P. J. Burke (ed.), *Contemporary social psychological theories* (pp. 111–36). Palo Alto, CA: Stanford University Press. An up-to-date and easily readable overview of contemporary social identity theory.

Hogg, M. A., & Abrams, D. (1988). *Social identifications: A social psychology of intergroup relations and group processes.* London: Routledge. Detailed coverage of theory and research on group processes and intergroup relations from the perspective of social identity theory – probably still the most comprehensive text-style overview of social identity theory.

Hogg, M. A., & Abrams, D. (eds) (2001). *Intergroup relations: Essential readings.* Philadelphia, PA: Psychology Press. Annotated collection of key publications on intergroup relations. There is an introductory overview chapter and commentary chapters introducing each reading.

Hogg, M. A., & Abrams, D. (2007). Intergroup behavior and social identity. In M. A. Hogg & J. Cooper (eds), *The SAGE handbook of social psychology: Concise student edition* (pp. 335–60). London: SAGE. A comprehensive overview of research on intergroup relations and social identity processes.

Robinson, W. P. (ed) (1996). *Social groups and identities: Developing the legacy of Henri Tajfel*. Oxford, UK: Butterworth-Heinemann. A collection of chapters from almost everyone who was closely associated with Tajfel's far-reaching insights on intergroup relations; although social identity and self-categorisation theory are well represented, there is also diversity and breadth in these chapters.

Stangor, C. (2004). *Social groups in action and interaction*. New York: Psychology Press. Comprehensive and accessible coverage of the social psychology of processes within and between groups.

Thompson, L. L. (2009). *The mind and heart of the negotiator* (4th ed.). Upper Saddle River, NJ: Prentice Hall. The most recent edition of this classic book on the psychology of negotiation.

Yzerbyt, V., & Demoulin, S. (2010). Intergroup relations. In S. T. Fiske, D. T. Gilbert, & G. Lindzey (eds), *Handbook of social psychology* (5th ed., Vol. 2, pp. 1024–1083). New York: Wiley. A thorough overview of the field of intergroup relations, in the most recent edition of the classic handbook – a primary source for theory and research.

Refresh your understanding, assess your progress and go further with interactive summaries, questions, podcasts and much more at **www.mypsychlab.co.uk**

## This chapter discusses

- Aggression and violence in the community
- Defining and measuring aggression
- Biological and social theories of aggression
- Personal and situational factors
- Effects of the mass media
- Domestic violence
- Institutionalised aggression
- Group-centred versus person-centred explanations
- Reducing aggression

## Focus questions

1. Mary is sarcastic to her boyfriend, Tony, and circulates nasty rumours about him, but she never pushes or shoves him. Tony is never sarcastic to Mary and never circulates rumours about her, but he does push and shove her. Who is more 'aggressive'?

2. We've all seen those nature movies – a nasty-looking pack of African hunting dogs viciously tearing some poor little creature to bits and snarling aggressively at each other. Are humans like this? How far does animal behaviour inform our understanding of human aggression?

3. According to your neighbour, watching violent movies and playing gory computer games is a good way to let off steam. Can you counter this view? For an example based on a correlation between childhood exposure to television violence and levels of aggressiveness ten years later, go to Chapter 12 of MyPsychLab at **www.mypsychlab.co.uk** (watch *Research methods*).

4. Tom has quite a collection of favourite porn sites. His girlfriend knows this and asks him to give up his habit. Tom says: 'It doesn't hurt anyone. I'm not turning into a rapist you know!' As a budding social psychologist, how would you advise him?

will use which involves getting you to decide to buy a car by giving you a very low price

Go to **mypsychlab** to explore video and test your understanding of key topics addressed in this chapter.

Refresh your understanding with interactive summaries, explore topics further with video and audio clips and assess your progress with quick test and essay questions by logging to the accompanying website at **www.mypsychlab.co.uk**

# Chapter 12
## Aggression

| Key terms | | |
|---|---|---|
| | Disinhibition | Neo-associationist analysis |
| | Ethology | Neo-Freudians |
| Abuse syndrome | Evolutionary social psychology | Operational definition |
| Agentic mode | Excitation-transfer model | Peace studies |
| Analogue | External validity | Priming |
| Belief in a just world | Fighting instinct | Relative deprivation |
| Biosocial theories | Frustration-aggression hypothesis | Releasers |
| Catharsis | General aggression model | Script |
| Cathartic hypothesis | Hate crime | Sexual selection theory |
| Collective aggression | Instinct | Social learning theory |
| Cultural norms | Institutionalised aggression | Social order |
| Culture of honour | Learning by direct experience | Social role theory |
| Dehumanisation | Learning by vicarious experience | Subculture of violence |
| Deindividuation | Machismo | Type A personality |
| Desensitisation | Modelling | Values |
| | Nature–nurture controversy | Weapons effect |

# Aggression in our community

What catches your attention about aggression? Is it the latest report of casualties in one of the world's ongoing wars or of civilians killed in a terrorist attack? What about a burglary in your neighbourhood, or reported serious injuries to a child by a close relative? How about a newspaper story of a rape in a nearby town? Some of these – but perhaps not all – are criminal acts against persons or property, and may be shockingly violent. Would unkind words between two people count as aggression? As we shall see, all of these are important issues in our daily lives and qualify to varying degrees as acts of aggression, some fairly trivial and others monstrous.

Let's talk about murder. In the period 1998–2000 the number of murders per 100,000 people was four in the United States and a staggering sixty-two in Colombia (see Figure 12.1). How does your country rate? Assuming national statistics are equally reliable murder rates may vary for many reasons; for example access to lethal weapons, conditions of poverty or war, and cultural and subcultural support for violence. We explore these influences in this chapter.

Many of us occasionally witness aggression and most of us regularly see evidence and symbols of aggressive acts or aggressive people: graffiti, vandalism, violent arguments, and weapons. Would you regard wearing a hoodie in a shopping mall as 'in your face'? The victims of aggression often have less power or are disadvantaged: the very young, the old, the sick and people from different ethnic backgrounds. In a survey of 11- and 12-year-old children, half had been punched, kicked, beaten or hit by other children, and two-thirds had been threatened with physical abuse or had been emotionally abused by their peers (Lind & Maxwell, 1996).

Most of us have 'played' aggressive games: shooting, hunting, fighting, video games. Again, we are often constrained by the potential for harm to occur. A survey of 10,000 women reported that 20 per cent felt 'very unsafe' when walking out at night, even though less that 1 per cent reported actually having been attacked in the last year – better 'safe than sorry' (Jones, Gray, Kavanagh, Moran, Norton, & Seldon, 1994). There is some evidence that the modern world may indeed have become a more dangerous place. Homicide rates have increased since the Second World War in industrialised countries, such as the United

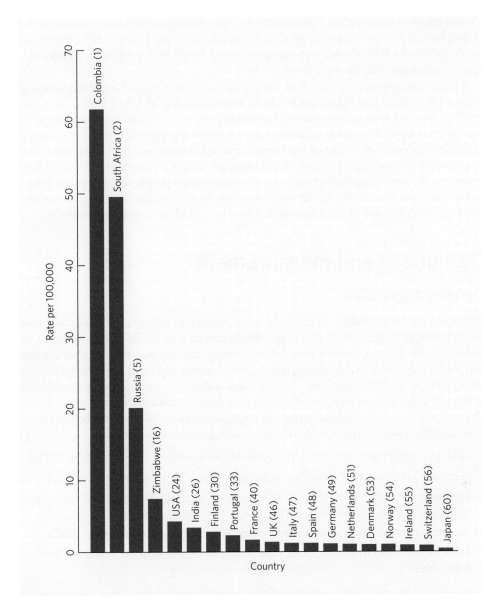

**Figure 12.1**  International murder rates per 100,000, 1998–2000

The rates are shown on the vertical axis. The numbers in parentheses are ranks for the countries, based on the sixty national murder rates originally included in the database

*Source:* Seventh United Nations Survey of Crime Trends, http://www.nationmaster.com/graph/cri_mur_percap

States (Anderson & Bushman, 2002a). Several factors have been implicated: violence against children in homes (Straus, 2001), high levels of exposure to violent media among children (Bushman & Huesmann, 2001), the availability of guns in some countries (O'Donnell, 1995), and even global warming (Anderson, Bushman & Groom, 1997). We would add to this list of causes the pervasive effects of relative deprivation, involving the widening gap perceived by very poor people when they compare themselves with those who are better off. It is also notable that vivid pictorial and video portrayals of violence and aggression are now inescapable. In the late 1960s and early 1970s the world was shocked by

TV and magazine images of the Vietnam War, but now images of aggression and violence are all over the scores of news and current affairs channels on TV and simply a click or two away on *YouTube* and a host of other web resources, not to mention video-games. Aggression is simply more accessible now than it used to be.

If aggression is omnipresent, is it an integral part of human nature? Some scholars (e.g. Ardrey, 1961) claim that aggression is a basic human instinct, an innate fixed action pattern that we share with other species. If aggression has a genetic basis, then presumably its expression is inevitable. Other scholars paint a less gloomy picture, arguing that even if aggressive tendencies are a part of our behavioural repertoire it may be possible to control and possibly prevent the expression of the tendency as actual behaviour. The immediate challenges for psychologists are to identify the reasons why people aggress against others and to find ways of reducing the harmful effects on the victims, the aggressor and society. But first, consider some of the attempts that have been made to define 'aggression'.

# Definitions and measurement

## Defining aggression

Aggression can be studied in experimental or in naturalistic settings, but researchers have found it difficult to agree about how to describe it, explain it, or isolate its components. One researcher may define aggression physically as pushing, shoving and striking, while another may add features such as threatening speech, verbal insults and facial expressions. What is 'aggressive' is partly shaped by societal and cultural norms. Among the Amish of Pennsylvania the bar is very low, whereas in most gang subcultures the bar is much higher. The part played by culture in the norms controlling aggression is covered in Chapter 16.

Social psychology is replete with definitions of aggression. Here are a few:

- behaviour that results in personal injury or destruction of property (Bandura, 1973);

- behaviour intended to harm another of the same species (Scherer, Abeles & Fischer, 1975);

- behaviour directed towards the goal of harming or injuring another living being who is motivated to avoid such treatment (Baron, 1977);

- the intentional infliction of some form of harm on others (Baron & Byrne, 2000);

- behaviour directed towards another individual carried out with the proximate (immediate) intent to cause harm (Anderson & Huesmann, 2003).

Conceptual differences between these definitions are apparent. What, then, should qualify as the key components of aggression? Carlson, Marcus-Newhall and Miller (1989) have argued that more common ground is achieved, across findings and contexts, by defining aggression as 'the intent to harm'. Are any of these views sufficiently inclusive for a definition (see Box 12.1)?

## Measuring aggression

In practice, scientists are like most of us – they use definitions that correspond to their **values**. As a result, the behaviour studied may differ from one researcher to another, and across different cultures, and yet be called 'aggression'. For example, are bodily cues of anger directed towards someone else the same as actually fighting? Are protests by indigenous peoples about their traditional lands comparable to acts of international terrorism; or is spanking a child in the same category as the grisly deeds of a serial killer?

Although the problem of definition is not fully resolved, researchers have been ready to operationalise aggression – they have developed an **operational definition** (see Chapter 1) So that they can manipulate and measure aggression in empirical research. However,

**Values**
A higher-order concept thought to provide a structure for organising attitudes.

**Operational definition**
Defines a theoretical term in a way that allows it to be manipulated or measured.

> ### Real world 12.1
> #### Components of definitions of aggression
>
> How much should a satisfactory definition of aggression include? Is motive important? What about the nature of the target? Are some situations more complex in reaching a decision? Consider whether the following would qualify as aggression:
>
> - actual harm, but not an unsuccessful act of violence;
> - physical injury, but not psychological harm (such as verbal abuse);
> - harm to people, but not to animals or property;
> - harm to people in war;
> - harm in a rule-governed context (such as a boxing match);
> - intentional harm, but not negligent harm;
> - belief by a victim that harm has occurred;
> - injury in a victim's alleged 'best interests' (such as smacking a child);
> - self-injury, such as self-mutilation or suicide.
>
> This list is not exhaustive. You may think of other elements of behaviour that may or may not render it aggressive, according to your perspective. Discuss some of these issues with a friend. Is it difficult to agree on a definition?

different researchers have used different measures for the same term. Consider the following attempts to operationalise aggression:

- punching an inflated plastic doll (Bandura, Ross & Ross, 1963);
- pushing a button that is supposed to deliver an electric shock to someone else (Buss, 1961);
- pencil-and-paper ratings by teachers and classmates of a child's level of aggressiveness (Eron, 1982);
- written self-report by institutionalised teenage boys about their prior aggressive behaviour (Leyens, Camino, Parke & Berkowitz, 1975);
- a verbal expression of willingness to use violence in an experimental laboratory setting (Geen, 1978).

Each of these measures has been used as an **analogue**, or substitute, for the real thing. The major reason for this is ethical (see Chapter 1) – it is very difficult to justify an actual physical assault against a person in an experimental setting.

A key question is whether we can generalise any of findings from analogue measures of aggression to a larger population in real-life settings. For example, what is the **external validity** of the aggression (electric shock) machine developed by Buss (1961), which is similar to the apparatus used by Milgram (1963) in his studies of obedience (see Chapter 7)? In a test of this device, prisoners with histories of violence administered higher levels of shock to a confederate (Cherek, Schnapp, Moeller & Dougherty, 1996). Anderson and Bushman (1997) have carried out a supportive validity check. Similarly, there is a parallel between the laboratory and real life for the effects on aggression of alcohol, high temperatures, direct provocation and violence in the media (topics dealt with below).

Even though this chapter explores only some of the extensive range of behaviour that is labelled 'aggressive', it will become clear that there can be no single definition for an array of complex, and perhaps qualitatively different, phenomena. (Are Mary and Tony each aggressive? Check the first focus question.)

**Analogue**
Device or measure intended to faithfully mimic the 'real thing'.

**External validity**
Similarity between circumstances surrounding an experiment and circumstances encountered in everyday life.

## What do the major theories say?

How we measure aggression is closely linked to how we define it, and both are determined by our theoretical position. Given aggression's impact on our lives, it should be no surprise to find that theories of aggression are plentiful.

Trying to understand why humans aggress against their own kind, and the factors that make them behave with viciousness and brutality towards one another in ways and degrees unparalleled in other animals, has led to much speculation since ancient times (Geen & Donnerstein, 1983). Explanations of aggression fall into two broad classes, the biological and the social, although this distinction is not entirely rigid. A debate over which of the two explanations is superior is an example of the **nature–nurture controversy**: is human action determined by our biological inheritance or by our social environment? (A related instance of this debate involves the origins of prosocial behaviour; see Chapter 13.)

Because our interest is social psychological it favours a focus on social factors, and therefore theories that incorporate a social learning component. However, a biological contribution to aggression cannot be ignored. After all, violence is a reaction of our bodily system. One issue is that some biological explanations are so biological that they might seem to be a threat to any form of theory that is social.

**Nature–nurture controversy**
Classic debate about whether genetic or environmental factors determine human behaviour. Scientists generally accept that it is an interaction of both.

## Biological explanations

The starting point for these explanations is that aggression is an innate action tendency. Although modification of the consequent behaviour is possible, the wellspring is not. Aggression is an instinct: that is, a pattern of responses that is genetically predetermined. If so, it should show the characteristics of an instinct. According to Riopelle (1987), an **instinct** is:

**Instinct**
Innate drive or impulse, genetically transmitted.

- *goal-directed* and terminates in a specific consequence (e.g. an attack);
- *beneficial* to the individual and to the species;
- *adapted* to a normal environment (although not to an abnormal one);
- *shared* by most members of the species (although its manifestation can vary from individual to individual);
- *developed* in a clear way as the individual matures;
- *unlearned* on the basis of individual experience (although it can become manifest in relation to learned aspects within a context).

Three approaches have shared most, if not all, of these biological attributes in their treatment of human aggression. All argue that aggressive behaviour is an inherent part of human nature, that we are programmed at birth to act in that way. The oldest is the psychodynamic approach, dating back to the early part of the twentieth century. This was followed a little later by the ideas of the ethologists, based on their studies of animal behaviour. The third approach, which is more recent, comes mainly from evolutionary social psychology.

### Psychodynamic theory

In *Beyond the pleasure principle* (1920/1990), Freud proposed that human aggression stems from an innate 'Death Instinct', *Thanatos,* which is in opposition to a 'Life Instinct', *Eros*. Thanatos is initially directed at self-destruction, but later in development it becomes redirected outwards towards other people. Freud's background as a physician influenced his; his notion of the death instinct was partly a response to the large-scale destruction of the First World War (see **http://www.historyguide.org/europe/freud_discontents.html**). Like the sexual urge, which stems from Eros, an aggressive urge stemming from Thanatos builds up from bodily tensions, and needs to be expressed. This is essentially a one-factor theory: aggression builds up naturally and must be released. Freud's ideas were revised by later theorists, known as **neo-Freudians**, sympathetic to his position who viewed aggression as a more rational, but nonetheless innate, process whereby people sought a healthy release for primitive survival instincts that are basic to all animal species (Hartmann, Kris & Loewenstein, 1949).

**Neo-Freudians**
Psychoanalytic theorists who modified the original theories of Freud.

## Ethology

In the 1960s, three books made a strong case for the instinctual basis of human aggression, on the grounds of a comparison with animal behaviour: Lorenz's *On Aggression* (1966), Ardrey's *The Territorial Imperative* (1966) and Morris's *The Naked Ape* (1967). The general perspective that underpins this explanation of aggression is referred to as **ethology**, a branch of biology devoted to the study of instincts, or fixed action patterns, among all members of a species when living in their natural environment.

Like the neo-Freudians, ethologists stressed the positive, functional aspects of aggression, but they also recognised that, while the potential or instinct for aggression may be innate, actual aggressive behaviour is elicited by specific stimuli in the environment, known as **releasers**. Lorenz invoked evolutionary principles to propose that aggression has survival value. An animal is considerably more aggressive towards other members of its species, which serves to distribute the individuals and/or family units in such a way as to make the most efficient use of available resources, such as sexual selection and mating, food and territory. Most of the time, intraspecies aggression may not even result in actual violence, as one animal will display instinctual threat gestures that are recognised by the other animal, which can then depart the scene – 'the Rottweiler growls so the Chihuahua runs'. Even if fighting does break out, it is unlikely to result in death, since the losing animal can display instinctual appeasement gestures that divert the victor from actually killing: for example, some animals will lie on the ground belly up in an act of subordination. Over time, in animals such as monkeys that live in colonies, appeasement gestures can help to establish dominance hierarchies or pecking orders. This is a two-factor theory: (1) there is an innate urge to aggress, which (2) depends upon appropriate stimulation by environmental releasers.

Lorenz (1966) extended the argument to humans, who must also have an inherited **fighting instinct**. Unfortunately, its survival value is much less clear than is the case for other animals. This is largely because humans lack well-developed killing appendages, such as large teeth or claws, so that clearly recognisable appeasement gestures seem not to have evolved (or may have disappeared over the course of evolution).

**Ethology**
Approach that argues that animal behaviour should be studied in the species' natural physical and social environment. Behaviour is genetically determined and is controlled by natural selection.

**Releasers**
Specific stimuli in the environment thought by ethologists to trigger aggressive responses.

**Fighting instinct**
Innate impulse to aggress which ethologists claim is shared by humans with other animals.

**Threat displays**
Nice little puppy! Aggression in animals is often limited by appeasement gestures. Do you think appeasement will work with 'Mad Max'?

There are two implications from this approach: (1) once we start being violent, we do not seem to know when to stop; and (2) in order to kill we generally need to resort to weapons. The advanced technology of our times has produced frightful devices that can slaughter people in large numbers. Furthermore, this can be accomplished at a great distance, so that even the visual and auditory feedback cues of the victim's anguish are not available to persuade the victor to desist. This insanity culminated in the hydrogen bomb – in October 1961 the Soviet Union detonated a 50-megaton device (equivalent to 50 million tons of TNT), three thousand times the force of the 1945 Hiroshima atom bomb that killed 200,000 people. At the height of the cold war there was a stockpile of 65,000 nuclear bombs ('down' to about 27,000 now). In short, humans have the ability to harm others easily, and with very little effort.

## Evolutionary social psychology

**Evolutionary social psychology**

An extension of evolutionary psychology that views complex social behaviour as adaptive, helping the individual, kin and the species as a whole to survive.

**Evolutionary social psychology** developed out of evolutionary theory and a field known as sociobiology (see Chapter 1) but has been promulgated as a revised perspective on the entire discipline of social psychology. Evolutionary social psychology is an ambitious approach that not only assumes an innate basis for aggression but also claims a biological basis for all social behaviour (Caporeal, 2007; Kenrick, Maner & Li, 2005; Neuberg, Kenrick & Schaller, 2010; Schaller, Simpson & Kenrick, 2006). Evolutionary treatments of altruism and interpersonal attraction are discussed in Chapters 13 and 14.

Derived from Darwinian theory, the evolutionary argument is provocative: specific behaviour has evolved because it promotes the survival of genes that allow the individual to live long enough to pass the same genes on to the next generation. Aggression is adaptive because it must be linked to living long enough to procreate. As such, it is helpful to the individual and to the species. Consider the situation where danger threatens the offspring of a species. Most animals, and usually the mother, will react with a high level of aggression, often higher than they would normally exhibit in other situations. A mother bird, for example, may take life-threatening risks to protect her young.

In territorial species, the defence of space is linked to aggression and being aggressive can also increase access to resources (Vaughan, 2010c). For humans, the goals for which aggressive behaviour is adaptive include social and economic advantage, either to defend the resources that we already have or to acquire new ones.

## Limitations of biological arguments

Biological explanations of aggression have considerable appeal, picking up as they do on the popular assumption that violence is part of human nature. The seventeenth-century philosopher Thomas Hobbes was one who saw fit to remark that people's lives are 'short, nasty and brutish'. Biological explanations also allow for our common experience of the power of strong bodily reactions that accompany some emotions – in this case, anger. Broadly speaking, however, social scientists (Goldstein, 1987; Rose & Rose, 2000; Ryan, 1985) question the sufficiency of the explanation of aggression when it is based totally on the cornerstone of instinct, on the grounds that this concept:

- depends on energy that is unknown, unknowable and immeasurable;
- is supported by only limited and biased empirical observation of actual human behaviour;
- has little utility in the prevention or control of aggression;
- relies on circular logic, proposing causal connections for which there is no evidence.

In summary, the view among most social psychologists who research human aggression is that evolutionary social psychology's overall contribution to an understanding of the incidence and maintenance of aggression (as distinct from its expression) is limited (Geen, 1998). (See the second focus question.) More recently, however, some evolutionary stalwarts have argued:

> . . . to say that an individual has a trait is not to say that his or her overt behavior is insensitive to the environment . . . Rather, the behavioral manifestation of a given genotype depends critically on inputs from, and reactions to, the environment. (*Kenrick, Li & Butner, 2003, p. 12*)

In other words, there is an interaction between what is inherited and the kinds of behaviour that a context permits. For example, if Igor is by nature an irritable person, it might be in his best interests not to be his usual confrontational self (a behavioural trait) when a gang of powerful bullies visits the neighbourhood bar. This is an interactionist argument and the view is in effect a biosocial approach. We now move to theories that are avowedly either social or biosocial in their sweep.

## Social and biosocial explanations

Generally, social psychologists have not favoured theories of aggression defined in terms of instinct, although modern evolutionary psychology has stimulated a renewed interest in a biological account (Bushman & Huesmann, 2010). We now consider approaches that emphasise the role of learning and of the social context. Some of these nevertheless incorporate a biological element and we refer to them as **biosocial theories**. The two outlined below propose that a drive (or state of arousal) is a precondition for aggression, although they differ in how internal and external factors are thought to interact to promote aggressive reactions.

**Biosocial theories**
In the context of aggression, theories that emphasise an innate component, though not the existence of a full-blown instinct.

### Frustration and aggression

In its original form, the **frustration–aggression hypothesis** linked aggression to an antecedent condition of frustration. It derived from the work of a group of psychologists at Yale University in the 1930s, and, as described in Chapter 10, it has been used to explain prejudice. The anthropologist John Dollard and his psychologist colleagues (Dollard, Doob, Miller, Mowrer & Sears, 1939) proposed that aggression was always caused by some kind of frustrating event or situation; conversely, frustration invariably led to aggression. This reasoning has been applied to the effects of job loss on violence (Catalano, Novaco & McConnell, 1997) and the role of social and economic deprivation in 'ethnic cleansing' of the Kurds in Iraq and of non-Serbs in Bosnia (Dutton, Boyanowsky & Bond, 2005; Staub, 1996, 2000). We might also speculate that terrorism is spawned by chronic and acute frustration over the ineffectiveness of other mechanisms to achieve socioeconomic and cultural goals – people are unlikely to become suicide bombers unless all other channels of social improvement have proved ineffective.

**Frustration–aggression hypothesis**
Theory that all frustration leads to aggression, and all aggression comes from frustration. Used to explain prejudice and intergroup aggression.

Frustration–aggression theory had considerable appeal, inasmuch as it was decidedly different from the Freudian approach. According to Goldstein (1980, pp. 262–3), 'it was a theory with no psychoanalytic mumbo jumbo. No need to bother about such phantoms as ids, egos, superegos, and ego defence mechanisms.' Later research revealed that the basic hypothesis was simplistic and far from a complete explanation for aggressive behaviour (see Berkowitz, 1993). One major flaw is the theory's loose definition of 'frustration' and the difficulty in predicting which kinds of frustrating circumstance may lead to aggression. As we shall see, there are many factors other than frustration that can cause violence between people.

**Road rage**

Sitting in traffic and dealing with discourteous drivers is a common frustration for many people that occasionally spills over into aggression

## Excitation transfer

**Excitation-transfer model**

The expression of aggression is a function of learned behaviour, some excitation from another source, and the person's interpretation of the arousal state.

A later approach that featured the concept of drive is Zillmann's (1979, 1988) **excitation-transfer model**. The expression of aggression (or any other emotion) is a function of:

- a learned aggressive behaviour;
- arousal or excitation from another source;
- the person's interpretation of the arousal state, such that an aggressive response seems appropriate.

Zillmann suggests that this residual arousal transfers from one situation to another in a way that promotes the likelihood of an aggressive response, especially if aggressive behaviour is well established in someone's usual repertoire. According to Zillmann, any experience that markedly increases the level of overall excitation can lead to unintended consequences.

Look at the example in Figure 12.2. A student has been exercising at the gym and is still physically aroused when driving to the local supermarket. Here, another customer's car sneaks forward into the parking space that the student is trying to reverse into. Although the event might ordinarily be mildly annoying, this time the residual excitation from the gym session (now forgotten) triggers verbal abuse from the student (not you, of course).

Heightened arousal can often lead us to be more aggressive than we are normally: for example, making gestures while driving in stressful traffic conditions; exclaiming with annoyance at our partner when we are already upset about dropping some crockery in the kitchen; severely scolding a child who accidentally gets lost. The extreme level of excitement that often occurs at football matches can erupt in violence between rival groups of fans (Kerr, 2005). All of these instances make some sense in terms of Zillmann's theory. It can be applied to the experience of sexual arousal as well (see the section on erotica below), or to any kind of former stimulation whose effects linger over time.

The concept of arousal is retained in Anderson and Bushman's (2002a) general aggression model, to which we return in a later section.

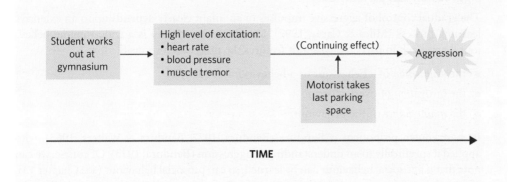

**Figure 12.2**  Applying the excitation-transfer model of aggression
*Source:* based on Zillman (1979)

## Hate crimes

Biological and social models of aggression can provide us with likely and plausible reasoning as to why people aggress against others. Sometimes, violence is linked to prejudice, as noted in our discussion of the frustration–aggression hypothesis above (see also Chapter 10). **Hate crimes** are an instance. However, some old targets of prejudice have been replaced: the lynchings of African Americans in the South during the 1930s have given way to different forms of persecution, and the persecution of other minorities (Green, Glaser, & Rich, 1998). In some countries, hate crimes now are a class of criminal offence (Vaughan 2010d). See Box 12.2 for an example of how a gay man was persecuted.

**Hate crime**
A class of violence against members of a stereotyped minority group.

---

### Real world 12.2
#### Hate crimes, gays and the case of Mathew Shepard

A sub-population whose members have been the victims of frequent and extreme hate crimes is the gay community. Aggression is frequently perpetrated against homosexuals by people who have no direct dealings with their victims other than being motivated by strong negative feelings towards homosexuality. Many homosexual people report being the victims of such hate crimes, and one study found that 94 per cent of its homosexual participants had been victimised for reasons associated with their sexuality (National Gay and Lesbian Task Force, 1990). Franklin (2000) surveyed 489 racially and economically diverse students at a community college in North Carolina in the United States: 10 per cent reported that they had physically assaulted or threatened to assault a person whom they knew or assumed to be homosexual; 24 per cent reported that they had verbally abused people they thought were homosexual.

Mathew Shepard was a 21-year-old gay college student in Wyoming who was the victim of a hate crime against gay people. He was murdered in 1998 by two 22-year-old men. Mathew was taken from a bar five days earlier to a remote prairie, where he was tied to a fence and whipped in the face with a gun until he lost consciousness. He was then left to die in the freezing weather. His killers admitted to laughing while they attacked Mathew. Each assailant received two life sentences. Attempts by the prosecution to secure the death penalty were thwarted by Mathew's mother, who appealed for clemency for the men. Both of the men's girlfriends were also charged with being an accessory to the crime.

This hate crime, although not uncommon, sparked worldwide outrage in gay and lesbian communities, and Matthew has become something of a symbol for the persecution that many minority group members experience. (See the Matthew Shepard Foundation website at **http://www.matthewshepard.org/**; but also see the Westborough Baptist anti-gay home page, some of whose members picketed his funeral, at **http://www. godhatesfags.com/**.)

## Aggression can be learned

The gradual control of aggressive impulses in an infant clearly depends upon an extensive learning process (Miles & Carey, 1997). **Social learning theory** is a wide-ranging behavioural approach in psychology, and it features the processes responsible for:

- the *acquisition* of a behaviour or a behavioural sequence;
- the *instigation* of overt acts; and
- the *maintenance* of the behaviour.

Its best known proponent is Bandura (Bandura, 1977; Bandura & Walters, 1963), who applied it specifically to an understanding of aggression (Bandura, 1973). Of course, we can note that if antisocial behaviour can be learned, so can prosocial behaviour (see Chapter 13). Although Bandura acknowledged the role of biological factors in relation to aggression, the theory's emphasis is on the role of experience, which can be direct or vicarious. Through socialisation, children learn to aggress because either they are directly rewarded or someone else appears to be rewarded for their actions.

The idea of **learning by direct experience** is based on Skinner's operant reinforcement principles: a behaviour is maintained by rewards and punishments actually experienced by the child. For example, if Jonathan takes Margaret's biscuit from her, and no one intervenes, then he is reinforced by now having the biscuit. The idea of **learning by vicarious experience** is a contribution made by social learning theorists, who argue that learning occurs through the processes of modelling and imitation of other people.

The concept of imitation is not new in social theory. The French sociologist Tarde (1890), for example, devoted a whole book, *Les lois de l'imitation,* to the subject and boldly asserted that 'Society *is* imitation'. What is unique in social learning theory is the proposition that the behaviour to be imitated must be seen to be rewarding in some way. Some models, such as parents, siblings and peers, are more appropriate for the child than others. The learning sequence of aggression can be extended beyond direct interactions between people to include media images, such as on television. It can also be applied to understanding how adults learn in later life.

According to Bandura, whether a person is aggressive in a particular situation depends on:

- the person's previous experiences of aggressive behaviour, including that both of the individual and of others;

**Social learning theory**
The view championed by Bandura that human social behaviour is not innate but learned from appropriate models.

**Learning by direct experience**
Acquiring a behaviour because we were rewarded for it.

**Learning by vicarious experience**
Acquiring a behaviour after observing that another person was rewarded for it.

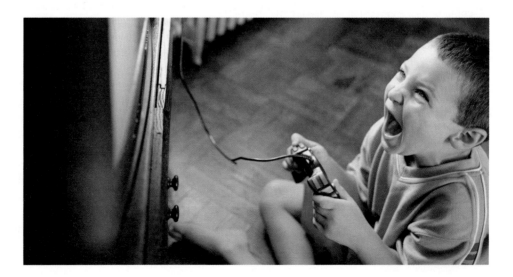

**Vicarious learning**
Children can learn to be aggressive by playing video games in which heroic characters are reinforced for aggression

- the success of aggressive behaviour in the past;
- the current likelihood of the aggression being either rewarded or punished;
- the complex array of cognitive, social and environmental factors in the situation.

Bandura's studies used a variety of experimental settings to show that children will quite readily mimic the aggressive acts of others. In particular, an adult makes a potent model, no doubt because children perceive their elders as responsible and authoritative figures (see also Chapters 5 and 14). The early findings pointed to a clear **modelling** effect when the adult was seen acting aggressively in a live setting. Even more disturbingly, this capacity to acquire aggression was also demonstrated when the adult model was seen acting violently on television (see Box 12.3 and Figure 12.3).

An interesting and recent theoretical development is a blending of social learning theory with the learning of a particular kind of cognitive schema – the **script** (see Chapter 2). Children learn rules of conduct from those around them, so that aggression becomes internalised. A situation is recognised as frustrating or threatening: for example, a human target is identified, and a learned routine of aggressive behaviour is enacted (Perry, Perry & Boldizar, 1990). Once established in childhood, an aggressive sequence is persistent (Huesmann, 1988; Anderson & Huesmann, 2003). Research on age trends for murder and manslaughter in the United States shows that this form of aggression quickly peaks among 15–25-year-olds and then declines systematically (US Department of Justice, 2001).

In summary, the social learning approach has had a major impact on research on aggression. It has also touched a chord in our community about the causes of aggression and has directly increased research into the effects of violence in the visual media on both children and adults. If violence is learned, exposure to aggressive and successful models leads people to imitate them. Being aggressive can become an established pattern of behaving, even a way of life, which is likely to repeat itself by imitation across generations (Huesmann, Eron, Lefkowitz & Walder, 1984). This does not necessarily mean that change is impossible. If aggression can be learned, presumably it can also be modified and remedied. This is the basis of behaviour modification programmes, such as anger management, used by clinical and community psychologists to help people to find more peaceful ways of dealing with others.

Finally, what effects does spanking have on the social development of children? Considering the thrust of social learning theory, you might deduce that children will learn that striking another is not punished, at least if the aggressor is more powerful! In a two-year longitudinal study of children and their parents, Straus, Sugarman and Giles-Sims (1997) recorded how often a child was spanked (none to three or more times) each week. Across a two-year span, they found an almost linear relationship over time between the rate of spanking and the level of antisocial behaviour. What is more, children who were not spanked at all showed less antisocial behaviour after two years.

## Does theory have any point?

As each chapter in this book attests, social psychology is replete with theory. In the case of aggression, theories are numerous and vigorously debated. There is no sign of change in the search for explanation – and little wonder, as aggression is part of a community's everyday experience and it is every person's wish to account for it (see Chapter 3). According to some, little theoretical progress has been made (Geen & Donnerstein, 1983), but others have seen merit in pulling 'mini-theories' of aggression together into a more general model (Anderson & Bushman, 2002a – see below).

None of the foregoing theories provides a full explanation for the diversity of aggression, and even when a precipitating event may be apparent, there will invariably be other, less obvious contributing factors. Consider how cultural values (see Chapter 16) and social

**Modelling**
Tendency for a person to reproduce the actions, attitudes and emotional responses exhibited by a real-life or symbolic model. Also called *observational learning*.

**Script**
A schema about an event.

### Research classic 12.3
### Sock it to the Bobo doll!

Can the mere observation of an act be sufficient to learn how to perform it? Albert Bandura and his colleagues addressed this question in a series of experiments at Stanford University. This work had a considerable impact on the acceptance of social factors within the narrower field of experimental research on learning, but it also had a long-term effect on wider thinking about the origins of aggression. According to the social learning theory of observational learning, observing a behaviour produces a cognitive representation in the observer, who then experiences vicarious reinforcement. This kind of reinforcement refers to a process whereby the outcome for the model, whether rewarding or punishing, becomes a remote reinforcement for the observer. If this is so, then aggression is likely to be one of many forms of behaviour that can be learned.

Bandura, Ross and Ross (1963) tested this idea in one study of 4- and 5-year-old children who watched a male or female adult play with a commercially popular inflated Bobo doll. There were four conditions:

1  *Live*. The adult model came into the room where the child was playing. After playing with some Tinker Toys, the adult then began to act aggressively towards the Bobo doll. The acts included sitting on the doll, hitting its nose, banging it on the head with a mallet and kicking it around the room. The words used were 'sock him in the nose', 'pow', 'kick him', 'hit him down' and the like. After this, the child was left to play with the Bobo doll.

2  *Videotape*. This was the same as the live sequence but had been filmed on videotape for the child to view.

3  *Cartoon*. The model acted in the same way but was dressed in a cat uniform, and the room was decorated as if it were in a cartoon.

4  *Control*. The child skipped all of these conditions and went directly to play with the Bobo doll.

The results in Figure 12.3 show that the children who watched an adult behave aggressively in any condition behaved more aggressively later. The most effective condition for modelling aggressive behaviour was the live sequence. However, the finding that the cartoon and videotaped conditions also increased imitative aggression in children provided fuel for critics who argued that graphic presentations of violence in films and television could have serious consequences for children's later behaviour.

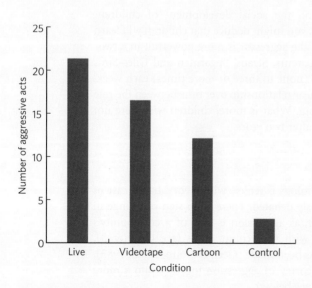

**Figure 12.3** How children learn aggression through mere observation

*Source*: based on data from Bandura & Walters (1963)

pressures may contribute to a pub brawl involving unemployed immigrants, even though intoxication may seem to be the cause. Other examples are the underlying effects of poverty, chronic frustration and social disadvantage, which cumulatively often lead to acts of both public and domestic violence. Some of these factors are explored next.

# Personal and situational variations

Although it is possible to distinguish conceptually between the person and the situation when dealing with any social behaviour, common sense suggests that an interaction of both determines how people behave (see Ross & Nisbett, 1991). Like an echo of Lewin's early field theory notion of a tension between the person and the environment (see Chapter 1), people bring to any situation their unique characteristics and their individual way of construing the situation. When we apply such thinking to the study of aggression, the separation of person variables from situation variables is may be an oversimplification and a matter of conceptual convenience. It reflects the way in which most research has been performed and belies the reality that the causes of aggression are complex and interactive.

Consider some contexts in which aggression occurs: reacting to being teased, a carryover from a near traffic accident, a continuing response to the burden of poverty, a method for dealing with a nagging partner, or a parent's control over a fractious child. Some of these appear to involve situational variables, but closer inspection suggests that some go with the person, or with a category of people (the poor, the partner, the parent). However, an important caveat is that not all people in a category respond in the same way in identical situations.

## Individual differences

### Personality

The tendency to aggress develops quite early in life and becomes a stable behavioural pattern. Huesmann and Guerra (1997) found that children who are aggressive at eight years of age are more likely to be aggressive in later years. It also seems likely that chronic aggression is linked to a tendency to attribute hostile intentions to others (Graham, Hudley & Williams, 1992).

When a behavioural pattern is both stable and found in children, it is easy to propose that people aggress because they have an 'aggressive personality'. Can you rate your friends according to how much or how little they typically tend towards aggressive behaviour? The ability to evaluate people in terms of their aggressiveness is an important part of some psychometric (i.e. psychological test-based) and clinical assessments (Sundberg, 1977): for example, in determining the likelihood of reoffending among violent offenders (Mullen, 1984).

It is simplistic to think that people are naturally aggressive. At the same time, some of us can be more aggressive than others because of our age, gender, culture and personal experiences. There are several individual characteristics that are common to violent offenders, including low self-esteem and poor frustration tolerance. However, narcissistic people who have high self-esteem and a sense of entitlement seem to be particularly prone to aggression (Bushman & Baumeister, 1998). Social workers often recognise children who have been exposed to above-average levels of violence, particularly in their homes, as being 'high risk' and in need of primary intervention.

## Type A personality

Research has identified the existence of a behaviour pattern called **Type A personality** (Matthews, 1982). This syndrome is associated with susceptibility to coronary heart disease. People evincing this pattern are overactive and excessively competitive in their encounters with others. Type A people may be more aggressive towards others perceived to be competing with them on an important task (Carver & Glass, 1978). Again, Type A people prefer to work alone rather than with others when they are under stress, probably to avoid exposure to incompetence in others and to feel in control of the situation (Dembroski & MacDougall, 1978). However, behaving in this way can be destructive. For example, Type A personalities were reported to be more prone to abuse children (Strube et al., 1984). In an organisational setting, Baron (1989) found that managers who were classified as Type A experienced more conflict with peers and subordinates, although not with their own supervisors. They apparently knew when to draw the line!

## Hormones

Is it a popular fallacy that hormonal activity could be related to aggression? There may be a real link. Gladue (1991) reported higher levels of overt aggression in males than in females. Moreover, this sex difference applied equally to both heterosexual and homosexual males when compared with females – biology (male/female) rather than gender orientation was the main contributing variable. In a second study, Gladue and his colleagues measured testosterone levels through saliva tests in their male participants and also assessed whether they were Type A or Type B personalities (Berman, Gladue & Taylor, 1993). The levels of shock administered to an opponent in an experimental setting were higher when the male was either higher in testosterone or a Type A personality, or both. Overall there is a small correlation of 0.14 between elevated testosterone (in both males and females) and aggression (Book, Starzyk & Quinsey, 2001) – if it was causal, testosterone would explain 2 per cent of variation in aggression.

However, a correlation between levels of testosterone and aggression does not establish causality. In fact, causality could operate in the opposite direction: for example, playing and winning at chess or tennis can cause a temporary elevation of testosterone level (Gladue, Boechler & McCall, 1989; Mazur, Booth & Dabbs, 1992). A more convincing link between the two was pinpointed by two studies in the Netherlands (Cohen-Kettenis & Van Goozen, 1997; Van Goozen, Cohen-Kettenis, Gooren, Frijda & Van der Poll, 1995). Transsexuals who were treated with sex hormones as part of their sex reassignment showed increased or decreased proneness to aggression according to whether the direction of change was female to male or male to female.

## Gender and socialisation

Both social and developmental psychology have traditionally emphasised the differential socialisation of gendered characteristics – homemaker versus worker. This is an explanation based on **social role theory**, and not on **sexual selection theory** based in evolutionary social psychology (Archer, 2004).

A wealth of research has confirmed this male–female difference: men tend to be more aggressive than women across cultures and socioeconomic groups. However, the size of the difference varies according to the kind and context of aggression. Men are more likely than women to be physically violent, whereas women are as likely as men to use verbal attack in similar contexts, although the degree to which they aggress may be less (Eagly & Steffen, 1986; Harris, 1992). As children mature, girls manipulate and boys fight – the essential gender difference is that boys aggress directly whereas girls aggress indirectly: for example, by gossip and social exclusion (Archer & Coyne, 2005; Björkvist, Lagerspetz & Kaukiainen, 1992).

A recent examination of meta-analyses of aggression in men and women has suggested that gender is confounded with status in many of the designs, and that this issue is important when the male–female interaction involves strangers (Conway, Irannejad & Giannopoulos, 2005). Aggression is often directed at the weaker person, who may be female or simply of lower status. Aggression may be more to do with status than sex or gender.

## Catharsis

An instrumental reason for aggression, with popular appeal, is **catharsis**, which refers to the process of using our behaviour as an outlet or release for pent-up emotion – the **cathartic hypothesis**. Although associated with Freud, the idea can be traced back to Aristotle and ancient Greek tragedy: by acting out their emotions, people can purify their feelings (Scherer, Abeles & Fischer, 1975). The idea has popular appeal. Perhaps 'letting off steam' from frustration can restore equanimity. The author of a popular book gave this advice:

> Punch a pillow or a punching bag. Punch with all the frenzy you can. If you are angry at a particular person, imagine his or her face on the pillow or punching bag, and vent your rage physically and verbally. You will be doing violence to a pillow or punching bag so that you can stop doing violence to yourself by holding in poisonous anger. (*Lee, 1993, p. 96*)

In Japan, some companies have already followed this principle, providing a special room with a toy replica of the boss upon which employees can relieve their tensions by 'bashing the boss!' (Middlebrook, 1980).

However, questions about the efficacy of the catharsis hypothesis were asked some years ago (Geen & Quanty, 1977; Konečni & Ebbesen, 1976). Recent experimental research has gone further to reject outright the basis of catharsis in the present for reducing later aggression. Bushman, Baumeister and Stack (1999) found that people who hit a punching bag, believing that it reduced stress, were more likely later to punish someone who had transgressed them (see Box 12.4).

**Catharsis**
A dramatic release of pent-up feelings: the idea that aggressive motivation is 'drained' by acting against a frustrating object (or substitute), or by a vicarious experience.

**Cathartic hypothesis**
The notion that acting aggressively, or even just viewing aggressive material, reduces feelings of anger and aggression.

**Catharsis**
This is an anger management centre where you can drop by to let it all hang out – in this case by beating someone up

## Research and applications 12.4
### Letting it 'all hang out' may be worse than useless

Have you ever felt really angry and then 'let it all out' by screaming, punching a pillow or breaking a plate? Did you feel better afterwards? There is a common perception that such 'designer outbursts' of aggression are an effective way of reducing anxiety and aggression. Wann and colleagues (Wann et al., 1999) found that many participants in their experiments believed that catharsis, achieved in particular by viewing violent sports, can lower the likelihood of subsequent aggression. However, the cathartic hypothesis has little support; research suggests that the opposite is true: cathartic aggression actually increases aggression in general. If so, then the common belief that catharsis is an effective remedy for pent-up anger and aggression is a dangerous misconception.

A study by Bushman, Baumeister and Stack (1999) tested the cathartic hypothesis by asking students to read one of three fake newspaper articles: (1) a pro-catharsis article in which a prominent university researcher claimed that cathartic behaviour relieved the tendency to aggress; (2) an anti-catharsis article quoting a research finding of no link between catharsis and a reduction in later aggression; and (3) a 'control' article completely unrelated to aggression or catharsis.

The students were then asked to write an essay that was critiqued by another student (in fact by the experimenter) while they waited. The essays were returned with very negative written comments designed to induce anger, such as 'this is one of the worst essays I have ever read!' Angered students who had read the pro-catharsis article were more inclined to choose a punching bag exercise as an optional task than those who had read either the anti-catharsis or the control article. Those who had not been angered by the critique of their essays were still more likely to choose to punch a bag if they had read the pro-catharsis article than those who had not. The results of this study highlight how the media or popular belief can influence people to choose cathartic stress relief, and how this choice is affected by the amount of anger people are feeling.

The initial study was extended to a situation where an essay writer could later interact with the essay critic. After reading one of the three articles, some students were asked to spend two minutes punching a punching bag. Next, they completed a competitive reaction time task in which they selected a degree of punishment (noise volume) to deliver to the competitor (supposedly in another room) when the competitor was slower. As a final twist, just before this encounter, a group of students were led to believe that this competitor was the person who had negatively critiqued their essay.

Those who expected to interact with their critic were more willing to engage in punching the bag before their 'meeting'. Also, those who had read the pro-catharsis article were more aggressive in the task (delivering louder noises) even after punching the bag – which, according to popular belief, should be a cathartic exercise and reduce aggression. This study suggests that catharsis does not relieve stress and is actually 'worse than useless'!

---

Anderson, Carnagey and Eubanks (2003) reported five experiments that demonstrated the effects of songs with violent lyrics on both aggressive feelings and thoughts. In the data in Figure 12.4, students listened to rock songs that were either violent or non-violent, and then rated pairs of words for their semantic similarity. The word meanings were either clearly aggressive (e.g., *blood, butcher, choke, gun*) or ambiguously aggressive (e.g. *alley, bottle, rock, stick*). The word pairs were either: aggressive–ambiguous or control (aggressive–aggressive or ambiguous–ambiguous). The researchers found that a priming effect (more similarity) from hearing violent lyrics occurred for aggressive–ambiguous pairs (e.g. *blood/stick*) than for control pairs (*butcher/gun* or *alley/rock*). This increase in aggressive thinking goes against the cathartic hypothesis. (Priming is discussed further below.)

Bushman delivered this parting shot to the cathartic hypothesis after one of his studies:

> Does venting anger extinguish or feed the flame? The results from the present research show that venting to reduce anger is like using gasoline to put out a fire – it only feeds the flame. (*Bushman, 2002, p. 729*)

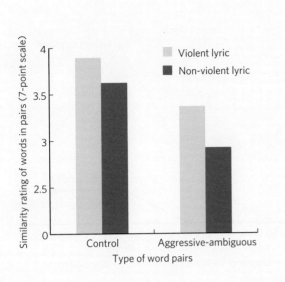

**Figure 12.4** Ratings of how similar aggressive or ambiguous word pairs are after hearing violent or non-violent lyrics

- Participants listened to songs with lyrics that were either violent or non-violent.

- Violent lyrics triggered aggressive associations in words previously ambiguous in meaning.

- This contradicts the cathartic hypothesis, since listening to violent lyrics should lessen rather than increase aggressive thinking.

*Source:* based on data from Anderson, Carnagey & Eubanks (2003)

## Alcohol

It is often assumed that alcohol befuddles the brain. This is a particular form of the *disinhibition hypothesis* (see below): that is, alcohol detracts from cortical control and increases activity in more primitive brain areas. The link between alcohol and aggressive behaviour seems firmly established (Bartholow, Pearson, Gratton & Fabiani, 2003; Bushman & Cooper, 1990; Giancola, 2003), and controlled behavioural studies suggest a causal relationship. Additionally, people who drink more are more aggressive (Bailey & Taylor, 1991). Even people who do not often consume alcohol can become aggressive when they do (LaPlace, Chermack & Taylor, 1994).

In an experimental study of the effects of alcohol on aggression, male students were assigned to either an alcohol or placebo condition (Taylor & Sears, 1988). They were placed in a competition involving reaction time with another participant. In each pair, the person who responded more slowly on a given trial would receive an electric shock from the opponent. The level of shock to be delivered could be set at various intensity levels and was selected by each person before that trial commenced. The opponent's shock settings were actually determined by the experimenter. The shocks were always low intensity (i.e. fairly passive) and the win/loss frequency was 50 per cent. The results in Figure 12.5 show the proportions of high-intensity shocks given by participants who were in either an alcohol or a placebo condition.

There were four sequential stages (none → mild → strong → none) of social pressure in which a confederate, who was watching the proceedings, sometimes encouraged the participant to give a shock. The results show an interaction between taking alcohol and being pressured to aggress: participants who had imbibed were more susceptible to influence and continued to give high-intensity shocks even after the pressure was later withdrawn. In an extension by Gustafson (1992), intoxicated males were more aggressive than those who were sober, and they delivered a more intense shock when they were provoked.

The analogy to real life is the *context* of social drinking, such as at a party or in a bar, where others may goad the drinker to be aggressive. Actual statistics on the connection

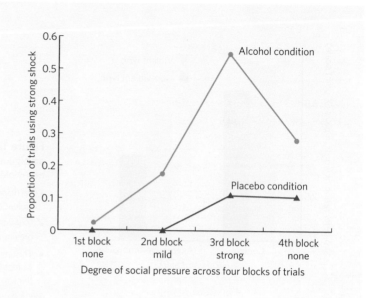

**Figure 12.5** Alcohol, social pressure and males' willingness to shock a passive opponent

*Source*: based on Taylor & Sears (1988)

between alcohol and aggression are suggestive, not clear-cut. Although alcohol consumption is disproportionately associated with physical violence, the causal pathways are complex.

Behaviour that is normally under control, such as acts that are antisocial, illegal or embarrassing, can be released by consuming alcohol. How many people sing karaoke only after a few drinks? Are they disinhibited?

It is well established that alcohol impairs various higher-order cognitive operations, such as attention, encoding information and retrieving information from memory. Bartholow, Pearson, Gratton and Fabiani (2003) carried out an experiment drawing on ideas and methods from social cognition and cognitive neuroscience. Their findings implied that alcohol might put people at risk in interpersonal encounters by:

- preventing changes to positive impressions when negative behaviours indicate that doing so would be adaptive; and
- promoting changes in negative impressions such that potentially threatening people are deemed less dangerous (Bartholow, Pearson, Gratton & Fabiani, 2003 p. 635).

The authors surmised that these effects were a likely precursor to disinhibited and socially inappropriate behaviour, regardless of the consequences.

## Disinhibition, deindividuation and dehumanisation

Sometimes people act 'out of character'. **Disinhibition** refers to a reduction in the usual social forces that operate to restrain us from acting antisocially, illegally or immorally. There are several ways in which people lose their normal inhibitions against aggression. In Box 12.5, we consider the case in which the *aggressor* experiences a state of **deindividuation**. This process (discussed in more detail in Chapter 11) involves changes in situational factors affecting an aggressor, such as the presence of others or lack of identifiability. As well, we include factors that focus on how the victim is perceived, such as being less than human – **dehumanisation**.

Mann (1981) applied the concept of deindividuation to a particular context relating to **collective aggression**, the 'baiting crowd'. The typical situation involves a person threatening

**Disinhibition**
A breakdown in the learned controls (social mores) against behaving impulsively or, in this context, aggressively. For some people, alcohol has a disinhibiting effect.

**Deindividuation**
Process whereby people lose their sense of socialised individual identity and engage in unsocialised, often antisocial, behaviours.

**Dehumanisation**
Stripping people of their dignity and humanity.

**Collective aggression**
Unified aggression by a group of individuals, who may not even know one another, against another individual or group.

## Real world 12.5
### Deindividuation and dehumanisation

### Being deindividuated

Deindividuation brings a sense of reduced likelihood of punishment for acting aggressively.

A dramatic example of how a real, or perceived, reduction in the likelihood of punishment can enhance aggression and violence was seen in the My Lai incident, during the Vietnam War, where American soldiers slaughtered an entire village of innocent civilians. In the official inquiry, it was revealed that the same unit had previously killed and tortured civilians without any disciplinary action; that the area was a designated 'free-fire' zone, so that it was considered legitimate to shoot at anything that moved; and indeed that the whole ethos of the war was one of glorified violence (Hersh, 1970).

In addition, there was a sense of anonymity, or *deindividuation,* that came from being part of a large group and this further enhanced the soldiers' perception that they would not be punished as individuals. (See the effects of deindividuation in Chapter 11.) This sense of anonymity is thought to contribute to the translation of aggressive emotion into actual violence: it may occur through being part of a large group or gathering, as in the crowd that baits a suicide to jump (Mann, 1981) or a pack rape at a gang convention; or it may happen through something that protects anonymity in another way, such as the white hoods worn by Ku Klux Klan members (Middlebrook, 1980), the stocking worn over the face of an armed robber or terrorist or the Hallowe'en masks that prompt children to steal sweets and money (Diener, Fraser, Beaman & Kelem, 1976). Malamuth (1981) found that almost one-third of male students questioned at an American university admitted there was a likelihood that they would rape if they were certain of not getting caught!

### Dehumanising the victim

A variation of deindividuation in the aggressor can occur when the victim, rather than the aggressor, is anonymous or dehumanised in some way (Haslam, 2006; Haslam, Loughnan & Kashima, 2008), so that the aggressor cannot easily see the personal pain and injury suffered by the victim. This can weaken any control that may be applied through feelings of shame and guilt.

Terrible examples of this phenomenon have been documented, such as the violent treatment of psychiatric patients and prisoners who were either kept naked or dressed identically so that they were indistinguishable as individuals (Steir, 1978). Again, having faceless and deindividuated victims in violent films and television programmes can disinhibit some viewers, encouraging them to play down the injury and thus be more likely to imitate the violent acts (Bandura, 1986).

Extreme and inhumane instances of disinhibition come from war: for example, the extermination of tens of thousands of people by a single atomic blast in Hiroshima and again in Nagasaki in 1945. Cohn (1987) presented a revealing analysis of the ways in which military personnel 'sanitise', and thereby justify, the use of nuclear weaponry by semantics that dehumanise the likely or actual victims, referring to them as 'targets', 'the aggressed' or even 'collateral damage'. American military personnel used the same semantic strategies during the Vietnam War to rationalise and justify the killing of Vietnamese civilians, who were known as 'gooks' (Sabini & Silver, 1982).

In 1993 Bosnian Serbs, in what was once part of Yugoslavia, referred to acts of genocide against the Muslim population as 'ethnic cleansing'. The media can also unwittingly lessen the impact of the horror of large-scale killing. A phrase often used on television during the Allied bombing campaigns in Iraq in 1991 was 'theatre of war', inviting the audience to sit back and be entertained.

See Chapter 10 for other examples of dehumanisation.

---

to jump from a high building, a crowd gathers below, and some begin to chant 'jump, jump'. In one dramatic case in New York in 1938, thousands of people waited at ground level, some for eleven hours, until a man jumped to his death from a seventeenth-floor hotel ledge.

Mann analysed twenty-one cases of suicides reported in newspapers in the 1960s and 1970s. He found that in ten out of the twenty-one cases where there had been a crowd watching, baiting had occurred. He examined other features of these reports that distinguished between crowds that bait and those that do not. Baiting was more likely to occur at night and when the crowd was large (more than 300 people). Also, the crowd was typically a long way from the victim, usually at ground level. These features are likely to produce a

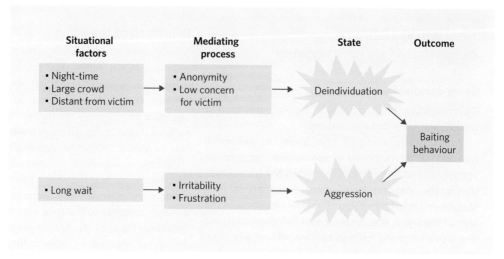

**Figure 12.6** The baiting crowd: an exercise in deindividuation and frustration
*Source:* based on Mann (1981)

state of deindividuation in the individual. The longer the crowd waited, the more likely they would bait, perhaps egged on by irritability and frustration (see Figure 12.6).

In a study in Israel, Struch and Schwartz (1989) investigated aggression among non-Orthodox Jews towards highly Orthodox Jews, measured in terms of strong opposition to Orthodox institutions. They found two contributing factors: a perception of inter-group conflict of interests (see also Chapter 11), and a tendency to regard Orthodox Jews as 'inhuman'.

Since the early 1970s, European, but particularly English, football became strongly associated with hooliganism – to such an extent, for example, that the violence of some English fans in Belgium associated with Euro 2000 undoubtedly contributed to England's failure to be chosen to host the World Cup in 2006. England was made to wait a little longer! Popular hysteria has characterised 'soccer hooliganism' in terms of the stereotyped images of football fans on the rampage (Murphy, Williams & Dunning, 1990).

It is tempting to apply an explanation in terms of deindividuation in a crowd setting, but a study of football hooliganism by Marsh, Russer and Harré (1978) suggested a different cause. Violence by fans is often orchestrated far away from the stadium and long before a given match. What might appear to be a motley crowd of supporters on match day can actually consist of several groups of fans with different status. By participating in ritualised aggression over a period of time, a faithful follower can be 'promoted' into a higher group and can continue to pursue a 'career structure'. Rival fans who follow their group's rules carefully can avoid real physical harm to themselves or others. For example, chasing the opposition after a match ('seeing the others off') need not end in violence; the agreed code is that no one is caught! Organised football hooliganism is a kind of staged production rather than an uncontrollable mob.

Football hooliganism can also be understood in more societal terms. For example, Murphy, Williams and Dunning (1990) described how football arose in Britain as a working-class sport. By the 1950s, a working-class value of masculine aggression was associated with the game. Attempts by a government (seen as middle class) to control this aspect of the sport would enhance class solidarity and encourage increased violence that generalises beyond matches. This account is societal (see below), and involves intergroup relations and the subcultural legitimation of aggression (see Chapter 10). Finally, hooliganism can be viewed in intergroup terms: in particular, the way hooligans behave towards the police and vice versa (Stott & Adang, 2004; Stott, Hutchison & Drury, 2001; see also Chapter 11).

## Situational variables

### Physical environment

Two aspects of our environment have been reliably implicated in increasing levels of aggression, *heat* and *crowding*.

You would not be surprised to hear that aggression is linked to ambient temperature, given that our language commonly links it to *body temperature*. We can be 'hot under the collar' or 'simmering with rage', or tell someone else to 'cool down'. As the ambient temperature rises, there are increases in domestic violence (Cohn, 1993), violent suicide (Maes, De Meyer, Thompson, Peeters & Cosyns, 1994) and collective violence (Carlsmith & Anderson, 1979).

Harries and Stadler (1983) examined the incidence of aggravated assault in Dallas over the twelve months of 1980. Assaults were more evident when it was hotter and more humid than normal, but not when it was excessively hot and humid. Another study, of the incidence of murders and rapes over a two-year period, found a positive relationship with fluctuations in the daily average temperature (Anderson & Anderson, 1984). Kenrick and MacFarlane (1986) gauged motorists' responses to a car blocking the road at a green light by recording the amount of horn honking. As the heat went up, so did the honking. The relationship between heat and aggression was even recorded in Ancient Rome (Anderson, Bushman & Groom, 1997). Even in normally very hot climates, such as in India, people report more negative moods on the hottest days (Ruback & Pandey, 1992).

Graphically, the relationship between heat and aggression follows an inverted U (Halpern, 1995): as the temperature rises, so does aggression, at least to a certain level. When it gets very hot, aggression levels out and then declines, a trend suggesting that extreme heat saps our energy. We should note here that the critical variable is likely to be the *ambient temperature*. Cohn and Rotton (1997) tracked rates of physical assault according to temperature throughout each day over a two-year period in Minneapolis (1987–88). Their data reflect an inverted U-curve (see Figure 12.7).

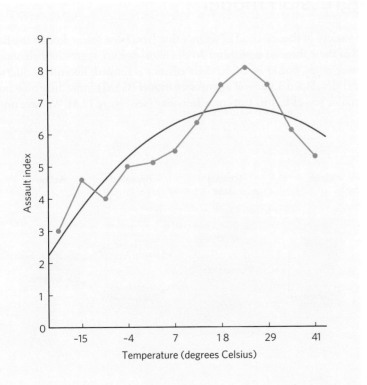

**Figure 12.7**  Relationship between rate of assaults and outdoor temperature

A curve has been fitted to the data. The effect appears as an inverted U-curve

*Source*: based on data from Cohn & Rotton (1997)

Cohn and Rotton also found that assaults were more frequent later in the evening than at other times. Most people in Minneapolis work in temperature-controlled environments during the day; as a result, the effects of ambient temperature did not show up until people left work. Further analysis revealed that it is temperature per se that accounts for the curvilinear trend, and not simply by time of day (Cohn & Rotton, 2005). Cohn and Rotton (1997) also reported a link between heat and *alcohol consumption*. When people drink more alcohol in the evening to quench their thirst, alcohol becomes a mediating variable leading to aggression.

*Crowding* that leads to fighting has long been recognised in a variety of animal species (e.g. Calhoun, 1962). For humans, crowding is a subjective state and is generally characterised by feeling that one's personal space has been encroached (see Chapter 15). There is a distinction between the invasion of personal space and a high level of population density, but in practical terms there is also an overlap. Urbanisation requires more people to share a limited amount of space, with elevated stress and potentially antisocial consequences. In a study conducted in Toronto, Regoeczi (2003) noted that population density as a gross measure can contribute to the overall level of crime in an area. However, variables crucial to a state of crowding are more finely grained – household density (persons per house) and neighbourhood density (detached housing versus high-rise housing). Her results showed that density on both measures correlated positively with self-reported feelings of aggression and also of withdrawal from interacting with strangers. In a prison context, Lawrence and Andrew (2004) confirmed a consistent finding in studies of the penal environment. Feeling crowded made it more likely that events in a UK prison were perceived as aggressive and the protagonists as more hostile and malevolent. In an acute psychiatric unit in New Zealand, Ng, Kumar, Ranclaud and Robinson (2001) found that 'crowding' (inferred from higher ward occupancy rates) was associated with a higher number of violent incidents and increased verbal aggression.

**General aggression model**

Anderson's model that includes both personal and situational factors, and cognitive and affective processes in accounting for different kinds of aggression.

# General aggression model

Let us reflect on the variety of theories and of factors that have been researched in the field of aggression. Are all of these theories useful and do all factors predict aggressive behaviour? On balance, the answer is yes, but in isolation their efficacy is limited. Recently, Anderson and Bushman (2002a) developed a **general aggression model** (GAM) indicating how both 'mini-theories' and major sets of factors can come into play (see Figure 12.8). We have noted

**Figure 12.8** A general model of aggression

Aggression is a social encounter that follows several steps. It starts with a person with specific characteristics in a particular context. The person and the situation are inputs that impact via affective, cognitive and arousal routes. The person's decision on how to act depends: is the appraisal thoughtful or impulsive?

*Source*: Anderson & Bushman (2002a)

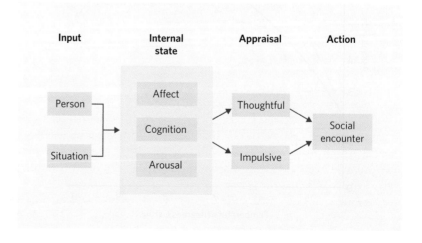

that the person–situation equation is an old concept in social psychology (e.g. Lewin, 1951). In the GAM, the kinds of personal and situational variables that we have reviewed are included. Their interplay activates three kinds of internal state (affect, cognition and arousal). A person's appraisal of the situation is predominantly either thoughtful or impulsive, and the consequence is the social encounter.

# Societal influences

## Disadvantaged groups

Social disadvantage can be an underlying cause of aggression, although the causal link can be reversed – deprived groups often become passive victims. In a review of youth violence in the United States, the rates of homicide and non-lethal violence are higher among young, urban-poor, minority males, a trend largely attributable to a mix of social and ecological factors (Tolan & Gorman-Smith, 2002). High-risk youth show signs of antisocial behaviour as children, but in inner-city areas they are likely to have dysfunctional families, rented accommodation, concentrated poverty and below-average neighbourhood facilities, and to be lacking norms that define acceptable social behaviour.

In Chapter 11, we explored in detail the relationship between disadvantage and intergroup behaviour. A key factor in the relationship between disadvantage and aggression is the extent to which a disadvantaged group has a sense of **relative deprivation**, and in particular a sense that it is deprived relative to other groups (called fraternalistic deprivation: Runciman, 1966), or that against a background of rising expectations the group has suddenly experienced a dramatic setback (Davies, 1969).

**Relative deprivation**
A sense of having less than we feel entitled to.

Relative deprivation is a sense of discontent associated with feeling that the chance of improving one's condition is slight. If improvement cannot be achieved legitimately, a deprived individual might commit vandalism, assault or burglary; at an intergroup level, this could extend to collective aggression, such as violent protest or rioting. The Los Angeles race riots of 1992 were ostensibly triggered by a jury verdict that acquitted White police officers of beating a Black motorist. Although this was the patent cause, there was also a marked undercurrent of relative deprivation among African Americans in the neighbourhoods of Los Angeles where the rioting occurred (see Box 11.1 in Chapter 11).

There is reasonable support for the validity of the concept of relative deprivation, from both experiments and historical analyses (Walker & Smith, 2002). Relative deprivation provides a plausible, partial explanation for events such as increased violence against immigrants – for example, Turkish migrants in the eastern part of Germany – when unemployment is at a very high level.

## Criminality and women

Gender stereotypes characterise men as being significantly more aggressive than women. It is possible that as gender roles in Western societies are re-orientated, women's inhibitions against violence are lowered – emancipation may be criminogenic. The redefinition of male and female roles (see also Chapter 14) in most Western societies in recent decades is correlated with a rise in alcohol and drug abuse among women. The return of women to the workforce coincided with widespread unemployment, a further trigger for increased offences against persons (and property).

Although criminal violence is still more prevalent among men than women, the *rate* of violent offending has increased more rapidly among women (see the trend for young American offenders in Figure 12.9).

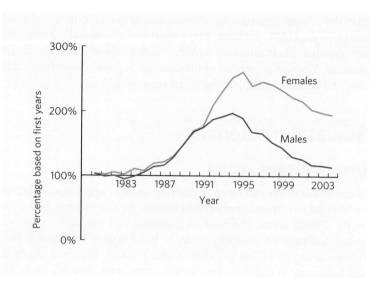

**Figure 12.9** US juvenile arrest rates for aggravated assault by sex, 1980–2004

- The original data set are arrest rates per 100,000 for males and females aged 10–17 years from 1980 to 2004.

- The data have been converted to percentages calculated on the base rates in 1980, 239 for males and 45 for females.

- The graph shows that the relative increase in percentages of the arrest rates for aggravated assault was considerably higher for females between 1987 and 1994.

*Source:* based on data from US Department of Justice (2006)

## Cultural variation

Attitudes towards aggression and violence vary over time and between cultures, and also between groups within cultures and nations. Western nations view democracy, human rights and non-violence as core cultural values. It is important to recognise these emphases for what they are: sociocultural artefacts. Throughout history, there have always been differences in **cultural norms** and **values** that have shaped some societies as more, and some as less, aggressive than others. The reasons are usually evident. A history of repeated invasions, a geography that made some settlements more competitive or more vulnerable, and a bio-evolutionary factor of physique that permitted successful raids by some groups, have all in part shaped the social philosophies of particular societies. These philosophies are dynamic and can change rapidly according to context. Examples of this in recent decades are the development of both aggressive Zionism and a radical Islam.

Vandello and Cohen (2003) studied the impact of a **culture of honour** (Nisbett & Cohen, 1996; see also Chapter 16) on domestic violence. Regions that place a value on violence to restore honour include some Mediterranean countries, the Middle East and Arab countries, central and southern America, and the southern United States. Their sample compared Brazil and US honour cultures participants with northern US participants. Their results supported three general propositions:

1   Female infidelity damages a man's reputation, particularly in honour cultures.

2   This reputation can be partly restored by using violence.

3   Women in honour cultures are expected to remain loyal in the face of jealousy-related violence.

Aggression against women is generally not a matter to display publicly. Hilton and her colleagues have suggested that, in patriarchal cultures, men and boys are proud of male-directed violence but ashamed of female-directed aggression (Hilton, Harris & Rice, 2000).

While interpersonal violence occurs in most societies, some actively practise a lifestyle of non-aggression. There may be as many as twenty-five societies with a world view based on cooperation rather than competition (Bonta, 1997). Among these are the Hutterite and Amish communities in the United States, the Inuit of the Arctic region, the !Kung of southern and central Africa, the Bushmen of Southern Africa and the Ladakhis of Tibet. Such

**Cultural norms**
Norms whose origin is part of the tradition of a culture.

**Culture of honour**
A culture that endorses male violence as a way of addressing threats to social reputation or economic position.

communities are small, sometimes scattered and relatively isolated, which suggests that these may be necessary preconditions for peaceful existence. The anthropologist Gorer (1968) argued that evidence of peaceful societies disproves the notion that humans have a 'killer' instinct.

Despite evidence of cross-cultural and cross-national variations in aggression, we need to retain a focus:

> it is individuals who hit, curse, challenge, ignore, fail to warn, testify against, gossip about, retaliate for being hurt by, and form alliances against others, either singly or as part of a group. (*Bond, 2004, p. 74*)

## Subculture of violence

A different kind of cultural variation is the **subculture of violence** (Toch, 1969). Many societies include minority subcultures in which violence is legitimised as a lifestyle. The norms of the group reflect an approval of aggressiveness, and there will be both rewards for violence and sanctions for non-compliance. In urban settings, these groups are often labelled and self-styled as gangs, and the importance of violence is reflected in their appearance and behaviour.

Nieburg (1969) provided a graphic example of the traditional initiation rite for the Sicilian Mafia. After a long lead-up period of observation, the new Mafia member would attend a candlelit meeting of other members and be led to a table showing the image of a saint, an emblem of high religious significance. Blood taken from his right hand would be sprinkled on the saint, and he would swear an oath of allegiance binding him to the brotherhood. In a short time, he would then prove himself worthy by executing a suitable person selected by the Mafia. Ingoldsby (1991) has pointed to the existence of **machismo** among Latin American families. In Italy, Tomada and Schneider (1997) report that aggression is still encouraged in adolescent boys from traditional villages in the belief that it shows sexual prowess and shapes a dominant male in the household. They link this in turn to a higher rate of male bullying at school than in England, Spain, Norway or Japan (Genta, Menesini, Fonzi, Costabile & Smith, 1996).

**Subculture of violence**
A subgroup of society in which a higher level of violence is accepted as the norm.

**Machismo**
A code in which challenges, abuse and even differences of opinion must be met with fists or other weapons.

**Culture of violence**
These young people are members of rival gangs whose norm for solving intergroup disputes is violence. Will the mums remain neutral?

# Mass media

The impact of *mass media* on aggression has been both a popular and controversial focus of inquiry. There are many examples of people emulating violent acts such as assault, rape and murder in almost identical fashion to portrayals in films or television programmes; and likewise of the disinhibitory effects of watching an excessive amount of sanitised violence, mostly on television. Some of the laboratory research has been flawed. For example, work on the effects of **desensitisation** to media violence has often involved exposure to rather mild forms of television violence for relatively short periods of time (Freedman, 1984; Geen & Donnerstein, 1983).

Interestingly, violence can be presented as if it is not actually harmful. Bandura (1973, 1986) has shown how film and television violence distorts its perceived outcomes by sanitising both the aggressive acts and the injuries sustained by the victim. Again, an aggressor may be portrayed as the good guy and go unpunished for acts of violence. Social learning theory has taken a strong position on this point: children will readily mimic the behaviour of a model who is reinforced for aggressing, or at least escapes punishment (Bandura, 1973). There has been considerable debate about whether violent video games can also have harmful effects on children (see Box 12.6 and then consider how you would deal with the third focus question).

**Desensitisation**
A serious reduction in a person's responsiveness to material that usually evokes a strong emotional reaction, such as violence or sexuality.

## Research and applications 12.6
### Do gory video games make young people more aggressive?

There is frequent and often heated debate about the effects of violence in video games. Some believe these games increase levels of aggression in children, whereas others argue that such games actually reduce aggression. Proponents claim that contact between characters in the games is often graphically violent, and that children will copy this in their everyday interactions with others; *social learning theory* is sympathetic to this view. We noted in Box 12.2, for example, that even cartoon characters might be imitated by young children. Those disagreeing with this view believe that children may experience the benefits of *catharsis* from playing the games, by venting some energy and by relaxing. Again, we have already called into question the efficacy of catharsis in this connection (see Box 12.3).

Will children become desensitised to the consequences of acting aggressively in real-life situations by playing out violent scenes? Certainly, the content of the games themselves is of some concern. Dietz (1998) examined thirty-three popular video games, and found that nearly 80 per cent contained aggression as part of either the immediate object or the long-term strategy.

Griffiths (1997) reviewed research into the effects of video games on aggression in children and concluded that aggression levels increase in younger children but not in teenage children. However, he cautioned on methodological grounds that most of the research in this field is restricted to observations of children's free play activity following game-playing.

In a large-scale study, Van Schie and Wiegman (1997) investigated game playing among more than 300 Dutch children. Their findings were multifaceted:

- There was no significant relationship between the amounts of time spent gaming and subsequent levels of aggression.
- Video gaming did not replace children's other leisure activities.
- The amount of time spent gaming was positively correlated with the child's measured level of intelligence.

On the other hand, they also found that children who spent more time playing video games were less likely to behave prosocially (see Chapter 13 for a full discussion of factors associated with prosocial behaviour in children).

Working with an older age range, Bushman and Anderson (2002) found that undergraduate students who played a violent video game later described the main character as behaving and thinking more aggressively, and feeling more angry. Further, Carnagey, Anderson and Bushman (2007) found that college students who had played a violent video game showed a desensitisation effect (lowered GSR and heart rate) when they later viewed videotape of real-life violence.

In a study of boys and girls at Australian primary schools in 1979–81, Sheehan (1983) presented evidence of a correlation between children's television viewing habits and their levels of aggressive behaviour. Correlations between viewing violent programmes and peer-rated aggression were consistently significant only among older children (approximately 8–10 years), mostly close to $r = 0.25$, and were stronger among boys than among girls. Other non-experimental studies have demonstrated connections between mass media violence and both intrapersonal and interpersonal aggression (see Phillips, 1986). As well, longitudinal research points to a correlation between the overall amount of violent television watched and aggressive behaviour (Huesmann & Miller, 1994). The effect is not simply one of the imitation of violence modelled on the screen or read about in newspapers and magazines, or just of desensitisation and disinhibition; there is evidence that seeing and reading about violence in general simply promotes greater aggression in some people.

Black and Bevan (1992) investigated reported levels of aggression among filmgoers who watched either a very violent or a non-violent film. The participants completed an aggression questionnaire either entering or leaving the cinema. The researchers found higher pre-viewing aggression scores among participants who chose the violent film, and their scores were even higher after seeing the film. Gender differences were minimal (see Figure 12.10). The bottom line from an extensive and rigorous meta-analysis by Anderson and Bushman (2002b) is that, regardless of how one studies the media violence/aggression link, the outcomes are the same – significant, substantial positive relations. The issue is not whether but *why* violent media increase aggression. Let us seek an answer in a social cognition framework.

## A cognitive analysis

Social cognition deals with how people process information (see Chapters 2, 5 and 6), and research suggests that the media can trigger violence as an automatic reaction to aggressive scenes or descriptions (Berkowitz, 1984; Eron, 1994; Huesmann, 1988). Berkowitz's (1984) **neo-associationist analysis** picked up on old themes in psychology, including the

**Neo-associationist analysis**
A view of aggression according to which mass media may provide images of violence to an audience that later translate into antisocial acts.

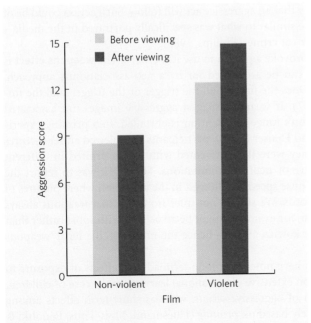

**Figure 12.10** Filmgoers' aggression scores before and after watching a non-violent or a violent film

- People who attend screenings of violent films may be generally more disposed to aggression, according to their scores on an aggression questionnaire.
- Viewing a violent film has an additional effect, because their aggression scores rise afterwards.

*Source*: based on data from Black & Bevan (1992)

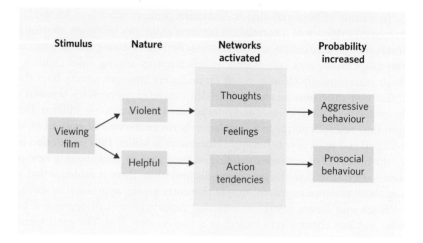

**Figure 12.11** 'Unconscious' effects of the media: a neo-associationist analysis

*Source:* based on Berkowitz (1984)

nineteenth-century notion of *ideomotor response* – that merely thinking about an act can facilitate its performance (see Chapter 1). According to neo-associationism, real or fictional images of violence that are presented to an audience can translate later into antisocial acts. Conversely, exposure to images of people helping others can lead later to prosocial acts (see Figure 12.11).

Berkowitz argued that memory can be viewed as a collection of networks, each consisting of nodes. A node can include substantive elements of thoughts and feelings, connected through associative pathways. When a thought comes into focus, its activation radiates out from that particular node via the associative pathways to other nodes, which in turn can lead to a **priming** effect (see Chapter 2). Consequently, if you have been watching a movie depicting a violent gang 'rumble', other semantically related thoughts can be primed, such as *punching, kicking* and *shooting a gun*. This process can be mostly automatic, without much conscious thinking involved. Similarly, feelings associated with aggression, such as some components of the emotion of anger, may likewise be activated. The outcome is an overall increase in the probability that an aggressive act will follow. Such action could be of a generalised nature, or it may be similar to what was specifically portrayed in the media – in which case, it could be a 'copy-cat crime' (Phillips, 1986).

Can the mere sight of a gun provoke a person to use it? Perhaps. The **weapons effect** is a particular phenomenon that can be accounted for by a neo-associationist approach. Berkowitz asked the question, 'Does the finger pull the trigger or the trigger pull the finger?' (Berkowitz & LePage, 1967). If weapons suggest aggressive images not associated with most other stimuli, a person's range of attention is curtailed. In a priming experiment by Anderson, Anderson and Deuser (1996), participants first viewed either pictures of guns or scenes of nature. They were then presented with words printed in different colours that had either aggressive or neutral connotations. Their task was to report the colours of the words. Their response speed was slowest in the condition where pictures of weapons preceded aggressive words. We should not infer from this that weapons always invite violent associations. A gun, for example, might be associated with sport rather than being a destructive weapon (Berkowitz, 1993) – hence the more specific term 'weapons effect'.

Huessman and his colleagues have noted that long-term adverse effects of exposure to media violence are likely based on extensive observational learning in the case of children, accompanied by the acquisition of aggressive *scripts*, whereas short-term effects among adults and children are more likely based on *priming* (Huesmann, Mois-Titus, Podolski & Eron, 2003).

**Priming**
Activation of accessible categories or schemas in memory that influence how we process new information.

**Weapons effect**
The mere presence of a weapon increases the probability that it will be used aggressively.

**The weapons effect**
Guns evoke images associated with few
other stimuli. They shoot, they kill. A firearm
is unlikely to have neutral connotations

## Erotica and aggression

If exposure to erotica in magazines and videos can lead to sexual arousal, might it also be
linked to aggression? A meta-analysis of forty-six studies by Oddone-Paolucci, Genuis and
Violato (2000) suggests so. Their evidence indicates that the exposure of men to *pornography*
is connected to sexual deviancy, sexual assault, and attitudes to intimate relationships and
rape myths.

Data based on experiments indicate that any effect on aggression depends on the kind
of erotica viewed. For example, viewing pictures of attractive nudes (mild erotica) have a
distracting effect – they seem to reduce aggression when compared with neutral pictures
(Baron, 1979; Ramirez, Bryant & Zillmann, 1983). On the other hand, viewing images of
explicit lovemaking (highly erotic) can increase aggression (Baron & Bell, 1977; Zillmann,
1984, 1996). We need to allow that sexually arousing non-violent erotica could lead to
aggression because of the excitation-transfer effect (see Figure 12.2 earlier in this chapter).
However, excitation-transfer includes the experience of a later frustrating event, which acts
as a trigger to aggress. In short, there has not been a convincing demonstration of a direct
link between erotica per se and aggression.

In a more dramatic experiment (Zillmann & Bryant, 1984), participants were first
exposed to a massive amount of violent pornography, and then were actively irritated by a
confederate. They became more callous about what they had seen: they viewed rape more
tolerantly and became more lenient about prison sentences that they would recommend
(see Figure 12.12). However, the experimental design involves a later provoking event, so
this outcome could be an instance of excitation transfer.

Correlational rather than experimental studies based on larger population samples open
up a different possibility. In examining the association between pornography and sexual
offending, Seto, Maric and Barbaree (2001) suggest that it is people who are already predisposed to sexually offend who are the most likely to be affected by pornography exposure
and are also the most likely to show the strongest consequences.

When violence is mixed with sex in films there is, at the very least, evidence of male desensitisation to aggression against women – callous and demeaning attitudes (Donnerstein &
Linz, 1994; Mullin & Linz, 1995). In a meta-analysis by Paik and Comstock (1994), sexually
violent TV programmes have been linked to later aggression, most clearly in male aggression against women (Donnerstein & Malamuth, 1997).

Linz, Donnerstein and Penrod (1988) reported that when women were depicted enjoying violent pornography, men were later more willing to aggress against women (although,

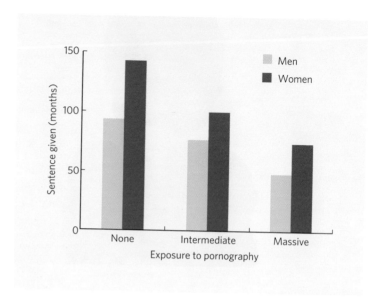

**Figure 12.12** Effect of number of pornographic films viewed on lenience in sentencing

*Source*: based on data from Zillmann & Bryant (1984)

interestingly, not against men). Perhaps just as telling are other consequences of such material: it can perpetuate the myth that women actually enjoy sexual violence. It has been demonstrated that portrayals of women apparently enjoying such acts reinforce rape myths and weaken social and cognitive restraints against violence towards women (Malamuth & Donnerstein, 1982). Zillmann and Bryant (1984) pointed out that the cumulative effect of exposure to violent pornography trivialises rape by portraying women as 'hyperpromiscuous and socially irresponsible'.

There has been a growth of resistance to such material by women's movements in recent years. A *feminist perspective* emphasises two concerns about continual exposure of men to media depicting violence and/or sexually explicit material involving women:

1   Exposure to violence will cause men to become callous or desensitised to violence against female victims.

2   Exposure to pornography will contribute to the development of negative attitudes towards women.

Some feminist writers (see Gubar & Hoff, 1989) maintain that pornography is a blight when it depicts women as subordinate to men and existing solely to satisfy men's sexual needs. In Geen's (1998) review, an attitude of callousness – perhaps a value – develops by using pornography over a long period. A woman is reduced to being a sexual reward for the conquering male (Mosher & Anderson, 1986). In her analysis of widely available pornography (videos, DVDs and internet sites), Corsianos (2007) found that the images and story lines most often portrayed are written by straight men for straight men. Further, sex scenes between men are rare in this genre, while lesbian acts are fantasies for straight men. (See the fourth focus question. What might you now tell Tom?)

In summary, Linz, Wilson and Donnerstein (1992) isolated two culprits in an otherwise confusing mix of violence, sex and women in the media:

1   The portrayal of violence can beget violence.

2   Degrading messages about women institutionalise a demeaning and one-dimensional image of women.

Issues concerning the links between media violence, media pornography and real-life violence extend to the role of the Internet (see Durkin & Bryant, 1995). This medium brings

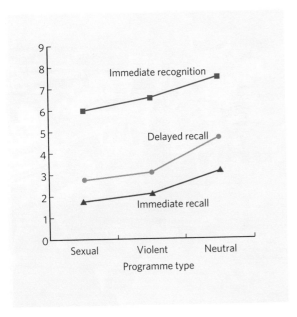

**Figure 12.13** Sex, violence and memory for television advertisements

- People watched TV programmes that were sexually explicit, violent or neutral.
- They then both recalled and identified nine brand advertisements contained in the programmes.
- More brands were remembered in the neutral programme.
- The moral: sex (and violence) does not always sell!

*Source*: Bushman & Bonacci (2002)

massive amounts of information directly into our homes. There have been revelations of international paedophilia and child pornography networks, and the likelihood of a connection between these networks and child sexual abuse. However, even if these variables are correlated, care must be exercised in drawing a causal inference.

Before we close this section, let us return to the issue of how sexual content is used in a particular medium – advertising. Exploiting sex (and violence) in advertising can sometimes backfire if it is intended that a product should be more memorable and therefore a commercial success. Bushman and Bonacci (2002) studied more than 300 young to middle-aged people who watched one of three television programmes, each containing nine brand advertisements. The programme themes were sexually explicit, violent or neutral. Later, the participants tried to recall the brands and to identify them from photographs. The lesson is salutary – see Figure 12.13.

# Domestic violence

Family violence is a major public health issue with an important psychological basis (Tolan, Gorman-Smith & Henry, 2006). Groups at risk are women, children and elders. It is partner abuse, however, that has come so much into focus that a specialised journal *Violence Against Women* was founded in 1995. Already we can detect a gender asymmetry here: the victims are mostly women.

Data relating to partner abuse have been available for many years. An American survey of more than 2,000 families revealed that an assault with intent to injure had occurred in three out of ten of married couples, and in one out of six within the past year (Straus, Gelles & Steinmetz, 1980). The acts were pushing, hitting with the fist, slapping, kicking, throwing something and beating up; and a few were threatened with a gun or knife. It may be surprising to learn that women are slightly more likely than men to use physical aggression against their partners in heterosexual relationships (Archer, 2000). However, female violence tends to do less harm – women account for 35 per cent of serious injuries and 44 per cent of deaths (*We Can Stop Domestic Violence*, 1994). Because male violence is usually more severe, the term *battered woman* is apt (Walker, 1993).

**Domestic violence**
Within relationships and families people can use whatever advantage they have (physical strength, verbal dexterity) as a means of control – which can sometimes spill over into aggression or violence

Here is a sobering statistic: about one-quarter of those homicides where the killer knows the victim are spousal. According to Shackelford (2001), American women in cohabiting relationships incur about nine times the risk of being murdered as women in marital relationships, a trend that is similar in Canada. The break-up rate is also higher for cohabiting partners. There are other correlates of cohabiting: being poorer, younger and having stepchildren. Archer (2000) also suggested a cultural effect clearly associated with female domestic violence – much higher rates are found in societies that are modern, secular and liberal, and where women are emancipated in both the local economy and the family.

Very different interpretations can be made of violence between partners (Archer, 2000). Family conflict researchers emphasise mutual combat between the partners, whereas feminist writers portray violent encounters between male perpetrators and female victims.

## Gender asymmetry?

Studies of same-sex relationships show that lesbians, bisexuals and gay men are also victims of acts of violence in the home (Klinger & Stein, 1996). Does this mean that earlier theories of domestic violence are insufficient and 'heterosexist' (Letellier, 1994)?

The image of a man being battered by a woman may be difficult to envisage. Harris and Cook (1994) investigated students' responses to three scenarios: a husband battering his wife, a wife battering her husband and a gay man battering his male partner, each in response to verbal provocation. The first scenario, a husband battering his wife, was rated as more violent than the other two scenarios. Further, 'victim blaming' – an example of **belief in a just world** (see Chapter 3) – was attributed most often to a gay victim, who was also judged most likely to leave the relationship. It seems that the one act takes on a different meaning according to the gender of the aggressor and the victim.

DeKeseredy (2006) and Renzetti (2006) are agreed in deciding that both gender and ethnic asymmetries underlie partner abuse:

**Belief in a just world**
Belief that the world is a just and predictable place where good things happen to 'good people' and bad things to 'bad people'.

- Most sexual assaults in heterosexual relationships are committed by men.
- Much of women's use of violence is in self-defence against their partner's assault.
- Men and women in different ethnic groups 'do gender' differently, including variations in perceptions of when it is appropriate to use violence.

## Hurting the one we 'love'

Why do people hurt those closest to them? There are no simple answers, but here are some influential factors:

- *learned patterns of aggression,* imitated from parents and significant others, together with low competence in responding non-aggressively; there is a generational cycle of child abuse (Straus, Gelles & Steinmetz, 1980), and the chronic repetition of violence in some families has been identified as an **abuse syndrome;**

- the *proximity* of family members, which makes them more likely to be sources of annoyance or frustration, and targets when these feelings are generated externally;

- *stresses,* especially financial difficulties, unemployment and illnesses (including postnatal depression; see Searle, 1987); this partly accounts for domestic violence being much more common in poorer families;

- the division of *power* in traditional nuclear families, favouring the man, which makes it easier for less democratic styles of interaction to predominate (Claes & Rosenthal, 1990); and

- a high level of *alcohol* consumption, which is a common correlate of male abuse of a spouse (Stith & Farley, 1993).

An interaction of these factors, heightened by the normal stresses of day-to-day living that we all encounter, means that those we live closest to are, ironically, the likely targets of our aggression. Visit the *United States Office of Violence Against Women* at **http://www.ovw. usdoj.gov/**.

> **Abuse syndrome**
> Factors of proximity, stress and power that are associated with the cycle of abuse in some families.

# Institutionalised aggression

## Role of society

Not all societies define aggression as an altogether bad thing. In our society, the emphasis on non-violence is an outcome of historical and sociocultural factors. It is an ethic that derives from a combination of politics, religion, philosophy and events in recent history, including the atrocities of the Second World War, the Vietnam War, the war in Iraq, and the threat of nuclear annihilation. An emphasis on non-violence is a sociocultural value judgement about the significance and purpose of aggression.

We have noted that biological theories generally argue that aggression has useful properties. Apart from personal self-defence, are there examples of human aggression that seem reasonable? Issues of definition reappear: there are ways in which some kinds of aggression are used to bring about positive outcomes. Where these involve groups or a whole society, they preserve the **social order** (Kelvin, 1970). Human societies depend for their continuity on social norms; those that are well established may become embedded as values that are widely shared in a community, such as caring for our fellows. Ultimately, law provides protection for a social system. Occasionally, the mechanisms of social order even sanction the use of violence. While the functions of some kinds of **institutionalised aggression** can be legitimate, there can also be both socially desirable and undesirable effects. The need for law and order can lead to arrests (desirable) but also prisoner abuse (undesirable). Parental discipline can lead to verbal criticism (desirable?) but also to severe physical punishment (undesirable).

Terrorism is an instance of extreme violence that comes vividly to mind. The most dramatic example has been 11 September 2001, in New York and Washington. Other scenes of horrific multiple deaths include the Bali bar and restaurant bombings aimed at Western tourists in 2002 and 2005, the 2004 train bombing in Madrid, the London train and bus

> **Social order**
> The balance and control of a social system, regulated by norms, values, rules and law.
>
> **Institutionalised aggression**
> Aggression that is given formal or informal recognition and social legitimacy by being incorporated into rules and norms.

**Institutionalised aggression**
Fight to the death? Boxing is a regulated sport with rules that govern aggression. These were applied in a world featherweight boxing title fight in Liverpool in 2007

bombings in 2005, the 2008 Mumbai Hotel attacks, and numerous bombings of crowded public places in Iraq, Afghanistan and Pakistan. Various political groups argue that their powerless position leaves no alternative – only deadly acts of terror will ensure that their fight for justice is taken seriously.

Significant moral and political issues underlie the judgements about aggression, as they do about suicide, abortion and euthanasia. All of these can be made to fit a definition of aggression.

## War

Tragically, large-scale aggression and war, which can be linked to the topics of prejudice and discrimination (discussed in Chapters 10 and 11), are part of the human condition. Two million years of human evolution, industrialisation, the communications revolution, philosophy, art and poetry have had no effect whatsoever – collective violence continues unabated. Recent years have witnessed monstrous violence in Somalia, Bosnia, Croatia, Kosovo, Rwanda, Chechnya, Afghanistan and Iraq. While we might like to think that we have evolved gracefully from the Renaissance period, the last century was by far the bloodiest in systematic human slaughter (Dutton, Boyanowski & Bond, 2005).

A way of glimpsing the continuing tragedy is to consider the incidence and severity of wars. Most of us will think of two world wars as the most obvious examples of widespread violence, but there are many others. The estimates in Figure 12.14 are drawn from a number of sources, and are limited to the twentieth century. The data include interstate wars, civil wars, wars of independence, genocide, massacres and atrocities. They remain selective by excluding other instances of mass death that numbered fewer than *one million* people!

A neglected consequence of war is its long-term effects. Ember and Ember (1994) noted that societies with more war have more warlike sports, beliefs in malevolent magic, and severe punishment for crime – and perhaps surprisingly, are causally implicated in population rates of homicide and assault.

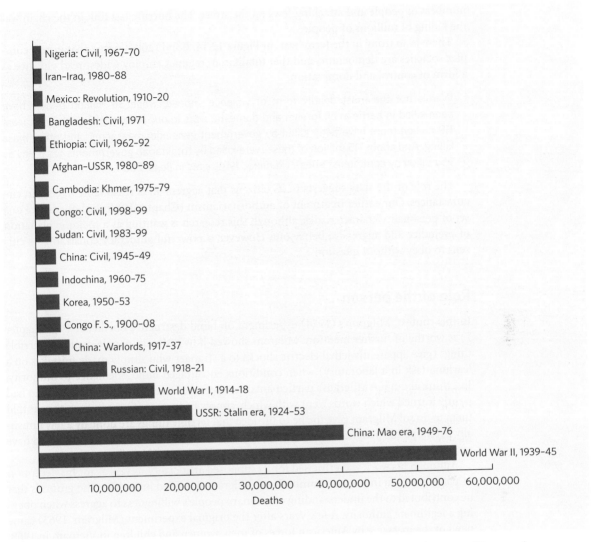

**Figure 12.14**  Wars, massacres and atrocities of the twentieth century: deaths exceeding one million people

*Source:* based on data from White (2004)

## Role of the state

The worst acts of inhumanity are committed against humanity itself. Warfare is not possible without a supporting psychological structure involving the beliefs and emotions of a people. If such a structure is lacking, leaders will use propaganda to create one (see Chapter 6). In times of war, both the soldiers who are fighting and the people at home need to maintain good morale. Genocide is a kind of legitimised prejudice translated into behaviour (see Chapter 11). Some political regimes have fostered beliefs in genetic differences between groups of people to justify oppression and slaughter. Ideologies of racial, moral and social inferiority were the cornerstones of the Nazi programmes directed against gypsies, political non-conformists, homosexuals, the mentally handicapped, ill people, and of course Jews. Antagonism expressed by Hitler led German citizens to avoid Jews, even those who were neighbours and friends. This created a climate for enacting the Nuremberg laws of discrimination. It was a small step towards burning synagogues, arresting huge numbers of people and attacking Jews on the street. The horrific last link in the chain was the killing of millions of people.

There is an irony in the term 'war' in Figure 12.14. Bond (2004) noted that not all complex societies are democratic, and that totalitarian regimes employ widespread violence as a form of control and domination.

> War is not the most deadly form of violence. Indeed, while 36 million people have been killed in battle in all foreign and domestic wars in our [twentieth] century, at least 119 million more have been killed by government genocide, massacres, and other mass killing. And about 115 million of these were killed by totalitarian governments (as many as 95 million by communist ones). (*Rummel, 1988; cited in Bond, 2004, p. 68*)

The role of the state suggests to its citizens that aggression is reasonable in certain circumstances. Our earlier treatment of authoritarianism (Chapter 10) linked obedience to a set of personality characteristics, although this research is wanting as a major explanation of prejudice and aggressive behaviour. However, a powerful autocracy constrains its citizens to obey without question.

## Role of the person

In this context, Milgram's (1974) experiment on blind destructive obedience (see Chapter 7) is worthy of further mention. Milgram showed how ordinary people could do terrible things (give apparently lethal electric shocks to a stranger who simply made mistakes on a learning task in a laboratory) when conditions encouraged blind obedience to authority. Just think about it – Milgram's participants were prepared to electrocute someone who had poorly learned which words went with which, simply because someone in a white coat told them to do so! Milgram gave the lie to the idea that terrible things are done by a few unusually psychopathic people: on the contrary, his results suggested that many of us would have responded in the same way (see Blass, 2004; **http://www.stanleymilgram.com**).

Although his work was criticised for its supposed artificiality, as well as for his deception of participants to induce an 'immoral act', Milgram defended himself on the grounds that he contributed to the understanding of ordinary people's willingness to aggress when obeying a legitimate authority. A few years after the original experiment (Milgram, 1963) came news of the massacre by American forces of men, women and children in Vietnam in 1969, at a village called My Lai (see details in Dutton, Boyanowski & Bond, 2005). This war scarred the American psyche, and this incident has acquired a unique reputation by exploding the myth that it is the 'enemy' that commits atrocities.

Milgram generalised to the everyday life. Citizens are taught from childhood to obey both the laws of the state and the orders of those who represent its authority. In so doing, citizens enter an **agentic state** of thinking and distance themselves from personal responsibility for their actions.

**Agentic state**
State of mind thought by Milgram to characterise unquestioning obedience, in which people transfer personal responsibility to the person giving orders.

## Levels of explanation

We have noted earlier that different levels of explanation are adopted to account for aggression and for a wide variety of social behaviour (see Chapter 1). In the context of war, psychological explanations have varied from being heavily person-centred to being group-centred. Studies of authoritarianism have argued that prejudice, discrimination, violence and war atrocities reside in extreme or deviant personalities. Milgram moved away from this by suggesting that ordinary people can feel they are agents of the state and will carry out orders that can harm others when the voice of authority seems legitimate. Sherif (Sherif & Sherif, 1953) moved even further away from an individual level of explanation by

## Research and applications 12.7
### Two different levels of explanation of aggression and war

An explanation of prejudice and discrimination was once offered by Adorno, Frenkel-Brunswik, Levinson and Sanford (1950) in terms of person characteristics, namely the authoritarian personality (see Chapter 10). The use of a similar individual level of explanation is clear in the views of Berkowitz (1962, p. 167) in his account of the causes of aggression:

> Granting all this, the present writer is still inclined to emphasise the importance of individualistic considerations in the field of group relations. Dealings between groups ultimately become problems of the psychology of the individual. Individuals decide to go to war; battles are fought by individuals; and peace is established by individuals. It is the individual who adopts the beliefs prevailing in his society, even though the extent to which these opinions are shared by many people is a factor governing his readiness to adopt them, and he transmits these views to other individuals. Ultimately, it is the single person who attacks the feared and disliked ethnic minority group, even though many people around him share his feelings and are very important in determining his willingness to aggress against this minority.

The social psychologist Tajfel, working at Bristol in the early 1970s, regarded this view as typical of the restricted level of explanation offered by American social psychology. In an unpublished paper written in 1974, he deliberately rewrote Berkowitz's words as follows, using words in italics to emphasise where an individual focus is replaced by a societal one:

> Granting all this, the present writer is still inclined to emphasise the importance of considering the field of group relations in terms of *social structure*. Dealings between groups cannot be accounted for by the psychology of the individual. *Governments* decide to go to war; battles are fought by *armies*; and peace is established by *governments*. The *social conditions* in which groups live largely determine their beliefs and the extent to which they are shared. Ultimately, a single person's attack on an ethnic minority group that he dislikes or fears would remain a trivial occurrence had it not been for the fact that he acts in unison with others who share his feelings and are very important in determining his willingness to aggress against this minority.

*Source:* Tajfel (1974); cited in Vaughan (1988)

relating large-scale conflict to the nature of *intergroup relations,* suggesting that discriminatory acts against an outgroup will flourish only when the objective interests of their group are threatened. Recently, Bond (2004) has emphasised the necessity to have both individual and societal levels of analysis of aggression and, very clearly, of war.

Tajfel (1974) outlined a group-centred approach to aggression and war by suggesting that the very existence of ingroups is the essential cause of prejudice, discrimination and conflict. Outgroups provide a reference and must be kept at bay (see Chapter 11). Tajfel contrasted an account of aggression based on the person with one based on the group. The first account is an individualist perspective offered by Berkowitz (1962). The second is by Tajfel, who took Berkowitz's own words and made crucial substitutions of terms that implicate society as the 'cause' (see Box 12.7).

# Reducing aggression

Levels of explanation of aggression show up different levels of its causes. Consequently, reducing aggression will be multifaceted.

At an individual level – where the person is our focus as the aggressor – effective interventions will involve political decisions, a budget and a community will. There are now effective technologies deriving from behavioural and counselling psychology that require

**Cyber bullying**
Bullying has long been a
problem – openly at school
but covertly at home. There
is a clear need for school
authorities and parent groups
to protect the victim and to
apply sanctions against the
perpetrators

the cooperation of regional agencies, schools and families for their implementation. Among younger people, there are clear-cut concerns with vandalism and bullying to be dealt with. There is the cycle of violence involving the family unit to be addressed. In families, parents can raise more peaceful children by not rewarding violent acts, by rewarding behaviour that is not compatible with violence, and by avoiding the use of punishing behaviour. At the interpersonal level, there is probably more optimism, and techniques of behaviour modification, social skills training, non-aggressive modelling, anger management and assertiveness training have been shown to be effective in teaching individuals self-control. In dealing with continuing and increasing violence in schools, Goldstein (1999) has noted that aggression is multicausal and that a preventative strategy must be both broad and flexible, including the techniques and target groups already referred to. A successful strategy should generally avoid punitive tactics that have proved ineffective in the past, such as corporal punishment and suspension.

There are direct educational opportunities to use our knowledge for the betterment of women. For example, a media studies course can help develop critical skills that evaluate whether and how women are demeaned, and in what way we might undermine rape myths (Linz, Wilson & Donnerstein, 1992).

At a societal level, there is the role of law. Take gun ownership law in the United States as an example. You now know something of the weapons effect. Consider this irony: guns may be kept in the home to confer protection. The same guns are used to kill a family member or an intimate acquaintance, particularly in homes with a history of the use of drugs and physical violence (Kellerman et al., 1993).

To make an impact on underlying causes, significant changes are required that improve the conditions of those groups plagued by cyclical violence and most likely to be involved in dangerous collective action. A major underlying factor is poverty (Belsky, 1993) and relative (intergroup) deprivation.

Mass violence such as genocide and war is a different matter (see Chapter 11). There is room for the introduction of **peace studies** into the formal education system. Peace education is more than an anti-war campaign: it has broadened to cover all aspects of peaceful relationships and coexistence. By teaching young children how to build and maintain self-esteem without being aggressive (the culture of self-esteem may nourish aggression – see Chapter 4), it is hoped that there will be a long-term impact that will expand into all areas of people's lives.

We cannot wave a magic wand and banish violence. At both individual and societal levels, there is room for social psychologists and others to work towards harmony in a world of increasing stress and dwindling resources.

**Peace studies**
Multidisciplinary movement dedicated to the study and promotion of peace.

## Summary

- Aggression has been defined in ways that reflect differences in underlying theories about its nature and causes. One simple definition is 'the intentional infliction of some type of harm on others'.

- There are two major classes of theory about the origins of aggression; one emphasising its biological origins and the other its social origins.

- Biological explanations can be traced to Darwinian theory and include the views of Freud, ethological theory and, more recently, evolutionary social psychology. These approaches emphasise genetically determined behaviour patterns shared by a species.

- Social explanations usually stress the role of societal influences and/or learning processes. Some incorporate a biological component as well, such as the frustration–aggression hypothesis and excitation-transfer theory. Social learning theory is a developmental approach that stresses reinforcement principles and the influence that models have on the young child.

- Some research into causes has concentrated on factors thought to be part of the person, such as personality and gender. Other work has focused on transitory states: the experience of frustration, the role of catharsis, the effects of provocation and alcohol, the role of brain injury or mental illness, and the experience of disinhibition.

- Other studies have focused on situational factors. These include stressors in the physical environment, such as heat and crowding. A significant societal variable is relative deprivation – the perceived disadvantage that some groups have in relation to those holding power.

- A social approach to aggression allows for the possibility of change in patterns over time and cultural context. For example, there is evidence for increased aggression in women over recent time, and that rates of physical aggression vary across cultures, reflecting long-standing differences in norms and values.

- The role of the mass media, particularly television, has been controversial. It is argued that the continued portrayal of violence may desensitise young people to the consequences of violence. A stronger argument is that it provides a model for future behaviour.

- Reports of domestic violence, particularly against a partner, have a high profile in our community. Whether domestic violence is actually more common is unclear.

- War is a shocking, massive stain on humanity. Arguments about its causes and its prevention that are defined purely in political terms miss many crucial points: the role of intergroup relations themselves, the fact that people actually hurt other people, and the perpetuation across generations of outgroup stereotypes and prejudice.

## Literature, film and TV

### The Great War for Civilisation

2005 book by journalist Robert Fiske. A personal but inside view of wars in the Middle East, it covers bloody events from the early part of the twentieth century through the Arab–Israeli wars of the 1960s and 1970s, the rise of the PLO and of the Taliban, the 9/11 atrocities, to the fall of Saddam Hussein in 2003.

### A Clockwork Orange

1971 film directed by Stanley Kubrick, based on the novel by Anthony Burgess, and starring Malcolm McDowell. A powerful and classic exploration of apparently mindless violence – acts of 'ultraviolence' to the accompaniment of Beethoven's Ninth Symphony. The movie also touches on ways to stop such extreme violence through flooding.

### Syriana

2005 geopolitical thriller directed by Stephen Gaghan and starring George Clooney and Matt Damon. Focused on the complexity and intrigue of petroleum politics and the Middle East, this film is also a powerful commentary on strategic state-sponsored aggression, individual suicide terrorism, and the personal cost of violence. Other recent films in the same genre include Gavin Hoods' 2007 film *Rendition,* and Peter Berg's 2007 film *The Kingdom.*

### Bowling for Columbine and Elephant

*Bowling for Columbine* is Michael Moore's 2000 documentary about gun crime and aggression in the United States, giving particular emphasis on aggression and adolescents in school settings. It centres on the Columbine high school shooting in Littleton, Colorado, on 20 April, 1999. Two students, 18-year-old Eric Harris and 17-year-old Dylan Klebold, walked into school dressed in trench coats and killed 12 of their classmates and one teacher, and then killed themselves. In the 2003 film *Elephant,* director Gus Van Sant approaches the same issues in a different way. Using unknown actors and a naturalistic approach, the audience witness the build-up to the massacre and the killings themselves from the students' point of view (victims, onlookers and culprits) encouraging us to make sense of the aggression and premeditated violence of the teenagers.

### City of God

2002 film by Fernando Meirelles portraying gang violence in the slums of Rio de Janeiro. We see how easily aggression and violence becomes a way of life when there is no protection on the streets and a gun can give you safety, power and popularity. This is most poignantly demonstrated by the story of 11-year-old Li'l Dice who murders everyone in a brothel, and goes on to become a powerful gang leader and drug dealer within a couple of years, thriving on the power afforded by his brutality.

### The Killing Fields

1984 film directed by Roland Joffé, starring Sam Waterston, John Malkovich and Haing S. Ngor. The film is a chilling and disturbing portrayal of the 1970s genocide in Cambodia. The Khmer Rouge, led by Pol Pot, exterminated between one and two million Cambodians (the actual figure may never be known) during the second half of the 1970s.

### Pulp Fiction

Quentin Tarantino's 1994 classic, starring John Travolta, Samuel T. Jackson and Uma Thurman. The violent lives of mobsters and small-time criminals in Los Angeles are graphically dramatised; but the film is also memorable for its clever and humorous dialogue and its focus on the characters' perspectives on life and on their essential humanness.

### Lock, Stock and Two Smoking Barrels and RocknRolla

Two classic Guy Ritchie films, from 1998 and 2008. Set in London's underbelly of organised, though often quite disorganised, crime, these films are not only graphic portrayals of chaotic violent lifestyles but they are also very, gruesomely, funny.

### Fatal Attraction and The War of the Roses

Two films that illustrate violence in relationships, but in different ways. *Fatal Attraction* is a 1987 film starring Michael Douglas and Glenn Close. A man has a one-night stand with his work colleague, who then stalks him. This is a very tense and scary movie about violence in a relationship. In contrast, *The War of the Roses* is a 1989 black comedy in which Danny DeVito is a divorce lawyer for Michael Douglas and Kathleen Turner, who were formerly deeply in love but now dedicate their lives to harming each other. Each refuses to leave the family home – in the process they wreck the home and each other.

## Guided questions

1  What is the *frustration–aggression hypothesis*? Does it help to account for the origins of aggression?

2  Can children really learn quite quickly how to be aggressive? See a portrayal of one of the scenarios used in Albert Bandura's famous Bobo doll experiment in Chapter 12 of MyPsychLab at **www.mypsychlab.co.uk** (watch *Bandura's Bobo doll experiment*).

3  Does the incidence of aggression vary in relation to gender or culture?

4  Does viewing television violence make people more aggressive?

5  In what ways can the tendency to aggress be reduced?

## Learn more

Anderson, C. A., & Huesmann, L. R. (2007). Human aggression: A social-cognitive view. In M. A. Hogg & J. Cooper (eds), *The SAGE handbook of social psychology: Concise student edition* (pp. 259–87). London: SAGE. Up-to-date and comprehensive overview of research on human aggression, by two of the world's leading aggression researchers.

Baron, R. A., & Richardson, D. R. (1994). *Human aggression* (2nd ed.). New York: Plenum. A heavily cited source for research on human aggression.

Berkowitz, L. (1993). *Aggression: Its causes, consequences and control*. Philadelphia, PA: Temple University Press. Another work by an authority in the field with a good coverage of the topic.

Buford, B. (1993). *Among the thugs*. New York: Vintage. An insider's perspective on the world of English football 'hooligans' in British and other European settings. The work is compelling – one reviewer described it as '*A Clockwork Orange* comes to life'.

Bushman, B. J., & Huesmann, L. R. (2010). Aggression. In S. T. Fiske, D. T. Gilbert, & G. Lindzey (eds), *Handbook of social psychology* (5th ed., Vol. 2, pp. 833–63). New York: Wiley. Currently the most up-to-date, detailed and comprehensive coverage of theory and research on all aspects of and perspectives on human aggression.

Campbell, A. (1993). *Men, women and aggression*. New York: Harper Collins. A discussion of sex, gender and aggression.

Glick, R. A., & Roose, S. P. (eds) (1993). *Rage, power, and aggression*. New Haven, CT: Yale University Press. A collection of chapters that review research, theory and clinical perspectives on the origins, nature and development of aggression.

Goldstein, A. P. (1994). *The ecology of aggression*. New York: Plenum. As the title suggests, the focus is on how aggression can be influenced by ecological factors, which can be both physical and social.

Krahé, B. (1996). Aggression and violence in society. In G. R. Semin & K. Fiedler (eds), *Applied social psychology* (pp. 343–73). London: SAGE. A compact introduction to problems of definition and explanation. Personal and situational variables are explored, as are topics such as domestic violence, rape and bullying.

Rose, H., & Rose, S. (eds) (2000). *Alas, poor Darwin: Arguments against evolutionary psychology*. London: Vintage. A group of scholars from a variety of biological, philosophical and social science backgrounds raise concerns about the adequacy of genetic accounts of social behaviour, including aggression.

Staub, E. (2010). *The panorama of mass violence: Origins, prevention, healing and reconciliation*. New York: Oxford University Press. Analysis of mass violence including genocide, with some thoughts on prevention and healing – Staub is the pre-eminent expert on group aggression.

 Refresh your understanding, assess your progress and go further with interactive summaries, questions, podcasts and much more at **www.mypsychlab.co.uk**

## This chapter discusses

- Categories of prosocial behaviour: helping and altruism
- The Kitty Genovese murder: a trigger for research
- Evolution's part in acting prosocially
- Empathy, arousal and bystander calculus
- Learning to be helpful; attribution and the just-world hypothesis
- The nature of emergencies, the role of cognition and the bystander effect
- The person in the equation: correlates of helpful people; being competent
- Applications: crime prevention, exam cheating, a health support network
- Who receives help?
- Norms and motives for helping
- Volunteers: the ultimate helpers

## Focus questions

1. Arthur spots this headline in his local newspaper: 'Altruistic dolphin saves surfer!' Interesting, he thinks, but that's not altruism . . . or is it?

2. Alex is fit and healthy, his whole life ahead of him. His twin brother's future is uncertain. He now needs dialysis more than once a week. After months of thinking, some of it agonising, Alex's mind is made up – he will donate a kidney to his brother. Would you want to help your really close kin? Does Alex's choice have implications for evolutionary theory?

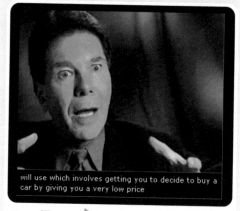

will use which involves getting you to decide to buy a car by giving you a very low price

Go to **mypsychlab** to explore video and test your understanding of key topics addressed in this chapter.

3. Lily is thirteen years old and tall for her age. One afternoon, she confronts a suspicious-looking stranger loitering near a young girl playing in the local park. The stranger takes to his heels when Lily challenges him. It's the talk of the neighbourhood, and there's mention of a medal for bravery. Hearing this, your social psychology classmate points out: 'It's just as well that Lily's usual playmates were not around, or that little girl might not have received any help.' What could your classmate mean? For an experimental re-enactment of a similar scenario go to Chapter 13 of MyPsychLab at www.mypsychlab.co.uk (watch *Research methods*).

4. You turn the corner of a city street to see a man sprawled across the footpath in front of you. What do you do? What things might you want to know more about before deciding on how to act?

Refresh your understanding with interactive summaries, explore topics further with video and audio clips and assess your progress with quick test and essay questions by logging to the accompanying website at www.mypsychlab.co.uk

# Chapter 13
## Prosocial behaviour

# Background

In Chapter 10, we saw how people can hate others simply because they are not members of their group. Chapter 11 looked at how groups can discriminate and compete destructively against each other, and in Chapter 12 we saw how aggressive human beings can be. One would be forgiven for gloomily concluding that people are basically full of hatred and aggression. It was the philosopher Thomas Hobbes who famously proclaimed in *Leviathan,* his 1651 treatise on the human condition, that life is 'solitary, poor, nasty, brutish and short'. This chapter stands in contrast as we turn to the positive and altruistic aspect of human nature. We now ask why, when and how people decide to help others even if they in turn pay the ultimate sacrifice.

We try to explain phenomena such as soldiers throwing themselves on live grenades to save their comrades, firefighters losing their own lives while rescuing people from the collapsing World Trade Center towers in New York on 11 September 2001, and people such as Oscar Schindler and Miep Gies taking huge personal risks to save Jews in Nazi Europe.

## Prosocial behaviour, helping behaviour and altruism

Researchers typically refer to acts that benefit another person as prosocial behaviour, helping behaviour or altruistic behaviour. Although people often use these three terms interchangeably, there are some distinctions, and there are differences in the way they are used in the scientific literature. In social psychology, the overall interest is long-standing (Schroeder, Penner, Dovidio & Piliavin, 1995).

**Prosocial behaviour**
Acts that are positively valued by society.

**Prosocial behaviour** is a broad category of acts that are valued positively by society – contrast it with antisocial behaviour. Wispé (1972) defined prosocial behaviour as behaviour that has positive social consequences, and contributes to the physical or psychological well-being of another person. It is voluntary and has the intention to benefit others (Eisenberg, et al., 1996). Being prosocial includes both being helpful and altruistic. It also embraces acts of charity, cooperation, friendship, rescue, sacrifice, sharing, sympathy and trust. What is thought to be prosocial is defined by a society's norms.

**Helping behaviour**
Acts that intentionally benefit someone else.

**Helping behaviour** is a subcategory of prosocial behaviour. Helping is intentional and it benefits another living being or group. If you accidentally drop ten pounds and someone finds it and uses it, you have not performed a helping behaviour. But if you gave ten pounds to Connie who really needed it, you have helped her. On the other hand, making a large public donation to a charity because you wanted to appear generous is not helping behaviour. Some corporate donations to a good cause may even be driven by product image, e.g. looking for a long-term increase in profit. Helping can even be antisocial, e.g. overhelping, when giving help is designed to make others look inferior (Gilbert & Silvera, 1996).

**Altruism** is another subcategory of prosocial behaviour, and refers to an act that is meant to benefit another rather than oneself. In this respect, Batson (1991) proposed that true altruism is selfless, although there is some difficulty with the concept. Can we demonstrate that an act does not stem from a long-term ulterior motive, such as ingratiation? Staub (1977) noted that there are sometimes 'private' rewards associated with acting prosocially, such as feeling good or being virtuous. There is a considerable and often controversial literature dealing with altruism, centring on the issue of how magnanimous human nature really is (Maner et al., 2002). Later, we will explore the link between altruism and empathy.

> **Altruism**
> A special form of helping behaviour, sometimes costly, that shows concern for fellow human beings and is performed without expectation of personal gain.

## The Kitty Genovese murder

Social psychological research into helping behaviour began in the late 1950s. Over a thousand articles dealing with altruism and helpfulness in the next 25 years (Dovidio, 1984), so that we now know a great deal more about why we sometimes turn our backs on people requiring assistance, but also why we often go out of our way to help those in need. A single event is credited with providing a major impetus to this research – the murder of a young woman called Kitty Genovese in New York in 1964. The report of her murder appalled New York residents (see Box 13.1).

Prosocial behaviour is difficult to explain using traditional theories of human behaviour. Probably the majority of psychologists, and philosophers before them, have conceptualised human behaviour as egoistic. Everything we do is ultimately done to benefit ourselves – self-interest reigns supreme. Prosocial behaviour is therefore unusual because it seems to be independent of reinforcement. It highlights an optimistic and positive view

---

### Research classic 13.1
#### The Kitty Genovese murder: a trigger for research on helping behaviour

#### A sad night in New York city

Late one night in March 1964, Kitty Genovese was on her way home from work at the time she was attacked by a knife-wielding maniac.

The scene was the Kew Gardens in the borough of Queens in New York, a respectable neighbourhood. Her screams and struggles drove off the attacker at first but, seeing no one come to the woman's aid, the man attacked again. Once more she escaped, shouting and crying for help. Yet her screams were to no avail and she was soon cornered again. She was stabbed eight more times and then sexually molested. In the half-hour or so that it took for the man to kill Kitty, not one of her neighbours helped her.

About half an hour after the attack began, the local police received a call from an anonymous witness. He reported the attack but would not give his name because he did not want to 'get involved'. The next day, when the police interviewed the area's residents, thirty-eight people openly admitted to hearing the screaming. They had all had time to do something but failed to act. It is perhaps understandable that some had not rushed out into the street for fear of also being attacked, but why did they not at least call the police?

This particularly tragic and horrific event received national media attention in America, all asking why none of the neighbours had helped. Not surprisingly, this resulted in heightened interest from social psychologists, including Latané and Darley (1976, p. 309):

> This story became the journalistic sensation of the decade. 'Apathy,' cried the newspapers. 'Indifference,' said the columnists and commentators. 'Moral callousness', 'dehumanisation', 'loss of concern for our fellow man', added preachers, professors and other sermonisers. Movies, television specials, plays and books explored this incident and many like it. Americans became concerned about their lack of concern.

Read how the story of Kitty's murder first broke at **http://www2.selu.edu/Academics/Faculty/scraig/gansberg.html**.

of human beings. How can effort and sacrifice for another person be reinforcing in the usual sense?

A recurring theme in psychology is the **nature-nurture controversy**, the debate over the roles of biological versus learned determinants of behaviour. We saw this in relation to aggression in Chapter 12, and it crops up again here in connection with prosocial behaviour.

**Nature-nurture controversy**
Classic debate about whether genetic or environmental factors determine human behaviour. Scientists generally accept that it is an interaction of both.

# The why and the when of helping

The question of why people help others is obviously an important one. We address two major viewpoints in the following sections, one grounded in evolutionary theory and the other in a social learning theory. This distinction is significant and represents important differences among psychologists generally, as well as among some social psychologists. Other views give a more biosocial account, reflecting the role of empathy, cognition, and characteristics of the situation in which help is either given or not.

## Helping: a phenomenon of nature?

The biological position is that, just as humans have innate tendencies to eat and drink, so they have innate tendencies to help others. If true, it could be a reason why human beings have been so successful in an evolutionary sense. The question whether altruism is a trait that has evolutionary survival value has been asked by social psychologists (e.g Campbell, 1975), sociobiologists (e.g. Wilson, 1975), and **evolutionary social psychologists** (e.g. Buss & Kenrick, 1998). Consider the next example.

**Evolutionary social psychology**
An extension of evolutionary psychology that views complex social behaviour as adaptive, helping the individual, kin and the species as a whole to survive.

A small child, Margaret, and her friend, Red, were seated in the back seat of Margaret's parents' car. Suddenly the car burst into flames. Red jumped from the car but realised that Margaret was still inside. He jumped back into the burning car, grabbed Margaret by the jacket and pulled her to safety (Batson, 1983). Should we view these actions as being caused by an altruistic impulse inherited from our ancestors? The answer is still being debated, but the fact that Red was an Irish setter – yes, a dog! – adds some weight to the argument that there is a genetic aspect to altruism and prosocial behaviour. It also begs the question: can other animals be altruistic? (Think back to Arthur's quandary in the first focus question.)

> Vampire bats regurgitate blood to others despite the possibility of dying if three days elapse without consuming blood. Ground squirrels give alarm calls even though they alert predators to their own presence. Cleaner fish enter the mouths of their hosts to remove parasites even at risk of being eaten. Florida scrub jays often stay at home with their parents, forgoing the benefits of personal reproduction to help rear their younger siblings. These cases of cooperation have generated a substantial amount of theoretical and empirical interest over the past several decades, primarily focusing on adaptive accounts of cooperative behaviors. (*Stevens, Cushman & Hauser, 2005, p. 499*)

Evolutionary biologists have grappled with these and other instances of cooperation in the animal world. Stevens, Cushman and Hauser have distinguished two reliable explanations of cooperative behaviour in animals and humans:

- *Mutualism* – cooperative behaviour benefits the cooperator as well as others; a defector will do worse than a cooperator.
- *Kin selection* – in which a cooperator is biased towards blood relatives because it helps propagate one's own genes; the lack of direct benefit to the cooperator indicates *altruism*.

Kin selection is the obvious candidate to be an evolutionary account of human altruism. Is there any such evidence?

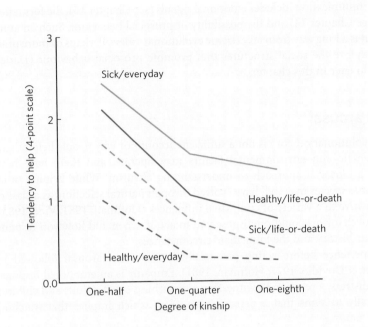

**Figure 13.1** Helping kin who are either healthy or sick: life-or-death versus everyday situations

- There is an interaction between health, kinship and willingness to help.
- Participants chose between people who varied in kinship in two conditions: healthy versus sick individuals, and giving help in a situation that was life-or-death versus merely 'everyday'.
- They were generally more willing to help closer kin than more distant kin.
- They also preferred to help people who were sick rather than healthy in an everyday situation, but who were healthy rather than sick in a perilous situation.

*Source:* Burnstein, Crandall & Kitayama (1994)

Burnstein and his colleagues investigated 'decision rules' for being altruistic that might deal with genetic overlap between persons. Participants rated how likely they would be to help others in several situations (see Figure 13.1). People favoured the sick over the healthy in everyday situations but favoured the healthy over the sick in life-or-death situations. They took more account of kinship in everyday situations and the healthy in life-or-death situations. Finally, people were more likely to assist the very young or the very old in everyday situations, but under famine conditions people prefer to help 10-year-olds or 18-year-olds rather than infants or older people. These data are consistent with the idea that close kin will get crucial help when 'the chips are down'. (Consider Vincenzo's decision in the second focus question.)

The notion that we are 'wired' to help others, as well as kin, is fascinating and has generated a great deal of debate: for example, between psychologists and sociobiologists (Vine, 1983). Few social psychologists accept an exclusively evolutionary explanation of human prosocial behaviour, and accept evolutionary explanations only to a limited extent. The philosopher Turner asked the question 'Is altruism an anomaly?' We can ask psychological questions about people's motives for helping others and philosophical questions also about moral obligations to do so. We can also ask biological questions about what we have inherited, but one concept is a sticking point – *fitness altruism*: 'how could natural selection ever smile upon organisms that sacrifice their own reproductive fitness for another's benefit?' (Turner, 2005, p. 317). If I adopt a child who is not kin, is that a strong case for fitness altruism? If so, what are its genetic mechanisms and how did they evolve?

A problem with evolutionary theory as a sole explanation of altruism is the lack of convincing human evidence; on the contrary, a case such as the failure to help Kitty Genovese is difficult to explain at a biological level. Another criticism is the scant attention afforded by evolutionary theorists to the work of social learning theorists, in particular to the role of modelling (see below).

Buck and Ginsburg (1991) softened the strong version of an 'altruistic gene' with a proposed 'communicative gene', according to which both animals and humans are disposed to communicate. Communication includes emotional signals (see Chapter 15), the formation of social bonds (see Chapter 14) and the possibility of prosocial behaviour. Such an argument has merit but is a long way from an extreme evolutionary view. Perhaps of more practical value is to explore the social structures that promote prosocial behaviour (Darley, 1991), as we will do later in this chapter.

## Empathy and arousal

In its own right, evolutionary theory is not a sufficient account of why people help others. However, both genetic and environmental factors may operate, and there have been attempts to forge a biosocial approach to understanding altruism. While helping other members of the same species may well have evolved through natural selection, as a class of behaviour it is sensitive to a variety of contextual influences (Hoffman, 1981; Vine, 1983). While biological mechanisms could predispose you to act, if, when and how you respond will depend on your history and the immediate circumstances.

A common experience before acting prosocially is a state of arousal followed by **empathy** (Gaertner & Dovidio, 1977; Hoffman, 1981). Empathy is an emotional response to someone else's distress, a reaction to witnessing a disturbing event. Adults and children respond empathically to signs that a person is troubled, which implies that watching

**Empathy**
Ability to feel another person's experiences; identifying with and experiencing another person's emotions, thoughts and attitudes.

**Empathy and perspective taking**
Michael Jackson endured scathing criticism during a long-running scandal of alleged child sexual abuse. He also suffered mishaps during repeated facial surgery. Did you feel his 'pain' through those years? Finally he died from a drug overdose. Did your feelings change at this point?

someone suffer is unpleasant. Have you ever looked away when a film shows someone being tortured? Censors warn us if a film depicts scenes of violence, and most of us have been in an audience when a few tears are not far away. Even infants one or two days old can respond to the distress of another infant (Sagi & Hoffman, 1976; Simner, 1971). In real life, people often fail to act prosocially because they are actively engaged in *avoiding* empathy (Shaw, Batson & Todd, 1994). However, when we really do help, are we merely trying to reduce our own unpleasant feelings? The extra ingredient suggested is empathy, an ability to identify with someone else's experiences, particularly their feelings (Krebs, 1975).

## Helping: doing the maths

The **bystander-calculus model** of helping involves body and mind, a mixture of physiological processes and cognitive processes. According to Piliavin, when we think someone is in trouble we work our way through three stages, or sets of calculations, before we respond (Piliavin et al., 1981). First, we are physiologically aroused by another's distress. Second, we label this arousal as an emotion. Third, we evaluate the consequences of helping. See Box 13.2.

Interestingly, *not* helping can also involve costs. Piliavin distinguished between **empathy costs of not helping** and **personal costs of not helping**. A critical intervening variable is the relationship between the bystander and the victim. We have already seen that empathic concern is one motive for helping a distressed person; conversely, not helping when you feel empathic concern results in empathy costs (e.g. anxiety) in response to the other's plight. Thus the clarity of the emergency, its severity and the closeness of the bystander to the victim will increase the costs of not helping. Anything that increases the impact of the victim's state on the bystander will increase the empathy costs if help is not given.

Personal costs of not helping are many and varied, such as public censure or self-blame. Certain characteristics of the person in distress also affect the costs of not helping: for instance, the greater the victim's need for help, the greater the costs of not helping (Piliavin et al., 1981). If you believe that a victim might die if you do not help, the personal costs are

**Bystander-calculus model**
In attending to an emergency, the bystander calculates the perceived costs and benefits of providing help compared with those associated with not helping.

**Empathy costs of not helping**
Piliavin's view that failing to help can cause distress to a bystander who empathises with a victim's plight.

**Personal costs of not helping**
Piliavin's view that not helping a victim in distress can be costly to a bystander (e.g. experiencing blame).

---

### Research highlight 13.2
#### Steps in the bystander-calculus model

There are three steps in Jane Piliavin's model, which is supported by the work of others:

#### 1 Physiological arousal

Our first reaction to someone in distress is physiological, an empathic response. The greater the arousal, the more chance that a bystander will help. How quickly we react is related to the level of our body's response: e.g. the quicker our heartbeat the quicker we respond (Gaertner & Dovidio, 1977). There is also a cognitive aspect. As the victim's plight becomes clearer and more severe our physiological arousal increases.

#### 2 Labelling the arousal

Being aroused is one thing, but feeling a specific emotion (fear, anger, love) is another. Generally, arousal does not automatically produce specific emotions; people's cognitions or thoughts about the arousal play a critical role in determining the nature of the emotions they feel. Sometimes our response is also to feel distressed. Dan Batson suggested further that situational cues often trigger another set of responses, *empathic concern* (Batson & Coke, 1981). He also argued that when bystanders believe they are similar to a victim they are more likely to experience empathic concern.

#### 3 Evaluating the consequences

Finally, bystanders evaluate the consequences of acting before they help a victim, choosing an action that will reduce their personal distress at the lowest cost (a cost-benefit analysis is also used in a social exchange approach to close relationships; see Chapter 10). The main costs of helping are time and effort: the greater these costs, the less likely that a bystander will help (Darley & Batson, 1973).

likely to be high. If a tramp in the street asked you for money to buy alcohol, the personal costs of refusing might not be high; but if the request was for money for food or medicine, the costs might be quite high.

Other things being equal, the more similar the victim is to the bystander, the more likely the bystander is to help (Krebs, 1975). Similarity causes greater physiological arousal in bystanders and thus greater empathy costs of not helping. Similar victims may also be friends, for whom the costs of not helping would probably be high. Recall the position based on evolutionary theory that preservation of our genes is the basis of protecting our kin. The Piliavin model would simply note the high level of similarity between bystander and victim, thereby increasing the cost of not helping to an excruciating level. Think of the agony if you did not try to enter a blazing house to rescue your own child.

With regard to the Genovese case, the bystander-calculus model suggests that, although the onlookers would have been aroused and felt personal distress and empathic concern, the empathy costs and personal costs were not sufficient. Personal costs, in particular, may have deterred people from intervening. What if they got killed? The costs of not helping could be either high or low, depending on how people interpreted the situation: for example, was it just a marital dispute? The impact of this approach is that situational influences are heavily involved when adults decide whether to help in an emergency. This point will be confirmed when we compare it with Latané and Darley's step-by-step decision approach in a later section.

Lest we conclude this section with the feeling that Piliavin's model is unacceptably mechanistic, consider a view expressed by Piliavin and Charng (1990, p. 27):

> There appears to be a 'paradigm' shift away from [an] earlier position that behaviour that appears to be altruistic must, under close scrutiny, be revealed as reflecting egoistic motives. Rather, theory and data now being advanced are more compatible with the view that true altruism – acting with the goal of benefiting another – does exist and is part of human nature.

## Empathy and altruism

According to the bystander-calculus model, people intervene in an emergency because they find it unpleasantly arousing and they seek relief (see reviews by Batson & Oleson, 1991; Dovidio et al., 1991). As a result, 'altruism' is a misnomer because it is really motivated by self-interest, or egoism, although we have just noted that Piliavin and Charng were having second thoughts about this.

Batson and his colleagues (Batson et al., 1981) argued that an act is truly altruistic only if people seek to help even when they will no longer be troubled by observing the suffering of another person (e.g. turning back to help after passing a stranded motorist). This approach offers a different perspective to the Genovese case, with the bystanders feeling disturbed, but not sufficiently so to act: perhaps they could not identify with the victim. More recently, Bierhoff and Rohmann (2004) have supported this view, that true altruism is most likely defined in situations where the potential helper can easily not help – just quietly escape or slip away.

## Perspective taking

Oswald (1996) has argued that empathy requires us to demonstrate *perspective taking* – being able to see the position of another person from that person's point of view. Maner and his colleagues (2002) went further to report a connection between perspective taking, increased empathy and increased helping. According to Decety and Lamm (2006), this capacity has evolutionary significance. Some nonhuman primates respond to the feelings of others, but humans can both feel and act intentionally on behalf of others. It is this capacity that may account for why **empathic concern** is thought by theorists such as Batson to be crucial for altruism.

Batson and his colleagues (Batson, Early & Salvarini, 1997; Batson et al., 2003) made a further distinction concerning perspective taking: between understanding and experiencing how another person feels and how you would feel in the same situation. Different kinds of empathy lead to different kinds of motivation to help. Their research has shown that actively imagining how *another* feels produces empathy, which leads to altruistic motivation. However, actively imagining how *you* would feel produces empathy, but it also produces self-oriented distress, and involves a mix of altruism and egoism. Perhaps people who have experienced something stressful will empathise more with a person who is in a similar situation. For example, people who have been homeless or extremely ill may empathise more with a person in the same condition.

Are women more empathic than men? In one study, participants read a same-sex adolescent's description of a stressful life event, such as being the object of ridicule and teasing because of acne, or being betrayed and rejected (Batson et al., 1996). Women reported more empathy with a same-sex teenager when they had had similar experiences during their adolescence, an effect not found with men (see Figure 13.2). Batson accounted for this sex difference in terms of socialisation: women value interdependence and are more other-oriented, while men value independence and are more self-oriented.

Finally, in another study by Batson (Batson, Charng, Orr & Rowland, 2002), students were induced to feel empathy towards a convicted drug addict and then generalised their reaction to voting for allocating university funds (not their own money, of course!) to help other drug addicts. In this instance, empathy for a person from a stigmatised group led to action and also to changing an attitude (attitude change is also discussed in Chapter 6).

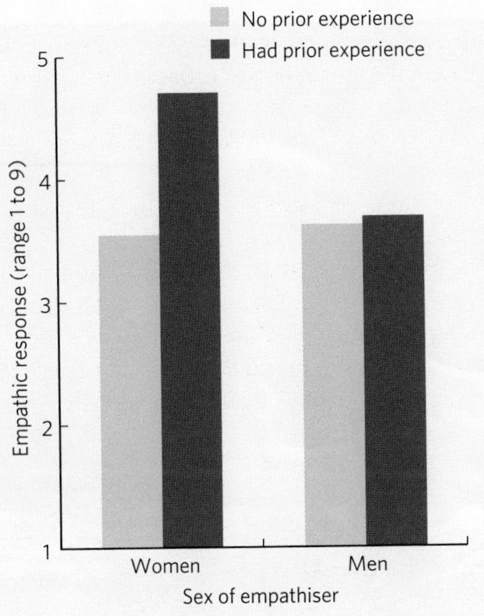

**Empathic concern**
An element in Batson's theory of helping behaviour. In contrast to personal distress (which may lead us to flee from the situation), it includes feelings of warmth, being soft-hearted, and having compassion for a person in need.

**Figure 13.2** Difference between women and men in empathising with a distressed teenager

- We might expect that people with prior experience of a stressful situation would empathise more with a same-sex teenager undergoing that same experience.

- In this study, only women with prior experience showed an increase in empathy.

*Source*: based on Batson et al. (1996)

## Learning to be helpful

A major explanation of helping is that displaying prosocial behaviour is intricately bound up with becoming socialised: it is learned, not inborn. Various theorists have argued that the processes of classical conditioning, instrumental conditioning and observational learning all contribute to being prosocial. In dealing with child development, Eisenberg noted a strand of research directed to the way that prosocial behaviour is acquired in childhood (Eisenberg et al., 1999). The application of learning theory to prosocial behaviour has been vigorously pursued within developmental and educational research fields in recent years.

However, traditional research carried out with adults in earlier decades, some of it experimental, dealt with a variety of conditions that control the display of helping. These are covered later in this chapter. First, we deal with studies of childhood, the period in which so much important learning takes place. Zahn-Waxler has studied the development of the emotions in children. She concluded that how we response to distress in others is connected to the way we learn to share, help and provide comfort, and that these patterns emerge between the ages of 1 and 2 (Zahn-Waxler, Radke-Yarrow, Wagner & Chapman, 1992). There are several ways in which these actions can be learned:

- **Giving instructions** In her studies of parenting, Grusec found that simply telling children to be helpful to others actually works (Grusec, Kuczynski, Rushton & Simutis, 1978). Telling a child what is appropriate establishes an expectation and a later guide for action. However, preaching about being good is of doubtful value unless a fairly strong form is used (Rice & Grusec, 1975). Furthermore, telling children to be generous if the 'preacher' behaves inconsistently is pointless: 'do as I say, not as I do' does not work. Grusec reported that when an adult acted selfishly but urged children to be generous, the children were actually less generous.

- **Using reinforcement** Acts that are rewarded are more likely to be repeated. When young children are rewarded for offering to help, they are more likely to offer help again later. Similarly, if they are not rewarded, they are less likely to offer help again (Grusec, 1991). Rushton has studied this field intensively. See an example of his work in Figure 13.3.

**Learning to be helpful**
Young children soon learn the value of sharing and helping one another

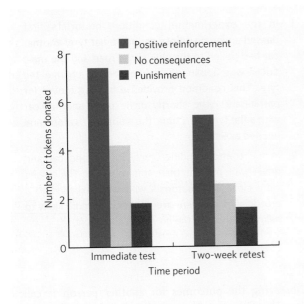

**Figure 13.3** The effects of reward and punishment on children's willingness to behave generously

- Boys aged 8–11years watched an adult who played a game to win tokens.
- Then the adult generously donated some by putting them in a bowl to be given later to a child pictured in a poster, a boy who was 'poor little Bobby, who had no Mommy or Daddy to look after him'.
- Next, the child played the game. In one condition, the adult used verbal reinforcers as rewards or punishments for behaving generously (e.g. either 'good for you', or 'that's kind of silly . . . now you will have less tokens for yourself').
- Both tactics had strong effects on how the boys behaved, immediately and after a two-week interval.
- While this study employed reinforcement principles, it clearly also featured the effects of watching a model.

*Source:* based on Rushton & Teachman (1978)

- **Exposure to models** In his review of factors that influence children to give help, Rushton (1976) concluded that while reinforcement is effective in shaping behaviour, **modelling** is even more effective. Watching someone else helping another is a powerful form of learning. This approach can be extended to other contexts. Take the case of young Johnny who first helps his mummy to carry some shopping into the house and then wants to help in putting it away, and then cleans up his/her bedroom. Well, maybe not the last bit!

Learning to be helpful through observation is a particular case of a process that can account for how people learn attitudes (Chapter 5) and to act aggressively (Chapter 12). In studies of the effects of viewing prosocial behaviour on television, the general finding has been that children's *attitudes* towards prosocial behaviour are improved (Coates, Pusser & Goodman, 1976; Rushton, 1979). However, there was a reduced effect on actual prosocial behaviour and even less effect over longer time periods.

Children who behave prosocially also tend to be able to tolerate a delay in gratification (Long & Lerner, 1974) and are more popular with their peers (Dekovic & Janssens, 1992). There are also close developmental links between prosocial skills, coping and social competence (Eisenberg et al., 1996), which suggests an underlying growth of a fully socialised being.

We can take some comfort that it's never too late – adults can also be influenced by the helpful model. Check the example in Box 13.3.

When a person observes a model and behaves in kind, is this just a matter of mechanical imitation? The work of Bandura (1973) suggests otherwise (see also Chapter 12). According to **social learning theory,** it is the knowledge of what happens to the model that largely determines whether or not the observer will help. As with direct learning experience, a positive outcome should increase a model's effectiveness in influencing the observer to help, while a negative outcome should decrease the model's effectiveness. Hornstein (1970) conducted an experiment where people saw a model returning a lost wallet. They either appeared pleased to be able to help, displeased at the bother of having to help or showed no strong reaction. Later, the participant came across another 'lost' wallet. Those who had seen the pleasant consequences helped the most; others who saw the unpleasant

**Modelling**
Tendency for a person to reproduce the actions, attitudes and emotional responses exhibited by a real-life or symbolic model. Also called *observational learning.*

**Social learning theory**
The view championed by Bandura that human social behaviour is not innate but learned from appropriate models.

### Research and applications 13.3
#### The case of the helpful motorist: the role of modelling

A model showing us how to perform a helpful act reminds us that helping is appropriate, increases our confidence in being able to help and gives us information about the consequences of helping others (Rushton, 1980).

In a study of the *modelling effect,* Bryan and Test (1967) investigated whether a model would influence the number of people who might stop to help a woman change a car tyre. There were two conditions:

1  In the experimental condition, motorists first passed a woman whose car had a flat tyre; another car had pulled to the side of the road and the male driver was apparently helping her to change the tyre. This condition provided a helping model for participants who shortly came upon another car with a flat tyre. This time, the woman was alone and needed assistance.

2  In the control condition, only the second car and driver were present; there was no model. The results were clear. The motorists who were exposed to a prosocial model were over 50 per cent more likely to help than those in the no-model condition.

---

**Learning by vicarious experience**
Acquiring a behaviour after observing that another person was rewarded for it.

consequences helped the least. Observing the outcomes for another person is called **learning by vicarious experience** (see also Chapter 12); it can increase the rates at which both selfishness and selflessness take place (Midlarsky & Bryan, 1972).

### Education and game playing

Obvious at it may seem, children can profit from a simple education in moral reasoning. Rosenkoetter (1999) found that children who watched television comedies that included a moral lesson engaged more frequently in prosocial behaviour than children who did not, provided they understood the principle involved. Gentile and his colleagues investigated the effects of playing video games featuring prosocial acts on prosocial behaviour measured by questionnaires (Gentile, Anderson, Yukawa, Ihori, Saleem et al., 2009). In a series of three developmental studies, three age groups of Singaporeans, Americans and Japanese (including longitudinal samples) played a variety of both prosocial and violent video games. A central finding was that when the video content was prosocial the participants acted in more helpful ways, but when it was violent they acted in more hurtful ways. These effects were consistent across cultures and age groups.

### The impact of attribution

People make attributions about helping or not helping others. To continue being helpful on more than one occasion requires a person to internalise the idea of 'being helpful' (see self-perception theory, Chapter 4). Helpfulness can then be a guide in the future when helping is an option. A self-attribution can be even more powerful than reinforcement for learning helping behaviour: young children who were told they were 'helpful people' donated more marbles to a needy child than those who were reinforced with verbal praise, and this effect persisted over time (Grusec & Redler, 1980). Indeed, Perry and his colleagues found that children may experience self-criticism and bad feelings when they fail to live up to the standards implied by their own attributions (Perry et al., 1980).

**Just-world hypothesis**
According to Lerner, and Miller people need to believe that the world is a just place where they get what they deserve. As evidence of undeserved suffering undermines this belief, people may conclude that victims deserve their fate.

If we are wondering if we should offer help to someone in need we usually try to figure out who or what this person might be. Some observers may even blame an innocent victim. According to the **just-world hypothesis** proposed by Lerner and Miller (1978), people need to believe – perhaps for their own security – that the world is a just place where people get what they deserve (see Chapter 3). For instance, someone who has an accident may have deserved it (Bulman & Wortman, 1977). Therefore, if some victims deserve their fate, we can think 'Good, they had that coming to them!' and not help them.

**Social responsibility norm**
Helping someone in need is a matter of compassion, not simply an act that reduces one's own sense of distress.

Some witnesses in the Kitty Genovese case may have believed that it was her fault for being out so late – a familiar response to many crimes. Take another example: perhaps a rape victim 'deserved' what happened because her clothing was too tight or revealing? Accepting that the world must necessarily be a just place begins in childhood and is a learned attribution.

Fortunately, most of us respond to evidence that suffering is undeserved. Accepting this undermines the power of belief in a just world and allows justice to be done. A necessary precondition of actually helping is to believe that the help will be effective. Miller (1977) isolated two factors that can convince a would-be helper: (1) the victim is a special case rather than one of many, and (2) the need is temporary rather than persisting. Each of these allows us to decide that giving aid 'right now' will be effective.

Using this line of thinking, Warren and Walker (1991) showed that if the needs of a person in distress can be specified, others can use this information to determine if giving help is justified. In a field study of more than 2,500 recipients, a letter mail-out solicited donations for a refugee family from Sudan. Cover letters with slightly different wording were used. More donations were recorded when the letter highlighted that: (1) the donation was restricted to this particular family rather than being extended to other people in Sudan; and (2) the family's need was only short term. In short, the case was just and action would be effective.

# The bystander effect

We noted at the outset that social psychologists were curious and concerned about the lack of involvement of witnesses and bystanders during the Kitty Genovese murder. The initial frenzy of research that followed was meant to discover when people would help in an emergency. More recently, the question has broadened: when will people help in non-emergencies by performing such deeds as giving money, donating blood or contributing their time or effort? The focus here is on the situational factors that affect **bystander intervention** in real-life situations in the real world, rather than on the origins or

**Bystander intervention**
This occurs when an individual breaks out of the role of a bystander and helps another person in an emergency.

learning of helping behaviour. Furthermore, there has been an attempt to develop models of the helping process, largely from a cognitive viewpoint. The initial emphasis was on helping in emergencies, but this has now widened to prosocial behaviour in general.

Perhaps the most influential and thoroughly studied factor that affects prosocial behaviour is whether the potential helper is alone or in the company of others. What is now known is that a lone bystander is more likely to help than any of several bystanders, a phenomenon known as the **bystander effect**. (Apply this to account for Lily's bravery in the third focus question.) Unlike Piliavin's account of helping based on empathy discussed above, the model suggested by Latané and Darley (1970) features a decision making process based on how other people respond.

**Bystander effect**
People are less likely to help in an emergency when they are with others than when alone. The greater the number, the less likely it is that anyone will help.

## Latané and Darley's cognitive model

Stemming directly from the wide public discussion and concern about the Genovese case, Latané and Darley began a programme of research (Darley & Latané, 1968), now considered a classic in social psychology. Surely, these researchers asked, empathy for another's suffering, or at the very least a sense of civic responsibility, should lead to an intervention in a situation of danger? Furthermore, where several bystanders are present, there should be a correspondingly greater probability that someone will help. Before dealing with this theory, consider first the elements of an **emergency situation**:

**Emergency situation**
Often involves an unusual event, can vary in nature, is unplanned and requires a quick response.

- It can involve danger, for person or property.
- It is an unusual event, rarely encountered by the ordinary person.
- It can differ widely in nature, from a bank on fire to a pedestrian being mugged.
- It is not foreseen, so that prior planning of how to cope is improbable.
- It requires instant action, so that leisurely consideration of options is not feasible.

At this juncture, note a similarity between the nature of an emergency and the autokinetic paradigm used by Sherif (e.g. Sherif, 1935) to study the development of social norms (see Chapters 7 and 8). Both involve uncertainty, ambiguity and a lack of structure when what we want is a proper basis for judgement or action. In both cases, we are more likely to look to others for guidance on how to think and act. So a core prediction about an emergency is that people will react quite differently according to whether others are present or absent.

Latané and Darley noted that it would be easy simply to label the failure to help a victim in an emergency as apathy – an uncaring response to the problems of others. However, they reasoned that the apparent lack of concern shown by the witnesses in the Genovese case could conceal other processes. An early finding was that failure to help occurred more often when the size of the group of witnesses increased. Latané and Darley's cognitive model of bystander intervention proposes that whether a person helps depends on the outcomes of a series of decisions. At any point along this path, a decision could be made that would terminate helping behaviour. The steps in this model are described in Box 13.4, and the decision process is illustrated in Figure 13.4. (Reflect now on your likely thought processes in the fourth focus question.) A series of experiments is outlined below to illustrate how this model works.

### 'Where there's smoke there's fire'

Latané and Darley (1970) invited male students to an interview room to discuss some of the problems involved in life at a large university. While the students were completing a preliminary questionnaire, smoke began to pour in from a wall vent. This continued for six minutes until the room was full of smoke. Participants were either alone, with two other participants they did not know, or with two confederates who completely ignored the

## Research classic 13.4
### Steps in Latané and Darley's cognitive model

**Deciding whether to help**

1  Do we even notice an event where helping may be required, such as an accident?

2  How do we interpret the event? We are most likely to define a situation as an emergency, and most likely to help, when we believe that the victim's condition is serious and is about to deteriorate rapidly. Shotland and Huston (1979) found that people were more likely to help in emergencies (e.g. someone needs an insulin shot for diabetes) than in non-emergencies (e.g. needing some allergy medicine). Verbal distress cues (e.g. screaming) are particularly effective and increase the likelihood of bystander intervention: the act of screaming can lead to receiving help 75 per cent or more of the time. Bystander apathy is markedly reduced once people interpret a situation as an emergency (Clark & Word, 1974; Gaertner & Dovidio, 1977).

3  Do we accept personal responsibility for helping? Sometimes a person witnessing an emergency knows that there are other onlookers but cannot see their reactions. This was clearly the case in the Genovese incident. Sometimes the decision to assume responsibility is determined by how competent the bystander feels in the particular situation. For both steps 2 and 3, the influence of other people is clearly a determining factor.

4  What do we decide to do?

5  Is help given? If we doubt whether the situation is an emergency, or we do not know what to do if it is, the way others behave can influence how we respond.

*Source:* based on Darley & Latané (1968)

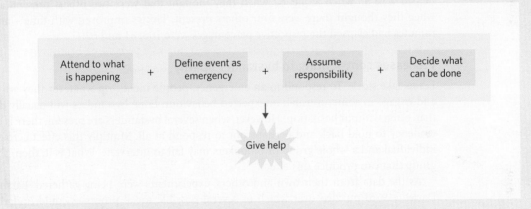

**Figure 13.4**  Deciding whether or not to help in Latané and Darley's cognitive model
*Source:* based on data from Latané & Darley (1970)

smoke. What would the participants do, and how long would they take to do it? The researchers wondered if people in such situations look to others as a guide. This is exactly what happened. Participants who were alone were more likely to report the smoke than were those with other strangers. While 75 per cent of the participants who were alone took positive action, only 38 per cent of the two-stranger groups intervened. Participants in the presence of two passive confederates were even less likely to report the situation, taking action only 10 per cent of the time! 

Latané and Darley suggested that the presence of others can inhibit people from responding to an emergency: the more people, the slower the response. Even worse, many of the people who did not respond were persuaded that if others were passive there is no emergency. Some later reported that there was no danger from the smoke. In a real emergency, this could easily have proved fatal.

### 'A lady in distress'

Latané and Rodin (1969) replicated these results, extending the argument to situations where others might be in danger. Male participants were alone or in pairs filling in a questionnaire and heard a woman in another room struggle to open a filing cabinet. They then heard a loud crash, followed by a cry of pain and moans and groans. Helping dropped from 70 per cent of the time among participants who were alone to 40 per cent among those in pairs. The presence of a passive confederate suggested that the situation was not critical, and helping plunged to 7 per cent. A refinement was added. Pairs of friends helped more often – 70 per cent of the time.

### 'He's having a fit'

Must bystanders be physically present to lessen the chance of helping? Darley and Latané (1968) devised an experiment where students could communicate with each other only via microphones while in separate cubicles. The students believed that the group consisted of two people (self and a victim), four people or six people. The 'victim' told the others over the intercom system that he was epileptic. Later he was heard to choke and gasp, apparently having a seizure, and then became quiet. Would the number of presumed bystanders who might help increase the time it took a participant to help?

The results showed that the more 'bystanders' an individual thought were present, the less likely they were to help. Before the end of the fit, the percentage of participants who helped was: 85 when alone, 62 when they thought that were two others present, and 31 when they thought there were four others present. Things improved with time – after six minutes had elapsed the respective percentages were 100, 81 and 62.

### Processes contributing to bystander apathy

Let us take stock. To respond to an emergency, people must stop whatever they are doing and engage in some unusual, unexpected behaviour. Lone bystanders will usually do just that, often without hesitation. However, when several bystanders are present, there is a clear tendency to hold back and perhaps not to respond at all. Multiply this effect across each individual and a whole group of onlookers may fail to intervene. What is it, then, about a group that can produce this effect?

As the data from their own and others' experiments were being gathered, Latané and Darley (1976) puzzled over which of several possible social processes could underlie the reluctance of groups to help a victim. Three major explanations were available. In distinguishing between them, we can use the analogy of the nature of the communication channel open to the onlookers. Three questions can be asked:

1   Is the individual aware that others are present?

2   Can the individual actually see or hear the others and be aware of how they are reacting?

3   Can these others monitor the behaviour of the individual?

Each of the following processes is distinctive in terms of how these questions are answered:

**Diffusion of responsibility**

Tendency of an individual to assume that others will take responsibility (as a result, no one does). This is a hypothesised cause of the bystander effect.

- **Diffusion of responsibility.** Think back to the phenomenon of social loafing (discussed in Chapter 8), in which a person who is part of a group often tends to offload responsibility for action to others. In the case of an emergency, the presence of other onlookers provides the opportunity to transfer the responsibility for acting, or not acting, on to them. The communication channel does not imply that the individual can be seen by the others or can see them. It is necessary only that they be available, somewhere, for action. People who are alone are most likely to help a victim because they believe they carry the entire responsibility for action. If they do not act, nobody else will. Ironically, the presence of just one other witness allows diffusion of responsibility to operate among all present.

- *Audience inhibition.* Other onlookers can make people self-conscious about an intended action; people do not want to appear foolish by overreacting. In the context of prosocial behaviour, this process is sometimes referred to as a **fear of social blunders**. Have you felt a dread of being laughed at for misunderstanding little crises involving others? What if it is not as it seems? What if someone is playing a joke? Am I on *Candid Camera*? The

**Fear of social blunders**
The dread of acting inappropriately or of making a foolish mistake witnessed by others. The desire to avoid ridicule inhibits effective responses to an emergency by members of a group.

---

## Research classic 13.5
### The three-in-one experiment: A shocking experience

Students who had agreed to take part in a study of 'repression' found that their task was to rate whether the way in which a target person responded to verbal stimuli indicated whether they had received an electric shock or not. When certain words were presented, the target person would receive a shock from the experimenter. The participant would watch this on closed-circuit television in another room and judge when shocks had been delivered by studying the target person's overall behaviour. The experiment was carried out at night in a deserted building at Princeton University. Participants were to work in pairs (except in the Alone condition), although in fact the second rater in each case was a confederate of the experimenter.

Each pair of participants was initially taken to a control room, where there was an antiquated shock generator. Commenting on it, the experimenter said that the parts were from army surplus and were not reliable. In front of the generator was a chair, with a TV camera pointing at it. The experimenter then noted that the target person was late and that time could be saved by filling in a background questionnaire. The participants were ushered to their individual cubicles, each of which contained two TV monitors and a camera. Monitor 1 was operating and showed the control room they had just left, with the shock generator in clear view. The experimenter apologised for the presence of monitor 2 and the camera, saying they belonged to another, absent, staff member and could not be touched. Both items were operating. This extra, supposedly superfluous, equipment provided the basis for several experimental conditions. Monitor 2 could show the neighbour in the next cubicle, and the camera could show the participant to the neighbour. There were five conditions:

1 *Alone.* This is a baseline condition in which no other person is present with the real participant. The camera in the real participant's room is pointing at the ceiling, and monitor 2 shows a shot of the ceiling of the second cubicle but no sign of anybody else.

2 *Diffusion of responsibility.* As in the remaining conditions, there are two people, but no communication. Monitor 2 shows only the ceiling of the other cubicle (where its camera is pointing). The camera in the real participant's room is pointing at the ceiling. It is different from the 'alone' condition, however, as the participant knows that a bystander is present.

3 *Diffusion plus social influence.* The participant sees the other's response, but not vice versa. One camera is trained on someone, in this case the bystander. The confederate can be seen working on a questionnaire on monitor 2.

4 *Diffusion plus audience inhibition.* The other sees the participant's response, but not vice versa. One camera is trained on someone, in this case the participant. Although the bystander cannot be seen, presumably the participant can.

5 *Diffusion plus social influence plus audience inhibition.* The two persons see each other. Both cameras are trained on them, and they can be seen on the respective monitors.

The emergency was created when the experimenter left the participant in the cubicle and returned to the control room to adjust the shock generator, visible on monitor 1. On the screen, the experimenter could be seen to pick up some wires. They must not have been the right wires, because the experimenter screamed, jumped in the air, threw himself against the wall, and fell to the floor out of camera range with his feet sticking up. About fifteen seconds later he began to moan softly, and he continued until help was received or for about six minutes (Latané & Darley, 1976, p. 327).

What will the real participant do in each condition? See the results in Figure 13.5.

communication channel implies that the others can see or hear the individual, but it is not necessary that they can be seen.

- *Social influence.* Other onlookers provide a model for action. If they are passive and unworried, the situation may seem less serious. The communication channel implies that the individual can see the others, but not vice versa.

### The three-in-one experiment

We are now ready to consider the most complicated of Latané and Darley's experiments, designed specifically to detect the operation of each of the three processes just outlined. By the use of TV monitors and cameras, participants were induced to believe that they were in one of four conditions with respect to other onlookers. They could (1) see and be seen; (2) see, but not be seen; (3) not see, but be seen; or (4) neither see nor be seen. This complexity was necessary in order to allow for the consequences of sequentially adding social influence and audience inhibition effects to that of diffusion of responsibility.

We should note here that diffusion of responsibility must always be involved if a bystander is, or is thought to be, present at the moment of the emergency. However, the additive effect of another process can be assessed and then compared with the effect of diffusion acting on its own. You will get a good idea of how this was done by studying Box 13.5.

### Limits to these effects

Bystanders who are strangers to each other inhibit helping even more because communication between them is slower. When bystanders are known to each other, there is much less inhibition of prosocial behaviour than in a group of strangers (Latané & Rodin, 1969; Rutkowski, Gruder & Romer, 1983). However, Gottlieb and Carver (1980) showed that even among strangers inhibition is reduced if they know that there will be an opportunity to interact later and possibly explain their actions. Overall, the bystander effect is strongest when the bystanders are anonymous strangers who do not expect to meet again, which could have been the situation in the Genovese case. Christy and Voigt (1994) found that bystander apathy is reduced if the victim is an acquaintance, friend or relative, or is a child being abused in a public place.

# The person in the equation

With so many situational factors affecting prosocial behaviour, we might wonder if aspects of the person have much effect. Let us re-establish some balance by noting the psychological maxim that 'behaviour is a product of the individual and the environment'.

Are there personal characteristics that are relatively independent of the situation? Research has concentrated on two areas: transitory psychological states and personality characteristics. The former includes passing moods and feelings, which all of us may experience; the latter implies relatively permanent attributes.

## Mood states

We have all experienced days where things seem to go perfectly and others when things go totally wrong, and we know that this can affect how we interact with other people. Prosocial research has shown that people who feel good are much more likely to help someone in need than are people who feel bad.

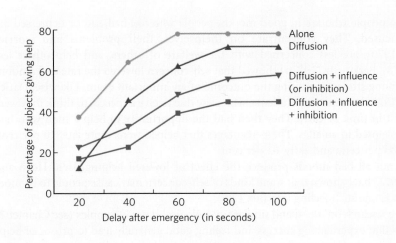

**Figure 13.5** The effects of three processes on willingness to help a victim

- The results measured in seconds the elapsed time before help was given to the prostrate experimenter.
- The graph shows the cumulative number of participants who helped as time went by.
- The analysis distinguishes between the Alone condition and three sets of Bystander conditions.
- The results were combined for two of these (diffusion of responsibility plus either audience inhibition or social influence); their effects did not differ and both involved one-way communication.
- As the degree of communication increased helping decreased: (a) simple diffusion of responsibility (no communication) reduced helping; (b) this declined further when either social influence or audience inhibition was added (one-way communication); (c) when all three processes operated (two-way communication) the least help is given.

*Source:* based on data from Latané & Darley (1976)

## Good moods

A typical experimental approach is to get participants to believe that they have succeeded or failed at a task they are asked to perform. It then transpires that those who believe they have been successful are more helpful than those who believe they have failed or those who have received no feedback. Isen (1970) found that teachers who were more successful on a task were more likely to contribute later to a school fundraising drive. Those who had done well in fact donated seven times as much as the others! So, such momentary feelings as success on a relatively innocuous task can dramatically affect prosocial behaviour.

Isen suggested that doing well creates a 'warm glow of success', which makes people more likely to help. (You can compare this effect with the *reinforcement–affect model* of interpersonal liking in Chapter 14.) When people feel good, they are less preoccupied with themselves and are more sensitive to the needs and problems of others. Being in a good mood means that people are more likely to focus on positive things (Isen, Clark & Schwartz, 1976), to have a more optimistic outlook on life and to see the world in pleasant ways (Isen & Stalker, 1982).

People who hear good news on the radio show greater attraction towards strangers and greater willingness to help than people who hear bad news (Holloway, Tucker & Hornstein, 1977); people are in better moods and are more helpful on sunny, temperate days than on overcast, cold days (Cunningham, 1979). Even experiences such as reading aloud statements expressing elation, or recalling pleasant events from our childhood, can increase the rate of helping. The evidence consistently demonstrates that good moods produce helpful behaviour under a variety of circumstances.

### Bad moods

In contrast to people who are in good moods, people who feel bad, sad or depressed are internally focused. They concentrate on themselves, their problems and worries (Berkowitz, 1970), are less concerned with the welfare of others, and help others less (Weyant, 1978). Berkowitz (1972b) showed that self-concern lowered the rate and amount of helping among students awaiting the outcome of an important exam. Likewise, Darley and Batson (1973) led seminary students, who were due to give a speech, to think they were quite late, just in time or early. They then had the opportunity to help a man who had apparently collapsed in an alley. The percentages that helped were: quite late, 10 per cent; just in time, 45 per cent; and early, 63 per cent.

However, not all bad moods produce the effect of lowered helping. Isen, Horn and Rosenhan (1973) have shown that some kinds of self-concern may cause people to be more helpful. Guilt is one such feeling (see Box 13.6).

Overall, the research on mood and similar psychological states is complex (see Chapter 2) and indicates that experiencing success and feeling good generally lead to prosocial helping behaviour, but that bad moods may or may not lead to helping, depending on whether they are moderated by self-concern. Nevertheless, a common feature derived from providing help is that the helper ends up *feeling good* (Williamson & Clark, 1989) and experiences, at least for a while, a more positive self-evaluation. A study of feedback on a verbal task performance by Klein (2003) was in a similar vein. When a student received positive feedback, such as having performed better than a second student, the process of **social comparison** was invoked. The participant reported feeling pleased (suggesting a more positive self-evaluation) and was more willing to give helpful hints to a third student about to undertake a similar task. This study is another example of the feeling-good factor triggering prosocial behaviour.

**Social comparison**
Comparing our behaviours and opinions with those of others in order to establish the correct or socially approved way of thinking and behaving.

---

## Real world 13.6
### The case of the guilty helper

#### 'Oh dear! You've smashed my camera'

People who have accidentally broken something or injured someone show increases in helping behaviour. When participants believed they had ruined an experiment, cheated on a test, broken expensive equipment or inflicted pain on another, they were much more likely to help the person against whom they had transgressed.

Regan, Williams and Sparling (1972) led a group of female participants to believe they had broken an expensive camera. Later, when they had the chance to help another woman who had dropped some groceries, 50 per cent of the 'guilty' participants intervened to help, whereas only 15 per cent of a control group did so.

One explanation offered to account for the guilty helper is the image-reparation hypothesis: people want to make amends. If you have hurt someone, you can restore self-esteem by making it up. However, the complication is that the guilty party will actually help anyone in need, not just the person towards whom they feel guilty. It is difficult to see how their self-esteem can be threatened in this way.

According to Cialdini's negative relief state model (e.g. Cialdini & Kenrick, 1976), hurting another person, or even seeing this happen, causes a bystander to experience a negative affect state. This motivates them to do something to relieve this feeling. We come to learn that helping can alleviate negative moods. Consequently, people are motivated to feel good rather than to look good. If so, this process is better described as hedonism than altruism, as it is motivated by self-interest.

This view gains support from the finding that people who have inflicted, or who have witnessed, harm or pain, and then receive an unexpected monetary reward or social approval immediately afterwards, are less helpful than participants who are left in a bad mood (Cialdini, Darby & Vincent, 1973; McMillen, 1971).

## Attributes of the person

Special interpersonal relationships can increase the feeling of personal responsibility that a bystander in an emergency will experience. This is more likely, for example, if there is a special bond with or commitment to the victim (Geer & Jarmecky, 1973; Moriarty, 1975; Tilker, 1970), or if the victim is especially dependent on the bystander (Berkowitz, 1978).

Are there other individual factors that can make people more helpful, even temporarily? Why are some people are consistently more helpful than others? Famous figures such as Florence Nightingale, Albert Schweitzer and Mother Teresa come to mind. This area of research has been described as trying to profile the 'Good Samaritan'. Supporting evidence is weak (Schwartz, 1977). However, people who are consistently helpful tend to be taller, heavier and physically stronger, and better trained to cope with crimes and emergencies (see Huston, Ruggiero, Conner & Geis, 1981) (How might any of these points throw additional light on Lily's bravery in focus question 3?)

We can also note that *forgiveness* is valued in many cultures and can help close relationships to survive (see Chapter 14). Karremans, van Lange and Holland (2005) have recently studied the 'spillover' effects of forgiveness. They found that people who are willing to forgive a significant other person (e.g. a partner) for offending them can later be more prosocial in general – such as volunteering to work for or donate money to a charity organisation (revisit the second focus question).

### Living in big cities

Latané and Darley (1970) found that fairly obvious demographic variables, such as a parent's occupation and number of siblings, were not correlated with helping behaviour. However, there was the intriguing suggestion that size of one's home town might be connected. People from small-town backgrounds were more likely to help than those from larger cities, a finding replicated by Gelfand, Hartmann, Walder and Page (1973).

Paul Amato (1983) studied size of population in a direct fashion. He investigated people's willingness to help in fifty-five Australian cities and towns, focusing on acts such as picking up fallen envelopes, giving a donation to charity, giving a favourite colour for a student project, correcting inaccurate directions that are overheard and helping a stranger who has hurt a leg and collapsed on the footpath. With the exception of picking up the fallen envelope, the results showed that as population size rose (i.e. in the larger towns and cities), acts of helping decreased. The results for four of the helping measures are shown in Figure 13.6. Best-fit regression lines for each set of data points are shown. You can see that there is a consistent trend downwards for helping a stranger as the population level rises.

Various reasons have been advanced for rural–urban differences in helping or not helping. Perhaps rural people care more because they feel less crowded, less rushed and less affected by noise; and generally feel less 'urban overload' and environmental stress than their fellows in a big and bustling city (Bonnes & Secchiaroli, 1995; Halpern, 1995).

### Individual differences

Latané and Darley (1970) reported that helping behaviour could not be predicted from *personality measures* including authoritarianism, alienation, trustworthiness, Machiavellianism (the tendency to manipulate others) and need for approval.

On the other hand, positive relationships have been reported between helping behaviour and the belief that our fate lies within our control, mature moral judgement, and the tendency to take responsibility for others' welfare (Eisenberg-Berg, 1979; Staub, 1974). However, even this evidence is not strong enough (i.e the correlations are small) to distinguish clearly Good Samaritans from the rest of humanity, and some doubt that the attempt is meaningful (Bar-Tal, 1976; Schwartz, 1977). More modern research by Mikulincer and his colleagues dealing with **attachment styles** (see Chapter 14) has reported that people

**Attachment styles**
Descriptions of the nature of people's close relationships, thought to be established in childhood.

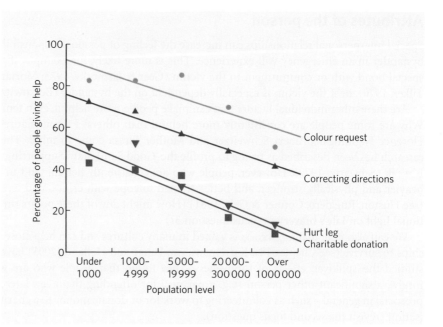

**Figure 13.6** Effect of population level on willingness to help a stranger

- In cities with large populations, strangers can expect less help from the inhabitants.

- Regression lines have been fitted to the original data points for each helping measure.

*Source:* based on data from Amato (1983)

who are securely attached are more likely to be compassionate and altruistic (Mikulincer & Shaver, 2005). This link to early childhood is echoed in a longitudinal study spanning from four years of age to early adulthood which pointed to stable differences – the child who shares, helps and offers emotional comfort to others continues to do so in adulthood (Eisenberg et al., 1999). Of course, stability could be attributed to environmental constancies, such as secure attachment.

The common view shared by researchers in this field is that there is no stand-alone, altruistic personality (Bierhoff & Rohmann, 2004). Whether a person will act prosocially might, at most, be determined by their personality acting in unison with the nature of the situation and of the person requiring help (Gergen, Gergen & Meter, 1972).

### The 'Scrooge effect'

Might people become more caring for others as they face their own mortality? There is a line of research on mortality salience suggesting that prosocial behaviour can be a side benefit of being reminded that our lives end in death – a case of 'Repent! Do good!'

> At Christmas time, one of the most cherished and frequently told stories in Western culture is Charles Dickens's *A Christmas Carol*. In this story, the ghost of Christmas past and the ghost of Christmas present show Ebenezer Scrooge how his cruelty and selfishness has adversely affected his own life and the lives of others. However, it is not until the ghost of Christmas future shows Scrooge a glimpse of his own future, inscribed on the head of a tombstone, that his stinginess and greed give way to benevolence and compassion for others. Dickens is telling us that one should value kindness and concern for others over selfishness and material riches or else die an insignificant and lonely death. (*Jonas, Schimel, Greenberg & Pyszczynski, 2002, p. 1342*)

**Terror management theory**
The notion that the most fundamental human motivation is to reduce the terror of the inevitability of death. Self-esteem may be centrally implicated in effective terror management.

Jonas and her colleagues put **terror management theory** to the test by interviewing pedestrians who were walking towards a funeral parlour marked with a large sign that read 'Howe's Mortuary'. Some interviews were carried out three blocks away while others took place right in front of the home and in full view of the sign. After the interview, the pedestrians rated several charities in terms of the benefits they provided people. A charity was rated more favourably when the pedestrians were in front of the funeral parlour. Like Scrooge, they saw *Christmas future*.

## Competence: 'have skills, will help'

Feeling competent to deal with an emergency makes it more likely that help will be given; there is the awareness that 'I know what I'm doing' (Korte, 1971). Specific kinds of competence have increased helping in these contexts:

- People who were told they had a high tolerance for electric shock, were more willing to help others move electrically charged objects (Midlarsky & Midlarsky, 1976).

- People who were told they were good at handling rats were more likely to help to recapture a 'dangerous' laboratory rat (Schwartz & David, 1976).

- The competence effect may even generalise beyond a restricted context. Kazdin and Bryan (1971) found that people who thought they had done well on a health examination or even on a creativity task were later more willing to donate blood.

Certain 'packages' of skills are perceived as being relevant to some emergencies. In reacting to a stranger who was bleeding, people with first-aid training intervened more often than those who were untrained (Shotland & Heinold, 1985).

Pantin and Carver (1982) improved the level of students' competence by showing them a series of films on first aid and emergencies. Three weeks later, they had the chance to help a confederate who was apparently choking. The bystander effect was reduced by having previously seen the films. Pantin and Carver also reported that the increase in helping persisted over time. This area of skill development is at the core of Red Cross first-aid training courses for ordinary people in many countries.

The impact of skill level was tested experimentally by comparing professional help with novice help (Cramer, McMaster, Bartell & Dragna, 1988). The participants were two groups of students, one being highly competent (registered nurses) and the other less competent (general-course students). In a contrived context, each participant waited in the company

**Competence in an emergency**
'Trust us — we know what we're doing.' This skilled civil defence team in Baghdad are both quick and efficient in helping a bomb victim

of a non-helping confederate. The nurses were more likely than the general students to help a workman, seen earlier, who had apparently fallen off a ladder in an adjoining corridor (a rigged accident, with pre-recorded moans). In responding to a post-experimental questionnaire, the nurses specified that they felt they had the skills to help.

To sum up: situations highlighting the fact that a person possesses relevant skills implies that these skills should be used. The self-perception is: 'I know what to do, so I have the responsibility to act.' Competence may be situation-specific, but there is the tantalising possibility that it may last over time and also generalise to non-related situations.

## Leaders and followers

A variation on the theme of competence is the case of acting as a leader. We might think that a leader is, by definition, more generally competent than followers and more likely to initiate all kinds of action, including helping in an emergency. The skills component of leadership could probably be used to account for some helping outcomes. Even so, a study by Baumeister and his colleagues (Baumeister, Chesner, Senders & Tice, 1988) specified an additional feature of the leadership role (see also Chapter 9) that goes beyond the 'have skills, will help' explanation: being a leader acts as a cue to generalised responsibility. In an emergency situation, Baumeister hypothesised, the leader does not experience the same degree of diffusion of responsibility as ordinary group members. Read how they tested for this in Box 13.7.

## Gender differences

Are men destined to be 'knights in shining armour'? The literature of romance but also of science indicates that men are more likely to help women than vice versa. Examples of research contexts include helping a motorist in distress (flat tyre, stalled car), or offering

### Research and applications 13.7
Acting like a leader counteracts diffusion of responsibility: 'Who's in charge around here?'

A major requirement of effective leadership is to guide decision making for a group (see Chapter 9) and, in an emergency, to provide control and direction for action. In an experiment by Baumeister, Chesner, Senders and Tice (1988) thirty-two male and female students (seven others were dropped because they suspected a deception) were led to believe they had been allocated to four-person groups, in which one member was thought to be randomly assigned to act as leader. The students were told that their task was to decide which survivors of a nuclear war should be allowed to join the group in its bomb shelter. The assistants could make recommendations, but their designated leader would make the final decision.

Participants were actually tested individually, half as leaders and half as followers, and group discussion was simulated using tape recordings over an intercommunication system. At a critical point, each participant was

exposed to a simulated emergency, when the recorded voice of a male group member faltered and said, 'Somebody come help me, I'm choking!' He then had a fit of coughing and went silent. The experimenter met those who came out of the test room to help, telling them there was no problem. All were later debriefed.

Those designated as leaders were much more likely to help than assistants: as high as 80 per cent (twelve of fifteen) leaders helped, but only 35 per cent (six of seventeen) followers did so.

Now, the leaders in this study were randomly allocated to their role, so the outcome cannot be explained in terms of their merely having a set of personal skills. In Baumeister's view, acting as a leader brings with it a generalised responsibility, which:

- goes beyond the immediate requirement of the group task to involve other external events;

- provides a buffer against the usual process of diffusion of responsibility to which ordinary members are prone, and which can mediate the seeming indifference to helping a victim.

## Research highlight 13.8
Prosocial behaviour and male-female interactions

Might men be motivated by sexual attraction to help women in trouble? Probably so, according to Benson who found that more physically attractive women received more help (Benson, Karabenick & Lerner, 1976). Przybyla (1985) clarified the effect of sexual arousal more directly. Male and female students watched either an erotic or non-erotic video, or none at all. When leaving the laboratory, they passed either a male or a female confederate who 'accidentally' knocked over a stack of papers and cried out 'oh no!' Will the passer-by help to clean up the mess? The results are shown in Figure 13.7. Almost all the males who had seen an erotic tape were motivated to

help a female. They also spent a relaxed six minutes helping a woman, but a man in need got short shrift – thirty seconds!

Przybyla noted that both men and women reported degrees of arousal when viewing the erotic tape. The more aroused the man felt, the longer he spent helping a woman, an effect not extended to another man. In contrast, the more aroused women spent less time helping anyone. It is possible that male altruism towards women is confounded with a desire to be romantic. However, women are less likely to initiate interactions with strangers (especially men), due perhaps to socialisation experiences. This is consistent with **social role theory** in accounting for cross-gender helping and has been supported in a recent study by Karakashian, Walter, Christopher & Lucas (2006).

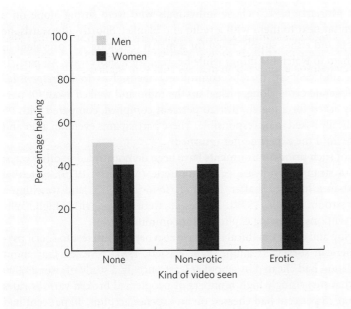

**Figure 13.7** Helping an opposite-sex stranger as a function of sexual arousal

- Male and female students watched either an erotic or non-erotic video, or none at all.
- The use of erotic material was to induce sexual arousal and explore its consequences on helping others.
- They then saw either a male or a female confederate who needed some help.
- There was one huge sex-difference: males, but not females, were very ready to help an opposite-sex stranger.

*Source*: based on data from Przybyla (1985)

a ride to a hitchhiker (Latané & Dabbs, 1975). When the person in need of such help is female, passing cars are much more likely to stop than for a man or for a male–female pair (Pomazal & Clore, 1973; West, Whitney & Schnedler, 1975). Those who stop are typically young men driving alone. A meta-analysis by Eagly and Crowley (1986) showed that the strongest combination was that of males being more helpful to women – and importantly, despite a baseline difference of women showing more empathy generally than men. Read about an interesting study that explored a connection between sexual arousal and the likelihood of helping someone of either sex who is in trouble (see Box 13.8 and Figure 13.7.)

**Social role theory**
The argument that sex differences in behaviour are determined by society rather than one's biology.

# Applied contexts

## Helping to prevent crime

An interesting line of research has focused on the causes and prevention of petty and non-violent crime, such as property theft and shoplifting, and of misdemeanours, such as classroom cheating. Preventing crime can involve a class of prosocial behaviour. The development of neighbourhood watch schemes and accompanying media campaigns are examples of the promotion of prosocial behaviour. People are most likely to engage in non-violent crime if the benefits are high and the costs are low. Fraud and tax evasion are often perceived in this way by offenders (Hassett, 1981; Lockard, Kirkevold & Kalk, 1980).

A riskier crime is property theft, which is statistically more common among younger men. As individuals mature, their assessment of the costs and benefits changes. Older people are more likely to deceive a customer or lie about a product or service than actually to steal something. However, research into property theft illustrates two important phenomena related to prosocial behaviour: responsibility and commitment.

People are most likely to be helpful to others if they have a feeling of *responsibility* for providing assistance. For example, we saw earlier that people feel responsible if they are the only witness to a crime or accident, or if they have been trained to deal with emergencies. Feeling responsible for providing aid increases the likelihood of prosocial behaviour. **Prior commitment** is a specific form of responsibility that can induce a prosocial act. In a series of real-life encounters, Moriarty (1975) chose individuals who were sitting alone on a crowded beach and then sat next to them with a radio and blanket. Shortly afterwards, he talked to the participants and either simply asked for a match (smoking was prevalent in those days!), or asked them to watch his things while he went for a short walk. All participants agreed to the second request, thereby committing themselves to be *responsible bystanders*. Then a confederate came along, picked up the radio and walked away. Of participants who were only asked for a match, just 20 per cent complied, compared with 95 per cent for those specifically asked to be responsible. These participants even ran after and grabbed the confederate until the experimenter returned!

The powerful effects of such prior commitments have been demonstrated in other ways: for example, watching a stranger's suitcase in a laundrette (Moriarty, 1975), watching another student's books in a library (Shaffer, Rogel & Hendrick, 1975) and watching a stranger's books in a classroom (Austin, 1979). The results were similar, with a high likelihood of prosocial interventions following explicit prior commitment.

Cheating, stealing, lying and other unethical acts have also been of interest to social psychologists. Massive American surveys (Gallup, 1978; Hassett, 1981) revealed that about two-thirds of the population had cheated in school at least once. In a study of over 24,000 people, Hassett found that surprisingly high numbers of people had broken various rules of ethical conduct. About 25 per cent had cheated on an expense account, 40 per cent had driven while drunk, and 65 per cent had stolen office supplies from their employers. Understanding the types of situation that can induce such behaviour or the types of people most likely to commit such acts could give clues to reduce their occurrence and even to replace them with prosocial alternatives.

## Shoplifting

Stealing goods from shops is a crime that has been of interest to psychologists investigating prosocial behaviour (Gelfand, Hartmann, Walder & Page, 1973). Bickman and Rosenbaum (1977) showed that most people would report a thief to the management, if reminded by

---

**Prior commitment**
An individual's agreement in advance to be responsible if trouble occurs: for example, committing oneself to protect the property of another person against theft.

an experimental confederate. In contrast, it is clear that posters or other mass media messages have not been effective in reducing shoplifting. It is possible that impersonal reminders such as these influence attitudes about shoplifting and about reporting thieves but do not change the behaviour itself (Bickman & Green, 1977).

A specific programme was developed to reduce shoplifting by informing people about its nature and its costs, in both financial and human terms. The most effective method for increasing prosocial interventions in shoplifting was found to be a lecture stressing how and why to report this crime and the reasons that bystanders are sometimes inhibited from taking action (Klentz & Beaman, 1981).

## Exam cheating

Are there personality correlates? Cheating in examinations has been well researched by social psychologists. In an early study, MacKinnon (1933) distinguished between cheaters and non-cheaters. He reported that cheaters more often express anger towards the task and were more destructive or aggressive in the exam room (kicking the table leg or pounding their fists on the table). On the other hand, non-cheaters more often blamed themselves for not solving the problems, tended to verbalise the problems and develop other strategies to help to solve them, and behaved more nervously and fidgeted more. Weeks later, the students were asked if they had cheated. Those who had not cheated readily said so; those who had cheated either denied it or admitted it but said they felt no guilt about it. Further, such guilt feelings appeared to be a critical variable in determining whether a person cheated or not: 84 per cent of the non-cheaters said they would feel guilty if they were to cheat. Those who did not cheat reported the most guilt at the thought of cheating; those who had cheated reported the least guilt. MacKinnon assumed that cheating was dispositional – a personality characteristic that was inherent in a 'cheater'.

Later studies pursued links between cheating and personality. Students who cheat tend to be low in the ability to delay gratification (Yates & Mischel, 1979), high in sociopathic tendencies (Lueger, 1980), high in the need for approval (Milham, 1974), low in interpersonal trust (Rotter, 1980), high in chronic self-destructive tendencies (Kelley et al., 1985), low in adherence to the work ethic and in the desire to perform tasks industriously (Eisenberger & Shank, 1985), and high in the belief that transgressions are not automatically punished (Karniol, 1982). Despite these findings, correlations for the general population are typically modest, suggesting that situational factors are more important, which may be just as well if remedial measures are to be found.

One short-term situational effect is *arousal* – a feeling of excitement or a thrill from taking a chance. Why not cheat, at least when there is little chance of being caught (Scitovsky, 1980)?

Lueger (1980) approached arousal differently: it is distracting and makes us less able to regulate our behaviour. In his study, participants saw either an arousing film or a relaxing one and then had the chance to cheat while taking a test. In the relaxed condition 43 per cent cheated, but in the aroused condition 70 per cent cheated. Warning students about to sit an exam of the penalties for being caught cheating paradoxically may increase cheating (Heisler, 1974), perhaps because they are also more aroused. Much of this research has pursued ways of *discouraging cheating*. A traditional reaction has been to increase the severity of punishments available. However, one estimate is that only about one in five self-reported cheaters are ever caught (Gallup, 1978).

Consider again MacKinnon's (1933) study: perhaps something that increases feelings of guilt may lead to a decrease in cheating? People usually agree that cheating is wrong, and those who do cheat disapprove as strongly as those who do not (Hughes, 1981). Some institutions have introduced programmes to raise the ethical awareness of their pupils and to

**Cheating**
Given the opportunity would you take a peek at your neighbour's exam script?

promote prosocial behaviour in various ways (see Britell, 1981; Dienstbier, Kahle, Willis & Tunnell, 1980). Dienstbier et al.'s study reported some success by focusing less on students' assumed lack of morality and more on how to make ethical standards salient. Similarly, reducing student cheating by activating socially approved norms of academic honesty continues to show promise as an intervention in recent experimental work (Lonsbary, 2007).

In summary, many people readily confess all kinds of occasional, unethical or illegal behaviour. Non-violent crimes such as fraud, tax evasion, insurance scams, shoplifting and exam cheating, which may have serious consequences for others, are prevalent in our society. Social psychologists sometimes work in these fields, seeking not only causes but also solutions, such as devising advertising campaigns, community interventions and deterrents based on surveillance techniques.

## A health support network

**Social support network**
People who know and care about us and who can provide back-up during a time of stress.

The use of the term 'victim' so often in this chapter reaches out to another field, the function of a **social support network**. We look at just one example from this extensive literature, a study by Dakof and Taylor (1990) dealing with cancer patients. A victimising event such as cancer has profound effects on how significant others (family, friends, workmates, medical staff) might interact with a patient: an initial reaction of aversion can give way to a façade projecting good cheer. Not surprisingly, the victim can feel stigmatised and

**A social support network**
Surrounding yourself with others who care can help you cope with life's trials and tribulations

unwanted. Dakof and Taylor argued that the reactions of members of a support network are moderated by the nature of the relationship that people have with the victim and, in a wider sense, by the cultural constraints imposed on social interactions. In most nuclear families, those close to a cancer victim are more likely to be overprotective than withdrawing. Their study concentrated on how a victim views the nature of help and how this interacts with its source.

Their participants were fifty-five cancer patients, mostly Whites, in Los Angeles. In terms of the source of help, patients generally valued as helpful acts by intimate providers (family, friends) that related to the victim's self-esteem and emotional support, such as concern, empathy and affection. In contrast, the acts of medical staff and other cancer patients that patients viewed as helpful were informational and tangible support, such as prognosis and technical or medical care. When either group stepped out of the appropriate role, the act became misguided and unhelpful. In the case of nursing staff, acts considered helpful tended to be those that were closer to the acts appreciated among people intimate to the victim.

# Receiving help

We have based this chapter around the psychology of the 'helper': when will we help, why do we hesitate, and how can we improve the rate of helping in our community? There is another angle that we should consider. Does the recipient always want help? Just as we have noted that there can be psychological costs in helping (Piliavin et al., 1981), does this extend to the person who is thought to need help? Nadler (1986, 1991) believes that it does. Western society encourages people to be self-reliant and to achieve as individuals. To ask for help, then, confronts people with a dilemma: the benefits of being aided are tempered by the costs of appearing dependent on others. In a study in Israel, Nadler (1986) introduced a sociocultural dimension to this issue by comparing the help-seeking tendencies of *kibbutz* dwellers with those of city dwellers. People in *kibbutzim* are socialised to cherish collectivism, and they sought help on a difficult task only when they thought the performance of their group as a whole was to be compared with other groups. However, Israeli city people are typically Western and individualistic, and sought help only when they thought their individual performance was to be compared with other individuals. (For details of this research, see Chapter 16, particularly Figure 16.4 and Box 16.4.)

Relative to studies of people who act prosocially, the responses of those who receive help have not been well researched. Most acts of help in our day-to-day lives do not involve strangers. Rather, they take place in ongoing relationships between partners and close relations. The recipient will make attributions about the helper's motives and interpret the help given in terms of what it means to the relationship: for example: 'my partner is wonderful!' or 'you can always count on Mum!' In a series of studies, Ames and his colleagues concluded that when we receive help we attend 'to help from the heart (*affect*), from the head (*cost–benefit*), or by the book (*roles*)' (Ames, Flynn & Weber, 2004, p. 472). In all of these cases, prosocial acts nourish a relationship and help to define the identities of those involved.

# Norms, motives and volunteering

## Norms for helping

Often we help others simply because 'something tells us' we should. We ought to help that little old lady cross the street, return a wallet we found, help a crying child. An important influence on developing and sustaining prosocial behaviour is a cultural norm. **Norms** provide a background influence on human behaviour (see Chapter 7) and are quintessentially learned rather than innate. A norm is a standard of action that specifies what is expected, 'normal' or proper.

Almost every culture has a norm that concern for others is good and that selfishness is bad. An unwritten rule is that when the cost is not very great and another person is in need, we should help. If a norm of social responsibility is universal, it indicates that it is functional and that it facilitates social life. One way to account for why we help others, therefore, is to say that it is *normative*. There are social rewards for behaving in accord with the norm and sanctions for violating the norm. Sanctions may range from mild disapproval to incarceration or worse, depending on the threat posed to the existing social order.

Two specific norms have been proposed as a basis for altruism:

1 *The reciprocity norm* – we should help those who help us. It is that this norm, also referred to as the **reciprocity principle**, is as universal as the incest taboo (Gouldner, 1960). However, the extent to which we should reciprocate varies. We feel deeply indebted when someone freely makes a big sacrifice for us but much less so if what they do is smaller and expected (Tesser, Gatewood & Driver, 1968). Further, people might give help only in return for help given in the past or anticipated in the future (see the concept of social exchange in Chapter 14). People driven by egoism are more likely to act prosocially when they believe their reputations are at stake (Simpson & Willer, 2008).

2 The **social responsibility norm**. We should give help freely to those in need without regard to future exchanges. Members of a community are often willing to help the needy, even when they remain anonymous donors and do not expect any social reward

## Marginal glossary

**Norms**
Attitudinal and behavioural uniformities that define group membership and differentiate between groups.

**Reciprocity principle**
The law of 'doing unto others as they do to you'. It can refer to an attempt to gain compliance by first doing someone a favour, or to mutual aggression or mutual attraction.

**Social responsibility norm**
The idea that we should help people who are dependent and in need. It is contradicted by another norm that discourages interfering in other people's lives.

(Berkowitz, 1972b). In practice, people usually apply this norm selectively, e.g. to those in need through no fault of their own rather than to callers at the front door. The extent to which people internalise as a norm beliefs about the future of our planet has been linked to environmental activism (Fielding, McDonald & Louis, 2008; Stern, Dietz & Guagnano, 1995).

Neither norm can realistically explain prosocial behaviour in animals (Stevens, Cushman & Hauser, 2005). If reciprocity applies to humans then it is distinctive to humans; and there is no room for a social responsibility norm in animals.

Teger (1970) has suggested that a norm of helping is often endorsed verbally but is really an ideal rather than actual behaviour, and even then it is not a very compelling force. As an ideal norm, the prosocial ethic is an expression of people paying lip service to being responsible citizens. When and why do people actually adhere to these norms? Situational variables covered later in this chapter give us an insight.

## The keys to being helpful

Batson has argued that what prompts helping is a question of motivation, and motives involve goals. Is the action an *instrumental goal,* and intermediate step on the way to a person's ultimate self-interest? Or is it an *ultimate goal* in its own right, with any self-benefit as an unintended side effect? We summarise his ideas in Box 13.9.

Some remain unconvinced that a true altruism exists and that so-called examples are forms of egoism. However, both collectivism and principlism allow us to view some prosocial behaviour as acting for the common good – for example, in the context of the **commons dilemma** (see Chapter 11).

**Commons dilemma**
Social dilemma in which cooperation by all benefits all, but competition by all harms all.

## Volunteers: the ultimate helpers

Many people now take an interest in another form of spontaneous helping – volunteering, an activity that has become more and more important for the common good in times of government retrenchment (Wilson, 2000). Gil Clary and Mark Snyder have noted that, for a community to retain a high level of volunteering, it must earmark situations and opportunities and enhance a sense of personal control among the volunteers. (Clary & Snyder, 1991, 1999). Volunteers commonly offer to others a sense of community, or civic

---

### Theory and concepts 13.9
#### Four motives for helping others

His research over many years has led Batson to conclude that four motives control prosocial behaviour. How often we help, and the various ways that we might help, depend on one of the following:

1  **Egoism**: Prosocial acts benefits one's self. We may help others to secure material, social and self-reward; and to escape punishment.

2  **Altruism**: Prosocial acts contribute to the welfare of others. Acting altruistically does not imply that

someone should reciprocate. This kind of prosocial motivation is esteemed in many cultures.

3  **Collectivism**: Prosocial acts contribute to the welfare of a social group, e.g one's family, ethnic group or country. Of course, actions that benefit one's ingroup may harm an outgroup (see Chapter 11).

4  **Principlism**: Prosocial acts follow a moral principle, such as 'the greatest good for the greatest number'. Although the link between moral reasoning and prosocial behaviour is not strong, the two processes are at least related (Underwood & Moore, 1982).

*Source:* based on Batson, 1994; Batson, Ahmad, & Tsang, 2002

participation (Omoto & Snyder, 2002). This can show itself by being a companion for the elderly, counselling troubled people, tutoring the illiterate, making home visits to the terminally ill through the hospice movement, or acting as a support person for AIDS victims. In the United States in 1998, more than one million people gave 3.5 hours per week acting in these and similar ways. Mark Davis and his colleagues have shown that voluntary activities that entail some distress, which is an example of a response invoking empathy discussed earlier, require well-designed training programmes to prepare the volunteer (Davis, Hall & Meyer, 2003). Sometimes the idea of volunteering involves high-profile individuals who can and have done much good for many people. The humanitarian gestures of Bob Geldof, the founder of Live Aid, and of Bono spring to mind. We must add that even what is arguably the noblest of motives, altruism, continues to be questioned. Is it real? Even volunteers, it seems, may in some senses be self-serving.

Batson allows that community involvement can be driven by an egoistic motive (Batson, Ahmad & Tsang, 2002), but argues that it is just one of four, as we have discussed earlier; and that all four have both strengths and weaknesses. In recruiting volunteers, an effective strategy is to steer them to supplement egoism with additional reasons based on altruism, principlism, or both. Evert van der Vliert and his colleagues also pointed other very broad features, not located with the person as such, that affect whether egoism or altruism comes into play. In a cross-cultural comparison of volunteers in thirty-three countries, they found the two motives can be separated in some countries but not in others. The picture they paint is complex. Put simply, the weight given to each motive depends on a country's ecology (the climate) and its overall wealth (van der Vliert, Huang & Levine, 2004).

## Concluding thought

In closing, let us reflect on what we have covered in this and the preceding chapter. We have seen that both brutal and charitable aspects of humanity – hurting others versus helping others – entail strong physical reactions that are rooted in our biology. There are ways that we can reduce aggression and promote prosocial behaviour. Moreover, acting in ways that contribute to the common good can be learned and, more importantly, entrenched as social norms. One thing that social psychologists can do is to spread this message.

# Summary

- Prosocial behaviour is a broad category that refers to all acts positively valued by society, including helping and altruistic behaviour. Helping behaviour refers to intentional acts designed to benefit another person. Altruistic behaviour refers to behaviour motivated by the desire to benefit another with no expectation of personal gain or reward. It is difficult to identify purely altruistic behaviour because motives or rewards may not be observable.

- The Kitty Genovese murder stimulated and heavily influenced the entire field of understanding prosocial behaviour in humans, and research into bystander intervention specifically.

- Two major accounts of the origin and nature of prosocial behaviour in humans stand in contrast. One is biological and is derived from evolutionary theory. The other is social and is based on reinforcement principles, with an added feature of modelling. Most social psychologists reject too heavy an emphasis on the biological approach.

- A third account is more integrative, featuring arousal, empathy and a cost–benefit analysis.

- Research into helping in an emergency highlighted the bystander effect: aid is more likely when just a solitary bystander is present. Situational factors are important determinants in the context of an emergency.

- Research into the individual attributes of helpers has presented a mixed picture. Personality correlates of helping are weak. However, people's mood, attachment style and competence can have considerable influence in some contexts.

- Other strands of research on prosocial behaviour touch on gender roles, preventing or reporting theft or shoplifting, and examination cheating.

- A less well-researched area deals with how a recipient interprets a prosocial act. This points to an overlooked subject: most help is actually given to people we know, and our actions contribute to how the relationship is defined.

- Important issues in research and theory include the guiding effect of social norms and the relevance of fundamental motives, such as principlism. There is also an increased public awareness of the work of volunteers.

## Literature, film and TV

### Schindler's Ark

Thomas Keneally's 1982 novel about how Otto Schindler, a German living in Cracow during the Second World War, took enormous risks to save Jews from the gas chambers of Auschwitz. The book was made into a 1993 film called *Schindler's List*, directed by Stephen Spielberg, and starring Liam Neeson and Ben Kingsley.

### The Girl in the Café

Although this 2005 film by David Yates, starring Bill Nighy and Kelly Macdonald, is largely a gentle love story it also has a sharper subtext. The setting is the 2005 G8 meeting in Reykjavik at which decisions were to be made about helping the developing world out of poverty. The film illustrates how difficult it can be to engineer collective prosocial behaviour.

### The Trial

Franz Kafka's prophetic 1935 novel about being trapped in a monstrous bureaucratic system where it is rare to encounter a real human being, and no one and nothing seems to be designed to help you. A world devoid of prosocial behaviour.

### Amélie

2001 French romantic comedy by Jean-Pierre Jeunet and starring Audrey Tautou. The film is a wonderfully whimsical and idealised depiction of contemporary Parisian life, set in Montmartre. Amélie is a young waitress whose life is directionless until she finds an old box of childhoood memorabilia that she is determined to return to its owner, now a grown man. She makes a deal with herself in the process; if she finds him and it makes him glad, she will devote her life to goodness and doing good.

### Pay it Forward

2000 'feel-good' film by Mimi Leder, with Kevin Spacey and Helen Hunt. A small boy, played by Haley Joel Osment, takes the opportunity to make the world a better place, by starting a chain where people do an altruistic act for three other people, and each of them does it to another three, and so forth.

### Secret Millionaire

A popular TV reality showed first aired in 2006 in the UK. Millionaires go incognito to live like locals in impoverished communities – they identify worthy projects and individuals to donate tens of thousands of pounds of their own fortune to. On their final day the millionaires come clean and reveal their identity to the lucky people they have chosen – lots of joy and tears ensue.

### The Bonfire of the Vanities and Wall Street

*The Bonfire of the Vanities* is the classic 1987 novel by Tom Wolfe. Set in the New York financial world of the 1980s, it is a powerful novel about greed, selfishness and unfettered personal ambition – the very antithesis of prosocial or altruistic behaviour. It was adapted into an eponymous 1990 film directed by Brian de Palma, and starring Tom Hanks, Bruce Willis and Melanie Griffiths. A better film in the same vein is *Wall Street* – written and directed by Oliver Stone, and starring Michael Douglas. This is the 1987 classic that brought us 'master of the universe' Gordon Gecko and his credo 'greed is good' – a credo that was an anthem of the 1980s, but is clearly alive and well in the 2000s.

# Guided Questions

**1** How has evolutionary theory influenced social psychology's approach to understanding the origins of altruism?

**2** What is *empathy* and how is it related to helping others who are in need?

**3** Is there evidence that children can learn to be helpful?

**4** What factors in the situation, or what kinds of individual differences between potential helpers, would increase the chances of help being given to a child who is being bullied? See some relevant examples in Chapter 13 of MyPsychLab at **www.mypsychlab.co.uk** (watch *Prosocial behaviour*).

**5** What advice could a social psychologist give to a school board to help reduce exam cheating?

## Learn more

Batson, C. D. (1998). Altruism and prosocial behaviour. In D. T. Gilbert, S. T. Fiske & G. Lindzey (eds), *The handbook of social psychology* (4th ed., Vol. 2, pp. 282–316). New York: McGraw-Hill. Authoritative overview of the field of prosocial behaviour – the most recent fifth edition of the handbook does not have a chapter on prosocial behaviour.

Batson, C. D., Van Lange, P. A. M., Ahmad, N., & Lishner, D. A. (2007). Altruism and helping behavior. In M. A. Hogg & J. Cooper (eds), *The SAGE handbook of social psychology: Concise student edition* (pp. 241–58). London: SAGE. Comprehensive, up-to-date and easily accessible overview of research on altruism and prosocial behaviour.

Clark, M. S. (ed.) (1991). *Prosocial behavior*. Newbury Park, CA: SAGE. A collection of chapters by major theorists who played a significant role in developing the social psychology of helping behaviour.

Eisenberg, N., & Mussen, P. H. (1989). *The roots of prosocial behaviour in children*. Cambridge, UK: Cambridge University Press. A concise introduction to the socialisation of prosocial behaviour in children, and its connection to moral reasoning.

Rose, H., & Rose, S. (2000). *Alas, poor Darwin: Arguments against evolutionary psychology*. London: Vintage. Scholars from a variety of biological, philosophical and social science backgrounds raise concerns about the adequacy of genetic accounts of social behaviour, including altruism.

Schroeder, D. A., Penner, L. A., Dovidio, J. F., & Piliavin, J. A. (1995). *The psychology of helping and altruism*. New York: McGraw-Hill. A good general overview of the literature dealing with prosocial behaviour.

Snyder, M., & Omoto, A. M. (2007). Social action. In A. W. Kruglanski & E. T. Higgins (eds), *Social psychology: Handbook of basic principles* (2nd ed., pp. 940–61). New York: Guilford Press. A comprehensive, up-to-date and detailed discussion of collective prosocial behaviour – how people can come together to do good.

Spacapan, S., & Oskamp, S. (eds) (1992). *Helping and being helped*. Newbury Park, CA: SAGE. The contributors deal with a wide range of real-life helping behaviour; including kidney donation, spouse support of stroke patients, and family support for people with Alzheimer's disease.

 Refresh your understanding, assess your progress and go further with interactive summaries, questions, podcasts and much more at **www.mypsychlab.co.uk**

# This chapter discusses

- How attraction evolved
- The appealing body
- Contextual cues and attraction
- Culture intervenes
- Rewards and costs in selecting a mate
- Why we get attached
- Liking and loving
- Close relationships and well-being
- Marriage: love or a contract?
- Relationships that work
- Ending a relationship

# Focus questions

1. Carol finds David more attractive than Paul but bumps into him less often. Who do you think Carol is most likely to get to like and perhaps have a relationship with?

2. Erik and Charles have been chatting over a few drinks when Erik remarks that he is 'profiting' from his latest romantic relationship. Charles doesn't know what to say, but thinks this a callous comment. Can you offer a more benign interpretation?

3. Even when they were dating, Kamesh felt that Aishani was mostly uncomfortable when they were with other people. She also avoided having other members of their families visit them. Now, Aishani does not seem very interested in their new baby. Are these events somehow connected?

will use which involves getting you to decide to buy a car by giving you a very low price

Go to **mypsychlab** to explore video and test your understanding of key topics addressed in this chapter.

4. Can we study love scientifically – or should we pack the statistics away and leave it to the poets? Robert Sternberg discusses his general approach and the main components of his triangular theory of love in Chapter 14 of MyPsychLab at **www.mypsychlab.co.uk**.

Refresh your understanding with interactive summaries, explore topics further with video and audio clips and assess your progress with quick test and essay questions by logging on to the accompanying website at **www.mypsychlab.co.uk**

# Chapter 14
## Attraction and close relationships

## Key terms

Archival research
Assortative mating
Attachment behaviour
Attachment styles
Automatic activation
Averageness effect
Behaviourism
Big Five
Commitment
Comparison level

Consummate love
Cost–reward ratio
Distributive justice
Emotion-in-relationships model
Equity theory
Evolutionary social psychology
Familiarity
Hospitalism
Instinct
Love
Mere exposure effect
Meta-analysis
Minimax strategy

Need to affiliate
Partner regulation
Procedural justice
Profit
Proximity
Reinforcement–affect model
Relationship dissolution model
Self-disclosure
Self-regulation
Similarity of attitudes
Social comparison (theory)
Social exchange
Three-factor theory of love

Collectively we are known as the species *Homo sapiens* – wise, knowing and judicious humans. Given the modern interest in the nature of cognition – how we think – this description might seem apt, but it is barely half the story. We live as social beings. We love and help, hate and fight. This chapter deals with the liking and the loving part, and more fundamentally with why we want to be with others. Perhaps there is a term missing from our dictionary: *Homo socius* – humans who can be allies, friends and partners. We start with the process of attraction, then take a step back to explore the reasons why we affiliate (i.e. choose the company) with and become attached to others, and ask the perennial question 'What is love?' We conclude with how our most intimate relationships can be maintained and what happens when they break down.

## Attractive people

We just *know* when we are attracted to someone. We are allured, perhaps charmed, captivated, even enthralled. We want to know and spend time with that person. At one level, attraction is necessary for friendships of any kind to begin, though many first meetings are by chance. At another level, attraction can be the precursor to an intimate relationship. Do you believe in love at first sight?

Perhaps you subscribe to other popular sayings such as: *never judge a book by its cover, beauty is only skin deep,* and *beauty is in the eye of the beholder.* Unfortunately for some of us, there is evidence that the primary cue in evaluating others is how they look. A systematic **meta-analysis** of more than one hundred studies by Langlois and her colleagues (2000) found that these sayings are myths rather than maxims. As a cautionary note, the overall impact of the findings is reduced because some studies focus on just two categories – the attractive and the unattractive. Bearing this in mind, Langlois et al. concluded that attractive people are different from those who are unattractive in how they are judged, how they are treated and how they behave. Here are some of the major findings:

**Meta-analysis**
Statistical procedure that combines data from different studies to measure the overall reliability and strength of specific effects.

- Attractive children received higher grades from their teachers, showed higher levels of intellectual competence, and were more popular and better adjusted than their unattractive counterparts.

- Attractive adults were more successful in their jobs, liked more, more physically healthy and more sexually experienced than unattractive adults. They had had more dates, held more traditional attitudes, had more self-confidence and self-esteem, and had slightly higher intelligence and mental health.

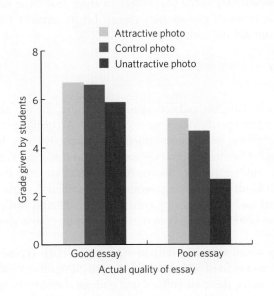

**Figure 14.1**  Being attractive can lead to better essay grades

*Source:* based on data from Landy & Sigall (1974)

We can add more to the advantages of having good looks:

- If you are female, babies will gaze longer (Slater et al., 1998)!

- In computer-simulation studies, attractiveness is associated with some feminisation of facial features, even for male faces (Rhodes, Hickford & Jeffrey, 2000), and with having a slimmer figure (Gardner & Tockerman, 1994);

- An attractive person is a youthful person (Buss & Kenrick, 1998), is judged as more honest (Yarmouk, 2000), and, if a female defendant, gets an easier time from jurors (Sigall & Ostrove, 1975).

We have noted that attractive children receive higher grades than unattractive children. Landy and Sigall (1974) studied the last effect experimentally in university students, asking the question 'Does beauty signal talent?' Male students graded one or other of two essays of different quality, attached to which was a photograph of the supposed writer, a female student. The same essays were also rated by control participants, but without any photograph. The 'good' and 'poor' essays were paired in turn with either an attractive photograph or a relatively unattractive photograph. The answer to the researchers' question was 'yes' – sad to relate, better grades were given to the attractive female student (see Figure 14.1).

With attractiveness being such an asset, those who spend big on cosmetics and fashion could be making a real investment in their future! Short of this, just a smile can also work wonders. Forgas, O'Connor and Morris (1983) found that students who smile are punished less after a misdemeanour than those who do not.

# Evolution and attraction

Evolutionary theory, derived in the main from Charles Darwin, has helped by teasing out biological factors that trigger aggression, altruism and the emotions (see Chapters 12, 13 and 15). It has also offered insights that can help us understand some aspects of why we are attracted to some people, and how we might go about choosing a long-term partner. In an

**Evolutionary social psychology**
An extension of evolutionary psychology that views complex social behaviour as adaptive, helping the individual, kin and the species as a whole to survive.

extreme form, Buss (2003) used **evolutionary social psychology** to argue that close relationships can only be understood in terms of evolutionary theory. Let us consider what modern research has told us about our natural endowment.

## The role of our genes

In the large-scale analysis of studies by Langlois and colleagues cited above, the way that interpersonal attraction develops is related partly to how we select a mate. According to the evolutionary concept of *reproductive fitness,* people guess whether a prospective mate has good genes, using cues such as physical health, youthful appearance, and body and facial symmetry. Good looks can also help, since attractive children receive extra care from their parents. Humans can respond to all kinds of cues – e.g., women who sniffed T-shirts of unknown origin preferred those that had been worn by symmetrical men! And further, according to Gangstead and Simpson (2000) this was even more likely among those about to ovulate!

As you know, males 'have a thing' about women's waist-to-hip ratio (WHR). Typically, men prefer the classic hourglass figure (a ratio of 0.70), probably because it signifies youthfulness, good health and fertility. However, there are cultural and ecological effects: in foraging societies, being thin may mean being ill and so men prefer their women to be heavier (i.e. larger WHRs). In Western societies, where heaviness may indicate ill health, men prefer slimmer women (i.e smaller WHRs) (Marlowe & Wetsman, 2001). These effects point to the role of social and contextual factors that go beyond a genetic account.

## Attractive faces

As well as acknowledging the role of biological explanation, Langlois et al. (2000) also tested the validity of three well-known maxims: *beauty is in the eye of the beholder, never judge a book by its cover,* and *beauty is only skin-deep.* These question the assumption that physical beauty is ultimately important in real-life decisions, implying that social factors must play some part in how relationships are formed. For example, socialisation theory emphasises the effects on judgements of beauty of social and cultural norms and of experience; and social expectancy theory argues that social stereotypes (see Chapter 2) create their own reality.

How would evolutionary theory deal with the maxim *beauty is in the eye of the beholder?* Is physical attractiveness a matter of personal preference, or of fashion in a particular society and its history, or is it something else – in our genes? As part of her research programme dealing with face perception, Gill Rhodes (2006) has extensively researched the social information that our faces convey, including the cues that make a face attractive. One interesting finding is the 'pulling power' of the **averageness effect** (see Box 14.1 and Figure 14.2).

**Averageness effect**
Humans have evolved to prefer average faces to those with unusual or distinctive features.

## The search for ideals

There are other characteristics of being attractive may derive *in part* from our genes. Garth Fletcher (Fletcher et al., 2004; also see Buss, 2003) studied the ideals (or standards) that college students look for in a partner. In long-term relationships, three 'ideal partner' dimensions appear to guide the preferences of both men and women:

- warmth–trustworthiness – showing care and intimacy;
- vitality–attractiveness – signs of health and reproductive fitness;
- status–resources – being socially prominent and financially sound.

## Research highlight 14.1
### Physical appeal – evolutionary or cultural?

What kind of face do we prefer? The preferences of very young children and a high degree of cross-cultural agreement challenge the notion that standards of beauty are dictated by culture. For example, body and facial *symmetry* (of right and left halves) in both women and men contributes to standards that most people have in judging beauty. Perhaps surprisingly, facial *averageness* is another plus.

Rhodes (2006), who has researched extensively how we process information about the human face, asked whether facial beauty depends more on common physical qualities than on striking features. Participants judged caricatures of faces, each of which was systematically varied from average to distinctive. She found that averageness, rather than distinctiveness, was correlated with facial attractiveness (see also Rhodes, Sumich & Byatt, 1999). The averageness effect has also been confirmed in other studies (e.g Langlois, Roggman & Musselman, 1994).

Rhodes (Rhodes & Tremewan, 1996) suggested an evolutionary basis for this effect: average faces draw the attention of infants to those objects in their environment that most resemble the human face – an average face is like a prototype. Face preferences may be adaptations that guide mate choice. Why would facial averageness (and also facial symmetry) make a person more attractive? One possibility is that these cues make a face seem more familiar and less strange. Another possibility is that both averageness and symmetry are signals of good health and therefore of 'good genes'– cues that we latch on to in searching for a potential mate.

See Figure 14.2 for examples of how averageness has been created by combining sets of real faces into composite faces.

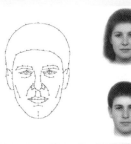    

**Figure 14.2** What makes a face attractive?
- Landmark points were used to align features across individual photographs.
- Face composites were created by averaging the features of 24 real faces.
- These four faces are composites and are usually rated as more attractive than a real individual face.

*Source*: Rhodes (2006)

A fair conclusion is that the physicality of the human is a major cue to initial attraction and that there is an evolutionary and universal basis for some of this. Let us turn now to a number of social and contextual factors also related to what we find attractive.

# What increases liking?

Suppose that someone has passed your initial 'attraction' test. What other factors encourage you to take another step? This question has been well researched and points to several crucial factors that determine how we come to like people even more:

- Proximity – do they live or work close by?
- Familiarity – do we feel that we know them?
- Similarity – are they people who are like us?

**Proximity**

Chatting with neighbours in the street is an important form of social interaction. It increases mutual liking and also promotes the willingness to be cooperative

## Proximity

**Proximity**

The factor of living close by is known to play an important role in the early stages of forming a friendship.

There is a good chance that you will get to like people who are in a reasonable **proximity** to where you live or work — think of this as the neighbourhood factor. In a famous study of a student housing complex led by Leon Festinger (who is also associated with the concept of cognitive dissonance discussed in Chapter 6), it emerged that people were more likely to choose as friends those living in the same building and even on the same floor (Festinger, Schachter & Back, 1950). Subtle architectural features, such as the location of a staircase, can also affect the process of making acquaintances and establishing friendships.

Look at the apartment block in Figure 14.3. Of the lower-floor residents, those in apartments 1 and 5 interacted most often with people living on the upper floor. Note that the residents in apartments 1 and 5 are close to the staircases used by upper-floor residents and are therefore more likely to encounter them. Friendships occurred more often between 1 and 6 than between 2 and 7; and likewise between 5 and 10 than between 4 and 9. Although the physical distance between residents within each pair is the same, the interaction rate varied: becoming acquainted depended on the traffic flow.

People who live close by are *accessible,* so that interacting with them requires little effort and the rewards of doing so have little cost. Consider your immediate neighbours: you expect to continue interacting with them and it is better that you are at ease when you do so rather than feeling stressed.

If at the outset you think that you are more likely to interact with John rather than Brian it is probable that you will anticipate (perhaps hope!) that you will like John more

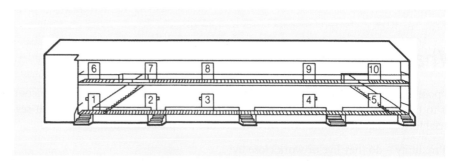

**Figure 14.3**   Friendship choice, physical proximity and housing design

*Source:* based on Festinger, Schachter & Back (1950)

## Real world 14.2
### Meeting on the net

Access to a computer and the Internet allows people to meet, form friendships, fall in love, live together or get married. A cyberspace relationship does not necessarily stop there, and some online friends actually meet.

In cyberspace, traditional variables that you would find interesting about someone else are often missing, such as seeing, hearing and touching them. Even so, cyber-relationships can progress rapidly from knowing little about the other person to being intimate; equally, they can be ended very quickly, literally with the 'click of a button'.

From the outset, Internet-mediated relationships differ markedly from offline relationships. A first meeting via the Internet does not give access to the usual range of physical and spoken linguistic cues that help to form an impression, unless the use of digital cameras to exchange images and live video over the Internet increases.

Jacobson (1999) investigated impression formation in comparing online expectation with offline experiences: that is, when people who had met online actually met in person. He found significant discrepancies – people had often formed erroneous impressions about characteristics such as talkativeness ('they seemed so quiet in person') and expansiveness ('they seemed so terse online but were very expressive offline'). People online often constructed images based on stereotypes, such as the vocation of the unseen person. One participant reported:

I had no idea what to expect with Katya. From her descriptions I got the impression she would be overweight, kinda hackerish, but when we met, I found her very attractive. Normal sized, nice hair, not at all the stereotypical programmer. (*Jacobson, 1999, p. 13*)

(Berscheid, Graziano, Monson, & Dermer, 1976). In the first focus question, who will Carol like more, David or Paul?

Proximity became a hazier psychological concept during the twentieth century. The potentially negative impact of having a 'long-distance lover' is lessened by a phone call, an email, or better still by video contact such as 'skyping' (see the review by Bargh & McKenna, 2004). Can we actually pursue a relationship on the net? (See Box 14.2.)

## Familiarity

Proximity generally leads to greater familiarity – a friend is rather like your favourite pair of shoes, something that you feel comfortable about. **Familiarity** can account for why we gradually come to like the faces of strangers if we encounter them more often (Moreland & Beach, 1992). In contrast, when something familiar seems different, people feel uncomfortable. For example, people do not usually like mirror reversals of photos of their own or others' faces (Mita, Dermer & Knight, 1977).

Further, Zajonc (1968) found that familiarity enhances liking just as repeatedly presenting stimuli increases liking for them – the basic **mere exposure effect** as used by advertisers to have us feel familiar with new products (see the effect of repetitive advertising in Chapter 6). In a classroom setting, Moreland and Beach (1992) found that students rated another new 'student' (actually, collaborating with the investigators) as more attractive the more often they saw her (see Figure 14.4). If you want to be liked, be around!

**Familiarity**
As we become more familiar with a stimulus (even another person), we feel more comfortable with it and we like it more.

**Mere exposure effect**
Repeated exposure to an object results in greater attraction to that object.

## Similarity

There are other important psychological factors that exert some control over attraction. In an early study by Theodore Newcomb (1961), students received rent-free housing in return for filling in questionnaires before they arrived about their attitudes and values. Changes

**Figure 14.4** Mere exposure and attraction

- This study tested the 'mere exposure' effect in a university class setting.
- Four new women 'students' took part in the class on 0, 5, 10 or 15 occasions.
- At the end of term, students in the class rated slides of the women for several characteristics.
- There was a weak effect for familiarity but a strong and increasing effect across visits for attractiveness.

*Source:* based on Moreland & Beach (1992)

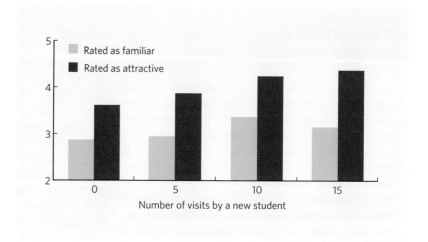

in interpersonal attraction were measured over the course of a semester. Initially, attraction went hand-in-hand with proximity – students liked those who lived close by. Then another factor came into play: having compatible attitudes.

## Similarity of attitudes

**Similarity of attitudes**
A powerful and positive determinant of attraction.

Newcomb found that, as the semester progressed, the focus shifted to **similarity of attitudes**. Students with similar pre-acquaintance attitudes became more attractive. This is logical, because in real life it usually takes some time to discover whether or not a house-mate thinks and feels in the same way about a variety of social issues.

Byrne and Clore have carried out extensive research dealing with the connection between sharing attitudes with another person and liking them (e.g. Byrne, 1971; Clore & Byrne, 1974). Attitudes that were markedly similar were an important ingredient in maintaining a relationship. The results were so reliable and consistent that Clore (1976) formulated a 'law of attraction' – attraction towards a person bears a linear relationship to the actual proportion of similar attitudes shared with that person. This law was thought to be applicable to more than just attitudes. Anything that other people do that agrees with your perception of things is rewarding, i.e. reinforcing. The more other people agree, the more they act as reinforcers for you and the more you like them. For example, if you suddenly discover that someone you are going out with likes the same obscure rock band as you, your liking for that person will increase.

Conversely, differences in attitudes and interests can lead to avoidance and dislike (Singh & Ho, 2000). The notion that we should be consistent in our thinking, as stressed in the theory of cognitive dissonance (see Chapter 4), may explain this. An inconsistency, such as recognising that we like something but that someone else does not, is cause for worry. A way to resolve this is to not like that person and re-establish consistency. Thus we usually choose or preserve the company of similar others – it makes us feel comfortable.

## Social matching

There is an extensive interest devoted to match-making where people are paired up based on having compatible attitudes, but also on sharing demographic characteristics that we discuss further below. But even a seemingly trivial similarity such as one's name can

## Research highlight 14.3
### What's in a name? A search in the marriage archives

Marriage records that included the names of brides and grooms were downloaded from the website 'Ancestry. com', dating back to the nineteenth century. Several common names were focused on: Smith, Johnson, Williams, Jones and Brown. The researchers predicted that people would seek out others who simply resemble them, and found that people disproportionately married someone whose first or last name resembles their own. It seems that we are egotists at heart. Someone who is similar enough to activate mental associations with 'me' must be a fairly good choice!

In some initial experimental work, the researchers found that people were more attracted to someone with: (a) a random experimental code number (such as

a PIN number) resembling their own birth date, (b) a surname containing letters from their own surname, and (c) a number on a sports jersey that had been paired subliminally, on a computer screen, with their own name.

These results prompted them to carry out an *archival study* of marriage among people with matching surnames. They found the most frequent choices of a marriage partner had the same last name. More than 60 per cent of the Smiths married another Smith, more than 50 per cent of the Joneses married another Jones, and more than 40 per cent of the Williamses married another Williams. All of these choices were well beyond chance.

We can note with passing interest that the senior researcher is named John Jones!

*Source*: based on Jones, Pelham, Carvallo & Mirenberg (2004, Study 2)

increase attraction. See the study by Jones et al. (2004) using an **archival research** method in Box 14.3, and Figure 14.5.

## Assortative mating

Life is not a lucky dip. People seeking a partner do not usually choose one at random, but try to *match* each other on several features. Peruse the personal columns in your local newspaper to see how people describe themselves and what they look for in a potential partner. We bring previously held beliefs to the situation – beliefs about appropriateness such as gender, physique, socioeconomic class and religion. Matching is a form of **assortative mating**.

**Archival research**
Non-experimental method involving the assembly of data, or reports of data, collected by others.

**Assortative mating**
A non-random coupling of individuals based on their resemblance to each other on one or more characteristics.

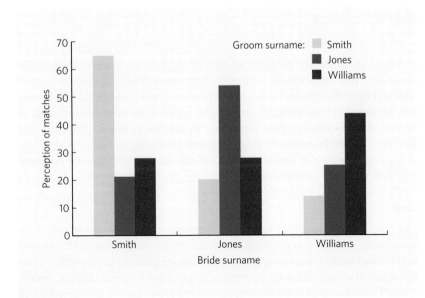

**Figure 14.5** 'Alias Smith and Jones': name matching and marriage

- A database of surnames was constructed based on early American archival marriage records.
- Commonly occurring names provided large enough samples to find those that were identical prior to marriage.
- Matched surnames – the Smiths, the Joneses and even the Williamses – were well beyond chance.

*Source*: based on data from Jones, Pelham, Carvallo & Mirenberg (2004), Study 2

Sprecher (1998) found that, in addition to the factors of proximity and familiarity, people who are evenly matched in their physical appearance, social background and personality, sociability and interests and leisure activities are more likely to be attracted to one another. There is perhaps some truth in the saying *birds of a feather flock together*.

Do cohort studies, conducted across time, support this? Gruber-Baldini and her colleagues carried out such a longitudinal study of married couples over twenty-one years (Gruber-Baldini, Schaie & Willis, 1995). At the time of first testing, they found similarities in age, education, intellectual aptitude and flexibility of attitudes. An additional and interesting finding was that some spouses became even more alike over time on attitude flexibility and word fluency. Thus initial similarity in the phase of assortative mating was enhanced by their experiences together. There is also a strong element of reality testing when it comes to looks, since most usually settle on a romantic partner who is similar to their own level of physical attractiveness (Feingold, 1988).

Studies of dating across ethnic or cultural groups reveal a complex interplay of factors involving *similarity of culture* that influence attraction. A study of heterosexual dating preferences among four ethnic groups in the United States (Asian, African, Latino and Euro/White Americans) showed that participants generally preferred partners from their own ethnic group (Liu, Campbell, & Condie, 1995). Gaining approval from one's social network was the most powerful predictor for partner preferences, followed by similarity of culture and physical attractiveness. Yancey (2007) compared the ethnic choices of White, Black, Hispanic and Asian contributors to the Internet site *Yahoo Personals*. Willingness to meet with partners of different race varied: women were less likely than men to date interracially, while Asians were more likely than Whites or Hispanics to date Blacks. Significantly, interracial dating was lower among those who were conservative politically or high in religiosity (the religious right). On the other hand, several demographic factors (age, city size, level of education) had little influence on ethnic dating preferences.

We can reasonably conclude that, while similarity of culture and ethnicity are important determinants of partner choice, interracial studies point to other factors, particularly values, that come into play. In a world where multi-ethnic societies are increasingly more prevalent, we need to take into account differences between cultures in dating practices and how intimate relationships develop, along with the more obvious factors of proximity and similarity.

## Personal characteristics

### Personality

Although similarity is an important predictor of attraction, there are other characteristics that people consistently find attractive. In a study of three kinds of relationship (romantic, and same-gender and opposite-gender friendship), Sprecher (1998) confirmed that having similar interests, leisure activities, attitudes, values and social skills were determinants of attraction. However, these factors were less important than other personal characteristics: for example, having a 'desirable personality', warmth and kindness, and reciprocal liking. Proximity and familiarity were also important; in contrast, intelligence, earning potential and competence were relatively unimportant.

### Self-disclosure

**Self-disclosure**

The sharing of intimate information and feelings with another person.

A willingness to reveal some aspects of oneself in conversation, or **self-disclosure**, is an important determinant of long-term intimacy in a relationship. According to Altman and Taylor's model (1973) of *social penetration,* people share more intimate topics with a close friend than with a casual acquaintance or a stranger. People tend to reveal more to people they like and trust. The converse is also true. People tend to prefer people who reveal more about their feelings and thoughts (Collins & Miller, 1994). Disclosing personal information and being sensitive and responsive to our partner's disclosures are central processes, both in developing relationships (Laurenceau, Barrett & Pietromonaco, 1998) and in maintaining them (Cross, Bacon & Morris, 2000).

In a study by Vittengl and Holt (2000), students who did not know one another engaged in brief conversations, before and after which they rated their positive and negative affect as well as their willingness to self-disclose. Greater self-disclosure led to an increase in positive affect. Despite this, self-disclosure is not universal; the amount and depth of information shared with another vary according to culture and gender. For example, a meta-analysis of 205 studies of self-disclosure showed that women reveal more about themselves than men (Dindia & Allen, 1992).

With respect to culture, Lewin (1936) long ago observed differences between Americans and Germans. Americans disclosed more than Germans in initial encounters but did not become as intimate as Germans as their relationships progressed. People from individualist cultures self-disclose more information than people from collectivist cultures (see Chapter 16). When information is shared, individualists give more personal information whereas collectivists share information about group membership (Gudykunst et al., 1996) (for a review of cultural differences in disclosure, see Goodwin, 1999).

Another reason why self-disclosure is important in relationships may be that trust sustains relationships. In life people try to reduce risk, but they also need and seek out relationships. The problem is that relationships are a risky business in which people make themselves vulnerable to others. People need to build interpersonal trust to manage relationship-based risk (Cvetkovich & Löfstedt, 1999). Self-disclosure plays an important role in reducing risk and building trust – the more that your friend or partner self-discloses, the safer you feel in the relationship and the greater you trust him or her. Trust and good relationships go hand-in-hand (Holmes, 2002; Rempel, Ross & Holmes, 2001).

## Cultural stereotypes

When collectivist societies are compared with individualistic societies, they are usually found to:

- nurture a self that is interdependent rather than independent;
- encourage interpersonal relationships that are harmonious rather than competitive.

These and related issues are discussed in detail in Chapters 4 and 16. Albright et al. (1997) queried whether a major cross-cultural difference really existed when they compared participants from the United States and China. The same method of data collection was used in each country. Within-culture data were based on face-to-face interactions, and across-culture data were based on photographs. The results showed that the **Big Five** personality dimensions (which contain a variety of more specific traits) were used in a consistent way in both countries and both within and across cultures. An attractive person was perceived positively regardless of the ethnicity of the judge or of the target.

Although research by Wheeler and Kim (1997) that compared Koreans and North Americans was to an extent supportive, they also reported some important cultural differences (see Figure 14.6). Stereotypes associated with attractiveness include several that are common to both cultures ('universal') and overlap with the Big Five dimensions. There were two categories of cultural difference correlated with being physically attractive:

- For North Americans, positive stereotypes include being assertive, dominant and strong – characteristics associated with *individualism*.
- For Koreans, positive stereotypes include being empathic, generous, sensitive, honest and trustworthy – characteristics associated with *collectivism*.

**Big Five**

The five major personality dimensions of extraversion/ surgency, agreeableness, conscientiousness, emotional stability, and intellect/openness to experience.

**Figure 14.6** Cultural variation and attraction

- Korean participants rated traits for their association with photographs of people who varied in physical beauty.
- Their ratings were compared with previously published American and Canadian data.
- Some traits were 'universal', associated with the three national groups.
- Other traits were specific either to individualistic cultures (North American) or to a collectivist culture (Korean).

*Source:* based on Wheeler & Kim (1997)

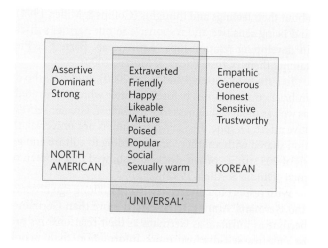

# Attraction and rewards

Rarely in psychology does a theory account for a phenomenon in its totality. More often, several theories contribute perspectives that focus on different aspects of the same process. Theories of attraction are no exception. At the broadest level, theories of attraction can be divided into those that view human nature as a striving to maintain cognitive consistency, and those that view human nature as the pursuit of pleasure and the avoidance of pain – behaviourist or reinforcement approaches. Consistency theories (e.g. balance theory in Chapter 5, cognitive dissonance theory in Chapter 6) allow a simple proposition. People normally like others who are similar to them – agreement is an affirming experience with positive affect. However, if people who like one another disagree, they experience tension, but could then try to modify their attitudes to make them more similar. If relative strangers disagree, an absence of continued interpersonal attraction should not lead to a sense of imbalance or dissonance, and they are unlikely to pursue contact.

We now turn to two approaches based directly on reinforcement, and two other approaches based on a social exchange model of people's behaviour, but also derived from reinforcement principles.

## A reinforcement approach

The general idea is simple. People who reward us directly become associated with pleasure and we learn to like them. People who punish us directly become associated with pain and we dislike them, ideas that have a long heritage in philosophy, literature and general psychology. They have also been applied in social psychology to help explain interpersonal attraction (Walster, Walster & Berscheid, 1978).

**Reinforcement–affect model**

Model of attraction which postulates that we like people who are around when we experience a positive feeling (which itself is reinforcing).

In a variation related to classical or Pavlovian conditioning (also see Chapter 5), Byrne and Clore (1970) proposed a **reinforcement–affect model** – just as Pavlov's dog learns to associate the sound of a bell with the positive reinforcement of food, so humans can associate another person with other positive or negative aspects of the immediate environment. They proposed that any *background* (and neutral) stimulus that may even be associated accidentally with reward becomes positively valued. However, if it is associated with punishment it becomes negatively valued.

## Research classic 14.4
### Evaluating a stranger when we feel hot and crowded

After completing a 24-item attitude scale designed to measure opinions on a variety of social issues, imagine that you were later invited to participate by completing a further series of questionnaires along with other students in an investigation of 'judgemental processes under altered environmental conditions'. You were not to know that you were in one of eight different experimental groups. Dressed lightly in cotton shorts and a cotton shirt, you and your group enter an 'environmental chamber', 3 metres long and 2.2 metres wide.

By using eight groups, the researchers were able to test three independent variables: (a) *heat*, the ambient temperature, which was either normal at 23C or hot at 34C; (b) *population density* which consisted of having either 3–5 group members or 12–16 group members in the chamber at one time; (c) *attitude similarity*. Note that some participants would really have experienced a degree of environmental stress by working on their questionnaires in an environment that was either hot or crowded. As a measure of attitude similarity, each

participant also rated an anonymous stranger after they had first inspected the stranger's responses to the 24-item attitude scale – the same scale that the participants had completed earlier. What they saw was fictitious. The stranger had made similar responses to a proportion of the items – to either 0.25 (low similarity) or 0.75 (high similarity) of them – as those made by that participant.

Finally, the stranger was also rated in order to calculate a measure of attraction based on two questions: how much the stranger would probably be liked, and how desirable would the stranger be as a work partner.

The result for attitude similarity was striking. Not surprisingly, the stranger who was more similar to a participant was considerably more attractive than one who was less similar, confirming the importance of attitude similarity in determining initial attraction, discussed in an earlier section.

The other results show that feeling hot or feeling crowded also affected how attractive a stranger was judged. In the context of classical conditioning, this means that the mere association of a negatively valued background stimulus, in this case two different environmental stressors, can make another person seem less attractive.

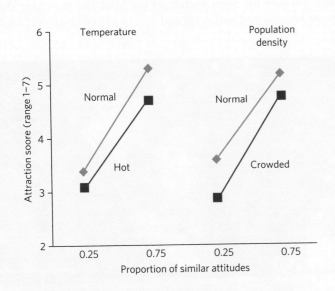

**Figure 14.7** Attraction and the reinforcing effects of background features

- Students rated a fictitious stranger as more attractive when they shared a higher proportion of similar attitudes.
- Stressful background factors, such as feeling hot or feeling crowded, reduced the attractiveness of the stranger.

*Source*: based on Griffitt & Veitch (1971)

An example of this was an early environmental experiment by William Griffitt and Russell Veitch (1971) who showed how simple background features, such as feeling hot or crowded, can reduce our attraction to a stranger (see Box 14.4 and Figure 14.7).

The study of how our feelings can be conditioned is connected to another important field in social psychology, the **automatic activation** of attitudes (see Chapter 5). In short, terms such as *affect, stimulus value* and *attitude* are related to the fundamental psychological dimensions of *good* versus *bad, positive* versus *negative,* and *approach* versus *avoidance* (De Houwer & Hermans, 2001).

**Automatic activation**
According to Fazio, attitudes that have a strong evaluative link to situational cues are more likely to automatically come to mind from memory.

## Relationships as a social exchange

As we have noted, reinforcement is based on patterns of rewards and punishments. When we look at how economics is applied to studying social behaviour, psychologists talk about **social exchange**: pay-offs, costs and rewards.

Is there a relationships marketplace out there, where we humans can satisfy our needs to interact, be intimate, 'love and be loved in return'? While social exchange theory is one of a family of theories based on **behaviourism**, it is also an approach to studying interpersonal relationships that incorporates *interaction*. Further, it deals directly with close relationships.

**Social exchange**
People often use a form of everyday economics when they weigh up costs and rewards before deciding what to do.

**Behaviourism**
An emphasis on explaining observable behaviour in terms of reinforcement schedules.

## Costs and benefits

If two people are to progress in a relationship it will be because they gain from the way that they exchange benefits (i.e. rewards). Social exchange is a model of behaviour introduced by the sociologist George Homans (1961): it accounts for our interpersonal relationships using economic concepts and is wedded to behaviourism. Whether we like someone is determined by the **cost–reward ratio**: 'What will it cost me to get a positive reward from that person?' Social exchange theory also argues that the each participant's outcomes are determined by their *joint* actions.

A relationship is an ongoing everyday activity. We seek to obtain, preserve or exchange things of value with other human beings. We bargain. What are we prepared to give in exchange for what they will give us? Some exchanges are brief and may have shallow meaning, while others are ongoing and long-term and may be extremely important. In all

**Cost–reward ratio**
Tenet of social exchange theory, according to which liking for another is determined by calculating what it will cost to be reinforced by that person.

**Social exchange**
Marriage is not entered into lightly. In long-term relationships, partners carefully weigh up the respective costs and benefits of the relationship

cases, we experience outcomes or payoffs that depend on what others do. Over time, we try to fashion a way of interacting that is rational and mutually beneficial. Social exchange is a give-and-take relationship between people, and relationships are examples of business transactions. So, is this a dry approach to the study of important relationships? If so, its proponents argue it is nevertheless valid.

Broadly speaking, resources exchanged include: goods, information, love, money, services and status (Foa & Foa, 1975). Each can be particular, so that its value depends on who gives the reward. So a hug (a specific case of 'love') will be more valued if it comes from a special person. Each reward can also be concrete, as money clearly is. There are also costs in a relationship, such as the time it takes to pursue it or the way one's friends may frown on it. Because resources are traded with a partner, we try to use a **minimax strategy** – minimise costs and maximise rewards. Of course, we may not be conscious of doing so and would probably object to the idea that we do!

Thibaut and Kelley's (1959) *The social psychology of groups* was a major work that underpinned much subsequent research. They argued that we must understand the *structure* of a relationship in order to deal with the behaviour that takes place, as it is this structure that defines the rewards and punishments available. According to the minimax strategy, what follows is that a relationship is unsatisfactory when the costs exceed the rewards. In practice, people exchange resources with one another in the hope that they will earn a **profit**: that is, one in which the rewards exceed the costs. This is a novel way of defining a 'good relationship'. How might you interpret what Erik meant in the second focus question?

**Minimax strategy**
In relating to others, we try to minimise the costs and maximise the rewards that accrue.

**Profit**
This flows from a relationship when the rewards that accrue from continued interaction exceed the costs.

## Comparison levels

A final and important concept in social exchange theory is the part played by each person's **comparison level** or CL – a standard against which all of one's relationships are judged. People's comparison levels are the product of their past experiences with other parties in similar exchanges. If the result in a present exchange is positive (i.e. a person's profit exceeds their CL), the relationship will be perceived as satisfying and the other person will seem attractive. However, dissatisfaction follows if the final result is negative (i.e. the profit falls below the CL). There is a blessing in this model because it is possible for both people in a relationship to be making a profit and therefore to be gaining satisfaction. The CL concept is helpful in accounting for why some relationships might be acceptable at some times but not at others (see Box 14.5).

**Comparison level**
A standard that develops over time, allowing us to judge whether a new relationship is profitable or not.

## Does exchange theory have a future?

In summary, the answer to this question is yes. A strong feature of exchange theory is that it accommodates variations in relationships, including:

- differences between people in how they perceive rewards and costs (you might think that free advice from your partner is rewarding, others might not);
- differences within the person based on varying CLs, both over time and across different contexts (I like companionship, but I prefer to shop for clothes alone).

The theory is frequently used. For example, Rusbult has shown how *investment* includes the way that rewards, costs and CLs are related to both satisfaction and commitment in a relationship (Rusbult, Martz & Agnew, 1998).

Its connections with how we view social justice are explored next, and a recent review (Le & Agnew, 2003) has shown that the breakdown of a relationship often follows a lack of commitment (discussed later).

## Real world 14.5
### What do you get from a relationship?
### An exercise in social exchange

An individual's comparison level or CL is an idiosyncratic judgement point, as each person has had unique experiences. Your CL is the average value of all outcomes of relationships with others in your past, and also of outcomes for others that you may have heard about. It can vary across different kinds of relationship, so your CL for your doctor will be different from that for a lover.

Your entry point into a new relationship is seen against a backdrop of the other people you have known (or known about) in that context, together with the profits and losses you have encountered in relating to them. This running average constitutes a baseline for your relationships in that particular sphere. A new encounter could only be judged as satisfactory if it exceeded this baseline.

Take as an example a date that you have had with another person. The outcome is defined as the rewards (having a nice time, developing a potential relationship) minus the costs (how much money it cost you, how difficult or risky it was to arrange, whether you feel you blew your chance to make a good impression). The actual outcome will be determined by how it compares with other dates you have had in similar circumstances in the past or at present, and perhaps by how successful other people's dates have seemed to you.

To complicate matters a little, your CL can change over time. Although age may not make you any wiser, as you get older you are likely to expect more of some future commitment to another person than when you were younger.

There is an additional concept – the *comparison level for alternatives*. Suppose that you are in an already satisfying relationship but then meet someone new, an enticing stranger. As the saying goes, 'the grass always looks greener on the other side of the fence'. In social exchange language, there is the prospect here of an increase in rewards over costs.

Does all this sound too calculating to you? Be honest, now! Whatever the outcome, the situation has become unstable. Decisions, decisions . . .

## Social exchange, equity and justice

Western society may actually be founded on a system of social exchange within which we strive for *equity*, or balance, in our relationships with others (Walster, Walster & Berscheid, 1978).

Most people believe that outcomes in an exchange should be fair and just, enshrined in a society's laws and norms: we should comply with the 'rules'. What is thought to be just and fair is a feature of group life (see the role of leader in Chapter 9) and of intergroup relations (see Chapter 11). Equity and equality are not identical concepts. In a work setting, *equality* requires that all people are paid the same, whereas *equity* requires that those who work hardest or do the most important jobs are paid more.

People are happiest in relationships when they believe that the give and take is approximately equal. **Equity theory** was developed in the context of workplace motivation and popularised in social psychology by Adams (1965) and covers two main situations:

**Equity theory**
A special case of social exchange theory that defines a relationship as equitable when the ratio of inputs to outcomes are seen to be the same by both partners.

1 a mutual exchange of resources (as in marriage);

2 an exchange where limited resources must be distributed (such as a judge awarding compensation for injury).

In both, equity theory predicts that people expect resources to be given out *fairly*, in proportion to their contribution. (See how a norm of equity has been applied to help understand *prosocial behaviour* in Chapter 13.) If we help others, it is fair to expect them to help us. Equity exists between Jack and Jill when:

$$\frac{\text{Jack's outcomes}}{\text{Jack's inputs}} = \frac{\text{Jill's outcomes}}{\text{Jill's inputs}}$$

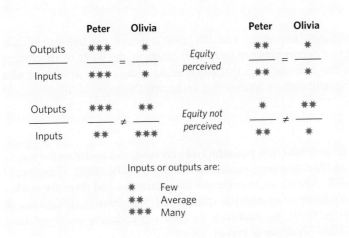

**Figure 14.8** Equity theory applied to two equitable and two inequitable relationships
*Source*: based on Baron & Byrne (1987)

First, Jack estimates the ratio between what he has put into his relationship with Jill and what he has been received in return. Next, Jack compares this ratio with the ratio applying to Jill (see Figure 14.8). If these ratios are equal, Jack will feel that each of them is being treated fairly or equitably. Jill, of course, will have her own ideas about what is fair. Perhaps Jack is living in a dream world!

When a relationship is equitable, the participants' outcomes (rewards minus costs) are proportional to their inputs or contributions to the relationship. The underlying concept is **distributive justice** (Homans, 1961). It is an aspect of social justice and refers more generally to practising a norm of fairness in the sharing of goods that each member of a group receives. Equity theory can be applied to many areas of social life, such as exploitative relationships, helping relationships and intimate relationships (Walster, Walster & Berscheid, 1978). The more inequitably people are treated, the more distress they will feel. When we experience continuing inequity, the relationship is likely to end (Adams, 1965), a topic dealt with at the end of this chapter.

**Distributive justice**
The fairness of the outcome of a decision.

## The role of norms

Although Adams (1965) thought that people always prefer an equity norm when allocating resources, this has been questioned (Deutsch, 1975). When resources are shared out according to inputs, we may evaluate our friend's inputs differently from a stranger's. Strangers tend to allocate resources on the basis of *ability*, whereas friends allocate on the basis of both *ability* and *effort* (Lamm & Kayser, 1978). A norm of mutual obligation, rather than equity, to contribute to a common cause may be triggered when a friendship is involved: we expect our friends more so than strangers to pull their weight – perhaps to help us paint our new house!

Gender plays an interesting role: women prefer an equality norm and men an equity norm (Major & Adams, 1983). Such a difference may be based on a sex-stereotyped role in which a woman strives for harmony and peace in interactions by treating people equally. In contrast, Tyler has suggested that in *groups* people actually consider **procedural justice** to be more important than distributive justice or equality (Tyler & Lind, 1992; also see Chapter 8).

**Procedural justice**
The fairness of the procedures used to make a decision.

# Attachment

Attachment is an increasingly important research area in social psychology. Initially focused on the bonding that occurs between infant and caregiver, the study of attachment has expanded to include the different ways that adults make connections with those who are close to them. First, we will explore an area that underpins this topic – affiliation.

## Affiliation

**Need to affiliate**
The urge to form connections and make contact with other people.

The **need to affiliate**, to be with others, is powerful and pervasive, and underlies the way in which we form positive and lasting interpersonal relationships (Leary, 2010). There are, of course, times when we wish to be alone, to enjoy our own company, and there are models that deal with people's attempts to regulate their need for privacy (O'Connor & Rosenblood, 1996; Pedersen, 1999). We start with the effects of enduring social isolation, an experience that can be dire (Perlman & Peplau, 1998).

## Forerunners in this field

There have been many stories of people being isolated for long periods of time, such as prisoners in solitary confinement and shipwreck survivors. However, in situations such as these, isolation is often accompanied by punishment or perhaps lack of food. For this reason, the record of Admiral Byrd is perhaps the most interesting example we have – his isolation was voluntary and planned, with adequate supplies to meet his physical needs. Byrd volunteered to spend six months alone at an Antarctic weather station observing and recording conditions. His only contact was by radio with the main expedition base. At first, he wanted to 'be by myself for a while and to taste peace and quiet and solitude long enough to find out how good they really are' (Byrd, 1938, p. 4). But in the fourth week he wrote of feeling lonely, lost and bewildered. He began to spice up his experience by imagining that he was among familiar people. After nine weeks Byrd became preoccupied with religious questions and, like Monty Python, dwelt on the 'meaning of life'. His thoughts turned to ways of believing that he was not actually by himself: 'The human race, then, is not alone in the universe. Though I am cut off from human beings, I am not alone' (p. 185). After three months, he became severely depressed, apathetic and assailed by hallucinations and bizarre ideas.

**Instinct**
Innate drive or impulse, genetically transmitted.

The early social psychologist William McDougall (1908) suggested that humans are innately motivated to gather together and to be part of a group, as some animals do that live in herds or colonies. This was a simplistic **instinct** theory and was roundly criticised by the behaviourist John Watson (1913). He argued that accounting for herding behaviour by calling it a herding instinct was a very weak position. Later biological arguments about social behaviour were much more sophisticated (note what we have covered already regarding evolutionary theory and attraction). Affiliation has been extensively researched, so we have been selective in choosing just two topics. Do people want company when they become anxious? How serious are the consequences of inadequate care-giving for infants?

## Modern research

**Social comparison (theory)**
Comparing our behaviours and opinions with those of others in order to establish the correct or socially approved way of thinking and behaving.

In his classic work *The Psychology of Affiliation* (1959), Stanley Schachter described a connection between being isolated and feeling anxious. Being alone can lead people to want to be with others, even with strangers for a short period. Schachter surmised that having company serves to reduce anxiety, noting that two factors could be involved, either that the other person might serve as a distraction from a worrying situation, or else as a yardstick for the process of **social comparison**. His results confirmed the latter explanation.

James Kulik has studied how social psychological processes can be used to promote recovery from surgery. See Box 14.6 for an example of how social comparison can be used to speed recovery for heart patients.

In summary, the need to affiliate can be affected by temporary states, such as fear. It is not just any person that we want to be with, but someone specific. Schachter's original assertion can be amended to read: 'Misery loves the company of those in the same miserable situation' (Gump & Kulik, 1997). The reduction of anxiety is only one condition that invokes the process of social comparison. In a broader context, we make these comparisons whenever we look to the views of a special group, our friends. How people come to be part of this special group is discussed below.

## Effects of social deprivation

A new insight into the nature of affiliation was provided by the study of the effects of *social deprivation in infancy*. According to the British psychiatrist John Bowlby (1988), the release of two movies had a profound effect on research workers studying children in the 1950s, one by René Spitz, *Grief: A peril in infancy* (1947), and the other by James Robertson, *A two-year-old goes to hospital* (1952). Survival, it transpired, depends on physical needs but also on a quite independent need for care and intimate interaction.

The psychoanalyst Spitz (1945) reported on babies who had been in an overcrowded institution for two years, left there by mothers unable to look after them. The babies were fed but rarely handled, and were mostly confined to their cots. Compared with other institutionalised children who had been given adequate care, they were less mentally and socially advanced, and their mortality rate was extremely high. Spitz coined the term **hospitalism** to describe the psychological condition in which he found these children. Hospitalism came to life vividly with heart-wrenching television footage of little children abandoned in Romanian orphanages in the early 1990s. Robertson was a psychiatric social worker and psychoanalyst working at the Tavistock Clinic and Institute in London, and was acknowledged by Bowlby as an inspiration. His remarkable film dealt with the emotional deterioration of a young girl separated from her mother for eight days while in hospital for minor surgery (see 'A Two-year-old Goes to Hospital' at **http://www.robertsonfilm.info/**).

Other work of that time by Harlow and his colleagues at the University of Wisconsin dealt with the devastating effects of social isolation on newborn rhesus monkeys

**Hospitalism**
A state of apathy and depression noted among institutionalised infants deprived of close contact with a caregiver.

---

### Research highlight 14.6
#### Heart to heart: effects of room sharing before surgery

Kulik, Mahler and Moore (1996) recorded the verbal interactions of heart patients, studying the effects of pre-operative room-mate assignments on patterns of affiliation, including how anxious they were before the operation and their speed of recovery afterwards. If social comparison were to play a part in this context then it should reveal itself if the other person is also a cardiac patient. The results indicated that the process of social comparison was at work:

- Patients were significantly more likely to clarify their thoughts, by talking about the surgery and the prospects of recovery afterwards, when their room-mate was a cardiac rather than a non-cardiac patient.

- This effect was strongest when the room-mate had already undergone the operation. When patient A was pre-operative and patient B was post-operative, patient A would be less anxious, as measured by the number of anxiety-reducing drugs and sedatives requested by patients the night before surgery.

- Patients were also more likely to be discharged sooner if assigned to a room-mate who was cardiac rather than non-cardiac, measured by the length of stay following the procedure.

- Patients without room-mates generally had the slowest recoveries.

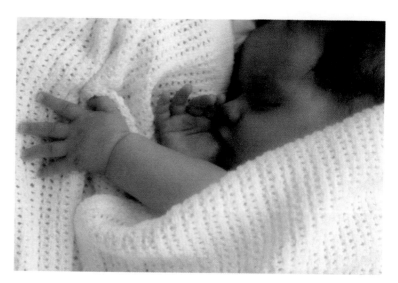

**Attachment**

Early studies by Harlow and Bowlby showed that babies need nurturing as well as food. Lots of cuddling, warmth, and softness works wonders

(Harlow, 1958; Harlow & Harlow, 1965). (Much later, an evolutionary approach to attachment and pair bonding in mammals was outlined by Fraley, Brumbaugh & Marks, 2005.) This included deprivation of contact with their mothers. A monkey mother provides more than contact, food, rocking and warmth: she is the first link in the chain of the baby's experience of socialisation. Harlow's investigation was extended to babies who were totally isolated from contact with any living being for up to 12 months. Such long periods of solitary confinement had drastic consequences. The infant monkeys would sometimes huddle in a corner, rock back and forth repetitively, and bite themselves. When later exposed to normal peers, they did not enter into the rough-and-tumble play of the others, and failed to defend themselves from attack. As adults, they were sexually incompetent.

## The link to attachment

**Attachment behaviour**

The tendency of an infant to maintain close physical proximity with the mother or primary caregiver.

Clearly, long-term social deprivation in infants is psychologically traumatic – in particular with a long-term caregiver, typically the mother. Bowlby (1969) and his colleagues at the Tavistock Institute in England focused on the **attachment behaviour** of infants to their mothers, noting that young children keep close to their mothers. Young children send signals to their caregiver by crying and smiling, and maintained proximity by clinging or following, all of which Bowlby attributed to an innate affiliative drive. Compared with affiliation, attachment involves that extra step of a close relationship at a particular point in time with just a few, perhaps one, other person.

For Bowlby and many other social psychologists, attachment behaviour is not limited to the mother–infant experience but can be observed throughout the life cycle. In Bowlby's words, it accompanies people 'from the cradle to the grave'.

## Attachment styles

**Attachment styles**

Descriptions of the nature of people's close relationships, thought to be established in childhood.

Stable adult relationships 'come from somewhere' (Berscheid, 1994). Modern research into the genesis of adult attachment in relationships is now clearly linked to the study of human social development in infancy, and Bowlby's work with young children in particular has moved on to include the study of **attachment styles** in their elders. In accounting for the way that we as adults experience both love and loneliness, Cindy Hazan and Phillip Shaver (1987) defined three attachment styles – *secure, avoidant* and *anxious* – that are also found in children (see Table 14.1).

**Table 14.1**  Characteristics of three attachment styles

| Attachment style | Characteristics |
| --- | --- |
| *Secure* | Trust in others; not worried about being abandoned; belief that one is worthy and liked; find it easy to be close to others; comfortable being dependent on others, and vice versa. |
| *Avoidant* | Suppression of attachment needs; past attempts to be intimate have been rebuffed; uncomfortable when close to others; find it difficult to trust others or to depend on them; feel nervous when anyone gets close. |
| *Anxious* | Concern that others will not reciprocate one's desire for intimacy; feel that a close partner does not really offer love, or may leave; want to merge with someone and this can scare people away. |

*Source*: based on Hazan & Shaver (1987)

Based on their studies of how important the family is to an individual's psychological development, Feeney and Noller (1990) found that attachment styles developed in childhood carry on to influence the way romantic relationships are formed in later life. They assessed the levels of attachment, communication patterns and relationship satisfaction of married couples, and

**Secure attachment style**
Children benefit from contact with compassionate caregivers. They are more likely to be both self-sufficient and trusting of others

found that securely attached individuals (comfortable with closeness and having low anxiety about relationships) were more often paired with similarly secure spouses. On the other hand, people with an avoidant style often report aversive sexual feelings and experiences, and are less satisfied and more stressed from parenting when a baby arrives (Birnbaum et al., 2006; Rholes, Simpson, & Friedman, 2006), and less close to their children as they grow older (Rholes, Simpson, & Blakely (1995). Now consider the third focus question. What might have happened in Aishani's life before she met Kamesh that could account for her current predicament?

Studies in this field suggest that Bowlby was right – attachment is a process that is active throughout life rather than simply a feature of infancy, and attachment styles adopted early in life can prevail in later relationships. One study by Brennan and Shaver (1995) of attachment styles and romantic relationships found that:

- Secure adults found it easier to get close to others and to enjoy affectionate and long-lasting relationships.
- Avoidant adults reported discomfort in getting close to others and their relationships were hampered by jealousy and a lack of self-disclosure.
- Anxious adults tended to fall in love easily; however, their subsequent relationships were full of emotional highs and lows, and they were more often unhappy.

Experimental data from Brumbaugh and Fraley (2006) show that an attachment style in one romantic relationship is likely to carry over to another relationship. However, people's styles may not be set in concrete. Kirkpatrick and Hazan's (1994) study carried out over a four-year period has shown that an insecure partner may become less so if a current partner is secure and the relationship engenders trust.

## Longitudinal research

Most research into attachment styles has not examined children and therefore is not genuinely developmental. The studies to which we have referred (excluding Kirkpatrick and Hazan's) typically measure the attachment style of adult participants and have no independent estimate of children's attachment style. Even cross-sectional studies of different age groups tested at the one time are not, strictly speaking, developmental. In contrast, Eva Klohnen spearheaded a genuine longitudinal programme of research across more than thirty years. Women who had been avoidant or secure in their attachment styles in their 20s were still so in their 40s and 50s. Differences in how they related were also maintained across the years. Compared with secure women, avoidant women were more distant from others, less confident, more distrustful, but more self-reliant (Klohnen & Bera, 1998).

Attachment theory has been increasingly researched since the 1980s and has become fashionable as well in the popular literature devoted to love, our next topic.

# Close relationships

What does a close relationship conjure up for you? Perhaps warm fuzzies, perhaps passion and maybe love. But when you search your memory banks, there can be other worrisome thoughts too – try jealousy for one.

**Emotion-in-relationships model**
Close relationships provide a context that elicits strong emotions due to the increased probability of behaviour interrupting interpersonal expectations.

Close relationships are a crucible for a host of strong emotions (Fitness, Fletcher & Overall, 2003). According to the **emotion-in-relationships model**, relationships pivot on strong, well-established and wide-ranging expectations about a partner's behaviour (Berscheid & Ammazzalorso, 2001). People who can express their emotions are generally valued in close relationships, particularly by others with a secure attachment style (Feeney, 1999). There is, however, a caveat. Fitness (2001) has reported that the elevated tendency to feel *all* emotions in close relationships makes it important for us to manage their expression, particularly negative emotions. If I engage in an orgy of uninhibited expression of all I feel for my partner the relationship may not be long for this world. The way that I show my feelings for my partner needs to be carefully, even strategically, managed.

## What is love?

We have discussed the general process of interpersonal attraction. We have explored the way we choose acquaintances and friends, the powerful need to affiliate with a range of people, and how we become attached to particular individuals. Can we extend these principles to the important topic of the very special people whom we love – and are liking and loving different? Once a neglected topic of empirical study, **love** is now a popular focus for research (Dion & Dion, 1996).

People commonly use terms such as passion, romance, companionship, infatuation and sexual attraction, but would have difficulty defining them. Couple this with the way that love is regarded as magical and mysterious – the stuff of poetry and song rather than science – and the difficulty of taking love into the laboratory becomes compounded. Despite this, our knowledge is growing (see the fourth focus question), but not surprisingly, most research on love has used survey and interview methods.

Rubin (1973) distinguished between *liking* and *loving* and developed scales to measure each separately. Take a few examples of some of Rubin's items. Julie thinks Artie is 'unusually well adjusted', 'is one of the most likeable people' she knows, and 'would highly recommend him for a responsible job'. When it comes to Frankie, Julie 'finds it easy to ignore his faults', 'if she could never be with him she would feel miserable', and 'feels very possessive towards him'. Which one does Julie like and which one does she love? Other researchers have added that *liking* involves the desire to interact with a person, *loving* adds the element of trust, and *being in love* implies sexual desire and excitement (Regan & Berscheid, 1999).

**Love**
A combination of emotions, cognitions and behaviours that can be involved in intimate relationships.

## Kinds of love

In a study of what kinds of love there might be, Fehr (1994) asked this question: do ordinary people and love researchers *think* of love in the same way? She answered this by analysing the factors underlying several love scales commonly used in psychological research, and also by having ordinary people generate ideas about the kinds of love that they thought best described various close relationships in a number of scenarios. Fehr found both a simple answer and a more complex one:

- There was reasonable agreement across her data sets that there are at least two broad categories of love: (a) companionate love and (b) passionate or romantic love. This result substantiated earlier, influential work by Hatfield and Walster (1981).
- The scales devised by love experts made relatively clear distinctions between types and sub-types of love, whereas the views of lay people were quite fuzzy.

Passionate love is an intensely emotional state and a confusion of feelings: tenderness, sexuality, elation and pain, anxiety and relief, altruism and jealousy. Companionate love, in contrast, is less intense, combining feelings of friendly affection and deep attachment (Hatfield, 1987). A distinction between passionate and companionate love makes good sense. There are many people with whom we are pleased and comforted by sharing time, and yet with whom we are not 'in love'. In general, love can trigger emotions such as sadness, anger, fear and happiness (Shaver, Morgan & Wu, 1996; see Chapter 15 for a discussion of 'primary' emotions). Hendrick and Hendrick (1995) also reported some gender differences in the meaning that people give to love: men are more inclined to treat love as a game; whereas women are more friendship-oriented, pragmatic, but also more possessive.

**Love**
Romantic love involves intense and occasionally confused emotions. Companionate love develops slowly from the continuous sharing of intimacy

## Love and romance

In 1932 the American songwriters Rodgers and Hart asked the question 'Isn't it romantic?' and also tried to tell us what love is. Social psychologists have mostly been more prosaic, sticking to descriptions of acts and thoughts that point to being 'in love'. People report that they think of their lover constantly; they want to spend as much time as possible with, and are often unrealistic about, their lover (Murstein, 1980). Not surprisingly, the lover becomes the focus of the person's life, to the exclusion of other friends (Milardo, Johnson & Huston, 1983). It is a very intense emotion and almost beyond control.

In pursuing the nature of romantic love, we should note that the concepts of love and friendship almost certainly share a common root of becoming acquainted and are generally triggered by the same factors – proximity, similarity, reciprocal liking and desirable personal characteristics. Our lover is very likely to be a friend, albeit a special one!

Have you ever fallen in love? We speak of 'falling in love' as though it is an accident, something that happens rather than a process in which we actively participate. What happens when we fall in this way? Aron and his colleagues addressed this in a short-term longitudinal study of undergraduate students who completed questionnaires about their love experiences and their concept of self every two weeks for ten weeks (Aron, Paris & Aron, 1995). Those who reported that they fell in love during this period reported positive experiences that were centred on their self-concept. Since somebody now loved them their self-esteem increased. Further, their self-concept had 'expanded' by incorporating aspects of the other person; and they also reported an increase in self-efficacy, e.g. not only making plans but making the plans work.

One widely accepted claim about falling in love is that it is culture-bound: for young people to experience it, a community needs to believe in love and offer it as an option, through fiction and real-life examples. If it is an accident, then at least some people from all cultures should fall in love – but is this the case? Attachment theory has argued that love is both a biological and a social process, and cannot be reduced to a historical or cultural invention (Hazan & Shaver, 1987). Indeed, there is evidence of romantic love, not necessarily linked to marriage, in the major literate civilisations of early historic times – Rome, Greece, Egypt and China (Mellen, 1981). For example, although romance was not an essential ingredient in choosing a spouse in Rome, love between a husband and wife could grow (see **http://www.womenintheancientworld.com**).

**Three-factor theory of love**
Hatfield and Walster distinguished three components of what we label 'love': a cultural concept of love, an appropriate person to love and emotional arousal.

## Love as a label

In Hatfield and Walster's (1981) **three-factor theory of love**, romantic love is a product of three interacting variables:

1 a cultural determinant that acknowledges love as a state;

2 an appropriate love object present – in most cultures, the norm is a member of the opposite sex and of similar age;

**3**   emotional arousal, self-labelled 'love', that is felt when interacting with, or even thinking about, an appropriate love object.

Label or not, those of us who have been smitten report powerful feelings. Although the idea of labelling arousal may not seem intuitively appealing, it has a basis in research. Our physiological reactions are not always well differentiated across the emotions, such as when we describe ourselves as angry, fearful, joyful or sexually aroused (Fehr & Stern, 1970).

Recall Schachter and Singer's (1962) argument that arousal prompts us to make a causal attribution (see Chapter 2). Some cues (e.g. heightened heart rate) suggest that the cause is internal and we then label the experience as an emotion. If we feel aroused following an insult we are likely to label the feeling as anger. However, if we are interacting with an attractive member of appropriate gender we will possibly label the arousal as sexual attraction, liking, and even a precursor to love. See Box 14.7 on how even danger, or at least excitement, can act as a precursor to romance!

The three-factor theory stresses that love depends on past learning of the concept of love, the presence of someone to love, and arousal. Even if these components are necessary, they are not sufficient for love to occur. If they were, love could easily be taken into the laboratory. The ingredients would require that John's culture includes a concept of love and that Janet provides arousal by being attractive, or by chasing John around the room, or by paying him a compliment – and hey presto! 'Love'!

We know that sexual arousal itself does not define love, and that lust and love can be distinguished. Think of the anecdote in which a person is called to account for an extramarital affair by a spouse and makes the classic response 'But, dear, it didn't *mean* anything!'

## Love and illusions

People bring various ideals or images into a love relationship that can impact on the way it might develop. A person can fall out of love quickly if the partner is not what (or who) they were first thought to be. The initial love was not for the partner but for some *ideal image* that the person had formed of this partner, such as 'the knight in shining armour'. Possible sources

---

### Research Classic 14.7
#### Excitement and attraction on a suspension bridge

Dutton and Aron (1974) conducted a famous experiment on a suspension bridge spanning Capilano canyon in British Columbia. They described the setting in this way:

> The 'experimental' bridge was the Capilano Canyon Suspension Bridge, a five-foot-wide, 450-foot-long, bridge constructed of wooden boards attached to wire cables that ran from one side to the other of the Capilano Canyon. The bridge has many arousal-inducing features such as a tendency to tilt, sway, and wobble, creating the impression that one is about to fall over the side; (b) very low handrails of wire cable which contribute to this impression; and (c) a 230-foot

drop to rocks and shallow rapids below the bridge.
(*Dutton & Aron, 1974, pp. 510–511*)

The participants were young men who crossed rather gingerly over a high and swaying suspension bridge, one at a time. An attractive young woman approached each one on the pretext of conducting research, asking if they would complete a questionnaire for her. Next, she gave them her name and her phone number in case they wanted to ask more questions later. Many called her. However, very few made the phone call if the interviewer was a man or if the setting was a lower and safer 'control' bridge. Arousal in a perilous situation, it seems, enhances romance!

The phenomenon of accidental arousal enhancing the attractiveness of an already attractive person described is reliable, according to a meta-analysis of thirty-three experimental studies (Foster, Witcher, Campbell & Green, 1998).

for these images are previous lovers, characters from fiction, and childhood love objects such as parents. A physical characteristic similar to one contained by the image can start a chain reaction whereby other characteristics from the image are transferred on to the partner.

It is the images we hold about an ideal partner (discussed further below) that seem best to differentiate love from liking. Some of these images may be based on illusions. One of these is the belief in romantic destiny – *We were meant for each other*. This illusion can be helpful, both in feeling initially satisfied and in maintaining a relationship longer (Knee, 1998). Romance in general is most likely entwined with fantasy and positive illusions (Martz et al., 1998; Murray & Holmes, 1997). A positive illusion may not be a bad thing when it comes to relationships. Probably, the reality is that we need to be in the right relationship with the right person. There is some conviction 'from maintaining a tight, coherent, evaluatively consistent story about one's partner' (Murray, Holmes & Griffin, 2003, p. 290). When a partner falls short of one's ideals, we could highlight virtues and minimise faults. Partner ideals are a feature of the work of Fletcher and his colleagues in maintaining relationships, discussed in a later section.

## No greater love

Robert Sternberg (1988) proposed what has become an influential model in which commitment and intimacy are factors as crucial as passion to some experiences of love. *Passion* is roughly equivalent to sexual attraction; *intimacy* refers to feelings of warmth, closeness and sharing; *commitment* is our resolve to maintain the relationship, even in moments of crisis. These same three dimensions have been confirmed as independent statistical factors (Aron & Westbay, 1996).

While sexual desire and romantic love are linked in experience, Diamond has pointed out that they may have evolved as different biological systems with different goals:

> Desire is governed by the *sexual mating* system, the goal of which is sexual union for the purpose of reproduction. Romantic love, however, is governed by the *attachment* or *pair-bonding* system. (*Diamond, 2003, p. 174*)

It would follow that affectional bonding can be directed towards both other-gender and same-gender partners.

**Consummate love**
Sternberg argues that this is the ultimate form of love, involving passion, intimacy and commitment.

In Sternberg's model, romance is exceeded by one other experience, **consummate love**, which includes all three factors. By systematically creating combinations of the presence or absence of each factor, we can distinguish eight cases, ranging in degree of bonding from no love at all to consummate love. Out of this some interesting relationships emerge. Fatuous love is characterised by passion and commitment but no intimacy (e.g. the 'whirlwind Hollywood romance'). The differentiation between varieties of love by Sternberg appears to be robust (Diamond, 2003). Have you experienced some of the relationships in Figure 14.9?

## Love and marriage

Love and romance being the essence of deciding to get married has long been a popular theme in literature. And yet, in Western culture there appears to have been a change in attitude over time, even across a single generation. Simpson and his colleagues compared three time samples (1967, 1976 and 1984) of people who answered this question: 'If a man (woman) had all the qualities you desired, would you marry this person if you were not in love with him (her)?' The answer 'No' was much higher in 1984, but in 1967 women were much more like to say 'Yes' (Simpson, Campbell & Berscheid, 1986). A later study documented a trend in Western cultures towards far more long-term relationships outside marriage (Hill & Peplau (1998). Even so, American data suggest that love is still an

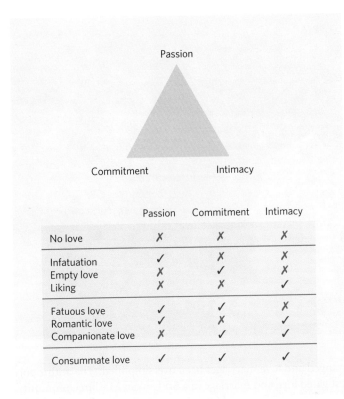

| | Passion | Commitment | Intimacy |
|---|---|---|---|
| No love | ✗ | ✗ | ✗ |
| Infatuation | ✓ | ✗ | ✗ |
| Empty love | ✗ | ✓ | ✗ |
| Liking | ✗ | ✗ | ✓ |
| Fatuous love | ✓ | ✓ | ✗ |
| Romantic love | ✓ | ✗ | ✓ |
| Companionate love | ✗ | ✓ | ✓ |
| Consummate love | ✓ | ✓ | ✓ |

**Figure 14.9**  Sternberg's (1988) triangle of love

- Three factors (passion, commitment and intimacy) are crucial in characterising different experiences of love. When all three are present we can speak of consummate love.
- When only one or two are present we have love in a different way. Two commonly experienced kinds include romantic love and companionate love.

accurate predictor of getting married or not, but is not enough to guarantee a happy and stable relationship.

Most research on marriage is Western, and may seem culturally myopic. In one sense, it is – because 'marriage', as a social contract, takes varying forms in different cultures and groups. However, almost all love relationships in all cultures and groups have some kind of public contract to identify the relationship.

## Arranged marriages

Some cultures have long preferred the careful arrangement of 'suitable' partners for their children. Arranged marriages can be very successful, particularly if we judge them by their duration and social function: having children, caring for aged parents, reinforcing the extended family and building a stronger community. They can also act as treaties between communities and tribal groups. Historically, this function has been critical – it became weaker in post-industrial societies that are organised around nuclear families, including Western societies in general.

There have been several studies of arranged marriages in India. In one, mutual love was rated lower by arranged couples than by 'love' couples – at first (Gupta & Singh, 1982). Over time, this trend reversed. In a second study, female students preferred the idea of an arranged marriage, provided they consented to it; but they endorsed the 'love marriage' provided their parents consented (Umadevi, Venkataramaiah & Srinivasulu, 1992). In a third study, students who preferred love marriages were liberal in terms of their mate's sociocultural background, whereas those who preferred arranged marriages would seek a partner from within their own kin group (Saroja & Surendra, 1991).

**Arranged marriages**
Marriage serves such an important function for the community that young people may not be able to choose their partner freely

Has the dichotomy of arranged and love marriages been oversimplified? The anthropologist De Munck (1996) investigated love and marriage in a Sri Lankan Muslim community. Arranged marriages were the cultural preference. However, romantic love also contributed to the final decision, even when parents officially selected the partner.

These studies highlight the importance and respect that some cultures afford their elders as legitimate matchmakers. Many Westerners believe that they would never consider an arranged marriage. However, dating and international marriage-match agencies are growing rapidly in popularity in Western culture, perhaps reflecting diminished opportunities for people to meet, particularly those with busy lives.

## Gay and lesbian relationships

Until recently, this important topic has been neglected in research, but an increase in the numbers of people 'coming out' has changed that. Lesbians and gay men are more evident in many societies, and research on same-sex couples has increased accordingly. Same-sex marriages, civil unions, gay adoption and gay/lesbian sexuality have been matters of public debate. There was once a view that same-sex couples were abnormal and their activities illegal. This has shifted – lesbians and gay men are minority groups who are now more confident in confronting social stigma and discrimination. For a discussion of psychological issues confronting people in gay and lesbian relationships, see the review by Peplau and Fingerhut (2007).

# Relationships that work (and those that don't)

## Maintaining relationships

This literature deals mostly with marriage, as researchers no doubt assume that this is the most obvious relationship to be preserved. However, in view of what we have discussed so far, marriage is only one of a number of love relationships. In this section we do not draw a distinction between de facto marriage relationships and other long-term intimate relationships.

External influences, such as pressure from in-laws, are other factors beyond love that can perpetuate a marriage relationship; alternatively, a progressive weakening of external obstacles to separation can be linked to an escalating divorce rate (Attridge & Berscheid, 1994). Karney and Bradbury (1995) studied some 200 variables in a longitudinal study of marital satisfaction and stability. Positive outcomes were predicted by groups of positively valued variables (e.g. education, employment and desirable behaviour), whereas negative outcomes were predicted by groups of negatively valued variables (e.g. neuroticism, an unhappy childhood and negative behaviour). However, no factor in isolation was a reliable predictor of satisfaction.

Cotton, Cunningham and Antill (1993) investigated the relationship between spousal marital satisfaction and couples' social and support networks. Wives reported more marital satisfaction when members of their network were related to one another, when their husband's network included some relatives, and when they themselves were friends of some members of their husband's network. Husbands reported more marital satisfaction when they were friends of some members of their wife's network, and when some members of their network were related to those in their wife's network. Marriage is more than a union of two individuals: it includes interaction of the partners with, and overlap between, two larger networks of people. Satisfaction is higher when people who might have been 'worlds apart' become 'worlds together'.

Clark and Grote (1998) have used equity theory based on benefits and costs to pinpoint actions that help or hinder a relationship:

- *Benefits* help. They can be intentional (e.g. 'My husband complimented me on my choice of clothing'), or unintentional (e.g. 'I like being in public with my wife because she is attractive').

- *Costs* hinder. They can be intentional (e.g. 'My wife corrected my grammar in front of other people'), or unintentional (e.g. 'My husband kept me awake at night by snoring').

- *Communal behaviour* helps. Sometimes it can be a benefit to one partner but a cost to the other (e.g. 'I listened carefully to something my wife wanted to talk about even though I had no interest in the issue').

Romance novels suggest that 'love endures', whereas TV soap operas often focus on relationship break-ups. A longitudinal study spanning ten years of American newly-weds found a steady decline in marital satisfaction among both husbands and wives (Kurdeck (1999). This decline included two accelerated downturns, one after the first year, 'the honeymoon is over', and the other in the eighth year, 'the seven year itch'!

A relationship that survives is one where partners adapt and change in what they expect of each other. Companionate love can preserve a relationship, based on deep friendship and caring, and arising from lives that are shared and the myriad experiences that only time can provide. In this way, we can get a glimpse of how both the Western 'love' marriage and the Eastern arranged marriage could each result in a similar perception of powerful bonding between partners.

The themes summarised in this section tally with Huston's (2009) recent description of the 'behavioural ecology' of marriages that work. His longitudinal studies show that spouses who get on are:

- *domestic partners* – with either traditional or workable and customised gender role patterns;

- *lovers* – since sex is a core element of most marriages;

- *companions and friends* – mostly in genial relationships with shared activities; and are supported by a:

- *social network* – consisting of friends and relatives with whom they visit and socialise.

## For better or for worse

When do partners live up to the maxim 'For better or for worse'? Adams and Jones (1997) pinpointed three factors that contribute to an ongoing relationship:

1 *personal dedication* – positive attraction to a particular partner and relationship;

2 *moral commitment* – a sense of obligation, religious duty or social responsibility, controlled by a person's values and moral principles;

3 *constraint commitment* – factors that make it costly to leave a relationship, such as lack of attractive alternatives, and various social, financial or legal investments in the relationship.

**Commitment**
The desire or intention to continue an interpersonal relationship.

**Commitment** is a concept we have referred to several times in this chapter. It increases the chance that partners will stay together, and even entertaining the idea of becoming committed is important (Berscheid & Reis, 1998). Wieselquist and her colleagues found a link between commitment and marital satisfaction, acts that promote a relationship, and trust (Wieselquist, Rusbult, Foster & Agnew, 1999).

There are a series of risk factors that predict a relationship break-up, such as use of negative forms of communication and lack of a social support network. As a counter to a risk approach, Arriaga and Agnew (2001) built on Rusbult's concept of investment referred to earlier. Their longitudinal investigation confirmed that a healthy relationship includes high levels of three components: (1) psychological attachment, (2) a long-term orientation, and (3) an intention to persist. These components put a positive slant on the nature of commitment.

Highly committed partners have a greater chance of staying together (Adams & Jones, 1997). The very idea of subjectively committing oneself to a relationship can be more important than the conditions that led to commitment (Berscheid & Reis, 1998). Subjective commitment may be related to our self-construal, the way we think about ourselves (see Chapter 4). In a study by Cross, Bacon and Morris (2000), people who construed themselves as being the sort of people who are interdependent with others were more committed to important relationships than individuals who did not.

Wieselquist and her colleagues found that commitment has been linked to marital satisfaction (Wieselquist, Rusbult, Foster & Agnew, 1999), to behaviour that promotes a relationship, and to trust. Promoting a relationship includes 'inspiring' acts, such as being accommodating to one's partner's needs and being willing to make some sacrifices. Wieselquist's model is *cyclical*: inspiring acts bring forth a partner's trust and reciprocal commitment, and subsequent interdependence for both in the relationship. Trust is a particular case of the way we attribute another's motives (see Chapter 3). It can preserve a relationship in the face of adversity (Miller & Rempel, 2004), whereas a lack of trust is associated with an insecure attachment style (Mikulincer, 1998).

## Forgiveness

*To err is human, to forgive divine*: sometimes it pays to turn the other cheek – forgive a partner who has transgressed. It is a benefit with high value (McCullough, Worthington & Rachal, 1997), as is its counterpart, apologising for giving offence (Azar, 1997). Fincham (2000) has characterised forgiveness as an interpersonal construct: *you* forgive *me*. It is a process and not an act, and resonates in histories, religions and values of many cultures. Forgiveness is a solution to estrangement, and a positive alternative to relationship breakdown. Forgiving a partner is also an act that can extend to later prosocial acts (see Karremans, Van Lange & Holland, 2005 in Chapter 13.)

## Does your partner meet your ideals?

How well do you match the expectations of your partner, and is this important to your relationship? These are questions that Fletcher and his colleagues have explored (Fletcher, Simpson,

Thomas & Giles, 1999). Our ideal image of a partner has developed over time and usually predates a relationship in the present. In a study of romantic relationships by Campbell, Simpson, Kashy and Fletcher (2001), people rated their ideal romantic partners on three dimensions: warmth–trustworthiness, vitality–attractiveness and status–resources, the same dimensions proposed by Fletcher as important when selecting a mate (discussed earlier). The results were in accord with the *ideal standards model*: people who think that their current partner closely matches their image of an ideal partner are more satisfied with their relationship.

This model has been extended to include how people maintain and perhaps improve a relationship by trying to regulate or control a partner's behaviour. See how Overall and her colleagues have expanded this idea in Box 14.8.

## Relationship breakdown

Levinger (1980) points to four factors that herald the end of a relationship, including those of same-gender partners (Schullo & Alperson, 1984):

1  A new life seems to be the only solution.
2  Alternative partners are available (also see Arriaga & Agnew, 2001).
3  There is an expectation that the relationship will fail.
4  There is a lack of commitment to a continuing relationship.

Rusbult and Zembrodt (1983) believe that once deterioration has been identified, it can be responded to in any of four ways. A partner can take a passive stance and show:

- *loyalty*, by waiting for an improvement to occur; or
- *neglect*, by allowing the deterioration to continue.

Alternatively, a partner can take an active stance and show:

- *voice behaviour*, by working at improving the relationship; or
- *exit behaviour*, by choosing to end the relationship.

**Self-regulation**
Strategies that we use to match our behaviour to an ideal or 'ought' standard.

**Partner regulation**
Strategy that encourages a partner to match an ideal standard of behaviour.

---

### Research highlight 14.8
#### Strategies for sustaining a long-term relationship

According to Overall, Fletcher & Simpson (2006), people use a variety of cognitive tactics to maintain their relationships when they judge their partner to be less than ideal. They may weather little storms along the way by:

- enhancing a partner's virtues and downplaying the faults (Murray & Holmes, 1999);
- lowering their expectations to fit more closely with what their partner offers (Fletcher, Simpson & Thomas, 2000);
- adjusting their perceptions so that their partner bears resemblance to their ideal (Murray, Holmes & Griffin, 1996).

Another approach is to work more directly on the partner. You will recall that people use **self-regulation** when they try to rationalise perceived self-concept discrepancies between how they are and how they want to be (see Chapter 4). Overall and her colleagues have used a similar, but more complex, concept based on the ideal standards model, with its pivotal dimensions of warmth–trustworthiness, vitality–attractiveness and status–resources. This model can throw new light on the way that we can try to improve and sustain a long-term relationship – **partner regulation**. Begin by comparing what we perceive with what we want relating to our partner – test the perception against our ideal standards. Regulation kicks in when the reality begins to fall short. Overall et al. give this example: Mary places considerable importance on one of the three dimensions, status/resources; but her partner John has limited potential to be financially secure; Mary encourages John to retrain or look for another job, perhaps a major challenge. But there are brownie points on offer – John's status and resources could come much closer to Mary's ideal and lift the quality of their relationship.

It is not clear whether the passive or the active approach leads to more pain at the final break-up. Other factors are involved, such as previous levels of attraction, the amount of time and effort invested and the availability of new partners. It can also depend on the person's available social contact, such as support from family and friends. It is often loneliness that adds to the pain and makes life seem unbearable; if this is minimised, recovery from the ending of a relationship can be faster.

## Consequences of failure

**Relationship dissolution model**

Duck's proposal of the sequence through which most long-term relationships proceed if they finally break down.

A break-up is a process, not a single event. Steve Duck (1982, 2007) has offered a detailed **relationship dissolution model** of four phases that partners pass through (see Box 14.9 and Figure 14.10). Each phase culminates in a threshold at which a typical form of action follows.

You may well think, 'This is pretty grim stuff.' It is. Most often, the break-up of long-term relationships and marriages is extremely distressing. Partners who were close have tried hard over a long period to make it work – they have mutually reinforced each other and have had good times along with the bad. In the break-up of marriage, at least one partner has reneged on a contract (Simpson, 1987). The consequences of a family break-up can be serious for children. Tucker et al. (1997) used **archival research** in a longitudinal study of more than 1,200 people in the period 1921–91, showing that men and women whose parents had divorced were more likely also to experience divorce (Tucker et al., 1997).

**Archival research**

Non-experimental method involving the assembly of data, or reports of data, collected by others.

Serious domestic conflict also undermines parent–child relationships. Riggio (2004) studied young adults from families affected by divorce or chronic and high levels of conflict, finding that they more often felt lacking in social support and more anxious in their own relationships. Add divorce to the mixture and the quality of the relationship with the father, though not with the mother, was also diminished, perhaps because interaction with mothers was expected to continue.

In short, most of us probably live in the hope that a long-term intimate relationship will involve loyalty, trust and commitment – forever. There is truth in the adage *Look before you leap*.

## Research highlight 14.9
### Phases in the break-up of a relationship

1 The *intrapsychic phase* starts as a period of brooding with little outward show, perhaps in the hope of putting things right. This can give way to needling the partner and seeking out a third party to be able to express one's concerns.

2 The *dyadic* (i.e two-person) phase leads to deciding that some action should be taken, short of leaving the partner, which is usually easier said than done. Arguments point to differences in attributing responsibility for what is going wrong. With luck, they may talk their problems through.

3 The *social phase* involves a new element: in saying that the relationship is near an end, the partners may

negotiate with friends, both for support for an uncertain future and for reassurance of being right. The social network will probably take sides, pronounce on guilt and blame and, like a court, sanction the dissolution.

4 The final *grave-dressing phase* can involve more than leaving a partner. It may include the division of property, access to children, and working to assure one's reputation. Each partner wants to emerge with a self-image of reliability for a future relationship. The metaphor for the relationship is death: there is its funeral, it is buried and marked by erecting a tablet. This 'grave-dressing' activity seeks a socially acceptable version of the life and death of the relationship.

*Source:* based on Duck (1982, 2007)

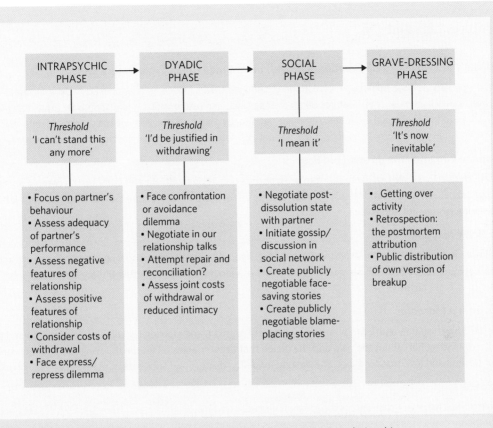

**Figure 14.10**  When things go wrong: phases in dissolving an intimate relationship

*Source:* based on Duck (1982)

## Summary

- Attraction is necessary for friendships to form and is a precursor to an intimate relationship.

- Evolutionary social psychology has made strong arguments for the power of human genetic inheritance in accounting for what attracts people to each other.

- Variables that play a significant role in determining why people are attracted towards each other include physical attributes, whether they live or work close by, how familiar they are and how similar they are, especially in terms of attitudes and values.

- Social psychological explanations of attraction include: reinforcement (a person who engenders positive feelings is liked more); social exchange (an interaction is valued if it increases benefits and reduces costs); and the experience of equitable outcomes for both parties in a relationship.

- Affiliation with others is a powerful form of human motivation. Long-term separation from others can have disturbing intellectual and social outcomes, and may lead to irreversible psychological damage in young children.

- Life-cycle studies of affiliation led to research into attachment and attachment styles. The ways that children connect psychologically to their caregiver can have long-term consequences for how they establish relationships in adulthood.

- Love is distinguished from mere liking. It also takes different forms, such as romantic love and companionate love.

- Maintaining a long-term relationship involves partner regulation, using strategies that bring a partner closer to one's expectations or standards.

- The break-up of a long-term relationship can be traced through a series of stages. The relationship dissolution model notes four phases: intrapsychic, dyadic (two-person), social and grave-dressing.

## Literature, film and TV

### Dr Tatiana's Sex Advice to All Creation: The Definitive Guide to the Evolutionary Biology of Sex

This 2006 popular science book by an evolutionary biologist, Olivia Judson, is hilarious. Dr Tatiana (Judson) receives letters from a truly bizarre array of creatures about their sex lives and relationships, and responds by explaining the surreal biology of sex to the concerned creatures. Although not directly about people, you will make comparisons, and this will make you examine your assumptions about how 'natural' the nature of human relationships and sexuality really are.

### Sex and the City and Friends and Cold Feet

These are classic TV series of a genre that explores, both seriously and with wit and humour, the complexity of friendships and sexual and love relationships. Although these series have finished, they did such an excellent job that we will be seeing re-runs for some time.

### When Harry met Sally

1989 film by Rob Reiner, starring Billy Crystal and Meg Ryan. Classic comedy showing how love and attraction can develop between very dissimilar people. There are lots of wonderful little vignettes of very long-term relationships and how they first started.

### Scenes from a Marriage

Classic 1973 Swedish film and TV mini-series by Ingmar Bergman, and starring Liv Ullmann. An intense and psychologically demanding film about the pain and the peace that accompanies a lifetime of loving – the film chronicles 10 years of turmoil and love that bind a couple despite infidelity, divorce and subsequent marriages.

### Casablanca

Many film critics feel that *Casablanca* is the greatest film ever – a 1942 all-time classic directed by Michael Curtiz, starring Humphrey Bogart (as Rick) and Ingrid Bergman (as Ilsa), and also with Sydney Greenstreet and Peter Lorré. A love affair between Rick and Ilsa is disrupted by the Nazi occupation of Paris – some years later Ilsa shows up in Rick's Café in Casablanca. The film is about love, friendship and close relationships, as well as hatred and jealousy, against the background of war, chaos and other impossible obstacles. Another absolute classic in the same vein is David Lean's 1965 film, *Dr Zhivago* – based on the novel by Boris Pasternak, and starring Omar Sharif and Julie Christie.

### Mamma Mia

A 2008 infectious romantic comedy is built on ABBA's hits, starring Meryl Streep, Amanda Seyfried, Pierce Brosnan and Colin Firth. Sophie, who has lived her life with her solo mother on a Greek island, is getting married. She has never met her father, but after unearthing her mother's secret diary from years ago, she narrows the 'culprit' down to three lovers. Without her mother's knowledge she invites three handsome men to her wedding. Chaos erupts and a mad round of parties ensues. Sophie, however, is determined to acquire a father. Attachment theory suggests that one Dad is enough, but she faces a dilemma – Sophie likes them all! Is it better to know who it is and have just one father? Or could she share all three in her life but never solve the secret?

### The Road

2009 John Hillcoat film based on a Cormac McCarthy novel, and starring Viggo Mortensen. A father and his young son trudge across a brutal and ruined post-apocalyptic world – the only thing that allows them to survive and keeps them sane and human is their relationship.

### Brokeback Mountain

This 2005 film by Ang Lee, starring Heath Ledger, Jake Gyllenhaal, Anne Hathaway and Michelle Williams is set in the period 1963–83 in the American West. A sexual encounter between two men deepens into a relationship that is not only sexual but also emotional and romantic. One of the men later marries, and his conflict between two relationships, one homosexual and the other heterosexual, is a key element in the story.

## Guided questions

1. What does evolutionary social psychology have to say about how humans select a mate?
2. How can a *cost-and-benefits* analysis be applied to predict the future of an intimate relationship?
3. How does a person's attachment *style* develop and can it continue later in life? A student discusses her experience of insecure attachment following years of physical and emotional abuse from her father in Chapter 14 of MyPsychLab at **www.mypsychlab.co.uk** (watch *Attachment style*).
4. Is romantic love universal, and is it the only kind of love?
5. What has social psychology told us about why some relationships work?

### Learn more

Clark, M. S., & Lemay, E. P. Jr (2010). Close relationships. In S. T. Fiske, D. T. Gilbert, & G. Lindzey (eds), *Handbook of social psychology* (5th ed., Vol. 2, pp. 898–940). New York: Wiley. Currently the most up-to-date, detailed and comprehensive coverage of theory and research on close relationships.

Duck, S. (2007). *Human relationships* (4th ed.). London: SAGE. A perspective by a major theorist on people's interactions, acquaintances, friendships and relationships. Students can use the resources provided to apply the concepts in their personal lives.

Fehr, B. (1996). *Friendship processes*. Thousand Oaks, CA: SAGE. An in-depth research-based analysis of friendship in modern society.

Fitness, J., Fletcher, G., & Overall, N. (2007). Interpersonal attraction and intimate relationships. In M. A. Hogg & J. Cooper (eds), *The SAGE handbook of social psychology: Concise student edition* (pp. 219–40). London: SAGE. Detailed overview of research on close relationships, which includes coverage of emotion in relationships and evolutionary dimensions of relationships.

Goodwin, R. (1999). *Personal relationships across cultures*. London: Routledge. Draws together research from around the world to explore how fundamental differences in cultural values influence how people form and maintain various kinds of relationship.

Leary, M. R. (2010). Affiliation, acceptance, and belonging: The pursuit of interpersonal connection. In S.

T. Fiske, D. T. Gilbert, & G. Lindzey (eds), *Handbook of social psychology* (5th ed., Vol. 2, pp. 864–97). New York: Wiley. This chapter includes detailed discussion of why people might be motivated to affiliate with others and thus form groups.

Mikulincer, M., & Goodman, G. S. (eds) (2006). *Dynamics of romantic love: Attachment, caregiving, and sex*. New York: Guilford. Topics such as intimacy, jealousy, self-disclosure, forgiveness and partner violence are examined from the perspective of attachment, caregiving and sex.

Rholes, W. S., & Simpson, J. A. (2004). *Adult attachment: Theory, research, and clinical implications*. New York: Guilford. Attachment theory is considered from physiological, emotional, cognitive and behavioural perspectives.

Rose, H., & Rose, S. (eds) (2000). *Alas, poor Darwin: Arguments against evolutionary psychology*. London: Vintage. Scholars from a variety of biological, philosophical and social science backgrounds raise major concerns about the adequacy of genetic accounts of social behaviour, including partner selection.

Shaver, P. R., & Mikulincer, M. (2007). Attachment theory and research: Core concepts, basic principles, conceptual bridges. In A. W. Kruglanski & E. T. Higgins (eds), *Social psychology: Handbook of basic principles* (2nd ed., pp. 650–77). New York: Guilford Press. A comprehensive coverage of research and theory on human attachment and affiliation.

Refresh your understanding, assess your progress and go further with interactive summaries, questions, podcasts and much more at **www.mypsychlab.co.uk**

# This chapter discusses

- The nature of communication
- How language arose and its connections to thought
- Paralinguistic cues, speech style and social markers
- Language, ethnolinguistic identity and speech accommodation
- Social issues in second-language learning
- Why language is crucial to a culture
- Speech style, power, gender and age

- The nature and function of non-verbal communication
- Communicating without words
- How the face conveys emotions
- Functions of gaze and eye contact
- Meaning in postures, gestures and touching
- Personal space: the bubble around our bodies
- Impressing and deceiving other people
- Having conversations and analysing discourse
- Using computers to communicate

# Focus questions

1. Kamalini lived most of her early life in Sri Lanka. When she shops for rice in a shop near you, she checks for colour, smell and whether it is free from grit, and she can put names to at least seven varieties. Are her senses more acute than yours? Is her vocabulary richer than yours?

2. En Li worked as a shop assistant in Shanghai after leaving school at fourteen years of age, and arrived in London at eighteen with just a smattering of English. What support factors might help her master English?

3. Pablo, his wife Diana and young son Paulo have recently moved from Colombia to the United States. They think it is important for their son to speak both Spanish and English. Will it be useful for Paulo to be bilingual? Watch these parents discuss this real-life issue in Chapter 15 of MyPsychLab at **www.mypsychlab.co.uk** (watch *Dev_bstate_03_Bilingual_Family*).

4. Santoso has recently arrived in The Hague after emigrating from Jakarta. At his first job interview, he did not make much eye contact with the human resources manager. Why might he have not done so, and will it hurt his prospects?

will use which involves getting you to decide to buy a car by giving you a very low price

Go to **mypsychlab** to explore video and test your understanding of key topics addressed in this chapter.

Refresh your understanding with interactive summaries, explore topics further with video and audio clips and assess your progress with quick test and essay questions by logging on to the accompanying website at **www.mypsychlab.co.uk**

# Chapter 15
## Language and communication

## Key terms

Ageism
Attachment styles
Back-channel communication
Bogus pipeline technique
Communication
Communication accommodation
　theory
Deindividuation
Discourse
Discourse analysis
Display rules
Emblems

Ethnolinguistic group
Ethnolinguistic identity theory
Ethnolinguistic vitality
Gaze
Gestures
Illocution
Kinesics
Language
Linguistic relativity
Locution
Matched-guise technique
Nature-nurture controversy
Non-verbal communication
Paralanguage
Personal space

Proxemics
Received pronunciation
Social identity theory
Social markers
Social representations
Speech
Speech accommodation
　theory
Speech convergence
Speech divergence
Speech style
Stereotype
Subjective vitality
Utterance
Visual dominance behaviour

# Communication

**Communication**

Transfer of meaningful
information from one
person to another.

**Gestures**

Meaningful body
movements and postures.

**Communication** is the essence of social interaction: when we interact we communicate. Try to think of any social interaction that is free of communication. We constantly transmit information about what we sense, think and feel – indeed even about our identity – and some of our 'messages' are unintentional. We communicate through words, facial expressions, signs, **gestures** and touch. We use phone calls, writing, emails and texts. Communication is social in several ways:

- It involves our relationships with others.
- It is built upon a shared understanding of meaning.
- It is how people influence each other.

Communication requires a sender, a message, a receiver and a channel of communication. However, any communicative event is enormously complex: a sender is also a receiver and vice versa, and there may be multiple, sometimes contradictory, messages travelling together via an array of different verbal and non-verbal channels.

Some social psychologists claim that communication is the dimension missing from treatments of social cognition, given that the latter is influenced by thought (see Chapter 2). However, research in social cognition has generally focused on individual information processing and storage, and has underemphasised the important role of communication in structuring cognition (Forgas, 1981; Markus & Zajonc, 1985; Zajonc, 1989).

The study of communication is potentially an enormous undertaking that can draw on a wide range of disciplines, such as psychology, social psychology, sociology, linguistics, sociolinguistics, philosophy and literary criticism. Social psychologists have tended broadly to distinguish between the study of language and the study of non-verbal communication. Recently, some social psychologists have focused on discourse. The structure of this chapter reflects the existence of these three overlapping areas of research. Scholars find that a full understanding of communication needs to incorporate both verbal and non-verbal communication (Ambady & Weisbuch, 2010; Holtgraves, 2010; Semin, 2007). We also touch briefly on computer-mediated communication (Hollingshead, 2001).

# Language

Spoken languages are based on rule-governed structuring of meaningless sounds (phonemes) into basic units of meaning (morphemes), which are further structured by morphological rules into words and by syntactic rules into sentences. The meanings of words, sentences and entire utterances are determined by semantic rules. Together, these rules represent grammar. It is because shared knowledge of morphological, syntactic and semantic rules permits the generation and comprehension of almost limitless meaningful utterances that **language** is such a powerful communication medium.

Meaning can be communicated by language at a number of levels. These range from a simple **utterance** (a sound made by one person to another) to a **locution** (words placed in sequence, e.g. 'It's hot in this room'), to an **illocution** (the locution and the context in which it is made: 'It's hot in this room' may be a statement, or a criticism of the institution for not providing cooled rooms, or a request to turn on the air conditioner, or a plea to move to another room) (Austin, 1962).

Mastery of language also requires us to know culturally rules appropriate for what to say – and when, where, how and to whom to say it. Recognising this opens to door to sociolinguistics (Fishman, 1972; see also Forgas, 1985), and more recently to the study of discourse as the basic unit of analysis (Edwards & Potter, 1992; Potter & Wetherell, 1987; see also below). Finally, Searle (1979) identifies five sorts of meaning that people can intentionally use language to communicate:

1 to say how something is;
2 to get someone to do something;
3 to express feelings and attitudes;
4 to make a commitment; and
5 to accomplish something directly.

Language is a distinctly human form of communication (see Box 15.4, 'The gestural origins of language'). Although young apes have been taught to combine basic signs in order to communicate meaningfully (Gardner & Gardner, 1971; Patterson, 1978), even the most precocious ape cannot match the complexity of hierarchical language structure used by a normal 3-year-old child (Limber, 1977). The species specificity of language has caused some theorists to believe that there must be an innate component to language. Specifically, Chomsky (1957) argued that the most basic universal rules of grammar are innate (called a 'language acquisition device') and are activated by social interaction to 'crack the code' of language. Others argue that the basic rules of language do not have to be innate. They can easily be learned through prelinguistic interaction between a child and its parents (Lock, 1978, 1980), and the meanings of utterances are so dependent on social context that they are unlikely to be innate (Bloom, 1970; Rommetveit, 1974; see Durkin, 1995).

## Language, thought and cognition

Language is social in all sorts of ways: as a system of symbols it lies at the heart of social life (Mead, 1934). It may be even more important than this. Perhaps thought itself is determined by language. We tend to perceive and think about the world in terms of linguistic categories, and thinking often involves a silent internal conversation with ourselves. Vygotsky (1962) believed that inner speech was the medium of thought, and that it was mutually interdependent with external speech (the medium of social communication). This interdependence suggests that cultural differences in language and speech are reflected

**Language**
A system of sounds that convey meaning because of shared grammatical and semantic rules.

**Utterance**
Sounds made by one person to another.

**Locution**
Words placed in sequence.

**Illocution**
Words placed in sequence and the context in which this is done.

**Linguistic relativity**
View that language determines thought and therefore people who speak different languages see the world in very different ways.

in cultural differences in thought. Sapir and Whorf proposed a more extreme version of this idea in their theory of **linguistic relativity** (Whorf, 1956).

The strong version of this theory is that language entirely determines thought, so people who speak different languages actually see the world in entirely different ways and effectively live in entirely different cognitive universes. Inuit (Eskimos) have a much more textured vocabulary for snow than other people; does this mean that they actually see more differences than we do? In English, we differentiate between living and non-living flying things, while the Hopi of North America do not; does this mean that they actually see no difference between a bee and an aeroplane? Japanese personal pronouns differentiate between interpersonal relationships more subtly than do English personal pronouns; does this mean that English speakers cannot tell the difference between different relationships? (To what would you attribute Kamalini's skills in the first focus question?)

The strong form of the Sapir–Whorf hypothesis is now considered too extreme (but see Box 15.1), and a weak form seems to accord better with the facts (Hoffman, Lau & Johnson, 1986). Language does not determine thought but rather permits us to communicate more easily about those aspects of the physical or social environment that are important for the community (e.g. Krauss & Chiu, 1998). If it is important to be able to communicate about snow, it is likely that a rich vocabulary concerning snow will develop. If you want or need to discuss wine in any detail and with any ease, it is useful to be able to master the arcane vocabulary of the wine connoisseur.

Although language may not determine thought, it certainly can constrain thought so that it is more or less easy to think about some things than others. If there is no simple word for something, it is more difficult to think about it. Nowadays, for this reason, there is a great deal of borrowing of words from one language by another: for example, English has borrowed *Zeitgeist* from German, *raison d'être* from French, *aficionado* from Spanish and *verandah* from Hindi. This idea is powerfully illustrated in George Orwell's novel *1984*, in which is described a fictional totalitarian regime based on Stalin's Soviet Union. The regime develops its own highly restricted language, called Newspeak, designed specifically to inhibit people from even thinking non-orthodox or heretical thoughts, because the relevant words do not exist.

## Real world 15.1
### Groups in space: the spatial agency bias

Maass and her colleagues have reported an intriguing study showing whether our culture writes from left to right or vice versa influences how we place people in pictures (Maass, Suitner, Favaretto & Cignacchi, 2009). Research has revealed a *spatial agency bias* in which people, from their visual perspective, tend to place/depict more agentic groups to the left of less agentic groups (e.g. pictures of men and women have the man on the left of the woman). However, this only happens for people whose language is written left-right (e.g. English); for those whose language is written right-left (e.g. Arabic) the spatial agency bias leads to more agentic groups being depicted to the right of less agentic groups. The way we scan the world as a consequence of the way our language is written affects the way we portray the world – what we scan first is given priority and is assumed to be more agentic and of higher status.

An intriguing implication of this is that in British culture men being positioned to the left of women, say in mixed-gender news reports or panel discussions, reinforces the assumption that men are more agentic and of higher status. Perhaps if this was switched so that the woman was on the left the perception would be challenged and the woman would be seen to have greater authority.

This research identifies an intriguing real world impact of language on cognition and perception.

## Paralanguage and speech style

Language communicates not only by *what* is said but also by *how* it is said. **Paralanguage** refers to all the non-linguistic accompaniments of speech – volume, stress, pitch, speed, tone of voice, pauses, throat clearing, grunts and sighs (Knapp, 1978; Trager, 1958). Timing, pitch and loudness (the *prosodic* features of language; Argyle, 1975) are particularly important, as they can dramatically change the meaning of utterances: a rising intonation at the end of a statement transforms it into a question or communicates uncertainty, doubt or need for approval (Lakoff, 1973). Prosodic features are important cues to underlying emotions: low pitch can communicate sadness or boredom, while high pitch can communicate anger, fear or surprise (Frick, 1985). Fast speech often communicates power and control (Ng & Bradac, 1993).

Scherer (1974) systematically varied, by means of a synthesiser, a range of paralinguistic features of short neutral utterances and then had people identify the emotion that was being communicated. Table 15.1 shows how different paralinguistic features communicate information about the speaker's feelings.

In addition to these paralinguistic cues, something can be said in different accents, different language varieties and different languages altogether. These are important **speech style**

**Paralanguage**
The non-linguistic accompaniments of speech (e.g. stress, pitch, speed, tone, pauses).

**Speech style**
The way in which something is said (e.g. accent, language), rather than the content of what is said.

**Table 15.1** Emotions displayed through paralinguistic cues

| Acoustic variable | Quality | Perceived as |
|---|---|---|
| Amplitude variation | Moderate | Pleasantness, activity, happiness |
| | Extreme | Fear |
| Pitch variation | Moderate | Anger, boredom, disgust, fear |
| | Extreme | Pleasantness, activity, happiness, surprise |
| Pitch contour | Down | Pleasantness, boredom, sadness |
| | Up | Potency, anger, fear, surprise |
| Pitch level | Low | Pleasantness, boredom, sadness |
| | High | Activity, potency, anger, fear, surprise |
| Tempo | Slow | Boredom, disgust, sadness |
| | Fast | Pleasantness, activity, potency, anger, fear, happiness, surprise |
| Duration (shape) | Round | Potency, boredom, disgust, fear, sadness |
| | Sharp | Pleasantness, activity, happiness, surprise |
| Filtration (no overtones) | Low | Pleasantness, happiness, boredom, sadness |
| | Moderate | Potency, activity |
| | Extreme | Anger, disgust, fear, surprise |
| | Atonal | Disgust |
| Tonality | Tonal – minor | Anger |
| | Tonal – major | Pleasantness, happiness |
| Rhythm | Not rhythmic | Boredom |
| | Rhythmic | Activity, fear, surprise |

*Source:* Scherer (1974)

differences that have been extensively researched in social psychology (Giles & Coupland, 1991). The social psychology of language tends to focus more on how something is said than on what is said, with speech style rather than speech content; whereas discourse analytic approaches (see later in this chapter) also place importance on what is said, speech content.

## Social markers in speech

Interpersonal differences in speech style are minor (Giles & Street, 1985). We have a repertoire of styles, and we automatically or deliberately tailor the way we speak to the context of the communicative event. For instance, we tend to speak slowly and use short words and simple grammatical constructions when we speak to foreigners and children (Clyne, 1981; Elliot, 1981). We use longer and more complex constructions, or more formalised language varieties or standard accents, when we are in a formal context such as an interview.

Brown and Fraser (1979) charted the different components of a communicative situation that may influence speech style, and distinguish between two broad features: (1) the scene (e.g. its purpose, time of day, whether there are bystanders); (2) the participants (e.g. their personality, ethnicity, whether they like each other). Since this is an objective classification of situations, we should remember that different people might not define the same objective situation in the same way. What is a formal context to one may seem quite informal to another. It is how the situation is subjectively perceived that influences speech style.

Furnham (1986) goes one step further in pointing out that not only do we cater speech style to perceived situational demands, but also we can seek out situations that are appropriate to a preferred speech style. If you want to have an informal chat, you are likely to choose a pleasant café rather than a seminar room as the venue.

Contextual variation in speech style means that speech style itself can tell us something about the context: in other words, speech contains clues to who is speaking to whom, in what context and about what. Speech contains **social markers** (Scherer & Giles, 1979). Some of the most researched markers are of group memberships such as social class, ethnicity, sex and age. Social markers are often clearly identifiable and act as very reliable clues to group membership. For instance, most Britons can quite easily identify Americans, Australians and South Africans from speech style alone, and are probably even better at identifying people who come from Exeter, Birmingham, Liverpool, Leeds and Essex! Speech style can elicit a listener's attitudes towards the group that the speaker represents. Recall the lengths to which Eliza Doolittle went in the film *My Fair Lady* to acquire a standard English accent in order to conceal her Cockney origins.

This idea is the basis of one of the most widely used research paradigms in the social psychology of language – the **matched-guise technique** – devised to investigate language attitudes based on speech alone (Lambert, Hodgson, Gardner & Fillenbaum, 1960). The method involves people rating short extracts of speech that are identical in all paralinguistic, prosodic and content respects, differing only in speech style (accent, dialect, language). All the speech extracts are spoken by the same person – someone who is fluently bilingual. The speaker is rated on a number of evaluative dimensions, which often fall into two distinct clusters that reflect competence and warmth (also see Fiske, Cuddy, Glick & Xu, 2002):

1 *status* variables (e.g. intelligent, competent, powerful);

2 *solidarity* variables (e.g. close, friendly, warm).

The matched-guise technique has been used extensively in a wide range of cultural contexts to investigate how speakers of standard and non-standard language varieties are evaluated. The standard language variety is the one that is associated with high economic status,

**Social markers**
Features of speech style that convey information about mood, context, status and group membership.

**Matched-guise technique**
Research methodology to measure people's attitudes towards a speaker based solely on speech style.

power and media usage – in Britain, for example, it is what has been called **received pronunciation** (RP) English. Non-standard varieties include regional accents (e.g. Yorkshire), non-standard urban accents (e.g. Birmingham) and minority ethnic languages (e.g. Hindi in Britain). Research reveals that standard varieties are more favourably evaluated on status and competence dimensions (such as intelligence, confidence, ambition) than non-standard varieties (e.g. Giles & Powesland, 1975).

There is also a tendency for non-standard speakers to be more favourably evaluated on solidarity dimensions. For example, Gallois, Callan and Johnstone (1984) found that both White Australians and Australian Aborigines upgraded Aboriginal-accented English on solidarity dimensions. In another study, Hogg, Joyce and Abrams (1984) found that Swiss Germans upgraded speakers of non-standard Swiss German relative to speakers of High German on solidarity dimensions.

## Language, identity and ethnicity

Matched-guise and other studies suggest that how we speak (our accent or even language) can affect how others evaluate us. This is unlikely to be because certain speech styles are intrinsically more pleasing than others, but rather because speech styles are associated with particular social groups that are consensually evaluated more or less positively in society. Use of a speech style that is associated with a lower-status group may cause people to regard you in terms of their evaluation of that group – with implications for how you may perceive yourself, your group and other groups, and how you may act in society. This suggests that processes associated with intergroup relations and group membership can affect language behaviour.

Giles and Bourhis and their colleagues have employed and extended principles from **social identity theory** (see Chapter 11) to develop an intergroup perspective on the social psychology of language (Giles, Bourhis, & Taylor, 1977; Giles & Johnson, 1981, 1987; see Giles, Reid & Harwood, 2009). Because the analysis focuses mainly on ethnic groups that differ in speech style, the theory is called **ethnolinguistic identity theory**.

### Speech style and ethnicity

Ethnic groups can differ in appearance, dress, cultural practices, and religious beliefs. However, language or speech style is often one of the most distinct and clear markers of *ethnic identity* (see Chapter 4) – social identity as a member of an **ethnolinguistic group** (an ethnic group defined by language or speech style). For instance, the Welsh and the English in the UK are most distinctive in terms of accent and language. Speech style, then, is an important and often central stereotypical or normative property of group membership: one of the most powerful ways to display your Welshness is to speak English with a marked Welsh accent – or, even better, to speak Welsh itself.

Language or speech style cues ethnic identity. Therefore, whether people accentuate or de-emphasise their ethnic language will be influenced by the extent to which they see their ethnic identity as being a source of self-respect and pride. This perception will in turn be influenced by the real nature of the power and status relations between ethnic groups in society. Almost all societies are multicultural, containing a single dominant high-status group whose language is the lingua franca of the nation, and a number of other ethnic groups whose languages are subordinate.

However, it is in new world immigrant countries such as the United States, Canada and Australia that the biggest variety of large ethnic minorities occurs. Not surprisingly, much of the research into ethnicity and language comes from these countries, particularly Australia and Canada. For example, in Australia, English is the lingua franca, but there are

**Received pronunciation**
Standard, high-status, spoken variety of English.

**Social identity theory**
Theory of group membership and intergroup relations based on self-categorisation, social comparison and the construction of a shared self-definition in terms of ingroup-defining properties.

**Ethnolinguistic identity theory**
Application and extension of social identity theory to deal with language behaviour of ethnolinguistic groups.

**Ethnolinguistic group**
Social group defined principally in terms of its language.

**Communication**
Communication involves spoken and written language and a rich mix of expressions, gestures and emblems — all contextualised by ethnicity and nationality

also large ethnic Chinese, Italian, Greek and Vietnamese Australian communities – language research has been conducted in all these communities (e.g. Gallois, Barker, Jones & Callan, 1992; Gallois & Callan, 1986; Giles, Rosenthal & Young, 1985; Hogg, D'Agata & Abrams, 1989; McNamara, 1987; Smolicz, 1983; see Box 16.5 in Chapter 16).

### Language and vitality

**Ethnolinguistic vitality**
Concept describing objective features of an interethnic context that influence language, and ultimately the cultural survival or disappearance of an ethnolinguistic group.

Giles, Bourhis and Taylor (1977) introduced the term **ethnolinguistic vitality** to describe those objective features of an inter-ethnic context that influence language behaviour (see Figure 15.1). Ethnic groups that are high on status, and demographic and institutional support variables, have high ethnolinguistic vitality. This encourages continued use of the language and thus ensures its survival and the survival of the ethnolinguistic group itself as a distinct entity in society. Low vitality is associated with declining use of the ethnic language, its gradual disappearance and often the disappearance of the ethnolinguistic group as a distinct entity: that is, there is language death or language suicide.

**Subjective vitality**
Individual group members' representation of the objective ethnolinguistic vitality of their group.

Objective ethnolinguistic vitality configurations can be calculated for different groups (Giles, 1978; Saint-Blancat, 1985), but it is **subjective vitality** – that is, people's *own* perception of the vitality of their group – that more directly influences language usage (Bourhis, Giles & Rosenthal, 1981; Harwood, Giles & Bourhis, 1994; Sachdev & Bourhis, 1993). In general, there is a correspondence between objective and subjective vitality, but the two need not be identical.

Ethnic minorities may consider their language to have more or less vitality than objective indices indicate. Under some circumstances, a dominant group may actively encourage a minority to underestimate the vitality of its language in order to inhibit ethnolinguistic revival movements that may threaten the status quo.

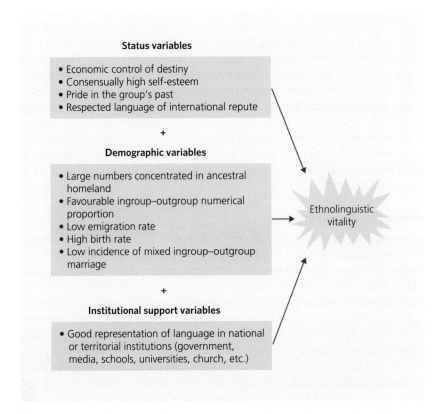

**Status variables**

- Economic control of destiny
- Consensually high self-esteem
- Pride in the group's past
- Respected language of international repute

+

**Demographic variables**

- Large numbers concentrated in ancestral homeland
- Favourable ingroup–outgroup numerical proportion
- Low emigration rate
- High birth rate
- Low incidence of mixed ingroup–outgroup marriage

+

**Institutional support variables**

- Good representation of language in national or territorial institutions (government, media, schools, universities, church, etc.)

Ethnolinguistic vitality

**Figure 15.1** When is a language vital?

- Ethnolinguistic vitality is influenced by status, demographic and institutional support variables

*Source*: Giles, Bourhis & Taylor (1977); based on Hogg & Abrams (1988)

Inter-ethnic relations, and subjective perceptions of these relations, may thus influence language behaviour. In Canada, the past forty years have witnessed a strong French-language revival in the province of Quebec, which can be understood in terms of changes in subjective vitality (Bourhis, 1984; Sachdev & Bourhis, 2005). Other revivals include Hebrew, considered a dead language half a century ago, in Israel; Flemish in Belgium; Welsh in the UK; Hindi in India; and again, Welsh in both Wales and beyond (see Coupland, Bishop, Evans & Garrett, 2006; Fishman, 1989). These studies converge on a major finding: ethnolinguistic vitality is strongest among speakers who are competent in the language.

A language can also die. A loss of ethnolinguistic identity has occurred in the following: in Canada, Italian and Scottish Canadians generally consider themselves Anglo-Canadian; third-generation Japanese in Brazil have entirely lost their Japanese culture; in Australia, linguistic vitality has declined from first- to second-generation Greek, Italian and Vietnamese Australians (see Edwards & Chisholm, 1987; Hogg, D'Agata & Abrams, 1989; Kanazawa & Loveday, 1988).

Allard and Landry (1994) have recently extended the subjective vitality notion to place greater emphasis on interpersonal communicative environments. They argue that what really counts for an ethnic language to thrive is not subjective beliefs about the vitality of the language but rather the interpersonal network of linguistic contacts that people have. This makes good sense: a language will not thrive unless it is used. However, perceived vitality may still be important – it influences linguistic opportunities, linguistic and identity motivations, and linguistic evaluations. A study of Italian Australians (Hogg & Rigoli, 1996) found that Italian-language competence was related not to interpersonal linguistic contacts but to subjective vitality. (Consider how En Li's command of English could improve in the second focus question.)

# Speech accommodation

**Speech accommodation theory**
Modification of speech style to the context (e.g. listener, situation) of a face-to-face inter-individual conversation.

Social categories such as ethnic groups may develop and maintain or lose their distinctive languages or speech styles as a consequence of intergroup relations. However, categories do not speak. People speak, and they speak to one another, usually in face-to-face interaction. As described above, when people speak they tend to adapt their speech style to the context – the situation, and in particular the listener. This idea is the foundation of **speech accommodation theory** (Giles, 1984; Giles, Taylor & Bourhis, 1973), which explains the ways in which people accommodate their speech style to those who are present, in terms of specific motivations. The motives that may be involved include a desire to help the listener to understand what you are saying or a desire to promote a specific impression of yourself in order to obtain social approval.

## Speech convergence and divergence

**Speech convergence**
Accent or speech style shift towards that of the other person.

Based on the assumption that most talk involves people who are potentially of unequal status, speech accommodation theory describes the type of accommodation that might occur as a function of the sort of social orientation that the speakers may have towards one another (see Table 15.2). Where a simple interpersonal orientation exists (e.g. between two friends), bilateral **speech convergence** occurs. Higher-status speakers shift their accent or speech style 'downwards' towards that of lower-status speakers, who in turn shift 'upwards'. In this context, convergence satisfies a need for approval or liking. Convergence increases interpersonal speech style similarity and thus enhances interpersonal approval and liking (Bourhis, Giles & Lambert, 1975), particularly if the convergence behaviour is clearly intentional (Simard, Taylor & Giles, 1976).

**Speech divergence**
Accent or speech style shift away from that of the other person.

Now consider the case where an intergroup orientation exists. If the lower-status group has low subjective vitality coupled with a belief in social mobility (i.e. that one can pass, linguistically, into the higher-status group), there is unilateral upward convergence on the part of the lower-status speaker and unilateral **speech divergence** on the part of the higher-status speaker. In intergroup contexts, divergence achieves psycholinguistic distinctiveness: it differentiates the speaker's ingroup on linguistic grounds from the outgroup. Where an intergroup orientation exists and the lower-status group has high subjective vitality coupled with a belief in social change (i.e. that one cannot pass into the higher-status group), bilateral divergence occurs. Both speakers pursue *psycholinguistic distinctiveness*.

Speech accommodation theory has been well supported empirically (Giles & Coupland, 1991). For example, Bourhis and Giles (1977) found that Welsh adults accentuated their Welsh accent in the presence of RP English speakers (i.e. the standard non-regional variety of English). Bourhis, Giles, Leyens and Tajfel (1979) obtained a similar finding in Belgium, with Flemish speakers in the presence of French speakers. In both cases, a language revival was under way at the time, and thus an intergroup orientation with high vitality was

**Table 15.2** Speech accommodation as a function of status, social orientation and subjective vitality

| | Social orientation and vitality of lower-status group | | |
|---|---|---|---|
| | Interpersonal | Intergroup | |
| Speaker status | | Low vitality (*Social mobility*) | High vitality (*Social change*) |
| Higher | Downward convergence | Upward divergence | Upward divergence |
| Lower | Upward convergence | Upward convergence | Downward divergence |

salient. In a low-vitality social mobility context, Hogg (1985) found that female students in Britain shifted their speech style 'upwards' towards that of their male partners.

Accommodation in intergroup contexts reflects an intergroup or social identity mechanism in which speech style is dynamically governed by the speakers' motivations to adopt ingroup or outgroup speech patterns. These motivations are in turn formed by perceptions of:

- the relative status and prestige of the speech varieties and their associated groups; and
- the vitality of their own ethnolinguistic group.

### Stereotyped speech

What may actually govern changes in speech style is conformity to stereotypical perceptions of the appropriate speech norm (see Chapter 7). Thakerar, Giles and Cheshire (1982) have recognised this in distinguishing between objective and subjective accommodation. People converge on or diverge from what they perceive to be the relevant speech style. Objective accommodation may reflect this, but in some circumstances it may not: for instance, subjective *con*vergence may look like objective *di*vergence if the speech style **stereotype** is different from the actual speech behaviour of the other speaker.

**Stereotype**
Widely shared and simplified evaluative image of a social group and its members.

Even the 'Queen's English' is susceptible to some accommodation towards a more popular stereotype (Harrington, 2006). A phonetic analysis of Queen Elizabeth II's speech contained in her Christmas broadcasts to the Commonwealth since 1952 point to a gradual change in the Royal vowels, moving from 'upper-class' RP to a more 'standard' and less aristocratic RP. Possibly this reflects a softening of the once strong demarcation between the social classes – social change can sometimes be a catalyst for speech change. Where once she might have said 'thet men in the bleck het', she would now say 'that man in the black hat'.

Recently, speech accommodation theory has been extended in recognition of the role of non-verbal behaviour in communication (non-verbal behaviour is discussed below). Now more accurately called **communication accommodation theory** (Giles, Mulac, Bradac & Johnson, 1987; Giles & Noels, 2002), it acknowledges that convergence and divergence can occur non-verbally as well as verbally. For instance, Mulac, Studley, Wiemann and Bradac (1987) found that women in mixed-sex dyads converged towards the amount of eye contact (now called 'gaze' – see below) made by their partner. While accommodation is often synchronised in verbal and non-verbal channels, this is not necessarily the case. Bilous and Krauss (1988) found that women in mixed-sex dyads converged towards men on some dimensions (e.g. total words uttered and interruptions) but diverged on others (e.g. laughter).

**Communication accommodation theory**
Modification of verbal and non-verbal communication styles to the context (e.g. listener, situation) of a face-to-face interaction – an extension of speech accommodation theory to incorporate non-verbal communication.

## Bilingualism and second-language acquisition

Most countries are bilingual or multilingual – in some instances, people need to be trilingual (see Box 15.2). Such countries contain a variety of ethnolinguistic groups, with a single dominant group whose language is the lingua franca. Very few countries (e.g. Japan and Portugal) are effectively monolingual.

Bilingualism or second-language acquisition for most people is not simply a recreational activity – it is a vital necessity for survival. For example, in Britain, Chinese immigrants really have to learn English in order to be educated and to be able to participate in employment, culture and day-to-day life in Britain. Acquisition of a second language is not so much a matter of acquiring basic classroom proficiency as the wholesale acquisition of a language imbedded in its cultural context (Gardner, 1979). Second-language acquisition requires native-like mastery (being able to speak like a native speaker), and this hinges more on the motivations of the second-language learner than on linguistic aptitude or pedagogical factors. Failure to acquire native-like mastery can undermine self-confidence and

**Bilingualism**
If you can't read Welsh enrol on a language course. Until then, how about English?

cause physical and social isolation, leading to material hardship and psychological suffering. For example, Noels, Pon and Clément (1996) found low self-esteem and marked symptoms of stress among Chinese Canadians with poor English skills.

Building on earlier models by Gardner (1979) and Clément (1980), Giles and Byrne (1982) proposed an intergroup model. There are five *socio-psychological dimensions* that influence a subordinate group member's motivational goals in learning the language of a dominant group (see Figure 15.2):

1 strength of ethnolinguistic identification;

2 number of alternative identities available;

3 number of high-status alternative identities available;

4 subjective vitality perceptions;

5 social beliefs regarding whether it is or is not possible to pass linguistically into the dominant group.

## Research highlight 15.2
### Being trilingual in Montreal

Since the 1970s, Montreal's population has become bilingual, whereas in earlier decades its residents were more likely to be bilingual Francophones than bilingual Anglophones (Lamarre & Paredes, 2003). This past asymmetry reflected the relative status of the two language groups – English was the dominant group. Social change, specifically in the use of French, was enacted in law as part of Quebec's language policy – its 1977 *Charte*

*de la langue française* gave French official status in schools alongside English – and in the following decades the perceived status of French improved.

This change in relative French–English status has had major consequences for the children of new immigrants: they are now mostly *trilingual*. At one time they would have preferred to learn English as their second language, on the basis that Anglophones were perceived to be the dominant group, but now they choose to speak three languages – a degree of their ancestral language at home and the two local languages in public.

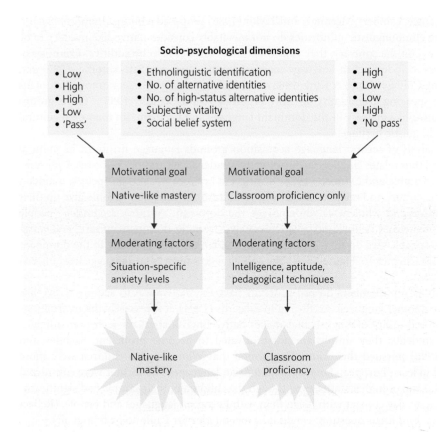

**Socio-psychological dimensions**

| | | |
|---|---|---|
| • Low<br>• High<br>• High<br>• Low<br>• 'Pass' | • Ethnolinguistic identification<br>• No. of alternative identities<br>• No. of high-status alternative identities<br>• Subjective vitality<br>• Social belief system | • High<br>• Low<br>• Low<br>• High<br>• 'No pass' |

| Motivational goal | Motivational goal |
|---|---|
| Native-like mastery | Classroom proficiency only |

| Moderating factors | Moderating factors |
|---|---|
| Situation-specific anxiety levels | Intelligence, aptitude, pedagogical techniques |

Native-like mastery      Classroom proficiency

**Figure 15.2**  Intergroup model of second-language acquisition

• Learning a second language is influenced by motivational goals formed by the wider context of social identity and intergroup relations.

*Source:* Giles & Byrne (1982)

Low identification with the ethnic ingroup, low subjective vitality and a belief that one can 'pass' linguistically, coupled with a large number of other potential identities of which many are high-status, are conditions that motivate someone to acquire native-like mastery in the second language. Proficiency in the second language is seen to be economically and culturally useful; it is considered *additive* to our identity. Realisation of this motivation will be facilitated or inhibited by the extent to which we are made to feel confident or anxious about using the second language in specific contexts. The converse set of socio-psychological conditions (see Figure 15.2) motivates people to acquire only classroom proficiency. Through fear of assimilation, the second language is considered *subtractive* in that it may attract ingroup hostility and accusations of ethnic betrayal. Intelligence and aptitude will also affect proficiency.

## Language, culture and migration

The intergroup model in Figure 15.2 found broad support in a study by Hall and Gudykunst (1986) in Arizona. The English-language ability of over 200 international students from a wide range of cultural and linguistic backgrounds could be explained in terms of Giles and Byrne's (1982) intergroup model. The model has subsequently been developed and modified somewhat in recognition of the enormous complexity of accurately modelling second-language learning in multicultural contexts (Garrett, Giles & Coupland, 1989; Giles & Coupland, 1991).

For instance, Lambert, Mermigis and Taylor (1986) proposed a *multiculturalism hypothesis*. Secure ethnolinguistic minorities do not inevitably consider native-like mastery to be subtractive – on the contrary, they can sometimes consider it to be additive. Examples of this process include English-language mastery among Japanese (San Antonio, 1987) and Hong Kong Chinese (Bond & King, 1985), and Italian language mastery among Valdotans (a French-speaking community in northern Italy; Saint-Blancat, 1985). These groups acquire native-like mastery in the dominant language and yet maintain their own cultural and ethnolinguistic heritage.

This analysis of second-language acquisition grounds language firmly in its cultural context and thus relates language acquisition to broader acculturation processes. For example, Berry, Trimble and Olmedo (1986) distinguish between *integration* (people maintain their ethnic culture and relate to the dominant culture), *assimilation* (people give up their ethnic culture and wholeheartedly embrace the dominant culture), *separation* (people maintain their ethnic culture and isolate themselves from the dominant culture) and *marginalisation* (people give up their ethnic culture and fail to relate properly to the dominant culture – see Chapter 16, Figure 16.5). The consequences for second-language learning can be dramatic.

Majority group members do not generally have the motivation to acquire native-like mastery of another language. According to Edwards (1994), it is precisely the international prestige and utility of English that makes native English speakers such poor foreign-language students: they simply are not motivated to become proficient. Sachdev and Wright (1996) pursued this point. They found that White English children were more motivated to learn European languages than Asian languages: the former were considered more useful and of higher status, even though the children in their sample had significantly more day-to-day contact with Asian than with European languages and people. (Reflect now on the third focus question: would it be a good idea for Paulo to be bilingual?)

## Gender, age and language

Much of the social psychology of language focuses on ethnicity and language. However, the general principles with language apply in an intergroup context and we now extend our treatment to gender and age effects.

### Gender

Speech style differences between women and men have been studied mostly in Western countries (Aries, 1996; Smith, 1985), where there are strong stereotypes about sex differences in speech (Haas, 1979; see Chapter 10). For example, women are often assumed to be more talkative, polite, emotional, positive, supportive and tentative, less assertive, and more likely to talk about home and family. Real speech differences are much smaller than stereotypes lead one to believe (Aries, 1997), and such differences are highly context-dependent. Even paralinguistic differences that are grounded in physiology (women's voices have a higher pitch, softer volume, greater variability, and more relaxed and mellifluous tone) are influenced by context and show marked within-sex variability (Montepare & Vega, 1988).

Because speech style has become stereotypically sex-typed (Weatherall, 1998), it is not surprising to discover that both men and women can adopt more or less masculine or feminine speech styles depending on whether they have a more or less traditional sex-role orientation (Smith, 1985). Non-traditional men tend to eschew more masculine speech styles, and non-traditional women eschew more feminine speech styles. In line with speech accommodation theory, speech style can also vary according to the immediate communicative context. In the case of gender differences, the way that men and women speak, particularly to each other, is sometimes linked to power (see Box 15.3).

## Research highlight 15.3
### Speech style, gender and power

There is some evidence that women can adopt a 'powerless' form of speech when addressing men or in the company of men (O'Barr & Atkins, 1980; Wiemann & Giles, 1988). Women tend to adopt a more masculine (more powerful) speech style when speaking to male strangers or acquaintances (Hall & Braunwald, 1981; Hogg, 1985) but a more feminine (less powerful) style when speaking to intimate male friends (Montepare & Vega, 1988).

The linguist Robin Lakoff's *Language and Woman's Place* (1975) outlined the nature of powerless speech: it involves greater use of *intensifiers* (e.g. 'very', 'really', 'so'), *hedges* (e.g. 'kind of', 'sort of', 'you know'), *tag questions* (e.g. '. . . didn't they?'), *empty adjectives* ('gorgeous', 'adorable', 'divine'), rising intonation, which transforms a declarative statement into a question, and *polite forms of address*.

Power can also be associated with the ability to interrupt and take control of the floor (Reid & Ng, 1999; Ng, Bell & Brooke, 1993; Ng & Bradac, 1993). In mixed-sex conversations, women have been shown to interrupt less often than men: Zimmerman and West (1975) reported that 98 per cent of interruptions were by men. However, other research suggests that women can interrupt more often than men (Dindia, 1987).

Powerless speech is not confined to women; it simply reflects status differences in interactions and has been shown to characterise low-status speakers in general (Lind & O'Barr, 1979). A study of stereotypical beliefs about speech styles by Popp and her colleagues found that women – and even more so, Blacks – have a less direct and more emotional style than that of White men (Popp, Donovan, Crawford, Marsh & Peele, 2003). In this sense, the speech of women is now better described as a powerless rather than a female linguistic style (Blankenship & Holtgraves, 2005).

When children are socialised in relatively sex-segregated groups, boys and girls acquire different kinds of interaction and communication styles that carry over into adulthood. Girls emphasise cooperation and equality, and attend sensitively to relationships and situations. Boys emphasise competition and hierarchical relations, and assert their individual identity. Much like interactions between cultural groups with different language communication norms, men and women interact with different assumptions and goals in a conversation. Since some of the same forms can carry different meanings and serve different functions for men and women, inter-sex miscommunication is almost inevitable (e.g. Mulac, Bradac & Gibbons, 2001).

Critics have pointed to difficulties in generalising about research on gender differences in language and communication: contextual factors are underplayed, and it is culturally constrained largely to men and women who are White, middle-class and Western (e.g. Crawford, 1995; Eckert & McConnell-Ginet, 1999).

## Age

Through life we all move into and out of a sequence of age groups – infant, child, teenager, youth, young adult, adult, middle-aged, old. Society has stereotypical beliefs and expectations about the attitudes and behaviour associated with these categories. In Western society, for instance, **ageism** is common – old people are generally considered to be frail, incompetent, of low status and largely worthless (Baker, 1985; Noels, Giles & Le Poire, 2003; see Chapter 10). In a perverse form of speech accommodation strategy, younger people might adopt a sort of 'baby talk' to communicate with both institutionalised and non-institutionalised elderly people (Caporael, Lukaszewski & Cuthbertson, 1983; Ryan, Giles, Bartolucci & Henwood, 1986). This can be accompanied by 'elderspeak' – the use of simple and short sentences (Kemper, 1994). While some elderly find this nurturant, many believe it is patronising (Nelson, 2005).

**Ageism**
Prejudice and discrimination against people based on their age.

At the same time, young people feel that the elderly fail to accommodate their speech, and they find this irritating (Fox & Giles, 1993; Williams, 1996). Intergenerational encounters between the young and the elderly are thus likely to reinforce stereotypes rather than disconfirm them (see discussion of intergroup contact in Chapter 11). These intergenerational effects are widespread, and some recent research by Giles and his associates has found, quite surprisingly, that they are more pronounced in East Asian settings (Giles, Noels, Ota, et al., 2001).

Because age categories are so pervasive, we all know what is expected of us once we reach a particular age. Indeed, along with race and gender, age is one of the primitive, well-learned and automatic forms of social categorisation (Mackie, Hamilton, Susskind & Rosselli, 1996; Nelson, 2005). Almost every official form you complete asks for your age and sex. As these experiences accumulate it makes it difficult for elderly people not to 'act their age'. The social costs of not acting our age can be extreme – as was entertainingly illustrated in the 1980s movie *Cocoon*. Perhaps, then, elderly people talk a great deal about their age, make painful disclosures about their health and exhibit other symptoms of elderly speech, not so much because of their age but because they are constrained to conform to social expectations (Coupland, Coupland, Giles & Henwood, 1988; Giles & Coupland, 1991). Intergenerational communication can certainly be problematic, and can even have effects on psychological and physical well-being (Williams & Nussbaum, 2001).

# Communicating without words

**Speech**
Vocal production of language.

**Speech** rarely occurs in isolation from non-verbal cues. Even on the phone, people tend automatically to use all sorts of gestures that cannot possibly be 'seen' by the person at the other end of the line. Similarly, phone and computer-mediated communication (CMC) conversations can often be difficult precisely because many non-verbal cues are not accessible. However, non-verbal channels do not necessarily work in concert with speech to facilitate understanding. Sometimes the non-verbal message starkly contradicts the verbal message (e.g. threats, sarcasm and other negative messages accompanied by a smile; Bugental, Love & Gianetto, 1971; Noller, 1984).

## Functions of non-verbal communication

Did you know that people can produce about 20,000 different facial expressions and about 1,000 different cues based on paralanguage? There are also about 700,000 different physical gestures, facial expressions and movements (see Birdwhistell, 1970; Hewes, 1957; Pei, 1965). How on earth do we cope? Even the briefest interaction can involve the fleeting and simultaneous use of a large number of these devices, making it very difficult even to code behaviour, let alone analyse the causes and consequences of particular **non-verbal communications**. Their importance is now well recognised in social psychology (Ambady & Weisbuch, 2010; Burgoon, Buller & Woodall, 1989; DePaulo & Friedman, 1998). However, doing research in this area is a major challenge. Non-verbal behaviour can serve a variety of purposes (Patterson, 1983). We can use it to:

**Non-verbal communication**
Transfer of meaningful information from one person to another by means other than written or spoken language (e.g. gaze, facial expression, posture, touch).

- glean information about feelings and intentions of others (e.g. non-verbal cues are often reliable indicators of whether someone likes you);
- regulate interactions (e.g. non-verbal cues can signal the approaching end of an utterance, or that someone else wishes to speak);
- express intimacy (e.g. touching and mutual eye contact);

- establish dominance or control (non-verbal threats);
- facilitate goal attainment (e.g. pointing).

## Variations in non-verbal behaviour

The functions referred to will become evident in our discussion of gaze, facial expressions, body language, touch and interpersonal distance. Perhaps partly because we acquire non-verbal behaviour unawares, we tend not to be conscious that we are using non-verbal cues or that we are being influenced by others' use of such cues: non-verbal communication goes largely unnoticed, yet it has enormous impact.

People acquire, without any formal training, consummate mastery of a rich repertoire of non-verbal behaviour very early in life. This suggests that there will be broad individual differences in the skills and uses people have in employing non-verbal communication.

This is not to say that non-verbal behaviour is completely uncontrolled. On the contrary, social norms can influence its expression. For example, even if delighted at the demise of a foe, we are unlikely to smile at his or her funeral. There are also individual and group differences, with some people being better than others at noticing and using non-verbal cues. Rosenthal and his colleagues (Rosenthal, Hall, DiMatteo, Rogers & Archer, 1979) devised a *profile of non-verbal sensitivity* (PONS) as a test to chart some of these individual and group differences. All things being equal, non-verbal sensitivity improves with age, is more advanced among successful people and is compromised among people with a range of psychopathologies.

We now consider two other areas of difference that have attracted attention.

### Gender differences

Reviews have concluded that women are generally better than men at decoding both visual cues and auditory cues, such as voice tone and pitch (E. T. Hall, 1979; J. A. Hall, 1978, 1984). The most likely interpretation is a social rather than evolutionary one (Manstead, 1992), including child-rearing strategies that encourage girls more than boys to be emotionally expressive and attentive. A question recently addressed is whether women's greater competence is due to greater knowledge about non-verbal cues. The answer, according to Rosip and Hall (2004), is yes – women have a slight advantage, based on results from their *test of non-verbal cue knowledge* (TONCK). A meta-analysis by Ickes, Gesn and Graham (2000) has shown that when motivated to do so, women can become even more accurate: for example, when they think they are being evaluated for their empathy or when gender-role expectations of empathy are brought to the fore.

There is scope for all of us to improve our non-verbal skills. As they can be useful for improving interpersonal communication, detecting deception, presenting a good impression and hiding our feelings, practical books and courses on communications skills are popular. Why not try yourself out on the TONCK?

### Relationships and attachment

People have different **attachment styles** that influence their relationships (see Chapter 14) and thus their non-verbal behaviour. In the case of an intimate relationship, we might expect that partners will enhance each other's emotional security by accurately decoding non-verbal cues and responding appropriately (Schachner, Shaver & Mikulincer, 2005). There are data dealing with non-verbal behaviour in parent–child interactions and how these relate to the development of attachment styles in children (Bugental, 2005) – the field is ripe to be broadened to understand better how adult attachment styles are reflected non-verbally in close relationships. For example, if Harry is vigilant to threat in his relationship with Sally, he may take her (ambiguous) silence as rejection.

**Attachment styles**
Descriptions of the nature of people's close relationships, thought to be established in childhood.

## Using the face to express emotions

You may have already surmised that the emotions play a major part in communicating our feelings, through our body and especially our facial expressions, and that there is a time and a place when we should do so. Keeping a 'stiff upper lip' is not always the smartest move.

The scientific study of facial expression has largely focused on the way in which different expressions communicate emotions. Darwin (1872) believed that there are a small number of universal emotions and that associated with these emotions are universal facial expressions. Subsequent research generally identified six basic emotions (happiness, surprise, sadness, fear, disgust and anger), from which more complex or blended emotions are derived (Ekman, 1982, 2003; Scherer, 1986; but see also Ortony & Turner, 1990). There are cross-cultural gender differences in how often both basic and complex emotions are experienced (Fischer, Mosquera, van Vienan & Manstead, 2004). Women report more often their powerless emotions (e.g. fear, sadness, shame, guilt), while men more often report their powerful emotions (e.g. anger, hostility).

A basic emotion has a quite distinctive pattern of facial muscle activity: for instance, surprise is associated with raised eyebrows, dropped jaw, horizontal wrinkles across the forehead, raised upper eyelids and lowered lower eyelids (Ekman & Friesen, 1975). Researchers have even developed a computer program that can simultaneously vary different facial components (e.g. roundness of eyes, thickness of lips, curve of eyebrows, distance between mouth and eyes) to reproduce recognisable emotional expressions on a computer screen (Katsikitis, Pilowsky & Innes, 1990).

The human facial expressions associated with basic emotions appear to be relatively universal. Ekman and his colleagues showed people a series of photographs of faces expressing the six basic emotions and had them report the emotions being expressed (Ekman, 1971; Ekman & Friesen, 1971; Ekman et al., 1987). People from a variety of Western cultures (Argentina, Brazil, Chile, Germany, Greece, Italy, Scotland, the United States), Asian cultures (Hong Kong, Japan, Sumatra, Turkey) and tribal cultures (Borneo, New Guinea) were remarkably accurate in identifying the six emotions from facial expression by people from both the same and different cultures.

There has been some criticism of Ekman's method, which depended on participants rating photographs of posed rather than natural (candid) emotional expressions. However, in contrast to Ekman's use of posed photographs, Robert Krauss and his colleagues adopted a more naturalistic technique in which people identified emotions as they occurred on videotapes of Japanese and American soap operas (Krauss, Curran & Ferleger, 1983). Like Ekman's findings, there was remarkable cross-cultural agreement.

Ekman's argument that the primary emotions are universal has also been criticised (e.g. Russell, Bachorowski & Fernandez-Dols, 2003), but his work has generated a large number

**Unlearned facial displays**

Crying and smiling — innate expressions of emotion. Later in life we learn when to display different feelings

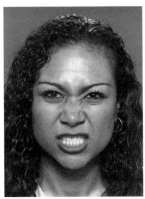

**Six basic emotions**
Anger, happiness, surprise, fear, sadness and disgust. But, which is which?

of studies and continues to do so. Undeterred, Ekman has developed a Facial Action Coding System (FACS), a standardised method to measure facial movement based on small units of muscles that reflect a variety of underlying emotional states (Ekman, Friesen & Hager, 2002). This technique has even been adapted to measure facial responses in chimpanzees (Vick et al., 2007). The aim of such work is to make a cross-species comparison of 'emotions' with humans, in an evolutionary quest for characteristics that are uniquely human and those that may be shared with other primates.

The apparent universality of facial expressions of emotion may either reflect universals of *ontogeny* (cross-cultural commonalities in early socialisation) or else *phylogeny* (an innate link between emotions and facial muscle activity). The contribution of phylogeny has some support from research among people born deaf, blind and without hands. Although these people have limited access to the normal cues that we would use to learn which facial expressions go with which emotions, they express basic emotions in much the same manner as people who are not handicapped in these ways (Eibl-Eibesfeldt, 1972).

## Facial display rules

Having made an argument for universals in the facial expression of the emotions, we must now make an important qualification. There are marked cultural and situational rules, called **display rules**, governing the expression of emotions (see Figure 15.3).

These rules exist because we also use our facial expressions to communicate with someone else (Gallois, 1993). There are shades of surprise: when we 'choose' one of these, we might accompany our facial display by vocalising with something like 'oh my god' or

**Display rules**
Cultural and situational rules that dictate how appropriate it is to express emotions in a given context.

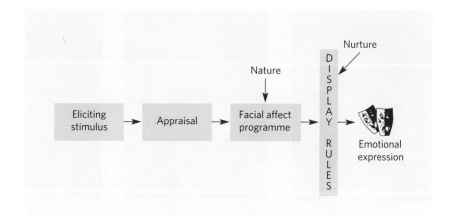

**Figure 15.3**  The facial affect programme: expressing an emotion

- Rapid facial signals accompany many affective states.
- These signals are the facial affect programme, or facial 'blueprints'.
- They distinguish primary emotions from their blends.
- There is an interplay between nature and nurture
  - Singnals have a genetic base, whereas
  - Display rules arise from experience and provide a little control over what we show others.

*Source:* based on Ekman (1971)

'whew'. In a fine-grained analysis of conversations, Sue Wilkinson and Celia Kitzinger (2006) have demonstrated that we are equipped to respond with surprise several turns in advance. Perhaps you can remember talking with a friend and can guess what is about to announced – your face begins to move ... oh gosh, the suspense!

There are cultural, gender and situational variations in display rules. The expression of emotion is encouraged for women and in Mediterranean cultures, but is discouraged for men and in northern European and Asian cultures (Argyle, 1975). In Japan, people are taught to control facial expressions of negative emotion and to use laughter or smiling to conceal anger or grief. In Western cultures, it is impolite to display happiness at beating an opponent in tennis by laughing, yet happy laughter is acceptable at a party. Similarly, it is fine to cry at a funeral but not on hearing disappointing news in a business setting. Ekman's approach has been described as 'one of the first theories to explain how a psychological process could be both universal and culture-specific' (Matsumoto, 2004, p. 49).

In short, we are dealing with the **nature–nurture controversy**, a point that is nicely illustrated by Russell's (1994) investigation of the varying success that people from different parts of the world have in decoding (or labelling) the six primary emotions (shown in the photo above). His results are shown in Figure 15.4.

A meta-analysis has confirmed that both universal and cultural components are involved in recognising the emotions (Elfenbein & Ambady, 2002), and also in how we experience them (Kitayama, Mesquita & Karasawa, 2006). One interesting finding was that people are more accurate at facial recognition and decoding emotions expressed by people from the same ethnic or regional group as themselves. Just as there are language dialects, there may be emotional dialects, shaped by geographic, national and social boundaries.

We have noted that we use our face to *express* our emotions; however, we use display rules to *communicate* with others. Thus distinction featured in a series of naturalistic studies of smiling, by Kraut and Johnston (1979). They studied the frequency of smiling in a range of settings, including bowling alleys, ice hockey arenas and public footpaths. People were more likely to smile when talking to others than when alone, and whether they were

**Nature–nurture controversy**
Classic debate about whether genetic or environmental factors determine human behaviour. Scientists generally accept that it is an interaction of both.

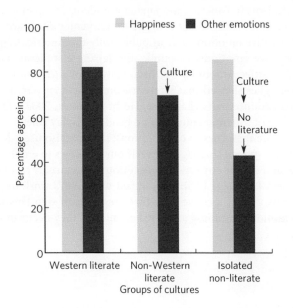

**Figure 15.4**  Cross-cultural success at decoding facial expressions of primary emotions

- People from three categories of cultures were compared: literate and from the West (20 studies) or elsewhere (11 studies), and non-literate from elsewhere (three studies).
- Recognition of happiness is high in all cultures.
- Agreement about other emotions falls away, depending on: (a) what is thought to be a culturally appropriate expression, and (b) exposure to a literature that provides models of how to express an emotion.

*Source*: based on data from Russell (1994)

really happy or not seemed to have little influence on whether they smiled or not: smiling was an even more important way of communicating happiness as expressing it. Figure 15.5 shows the percentage of bowlers in competition who smiled either when facing their teammates (social interaction) or facing the pins (no social interaction), as an outcome of bowling well or poorly. These findings were replicated in a study of football fans as well as bowlers (Ruiz-Belda, Fernández-Dols, Carrera & Barchard, 2003): our smiles usually require an audience.

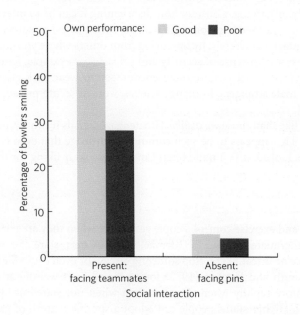

**Figure 15.5**  People smile more when they are interacting with others rather than when they perform well

- Players at a bowling alley smiled much more when facing their teammates than facing the pins.
- Smiling was much less strongly related to whether they were performing well or not.

*Source*: based on data from Kraut & Johnston (1979)

Focusing on cross-cultural differences in emotional displays, Ekman (1973) monitored facial expressions of American students in America and Japanese students in Japan watching a very stressful film in private and talking about it to the experimenter afterwards. In private, both groups displayed negative emotions, but in public only the Americans gave facial expressions indicating negative emotions. In public, the Japanese students' facial expressions were indicative of positive emotions. A meta-analysis of 162 studies by Maryanne LaFrance and her colleagues showed that Western women were encouraged to smile more often than their Asian counterparts (LaFrance, Hecht & Paluck, 2003). These findings clearly reflect the existence of different cultural (and gender) display rules.

Finally, facial movements are more than cues to our emotions; they are also used deliberately to support or even to replace spoken language. We raise our eyebrows to emphasise a question, or furrow our brows and squint our eyes to reflect doubt or scorn. A relatively new development – American Sign Language (ASL) – is linked to Ekman's work on the facial expression of basic emotions. ASL is a convention that uses a set of sign language facial expressions, which have emotional meaning and are dynamic, i.e. they occur in real time (Grossman & Kegl, 2007).

## Gaze and eye contact

There are often voice and words in a silent look. (*Ovid; cited in Kleinke, 1986, p. 78*)

**Gaze**
Looking at someone's eyes.

It will not surprise you to learn that we spend a great deal of time gazing at each other's eyes. In two-person settings, people spend 61 per cent of the time gazing, and a **gaze** lasts about three seconds (Argyle & Ingham, 1972). Eye contact refers more precisely to mutual gaze. People in pairs spend about 30 per cent of their time engaging in mutual gaze, and a mutual gaze lasts less than a second.

According to Kleinke (1986), gaze is perhaps the most information-rich and important of the non-verbal communication channels. We make inferences about their feelings, credibility, honesty, competence and attentiveness. We are driven to seek out the information communicated by others' eyes, even though under certain circumstances (e.g. passing a stranger in the street) eye contact itself is uncomfortable and even embarrassing. Absence of eye behaviour can be equally unnerving. Consider how disorienting it can be to interact with someone whose eyes you cannot see (e.g. someone wearing dark glasses) or someone who continually avoids eye contact. Conversely, by obscuring from others where your own eyes are looking can increase your own sense of security and privacy: for example, female tourists visiting notably chauvinistic societies are often encouraged to wear dark glasses and to avoid eye contact with male strangers. In many societies, women secure privacy in public places by wearing a veil.

We look more at people we like than those we dislike. Greater gaze signals intimacy, particularly if the gaze is mutual. This appears to be such common knowledge that even false information that someone has looked at you quite often can increase your liking for that person (Kleinke, 1986).

### Visual dominance

Gaze can communicate status and exercise control. People gaze more when they are trying to be persuasive or trying to ingratiate themselves (Kleinke, 1986). A stern stare can also express disapproval, dominance or threat. It can stop someone talking or even cause flight. For instance, Ellsworth, Carlsmith and Henson (1972) found that drivers waiting at an intersection departed much more rapidly when stared at than when not stared at by a person standing on the corner. Higher-status people can adopt a specific pattern of gaze behaviour in order to exert control. They generally gaze less than lower-status people at a partner (Dovidio & Ellyson, 1985; Exline, 1971). This is **visual dominance behaviour**, a tendency to gaze fixedly at a lower-status speaker. Leaders who adopt this visual dominance pattern tend to be given higher leadership ratings than leaders who do not (Exline, Ellyson & Long, 1975). Overall, the powerless tend to pay more attention to the powerful than vice versa, because people without power are highly motivated to learn about those who have power over them (Fiske & Dépret, 1996; also see Fiske, 2010; Fiske & Berdahl, 2007).

**Visual dominance behaviour**
Tendency to gaze fixedly at a lower-status speaker.

## Status and gender

Women generally engage in more eye contact than men, and in some contexts it likely reflects a traditional, lower-status power difference (Duncan, 1969; Henley, 1977; Henley & Harmon, 1985).

Dovidio and colleagues investigated the role of power in gender-related differences in gaze by having mixed-sex pairs discuss three topics of conversation – one where the man had more expertise, one where the woman had more expertise and one where the partners had equal expertise (Dovidio, Ellyson, Keating, Heltman & Brown, 1988). The percentage of speaking time, and separately of listening time, spent gazing was recorded. The results in Figure 15.6 show that when the man or the woman was an expert (high status) they dominated – gazing almost as much or more while speaking as listening). When the man

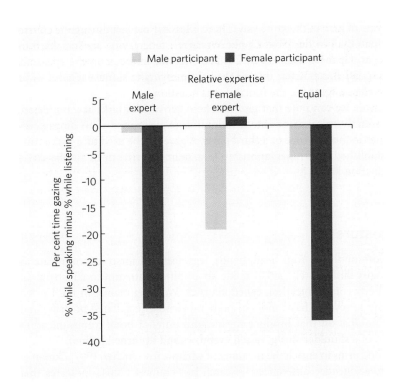

**Figure 15.6** Gaze, gender expertise and dominance

- A dominant gaze pattern occurs when people gaze more when speaking than listening. See the vertical axis to check how this was calculated.
- In this graph, the less negative the bars the more they indicate a dominant gaze pattern.
- Both men and women in male–female dyads assumed the dominant gaze pattern when they were in the high-status, expert role.
- When status was not specified, men simply assumed the dominant gaze pattern.

*Source*: based on data from Dovidio et al. (1988)

or the woman was not an expert (low status) they showed the low-status pattern – gazing more while listening than speaking. The interesting finding in this study is that when the man and the woman were equally expert, the man would dominate whereas the woman showed the low-status pattern.

### Status and ethnicity

Gaze regulates interaction. Mutual gaze, making eye contact, is an important means of initiating conversation (Argyle, 1971; Cary, 1978), and we tend to avoid eye contact if we do not wish to be drawn into conversation. Gaze plays an important role in regulating the course of a conversation once started. White adults spend on average 75 per cent of the time gazing when listening and 41 per cent of the time gazing when speaking (Argyle and Ingham, 1972), and thus a listener can decrease gaze in order to signal an intention to gain the floor, while a speaker can increase gaze to indicate an intention to stop speaking.

LaFrance and Mayo (1976) have shown that this pattern is reversed among African Americans, who gaze more when speaking than when listening. This complicates communication in interracial interactions. For example, a White speaker may interpret a Black listener's *low* rate of gaze as lack of interest, rudeness or an attempt to butt in and take the floor, while a Black speaker may interpret a White listener's *high* rate of gaze in the same way. From the perspective of the listener, a White may interpret a Black speaker's high rate of gaze as arrogance and/or an invitation to take the floor, while a Black may interpret a White speaker's low rate of gaze in the same way. There is less eye contact during the course of an interview in Japan than in the West. Unlike Western listeners, who are socialised to look at a speaker's eyes, Japanese listeners find it less stressful to focus on the speaker's knees (Bond & Komai, 1976), a practice that might be unnerving to some! (What do you now think about Santoso's plight? See the fourth focus question.)

In closing this section, we can note that gaze can help get various tasks accomplished. A gaze can be used secretly to communicate information (e.g. surprise at an outrageous statement) to a partner in the presence of a third party. A gaze can be used to signal a routine activity in an established working relationship (e.g. sailing a boat) or in a noisy environment (e.g. a production line).

### Postures and gestures

**Kinesics**
Linguistics of body communication.

Your eyes and face communicate. Your head, hands, legs, feet and torso communicate as well. The anthropologist Birdwhistell (1970) made an ambitious attempt to construct an entire linguistics of body communication, called **kinesics**. Working mainly in the United States, he identified up to seventy basic units of body movement (e.g. flared nostrils) and described rules of combination that produce meaningful units of body communication (e.g. the combination of a shoulder shrug, raised eyebrows and upturned palms).

We use our hands and arms to enrich the meaning of what we say (Archer, 1997; Ekman & Friesen, 1972). There are gender differences: research by Schubert (2004) indicates that men are more likely than women to raise a clenched fist as a symbol of pride or power. Some gestures are universal, such as giving directions by moving the arm and pointing with a finger or thumb. Sometimes we even continue to do so when talking on the telephone – why should technology get in our way?

The evolutionary psychologist Corballis believes that hand gestures preceded spoken language in humans, and research in neuroscience indicates that only a brain as complex as yours and mine can handle what a real language depends on – syntax. See Box 15.4 for a short evolutionary history of how language came about.

**Phone language**
Not another
automated menu! Body
movements and facial
expressions are
superfluous when we
talk on the telephone

## Research highlight 15.4
### The gestural origins of language

#### The hands have it

Can chimps talk? Not as we know it. Animal vocalisation in general is stimulus-bound – a relatively small number of utterances connected to specific cues, such as a food source or a predator. Our own cries that sometimes accompany the primary emotions (see 'Using the face to express emotions' earlier in this chapter) may be the vestiges of the utterances of our primate ancestors.

Corballis has argued that language evolved something like this:

1 Hominids diverged from the other great apes (6–7 million years ago).

2 Bipedal hominids, such as *Australopithecus*, used hand gestures (5 million years ago).

3 Syntax was added to gestures, and then vocalisation (2 million years ago).

4 Speech now dominated gesture in *Homo sapiens* (100,000 years ago).

Chimpanzees and the early hominids could undoubtedly vocalise well before the arrival of *Homo sapiens,* but vocal control was largely involuntary. Anatomical and cortical changes necessary for voluntary control of vocalisation were probably not complete until the emergence of *Homo sapiens*. Vocal language freed the hands for manufacture, allowing the development of pedagogy through combined speech and manual action, and permitted communication at night. These developments may explain the so-called 'human revolution' within the past 100,000 years, characterised by increasing technological innovation and the demise of all other hominids.

A limited use of gesture to communicate may extend back more than 25 million years to the common ancestors of humans, apes and monkeys. However, when hominids (our human line) stood up and walked, their hands were no longer instruments of locomotion and could serve extensively as tools for gestural communication. Like speech, gestural language depends on the left side of the brain.

Today, examples of gestural language include:

- sign languages used by the deaf;
- communicating with someone who speaks a different language;
- hand gestures that accompany speech, often superfluously, as when talking on the phone;
- religious communities bound by a vow of silence;
- sophisticated manual hand signs among Australian Aborigines and American Plains Indians.

*Source:* based on Corballis, 1999, 2004

**Gestures**
Rude gestures can cross cultural boundaries. Does the double gesture make it twice as bad?

**Emblems**
Gestures that replace or stand in for spoken language.

**Emblems**, on the other hand, are special kinds of gesture that replace or stand in for spoken language, such as the wave of the hand in greeting, or less friendly hand signals. Some emblems are widely understood across cultures, but many are culture-specific. The same thing can be indicated by different gestures in different cultures, and the same gesture can mean different things in different cultures. For instance, we refer to 'self' by pointing at our chest, while in Japan they put a finger to the nose (DeVos & Hippler, 1969). A sideways nod of the head means 'no' in Britain but 'yes' in India, and in Turkey 'no' is indicated by moving the head backwards and rolling the eyes upwards (Rubin, 1976). In Britain, we invite people to approach by beckoning with an upturned finger, while Indians use all four down-turned fingers. In Britain, if you were to draw your finger across your throat it would mean that someone was in big trouble. The same gesture in Swaziland means 'I love you', or 'I've lost my job' in Japan. Cross-cultural differences in the meaning of gestures can have serious consequences. Be careful when and where you gesture with a forefinger and thumb forming a circle: you would probably think they meant 'it's okay' or 'great'. In Brazil this means 'screw you!' (Burgoon, Buller & Woodall, 1989).

### Status differences

Body language can serve other functions apart from illustrating or replacing spoken language. The relative status of interactants may be evident from body cues (Mehrabian, 1972). In a study of people interacting in dyads, Tiedens & Fragale (2003) found that higher-status or dominant individuals took up more space by adopting an expansive posture: relaxed, open, with arms and legs akimbo, and a backward lean to the body. Those who were lower-status or submissive made responses that were complementary: they took up less space and adopted a constricted posture, with arms and legs in, and a curved torso. This status effect may surface in interactions between men and women, since men often use an expansive posture and women a submissive posture (Henley, 1977). As another example, people who like one another tend to lean forward, maintain a relaxed posture and face one another (Mehrabian, 1972). There is a cautionary aspect to some other studies in this area: several are based on ratings of a person's actions by others, and can therefore reflect what is perceived – stereotypes – rather than what actually happened (Hall, Coats & LeBeau, 2005).

In real life, non-verbal cues to status usually operate in combination (Hall, Coats & LeBeau, 2005). Consider these composites:

- A sense of *immediacy* involves eye contact, body relaxation, direct orientation, smiling, vocal expressiveness, close physical distance and hand gesturing (Prisbell, 1985).
- An impression of *dominance* involves touching, pointing, invading space and standing over another person (Henley & Harmon, 1985).

## Touch

Social touch is perhaps the earliest form of communication we learn. Do you have flashes from your childhood, or have you watched very young children? Long before we learn language, and even before we are adept at using body illustrators or gestures, we give and receive information by touch. There are many different types of touch (e.g. brief, enduring, firm, gentle) to different parts of the body (e.g. hand, shoulder, chest). The meaning of a touch varies as a function of the type of touch, the context within which the touch occurs, who touches whom, and what the relationship is between the interactants (e.g. husband and wife, doctor and patient, strangers). As Thayer (1986) had noted, our language reflects facets of its meaning – e.g. 'a soft touch', 'a gripping experience', 'deeply touched'.

From an analysis of 1,500 bodily contacts between people, Jones and Yarbrough (1985) identified five discrete categories of touch:

- *Positive affect* – to communicate appreciation, affection, reassurance, nurturance or sexual interest.
- *Playful* – to communicate humour and playfulness.
- *Control* – to draw attention or induce compliance.
- *Ritualistic* – to satisfy ritualised requirements (e.g. greetings and departures).
- *Task-related* – to accomplish tasks (e.g. a nurse taking one's pulse, or a violin teacher positioning a student's hand).

To these can be added *negative affect* (gently pushing an annoying hand away) and *aggressive touches* (slaps, kicks, shoves, punches) (Burgoon, Buller & Woodall, 1989).

Even the most incidental and fleeting touches can have significant effects. Male and female customers in a restaurant gave larger tips after their female waiting person touched them casually on the hand (Crusco & Wetzel, 1984). In another study, university library clerks briefly touched the hand of students checking out books. Women who had been touched indicated greater liking for the clerk, and even for the library, than those who had not been touched (Fisher, Rytting & Heslin, 1976). Male students were stolidly unaffected in this instance.

Whitcher and Fisher (1979) also reported a gender difference, this time in a health setting. They arranged for patients to be touched or not touched by a female nurse during a pre-operative teaching interaction. Although the touches were brief and 'professional', they had significant effects on post-operative physiological and questionnaire measures. Female patients who had been touched reported less fear and anxiety, and had lower blood pressure readings, than those who had not been touched. Unfortunately, male patients who had been touched were more anxious and had higher blood pressure! Let us explore gender differences a little further.

### Gender differences

In general, men touch women more often than women touch men, and people are more likely to touch members of the opposite than the same sex (Henley, 1973). Women derive greater pleasure from being touched than men (Major, 1981), but the circumstances of the touch are important. Heslin (1978) asked men and women how much they would enjoy having various parts of the body 'squeezed and patted' by strangers or close friends of the same or the opposite sex. Figure 15.7 shows that both sexes agreed that being touched by someone of the same sex was relatively unpleasant, and that being touched by an opposite-sex close friend was relatively pleasant, but they disagreed about the pleasantness of being touched by an opposite-sex stranger. Women did not enjoy being touched by strange men, but men enjoyed being touched by strange women! Heslin (1978) also found that men were much more likely than women to read sexual connotations into touch, with all sorts of obvious implications for miscommunication and misinterpretation (Heslin & Alper, 1983).

Apparent gender differences in touch may reflect more general status differences in touch: people who initiate touch are perceived to be of higher status than those who receive a touch (Major & Heslin, 1982). Major (1981) has argued that the usual gender differences in touch (women react more positively than men) occur only when status differences between

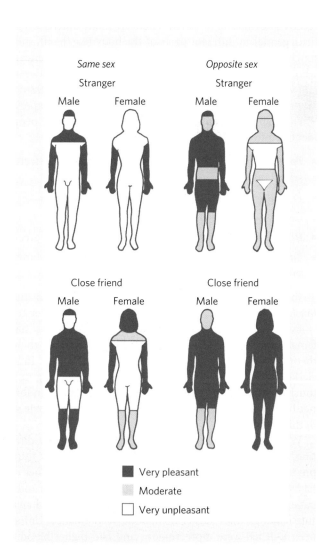

**Figure 15.7**  How pleasant is it to be touched?

- Men and women differ in how pleasant they find being touched on different parts of the body.
- The degree of pleasantness varies according to whether people are touched by same-sex or opposite-sex strangers or friends.
- The figures at the top left are men and women being touched by a same-sex stranger.
- The figures at the top right are men and women being touched by an opposite-sex stranger, etc.
- There was no breakdown in these results by sexual orientation.

*Source*: Burgoon, Buller & Woodall (1989)

interactants are ambiguous or negligible: under these circumstances, wider societal assumptions about sex-linked status differences come into play. When the toucher is clearly higher in status than the recipient, both men and women react positively to being touched.

## Cultural differences

Finally, there is substantial cross-cultural variation in the amount of actual use made of touch. People from Latin American, Mediterranean and Arab countries touch a great deal, while people from northern Europe, North America, Australia and Asia do not (Argyle, 1975). From a study of the touching behaviour of couples in cafés in different countries, Jourard (1966) observed, in a one-hour period, no touching in London, 2 touches in Florida, 110 touches in Paris and 180 in Puerto Rico. Perhaps a Londoner dating in Puerto Rico or a Parisian dating in Florida might feel uncomfortable!

## Up close and personal

We have seen how parts of our bodies can send messages. The distance between our bodies, or interpersonal distance does this as well and its study is called **proxemics**. Furthermore, the closer two people are, the greater the number of non-verbal cues that can be detected

**Proxemics**
Study of interpersonal distance.

**Interpersonal distance**
Her personal space is being invaded — or is it?

**Table 15.3** Four zones of space in social interaction: how close is comfortable?

| Zone | Distance | Description |
|---|---|---|
| Intimate distance | Up to 0.5 m | Physical contact can take place. Much is exposed about a person. Cues come from sight, sound, smell, body temperature, and depth and pace of breathing. |
| Personal distance | 0.5–1.25 m | This transitional area between intimate contact and formal behaviour is the norm in Western countries for everyday interactions with friends and acquaintances. Touching is still possible. Although many cues are still available, the effects of body temperature, smell and breathing are greatly reduced. |
| Social distance | 1.25–4 m | This is typical for both casual and business interactions. Many cues are lost, but verbal contact is easily maintained. Furniture arrangement helps to achieve this. In an office, the desk is about 75 cm deep, and allowing for chair space, people interacting across the desk are just over one metre apart. A bigger desk can signal rank. |
| Public distance | 4–8 m | Communication cues now lose some impact. It is a common distance for public speakers, celebrities and lecturers. In a lecture hall, lecterns are usually placed about 3.5 m back from the first row of seats. Courtrooms use this intervening space to prevent easy exchanges with the judge. The message? Interaction is not wanted. |

*Source*: Hall (1966)

and 'talking' becomes richer. We use interpersonal distance to regulate privacy and intimacy: the greater the distance, the more private you can be. The anthropologist Edward Hall's (1966) work *The Hidden Dimension* identified four *interpersonal distance zones* found mainly in the United States– ranging from high to low intimacy, each a little more removed from our bodies (see Table 15.3).

If you feel more intimate towards someone you will move closer, but if you feel a difference in status you will keep physically further away – see Hayduk's (1983) review. Being physically near to a person can occasionally be 'too close for comfort'. **Personal space**, a now-popular term also introduced by Hall (1966), reflects the importance that people place on their perceived body buffer zone. Here are two research examples, one experimental and the other observational, relating to liking and status.

**Personal space**
Physical space around people's bodies which they treat as a part of themselves.

- *Liking* – Female students talked with a female confederate (i.e. a collaborator of the experimenter), with the goal of either appearing friendly or of avoiding the appearance of friendliness. The friendly ones placed their chairs on average 1.5 metres from the confederate, while those who did not want to appear friendly placed their chairs 2.25 metres away (Rosenfeld, 1965).

- *Status* – Navy personnel maintained greater interpersonal distance when interacting with someone of a different rank than with someone of the same rank, and the effect was stronger as the difference in rank increased (Dean, Willis & Hewitt, 1975).

### Protecting personal space

Interpersonal distance is such a potent cue to intimacy that if it seems inappropriate we can feel disconcerted. Argyle and Dean (1965) proposed an intimacy–equilibrium theory, which predicts that when intimacy signals are increased in one modality, they are decreased in other modalities (e.g. eye contact). For instance, on approaching a stranger who is still some distance away, you might gaze discreetly; as soon the approaching stranger enters your social zone (about 3.5 metres), you look away; or on your own turf you might show a ritualised recognition (a smile or mumbled greeting).

Have you had that crowded feeling in a lift? According to intimacy–equilibrium theory, we can reduce intimacy cues by assiduously staring at the numbers for each floor level flashing away (Zuckerman, Miserandino & Bernieri, 1983). Close seating arrangements can have a similar effect (Sommer, 1969). Look at how people usually try to create space between themselves and other passengers in an airport terminal, or read or listen to their iPods more as numbers build up.

People are often stressed when their personal space is invaded. Middlemist, Knowles and Mutter (1976) conducted a memorable study in which a male confederate loitered outside a men's urinal until someone entered. The confederate followed the man into the urinal and stood in another cubicle that varied in distance from him. The closer they were, the longer the man took to begin urinating and the faster the act was completed! (We doubt that this study would get past a university research ethics committee today.)

Individual differences in perceived personal space, which vary dramatically across age, gender and cultures, frequently lead to violations. For instance, Aiello and Jones (1971) found that African American and working-class children in the United States tend to stand closer to people than do White or non-working-class children. Likewise, people in Southern Europe, the Middle East and Latin America also stand closer, while in some tribal communities in Africa and Indonesia people will often touch while talking (Argyle & Dean, 1965).

## Impression management and deception

Non-verbal communication can be subliminal and automatic, in that we are often unaware that we or other people are using it. However, we do have some control and awareness, and we can use non-verbal cues strategically to create an impression of ourselves or to influence other people's beliefs, attitudes and behaviour (DePaulo, 1992). We can also sometimes detect others' strategic use of non-verbal cues. This raises the possibility that people may try to hide their true feelings or communicate false feelings or information by controlled use of appropriate non-verbal cues. In general, such attempts at deception are not completely successful, as there is information leakage via non-verbal channels. As Freud (1905) so eloquently remarked: 'He that has eyes to see and ears to hear may convince himself that no mortal can keep a secret. If his lips are silent, he chatters with his fingertips; betrayal oozes out of him at every pore.'

Research indicates that people are relatively good at controlling the verbal content of a message to conceal deception. Liars try to avoid saying things that might give them away, so they tend to make fewer factual statements, they are prone to making vague, sweeping statements, and they leave gaps in the conversation (Knapp, Hart & Dennis, 1974). There is also a tendency for attempts at deception to be accompanied by a slightly raised vocal pitch (Ekman, Friesen & Scherer, 1976). Facial expressions are generally not very 'leaky': people tend to make a special and concerted effort to control facial cues to deception. However, with so much attention diverted to facial cues, other channels of non-verbal communication are left unguarded. For example, deceivers tend to touch their face more often (Ekman & Friesen, 1974) or to fiddle with their hands, their glasses or other external objects (Knapp, Hart & Dennis, 1974). A recent meta-analysis has revealed that people are more accurate at judging audible than visible lies (Bond & DePaulo, 2006). Despite all of this, there are some effective professional lie catchers out there! In an American study (Ekman, O'Sullivan & Frank, 1999), Federal police officers and sheriffs were more accurate in detecting lies than judges; and clinical psychologists with an interest in deception techniques were more accurate than academic and regular clinical psychologists.

Some people are better than others at concealing deception. For instance, people who habitually monitor their own behaviour carefully tend to be better liars (Siegman & Reynolds, 1983; see Chapter 4 for further information about self-monitoring). People who are highly motivated to deceive because, for instance, they believe it to be necessary for career advancement, tend to be adept at controlling verbal channels (DePaulo, Lanier & Davis, 1983) but, ironically, poor at controlling other channels. This is often their downfall.

However, people are generally rather poor at detecting deception (DePaulo, 1994). Even those whose jobs are, in essence, the detection of deception (e.g. in the customs, police, legal and intelligence professions) are often not significantly better than the general population (Kraut & Poe, 1980). People who do detect deception tend to feel only generally suspicious and are not sure exactly what false information is being communicated (DePaulo & Rosenthal, 1979; DePaulo & DePaulo, 1989). Interestingly, although women are superior to men at reading other people's non-verbal cues (Hall, 1978), they are no better than men at detecting deception (Rosenthal & DePaulo, 1979). Does this discussion of deception lead to the conclusion that we are more likely to get away with a lie than be detected? Zuckerman, DePaulo and Rosenthal (1981) have reviewed research on deception and conclude that, overall, receivers have the edge: they are slightly better at detecting deception than senders are at concealing it.

Impression management and deception have another consequence, which we have already discussed (see Chapters 4, 5 and 10). Social psychology often tries to gain insight into people's underlying attitudes and feelings by administering questionnaires or conducting surveys or interviews. In the context of our discussion of impression management and deception, we can see that this enterprise is fraught with difficulties. Social psychologists are continually seeking non-reactive unobtrusive measures. For example, there is the **bogus pipeline technique** (Jones & Sigall, 1971), where research participants are led to believe that the researchers have unambiguous physiological measures against which to check the validity of their attitudinal responses (see Chapter 5 for details).

Another example: Maass and her associates take advantage of the linguistic intergroup bias effect (Franco & Maass, 1996; Maass, 1999; Maass & Arcuri, 1996; Maass, Salvi, Arcuri & Semin, 1989) to detect underlying prejudices through speech style. Prejudiced people talk about the negative attributes of outgroups in broad and general terms that nevertheless make the attributes appear to be enduring and immutable, whereas they talk about the positive attributes of outgroups in very concrete, specific terms that are transitorily tied to the specific context.

**Bogus pipeline technique**
A measurement technique that leads people to believe that a 'lie detector' can monitor their emotional responses, thus measuring their true attitudes.

# Conversation and discourse

Although language and non-verbal communication are considered separately in this chapter, they usually occur together in communication (Cappella & Palmer, 1993). Non-verbal and paralinguistic behaviour can influence the meaning of what is said and can also serve important functions in regulating the flow of conversation.

## Conversation

Conversations have distinct phases (e.g. opening and closing) and an array of complex cultural rules that govern every phase of the interaction (Clark, 1985). For instance, there are ritualistic openings (e.g. 'Hello') and closings (e.g. 'Well, I must go'). We can signal the end of a face-to-face conversation non-verbally by moving apart and looking away (looking at your watch is a common but unsubtle way of doing this), and end a telephone conversation by lengthening pauses before responding. During a conversation, it is important to have rules about turn taking, otherwise there would be conversational chaos. Argyle (1975) describes a number of signals that people use to indicate that they are ending their turn and giving the listener an opportunity to take the floor:

- coming to the end of a sentence;
- raising or lowering the intonation of the last word;
- drawing out the last syllable;
- leaving a sentence unfinished to invite a continuation (e.g. 'I was going to go to the beach, but, uh . . .');
- body motions such as ceasing hand gestures, opening the eyes wide or lifting the head with the last note of a question, sitting back, or looking directly at the listener.

Attempts to butt in before the speaker is ready to yield the floor invite *attempt-suppressing* signals. The voice maintains the same pitch, the head remains straight, the eyes remain unchanged, the hands maintain the same gesture, the speaker may speak louder or faster and may keep a hand in mid-gesture at the end of sentences. At the same time, listeners may regularly signal that they are still listening and not seeking to interrupt. We do this by using **back-channel communication**: the listener nods or says 'mm-hmm' or 'okay' or 'right'. Ng reviewed and extended the relationship between conversational turn taking and power to show that interruptions can convey different information. Depending on context, an interruption may be considered rude, may signify greater influence and power, and can also signify involvement, interest and support (Dindia, 1987; Ng, 1996; Ng, Bell & Brooke, 1993; Ng & Bradac, 1993; Reid & Ng, 1999). See Box 15.5 for an example between persons of unequal power.

**Back-channel communication**
Verbal and non-verbal ways in which listeners let speakers know they are still listening.

The course of conversation differs depending on how well the interactants know one another. Close friends are more interpersonally responsive and tend to raise more topics and disclose more about themselves (Hornstein, 1985). Under these circumstances, women are more likely than men to talk about and self-disclose relational and personal topics (Davidson & Duberman, 1982; Jourard, 1971), but both sexes adhere to a reciprocity norm

---

## Applied context 15.5
### Speaking with your doctor

**Power imbalance in doctor–patient communication**

Effective communication is of paramount importance in the doctor–patient consultation. In order to make a correct diagnosis and provide proper treatment, the communicative context should be one in which the doctor can obtain as much relevant information as possible. To do this, the doctor should develop rapport with the patient, appear empathic, encourage the patient to speak frankly and openly and, generally, do a substantial amount of listening. Is this your experience of visiting a doctor?

Research in the United States revealed a marked conversational imbalance, with the doctor controlling the conversation (Fisher & Todd, 1983; West, 1984). The doctor did most of the talking, initiated 99 per cent of utterances, left only 9 per cent of questions to be asked by the patient, asked further questions before the patient finished answering the last one, interrupted the patient more, determined agenda and topic shifts, and controlled the termination of the consultation.

This communication pattern reflects a power and status imbalance between doctor and patient that resides in social status differences, unshared expertise and knowledge, and uncertainty and to some extent anxiety on the part of the patient. This is all accentuated by the context of the consultation – the doctor's surgery. Far from encouraging communicative openness, this conversational imbalance may inhibit it, and communication may in many instances be counterproductive as far as diagnosis and treatment are concerned.

governing the intimacy of self-disclosure (Cozby, 1973). The reciprocity norm is relaxed in longer-term relationships (Morton, 1978).

In marriage, one of the most intimate of relationships, communication is a central process – and, as we have seen above, there is genuine potential for miscommunication between men and women (e.g. Mulac, Bradac & Gibbons, 2001). Effective communication is one of the strongest correlates of marital satisfaction (Snyder, 1979), and marital therapists identify communication problems as one of the major features of marital distress (Craddock, 1980).

Noller (1984) has analysed communication between married partners in detail by asking people to imagine situations in which they have to communicate something to their partners and to verbalise the communication (i.e. encode what they intend to communicate). The partner then has to decode the communication to discover what was intended; several choices are given, and only one can be selected.

Using this paradigm, Noller was able to discover that couples who scored high on a scale of marital adjustment were much more accurate at encoding their own and decoding their partner's communications than were couples who scored low. In general, women were better than men at encoding messages, particularly positive ones. Maritally dissatisfied couples tended to spend more time arguing, nagging, criticising and being coercive, and were poor and unresponsive listeners. On balance, it seems that poor marital communication may be a symptom of a distressed relationship rather than something brought to the relationship by partners (Noller, 1984; Noller & Fitzpatrick, 1990). People who have problems encoding and decoding messages within the marriage may have no such problems in their relationships with others.

The analysis of conversation, or talk-in-interaction, as we have just explored, focuses on what is said but does not generally focus on the semantic and motivational subtleties of what is said, why and to what ends – conversation analysis does not generally delve into the subtext of the interaction, whereas discourse analysis and discursive psychology, to which we now turn, do (Wilkinson & Kitzinger, 2006).

## Discourse

The social psychology of language and communication tends to analyse speech styles and non-verbal communication rather than the actual text of the communication. It also tends to break the communicative act down into component parts and then reconstructs more complex communications from the interaction of different channels. This approach may have some limitations. For example, a great deal of language research has rested on the use of the matched-guise technique (Lambert, Hodgson, Gardner & Fillenbaum, 1960; see above). This technique isolates the text of a speech from the speech style (i.e. non-text), in order to see how the speaker is evaluated on the basis of the group that is marked by the speech style. However, the text of a speech is rarely truly neutral: that is, it rarely carries no information on group membership (e.g. older and younger people talk about different things). Furthermore, the meaning of the text can itself be changed by speech style. Thus text and non-text features of utterances are inextricable, together conveying meaning, which influences attitude (Giles et al., 1990). This suggests that we might need to look to the entire **discourse** (what is said, in what way, by whom and for what purpose) in order to understand the contextualised attitudes that emerge (e.g. Billig, 1987; Edwards & Potter, 1992; Giles & Coupland, 1991; Potter & Wetherell, 1987).

This idea has been taken up by a number of researchers in the study of racism and sexism as they are imbedded in and created by discourse (Condor, 1988; Potter & Wetherell, 1987; van Dijk, 1987, 1993; also see Chapter 10). It has also been employed in the study of youth language (Widdicombe & Wooffitt, 1990, 1994), intergenerational talk (Giles &

**Discourse**
Entire communicative event or episode located in a situational and sociohistorical context.

Coupland, 1991), homophobia and prejudice against people with HIV (Pittam and Gallois, 1996), political rhetoric (Billig, 1987, 1991, 1996), and collective action and protest (Reicher, 1996, 2001). The entire discourse is considered the unit of analysis, and it is through discourse that people construct categories of meaning. For instance, 'the economy' does not really exist for most of us. It is something that we bring into existence through talk (see discussion of **social representations** in Chapters 3 and 5).

A good example of **discourse analysis** is Rapley's (1998) analysis of Pauline Hanson's maiden speech to the Australian Federal Parliament in September 1996. Hanson suddenly rose to prominence in Australia in 1996 when she was unexpectedly elected to the federal parliament. She immediately formed, and was leader of, the eponymous political party 'Pauline Hanson's One Nation Party'. One Nation's platform was nationalism, monoculturalism, opposition to affirmative action, anti-immigration, anti-intellectualism, anti-arts, economic isolationism, and promotion of the right to own and bear arms – an ultraconservative platform that was mirrored in the party's organisational structure, which was highly authoritarian. Rapley conducted a careful analysis of Hanson's speeches to identify One Nation's true agenda. Rapley believed, and was able to show, that a relatively thin veneer of modern prejudice (see Chapter 10) concealed an underlying current of old-fashioned prejudice.

The analysis of discourse is clearly a useful tool for revealing hidden agendas and laying bare concealed prejudices (Wetherell, Taylor & Yates, 2001). However, the discourse analysis approach in social psychology often goes one step further by arguing that many social psychological concepts such as attitude, motivation, cognition and identity may likewise be constituted through discourse, and therefore any discussion of them as real causal processes or structures is misguided. If accepted in its extreme form, this idea necessarily rejects much of social psychology and invites a new social psychology that focuses on talk, not people, groups or cognition, as the basic social psychological unit (also see Chapter 1). This is an interesting and provocative idea, which forms the core of the *discourse analysis* approach to social psychology (e.g. Edwards, 1997; Potter, 1996; Potter & Wetherell, 1987; Potter, Wetherell, Gill & Edwards, 1990). It has its origins in poststructuralism (Foucault, 1972), ethnomethodology (Garfinkel, 1967), ethogenics (Harré, 1979) and dramaturgical perspectives (Goffman, 1959). However, critics believe that it can be too extreme in its rejection of cognitive processes and structures (Abrams & Hogg, 1990b; Zajonc, 1989), and that it may be more profitable to retain cognition and theorise how it articulates with language (Giles & Coupland, 1991).

**Social representations**
Collectively elaborated explanations of unfamiliar and complex phenomena that transform them into a familiar and simple form.

**Discourse analysis**
A set of methods used to analyse text, in particular, naturally occurring language, in order to understand its meaning and significance.

# Computer-mediated communication

No chapter on communication would be complete without recognition that people in the developed world increasingly communicate electronically with one another via phone, e-mail, and a huge variety of Internet formats. The biggest development is the explosion of *computer-mediated communication* (CMC) over the past fifteen years. Not surprisingly, research in this area is in its infancy – it is as yet relatively fragmented, un-programmatic and a-theoretical (Hollingshead, 2001; McGrath & Hollingshead, 1994). There are, however, five general findings:

1 CMC, in the absence of video, restricts paralanguage and non-verbal communication channels. This has little effect on communication between strangers, but adversely affects interaction between people who have a closer relationship (Hollingshead, 1998). However, non-verbal and paralanguage cues can be introduced into CMC by emphasis: for example 'YES!!!' or by means of what are called emoticons: for example, the sideways 'smiley' :-). Video chat clearly brings the communication channels much closer to real life.

**Gender-specific texting**
'I don't know who it is, but only a guy would text like that!'

2  CMC can suppress the amount of information that is exchanged, such as non-verbal vocal and physical cues. Generally, procedural aspects of group discussion that improve information exchange and group decisions in face-to-face settings may not have the same effect in computer-mediated settings (Hollingshead, 1996; Straus & McGrath, 1994). However, this not an inevitable outcome, because people can still infuse a message with contextual and stylistic cues about gender (see below), individual attributes, attitudes and their emotional state (Walther, Loh & Granka, 2005; Walther & Parks, 2002).

3  CMC has a 'participation-equalisation effect', which evens out many of the status effects that occur in face-to-face communicative contexts. People may feel less inhibited because they are less personally identifiable (see **deindividuation** in Chapter 11). The effect depends on how effectively identity and status markers are concealed by the electronic medium (Spears & Lea, 1994). For example, e-mails usually have a signature that clearly indicates the identity and status of the communicator. According to the social identity analysis of deindividuation phenomena (Klein, Spears & Reicher, 2007; Reicher, Spears & Postmes, 1995) personal anonymity in the presence of a highly salient social identity will make people conform strongly to identity-congruent norms, and be easily influenced by group leaders and normative group members. CMC research has confirmed this (Postmes, Spears & Lea, 1998; Postmes, Spears, Sakhel & de Groot, 2001; Sassenberg & Boos, 2003).

4  Although, on balance, CMC hinders interaction and group performance initially, over time people adapt quite successfully to their mode of communication (Arrow et al., 1996; Walther, 1996). Indeed, in many ways people gradually respond to CMC as if it was not computer-mediated. For example, Williams and his associates found that when people are ignored in e-mail interactions or chat rooms, they can interpret it as

**Deindividuation**
Process whereby people lose their sense of socialised individual identity and engage in unsocialised, often antisocial, behaviours.

ostracism (called cyber-ostracism) and can react much as they would in face-to-face settings (Williams, Cheung & Choi, 2000; see Chapter 8 for more on social ostracism).

5 Using the Internet to 'surf' does not impact negatively on users. They do not become lonely or depressed, or withdraw from interacting socially with others in real-life settings. Internet users in general have no less contact with friends and family than non-users; it seems that users do, however, spend less time watching television and reading newspapers (see the review by Bargh & McKenna, 2004).

We have already noted that men and women differ in how they communicate non-verbally when interacting with each other. A controlled laboratory study by Thomson and Murachver (2001) showed that a gender difference could also be detected in language used in students' e-mail messages, even when the sex of the recipient is unknown to the sender. A gender effect is clearest when the topic of discussion is sex stereotypic (Thomson, 2006). Here are some differences reported in the Thomson and Murachver study. Females used more intensive adverbs (e.g. 'it was *really* good'), hedges (e.g. 'it was sort of interesting') and emotive references (e.g. 'I was *upset*'), and they provided more personal information (e.g. where they worked). On the other hand, males were more insulting (e.g. 'you were *stupid* to take that course') and offered more opinions (e.g. 'the protest was worthwhile'). Perhaps with your own knowledge of sex-stereotypical behaviour you are not surprised at these findings after all!

## Summary

- Language is a shared, rule-governed and meaningfully structured system of elementary sounds. Speech is the articulation of language.

- Language does not determine thought, but it eases how we communicate with others about what is important.

- The way we speak informs others about our feelings, motives and our membership of social groups, such as gender, status, nationality and ethnicity.

- Ethnic groups may actively promote their own language, or gradually abandon it, depending on the degree of vitality they consider their ethnolinguistic group to possess in a multi-ethnic context.

- People tailor their speech style to the context in which they communicate. Minority ethnic groups tend to converge on higher-status speech styles unless they believe the status hierarchy illegitimate and the vitality of their own group to be high.

- For a minority ethnolinguistic group, motivation is crucial if its members wish to master the dominant group's language as a second language.

- Non-verbal channels of communication (e.g. gaze, facial expression, posture, gesture, touch, interpersonal distance) carry important information about our attitudes, emotions and relative status.

- People communicate non-verbally, with gender, status and cultural differences, through their postures, gestures and touch. Interpersonal distance is a cue to the nature of an interpersonal relationship.

- We are less aware of and have less control over non-verbal communication than spoken language. Non-verbal cues in a face-to-face setting can often give away attempts to conceal information.

- Non-verbal cues play an important role in regulating turn taking and other features of conversation.

- Much can be learned from analysing discourse, by focusing on complete communicative events.

- Studies of computer-mediated communication point to some consistencies with other ways of conversing and transmitting information (e.g. ostracising others in a chat room, unknowingly providing cues to one's gender).

## Literature, film and TV

### Pygmalion

1938 play directed by Anthony Asquith and Leslie Howard, based on the play by George Bernard Shaw. There are many variants on this perennial theme of changing your accent and the way you speak in order to change your status in society: for example, the 1964 film *My Fair Lady,* directed by George Cukor (again based on Shaw's play), and starring Audrey Hepburn and Rex Harrison; and the 1983 film *Educating Rita,* directed by Lewis Gilbert, written by Willy Russell and starring Michael Caine and Julie Walters.

### Yes Minister and Yes Prime Minister

These 1980s BBC TV series, starring Paul Eddington, Nigel Hawthorne and Derek Fowlds, are absolutely hilarious and extremely clever. Sir Humphrey's use of language to conceal reality from James Hacker (the Prime Minister) is breathtakingly accurate. The series show the way that language can be used to say something entirely different from what is intended – and can be used to manipulate people. There are books of both series – written by Jonathan Lynn and Anthony Jay and published by BBC books.

### Babel

2006 film by Alejandro González Inárritu, with Brad Pitt, Cate Blanchett and Gael Garcia Bernal. It is a powerful, atmospheric multi-narrative drama exploring the theme that cross-cultural assumptions prevent people from understanding and communicating with one another. Each sub-plot features people out of their familiar cultural context: American children lost in the Mexican borderlands, a deaf Japanese girl mourning and alone in a hearing world, and two Americans stranded in the Moroccan desert.

### Lost in Translation

2003 film written and directed by Sofia Coppola, starring Bill Murray and Scarlet Johansson. A film, which is also relevant to Chapter 16, that illustrates how you can feel like a fish out of water in a foreign culture where you do not speak the language and do not really understand the culture. This is also a film about life crises – two Americans at very different stages in their lives but with similar relationship problems are marooned in a large Japanese city and are drawn to each other.

## Guided questions

1 How does language shape a person's identity?

2 What motivates a person to learn a second language? How can the challenge of adapting to a host culture for an immigrant group be eased?

3 How do non-verbal cues help to inform us about another person?

 4 How accurate are people in recognising basic emotions? See how students fared on this task in Chapter 15 of MyPsychLab at **www.mypsychlab.co.uk** (watch *Recognising basic emotions*).

5 What is personal space? How and why do we use it?

## Learn more

Ambady, N., & Weisbuch. M. (2010). Nonverbal behavior. In S. T. Fiske, D. T. Gilbert, & G. Lindzey (eds), *Handbook of social psychology* (5th ed., Vol. 1, pp. 464–97). New York: Wiley. Up-to-date comprehensive and detailed coverage of theory and research on non-verbal communication.

Bayley, B., & Schechter, S. R. (eds) (2003). *Language socialization in bilingual and multilingual societies*. Clevedon, UK: Multilingual Matters. Sociolinguists, educationalists and other social scientists take an international perspective on language socialisation and bilingualism from early childhood to adulthood. Contexts include home, schools, communities and the workplace.

Comrie, B., Matthews, S., & Polinsky, M. (eds) (2003). *The atlas of languages* (rev. ed.). New York: Facts on File. A richly illustrated treatment of the origin and development of languages throughout the world.

Giles, H., & Coupland, N. (1991). *Language: Contexts and consequences*. Milton Keynes, UK: Open University Press. Readable introduction and overview of the social psychology of language, with an emphasis on intergroup dimensions and a balanced coverage of discourse perspectives.

Giles, H., Reid, S., & Harwood, J. (eds) (2009). *The dynamics of intergroup communication*. New York: Peter Lang. A collection of thoroughly up-to-date chapters by leading communication scholars and social psychologists on communication between groups and the impact of intergroup relations on communication.

Giles, H., & Robinson, W. P. (eds) (1993). *Handbook of language and social psychology*. Oxford, UK: Pergamon Press. Comprehensive collection of critical and review chapters, covering interpersonal communication from a language and social psychology perspective.

Grasser, A. C., Millis, K. K., & Swan, R. A. (1997). Discourse comprehension. *Annual Review of Psychology, 48*, 163–189. A dispassionate overview of the technical contributions of discourse analysis to psychology in general.

Holtgraves, T. (2010). Social psychology and language: Words, utterances and conversations. In S. T. Fiske, D. T. Gilbert, & G. Lindzey (eds), *Handbook of social psychology* (5th ed., Vol. 2, pp. 1386–1422). New York: Wiley. Up-to-date comprehensive and detailed coverage of social psychological theory and research on the role of language in communication.

Knapp, M. L., & Miller, G. R. (eds) (1994). *The handbook of interpersonal communication* (2nd ed.). Thousand Oaks, CA: SAGE. Invaluable source book for in-depth knowledge of virtually all areas of interpersonal communication.

Noels, K. A., Giles, H., & Le Poire, B. (2003). Language and communication processes. In M. A. Hogg & J. Cooper (eds), *The SAGE handbook of social psychology* (pp. 232–57). London: SAGE. A very accessible review, from a social psychological perspective, of research on language and communication – includes both verbal and non-verbal communication.

Russell, J. A., & Fernandez-Dols, J. M. (eds) (1997). *The psychology of facial expression*. Cambridge, UK: Cambridge University Press. A critical overview of theoretical perspectives on facial expression. These include ethological, neurobehavioural and developmental views.

Semin, G. (2007). Grounding communication: Synchrony. In A. W. Kruglanski & E. T. Higgins (eds), *Social psychology: Handbook of basic principles* (2nd ed., pp. 630–49). New York: Guilford Press. A conceptually ambitious chapter – it sets an agenda for integrating levels of explanation to provide a full framework for understanding human communication.

Refresh your understanding, assess your progress and go further with interactive summaries, questions, podcasts and much more at **www.mypsychlab.co.uk**

## This chapter discusses

- Culture's contribution
- Historical links with cultural anthropology
- Rise of cross-cultural psychology
- Culture and thought processes
- Culture and behaviour
- Individualistic and collectivist cultures
- The two psyches: East and West

- Can we compare cultures?
- Culture, norms and identity
- Culture contact
- The nature of acculturation
- The cross-cultural challenge
- Multiculturalism

## Focus questions

1. Daan is Dutch and has been brought up to defend openly what he believes to be true. After living in South Korea for a few months, he has noticed that the locals are more concerned about maintaining harmony in their social relationships than in deciding who is right and who is wrong. Why, he wonders, can they not just speak their minds?

2. Bernice and Joeli are indigenous Fijians who have studied social psychology at the University of the South Pacific in Suva. They are concerned that what they have studied is based on Western theory, with limited relevance to the traditional group-centred values of their community. Do they have a point?

3. Horacio is a researcher from Brazil. He argues that negotiating with a shy business executive in Hong Kong may be no more challenging than communicating with a Brazilian teenager, since to an adult a teenager might just as well be from another culture. What point is he making? See Horacio Falcao explain what he means in Chapter 16 of MyPsychLab at **www.mypsychlab.co.uk** (watch *Cross-cultural negotiations: Avoiding the pitfalls*; see **http://tv.insead.edu/** – 6 in the section 'Networking and organizations').

4. Keiko and her new husband are Japanese. After a traditional wedding in Hokkaido, they emigrated to Oslo. Then a dilemma arose – should they maintain the customs of their homeland, or should they become entirely Norwegian? Do they have any other options?

will use which involves getting you to decide to buy a car by giving you a very low price

Go to **mypsychlab** to explore video and test your understanding of key topics addressed in this chapter.

5. Jessica is a social psychology student who lives in London and is proud of her Cornish heritage. She has read about the paths that migrants might choose in adapting to a host culture. Then an idea occurs to her – to apply the concept of being a migrant to being Cornish. They are a minority group in a predominantly English culture. So what is the status of Cornish culture: integrated, assimilated, separated or marginalised?

Refresh your understanding with interactive summaries, explore topics further with video and audio clips and assess your progress with quick test and essay questions by logging on to the accompanying website at **www.mypsychlab.co.uk**

# Chapter 16
## Culture

# The cultural context

Culture is a pervasive but slippery construct. It has been 'examined, poked at, pushed, rolled over, killed, revived and reified ad infinitum' (Lonner, 1984, p. 108). There is a great deal of popular talk about culture, cultural differences, cultural sensitivity, cultural change, culture shock, subcultures and culture contact; but what precisely is culture, and how much and through what processes does it affect people, and how in turn is it affected by people? In his presidential address to the American Association for the Advancement of Science in 1932, the sociologist Franz Boas made a plea for his own discipline to pay much greater attention to cultural variation in behaviour:

> It seems a vain effort to search for sociological laws disregarding what should be called social psychology, namely, the reaction of the individual to culture. They can be no more than empty formulas that can be imbued with life only by taking account of individual behaviour in cultural settings. (*Cited in Kluckhohn, 1954, p. 921*)

Boas believed culture to be central to social science, and that the study of culture's influence on people is the definition of the discipline of social psychology. This is not an isolated view. Wundt (1897, 1916), the founder of psychology as an experimental science, believed that social psychology was all about collective phenomena such as culture – a position shared by Durkheim (1898), one of the founders of sociology (see Farr, 1996; Hogg & Williams, 2000; see also Chapter 1).

Throughout this book, we have repeatedly drawn attention to the impact of culture on behaviour: for example, in Chapter 3 we discussed how culture intrudes upon intergroup attributions (see Figure 3.7). In this chapter, we draw together and integrate these observations but go further to ask some fundamental questions about the universality of social psychological laws and about the relevance of social psychological principles to cultures in which such principles were not developed.

Cross-cultural psychologists, and some social psychologists, have provided evidence for considerable cultural variation in a range of quite basic human behaviour and social psychological processes. Most of this research identifies a general difference between Eastern and Western cultures – indeed, the contemporary debate in social psychology about 'culture' has been largely restricted to this contrast, or more accurately the contrast between (Eastern) collectivism and (Western) individualism.

The big question then is 'how deep do these differences go?' – are they simply differences in normative practices, or do they go much deeper to affect basic cognitive and perceptual processes? In this chapter, we also explore the role of language barriers to effective communication, the nature of acculturation, and what role social and cross-cultural psychologists can play in helping to improve intercultural relations. Think of psychological processes and culture at opposite ends of a closed street:

> Individual thoughts and actions influence cultural norms and practices as they evolve over time, and these cultural norms and practices influence the thoughts and actions of individuals. (*Lehman, Chiu & Schaller, 2004, p. 689*)

The issues discussed in this final chapter of our book build upon and reflect on many of the themes and ideas explored earlier in the book – we hope that this chapter provides a cultural context and a cultural challenge to earlier chapters.

# Locating culture in social psychology

## Has social psychology neglected culture?

How far have you travelled recently? With cheap airfares the world is increasingly at your doorstep. Most Europeans have travelled extensively within Europe; Americans have explored Mexico, and Australians and New Zealanders check out Indonesia and Thailand. Russians live in London, Japanese chill out in Hawaii, and the Dutch head for Tuscany. In addition almost all of us, particularly if we live in capital cities like London, Paris or Amsterdam, rub shoulders with a rich cultural mix of people from all over the world in our daily life.

One of the first things that strikes you in a foreign land is the different language or accent, along with the appearance and dress of the local people. Other differences may be more subtle and slower to emerge – they are to do with underlying values, attitudes, and representational and explanatory systems. Culture infuses behaviour and is the lifeblood of ethnic and national groups. In unravelling the properties and processes of groups, social psychologists have usually eschewed culture, focusing instead on normative differences between groups and subgroups (see Chapter 8). Farr (1996) has argued that psychological theory and research in social psychology have been dominated by one cultural perspective – that of middle-class, largely White, America. In itself this is not surprising, as so many psychologists have been middle-class White Americans. A leading cross-cultural psychologist once noted that:

> One of the key facts about psychology is that most of the psychologists who have ever lived and who are now living can be found in the United States . . . The rest of the world has only about 20 per cent of the psychologists that are now or have ever been alive. (*Triandis, 1980, p. ix*)

There is a natural tendency for people to fail to recognise that their life is only one of many possible lives – that what may appear natural may merely be normative (Garfinkel, 1967). The problem for social psychology is that this cultural perspective is dominant – social psychology is **culture-bound**, and also, to a notable extent, **culture-blind**. For example, most major introductory social psychology texts are American (one reason we wrote this book was to balance this – see the Preface and Chapter 1). They are beautifully produced and highly scholarly, but they are written by Americans for Americans – and yet these are authoritative texts in European and other countries around the world.

However, it should be noted that over the past 20 years there has been a rebalancing – the relative hegemony of White American social psychology has waned somewhat with the continuing ascendance of European social psychology and the growing number of influential social psychologists, particular in America, who have East Asian and other ethnic backgrounds.

Another reason why social psychologists have underemphasised culture may be the experimental method (Vaughan & Guerin, 1997). As explained in Chapter 1, social psychologists generally, and with good cause, consider laboratory experiments to be the most

**Culture-blind**
Theory and data untested outside the host culture.

**Culture-bound**
Theory and data conditioned by a specific cultural background.

rigorous way to test causal theories – a love affair with laboratory experimentation that dates back to the early twentieth century. Laboratory experiments tend, by definition, to focus on the manipulation of focal variables in isolation from other variables, such as participants' biographical and cultural backgrounds. However, people *do* bring their autobiographical and cultural baggage into the laboratory – as Tajfel (1972) so eloquently put it, you simply cannot do experiments in a social vacuum. This is not a trivial problem. Because experiments regard culture as the unproblematic backdrop to research, this method may prevent researchers realising that culture may itself be a variable that influences the processes being studied. This point is recognised by Heine, who sees that the experiment can cast much-needed light on cultural difference:

> If culture is the social situation writ large, then it perhaps follows that the experimental methods applied by social psychologists would be most appropriate for studying many questions regarding how culture affects people's thoughts and behaviors. (*Heine, 2010, p. 1427*)

## Defining culture

Boas (1930, p. 30) defined culture as 'the social habits of a community', and Smith and Bond (1998, p. 69) as 'systems of shared meanings'. These elements, shared activity and shared meaning, should both be included in a definition of culture, according to Greenfield and her colleagues (Greenfield, Keller, Fuligni & Maynard, 2003). In discussing variations in definition, Brislin noted:

> Kroeber and Kluckhohn [1952] concluded that many definitions contained 'patterns . . . of behaviour transmitted by symbols, constituting the distinctive achievements of human groups . . . [and] ideas and their attached values'. Herskovits proposed the equally influential generalization that culture is 'the man-made part of the human environment'. Triandis made a distinction between physical [e.g. houses and tools] and subjective culture [e.g. people's values, roles, and attitudes]. (*Brislin, 1987, p. 275*)

Although definitions vary, they tend to share the broad view that culture is an enduring product of and influence on human interaction. In line with this broad perspective, we view culture as the set of cognitions and practices that characterise a specific social group and distinguish it from others. In the same vein, Hofstede (2001, p. 9) referred to culture as 'the collective programming of the mind that distinguishes the members of one group or category of people from another'. In essence, culture is the expression of *group norms* at the national, racial and ethnic level (see Chapter 8 on norms, Chapter 4 on self and identity, and Chapter 11 on intergroup behaviour).

This view is consistent with that of Moreland and Levine (Moreland, Argote & Krishnan 1996; Levine & Moreland, 1991; see also Chapter 9), who argue that culture is an instance of group memory and so culture can apply to social collectives of all sizes – including families, work groups and organisations (Smith, Bond & Kağitçibaşi, 2006). This perspective sets the scene for an analysis of culture and cultural phenomena that uses the language and concepts of the social psychology of social influence, group processes, intergroup relations, and self and identity.

**Völkerpsychologie**
Early precursor of social psychology, as the study of the collective mind, in Germany in the mid- to late nineteenth century.

# Culture, history and social psychology

The early origins of social psychology in nineteenth-century Germany were marked by a concern to describe collective phenomena (see Chapter 1). The work of these folk psychologists, their **Völkerpsychologie**, recognized that groups differ in their beliefs and practices and that describing and explaining these differences should be a focus of social psychology. However, as it gathered momentum social psychology very quickly focused on the individual rather than the group. In contrast, by the beginning of the twentieth century anthropologists were increasingly focusing on group phenomena and differences; devoting time to the concept of culture and to the process of cultural transmission.

## Origins in cultural anthropology

During and after the sixteenth century, there was a confluence of factors that contributed to new ways of construing the self, the individual and the social group (see Chapter 4):

- *Secularisation* – a new focus on the here and now rather than the afterlife.
- *Industrialisation* – people were required to be mobile in order to seek work, and therefore they needed to have a portable personal identity rather than one imbedded in a social structure based on the geographically fixed extended family.
- *Enlightenment* – a philosophy that endowed individuals with rationality and the ability and intellect to manage their social lives and to construct and maintain complex systems of normative social behaviour: culture (see also Allport, 1954a; Fromm, 1941; Weber, 1930).

By the late nineteenth and early twentieth centuries, cross-cultural research had formed the basis of modern cultural anthropology. Some of the key works that shaped cultural anthropology were, in the United Kingdom, Frazer's (1890) *The golden bough* and Malinowski's (1927) *Sex and repression in savage society* and, in the United States, Boas's (1911) *The mind of primitive man*. In terms of what was to follow, the most influential of these early figures was Franz Boas at Columbia University, who single-mindedly championed the proposition that personality is formed by culture. This was not an easy sell in an intellectual milieu where social behaviour was thought to be biologically determined: for example, by Freud and fellow psychodynamic theorists (see Chapter 12).

Boas's ideas were promoted further by two of his students, Margaret Mead (1928/1961) and Ruth Benedict (1934). On the basis of detailed **ethnographic research**, they provided rich and graphic descriptions of cultures that differed enormously in terms of the behavioural practices that were sanctioned or proscribed by social norms. Mead, who was also trained in psychology, made a concerted effort to divert anthropology from studying the universal biological bases of behaviour to a study of how culture impacts psychological development (Price-Williams, 1976). As a consequence of this, by the 1950s cross-cultural research had made a significant contribution to theories of child development and socialisation (Child, 1954).

There have been other isolated but influential instances of early psychological studies that drew from cultural anthropology. At Cambridge University, Bartlett conducted a series of experiments (e.g. Bartlett, 1923, 1932) on social and cultural factors affecting memory. In one, he borrowed a folk tale, *The war of the ghosts*, from Boas. His participants read the tale and later reconstructed it as precisely as possible from memory. In a variation using serial reproduction, each participant in a group passed a recalled version on to the next participant, in an analogue of spreading a rumour (see Chapter 3). In both cases, the original story was systematically reconstructed to bring it more into line with what they would remember easily. The consequence was a 'cultural' transformation of the tale.

This early research is remarkably consistent with Moscovici's (e.g. 1988) more recent notion of social representations (see Lorenzi-Cioldi & Clémence, 2001), which is discussed in Chapters 3 and 5. You will recall that social representations are shared frameworks for rendering the world meaningful, and that they are developed and maintained by social interaction.

**Ethnographic research**
Descriptive study of a specific society, based on fieldwork, and requiring immersion of the researcher in the everyday life of its people.

In 1940 Klineberg published an influential text, *Social psychology,* in which he introduced findings from ethnology (the 'science of races') and comparative sociology. This was an unusual innovation, well ahead of its time – for much of the twentieth century social psychologists often distanced themselves from cross-cultural research. There were two reasons: they were unwilling to be seen as 'tender-minded', particularly since anthropologists were often wedded to psychoanalytic theory and methods (Segall, 1965); they were also increasingly committed to using experimental methods and felt that cross-cultural research was merely descriptive (Vaughan & Guerin, 1997; see above and Chapter 1).

## Rise of cross-cultural psychology

The public coming-out of cross-cultural psychology was marked by publication of the *International Journal of Psychology* in Paris in 1966 and the *Journal of Cross-Cultural Psychology* in the United States in 1970. In the opening article of the inaugural issue of this latter journal, two eminent social psychologists, Lois and Gardner Murphy (Murphy & Murphy, 1970) discussed the promise of cross-cultural psychology and what it might achieve. The arrival of cross-cultural psychology has also been marked by publication of authoritative handbooks dedicated to cross-cultural psychology (e.g., Berry, Dasen & Saraswathi, 1997; Berry, Poortinga & Pandey, 1997; Triandis et al., 1980). Cross-cultural psychologists sought answers to three questions:

1   Are Western psychological theories valid in other cultures?

2   Are there psychological constructs that are culture-specific?

3   How can we evolve a psychology with universal relevance?

Cultural anthropologists have long been interested in the second and third of these questions (Kluckhohn, 1954). With the arrival of the new subdiscipline came new terminology and a new distinction: the **etic–emic distinction**, drawn by analogy with the linguistic distinction between phonetics and phonemics (see Chapter 15). As Smith and Bond (1998, p. 57) noted:

> Berry . . . argues that 'etic' analyses of behaviour are those that focus on universals, principally those that . . . are either simple or variform. For example, we all eat, we almost all have intimate relations with certain others, and we all have ways of attacking enemies. An 'emic' analysis of these behaviours, on the other hand, would focus on the different, varied ways in which each of these activities was carried out in any specific cultural setting. Successful emic analyses could be expected to establish generalisations that were only valid locally. (*Smith & Bond, 1998, p. 57*)

Power distance, for example, is an etic construct because it can be observed in most cultures, while *amae,* or passive love, is an emic construct that is probably limited to Japanese culture. (Power distance and *amae* are discussed below.) Emic constructs may 'grow' into etic ones if they are appropriately investigated and established across cultures.

The formal recognition of the subdiscipline is complete. In addition to the journals and books, there are now university courses devoted to cross-cultural psychology. Some distinguish between what *cross-cultural psychologists* do and what *cultural psychologists* do. The cross-cultural psychologist might use traditional social psychological (questionnaires, interviews) and statistical methods to compare and contrast ethnic and national groups (see Smith, Bond & Kağitçibaşi, 2006). On the other hand, the cultural psychologist might study how people extract meaning from their sociocultural environment and emphasise that the person as an entity cannot be extracted from the culture, which is also an entity; and might also to prefer qualitative methods and sometimes use discourse analysis (Shweder, 1991). However, it is unlikely that cultural psychology can be defined as a

**Etic–emic distinction**
Contrast between psychological constructs that are relatively culture-universal and those that are relatively culture-specific.

separate discipline simply in terms of method – we have already noted that Heine (2010) regards cultural psychology as fit to profit from the use of the experimental method. In practice, the boundary between cross-cultural and cultural psychology is likely to remain fluid.

Much of what follows in the following sections centres on cross-cultural, and sometimes cross-national, comparisons. But if our data are cross-cultural, can we do justice to the complexities inherent in an individual culture? The cross-cultural psychologist Michael Bond has suggested that the cross-cultural challenge may be beyond us: 'Cross-cultural psychologists will never get it culturally right, only cross-culturally right' (Bond, 2003, p. 281). We return to the topic of this challenge later in this chapter.

# Culture, thinking and behaving

## Culture, cognition and attribution

In Chapter 3 we saw how it is cultural knowledge that allows us to make a causal attribution of behaviour that is appropriate to the context – failure to pay attention to culture would have 'interesting' consequences for the unfortunate attributor. We also saw that there are cultural variations in *attributional style,* such as differences in ethnocentric bias between Malay and Chinese people in Singapore (Hewstone & Ward, 1985) – a case of the **ultimate attribution error** (see Chapter 3, Figure 3.7). In another example, Hindu Indians were much less likely than North Americans to make dispositional rather than situational attributions (Miller, 1984; see Chapter 3, Figure 3.8) – a case of the **fundamental attribution error**.

A review by Lehman pointed to subtle but consistent differences in *thought processes* between East Asians and Americans (Lehman, Chiu & Schaller, 2004). The intellectual tradition of East Asians (and other collectivist cultures) has evolved to be generally more holistic and relationship-oriented, whereas Americans (and other individualistic cultures) are usually more analytic and linear in their thinking. In Box 16.1 we include some findings

**Ultimate attribution error**
Tendency to attribute bad outgroup and good ingroup behaviour internally, and to attribute good outgroup and bad ingroup behaviour externally.

**Fundamental attribution error**
Bias in attributing another's behaviour more to internal than to situational causes.

---

### Real world 16.1
### East Asian and American differences in thinking and in explaining behaviour

Is it possible that thought processes among East Asian peoples differ from those in the West? Studies by Nisbett, Peng and Choi suggest they do in subtle ways. East Asians more often:

- have a better memory for objects in their context (e.g. the *wolf* is in the *dark forest*);

- are prone to perceptual error when a stimulus object needs to be judged against a distracting background (e.g. judging if a fixed rod remains perpendicular as a frame behind it starts to rotate);

- are sensitive to people's social backgrounds when judging them;

- accept deductions when the premises are believable;

- take notice of typical examples when solving tasks based on categories;

- accept apparent contradictions about themselves (e.g. agreeing *that equality is more important than ambition* at one moment in time but then disagreeing with this later);

- are less surprised by unexpected behaviour;

- look at arguments from both sides and compromise when there is conflict;

- expect trends in behaviour in the future to be variable rather than consistent.

*Source:* based on Choi & Nisbett, 2000; Masuda & Nisbett, 2001; Peng & Nisbett, 1999

suggesting that East Asians differ in subtle ways of thinking and of attributing causes when they are compared with North Americans. We shall see in a later section that this broad East–West difference is reflected in different conceptions of the self and in the way that values are expressed. Nisbett has referred to the 'geography of thought' and suggests that people from East Asia and those from the West have had different systems for thinking for thousands of years.

This last finding in Box 16.1 has an interesting implication. Westerners often have difficulty with the notion of regression to the mean because they assume permanence, that what happens at time-1 will happen at time-2 or that an existing trend will continue (Nisbett, Krantz, Jepson & Kunda, 1983; see Chapter 1). This follows because Westerners play down the role of situational influences on events and behaviours. However, East Asians focus more on the situation and do not assume permanence – so instead of expecting what happens at time-1 to be the same as what happens at time-2 they realise that as the situation changes so will the behaviour. They expect behaviour to vary across time and that trends are not linear – they have a better intuitive understanding of regression to the mean.

Another interesting cultural difference is in the stereotype rebound effect – the tendency for people who are instructed to suppress their stereotypes to subsequently show evidence of stronger stereotype expression. Zhang and Hunt (2008) had US and Chinese participants write about a gay man under instructions to suppress their stereotypes, or with no instruction – both instructed groups successfully suppressed their stereotypes. After a filler task they were asked, without instruction, to write another essay about a gay man. The predicted stereotype rebound effect emerged, but only for the US participants; the Chinese still managed to suppress their anti-gay stereotypes. The explanation is that collectivist/interdependent cultures help people learn to suppress (the expression of) their feelings and attitudes in order to maintain social harmony – thus Asians who suppress stereotypes do not experience a rebound.

Finally Kitayama and his colleagues (Kitayama, Snibbe, Markus & Suzuki, 2004) have reported differences between Japanese and American participants in their experience of cognitive dissonance (see Chapter 6). Japanese may feel dissonance only when social cues are active, such as becoming aware of their peers' opinions when making a decision. Again, see differences in East–West self-concept later in this chapter.

## Culture, conformity and obedience

**Meta-analysis**
Statistical procedure that combines data from different studies to measure the overall reliability and strength of specific effects.

Asch's (1951) study of conformity to group pressure (see Chapter 7) is one of the most widely replicated social psychology experiments of all time. Smith and Bond (1998) report a **meta-analysis** of Asch-type studies carried out in the United States and sixteen other countries, which reveals considerable variation in the degree of conformity across different cultures. Conformity was generally stronger outside Western Europe and North America (see Figure 16.1). The reason why conformity in the Asch paradigm is greater in non-Western cultures is probably that participants did not wish to cause embarrassment by disagreeing with the majority's erroneous responses – conforming to the majority was a way to allow the majority to 'save face'. (For a defence of the continued use of experiments in cross-cultural research see Heine, 2010.)

### Conformity in subsistence cultures

The way in which people function interpersonally and in groups can be profoundly affected by where they work and live. For example, people from both Western and Eastern cultures experience considerable physical and psychological stress when they live for extended periods of time in polar regions (Taylor, 1987). Furthermore, our geographical

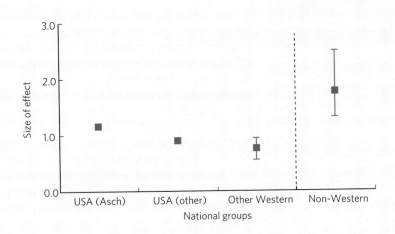

**Figure 16.1**  Variations in size of conformity effect across cultures

- This analysis of 'effect size' shows that conformity rates were lower in American and other Western samples than in samples from other parts of the world.
- The rates among Americans have also dropped since Asch conducted his studies.

*Source:* based on Smith & Bond (1998)

location can interact with kinship and family structure, child development and group norms regarding economic practices (e.g. Price-Williams, 1976; Smith & Bond, 1998).

An early study of two subsistence cultures compared response differences in an Asch-type conformity setting. One was a food-accumulating culture, the Temne from Sierra Leone, and the other a hunter–gatherer society, the Canadian Eskimos (Inuit) (Berry, 1967; see Box 16.2).

**Conformity as a necessity**
This young Laplander lives in a harsh environment where survival depends on strict adherence to communal norms

## Real world 16.2
### No room for dissenters among the Temne

**The Temne of Sierra Leone provide an intriguing example of how culture can influence conformity**

Using a variant of Asch's conformity paradigm, Berry (1967) hypothesised that a people's hunting and food-gathering practices should affect the extent that individuals conform to their group. On this basis, he compared the Temne people of Sierra Leone with the Eskimos (Inuit) of Canada and found much greater conformity among the Temne.

The Temne subsist on a single crop, which they harvest in one concerted effort once a year. As this requires enormous cooperation and coordination of effort, consensus and agreement are strongly valued and represented in Temne culture. Berry quotes one participant as saying, 'When Temne people choose a thing, we must all agree with the decision – this is what we call cooperation' (Berry, 1967, p. 417).

In contrast, the Eskimo economy involves continual hunting and gathering on a relatively individual basis. An Inuit looks after himself and his immediate family; thus, consensus is less strongly emphasised in Eskimo culture.

### Obedience to authority

In considering some of the major findings of social psychology, Smith and Bond (1998) concluded that the solitary finding that clearly replicated across cultures is obedience to authority (see Chapter 7). This would hardly be surprising, given that authority is a cornerstone of any major social system. Below, we touch on some more substantial differences, and several interesting variations by culture. These are by no means exhaustive. A target for the future is for psychologists who are social, cross-cultural and cultural to be alive to processes that are relatively universal and those that are relatively culture-specific.

### Culture and becoming socialised

By the 1930s, anthropologists at Columbia University (Boas, Benedict, Mead) had established that child development was inextricably bound up with cultural norms. According to Margaret Mead, Samoan norms dictate that young people 'should keep quiet, wake up early, obey, and work hard and cheerfully' (Mead, 1928/1961, p. 130), whereas among the Manus in New Guinea there was a culturally induced disposition towards being 'the aggressive, violent, overbearing type' (Mead, 1930/1962, p. 233).

Recent work on socialisation has been extended by Kağitçibaşi to include explorations of family structure and values, and what kind of value is placed upon children in different cultures – and how these interact with a society's economy (see Smith, Bond & Kağitçibaşi, 2006). These issues, centred on the family, affect how a person relates to others and how the self develops: will an individual become more independent or interdependent?

### Families and aggression

'It is a fundamental aspect of human nature; people live in a dog-eat-dog world; people need to compete to survive and prosper' (Bonta, 1997, p. 299). Bonta was quoting another author and noted up to twenty-five striking exceptions to this so-called rule. In contrast to comparisons of socialised aggression often featured in cross-cultural commentaries, there are societies that emphasise the importance of cooperation; they devalue achievement because they believe it leads to violence. They are usually non-Western communities and are mostly small and isolated (see also Chapter 12).

Norms that support a **subculture of violence** are also channelled through the family, which is why rates of violence have traditionally been higher in the American South than

**Subculture of violence**
A subgroup of society in which a higher level of violence is accepted as the norm.

## Research highlight 16.3
### Southern honour

Historically, the Southern United States has had higher homicide rates than the rest of the country. Nisbett and his colleagues link greater violence in the South to the herding economy that developed in its early settlements. In other parts of the world, herders have typically resorted to force more readily when they needed to protect their property, especially in contexts where their animals can roam widely.

When self-protection can be so important, a culture of honour may develop. An individual must let an adversary know that intrusion will not be tolerated. In old Louisiana, a wife and her lover were surrendered by law to the husband, who might punish as he saw fit, including killing them. Even today, laws in the South relating to violent actions are more tolerant of violence than those

in the North – for example, relating to gun ownership, spouse abuse, corporal punishment and capital punishment. According to Fischer (1989), Southern violence is not indiscriminate. For example, rates for robbery in the South are no higher than those in the North. The culture of honour would apply to self-protection, protection of the family, or when affronted.

The persistence of higher levels of violence so long after the pioneering days may follow from the use of more violent child-rearing in the South (see the discussion of learned patterns of aggression and the abuse syndrome in Chapter 12). Boys are told to stand up for themselves and to use force in so doing, while spanking is regarded as the normal solution for misbehaviour. Table 16.1 shows comparative responses, from the South and elsewhere, of appropriate ways of using violence for self-protection.

*Source*: Cohen & Nisbett, 1997; Nisbett & Cohen 1996; Vandello & Cohen, 2003

in other parts of the United States – the trends are confined to situations involving oneself, one's family or one's possessions (see Box 16.3 and Table 16.1). The studies use the concept of **culture of honour** (Nisbett & Cohen, 1996) to give meaning to a regional pattern of behaviour. In this instance, it is linked to a tradition of aggression in dealing with threat and is related clearly to **machismo** in Latin American families (see Chapter 12). It can also be linked to acts of beneficence, however: a person can be honour-bound to help as well as to hurt. The Arabic term *izzat* has the same sense.

**Culture of honour**
A culture that endorses male violence as a way of addressing threats to social reputation or economic position.

**Machismo**
A code in which challenges, abuse and even differences of opinion must be met with fists or other weapons.

**Table 16.1** Males using violence in self-defence: differences in the United States between Southern and non-Southern views

| Question and region | Percentage agreeing | Percentage agreeing strongly |
|---|---|---|
| A man has a right to kill: | | |
| (a) *in self-defence* | | |
| South | 92 | 70 |
| Non-South | 88 | 57 |
| (b) *to defend his family* | | |
| South | 97 | 80 |
| Non-South | 92 | 67 |
| (c) *to defend his house* | | |
| South | 69 | 56 |
| Non-South | 52 | 18 |

*Source*: based on Blumenthal, Kahn, Andrews & Head (1972); cited in Taylor, Peplau, & Sears (2000)

# Two psyches: East meets West

Fiske, Kitayama, Markus and Nisbett (1998) refer to two very different culturally patterned social systems, or psyches: the European American (called loosely, Western) and East Asian (called loosely, Eastern). These groupings best reflect the spectrum of available research findings when dealing with cultural differences at the broadest level, but they may be insufficiently textured to capture more subtle cultural differences between subgroups. A further description of the two regions is that people in Western cultures have an *independent* self-concept and people in Eastern cultures have an *interdependent* self-concept (Markus & Kityama, 1991, 2003; Schimmack, Oishi & Diener, 2005). Indeed, much of the focus of contemporary cross-cultural psychology often seems to be on this general distinction between the interdependent self of collectivist societies and the independent self of individualistic societies (Nisbett, 2003).

Using a cognitive metaphor, Triandis (Triandis, 1989, 1994a; Triandis & Suh, 2002) has suggested that cultures provide conventions for people to sample information in their environment. When sampling for clues, those from Western cultures use elements of the personal self, such as 'I am kind', whereas those from Eastern cultures use elements of the collective self, such as 'my co-workers think I am kind'. Nevertheless, the general distinctions, East–West and independent–interdependent, are useful. For example, Latin American cultures, such as that found in Mexico, are usually strongly based on interdependence among individuals (Diaz-Guerrero, 1987). We should note that the terms 'collectivism' and 'individualism' have not been used in a consistent way (Oyserman, Coon & Kemmelmeier, 2002) and that other terms are used interchangeably to define these orientations (e.g. independence versus interdependence; private self versus collective self) – also see Brewer & Chen (2007).

These cultural-level distinctions may be reflected in differences in the way in which the self is construed and how social relationships are understood. Both the self and the basis on which social relations are conducted are relatively independent in historically newer and market-oriented, person-centred societies. However, they are interdependent in historically older and traditional, group-centred societies. In Chapter 4, on self and identity, we discussed the nature of self and focused on whether or when the self is best described as independent, interdependent, collective, relational, autonomous and so forth; however, it is worth revisiting several points here in the context of culture (see Chapter 4 for full exposition).

## Two kinds of self

**Independent self**
A self that is relatively separate, internal and unique.

**Interdependent self**
A self that is relatively dependent on social relations and has more fuzzy boundaries.

Markus and Kitayama (1991) introduced the concepts of **independent self** and **interdependent self** to distinguish between the different kinds of self found in different cultures (see Table 16.2).

People in individualistic (Western) cultures generally have an independent self, whereas people in collectivist (Eastern) cultures have an interdependent self. The independent self is an autonomous entity with clear boundaries between self and others. Internal attributes, such as thoughts, feelings and abilities, are stable and largely unaffected by social context. The behaviour of the independent self is governed and constituted primarily according to one's inner and dispositional characteristics. In contrast, the interdependent self has flexible and diffuse boundaries between self and others. It is tied into relationships and is highly responsive to social context. Others are seen as a part of the self, and the self is seen as a part of other people. There is no self without the collective. One's behaviour is governed and organised primarily according to perception of other people's thoughts, feelings and actions.

**Table 16.2**  Western and Eastern cultural models of the person

| The independent person | The interdependent person |
| --- | --- |
| is bounded, stable, autonomous | is connected, fluid, flexible |
| has personal attributes that guide action | participates in social relationships that guide action |
| is achievement-oriented | is oriented to the collective |
| formulates personal goals | meets obligations and conforms to norms |
| defines life by successful goal achievement | defines life by contributing to the collective |
| is responsible for own behaviour | is responsible with others for joint behaviour |
| is competitive | is cooperative |
| strives to feel good about the self | subsumes self in the collective |

*Source*: based on Fiske, Kitayama, Markus & Nisbett (1998)

The distinction between two kinds of self is further elaborated in Figure 16.2 and has important implications for how individuals may relate to significant others in their cultures. Think back now to Daan's concern about 'speaking out' in South Korea (the first focus question). (Brewer & Gardner, 1996, make a similar distinction between the individual self, which is defined by personal traits that differentiate the self from all others, and the relational self, which is defined in relation to specific other people with whom one interacts in a group context.) These cultural differences in how the self is construed are probably implicit – we operate the way we do with little conscious awareness (Kitayama, Snibbe, Markus & Suzuki, 2004).

From a recent review, Vignoles, Chryssochoou and Breakwell (2000) conclude that despite cultural differences in self-conception, the need to have a distinctive and integrated sense of self may be universal; however, self-distinctiveness means something different in individualist and in collectivist cultures. In one it is the isolated and bounded self that gains meaning from separateness, whereas in the other it is the relational self that gains meaning from its relations with others. Cross, Bacon and Morris (2000) suggest that the interdependent self is based on different relations in individualistic and collectivist cultures. In the former it is based on close interpersonal relationships, whereas in the latter it is based on a relationship with the group as a whole. Consider a different context: in organisational settings, Chinese employees are selected according to their ties to current employees rather than traditional selection tools, such as tests and interviews (Markus, 2004).

People from individualist cultures consistently generate primarily independent descriptions of themselves when answering the question 'Who am I?' whereas those from collectivist cultures generate interdependent descriptions (Hannover & Kühnen, 2004). Furthermore, when people from East Asia are compared with those from the West, there are other differences in how they make moral judgements, attribute causes, process information and seek happiness (Choi & Choi, 2002). Remaining within a broad East–West cultural dichotomy, we now turn to other ways in which different cultures can be compared.

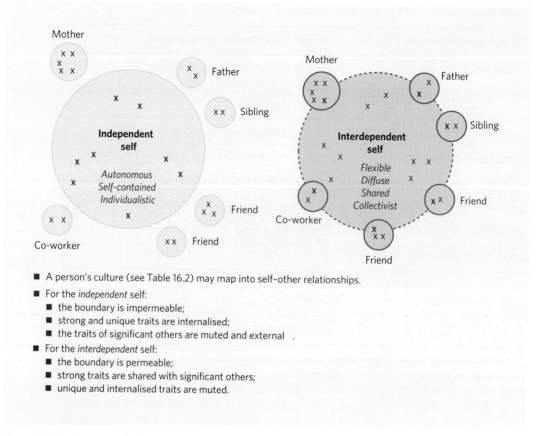

- A person's culture (see Table 16.2) may map into self–other relationships.
- For the *independent* self:
  - the boundary is impermeable;
  - strong and unique traits are internalised;
  - the traits of significant others are muted and external .
- For the *interdependent* self:
  - the boundary is permeable;
  - strong traits are shared with significant others;
  - unique and internalised traits are muted.

**Figure 16.2** Representations of the self: independent versus interdependent

*Source*: based on Markus & Kitayama (1991)

# Systems for comparing cultures

## Characterising cultures by values

**Values**
A higher-order concept thought to provide a structure for organising attitudes.

**Level of analysis (or explanation)**
The types of concepts, mechanisms and language used to explain a phenomenon.

The study of **values** has a long history in the social sciences, with psychology adopting a different **level of analysis** to sociology. Psychology has tended to explore values at the level of the individual (see Chapter 5), whereas sociology has adopted a societal perspective. Within both disciplines, however, values are broad constructs used by individuals and societies to orient people's specific attitudes and behaviour in an integrated and meaningful manner. Values are tied to groups, social categories and cultures, and are thus socially constructed and socially maintained. Not surprisingly, the study of values is central to the analysis of culture (Fiske, Kitayama, Markus & Nisbett, 1998). In this section, we consider the research of Hofstede and Schwartz.

Hofstede's (1980) work was a *tour de force* that contributed to the development of cross-cultural psychology (Smith, Bond & Kağıtçıbaşı, 2006). Hofstede distributed a questionnaire to 117,000 managers of a large multinational company in forty different countries. Using factor analysis, he isolated four dimensions on which these countries could be compared (although in 1991, on the basis of an expanded sample of fifty countries, he added a fifth dimension – time perspective):

**Collective decision making**

In making group decisions people can be concerned not to damage their relationships with fellow group members — this is particularly true of Eastern cultures

1  *Power distance* – the degree to which unequal power in institutions and practices is accepted, or, alternatively, egalitarianism is endorsed (e.g. can employees freely express disagreement with their manager?).

2  *Uncertainty avoidance* – planning for stability in dealing with life's uncertainties (e.g. believing that company rules should never be broken).

3  *Masculinity–femininity* – valuing attributes that are either typically masculine (e.g. achieving, gaining material success) or typically feminine (e.g. promoting interpersonal harmony, caring).

4  *Individualism–collectivism* – whether one's identity is determined by personal choices or by the collective (e.g. having the freedom to adapt your approach to the job).

These four dimensions are the basis of the data shown in Table 16.3. The top and bottom quartiles among the forty countries have been ranked by an index on each dimension. Take the following examples:

- Denmark is low on power distance (0.18), uncertainty avoidance (0.23) and masculinity (0.16), but high on individualism (0.74) – Danes do not easily accept hierarchical relationships, they tolerate uncertain outcomes, are caring and egalitarian, but individualistic.

- Japan is high on uncertainty avoidance (0.92) and masculinity (0.95) – Japanese seek clear-cut outcomes, want to reduce life's uncertainties, and want to achieve and gain material success.

- Singapore is high on power distance (0.74) but low on individualism (0.20) – Singaporeans tend to accept hierarchical relationships and are collectivist.

An interesting aspect of this analysis is that Eastern and Western countries do not always follow an East–West dichotomy. Of these dimensions, by far the most popular for the work that was to follow was individualism–collectivism (Fiske, Kitayama, Markus & Nisbett, 1998; Smith & Bond, 1998). It was the one deemed to capture the essence of the East–West dichotomy discussed above.

**Table 16.3** Cross-cultural differences in work-related values

| | Power distance | | Uncertainty avoidance | | Individualism | | Masculinity | |
|---|---|---|---|---|---|---|---|---|
| Lowest quartile | Austria | 0.11 | Singapore | 0.08 | Venezuela | 0.12 | Sweden | 0.05 |
| | Israel | 0.13 | Denmark | 0.23 | Colombia | 0.13 | Norway | 0.08 |
| | Denmark | 0.18 | Hong Kong | 0.29 | Pakistan | 0.14 | Netherlands | 0.14 |
| | New Zealand | 0.22 | Sweden | 0.29 | Peru | 0.16 | Denmark | 0.16 |
| | Ireland | 0.28 | Great Britain | 0.35 | Taiwan | 0.17 | Yugoslavia | 0.21 |
| | Norway | 0.31 | Ireland | 0.35 | Singapore | 0.20 | Finland | 0.26 |
| | Sweden | 0.31 | India | 0.40 | Thailand | 0.20 | Chile | 0.28 |
| | Finland | 0.33 | Philippines | 0.44 | Chile | 0.23 | Portugal | 0.31 |
| | Switzerland | 0.34 | USA | 0.46 | Hong Kong | 0.25 | Thailand | 0.34 |
| | Great Britain | 0.35 | Canada | 0.48 | Portugal | 0.27 | Spain | 0.42 |
| | Turkey | 0.66 | Turkey | 0.85 | France | 0.71 | Colombia | 0.64 |
| | Colombia | 0.67 | Argentina | 0.86 | Sweden | 0.71 | Philippines | 0.64 |
| | France | 0.68 | Chile | 0.86 | Denmark | 0.74 | Germany (FR) | 0.66 |
| | Hong Kong | 0.68 | France | 0.86 | Belgium | 0.75 | Great Britain | 0.66 |
| | Brazil | 0.69 | Spain | 0.86 | Italy | 0.76 | Ireland | 0.68 |
| | Singapore | 0.74 | Peru | 0.87 | New Zealand | 0.79 | Mexico | 0.69 |
| | Yugoslavia | 0.76 | Yugoslavia | 0.88 | Canada | 0.80 | Italy | 0.70 |
| | India | 0.77 | Japan | 0.92 | Netherlands | 0.80 | Switzerland | 0.70 |
| | Mexico | 0.81 | Belgium | 0.94 | Great Britain | 0.89 | Venezuela | 0.73 |
| Highest quartile | Venezuela | 0.81 | Portugal | 1.04 | Australia | 0.90 | Austria | 0.70 |
| | Philippines | 0.94 | Greece | 1.12 | USA | 0.91 | Japan | 0.95 |

*Source*: based on Hofstede (1980)

Schwartz, in a 1992 study, and in a Polish study (Schwartz & Bardi, 1997), offered an alternative approach, based on a tradition dating back to the work of Rokeach (1973; see Chapter 5). Schwartz started with fifty-six values thought to exist in different cultures. He then had more that 40,000 teachers and students from fifty-six nations rate these values for their relevance to themselves. Using a multidimensional scaling analysis, he found two dimensions with stable meanings:

1 *openness to change versus conservatism*, e.g. ranging from autonomy to security and tradition;

2 *self-enhancement versus self-transcendence*, e.g. ranging from mastery and power to egalitarianism and harmony with nature.

There are similarities between Schwartz's first dimension and Hofstede's individualism–collectivism, and between Schwartz's second dimension and Hofstede's power distance. An advantage of Schwartz's approach is that he carried out separate analyses, one at the level of individuals and another at the level of cultures.

Fiske, Kitayama, Markus and Nisbett (1998) concluded that the body of cross-cultural work on values, together with other research (e.g. Smith, Dugan & Trompenaars, 1996), indicated three groupings of European nations in terms of value orientations:

1  Western European nations are individualistic and egalitarian;

2  Eastern European nations are individualistic and hierarchical;

3  Asian nations are collectivist and hierarchical.

Research into the nature of values expressed through culture continues to flourish, and some connections between various approaches have been identified. For example, Smith and Bond (1998) pointed to a similarity between the concepts of power distance in Hofstede's theory covered above, and authority ranking (where relationships are defined by power and status) covered below in Fiske's relationship models theory. Bond (1996) has suggested that there is a fundamental Chinese value not captured by Western research: Confucian work dynamism which highlights role obligations towards the family. (See the second focus question.)

## Individualism and collectivism

The study of cultural values – for example, Hofstede's work – focuses on value systems that differentiate between societies. The sensible assumption is that (most) people in those societies subscribe to the relevant values: that is, the values are internalised by individuals as part of their personal value system. Triandis and his colleagues (Triandis, 1994b; Triandis, Leung, Villareal & Clack, 1985) explicitly addressed this assumption. They introduced the concepts of *allocentrism* and *idiocentrism* to describe collectivism and individualism, respectively, at the individual level of analysis. Allocentric people tend towards cooperation, social support, equality and honesty, whereas idiocentric people tend towards need for achievement, anomie, alienation, loneliness, and values such as a comfortable life, pleasure and social recognition.

Triandis and his associates found that people could be more or less allocentric or more or less idiocentric in different situations. The reason why cultures as a whole differ is that they differ in the prevalence of situations that call for either allocentrism or idiocentrism. Collectivist cultures have a higher proportion of situations requiring allocentrism than idiocentrism, whereas the opposite is true for individualistic cultures.

We have already noted that traditional and agrarian societies were collectivist. The very term 'tribe' has the sense of a collective. As far as we know, **collectivism** characterised pre-literate communities as well. A shift to **individualism** has been gradual (see our earlier treatment of the development of cultural anthropology).

We consider below two examples of research based on individualism and collectivism selected from topics that have featured in earlier chapters.

## Cooperate or compete? Role of social identity

A social situation may be structured in ways that favour cooperative or competitive interactions, involving individuals or groups. In gaming research, this was encapsulated in the **prisoner's dilemma** (see Chapter 11).

Hinkle and Brown (1990) pursued this idea further and have suggested an interesting qualification to **social identity theory** (see Chapter 11). They argue that groups can vary in

**Collectivism**
Societal structure and world-view in which people prioritise group loyalty, commitment and conformity, and belonging and fitting in to groups, over standing out as an isolated individual.

**Individualism**
Societal structure and world-view in which people prioritise standing out as an individual over fitting in as a group member.

**Prisoner's dilemma**
Two-person game in which both parties are torn between competition and cooperation and, depending on mutual choices, both can win or both can lose.

**Social identity theory**
Theory of group membership and intergroup relations based on self-categorisation, social comparison and the construction of a shared self-definition in terms of ingroup-defining properties.

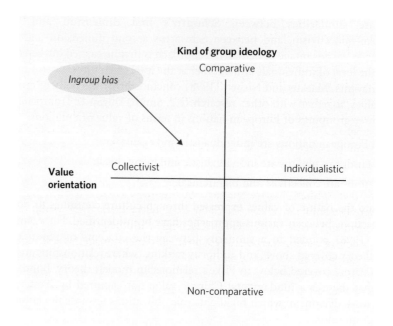

**Figure 16.3** Individuals' values and intergroup comparison can impact ingroup bias

- Groups may have a comparative or non-comparative ideology, depending on whether intergroup comparisons are important in sustaining identity or not.
- Ingroup bias occurs when a person has a collectivist value orientation and is a member of a group with a comparative ideology.
- This combination occurs in the figure's upper-left quadrant.

*Source:* based on Hinkle & Brown (1990, p. 48)

terms of their social orientation from *collectivist* to *individualist*. However, groups can also vary in their orientation towards defining themselves through comparisons or not – they can vary from a *comparative ideology* to a *non-comparative ideology*. For example, some groups, such as sports teams, are intrinsically comparative – they often require a comparison group to estimate their worth. Other groups are non-comparative, such as a family whose members are close and would think it unnecessary to compare their group's qualities with, say, those of their neighbours (see Figure 16.3).

The implication of this analysis is that not all intergroup contexts generate discrimination – groups vary in the extent to which they engage in intergroup discrimination. Those located in the top left-hand quadrant of Figure 16.3 show most (or any) discrimination.

Brown and his colleagues (Brown, Hinkle, Ely, Fox-Cardamone, Maras & Taylor, 1992) confirmed this idea in a study in which they measured individualistic and collectivist values among British participants who were members of groups that were either relatively comparative or non-comparative. They found that outgroup discrimination was highest when an individual's orientation was collectivist and the ingroup was comparative. (We should note here that conformity rates are also higher in non-Western, collectivist cultures – refer back to Figure 16.1 – which might be expected if collectivism implies greater ingroup identification.)

The relationship between cultural orientation and social identity has been taken further in three studies designed to show that the more strongly people identify with a (cultural) group, the more strongly they will endorse and conform to the norms of individualism or collectivism that define the relevant (cultural) group.

In the first study (Jetten, Postmes & McAuliffe, 2002), North Americans (individualist culture) were more individualistic when they highly identified with their culture than when

**Ideology**
A systematically interrelated set of beliefs whose primary function is explanation. It circumscribes thinking, making it difficult for the holder to escape from its mould.

they did not; Indonesians (collectivist culture) were less individualistic when they identified more strongly with their culture.

In the second and third studies (McAuliffe, Jetten, Hornsey & Hogg, 2003) participants were categorised as members of an ad hoc group described as having either an individualist or a collectivist group culture. They then evaluated a group member based on a series of statements, manipulated to reflect individualism or collectivism, ostensibly made by the group member. It was found that collectivist behaviour was evaluated more positively than individualist behaviour when the group norm prescribed collectivism, but that this preference was attenuated when group norms prescribed individualism. Furthermore, consistent with the idea that evaluations were driven by conformity to *salient norms*, attenuation occurred only for high identifiers, not for low identifiers.

In two further studies (Hornsey, Jetten, McAuliffe & Hogg, 2006), dissenting group members were better tolerated and less likely to be rejected when the group had an individualistic norm and participants identified strongly with the group.

Recently, a note of caution has been aired: no single dimension, in this case individualism–collectivism, can hope to do justice to the world's complex and varied cultures (Smith, Bond & Kağıtçıbaşı, 2006). By comparison, the impact of religion has been neglected in cross-cultural research despite its obvious historical and contemporary importance in national and international affairs.

## Collectivism and being prosocial

We noted in Chapter 13 that **prosocial behaviour** is more likely to occur in rural areas than in cities. It is tempting to ask on this basis whether people whose orientation is collectivist rather than individualistic are more likely to help others and to receive help from them. According to Nadler (1986, 1991), self-reliance and individual achievement are fostered by Western cultures.

Nadler (1986) compared the help-seeking tendencies of Israeli high-school students living in *kibbutzim* with those dwelling in cities. In Israel, socialisation in a *kibbutz* stresses collectivist values, a lifestyle in which a communal and egalitarian outlook is important, and being cooperative with peers is crucial (Bettleheim, 1969). *Kibbutz* dwellers rely on being comrades – they depend heavily on group resources, and they treat group goals as paramount. In contrast, the Israeli city context is typically Western, with an emphasis on individualist values, including personal independence and individual achievement.

Seeking help has a strong sociocultural component. Nadler found that the two groups treated a request for aid in dramatically different ways. If it was clear that the situation affected the outcome for a group as a whole, *kibbutz* dwellers were much more likely than city dwellers to seek help, and vice versa if the benefit was defined in individual terms. There were no differences between men and women in these trends. See how Nadler tested this idea, as described in Box 16.4, and check the results in Figure 16.4.

## Characterising cultures by relationships

A thoroughgoing cultural psychology might argue that one's psyche works in tandem with one's social relationships. A. P. Fiske (Fiske, 1992; Fiske & Haslam, 1996; Haslam, 1994) developed a **relational theory** based on the core social cognition concept of **schema** (see Chapter 2 for discussion of schemas):

> People in every culture use just four elementary models to generate, understand, coordinate, evaluate, and contest most social interaction. Each of these four models is a motivated, affectively colored, cognitive schema . . . [by] which people jointly construct meaningful social relations. (*Fiske, Kitayama, Markus & Nisbett, 1998, p. 950*)

**Prosocial behaviour**
Acts that are positively valued by society.

**Relational theory**
An analysis based on structures of meaningful social relationships that recur across cultures.

**Schema**
Cognitive structure that represents knowledge about a concept or type of stimulus, including its attributes and the relations among those attributes.

---

**Research and applications 16.4**
Sociocultural values and the tendency to
seek help

**'For my comrade's sake, will you help me?'**

The participants were high-school students in Israel. Half
grew up and lived with their families on various *kibbutzim*
and attended a high school catering to the needs of
*kibbutz* dwellers. The city dwellers grew up and lived with
their families in two middle-sized towns in northern
Israel, and attended their local high school. The study
was conducted in the students' classrooms.

The students tried to solve twenty anagrams and the
task's importance was made salient by suggesting that
performance could predict success in other domains in
life. They were told that: (1) some anagrams had never

been solved; (2) if they could not solve one, they could
seek help from the investigator. The percentage of occasions on which help was requested was recorded (e.g. if
help was sought on five out of ten unsolved anagrams,
the help-seeking score was 50 per cent).

In a 2 × 2 design, half the *kibbutz* group and half of the city
group had first received a *group-oriented task* instruction –
their scores would be compared with the average of other
classes. The other half had an *individual-oriented task* instruction – their scores would be compared with other individuals.

Would help be sought according to the nature of the
group and of the instruction? Perhaps *kibbutz* dwellers
would seek help more often if they were group-oriented,
while city dwellers would look for help if they were individual-oriented.

See the results in Figure 16.4.

*Source:* based on Nadler (1986)

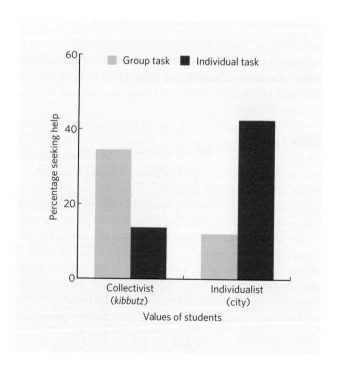

**Figure 16.4** Collectivist
values, individualist values
and when to seek help

*Source:* based on data from Nadler
(1986)

Fiske's four models were as follows:

1  *Communal sharing* (CS) – the group transcends the individual. People in a CS relationship experience solidarity and a corporate identity. Examples are lovers, teams and
   families.

2  *Authority ranking* (AR) – the AR relationship is defined by precedence and a linear hierarchy. Examples are how a subordinate individual relates to an army officer and, in
   Chinese society, the tradition of filial piety.

## Real world 16.5
### Four relationship models for a mother and son

In practice, people may use any of Fiske's four relationship models in accordance with the multiple roles that people play at different moments in time. Sally is John's mother. In the course of a normal day, they adopt different ways of relating to each other without being very conscious of the changes that take place. At home in the morning, Sally prepares breakfast with John. She makes the drinks, while he checks the food and places utensils on the table – neither one minding who puts in more effort (CS). Later that morning Sally goes to work, where she is a company manager. John, a sales representative in the same company, is told by his mother that his sales figures are improving (AR). After dinner that night they play a game of chess, which the better player will win (EM). Before going to bed, John asks Sally for a loan to buy a car. She thinks carefully and they discuss his proposition. Finally she agrees, provided that he paints the house and makes a good job of it (MP). Together, they feel that their overall relationship is complex and that life is rich.

3 *Equality matching* (EM) – based on attending to balance in a social exchange. Examples of an EM relationship are reciprocating in a tit-for-tat manner, taking biblical vengeance, being egalitarian and car-pooling.

4 *Market pricing* (MP) – based on a sense of proportional outcomes. Examples of MP are prices, rents, salaries and taxes. In an MP interpersonal relationship, the partners calculate their relative costs and benefits (see the discussion of the cost–reward ratio in Chapter 14).

Before linking relational theory to cultural variation, first consider how they can operate within the same culture. An example of how the four relationship models work is given in Box 16.5.

**Authority ranking**
This 105-year-old lady in northern India has just cast her vote. Respect for elders is a cornerstone of collective societies

Since the models operate as schemas, they are available for use in ways that make sense within a culture, and they are not necessarily used identically across cultures. They provide a 'grammar' for defining work, distributing resources and giving meaning to time and land. Fiske and colleagues (Fiske, Kitayama, Markus & Nisbett, 1998) provide this illustration with respect to land: it can be an investment (MP), a kingdom (AR), a mark of equal status if all citizens can own it or not own it (EM), and a motherland, or even a commons, defining a collective identity (CS). Relational theory is an innovative and promising approach to understanding fundamental ways in which cultures can be similar or different.

Fiske and his colleagues (e.g. Fiske & Haslam, 1996) also made a strong claim. The four relationship models are not commensurate: there is no higher-order schema that mediates between them. Although the models are 'in the culture', they are also 'in the head' – if a person is in CS mode, it is not easy to switch into AR mode. It can affect the ease or the difficulty of retrieving people from memory (see person memory in Chapter 2). If you are thinking in AR terms about your present boss, for example, you are more likely to recall your last boss and other bosses before that.

Finally, there is a link between the relational models and cultural variations in independence–interdependence. MP is more common in individualistic cultures and CS in collectivist cultures. Furthermore, AR occurs more frequently in East Asian cultures, as it once did in feudal Europe. Likewise, the incidence of EM is higher in interdependent cultures, in some Asian countries and in Melanesia. This points to some convergence between the two major systems we have discussed. There are common features in characterising cultures, whether we use *values* or use *relational models*.

# Understanding culture through norms and identity

We can approach culture from a number of perspectives. We have noted that the physical environment can impact many aspects of how people live (see Box 16.2) and how a community's families are organised. For a whole culture to flourish, it needs a network of supportive systems – legal, political and economic (Cohen, 2001). Sometimes, religious dogma and a nation's history combine to justify the use of force through 'codes of legitimation' and 'ideologies of antagonism' towards some outgroups (Bond, 2004).

We can also approach culture from a social psychological perspective: culture does not just influence social psychological processes but is also a product of social psychological processes. In this short section, we elaborate this point by reflecting back on the way in which some of the basic social psychological processes discussed in earlier chapters may generate and influence culture.

Our culture provides us with an identity and a set of attributes that define that identity. Culture influences what we think, how we feel, how we dress, what and how we eat, how we speak, what values and moral principles we hold, how we interact with one another and how we understand the world around us. Culture pervades almost all aspects of our existence. Perhaps because of this, culture is often the taken-for-granted background to everyday life (e.g. Garfinkel, 1967), and we may only really become aware of features of our culture when we encounter other cultures or when our own culture is threatened. Culture, like other entrenched normative systems, may only be revealed to us by intercultural exposure, or by intercultural conflict.

A key feature of cultural attributes is that they are tightly integrated in a logical way that makes our lives and the world we live in meaningful. In this sense, culture has some of the attributes of social attributions (see Hewstone, 1989), social representations (see

Lorenzi-Cioldi & Clémence, 2001) and ideologies (Thompson, 1990) – see Chapters 3 and 5. At the cognitive level, our own culture might be represented schematically as a well-organised and compact prototype (see Chapter 2).

Because culture makes the world meaningful, we might expect cultural revivals to occur under conditions of societal uncertainty (e.g. Hogg, 2007b, in press): for example, prolonged economic crises. Because culture defines identity, we would also expect cultural revivals when the prestige or distinctiveness of our culture is threatened by other cultural groups – in these respects, culture would be expected to obey the principles of intergroup behaviour described by social identity theory (see Chapter 11). Indeed, research on language revivals, where language is central to culture, shows precisely this (e.g. Giles & Johnson, 1987; see Chapter 15).

Another key feature of cultural attributes is that they are shared among members of the culture, and they differentiate between cultures – they are normative and thus obey the general principles of norms (Chapter 8). For example, cultural leaders may be allowed greater latitude for cultural divergence than are other members of the culture (e.g. Sherif & Sherif, 1964; see Chapter 8). Cultural forms may emerge and be sustained or modified through human interaction, as described by Moscovici's (e.g. 1988) theory of social representations (see Chapter 3), and through talk, as described by discourse perspectives on social psychology (e.g. Potter, 1996; see also Chapter 15).

The dynamics of large-scale cultures may be very similar to the dynamics of small-scale cultures in organisations and small groups. In such cases the processes of group socialisation (e.g. Levine & Moreland, 1994; see Chapter 8) and group memory (e.g. Moreland, Argote, & Krishnan, 1996; see Chapter 9) may operate at the societal level.

The main message of this, necessarily brief, section is that while culture can be studied as an independent topic in its own right, there is a real sense in which it is actually an integral part of social psychology as a whole.

# Contact between cultures

Cultural groups do not live in isolation – they come into contact with one another, increasingly so with each passing decade. You do not need to be a tourist to taste another culture. New York is probably the best example of a cultural mélange, although the same can be seen in other Western gateway cities such as London, Paris, Los Angeles and Amsterdam. Intercultural contact should be an enriching experience, a force for good and for beneficial change, but it can also be a pressure cooker, in which perceived threats and ancient animosities boil over into conflict (see Prentice & Miller, 1999).

Most intercultural contact does not last long enough to cause a permanent change in behaviour or in people's attitudes towards another cultural group. Recall the complexities of the **contact hypothesis** – it can be very difficult to create conditions of contact that will produce enduring improvement in intergroup attitudes and feelings (see Chapter 11 for details). Even a brief face-to-face encounter between people from different cultures is actually more likely to produce or strengthen stereotypes and prejudices (see Chapters 2, 10 and 11). A variety of factors are likely to lead to negative outcomes: for example, language differences, pre-existing prejudice, ethnocentrism, intergroup anxiety or a history of intergroup conflict.

**Contact hypothesis**
The view that bringing members of opposing social groups together will improve intergroup relations and reduce prejudice and discrimination.

## Communication, language and speech style

We have noted elsewhere that multilingual, and therefore multicultural, societies usually have a high-status dominant group (see Chapter 15). Consequently, a language barrier can be a major obstacle to a comfortable intercultural encounter. Quite clearly, if you are in

**The global village**
Multinationals and cheap air travel are two factors that may contribute to the dilution of cultural difference

France and cannot speak French very well, you have a major hurdle in communicating with the locals. Phrase books and sign language can take you only so far.

Even accent and speech style present a problem – native speakers may be less attentive to people with a foreign accent. For example, in an Australian study Gallois and Callan (1986) found that native speakers of Australian English tended to be less engaged in listening to speakers with an Italian accent – an effect probably compounded by negative stereotypes of immigrants from southern Europe. In another Australian study, Gallois, Barker, Jones and Callan (1992) found that the communication style of overseas Chinese students might reinforce unfavourable stereotypes of that group (see Box 16.6).

The magnitude of perceived cultural difference can influence *intercultural contact*. The extent to which a culture is perceived to be dissimilar to our own can affect intercultural interaction. An early social distance study by Vaughan (1962) showed that the more dissimilar a culture is perceived to be, the more people wish to distance themselves from members of that cultural group. Thus, the likelihood of developing intercultural contacts is reduced.

The setting of any intergroup contact is also important. In discussing the contact hypothesis (see Chapter 11), we noted several elements of group relations that can make contact a more positive experience, such as cooperation, shared goals and equal status. These are likely to apply to intercultural contact within the same society. However, there are other features of intercultural contact that can act as a barrier. For example, Kochman (1987) has shown that African Americans use an intonation and expressive intensity in their speech that marks them out from the White majority. This can be an intentional sociolinguistic marker, drawing an intergroup line and acting to protect their ethnic identity (see Chapters 11 and 15).

International contact can add further barriers – we are now dealing with different nations, territories, political institutions and the norms that relate to these (Smith, Bond & Kağitçibaşi, 2006). International contact is also often shorter-term, less frequent, and more variable in intimacy, relative status and power. In the remainder of this section, we deal with intercultural communication that is cross-national.

A quite substantial East–West difference is that Asians are more likely to use 'code' – messages with implicit meanings for each communicator (Burgoon, Buller & Woodall,

## Research highlight 16.6
### Ethnic differences in communication style can affect a student's perceived academic ability

Chinese students have become the largest single ethnic group of overseas students enrolled in Australian universities. Owing to cultural differences in communication styles, these students have sometimes found it difficult to adjust to local communication norms, which encourage students to speak out in class and in interaction with academic staff.

Gallois and her associates (Gallois, Barker, Jones & Callan, 1992) studied this phenomenon. They prepared twenty-four carefully scripted videotapes of communications between a student and a lecturer, in which the student adopted a submissive, assertive or aggressive communication style to ask for help with an assignment or to complain about a grade. The student was either a male or a female Anglo-Australian or an ethnic Chinese (the lecturer was always Anglo-Australian and the same sex as the student).

Gallois and colleagues had Australian students, ethnic Chinese students (i.e. from Hong Kong, Singapore or Malaysia) and lecturers view the videotaped vignettes and rate the students on a number of behavioural dimensions and on the effectiveness of their communication style. All participants agreed that the aggressive style was inappropriate, ineffective and atypical of students of any ethnic background. Consistent with stereotypes, submissiveness was considered more typical of Chinese than Australian students, and assertiveness more typical of Australian than Chinese students. Chinese students felt that the submissive style was more effective than the assertive style. However, lecturers and Australian students interpreted the submissive style as being less effective and indicating less need for assistance.

Clearly, this assumption that a submissive style indicates lack of need and interest could nourish a view that Chinese students are less talented than their Australian counterparts.

1989). This is recognised in Chinese society, for example, as *hanxu* (Gao, Ting-Toomey & Gudykunst, 1996). Consequently, an East–West interaction can sometimes generate misunderstandings (Gallois & Callan, 1997). In a conversation between an American and a Japanese, for example, the American might seem blunt and the Asian evasive.

We have noted earlier in this book that there are cultural differences in non-verbal behaviour (see Chapter 15). Culturally relevant facial **display rules** are used to communicate our emotions, and **kinesics** point to our cultural background, as do variations in touching and in interpersonal distance. There are some differences between Eastern and Western cultures in the rate of mutual gaze in certain social contexts. For example, Bond and Komai (1976) found that young Japanese males made less eye contact than Western samples with an interviewer during the course of an interview.

As another example, suppose that someone gestured to you with a forefinger and thumb forming a circle: you would probably think they meant 'it's okay' or 'great'. However, there are cultures where this is the symbol for 'money', 'worthless' or even 'screw you!' (Burgoon, Buller & Woodall, 1989; Morris, Collett, Marsh & O'Shaughnessy, 1979).

Sometimes an action that is normal in one culture violates a moral standard in another. Western women, for example, should avoid wearing revealing clothing in some Islamic countries. Unfortunately, breaches of a cultural norm are often committed in ignorance, such as sitting or standing on a table in an area where food is served, which offends Maori custom in New Zealand. Intergroup and therefore intercultural contact can be severely curtailed if it leads to anxiety and uncertainty (Hogg, 2007b; Stephan & Stephan, 2000; see Chapter 11).

**Display rules**
Cultural and situational rules that dictate how appropriate it is to express emotions in a given context.

**Kinesics**
Linguistics of body communication.

## Language and understanding

Language itself poses a problem. The direct translation of words from one language to another does not necessarily preserve meaning. Glenn (1976) provided examples of differences in word meanings when changing from English to French or Russian. The use of the personal pronoun 'I', for example, usually has a subjective connotation in English but extends to objective connotations in French or Russian. In English, 'as long as I understand that' could be rendered in French as '*s'il s'agit de*', an idiom meaning 'if what is being dealt with is'. In English there is a single word for 'here', whereas in Spanish there is a distinction between right here (*aquí*) and hereabouts (*acá*).

In addition to seeking words or idioms to communicate meaning accurately across cultures, a language can pose a larger problem when words, or word usage, are entwined with culturally specific concepts. For example, Kashima and Kashima (1998) show that, for certain statements, the first personal pronoun 'I' is dropped in Japanese but not in English. What is intriguing is that this may reflect the self-conceptual difference between the independent self and the interdependent self dealt with above (see Table 16.2 and Figure 16.2). This implies that individualistic English speakers use 'I' to represent the self as separate from all others, whereas collectivist Japanese speakers drop 'I' to incorporate significant others into the self. Another example, again from Japanese: the Japanese have a word, *amae*, to identify an emotional state with communicative implications that are fundamental in traditional Japanese culture. According to Doi:

> *Amaeru* [*amae* is its noun form] can be translated as 'to depend and presume upon another's love' . . . [It] has a distinct feeling of sweetness, and is generally used to express a child's attitude toward an adult, especially his parents. I can think of no English word equivalent to *amaeru* except for 'spoil', which, however, is a transitive verb and definitely has a bad connotation . . . I think most Japanese adults have a dear memory of the taste of sweet dependency as a child and, consciously or unconsciously, carry a lifelong nostalgia for it. (*Doi, 1976, p. 188*)

In this quotation, the context is that of adult and child, but *amae* also applies to students and professors, and to work teams and their supervisors. By custom, Japanese people have a powerful need to experience *amae*, and knowledge of this state provides an emotional basis for interpersonal communication. A person who experiences *amae* during conversation will provide non-verbal cues (e.g. silences, pensive looks and even unnatural smiles) to 'soften the atmosphere' for the other person. It follows that these cues are not likely to be interpreted appropriately by someone unfamiliar with both the language and the culture. (Reflect on the irony in the third focus question).

At a political level, intercultural communication can sometimes involve subtle word games in negotiating outcomes that minimise public humiliation (see Box 16.7).

### Real world 16.7
#### When is being 'sorry' an apology?

An international event in April 2001 highlighted how language differences can reflect conceptual differences. An American surveillance aircraft was damaged in an accident with a Chinese plane off the coast of China and was forced to land in Chinese territory. The Chinese pilot was lost at sea. The Chinese government insisted that the American government make a formal apology before they would return the American crew. Such an apology (*dao qian*) is an admission of responsibility and an expression of remorse.

At first, the American expression was one of 'regret' (*yihan*), which carries no acknowledgement of guilt. The American president next expressed 'sincere regret' (*shen biao qian yi*) for the missing pilot and said he was 'very sorry' (*zhen cheng yihan*) for the unauthorised landing. Both expressions are ambiguous with respect to implying blame.

The American crew was finally released and both governments may have felt that face was saved.

## Acculturation and culture change

When people migrate, they find it almost impossible to avoid close contact with members of the host culture and with other immigrant cultural groups. Extended contact inevitably produces changes in behaviour and thinking among new migrants. The process of internalising the rules of behaviour characteristic of another culture is **acculturation**, and when it applies to a whole group we have large-scale culture change. However, immigrant groups have some choice about the form that these changes take – the starkest choice is between assimilation and separatism. We should note that culture change is not restricted to immigrants; it also applies to indigenous peoples. Culture change can lead to acculturative stress. For example, look again at how ethnic minorities can suffer depression when their culture is eroded by an ethnic majority (see Box 4.4 in Chapter 4).

An acculturating individual can have *dual identities*: for example, a feeling that one is both a Mexican American and an Anglo-American (Buriel, 1987), a Greek and an Australian (Rosenthal, 1987). A similar concept, *bicultural identity,* is used in research into ethnic socialisation in children (see Phinney & Rotheram, 1987). Heine (2010) has noted that, when the self is derived from multiple cultural backgrounds, individuals can have multicultural minds, i.e. access more than one self-concept. They can, on occasion, draw on a blend of these or else frame switch, i.e. alternate between different self-concepts: a given self-concept can be accessed depending on the context or on which one is primed (see also Hong, Morris, Chiu, & Benet-Martínez, 2000).

Immigrants who arrive in a new country face a dilemma: will they maintain their social identity as defined by their home culture identity, or will it be defined by the host culture? How can this be resolved? The cross-cultural psychologist Berry (e.g. Berry, Trimble & Olmedo, 1986) identified four different paths to acculturation. In weighing up home culture and dominant culture, immigrants can choose between:

1 *integration* – maintaining home culture but also relating to dominant culture;
2 *assimilation* – giving up home culture and embracing dominant culture;

**Acculturation**
The process whereby individuals learn about the rules of behaviour characteristic of another culture.

**Acculturative stress**
These newly-naturalised German citizens may face further hurdles. As well as aiming for language fluency they must also address subtleties in the social mores of their new country

**Figure 16.5** Four paths to acculturation

- Berry *et al.* pinpointed four options that immigrants can follow in reconciling their ancestral culture with the new host culture.
- The positive valence (**+**) indicates that, to an extent, an immigrant adopts the host culture or retains the ancestral culture – or both.
- The negative valence (**-**) indicates that, to an extent, an immigrant fails to adopt the host culture or to retain elements of the ancestral culture – or both.
- The optimal outcome for an immigrant is integration.

*Source:* based on Berry, Trimble & Olmedo, 1986

|  | Host culture + | - |
|---|---|---|
| Ancestral culture + | Integration | Separation |
| - | Assimilation | Marginalisation |

**3** *separation* – maintaining home culture and being isolated from dominant culture;

**4** *marginalisation* – giving up home culture and failing to relate properly to dominant culture.

These choices are shown in Figure 16.5. (Reflect on the dilemma faced by Keiko and her husband in the fourth focus question at the beginning of this chapter. Then consider how you might respond to Jessica's poser in the fifth focus question.)

Leaving aside issues of learning a second language (see Chapter 15), the most popular path for immigrants is integration, and is the one associated with the least stress in acculturating (Berry, Kim, Minde & Mok, 1987). A key factor in stress reduction is the availability

**The path of separation?**
This French girl solved an immigrant's dilemma by refusing to remove her headdress – she was not willing to assimilate entirely to a new culture. Or has she chosen to integrate?

of a **social support network**, just as it is in dealing with the breakdown of a close relationship (see Chapter 14). Choosing to integrate makes sense based on theories of intergroup relations that maximise harmony and stability (e.g. Hornsey & Hogg, 2000a; Vescio, Hewstone, Crisp & Rubin, 1999; see also Chapter 11). Groups tend to get on better together when their cherished identities and practices are respected and allowed to flourish within a superordinate culture – one that also allows groups to feel that their relations to one another are not competitive but are more akin to different teams that 'pull together'.

However, choosing to integrate is a process that takes considerable time, and in many instances, competes with a host culture's frequent expectation of assimilation. For the second generation immigrants (the children of the settlers), conflict with their elders is minimised if all actually integrate. If integration is a 'good' solution for the individual immigrant – is it also good for whole groups of immigrants, and indeed for the host culture? Before we return to the challenge of posed by multiculturalism we ask the question: how has social psychology fared in pursuing cross-cultural research?

> **Social support network**
> People who know and care about us and who can provide backup during a time of stress.

# Testing social psychology cross-culturally

The publication of Bond's (1988) *The cross-cultural challenge to social psychology* was a call to arms. When would social psychologists pay heed to the limitations of untested universal assumptions in developing their theories? The challenges are multiple, occurring across cultures as nations, and within a culture when addressing majority–minority group relations. We dealt with the latter topic in the context of intergroup theory (see Chapter 11). Later, we revisit it in the setting of the consequences of policy making for ethnic minorities.

## The cross-cultural challenge

Although the cross-cultural challenge is typically targeted at social psychology, it actually cuts both ways. Cross-cultural and cultural psychologists can and should draw on principles from social psychology and use them beyond the culture in which they were developed (Moghaddam, 1998; Smith, Bond & Kağitçibaşi, 2006). Take the instance of planning to improve intercultural relations. Social psychologists can argue that intercultural relations are a special case of intergroup relations. As such, an understanding of what drives intercultural conflict, discrimination and stereotyping is informed by the social psychology of intergroup behaviour (Chapter 11), of the self-concept (Chapter 4), of prejudice and discrimination (Chapter 10), and of stereotyping (Chapters 2 and 10). What are the challenges, in the reverse direction, to social psychologists?

## Indigenous social psychologies

Should we promulgate an **indigenous psychology**? Or put differently, should each culture have its own social psychology that reflects its unique perspective in its topics and constructs? Middle Eastern and South-East Asian countries in particular can have legitimate concerns about a pervasive and encroaching Western-centric world-view:

> the ideology and techniques of modern psychology [in general] are being overlaid upon already highly developed systems of psychological belief, derived from Hinduism, Islam, Buddhism, Taoism, Confucianism, Shintoism and Marxism-Leninism, or varying combinations of these. (*Turtle, 1994, pp. 9–10*)

Until recently, the most successful example of an indigenous *social* psychology is the development of a relatively distinct European social psychology (see Chapter 1). As a

> **Indigenous psychology**
> A psychology created by and for a specific cultural group – based on the claim that culture can be understood only from within its own perspective.

consequence of fascism and the Second World War, social psychology in Europe in the 1940s, 1950s and early 1960s was largely an outpost of American social psychology. In this context, Moscovici (1972) worried that American social psychology was culturally alien for Europeans because it did not address European priorities and interests, and it adopted an interpretative framework or **metatheory** that clashed with European metatheory. He advocated a European social psychology grounded specifically in the cultural context of Europe.

**Metatheory**
Set of interrelated concepts and principles concerning which theories or types of theory are appropriate.

Although Europe (particularly north-west Europe) and the United States have different traditions, histories and world-views, as cultures they are remarkably similar – both are industrialised, individualistic Western democratic cultures. They can largely be grouped together and contrasted with non-industrialised and collectivist cultures around the world. Thus, even if we make a distinction between European and American social psychology, the difference is not really that great.

Malpass (1988), an American, reminds us that scientific psychology is a Euro-American enterprise (see also the historical origins of social psychology in Chapter 1). As such, people from Western cultures are the objects of study. Thus we should not be surprised at a call for indigenous psychologies from the Asian region – for Filipinos by Enriquez (1993), for Chinese by Yang (Yang & Bond, 1990) and for Indians by Sinha (1997). The formation of both the Asian Association of Social Psychology and the *Asian Journal of Social Psychology* in 1995 has, in the ensuing years, nurtured social psychology in East Asia, stimulating research using indigenous themes and raising issues about the nature of indigenous psychologies (Kashima, 2005; Kim, 2000; Ng & Liu, 2000; Yang, 2000).

A starting point for an indigenous social psychology is to develop theories and apply them within the same culture. This issue is particularly relevant for developing nations that have serious social problems to solve – the well-meaning application of theories that are developed, say, in Europe or the United States may simply not work. For example, Moghaddam (1998) describes how the application of the Western idea that modernisation can be achieved by motivating people to act like entrepreneurs has backfired – it brought about a collapse of traditional communities (e.g. among Pygmies in central Africa) and ecologies (e.g. in parts of Brazil). Indeed, one of the fundamental problems of globalisation is precisely the assumption that people in developing nations have the same social psychological resources as people in the West (Stiglitz, 2002).

Another problem is the tendency for social psychological theory, and social action, to focus on static social relations rather than on dynamic processes that may change those relations (Moghaddam, 1990). There have been some notable exceptions, such as social identity theory (e.g. Tajfel & Turner, 1979; Hogg & Abrams, 1988; see Chapter 11) and minority influence theory (e.g. Moscovici, 1976; see Chapter 7). These theoretical orientations, from Europe, were part of a deliberate strategy to address a European scientific and social agenda and to differentiate European from American social psychology (see Chapter 1; also Israel & Tajfel, 1972).

Whether independent indigenous psychologies are required to solve problems in each and every culture is a moot point. Neglected in the current debate is an older question of linking theory to practice, culture notwithstanding. The question arises as to whether an **action research** approach (see Chapter 6), which is oriented towards practical outcomes, is more useful. In a similar vein, Moghaddam (1990, 1998) has advocated a **generative psychology** – he cites examples of the success of such an approach in the 1990s in Latin America and Turkey.

**Action research**
The simultaneous activities of undertaking social science research, involving participants in the process, and addressing a social problem.

**Generative psychology**
Psychology intended to generate positive social change through direct intervention.

## The search for universals

We have already noted that tabulating human attributes and classes of behaviour with universal application was a characteristic of early cultural anthropology. This is still the case today with respect to most social psychologists, who are generally committed to the search that concerned Boas, a quest for universal laws of social behaviour. A call for multiple indigenous psychologies that apply to a host of specific cultural groups raises issues that touch on the relationship between science and ideology, issues of epistemology and the constitution of valid knowledge, and the role of abstract scientific inquiry in society. For every new indigenous psychology, there may be a different set of laws and principles. Do we run the risk of scientific Balkanisation? In addition, associated with the drive for locally relevant theory is usually the poststructuralist assumption of cultural relativism – the view that all cultural belief systems and practices are equally acceptable, and that there are no universal psychological truths. There are no easy answers to or resolutions of these issues.

A realistic target is to encourage social psychologists to broaden their discipline to articulate fundamental social cognition and perception, such as social categorisation (see Chapter 2), with emergent social properties, such as group norms and social representations (see Chapters 5, 7 and 9). It is in this way that we can gain an insight into human behaviour in its general form and in its context-specific cultural and historical expression. The *universal* and the *cultural* are the two interdependent moments of the dialectic of a mature social psychology. (See Heine and Buchtel's (2009) recent review for a treatment of universality versus variability of personality traits across cultures.)

The challenge of cross-cultural research for social psychologists is not that it can be difficult to do cross-cultural research. Although cross-cultural research presents its challenges, so too does social cognition research (Devine, Hamilton & Ostrom, 1994; see also Chapter 2) and research into small interactive task-oriented groups (e.g. Moreland, Hogg & Hains, 1994; see also Chapters 2 and 8).

The real challenge is to try to overcome our own cultural perspective – to try to see things from different cultural perspectives as well as to be aware of the cultural limitations of our own thinking (see Smith, Bond & Kağitçibaşi, 2006). Social psychologists, like all people, are blinkered by their own cultural parameters, adopting perspectives and addressing questions that are culturally relevant. They incline us towards culture-specific psychologies rather than a universal science. A collateral problem of this is that the psychology of the dominant scientific culture can oust all other psychologies and hinder the development of true universalism.

A social psychology that is relevant to all peoples would have a laudable sociopolitical role to play on the global stage, perhaps guiding humanitarians dedicated to solving widespread and pressing problems in the developing world. As well, social psychology could help to explain how basic social psychological processes interact with socioculturally specific processes. Activities like these may help us to understand destructive blind obedience, intergroup conflict, family violence, social dilemmas and social change. They may also tell us why noble attitudes rarely translate into noble acts.

## The multicultural challenge

There is also a wider challenge to the many societies of the world – can multiple cultures coexist? In a society of diverse cultures, should all cultural forms be permitted to flourish (even if they engage in such practices as infanticide or genital mutilation), or should cultures change with changing global values? For example, as an extreme case, consider the campaign in Afghanistan against Al-Qaeda and the Taliban. Is this a struggle against universal evil, or is it the forceful imposition of one cultural world-view over another? This is, of course, a highly politicised question, which is beyond the scope of a scientific text. It confronts issues of cultural relativism and what has been called the *postmodern paradox* (Dunn, 1998) – the tendency for people to embrace fundamentalist belief systems in order to find a distinct and prescriptive identity that resolves the sense of anomie and moral vacuum in modern industrialised society.

**Cultural diversity**
These workmates have different ethnic origins and clearly enjoy each others' company

## Managing cultural diversity

A lesser problem is the 'simple' question of how to manage cultural diversity in pluralistic societies. This is the cultural application of resolving intergroup conflict that we discussed in Chapter 11 and touched on earlier in this chapter. At the intergroup level, you will recall, there is increasing support for the idea that groups live more harmoniously together if their cherished identities and practices are respected. Groups will flourish within a superordinate culture that also allows them to feel that their relations to one another are cooperative rather than competitive.

At the cultural level, the debate is largely over the relative merits of assimilationism and multiculturalism (see Prentice & Miller, 1999). For example, Moghaddam (1998, 2008) has contrasted assimilationist policies with those that manage cultural diversity by promoting multiculturalism (see Figure 16.6). Assimilation can be of two kinds, total and 'melting-pot'. The former implies the obliteration of a culture, whereas the latter is less extreme and allows a new form of the dominant culture to emerge.

Multiculturalism is a more positive and embracing view of both dominant and minority cultures. In its laissez-faire form, cultural diversity can continue without help from the host culture. Ethnic enclaves, such as the many Chinatowns that can be found in various cities of the world, Little India in Singapore and expatriate European communities in some Asian cities are examples of laissez-faire multiculturalism. In its active form, a nation's policy sustains cultural diversity. For example, there is government support in Canada and Australia for a variety of activities designed to sustain, to some degree, the cultural integrity of various immigrant groups. At the psychological level, active multiculturalism

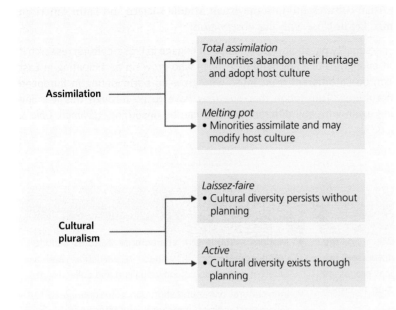

**Figure 16.6** Types of assimilation and multiculturalism

- Cultural diversity is a challenge to society.
- Immigrant or indigenous minorities may assimilate fully or may leave some mark on the host culture in the process.
- Alternatively, cultural pluralism may flourish, either by accident or design.

*Source*: based on Allport (1954b) and Moghaddam (1998)

sustains cultural units that can be either individualistic or collectivist. Belanger and Pinard (1991) have suggested that there is a worldwide trend to sustain collectivist cultures.

There is, of course, another face to cultural diversity. In western European cities such as London, Paris and Rome, high levels of immigration have coincided with a growth of intergroup confrontation and in some cases frightening acts of individual or collective terror. The finger of blame has been pointed at many groups, for example North Africans, Muslims, and Eastern Europeans. However, the root problem is unlikely to be solely cultural difference – unemployment, economic disadvantage, inadequate education and housing and so forth all play a very significant role.

Multiculturalism is not only evident but is increasing in many parts of the world. Take two instances: more business is being transacted between China and the West, and the expansion of the European community has large numbers of people relocating from Eastern to Western Europe. In addition, Internet access has made business, governmental, academic and personal communication very easy. In short, globalisation has accelerated. More than ever, these changes require psychologists to have more accurate definitions of culture, and of how it can influence how people think, feel and behave (Hong & Mallorie, 2004). Furthermore, cultures are not set in stone. Cultures in contact, especially living side by side, are probably cultures that will change. A vibrant social psychology is one that can track change both within and between cultures and contribute to cooperative development.

## Where to from here?

In making cross-cultural comparisons, we have referred most frequently to those between Western and East Asian cultures. One might say that these cultures provide the most extreme psychological contrasts, but at a more prosaic level the reason is simple: there has been an upsurge of research by social psychologists in China, Japan and Korea or who work in the West but are ethnically East Asian. This does, however, raise the question of where

African and South Asian cultures and to some extent Middle Eastern and Latin American cultures fit in the mix. Let us close with this observation:

> For many social-personality psychologists who do not engage in cross-cultural research it has been difficult enough to be convinced that those who grow up participating in East Asian cultures can be so different from those who grow up participating in European North American cultures. The notion that one may have to go through this learning process again and again with still different cultures can be unsettling. (*Lehman, Chiu & Schaller, 2004, p. 689*)

## Summary

- The roots of social psychology are Western, and the discipline had until recently underemphasised the impact of culture. If social psychological processes are really universal, they should stand up to cross-cultural scrutiny.

- People, including psychologists, often use their own cultural standards to interpret the behaviour of people from different cultural backgrounds.

- Anthropologists rather than psychologists conducted almost all research dealing with culture and behaviour in the early twentieth century.

- Cultures vary considerably in social behaviour, including cognitive processes and attributional style. Norms that govern conformity and aggression also differ across cultures.

- People in the East have a different way of viewing themselves and relating to each other from people in the West. Eastern people are collectivist and nurture interdependence, whereas Western people are individualistic and nurture independence.

- Modern systems that characterise cultures include crucial differences in values, in particular, and a different distribution of individualism and collectivism.

- Intercultural communication can sometimes lead to misunderstandings in meaning and intentions.

- Acculturating groups such as migrants face different acculturative choices, varying from retaining their ethnic identity to merging with the dominant culture. Acculturative stress is a common problem.

- Some social psychological principles may be applied across cultures and some may not. There is a tension between fostering principles that may apply only to an indigenous people and the pursuit of principles that are universal.

- The world's societies are increasingly multicultural. To both foster cultural diversity and maintain intergroup harmony is a challenge.

# Literature, film and TV

### *Bend It Like Beckham* and *East is East*

A 2002 film directed by Gurinder Chadha, starring Parminder Nagra as the Indian girl 'Jess', *Bend it Like Beckham* is a light-hearted film about the clashing of different cultures in the UK, and about how culture creates expectations and ways of doing things that seem normal – Jess is at the intersection of different role expectations based on culture and gender. In a very similar vein, *East is East* is a 1999 culture-clash comedy set in Salford in the 1970s – George Kahn is a Pakistani immigrant who runs a fish-and-chip shop and tries to bring up his sons in traditional Pakistani ways. He gradually comes to realise that his sons see themselves as British and will never conform to his strict rules on marriage, food, dress and religion

### *Rachel Getting Married*

2008 film by Jonathan Demme, starring Anne Hathaway. This superbly powerful commentary on, among other things, culture as commodity has as its setting a wealthy wedding party at a country mansion in the eastern US. The wedding hosts and guests are liberal, educated and politically correct – but they are cringingly pretentious and inauthentic as they cycle through different cultural practices and symbols as mere decoration and entertainment. The only authentic and genuinely human character at the wedding is the younger daughter Kym, played by Hathaway, who is just out of rehab.

### *Changing Places*

1975 comic novel by David Lodge. Two academics, the American Morris Zap and the Englishman Phillip Swallow, do a sabbatical swap between Berkeley in California and Birmingham in the UK. This is a book about culture differences – it shows how even relatively small cultural differences, between the UK and the USA, can create hilarious problems. This is a good story and a very funny book, which highlights the strangeness of UK and US cultural practices from the perspective of the other country.

### *The Kitchen God's Wife*

1991 Amy Tan novel about second-generation Chinese in San Francisco who are pulled between traditional Chinese culture and liberal US culture. It focuses on women, who feel the contrast more strongly because the pressure and expectations to retain relatively traditional and repressive Chinese culture are very strong.

### *Coming to America*

1988 John Landis comedy, with Eddy Murphy as a wealthy African prince coming to America to find a wife. This is a very light-hearted treatment of culture clash and stereotypical expectations, violation of norms, and so forth.

### *Persepolis*

2007 French film that explores cultural anomie. The young Marji Statrapi celebrates the removal of the Shah in the 1979 Iranian revolution, but quickly finds herself an outsider as Iran lurches towards Islamic fundamentalism and a new form of tyranny. For her own protection her family sends her to Vienna to study and build a new life, but Marji finds it an abrasive and difficult culture that is hard to fit into. When she returns to Iran things have changed so much that she feels like a stranger in her own culture – she must decide where she belongs.

### *Crash*

An incredibily powerful and sophisticated 2004 Paul Haggis film about cultural diversity, starring Don Cheadle, Sandra Bullock, Matt Dillon and Jennifer Esposito. Set in the cultural melting pot of Los Angeles, a sprawling city of 17 million, it shows how different cultures are often suspicious of one another and how all cultures have stereotypes of one another that can turn ugly when people are anxious and stressed. A sobering film that moves away from the old-fashioned 'white male redneck' caricature of prejudice and raises challenging questions about how and if cultures really can live in harmony in the global village.

## Guided questions

1  Can culture constrain the way we think?
2  What do you understand by the *independent* and *interdependent self,* and how is this related to culture?
3  How are *individualism* and *collectivism* connected to the world's cultures?

4  What is *acculturative stress* and what are the main contributory factors? See Melody discuss her fears about her future husband's job prospects when he changes his country of residence in Chapter 16 of MyPsychLab at **www.mypsychlab.co.uk** (watch I*mmigration stress*; see **http://www.youtube.com/watch?v=JI4Neq-RB1Y**).
5  Should the development of indigenous social psychologies be pursued vigorously?

## Learn more

Adamopoulos, J., & Kashima, Y. (eds) (1999). *Social psychology and cultural context.* London: Sage. Social and cross-cultural psychologists from various countries discuss the cultural context of social psychology and how social psychological phenomena are influenced by culture.

Berry, J. W., Segall, M. H., & Kağitçibaşi, C. (eds) (1997). *Handbook of cross-cultural psychology* (2nd ed.). Boston, MA: Allyn and Bacon. A three-volume review of all major areas of cross-cultural psychology.

Brislin, R. (1993). *Understanding culture's influence on behavior.* Fort Worth, TX: Harcourt Brace. An undergraduate text treating both cross-cultural psychology and intercultural psychology.

Chiu, C.-Y., & Hong, Y.-Y. (2007). Cultural processes: Basic principles. In A. W. Kruglanski & E. T. Higgins (eds), *Social psychology: Handbook of basic principles* (2nd ed., pp. 785–804). New York: Guilford Press. Comprehensive and detailed coverage of the social psychology of culture.

Chryssochoou, X. (2004). *Cultural diversity: Its social psychology.* Oxford, UK: Blackwell. An accessible and well illustrated social psychological discussion of processes, for example migration, in multicultural societies.

Fiske, A. P., Kitayama, S., Markus, H. R., & Nisbett, R. E. (1998). The cultural matrix of social psychology. In D. T. Gilbert, S. T. Fiske, & G. Lindzey (eds), *The handbook of social psychology* (4th ed., Vol. 2, pp. 915–81). New York:

McGraw-Hill. A major review of theories and processes underlying the connection between social psychology and culture.

Heine, S. J. (2010). Cultural psychology. In S. T. Fiske, D. T. Gilbert, & G. Lindzey (eds), *Handbook of social psychology* (5th ed., Vol. 2, pp. 1423–64). New York: Wiley. Up-to-date comprehensive and detailed coverage of the social psychology of culture and the cultural context of social psychology. It includes an excellent treatment of theoretical and methodological issues.

Moghaddam, F. M. (1998). *Social psychology: Exploring universals across cultures.* New York: Freeman. A general text that explicitly builds cultural constructs and analysis into the treatment of traditional social psychological topics.

Moghaddam, F. M. (2008). *Multiculturalism and intergroup relations: Psychological implications for democracy in global context.* Washington, DC: American Psychological Association. A thoughtful and detailed social psychological examination of contemporary multicultural society – dangers, opportunities and potential benefits.

Schaller, M., & Crandall, C. S. (eds) (2004). *The psychological foundations of culture.* Mahwah, NJ: Erlbaum. Questions about the origins, evolution and nature of culture are examined in relation to cognition, motivation and social interaction.

Smith, P. B., Bond, M. H., & Kağitçibaşi, C. (2006). *Understanding social psychology across cultures.* Thousand Oaks, CA: SAGE. This book is a substantially revised version of an earlier work (Smith & Bond, 1998), organised around three sections: an overall framework, core issues and global change.

Triandis, H. (1994). *Culture and social behavior*. New York: McGraw-Hill. Still a good source of material documenting cross-cultural differences in behaviour.

 Refresh your understanding, assess your progress and go further with interactive summaries, questions, podcasts and much more at **www.mypsychlab.co.uk**

# Glossary

**Abuse syndrome** Factors of proximity, stress and power that are associated with the cycle of abuse in some families.

**Accentuation effect** Overestimation of similarities among people within a category and dissimilarities between people from different categories.

**Accentuation principle** Categorisation accentuates perceived similarities within and differences between groups on dimensions that people believe are correlated with the categorisation. The effect is amplified where the categorisation and/or dimension has subjective importance, relevance or value.

**Accessibility** Ease of recall of categories or schemas that we already have in mind.

**Acculturation** The process whereby individuals learn about the rules of behaviour characteristic of another culture.

**Acquiescent response set** Tendency to agree with items in an attitude questionnaire. This leads to an ambiguity in interpretation if a high score on an attitude questionnaire can be obtained only by agreeing with all or most items.

**Action research** The simultaneous activities of undertaking social science research, involving participants in the process, and addressing a social problem.

**Actor–observer effect** Tendency to attribute our own behaviours externally and others' behaviours internally.

**Affect-infusion model** Cognition is infused with affect such that social judgements reflect current mood.

**Ageism** Prejudice and discrimination against people based on their age.

**Agentic state** A frame of mind thought by Milgram to characterise unquestioning obedience, in which people as agents transfer personal responsibility to the person giving orders.

**Altruism** A special form of *helping behaviour,* sometimes costly, that shows concern for fellow human beings and is performed without expectation of personal gain.

**Analogue** Device or measure intended to faithfully mimic the 'real thing'.

**Anchoring and adjustment** A cognitive short cut in which inferences are tied to initial standards or schemas.

**Arbitration** Process of intergroup conflict resolution in which a neutral third party is invited to impose a mutually binding settlement.

**Archival research** Non-experimental method involving the assembly of data, or reports of data, collected by others.

**Associative meaning** Illusory correlation in which items are seen as belonging together because they 'ought' to, on the basis of prior expectations.

**Associative network** Model of memory in which nodes or ideas are connected by associative links along which cognitive activation can spread.

**Assortative mating** A non-random coupling of individuals based on their resemblance to each other on one or more characteristics.

**Attachment behaviour** The tendency of an infant to maintain close physical proximity with the mother or primary caregiver.

**Attachment styles** Descriptions of the nature of people's close relationships, thought to be established in childhood.

**Attitude** (a) A relatively enduring organisation of beliefs, feelings and behavioural tendencies towards socially significant objects, groups, events or symbols. (b) A general feeling or evaluation – positive or negative – about some person, object or issue.

**Attitude change** Any significant modification of an individual's attitude. In the persuasion process this involves the communicator, the communication, the medium used, and the characteristics of the audience. Attitude change can also occur by inducing someone to perform an act that runs counter to an existing attitude.

**Attitude formation** The process of forming our attitudes, mainly from our own experiences, the influences of others and our emotional reactions.

**Attribution** The process of assigning a cause to our own behaviour, and that of others.

**Attributional style** An individual (personality) predisposition to make a certain type of causal attribution for behaviour.

**Audience** Intended target of a persuasive communication.

**Audience effects** Impact of the presence of others on individual task performance.

**Authoritarian personality** Personality syndrome originating in childhood that predisposes individuals to be prejudiced.

**Autocratic leaders** Leaders who use a style based on giving orders to followers.

**Autokinesis** Optical illusion in which a pinpoint of light shining in complete darkness appears to move about.

**Automatic activation** According to Fazio, attitudes that have a strong evaluative link to situational cues are more likely to automatically come to mind from memory.

**Availability heuristic** A cognitive short cut in which the frequency or likelihood of an event is based on how quickly instances or associations come to mind.

**Averageness effect** Humans have evolved to prefer average and symmetrical faces to those with unusual or distinctive features.

**Averaging** A method of forming positive or negative impressions by averaging the valence of all the constituent attributes.

**Back-channel communication** Verbal and non-verbal ways in which listeners let speakers know they are still listening.

**Balance theory** According to Heider, people prefer attitudes that are consistent with each other over those that are inconsistent. A person (P) tries to maintain consistency in attitudes to, and relationships with, other people (O) and elements of the environment (X).

**Bargaining** Process of intergroup conflict resolution where representatives reach agreement through direct negotiation.

**Base-rate information** Pallid, factual, statistical information about an entire class of events.

**Behaviour** What people actually do that can be objectively measured.

**Behavioural decision theory** Set of normative models (ideal processes) for making accurate social inferences.

**Behaviourism** An emphasis on explaining observable behaviour in terms of reinforcement schedules.

**Belief congruence theory** The theory that similar beliefs promote liking and social harmony among people while dissimilar beliefs produce dislike and prejudice.

**Belief in a just world** Belief that the world is a just and predictable place where good things happen to 'good people' and bad things to 'bad people'.

**Big Five** The five major personality dimensions of extraversion/surgency, agreeableness, conscientiousness, emotional stability, and intellect/openness to experience.

**Biosocial theories** In the context of aggression, theories that emphasise an innate component, though not the existence of a full-blown instinct.

**BIRGing** Basking In Reflected Glory; that is, name-dropping to link yourself with desirable people or groups and thus improve other people's impression of you.

**Bogus pipeline technique** A measurement technique that leads people to believe that a 'lie detector' can monitor their emotional responses, thus measuring their true attitudes.

**Bookkeeping** Gradual schema change through the accumulation of bits of schema-inconsistent information.

**Brainstorming** Uninhibited generation of as many ideas as possible in a group, in order to enhance group creativity.

**Bystander-calculus model** In attending to an emergency, the bystander calculates the perceived costs and benefits of providing help compared with those associated with not helping.

**Bystander effect** People are less likely to help in an emergency when they are with others than when alone. The greater the number, the less likely it is that anyone will help.

**Bystander intervention** This occurs when an individual breaks out of the role of a bystander and helps another person in an emergency.

**Case study** In-depth analysis of a single case (or individual).

**Catharsis** A dramatic release of pent-up feelings: the idea that aggressive motivation is 'drained' by acting against a frustrating object (or substitute), or by a vicarious experience.

**Cathartic hypothesis** The notion that acting aggressively, or even just viewing aggressive material, reduces feelings of anger and aggression.

**Causal schemata** Experience-based beliefs about how certain types of causes interact to produce an effect.

**Central traits** Traits that have a disproportionate influence on the configuration of final impressions, in Asch's configural model of impression formation.

**Charismatic leadership** Leadership style based upon the leaders (perceived) possession of charisma.

**Cognition** The knowledge, beliefs, thoughts and ideas that people have about themselves and their environment. May also refer to mental processes through which knowledge is acquired, including perception, memory and thinking.

**Cognitive algebra** Approach to the study of impression formation that focuses on how people combine attributes that have valence into an overall positive or negative impression.

**Cognitive alternatives** Belief that the status quo is unstable and illegitimate, and that social competition with the dominant group is the appropriate strategy to improve social identity.

**Cognitive consistency** A model of social cognition in which people try to reduce inconsistency among their cognitions, because they find inconsistency unpleasant.

**Cognitive consistency theories** A group of attitude theories stressing that people try to maintain internal consistency, order and agreement among their various cognitions.

**Cognitive dissonance** State of psychological tension produced by simultaneously having two opposing cognitions. People are motivated to reduce the tension, often by changing or rejecting one of the cognitions. Festinger proposed that we seek harmony in our attitudes, beliefs and behaviours, and try to reduce tension from inconsistency among these elements.

**Cognitive miser** A model of social cognition that characterises people as using the least complex and demanding cognitions that are able to produce generally adaptive behaviours.

**Cognitive theories** These attempt to explain behaviour in terms of the way people actively interpret and represent their experiences and then plan action.

**Cohesiveness** The property of a group that affectively binds people, as group members, to one another and to the group as a whole, giving the group a sense of solidarity and oneness.

**Collective aggression** Unified aggression by a group of individuals, who may not even know one another, against another individual or group.

**Collective behaviour** The behaviour of people en masse – such as in a crowd, protest or riot.

**Collectivism** Societal structure and world-view in which people prioritise group loyalty, commitment and conformity, and belonging and fitting in to groups, over standing out as an isolated individual.

**Commitment** The desire or intention to continue an interpersonal relationship.

**Commons dilemma** Social dilemma in which cooperation by all benefits all, but competition by all harms all.

**Communication** Transfer of meaningful information from one person to another.

**Communication accommodation theory** Modification of verbal and non-verbal communication styles to the context (e.g. listener, situation) of a face-to-face interaction – an extension of speech accommodation theory to incorporate non-verbal communication.

**Communication network** Set of rules governing the possibility or ease of communication between different roles in a group.

**Companionate love** The caring and affection for another person that usually arises from sharing time together.

**Comparison level** A standard that develops over time, allowing us to judge whether a new relationship is profitable or not.

**Compliance** Superficial, public and transitory change in behaviour and expressed attitudes in response to requests, coercion or group pressure.

**Conciliation** Process whereby groups make cooperative gestures to one another in the hope of avoiding an escalation of conflict.

**Configural model** Asch's *Gestalt*-based model of impression formation, in which central traits play a disproportionate role in configuring the final impression.

**Conformity** Deep-seated, private and enduring change in behaviour and attitudes due to group pressure.

**Conformity bias** Tendency for social psychology to treat group influence as a one-way process in which individuals or minorities always conform to majorities.

**Confounding** Where two or more independent variables covary in such a way that it is impossible to know which has caused the effect.

**Consensus information** Information about the extent to which other people react in the same way to a stimulus X.

**Consistency information** Information about the extent to which a behaviour Y always co-occurs with a stimulus X.

**Conspiracy theory** Explanation of widespread, complex and worrying events in terms of the premeditated actions of small groups of highly organised conspirators.

**Consummate love** Sternberg argues that this is the ultimate form of love, involving passion, intimacy and commitment.

**Contact hypothesis** The view that bringing members of opposing social groups together will improve intergroup relations and reduce prejudice and discrimination.

**Contingency theories** Theories of leadership that consider the leadership effectiveness of particular behaviours or behavioural styles to be contingent on the nature of leadership situation.

**Conversion** Sudden schema change as a consequence of gradual accumulation of schema-inconsistent information.

**Conversion effect** When minority influence brings about a sudden and dramatic internal and private change in the attitudes of a majority.

**Coordination loss** Deterioration in group performance compared with individual performance, due to problems in coordinating behaviour.

**Correlation** Where changes in one variable reliably map onto changes in another variable, but it cannot be determined which of the two variables *caused* the change.

**Correspondence bias** A general attribution bias in which people have an inflated tendency to see behaviour as reflecting (corresponding to) stable underlying personality attributes.

**Correspondent inference** Causal attribution of behaviour to underlying dispositions.

**Cost–reward ratio** Tenet of social exchange theory, according to which liking for another is determined by calculating what it will cost to be reinforced by that person.

**Covariation model** Kelley's theory of causal attribution – people assign the cause of behaviour to the factor that covaries most closely with the behaviour.

**Cultural norms** Norms whose origin is part of the tradition of a culture.

**Cultural values theory** The view that people in groups use members' opinions about the position valued in the wider culture, and then adjust their views in that direction for social approval reasons.

**Culture of honour** A culture that endorses male violence as a way of addressing threats to social reputation or economic position.

**Culture-blind** Theory and data untested outside the host culture.

**Culture-bound** Theory and data conditioned by a specific cultural background.

**Data** Publicly verifiable observations.

**Dehumanisation** Stripping people of their dignity and humanity.

**Deindividuation** Process whereby people lose their sense of socialised individual identity and engage in unsocialised, often antisocial, behaviours.

**Demand characteristics** Features of an experiment that seem to 'demand' a certain response.

**Democratic leaders** Leaders who use a style based on consultation and obtaining agreement and consent from followers.

**Dependent variables** Variables that change as a consequence of changes in the independent variable.

**Depersonalisation** The perception and treatment of self and others not as unique individual persons but as prototypical embodiments of a social group.

**Desensitisation** A serious reduction in a person's responsiveness to material that usually evokes a strong emotional reaction, such as violence or sexuality.

**Diffuse status characteristics** Information about a person's abilities that are only obliquely relevant to the group's task, and derive mainly from large-scale category memberships outside the group.

**Diffusion of responsibility** Tendency of an individual to assume that others will take responsibility (as a result, no one does). This is a hypothesised cause of the bystander effect.

**Disconfirmation bias** The tendency to notice, refute and regard as weak, arguments that contradict our prior beliefs.

**Discount** If there is no consistent relationship between a specific cause and a specific behaviour, that cause is discounted in favour of some other cause.

**Discourse** Entire communicative event or episode located in a situational and socio-historical context.

**Discourse analysis** A set of methods used to analyse text – in particular, naturally occurring language – in order to understand its meaning and significance.

**Discrimination** The behavioural expression of prejudice.

**Disinhibition** A breakdown in the learned controls (social mores) against behaving impulsively or, in this context, aggressively. For some people, alcohol has a disinhibiting effect.

**Displacement** Psychodynamic concept referring to the transfer of negative feelings on to an individual or group other than that which originally caused the negative feelings.

**Display rules** Cultural and situational rules that dictate how appropriate it is to express emotions in a given context.

**Distinctiveness information** Information about whether a person's reaction occurs only with one stimulus, or is a common reaction to many stimuli.

**Distraction–conflict theory** The physical presence of members of the same species causes drive because people are distracting and produce conflict between attending to the task and to the audience.

**Distributive justice** The fairness of the outcome of a decision.

**Dogmatism** Cognitive style that is rigid and intolerant and predisposes people to be prejudiced.

**Door-in-the-face tactic** Multiple-request technique to gain compliance, in which the focal request is preceded by a larger request that is bound to be refused.

**Double-blind** Procedure to reduce experimenter effects, in which the experimenter is unaware of the experimental conditions.

**Drive theory** Zajonc's theory that the physical presence of members of the same species instinctively causes arousal that motivates performance of habitual behaviour patterns.

**Dual-process dependency model** General model of social influence in which two separate processes operate – dependency on others for social approval and for information about reality.

**Effort justification** A special case of cognitive dissonance: inconsistency is experienced when a person makes a considerable effort to achieve a modest goal.

**Egoistic relative deprivation** A feeling of personally having less than we feel we are entitled to, relative to our aspirations or to other individuals.

**Elaboration–likelihood model** Petty and Cacioppo's model of attitude change: when people attend to a message carefully, they use a central route to process it; otherwise they use a peripheral route. This model competes with the heuristic–systematic model.

**Emblems** Gestures that replace or stand in for spoken language.

**Emergency situation** Often involves an unusual event, can vary in nature, is unplanned, and requires a quick response.

**Emergent norm theory** Collective behaviour is regulated by norms based on distinctive behaviour that arises in the initially normless crowd.

**Emotion-in-relationships model** Close relationships provide a context that elicits strong emotions due to the increased probability of behaviour interrupting interpersonal expectations.

**Empathic concern** An element in Batson's theory of helping behaviour. In contrast to personal distress (which may lead us to flee from the situation), it includes feelings of warmth, being soft-hearted, and having compassion for a person in need.

**Empathy** Ability to feel another person's experiences; identifying with and experiencing another person's emotions, thoughts and attitudes.

**Empathy costs of not helping** Piliavin's view that failing to help can cause distress to a bystander who empathises with a victim's plight.

**Entitativity** The property of a group that makes it seem like a coherent, distinct and unitary entity.

**Equity theory** A special case of social exchange theory that defines a relationship as equitable when the ratio of inputs to outcomes are seen to be the same by both partners.

**Essentialism** Pervasive tendency to consider behaviour to reflect underlying and immutable, often innate, properties of people or the groups they belong to.

**Ethnocentrism** Evaluative preference for all aspects of our own group relative to other groups.

**Ethnographic research** Descriptive study of a specific society, based on fieldwork, and requiring immersion of the researcher in the everyday life of its people.

**Ethnolinguistic group** Social group defined principally in terms of its language.

**Ethnolinguistic identity theory** Application and extension of social identity theory to deal with language behaviour of ethnolinguistic groups.

**Ethnolinguistic vitality** Concept describing objective features of an interethnic context that influence language, and ultimately the cultural survival or disappearance of an ethnolinguistic group.

**Ethnomethodology** Method devised by Garfinkel, involving the violation of hidden norms to reveal their presence.

**Ethology** Approach that argues that animal behaviour should be studied in the species' natural physical and social environment. Behaviour is genetically determined and is controlled by natural selection.

**Etic–emic distinction** Contrast between psychological constructs that are relatively culture-universal and those that are relatively culture-specific.

**Evaluation apprehension model** The argument that the physical presence of members of the same species causes drive because people have learned to be apprehensive about being evaluated.

**Evolutionary psychology** A theoretical approach that explains 'useful' psychological traits, such as memory, perception or language, as adaptations through natural selection.

**Evolutionary social psychology** An extension of evolutionary psychology that views complex social behaviour as adaptive, helping the individual, kin and the species as a whole to survive.

**Excitation-transfer model** The expression of aggression is a function of learned behaviour, some excitation from another source, and the person's interpretation of the arousal state.

**Exemplars** Specific instances of a member of a category.

**Expectancy-value model** Direct experience with an attitude object informs a person how much that object should be liked or disliked in the future.

**Expectation states theory** Theory of the emergence of roles as a consequence of people's status-based expectations about others' performance.

**Experimental method** Intentional manipulation of independent variables in order to investigate effects on one or more dependent variables.

**Experimental realism** Psychological impact of the manipulations in an experiment.

**Experimenter effect** Effect that is produced or influenced by clues to the hypotheses under examination, inadvertently given by the experimenter.

**Extended contact effect** Knowing about an ingroup member who shares a close relationship with an outgroup member can improve one's own attitudes towards the outgroup.

**External (or situational) attribution** Assigning the cause of our own or others' behaviour to external or environmental factors.

**External validity** Similarity between circumstances surrounding an experiment and circumstances encountered in everyday life.

**Face-ism** Media depiction that gives greater prominence to the head and less prominence to the body for men, but vice versa for women.

**False consensus effect** Seeing our own behaviour as being more typical than it really is.

**Familiarity** As we become more familiar with a stimulus (even another person), we feel more comfortable with it and we like it more.

**Family resemblance** Defining property of category membership.

**Fear of social blunders** The dread of acting inappropriately or of making a foolish mistake witnessed by others. The desire to avoid ridicule inhibits effective responses to an emergency by members of a group.

**Fighting instinct** Innate impulse to aggress which ethologists claim is shared by humans with other animals.

**Foot-in-the-door tactic** Multiple-request technique to gain compliance, in which the focal request is preceded by a smaller request that is bound to be accepted.

**Forewarning** Advance knowledge that one is to be the target of a persuasion attempt. Forewarning often produces resistance to persuasion.

**Frame of reference** Complete range of subjectively conceivable positions on some attitudinal or behavioural dimension, which relevant people can occupy in that context.

**Fraternalistic relative deprivation** Sense that our group has less than it is entitled to, relative to its aspirations or to other groups.

**Free-rider effect** Gaining the benefits of group membership by avoiding costly obligations of membership and by allowing other members to incur those costs.

**Frustration–aggression hypothesis** Theory that all frustration leads to aggression, and all aggression comes from frustration. Used to explain prejudice and intergroup aggression.

**Fundamental attribution error** Bias in attributing another's behaviour more to internal than to situational causes.

**Fuzzy sets** Categories are considered to be fuzzy sets of features organised around a prototype.

**Gaze** Looking at someone's eyes.

**Gender** Sex-stereotypical attributes of a person.

**General aggression model** Anderson's model that includes both personal and situational factors, and cognitive and affective processes in accounting for different kinds of aggression.

**Generative psychology** A psychology intended to generate positive social change through direct intervention.

**Genocide** The ultimate expression of prejudice by exterminating an entire social group.

**Gestalt psychology** Perspective in which the whole influences constituent parts rather than vice versa.

**Gestures** Meaningful body movements and postures.

**Glass ceiling** An invisible barrier that prevents women, and other minorities, from attaining top leadership positions.

**Great person theory** Perspective on leadership that attributes effective leadership to innate or acquired individual characteristics.

**Group** Two or more people who share a common definition and evaluation of themselves and behave in accordance with such a definition.

**Group mind** McDougall's idea that people adopt a qualitatively different mode of thinking when in a group.

**Group polarisation** Tendency for group discussion to produce more extreme group decisions than the mean of members' pre-discussion opinions, in the direction favoured by the mean.

**Group socialisation** Dynamic relationship between the group and its members that describes the passage of members through a group in terms of commitment and of changing roles.

**Group structure** Division of a group into different roles that often differ with respect to status and prestige.

**Group value model** View that procedural justice within groups makes members feel valued, and thus leads to enhanced commitment to and identification with the group.

**Groupthink** A mode of thinking in highly cohesive groups in which the desire to reach unanimous agreement overrides the motivation to adopt proper rational decision-making procedures.

**Guttman scale** A scale that contains either favourable or unfavourable statements arranged hierarchically. Agreement with a strong statement implies agreement with weaker ones; disagreement with a weak one implies disagreement with stronger ones.

**Hate crimes** A class of violence against members of a stereotyped minority group.

**Hedonic relevance** Refers to behaviour that has important direct consequences for self.

**Helping behaviour** Acts that intentionally benefit someone else.

**Heuristics** Cognitive short cuts that provide adequately accurate inferences for most of us most of the time.

**Heuristic–systematic model** Chaiken's model of attitude change: when people attend to a message carefully, they use systematic processing; otherwise they process information by using heuristics, or 'mental short cuts'. This model competes with the elaboration–likelihood model.

**Hospitalism** A state of apathy and depression noted among institutionalised infants deprived of close contact with a caregiver.

**Hypotheses** Empirically testable predictions about what goes with what, or what causes what.

**Ideology** A systematically interrelated set of beliefs whose primary function is explanation. It circumscribes thinking, making it difficult for the holder to escape from its mould.

**Idiosyncrasy credit** Hollander's transactional theory, in which followers reward leaders for achieving group goals by allowing them to be relatively idiosyncratic.

**Illocution** Words placed in sequence and the context in which this is done.

**Illusion of control** Belief that we have more control over our world than we really do.

**Illusion of group effectivity** Experience-based belief that we produce more and better ideas in groups than alone.

**Illusory correlation** Cognitive exaggeration of the degree of co-occurrence of two stimuli or events, or the perception of a co-occurrence where none exists.

**Implicit association test** Reaction-time test to measure attitudes – particularly unpopular attitudes that people might conceal.

**Implicit personality theories** Idiosyncratic and personal ways of characterising other people and explaining their behaviour.

**Impression management** People's use of various strategies to get other people to view them in a positive light.

**Independent self** A self that is relatively separate, internal and unique.

**Independent variables** Features of a situation that change of their own accord, or can be manipulated by an experimenter to have effects on a dependent variable.

**Indigenous psychology** A psychology created by and for a specific cultural group – based on the claim that culture can be understood only from within its own perspective.

**Individualism** Societal structure and world view in which people prioritise standing out as an individual over fitting in as a group member.

**Induced compliance** A special case of cognitive dissonance: inconsistency is experienced when a person is persuaded to behave in a way that is contrary to an attitude.

**Information integration theory** The idea that a person's attitude can be estimated by averaging across the positive and negative ratings of the object.

**Information processing** The evaluation of information; in relation to attitudes, the means by which people acquire knowledge and form and change attitudes.

**Informational influence** An influence to accept information from another as evidence about reality.

**Ingratiation** Strategic attempt to get someone to like you in order to obtain compliance with a request.

**Ingroup favouritism** Behaviour that favours one's own group over other groups.

**Initiation rites** Often painful or embarrassing public procedure to mark group members' movements from one role to another.

**Inoculation** A way of making people resistant to persuasion. By providing them with a diluted counter-argument, they can build up effective refutations to a later, stronger argument.

**Instinct** Innate drive or impulse, genetically transmitted.

**Institutionalised aggression** Aggression that is given formal or informal recognition and social legitimacy by being incorporated into rules and norms.

**Interdependent self** A self that is relatively dependent on social relations and has more fuzzy boundaries.

**Intergroup attributions** Process of assigning the cause of one's own or others' behaviour to group membership.

**Intergroup behaviour** Behaviour among individuals that is regulated by those individuals' awareness of and identification with different social groups.

**Intergroup differentiation** Behaviour that emphasises differences between our own group and other groups.

**Intergroup emotions theory (IET)** Theory that, in group contexts, appraisals of personal harm or benefit in a situation operate at the level of social identity and thus produce mainly positive ingroup and negative outgroup emotions.

**Internal (or dispositional) attribution** Process of assigning the cause of our own or others' behaviour to internal or dispositional factors.

**Internal validity** Psychological impact of the manipulations in an experiment.

**J-curve** A graphical figure that captures the way in which relative deprivation arises when attainments suddenly fall short of rising expectations.

**Just-world hypothesis** According to Lerner and Miller, people need to believe that the world is a just place where they get what they deserve. As evidence of undeserved suffering undermines this belief, people may conclude that victims deserve their fate.

**Kinesics** Linguistics of body communication.

**Laboratory** A place, usually a room, in which data are collected, usually by experimental methods.

**Laissez-faire leaders** Leaders who use a style based on disinterest in followers.

**Language** A system of sounds that convey meaning because of shared grammatical and semantic rules.

**Leader categorisation theory** We have a variety of schemas about how different types of leaders behave in different leadership situations. When a leader is categorised as a particular type of leader, the schema fills in details about how that leader will behave.

**Leader behaviour description questionnaire (LBDQ)** Scale devised by the Ohio State leadership researchers to measure leadership behaviour and distinguish between 'initiating structure' and 'consideration' dimensions.

**Leader–member exchange (LMX) theory** Theory of leadership in which effective leadership rests on the ability of the leader to develop good-quality personalised exchange relationships with individual members.

**Leadership** Getting group members to achieve the group's goals.

**Learning by direct experience** Acquiring a behaviour because we were rewarded for it.

**Learning by vicarious experience** Acquiring a behaviour after observing that another person was rewarded for it.

**Least-preferred co-worker (LPC) scale** Fiedler's scale for measuring leadership style in terms of favourability of attitude towards one's least-preferred co-worker.

**Level of analysis (or explanation)** The types of concepts, mechanisms and language used to explain a phenomenon.

**Likert scale** Scale that evaluates how strongly people agree/disagree with favourable/unfavourable statements about an attitude object. Initially, many items are tested. After item analysis, only those items that correlate with each other are retained.

**Linguistic relativity** View that language determines thought and therefore people who speak different languages see the world in very different ways.

**Locution** Words placed in sequence.

**Looking-glass self** The self derived from seeing ourselves as others see us.

**Love** A combination of emotions, cognitions and behaviours that can be involved in intimate relationships.

**Low-ball tactic** Technique for inducing compliance in which a person who agrees to a request still feels committed after finding that there are hidden costs.

**Machismo** A code in which challenges, abuse and even differences of opinion must be met with fists or other weapons.

**Matched-guise technique** Research methodology to measure people's attitudes towards a speaker based solely on speech style.

**Mediation** Process of intergroup conflict resolution where a neutral third party intervenes in the negotiation process to facilitate a settlement.

**Membership group** Kelley's term for a group to which we belong by some objective external criterion.

**Mere exposure effect** Repeated exposure to an object results in greater attraction to that object.

**Mere presence** Refers to an entirely passive and unresponsive audience that is only physically present.

**Message** Communication from a source directed to an audience.

**Meta-analysis** Statistical procedure that combines data from different studies to measure the overall reliability and strength of specific effects.

**Metacontrast principle** The prototype of a group is that position within the group that has the largest ratio of 'differences to ingroup positions' to 'differences to outgroup positions'.

**Metatheory** Set of interrelated concepts and principles concerning which theories or types of theory are appropriate.

**Mindlessness** The act of agreeing to a request without giving it a thought. A small request is likely to be agreed to, even if a spurious reason is provided.

**Minimal group paradigm** Experimental methodology to investigate the effect of social categorisation alone on behaviour.

**Minimax strategy** In relating to others, we try to minimise the costs and maximise the rewards that accrue.

**Minority influence** Social influence processes whereby numerical or power minorities change the attitudes of the majority.

**Modelling** Tendency for a person to reproduce the actions, attitudes and emotional responses exhibited by a real-life or symbolic model. Also called *observational learning*.

**Moderator variable** A variable that qualifies an otherwise simple hypothesis with a view to improving its predictive power (e.g. A causes B, but only when C (the moderator) is present).

**Motivated tactician** A model of social cognition that characterises people as having multiple cognitive strategies available, which they choose among on the basis of personal goals, motives and needs.

**Multifactor leadership questionnaire (MLQ)** The most popular and widely used scale to measure transactional and transformational leadership.

**Multiple-act criterion** Term for a general behavioural index based on an average or combination of several specific behaviours.

**Multiple requests** Tactics for gaining compliance using a two-step procedure: the first request functions as a set-up for the second, real request.

**Mundane realism** Similarity between circumstances surrounding an experiment and circumstances encountered in everyday life.

**Naive psychologist (or scientist)** Model of social cognition that characterises people as using rational, scientific-like, cause–effect analyses to understand their world.

**Nature–nurture controversy** Classic debate about whether genetic or environmental factors determine human behaviour. Scientists generally accept that it is an interaction of both.

**Need to affiliate** The urge to form connections and make contact with other people.

**Neo-associationist analysis** A view of aggression according to which mass media may provide images of violence to an audience that later translate into antisocial acts.

**Neo-behaviourist** One who attempts to explain observable behaviour in terms of contextual factors and unobservable intervening constructs such as beliefs, feelings and motives.

**Neo-Freudians** Psychoanalytic theorists who modified the original theories of Freud.

**Non-common effects** Effects of behaviour that are relatively exclusive to that behaviour rather than other behaviours.

**Non-verbal communication** Transfer of meaningful information from one person to another by means other than written or spoken language (e.g. gaze, facial expression, posture, touch).

**Normative decision theory (NDT)** A contingency theory of leadership that focuses on the effectiveness of different leadership styles in group decision making contexts.

**Normative influence** An influence to conform with the positive expectation of others, to gain social approval or to avoid social disapproval.

**Normative models** Ideal processes for making accurate social inferences.

**Norms** Attitudinal and behavioural uniformities that define group membership and differentiate between groups.

**One-component attitude model** An attitude consists of affect towards or evaluation of the object.

**Operational definition** Defines a theoretical term in a way that allows it to be to manipulated or measured.

**Optimal distinctiveness** People strive to achieve a balance between conflicting motives for inclusiveness and separateness, expressed in groups as a balance between intragroup differentiation and intragroup homogenisation.

**Outcome bias** Belief that the outcomes of a behaviour were intended by the person who chose the behaviour.

**Overjustification effect** In the absence of obvious external determinants of our behaviour, we assume that we freely choose the behaviour because we enjoy it.

**Paired distinctiveness** Illusory correlation in which items are seen as belonging together because they share some unusual feature.

**Paralanguage** The non-linguistic accompaniments of speech (e.g. stress, pitch, speed, tone, pauses).

**Partner regulation** Strategy that encourages a partner to match an ideal standard of behaviour.

**Passionate (or romantic) love** State of intense absorption in another person involving physiological arousal.

**Path-goal theory (PGT)** A contingency theory of leadership that can also be classified as a transactional theory – it focuses on how 'structuring' and 'consideration' behaviours motivate followers.

**Peace studies** Multidisciplinary movement dedicated to the study and promotion of peace.

**Peripheral traits** Traits that have an insignificant influence on the configuration of final impressions, in Asch's configural model of impression formation.

**Personal attraction** Liking for someone based on idiosyncratic preferences and interpersonal relationships.

**Personal constructs** Idiosyncratic and personal ways of characterising other people.

**Personal costs of not helping** Piliavin's view that not helping a victim in distress can be costly to a bystander (e.g. experiencing blame).

**Personal identity** The self defined in terms of unique personal attributes or unique interpersonal relationships.

**Personal space** Physical space around people's bodies which they treat as a part of themselves.

**Personalism** Behaviour that appears to be directly intended to benefit or harm oneself rather than others.

**Persuasive arguments theory** View that people in groups are persuaded by novel information that supports their initial position, and thus become more extreme in their endorsement of their initial position.

**Persuasive communication** Message intended to change an attitude and related behaviours of an audience.

**Positivism** Non-critical acceptance of science as the only way to arrive at true knowledge: science as religion.

**Post-decisional conflict** The dissonance associated with behaving in a counter-attitudinal way. Dissonance can be reduced by bringing the attitude into line with the behaviour.

**Power** Capacity to influence others while resisting their attempts to influence.

**Prejudice** Unfavourable attitude towards a social group and its members.

**Primacy** An order of presentation effect in which earlier presented information has a disproportionate influence on social cognition.

**Priming** Activation of accessible categories or schemas in memory that influence how we process new information.

**Prior commitment** An individual's agreement in advance to be responsible if trouble occurs: for example, committing oneself to protect the property of another person against theft.

**Prisoner's dilemma** Two-person game in which both parties are torn between competition and cooperation and, depending on mutual choices, both can win or both can lose.

**Procedural justice** The fairness of the procedures used to make a decision.

**Process loss** Deterioration in group performance in comparison to individual performance due to the whole range of possible interferences among members.

**Production blocking** Reduction in individual creativity and productivity in brainstorming groups due to interruptions and turn-taking.

**Profit** This flows from a relationship when the rewards that accrue from continued interaction exceed the costs.

**Prosocial behaviour** Acts that are positively valued by society.

**Protection motivation theory** Adopting a healthy behaviour requires cognitive balancing between the perceived threat of illness and one's capacity to cope with the health regimen.

**Prototype** Cognitive representation of the typical/ideal defining features of a category.

**Proxemics** Study of interpersonal distance.

**Proximity** The factor of living close by is known to play an important role in the early stages of forming a friendship.

**Racism** Prejudice and discrimination against people based on their ethnicity or race.

**Radical behaviourist** One who explains observable behaviour in terms of reinforcement schedules, without recourse to any intervening unobservable (e.g. cognitive) constructs.

**Reactance** Brehm's theory that people try to protect their freedom to act. When they perceive that this freedom has been curtailed, they will act to regain it.

**Realistic conflict theory** Sherif's theory of intergroup conflict that explains intergroup behaviour in terms of the nature of goal relations between groups.

**Received pronunciation (RP)** Standard, high-status, spoken variety of English.

**Recency** An order of presentation effect in which later presented information has a disproportionate influence on social cognition.

**Reciprocity norm** The principle of 'doing unto others as they do to you'. It can refer to returning a favour, mutual aggression, mutual attraction or mutual help.

**Reciprocity principle** See 'Reciprocity norm'.

**Reductionism** A phenomenon in terms of the language and concepts of a lower level of analysis, usually with a loss of explanatory power.

**Reference group** Kelley's term for a group that is psychologically significant for our behaviour and attitudes.

**Referent informational influence** Pressure to conform with a group norm that defines oneself as a group member.

**Regression** Tendency for initial observations of instances from a category to be more extreme than subsequent observations.

**Regulatory focus theory** A promotion focus causes people to be approach-oriented in constructing a sense of self; a prevention focus causes people to be more cautious and avoidant in constructing a sense of self.

**Reinforcement–affect model** Model of attraction which postulates that we like people who are around when we experience a positive feeling (which itself is reinforcing).

**Relational model of authority in groups** Tyler's account of how effective authority in groups rests upon fairness- and justice-based relations between leader and followers.

**Relational theory** An analysis based on structures of meaningful social relationships that recur across cultures.

**Relationship dissolution model** Duck's proposal of the sequence through which most long-term relationships proceed if they finally break down.

**Relative deprivation** A sense of having less than we feel entitled to.

**Relative homogeneity effect** Tendency to see outgroup members as all the same, and ingroup members as more differentiated.

**Releasers** Specific stimuli in the environment thought by ethologists to trigger aggressive responses.

**Representativeness heuristic** A cognitive short cut in which instances are assigned to categories or types on the basis of overall similarity or resemblance to the category.

**Reverse discrimination** The practice of publicly being prejudiced in favour of a minority group in order to deflect accusations of prejudice and discrimination against that group.

**Ringelmann effect** Individual effort on a task diminishes as group size increases.

**Risky shift** Tendency for group discussion to produce group decisions that are more risky than the mean of members' pre-discussion opinions, but only if the pre-discussion mean already favoured risk.

**Role congruity theory** Mainly applied to the gender gap in leadership – because social stereotypes of women are inconsistent with people's schemas of effective leadership, women are evaluated as poor leaders.

**Roles** Patterns of behaviour that distinguish between different activities within the group, and that interrelate to one another for the greater good of the group.

**Salience** Property of a stimulus that makes it stand out in relation to other stimuli and attract attention.

**Scapegoat** Individual or group that becomes the target for anger and frustration caused by a different individual or group or some other set of circumstances.

**Schema** Cognitive structure that represents knowledge about a concept or type of stimulus, including its attributes and the relations among those attributes.

**Schism** Division of a group into subgroups that differ in their attitudes, values or ideology.

**Science** Method for studying nature that involves the collecting of data to test hypotheses.

**Script** A schema about an event.

**Selective exposure hypothesis** People tend to avoid potentially dissonant information.

**Self-affirmation theory** The theory that people reduce the impact of threat to their self-concept by focusing on and affirming their competence in some other area.

**Self-assessment** The motivation to seek out new information about ourselves in order to find out what sort of person we really are.

**Self-categorisation theory** Turner and associates' theory of how the process of categorising oneself as a group member produces social identity and group and intergroup behaviours.

**Self-disclosure** The sharing of intimate information and feelings with another person.

**Self-discrepancy theory** Higgins' theory about the consequences of making actual–ideal and actual–'ought' self-comparisons that reveal self-discrepancies.

**Self-efficacy** Expectations that we have about our capacity to succeed in particular tasks.

**Self-enhancement** The motivation to develop and promote a favourable image of self.

**Self-esteem** Feelings about and evaluations of oneself.

**Self-evaluation maintenance model** People who are constrained to make esteem-damaging upward comparisons can underplay or deny similarity to the target, or they can withdraw from their relationship with the target.

**Self-fulfilling prophecy** Expectations and assumptions about a person that influence our interaction with that person and eventually change their behaviour in line with our expectations.

**Self-handicapping** Publicly making advance external attributions for our anticipated failure or poor performance in a forthcoming event.

**Self-monitoring** Carefully controlling how we present ourselves. There are situational differences and individual differences in self-monitoring.

**Self-perception theory** Bem's idea that we gain knowledge of ourselves only by making self-attributions; for example, we infer our own attitudes from our own behaviour.

**Self-presentation** A deliberate effort to act in ways that create a particular impression, usually favourable, of ourselves.

**Self-regulation** Strategies that we use to match our behaviour to an ideal or 'ought' standard.

**Self-serving biases** Attributional distortions that protect or enhance self-esteem or the self-concept.

**Self-verification** Seeking out information that verifies and confirms what we already know about ourselves.

**Semantic differential** An attitude measure that asks for a rating on a scale composed of bipolar (opposite) adjectives. (Also a technique for measuring the connotative meaning of words or concepts.)

**Sex role** Behaviour deemed sex-stereotypically appropriate.

**Sexism** Prejudice and discrimination against people based on their gender.

**Sexual selection theory** The argument that sex differences in behaviour are determined by evolutionary history rather than society.

**Similarity of attitudes** One of the most important positive, psychological determinants of attraction.

**Situational control** Fiedler's classification of task characteristics in terms of how much control effective task performance requires.

**Sleeper effect** The impact of a persuasive message can increase over time when a discounting cue, such as an invalid source, can no longer be recalled.

**Social attraction** Liking for someone based on common group membership and determined by the person's prototypicality of the group.

**Social categorisation** Classification of people as members of different social groups.

**Social change belief system** Belief that intergroup boundaries are impermeable. Therefore, a lower-status individual can improve social identity only by challenging the legitimacy of the higher-status group's position.

**Social cognition** Cognitive processes and structures that influence and are influenced by social behaviour.

**Social comparison (theory)** Comparing our behaviours and opinions with those of others in order to establish the correct or socially approved way of thinking and behaving.

**Social compensation** Increased effort on a collective task to compensate for other group members' actual, perceived or anticipated lack of effort or ability.

**Social competition** Group-based behavioural strategies that improve social identity by directly confronting the dominant group's position in society.

**Social creativity** Group-based behavioural strategies that improve social identity but do not directly attack the dominant group's position.

**Social decisions schemes** Explicit or implicit decision-making rules that relate individual opinions to a final group decision.

**Social dilemmas** Situations in which short term personal gain is at odds with the long term good of the group.

**Social dominance theory** Theory that attributes prejudice to an individual's acceptance of an ideology that legitimises ingroup-serving hierarchy and domination, and rejects egalitarian ideologies.

**Social exchange** People often use a form of everyday economics when they weigh up costs and rewards before deciding what to do.

**Social facilitation** An improvement in the performance of well-learned/easy tasks and a deterioration in the performance of poorly learned/difficult tasks in the mere presence of members of the same species.

**Social identity** That part of the self-concept that derives from our membership of social groups.

**Social identity theory** Theory of group membership and intergroup relations based on self-categorisation, social comparison and the construction of a shared self-definition in terms of ingroup defining properties.

**Social identity theory of leadership** Development of social identity theory to explain leadership as an identity process whereby in salient groups prototypical leaders are more effective than less prototypical leaders.

**Social impact** The effect that other people have on our attitudes and behaviour, usually as a consequence of factors such as group size, and temporal and physical immediacy.

**Social influence** Process whereby attitudes and behaviour are influenced by the real or implied presence of other people.

**Social judgeability** Perception of whether it is socially acceptable to judge a specific target.

**Social learning theory** The view championed by Bandura that human social behaviour is not innate but learned from appropriate models.

**Social loafing** A reduction in individual effort when working on a collective task (one in which our outputs are pooled with those of other group members) compared with working either alone or co-actively (our outputs are not pooled).

**Social markers** Features of speech style that convey information about mood, context, status and group membership.

**Social mobility belief system** Belief that intergroup boundaries are permeable. Thus, it is possible for someone to pass from a lower-status into a higher-status group to improve social identity.

**Social neuroscience** The exploration of the neurological underpinnings of the processes traditionally examined by social psychology.

**Social order** The balance and control of a social system, regulated by norms, values, rules and law.

**Social ostracism** Exclusion from a group by common consent.

**Social psychology** Scientific investigation of how the thoughts, feelings and behaviour of individuals are influenced by the actual, imagined or implied presence of others.

**Social representations** Collectively elaborated explanations of unfamiliar and complex phenomena that transform them into a familiar and simple form.

**Social responsibility norm** The idea that we should help people who are dependent and in need. It is contradicted by another norm that discourages interfering in other people's lives.

**Social role theory** The argument that sex differences in behaviour are determined by society rather than one's biology.

**Social support network** People who know and care about us and who can provide back-up during a time of stress.

**Social transition scheme** Method for charting incremental changes in member opinions as a group moves towards a final decision.

**Sociocognitive model** Attitude theory highlighting an evaluative component. Knowledge of an object is represented in memory along with a summary of how to appraise it.

**Source** The point of origin of a persuasive communication.

**Specific status characteristics** Information about those abilities of a person that are directly relevant to the group's task.

**Speech** Vocal production of language.

**Speech accommodation theory** Modification of speech style to the context (e.g. listener, situation) of a face-to-face interindividual conversation.

**Speech convergence** Accent or speech style shift towards that of the other person.

**Speech divergence** Accent or speech style shift away from that of the other person.

**Speech style** The way in which something is said (e.g. accent, language), rather than the content of what is said.

**Spreading attitude effect** A liked or disliked person (or attitude object) may affect not only the evaluation of a second person directly associated but also others merely associated with the second person.

**Statistical significance** An effect is statistically significant if statistics reveal that it, or a larger effect, is unlikely to occur by chance more often than 1 in 20 times.

**Statistics** Formalised numerical procedures performed on data to investigate the magnitude and/or significance of effects.

**Status** Consensual evaluation of the prestige of a role or role occupant in a group, or of the prestige of a group and its members as a whole.

**Status characteristics theory** Theory of influence in groups that attributes greater influence to those who possess both task-relevant characteristics (specific status characteristics) and characteristics of a high-status group in society (diffuse status characteristics). Also called expectation states theory.

**Stereotype** Widely shared and simplified evaluative image of a social group and its members.

**Stereotype threat** Feeling that we will be judged and treated in terms of negative stereotypes of our group, and that we will inadvertently confirm these stereotypes through our behaviour.

**Stigma** Group attributes that mediate a negative social evaluation of people belonging to the group.

**Subculture of violence** A subgroup of society in which a higher level of violence is accepted as the norm.

**Subject effects** Effects that are not spontaneous, owing to demand characteristics and/or participants wishing to please the experimenter.

**Subjective vitality** Individual group members' representation of the objective ethnolinguistic vitality of their group.

**Subtyping** Schema change as a consequence of schema-inconsistent information, causing the formation of subcategories.

**Summation** A method of forming positive or negative impressions by summing the valence of all the constituent person attributes.

**Superordinate goals** Goals that both groups desire but that can be achieved only by both groups cooperating.

**Symbolic interactionism** Theory of how the self emerges from human interaction that involves people trading symbols (through language and gesture) that are usually consensual, and represent abstract properties rather than concrete objects.

**System justification theory** Theory that attributes social stasis to people's adherence to an ideology that justifies and protects the status quo.

*t* **test** Statistical procedure to test the statistical significance of an effect in which the mean for one condition is greater than the mean for another.

**Task taxonomy** Group tasks can be classified according to whether a division of labour is possible; whether there is a predetermined standard to be met; and how an individual's inputs can contribute.

**Terror management theory** The notion that the most fundamental human motivation is to reduce the terror of the inevitability of death. Self-esteem may be centrally implicated in effective terror management.

**Theory** Set of interrelated concepts and principles that explain a phenomenon.

**Theory of planned behaviour** Modification by Ajzen of the *theory of reasoned action*. It suggests that predicting a behaviour from an attitude measure is improved if people believe they have control over that behaviour.

**Theory of reasoned action** Fishbein and Ajzen's model of the links between attitude and behaviour. A major feature is the proposition that the best way to predict a behaviour is to ask whether the person intends to do it.

**Third-person effect** Most people think that they are less influenced than others by advertisements.

**Three-component attitude model** An attitude consists of cognitive, affective and behavioural components. This three-fold division has an ancient heritage, stressing thought, feeling and action as basic to human experience.

**Three-factor theory of love** Hatfield and Walster distinguished three components of what we label 'love': a cultural concept of love an appropriate person to love and emotional arousal.

**Thurstone scale** An 11-point scale with 22 items, 2 for each point. Each item has a value ranging from very unfavourable to very favourable. Respondents check the items with which they agree. Their attitude is the average scale value of these items.

**Tokenism** The practice of publicly making small concessions to a minority group in order to deflect accusations of prejudice and discrimination.

**Transactional leadership** Approach to leadership that focuses on the transaction of resources between leader and followers. Also a style of leadership.

**Transactive memory** Group members have a shared memory for who within the group remembers what and is the expert on what.

**Transformational leadership** Approach to leadership that focuses on the way that leaders transform group goals and actions – mainly through the exercise of charisma. Also a style of leadership based on charisma.

**Two-component attitude model** An attitude consists of a mental readiness to act. It also guides evaluative (judgemental) responses.

**Type A personality** The 'coronary-prone' personality – a behavioural correlate of heart disease characterised by striving to achieve, time urgency, competitiveness and hostility.

**Ultimate attribution error** Tendency to internally attribute bad outgroup and good ingroup behaviour, and to externally attribute good outgroup and bad ingroup behaviour.

**Uncertainty-identity theory** To reduce uncertainty and to feel more comfortable about who they are, people choose to identify with groups that are distinctive, clearly defined, and have consensual norms.

**Unidimensionality** A Guttman scale consists of a single (low to high) dimension. It is also cumulative; that is, agreement with the highest-scoring item implies agreement with all lower-scoring items.

**Unobtrusive measures** Observational approaches that neither intrude on the processes being studied nor cause people to behave unnaturally.

**Utterance** Sounds made by one person to another.

**Values** A higher-order concept thought to provide a structure for organising attitudes.

**Vertical dyad linkage (VDL) model** An early form of leader–member exchange (LMX) theory in which a sharp distinction is drawn between dyadic leader–member relations: the subordinate is treated as either an ingroup member or an outgroup member.

**Visual dominance behaviour** Tendency to gaze fixedly at a lower-status speaker.

**Vividness** An intrinsic property of a stimulus on its own that makes it stand out and attract attention.

**Völkerpsychologie** Early precursor of social psychology, as the study of the collective mind, in Germany in the mid- to late nineteenth century.

**Weapons effect** The mere presence of a weapon increases the probability that it will be used aggressively.

**Weighted averaging** Method of forming positive or negative impressions by first weighting and then averaging the valence of all the constituent person attributes.

# References

Abeles, R. P. (1976). Relative deprivation, rising expectations, and black militancy. *Journal of Social Issues, 32,* 119–137.

Abelson, R. P. (1968). Computers, polls and public opinion – some puzzles and paradoxes. *Transaction, 5,* 20–27.

Abelson, R. P. (1972). Are attitudes necessary? In B. T. King (Ed.), *Attitudes, conflict and social change* (pp. 19–32). New York: Academic Press.

Abelson, R. P. (1981). The psychological status of the script concept. *American Psychologist, 36,* 715–729.

Abelson, R. P., Aronson, E., McGuire, W. J., Newcomb, T. M., Rosenberg, M. J., & Tannenbaum, P. H. (Eds.) (1968). *Theories of cognitive consistency: A sourcebook.* Chicago: Rand McNally.

Aboud, F. (1988). *Children and prejudice.* Oxford, UK: Blackwell.

Aboud, F. E. (1987). The development of ethnic self-identification and attitudes. In J. S. Phinney & M. J. Rotheram (Eds.), *Children's ethnic socialization: Pluralism and development* (pp. 32–55). Beverly Hills, CA: SAGE.

Abrams, D. (1990). Political identity: Relative deprivation, social identity and the case of Scottish Nationalism. *ESRC 16–19 Initiative Occasional Papers.* London: Economic and Social Research Council.

Abrams, D. (1994). Social self-regulation. *Personality and Social Psychology Bulletin, 20,* 473–483.

Abrams, D., & Hogg, M. A. (1988). Comments on the motivational status of self-esteem in social identity and intergroup discrimination. *European Journal of Social Psychology, 18,* 317–334.

Abrams, D., & Hogg, M. A. (1990a). Social identification, self-categorisation, and social influence. *European Review of Social Psychology, 1,* 195–228.

Abrams, D., & Hogg, M. A. (1990b). The social context of discourse: Let's not throw out the baby with the bath water. *Philosophical Psychology, 3,* 219–225.

Abrams, D., & Hogg, M. A. (2001). Collective identity: Group membership and self-conception. In M. A. Hogg & R. S. Tindale (Eds.), *Blackwell handbook of social psychology: Group processes* (pp. 425–60). Oxford, UK: Blackwell.

Abrams, D., & Hogg, M. A. (2004). Metatheory: Lessons from social identity research. *Personality and Social Psychology Review, 8,* 98–106.

Abrams, D., & Hogg, M. A. (Eds.) (1999). *Social identity and social cognition.* Oxford, UK: Blackwell.

Abrams, D., & Hogg, M. A. (in press). Social identity and self-categorization. In J. F. Dovidio, M. Hewstone, P. Glick & V. M. Esses (Eds.), *Handbook of prejudice, stereotyping, and discrimination.* London: SAGE.

Abrams, D., Wetherell, M. S., Cochrane, S., Hogg, M. A., & Turner, J. C. (1990). Knowing what to think by knowing who you are: Self-categorization and the nature of norm formation, conformity, and group polarization. *British Journal of Social Psychology, 29,* 97–119.

Abramson, L. Y., Seligman, M. E. P., & Teasdale, J. D. (1978). Learned helplessness in humans: Critique and reformulation. *Journal of Abnormal and Social Psychology, 87,* 49–74.

Abric, J. C., & Vacherot, C. (1976). The effects of representations of behaviour in experimental games. *European Journal of Social Psychology, 6,* 129–144.

Acorn, D. A., Hamilton, D. L., & Sherman, S. J. (1988). Generalization of biased perceptions of groups based on illusory correlations. *Social Cognition, 6,* 345–372.

Adair, J., Dushenko, T. W., & Lindsay, R. C. L. (1985). Ethical regulations and their impact on research practice. *American Psychologist, 40,* 59–72.

Adamopoulos, J., & Kashima, Y. (1999). *Social psychology and cultural context.* London: SAGE.

Adams, J. S. (1965). Inequity in social exchange. In L. Berkowitz (Ed.), *Advances in experimental social psychology* (Vol. 2, pp. 267–299). New York: Academic Press.

Adams, J. M., & Jones, W. H. (1997). The conceptualization of marital commitment: An integrative analysis. *Journal of Personality and Social Psychology, 11,* 1177–1196.

Adorno, T. W., Frenkel-Brunswik, E., Levinson, D. J., & Sanford, R. M. (1950). *The authoritarian personality.* New York: Harper.

Ahlstrom, W., & Havighurst, R. (1971). *400 losers: Delinquent boys in high school.* San Francisco, CA: Jossey-Bass.

Aiello, J. R., & Jones, S. E. (1971). Field study of the proxemic behavior of young children in three subcultural groups. *Journal of Personality and Social Psychology, 19,* 351–356.

Ajzen, I. (1989). Attitude structure and behavior. In A. R. Pratkanis, S. J. Breckler & A. G. Greenwald (Eds.), *Attitude structure and function* (pp. 241–274). Hillsdale, NJ: Erlbaum.

Ajzen, I. (1998). Models of human social behavior and their application to health psychology. *Psychology and Health, 13,* 735–739.

Ajzen, I. (2001). Nature and operation of attitudes. *Annual Review of Psychology, 52,* 27–58.

Ajzen, I. (2002). Residual effects of past on later behavior: Habituation and reasoned action perspectives. *Personality and Social Psychology Review, 6,* 107–122.

Ajzen, I., & Fishbein, M. (1980). *Understanding attitudes and predicting social behavior.* Englewood Cliffs, NJ: Prentice Hall.

Ajzen, I., & Fishbein, M. (2005). The influence of attitudes on behavior. In D. Albarracín, B. T. Johnson, & M. P. Zanna (Eds.), *The handbook of attitudes* (pp. 173–221). Mahwah, NJ: Erlbaum.

Ajzen, I., & Madden, T. J. (1986). Prediction of goal-directed behavior: Attitudes, intentions and perceived behavioral control. *Journal of Experimental Social Psychology, 22,* 453–474.

Albarracín, D., Cohen, J. B., & Kumkale, G. T. (2003). When communications collide with recipients' actions: Effects of post-message behavior on intentions to follow the message recommendation. *Personality and Social Psychology Bulletin, 29,* 834–845.

Albarracín, D., & Vargas, P. (2010). Attitudes and persuasion: From biology to social responses to persuasive intent. In S. T. Fiske, D. T. Gilbert, & G. Lindzey (Eds.), *Handbook of social psychology* (5th ed., Vol. 1, pp. 394-427). New York: Wiley.

Albion, M. S., & Faris, P. W. (1979). *Appraising research on advertising's economic impacts* (Report no. 79–115). Cambridge, MA: Marketing Science Institute.

Albright, L., Malloy, T. E., Dong, Q., Kenny, D. A., Fang, X., Winquist, L., et al. (1997). Cross-cultural consensus in personality judgments. *Journal of Personality and Social Psychology, 72,* 558–569.

Aldag, R. J., & Fuller, S. R. (1993). Beyond fiasco: A reappraisal of the groupthink phenomenon and a new model of group decision processes. *Psychological Bulletin, 113,* 533–552.

Alexander, C. N., Zucker, L. G., & Brody, C. L. (1970). Experimental expectations and autokinetic experiences: Consistency theories and judgmental convergence. *Sociometry, 33,* 108–122.

Allard, R., & Landry, R. (1994). Subjective ethnolinguistic vitality: A comparison of two measures. *International Journal of the Sociology of Language, 108,* 117–144.

Allen, M., Mabry, E., & McKelton, D. (1998). Impact of juror attitudes about the death penalty on juror evaluations of guilt and punishment. *Law and Human Behavior, 23,* 715–732.

Allen, N. J., & Hecht, T. D. (2004). The 'romance of teams': Towards an understanding of its psychological underpinnings and implications. *Journal of Occupational and Organizational Psychology, 77,* 439–461.

Allen, V. L. (1965). Situational factors in conformity. In L. Berkowitz (Ed.), *Advances in experimental social psychology* (Vol. 2, pp. 133–75). New York: Academic Press.

Allen, V. L. (1975). Social support for non-conformity. In L. Berkowitz (Ed.), *Advances in experimental social psychology* (Vol. 8, pp. 1–43). New York: Academic Press.

Allen, V. L., & Levine, J. M. (1971). Social support and conformity: The role of independent assessment of reality. *Journal of Experimental Social Psychology, 7,* 48–58.

Allen, V. L., & Wilder, D. A. (1975). Categorization, belief similarity, and group similarity. *Journal of Personality of Social Psychology, 32,* 971–977.

Allison, S. T., Mackie, D. M., & Messick, D. M. (1996). Outcome biases in social perception: Implications for dispositional inference, attitude change, stereotyping, and social behavior. In M. Zanna (Ed.), *Advances in experimental social psychology* (Vol. 28, pp. 53–93). New York: Academic Press.

Alloy, L. B., & Tabachnik, N. (1984). Assessment of covariation by humans and animals: The joint influence of prior expectations and current situational information. *Psychological Review, 91,* 112–149.

Allport, F. H. (1920). The influence of the group upon association and thought. *Journal of Experimental Psychology, 3,* 159–182.

Allport, F. H. (1924). *Social psychology*. Boston, MA: Houghton-Mifflin.

Allport, G. W. (1935). Attitudes. In C. M. Murchison (Ed.), *Handbook of social psychology* (pp. 789–844). Worcester, MA: Clark University Press.

Allport, G. W. (1954a/1968). The historical background of modern social psychology. In G. Lindzey (Ed.), *Handbook of social psychology* (Vol. 1, pp. 3–56). Reading, MA: Addison-Wesley.

Allport, G. W. (1954b). *The nature of prejudice*. Reading, MA: Addison-Wesley.

Allport, G. W., & Postman, L. J. (1945). Psychology of rumor. *Transactions of the New York Academy of Sciences, 8,* 61–81.

Allport, G. W., & Postman, L. J. (1947). *The psychology of rumor*. New York: Holt, Rinehart & Winston.

Allport, G. W., & Vernon, P. E. (1931). *A study of values*. Boston, MA: Houghton-Mifflin.

Allyn, J., & Festinger, L. (1961). The effectiveness of unanticipated persuasive communications. *Journal of Abnormal and Social Psychology, 62,* 35–40.

Altemeyer, B. (1981). *Right-wing authoritarianism*. Winnipeg, Canada: University of Manitoba Press.

Altemeyer, B. (1988). *Enemies of freedom: Understanding right-wing authoritarianism*. San Francisco, CA: Jossey-Bass.

Altemeyer, B. (1994). Reducing prejudice in right-wing authoritarians. In M. P. Zanna & J. M. Olsen (Eds.), *The psychology of prejudice: The Ontario symposium* (pp. 131–148). Hillsdale, NJ: Erlbaum.

Altemeyer, B. (1998). The other 'authoritarian personality'. In M. Zanna (Ed.), *Advances in experimental social psychology* (Vol. 30, pp. 47–92). Orlando, FL: Academic Press.

Altman, D. (1986). *AIDS and the new puritanism*. London and Sydney: Pluto Press.

Altman, I., & Taylor, D. A. (1973). *Social penetration: The development of interpersonal relationships*. New York: Holt, Rinehart & Winston.

Amato, P. R. (1983). Helping behavior in urban and rural environments: Field studies based on a taxonomic organisation of helping episodes. *Journal of Personality and Social Psychology, 45,* 571–586.

Ambady, N., & Weisbuch. M. (2010). Nonverbal behavior. In S. T. Fiske, D. T. Gilbert, & G. Lindzey (Eds.), *Handbook of social psychology* (5th ed., Vol. 1, pp. 464-497). New York: Wiley.

American Psychological Association (2002). Ethical principles of psychologists and code of conduct. *American Psychologist, 57(12).*

Ames, D. R., Flynn, F. J., & Weber, E. U. (2004). It's the thought that counts: On perceiving how helpers decide to lend a hand. *Personality and Social Psychology Bulletin, 30,* 461–474.

Amichai-Hamburger, Y., & McKenna, K. Y. A. (2006). The contact hypothesis reconsidered: Interacting via the Internet. *Journal of Computer-Mediated Communication, 11(3),* article 7. [http://jcmc.indiana.edu/vol11/issue3/amichai-hamburger.html]

Amir, Y. (1976). The role of intergroup contact in change of prejudice and ethnic relations. In P. A. Katz (Ed.), *Towards the elimination of racism* (pp. 245–308). Elmsford, NY: Pergamon Press.

Anderson, C. A., & Anderson, D. C. (1984). Ambient temperature and violent crime: Tests of the linear and curvilinear hypothesis. *Journal of Personality and Social Psychology, 46,* 91–97.

Anderson, C. A., Anderson, K. B., & Deuser, W. E. (1996). Examining an affective framework: Weapon and temperature effects on aggressive thoughts, affect, and attitudes. *Personality and Social Psychology Bulletin, 22,* 366–376.

Anderson, C. A., & Bushman, B. J. (1997). External validity of trivial experiments: The case of laboratory aggression. *Review of General Psychology, 1,* 19–41.

Anderson, C. A., & Bushman, B. J. (2002a). Human aggression. *Annual Review of Psychology, 53,* 27–51.

Anderson, C. A., & Bushman, B. J. (2002b). The effects of media violence on society. *Science, 295,* 2377–2378.

Anderson, C. A., Bushman, B. J., & Groom, R. W. (1997). Hot years and serious and deadly assault: Empirical tests of the heat hypothesis. *Journal of Personality and Social Psychology, 73,* 1213–1223.

Anderson, C. A., Carnagey, N. L., & Eubanks, J. (2003). Exposure to violent media: The effects of songs with violent lyrics on aggressive thoughts and feelings. *Journal of personality and social psychology, 84,* 960–971.

Anderson, C. A., & Godfrey, S. S. (1987). Thoughts about actions: The effects of specificity and availability of imagined behavioral scripts on expectations about oneself and others. *Social Cognition, 5,* 238–258.

Anderson, C. A., & Huesmann, L. R. (2003). Human aggression: A social-cognitive view. In M. A. Hogg & J. Cooper (Eds.), *The SAGE handbook of social psychology* (pp. 296–323). London: SAGE.

Anderson, C. A., & Huesmann, L. R. (2007). Human aggression: A social-cognitive view. In M. A. Hogg & J. Cooper (Eds.), *The SAGE handbook of social psychology: Concise student edition* (pp. 259-287). London: SAGE.

Anderson, C. A., & Slusher, M. P. (1986). Relocating motivational effects: A synthesis of cognitive and motivational effects on attributions for success and failure. *Social Cognition, 4,* 250–292.

Anderson, J., & McGuire, W. J. (1965). Prior reassurance of group consensus as a factor in producing resistance to persuasion. *Sociometry, 28,* 44–56.

Anderson, J. R. (1990). *Cognitive psychology and its implications* (3rd ed.). New York: Freeman.

Anderson, N. H. (1965). Adding versus averaging as a stimulus combination rule in impression formation. *Journal of Experimental Psychology, 70,* 394–400.

Anderson, N. H. (1971). Integration theory and attitude change. *Psychological Review, 78,* 171–206.

Anderson, N. H. (1978). Cognitive algebra: Integration theory applied to social attribution. In L. Berkowitz (Ed.), *Cognitive theories in social psychology* (pp. 1–126). New York: Academic Press.

Anderson, N. H. (1981). *Foundations of information integration theory.* New York: Academic Press.

Andreeva, G. (1984). Cognitive processes in developing groups. In L. H. Strickland (Ed.), *Directions in Soviet social psychology* (pp. 67–82). New York: Springer.

Antonakis, J., & House, R. J. (2003). An analysis of the full-range leadership theory: The way forward. In B. J. Avolio & F. J. Yammarino (Eds.), *Transformational and charismatic leadership: The road ahead* (pp. 3–33). New York: Elsevier.

Apfelbaum, E. (1974). On conflicts and bargaining. *Advances in Experimental Social Psychology, 7,* 103–156.

Apfelbaum, E., & Lubek, I. (1976). Resolution vs. revolution? The theory of conflicts in question. In L. Strickland, F. Aboud & K. J. Gergen (Eds.), *Social psychology in transition* (pp. 71–94). New York: Plenum.

Apfelbaum, E., & McGuire, G. R. (1986). Models of suggestive influence and the disqualification of the social crowd. In C. F. Graumann & S. Moscovici (Eds.), *Changing conceptions of crowd mind and behavior* (pp. 27–50). New York: Springer.

Archer, D. (1997). Unspoken diversity: Cultural differences in gestures. *Qualitative Sociology, 20,* 79–105.

Archer, D., Iritani, B., Kimes, D. D., & Barrios, M. (1983). Face-ism: Five studies of sex differences in facial prominence. *Journal of Personality and Social Psychology, 45,* 725–735.

Archer, J. (2000). Sex differences in aggression between heterosexual partners: A meta-analytic review. *Psychological Bulletin, 126,* 697–702.

Archer, J. (2004). Sex differences in aggression in real-world settings: A meta-analytic review. *Review of General Psychology, 8,* 291–322.

Archer, J., & Coyne, S. M. (2005). An integrated review of indirect, relational, and social aggression. *Personality and Social Psychology Review, 9,* 212–230.

Ardrey, R. (1961). *African genesis.* New York: Delta Books.

Ardrey, R. (1966). *The territorial imperative.* New York: Atheneum.

Arendt, H. (1963). *Eichmann in Jerusalem: A report on the banality of evil.* New York: Viking.

Argote, L., Insko, C. A., Yovetich, N., & Romero, A. A. (1995). Group learning curves: The effects of turnover and task complexity on group performance. *Journal of Applied Social Psychology, 25,* 512–529.

Argyle, M. (1971). *The psychology of interpersonal behaviour.* Harmondsworth, UK: Penguin.

Argyle, M. (1975). *Bodily communication*. London: Methuen.

Argyle, M. (1980). The development of applied social psychology. In R. Gilmour & S. Duck (Eds.), *The development of social psychology*. New York: Academic Press.

Argyle, M., & Dean, J. (1965). Eye-contact, distance and affiliation. *Sociometry, 28,* 289–304.

Argyle, M., & Ingham, R. (1972). Gaze, mutual gaze, and proximity. *Semiotica, 6,* 32–49.

Aries, E. (1996). *Men and women in interaction: Considering the differences.* New York: Oxford University Press.

Aries, E. (1997). Women and men talking: Are they worlds apart? In W. R. Walsh (Ed.), *Women, men and gender: Ongoing debates* (pp. 79–100). New Haven, CT: Yale University Press.

Arkes, H. R., Boehm, L. E., & Xu, G. (1991). Determinants of judged validity. *Journal of Experimental Social Psychology, 27,* 576–605.

Armitage, C. J., & Conner, M., (2001). Efficacy of the theory of planned behavior: A meta-analytic review. *British Journal of Social Psychology, 40,* 471–499.

Aron, A., Paris, M., & Aron, E. N. (1995). Falling in love: Prospective studies of self-concept change. *Journal of Personality and Social Psychology, 69,* 1102–1112.

Aron, A., & Westbay, L. (1996). Dimensions of the prototype of love. *Journal of Personality and Social Psychology, 70,* 535–551.

Aronson, E. (1984). *The social animal* (4th ed.). New York: Freeman.

Aronson, E. (1999). Dissonance, hypocrisy, and the self-concept. In E. Harmon-Jones & J. Mills (Eds.), *Cognitive dissonance: Progress on a pivotal theory in social psychology* (pp. 103–126). Washington, DC: American Psychological Association.

Aronson, E., Ellsworth, P. C., Carlsmith, J. M., & Gonzales, M. H. (1990). *Methods of research in social psychology* (2nd ed.). New York: McGraw-Hill.

Aronson, E., & Mills, J. (1959). The effects of severity of initiation on liking for a group. *Journal of Abnormal and Social Psychology, 59,* 177–181.

Arriaga, X. B., & Agnew, C. R. (2001). Being committed: Affective, cognitive, and conative components of relationship commitment. *Personality and Social Psychology Bulletin, 27,* 1190–1203.

Arrow, H., Berdahl, J. L., Bouas, K. S., Craig, K. M., Cummings, A., Lebie, L., McGrath, J. E., O'Connor, K. M., Rhoades, J. A., & Schlosser, A. (1996). Time, technology, and groups: An integration. *Computer Supported Cooperative Work, 4,* 253–261.

Arrow, H., McGrath, J. E., & Berdahl, J. L. (2000). *Small groups as complex systems: Formation, coordination, development, and adaptation.* Thousand Oaks, CA: SAGE.

Asch, S. E. (1946). Forming impressions of personality. *Journal of Abnormal and Social Psychology, 41,* 258–290.

Asch, S. E. (1951). Effects of group pressure upon the modification and distortion of judgements. In H. Guetzkow (Ed.), *Groups, leadership and men* (pp. 177–190). Pittsburgh, PA: Carnegie Press.

Asch, S. E. (1952). *Social psychology*. Englewood Cliffs, NJ: Prentice Hall.

Asch, S. E. (1956). Studies of independence and conformity: A minority of one against a unanimous majority. *Psychological Monographs: General and Applied, 70,* 1–70 (whole no. 416).

Aschenbrenner, K. M., & Schaefer, R. E. (1980). Minimal group situations: Comments on a mathematical model and on the research paradigm. *European Journal of Social Psychology, 10,* 389–398.

Ashburn-Nardo, L., Voils, C. I., & Monteith, M. J. (2001). Implicit associations as the seeds of intergroup bias: How easily do they take root? *Journal of Personality and Social Psychology, 81,* 789–799.

Ashmore, R. D. (1981). Sex stereotypes and implicit personality theory. In D. L. Hamilton (Ed.), *Cognitive processes in stereotyping and intergroup behavior* (pp. 37–81). Hillsdale, NJ: Erlbaum.

Ashmore, R. D., & Jussim, L. (1997). Towards a second century of the scientific analysis of self and identity. In R. Ashmore & L. Jussim (Eds.), *Self and identity: Fundamental issues* (pp. 3–19). New York: Oxford University Press.

Assael, H. (1981). *Consumer behavior and marketing action.* Boston, MA: Kent.

Atkin, C. K. (1977). Effects of campaign advertising and newscasts on children. *Journalism Quarterly, 54,* 503–558.

Atkin, C. K. (1980). *Effects of the mass media.* New York: McGraw-Hill.

Attridge, M., & Berscheid, E. (1994). Entitlement in romantic relationships in the United States: A social exchange perspective. In M. J. Lerner and G. Mikula (Eds.), *Entitlement and the affectional bond: Justice in close relationships* (pp. 117–148). New York: Plenum.

Augoustinos, M., & Innes, J. M. (1990). Towards an integration of social representations and social schema theory. *British Journal of Social Psychology, 29,* 213–231.

Austin, J. L. (1962). *How to do things with words.* Oxford, UK: Clarendon Press.

Austin, W. (1979). Sex differences in bystander intervention in a theft. *Journal of Personality and Social Psychology, 37,* 2110–20.

Avolio, B. J. (1999). *Full leadership development: Building the vital forces in organizations.* Thousand Oaks, CA: SAGE.

Avolio, B. J., & Bass, B. M. (1987). Transformational leadership, charisma and beyond. In J. G. Hunt, B. R. Balaga, H. P. Dachler & C. A. Schriesheim (Eds.), *Emerging leadership vistas* (pp. 29–50). Elmsford, NY: Pergamon Press.

Avolio, B. J., & Yammarino, F. J. (Eds.) (2003). *Transformational and charismatic leadership: The road ahead.* New York: Elsevier.

Axelrod, R., & Dion, D. (1988). The further evolution of cooperation. *Science, 242,* 1385–1390.

Azar, B. (1997). Forgiveness helps keep relationships steadfast. *APA Monitor,* November 14.

Bailey, D. S., & Taylor, S. P. (1991). Effects of alcohol and aggressive disposition on human physical aggression. *Journal of Research in Personality, 25,* 334–342.

Bain, P. G., Kashima, Y., & Haslam, N. (2006) Conceptual beliefs about human values and their implications: Human nature beliefs predict value importance, value trade-offs, and responses to value-laden rhetoric. *Journal of Personality and Social Psychology, 91*, 351–367.

Bains, G. (1983). Explanations and the need for control. In M. Hewstone (Ed.), *Attribution theory: Social and functional extensions* (pp. 126–143). Oxford, UK: Blackwell.

Bakan, D. (1966). *The duality of human existence.* Chicago: Rand McNally.

Baker, P. M. (1985). The status of age: Preliminary result. *Journal of Gerontology, 40*, 506–508.

Baldwin, J. M. (1897/1901). *Social and ethical interpretations in mental development.* New York: Macmillan.

Bales, R. F. (1950). *Interaction process analysis: A method for the study of small groups.* Reading, MA: Addison-Wesley.

Banaji, M. R., & Heiphetz, L. (2010). Attitudes. In S. T. Fiske, D. T. Gilbert, & G. Lindzey (Eds.), *Handbook of social psychology* (5th ed., Vol. 1, pp. 353-393). New York: Wiley.

Bandura, A. (1973). *Aggression: A social learning analysis.* Englewood Cliffs, NJ: Prentice Hall.

Bandura, A. (1977). *Social learning theory.* Englewood Cliffs, NJ: Prentice Hall.

Bandura, A. (1986). *Social foundations of thought and action: A social cognitive theory.* Englewood Cliffs, NJ: Prentice Hall.

Bandura, A. (1992). Exercise of personal agency through the self-efficacy mechanism. In R. Schwarzer (Ed.), *Self-efficacy: Thought control of action* (pp. 3–38). Washington: Hemisphere Press.

Bandura, A., Ross, D., & Ross, S. A. (1963). Imitation of film-mediated aggressive models. *Journal of Abnormal and Social Psychology, 66*, 3–11.

Bandura, A., & Walters, R. H. (1963). *Social learning and personality development.* New York: Holt, Rinehart & Winston.

Banks, W. C. (1976). White preference in Blacks: A paradigm in search of a phenomenon. *Psychological Bulletin, 83*, 1179–1186.

Banuazizi, A., & Movahedi, S. (1975). Interpersonal dynamics in a simulated prison: A methodological analysis. *American Psychologist, 30*, 152–160.

Bardi, A., & Schwartz, S. H. (2003). Values and behavior: Strength and structure of relations. *Personality and Social Psychology Bulletin, 29*, 1207–1220.

Bargh, J. A. (1984). Automatic and conscious processing of social information. In R. S. Wyer, Jr, & T. K. Srull (Eds.), *Handbook of social cognition* (Vol. 3, pp. 1–44). Hillsdale, NJ: Erlbaum.

Bargh, J. A. (1989). Conditional automaticity: Varieties of automatic influence in social perception and cognition. In J. S. Uleman & J. A. Bargh (Eds.), *Unintended thought* (pp. 3–51). New York: Guilford Press.

Bargh, J. A., Chaiken, S., Govender, R., & Pratto, F. (1992). The generality of the automatic attitude activation effect. *Journal of Personality and Social Psychology, 62*, 893–912.

Bargh, J. A., Lombardi, W. J., & Higgins, E. T. (1988). Automaticity of chronically accessible constructs in person X situation effects on person perception: It's just a matter of time. *Journal of Personality and Social Psychology, 55*, 599–605.

Bargh, J. A., & McKenna, K. Y. A. (2004). The internet and social life. *Annual Review of Psychology, 55*, 573–590.

Bargh, J. A., & Pratto, F. (1986). Individual construct accessibility and perceptual selection. *Journal of Experimental Social Psychology, 22*, 293–311.

Bargh, J. A., & Tota, M. E. (1988). Context-dependent automatic processing in depression: Accessibility of negative constructs with regard to self but not others. *Journal of Personality and Social Psychology, 54*, 925–939.

Bar-Hillel, M. (1980). The base-rate fallacy in probability judgements. *Acta Psychologica, 44*, 211–233.

Barjonet, P. E. (1980). L'influence sociale et des représentations des causes de l'accident de la route. *Le Travail Humain, 43*, 243–253.

Barocas, R., & Gorlow, L. (1967). Self-report personality measurement and conformity behaviour. *Journal of Social Psychology, 71*, 227–234.

Baron, R. A. (1977). *Human aggression.* New York: Plenum.

Baron, R. A. (1979). Aggression, empathy, and race: Effects of victim's pain cues, victim's race, and level of instigation on physical aggression. *Journal of Applied Social Psychology, 9*, 103–114.

Baron, R. A. (1989). Personality and organisational conflict: The type A behavior pattern and self-monitoring. *Organisational Behavior and Human Decision Processes, 44*, 281–297.

Baron, R. A., & Bell, P. (1977). Sexual arousal and aggression by males: Effects of types of erotic stimuli and prior provocation. *Journal of Personality and Social Psychology, 35*, 79–87.

Baron, R. A., & Byrne, D. (1987). *Social psychology: Understanding human interaction* (5th ed.). Boston, MA: Allyn & Bacon.

Baron, R. A., & Byrne, D. (1994). *Social psychology: Understanding human interaction* (7th ed.). Boston, MA: Allyn & Bacon.

Baron, R. A., & Byrne, D. (2000). *Social psychology: Understanding human interaction* (9th ed.). Boston, MA: Allyn & Bacon.

Baron, R. A., & Ransberger, V. M. (1978). Ambient temperature and the occurrence of collective violence: The 'long hot summer' revisited. *Journal of Personality and Social Psychology, 36*, 351–360.

Baron, R. S. (1986). Distraction–conflict theory: Progress and problems. In L. Berkowitz (Ed.), *Advances in experimental social psychology* (Vol. 20, pp. 1–40). New York: Academic Press.

Baron, R. S., & Kerr, N. (2003). *Group process, group decision, group action* (2nd ed.). Buckingham, UK: Open University Press.

Baron, R. S., & Roper, G. (1976). Reaffirmation of social comparison views of choice shifts: Averaging and extremity effects in an autokinetic situation. *Journal of Personality and Social Psychology, 33*, 521–530.

Barrett, M., & Short, J. (1992). Images of European people in a group of 5–10-year-old English school children. *British Journal of Developmental Psychology, 10,* 339–363.

Barrick, M. R., Day, D. V., Lord, R. G., & Alexander, R. A. (1991). Assessing the utility of executive leadership. *The Leadership Quarterly, 2,* 9–22.

Barron, F. (1953). Some personality correlates of independence of judgment. *Journal of Personality, 21,* 287–297.

Bar-Tal, D. (1976). *Prosocial behavior: Theory and research.* Washington: Hemisphere Press.

Bartholow, B. D., Pearson, M. A., Gratton, G., & Fabiani, M. (2003). Effects of alcohol on person perception: A social cognitive neuroscience approach. *Journal of Personality and Social Psychology, 85,* 627–638.

Bartlett, F. C. (1923). *Psychology and primitive culture.* Cambridge, UK: Cambridge University Press.

Bartlett, F. C. (1932). *Remembering: A study in experiential and social psychology.* Cambridge, UK: Cambridge University Press.

Bartol, K. M., & Butterfield, D. A. (1976). Sex effects in evaluating leaders. *Journal of Applied Psychology, 61,* 446–454.

Bartsch, R. A., & Judd, C. M. (1993). Majority–minority status and perceived ingroup variability revisited. *European Journal of Social Psychology, 23,* 471–483.

Bass, B. M. (1985). *Leadership and performance beyond expectations.* New York: Free Press.

Bass, B. M., & Avolio, B. J. (1990). *Transformational leadership development: Manual for the Multifactor Leadership Questionnaire.* Palo Alto, CA: Consulting Psychologists Press.

Batson, C. D. (1983). Sociobiology and the role of religion in promoting prosocial behavior: An alternative view. *Journal of Personality and Social Psychology, 45,* 1380–1385.

Batson, C. D. (1991). *The altruism question: Toward a social-psychological answer.* Hillsdale, NJ: Lawrence Erlbaum.

Batson, C. D. (1994). Why act for the public good? Four answers. *Personality and Social Psychology Bulletin, 20,* 603–610.

Batson, C. D. (1998). Altruism and prosocial behaviour. In D. T. Gilbert, S. T. Fiske & G. Lindzey (Eds.), *The handbook of social psychology* (4th ed., Vol. 2, pp. 282–316). New York: McGraw-Hill.

Batson, C. D., Ahmad, N., & Tsang, J. A. (2002). Four motives for community involvement. *Journal of Social Issues, 58,* 429–445.

Batson, C. D., Charng, J., Orr, R., & Rowland, J. (2002). Empathy, attitudes, and action: Can feeling for a member of a stigmatized group motivate one to help the group? *Personality and Social Psychology Bulletin, 28,* 1656–1666.

Batson, C. D., & Coke, J. S. (1981). Empathy: A source of altruistic motivation for helping? In J. P. Rushton & R. M. Sorrentino (Eds.), *Altruism and helping behavior: Social, personality, and developmental perspectives* (pp. 167–183). Hillsdale, NJ: Erlbaum.

Batson, C. D., Duncan, B., Ackerman, P., Buckley, T., & Birch, K. (1981). Is empathic emotion a source of altruistic motivation? *Journal of Personality and Social Psychology, 40,* 290–302.

Batson, C. D., Early, S., & Salvarani, G. (1997). Perspective taking: Imagining how another feels versus imagining how you would feel. *Personality and Social Psychology Bulletin, 23,* 751–758.

Batson, C. D., & Oleson, K. C. (1991). Current status of the empathy–altruism hypothesis. In M. S. Clark (Ed.), *Prosocial behaviour* (pp. 62–85). Newbury Park, CA: SAGE.

Batson, C. D., Schoenrade, P., & Ventis, W. L. (1993). *Religion and the individual: A social-psychological perspective.* New York: Oxford University Press.

Batson, C. D., Sympson, S. C., Hindman, J. L., Decruz, P., Todd, R. M., Weeks, J. L., Jennings, G., & Burris, C. T. (1996). 'I've been there, too': Effect on empathy of prior experience with a need. *Personality and Social Psychology Bulletin, 22,* 474–482.

Batson, C. D., Van Lange, P. A. M., Ahmad, N., & Lishner, D. A. (2003). Altruism and helping behavior. In M. A. Hogg & J. Cooper (Eds.), *The SAGE handbook of social psychology* (pp. 279–295). London: SAGE.

Battisch, V. A., Assor, A., Messé, L. A., & Aronoff, J. (1985). Personality and person perception. In P. Shaver (Ed.), *Review of personality and social psychology* (Vol. 6, pp. 185–208). Beverly Hills, CA: SAGE.

Baumeister, R. F. (1987). How the self became a problem: A psychological review of historical research. *Journal of Personality and Social Psychology, 52,* 163–176.

Baumeister, R. F. (1989). The optimal margin of illusion. *Journal of Social and Clinical Psychology, 8,* 176–189.

Baumeister, R. F. (1991). *Escaping the self: Alcoholism, spirituality, masochism, and other flights from the burden of selfhood.* New York: Basic Books.

Baumeister, R. F. (1998). The self. In D. T. Gilbert, S. T. Fiske & G. Lindzey (Eds.), *Handbook of social psychology* (4th ed., Vol. 1, pp. 680–740). New York: McGraw-Hill.

Baumeister, R. F., & Covington, M. V. (1985). Self-esteem, persuasion, and retrospective distortion of initial attitudes. *Electronic Social Psychology, 1,* 1–22.

Baumeister, R. F., Chesner, S. P., Senders, P. S., & Tice, D. M. (1988). Who's in charge here? Group leaders do lend help in emergencies. *Personality and Social Psychology Bulletin, 14,* 17–22.

Baumeister, R. F., Dale, K., & Sommer, K. L. (1998). Freudian defense mechanisms and empirical findings in modern social psychology: Reaction formation, projection, displacement, undoing, isolation, sublimation, and denial. *Journal of Personality, 66,* 1081–1124.

Baumeister, R. F., & Darley, J. M. (1982). Reducing the biasing effect of perpetrator attractiveness in jury simulation. *Personality and Social Psychology Bulletin, 8,* 286–292.

Baumeister, R. F., & Leary, M. R. (1995). The need to belong: Desire for interpersonal attachments as a fundamental human motivation. *Psychological Bulletin, 117,* 497–529.

Baumeister, R. F., Smart, L., & Boden, J. M. (1996). Relation of threatened egotism to violence and aggression: The dark side of high self-esteem. *Psychological Review, 103,* 5–33.

Baumeister, R. F., & Sommer, K. L. (1997). What do men want? Gender differences and two spheres of belongingness: Comment on Cross and Madson. *Psychological Bulletin, 122,* 38–44.

Baumeister, R. F., Tice, D. M., & Hutton, D. G. (1989). Self-presentational motivations and personality differences in self-esteem. *Journal of Personality, 57,* 547–579.

Baumeister, R. F., & Vohs, K. D. (Eds.) (2007). *Encyclopedia of social psychology.* Thousand Oaks, CA: SAGE.

Baumgarten-Tramer, F. (1948). German psychologists and recent events. *Journal of Abnormal and Social Psychology, 43,* 452–465.

Baumrind, D. (1964). Some thoughts on ethics of research: After reading Milgram's 'Behavioral study of obedience'. *American Psychologist, 19,* 421–443.

Baumrind, D. (1985). Research using intentional deception: Ethical issues revisited. *American Psychologist, 40,* 165–174.

Bavelas, A. (1968). Communications patterns in task-oriented groups. In D. Cartwright & A. Zander (Eds.), *Group dynamics: Research and theory* (3rd ed., pp. 503–511). London: Tavistock.

Baxter, T. L., & Goldberg, L. R. (1988). Perceived behavioral consistency underlying trait attributions to oneself and another: An extension of the actor–observer effect. *Personality and Social Psychology Bulletin, 13,* 437–447.

Beattie, A. E., & Mitchell, A. A. (1985). The relationship between advertising recall and persuasion: An experimental investigation. In L. F. Alwitt & A. A. Mitchell (Eds.), *Psychological processes and advertising effects: Theory, research and applications.* Hillsdale, NJ: Erlbaum.

Beauvois, J. L., & Dubois, N. (1988). The norm of internality in the explanation of psychological events. *European Journal of Social Psychology, 18,* 299–316.

Beauvois, J. L., & Joule, R. V. (1996). *A radical dissonance theory.* London: Taylor & Francis.

Beck, L., & Ajzen, I. (1991). Predicting dishonest actions using the theory of planned behavior. *Journal of Research in Personality, 25,* 285–301.

Belanger, S., & Pinard, M. (1991). Ethnic movements and the competition model: Some missing links. *American Sociological Review, 56,* 446–457.

Belch, G. E., & Belch, M. A. (2007). *Advertising and promotion: An integrated marketing communications perspective* (7th ed.). New York: McGraw-Hill/Irwin.

Bell, L. G., Wicklund, R. A., Manko, G., & Larkin, C. (1976). When unexpected behavior is attributed to the environment. *Journal of Research in Personality, 10,* 316–327.

Belsky, J. (1993). Etiology of child maltreatment: A developmental–ecological analysis. *Psychological Bulletin, 114,* 413–434.

Bem, D. J. (1967). Self perception: An alternative interpretation of cognitive dissonance. *Psychological Review, 74,* 183–200.

Bem, D. J. (1972). Self-perception theory. In L. Berkowitz (Ed.), *Advances in experimental social psychology* (Vol. 6, pp. 1–62). New York: Academic Press.

Bem, D. J., & Allen, A. A. (1974). On predicting some of the people some of the time: The search for cross-situational consistencies in behavior. *Psychological Review, 81,* 506–520.

Bem, D. J., & McConnell, H. K. (1970). Testing the self-perception explanation of dissonance phenomena: On the salience of premanipulation attitudes. *Journal of Personality and Social Psychology, 14,* 23–31.

Bem, S. L. (1981). Gender schema theory: A cognitive account of sex typing. *Psychological Review, 88,* 354–364.

Benedict, R. (1934). *Patterns of culture.* Boston, MA: Houghton Mifflin.

Bennett, E. B. (1955). Discussion, decision, commitment and consensus in group decision. *Human Relations, 8,* 25–73.

Bennett, M., & Sani, F. (Eds.) (2004). *The development of the social self.* New York: Psychology Press.

Benson, P. L., Karabenick, S. A., & Lerner, R. M. (1976). Pretty pleases: The effects of physical attractiveness, race, and sex on receiving help. *Journal of Experimental Social Psychology, 12,* 409–415.

Benton, A. A., & Druckman, D. (1974). Constituent's bargaining orientation and intergroup negotiations. *Journal of Applied Social Psychology, 4,* 141–150.

Berger, J., Fisek, M. H., Norman, R. Z., & Zelditch, M. Jr. (1977). *Status characteristics and social interaction.* New York: Elsevier.

Berger, J., Wagner, D., & Zelditch, M. Jr. (1985). Expectation states theory: Review and assessment. In J. Berger & M. Zelditch Jr (Eds.), *Status, rewards and influence* (pp. 1–72). San Francisco, CA: Jossey–Bass.

Berglas, S. (1987). The self-handicapping model of alcohol abuse. In H. T. Blane and K. E. Leonard (Eds.), *Psychological theories of drinking and alcoholism* (pp. 305–345). New York: Guilford Press.

Berglas, S., & Jones, E. E. (1978). Drug choice as a self-handicapping strategy in response to noncontingent success. *Journal of Personality and Social Psychology, 36,* 405–417.

Berkowitz, L. (1962). *Aggression: A social psychological analysis.* New York: McGraw-Hill.

Berkowitz, L. (1970). The self, selfishness and altruism. In J. Macaulay & L. Berkowitz (Eds.), *Altruism and helping behaviour.* New York: Academic Press.

Berkowitz, L. (1972a). Frustrations, comparisons, and other sources of emotion arousal as contributors to social unrest. *Journal of Social Issues, 28,* 77–91.

Berkowitz, L. (1972b). Social norms, feelings, and other factors affecting helping and altruism. In L. Berkowitz (Ed.), *Advances in experimental social psychology* (Vol. 6, pp. 63–108). New York: Academic Press.

Berkowitz, L. (1974). Some determinants of impulsive aggression: Role of mediated associations with reinforcements for aggression. *Psychological Review, 81,* 165–176.

Berkowitz, L. (1978). Decreased helpfulness with increased group size through lessening the effects of the needy individual's dependency. *Journal of Personality, 46,* 299–310.

Berkowitz, L. (1984). Some effects of thoughts on anti- and pro-social influences of media events: A cognitive-neo-association analysis. *Psychological Bulletin, 95,* 410–27.

Berkowitz, L. (1993). *Aggression: Its causes, consequences and control.* Philadelphia, PA: Temple University Press.

Berkowitz, L., & LePage, A. (1967). Weapons as aggression-eliciting stimuli. *Journal of Personality and Social Psychology, 7,* 202–207.

Berman, M., Gladue, B., & Taylor, S. (1993). The effects of hormones, type A behavior pattern, and provocation on aggression in men. *Motivation and Emotion, 17,* 125–138.

Bernard, M. M., Maio, G. R., & Olson, J. M. (2003). The vulnerability of values to attack: Inoculation of values and value-relevant attitudes. *Personality and Social Psychology Bulletin, 29,* 63–75.

Bernbach, W. (2002). *Bill Bernbach said.* New York: DDB Needham Worldwide.

Berry, J. W. (1967). Independence and conformity in subsistence level societies. *Journal of Personality and Social Psychology, 7,* 415–418.

Berry, J. W. (1984). Multicultural policy in Canada: A social psychological analysis. *Canadian Journal of Behavioural Science, 16,* 353–370.

Berry, J. W., Dasen, P. R., & Saraswathi, T. S. (Eds.) (1997). *Handbook of cross-cultural psychology, Vol. 2: Basic processes and human development* (2nd ed.). Needham Heights, MA: Allyn & Bacon.

Berry, J. W., Kim, U., Minde, T., & Mok, D. (1987). Comparative studies of acculturative stress. *International Migration Review, 21,* 491–511.

Berry, J. W., Poortinga, Y. P., & Pandey, J. (Eds.) (1997). *Handbook of cross-cultural psychology, Vol. 1: Theory and method (2nd ed.).* Needham Heights, MA: Allyn & Bacon.

Berry, J. W., Trimble, J. E., & Olmedo, E. L. (1986). Assessment of acculturation. In W. J. Lonner & J. W. Berry (Eds.), *Field methods in cross-cultural research* (pp. 290–327). Beverly Hills, CA: SAGE.

Berscheid, E. (1994). Interpersonal relationships. *Annual Review of Psychology, 45,* 79–129.

Berscheid, E., & Ammazzalorso, H. (2001). Emotional experience in close relationships. In G. J. O. Fletcher & M. Clark (Eds.), *Blackwell handbook of social psychology: Interpersonal processes* (pp. 253–278). Oxford, UK: Blackwell Publishers.

Berscheid, E., Graziano, W., Monson, T., & Dermer, M. (1976). Outcome dependency: Attention, attribution, and attraction. *Journal of Personality and Social Psychology, 34,* 978–989.

Berscheid, E., & Reis, H. T. (1998). Attraction and close relationships. In D. T. Gilbert, S. T. Fiske & G. Lindzey (Eds.), *The handbook of social psychology* (4th ed., Vol. 2, pp. 193–281). New York: McGraw-Hill.

Bettleheim, B. (1969). *The children of the dream.* London: Thames and Hudson.

Bickman, L., & Green, S. K. (1977). Situational cues and crime reporting: Do signs make a difference? *Journal of Applied Social Psychology, 7,* 1–8.

Bickman, L., & Rosenbaum, D. P. (1977). Crime reporting as a function of bystander encouragement, surveillance, and credibility. *Journal of Personality and Social Psychology, 35,* 577–586.

Biener, L., & Abrams, D. (1991). The contemplation ladder: Validation of a measure of readiness to consider smoking cessation. *Health Psychology, 10,* 360–365.

Bierhoff, H.-W., & Rohmann, E. (2004). Altruistic personality in the context of the empathy–altruism hypothesis. *European Journal of Personality, 18,* 351–365.

Billig, M. (1973). Normative communication in a minimal inter-group situation. *European Journal of Social Psychology, 3,* 339–343.

Billig, M. (1976). *Social psychology and intergroup relations.* London: Academic Press.

Billig, M. (1978). *Fascists: A social psychological view of the National Front.* London: Harcourt Brace Jovanovich.

Billig, M. (1987). *Arguing and thinking: A rhetorical approach to social psychology.* Cambridge, UK: Cambridge University Press.

Billig, M. (1991). *Ideology and opinions: Studies in rhetorical psychology.* London: SAGE.

Billig, M. (1996). *Arguing and thinking: A rhetorical approach to social psychology.* Cambridge, UK: Cambridge University Press.

Billig, M., & Cochrane, R. (1979). Values of political extremists and potential extremists: A discriminant analysis. *European Journal of Social Psychology, 9,* 205–222.

Billig, M., & Tajfel, H. (1973). Social categorisation and similarity in intergroup behaviour. *European Journal of Social Psychology, 3,* 27–52.

Bilous, F. R., & Krauss, R. M. (1988). Dominance and accommodation in the conversational behaviours of same- and mixed-gender dyads. *Language and Communication, 8,* 183–194.

Birdwhistell, R. (1970). *Kinesics and context: Essays on body movement communication.* Philadelphia, PA: University of Pennsylvania Press.

Birnbaum, G. E., Reis, H. T., Mikulincer, M., Gillath, O., & Orpaz, A. (2006). When sex is more than just sex: Attachment orientations, sexual experience, and relationship quality. *Journal of Personality and Social Psychology, 91,* 929–943.

Björkvist, K., Lagerspetz, K. M. J., & Kaukiainen, A. (1992). Do girls manipulate and boys fight? Developmental trends in regard to direct and indirect aggression. *Aggressive Behavior, 18,* 117–127.

Black, S. L., & Bevan, S. (1992). At the movies with Buss and Durkee: A natural experiment on film violence. *Aggressive Behavior, 18,* 37–45.

Blake, R. R., & Mouton, J. S. (1961). Reactions to intergroup competition under win/lose conditions. *Management Science, 7,* 420–435.

Blake, R. R., Shepard, H. A., & Mouton, J. S. (1964). *Managing intergroup conflict in industry.* Texas: Gulf Publishing.

Blankenship, K. L., & Holtgraves, T. (2005). The role of different markers of linguistic powerlessness in persuasion. *Journal of Language and Social Psychology, 24,* 3–24.

Blascovich, J. (2008). Challenge and threat. In A. J. Elliot (Ed.), *Handbook of approach and avoidance motivation* (pp. 431-446). New York: Erlbaum.

Blascovich, J., & Seery, M. D. (2007). Visceral and somatic indexes of social psychological constructs. In A. W. Kruglanski & E. T. Higgins (Eds.), *Social psychology: Handbook of basic principles* (2nd ed., pp. 19-38). New York: Guilford Press.

Blascovich, J., & Tomaka, J. (1996). The biopsychosocial model of arousal regulation. In M. Zanna (Ed.), *Advances in experimental social psychology* (Vol. 28, pp. 1-51). New York: Academic Press.

Blass, T. (2004). *The man who shocked the world: The life and legacy of Stanley Milgram*. New York: Basic Books.

Bloom, L. (1970). *Language development: Form and function in emerging grammars*. Cambridge, MA: MIT Press.

Bluic, A. M., McGarty, C., Reynolds, K., & Muntele, D. (2007). Opinion-based group membership as a predictor of commitment to political action. *European Journal of Social Psychology, 37,* 19-32

Blumenthal, M. D., Kahn, R. L., Andrews, F. M., & Head, K. B. (1972). *Justifying violence: Attitudes of American men*. Ann Arbor, MI: Institute for Social Research.

Blumer, H. (1969). *Symbolic interactionism: Perspective and method*. Englewood Cliffs, NJ: Prentice Hall.

Boas, F. (1911). *The mind of primitive man*. New York: Macmillan.

Boas, F. (1930). Anthropology. *Encyclopedia of the Social Sciences, 2,* 73–110.

Bochner, S. (1982). The social psychology of cross-cultural relations. In S. Bochner (Ed.), *Cultures in contact: Studies in cross-cultural interaction* (pp. *****). Oxford, UK: Pergamon Press.

Bochner, S., & Insko, C. A. (1966). Communicator discrepancy, source credibility, and opinion change. *Journal of Personality and Social Psychology, 4,* 614–621.

Bodenhausen, G. V., & Lichtenstein, M. (1987). Social stereotypes and information-processing strategies: The impact of task complexity. *Journal of Personality and Social Psychology, 52,* 871–880.

Bogardus, E. S. (1925). Measuring social distances. *Journal of Applied Sociology, 9,* 299–308.

Bohner, G., Bless, H., Schwarz, N., & Strack, F. (1988). What triggers causal attributions? The impact of valence and subjective probability. *European Journal of Social Psychology, 18,* 335–345.

Bohner, G., Chaiken, S., & Hunyadi, P. (1994). The role of mood and message ambiguity in the interplay of heuristic and systematic processing. Special issue: Affect in social judgments and cognition. *European Journal of Social Psychology, 24,* 207–221.

Bohner, G., Moskowitz, G. B., & Chaiken, S. (1995). The interplay of heuristic and systematic processing of social information. *European Review of Social Psychology, 6,* 33–68.

Bond, C. F., Jr. (1982). Social facilitation: A self-presentational view. *Journal of Personality and Social Psychology, 42,* 1042–1050.

Bond, C. F., & DePaulo, B. M. (2006). Accuracy of deception judgments. *Personality and Social Psychology Review, 10,* 214–234.

Bond, C. F., Jr., & Titus, L. J. (1983). Social facilitation: A meta-analysis of 241 studies. *Psychological Bulletin, 94,* 265–292.

Bond, M. H. (1996). Chinese values. In M. H. Bond (Ed.), *The handbook of Chinese psychology* (pp. 208–27). Hong Kong: Oxford University Press.

Bond, M. H. (2003). Marrying the dragon to the phoenix: Twenty-eight years of doing a psychology of the Chinese people. *Journal of Psychology in Chinese Societies, 4,* 269–283.

Bond, M. H. (2004). Culture and aggression: From context to coercion. *Personality and Social Psychology Review, 8,* 62–78.

Bond, M. H. (Ed.) (1988). *The cross-cultural challenge to social psychology*. Newbury Park, CA: SAGE.

Bond, M. H., & King, A. Y. C. (1985). Coping with the threat of Westernisation in Hong Kong. *International Journal of Intercultural Relations, 9,* 351–364.

Bond, M. H., & Komai, H. (1976). Targets of gazing and eye contact during interviews: Effects on Japanese nonverbal behaviour. *Journal of Personality and Social Psychology, 34,* 1276–1284.

Bond, R., & Smith, P. B. (1996). Culture and conformity: A meta-analysis of the Asch line judgment task. *Psychological Bulletin, 119,* 111–137.

Bonnes, M., & Secchiaroli, G. (1995). *Environmental psychology: A psycho-social introduction*. London: Sage.

Bonta, B. D. (1997). Cooperation and competition in peaceful societies. *Psychological Bulletin, 121,* 299–320.

Book, A. S., Starzyk, K. B., & Quinsey, V. L. (2001). The relationship between testosterone and aggression: A meta-analysis. *Aggression and Violent Behavior, 6,* 579–599.

Borden, R. J. (1980). Audience influence. In P. B. Paulus (Ed.), *Psychology of group influence* (pp. 99–131). Hillsdale, NJ: Erlbaum.

Bornstein, G., Crum, L., Wittenbraker, J., Harring, K., Insko, C. A., & Thibaut, J. (1983). On the measurement of social orientations in the minimal group paradigm. *European Journal of Social Psychology, 13,* 321–350.

Bornstein, R. F. (1989). Exposure and affect: Overview and meta-analysis of research, 1968–1987. *Psychological Bulletin, 106,* 265–289.

Bosveld, W., Koomen, W., & Vogelaar, R. (1997). Construing a social issue: Effects on attitudes and the false consensus effect. *British Journal of Social Psychology, 36,* 263–272.

Bothwell, R. K., Brigham, J. C., & Malpass, R. S. (1989). Cross-racial identification. *Personality and Social Psychology Bulletin, 15,* 19–25.

Bouas, K. S., & Komorita, S. S. (1996). Group discussion and cooperation in social dilemmas. *Personality and Social Psychology Bulletin, 22,* 1144–1150.

Bourhis, R. Y. (1984). *Conflict and language planning in Quebec*. Clevedon, UK: Multilingual Matters.

Bourhis, R. Y., & Giles, H. (1977). The language of intergroup distinctiveness. In H. Giles (Ed.), *Language, ethnicity and intergroup relations* (pp. 119–135). London: Academic Press.

Bourhis, R. Y., Giles, H., & Lambert, W. E. (1975). Social consequences of accommodating one's style of speech: A cross-national investigation. *International Journal of the Sociology of Language, 6,* 55–72.

Bourhis, R. Y., Giles, H., Leyens, J. P., & Tajfel, H. (1979). Psycholinguistic distinctiveness: Language divergence in Belgium. In H. Giles & R. St Clair (Eds.), *Language and social psychology* (pp. 158–185). Oxford, UK: Blackwell.

Bourhis, R. Y., Giles, H., & Rosenthal, D. (1981). Notes on the construction of a 'subjective vitality questionnaire' for ethnolinguistic groups. *Journal of Multilingual and Multicultural Development, 2,* 144–155.

Bourhis, R. Y., Sachdev, I., & Gagnon, A. (1994). Intergroup research with the Tajfel matrices: Methodological notes. In M. Zanna & J. Olson (Eds.), *The psychology of prejudice: The Ontario symposium* (Vol. 7, pp. 209–232). Hillsdale, NJ: Erlbaum.

Bowlby, J. (1969). *Attachment and loss:* (Vol. 1) *Attachment.* London: Hogarth Press.

Bowlby, J. (1988). *A secure base: Parent–child attachment and healthy human development.* New York: Basic Books.

Bowles, H. R., & McGinn, K. L. (2005). Claiming authority: Negotiating challenges for women leaders. In D. M. Messick & R. M. Kramer (Eds.), *The psychology of leadership: New perspectives and research* (pp. 191–208). Mahwah, NJ: Erlbaum.

Bowman, C. H., & Fishbein, M. (1978). Understanding public reaction to energy proposals: An application of the Fishbein model. *Journal of Applied Social Psychology, 8,* 319–340.

Branthwaite, A., Doyle, S., & Lightbown, N. (1979). The balance between fairness and discrimination. *European Journal of Social Psychology, 9,* 149–163.

Brauer, M., Judd, C. M., & Gliner, M. D. (1995). The effects of reoperated expressions on attitude polarization during group discussion. *Journal of Personality and Social Psychology, 68,* 1014–1029.

Bray, R. M., & Noble, A. M. (1978). Authoritarianism and decisions of mock juries: Evidence of jury bias and group polarization. *Journal of Personality and Social Psychology, 36,* 1424–1430.

Breakwell, G. M., & Canter, D. V. (1993). *Empirical approaches to social representations.* Oxford, UK: Clarendon Press.

Breaugh, J. A., & Klimoski, R. J. (1981). Social forces in negotiation simulations. *Personality and Social Psychology Bulletin, 7,* 290–295.

Breckler, S. J. (1984). Empirical validation of affect, behavior, and cognition as distinct components of attitude. *Journal of Personality and Social Psychology, 47,* 1191–1205.

Breckler, S. J., & Wiggins, E. C. (1989a). On defining attitude and attitude theory: Once more with feeling. In A. R. Pratkanis, S. J. Breckler, & A. G. Greenwald (Eds.), *Attitude structure and function* (pp. 407–427). Hillsdale, NJ: Erlbaum.

Breckler, S. J., & Wiggins, E. C. (1989b). Affect versus evaluation in the structure of attitudes. *Journal of Experimental Social Psychology, 25,* 253–271.

Breckler, S. J., Pratkanis, A. R., & McCann, C. D. (1991). The representation of self in multidimensional cognitive space. *British Journal of Social Psychology, 30,* 97–112.

Brehm, J. W. (1966). *A theory of psychological reactance.* New York: Academic Press.

Brennan, K. A., & Shaver, P. R. (1995). Dimensions of adult attachment, affect regulation, and romantic relationship functioning. *Personality and Social Psychology Bulletin, 21,* 267–283.

Brewer, M. B. (1981). Ethnocentrism and its role in interpersonal trust. In M. B. Brewer & B. Collins (Eds.), *Scientific inquiry and the social sciences* (pp. 345–360). San Francisco, CA: Jossey-Bass.

Brewer, M. B. (1988). A dual process model of impression formation. In T. K. Srull & R. S. Wyer (Eds.), *Advances in social cognition: A dual process model of impression formation* (Vol. 1, pp. 1–36). Hillsdale, NJ: Erlbaum.

Brewer, M. B. (1991). The social self: On being the same and different at the same time. *Personality and Social Psychology Bulletin, 17,* 475–482.

Brewer, M. B. (1994). Associated systems theory: If you buy two representational systems, why not many more? In R. Wyer & T. Srull (Eds.), *Advances in social cognition* (Vol. 7, pp. 141–147). Hillsdale, NJ: Erlbaum.

Brewer, M. B. (2001). The many faces of social identity: Implications for political psychology. *Political Psychology, 22,* 115–125.

Brewer, M. B. (2003). *Intergroup relations* (2nd ed.). Philadelphia, PA: Open University Press.

Brewer, M. B. (2007). The social psychology of intergroup relations: Social categorization, ingroup bias, and outgroup prejudice. In A. W. Kruglanski & E. T. Higgins (Eds.), *Social psychology: Handbook of basic principles* (2nd ed., pp. 785–804). New York: Guilford Press.

Brewer, M. B., & Campbell, D. T. (1976). *Ethnocentrism and intergroup attitudes: East African evidence.* New York: Halsted-Press (Sage).

Brewer, M. B., & Chen, Y-R. (2007). Where (who) are collectives in collectivism? Toward conceptual clarification of individualism and collectivism. *Psychological Review, 114,* 133–151.

Brewer, M. B., Dull, V., & Lui, L. (1981). Perceptions of the elderly: Stereotypes as prototypes. *Journal of Personality and Social Psychology, 41,* 656–670.

Brewer, M. B., & Gardner, W. (1996). Who is this 'We'? Levels of collective identity and self representation. *Journal of Personality and Social Psychology, 71,* 83–93.

Brewer, M. B., & Kramer, R. M. (1986). Choice behavior in social dilemmas: Effects of social identity, group size, and decision framing. *Journal of Personality and Social Psychology, 50,* 543–549.

Brewer, M. B., & Lui, L. L. (1989). The primacy of age and sex in the structure of person categories. *Social Cognition, 7,* 262–274.

Brewer, M. B., & Miller, N. (1996). *Intergroup relations.* Buckingham, UK: Open University Press.

Brewer, M. B., & Pierce, K. P. (2005). Social identity complexity and outgroup tolerance. *Personality and Social Psychology Bulletin, 31*, 428-437.

Brewer, M. B., & Schneider, S. (1990). Social identity and social dilemmas: A double-edged sword. In D. Abrams & M. A. Hogg (Eds.), *Social identity theory: Constructive and critical advances* (pp. 169–184). London: Harvester Wheatsheaf.

Brickner, M. A., Harkins, S. G., & Ostrom, T. M. (1986). Effects of personal involvement: Thought provoking implications of social loafing. *Journal of Personality and Social Psychology, 51*, 763–770.

Brief, A. P., Dukerich, J. M., & Doran, L. I. (1991). Resolving ethical dilemmas in management: Experimental investigation of values, accountability, and choice. *Journal of Applied Social Psychology, 21*, 380–396.

Brigham, J. C. (1971). Ethnic stereotypes. *Psychological Bulletin, 76*, 15–38.

Brigham, J. C. (1991). *Social psychology*. New York: HarperCollins.

Brigham, J. C., & Barkowitz, P. B. (1978). Do 'they all look alike'? The effect of race, sex, experience and attitudes on the ability to recognise face. *Journal of Applied Social Psychology, 8*, 306–318.

Brigham, J. C., & Malpass, R. S. (1985). The role of experience and contact in the recognition of faces of own- and other-race persons. *Journal of Social Issues, 41*, 139–156.

Brinthaupt, T. M., Moreland, R. L., & Levine, J. M. (1991). Sources of optimism among prospective group members. *Personality and Social Psychology Bulletin, 17*, 36–43.

Brislin, R. W. (1987). Cross-cultural psychology. In R. J. Corsini (Ed.), *Concise encyclopedia of psychology* (pp. 274–287). New York: Wiley.

Britell, J. K. (1981). Ethics courses are making slow inroads. *New York Times, Education Section*, 26 April, p. 44.

Broadbent, D. E. (1985). *Perception and communication*. London: Pergamon Press.

Brockner, J., & Wiesenfeld, B. M. (1996). The interactive impact of procedural and outcome fairness on reactions to a decision: The effects of what you do depend on how you do it. *Psychological Bulletin, 120*, 189–208.

Brockner, J., Chen, Y.-R., Mannix, E. A., Leung, K., & Skarlicki, D. P. (2000). Culture and procedural fairness: When the effects of what you do depend on how you do it. *Administrative Science Quarterly, 45*, 138–159.

Broverman, I. K., Broverman, D. M., Clarkson, F., Rosencrantz, P. S., & Vogel, S. (1970). Sex-role stereotypes and clinical judgments of mental health. *Journal of Consulting and Clinical Psychology, 34*, 1–7.

Broverman, I. K., Vogel, S. R., Broverman, D. M., Clarkson, F. E., & Rosenkrantz, P. S. (1972). Sex-role stereotypes and clinical judgments of mental health: A current appraisal. *Journal of Social Issues, 28*, 59–78.

Brown, P., & Fraser, C. (1979). Speech as a marker of situation. In K. R. Scherer & H. Giles (Eds.), *Social markers in speech* (pp. 33–108). Cambridge, UK: Cambridge University Press.

Brown, R. (1965). *Social psychology*. New York: Free Press.

Brown, R., & Fish, D. (1983). The psychological causality implicit in language. *Cognition, 14*, 237–73.

Brown, R. J. (1978). Divided we fall: An analysis of relations between sections of a factory workforce. In H. Tajfel (Ed.), *Differentiation between social groups: Studies in the social psychology of intergroup relations* (pp. 395–429). London: Academic Press.

Brown, R. J. (1995). *Prejudice: Its social psychology*. Oxford, UK: Blackwell.

Brown, R. J. (1996). Tajfel's contribution to the reduction of intergroup conflict. In W. P. Robinson (Ed.), *Social groups and identities: Developing the legacy of Henri Tajfel* (pp. 169–189). Oxford, UK: Butterworth-Heinemann.

Brown, R. J. (2000). *Group processes* (2nd ed.). Oxford, UK: Blackwell.

Brown, R. J., & Abrams, D. (1986). The effects of intergroup similarity and goal interdependence on intergroup attitudes and task performance. *Journal of Experimental Social Psychology, 22*, 78–92.

Brown, R. J., & Gaertner, S. (Eds.) (2001). *Blackwell handbook of social psychology: Intergroup processes*. Oxford, UK: Blackwell.

Brown, R. J., & Hewstone, M. (2005). An integrative theory of intergroup contact. In M. Zanna (Ed.), *Advances in experimental social psychology* (Vol. 37, pp. 255–343). San Diego, CA: Academic Press.

Brown, R. J., Hinkle, S., Ely, P. C., Fox-Cardamone, L., Maras, P., & Taylor, L. A. (1992). Recognising group diversity: Individualist–collectivist and autonomous–relational social orientations and their implications for intergroup processes. *British Journal of Social Psychology, 31*, 327–342.

Brown, R. J., & Turner, J. C. (1981). Interpersonal and intergroup behaviour. In J. C. Turner & H. Giles (Eds.), *Intergroup behaviour* (pp. 33–65). Oxford, UK: Blackwell.

Brown, R. J., & Wade, G. S. (1987). Superordinate goals and intergroup behavior: The effects of role ambiguity and status on intergroup attitudes and task performance. *European Journal of Social Psychology, 17*, 131–142.

Brumbaugh, C. C., & Fraley, R. C. (2006). Transference and attachment: How do attachment patterns get carried forward from one relationship to the next? *Personality and Social Psychology Bulletin, 32*, 552–560.

Bruner, J. S. (1957). On perceptual readiness. *Psychological Review, 64*, 123–52.

Bruner, J. S. (1958). Social psychology and perception. In E. E. Maccoby, T. M. Newcomb, & E. L. Hartley (Eds.), *Readings in social psychology* (3rd ed., pp. 85–94). New York: Henry Holt & Co.

Bruner, J. S., & Goodman, C. C. (1947). Value and need as organising factors in perception. *Journal of Abnormal and Social Psychology, 42*, 33–44.

Bruner, J. S., & Tagiuri, R. (1954). The perception of people. In G. Lindzey (Ed.), *Handbook of social psychology* (Vol. 2, pp. 634–654). Reading, MA: Addison-Wesley.

Brunswik, E. (1956). *Perception and the representative design of psychological experiments* (2nd ed.). Berkeley, CA: University of California Press.

Bryan, J. H., & Test, M. A. (1967). Models and helping: Naturalistic studies in aiding behavior. *Journal of Personality and Social Psychology, 6,* 400–407.

Bryman, A. (1992). *Charisma and leadership in organizations.* London: SAGE.

Buchanan, G. M., & Seligman, M. E. P. (1995). *Explanatory style.* Hillsdale, NJ: Erlbaum.

Buchanan, P. J. (1987). AIDS and moral bankruptcy. *New York Post,* 2 December, p. 23.

Buck, R., & Ginsburg, B. (1991). Spontaneous communication and altruism: The communicative gene hypothesis. In M. S. Clark (Ed.), *Prosocial behaviour* (pp. 149–75). Newbury Park, CA: SAGE.

Buckner, H. T. (1965). A theory of rumour transmission. *Public Opinion Quarterly, 29,* 54–70.

Budd, R. J., North, D., & Spencer, C. (1984). Understanding seat-belt use: A test of Bentler and Speckart's extension of the 'theory of reasoned action'. *European Journal of Social Psychology, 14,* 69–78.

Bugental, D. B. (2005). Interdisciplinary insights on nonverbal responses within attachment relationships *Journal of Nonverbal Behavior, 29,* 177–186.

Bugental, D. E., Love, L. R., & Gianetto, R. M. (1971). Perfidious feminine faces. *Journal of Personality and Social Psychology, 17,* 314–318.

Bulman, R. J., & Wortman, C. B. (1977). Attributions of blame and coping in the 'real world': Severe accident victims react to their lot. *Journal of Personality and Social Psychology, 35,* 351–363.

Bunge, C. (1903). *Principes de psychologie individuelle et sociale.* Paris: Alcan.

Burger, J. M. (1981). Motivational biases in the attribution of responsibility for an accident: A meta-analysis of the defensive attribution hypothesis. *Psychological Bulletin, 90,* 496–513.

Burger, J. M. (1986). Increasing compliance by improving the deal: The that's-not-all technique. *Journal of Personality and Social Psychology, 51,* 277–283.

Burgoon, J. K., Buller, D. B., & Woodall, W. G. (1989). *Nonverbal communication: The unspoken dialogue.* New York: Harper and Row.

Burgoon, M., Pfau, M., & Birk, T. S. (1995). An inoculation theory explanation for the effects of corporate issue/advocacy advertising campaigns. *Communication Research, 22,* 485–505.

Buriel, R. (1987). Ethnic labelling and identity among Mexican Americans. In J. S. Phinney & M. J. Rotheram (Eds.), *Children's ethnic socialization: Pluralism and development* (pp. 134–152). Newbury Park, CA: SAGE.

Burnham, W. H. (1910). The group as a stimulus to mental activity. *Science, 31,* 761–7.

Burns, J. M. (1978). *Leadership.* New York: Harper & Row.

Burnstein, E., & McRae, A. (1962). Some effects of shared threat and prejudice in racially mixed groups. *Journal of Abnormal and Social Psychology, 64,* 257–263.

Burnstein, E., & Vinokur, A. (1977). Persuasive argumentation and social comparison as determinants of attitude polarization. *Journal of Experimental Social Psychology, 13,* 315–332.

Burnstein, E., Crandall, C., & Kitayama, S. (1994). Some neo-Darwinian decision rules for altruism: Weighing cues for inclusive fitness as a function of the biological importance of the decision. *Journal of Personality and Social Psychology, 67,* 773–789.

Bushman, B. J. (1984). Perceived symbols of authority and their influence on compliance. *Journal of Applied Social Psychology, 14,* 501–508.

Bushman, B. J. (1988). The effects of apparel on compliance: A field experiment with a female authority figure. *Personality and Social Psychology Bulletin, 14,* 459–467.

Bushman, B. J. (2002). Does venting anger feed or extinguish the flame? Catharsis, rumination, distraction, anger, and aggressive responding. *Personality and Social Psychology Bulletin, 28,* 724–731.

Bushman, B. J., & Anderson, C. A. (2002). Violent video games and hostile expectations: A test of the general aggression model. *Personality and Social Psychology Bulletin, 28,* 1679–1686.

Bushman, B. J., & Baumeister, R. F. (1998). Threatened egotism, narcissism, self-esteem, and direct and displaced aggression: Does self-love or self-hate lead to violence? *Journal of Personality and Social Psychology, 75,* 219–229.

Bushman, B. J., Baumeister, R. F., & Stack, A. D. (1999). Catharsis, aggression, and persuasive influence: Self-fulfilling or self-defeating prophecies? *Journal of Personality and Social Psychology, 76,* 367–376.

Bushman, B. J., & Bonacci, A. M. (2002). Violence and sex impair memory for television ads. *Journal of Applied Psychology, 87,* 557–564.

Bushman, B. J., & Cooper, H. M. (1990). Effects of alcohol on human aggression: An integrative research review. *Psychological Bulletin, 107,* 341–354.

Bushman, B. J., & Huesmann, L. R. (2001). Effects of televised violence on aggression. In D. Singer (Ed.), *Handbook of children and the media* (pp. 223–254). Thousand Oaks, CA: SAGE.

Bushman, B. J., & Huesmann, L. R. (2010). Aggression. In S. T. Fiske, D. T. Gilbert, & G. Lindzey (Eds.), *Handbook of social psychology* (5th ed., Vol. 2, pp. 833-863). New York: Wiley.

Buss, A. H. (1961). *The psychology of aggression.* New York: Wiley.

Buss, D. M. (2003). *The evolution of desire: Strategies of human mating* (rev. ed.). New York: Free Press.

Buss, D. M., & Kenrick, D. T. (1998). Evolutionary social psychology. In D. T. Gilbert, S. T. Fiske & G. Lindzey (Eds.), *The handbook of social psychology* (4th ed., Vol. 2, pp. 982–1026). New York: McGraw-Hill.

Buss, D. M., & Reeve, H. K. (2003). Evolutionary psychology and developmental dynamics: Comment on Lickliter and Honeycutt (2003). *Psychological Bulletin, 129,* 848–853.

Butera, F., Mugny, G., Legrenzi, P., & Pérez, J. A. (1996). Majority and minority influence, task representation and inductive reasoning. *British Journal of Social Psychology, 35,* 123–136.

Byrd, R. E. (1938). *Alone*. New York: Putnam.

Byrne, D. (1971). *The attraction paradigm*. New York: Academic Press.

Byrne, D., & Clore, G. L. (1970). A reinforcement model of evaluative responses. *Personality: An International Journal, 1*, 103–128.

Byrne, D., & Wong, T. J. (1962). Racial prejudice, interpersonal attraction, and assumed dissimilarity of attitudes. *Journal of Abnormal and Social Psychology, 65*, 246–252.

Cacioppo, J. T., & Petty, R. E. (1979). Attitudes and cognitive response: An electrophysiological approach. *Journal of Personality and Social Psychology, 37*, 2181–2199.

Cacioppo, J. T., & Petty, R. E. (1981). Electromyograms as measures of extent and affectivity of information processing. *American Psychologist, 36*, 441–456.

Cacioppo, J. T., & Petty, R. E. (1982). The need for cognition. *Journal of Personality and Social Psychology, 42*, 116–131.

Cacioppo, J. T., & Tassinary, L. G. (1990). Inferring psychological significance from physiological signals. *American Psychologist, 45*, 16–28.

Calder, B. J., & Ross, M. (1973). *Attitudes and behavior*. Morristown, NJ: General Learning Press.

Calhoun, J. B. (1962). Population density and social pathology. *Scientific American, 206*, 139–148.

Callaway, M. R., & Esser, J. K. (1984). Groupthink: Effects of cohesiveness and problem-solving procedures on group decision making. *Social Behavior and Personality, 12*, 157–164.

Callaway, M. R., Marriott, R. G., & Esser, J. K. (1985). Effects of dominance on group decision making: Towards a stress-reduction explanation of groupthink. *Journal of Personality and Social Psychology, 49*, 949–952.

Campbell, D. T. (1957). Factors relevant to the validity of experiments in social settings. *Psychological Bulletin, 54*, 297–312.

Campbell, D. T. (1958). Common fate, similarity, and other indices of the status of aggregates of persons as social entities. *Behavioral Science, 3*, 14–25.

Campbell, D. T. (1975). On the conflict between biological and social evolution and between psychology and moral tradition. *American Psychologist, 30*, 1103–1126.

Campbell, J. D. (1986). Similarity and uniqueness: The effects of attribute type, relevance, and individual differences in self-esteem and depression. *Journal of Personality and Social Psychology, 50*, 281–94.

Campbell, J. D. (1990). Self-esteem and clarity of the self-concept. *Journal of Personality and Social Psychology, 59*, 538–49.

Campbell, J. D., & Fairey, P. J. (1985). Effects of self-esteem, hypothetical explanations, and verbalisations of expectancies on future performance. *Journal of Personality and Social Psychology, 48*, 1097–1111.

Campbell, J. D., & Fairey, P. J. (1989). Informational and normative routes to conformity: The effect of faction size as a function of norm extremity and attention to the stimulus. *Journal of Personality and Social Psychology, 57*, 457–468.

Campbell, J. D., Tesser, A., & Fairey, P. J. (1986). Conformity and attention to the stimulus: Some temporal and contextual dynamics. *Journal of Personality and Social Psychology, 51*, 315–324.

Campbell, L., Simpson, J. A., Kashy, D. A., & Fletcher, G. J. O. (2001). Ideal standards, the self, and flexibility of ideals in close relationships. *Personality and Social Psychology Bulletin, 27*, 447–462.

Campbell, M. C., & Keller, K. L. (2003). Brand familiarity and advertising repetition effects. *Journal of Consumer Research, 30*, 292–304.

Cannavale, F. J., Scarr, H. A., & Pepitone, A. (1970). Deindividuation in the small group: Further evidence. *Journal of Personality and Social Psychology, 16*, 141–147.

Cantor, N., & Kihlstrom, J. F. (1987). *Personality and social intelligence*. Englewood Cliffs, NJ: Prentice Hall.

Cantor, N., & Mischel, W. (1977). Traits as prototypes: Effects on recognition memory. *Journal of Personality and Social Psychology, 35*, 38–48.

Cantor, N., & Mischel, W. (1979). Prototypes in person perception. In L. Berkowitz (Ed.), *Advances in experimental social psychology* (Vol. 12, pp. 3–52). New York: Academic Press.

Caplow, T. (1947). Rumours in war. *Social Forces, 25*, 298–302.

Caporael, L. R. (2007). Evolutionary theory for social and cultural psychology. In A. W. Kruglanski & E. T. Higgins (Eds.), *Social psychology: Handbook of basic principles* (2nd ed., pp. 3- 18). New York: Guilford Press.

Caporael, L. R., Dawes, R., Orbell, J., & Van de Kragt, A. (1989). Selfishness examined: Cooperation in the absence of egoistic incentives. *Behavioral and Brain Sciences, 12*, 683–699.

Caporael, L. R., Lukaszewski, M. P., & Cuthbertson, G. H. (1983). Secondary baby talk: Judgments by institutionalized elderly and their caregivers. *Journal of Personality and Social Psychology, 44*, 746–754.

Cappella, J. N., & Palmer, M. (1993). The structure and organisation of verbal and non-verbal behavior: Data for models of production. In H. Giles & W. P. Robinson (Eds.), *Handbook of language and social psychology* (pp. 141–61). Oxford, UK: Pergamon Press.

Carli, L. L. (1990). Gender, language, and influence. *Journal of Personality and Social Psychology, 59*, 941–951.

Carlsmith, J. M., & Anderson, C. A. (1979). Ambient temperature and the occurrence of collective violence: A new analysis. *Journal of Personality and Social Psychology, 37*, 337–344.

Carlsmith, J. M., & Gross, A. E. (1969). Some effects of guilt on compliance. *Journal of Personality and Social Psychology, 11*, 232–239.

Carlson, M., Marcus-Newhall, A., & Miller, N. (1989). Evidence for a general construct of aggression. *Personality and Social Psychology Bulletin, 15*, 377–389.

Carlyle, T. (1841). *On heroes, hero-worship, and the heroic*. London: Fraser.

Carnagey, N. L., Anderson, C. A., & Bushman, B. J. (2007). The effect of video game violence on physiological desensitization to real-life violence. *Journal of Experimental Social Psychology, 43*, 489–496.

Carnevale, P. J. D., Pruitt, D. G., & Britton, S. D. (1979). Looking tough: The negotiator under constituent surveillance. *Personality and Social Psychology Bulletin, 5*, 118–121.

Carnevale, P. J., & Leung, K. (2001). Cultural dimensions of negotiation. In M. A. Hogg & R. S. Tindale (Eds.), *Blackwell handbook of social psychology: Group processes* (pp. 482–496). Oxford, UK: Blackwell.

Carrithers, M., Collins, S., & Lukes, S. (Eds.) (1986). *The category of the person.* Cambridge, UK: Cambridge University Press.

Carroll, J. S., Bazerman, M. H., & Maury, R. (1988). Negotiator cognitions: A descriptive approach to negotiators' understanding of their opponents. *Organizational Behavior and Human Decision Processes, 41,* 352–370.

Carter, L. F., & Nixon, M. (1949). An investigation of the relationship between four criteria of leadership ability for three different tasks. *The Journal of Psychology, 27,* 245–261.

Cartwright, D. (1968). The nature of group cohesiveness. In D. Cartwright & A. Zander (Eds.), *Group dynamics: Research and theory* (3rd ed., pp. 91–109). London: Tavistock.

Cartwright, D., & Harary, F. (1956). Structural balance: A generalisation of Heider's theory. *Psychological Review, 63,* 277–293.

Carver, C. S., & Glass, D. C. (1978). Coronary-prone behavior pattern and interpersonal aggression. *Journal of Personality and Social Psychology, 36,* 361–366.

Carver, C. S., & Scheier, M. F. (1981). *Attention and self-regulation: A control theory approach to human behavior.* New York: Springer.

Carver, C. S., Glass, D. C., & Katz, I. (1977). Favorable evaluations of Blacks and the disabled: Positive prejudice, unconscious denial, or social desirability. *Journal of Applied Social Psychology, 8,* 97–106.

Cary, M. S. (1978). The role of gaze in the initiation of conversation. *Social Psychology, 41,* 269–271.

Casas, J. M., Ponterotto, J. G., & Sweeney, M. (1987). Stereotyping the stereotyper: A Mexican American perspective. *Journal of Cross-cultural Psychology, 18,* 45–57.

Catalano, R., Novaco, R., & McConnell, W. (1997). A model of the net effect of job loss on violence. *Journal of Personality and Social Psychology, 72,* 1440–1447.

Chacko, T. I. (1982). Women and equal employment opportunity: Some unintended effects. *Journal of Applied Psychology, 67,* 119–123.

Chaffee, S. H., Jackson-Beeck, M., Durall, J., & Wilson, D. (1977). Mass communication in political communication. In S. A. Renshon (Ed.), *Handbook of political socialization: Theory and research* (pp. 223–258). New York: Free Press.

Chaiken, S. (1979). Communicator physical attractiveness and persuasion. *Journal of Personality and Social Psychology, 37,* 1387–1397.

Chaiken, S. (1983). Physical appearance variables and social influence. In C. P. Herman, E. T. Higgins & M. P. Zanna (Eds.), *Physical appearance, stigma, and social behavior: Third Ontario symposium* (pp. 143–178). Hillsdale, NJ: Erlbaum.

Chaiken, S. (1987). The heuristic model of persuasion. In M. P. Zanna, J. M. Olsen & C. P. Herman (Eds.), *Social influence: The Ontario symposium* (Vol. 5, pp. 3–39). Hillsdale, NJ: Erlbaum.

Chaiken, S., & Eagly, A. H. (1983). Communication modality as a determinant of persuasion: The role of communicator salience. *Journal of Personality and Social Psychology, 45,* 241–256.

Chaiken, S., Liberman, A., & Eagly, A. H. (1989). Heuristic and systematic processing within and beyond the persuasion context. In J. S. Uleman & J. A. Bargh (Eds.), *Unintended thought* (pp. 215–252). New York: Guilford Press.

Chaiken, S., & Maheswaran, D. (1994). Heuristic processing can bias systematic processing: Effects of source credibility, argument ambiguity, and task importance on attitude judgement. *Journal of Personality and Social Psychology, 66,* 460–473.

Chance, J. E. (1985). *Faces, folklore, and research hypotheses.* Presidential address to the Midwestern Psychological Association convention, Chicago.

Chandra, S. (1973). The effects of group pressure in perception: A cross-cultural conformity study. *International Journal of Psychology, 8,* 37–39.

Chaplin, W. F., John, O. P., & Goldberg, L. R. (1988). Conceptions of states and traits: Dimensional attributes with ideals as prototypes. *Journal of Personality and Social Psychology, 54,* 541–557.

Chapman, L. J. (1967). Illusory correlation in observational report. *Journal of Verbal Learning and Verbal Behavior, 6,* 151–155.

Charng, H.-W., Piliavin, J. A., & Callero, P. L. (1988). Role identity and reasoned action in the prediction of repeated behavior. *Social Psychology Quarterly, 51,* 303–317.

Chemers, M. M. (2001). Leadership effectiveness: An integrative review. In M. A. Hogg & R. S. Tindale (Eds.), *Blackwell handbook of social psychology: Group processes* (pp. 376–399). Oxford, UK: Blackwell.

Chen, H., Yates, B. T., & McGinnies, E. (1988). Effects of involvement on observers' estimates of consensus, distinctiveness, and consistency. *Personality and Social Psychology Bulletin, 14,* 468–478.

Chen, S., Boucher, H. C., & Tapias, M. P. (2006). The relational self revealed: Integrative conceptualization and implications for interpersonal life. *Psychological Bulletin, 132,* 151–179.

Chen, S., Shechter, D., & Chaiken, S. (1996). Getting at the truth or getting along: Accuracy versus impression motivated heuristic and systematic processing. *Journal of Personality and Social Psychology, 71,* 2.

Cherek, D. R., Schnapp, W., Moeller, F., & Dougherty, D. M. (1996). Laboratory measures of aggressive responding in male parolees with violent and nonviolent histories. *Aggressive Behaviour, 22,* 27–36.

Chesler, P. (1972). *Women and madness.* Garden City, NY: Doubleday.

Chidester, T. R. (1986). Problems in the study of inter-racial interaction: Pseudo-interracial dyad paradigm. *Journal of Personality and Social Psychology, 50,* 74–79.

Child, I. L. (1954). Socialization. In G. Lindzey (Ed.), *The handbook of social psychology* (Vol. 2, pp. 655–692). Cambridge, MA: Addison-Wesley.

Chiu, C.-Y., & Hong, Y.-Y. (2007). Cultural processes: Basic principles. In A. W. Kruglanski & E. T. Higgins (Eds.), *Social psychology: Handbook of basic principles* (2nd ed., pp. 785-804). New York: Guilford Press.

Choi, I., & Choi, Y. (2002). Culture and self-concept flexibility. *Personality and Social Psychology Bulletin, 28,* 1508–1517.

Choi, I., & Nisbett, R. E. (2000). Cultural psychology of surprise: Holistic theories and recognition of contradiction. *Journal of Personality and Social Psychology, 79,* 890–905.

Chomsky, N. (1957). *Syntactic structures.* The Hague: Mouton.

Chomsky, N. (1959). Verbal behavior [review of Skinner's book]. *Language, 35,* 26–58.

Christensen, L. (1988). Deception in psychological research: When is its use justified? *Personality and Social Psychology Bulletin, 14,* 664–675.

Christie, R., & Jahoda, M. (Eds.) (1954). *Studies in the scope and method of 'the authoritarian personality'.* New York: Free Press.

Christy, C. A., & Voigt, H. (1994). Bystander responses to public episodes of child abuse. *Journal of Applied Social Psychology, 24,* 824–847.

Chryssochoou, X. (2000). The representation(s) of a new superordinate category: Studying the stereotype of the European in the context of European integration. *European Psychologist, 5,* 269–277.

Chryssochoou, X. (2004). *Cultural diversity: Its social psychology.* Oxford, UK: Blackwell.

Cialdini, R. B., Borden, R. J., Thorne, A., Walker, M. R., Freeman, S., & Sloan, L. R. (1976). Basking in reflected glory: Three (football) field studies. *Journal of Personality and Social Psychology, 34,* 366–375.

Cialdini, R. B., Cacioppo, J. T., Bassett, R., & Miller, J. A. (1978). Low-balling procedure for producing compliance: Commitment then cost. *Journal of Personality and Social Psychology, 36,* 463–476.

Cialdini, R. B., Darby, B. L., & Vincent, J. E. (1973). Transgression and altruism: A case for hedonism. *Journal of Personality and Social Psychology, 9,* 502–516.

Cialdini, R. B., & Goldstein, N. J. (2004). Social influence: Compliance and conformity. *Annual Review of Psychology, 55,* 591–621.

Cialdini, R. B., Kallgren, C. A., & Reno, R. R. (1991). A focus theory of normative conduct: Theoretical refinement and reevaluation of the role of norms in human behavior. In L. Berkowitz (Ed.), *Advances in experimental social psychology* (Vol. 21, pp. 201-234). New York: Academic Press.

Cialdini, R. B., & Kenrick, D. T. (1976). Altruism as hedonism: A social development perspective on the relationship of

negative mood state and helping. *Journal of Personality and Social Psychology, 34,* 907–914.

Cialdini, R. B., & Petty, R. E. (1979). Anticipatory opinion effects. In R. Petty, T. Ostrom & T. Brock (Eds.), *Cognitive responses in persuasion.* Hillsdale, NJ: Erlbaum.

Cialdini, R. B., & Trost, M. R. (1998). Social influence: Social norms, conformity, and compliance. In D. Gilbert, S. T. Fiske & G. Lindzey (Eds.), *The handbook of social psychology* (4th ed., Vol. 2, pp. 151–192). New York: McGraw-Hill.

Cialdini, R. B., Trost, M. R., & Newsom, J. T. (1995). Preference for consistency: The development of a valid measure and the discovery of surprising behavioral implications. *Journal of Personality and Social Psychology, 69,* 318–328.

Cialdini, R. B., Vincent, J. E., Lewis, S. K., Catalan, J., Wheeler, D., & Darby, B. L. (1975). Reciprocal concessions procedure for inducing compliance: The door-in-the-face technique. *Journal of Personality and Social Psychology, 31,* 206–215.

Cinnirella, M. (1997). Towards a European identity? Interactions between the national and European social identities manifested by university students in Britain and Italy. *British Journal of Social Psychology, 36,* 19–31.

Citrin, J., Green, D. P., Muste, C., & Wong, C. (1997). Public opinion toward immigration reform: The role of economic motivations. *The Journal of Politics, 59,* 858-881.

Citrin, J., Wong, C., & Duff, B. (2001). The meaning of American national identity: Patterns of ethnic conflict and consensus. In R. D. Ashmore, L. Jussim & D. Wilder (Eds.), *Social identity, intergroup conflict, and conflict reduction* (Vol. 3, pp. 71–100). New York: Oxford University Press.

Claes, J. A., & Rosenthal, D. M. (1990). Men who batter women: A study in power. *Journal of Family Violence, 5,* 215–224.

Clark, H. H. (1985). Language use and language users. In G. Lindzey & E. Aronson (Eds.), *Handbook of social psychology* (3rd ed., Vol. 2, pp. 179–232). New York: Random House.

Clark, K. B., & Clark, M. P. (1939a). The development of consciousness of self and the emergence of racial identification in Negro preschool children. *Journal of Social Psychology, 10,* 591–599.

Clark, K. B., & Clark, M. P. (1939b). Segregation as a factor in the racial identification of Negro preschool children. *Journal of Experimental Education, 8,* 161–163.

Clark, K. B., & Clark, M. P. (1940). Skin color as a factor in racial identification and preference in Negro children. *Journal of Negro Education, 19,* 341–358.

Clark, M. S., & Grote, N. K. (1998). Why aren't indices of relationship costs always negatively related to indices of relationship quality? *Personality and Social Psychology Review, 2,* 2–17.

Clark, M. S., & Lemay, E. P. Jr. (2010). Close relationships. In S. T. Fiske, D. T. Gilbert, & G. Lindzey (Eds.), *Handbook of social psychology* (5th ed., Vol. 2, pp. 898-940). New York: Wiley.

Clark, N. K., & Stephenson, G. M. (1989). Group remembering. In P. B. Paulus (Ed.), *Psychology of group influence* (2nd ed., pp. 357–391). Hillsdale, NJ: Erlbaum.

Clark, N. K., & Stephenson, G. M. (1995). Social remembering: Individual and collaborative memory for social information. *European Review of Social Psychology, 6,* 127–160.

Clark, N. K., Stephenson, G. M., & Rutter, D. R. (1986). Memory for a complex social discourse: The analysis and prediction of individual and group remembering. *Journal of Memory and Language, 25,* 295–313.

Clark, R. D. III, & Word, I. E. (1974). Where is the apathetic bystander? Situational characteristics of the emergency. *Journal of Personality and Social Psychology, 29,* 279–287.

Clark, T. N. (1969). *Gabriel Tarde: On communication and social influence.* Chicago: University of Chicago Press.

Clary, E. G., & Snyder, M. (1991). A functional analysis of altruism and prosocial behaviour: The case of volunteerism. In M. S. Clarke (Ed.), *Prosocial behaviour* (pp. 119–147). Newbury Park, CA: SAGE.

Clary, E. G., & Synder, M. (1999). Considerations of community: The context and process of volunteerism. *Current Directions in Psychological Science, 8,* 156–159.

Clément, R. (1980). Ethnicity, contact and communication competence in a second language. In H. Giles, W. P. Robinson & P. M. Smith (Eds.), *Language: Social psychological perspectives* (pp. 147–154). Oxford, UK: Pergamon Press.

Clore, G. L. (1976). Interpersonal attraction: An overview. In J. W. Thibaut, J. T. Spence & R. C. Carson (Eds.), *Contemporary topics in social psychology* (pp. 135–175). Morristown, NJ: General Learning Press.

Clore, G. L., & Byrne, D. (1974). A reinforcement–affect model of attraction. In T. L. Huston (Ed.), *Foundations of interpersonal attraction* (pp. 143–165). New York: Academic Press.

Clover, C. (2004). *The end of the line: How over-fishing is changing the world and what we eat.* London: Ebury Press.

Clyne, M. G. (1981). 'Second generation' foreigner talk in Australia. *International Journal of the Sociology of Language, 28,* 69–80.

Coates, B., Pusser, H. E., & Goodman, I. (1976). The influence of 'Sesame Street' and 'Mister Rogers' Neighbourhood' on children's prosocial behavior in preschool. *Child Development, 47,* 138–144.

Coch, L., & French, J. R. P., Jr (1948). Overcoming resistance to change. *Human Relations, 1,* 512–32.

Codol, J.-P. (1975). On the so-called 'superior conformity of the self' behaviour: Twenty experimental investigations. *European Journal of Social Psychology, 5,* 457–501.

Cohen, D. (2001). Cultural variation: Considerations and implications. *Psychological Bulletin, 127,* 451–471.

Cohen, D., & Nisbett, R. E. (1997). Field experiments examining the culture of honor: The role of institutions in perpetuating norms about violence. *Personality and Social Psychology Bulletin, 23,* 1188–1199.

Cohen-Kettenis, P. T., & Van Goozen, S. H. M. (1997). Sex reassignment of adolescent transsexuals: A follow-up study. *Journal of the American Academy of Child and Adolescent Psychiatry, 36,* 263–71.

Cohn, C. (1987). Nuclear language. *Bulletin of the Atomic Scientists,* June, 17–24.

Cohn, E. G. (1993). The prediction of police calls for service: The influence of weather and temporal variables on rape and domestic violence. *Journal of Environmental Psychology, 13,* 71–83.

Cohn, E. G., & Rotton, J. (1997). Assault as a function of time and temperature: A moderator-variable time-series analysis. *Journal of Personality and Social Psychology, 72,* 1322–1334.

Cohn, E. G., & Rotton, J. (2005). The curve is still out there: A reply to Bushman, Wang, and Anderson's (2005) 'is the curve relating temperature to aggression linear or curvilinear?' *Journal of Personality and Social Psychology, 89,* 67–70.

Cohn, N. (1966). *Warrant for genocide: The myth of the Jewish world conspiracy and the Protocol of the Elders of Zion.* New York: Harper & Row.

Cohn, N. (1975). *Europe's inner demons: An enquiry inspired by the great witch hunt.* London: Chatto.

Collins, B. E. (1974). Four separate components of the Rotter I–E sale: Belief in a difficult world, a just world, a predictable world, and a politically responsive world. *Journal of Personality and Social Psychology, 29,* 381–391.

Collins, B. E., & Raven, B. H. (1969). Group structure: Attraction, coalitions, communication, and power. In G. Lindzey & E. Aronson (Eds.), *Handbook of social psychology* (Vol. 4, pp. 102–204). Reading, MA: Addison-Wesley.

Collins, N. L., & Miller, L. C. (1994). Self-disclosure and liking: A meta-analytic review. *Psychological Bulletin, 116,* 457–475.

Colvin, C. R., & Block, J. (1994). Do positive illusions foster mental health? An examination of the Taylor and Brown formulation. *Psychological Bulletin, 116,* 3–20.

Colvin, C. R., Block, J., & Funder, D. C. (1995). Overly positive evaluations and personality: Negative implications for mental health. *Journal of Personality and Social Psychology, 68,* 1152–1162.

Condor, S. (1988). Race stereotypes and racist discourse. *Text, 8,* 69–90.

Condor, S. (1996). Social identity and time. In W. P. Robinson (Ed.), *Social groups and identities: Developing the legacy of Henri Tajfel* (pp. 285–315). Oxford, UK: Butterworth-Heinemann.

Condry, J. (1977). Enemies of exploration: Self-initiated versus other-initiated learning. *Journal of Personality and Social Psychology, 35,* 459–477.

Conger, J. A., & Kanungo, R. N. (1998). *Charismatic leadership in organizations.* Thousand Oaks, CA: SAGE.

Conley, T. D., Collins, B. E., & Garcia, D. (2000). Perceptions of women condom proposers among Chinese Americans, Japanese Americans, and European Americans, *Journal of Applied Social Psychology, 30,* 389–406.

Connell, R. W. (1972). Political socialization in the American family: The evidence reexamined. *Public Opinion Quarterly, 36,* 323–333.

Conner, M., Warren, R., Close, S., & Sparks, P. (1999). Alcohol consumption and the theory of planned behaviour: An examination of the cognitive mediation of past behaviour. *Journal of Applied Social Psychology, 28,* 1676–1704.

Conway, M., Irannejad, S., & Giannopoulos, C. (2005). Status-based expectancies for aggression, with regard to gender differences in aggression in social psychological research. *Aggressive Behaviour, 31,* 381–398.

Cook, S. W. (1978). Interpersonal and attitudinal outcomes in cooperating interracial groups. *Journal of Research and Development in Education, 12,* 97–113.

Cook, S. W. (1985). Experimenting on social issues: The case of school desegregation. *American Psychologist, 40,* 452–460.

Cooke, R., & Sheeran, P. (2004). Moderation of cognition–intention and cognition–behaviour relations: A meta-analysis of properties of variables from the theory of planned behaviour. *British Journal of Social Psychology, 43,* 159–186.

Cooper, H. M. (1979). Statistically combining independent studies: Meta-analysis of sex differences in conformity. *Journal of Personality and Social Psychology, 37,* 131–146.

Cooper, J. (1999). Unwanted consequences and the self: In search of the motivation for dissonance reduction. In E. Harmon-Jones & J. Mills (Eds.), *Cognitive dissonance: Progress on a pivotal theory in social psychology* (pp. 149–174). Washington, DC: American Psychological Association.

Cooper, J. (2007). *Cognitive dissonance: 50 years of a classic theory.* London: SAGE.

Cooper, J., & Axsom, D. (1982). Effort justification in psychotherapy. In G. Weary & H. Mirels (Eds.), *Integrations of Clinical and Social Psychology.* London: Oxford University Press.

Cooper, J., & Croyle, R. T. (1984). Attitudes and attitude change. *Annual Review of Psychology, 35,* 395–426.

Cooper, J., & Fazio, R. H. (1984). A new look at dissonance theory. In L. Berkowitz (Ed.), *Advances in experimental social psychology* (Vol. 17, pp. 229–265). New York: Academic Press.

Cooper, J., & Hogg, M. A. (2007). Feeling the anguish of others: A theory of vicarious dissonance. In M. P. Zanna (Ed.), *Advances in experimental social psychology* (Vol. 39, pp. 359–403). San Diego, CA: Academic Press.

Corballis, M. C. (1999). The gestural origins of language. *American Scientist, 87,* 138–145.

Corballis, M. C. (2004). The origins of modernity: Was autonomous speech the critical factor? *Psychological Review, 111,* 543–552.

Cordery, J. L., Mueller, W. S., & Smith, L. M. (1991). Attitudinal and behavioral effects of autonomous group working: A longitudinal field study. *Academy of Management Journal, 34,* 464–476.

Corneille, O., Klein, O., Lambert, S., & Judd, C. M. (2002). On the role of familiarity with units of measurement in categorical accentuation: Tajfel and Wilkes (1963) revisited and replicated. *Psychological Science, 13(4),* 380–83.

Corsianos, M. (2007). Mainstream pornography and "women": Questioning sexual agency. *Critical Sociology, 33,* 863-885.

Cortes, B. P., Demoulin, S., Rodriguez, R. T., Rodriguez, A. P., & Leyens, J.-P. (2005). Infrahumanization or familiarity? Attribution of uniquely human emotions to the self, the ingroup, and the outgroup. *Personality and Social Psychology Bulletin, 31,* 253-263.

Cose, E. (1993). *Rage of a privileged class.* New York: HarperCollins.

Costanzo, P. R. (1970). Conformity development as a function of self-blame. *Journal of Personality and Social Psychology, 14,* 366–374.

Cotton, S., Cunningham, J. D., & Antill, J. (1993). Network structure, network support and the marital satisfaction of husbands and wives. *Australian Journal of Psychology, 45,* 176–181.

Cottrell, N. B. (1972). Social facilitation. In C. McClintock (Ed.), *Experimental social psychology* (pp. 185–236). New York: Holt, Rinehart & Winston.

Cottrell, N. B., Wack, D. L., Sekerak, G. J., & Rittle, R. H. (1968). Social facilitation of dominant responses by the presence of others. *Journal of Personality and Social Psychology, 9,* 245–50.

Counselman, E. (1991). Leadership in a long-term leaderless women's group. *Small Group Research, 22,* 240–257.

Coupland, N., Bishop, H., Evans, B., & Garrett, P. (2006). Imagining Wales and the Welsh language: Ethnolinguistic subjectivities and demographic flow. *Journal of Language and Social Psychology, 25,* 351–376.

Coupland, N., Coupland, J., Giles, H., & Henwood, K. (1988). Accommodating the elderly: Invoking and extending a theory. *Language in Society, 17,* 1–41.

Courtright, J. A. (1978). A laboratory investigation of groupthink. *Communication Monographs, 45,* 229–246.

Covell, K., Dion, K. L., & Dion, K. K. (1994). Gender differences in evaluations of tobacco and alcohol advertisements. *Canadian Journal of Behavioural Science, 26,* 404–420.

Cowen, W. L., Landes, J., & Schaet, D. E. (1958). The effects of mild frustration on the expression of prejudiced attitudes. *Journal of Abnormal and Social Psychology, 58,* 33–38.

Cozby, P. C. (1973). Self-disclosure: A literature review. *Psychological Bulletin, 79,* 73–91.

Craddock, A. (1980). The impact of social change on Australian families. *Australian Journal of Sex, Marriage and the Family, 1,* 4–14.

Cramer, R. E., McMaster, M. R., Bartell, P. A., & Dragna, M. (1988). Subject competence and minimization of the bystander effect. *Journal of Applied Social Psychology, 18,* 1133–1148.

Crandall, C. S. (1994). Prejudice against fat people: Ideology and self-interest. *Journal of Personality and Social Psychology, 66,* 882–894.

Crano, W. D. (2001). Social influence, social identity, and ingroup leniency. In C. W. K. de Dreu & N. K. de Vries (Eds.), *Group consensus and minority influence: Implications for innovation* (pp. 122–143). Oxford, UK: Blackwell.

Crano, W. D., & Alvaro, E. M. (1998). The context/comparison model of social influence: Mechanisms, structure, and linkages that underlie indirect attitude change. In W. Stroebe & M. Hewstone (Eds.), *European review of social psychology* (Vol. 8, pp. 175–202). Chichester, UK: Wiley.

Crano, W. D., & Chen, X. (1998). The leniency contract and persistence of majority and minority influence. *Journal of Personality and Social Psychology, 74*, 1437–1450.

Crano, W. D., & Prislin, R. (2006). Attitudes and persuasion. *Annual Review of Psychology, 57*, 345–374.

Crano, W. D., & Seyranian, V. (2009). How minorities prevail: The context/comparison-leniency contract model. *Journal of Social Issues, 65*, 335–363.

Crawford, M. (Ed.) (1995). *Talking difference: On gender and language*. London: SAGE.

Crisp, R. J., Ensari, N., Hewstone, M., & Miller, N. (2003). A dual-route model of crossed categorization effects. In W. Stroebe & M. Hewstone (Eds.), *European review of social psychology* (Vol. 13, pp. 35–74). New York: Psychology Press.

Crisp, R. J., & Hewstone, M. (2007). Multiple social categorization. In M. P. Zanna (Ed.). *Advances in experimental social Psychology* (Vol. 39, pp. 163-254). San Diego, CA: Academic Press.

Crocker, J. (1981). Judgement of covariation by social perceivers. *Psychological Bulletin, 90*, 272–292.

Crocker, J., Alloy, L. B., & Kayne, N. T. (1988). Attributional style, depression, and perceptions of consensus for events. *Journal of Personality and Social Psychology, 54*, 840–846.

Crocker, J., Fiske, S. T., & Taylor, S. E. (1984). Schematic bases of belief change. In J. R. Eiser (Ed.), *Attitudinal judgment* (pp. 197–226). New York: Springer.

Crocker, J., & Luhtanen, R. (1990). Collective self-esteem and ingroup bias. *Journal of Personality and Social Psychology, 58*, 60–67.

Crocker, J., & Major, B. (1989). Social stigma and self-esteem: The self-protective properties of stigma. *Psychological Review, 96*, 608–630.

Crocker, J., & Major, B. (1994). Reactions to stigma: The moderating role of justifications. In M. P. Zanna and J. M. Olson (Eds.), *The psychology of prejudice: The Ontario symposium* (Vol. 7, pp. 289–314). Hillsdale, NJ: Erlbaum.

Crocker, J., Major, B., & Steele, C. (1998). Social stigma. In D. T. Gilbert, S. T. Fiske & G. Lindzey (Eds.), *The handbook of social psychology* (4th ed., Vol. 2, pp. 504–553). New York: McGraw-Hill.

Crockett, W. H. (1965). Cognitive complexity and impression formation. In B. A. Maher (Ed.), *Progress in experimental personality research* (Vol. 2, pp. 47–90). New York: Academic Press.

Crosby, F. (1982). *Relative deprivation and working women*. New York: Oxford University Press.

Crosby, F. (1984). The denial of personal discrimination. *American Behavioral Scientist, 27*, 371–386.

Crosby, F., Bromley, S., & Saxe, L. (1980). Recent unobtrusive studies of black and white discrimination and prejudice: A literature review. *Psychological Bulletin, 87*, 546–563.

Crosby, F., Cordova, D., & Jaskar, K. (1993). On the failure to see oneself as disadvantaged: Cognitive and emotional components. In M. A. Hogg & D. Abrams (Eds.), *Group motivation: Social psychological perspectives* (pp. 87–104). London: Harvester Wheatsheaf.

Crosby, F., Pufall, A., Snyder, R. C., O'Connell, M., & Whalen, P. (1989). The denial of personal disadvantage among you, me, and all the other ostriches. In M. Crawford & M. Gentry (Eds.), *Gender and thought* (pp. 79–99). New York: Springer.

Cross, K. P. (1977). Not can but will college teaching be improved? *New Directions for Higher Education, 17*, 1–15.

Cross, S. E., & Madson, L. (1997). Models of the self: Self-construals and gender. *Psychological Bulletin, 122*, 5–37.

Cross, S. E., Bacon, P. L., & Morris, M. L. (2000). The relational–interdependent self-construal and relationships. *Journal of Personality and Social Psychology, 78*, 791–808.

Cross, W. E. (1987). A two-factor theory of black identity: Implications for the study of identity development in minority children. In J. S. Phinney & M. J. Rotheram (Eds.), *Children's ethnic socialization: Pluralism and development* (pp. 117–33). Beverly Hills, CA: SAGE.

Crusco, A. H., & Wetzel, C. G. (1984). The Midas touch: The effects of interpersonal touch on restaurant tipping. *Personality and Social Psychology Bulletin, 10*, 512–517.

Crutchfield, R. A. (1955). Conformity and character. *American Psychologist, 10*, 191–198.

Cunningham, M. R. (1979). Weather, mood, and helping behavior: Quasi-experiments with the sunshine samaritan. *Journal of Personality and Social Psychology, 37*, 1947–1956.

Cunningham, W. A., Preacher, K. J., & Banaji, M. R. (2001). Implicit attitude measures: Consistency, stability, and convergent validity. *Psychological Science, 12*, 163–170.

Cutrona, C. E., Russell, D., & Jones, R. D. (1985). Cross-situational consistency in causal attributions: Does attributional style exist? *Journal of Personality and Social Psychology, 47*, 1043–1058.

Cvetkovich, G., & Löfstedt, R. E. (Eds.) (1999). *Social trust and the management of risk*. London: Earthscan.

Dakof, G. A., & Taylor, S. E. (1990). Victims' perceptions of social support: What is helpful from whom? *Journal of Personality and Social Psychology, 58*, 80–89.

Danserau, F., Jr., Graen, G., & Haga, W. J. (1975). A vertical dyad linkage approach to leadership within formal organizations: A longitudinal investigation of the role-making process. *Organizational Behavior and Human Performance, 13*, 46–78.

Darley, J. M. (1991). Altruism and prosocial behavior: Reflections and prospects. In M. S. Clark (Ed.), *Prosocial behavior* (pp. 312–327). Newbury Park, CA: SAGE.

Darley, J. M., & Batson, C. D. (1973). From Jerusalem to Jericho: A study of situational and dispositional variables in helping behavior. *Journal of Personality and Social Psychology, 27*, 100–108.

Darley, J. M., & Latané, B. (1968). Bystander intervention in emergencies: Diffusion of responsibility. *Journal of Personality and Social Psychology, 8*, 377–383.

Darlington, R. B., & Macker, D. F. (1966). Displacement of guilt-produced altruistic behavior. *Journal of Personality and Social Psychology, 4,* 442–443.

Darwin, C. (1872). *The expression of emotions in man and animals.* Chicago: University of Chicago Press.

Das, E. H. H., de Wit, J. B. F., & Stroebe, W. (2003). Fear appeals motivate acceptance of action recommendations: Evidence for a positive bias in the processing of persuasive messages. *Personality and Social Psychology Bulletin, 29,* 650–664.

David, B., & Turner, J. C. (1996). Studies in self-categorization and minority conversion. Is being a member of the outgroup an advantage? *British Journal of Social Psychology, 35,* 179–199.

David, B., & Turner, J. C. (1999). Studies in self-categorization and minority conversion. The ingroup minority in intragroup and intergroup contexts. *British Journal of Social Psychology, 38,* 115–134.

David, B., & Turner, J. C. (2001). Majority and minority influence: A single process self-categorization analysis. In C. K. W. De Dreu & N. K. De Vries (Eds.), *Group consensus and innovation* (pp. 91–121). Oxford, UK: Blackwell.

Davidowicz, L. C. (1975). *The war against the Jews, 1933–1945.* New York: Holt, Rinehart & Winston.

Davidson, A. R., & Jacard, J. (1979). Variables that moderate the attitude–behavior relation: Results of a longitudinal survey. *Journal of Personality and Social Psychology, 37,* 1364–1376.

Davidson, L. R., & Duberman, L. (1982). Friendship: Communication and interactional patterns in same-sex dyads. *Sex Roles, 8,* 809–822.

Davies, J. C. (1969). The J-curve of rising and declining satisfaction as a cause of some great revolutions and a contained rebellion. In H. D. Graham & T. R. Gurr (Eds.), *The history of violence in America: Historical and comparative perspectives* (pp. 690–730). New York: Praeger.

Davis, J. A. (1959). A formal interpretation of the theory of relative deprivation. *Sociometry, 22,* 280–96.

Davis, J. H. (1973). Group decision and social interaction: A theory of social decision schemes. *Psychological Review, 80,* 97–125.

Davis, M. H., Hall, J. A., & Meyer, M. (2003). The first year: Influences on the satisfaction, involvement, and persistence of new community volunteers. *Personality and Social Psychology Bulletin, 29,* 248–260.

Dawes, R. M. (1991). Social dilemmas, economic self-interest, and evolutionary self-interest. In D. R. Brown & J. E. Keith-Smith (Eds.), *Frontiers of mathematical psychology: Essays in honour of Clyde Coombs* (pp. 53–79). New York: Springer.

Dawes, R. M., Faust, D., & Meehl, P. E. (1989). Clinical versus actuarial judgment. *Science, 243,* 1668–1674.

Dawes, R. M., & Messick, D. M. (2000). Social dilemmas. *International Journal of Psychology, 35,* 111–116.

De Cremer, D. (2000). Leadership selection in social dilemmas – not all prefer it: The moderating effect of social value orientation. *Group Dynamics, 4,* 330–337.

De Cremer, D. (2002). Charismatic leadership and cooperation in social dilemmas: A matter of transforming motives? *Journal of Applied Social Psychology, 32,* 997–1016.

De Cremer, D. (2003). A relational perspective on leadership and cooperation: Why it matters to care and be fair. In D. van Knippenberg & M. A. Hogg (Eds.), *Leadership and power: Identity processes in groups and organizations* (pp. 109–122). London: SAGE.

De Cremer, D., & Tyler, T. R. (2005). Managing group behavior: The interplay between procedural fairness, self, and cooperation. In M. Zanna (Ed.), *Advances in experimental social psychology* (Vol. 37, pp. 151-218). New York: Academic Press.

De Cremer, D., & Van Knippenberg, D. (2003). Cooperation with leaders in social dilemmas: On the effects of procedural fairness and outcome favorability in structural cooperation. *Organizational Behavior and Human Decision Processes, 91,* 1–11.

De Cremer, D., & Van Vugt, M. (1999). Social identification effects in social dilemmas: A transformation of motives. *European Journal of Social Psychology, 29,* 871–893.

De Cremer, D., & Van Vugt, M. (2002). Intergroup and intragroup aspects of leadership in social dilemmas: A relational model of cooperation. *Journal of Experimental Social Psychology, 38,* 126–136.

De Dreu, C. K. W. (2010). Social conflict: The emergence and consequences of struggle and negotiation. In S. T. Fiske, D. T. Gilbert, & G. Lindzey (Eds.), *Handbook of social psychology* (5th ed., Vol. 2, pp. 983-1023). New York: Wiley.

De Dreu, C. K. W., De Vries, N. K., Gordijn, E., & Schuurman, M. (1999). Convergent and divergent processing of majority and minority arguments: Effects on focal and related attitudes. *European Journal of Social Psychology, 29,* 329–348.

De Gilder, D., & Wilke, H. A. M. (1994). Expectation states theory and motivational determinants of social influence. *European Review of Social Psychology, 5,* 243–269.

De Houwer, J., & Hermans, D. (2001). Editorial: Automatic affective processing. *Cognition and Emotion, 15,* 113-114.

De Houwer, J., Thomas, S., & Baeyens, F. (2001). Associative learning of likes and dislikes: A review of 25 years of research on human evaluative conditioning. *Psychological Bulletin, 127,* 853–869.

De Jong, P. F., Koomen, W., & Mellenbergh, G. J. (1988). Structure of causes for success and failure: A multidimensional scaling analysis of preference judgments. *Journal of Personality and Social Psychology, 55,* 1024–1037.

De Munck, V. C. (1996). Love and marriage in a Sri Lankan Muslim community: Toward an evaluation of Dravidian marriage practices. *American Ethnologist, 23,* 698–716.

Dean, L. M., Willis, F. N., & Hewitt, J. (1975). Initial interaction distance among individuals equal and unequal in military rank. *Journal of Personality and Social Psychology, 32,* 294–299.

Deaux, K. (1976). *The behavior of women and men.* Monterey, CA: Brooks/Cole.

Deaux, K. (1984). From individual differences to social categories. *American Psychologist, 39,* 105–116.

Deaux, K. (1985). Sex and gender. *Annual Review of Psychology, 36,* 49–81.

Deaux, K., & Emswiller, T. (1974). Explanations of successful performance on sex-linked tasks: What is skill for the male is luck for the female. *Journal of Personality and Social Psychology, 29,* 80–85.

Deaux, K., & LaFrance, M. (1998). Gender. In D. T. Gilbert, S. T. Fiske & G. Lindzey (Eds.), *The handbook of social psychology* (4th ed., Vol. 1, pp. 788–827). New York: McGraw-Hill.

Deaux, K., & Philogene, G. (2001). *Representations of the social: Bridging theoretical traditions.* Oxford: Blackwell.

Deaux, K., Reid, A., Mizrahi, K. & Ethier, K. A. (1995). Parameters of social identity. *Journal of Personality and Social Psychology, 68,* 280–291.

Deaux, K., & Wrightsman, L. S. (1988). *Social psychology* (5th ed.). Belmont, CA: Brooks/Cole.

Decety, J., & Lamm, C. (2006). Human empathy through the lens of social neuroscience. *The Scientific World Journal, 6,* 1146-1163.

Deci, E. L., & Ryan, R. M. (1985). *Intrinsic motivation and self-determination in human behavior.* New York: Plenum.

DeJong, W. (1979). An examination of self-perception mediation of the foot in the door effect. *Journal of Personality and Social Psychology, 37,* 2221–2239.

DeKeseredy, W. S. (2006). Future directions. *Violence against women, 12,* 1078–1085.

Dekovic, M., & Janssens, J. M. (1992). Parents' child-rearing style and child's sociometric status. *Developmental Psychology, 28,* 925–932.

Delamater, J. (Ed.) (2003). *Handbook of social psychology.* New York: Kluwer Academic/Plenum.

Dembroski, T. M., & MacDougall, J. M. (1978). Stress effects on affiliation preferences among subjects possessing the Type A coronary-prone behavior pattern. *Journal of Personality and Social Psychology, 36,* 23–33.

D'Emilio, J. (1983). *Sexual politics, sexual communities: The making of a homosexual minority in the United States, 1940–1979.* Chicago: University of Chicago Press.

Dennis, A. R., & Valacich, J. S. (1993). Computer brainstorms: More heads are better than one. *Journal of Applied Psychology, 78,* 531–537.

DePaulo, B. (1992). Nonverbal behavior and self-presentation. *Psychological Bulletin, 111,* 203–243.

DePaulo, B. (1994). Spotting lies: Can humans learn to do better? *Current Directions in Psychological Science, 3,* 83–86.

DePaulo, B., & Friedman, H. S. (1998). Nonverbal communication. In D. T. Gilbert, S. T. Fiske & G. Lindzey (Eds.), *The handbook of social psychology* (4th ed., Vol. 2, pp. 3–40). New York: McGraw-Hill.

DePaulo, B. M., Lanier, K., & Davis, T. (1983). Detecting the deceit of the motivated liar. *Journal of Personality and Social Psychology, 45,* 1096–1103.

DePaulo, B. M., & Rosenthal, R. (1979). Telling lies. *Journal of Personality and Social Psychology, 37,* 1713–1722.

DePaulo, P. J., & DePaulo, B. M. (1989). Can deception by salespersons and customers be detected through non-verbal behavioral cues? *Journal of Applied Social Psychology, 19,* 1552–1577.

Deschamps, J.-C. (1983). Social attribution. In J. Jaspars, F.D. Fincham & M. Hewstone (Eds.), *Attribution theory and research: Conceptual, developmental and social dimensions* (pp. 223–240). London: Academic Press.

Deschamps, J.-C., & Brown, R. J. (1983). Superordinate goals and intergroup conflict. *British Journal of Social Psychology, 22,* 189–195.

Deutsch, M. (1975). Equity, equality and need: What determines which value will be used as a basis of distributive justice? *Journal of Social Issues, 31,* 137–149.

Deutsch, M., & Gerard, H. B. (1955). A study of normative and informational social influences upon individual judgment. *Journal of Abnormal and Social Psychology, 51,* 629–636.

Deutsch, M., & Krauss, R. M. (1960). The effect of threat upon interpersonal bargaining. *Journal of Abnormal and Social Psychology, 61,* 181–189.

Devine, P. G. (1989). Stereotypes and prejudice: Their automatic and controlled components. *Journal of Personality and Social Psychology, 56,* 5–18.

Devine, P. G., & Elliot, A. (1995). Are racial stereotypes really fading? The Princeton trilogy revisited. *Personality and Social Psychology Bulletin, 21,* 1139-1150.

Devine, P. G., Hamilton, D. L., & Ostrom, T. M. (Eds.) (1994). *Social cognition: Impact on social psychology.* San Diego, CA: Academic Press.

Devine, P. G., & Malpass, R. S. (1985). Orienting strategies in differential face recognition. *Personality and Social Psychology Bulletin, 11,* 33–40.

DeVos, G. A., & Hippler, A. E. (1969). Cultural psychology: Comparative studies of human behavior. In G. Lindzey & E. Aronson (Eds.), *Handbook of social psychology* (2nd ed., Vol. 4, pp. 322–417). Reading, MA: Addison-Wesley.

Diab, L. N. (1970). A study of intragroup and intergroup relations among experimentally produced small groups. *Genetic Psychology Monographs, 82,* 49–82.

Diamond, L. M. (2003). What does sexual orientation orient? A biobehavioral model distinguishing romantic love and sexual desire. *Psychological Review, 110,* 173–192.

Diaz-Guerrero, R. (1987). Historical sociocultural premises and ethnic socialization. In M. J. Rotheram (Ed.), *Children's ethnic socialization: Pluralism and development* (pp. 239–250). Newbury Park, CA: SAGE.

Dickens, C. (1854). *Hard times.* Harmondsworth, UK: Penguin.

Diehl, M. (1988). Social identity and minimal groups: The effects of interpersonal and intergroup attitudinal similarity on intergroup discrimination. *British Journal of Social Psychology, 27,* 289–300.

Diehl, M. (1990). The minimal group paradigm: Theoretical explanations and empirical findings. *European Review of Social Psychology, 1,* 263–292.

Diehl, M., & Stroebe, W. (1987). Productivity loss in brainstorming groups: Toward the solution of a riddle. *Journal of Personality and Social Psychology, 53,* 497–509.

Diehl, M., & Stroebe, W. (1991). Productivity loss in idea-generating groups: Tracking down the blocking effect. *Journal of Personality and Social Psychology, 61*, 392–403.

Diener, E. (1976). Effects of prior destructive behavior, anonymity, and group presence on deindividuation and aggression. *Journal of Personality and Social Psychology, 33*, 497–507.

Diener, E. (1980). Deindividuation: The absence of self-awareness and self-regulation in group members. In P. B. Paulus (Ed.), *Psychology of group influence* (pp. 209–242). Hillsdale, NJ: Erlbaum.

Diener, E., & Crandall, R. (1979). An evaluation of the Jamaican anticrime program. *Journal of Applied Social Psychology, 9*, 135–146.

Diener, E., Fraser, S. C., Beaman, A. L., & Kelem, R. T. (1976). Effects of deindividuation variables on stealing by Halloween trick-or-treaters. *Journal of Personality and Social Psychology, 33*, 178–183.

Dienstbier, R. A., Kahle, L. R., Willis, K. A., & Tunnell, G. B. (1980). The impact of moral theories on cheating: Studies of emotion attribution and schema activation. *Motivation and Emotion, 4*, 193–216.

Dietz, T. L. (1998). An examination of violence and gender role portrayals in video games: Implications for gender socialization and aggressive behavior. *Sex Roles, 38*, 425–442.

DiFonzo, N., & Bordia, P. (2007). Rumor psychology: Social and organizational approaches. Washington, DC: American Psychological Association.

Dijksterhuis, A. (2010). Automaticity and the unconscious. In S. T. Fiske, D. T. Gilbert, & G. Lindzey (Eds.), *Handbook of social psychology* (5th ed., Vol. 1, pp. 228-267). New York: Wiley.

Dindia, K. (1987). The effects of sex of subject and sex of partner in interruptions. *Human Communication Research, 13*, 345–371.

Dindia, K., & Allen, M. (1992). Sex differences in self-disclosure: A meta-analysis. *Psychological Bulletin, 112*, 106–124.

Dion, K. K., & Dion, K. L. (1996). Toward understanding love. *Personal Relationships, 3*, 1–3.

Dion, K. K., Berscheid, E., & Walster, E. (1972). What is beautiful is good. *Journal of Personality and Social Psychology, 24*, 285–290.

Dion, K. L. (1979). Intergroup conflict and intragroup cohesiveness. In W. G. Austin & S. Worchel (Eds.), *The social psychology of intergroup relations* (pp. 211–224). Monterey, CA: Brooks/Cole.

Dion, K. L. (2000). Group cohesion: From 'field of forces' to multidimensional construct. *Group Dynamics, 4*, 7–26.

Dion, K. L., & Earn, B. M. (1975). The phenomenology of being a target of prejudice. *Journal of Personality and Social Psychology, 32*, 944–950.

Dion, K. L., Earn, B. M., & Yee, P. H. N. (1978). The experience of being a victim of prejudice: An experimental approach. *International Journal of Psychology, 13*, 197–214.

Dipboye, R. L. (1977). Alternative approaches to deindividuation. *Psychological Bulletin, 84*, 1057–1075.

Dirks, K. T., & Ferrin, D. L. (2002). Trust in leadership: Meta-analytic findings and implications for research and practice. *Journal of Applied Psychology, 87*, 611–628.

Doi, L. T. (1976). The Japanese patterns of communication and the concept of amae. In L. A. Samovar & R. E. Porter (Eds.), *Intercultural communication: A reader* (2nd ed., pp. 188–193). Belmont, CA: Wadsworth.

Doise, W. (1978). *Groups and individuals: Explanations in social psychology*. Cambridge, UK: Cambridge University Press.

Doise, W. (1982). Report on the European Association of Experimental Social Psychology. *European Journal of Social Psychology, 12*, 105–111.

Doise, W. (1986). *Levels of explanation in social psychology*. Cambridge, UK: Cambridge University Press.

Doise, W., Clémence, A., & Lorenzi-Cioldi, F. (1993). *The quantitative analysis of social representations*. London: Harvester Wheatsheaf.

Dolinski, D. (2000). On inferring one's beliefs from one's attempt and consequences for subsequent compliance. *Journal of Personality and Social Psychology, 78*, 260–272.

Doll, J., & Ajzen, I. (1992). Accessibility and stability of predictors in the theory of planned behaviour. *Journal of Personality and Social Psychology, 63*, 754–765.

Dollard, J., Doob, L. W., Miller, N. E., Mowrer, O. H., & Sears, R. R. (1939). *Frustration and aggression*. New Haven, CT: Yale University Press.

Doms, M. (1983). The minority influence effect: An alternative approach. In W. Doise & S. Moscovici (Eds.), *Current issues in European social psychology* (Vol. 1, pp. 1–32). Cambridge, UK: Cambridge University Press.

Doms, M., & Van Avermaet, E. (1980). Majority influence, minority influence, and conversion behavior: A replication. *Journal of Experimental Social Psychology, 16*, 283–292.

Donnerstein, E., & Linz, D. (1994). Sexual violence in the mass media. In M. Costanzo & S. Oskamp (Eds.), *Violence and the law* (pp. 9–36). Thousand Oaks, CA: SAGE.

Donnerstein, E., & Malamuth, N. (1997). Pornography: Its consequences on the observer. In L. B. Schlesinger & E. Revitch (Eds.), *Sexual dynamics of anti-social behaviour* (2nd ed., pp. 30–49). Springfield, IL: Charles C. Thomas.

Doosje, B., Branscombe, N. R., Spears, R., & Manstead, A. S. R. (1998). Guilty by association: When one's group has a negative history. *Journal of Personality and Social Psychology, 75*, 872–886.

Dovidio, J. F. (1984). Helping behaviour and altruism: An empirical and conceptual overview. In L. Berkowitz (Ed.), *Advances in experimental social psychology* (Vol. 17, pp. 361–427). New York: Academic Press.

Dovidio, J. F., Brigham, J. C., Johnson, B. T., & Gaertner, S. L. (1996). Stereotyping, prejudice, and discrimination: Another look. In C. N. Macrae, C. Stangor & M. Hewstone (Eds.), *Stereotypes and stereotyping* (pp. 276–319). New York: Guilford Press.

Dovidio, J. F., & Ellyson, S. L. (1985). Patterns of visual dominance behavior in humans. In S. Ellyson & J. Dovidio (Eds.), *Power, dominance, and nonverbal behavior* (pp. 129–149). New York: Springer.

Dovidio, J. F., Ellyson, S. L., Keating, C. J., Heltman, K., & Brown, C. E. (1988). The relationship of social power to visual displays of dominance between men and women. *Journal of Personality and Social Psychology, 54*, 233–242.

Dovidio, J. F., & Gaertner, S. L. (2010). Intergroup bias. In S. T. Fiske, D. T. Gilbert, & G. Lindzey (Eds.), *Handbook of social psychology* (5th ed., Vol. 2, pp. 1084-1121). New York: Wiley.

Dovidio, J., Glick. P. Hewstone, M., & Esses, V. (Eds.) (2010). *Handbook of prejudice, stereotyping and discrimination.* London: SAGE.

Dovidio, J. F., Glick, P. G., & Rudman, L. (Eds.) (2005). *On the nature of prejudice: Fifty years after Allport.* Malden, MA: Blackwell.

Dovidio, J. F., Kawakami, K., & Beach, K. R. (2001). Implicit and explicit attitudes: Examination of the relationship between measures of intergroup bias. In R. Brown & S. Gaertner (Eds.), *Blackwell handbook of social psychology: Intergroup processes* (Vol. 4, pp. 175–197). Oxford, UK: Blackwell.

Dovidio, J. F., Pearson, A. R., & Orr, P. (2008). Social psychology and neuroscience: Strange bedfellows or a healthy marriage? *Group Processes and Intergroup Relations, 11*, 247-263.

Dovidio, J. F., Piliavin, J. A., Gaertner, S. L., Schroeder, D. A., & Clark, R. D., III (1991). The arousal: Cost–reward model and the process of intervention: A review of the evidence. In M. S. Clark (Ed.), *Prosocial behaviour* (pp. 86–118). Newbury Park, CA: SAGE.

Downton, J. V. (1973). *Rebel leadership.* New York: Free Press.

Duck, J. M., & Fielding, K. S. (1999). Leaders and sub-groups: One of us or one of them? *Group Processes and Intergroup Relations, 2*, 203–230.

Duck, J. M., & Fielding, K. S. (2003). Leaders and their treatment of subgroups: Implications for evaluations of the leader and the superordinate group. *European Journal of Social Psychology, 33*, 387–401.

Duck, J. M., Hogg, M. A., & Terry, D. J. (1999). Social identity and perceptions of media persuasion: Are we always less influenced than others? *Journal of Applied Social Psychology, 29*, 1879–1899.

Duck, J. M., Hogg, M. A., & Terry, D. J. (2000). The perceived impact of persuasive messages on 'us' and 'them'. In D. J. Terry & M. A. Hogg (Eds.), *Attitudes, behavior, and social context: The role of norms and group membership* (pp. 265–291). Mahwah, NJ: Erlbaum.

Duck, S. (2007). *Human relationships* (4th ed.). Thousand Oaks, CA: SAGE.

Duck, S. (Ed.) (1982). *Personal relationships, 4: Dissolving personal relationships.* London: Academic Press.

Duckitt, J. (1989). Authoritarianism and group identification: A new view of an old construct. *Political Psychology, 10*, 63–84.

Duckitt, J. (2000). Culture, personality and prejudice. In S. A. Renshon & J. Duckitt (Eds.), *Political psychology* (pp. 89–107). London: Macmillan.

Duckitt, J. (2006). Differential Effects of Right Wing Authoritarianism and Social Dominance Orientation on Outgroup Attitudes and Their Mediation by Threat From and Competitiveness to Outgroups. *Personality and Social Psychology Bulletin, 32*, 684-696.

Duckitt, J., Wagner, C., du Plessis, I., & Birum, I. (2002). The psychological bases of ideology and prejudice: Testing a dual process model. *Journal of Personality and Social Psychology, 83*, 75–93.

Duncan, S. (1969). Nonverbal communication. *Psychological Bulletin, 72*, 118–137.

Duncan, S. L. (1976). Differential social perception and attribution of intergroup violence: Testing the lower limits of stereotyping of blacks. *Journal of Personality and Social Psychology, 34*, 590–98.

Dunn, R. G. (1998). *Identity crises: A social critique of postmodernity.* Minneapolis, MN: University of Minnesota Press.

Dunning, D., Meyerowitz, J. A., & Holzberg, A. (1989). Ambiguity and self-evaluation: The role of idiosyncratic trait definitions in self-serving assessments of ability. *Journal of Personality and Social Psychology, 57*, 1082–1090.

Durkheim, E. (1898). Représentations individuelles et représentations collectives. *Revue de Metaphysique et de Morale, 6*, 273–302.

Durkheim, E. (1912/1995). *The elementary forms of the religious life.* New York: Free Press.

Durkin, K. (1995). *Developmental social psychology: From infancy to old age.* Oxford, UK: Blackwell.

Durkin, K. F., & Bryant, C. D. (1995). 'Log on to sex': Some notes on the carnal computer and erotic cyberspace as an emerging research frontier. *Deviant Behavior, 16*, 179–200.

Dutton, D. G., & Aron, A. P. (1974). Some evidence for heightened sexual attraction under conditions of high anxiety. *Journal of Personality and Social Psychology, 30*, 510-517.

Dutton, D. G., & Lake, R. (1973). Threat of own prejudice and reverse discrimination in interracial situations. *Journal of Personality and Social Psychology, 28*, 94–100.

Dutton, D. G., Boyanowsky, E. H., & Bond, M. H. (2005). Extreme mass homicide: From military massacre to genocide. *Aggression and Violent Behavior, 10*, 437–473.

Duval, S., & Wicklund, R. A. (1972). *A theory of objective self-awareness.* New York: Academic Press.

Dvir, T., Eden, D., Avolio, B. J., & Shamir, B. (2002). Impact of transformational leadership training on follower development and performance: A field experiment. *Academy of Management Journal, 45*, 735–744.

Eagly, A. H. (1978). Sex differences in influenceability. *Psychological Bulletin, 85*, 86–116.

Eagly, A. H. (1983). Gender and social influence: A social psychological analysis. *American Psychologist, 38*, 971–981.

Eagly, A. H. (1995). The science and politics of comparing women and men. *American Psychologist, 50*, 145–158.

Eagly, A. H. (2003). Few women at the top: How role incongruity produces prejudice and the glass ceiling. In D. van Knippenberg & M. A. Hogg (Eds.), *Leadership and power: Identity processes in groups and organizations* (pp. 79–93). London: SAGE.

Eagly, A. H., Beall, A. E., & Sternberg, R. J. (Eds.) (2005). *The psychology of gender.* New York: Guilford Press.

Eagly, A. H., & Carli, L. (1981). Sex of researcher and sex-typed communications as determinants of sex differences in influenceability: A meta-analysis of social influence studies. *Psychological Bulletin, 90*, 1–20.

Eagly, A. H., & Chaiken, S. (1984). Cognitive theories of persuasion. In L. Berkowitz (Ed.), *Advances in experimental social psychology* (Vol. 17, pp. 268–359). New York: Academic Press.

Eagly, A. H., & Chaiken, S. (1998). Attitude structure and function. In D. T. Gilbert, S. T. Fiske & G. Lindzey (Eds.), *The handbook of social psychology* (Vol. 1, pp. 269–322). Boston, MA: McGraw-Hill.

Eagly, A. H., & Chaiken, S. (2005). Attitude research in the 21st century: The current state of knowledge. In D. Albarracín, B. T. Johnson & M. P. Zanna (Eds.), *The handbook of attitudes* (pp. 742–767). Mahwah, NJ: Erlbaum.

Eagly, A. H., & Chrvala, C. (1986). Sex differences in conformity: Status and gender role interpretations. *Psychology of Women Quarterly, 10*, 203–220.

Eagly, A. H., & Crowley, M. (1986). Gender and helping behavior: A meta-analytic review of the social psychological literature. *Psychological Review, 100*, 283–308.

Eagly, A. H., Johannesen-Schmidt, M., Van Engen, M. L., & Vinkenburg, C. (2002). Transformational, transactional, and laissez-faire styles: A meta-analysis comparing men and women. *Psychological Bulletin, 129*, 569–591.

Eagly, A. H., & Karau, S. (1991). Gender and the emergence of leaders: A meta-analysis. *Journal of Personality and Social Psychology, 60*, 685–710.

Eagly, A. H., & Karau, S. J. (2002). Role congruity theory of prejudice toward female leaders. *Psychological Review, 109*, 573–598.

Eagly, A. H., Karau, S. J., & Makhijani, M. G. (1995). Gender and the effectiveness of leaders: A meta-analysis. *Psychological Bulletin, 117*, 125–145.

Eagly, A. H., Makhijani, M. G., & Klonsky, B. G. (1992). Gender and the evaluation of leaders: A meta-analysis. *Psychological Bulletin, 111*, 3–22.

Eagly, A. H., & Mladinic, A. (1994). Are people prejudiced against women? Some answers from research on attitudes, gender stereotypes, and judgments of competence. *European Review of Social Psychology, 5*, 1–35.

Eagly, A. H., & Steffen, V. J. (1984). Gender stereotypes stem from the distribution of women and men into social roles. *Journal of Personality and Social Psychology, 46*, 735–754.

Eagly, A. H., & Steffen, V. J. (1986). Gender and aggressive behavior: A meta-analytic review of the social psychological literature. *Psychological Bulletin, 100*, 309–330.

Eagly, A. H., & Wood, W. (1991). Explaining sex differences in social behaviour: A meta-analytic perspective. *Personality and Social Psychology Bulletin, 17*, 306–315.

Eagly, A. H., Wood, W., & Fishbaugh, L. (1981). Sex differences in conformity: Surveillance by the group as a determinant of male nonconformity. *Journal of Personality and Social Psychology, 40*, 384–394.

Earley, P. C. (1989). Social loafing and collectivism: A comparison of the United States and the People's Republic of China. *Administrative Science Quarterly, 34*, 565–581.

Earley, P. C. (1994). Self or group: Cultural effects of training on self-efficacy and performance. *Administrative Science Quarterly, 39*, 89–117.

Easterbrook, J. A. (1959). The effect of emotion on cue utilization and organization of behavior. *Psychological Review, 66*, 183–201.

Ebbinghaus, H. (1885). *Memory: A contribution to experimental psychology*. H. A. Ruger & C. E. Bussenius (trans.). New York: Dover, 1964.

Eckert, P., & McConnell-Ginet, S. (1999). New generalizations and explanations in language and gender research. *Language in Society, 28*, 185–201.

Eden, D. (1990). Pygmalion without interpersonal contrast effects: Whole groups gain from raising manager expectations. *Journal of Applied Psychology, 75*, 394–398.

Edney, J. J. (1979). The nuts game: A concise commons dilemma analog. *Environmental Psychology and Nonverbal Behavior, 3*, 252–254.

Edwards, A. L. (1957). *Techniques of attitude scale construction*. New York: Appleton-Century-Crofts.

Edwards, D. (1997). *Discourse and cognition*. London: SAGE.

Edwards, D., & Potter, J. (Eds.) (1992). *Discursive psychology*. London: SAGE.

Edwards, J. (1994). *Multilingualism*. London: Routledge.

Edwards, J., & Chisholm, J. (1987). Language, multi-culturalism and identity: A Canadian study. *Journal of Multilingual and Multicultural Development, 8*, 391–407.

Edwards, K. (1990). The interplay of affect and cognition in attitude formation and change. *Journal of Personality and Social Psychology, 59*, 202–216.

Edwards, K., & Smith, E. E. (1996). A disconfirmation bias in the evaluation of arguments. *Journal of Personality and Social Psychology, 71*, 5–24.

Ehrlich, H. J. (1973). *The social psychology of prejudice*. New York: Wiley.

Eibl-Eibesfeldt, I. (1972). Similarities and differences between cultures in expressive movements. In R. Hinde (Ed.), *Nonverbal communication* (pp. 297–314). Cambridge, UK: Cambridge University Press.

Eichler, M. (1980). *The double standard: A feminist critique of feminist social science*. London: Croom Helm.

Einhorn, H. J., & Hogarth, R. M. (1981). Behavioral decision theory: Processes of judgment and choice. *Annual Review of Psychology, 32*, 53–88.

Eisen, S. V. (1979). Actor–observer differences in information inference and causal attribution. *Journal of Personality and Social Psychology, 37*, 261–272.

Eisenberg, N., Fabes, R. A., Karbon, M., Murphy, B. C., Wosinski, M., Polazzi, L., et al. (1996). The relationship of children's dispositional prosocial behaviour to emotionality, regulation, and social functioning. *Child Development, 67*, 974–992.

Eisenberg, N., Guthrie, I. K., Murphy, B. C., Shepard, S. A., Cumberland, A., & Carlo, G. (1999). Consistency and development of prosocial dispositions: A longitudinal study. *Child Development, 70*, 1360–1372.

Eisenberg-Berg, N. (1979). Relationship of prosocial moral reasoning to altruism, political liberalism and intelligence. *Developmental Psychology, 15,* 87–89.

Eisenberger, N. I., Lieberman, M. D., & Williams, K. D. (2003). Does rejection hurt? An fMRI study of social exclusion. *Science, 302,* 290-292.

Eisenberger, R., & Shank, D. M. (1985). Personal work ethic and effort training affect cheating. *Journal of Personality and Social Psychology, 49,* 520–528.

Eiser, J. R. (1986). *Social psychology: Attitudes, cognition and social behaviour.* Cambridge, UK: Cambridge University Press.

Eiser, J. R., & Bhavnani, K. K. (1974). The effects of situational meaning on the behaviour of subjects in the prisoner's dilemma game. *European Journal of Social Psychology, 4,* 93–97.

Eiser, J. R., & Stroebe, W. (1972). *Categorization and social judgement.* London: Academic Press.

Ekman, P. (1971). Universals and cultural differences in facial expressions of emotion. In J. K. Cole (Ed.), *Nebraska symposium on motivation* (Vol. 19, pp. 207–284). Lincoln, NE: University of Nebraska Press.

Ekman, P. (1973). Cross-cultural studies of facial expression. In P. Ekman (Ed.), *Darwin and facial expression* (pp. 169–222). New York: Academic Press.

Ekman, P. (1982). *Emotion in the human face.* New York: Cambridge University Press.

Ekman, P. (2003). *Emotions revealed.* New York: Times Books.

Ekman, P., & Friesen, W. V. (1971). Constants across cultures in the face and emotion. *Journal of Personality and Social Psychology, 17,* 124–129.

Ekman, P., & Friesen, W. V. (1972). Hand movements. *Journal of Communication, 22,* 353–374.

Ekman, P., & Friesen, W. V. (1974). Detecting deception from the body or face. *Journal of Personality and Social Psychology, 29,* 188–198.

Ekman, P., & Friesen, W. V. (1975). *Unmasking the face.* Englewood Cliffs, NJ: Prentice Hall.

Ekman, P., Friesen, W. V., & Hager, J. C. (2002). *Facial action coding system.* Salt Lake City: Research Nexus.

Ekman, P., Friesen, W. V., O'Sullivan, M., Chan, A., Diacoyanni-Tarlatzis, I., Heider, K., Krause, R., Lecompte, W. A., Pitcairn, T., Riccibitti, P. E., Scherer, K., Tomita, M., & Tzavaras, A. (1987). Universals and cultural differences in the judgements of facial expressions of emotion. *Journal of Personality and Social Psychology, 53,* 712–717.

Ekman, P., Friesen, W. V., & Scherer, K. R. (1976). Body movement and voice pitch in deceptive interaction. *Semiotica, 16,* 23–27.

Ekman, P., O'Sullivan, M., & Frank, M. G. (1999). A few can catch a liar. *Psychological Science, 10,* 263–266.

Elfenbein, H. A., & Ambady, N. (2002). On the universality and cultural specificity of emotion recognition: A meta-analysis. *Psychological Bulletin, 128,* 203–235.

Ellemers, N. (1993). The influence of socio-structural variables on identity management strategies. *European Review of Social Psychology, 4,* 27–57.

Ellemers, N., De Gilder, D., & Haslam, S. A. (2004). Motivating individuals and groups at work: A social identity perspective on leadership and group performance. *Academy of Management Review, 29,* 459–478.

Ellemers, N., Spears, R., & Doosje, B. (Eds.) (1999). *Social identity.* Oxford, UK: Blackwell.

Elliot, A. J. (1981). *Child language.* Cambridge, UK: Cambridge University Press.

Ellis, R. J., Olson, J. M., & Zanna, M. P. (1983). Stereotypic personality inferences following objective versus subjective judgments of beauty. *Canadian Journal of Behavioral Science, 15,* 35–42.

Ellsworth, P. C., Carlsmith, J. M., & Henson, A. (1972). The stare as a stimulus to flight in human subjects: A series of field experiments. *Journal of Personality and Social Psychology, 21,* 302–311.

Ellsworth, P. C., & Gonzales, R. (2003). Questions and comparisons: Methods of research in social psychology. In M. A. Hogg & J. Cooper (Eds.), *The SAGE handbook of social psychology* (pp. 24–42). London: SAGE.

Elms, A. C. (1975). The crisis of confidence in social psychology. *American Psychologist, 30,* 967–76.

Elms, A. C. (1982). Keeping deception honest: Justifying conditions for social scientific research strategies. In T. L. Beauchamp & R. Faden (Eds.), *Ethical issues in social science research* (pp. 232-245). Baltimore, MD: Johns Hopkins University Press.

Elms, A. C., & Milgram, S. (1966). Personality characteristics associated with obedience and defiance toward authoritative command. *Journal of Experimental Research in Personality, 1,* 282–289.

Ember, C. R., & Ember, M. (1994). War, socialization, and interpersonal violence. *Journal of Conflict Resolution, 38,* 620–646.

Emler, N., & Hopkins, N. (1990). Reputation, social identity and the self. In D. Abrams & M. A. Hogg (Eds.), *Social identity theory: Constructive and critical advances* (pp. 113–130). London: Harvester Wheatsheaf.

Emler, N., Ohana, J., & Moscovici, S. (1987). Children's beliefs about institutional roles: A cross-national study of representations of the teacher's role. *British Journal of Educational Psychology, 57,* 26–37.

Emler, N., & Reicher, S. D. (1995). *Adolescence and delinquency: The collective management of reputation.* Oxford, UK: Blackwell.

Enriquez, V. G. (1993). Developing a Filipino psychology. In U. Kim & J. W. Berry (Eds.), *Indigenous psychologies: Research and experience in cultural context* (pp. 252–269). Newbury Park, CA: SAGE.

Erber, R. (1991). Affective and semantic priming: Effects of mood on category accessibility and inference. *Journal of Experimental Social Psychology, 27,* 480–498.

Erber, R., & Fiske, S. T. (1984). Outcome dependency and attention to inconsistent information. *Journal of Personality and Social Psychology, 47,* 709–726.

Eron, L. D. (1982). Parent–child interaction, television violence, and aggression of children. *American Psychologist, 37,* 197–211.

Eron, L. D. (1994). Theories of aggression: From drives to cognitions. In L. R. Huesmann (Ed.), *Aggressive behavior: Current perspectives* (pp. 3–11). New York: Plenum.

Esser, J. K., & Komorita, S. S. (1975). Reciprocity and concession making in bargaining. *Journal of Personality and Social Psychology, 31*, 864–872.

Esses, V. M., Dovidio, J. F., Semenya, A. H., & Jackson, L. M. (2005). Attitudes toward immigrants and immigration: The role of national and international identities. In D. Abrams, J. M. Marques, & M.A. Hogg (Eds.), *The social psychology of inclusion and exclusion* (pp. 317-337). Philadelphia: Psychology Press.

Esses, V. M., Jackson, L. M., Dovidio, J. F., & Hodson, G. (2005). Instrumental relations among groups: Group competition, conflict, and prejudice. In J. F. Dovidio, P. Glick,, & L. Rudman (Eds.), *Reflecting on the Nature of Prejudice* (pp. 227-243). Oxford, UK: Blackwell.

Evans, B. K., & Fischer, D. G. (1992). A hierarchical model of participatory decision-making, job autonomy, and perceived control. *Human Relations, 45*, 1169–1189.

Evans, N. J., & Jarvis, P. A. (1980). Group cohesion: A review and re-evaluation. *Small Group Behavior, 11*, 359–370.

Evans-Pritchard, E. E. (1937). *Witchcraft, oracles and magic among the Azande.* Oxford, UK: Oxford University Press.

Exline, R. V. (1971). Visual interaction: The glances of power and preference. In J. K. Cole (Ed.), *Nebraska symposium on motivation* (Vol. 19, pp. 163–206). Lincoln, NE: University of Nebraska Press.

Exline, R. V., Ellyson, S. L., & Long, B. (1975). Visual behavior as an aspect of power role relationships. In P. Pliner, L. Krames & T. Alloway (Eds.), *Nonverbal communication of aggression* (Vol. 2, pp. 21–52). New York: Plenum.

Fajardo, D. M. (1985). Author race, essay quality, and reverse discrimination. *Journal of Applied Social Psychology, 15*, 255–268.

Farr, R. M. (1996). *The roots of modern social psychology: 1872–1954.* Oxford, UK: Blackwell.

Farr, R. M., & Moscovici, S. (Eds.) (1984). *Social representations.* Cambridge: Cambridge University Press.

Fazio, R. H. (1986). How do attitudes guide behavior? In R. M. Sorrentino & E. T. Higgins (Eds.), *The handbook of motivation and cognition: Foundations of social behavior* (pp. 204-243). New York: Guilford Press.

Fazio, R. H. (1989). On the power and functionality of attitudes: The role of attitude accessibility. In A. R. Pratkanis, S. Breckler & A. G. Greenwald (Eds.), *Attitude structure and function* (pp. 153–179). Hillsdale, NJ: Erlbaum.

Fazio, R. H. (1995). Attitudes as object-evaluation associations: Determinants, consequences, and correlates of attitude accessibility. In R. E. Petty & J. A. Krosnick (Eds.), *Attitude strength: Antecedents and consequences* (pp. 247–282). Mahwah, NJ: Erlbaum.

Fazio, R. H., Blascovich, J., & Driscoll, D. M. (1992). On the functional value of attitudes: The influence of accessible attitudes upon the ease and quality of decision making. *Personality and Social Psychology Bulletin, 18*, 388–401.

Fazio, R. H., Effrein, E. A., & Falender, V. J. (1981). Self-perceptions following social interactions. *Journal of Personality and Social Psychology, 41*, 232–242.

Fazio, R. H., Jackson, J. R., Dunton, B. C., & Williams, C. J. (1995). Variability in automatic activation as an unobtrusive measure of racial attitudes: A bona fide pipeline. *Journal of Personality and Social Psychology, 69*, 1013–1027.

Fazio, R. H., Ledbetter, J. E., & Towles-Schwen, T. (2000). On the costs of accessible attitudes: Detecting that the attitude object has changed. *Journal of Personality and Social Psychology, 78*, 197–210.

Fazio, R. H., & Olson, M. A. (2003a). Attitudes: Foundations, functions, and consequences. In M. A. Hogg & J. Cooper (Eds.), *The SAGE handbook of social psychology* (pp. 139–160). London: SAGE.

Fazio, R. H., & Olson, M. A. (2003b). Implicit measures in social cognition research: Their meaning and use. *Annual Review of Psychology, 54*, 297–327.

Fazio, R. H., & Powell, M. C. (1997). On the value of knowing one's likes and dislikes: Attitude accessibility, stress and health in college. *Psychological Science, 8*, 430–436.

Fazio, R. H., Sanbonmatsu, D. M., Powell, M. C., & Kardes, F. R. (1986). On the automatic activation of attitudes. *Journal of Personality and Social Psychology, 50*, 229–238.

Fazio, R. H., & Zanna, M. P. (1978). Attitudinal qualities relating to the strength of the attitude–behaviour relation. *Journal of Experimental Social Psychology, 14*, 398–408.

Fazio, R. H., Zanna, M. P., & Cooper, J. (1977). Dissonance and self-perception: An integrative view of each theory's proper domain of application. *Journal of Experimental Social Psychology, 13*, 464–79.

Feagin, J. (1972). Poverty: We still believe that God helps them who help themselves. *Psychology Today, 6*, 101–129.

Feather, N. T. (1974). Explanations of poverty in Australian and American samples: The person, society and fate. *Australian Journal of Psychology, 26*, 199–216.

Feather, N. T. (1985). Attitudes, values, and attributions: Explanations of unemployment. *Journal of Personality and Social Psychology, 48*, 876–889.

Feather, N. T. (1991). Human values, global self-esteem, and belief in a just world. *Journal of Personality, 59*, 83–106.

Feather, N. T. (1994). Attitudes toward high achievers and reactions to their fall: Theory and research toward tall poppies. In L. Berkowitz (Ed.), *Advances in experimental social psychology* (Vol. 26, pp. 1–73). New York: Academic Press.

Feather, N. T. (2002). Values and value dilemmas in relation to judgments concerning outcomes of an industrial conflict. *Personality and Social Psychology Bulletin, 28*, 446–459.

Feather, N. T., & Barber, J. G. (1983). Depressive reactions and unemployment. *Journal of Abnormal Psychology, 92*, 185–195.

Feather, N. T., & Davenport, P. R. (1981). Unemployment and depressive affect: A motivational and attributional analysis. *Journal of Personality and Social Psychology, 41*, 422–436.

Feather, N. T., & Simon, J. G. (1975). Reactions to male and female success and failure in sex-linked occupations: Impressions of personality, causal attributions, and perceived likelihood of different consequences. *Journal of Personality and Social Psychology, 31,* 20–31.

Feeney, J. A. (1999). Adult attachment, emotional control, and marital satisfaction. *Personal Relationships, 6,* 169–185.

Feeney, J. A., & Noller, P. (1990). Attachment style as a predictor of adult romantic relationships. *Journal of Personality and Social Psychology, 58,* 281–291.

Fehr, B. (1994). Prototype based assessment of laypeople's views of love. *Personal Relationships, 1,* 309–331.

Fehr, R. S., & Stern, J. A. (1970). Peripheral physiological variables and emotion: The James–Lange theory revisited. *Psychological Bulletin, 74,* 411–424.

Feingold, A. (1988). Cognitive gender differences are disappearing. *American Psychologist, 43,* 95–103.

Fenigstein, A. (1984). Self-consciousness and the overperception of self as a target. *Journal of Personality and Social Psychology, 47,* 860–870.

Ferguson, C. K., & Kelley, H. H. (1964). Significant factors in overevaluation of own group's product. *Journal of Abnormal and Social Psychology, 69,* 223–228.

Fernández-Armesto, F. (2000). *Civilizations.* London: Macmillan.

Festinger, L. (1950). Informal social communication. *Psychological Review, 57,* 271–282.

Festinger, L. (1954). A theory of social comparison processes. *Human Relations, 7,* 117–140.

Festinger, L. (1957). *A theory of cognitive dissonance.* Stanford, CA: Stanford University Press.

Festinger, L. (1964). *Conflict, decision and dissonance.* Stanford, CA: Stanford University Press.

Festinger, L. (1980). *Retrospections on social psychology.* New York: Oxford University Press.

Festinger, L., & Carlsmith, J. M. (1959). Cognitive consequences of forced compliance. *Journal of Abnormal and Social Psychology, 58,* 203–210.

Festinger, L., Pepitone, A., & Newcomb, T. M. (1952). Some consequences of deindividuation in a group. *Journal of Personality and Social Psychology, 47,* 382–9.

Festinger, L., Schachter, S., & Back, K. (1950). *Social pressures in informal groups: A study of human factors in housing.* New York: Harper.

Fidell, L. S. (1970). Empirical verification of sex discrimination in hiring practices in psychology. *American Psychologist, 25,* 1094–1098.

Fiedler, F. E. (1964). A contingency model of leadership effectiveness. In L. Berkowitz (Ed.), *Advances in experimental social psychology* (Vol. 1, pp. 149–190). New York: Academic Press.

Fiedler, F. E. (1965). The contingency model of leadership effectiveness. In H. Proshansky, B. Seidenberg (Eds.), *Basic studies in social psychology* (pp. 538-551). New York: Holt, Rinehart, and Winston.

Fiedler, K. (1982). Causal schemata: Review and criticism of research on a popular construct. *Journal of Personality and Social Psychology, 42,* 1001–1013.

Fiedler, K., Messner, C., & Bluemke, M. (2006). Unresolved problems with the I, the A, and the T: A logical and psychometric critique of the Implicit Association Test (IAT). *European Review of Psychology, 17,* 74–147.

Field, R. H. G., & House, R. J. (1990). A test of the Vroom–Yetton model using manager and subordinate reports. *Journal of Applied Psychology, 75,* 362–366.

Fielding, K. S., & Hogg, M. A. (1997). Social identity, self-categorisation and leadership: A field study of small interactive groups. *Group Dynamics, Theory, Research, and Practice, 1,* 39–51.

Fielding, K. S., & Hogg, M. A. (2000). Working hard to achieve self-defining group goals: A social identity analysis. *Zeitschrift für Sozialpsychologie, 31,* 191–203.

Fielding, K. S., McDonald R., & Louis, W. R. (2008). Theory of planned behaviour, identity and intentions to engage in environmental activism. *Journal of Environmental Psychology, 28,* 318–326.

Fincham, F. D. (1985). Attributions in close relationships. In J. H. Harvey & G. Weary (Eds.), *Attribution: Basic issues and applications* (pp. 203–234). Orlando, FL: Academic Press.

Fincham, F. D. (2000). The kiss of the porcupines: From attributing responsibility to forgiving. *Personal Relationships, 7,* 1–23.

Fincham, F. D., & Bradbury, T. N. (1987). Cognitive processes and conflict in close relationships: An attribution–efficacy model. *Journal of Personality and Social Psychology, 53,* 1106–1118.

Fincham, F. D., & Bradbury, T. N. (1993). Marital satisfaction, depression, and attributions: A longitudinal analysis. *Journal of Personality and Social Psychology, 64,* 442–452.

Fincham, F. D., & O'Leary, K. D. (1983). Causal inferences for spouse behavior in maritally distressed and non-distressed couples. *Journal of Social and Clinical Psychology, 1,* 42–57.

Fiol, C. M. (2002). Capitalizing on paradox: The role of language in transforming organizational identities. *Organization Science, 13,* 653–666.

Fischer, A. H., Mosquera, P. M. R., Van Vienan, A. E. M., & Manstead, A. S. R. (2004). Gender and culture differences in emotion. *Emotion, 4,* 87–94.

Fischer, D. (1989). *Albion's seed: Four British folkways in America.* New York: Oxford University Press.

Fishbein, M. (1967a). A behavior theory approach to the relation between beliefs about an object and the attitude toward the object. In M. Fishbein (Ed.), *Readings in attitude theory and measurement* (pp. 389–400). New York: Wiley.

Fishbein, M. (1967b). A consideration of beliefs and their role in attitude measurement. In M. Fishbein (Ed.), *Readings in attitude theory and measurement* (pp. 257–266). New York: Wiley.

Fishbein, M. (1971). Attitudes and the prediction of behaviour. In K. Thomas (Ed.), *Attitudes and behaviour* (pp. 52–83). London: Penguin.

Fishbein, M., & Ajzen, I. (1974). Attitudes toward objects as predictors of single and multiple behavior criteria. *Psychological Review, 81,* 59–74.

Fishbein, M., & Ajzen, I. (1975). *Belief, attitude, intention and behavior: An introduction to theory and research.* Reading, MA: Addison-Wesley.

Fishbein, M., Ajzen, I., & Hinkle, R. (1980). Predicting and understanding voting in American elections: Effects of external variables. In I. Ajzen & M. Fishbein (Eds.), *Understanding attitudes and predicting human behavior* (pp. 173–195). Englewood Cliffs, NJ: Prentice Hall.

Fishbein, M., Bowman, C. H., Thomas, K., Jacard, J. J., & Ajzen, I. (1980). Predicting and understanding voting in British elections and American referenda: Illustrations of the theory's generality. In I. Ajzen & M. Fishbein (Eds.), *Understanding attitudes and predicting human behavior* (pp. 196–216). Englewood Cliffs, NJ: Prentice Hall.

Fishbein, M., & Coombs, F. S. (1974). Basis for decision: An attitudinal analysis of voting behavior. *Journal of Applied Social Psychology, 4,* 95–124.

Fishbein, M., & Feldman, S. (1963). Social psychological studies in voting behavior: I. Theoretical and methodological considerations. *American Psychologist, 18,* 388.

Fisher, J. D., Rytting, M., & Heslin, R. (1976). Hands touching hands: Affective and evaluative effects of an interpersonal touch. *Sociometry, 39,* 416–421.

Fisher, R. J. (1990). *The social psychology of intergroup and international conflict resolution.* New York: Springer.

Fisher, S., & Todd, A. D. (1983). *The social organization of doctor–patient communication.* Washington, DC: Center for Applied Linguistics.

Fishman, J. A. (1972). *Language and nationalism.* Rowley, MA: Newbury House.

Fishman, J. A. (1989). *Language and ethnicity in minority sociolinguistic perspective.* Clevedon, UK: Multilingual Matters.

Fiske, A. P. (1992). The four elementary forms of sociality: Framework for a unified theory of social relations. *Psychological Review, 99,* 689–723.

Fiske, A. P., & Haslam, N. (1996). Social cognition is thinking about relationships. *Current Directions in Psychological Science, 5,* 143–148.

Fiske, A. P., Kitayama, S., Markus, H. R., & Nisbett, R. E. (1998). The cultural matrix of social psychology. In D. T. Gilbert, S. T. Fiske & G. Lindzey (Eds.), *The handbook of social psychology* (4th ed., Vol. 2, pp. 915–981). New York: McGraw-Hill.

Fiske, S. T. (1980). Attention and weight on person perception. *Journal of Personality and Social Psychology, 38,* 889–906.

Fiske, S. T. (1993a). Social cognition and social perception. *Annual Review of Psychology, 44,* 155–194.

Fiske, S. T. (1993b). Controlling other people: The impact of power on stereotyping. *American Psychologist, 48,* 621–628.

Fiske, S. T. (1998). Stereotyping, prejudice, and discrimination. In D. T. Gilbert, S. T. Fiske, & G. Lindzey (Eds.), *The handbook of social psychology* (4th ed., Vol. 2, pp. 357–414). New York: McGraw-Hill.

Fiske, S. T. (2010). Interpersonal stratification: Status, power, and subordination. In S. T. Fiske, D. T. Gilbert, & G. Lindzey (Eds.), *Handbook of social psychology* (5th ed., Vol. 2, pp. 941-982). New York: Wiley.

Fiske, S. T., & Berdahl, J. (2007) Social power. In A. W. Kruglanski & E. T. Higgins (Eds.), *Social psychology: Handbook of basic principles* (2nd ed., pp. 678-692). New York: Guilford.

Fiske, S., Cuddy, A., Glick, P., & Xu, J. (2002). A model of (often mixed) stereotype content: Competence and warmth respectively follow from perceived status and competition. *Journal of Personality and Social Psychology, 82,* 878-902.

Fiske, S. T., & Dépret, E. (1996). Control, interdependence and power: Understanding social cognition in its social context. *European Review of Social Psychology, 7,* 31–61.

Fiske, S. T., Gilbert, D. T., & Lindzey, G. (Eds.) (2010). *Handbook of social psychology* (5th ed.). New York: Wiley.

Fiske, S. T., Lau, R. R., & Smith, R. A. (1990). On the varieties and utilities of political expertise. *Social Cognition, 8,* 31–48.

Fiske, S. T., & Neuberg, S. L. (1990). A continuum of impression formation, from category-based to individuating processes: Influences of information and motivation on attention and interpretation. In L. Berkowitz (Ed.), *Advances in experimental social psychology* (Vol. 23, pp. 1–74). New York: Academic Press.

Fiske, S. T., & Taylor, S. E. (1991). *Social cognition* (2nd ed.). New York: McGraw-Hill.

Fiske, S. T., & Taylor, S. E. (2008). *Social cognition: From brains to culture.* New York: McGraw-Hill.

Fitness, J. (2001). Emotional intelligence in intimate relationships. In J. Ciarrochi, J. Forgas & J. Mayer (Eds.), *Emotional intelligence in everyday life: A scientific enquiry* (pp. 98–112). Philadelphia, PA: Taylor & Francis.

Fitness, J., Fletcher, G., & Overall, N. (2003). Interpersonal attraction and intimate relationships. In M. A. Hogg & J. Cooper (Eds.), *The SAGE handbook of social psychology* (pp. 258–278). London: SAGE.

Fleishman, E. A. (1973). Twenty years of consideration and structure. In E. A. Fleishman & J. F. Hunt (Eds.), *Current developments in the study of leadership.* Carbondale, IL: South Illinois University Press.

Fletcher, G. J. O., & Clark, M. S. (Eds.) (2001). *Blackwell handbook of social psychology: Interpersonal processes.* Oxford, UK: Blackwell.

Fletcher, G. J. O., Danilovics, P., Fernandez, G., Peterson, D., & Reeder, G. D. (1986). Attributional complexity: An individual differences measure. *Journal of Personality and Social Psychology, 51,* 875–884.

Fletcher, G. J. O., Fincham, F. D., Cramer, L., & Heron, N. (1987). The role of attributions in the development of dating relationships. *Journal of Personality and Social Psychology, 53,* 481–489.

Fletcher, G. J. O., Simpson, J. A., & Thomas, G. (2000). Ideals, perceptions, and evaluations in early relationship development. *Journal of Personality and Social Psychology, 79,* 933–940.

Fletcher, G. J. O., Simpson, J. A., Thomas, G., & Giles, L. (1999). Ideals in intimate relationships. *Journal of Personality and Social Psychology, 76,* 72–89.

Fletcher, G. J. O., Tither, J. M., O'Loughlin, C., Friesen, M., & Overall, N. (2004). Warm and homely or cold and beautiful? Sex differences in trading off traits in mate selection. *Personality and Social Psychology Bulletin, 30,* 659–672.

Fletcher, G. J. O., & Thomas, G. (2000). Behavior and on-line cognition in marital interaction. *Personal Relationships, 7,* 111–130.

Fletcher, G. J. O., & Ward, C. (1988). Attribution theory and processes: A cross-cultural perspective. In M. H. Bond (Ed.), *The cross-cultural challenge to social psychology* (pp. 230–244). Newbury Park, CA: SAGE.

Flowers, M. L. (1977). A laboratory test of some implications of Janis's groupthink hypothesis. *Journal of Personality and Social Psychology, 35,* 888–896.

Floyd, D. L., Prentice-Dunn, S., & Rogers, R. W. (2000). A meta-analysis of research on protection motivation theory. *Journal of Applied Social Psychology, 30,* 407–429.

Foa, E. B., & Foa, U. G. (1975). *Resource theory of social exchange.* Morristown NJ: General Learning Press.

Foddy, M., Smithson, M., Schneider, S., & Hogg, M. A. (Eds.) (1999). *Resolving social dilemmas: Dynamic, structural, and intergroup aspects.* Philadelphia, PA: Psychology Press.

Fodor, E. M., & Smith, T. (1982). The power motive as an influence on group decision making. *Journal of Personality and Social Psychology, 42,* 178–185.

Fogelson, R. M. (1970). Violence and grievances: Reflections on the 1960s riots. *Journal of Social Issues, 26,* 141–163.

Fong, G. T., Krantz, D. H., & Nisbett, R. E. (1986). The effects of statistical training on thinking about everyday problems. *Cognitive Psychology, 18,* 253–292.

Forgas, J. P. (Ed.) (1981). *Social cognition: Perspectives on everyday understanding.* London: Academic Press.

Forgas, J. P. (1983). The effects of prototypicality and cultural salience on perceptions of people. *Journal of Research in Personality, 17,* 153–173.

Forgas, J. P. (1985). *Interpersonal behaviour.* Sydney: Pergamon Press.

Forgas, J. P. (1994). The role of emotion in social judgments: An introductory review and an affect infusion model (AIM). *European Journal of Social Psychology, 24,* 1–24.

Forgas, J. P. (1995). Mood and judgment: The affect infusion model. *Psychological Bulletin, 117,* 39–66.

Forgas, J. P. (2002). Feeling and doing: Affective influences on interpersonal behavior. *Psychological Inquiry, 13,* 1–28.

Forgas, J. P. (Ed.) (2006). *Affect, cognition and social behavior.* New York: Psychology Press.

Forgas, J. P., & Fiedler, K. (1996). Us and them: Mood effects on intergroup discrimination. *Journal of Personality and Social Psychology, 70,* 36–52.

Forgas, J. P., Morris, S., & Furnham, A. (1982). Lay explanations of wealth: Attributions for economic success. *Journal of Applied Social Psychology, 12,* 381–397.

Forgas, J. P., O'Connor, K., & Morris, S. (1983). Smile and punishment: The effects of facial expression on responsibility attributions by groups and individuals. *Personality and Social Psychology Bulletin, 9,* 587–596.

Forgas, J. P., & Smith, C. A. (2007). Affect and emotion. In M. A. Hogg & J. Cooper (Eds.), *The SAGE handbook of social psychology: Concise student edition* (pp. 146-175). London: SAGE.

Forsterling, F. (1988). *Attribution theory in clinical psychology.* Chichester, UK: Wiley.

Forsterling, F., & Rudolph, U. (1988). Situations, attributions and the evaluation of reactions. *Journal of Personality and Social Psychology, 54,* 225–232.

Foss, R. D., & Dempsey, C. B. (1979). Blood donation and the foot-in-the-door technique. *Journal of Personality and Social Psychology, 37,* 580–590.

Foster, C. A., Witcher, B. S., Campbell, W. K., & Green, J. D. (1998). Arousal and Attraction: Evidence for Automatic and Controlled Processes. *Journal of Personality and Social Psychology, 74,* 86-101.

Foucault, M. (1972). *The archaeology of knowledge.* London: Tavistock.

Fox, S. A., & Giles, H. (1993). Accommodating intergenerational contact: A critique and theoretical model. *Journal of Aging Studies, 7,* 423–451.

Fox, S. A., & Giles, H. (1996a). 'Let the wheelchair through!' An intergroup approach to interability communication. In W. P. Robinson (Ed.), *Social groups and identities: Developing the legacy of Henri Tajfel* (pp. 215–248). Oxford, UK: Butterworth-Heinemann.

Fox, S. A., & Giles, H. (1996b). Interability communication: Evaluating patronizing encounters. *Journal of Language and Social Psychology, 15,* 265–90.

Fox, S., & Hoffman, M. (2002). Escalation behavior as a specific case of goal-directed activity: A persistence paradigm. *Basic and Applied Social Psychology, 24,* 273–285.

Fox-Cardamone, L., Hinkle, S., & Hogue, M. (2000). The correlates of antinuclear activism: Attitudes, subjective norms, and efficacy. *Journal of Applied Social Psychology, 30,* 484–498.

Fraley, R. C., Brumbaugh, C. C., & Marks, M. M. (2005). The evolution and function of adult attachment: A comparative and phylogenetic analysis. *Journal of Personality and Social Psychology, 89,* 731–746.

Franco, F. M., & Maass, A. (1996). Implicit versus explicit strategies of outgroup discrimination: The role of intentional control in biased language use and reward allocation. *Journal of Language and Social Psychology, 15,* 335–359.

Frank, M. G., & Gilovich, T. (1989). Effect of memory perspective on retrospective causal attributions. *Journal of Personality and Social Psychology, 57,* 399–403.

Franklin, K. (2000). Antigay behaviours among young adults: Prevalence, patterns, and motivators in a noncriminal population. *Journal of Interpersonal Violence, 15,* 339-362.

Frazer, J. G. (1890). *The golden bough.* London: Macmillan.

Fredericks, A. J., & Dossett, D. L. (1983). Attitude–behavior relations: A comparison of the Fishbein–Ajzen and the Bentler–Speckart models. *Journal of Personality and Social Psychology, 45,* 501–512.

Freed, R. S., & Freed, S. A. (1989). Beliefs and practices resulting in female deaths and fewer females than males in India. *Population and Environment, 10,* 144–161.

Freedman, J. L. (1984). Effect of television violence on aggressiveness. *Psychological Bulletin, 96,* 227–246.

Freedman, J. L., & Fraser, S. C. (1966). Compliance without pressure: The foot-in-the-door technique. *Journal of Personality and Social Psychology, 4,* 195–202.

Freedman, J. L., Wallington, S. A., & Bless, E. (1967). Compliance without pressure: The effect of guilt. *Journal of Personality and Social Psychology, 7,* 117–124.

Freeman, S., Walker, M. R., Bordon, R., & Latané, B. (1975). Diffusion of responsibility and restaurant tipping: Cheaper by the bunch. *Personality and Social Psychology Bulletin, 1,* 584–587.

Freides, D. (1974). Human information processing and sensory modality: Cross-modal functions, information complexity, memory, and deficit. *Psychological Bulletin, 81,* 284–310.

French, J. R. P. (1944). Organized and unorganized groups under fear and frustration. *University of Iowa Studies of Child Welfare, 20,* 231–308.

French, J. R. P., & Raven, B. H. (1959). The bases of social power. In D. Cartwright (Ed.), *Studies in social power* (pp. 118–49). Ann Arbor, MI: Institute for Social Research.

Freud, S. (1905). *Three contributions to the theory of sex.* New York: Dutton.

Freud, S. (1921). Group psychology and the analysis of the ego. In J. Strachey (Ed.), *Standard edition of the complete psychological works* (Vol. 18, pp. 65–143). London: Hogarth Press.

Freud, S. (1920/1990). *Beyond the pleasure principle.* New York: W. W. Norton.

Frey, D. (1986). Recent research on selective exposure to information. In L. Berkowitz (Ed.), *Advances in experimental psychology* (Vol. 19, pp. 41–80). New York: Academic Press.

Frey, D., & Rosch, M. (1984). Information seeking after decisions: The roles of novelty of information and decision reversibility. *Personality and Social Psychology Bulletin, 10,* 91–98.

Frick, R. W. (1985). Communication emotions: The role of prosodic features. *Psychological Bulletin, 97,* 412–429.

Frieze, I., & Weiner, B. (1971). Cue utilisation and attributional judgments for success and failure. *Journal of Personality, 39,* 591–605.

Frohlich, N., & Oppenheimer, J. (1970). I get by with a little help from my friends. *World Politics, 23,* 104–120.

Fromm, E. (1941). *Escape from freedom.* New York: Farrar & Rinehart.

Funder, D. C. (1982). On the accuracy of dispositional vs situational attributions. *Social Cognition, 1,* 205–222.

Funder, D. C. (1987). Errors and mistakes: Evaluating the accuracy of social judgment. *Psychological Bulletin, 101,* 75–90.

Funder, D. C., & Fast, L. A. (2010). Personality in social psychology. In S. T. Fiske, D. T. Gilbert, & G. Lindzey (Eds.), *Handbook of social psychology* (5th ed., Vol. 1. pp. 668-697). New York: Wiley.

Furnham, A. (1982). Explanations for unemployment in Britain. *European Journal of Social Psychology, 12,* 335–352.

Furnham, A. (1983). Attributions for affluence. *Personality and Individual Differences, 4,* 31–40.

Furnham, A. (1986). Some explanations for immigration to, and emigration from, Britain. *New Community, 13,* 65–78.

Furnham, A. (2003). Belief in a just world: Research progress over the past decade. *Personality and Individual Differences, 34,* 795–817.

Furnham, A., & Bond, M. H. (1986). Hong Kong Chinese explanations for wealth. *Journal of Economic Psychology, 7,* 447–460.

Gaertner, S. L., & Dovidio, J. F. (1977). The subtlety of white racism, arousal, and helping behavior. *Journal of Personality and Social Psychology, 35,* 691–707.

Gaertner, S. L., & Dovidio, J. F. (1986). The aversive form of racism. In J. F. Dovidio & S. L. Gaertner (Eds.), *Prejudice, discrimination, and racism* (pp. 61–89). New York: Academic Press.

Gaertner S. L., & Dovidio, J. F. (2000). *Reducing intergroup bias: The common ingroup identity model.* New York: Psychology Press.

Gaertner, S. L., Dovidio, J., Anastasio, P., Bachman, B., & Rust, M. (1993). The common ingroup identity model: Recategorization and the reduction of intergroup bias. *European Review of Social Psychology, 4,* 1–26.

Gaertner, S. L., Mann, J., Murrell, A., & Dovidio, J. F. (1989). Reducing intergroup bias: The benefits of recategorization. *Journal of Personality and Social Psychology, 57,* 239–249.

Gaertner, S. L., & McLaughlin, J. P. (1983). Racial stereotypes: Associations and ascriptions of positive and negative characteristics. *Social Psychology Quarterly, 46,* 23–40.

Gaertner, S. L., Rust, M. C., Dovidio, J. F., Bachman, B. A., & Anastasio, P. A. (1996). The contact hypothesis: The role of a common ingroup identity on reducing intergroup bias among majority and minority group members. In J. L. Nye & A. M. Bower (Eds.), *What's social about social cognition: Research on socially shared cognition in small groups* (pp. 230–260). Thousand Oaks, CA: SAGE.

Galinsky, A. D. (2002). Creating and reducing intergroup conflict: The role of perspective-taking in affecting out-group evaluations. In H. Sondak (Ed.), *Toward phenomenology of groups and group membership. Research on managing groups and teams* (Vol. 4, pp. 85–113). New York: Elsevier.

Galinsky, A. D., & Moskowitz, G. B. (2000). Perspective-taking: Decreasing stereotype expression, stereotype accessibility, and in-group favoritism. *Journal of Personality and Social Psychology, 78,* 708–724.

Galinsky, A. D., & Mussweiler, T. (2001). First offers as anchors: The role of perspective-taking and negotiator focus. *Journal of Personality and Social Psychology, 81,* 657–669.

Galizio, M., & Hendrick, C. (1972). Effect of musical accompaniment on attitude: The guitar as a prop for persuasion. *Journal of Applied Social Psychology, 2,* 350–359.

Gallois, C. (1993). The language and communication of emotion: Interpersonal, intergroup, or universal. *American Behavioral Scientist, 36,* 309–338.

Gallois, C., & Callan, V. J. (1986). Decoding emotional messages: Influence of ethnicity, sex, message type, and channel. *Journal of Personality and Social Psychology, 51,* 755–762.

Gallois, C., & Callan, V. J. (1997). *Communication and culture: A guide for practice.* Chichester, UK: Wiley.

Gallois, C., Callan, V. J., & Johnstone, M. (1984). Personality judgements of Australian Aborigine and white speakers: Ethnicity, sex and context. *Journal of Language and Social Psychology, 3,* 39–57.

Gallois, C., Barker, M., Jones, E., & Callan, V. J. (1992). Intercultural communication: Evaluations of lecturers and Australian and Chinese students. In S. Iwawaki, Y. Kashima & K. Leung (Eds.), *Innovations in cross-cultural psychology* (pp. 86–102). Amsterdam: Swets & Zeitlinger.

Gallup, G. (1978). Gallup youth survey. *Indianapolis Star,* 18 October.

Gallupe, R. B., Cooper, W. H., Grise, M.-L., & Bastianutti, L. M. (1994). Blocking electronic brainstorms. *Journal of Applied Psychology, 79,* 77–86.

Galton, F. (1892). *Heredity genius: An inquiry into its laws and consequences.* London: Macmillan.

Gangestad, S. W., & Simpson, J. A. (2000). The evolution of human mating: Trade-offs and strategic pluralism. *Behavioral and Brain Sciences, 23,* 573–644.

Gao, G. (1996). Self and other: A Chinese perspective on interpersonal relationships. In W. B. Gudykunst, S. Ting-Toomey & T. Nishida (Eds.), *Communication in personal relationships across cultures* (pp. 81–101). Thousand Oaks, CA: SAGE.

Gao, G., Ting-Toomey, S., & Gudykunst, W. B. (1996). Chinese communication processes. In M. H. Bond (Ed.), *Handbook of Chinese psychology* (pp. 280–293). Hong Kong: Oxford University Press.

Gardner, M. J., Paulsen, N., Gallois, C., Callan, V. J., & Monaghan, P. (2001). Communication in organizations: An intergroup perspective. In W. P. Robinson & H. Giles (Eds.), *The new handbook of language and social psychology* (pp. 561–584). Chichester, UK: Wiley.

Gardner, R. A., & Gardner, B. T. (1971). Teaching sign language to a chimpanzee. *Science, 165,* 664–672.

Gardner, R. C. (1979). Social psychological aspects of second language acquisition. In H. Giles & R. St Clair (Eds.), *Language and social psychology* (pp. 193–220). Oxford, UK: Blackwell.

Gardner, R. M., & Tockerman, Y. R. (1994). A computer–TV methodology for investigating the influence of somatotype on perceived personality traits. *Journal of Social Behavior and Personality, 9,* 555–563.

Gardner, W. L., Gabriel, S., & Diekman, A. B. (2000). Interpersonal approaches. In J. T. Cacioppo, L. G. Tassinary & G. C. Berntson (Eds.), *Handbook of psychophysiology* (2nd ed., pp. 643–664). New York: Cambridge University Press.

Garfinkel, H. (1967). *Studies in ethnomethodology.* Englewood Cliffs, NJ: Prentice Hall.

Garrett, P., Giles, H., & Coupland, N. (1989). The contexts of language learning: Extending the intergroup model of second language acquisition. In S. Ting-Toomey & F. Korzenny (Eds.), *Language, communication, and culture* (pp. 201–221). Newbury Park, CA: SAGE.

Gaskell, G., & Smith, P. (1985). An investigation of youths' attributions for unemployment and their political attitudes. *Journal of Economic Psychology, 6,* 65–80.

Geen, R. G. (1978). Some effects of observing violence on the behaviour of the observer. In B. A. Maher (Ed.), *Progress in experimental personality research* (Vol. 8, pp. 49–93). New York: Academic Press.

Geen, R. G. (1989). Alternative conceptions of social facilitation. In P. B. Paulus (Ed.), *Psychology of group influence* (2nd ed., pp. 15–51). Hillsdale, NJ: Erlbaum.

Geen, R. G. (1991). Social motivation. *Annual Review of Psychology, 42,* 377–399.

Geen, R. G. (1998). Aggression and antisocial behaviour. In D. T. Gilbert, S. T. Fiske & G. Lindzey (Eds.), *The handbook of social psychology* (4th ed., Vol. 2, pp. 317–356). New York: McGraw-Hill.

Geen, R. G., & Donnerstein, E. (Eds.) (1983). *Aggression: Theoretical and empirical reviews.* New York: Academic Press.

Geen, R. G., & Gange, J. J. (1977). Drive theory of social facilitation: Twelve years of theory and research. *Psychological Bulletin, 84,* 1267–1288.

Geen, R. G., & Quanty, M. (1977). The catharsis of aggression: An evaluation of a hypothesis. In L. Berkowitz (Ed.), *Advances in experimental social psychology* (Vol. 10, pp. 2–37). New York: Academic Press.

Geer, J. H., & Jarmecky, L. (1973). The effect of being responsible for reducing another's pain on subject's response and arousal. *Journal of Personality and Social Psychology, 26,* 232–237.

Geertz, C. (1975). On the nature of anthropological understanding. *American Scientist, 63,* 47–53.

Gelfand, D. M., Hartmann, D. P., Walder, P., & Page, B. (1973). Who reports shoplifters? A field-experimental study. *Journal of Personality and Social Psychology, 25,* 276–285.

Genta, M. L., Menesini, E., Fonzi, A., Costabile, A., & Smith, P. K. (1996). Bullies and victims in schools in central and south Italy. *European Journal of Psychology of Education, 11,* 97–110.

Gentile, D. A., Anderson, C. A., Yukawa, S., Ihori, N., Saleem, M. et al. (2009). The effects of prosocial video games on prosocial behaviors: international evidence from correlational, longitudinal, and experimental studies. *Personality and Social Psychology Bulletin, 35,* 752-763.

Gerard, H. B., & Hoyt, M. F. (1974). Distinctiveness of social categorisation and attitude toward ingroup members. *Journal of Personality and Social Psychology, 29,* 836–842.

Gerard, H. B., & Mathewson, G. C. (1966). The effects of severity of initiation on liking for a group: A replication. *Journal of Experimental Social Psychology, 2,* 278–287.

Gergen, K. J. (1971). *The concept of self*. New York: Holt, Rinehart & Winston.

Gergen, K. J. (1973). Social psychology as history. *Journal of Personality and Social Psychology, 26*, 309–320.

Gergen, K. J., Gergen, M. M., & Meter, K. (1972). Individual orientations to prosocial behavior. *Journal of Social Issues, 28*, 105–130.

Gersick, C. J., & Hackman, J. R. (1990). Habitual routines in task performing groups. *Organizational Behavior and Human Decision Processes, 47*, 65–97.

Giancola, P. R. (2003). Individual difference and contextual factors contributing to the alcohol–aggression relation: diverse populations, diverse methodologies: An introduction to the special issue. *Aggressive Behavior, 29*, 285–287.

Gigone, D., & Hastie, R. (1993). The common knowledge effect: Information sharing and group judgment. *Journal of Personality and Social Psychology, 65*, 959–974.

Gilbert, D. T. (1995). Attribution and interpersonal perception. In A. Tesser (Ed.), *Advanced social psychology* (pp. 99–147). New York: McGraw-Hill.

Gilbert, D. T. (1998). Ordinary personology. In D. T. Gilbert, S. T. Fiske & G. Lindzey (Eds.), *The handbook of social psychology* (4th ed., Vol. 2, pp. 89–150). New York: McGraw-Hill.

Gilbert, D. T., Fiske, S. T., & Lindzey, G. (Eds.) (1998). *The handbook of social psychology* (4th ed.). New York: McGraw-Hill.

Gilbert, D. T., & Malone, P. S. (1995). The correspondence bias. *Psychological Bulletin, 117*, 21–38.

Gilbert, D. T., & Silvera, D. H. (1996). Overhelping. *Journal of Personality and Social Psychology, 70*, 678–690.

Giles, H. (1978). Linguistic differentiation in ethnic groups. In H. Tajfel (Ed.), *Differentiation between social groups: Studies in the social psychology of intergroup relations* (pp. 361–393). London: Academic Press.

Giles, H. (Ed.) (1984). The dynamics of speech accommodation theory. *International Journal of the Sociology of Language, 46*, whole issue.

Giles, H., Bourhis, R. Y., & Taylor, D. M. (1977). Towards a theory of language in ethnic group relations. In H. Giles (Ed.), *Language, ethnicity, and intergroup relations* (pp. 307–48). London: Academic Press.

Giles, H., & Byrne, J. L. (1982). The intergroup model of second language acquisition. *Journal of Multilingual and Multicultural Development, 3*, 17–40.

Giles, H., & Coupland, N. (1991). *Language: Contexts and consequences*. Milton Keynes, UK: Open University Press.

Giles, H., Coupland, N., Henwood, K., Harriman, J., & Coupland, J. (1990). The social meaning of RP: An intergenerational perspective. In S. Ramsaran (Ed.), *Studies in the pronunciation of English: A commemorative volume in honour of A. C. Gimson* (pp. 191–211). London: Routledge.

Giles, H., & Johnson, P. (1981). The role of language in ethnic group relations. In J. C. Turner & H. Giles (Eds.), *Intergroup behaviour* (pp. 199–243). Oxford, UK: Blackwell.

Giles, H., & Johnson, P. (1987). Ethnolinguistic identity theory: A social psychological approach to language maintenance. *International Journal of the Sociology of Language, 68*, 66–99.

Giles, H., Mulac, A., Bradac, J. J., & Johnson, P. (1987). Speech accommodation theory: The next decade and beyond. In M. McLaughlin (Ed.), *Communication yearbook* (Vol. 10, pp. 13–48). Newbury Park, CA: SAGE.

Giles, H., & Noels, K. A. (2002). Communication accommodation in intercultural encounters. In T. K. Nakayama & L. A. Flores (Eds.), *Readings in cultural contexts* (pp. 117–126). Boston, MA: McGraw-Hill.

Giles, H., Noels, K., Ota, H., Ng, S. H., Gallois, C., Ryan, E. B., et al. (2001). Age vitality in eleven nations. *Journal of Multilingual and Multicultural Development, 21*, 308–323.

Giles, H., & Powesland, P. F. (1975). *Speech style and social evaluation*. London: Academic Press.

Giles, H., Reid, S., & Harwood, J. (Eds.) (2010). *The dynamics of intergroup communication*. New York: Peter Lang.

Giles, H., Rosenthal, D., & Young, L. (1985). Perceived ethnolinguistic vitality: The Anglo- and Greek-American setting. *Journal of Multilingual and Multicultural Development, 6*, 253–69.

Giles, H., & Street, R. (1985). Communicator characteristics and behaviour. In M. L. Knapp & G. R. Miller (Eds.), *Handbook of interpersonal communication* (pp. 205–261). Beverly Hills, CA: SAGE.

Giles, H., Taylor, D. M., & Bourhis, R. Y. (1973). Towards a theory of interpersonal accommodation through language: Some Canadian data. *Language in Society, 2*, 177–192.

Gillig, P. M., & Greenwald, A. G. (1974). Is it time to lay the sleeper effect to rest? *Journal of Personality and Social Psychology, 29*, 132–139.

Gladue, B. A. (1991). Aggressive behavioural characteristics, hormones, and sexual orientation in men and women. *Aggressive Behavior, 17*, 313–326.

Gladue, B. A., Boechler, M., & McCall, K. D. (1989). Hormonal response to competition in human males. *Aggressive Behaviour, 15*, 409–422.

Glaser, J., & Banaji, M. R. (1999). When fair is foul and foul is fair: Reverse priming in automatic evaluation. *Journal of Personality and Social Psychology, 77*, 669–687.

Glassman, L. R., & Albarracín, D. (2006). Forming attitudes that predict future behavior: A meta-analysis of the attitude–behavior relation. *Psychological Bulletin, 132*, 788–822.

Glenn, E. S. (1976). Meaning and behaviour: Communication and culture. In L. A. Samovar & R. E. Porter (Eds.), *Intercultural communication: A reader* (2nd ed., pp. 170–193). Belmont, CA: Wadsworth.

Glick, P., & Fiske, S. T. (1996). The ambivalent sexism inventory: Differentiating hostile and benevolent sexism. *Journal of Personality and Social Psychology, 70*, 491–512.

Glick, P., & Fiske, S. T. (1997). Hostile and benevolent sexism: Measuring ambivalent sexist attitudes toward women. *Psychology of Women Quarterly, 21*, 119–135.

Godin, G. R., Valois, P., Lepage, L., & Desharnais, R. (1992). Predictors of smoking behaviour: An application of Ajzen's theory of planned behaviour. *British Journal of Addiction, 87*, 1335–1343.

Goethals, G. R., & Darley, J. M. (1987). Social comparison theory: Self-evaluation and group life. In B. Mullen & G. Goethals (Eds.), *Theories of group behavior* (pp. 21–48). New York: Springer.

Goethals, G. R., & Nelson, R. E. (1973). Similarity in the influence process: The belief–value distinction. *Journal of Personality and Social Psychology, 25,* 117–122.

Goethals, G. R., & Sorenson, G. (Eds.) (2004), *Encyclopedia of leadership.* Thousand Oaks, CA: SAGE.

Goethals, G. R., & Zanna, M. P. (1979). The role of social comparison in choice shifts. *Journal of Personality and Social Psychology, 37,* 1469–1476.

Goff, P. A., Steele, C. M., & Davies, P. G. (2008). The space between us: Stereotype threat and distance in interracial contexts. *Journal of Personality and Social Psychology, 94,* 91–107.

Goffman, E. (1959). *The presentation of self in everyday life.* New York: Doubleday/Anchor Books.

Goffman, E. (1963). *Stigma: Notes on the management of spoiled identity.* Englewood Cliffs, NJ: Prentice Hall.

Goldberg, M. E., & Gorn, G. J. (1974). Children's reactions to television advertising: An experimental approach. *Journal of Consumer Research, 1,* 69–75.

Goldberg, P. (1968). Are some women prejudiced against women? *Trans-Action, 5,* 28–30.

Goldman, M., Creason, C. R., & McCall, C. G. (1981). Compliance employing a two-feet-in-the-door procedure. *Journal of Social Psychology, 114,* 259–265.

Goldstein, A. P. (1987). Aggression. In R. J. Corsini (Ed.), *Concise encyclopedia of psychology* (pp. 35–39). New York: Wiley.

Goldstein, A. P. (1999). Aggression reduction strategies: Effective and ineffective. *School Psychology Quarterly, 14,* 40–58.

Goldstein, J. H. (1980). *Social psychology.* New York: Academic Press.

Golec de Zavala, A., Cichocka, A., Eidelson, R., & Jayawickreme, N. (in press). Collective narcissism and its social consequences. *Journal of Personality and Social Psychology.*

Gollwitzer, P. M., & Bargh, J. A. (Eds.) (1996). *The psychology of action: Linking cognition and motivation to behavior.* New York: Guilford Press.

Gollwitzer, P. M., & Kinney, R. F. (1989). Effects of deliberative and implemental mind-sets on illusion of control. *Journal of Personality and Social Psychology, 56,* 531–542.

Goodman, M. (1964). *Race awareness in young children* (2nd ed.). New York: Cromwell-Collier.

Goodman, M. E. (1946). Evidence concerning the genesis of interracial attitudes. *American Anthropologist, 38,* 624–630.

Goodman, M. E. (1952). *Race awareness in young children.* Cambridge, MA: Addison-Wesley.

Goodwin, R. (1999). *Personal relationships across cultures.* London: Routledge.

Goodwin, S. A., Gubin, A., Fiske, S. T., & Yzerbyt, V. Y. (2000). Power can bias impression processes: Stereotyping subordinates by default and by design. *Group Processes and Intergroup Relations, 3,* 227–256.

Gorassini, D. R., & Olson, J. M. (1995). Does self-perception change explain the foot-in-the-door effect? *Journal of Personality and Social Psychology, 69,* 91–105.

Gordon, R. A. (1996). Impact of ingratiation on judgments and evaluations: A meta-analytic investigation. *Journal of Personality and Social Psychology, 71,* 54–70.

Gorer, G. (1968). Man has no 'killer' instinct. In M. F. A. Montagu (Ed.), *Man and aggression* (pp. 27–36). New York: Oxford University Press.

Gorn, G. J. (1982). The effects of music in advertising on choice: A classical conditioning approach. *Journal of Marketing, 46,* 94–101.

Gorsuch, R. L., & Ortbergh, J. (1983). Moral obligation and attitudes: Their relation to behavioral intentions. *Journal of Personality and Social Psychology, 44,* 1025–1028.

Gosselin, C., & Wilson, G. (1980). *Sexual variations.* New York: Simon & Schuster.

Gottlieb, J., & Carver, C. S. (1980). Anticipation of future interaction and the bystander effect. *Journal of Experimental Social Psychology, 16,* 253–260.

Gouldner, A. W. (1960). The norm of reciprocity: A preliminary statement. *American Sociological Review, 25,* 161–178.

Graen, G. B., & Uhl-Bien, M. (1995). Relationship-based approach to leadership: Development of leader–member exchange (LMX) theory of leadership over 25 years: Applying a multi-level multi-domain approach. *The Leadership Quarterly, 6,* 219–247.

Graham, S., Hudley C., & Williams, E. (1992). An attributional approach to aggression in African-American children. *Developmental Psychology, 28,* 731–740.

Granberg, D. (1987). Candidate preference, membership group, and estimates of voting behavior. *Social Cognition, 5,* 323–335.

Graumann, C. F., & Moscovici, S. (Eds.) (1986). *Changing conceptions of crowd mind and behavior.* New York: Springer.

Graumann, C. F., & Moscovici, S. (Eds.) (1987). *Changing conceptions of conspiracy.* New York: Springer.

Green, D. P., Glaser, J., & Rich, A. (1998). From lynching to gay bashing: The elusive connection between economic conditions and hate crime. *Journal of Personality and Social Psychology, 75,* 82-92.

Greenberg, J., & Rosenfield, D. (1979). Whites' ethnocentrism and their attributions for the behavior of blacks: A motivational bias. *Journal of Personality, 47,* 643–657.

Greenberg, J., Pyszczynski, T., & Solomon, S. (1986). The causes and consequences of self-esteem: A terror management theory. In R. Baumeister (Ed.), *Public self and private self* (pp. 189–212). New York: Springer.

Greenberg, J., Solomon, S., & Pyszczynski, T. (1997). Terror management theory of self-esteem and cultural worldviews: Empirical assessments and conceptual refinements. In M. Zanna (Ed.), *Advances in experimental social psychology* (Vol. 29, pp. 61–139). Orlando, FL: Academic Press.

Greenberg, J., Solomon, S., Pyszczynski, T., Rosenblatt, A., Burling, J., Lyon, D., Simon, L., & Pinel, E. (1992). Why do people need self-esteem? Converging evidence that self-esteem serves an anxiety-buffering function. *Journal of Personality and Social Psychology, 63*, 913–922.

Greenberg, J., Williams, K. D., & O'Brien, M. K. (1986). Considering the harshest verdict first: Biasing effects on mock juror verdict. *Personality and Social Psychology Bulletin, 12*, 41–50.

Greenfield, P. M., Keller, H., Fuligni, A., & Maynard, A. (2003). Cultural pathways through universal development. *Annual Review of Psychology, 54*, 461–490.

Greenglass, E. R. (1982). *A world of difference: Gender roles in perspective*. Toronto: Wiley.

Greenwald, A. G. (1980). The totalitarian ego: Fabrication and revision of personal history. *American Psychologist, 35*, 603–618.

Greenwald, A. G., & Banaji, M. R. (1995). Implicit social cognition: Attitudes, self-esteem, and stereotypes. *Psychological Review, 102*, 4–27.

Greenwald, A. G., Banaji, M. R., Rudman, L. A., Farnham, S. D., Nosek, B. A., & Mellott, D. S. (2002). A unified theory of implicit attitudes, stereotypes, self-esteem, and self-concept. *Psychological Review, 109*, 3–25.

Greenwald, A. G., & Pratkanis, A. R. (1984). The self. In R. S. Wyer Jr & T. K. Srull (Eds.), *Handbook of social cognition* (Vol. 3, pp. 129–178). Hillsdale, NJ: Erlbaum.

Greenwald, A. G., & Pratkanis, A. R. (1988). On the use of 'theory' and the usefulness of theory. *Psychological Review, 95*, 575–579.

Greenwald, A. G., McGhee, D. E., & Schwartz, J. L. K. (1998). Measuring individual differences in implicit cognition: The implicit association test. *Journal of Personality and Social Psychology, 74*, 1464–1480.

Gregg, A. P., Seibt, B., & Banaji, M. R. (2006). Easier done than undone: Asymmetry in the malleability of implicit preferences. *Journal of Personality and Social Psychology, 90*, 1–20.

Gregson, R. A. M., & Stacey, B. G. (1981). Attitudes and self-reported alcohol consumption in New Zealand. *New Zealand Psychologist, 10*, 15–23.

Grieve, P., & Hogg, M. A. (1999). Subjective uncertainty and intergroup discrimination in the minimal group situation. *Personality and Social Psychology Bulletin, 25*, 926–940.

Griffitt, W. B., & Veitch, R. (1971). Hot and crowded: Influence of population density and temperature on interpersonal affective behavior. *Journal of Personality and Social Psychology, 17*, 92–98.

Griffiths, M. (1997). Video games and aggression. *The Psychologist*, September, 397–401.

Groff, B. D., Baron, R. S., & Moore, D. L. (1983). Distraction, attentional conflict, and drivelike behavior. *Journal of Experimental Social Psychology, 19*, 359–380.

Gross, A. E., & Fleming, J. (1982). Twenty years of deception in social psychology. *Personality and Social Psychology Bulletin, 8*, 402–408.

Grossman, R. B., & Kegl, J. (2007). Moving faces: Categorization of dynamic facial expressions in American Sign Language by deaf and hearing participants. *Journal of Nonverbal Behavior, 31*, 23–38.

Gruber-Baldini, A. L., Schaie, K. W., & Willis, S. L. (1995). Similarity in married couples: A longitudinal study of mental abilities and rigidity–flexibility. *Journal of Personality and Social Psychology, 69*, 191–203.

Gruenfeld, D. H., & Tiedens, L. Z. (2010). Organizational preferences and their consequences. In S. T. Fiske, D. T. Gilbert, & G. Lindzey (Eds.), *Handbook of social psychology* (5th ed., Vol. 2, pp. 1252-1287). New York: Wiley.

Grusec, J. E. (1991). The socialisation of altruism. In M. S. Clark (Ed.), *Prosocial behaviour* (pp. 9–33). Newbury Park, CA: SAGE.

Grusec, J. E., & Redler, E. (1980). Attribution, reinforcement and altruism: A developmental analysis. *Developmental Psychology, 16*, 525–534.

Grusec, J. E., Kuczynski, L., Rushton, J. P., & Simutis, Z. M. (1978). Modelling, direct instruction, and attributions: Effects on altruism. *Developmental Psychology, 14*, 51–57.

Gubar, S., & Hoff, J. (Eds.) (1989). *For adult users only: The dilemma of violent pornography*. Bloomington, IN: Indiana University Press.

Gudykunst, W. B., Matsumoto, Y., Ting-Toomey, S., Nishida, T., Kim, K., & Heyman, S. (1996). The influence of cultural individualism–collectivism, self-construals, and individual values on communication styles across cultures. *Human Communication Research, 22*, 510–543.

Guerin, B. (1986). Mere presence effects in humans: A review. *Journal of Experimental Social Psychology, 22*, 38–77.

Guerin, B. (1989). Reducing evaluation effects in mere presence. *Journal of Social Psychology, 129*, 183–190.

Guerin, B. (1993). *Social facilitation*. Cambridge: Cambridge University Press.

Guerin, B., & Innes, J. M. (1982). Social facilitation and social monitoring: A new look at Zajonc's mere presence hypothesis. *British Journal of Social Psychology, 21*, 7–18.

Guimond, S., & Dubé-Simard, L. (1983). Relative deprivation theory and the Québec Nationalist Movement: The cognitive–emotion distinction and the personal–group deprivation issue. *Journal of Personality and Social Psychology, 44*, 526–535.

Gump, B. B., & Kulik, J. A. (1997). Stress, affiliation, and emotional contagion, *Journal of Personality and Social Psychology, 72*, 305–319.

Gupta, U., & Singh, P. (1982). An exploratory study of love and liking and types of marriages. *Indian Journal of Applied Psychology, 19*, 92–97.

Gurr, T. R. (1970). *Why men rebel*. Princeton, NJ: Princeton University Press.

Gustafson, R. (1992). Alcohol and aggression: A replication study controlling for potential confounding variables. *Aggressive Behavior, 18*, 21–28.

Gutek, B. A. (1985). *Sex and the workplace*. San Francisco, CA: Jossey-Bass.

Guttman, L. A. (1944). A basis for scaling qualitative data. *American Sociological Review, 9*, 139–150.

Guzzo, R. A., & Dickson, M. W. (1996). Teams in organizations: Recent research on performance and effectiveness. *Annual Review of Psychology, 47*, 307–338.

Guzzo, R. A., Jost, P. R., Campbell, R. J., & Shea, G. P. (1993). Potency in groups: Articulating a construct. *British Journal of Social Psychology, 32*, 87–106.

Haas, A. (1979). Male and female spoken language differences: Stereotypes and evidence. *Psychological Bulletin, 86*, 616–626.

Hackman, J. R. (2002). *Leading teams: Setting the stage for great performances.* Boston, MA: Harvard Business School Press.

Hackman, J. R., & Katz, N. (2010). Group behavior and performance. In S. T. Fiske, D. T. Gilbert, & G. Lindzey (Eds.), *Handbook of social psychology* (5th ed., Vol. 2, pp. 1208-1251). New York: Wiley.

Haddock, G., & Zanna, M. P. (1999). Affect, cognition, and social attitudes. In W. Stroebe & M. Hewstone (Eds.), *European review of social psychology* (Vol. 10, pp. 75–100). Chichester, UK: Wiley.

Haddock, G., Rothman, A. J., Reber, R., & Schwarz, N. (1999). Forming judgements of attitude certainty, intensity, and importance: The role of subjective experiences. *Personality and Social Psychology Bulletin, 25*, 231–232.

Hagger, M. S., & Chatzisarantis, N. L. D. (2006). Self-identity and the theory of planned behaviour: Between- and within-participants analyses. *British Journal of Social Psychology, 45*, 731–757.

Haines, H., & Vaughan, G. M. (1979). Was 1898 a great date in the history of social psychology? *Journal for the History of the Behavioural Sciences, 15*, 323–332.

Hains, S. C., Hogg, M. A., & Duck, J. M. (1997). Self-categorization and leadership: Effects of group prototypicality and leader stereotypicality. *Personality and Social Psychology Bulletin, 23*, 1087–1100.

Haire, M., & Grune, W. E. (1950). Perceptual defenses: Processes protecting an organized perception of another personality. *Human Relations, 3*, 403–412.

Hale, J. L., Lemieux, R., & Mongeau, P. A. (1995). Cognitive processing of fear-arousing message content. *Communication Research, 22*, 459–474.

Hall, B. J., & Gudykunst, W. B. (1986). The intergroup theory of second language ability. *Journal of Language and Social Psychology, 5*, 291–302.

Hall, E. T. (1966). *The hidden dimension.* New York: Doubleday.

Hall, E. T. (1979). Gender, gender roles, and nonverbal communication. In R. Rosenthal (Ed.), *Skill in nonverbal communication* (pp. 32–67). Cambridge, MA: Oelgeschlager, Gunn & Hain.

Hall, E. T., & Braunwald, K. G. (1981). Gender cues in conversations. *Journal of Personality and Social Psychology, 40*, 99–110.

Hall, J. A. (1978). Gender effects in decoding nonverbal cues. *Psychological Bulletin, 85*, 845–857.

Hall, J. A. (1984). *Nonverbal sex differences: Communication accuracy and expressive style.* Baltimore, MD: Johns Hopkins University Press.

Hall, J. A., Coats, E. J., & LeBeau, L. S. (2005). Nonverbal behavior and the vertical dimension of social relations: A meta-analysis. *Psychological Bulletin, 131*, 898–924.

Halpern, D. (1995). *Mental health and the built environment: More than bricks and mortar?* London: Taylor & Francis.

Hamburger, Y. (1994). The contact hypothesis reconsidered: Effects of the atypical outgroup member on the outgroup stereotype. *Basic and Allied Social Psychology, 15*, 339–358.

Hamilton, D. L. (1979). A cognitive attributional analysis of stereotyping. In L. Berkowitz (Ed.), *Advances in experimental social psychology* (Vol. 12, pp. 53–84). New York: Academic Press.

Hamilton, D. L. (Ed.) (2004). *Social cognition: Essential readings.* New York: Psychology Press.

Hamilton, D. L., & Gifford, R. K. (1976). Illusory correlation in interpersonal personal perception: A cognitive basis of stereotypic judgments. *Journal of Experimental Social Psychology, 12*, 392–407.

Hamilton, D. L., & Sherman, J. W. (1989). Illusory correlations: Implications for stereotype theory and research. In D. Bar-Tal, C. F. Graumann, A. W. Kruglanski & W. Stroebe (Eds.), *Stereotyping and prejudice: Changing conceptions* (pp. 59–82). New York: Springer.

Hamilton, D. L., & Sherman, J. W. (1994). Stereotypes. In R. S. Wyler, Jr, & T. K. Srull (Eds.), *Handbook of social cognition* (Vol. 2, pp. 1–68). Hillsdale, NJ: Erlbaum.

Hamilton, D. L., & Sherman, S. J. (1996). Perceiving persons and groups. *Psychological Review, 103*, 336–335.

Hamilton, D., & Stroessner, S. J. (in press). *Social cognition.* London: SAGE.

Hamilton, D. L., Stroesser, S. J., & Driscoll, D. M. (1994). Social cognition and the study of stereotyping. In P. G. Devine, D. L. Hamilton, & T. M. Ostrom (Eds.), *Social cognition: Impact on social psychology* (pp. 291–321). San Diego, CA: Academic Press.

Hamilton, D. L., & Zanna, M. P. (1974). Context effects in impression formation: Changes in connotative meaning. *Journal of Personality and Social Psychology, 29*, 649–654.

Hampson, S. E., John, O. P., & Goldberg, L. R. (1986). Category breadth and hierarchical structure in personality: Studies in asymmetries in judgments of trait implications. *Journal of Personality and Social Psychology, 51*, 37–54.

Haney, C., Banks, C., & Zimbardo, P. (1973). A study of prisoners and guards in a simulated prison. *Naval Research Review, 9*, 1–17 [Reprinted in E. Aronson (Ed.), *Readings about the social animal* (3rd ed., pp. 52–67). San Francisco, CA: W. H. Freeman].

Hannover, B., & Kühnen, U. (2004). Culture, context, and cognition: The semantic procedural interface model of the self. *European Review of Social Psychology, 15*, 297–333.

Hardin, G. (1968). The tragedy of the commons. *Science, 162*, 1243–1248.

Harkins, S. G. (1987). Social loafing and social facilitation. *Journal of Experimental Social Psychology, 23*, 1–18.

Harkins, S. G., & Szymanski, K. (1987). Social loafing and social facilitation: New wine in old bottles. In C. Hendrick (Ed.), *Review of personality and social psychology: Group processes and intergroup relations* (Vol. 9, pp. 167–188). Newbury Park, CA: SAGE.

Harkins, S. G., & Szymanski, K. (1989). Social loafing and group evaluation. *Journal of Personality and Social Psychology, 56,* 934–941.

Harlow, H. F. (1958). The nature of love. *American Psychologist, 13,* 673–685.

Harlow, H. F., & Harlow, M. K. (1965). The affectional systems. In A. M. Schrier, H. F. Harlow & F. Stollnitz (Eds.), *Behavior of non-human primates* (Vol. 2). New York: Academic Press.

Harmon-Jones, E. (2000). Cognitive dissonance and experienced negative affect: Evidence that dissonance increases experienced negative affect even in the absence of aversive consequences. *Personality and Social Psychology Bulletin, 27,* 889–898.

Harmon-Jones, E., & Winkielman, P. (Eds.) (2007). *Social neuroscience: Integrating biological and psychological explanations of social behavior.* New York: Guilford Press.

Harré, N., Foster, S., & O'Neill, M. (2005). Self-enhancement, crash-risk optimism and the impact of safety advertisements on young dirvers. *British Journal of Psychology, 96,* 215–30.

Harré, R. (1979). *Social being: A theory for social psychology.* Oxford, UK: Blackwell.

Harries, K. D., & Stadler, S. J. (1983). Determinism revisited: Assault and heat stress in Dallas, 1980. *Environment and Behavior, 15,* 235–256.

Harrington, J. (2006). An acoustic analysis of 'happy-tensing' in the Queen's Christmas broadcasts. *Journal of Phonetics, 34,* 439–457.

Harris, E. E. (1970). *Hypothesis and perception.* London: Allen & Unwin.

Harris, N. B. (1992). Sex, race, and experiences of aggression. *Aggressive Behavior, 18,* 201–217.

Harris, R. J., & Cook, C. A. (1994). Attributions about spouse abuse: It matters who the batterers and victims are. *Sex Roles, 30,* 553–564.

Hart, P. T. (1990). *Groupthink in government: A study of small groups and policy failure.* Amsterdam: Swets & Zeitlinger.

Hartley, J. F., & Stephenson, G. M. (Eds.) (1992). *Employment relations: The psychology of influence and control at work.* Oxford, UK: Blackwell.

Hartmann, H., Kris, E., & Loewenstein, R. M. (1949). Notes on a theory of aggression. *Psychoanalytic Study of the Child, 3–4,* 9–36.

Harvey, J. H. (1987). Attributions in close relationships: Research and theoretical developments. *Journal of Social and Clinical Psychology, 5,* 420–434.

Harvey, J. H., & Weary, G. (1981). *Perspectives on attributional processes.* Dubuque, IA: W. C. Brown.

Harwood, J., Giles, H., & Bourhis, R. Y. (1994). The genesis of vitality theory: Historical patterns and discoursal dimensions. *International Journal of the Sociology of Language, 108,* 167–206.

Harwood, J., Giles, H., & Ryan, E. B. (1995). Aging, communication, and intergroup theory: Social identity and intergenerational communication. In J. Nussbaum & J. Coupland (Eds.), *Handbook of communication and aging research* (pp. 133–159). Mahwah, NJ: Erlbaum.

Haslam, N. (1994). Categories of social relationship. *Cognition, 53,* 59–90.

Haslam, N. (2006). Dehumanization: An Integrative Review. *Personality and Social Psychology Review, 10,* 252–264

Haslam, N., Bastian, B., Bain, P., & Kashima, Y. (2006). Psychological essentialism, implicit theories, and intergroup relations. *Group Processes and Intergroup Relations, 9,* 63–76.

Haslam, N., Bastian, B., & Bissett, M. (2004). Essentialist beliefs about personality and their implications. *Personality and Socia Psychology Bulletin, 30,* 1661-1673.

Haslam, N., Loughnan, S., & Kashima, Y. (2008). Attributing and denying humanness to others. *European Review of Social Psychology, 19,* 55-85.

Haslam, N., Rothschild, L., & Ernst, D. (1998). Essentialist beliefs about social categories. *British Journal of Social Psychology, 39,* 113–127.

Haslam, S. A. (2004). *Psychology in organisations: The social identity approach* (2nd ed.). London: SAGE.

Haslam, S. A., & Platow, M. J. (2001). Your wish is our command: The role of shared social identity in translating a leader's vision into followers' action. In M. A. Hogg & D. J. Terry (Eds.), *Social identity processes in organizational contexts* (pp. 213–228). Philadelphia, PA: Psychology Press.

Haslam, S. A., & Reicher, S. D. (2005). The psychology of tyranny. *Scientific American, 16,* 44–51.

Haslam, S. A., Turner, J. C., Oakes, P. J., McGarty, C., & Hayes, B. K. (1992). Context-dependent variation in social stereotyping 1: The effects of intergroup relations as mediated by social change and frame of reference. *European Journal of Social Psychology, 22,* 3–20.

Hass, R. G., Katz, I., Rizzo, N., Bailey, J., & Eisenstadt, D. (1991). Cross-racial appraisal as related to attitude ambivalence and cognitive complexity. *Personality and Social Psychology Bulletin, 17,* 83–92.

Hassett, J. (1981). But that would be wrong . . . *Psychology Today,* November, 34–50.

Hastie, R. (1984). Causes and effects of causal attribution. *Journal of Personality and Social Psychology, 46,* 44–56.

Hastie, R. (1988). A computer simulation model of person memory. *Journal of Experimental Social Psychology, 24,* 423–447.

Hastie, R. (Ed.) (1993). *Inside the juror: The psychology of juror decision making.* Cambridge, UK: Cambridge University Press.

Hastie, R., & Park, B. (1986). The relationship between memory and judgment depends on whether the judgment task is memory-based or on-line. *Psychological Review, 93,* 258–268.

Hastie, R., Penrod, S. D., & Pennington, N. (1983). *Inside the jury.* Cambridge, MA: Harvard University Press.

Hatfield, E. (1987). Love. In R. J. Corsini (Ed.), *Concise encyclopedia of psychology* (pp. 676–677). New York: Wiley.

Hatfield, E., & Walster, G. W. (1981). *A new look at love.* Reading, MA: Addison-Wesley.

Haugtvedt, C. P., & Petty, R. E. (1992). Personality and persuasion: Need for cognition moderates the persistence and resistance of attitude changes. *Journal of Personality and Social Psychology, 63,* 308–319.

Hawking, S. W. (1988). *A brief history of time: From the Big Bang to black holes*. London: Bantam.

Hayduk, L. A. (1983). Personal space: Where we now stand. *Psychological Bulletin, 94,* 293–335.

Hazan, C., & Shaver, P. (1987). Romantic love conceptualized as an attachment process. *Journal of Personality and Social Psychology, 52,* 511–524.

Heaven, P. C. L. (1990). Human values and suggestions for reducing unemployment. *British Journal of Social Psychology, 29,* 257–264.

Hebb, D. O., & Thompson, W. R. (1968). The social significance of animal studies. In G. Lindzey & E. Aronson (Eds.), *Handbook of social psychology* (2nd ed., Vol. 2, pp. 729–774). Reading, MA: Addison-Wesley.

Heider, F. (1946). Attitudes and cognitive organisation. *Journal of Psychology, 21,* 107–112.

Heider, F. (1958). *The psychology of interpersonal relations*. New York: Wiley.

Heider, F., & Simmel, M. (1944). An experimental study of apparent behavior. *American Journal of Psychology, 57,* 243–259.

Heilman, M. E. (1983). Sex bias in work settings: The lack of fit model. *Research in Organizational Behavior, 5,* 269–298.

Heilman, M. E., & Parks-Stamm, E. J. (2007). Gender stereotypes in the workplace: Obstacles to women's career progress. *Advances in group Processes, 24,* 47-77.

Heilman, M. E., & Stopeck, M. H. (1985). Attractiveness and corporate success: Different causal attributions for males and females. *Journal of Applied Psychology, 70,* 379–388.

Heilman, M. E., Wallen, A. S., Fuchs, D., & Tamkins, M. M. (2004). Penalties for success: Reactions to women who succeed at male gender-typed tasks. *Journal of Applied Psychology, 89,* 416–427.

Heine, S. J., & Buchtel, E. E. (2009). Personality: The universal and the culturally specific. *Annual Review of Psychology, 60,* 369-394.

Heine, S. J. (2010). Cultural psychology. In S. T. Fiske, D. T. Gilbert, & G. Lindzey (Eds.), *Handbook of social psychology* (5th ed., Vol. 2, pp. 1423-1464). New York: Wiley.

Heinemann, W. (1990). Meeting the handicapped: A case of affective–cognitive inconsistency. *European Review of Social Psychology, 1,* 323–338.

Heisler, G. (1974). Ways to deter law violators: Effects of levels of threat and vicarious punishment on cheating. *Journal of Consulting and Clinical Psychology, 42,* 577–582.

Henderson, J., & Taylor, J. (1985). Study finds bias in death sentences: Killers of Whites risk execution. *Times Union,* 17 November, p. A19.

Hendrick, C., & Hendrick, S. S. (1995). Gender differences and similarities in sex and love. *Personal Relationships, 2,* 55–65.

Hendrick, C., Bixenstine, V. E., & Hawkins, G. (1971). Race vs belief similarities as determinants of attraction: A search for a fair test. *Journal of Personality and Social Psychology, 17,* 250–258.

Henley, N. M. (1973). The politics of touch. In P. Brown (Ed.), *Radical psychology* (pp. 421–433). New York: Harper & Row.

Henley, N. M. (1977). *Body politics: Power, sex, and nonverbal communication*. Englewood Cliffs, NJ: Prentice Hall.

Henley, N. M., & Harmon, S. (1985). The nonverbal semantics of power and gender: A perceptual study. In S. L. Ellyson & J. F. Dovidio (Eds.), *Power, dominance, and nonverbal behavior* (pp. 151–164). New York: Springer.

Henriques, J., Holloway, W., Urwin, C., Venn, C., & Walkerdine, V. (1984). *Changing the subject: Psychology, social regulation, and subjectivity*. London: Methuen.

Henry, W. A., III (1994). Pride and prejudice. *Time,* 27 June, 54–59.

Hensley, T. R., & Griffin, G. W. (1986). Victims of groupthink: The Kent State University Board of Trustees and the 1977 gymnasium controversy. *Journal of Conflict Resolution, 30,* 497–531.

Herek, G. M., & Glunt, E. K. (1988). An epidemic of stigma: Public reaction to AIDS. *American Psychologist, 43,* 886–891.

Herman, C. P., Roth, D. A., & Polivy, J. (2003). Effects of the presence of others on food intake: A normative interpretation. *Psychological Bulletin, 129,* 873–886.

Herr, P. M., Sherman, S. J., & Fazio, R. H. (1983). On the consequences of priming: Assimilation and contrast effects. *Journal of Experimental Social Psychology, 19,* 323–340.

Hersh, S. M. (1970). *My Lai: A report on the massacre and its aftermath*. New York: Vintage Books.

Heslin, R. (1978). Responses to touching as an index of sex-role norms and attitudes. Paper presented at the annual meeting of the American Psychological Association, Toronto, August.

Heslin, R., & Alper, T. (1983). Touch: A bonding gesture. In J. M. Wiemann & R. P. Harrison (Eds.), *Nonverbal interaction* (pp. 47–75). Beverly Hills, CA: SAGE.

Hess, E. H. (1965). The pupil responds to changes in attitude as well as to changes in illumination. *Scientific American, 212,* 46–54.

Heuer, L., & Penrod, S. (1994). Trial complexity: A field investigation of its meaning and its effect. *Law and Human Behavior, 18,* 29–51.

Hewes, G. W. (1957). The anthropology of posture. *Scientific American, 196,* 123–132.

Hewstone, M. (1986). *Understanding attitudes to the European Community: A social-psychological study in four member states*. Cambridge, UK: Cambridge University Press.

Hewstone, M. (1989). *Causal attribution: From cognitive processes to collective beliefs*. Oxford, UK: Blackwell.

Hewstone, M. (1990). The 'ultimate attribution error': A review of the literature on intergroup causal attribution. *European Journal of Social Psychology, 20,* 311–335.

Hewstone, M. (1994). Revision and change of stereotypic beliefs: In search of the elusive subtyping model. *European Review of Social Psychology, 5,* 69–109.

Hewstone, M. (1996). Contact and categorization: Social psychological interventions to change intergroup relations. In C. N. Macrae, C. Stangor & M. Hewstone (Eds.), *Stereotypes and stereotyping* (pp. 323–368). New York: Guilford Press.

Hewstone, M., & Antaki, C. (1988). Attribution theory and social explanations. In M. Hewstone, W. Stroebe, J.-P. Codol & G. M. Stephenson (Eds.), *Introduction to social psychology: A European perspective* (pp. 111–141). Oxford, UK: Blackwell.

Hewstone, M., & Brown, R. J. (Eds.) (1986). *Contact and conflict in intergroup encounters.* Oxford, UK: Blackwell.

Hewstone, M., Cairns, E., Voci, A., Paolini, S., McLernon, F., Crisp, R. J., et al. (2005). Intergroup contact in a divided society: Challenging segregation in Northern Ireland. In D. Abrams, J. M. Marques & M. A. Hogg (Eds.), *The social psychology of inclusion and exclusion* (pp. 265–292). New York: Psychology Press.

Hewstone, M., & Jaspars, J. M. F. (1982). Intergroup relations and attribution processes. In H. Tajfel (Ed.), *Social identity and intergroup relations* (pp. 99–133). Cambridge, UK: Cambridge University Press.

Hewstone, M., & Jaspars, J. M. F. (1984). Social dimensions of attribution. In H. Tajfel (Ed.), *The social dimension* (pp. 379–404). Cambridge, UK: Cambridge University Press.

Hewstone, M., Jaspars, J. M. F., & Lalljee, M. (1982). Social representations, social attribution and social identity: The intergroup images of 'public' and 'comprehensive' schoolboys. *European Journal of Social Psychology, 12,* 241–269.

Hewstone, M., & Stroebe, W. (Eds.) (2001). *Introduction to social psychology* (3rd ed.). Oxford, UK: Blackwell.

Hewstone, M., Stroebe, W., & Jonas, K. (Eds.). (2008). *Introduction to Social Psychology: A European Perspective* (4th ed.). London: Blackwell.

Hewstone, M., & Ward, C. (1985). Ethnocentrism and causal attribution in Southeast Asia. *Journal of Personality and Social Psychology, 48,* 614–623.

Higgins, E. T. (1981). The 'communication game': Implications for social cognition. In E. T. Higgins, C. P. Herman & M. Zanna (Eds.), *Social cognition: The Ontario symposium* (Vol. 1, pp. 343–392). Hillsdale, NJ: Erlbaum.

Higgins, E. T. (1987). Self-discrepancy: A theory relating self and affect. *Psychological Review, 94,* 319–340.

Higgins, E. T. (1996). Knowledge activation: Accessibility, applicability, and salience. In E. T. Higgins & A. W. Kruglanski (Eds.), *Social psychology: Handbook of basic principles* (pp. 133–168). New York: Guilford Press.

Higgins, E. T. (1997). Beyond pleasure and pain. *American Psychologist, 52,* 1280–1300.

Higgins, E. T. (1998). Promotion and prevention: Regulatory focus as a motivational principle. In M. P. Zanna (Ed.), *Advances in experimental social psychology* (Vol. 30, pp. 1–46). New York: Academic Press.

Higgins, E. T., Bargh, J. A., & Lombardi, W. (1985). The nature of priming effects on categorization. *Journal of Experimental Psychology: Learning, Memory, and Cognition, 11,* 59–69.

Higgins, E. T., Bond, R. N., Klein, R., & Strauman, T. (1986). Self-discrepancies and emotional vulnerability: How magnitude, accessibility, and type of discrepancy influence affect. *Journal of Personality and Social Psychology, 51,* 5–15.

Higgins, E. T., Roney, C., Crowe, E., & Hymes, C. (1994). Ideal versus ought predilections for approach and avoidance: Distinct self-regulatory systems. *Journal of Personality and Social Psychology, 66,* 276–286.

Higgins, E. T., & Silberman, I. (1998). Development of regulatory focus: Promotion and prevention as ways of living. In J. Heckhausen & C. S. Dweck (Eds.), *Motivation and self-regulation across the lifespan* (pp. 78–113). New York: Cambridge University Press.

Higgins, E. T., & Tykocinski, O. (1992). Self-discrepancies and biographical memory: Personality and cognition at the level of psychological situation. *Personality and Social Psychology Bulletin, 18,* 527–535.

Higgins, E. T., Van Hook, E., & Dorfman, D. (1988). Do self-attributes form a cognitive structure? *Social Cognition, 6,* 177–207.

Hill, C., & Peplau, L. (1998). Premarital predictors of relationship outcomes: A 15-year follow up of the Boston couples study. In T. N. Bradbury et al. (Eds.), *The developmental course of marital dysfunction* (pp. 237–278). New York: Cambridge University Press.

Hill, D., White, V., Marks, R., & Borland, R. (1993). Changes in sun-related attitudes and behaviours and reduced sunburn prevalence in a population at high risk of melanoma. *European Journal of Cancer Prevention, 1,* 447–456.

Hilton, D. J. (1988). Logic and causal attribution. In D. J. Hilton (Ed.), *Contemporary science and natural explanation: Commonsense conceptions of causality* (pp. 33–65). Brighton, UK: Harvester Press.

Hilton, D. J. (1990). Conversational processes and causal explanation. *Psychological Bulletin, 107,* 65–81.

Hilton, D. J. (2007). Causal explanation: from social perception to knowledge-based causal attribution. In A. W. Kruglanski & E. T. Higgins (Eds.), *Social psychology: Handbook of basic principles* (2nd ed., pp. 232-253). New York: Guilford.

Hilton, D. J., & Karpinski, A. (2000). *Attitudes and the implicit associations test.* Ann Arbor, MI: University of Michigan Press.

Hilton, J. L., & von Hippel, W. (1996). Stereotypes. *Annual Review of Psychology, 47,* 237–271.

Hilton, N. Z., Harris, G. T., & Rice, M. E. (2000). The functions of aggression by male teenagers. *Journal of Personality and Social Psychology, 79,* 988–994.

Himmelfarb, S., & Eagly, A. H. (Eds.) (1974). *Readings in attitude change.* New York: Wiley.

Himmelweit, H. T., Humphreys, P., & Jaeger, M. (1985). *A model of vote choice based on a special longitudinal study extending over 15 years and the British election surveys of 1970–83,* Milton Keynes, UK: Open University Press.

Hinde, R. A. (1982). *Ethology: Its nature and relations with other sciences.* London: Fontana.

Hinkle, S., & Brown, R. (1990). Intergroup comparisons and social identity: Some links and lacunae. In D. Abrams & M. Hogg (Eds.), *Social identity theory: Constructive and critical advances* (pp. 48–70). Hemel Hempstead, UK: Harvester Wheatsheaf.

Hitler, A. (1933). *Mein Kampf*. Retrieved November 11, 2003, from http://www.stormfront.org/books/meinkampf/mkv1ch06.html

Hodges, S. D., Klaaren, K. J., & Wheatley, T. (2000). Talking about safe sex: The role of expectations and experience. *Journal of Applied Social Psychology, 30,* 330–349.

Hoffman, C., Lau, I., & Johnson, D. R. (1986). The linguistic relativity of person cognition: An English–Chinese comparison. *Journal of Personality and Social Psychology, 51,* 1097–1105.

Hoffman, C., Mischel, W., & Mazze, K. (1981). The role of purpose in the organisation of information about behavior: Trait-based versus goal-based categories in person cognition. *Journal of Personality and Social Psychology, 40,* 211–225.

Hoffman, M. L. (1981). Is altruism part of human nature? *Journal of Personality and Social Psychology, 40,* 121–137.

Hofstede, G. (1980). *Culture's consequences: International differences in work-related values.* Beverly Hills, CA: SAGE.

Hofstede, G. (2001). *Culture's consequences: Comparing values, behaviours, institutions and organizations across nations* (2nd ed.). Thousand Oaks, CA: SAGE.

Hogan, R., & Kaiser, R. (2006). What we know about leadership. *Review of General Psychology, 9,* 169–180.

Hogg, M. A. (1985). Masculine and feminine speech in dyads and groups: A study of speech style and gender salience. *Journal of Language and Social Psychology, 4,* 99–112.

Hogg, M. A. (1992). *The social psychology of group cohesiveness: From attraction to social identity.* London: Harvester Wheatsheaf.

Hogg, M. A. (1993). Group cohesiveness: A critical review and some new directions. *European Review of Social Psychology, 4,* 85–111.

Hogg, M. A. (2000a). Social processes and human behavior: Social psychology. In K. Pawlik & M. R. Rosenzweig (Eds.), *International handbook of psychology* (pp. 305–327). London: SAGE.

Hogg, M. A. (2000b). Social identity and social comparison. In J. Suls & L. Wheeler (Eds.), *Handbook of social comparison: Theory and research* (pp. 401–421). New York: Kluwer/Plenum.

Hogg, M. A. (2000c). Subjective uncertainty reduction through self-categorization: A motivational theory of social identity processes. *European Review of Social Psychology, 11,* 223-255.

Hogg, M. A. (2001a). Social categorization, depersonalization, and group behavior. In M. A. Hogg & R. S. Tindale (Eds.), *Blackwell handbook of social psychology: Group processes* (pp. 56–85). Oxford, UK: Blackwell.

Hogg, M. A. (2001b). A social identity theory of leadership. *Personality and Social Psychology Review, 5,* 184–200.

Hogg, M. A. (2003a). Intergroup relations. In J. Delamater (Ed.), *Handbook of social psychology* (pp. 479–501). New York: Kluwer Academic/Plenum.

Hogg, M. A. (Ed.) (2003b). *SAGE benchmarks in psychology: Social psychology.* London: SAGE.

Hogg, M. A. (2006). Social identity theory. In P. J. Burke (Ed.), *Contemporary social psychological theories* (pp. 111–136). Palo Alto, CA: Stanford University Press.

Hogg, M. A. (2007a). Social psychology of leadership. In A. W. Kruglanski & E. T. Higgins (Eds.), *Social psychology: A handbook of basic principles* (2nd ed., pp. 716-733). New York: Guilford Press.

Hogg, M. A. (2007b). Uncertainty-identity theory. In M. P. Zanna (Ed.), *Advances in experimental social psychology* (Vol. 39, pp. 69-126). San Diego, CA: Academic Press.

Hogg, M. A. (2009). From group conflict to social harmony: Leading across diverse and conflicting social identities. In T. Pittinsky (Ed.), *Crossing the divide: Intergroup leadership in a world of difference* (pp. 17–30). Cambridge, MA: Harvard Business Publishing.

Hogg, M. A. (2010). Influence and leadership. In S. T. Fiske, D. T. Gilbert, & G. Lindzey (Eds.), *Handbook of social psychology* (5th ed., Vol. 2, pp. 1166-1207). New York: Wiley.

Hogg, M. A. (in press). Uncertainty-identity theory. In P. A. M. van Lange, A. W. Kruglanski, & E. T. Higgins (Eds.), *Handbook of theories of social psychology.* Thousand Oaks, CA: SAGE.

Hogg, M. A., & Abrams, D. (1988). *Social identifications: A social psychology of intergroup relations and group processes.* London: Routledge.

Hogg, M. A., & Abrams, D. (1990). Social motivation, self-esteem and social identity. In D. Abrams & M. A. Hogg (Eds.), *Social identity theory: Constructive and critical advances* (pp. 28–47). London: Harvester Wheatsheaf.

Hogg, M. A., & Abrams, D. (1999). Social identity and social cognition: Historical background and current trends. In D. Abrams & M. A. Hogg (Eds.), *Social identity and social cognition* (pp. 1–25). Oxford, UK: Blackwell.

Hogg, M. A., & Abrams, D. (2003). Intergroup behavior and social identity. In M. A. Hogg & J. Cooper (Eds.), *The SAGE handbook of social psychology* (pp. 407–431). London: SAGE.

Hogg, M. A., Adelman, J. R., & Blagg, R. D. (in press). Religion in the face of uncertainty: An uncertainty-identity theory account of religiousness. *Personality and Social Psychology Review.*

Hogg, M. A., & Cooper, J. (Eds.) (2007). *The SAGE handbook of social psychology: Concise student edition.* London: SAGE.

Hogg, M. A., Cooper-Shaw, L., & Holzworth, D. W. (1993). Group prototypicality and depersonalised attraction in small interactive groups. *European Journal of Social Psychology, 24,* 452–465.

Hogg, M. A., D'Agata, P., & Abrams, D. (1989). Ethnolinguistic betrayal and speaker evaluations among Italian Australians. *Genetic, Social and General Psychology Monographs, 115,* 153–181.

Hogg, M. A., Fielding, K. S., Johnson, D., Masser, B., Russell, E., & Svensson, A. (2006). Demographic category membership and leadership in small groups: A social identity analysis. *The Leadership Quarterly, 17,* 335–350.

Hogg, M. A., & Hains, S. C. (1996). Intergroup relations and group solidarity: Effects of group identification and social beliefs on depersonalized attraction. *Journal of Personality and Social Psychology, 70*, 295-309.

Hogg, M. A., & Hains, S. C. (1998). Friendship and group identification: A new look at the role of cohesiveness in groupthink. *European Journal of Social Psychology, 28*, 323-341.

Hogg, M. A., Hains, S. C., & Mason, I. (1998). Identification and leadership in small groups: Salience, frame of reference, and leader stereotypicality effects on leader evaluations. *Journal of Personality and Social Psychology, 75*, 1248-1263.

Hogg, M. A., & Hardie, E. A. (1991). Social attraction, personal attraction, and self-categorisation: A field study. *Personality and Social Psychology Bulletin, 17*, 175-180.

Hogg, M. A., & Hornsey, M. J. (2006). Self-concept threat and multiple categorization within groups. In R. J. Crisp & M. Hewstone (Eds.), *Multiple social categorization: Processes, models, and applications* (pp. 112-135). New York: Psychology Press.

Hogg, M. A., Joyce, N., & Abrams, D. (1984). Diglossia in Switzerland? A social identity analysis of speaker evaluations. *Journal of Language and Social Psychology, 3*, 185-196.

Hogg, M. A., Martin, R., & Weeden, K. (2004). Leader–member relations and social identity. In D. van Knippenberg & M. A. Hogg (Eds.), *Leadership and power: Identity processes in groups and organizations* (pp. 18-33). London: SAGE.

Hogg, M. A., Martin, R., Epitropaki, O., Mankad, A., Svensson, A., & Weeden, K. (2005). Effective leadership in salient groups: Revisiting leader–member exchange theory from the perspective of the social identity theory of leadership. *Personality and Social Psychology Bulletin, 31*, 991-1004.

Hogg, M. A., & Reid, S. A. (2001). Social identity, leadership, and power. In A. Y. Lee-Chai & J. A. Bargh (Eds.), *The use and abuse of power: Multiple perspectives on the causes of corruption* (pp. 159-180). Philadelphia, PA: Psychology Press.

Hogg, M. A., & Reid, S. A. (2006). Social identity, self-categorization, and the communication of group norms. *Communication Theory, 16*, 7-30.

Hogg, M. A., & Rigoli, N. (1996). Effects of ethnolinguistic vitality, ethnic identification, and linguistic contacts on minority language use. *Journal of Language and Social Psychology, 15*, 76-89.

Hogg, M. A., Sherman, D. K., Dierselhuis, J., Maitner, A. T., & Moffitt, G. (2007). Uncertainty, entitativity, and group identification. *Journal of Experimental Social Psychology, 43*, 135-142.

Hogg, M. A., & Smith, J. R. (2007). Attitudes in social context: A social identity perspective. *European Review of Social Psychology, 18*, 89-131.

Hogg, M. A., Terry, D. J., & White, K. M. (1995). A tale of two theories: A critical comparison of identity theory with social identity theory. *Social Psychology Quarterly, 58*, 255-269.

Hogg, M. A., & Tindale, R. S. (Eds.) (2001). *Blackwell handbook of social psychology: Group processes.* Oxford, UK: Blackwell.

Hogg, M. A., & Tindale, R. S. (2005). Social identity, influence, and communication in small groups. In J. Harwood & H. Giles (Eds.), *Intergroup communication: Multiple perspectives* (pp. 141-164). New York: Peter Lang.

Hogg, M. A., & Turner, J. C. (1985). Interpersonal attraction, social identification and psychological group formation. *European Journal of Social Psychology, 15*, 51-66.

Hogg, M. A., & Turner, J. C. (1987a). Social identity and conformity: A theory of referent informational influence. In W. Doise & S. Moscovici (Eds.), *Current issues in European social psychology* (Vol. 2, pp. 139-182). Cambridge: Cambridge University Press.

Hogg, M. A., & Turner, J. C. (1987b). Intergroup behaviour, self-stereotyping and the salience of social categories. *British Journal of Social Psychology, 26*, 325-40.

Hogg, M. A., Turner, J. C., & Davidson, B. (1990). Polarized norms and social frames of reference: A test of the self-categorization theory of group polarization. *Basic and Applied Social Psychology, 11*, 77-100.

Hogg, M. A., Turner, J. C., Nascimento-Schulze, C., & Spriggs, D. (1986). Social categorization, intergroup behaviour and self-esteem: Two experiments. *Revista de Psicología Social, 1*, 23-37.

Hogg, M. A., & Van Knippenberg, D. (2003). Social identity and leadership processes in groups. In M. P. Zanna (Ed.), *Advances in experimental social psychology* (Vol. 35, pp. 1-52). San Diego, CA: Academic Press.

Hogg, M. A., & Vaughan, G. M. (2010). *Essentials of social psychology.* London: Pearson Education.

Hogg, M. A., & Williams, K. D. (2000). From I to we: Social identity and the collective self. *Group Dynamics: Theory, Research, and Practice, 4*, 81-97.

Hohman, Z. P., Hogg, M. A., & Bligh, M. C. (2010). Identity and intergroup leadership: Asymmetrical political and national identification in response to uncertainty. *Self and Identity, 9*, 113-128.

Holland, R. W., Verplanken, B., & Van Knippenberg, A. (2002). On the nature of attitude–behavior relations: The strong guide, the weak follow. *European Journal of Social Psychology, 32*, 869-876.

Hollander, E. P. (1958). Conformity, status, and idiosyncrasy credit. *Psychological Review, 65*, 117-127.

Hollander, E. P. (1967). *Principles and methods of social psychology.* New York: Oxford University Press.

Hollander, E. P. (1985). Leadership and power. In G. Lindzey & E. Aronson (Eds.), *Handbook of social psychology* (3rd ed., Vol. 2, pp. 485-537). New York: Random House.

Hollander, E. P., & Julian, J. W. (1970). Studies in leader legitimacy, influence, and innovation. In L. Berkowitz (Ed.), *Advances in experimental social psychology* (Vol. 5, pp. 34-69). New York: Academic Press.

Hollingshead, A. B. (1996). The rank order effect: Decision procedure, communication technology and group decisions. *Organizational Behavior and Human Decision Processes, 68*(3), 1-13.

Hollingshead, A. B. (1998). Retrieval processes in transactive memory systems. *Journal of Personality and Social Psychology, 74,* 659–671.

Hollingshead, A. B. (2001). Communication technologies, the internet, and group research. In M. A. Hogg & R. S. Tindale (Eds.), *Blackwell handbook of social psychology: Group processes* (pp. 557–573). Oxford, UK: Blackwell.

Hollingshead, A. B., & McGrath, J. E. (1995). Computer-assisted groups: A critical review of the empirical research. In R. A. Guzzo & E. Salas (Eds.), *Team effectiveness and decision making in organizations* (pp. 46–78). San Francisco, CA: Jossey-Bass.

Holloway, S., Tucker, L., & Hornstein, H. A. (1977). The effects of social and nonsocial information on interpersonal behavior of males: The news makes news. *Journal of Personality and Social Psychology, 35,* 514–522.

Holmes, J. G. (2002). Interpersonal expectations as the building blocks of social cognition: An interdependence theory perspective. *Personal Relationships, 9,* 1–26.

Holtgraves, T. (2010). Social psychology and language: Words, utterances and conversations. In S. T. Fiske, D. T. Gilbert, & G. Lindzey (Eds.), *Handbook of social psychology* (5th ed., Vol. 2, pp. 1386-1422). New York: Wiley.

Holtzworth-Munroe, A., & Jacobson, N. S. (1985). Causal attributions of married couples. When do they search for causes? What do they conclude when they do? *Journal of Personality and Social Psychology, 48,* 1398–1412.

Homans, G. C. (1961). *Social behavior: Its elementary forms.* New York: Harcourt, Brace and World.

Hong, Y.-Y., & Mallorie, L. M. (2004). A dynamic constructivist approach to culture: Lessons learned from personality psychology. *Journal of Research in Personality, 38,* 59–67.

Hong, Y.-Y., Morris, M. W., Chiu,. C, & Benet-Martínez, V. (2000). Multicultural minds: A dynamic constructivist approach to culture and cognition. *American Psychologist, 55,* 705–720.

Hopkins, N., & Moore, C. (2001). Categorizing the neighbors: Identity, distance, and stereotyping. *Social Psychology Quarterly, 64,* 239–252.

Horai, J. (1977). Attributional conflict. *Journal of Social Issues, 33,* 88–100.

Hornsey, M. J. (2005). Why being right is not enough: Predicting defensiveness in the face of group criticism. *European Review of Social Psychology, 16,* 301–334.

Hornsey, M. J., & Hogg, M. A. (2000a). Assimilation and diversity: An integrative model of subgroup relations. *Personality and Social Psychology Review, 4,* 143–156.

Hornsey, M. J., & Hogg, M. A. (2000b). Subgroup relations: A comparison of mutual intergroup differentiation and common ingroup identity models of prejudice reduction. *Personality and Social Psychology Bulletin, 26,* 242–256.

Hornsey, M. J., & Hogg, M. A. (2000c). Intergroup similarity and subgroup relations: Some implications for assimilation. *Personality and Social Psychology Bulletin, 26,* 948–958.

Hornsey, M. J., & Imani, A. (2004). Criticising groups from the inside and the outside: An identity perspective on the intergroup sensitivity effect. *Personality and Social Psychology Bulletin, 30,* 365–383.

Hornsey, M. J., Jetten, J., McAuliffe, B. J., & Hogg, M. A. (2006). The impact of individualist and collectivist group norms on evaluations of dissenting group members. *Journal of Experimental Social Psychology, 42,* 57–68.

Hornsey, M. J., Oppes, T., & Svensson, A. (2002). 'It's OK if we say it, but you can't': Responses to intergroup and intra-group criticism. *European Journal of Social Psychology, 32,* 293–307.

Hornsey, M. J., Spears, R., Cremers, I., & Hogg, M. A. (2003). Relations between high and low power groups: The importance of legitimacy. *Personality and Social Psychology Bulletin, 29,* 216–227.

Hornstein, G. A. (1985). Intimacy in conversational style as a function of the degree of closeness between members of a dyad. *Journal of Personality and Social Psychology, 49,* 671–681.

Hornstein, H. A. (1970). The influence of social models on helping. In J. Macaulay & L. Berkowitz (Eds.), *Altruism and helping behavior* (pp. 29–42). New York: Academic Press.

Horowitz, D. L. (1973). Direct, displaced and cumulative ethnic aggression. *Comparative Politics, 6,* 1–16.

Horowitz, E. L. (1936). The development of attitudes towards the Negro. *Archives of Psychology, 194.*

Horowitz, E. L. (1939). Racial aspects of self-identification in nursery school children. *Journal of Psychology, 7,* 91–99.

Horowitz, I. A., & Bordens, K. S. (1990). An experimental investigation of procedural issues in complex tort trials. *Law and Human Behavior, 14,* 269–285.

House, R. J. (1977). A 1976 theory of charismatic leadership. In J. G. Hunt & L. Larson (Eds.), *Leadership: The cutting edge* (pp. 189–207). Carbondale, IL: Southern Illinois University Press.

House, R. J. (1996). Path–goal theory of leadership: Lessons, legacy, and a reformulated theory. *The Leadership Quarterly, 7,* 323–352.

House, R. J., Spangler, W. D., & Woycke, J. (1991). Personality and charisma in the U.S. presidency: A psychological theory of leader effectiveness. *Administrative Science Quarterly, 36,* 364–396.

Hovland, C. I., & Sears, R. R. (1940). Minor studies in aggression: VI. Correlation of lynchings with economic indices. *Journal of Psychology, 9,* 301–310.

Hovland, C. I., & Weiss, W. (1952). The influence of source credibility in communication effectiveness. *Public Opinion Quarterly, 15,* 635–650.

Hovland, C. I., Janis, I. L., & Kelley, H. H. (1953). *Communication and persuasion.* New Haven, CT: Yale University Press.

Hovland, C. I., Lumsdaine, A. A., & Sheffield, F. D. (1949). *Experiments in mass communication.* Princeton, NJ: Princeton University Press.

Howard, J. A. (1985). Further appraisal of correspondent inference theory. *Personality and Social Psychology Bulletin, 11,* 467–477.

Howard, J. W., & Rothbart, M. (1980). Social categorization and memory for ingroup and outgroup behavior. *Journal of Personality and Social Psychology, 38,* 301–310.

Howell, D. C. (2007). *Statistical methods for psychology* (6th ed.). Belmont, CA: Duxbury.

Hraba, J. (1972). A measure of ethnocentrism? *Social Forces, 50,* 522–527.

Hraba, J., & Grant, G. (1970). Black is beautiful: A re-examination of racial preference and identification. *Journal of Personality and Social Psychology, 16,* 398–402.

Huesmann, L. R. (1988). An information processing model for the development of aggression. *Aggressive Behavior, 14,* 13–24.

Huesmann, L. R., & Guerra, N. G. (1997). Children's normative beliefs about aggression and aggressive behaviour. *Journal of Personality and Social Psychology, 72,* 408–419.

Huesmann, L. R., & Miller, L. S. (1994). Long-term effects of repeated exposure to media violence in childhood. In L. R. Huesmann (Ed.), *Aggressive behaviour: Current perspectives* (pp. 153–186). New York: Plenum.

Huesmann, L. R., Eron, L. D., Lefkowitz, M. M., & Walder, L. O. (1984). Stability of aggression over time and generations. *Developmental Psychology, 20,* 1120–1134.

Huesmann, L. R., Mois-Titus, J., Podolski, C. L., & Eron, L. D. (2003). Longitudinal relations between children's exposure to TV violence and their aggressive and violent behavior in young adulthood: 1977–1992. *Developmental Psychology, 39,* 201–221.

Hughes, M. T. (1981). To cheat or not to cheat? *Albany Times–Union,* 26 July, pp. B-1, B-3.

Huici, C., Ros, M., Cano, I., Hopkins, N., Emler, N., & Carmona, M. (1997). Comparative identity and evaluation of socio-political change: Perceptions of the European Community as a function of the salience of regional identities. *European Journal of Social Psychology, 27,* 97–113.

Hummert, M. L. (1990). Multiple stereotypes of elderly and young adults: A comparison of structure and evaluations. *Psychology and Aging, 5,* 182–193.

Huston, T. l. (2009). What's love got to do with it? Why some marriages succeed and others fail. *Personal relationships, 16,* 301-327.

Huston, T. L., Ruggiero, M., Conner, R., & Geis, G. (1981). Bystander intervention into crime: A study based on naturally-occurring episodes. *Social Psychology Quarterly, 44,* 14–23.

Ickes, W., Gesn, P. R., & Graham, T. (2000). Gender differences in empathic accuracy: Differential ability or differential motivation? *Personal Relationships, 7,* 95–109.

Ingham, A. G., Levinger, G., Graves, J., & Peckham, V. (1974). The Ringelmann effect: Studies of group size and group performance. *Journal of Experimental Social Psychology, 10,* 371–384.

Ingoldsby, B. B. (1991). The Latin American family: Familism vs machismo. *Journal of Comparative Family Studies, 23,* 47–62.

Insko, C. A. (1965). Verbal reinforcement of attitude. *Journal of Personality and Social Psychology, 2,* 621–623.

Insko, C. A. (1967). *Theories of attitude change.* New York: Appleton-Century-Crofts.

Insko, C. A., Nacoste, R. W., & Moe, J. L. (1983). Belief congruence and racial discrimination: Review of the evidence and critical evaluation. *European Journal of Social Psychology, 13,* 153–174.

Inzlicht, M., McGregor, I., Hirsh, J. B., & Nash, K. (2009). Neural markers of religious conviction. *Psychological Science, 20,* 385–392.

Isen, A. M. (1970). Success, failure, attention, and reaction to others: The warm glow of success. *Journal of Personality and Social Psychology, 15,* 294–301.

Isen, A. M., & Stalker, T. E. (1982). The effect of feeling state on evaluation of positive, neutral, and negative stimuli when you 'accentuate the positive': Do you 'eliminate the negative'? *Social Psychology Quarterly, 45,* 58–63.

Isen, A. M., Clark, M., & Schwartz, M. (1976). Duration of the effect of good mood on helping: 'footprints on the sands of time'. *Journal of Personality and Psychology, 34,* 385–393.

Isen, A. M., Horn, N., & Rosenhan, D. L. (1973). Effects of success and failure on children's generosity. *Journal of Personality and Social Psychology, 27,* 239–247.

Isenberg, D. J. (1986). Group polarization: A critical review. *Journal of Personality and Social Psychology, 50,* 1141–1151.

Islam, M., & Hewstone, M. (1993). Intergroup attributions and affective consequences in majority and minority groups. *Journal of Personality and Social Psychology, 65,* 936–950.

Israel, J., & Tajfel, H. (Eds.) (1972). *The context of social psychology: A critical assessment.* London: Academic Press.

Ito, T. A., Thompson, E., & Cacioppo, J. T. (2004). Tracking the timecourse of social perception: The effects of racial cues on event-related brain potentials. *Personality and Social Psychology Bulletin, 30,* 1267–1280.

Izraeli, D. N., & Izraeli, D. (1985). Sex effects in evaluating leaders: A replication study. *Journal of Applied Psychology, 70,* 540–546.

Izraeli, D. N., Izraeli, D., & Eden, D. (1985). Giving credit where credit is due: A case of no sex bias in attribution. *Journal of Applied Social Psychology, 15,* 516–530.

Jacks, Z. J., & Cameron, K. A. (2003). Strategies for resisting persuasion. *Basic and Applied Social Psychology, 25,* 145–61

Jackson, J., & Harkins, S. G. (1985). Equity in effort: An explanation of the social loafing effect. *Journal of Personality and Social Psychology, 49,* 1199–1206.

Jacobs, D., & Singell, L. (1993). Leadership and organisational performance: Isolating links between managers and collective success. *Social Science Research, 22,* 165–189.

Jacobs, R., & Campbell, D. T. (1961). The perpetuation of an arbitrary tradition through several generations of a laboratory microculture. *Journal of Abnormal and Social Psychology, 62,* 649–658.

Jacobson, D. (1999). Impression formation in cyberspace: Online expectations and offline experiences in textbased virtual communities. *Journal of Computer-Mediated Communication* [online serial], *5* (1). http://www/ ascusc. org/jcmc/vol5/issue1/jacobson.html

Jacoby, L. L., Kelly, C., Brown, J., & Jasechko, J. (1989). Becoming famous overnight: Limits on the ability to avoid unconscious influences of the past. *Journal of Personality and Social Psychology, 56,* 326–338.

Jahoda, G. (1979). A cross-cultural perspective on experimental social psychology. *Personality and Social Psychology Bulletin, 5,* 142–148.

Jahoda, G. (1982). *Psychology and anthropology: A psychological perspective.* London: Academic Press.

James, W. (1890). *The principles of psychology* (Vol. 1). New York: Holt.

Jamieson, D. W., & Zanna, M. P. (1989). Need for structure in attitude formation and expression. In A. R. Pratkanis, S. J. Breckler & A. G. Greenwald (Eds.), *Attitude structure and function* (pp. 383–406). Hillsdale, NJ: Erlbaum.

Janis, I. L. (1954). Personality correlates of susceptibility to persuasion. *Journal of Personality, 22,* 504–518.

Janis, I. L. (1967). Effects of fear arousal on attitude change: Recent developments in theory and experimental research. In L. Berkowitz (Ed.), *Advances in experimental social psychology* (Vol. 3, pp. 167–224). New York: Academic Press.

Janis, I. L. (1972). *Victims of groupthink: A psychological study of foreign policy decisions and fiascoes.* Boston, MA: Houghton Mifflin.

Janis, I. L. (1982). *Groupthink: Psychological studies of policy decisions and fiascoes* (2nd ed.). Boston, MA: Houghton Mifflin.

Janis, I. L., & Feshbach, S. (1953). Effects of fear-arousing communications. *Journal of Abnormal and Social Psychology, 48,* 78–92.

Janis, I. L., & Hovland, C. I. (1959). An overview of persuasibility research. In C. I. Hovland & I. L. Janis (Eds.), *Personality and persuasibility* (pp. 1–26). New Haven, CT: Yale University Press.

Janis, I. L., Kaye, D., & Kirschner, P. (1965). Facilitating effects of 'eating-while-reading' on responsiveness to persuasive communications. *Journal of Personality and Social Psychology, 1,* 181–186.

Janis, I. L., & King, B. T. (1954). The influence of roleplaying on opinion change. *Journal of Abnormal and Social Psychology, 49,* 211–218.

Janis, I. L., & Mann, L. (1977). *Decision making.* New York: Free Press.

Jarvis, W. B. G., & Petty, R. E. (1995). The need to evaluate. *Journal of Personality and Social Psychology, 70,* 172–192.

Jaspars, J. M. F. (1980). The coming of age of social psychology in Europe. *European Journal of Social Psychology, 10,* 421–428.

Jaspars, J. M. F. (1986). Forum and focus: A personal view of European social psychology. *European Journal of Social Psychology, 16,* 3–15.

Jellison, J., & Arkin, R. (1977). Social comparison of abilities: A self-presentation approach to decision making in groups. In J. M. Suls & R. L. Miller (Eds.), *Social comparison processes: Theoretical and empirical perspectives* (pp. 235–257). Washington, DC: Hemisphere Press.

Jellison, J. M., & Green, J. (1981). A self-presentation approach to the fundamental attribution error: The norm of internality. *Journal of Personality and Social Psychology, 40,* 643–649.

Jennings, M. K., & Niemi, R. G. (1968). The transmission of political values from parent to child. *American Political Science Review, 62,* 546–575.

Jetten, J., Postmes, T., & McAuliffe, B. J. (2002). We're all individuals: Group norms of individualism and collectivism, levels of identification, and identity threat. *European Journal of Social Psychology, 32,* 189–207.

Jodelet, D. (1991). *Madness and social representations.* Hemel Hempstead, UK: Harvester Wheatsheaf.

Johnson, B. T. (1994). Effects of outcome-relevant involvement and prior information on persuasion. *Journal of Experimental Social Psychology, 30,* 556–579.

Johnson, B. T., & Eagly, A. H. (1989). Effects of involvement on persuasion: Meta-analysis. *Psychological Bulletin, 106,* 290–314.

Johnson, D. W., & Johnson, F. P. (1987). *Joining together: Group theory and group skills* (3rd ed.). Englewood Cliffs, NJ: Prentice Hall.

Johnson, E. J., Pham, M. T., & Johar, G. V. (2007). Consumer behavior and marketing. In A. W. Kruglanski & E. T. Higgins (Eds.), *Social psychology: A handbook of basic principles* (2nd ed., pp. 869–887). New York: Guilford Press.

Johnson, R. D., & Downing, L. L. (1979). Deindividuation and valence of cues: Effects on prosocial and antisocial behavior. *Journal of Personality and Social Psychology, 37,* 1532–1538.

Johnston, L., & Hewstone, M. (1990). Intergroup contact: Social identity and social cognition. In D. Abrams & M. A. Hogg (Eds.), *Social identity theory: Constructive and critical advances* (pp. 185–210). London: Harvester Wheatsheaf.

Jonas, E., Schimel, J., Greenberg, J., & Pyszczynski, T. (2002). The Scrooge effect: Evidence that mortality salience increases prosocial attitudes and behavior. *Personality and Social Psychology Bulletin, 28,* 1342–1353.

Jones, B., Gray, A., Kavanagh, D., Moran, M., Norton, P., & Seldon, A. (1994). *Politics UK* (2nd ed.). Hemel Hempstead, UK: Harvester Wheatsheaf.

Jones, E. E. (1964). *Ingratiation: A social psychological analysis.* Des Moines, IA: Meredith Publishing Company.

Jones, E. E. (1979). The rocky road from acts to dispositions. *American Psychologist, 34,* 107–117.

Jones, E. E. (1990). *Interpersonal perception.* New York: Freeman.

Jones, E. E. (1998). Major developments in five decades of social psychology. In D. T. Gilbert, S. T. Fiske & G. Lindzey (Eds.), *The handbook of social psychology* (4th ed., Vol. 1, pp. 3–57). New York: McGraw-Hill.

Jones, E. E., & Davis, K. E. (1965). From acts to dispositions: The attribution process in person perception. In L. Berkowitz (Ed.), *Advances in experimental social psychology* (Vol. 2, pp. 219–266). New York: Academic Press.

Jones, E. E., Davis, K. E., & Gergen, K. (1961). Role playing variations and their informational value for person perception. *Journal of Abnormal and Social Psychology, 63,* 302–310.

Jones, E. E., & Goethals, G. R. (1972). Order effects in impression formation: Attribution context and the nature of the entity. In E. E. Jones, D. E. Kanouse, H. H. Kelley, R. E. Nisbett, S. Valins, & B. Weiner (Eds.), *Attribution: Perceiving the causes of behavior* (pp. 27–46). Morristown, NJ: General Learning Press.

Jones, E. E., & Harris, V. A. (1967). The attribution of attitudes. *Journal of Experimental Social Psychology, 3,* 1–24.

Jones, E. E., & McGillis, D. (1976). Correspondent inferences and the attribution cube: A comparative reappraisal. In J. H. Harvey, W. J. Ickes & R. F. Kidd (Eds.), *New directions in attribution research* (Vol. 1, pp. 389–420). Hillsdale, NJ: Erlbaum.

Jones, E. E., & Nisbett, R. E. (1972). The actor and the observer: Divergent perceptions of the causes of behavior. In E. E. Jones, D. E. Kanouse, H. H. Kelley, R. E. Nisbett, S. Valins & B. Weiner (Eds.), *Attribution: Perceiving the causes of behavior* (pp. 79–94). Morristown, NJ: General Learning Press.

Jones, E. E., & Pittman, T. S. (1982). Toward a general theory of strategic self-presentation. In J. Suls (Ed.), *Psychological perspectives on the self* (Vol. 1, pp. 231–262). Hillsdale, NJ: Erlbaum.

Jones, E. E., & Sigall, H. (1971). The bogus pipeline: A new paradigm for measuring affect and attitude. *Psychological Bulletin, 76,* 349–364.

Jones, E. E., Wood, G. C., & Quattrone, G. A. (1981). Perceived variability of personal characteristics in ingroups and outgroups: The role of knowledge and evaluation. *Personality and Social Psychology Bulletin, 7,* 523–528.

Jones, J. M. (1996). *The psychology of racism and prejudice.* New York: McGraw Hill.

Jones, J. T., Pelham, B. W., Carvallo, M., & Mirenberg, M. C. (2004). How do I love thee? Let me count the Js: Implicit egotism and interpersonal attraction. *Journal of Personality and Social Psychology, 87,* 665–683.

Jones, S. E., & Yarbrough, A. E. (1985). A naturalistic study of the meanings of touch. *Communication Monographs, 52,* 19–56.

Jost, J. T., & Banaji, M. R. (1994). The role of stereotyping in system-justification and the production of false consciousness. *British Journal of Social Psychology, 33,* 1–27.

Jost, J. T., & Hunyadi, O. (2002). The psychology of system justification and the palliative function of ideology. *European Review of Social Psychology, 13,* 111–153.

Jost, J. T., & Kramer, R. M. (2002). The system justification motive in intergroup relations. In D. M. Mackie & E. R. Smith (Eds.), *From prejudice to intergroup emotions: Differentiated reactions to social groups* (pp. 227–246). New York: Psychology Press.

Jost, J. T., & Kruglanski, A. (2002). The estrangement of social constructionism and experimental social psychology: History of the rift and prospects for reconciliation. *Personality and Social Psychology Review, 6,* 168–187.

Jost, J. T., & Major, B. (Eds.) (2001). *The psychology of legitimacy: Emerging perspectives on ideology, justice, and intergroup relations.* New York: Cambridge University Press.

Joule, R.-V., & Beauvois, J.-L. (1998). Cognitive dissonance theory: A radical view. *European Review of Social Psychology, 8,* 1–32.

Jourard, S. M. (1966). An exploratory study of body-accessibility. *British Journal of Social and Clinical Psychology, 5,* 221–231.

Jourard, S. M. (1971). *The transparent self.* New York: Van Nostrand.

Joyce, W. F., Nohria, N., & Roberson, B. (2003). *What really works: The 4+2 formula for sustained business success.* New York: Harper Business.

Judd, C. M., & Park, B. (1988). Out-group homogeneity: Judgments of variability at the individual and group levels. *Journal of Personality and Social Psychology, 54,* 778–788.

Judge, T. A., & Bono, J. E. (2000). Five-factor model of personality and transformational leadership. *Journal of Applied Psychology, 85,* 751–765.

Judge, T. A., Bono, J. E., Ilies, R., & Gerhardt, M. W. (2002). Personality and leadership: A qualitative and quantitative review. *Journal of Applied Psychology, 87,* 765–780.

Jung, C. G. (1946). *Psychological types or the psychology of individuation.* New York: Harcourt Brace. (Originally published 1922.)

Jussim, L., Eccles, J., & Madon, S. (1996). Social perception, social stereotypes, and teacher expectations: Accuracy and the quest for the powerful self-fulfilling prophecy. *Advances in experimental social psychology, 28,* 281–388.

Jussim, L., & Fleming, C. (1996). Self-fulfilling prophecies and the maintenance of social stereotypes: The role of dyadic interactions and social forces. In C. N. Macrae, C. Stangor & M. Hewstone (Eds.), *Stereotypes and stereotyping* (pp. 161–192). New York: Guilford Press.

Kafka, F. (1925). *The trial.* Harmondsworth, UK: Penguin.

Kahn, A., & Ryen, A. H. (1972). Factors influencing the bias towards one's own group. *International Journal of Group Tensions, 2,* 33–50.

Kahneman, D., & Tversky, A. (1973). On the psychology of prediction. *Psychological Review, 80,* 237–251.

Kanazawa, H., & Loveday, L. (1988). The Japanese immigrant community in Brazil: Language contact and shift. *Journal of Multilingual and Multicultural Development, 9,* 423–435.

Kanouse, D. E., & Hanson, L. R. Jr (1972). Negativity in evaluations. In E. E. Jones, D. E. Kanouse, H. H. Kelley, R. E. Nisbett, S. Valins & B. Weiner (Eds.), *Attribution: Perceiving the causes of behavior* (pp. 47–62). Morristown, NJ: General Learning Press.

Kanter, R. M. (1977). Numbers: Minorities and majorities. In *Men and women of the corporation* (pp. 206-242). New York: Basic Books.

Kaplan, M. F. (1977). Discussion polarization effects in a modified jury decision paradigm: Informational influence. *Sociometry, 40,* 262–271.

Kaplan, M. F., & Miller, L. E. (1978). Reducing the effects of juror bias. *Journal of Personality and Social Psychology, 36,* 1443–55.

Karakashian, L. M., Walter, M. I., Christopher, A. N., & Lucas, T. (2006). Fear of negative evaluation affects helping behavior: The bystander effect revisited. *North American Journal of Psychology, 8,* 13–32.

Karau, S. J., & Hart, J. W. (1998). Group cohesiveness and social loafing: Effects of a social interaction manipulation on individual motivation within groups. *Group Dynamics, 2,* 185–191.

Karau, S. J., & Williams, K. D. (1993). Social loafing: A meta-analytic review and theoretical integration. *Journal of Personality and Social Psychology, 65,* 681–706.

Karney, B. R., & Bradbury, T. N. (1995). Assessing longitudinal change in marriage: An introduction to the analysis of growth curves. *Journal of Marriage and the Family, 57,* 1091–1108.

Karniol, R. (1982). Behavioral and cognitive correlates of various immanent justice responses in children: Deterrent versus punitive moral systems. *Journal of Personality and Social Psychology, 43,* 881–920.

Karremans, J. C., Van Lange, P. A. M., & Holland, R. W. (2005). Forgiveness and its associations with prosocial thinking, feeling, and doing beyond the relationship with the offender. *Personality and Social Psychology Bulletin, 31,* 1315–1326.

Kashima, Y. (2005). Is culture a problem for social psychology? *Asian Journal of Social Psychology, 8,* 19–38.

Kashima, Y., & Kashima, E. (1998). Culture, connectionism, and the self. In J. Adamopoulos & Y. Kashima (Eds.) (1999). *Social psychology and cultural context* (pp. 77–92). London: SAGE.

Kasser, T., Koestner, R., & Lekes, N. (2002). Early family experiences and adult values: A 26-year, prospective longitudinal study. *Personality and Social Psychology Bulletin, 28,* 826–835.

Kassin, S. M. (1979). Consensus information, prediction and causal attribution: A review of the literature and issues. *Journal of Personality and Social Psychology, 37,* 1966–1981.

Kassin, S. M., & Pryor, J. B. (1985). The development of attribution processes. In J. Pryor & J. Day (Eds.), *The development of social cognition* (pp. 3–34). New York: Springer.

Kassin, S. M., Ellsworth, P. C., & Smith, V. L. (1989). The 'general acceptance' of psychological research on eyewitness testimony. *American Psychologist, 44,* 1089–1098.

Katsikitis, M., Pilowsky, I., & Innes, J. M. (1990). The quantification of smiling using a microcomputer-based approach. *Journal of Nonverbal Behavior, 14,* 3–17.

Katz, D. (1960). The functional approach to the study of attitudes. *Public Opinion Quarterly, 24,* 163–204.

Katz, D., & Braly, K. (1933). Racial stereotypes of one hundred college students. *Journal of Abnormal and Social Psychology, 28,* 280–290.

Katz, I., Glass, D. C., Lucido, D., & Farber, J. (1979). Harm-doing and victim's racial or orthopaedic stigma as determinants of helping behavior. *Journal of Personality, 47,* 340–364.

Katz, I., & Hass, R. G. (1988). Racial ambivalence and American value conflict: Correlational and priming studies of dual cognitive structures. *Journal of Personality and Social Psychology, 55,* 893–905.

Katz, P. A. (1976). *Towards the elimination of racism.* New York: Pergamon Press.

Kawakami, K., Young, H., & Dovidio, J. F. (2002). Automatic stereotyping: Category, trait, and behavioral activations. *Personality and Social Psychology Bulletin, 28,* 3–15.

Kazdin, A. E., & Bryan, J. H. (1971). Competence and volunteering. *Journal of Experimental Social Psychology, 7,* 87–97.

Keller, P. A., & Block, L. G. (1995). Increasing the persuasiveness of fear appeals: The effect of arousal and elaboration. *Journal of Consumer Research, 22,* 448–459.

Kellerman, A. L., Rivara, F. P., Rushforth, N. B., Banton, J. G., Reay, D. T., Francisco, J. T., et al. (1993). Gun ownership as a risk factor for homicide in the home. *New England Journal of Medicine, 329,* 1084–1091.

Kellerman, B. (2004). *Bad leadership: What it is, how it happens, why it matters.* Cambridge, MA: Harvard Business School Press.

Kelley, H. H. (1950). The warm–cold variable in first impressions of persons. *Journal of Personality, 18,* 431–439.

Kelley, H. H. (1952). Two functions of reference groups. In G. E. Swanson, T. M. Newcomb, & E. L. Hartley (Eds.), *Readings in social psychology* (2nd ed., pp. 410–414). New York: Holt, Rinehart & Winston.

Kelley, H. H. (1967). Attribution theory in social psychology. In D. Levine (Ed.), *Nebraska symposium on motivation* (pp. 192–238). Lincoln, NE: University of Nebraska Press.

Kelley, H. H. (1972a). Causal schemata and the attribution process. In E. E. Jones, D. E. Kanouse, H. H. Kelley, R. E. Nisbett, S. Valins & B. Weiner (Eds.), *Attribution: Perceiving the causes of behavior* (pp. 151–174). Morristown, NJ: General Learning Press.

Kelley, H. H. (1972b). Attribution in social interaction. In E. E. Jones, D. E. Kanouse, H. H. Kelley, R. E. Nisbett, S. Valins & B. Weiner (Eds.), *Attribution: Perceiving the causes of behavior* (pp. 1–26). Morristown, NJ: General Learning Press.

Kelley, H. H. (1973). The process of causal attribution. *American Psychologist, 28,* 107–128.

Kelley, H. H. (1979). *Personal relationships: Their structures and processes.* Hillsdale, NJ: Erlbaum.

Kelley, H. H., & Michela, J. L. (1980). Attribution theory and research. *Annual Review of Psychology, 31,* 457–501.

Kelley, H. H., & Thibaut, J. (1978). *Interpersonal relations: A theory of interdependence.* New York: Wiley.

Kelley, K., Byrne, D., Przybyla, D. P. J., Eberly, C. C., Eberly, B. W., Greenlinger, V., Wan, C. K., & Grosky, J. (1985). Chronic self-destructiveness: Conceptualisation, measurement, and initial validation of the construct. *Motivation and Emotion, 9,* 35–151.

Kelley, R. E. (1992). *The power of followership.* New York: Doubleday.

Kellstedt, P. M. (2003). *The mass media and the dynamics of American racial attitudes.* Cambridge, UK: Cambridge University Press.

Kelly, C., & Breinlinger, S. (1996). *The social psychology of collective action*. London: Taylor & Francis.

Kelly, G. A. (1955). *The psychology of personal constructs*. New York: Norton.

Kelman, H. C. (1967). Human use of human subjects: The problem of deception in social psychology. *Psychological Bulletin, 67*, 1–11.

Kelman, H. C. (1976). Violence without restraint: Reflections on the dehumanization of victims and victimizers. In G. M. Kren & L. H. Rappoport (Eds.), *Varieties of psychohistory* (pp. 282-314). New York: Springer.

Kelman, H. C., & Hovland, C. I. (1953). 'Reinstatement' of the communicator in delayed measurement of opinion change. *Journal of Abnormal and Social Psychology, 48*, 327–335.

Keltner, D., Gruenfeld, D. H., & Anderson, C. (2003). Power, approach, and inhibition. *Psychological Review, 110*, 265–284.

Keltner, D., & Lerner, J. S. (2010). Emotion. In S. T. Fiske, D. T. Gilbert, & G. Lindzey (Eds.), *Handbook of social psychology* (5th ed., Vol. 1, pp. 317-352). New York: Wiley.

Kelvin, P. (1970). *The bases of social behaviour: An approach in terms of order and value*. London: Holt, Rinehart & Winston.

Kemper, S. (1994). Elderspeak: Speech accommodations to older adults. *Aging and Cognition, 1*, 17–28.

Keneally, T. (1982). *Schindler's ark*. Washington, DC: Hemisphere Press.

Kennedy, J. (1982). Middle LPC leaders and the contingency model of leader effectiveness. *Organizational Behavior and Human Performance, 30*, 1–14.

Kenny, D. A., & DePaulo, B. M. (1993). Do people know how others view them? An empirical and theoretical account. *Psychological Bulletin, 114*, 145–161.

Kenrick, D. T., Li, N. P., & Butner, J. (2003). Dynamical evolutionary psychology: Individual decision rules and emergent social norms. *Psychological Review, 110*, 3–28.

Kenrick, D. T., & MacFarlane, S. W. (1986). Ambient temperature and horn honking: A field study of the heat/aggression relationship. *Environment and Behavior, 18*, 179–191.

Kenrick, D. T., Maner, J. K., & Li, N. P. (2005). Evolutionary social psychology. In D. M. Buss (Ed.), *Handbook of evolutionary psychology* (pp. 803-827). New York: Wiley.

Kernis, M. H., Granneman, B. D., & Barclay, L. C. (1989). Stability and level of self-esteem as predictors of anger arousal and hostility. *Journal of Personality and Social Psychology, 56*, 1013–1022.

Kerr, J. H. (2005). *Rethinking aggression and violence in sport*. London: Routledge.

Kerr, N. L. (1978). Beautiful and blameless: Effects of victim attractiveness and responsibility on mock jurors' verdicts. *Journal of Personality and Social Psychology, 4*, 479–482.

Kerr, N. L. (1981). Social transition schemes: Charting the group's road to agreement. *Journal of Personality and Social Psychology, 41*, 684–702.

Kerr, N. L. (1983). Motivation losses in small groups: A social dilemma analysis. *Journal of Personality and Social Psychology, 45*, 819–828.

Kerr, N. L. (1995). Norms in social dilemmas. In D. A. Schroeder (Ed.), *Social dilemmas: Perspectives on individuals and groups* (pp. 31-47). Westport, CT: Praeger.

Kerr, N. L., & Bruun, S. (1981). Ringelmann revisited: Alternative explanations for the social loafing effect. *Personality and Social Psychology Bulletin, 7*, 224–231.

Kerr, N. L., & Bruun, S. (1983). The dispensability of member effort and group motivation losses: Free rider effects. *Journal of Personality and Social Psychology, 44*, 78–94.

Kerr, N. L., & MacCoun, R. J. (1985). The effects of jury size and polling method on the process and product of jury deliberation. *Journal of Personality and Social Psychology, 48*, 349–363.

Kerr, N. L., & Park, E. S. (2001). Group performance in collaborative and social dilemma tasks: Progress and prospects. In M. A. Hogg & R. S. Tindale (Eds.), *Blackwell handbook of social psychology: Group processes* (pp. 107–138). Oxford, UK: Blackwell.

Kiesler, C. A., & Kiesler, S. B. (1969). *Conformity*. Reading, MA: Addison-Wesley.

Kihlstrom, J. F. (2004). Implicit methods in social psychology. In C. Sansone, C. C. Morf & A. T. Panter (Eds.), *The SAGE handbook of methods in social psychology* (pp. 195–212). London: SAGE.

Kilham, W., & Mann, L. (1974). Level of destructive obedience as a function of transmitter and executant roles in the Milgram obedience paradigm. *Journal of Personality and Social Psychology, 29*, 696–702.

Kim, H. S., & Baron, R. S. (1988). Exercise and the illusory correlation: Does arousal heighten stereotypic processing? *Journal of Experimental Social Psychology, 24*, 366–380.

Kim, U. (2000). Indigenous, cultural, and cross-cultural psychology: A theoretical, conceptual, and epistemological analysis. *Asian Journal of Social Psychology, 3*, 265–288.

Kimble, G. A. (1961). *Hilgard and Marquis' conditioning and learning* (2nd ed.). New York: Appleton-Century-Crofts.

Kimmel, P. R. (1994). Cultural perspectives on inter-national negotiations. *Journal of Social Issues, 50*, 179–196.

Kinder, D. R., & Sears, D. O. (1981). Symbolic racism vs. threats to the good life. *Journal of Personality and Social Psychology, 40*, 414–431.

Kirkpatrick, L. A., & Hazan, C. (1994). Attachment styles and close relationships: A four-year prospective study. *Personal Relationships, 1*, 123–142.

Kitayama, S., Markus, H. R., Matsumoto, H., and Norasakkunkit, V. (1997). Individual and collective processes in the construction of the self: Self-enhancement in the United States and self-criticism in Japan. *Journal of Personality and Social Psychology, 72*, 1245–1267.

Kitayama, S., Mesquita, B., & Karasawa, M. (2006). Cultural affordances and emotional experience: Socially engaging and disengaging emotions in Japan and the United States. *Journal of Personality and Social Psychology, 91*, 890–903.

Kitayama, S., Snibbe, A. C., Markus, H. M., & Suzuki, T. (2004). Is there any 'free' choice? Self and dissonance in two cultures. *Psychological Science, 15,* 527–533.

Kite, M. E., & Johnson, B. T. (1988). Attitudes toward older and younger adults: A meta-analysis. *Psychology and Aging, 3,* 233–244.

Klandermans, B. (1997). *The social psychology of protest.* Oxford, UK: Blackwell.

Klandermans, B. (2002). How group identification helps to overcome the dilemma of collective action. *American Behavioral Scientist, 45,* 887-900.

Klandermans, B. (2003). Collective political action. In D. O. Sears, L. Huddy., & R. Jervis, (Eds.), *Oxford handbook of political psychology* (pp. 670-709). Oxford, UK: Oxford University Press.

Klapp, O. E. (1972). *Currents of unrest.* New York: Holt, Rinehart & Winston.

Klasen, S. (1994). 'Missing women' re-considered. *World Development, 22,* 1061–1071.

Klein, O., Spears, R., & Reicher, S. (2007) Social identity performance: Extending the strategic side of SIDE. *Personality and Social Psychology Review, 11,* 28-45.

Klein, S. B., Loftus, J., Trafton, J. G., & Fuhrman, R. W. (1992). Use of exemplars and abstractions in trait judgments: A model of trait knowledge about self and others. *Journal of Personality and Social Psychology, 63,* 739–753.

Klein, W. M. P. (2003). Effects of objective feedback and 'single other' or 'average other' social comparison feedback on performance judgments and helping behavior. *Personality and Social Psychology Bulletin, 29,* 418–429.

Kleinke, C. L. (1986). Gaze and eye contact: A research review. *Psychological Bulletin, 100,* 78–100.

Klentz, B., & Beaman, A. L. (1981). The effects of type of information and method of dissemination on the reporting of a shoplifter. *Journal of Applied Psychology, 11,* 64–82.

Klineberg, O. (1940). *Social psychology.* New York: Holt.

Klineberg, O., & Hull, W. F. (1979). *At a foreign university: An international study of adaptation and coping.* New York: Praeger.

Klinger, R. L., & Stein, T. S. (1996). Impact of violence, childhood sexual abuse, and domestic violence and abuse on lesbians, bisexuals, and gay men. In R. P. Cabaj & T. S. Stein (Eds.), *Textbook of homosexuality and mental health* (pp. 801–818). Washington, DC: American Psychiatric Press.

Klohnen, E. C., & Bera, S. (1998). Behavioural and experiential patterns of avoidantly and securely attached women across adulthood: A 31-year longitudinal perspective. *Journal of Personality and Social Psychology, 74,* 211–223.

Kluckhohn, C. (1954). Culture and behavior. In G. Lindzey (Ed.), *A handbook of social psychology* (Vol. 2, pp. 921–976). Cambridge, MA: Addison-Wesley.

Knapp, M. L. (1978). *Nonverbal communication in human interaction* (2nd ed). New York: Holt, Rinehart & Winston.

Knapp, M. L., Hart, R. P., & Dennis, H. S. (1974). An exploration of deception as a communication construct. *Human Communication Research, 1,* 15–29.

Knee, C. R. (1998). Implicit theories of relationships: Assessment and prediction of romantic relationship initiation, coping, and longevity. *Journal of Personality and Social Psychology, 74,* 360–370.

Knottnerus, J. D., & Greenstein, T. N. (1981). Status and performance characteristics: A theory of status validation. *Social Psychology Quarterly, 44,* 338–49.

Knowles, E. S., & Linn, J. A. (Eds.) (2004). *Resistance and persuasion.* Mahwah, NJ: Erlbaum.

Kochman, T. (1987). The ethnic component in Black language and culture. In M. J. Rotheram (Ed.), *Children's ethnic socialization: Pluralism and development* (pp. 219–238). Newbury Park, CA: SAGE.

Koffka, K. (1935). *Principles of Gestalt psychology.* New York: Harcourt, Brace & World.

Kogan, N., & Wallach, M. A. (1964). *Risktaking: A study in cognition and personality.* New York: Holt.

Komorita, S. S., & Esser, J. K. (1975). Frequency of reciprocated concessions in bargaining. *Journal of Personality and Social Psychology, 32,* 699–705.

Komorita, S. S., Parks, C. D., & Hulbert, L. G. (1992). Reciprocity and the induction of cooperation in social dilemmas. *Journal of Personality and Social Psychology, 62,* 607–617.

Konečni, V. J. (1979). The role of aversive events in the development of intergroup conflict. In W. G. Austin & S. Worchel (Eds.), *The social psychology of intergroup relations* (pp. 85–102). Monterey, CA: Brooks/Cole.

Konečni, V. J., & Ebbesen, E. (1976). Disinhibition versus the cathartic effect: Artifact and substance. *Journal of Personality and Social Psychology, 34,* 352–165.

Korte, C. (1971). Effects of individual responsibility and group communication on help-giving in an emergency. *Human Relations, 24,* 149–159.

Kovera, M. B., & Borgida, E. (2010). Social psychology and law. In S. T. Fiske, D. T. Gilbert, & G. Lindzey (Eds.), *Handbook of social psychology* (5th ed., Vol. 2, pp. 1343–1385). New York: Wiley.

Kramer, R. M., & Brewer, M. B. (1984). Effects of identity on resource use in a simulated commons dilemma. *Journal of Personality and Social Psychology, 46,* 1044–1057.

Kramer, R. M., & Brewer, M. B. (1986). Social group identity and the emergence of cooperation in resource conservation dilemmas. In H. A. Wilke, D. M. Messick & C. G. Rutte (Eds.), *Psychology of decisions and conflict: Experimental social dilemmas* (pp. 205-234). Frankfurt, Germany: Verlag Peter Lang.

Kraus, S. J. (1995). Attitudes and the prediction of behaviour. A meta-analysis of the empirical literature. *Personality and Social Psychology Bulletin, 21,* 58–75.

Krauss, R. M., & Chiu, C. Y. (1998). Language and social behavior. In D. T. Gilbert, S. T. Fiske, & G. Lindzey (Eds.), *The handbook of social psychology* (4th ed., Vol. 2, pp. 41–88). New York: McGraw-Hill.

Krauss, R. M., Curran, N. M., & Ferleger, N. (1983). Expressive conventions and the cross-cultural perception of emotion. *Basic and Applied Social Psychology, 4,* 295–305.

Kraut, R. E., & Higgins, E. T. (1984). Communication and social cognition. In R. S. Wyer Jr & T. K. Srull (Eds.), *Handbook of social cognition* (Vol. 3, pp. 87–127). Hillsdale, NJ: Erlbaum.

Kraut, R. E., & Johnston, R. E. (1979). Social and emotional messages of smiling: An ethological approach. *Journal of Personality and Social Psychology, 37,* 1539–1553.

Kraut, R. E., & Poe, D. (1980). Behavioral roots of person perceptions: The deception judgments of the customs inspectors and laymen. *Journal of Personality and Social Psychology, 39,* 784–798.

Kravitz, D. A., & Martin, B. (1986). Ringelmann rediscovered: The original article. *Journal of Personality and Social Psychology, 50,* 936–941.

Krebs, D. L. (1975). Empathy and altruism. *Journal of Personality and Social Psychology, 32,* 1134–1146.

Krech, D., & Crutchfield, R. S. (1948). *Theory and problems of social psychology.* New York: McGraw-Hill.

Krech, D., Crutchfield, R., & Ballachey, R. (1962). *Individual in society.* New York: McGraw-Hill.

Kroeber, A. L., & Kluckhohn, L. (1952). *Culture: A critical review of concepts and definitions.* Cambridge, MA: Peabody Museum.

Krosnick, J. A. (1990). Expertise and political psychology. *Social Cognition, 8,* 1–8.

Krosnick, J. A., & Alwin, D. F. (1989). Aging and susceptibility to attitude change. *Journal of Personality and Social Psychology, 57,* 416–425.

Krosnick, J. A., Boninger, D. S., Chuang, Y. C., Berent, M. K., & Carnot, C. G. (1993). Attitude strength: One construct or many related constructs? *Journal of Personality and Social Psychology, 65,* 1132–1151.

Krosnick, J. A., Visser, P. S., & Harder, J. (2010). The psychological underpinnings of political behavior. In S. T. Fiske, D. T. Gilbert, & G. Lindzey (Eds.), Handbook of social psychology (5th ed., Vol. 2, pp. 1288-1342). New York: Wiley.

Kruger, J., & Dunning, D. (1999). Unskilled and unaware of it: How difficulties in recognizing one's own incompetence lead to inflated self-assessments. *Journal of Personality and Social Psychology, 77,* 1121–1134.

Kruglanski, A. W., & Higgins, E. T. (Eds.) (2007). *Social psychology: Handbook of basic principles* (2nd ed.). New York: Guilford Press.

Kruglanski, A. W. (1975). The endogenous–exogenous partition in attribution theory. *Psychological Review, 82,* 387–406.

Kruglanski, A. W., & Mackie, D. M. (1990). Majority and minority influence: A judgmental process analysis. *European Review of Social Psychology, 1,* 229–261.

Kruglanski, A. W., Webster, D. W., & Klem, A. (1993). Motivated resistance and openness to persuasion in the presence or absence of prior information. *Journal of Personality and Social Psychology, 65,* 861–876.

Krull, D. S. (1993). Does the grist change the mill? The effect of the perceiver's inferential goal on the process of social inference. *Personality and Social Psychology Bulletin, 19,* 340–348.

Kuhn, T. S. (1962). *The structure of scientific revolutions.* Chicago: University of Chicago Press.

Kuhnen U., Schiessl M., Bauer M., Paulig N., Poehlmann C., et al. (2001). How robust is the IAT? Measuring and manipulating attitudes of East and West-Germans. *Zeitschrift fur Experimentelle Psychologie, 48,* 135-144.

Kulik, J. A. (1983). Confirmatory attribution and the perpetuation of social beliefs. *Journal of Personality and Social Psychology, 44,* 1171–1181.

Kulik, J. A., Mahler, H. I. M., & Moore, P. J. (1996). Social comparison and affiliation under threat: Effects on recovery from major surgery. *Journal of Personality and Social Psychology, 71,* 967–979.

Kumkale, G. T., & Albarracín, D. (2004). The sleeper effect in persuasion: A meta-analytic review. *Psychological Bulletin, 130,* 143–172.

Kun, A., & Weiner, B. (1973). Necessary versus sufficient causal schemata for success and failure. *Journal of Research on Psychology, 7,* 197–207.

Kunda, Z. (1990). The case for motivated reasoning. *Psychological Bulletin, 108,* 480–498.

Kunda, Z., & Sanitoso, R. (1989). Motivated changes in the self-concept. *Journal of Experimental Social Psychology, 25,* 272–285.

Kurdeck, L. A. (1999). The nature and predictors of the trajectory of change in marital quality for husbands and wives over the first 10 years of marriage. *Developmental Psychology, 35,* 1283-1296.

Kurzban, R., & Leary, M. R. (2001). Evolutionary origins of stigmatization: The functions of social exclusion. *Psychological Bulletin, 127,* 187–208.

LaFrance, M., Hecht, M. A., & Paluck, E. L. (2003). The contingent smile: A meta-analysis of sex differences in smiling. *Psychological Bulletin, 129,* 305-334.

LaFrance, M., & Mayo, C. (1976). Racial differences in gaze behavior during conversations: Two systematic observational studies. *Journal of Personality and Social Psychology, 33,* 547–552.

Lakoff, R. (1973). Language and women's place. *Language in Society, 2,* 45–80.

Lalljee, M. (1981). Attribution theory and the analysis of explanations. In C. Antaki (Ed.), *The psychology of ordinary explanations of social behaviour* (pp. 119–138). London: Academic Press.

Lamarre, P., & Paredes, J. R. (2003). Growing up trilingual in Montreal: Perceptions of college students. In B. Bayley & S. R. Schechter (Eds.), *Language socialization in bilingual and multilingual societies* (pp. 62–80). Clevedon, UK: Multilingual Matters.

Lambert, W. E., Hodgson, R. C., Gardner, R. C., & Fillenbaum, S. (1960). Evaluation reactions to spoken language. *Journal of Abnormal and Social Psychology, 60,* 44–51.

Lambert, W. E., Mermigis, L., & Taylor, D. M. (1986). Greek Canadians' attitudes toward own group and other Canadian ethnic groups: A test of the multiculturalism hypothesis. *Canadian Journal of Behavioural Sciences, 18,* 35–51.

Lambert, W. W., Solomon, R. L., & Watson, P. D. (1949). Reinforcement and extinction as factors in size estimation. *Journal of Experimental Psychology, 39,* 637–641.

Lamm, H., & Kayser, E. (1978). The allocation of monetary gain and loss following dyadic performance: The weight given effort and ability under conditions of low and high intradyadic attraction. *European Journal of Social Psychology, 8,* 275–278.

Lander, E. S., Linton, L. M., Birren, B., Nusbaum, C., Zody, M. C., Baldwin, J., et al. (2001). Initial sequencing and analysis of the human genome. *Nature, 409,* 860–921.

Landman, J., & Manis, M. (1983). Social cognition: Some historical and theoretical perspectives. In L. Berkowitz (Ed.), *Advances in experimental social psychology* (Vol. 16, pp. 49–123). New York: Academic Press.

Landy, D., & Sigall, H. (1974). Beauty is talent: Task evaluation as a function of the performer's physical attractiveness. *Journal of Personality and Social Psychology, 29,* 299–304.

Langer, E. J. (1975). The illusion of control. *Journal of Personality and Social Psychology, 32,* 311–328.

Langer, E. J. (1978). Rethinking the role of thought in social interaction. In J. H. Harvey, W. I. Ickes & R. F. Kidd (Eds.), *New directions in attribution research* (Vol. 2, pp. 35–58). Hillsdale, NJ: Erlbaum.

Langer, E. J., Bashner, R. S., & Chanowitz, B. (1985). Decreasing prejudice by increasing discrimination. *Journal of Personality and Social Psychology, 49,* 113–120.

Langer, E. J., Blank, A., & Chanowitz, B. (1978). The mindlessness of ostensibly thoughtful action. *Journal of Personality and Social Psychology, 36,* 635–642.

Langlois, J. H., Kalakanis, L., Rubenstein, A. J., Larson, A., Hallam, M., & Smoot, M. (2000). Maxims or myths of beauty? A meta-analytic and theoretical review. *Psychological Bulletin, 126,* 390–423.

Langlois, J. H., Roggman, L. A., & Musselman, L. (1994). What is average and what is not average about attractive faces? *Psychological Science, 5,* 214–220.

LaPiere, R. T. (1934). Attitudes vs actions. *Social Forces, 13,* 230–237.

LaPiere, R. T., & Farnsworth, P. R. (1936). *Social psychology.* New York: McGraw-Hill.

LaPiere, R. T., & Farnsworth, P. R. (1949). *Social psychology* (3rd. ed). New York: McGraw-Hill.

LaPlace, A. C., Chermack S. T., & Taylor, S. P. (1994). Effects of alcohol and drinking experience on human physical aggression. *Personality and Social Psychology Bulletin, 20,* 439–444.

Lariscy, R. A. W., & Tinkham, S. F. (1999). The sleeper effect and negative political advertising. *Journal of Advertising, 28,* 13–30.

Larson, J. R., Jr, Foster-Fishman, P. G., & Keys, C. B. (1994). Discussion of shared and unshared information in decision-making group. *Journal of Personality and Social Psychology, 67,* 446–461.

Latané, B. (1981). The psychology of social impact. *American Psychologist, 36,* 343–356.

Latané, B., & Dabbs, J. M. Jr. (1975). Sex, group size and helping in three cities. *Sociometry, 38,* 180–194.

Latané, B., & Darley, J. M. (1970). *The unresponsive bystander: Why doesn't he help?* New York: Appleton-Century-Crofts.

Latané, B., & Darley, J. M. (1976). Help in a crisis: Bystander response to an emergency. In J. W. Thibaut & J. T. Spence (Eds.), *Contemporary topics in social psychology* (pp. 309–332). Morristown, NJ: General Learning Press.

Latané, B., & Rodin, J. (1969). A lady in distress: Inhibiting effects of friends and strangers on bystander intervention. *Journal of Experimental Social Psychology, 5,* 189–202.

Latané, B., & Wolf, S. (1981). The social impact of majorities and minorities. *Psychological Review, 88,* 438–453.

Latané, B., Williams, K. D., & Harkins, S. G. (1979). Many hands make light the work: The causes and consequences of social loafing. *Journal of Personality and Social Psychology, 37,* 822–832.

Latin American Bureau (1982). *Falklands/Malvinas: Whose crisis?* London: Latin American Bureau.

Laughlin, P. R. (1980). Social combination processes of cooperative problem solving groups on verbal intellective tasks. In M. Fishbein (Ed.), *Progress in social psychology* (Vol. 1, pp. 127–155). Hillsdale, NJ: Erlbaum.

Laughlin, P. R., & Ellis, A. L. (1986). Demonstrability and social combination processes on mathematical intellective tasks. *Journal of Experimental Social Psychology, 22,* 177–189.

Laurenceau, J. P., Barrett, L. F., & Pietromonaco, P. R. (1998). Intimacy as an interpersonal process: The importance of self-disclosure, partner disclosure, and perceived partner responsiveness in interpersonal exchanges. *Journal of Personality and Social Psychology, 74,* 1238–1251.

Lavine, H., Huff, J. W., Wagner, S. H., & Sweeney, D. (1998). The moderating influence of attitude strength on the susceptibility to context effects in attitude surveys. *Journal of Personality and Social Psychology, 75,* 359–373.

Lawrence, C., & Andrew, K. (2004). The influence of perceived prison crowding on male inmates' perception of aggressive events. *Aggressive Behavior, 30,* 273–283.

Le, B., & Agnew, C. R. (2003). Commitment and its theorized determinants: A meta-analysis of the investment model. *Personal Relationships, 10,* 37–57.

Leana, C. R. (1985). A partial test of Janis's groupthink model: Effects of group cohesiveness and leader behavior on defective decision making. *Journal of Management, 11,* 5–17.

Leary, M. R. (1995). *Self-presentation: Impression management and interpersonal behavior.* Madison, WI: Brown & Benchmark.

Leary, M. R. (2010). Affiliation, acceptance, and belonging: The pursuit of interpersonal connection. In S. T. Fiske, D. T. Gilbert, & G. Lindzey (Eds.), *Handbook of social psychology* (5th ed., Vol. 2, pp. 864-897). New York: Wiley.

Leary, M. R., & Kowalski, R. (1995). *Social anxiety.* New York: Guilford Press.

Leary, M. R., Tambor, E. S., Terdal, S. K., & Downs, D. L. (1995). Self-esteem as an interpersonal monitor: The sociometer hypothesis. *Journal of Personality and Social Psychology, 68,* 518–530.

Leary, M. R., & Tangney, J. P. (2003). *Handbook of self and identity.* New York: Guilford Press.

Leavitt, H. J. (1951). Some effects of certain communication patterns on group performance. *Journal of Abnormal and Social Psychology, 46,* 38–50.

LeBon, G. (1896/1908). *The crowd: A study of the popular mind.* London: Unwin.

Lee, J. (1993). *Facing the fire: Experiencing and expressing anger appropriately.* New York: Bantam.

Lee, Y. T., & Ottati, V. (1993). Determinants of ingroup and outgroup perceptions of heterogeneity. *Journal of Cross-cultural Psychology, 24,* 298–318.

Lehman, D. R., Chiu, C.-Y., & Schaller, M. (2004). Psychology and culture. *Annual Review of Psychology, 55,* 689–714.

Lemaine, G. (1966). Inégalité, comparison et incomparabilité: Esquisse d'une théorie de l'originalité sociale. *Bulletin de Psychologie, 20,* 24–32.

Lemaine, G. (1974). Social differentiation and social originality. *European Journal of Social Psychology, 4,* 17–52.

Lepore, L., & Brown, R. (1997). Category and stereotype activation: Is prejudice inevitable? *Journal of Personality and Social Psychology, 72,* 275–287.

Lepper, M. R., Greene, D., & Nisbett, R. E. (1973). Undermining children's intrinsic interest with extrinsic reward: A test of the over-justification hypothesis. *Journal of Personality and Social Psychology, 28,* 129–137.

Lerner, M. J. (1977). The justice motive: Some hypotheses as to its origins and forms. *Journal of Personality, 45,* 1–52.

Lerner, M. J., & Miller, D. T. (1978). Just-world research and the attribution process: Looking back and ahead. *Psychological Bulletin, 85,* 1030–1051.

Lesar, T. S., Briceland, L., & Stein, D. S. (1997). Factors related to errors in medication prescribing. *Journal of the American Medical Association, 277,* 312–317.

Leslie, J. B., & Van Velsor, E. (1996). *A look at derailment today.* Greensboro, NC: Centre for Creative Leadership.

Letellier, P. (1994). Gay and bisexual domestic violence victimisation: Challenges to feminist theories and responses to violence. *Violence and Victims, 9,* 95–106.

Leventhal, H., Singer, R., & Jones, S. (1965). Effects of fear and specificity of recommendations upon attitudes and behavior. *Journal of Personality and Social Psychology, 2,* 20–29.

Leventhal, H., Watts, J. C., & Pagano, R. (1967). Effects of fear and instructions on how to cope with danger. *Journal of Personality and Social Psychology, 6,* 313–321.

Levin, D. T. (2000). Race as a visual feature: Using visual search and perceptual discrimination tasks to understand face categories and the cross-race recognition deficit. *Journal of Experimental Psychology: General, 129,* 559–574.

Levine, J. M., & Hogg, M. A. (Eds.) (2010) *Encyclopedia of group processes and intergroup relations.* Thousand Oaks, CA: SAGE.

Levine, J. M., & Moreland, R. L. (1990). Progress in small group research. *Annual Review of Psychology, 41,* 585–634.

Levine, J. M., & Moreland, R. L. (1991). Culture and socialization in work groups. In L. B. Resnick, J. M. Levine, & S. D. Teasley (Eds.), *Perspectives on socially shared cognition* (pp. 257–279). Washington, DC: American Psychological Association.

Levine, J. M., & Moreland, R. L. (1994). Group socialization: Theory and research. *European Review of Social Psychology, 5,* 305–336.

Levine, J. M., & Moreland, R. L. (2002). Group reactions to loyalty and disloyalty. In E. Lawler & S. Thye (Eds.), *Advances in group processes* (Vol. 19, pp. 203–228). Amsterdam: Elsevier.

Levine, J. M., Moreland, R. L., & Choi, H.-S. (2001). Group socialization and newcomer innovation. In M. A. Hogg & R. S. Tindale (Eds.), *Blackwell handbook of social psychology: Group processes* (pp. 86–106). Oxford, UK: Blackwell.

Levine, J. M., Resnick, L. B., & Higgins, E. T. (1993). Social foundations of cognition. *Annual Review of Psychology, 44,* 585–612.

LeVine, R. A., & Campbell, D. T. (1972). *Ethnocentrism: Theories of conflict, ethnic attitudes and group behavior.* New York: Wiley.

Levinger, G. (1980). Toward the analysis of close relationships. *Journal of Experimental Social Psychology, 16,* 510–44.

Levitt, E., & Klassen, A. (1974). Public attitudes towards homosexuality: Part of the 1970 national survey by the Institute for Sex Research. *Journal of Homosexuality, 1,* 29–43.

Lévy-Bruhl, L. (1925). *How natives think.* New York: Alfred A. Knopf.

Lewin, A. Y., & Duchan, L. (1971). Women in academia. *Science, 173,* 892–895.

Lewin, K. (1936). Some socio-psychological differences between the United States and Germany. *Character and Personality, 4,* 265–293.

Lewin, K. (1943). Forces behind food habits and methods of change. *Bulletin of National Research Council, 108,* 35–65.

Lewin, K. (1947). Frontiers in group dynamics. *Human Relations, 1,* 5–42.

Lewin, K. (1951). *Field theory in social science.* New York: Harper.

Lewin, K., Lippitt, R., & White, R. K. (1939). Patterns of aggressive behavior in experimentally created 'social climates'. *Journal of Social Psychology, 10,* 271–299.

Lewis, A., Snell, M., & Furnham, A. (1987). Lay explanations for the causes of unemployment in Britain: Economic, individualistic, societal or fatalistic? *Political Psychology, 8,* 427–439.

Lewis, B. (2004). *The crisis of Islam: Holy war and unholy terror.* London: Phoenix.

Lewis, O. (1969). *A death in the Sanchez family.* New York: Secker & Warburg.

Leyens, J.-P., Camino, L., Parke, R. D., & Berkowitz, L. (1975). Effects of movie violence on aggression in a field setting as a function of group dominance and cohesion. *Journal of Personality and Social Psychology, 32,* 346–60.

Leyens, J.-P., Demoulin, S., Vaes, J., Gaunt, R., & Paladino, M. P. (2007). Infrahumanization: The wall of group differences. *Journal of Social Issues and Policy Review, 1,* 139–172.

Leyens, J.-P., Rodriguez-Perez, A., Rodriguez-Torres, R., Gaunt, R., Paladino, M.-P., Vaes, J., et al. (2001). Psychological essentialism and the differential attribution of uniquely human emotions to ingroups and outgroups. *European Journal of Social Psychology, 31,* 395–411.

Leyens, J.-P., Yzerbyt, V. Y., & Schadron, G. (1992). Stereotypes and social judgeability. *European Review of Social Psychology, 3,* 91–120.

Leyens, J.-P., Yzerbyt, V., & Schadron, G. (1994). *Stereotypes and social cognition.* London: SAGE.

Lickel, B., Hamilton, D. L., Wieczorkowska, G., Lewis, A. C., & Sherman, S. (2000). Varieties of groups and the perception of group entitativity. *Journal of Personality and Social Psychology, 78,* 223–246.

Lieberman, M. D. (2000). Intuition: A social cognitive neuroscience approach. *Psychological Bulletin, 126,* 109–137.

Lieberman, M. D. (2010). Social cognitive neuroscience. In S. T. Fiske, D. T. Gilbert, & G. Lindzey (Eds.), *Handbook of social psychology* (5th ed., Vol. 1, pp. 143-193). New York: Wiley.

Lieberman, M. D., Gaunt, R., Gilbert, D. T., & Trope, Y. (2002). Reflexion and reflection: A social cognitive neuroscience approach to attributional inference. In M. P. Zanna (Ed.), *Advances in experimental social psychology* (Vol. 34, pp. 199–249). San Diego, CA: Academic Press.

Liebrand, W. B. G. (1984). The effect of social motives, communication and group size in an n-person multistage mixed-motive game. *European Journal of Social Psychology, 14,* 239–64.

Liebrand, W., Messick, D., & Wilke, H. (Eds.) (1992). *A social psychological approach to social dilemmas.* New York: Pergamon Press.

Likert, R. (1932). A technique for the measurement of attitudes. *Archives of Psychology, 22,* no. 140, 44–53.

Lim, R. G., & Carnevale, P. J. D. (1990). Contingencies in the mediation of disputes. *Journal of Personality and Social Psychology, 58,* 259–272.

Limber, J. (1977). Language in child and chimp? *American Psychologist, 32,* 280–295.

Lind, E. A., & O'Barr, W. M. (1979). The social significance of speech in the courtroom. In H. Giles & R. N. St Clair (Eds.), *Language and social psychology.* Oxford, UK: Blackwell.

Lind, E. A., & Tyler, T. R. (1988). *The social psychology of procedural justice.* New York: Plenum Press.

Lind, J., & Maxwell, G. (1996). Children's experiences of violence in schools. *Children,* March. Wellington: Office of the Commissioner for Children.

Lindstrom, P. (1997). Persuasion via facts in political discussion. *European Journal of Social Psychology, 27,* 145–163.

Linskold, S. (1978). Trust development, the GRIT proposal, and the effects of conciliatory acts on conflict and cooperation. *Psychological Bulletin, 85,* 772–793.

Linskold, S., & Han, G. (1988). GRIT as a foundation for integrative bargaining. *Personality and Social Psychology Bulletin, 14,* 335–345.

Linssen, H., & Hagendoorn, L. (1994). Social and geographical factors in the explanation of European nationality stereotypes. *British Journal of Social Psychology, 23,* 165–182.

Linville, P. W. (1982). Affective consequences of complexity regarding the self and others. In M. S. Clark & S. T. Fiske (Eds.), *Affect and cognition: The 17th annual Carnegie symposium on cognition* (pp. 79–109). Hillsdale, NJ: Erlbaum.

Linville, P. W. (1985). Self-complexity and affective extremity: Don't put all of your eggs in one cognitive basket. *Social Cognition, 3,* 94–120.

Linville, P. W. (1987). Self-complexity as a cognitive buffer against stress-related depression and illness. *Journal of Personality and Social Psychology, 52,* 663–676.

Linville, P. W., Fischer, G. W., & Salovey, P. (1989). Perceived distributions of the characteristics of ingroup and outgroup members: Empirical evidence and a computer simulation. *Journal of Personality and Social Psychology, 57,* 165–188.

Linz, D. G., Donnerstein, E., & Penrod, S. (1988). Effects of long-term exposure to violent and sexually degrading depictions of women. *Journal of Personality and Social Psychology, 55,* 758–768.

Linz, D., Wilson, B. J., & Donnerstein, E. (1992). Sexual violence in the mass media: Legal solutions, warnings, and mitigation through education. *Journal of Social Issues, 48,* 145–171.

Lippa, R. A. (1990). *Introduction to social psychology.* Belmont, CA: Brooks/Cole.

Lippitt, R., & White, R. (1943). The 'social climate' of children's groups. In R. G. Barker, J. Kounin & H. Wright (Eds.), *Child behavior and development* (pp. 485–508). New York: McGraw-Hill.

Lippman, W. (1922). *Public opinion.* New York: Harcourt and Brace.

Litton, I., & Potter, J. (1985). Social representations in the ordinary explanation of a 'riot'. *European Journal of Social Psychology, 15,* 371–388.

Liu, J. H., Campbell, S. M., & Condie, H. (1995). Ethnocentrism in dating preferences for an American sample: The ingroup bias in social context. *European Journal of Social Psychology, 25,* 95–115.

Liu, T. J., & Steele, C. M. (1986). Attributional analysis and self-affirmation. *Journal of Personality and Social Psychology, 51,* 531–540.

Lock, A. (1980). *The guided reinvention of language.* London: Academic Press.

Lock, A. (Ed.) (1978). *Action, gesture and symbol: The emergence of language.* London: Academic Press.

Lockard, J. S., Kirkevold, B. C., & Kalk, D. F. (1980). Cost–benefit indexes of deception in nonviolent crime. *Bulletin of the Psychonomic Society, 16,* 303–306.

Lockwood, P., Jordan, C. H., & Kunda, Z. (2002). Motivation by positive or negative role models: Regulatory focus determines who will best inspire us. *Journal of Personality and Social Psychology, 83,* 854–864.

Loftin, C., McDowall, D., Wiersema, B., & Cottey, T. J. (1991). Effects of restrictive licensing of handguns on homicide and suicide in the District of Columbia. *New England Journal of Medicine, 325,* 1615–20.

Loftus, E. F. (1979). *Eyewitness testimony*. Cambridge, MA: Harvard University Press.

Long, G. T., & Lerner, M. J. (1974). Deserving the 'personal contract' and altruistic behaviour by children. *Journal of Personality and Social Psychology, 29,* 551–556.

Long, K., & Spears, R. (1997). The self-esteem hypothesis revisited: Differentiation and the disaffected. In R. Spears, P. J. Oakes, N. Ellemers & S. A. Haslam (Eds.), *The social psychology of stereotyping and group life* (pp. 296–317). Oxford, UK: Blackwell.

Longley, J., & Pruitt, D. G. (1980). Groupthink: A critique of Janis's theory. In L. Wheeler (Ed.), *Review of personality and social psychology* (Vol. 1, pp. 74–93). Beverly Hills, CA: SAGE.

Lonner, W. J. (Ed.) (1984). Differing views on 'culture.' *Journal of Cross-Cultural Psychology, 15,* 107–109.

Lonsbary, C. E. (2007). Using social norms to reduce academic dishonesty. *Dissertation Abstracts International: Section B: The Sciences and Engineering, 67,* (7B), 4159.

Lord, R. G., & Brown, D. J. (2004). *Leadership processes and follower identity*. Mahwah, NJ: Erlbaum.

Lord, R. G., Brown, D. J., & Harvey, J. L. (2001). System constraints on leadership perceptions, behavior and influence: An example of connectionist level processes. In M. A. Hogg & R. S. Tindale (Eds.), *Blackwell handbook of social psychology: Group processes* (pp. 283–310). Oxford, UK: Blackwell.

Lord, R. G., Brown, D. J., Harvey, J. L., & Hall, R. J. (2001). Contextual constraints on prototype generation and their multilevel consequences for leadership perceptions. *Leadership Quarterly, 12,* 311–338.

Lord, R. G., & Hall, R. (2003). Identity, leadership categorization, and leadership schema. In D. van Knippenberg & M. A. Hogg (Eds.) *Leadership and power: Identity processes in groups and organizations* (pp. 48–64). London: SAGE.

Lorenz, K. (1966). *On aggression*. New York: Harcourt, Brace and World.

Lorenzi-Cioldi, F., & Clémence, A. (2001). Group processes and the construction of social representations. In M. A. Hogg & R. S. Tindale (Eds.), *Blackwell handbook of social psychology: Group processes* (pp. 311–333). Oxford, UK: Blackwell.

Lorenzi-Cioldi, F., & Doise, W. (1990). Levels of analysis and social identity. In D. Abrams & M. A. Hogg (Eds.), *Social identity theory: Constructive and critical advances* (pp. 71–88). London: Harvester Wheatsheaf.

Lorenzi-Cioldi, F., Eagly, A. H., & Stewart, T. L. (1995). Homogeneity of gender groups in memory. *Journal of Experimental Social Psychology, 31,* 193–217.

Lorge, I., & Solomon, H. (1955). Two models of group behavior in the solution of eureka-type problems. *Psychometrika, 20,* 139–148.

Lott, A. J., & Lott, B. E. (1965). Group cohesiveness as interpersonal attraction. *Psychological Bulletin, 64,* 259–309.

Lott, B. E. (1961). Group cohesiveness: A learning phenomenon. *Journal of Social Psychology, 55,* 275–286.

Lowe, K. B., Kroeck, K. G., & Sivasubramaniam, N. (1996). Effectiveness correlates of transformational and transactional leadership: A meta-analytic review. *The Leadership Quarterly, 7,* 385–425.

Luce, R. D., & Raiffa, H. (1957). *Games and decisions*. New York: Wiley.

Lueger, R. J. (1980). Person and situation factors influencing transgression in behavior-problem adolescents. *Journal of Abnormal Psychology, 89,* 453–458.

Lumsdaine, A. A., & Janis, I. L. (1953). Resistance to 'counter-propaganda' produced by one-sided and two-sided 'propaganda' presentations. *Public Opinion Quarterly, 17,* 311–318.

Lydon, J., & Dunkel-Schetter, C. (1994). Seeing is committing: A longitudinal study of bolstering commitment in amniocentesis patients. *Personality and Social Psychology Bulletin, 20,* 218–227.

Maass, A. (1999). Linguistic intergroup bias: Stereotype-perpetuation through language. In M. P. Zanna (Ed.), *Advances in experimental social psychology* (Vol. 31, pp. 79–121). San Diego, CA: Academic Press.

Maass, A., & Arcuri, L. (1996). Language and stereotyping. In C. N. Macrae, C. Stangor & M. Hewstone (Eds.), *Stereotypes and stereotyping* (pp. 193–226). New York: Guilford Press.

Maass, A., & Clark, R. D., III (1983). Internalisation versus compliance: Differential processes underlying minority influence and conformity. *European Journal of Social Psychology, 13,* 197–215.

Maass, A., & Clark, R. D., III (1984). Hidden impact of minorities: Fifteen years of minority influence research. *Psychological Bulletin, 95,* 428–450.

Maass, A., & Clark, R. D., III (1986). Conversion theory and simultaneous majority/minority influence: Can reactance offer an alternative explanation. *European Journal of Social Psychology, 16,* 305–309.

Maass, A., Clark, R. D., III and Haberkorn, G. (1982). The effects of differential ascribed category membership and norms on minority influence. *European Journal of Social Psychology, 12,* 89–104.

Maass, A., Salvi, D., Arcuri, L., & Semin, G. (1989). Language use in intergroup contexts: The linguistic intergroup bias. *Journal of Personality and Social Psychology, 57,* 981–993.

Maass, A., Suitner, C., Favaretto, X., & Cignacchi, M. (2009). Groups in space: Stereotypes and the spatial agency bias. *Journal of Experimental Social Psychology, 45,* 496-504.

McArthur, L. A. (1972). The how and what of why: Some determinants of consequences of causal attributions. *Journal of Personality and Social Psychology, 22,* 171–193.

McArthur, L. Z. (1981). What grabs you? The role of attention in impression formation and causal attribution. In E. T. Higgins, C. P. Herman & M. P. Zanna (Eds.), *Social cognition: The Ontario symposium* (Vol. 1, pp. 201–246). Hillsdale, NJ: Erlbaum.

McArthur, L. Z., & Baron, R. (1983). Toward an ecological theory of social perception. *Psychological Review, 90,* 215–238.

McArthur, L. Z., & Friedman, S. A. (1980). Illusory correlation in impression formation: Variations in the shared distinctiveness effect as a function of the distinctive person's age, race, and sex. *Journal of Personality and Social Psychology, 39,* 615–624.

McArthur, L. Z., & Post, D. L. (1977). Figural emphasis and person perception. *Journal of Experimental Social Psychology, 13,* 520–535.

McAuliffe, B. J., Jetten, J., Hornsey, M. J., & Hogg, M. A. (2003). Individualist and collectivist group norms: When it's OK to go your own way. *European Journal of Social Psychology, 33,* 57–70.

McCall, G., & Simmons, R. (1978). *Identities and interactions* (2nd ed.). New York: Free Press.

McCauley, C. (1989). The nature of social influence in groupthink: Compliance and internalization. *Journal of Personality and Social Psychology, 57,* 250–260.

McClintock, C. G., & Van Avermaet, E. (1982). Social values and rules of fairness: A theoretical perspective. In V. Derlaga & J. L. Grzelak (Eds.), *Cooperation and helping behavior: Theories and research* (pp. 43–71). New York: Academic Press

McClure, J. (1998). Discounting causes of behavior: Are two reasons better than one? *Journal of Personality and Social Psychology, 74,* 1–14.

McConahay, J. G. (1986). Modern racism, ambivalence, and the modern racism scale. In J. F. Dovidio & S. L. Gaertner (Eds.), *Prejudice, discrimination, and racism* (pp. 91–125). New York: Academic Press.

McConnell, A. R., Sherman, S. J., & Hamilton, D. L. (1994). On-line and memory-based aspects of individual and group target judgments. *Journal of Personality and Social Psychology, 67,* 173–185.

McCullough, M. E., Worthington, E. L., & Rachal, K. C. (1997). Interpersonal forgiving in close relationships, *Journal of Personality and Social Psychology, 73,* 321–336.

McDougall, W. (1908). *An introduction to social psychology.* London: Methuen.

McDougall, W. (1920). *The group mind.* London: Cambridge University Press.

McGarty, C., Haslam, S. A., Turner, J. C., & Oakes, P. J. (1993). Illusory correlation as accentuation of actual intercategory difference: Evidence for the effect with minimal stimulus information. *European Journal of Social Psychology, 23,* 391–410.

McGarty, C., & Penny, R. E. C. (1988). Categorization, accentuation and social judgement. *British Journal of Social Psychology, 27,* 147–157.

McGarty, C., & Turner, J. C. (1992). The effects of categorization on social judgement. *British Journal of Social Psychology, 31,* 147–157.

McGillicuddy, N. B., Welton, G. L., & Pruitt, D. G. (1987). Third-party intervention: A field experiment comparing three different models. *Journal of Personality and Social Psychology, 53,* 104–112.

McGinnies, E. (1966). Studies in persuasion: III. Reactions of Japanese students to one-sided and two-sided communications. *Journal of Social Psychology, 70,* 87–93.

McGrath, J. E., & Hollingshead, A. B. (1994). *Groups interacting with technology.* Newbury Park, CA: SAGE.

McGuire, W. J. (1964). Inducing resistance to persuasion. In L. Berkowitz (Ed.), *Advances in experimental social psychology* (Vol. 1, pp. 191–229). New York: Academic Press.

McGuire, W. J. (1968). Personality and susceptibility to social influence. In E. F. Borgatta & W. W. Lambert (Eds.), *Handbook of personality: Theory and research* (pp. 1130–1187). Chicago: Rand McNally.

McGuire, W. J. (1969). The nature of attitudes and attitude change. In G. Lindzey & E. Aronson (Eds.), *Handbook of social psychology* (2nd ed., Vol. 3, pp. 136–314). Reading, MA: Addison-Wesley.

McGuire, W. J. (1986). The vicissitudes of attitudes and similar representational constructs in twentieth-century psychology. *European Journal of Social Psychology, 16,* 89–130.

McGuire, W. J. (1989). The structure of individual attitudes and attitude systems. In A. R. Pratkanis, S. J. Breckler, & A. G. Greenwald (Eds.), *Attitude structure and function* (pp. 37–69). Hillsdale, NJ: Erlbaum.

McGuire, W. J., & Papageorgis, D. (1961). The relative efficacy of various types of prior belief-defence in producing immunity against persuasion. *Journal of Abnormal and Social Psychology, 62,* 327–337.

MacKay, N. J., & Covell, K. (1997). The impact of women in advertisements on attitudes toward women. *Sex Roles, 36,* 573–579.

Mackie, D. M. (1986). Social identification effects in group polarization. *Journal of Personality and Social Psychology, 50,* 720–728.

Mackie, D. M., & Ahn, M. N. (1998). In-group and out-group inferences: When in-group bias overwhelms out-group bias. *European Journal of Social Psychology, 28,* 343–360.

Mackie, D. M., & Cooper, J. (1984). Attitude polarization: The effects of group membership. *Journal of Personality and Social Psychology, 46,* 575–585.

Mackie, D. M., Devos, T., & Smith, E. R. (1999). Intergroup emotions: Explaining offensive action tendencies in an intergroup context. *Journal of Personality and Social Psychology, 79,* 602–616.

Mackie, D. M., Hamilton, D. L., Susskind, J., & Rosselli, F. (1996). Social psychological foundations of stereotype formation. In C. N. Macrae, C. Stangor & M. Hewstone (Eds.), *Stereotypes and stereotyping* (pp. 41–78). New York: Guilford Press.

Mackie, D. M., Maitner, A. T., & Smith, E. R. (2009). Intergroup emotions theory. In T. D. Nelson (Ed.), *Handbook of prejudice, stereotyping and discrimination* (pp. 285-308). New York: Psychology Press.

Mackie, D. M., & Smith, E. R. (2002a). Intergroup emotions and the social self: Prejudice reconceptualized as differentiated reactions to outgroups. In J. P. Forgas & K. D. Williams (Eds.), *The social self: Cognitive, interpersonal, and intergroup perspectives* (pp. 309–326). New York: Psychology Press.

Mackie, D. M., & Smith, E. R. (Eds.) (2002b). *From prejudice to intergroup emotions: Differentiated reactions to social groups.* New York: Psychology Press.

Mackie, D. M., & Worth, L. T. (1989). Processing deficits and the mediation of positive affect in persuasion. *Journal of Personality and Social Psychology, 57,* 27–40.

Mackie, D. M., Worth, L. T., & Asuncion, A. G. (1990). Processing of persuasive in-group messages. *Journal of Personality and Social Psychology, 58,* 812–822.

McKiethen, K. B., Reitman, J. S., Rueter, H. H., & Hirtle, S. C. (1981). Knowledge organisation and skill differences in computer programmers. *Cognitive Psychology, 13,* 307–325.

McKimmie, B. M., Terry, D. J., Hogg, M. A. Manstead, A. S. R., Spears, R., & Doosje, B. (2003). I'm a hypocrite, but so is everyone else: Group support and the reduction of cognitive dissonance. *Group Dynamics: Theory, Research and Practice, 7,* 214–224.

MacKinnon, D. W. (1933). *The violation of prohibitions in the solving of problems.* Unpublished doctoral dissertation, Harvard University.

McMillen, D. L. (1971). Transgression, self-image, and complaint behaviour. *Journal of Personality and Social Psychology, 20,* 176–179.

McNamara, T. F. (1987). Language and social identity: Israelis abroad. *Journal of Language and Social Psychology, 6,* 215–28.

MacNeil, M., & Sherif, M. (1976). Norm change over subject generations as a function of arbitrariness of prescribed norms. *Journal of Personality and Social Psychology, 34,* 762–773.

Macrae, C. N., & Quadflieg, S. (2010). Perceiving people. In S. T. Fiske, D. T. Gilbert, & G. Lindzey (Eds.), *Handbook of social psychology* (5th ed., Vol. 1, pp. 428-463). New York: Wiley.

Macrae, C. N., Stangor, C., & Hewstone, M. (Eds.) (1996). *Stereotypes and stereotyping.* New York: Guilford Press.

Madden, T. J., Ellen, P. S., & Ajzen, I. (1992). A comparison of the theory of planned behavior and the theory of reasoned action. *Personality and Social Psychology Bulletin, 18,* 3–9.

Maes, M., De Meyer, F., Thompson, P., Peeters D., & Cosyns, P. (1994). Synchronised annual rhythms in violent suicide rate, ambient temperature and the light–dark span. *Acta Psychiatrica Scandinavica, 90,* 391–396.

Maio, G. R., & Haddock, G. (2007). Attitude change. In A. W. Kruglanski & E. T. Higgins (Eds.), Social psychology: Handbook of basic principles (2nd ed., pp. 565-586). New York: Guilford.

Maio, G., & Haddock, G. (2010). *The science of attitudes.* London: SAGE.

Maio, G. R., & Olson, J. M. (1994). Value–attitude–behaviour relations: The moderating role of attitude functions. *British Journal of Social Psychology, 33,* 301–312.

Maio, G. R., & Olson, J. M. (1995). Relations between values, attitudes, and behavioral intentions: The moderating role of attitude function. *Journal of Experimental Social Psychology, 31,* 266–285.

Major, B. (1981). Gender patterns in touching behavior. In C. Mayo & N. M. Henley (Eds.), *Gender and nonverbal behavior* (pp. 15–37). New York: Springer.

Major, B. (1994). From social inequality to personal entitlement: The role of social comparisons, legitimacy appraisals and group memberships. In M. P. Zanna (Ed.), *Advances in experimental social psychology* (Vol. 26, pp. 293–355). San Diego, CA: Academic Press.

Major, B., & Adams, J. B. (1983). Role of gender, interpersonal orientation, and self-presentation in distributive justice behaviour. *Journal of Personality and Social Psychology, 45,* 598–608.

Major, B., & Heslin, R. (1982). Perceptions of same-sex and cross-sex reciprocal touch: It's better to give than to receive. *Journal of Nonverbal Behavior, 3,* 148–163.

Major, B., & Konar, E. (1984). An investigation of sex differences in pay expectations and their possible causes. *Academy of Management Journal, 27,* 777–792.

Major, B., Quinton, W. J., & McCoy, S. K. (2002) Antecedents and consequences of attributions to discrimination: Theoretical and empirical advances. In M. P. Zanna (Ed.), *Advances in experimental social psychology* (Vol. 34, pp. 251–330). San Diego, CA: Academic Press.

Major, B., & Schmader, T. (1998). Coping with stigma through psychological disengagement. In J. K. Swim & C. Stangor (Eds.), *Prejudice: The target's perspective* (pp. 219–242). San Diego, CA: Academic Press.

Malamuth, N. M. (1981). Rape proclivity among males. *Journal of Social Issues, 37,* 138–157.

Malamuth, N. M., & Donnerstein, E. (1982). The effects of aggressive-pornographic mass media stimuli. In L. Berkowitz (Ed.), *Advances in experimental social psychology* (Vol. 15, pp. 104–136). New York: Academic Press.

Malinowski, B. (1927). *Sex and repression in savage society.* New York: Harcourt Brace.

Malkin, P. Z., & Stein, H. (1990). *Eichmann in my hands.* New York: Warner Books.

Malpass, R. S. (1988). Why not cross-cultural psychology? A characterization of some mainstream views. In M. H. Bond (Ed.), *The cross-cultural challenge to social psychology* (pp. 29–35). Newbury Park, CA: SAGE.

Malpass, R. S., & Kravitz, J. (1969). Recognition for faces of own and other race. *Journal of Personality and Social Psychology, 13,* 330–334.

Mandela, N. (1994). *The long walk to freedom: The autobiography of Nelson Mandela,* London: Little, Brown.

Maner, J. K., Luce, C. L., Neuberg, S. L., Cialdini, R. B., Brown, S., & Sagarin, B. J. (2002). The effects of perspective taking on motivations for helping: Still no evidence for altruism. *Personality and Social Psychology Bulletin, 28,* 1601–1610.

Manis, M. (1977). Cognitive social psychology. *Personality and Social Psychology Bulletin, 3,* 550–566.

Mann, L. (1981). The baiting crowd in episodes of threatened suicide. *Journal of Personality and Social Psychology, 41,* 703–709.

Mann, L. (1977). The effect of stimulus queues on queue-joining behavior. *Journal of Personality and Social Psychology, 35,* 437–442.

Mann, L., Newton, J. W., & Innes, J. M. (1982). A test between deindividuation and emergent norm theories of crowd aggression. *Journal of Personality and Social Psychology, 42,* 260–272.

Manstead, A. S. R. (1992). Gender differences in emotion. In A. Gale & M. W. Eysenck (Eds.), *Handbook of individual differences: Biological perspectives* (pp. 355–387). Oxford, UK: Wiley.

Manstead, A. S. R. (2000). The role of moral norm in the attitude–behavior relation. In D. J. Terry & M. A. Hogg (Eds.), (1995). *Attitudes, behavior, and social context: The role of norms and group membership* (pp. 11–30). Mahwah, NJ: Erlbaum.

Manstead, A. S. R., & Parker, D. (1995). Evaluating and extending the theory of planned behaviour. *European Review of Social Psychology, 6,* 69–95.

Manstead, A. S. R., Proffitt, C., & Smart, J. L. (1983). Predicting and understanding mother's infant-feeding intentions and behavior: Testing the theory of reasoned action. *Journal of Personality and Social Psychology, 44,* 657–671.

Manstead, A. S. R., & Semin, G. R. (1980). Social facilitation effects: Mere enhancement of dominant responses? *British Journal of Social and Clinical Psychology, 19,* 119–136.

Mantell, D. M. (1971). The potential for violence in Germany. *Journal of Social Issues, 27,* 101–12.

Marks, G., & Miller, N. (1985). The effect of certainty on consensus judgments. *Personality and Social Psychology Bulletin, 2,* 165–177.

Marks, G., & Miller, N. (1987). Ten years of research on the false-consensus effect: An empirical and theoretical review. *Psychological Bulletin, 102,* 72–90.

Markus, H. (1977). Self-schemata and processing information about the self. *Journal of Personality and Social Psychology, 35,* 63–78.

Markus, H. (1978). The effect of mere presence on social facilitation: An unobtrusive test. *Journal of Experimental Social Psychology, 14,* 389–397.

Markus, H. (2004). Culture and personality: Brief for an arranged marriage. *Journal of Research in Personality, 38,* 75–83.

Markus, H., & Kitayama, S. (1991). Culture and the self: Implications for cognition, emotion, and motivation. *Psychological Review, 98,* 224–253.

Markus, H., & Kitayama, S. (2003). Models of agency: Sociocultural diversity in the construction of action. In V. Murphy-Berman & J. J. Berman (Eds.), *Cross-cultural differences in perspectives on the self* (Vol. 49, pp. 18–74). Lincoln, NE: University of Nebraska Press.

Markus, H., Kitayama, S., & Heiman, R. J. (1996). Culture and basic psychological principles. In E. T. Higgins & A. W. Kruglanski (Eds.), *Social psychology: Handbook of basic principles* (pp. 857–914). New York: Guilford Press.

Markus, H., & Nurius, P. (1986). Possible selves. *American Psychologist, 41,* 954–969.

Markus, H., & Sentis, K. P. (1982). The self in social information processing. In J. Suls (Ed.), *Psychological perspectives on the self* (Vol. 1, pp. 41–70). Hillsdale, NJ: Erlbaum.

Markus, H., Smith, J., & Moreland, R. L. (1985). Role of the self-concept in the social perception of others. *Journal of Personality and Social Psychology, 49,* 1494–1512.

Markus, H., & Zajonc, R. B. (1985). The cognitive perspective in social psychology. In G. Lindzey & E. Aronson (Eds.), *Handbook of social psychology* (3rd ed., Vol. 1, pp. 137–230). New York: Random House.

Marlowe, F., & Wetsman, A. (2001). Preferred waist-to-hip ratio and ecology. *Personality and Individual Differences, 30,* 481–489.

Marques, J. M., Abrams, D., Páez, D., & Hogg, M. A. (2001). Social categorization, social identification, and rejection of deviant group members. In M. A. Hogg & R. S. Tindale (Eds.), *Blackwell handbook of social psychology: Group processes* (pp. 400–424). Oxford, UK: Blackwell.

Marques, J. M, Abrams, D., & Serodio, R. (2001). Being better by being right: Subjective group dynamics and derogation of in-group deviants when generic norms are undermined. *Journal of Personality and Social Psychology, 81,* 436–447.

Marques, J. M., & Páez, D. (1994). The 'black sheep effect': Social categorisation, rejection of ingroup deviates and perception of group variability. *European Review of Social Psychology, 5,* 37–68.

Marrow, A. J. (1969). *The practical theorist: The life and work of Kurt Lewin.* New York: Basic Books.

Marsh, P., Russer, E., & Harré, R. (1978). *The rules of disorder.* Milton Keynes, UK: Open University Press.

Martell, R. F., Parker, C., Emrich, C. G., & Crawford, M. S. (1998). Sex stereotyping in the executive suite: 'Much ado about something'. *Journal of Social Behavior and Personality, 13,* 127–138.

Martin, C. L. (1986). A ratio measure of sex stereotyping. *Journal of Personality and Social Psychology, 52,* 489–499.

Martin, J., & Murray, A. (1983). Distributive injustice and unfair exchange. In K. S. Cook & D. M. Messick (Eds.), *Theories of equity: Psychological and sociological perspectives.* New York: Praeger.

Martin, J., Brickman, P., & Murray, A. (1984), Moral outrage and pragmatism: Explanations for collective action. *Journal of Experimental Social Psychology, 20,* 484–496.

Martin, L. L., & Clark, L. F. (1990). Social cognition: Exploring the mental processes involved in human social interaction. In M. W. Eysenck (Ed.), *Cognitive psychology: An international review* (Vol. 1, pp. 266–310). Chichester, UK: Wiley.

Martin, R. (1987). Influence minorité et relations entre groupe. In S. Moscovici & G. Mugny (Eds.), *Psychologie de la conversion.* Paris: Cossett de Val.

Martin, R. (1988). Ingroup and outgroup minorities: Differential impact upon public and private response. *European Journal of Social Psychology, 18,* 39–52.

Martin, R. (1996). Minority influence and argument generation. *British Journal of Social Psychology, 35,* 91–103.

Martin, R. (1998). Majority and minority influence using the afterimage paradigm: A series of attempted replications. *Journal of Experimental Social Psychology, 34,* 1–26.

Martin, R., & Hewstone, M. (1999). Minority influence and optimal problem solving. *European Journal of Social Psychology, 29,* 825–832.

Martin, R., & Hewstone, M. (2003). Social influence processes of control and change: Conformity, obedience to authority, and innovation. In M. A. Hogg & J. Cooper (Eds.), *The SAGE handbook of social psychology* (pp. 347–366). London: SAGE.

Martin, R., & Hewstone, M. (2007). Social influence processes of control and change: Conformity, obedience to authority, and innovation. In M. A. Hogg & J. Cooper (Eds.), *The SAGE handbook of social psychology: Concise student edition* (pp. 312-332). London: SAGE.

Martin, R., & Hewstone, M. (2008). Majority versus minority influence, message processing and attitude change: The source-context-elaboration model. In M. P. Zanna (Ed.), *Advances in experimental social psychology* (Vol. 40, pp. 237–326). San Diego, CA: Elsevier.

Martin, R., Hewstone, M., Martin, P. Y., & Gardikiotis, A. (2008). Persuasion from majority and minority groups. In W. Crano & R. Prislin (Eds.), *Attitudes and attitude change* (pp. 361–384). New York: Psychology Press.

Martz, J. M., Verette, J., Arriaga, X. B., Slovic, L. F., Cox, C. L., & Rusbult, C. E. (1998). Positive illusion in close relationships. *Personal Relationships, 5,* 159–181.

Maslach, C. (1979). Negative emotional biasing of unexplained arousal. *Journal of Personality and Social Psychology, 37,* 953–969.

Masuda, T., & Nisbett, R. E. (2001). Attending holistically versus analytically: Comparing the context sensitivity of Japanese and Americans. *Journal of Personality and Social Psychology, 81,* 922–934.

Matsui, T., Kakuyama, T., & Onglatco, M. L. (1987). Effects of goals and feedback on performance in groups. *Journal of Applied Psychology, 72,* 407–415.

Matsumoto, D. (2004). Paul Ekman and the legacy of universals. *Journal of Research in Personality, 38,* 45–51.

Matthews, K. A. (1982). Psychological perspectives on the type-A behavior pattern. *Psychological Bulletin, 91,* 293–323.

Mayer, J. D. (1993). The emotional madness of the dangerous leader. *Journal of Psychohistory, 20,* 331–348.

Mazur, A., Booth, A., & Dabbs, J. M. (1992). Testosterone and chess competition. *Social Psychology Quarterly, 55,* 70–77.

Mead, G. H. (1934). *Mind, self and society.* Chicago: University of Chicago Press.

Mead, M. (1928/1961). *Coming of age in Samoa.* New York: Morrow.

Mead, M. (1930/1962). *Growing up in New Guinea.* New York: Morrow.

Medin, D. L., & Ortony, A. (1989). Psychological essentialism. In S. Vosniadou & A. Ortony (Eds.), *Similarity and analogical reasoning* (pp. 179–195). Cambridge, UK: Cambridge University Press.

Medvec, V. H., Madley, S. F., & Gilovich, T. (1995). When less is more: Counterfactual thinking and satisfaction among Olympic medalists. *Journal of Personality and Social Psychology, 69,* 603–610.

Meeus, W., & Raaijmakers, Q. (1986). Administrative obedience as a social phenomenon. In W. Doise & S. Moscovici (Eds.), *Current issues in European social psychology* (Vol. 2, pp. 183–230). Cambridge, UK: Cambridge University Press.

Mehrabian, A. (1972). Nonverbal communication. In J. Cole (Ed.), *Nebraska symposium on motivation* (Vol. 19, pp. 107–162). Lincoln, NE: University of Nebraska Press.

Meindl, J. R. (1995). The romance of leadership as a follower-centric theory: A social constructionist approach. *The Leadership Quarterly, 6,* 329–341.

Meindl, J. R., Ehrlich, S. B., & Dukerich, J. M. (1985). The romance of leadership. *Administrative Science Quarterly, 30,* 78–102.

Meindl, J. R., & Lerner, M. (1983). The heroic motive: Some experimental demonstrations. *Journal of Experimental Social Psychology, 19,* 1–20.

Mellen, S. L. W. (1981). *The evolution of love.* Oxford, UK: W. H. Freeman.

Merei, F. (1949). Group leadership and institutionalization. *Human Relations, 2,* 23–39.

Mervis, C. B., & Rosch, E. (1981). Categorization of natural objects. *Annual Review of Psychology, 32,* 89–115.

Messick, D. M. (2005). On the psychological exchange between leaders and followers. In D. M. Messick & R. M. Kramer (Eds.), *The psychology of leadership: New perspectives and research* (pp. 81–96). Mahwah, NJ: Erlbaum.

Metalsky, G. I., & Abramson, L. Y. (1981). Attributional styles: Toward a framework for conceptualization and assessment. In P. C. Kendall & S. D. Hollon (Eds.), *Cognitive–behavioral intentions: Assessment methods* (pp. 13-58). New York: Academic Press.

Michelini, R. L., & Snodgrass, S. R. (1980). Defendant characteristics and juridic decisions. *Journal of Research in Personality, 14,* 340–350.

Middlebrook, P. N. (1980). *Social psychology and modern life* (2nd ed.). New York: Alfred A. Knopf.

Middlemist, R. D., Knowles, E. S., & Mutter, C. F. (1976). Personal space invasions in the lavatory: Suggestive evidence for arousal. *Journal of Personality and Social Psychology, 33,* 541–546.

Middleton, D., & Edwards, D. (Eds.) (1990). *Collective remembering.* London: SAGE.

Midlarsky, E., & Bryan, J. H. (1972). Affect expressions and children's imitative altruism. *Journal of Experimental Research in Personality, 6,* 195–203.

Midlarsky, M., & Midlarsky, E. (1976). Status inconsistency, aggressive attitude, and helping behavior. *Journal of Personality, 44,* 371–391.

Mikula, G. (1980). On the role of justice in allocation decisions. In G. Mikula (Ed.), *Justice and social interaction: Experimental and theoretical contributions from psychological research* (pp. 127-166). Bern, Switzerland: Hans Huber.

Mikulincer, M. (1998). Attachment working models and the sense of trust: An exploration of interaction goals and affect regulation. *Journal of Personality and Social Psychology, 74,* 1209–1224.

Mikulincer, M., & Shaver, P. (2005). Attachment security, compassion, and altruism. *Current Directions in Psychological Science, 14,* 34–38.

Milardo, R. M., Johnson, M. P., & Huston, T. L. (1983). Developing close relationships: Changing patterns of interaction between pair members and social networks. *Journal of Personality and Social Psychology, 44,* 964–976.

Miles, D. R., & Carey, G. (1997). Genetic and environmental architecture of human aggression. *Journal of Personality and Social Psychology, 72,* 207–217.

Milgram, S. (1961). Nationality and conformity. *Scientific American, 205(6),* 45–51.

Milgram, S. (1963). Behavioral study of obedience. *Journal of Abnormal and Social Psychology, 67,* 371–378.

Milgram, S. (1974). *Obedience to authority.* London: Tavistock.

Milgram, S. (1992). *The individual in a social world: Essays and experiments* (2nd ed.). New York: McGraw-Hill.

Milgram, S., & Toch, H. (1969). Collective behavior: Crowds and social movements. In G. Lindzey & E. Aronson (Eds.), *Handbook of social psychology* (2nd ed., Vol. 4, pp. 507–610). Reading, MA: Addison-Wesley.

Milham, J. (1974). Two components of need for approval score and their relationship to cheating following success and failure. *Journal of Research in Personality, 8,* 378–392.

Mill, J. S. (1869). *The analysis of the phenomenon of the human mind.* New York: Kelley.

Millar, M. G., & Millar, K. U. (1990). Attitude change as a function of attitude type and argument type. *Journal of Personality and Social Psychology, 59,* 217–228.

Millar, M. G., & Tesser, A. (1986). Effects of affective and cognitive focus on the attitude–behavior relation. *Journal of Personality and Social Psychology, 51,* 270–276.

Miller, C. E. (1989). The social psychological effects of group decision rules. In P. B. Paulus (Ed.), *Psychology of group influence* (2nd ed., pp. 327–55). Hillsdale, NJ: Erlbaum.

Miller, D. T. (1977). Altruism and the threat to a belief in a just world. *Journal of Experimental Social Psychology, 13,* 113–124.

Miller, D. T., & McFarland, C. (1987). Pluralistic ignorance: When similarity is interpreted as dissimilarity. *Journal of Personality and Social Psychology, 53,* 298–305.

Miller, D. T., & Porter, C. A. (1980). Effects of temporal perspective on the attribution process. *Journal of Personality and Social Psychology, 39,* 532–541.

Miller, D. T., & Porter, C. A. (1983). Self-blame in victims of violence. *Journal of Social Issues, 39,* 139–152.

Miller, D. T., & Ross, M. (1975). Self-serving biases in the attribution of causality: Fact or fiction? *Psychological Bulletin, 82,* 213–225.

Miller, J. G. (1984). Culture and the development of everyday social explanation. *Journal of Personality and Social Psychology, 46,* 961–978.

Miller, N., & Brewer, M. B. (Eds.) (1984). *Groups in contact: The psychology of desegregation.* New York: Academic Press.

Miller, N., Brewer, M. B., & Edwards, K. (1985). Cooperative interaction in desegregated settings: A laboratory analogue. *Journal of Social Issues, 41,* 63–79.

Miller, N., Maruyama, G., Beaber, R. J., & Valone, K. (1976). Speed of speech and persuasion. *Journal of Personality and Social Psychology, 34,* 615–625.

Miller, N. E. (1948). Theory and experiment relating psycho-analytic displacement to stimulus–response generalisation. *Journal of Abnormal and Social Psychology, 43,* 155–178.

Miller, N. E., & Bugelski, R. (1948). Minor studies in aggression: The influence of frustrations imposed by the ingroup on attitudes toward outgroups. *Journal of Psychology, 25,* 437–442.

Miller, P. A., & Eisenberg, N. (1988). The relation of empathy to aggressive and externalizing/antisocial behavior. *Psychological Bulletin, 103,* 324–344.

Miller, P. J. E., & Rempel, J. K. (2004). Trust and partner-enhancing attributions in close relationships. *Personality and Social Psychology Bulletin, 30,* 695–705.

Milner, D. (1996). Children and racism: Beyond the value of the dolls. In W. P. Robinson (Ed.), *Social groups and identities: Developing the legacy of Henri Tajfel* (pp. 246–268). Oxford, UK: Butterworth-Heinemann.

Minard, R. D. (1952). Race relations in the Pocahontas coal field. *Journal of Social Issues, 8,* 29–44.

Mischel, W. (1968). *Personality and assessment.* New York: Wiley.

Mischel, W., Ebbesen, E. B., & Zeiss, A. R. (1976). Determinants of selective memory about the self. *Journal of Consulting and Clinical Psychology, 44,* 92–103.

Misumi, J., & Peterson, M. F. (1985). The performance-maintenance (P-M) theory of leadership: Review of a Japanese research program. *Administrative Science Quarterly, 30,* 198–223.

Mita, T. H., Dermer, M., & Knight, J. (1977). Reversed facial images and the mere exposure hypothesis. *Journal of Personality and Social Psychology, 35,* 597–601.

Mitchell, H. E. (1979). *Informational and affective determinants of juror decision making.* Doctoral dissertation, Purdue University.

Mitchell, S. (2002). *American generations: Who they are, how they live, what they think.* Ithica, NY: New Strategists Publications.

Moghaddam, F. M. (1990). Modulative and generative orientations in psychology: Implications for psychology in the three worlds. *Journal of Social Issues, 46,* 21–41.

Moghaddam, F. M. (1998). *Social psychology: Exploring universals across cultures.* New York: Freeman.

Moghaddam, F. M. (2008). *Multiculturalism and intergroup relations: Psychological implications for democracy in global context.* Washington, DC: American Psychological Association.

Moliner, P., & Tafani, E. (1997). Attitudes and social representations: A theoretical and experimental approach. *European Journal of Social Psychology, 27,* 687–702.

Monson, T. C., & Hesley, J. W. (1982). Causal attributions for behavior consistent or inconsistent with an actor's personality traits: Differences between those offered by actors and observers. *Journal of Experimental Social Psychology, 18,* 426–432.

Monteil, J.-M., & Huguet, P. (1999). *Social context and cognitive performance*. Philadelphia: Psychology Press.

Monteith, M. J. (1993). Self-regulation of prejudiced responses: Implication for progress in prejudice-reduction efforts. *Journal of Personality and Social Psychology, 65,* 469–485.

Montepare, J. M., & Vega, C. (1988). Women's vocal reactions to intimate and casual male friends. *Personality and Social Psychology Bulletin, 14,* 103–12.

Moore, B. S., Sherrod, D. R., Liu, T. J., & Underwood, B. (1979). The dispositional shift in attribution over time. *Journal of Experimental Social Psychology, 15,* 553–569.

Moreland, R. L. (1985). Social categorization and the assimilation of 'new' group members. *Journal of Personality and Social Psychology, 48,* 1173–1190.

Moreland, R. L., Argote, L., & Krishnan, R. (1996). Socially shared cognition at work: Transactive memory and group performance. In J. L. Nye & A. M. Bower (Eds.), *What's social about social cognition: Research on socially shared cognition in small groups* (pp. 57–84). Thousand Oaks, CA: SAGE.

Moreland, R. L., & Beach, S. R. (1992). Exposure effects in the classroom: The development of affinity among students. *Journal of Experimental Social Psychology, 28,* 255–276.

Moreland, R. L., Hogg, M. A., & Hains, S. C. (1994). Back to the future: Social psychological research on groups. *Journal of Experimental Social Psychology, 30,* 527–555.

Moreland, R. L., & Levine, J. M. (1982) Socialization in small groups: Temporal changes in individual–group relations. In L. Berkowitz (Ed.), *Advances in experimental social psychology* (Vol. 15, pp. 137–192). New York: Academic Press.

Moreland, R. L., & Levine, J. M. (1984). Role transitions in small groups. In V. Allen and E. van de Vliert (Eds.), *Role transitions: Explorations and explanations* (pp. 181–195). New York: Plenum.

Moreland, R. L., & Levine, J. M. (1989). Newcomers and oldtimers in small groups. In P. B. Paulus (Ed.), *Psychology of group influence* (2nd ed., pp. 143–186). Hillsdale, NJ: Erlbaum.

Moreland, R. L., Levine, J. M., & Cini, M. (1993). Group socialisation: The role of commitment. In M. A. Hogg & D. Abrams (Eds.), *Group motivation: Social psychological perspectives* (pp. 105–129). London: Harvester Wheatsheaf.

Moriarty, T. (1975). Crime, commitment and the responsive bystander: Two field experiments. *Journal of Personality and Social Psychology, 31,* 370–376.

Morley, I. E., & Stephenson, G. M. (1977). *The social psychology of bargaining*. London: Allen and Unwin.

Morley, I. E., Webb, J., & Stephenson, G. M. (1988) Bargaining and arbitration in the resolution of conflict. In W. Stroebe, A. W. Kruglanski, D. Bar-Tal & M. Hewstone (Eds.), *The social psychology of intergroup conflict: Theory, research and applications* (pp. 117–134). Berlin: Springer-Verlag.

Morris, D. (1967). *The naked ape*. New York: McGraw-Hill.

Morris, D., Collett, P., Marsh, P., & O'Shaughnessy, M. (1979). *Gestures: Their origins and distribution*. New York: Stein & Day.

Morris, M. W., & Peng, K. P. (1994). Culture and cause: American and Chinese attributions for social and physical events. *Journal of Personality and Social Psychology, 67,* 949–971.

Morris, W. N., & Miller, R. S. (1975). The effects of consensus-breaking and consensus preempting partners on reduction of conformity. *Journal of Experimental Social Psychology, 11,* 215–223.

Morton, T. L. (1978). Intimacy and reciprocity of exchange: A comparison of spouses and strangers. *Journal of Personality and Social Psychology, 36,* 72–81.

Moscovici, S. (1961). *La psychanalyse: Son image et son public*. Paris: Presses Universitaires de France.

Moscovici, S. (1972). Society and theory in social psychology. In J. Israel & H. Tajfel (Eds.), *The context of social psychology: A critical assessment* (pp. 17–68). New York: Academic Press.

Moscovici, S. (Ed.) (1973). *Introduction à la psychologie sociale* (Vol. 1). Paris: Larousse.

Moscovici, S. (1976). *Social influence and social change*. London: Academic Press.

Moscovici, S. (1980). Toward a theory of conversion behavior. In L. Berkowitz (Ed.), *Advances in experimental social psychology* (Vol. 13, pp. 202–239). New York: Academic Press.

Moscovici, S. (1981). On social representation. In J. P. Forgas (Ed.), *Social cognition: Perspectives on everyday understanding* (pp. 181–209). London: Academic Press.

Moscovici, S. (1982). The coming era of representations. In J.-P. Codol & J. P. Leyens (Eds.), *Cognitive analysis of social behaviour* (pp. 115–150). The Hague: Martinus Nijhoff.

Moscovici, S. (1983). The phenomenon of social representations. In R. M. Farr & S. Moscovici (Eds.), *Social Representations* (pp. 3–69). Cambridge, UK: Cambridge University Press.

Moscovici, S. (1984). *Psychologie Sociale*. Paris: Presses Universitaires de France.

Moscovici, S. (1985a). Social influence and conformity. In G. Lindzey & E. Aronson (Eds.), *Handbook of social psychology* (3rd ed., Vol. 2, pp. 347–412). New York: Random House.

Moscovici, S. (1985b). *The age of the crowd*. Cambridge, UK: Cambridge University Press.

Moscovici, S. (1988). Notes towards a description of social representations. *European Journal of Social Psychology, 18,* 211–250.

Moscovici, S. (2000). *Social representations: Explorations in social psychology*. Oxford: Blackwell.

Moscovici, S., & Faucheux, C. (1972). Social influence, conforming bias, and the study of active minorities. In L. Berkowitz (Ed.), *Advances in experimental social psychology* (Vol. 6, pp. 149–202). New York: Academic Press.

Moscovici, S., & Lage, E. (1976). Studies in social influence: III. Majority vs minority influence in a group. *European Journal of Social Psychology, 6,* 149–174.

Moscovici, S., Lage, E., & Naffrechoux, M. (1969). Influence of a consistent minority on the responses of a majority in a colour perception task. *Sociometry, 32,* 365–380.

Moscovici, S., & Personnaz, B. (1980). Studies in social influence: V. Minority influence and conversion behavior in a perceptual task. *Journal of Experimental Social Psychology, 16,* 270–282.

Moscovici, S., & Personnaz, B. (1986). Studies on latent influence by the spectrometer method: I. The impact of psychologization in the case of conversion by a minority or a majority. *European Journal of Social Psychology, 16,* 345–360.

Moscovici, S., & Zavalloni, M. (1969). The group as a polarizer of attitudes. *Journal of Personality and Social Psychology, 12,* 125–135.

Mosher, D. L., & Anderson, R. D. (1986). Macho personality, sexual aggression, and reactions to guided imagery of realistic rape. *Journal of Research in Personality, 20,* 77–94.

Moskowitz, G. B. (2005). *Social cognition: Understanding self and others.* New York: Guilford Press.

Mowday, R. T., & Sutton, R. I. (1993). Organisational behavior: Linking individuals and groups to organizational contexts. *Annual Review of Psychology, 44,* 195–229.

Mucchi-Faina, A., Maass, A., & Volpato, C. (1991). Social influence: The role of originality. *European Journal of Social Psychology, 21,* 183–197.

Mudrack, P. E. (1989). Defining group cohesiveness: A legacy of confusion. *Small Group Behavior, 20,* 37–49.

Mugny, G. (1982). *The power of minorities.* London: Academic Press.

Mugny, G., & Papastamou, S. (1981). When rigidity does not fail: Individualization and psychologization as resistance to the diffusion of minority innovations. *European Journal of Social Psychology, 10,* 43–62.

Mugny, G., & Papastamou, S. (1982). Minority influence and psychosocial identity. *European Journal of Social Psychology, 12,* 379–394.

Mulac, A., Bradac, J. J., & Gibbons, P. (2001). Empirical support for the gender-as-culture hypothesis: An intercultural analysis of male/female language differences. *Human Communication Research, 27,* 121–152.

Mulac, A., Studley, L. B., Wiemann, J. M., & Bradac, J. J. (1987). Male/female gaze in same-sex and mixed-sex dyads: Gender-linked differences and mutual influence. *Human Communication Research, 13,* 323–343.

Mulder, M. (1960). Communication structure, decision structure and group performance. *Sociometry, 23,* 1–14.

Mullen, B. (1983). Operationalizing the effect of the group on the individual: A self-attention perspective. *Journal of Experimental Social Psychology, 19,* 295–322.

Mullen, B. (1986). Atrocity as a function of lynch mob composition: A self-attention perspective. *Personality and Social Psychology Bulletin, 12,* 187–197.

Mullen, B., Atkins, J. L., Champion, D. S., Edwards, C., Hardy, D., Story, J. E., & Vanderklok, M. (1985). The false consensus effect: A meta-analysis of 115 hypothesis tests. *Journal of Experimental Social Psychology, 21,* 262–283.

Mullen, B., & Hu, L. (1989). Perceptions of ingroup and outgroup variability: A meta-analytic integration. *Basic and Applied Social Psychology, 10,* 233–252.

Mullen, B., & Johnson, C. (1990). Distinctiveness-based illusory correlations and stereotyping: A meta-analytic integration. *British Journal of Social Psychology, 29,* 11–28.

Mullen, B., Johnson, C., & Salas, E. (1991). Productivity loss in brainstorming groups. *Basic and Applied Social Psychology, 12,* 3–24.

Mullen, B., & Riordan, C. A. (1988). Self-serving attributions for performance in naturalistic settings: A meta-analytic review. *Journal of Applied Social Psychology, 18,* 3–22.

Mullen, P. E. (1984). Mental disorder and dangerousness. *Australian and New Zealand Journal of Psychiatry, 18,* 8–17.

Mullin, C. R., & Linz, D. (1995). Desensitisation and resensitisation to violence against women: Effects of exposure to sexually violent films on judgments of domestic violence victims. *Journal of Personality and Social Psychology, 69,* 449–459.

Mummendey, A., & Otten, S. (1998). Positive–negative asymmetry in social discrimination. *European Review of Social Psychology, 19,* 107–143.

Mummendey, A., & Wenzel, M. (1999). Social discrimination and tolerance in intergroup relations: Reactions to intergroup difference. *Personality and Social Psychology Review, 3,* 158–174.

Murchison, C. (Ed.) (1935). *Handbook of social psychology.* Worcester, MA: Clark University Press.

Murphy, G., & Murphy, L. B. (1931). *Experimental social psychology.* New York: Harper (rev. ed. published with T. M. Newcomb in 1937).

Murphy, L., & Murphy, G. (1970). Perspectives in cross-cultural research. *Journal of Cross-Cultural Psychology, 1,* 1–4.

Murphy, P., Williams, J., & Dunning, E. (1990). *Football on trial: Spectator violence and development in the football world.* London: Routledge.

Murphy, S. T., Monahan, J. L., & Zajonc, R. B. (1995). Additivity of nonconscious affect: Combined effects of priming and exposure. *Journal of Personality and Social Psychology, 69,* 589–602.

Murray, S. L., & Holmes, J. G. (1997). A leap of faith? Positive illusions in romantic relationships. *Personality and Social Psychology Bulletin, 23,* 586–604.

Murray, S. L., & Holmes, J. G. (1999). The mental ties that bind: Cognitive structures that predict relationship resilience. *Journal of Personality and Social Psychology, 77,* 1228–1244.

Murray, S. L., Holmes, J. G., & Griffin, D. W. (1996). The self-fulfilling nature of positive illusions in romantic relationships: Love is not blind, but prescient. *Journal of Personality and Social Psychology, 71,* 1155–1180.

Murray, S. L., Holmes, J. G., & Griffin, D. W. (2003). Reflections on the self-fulfilling effects of positive illusions. *Psychological Inquiry, 14,* 289–295.

Murstein, B. I. (1980). Love at first sight: A myth. *Medical Aspects of Human Sexuality, 14* (34), 39–41.

Myers, D. G., & Lamm, H. (1975). The polarizing effect of group discussion. *American Scientist, 63,* 297–303.

Myers, D. G., & Lamm, H. (1976). The group polarization phenomenon. *Psychological Bulletin, 83,* 602–627.

Nadler, A. (1986). Help seeking as a cultural phenomenon: Differences between city and kibbutz dwellers. *Journal of Personality and Social Psychology, 51,* 976–982.

Nadler, A. (1991). Help-seeking behavior: Psychological costs and instrumental benefits. In M. S. Clark (Ed.), *Prosocial behavior* (pp. 290–311). Newbury Park, CA: SAGE.

Nahem, J. (1980). *Psychology and psychiatry today: A Marxist view*. New York: International Publishers.

Nail, P. R. (1986). Toward an integration of some models and theories of social response. *Psychological Bulletin, 100,* 190–206.

National Gay and Lesbian Task Force (1990). *Anti-gay violence, victimization & defamation in 1989*. Washington DC: Author.

Neisser, U. (1967). *Cognitive psychology*. Englewood Cliffs, NJ: Prentice Hall.

Nelson, T. D. (2005). Ageism: Prejudiced against our feared future self. *Journal of Social Issues, 61,* 207-221.

Nemeth, C. (1970). Bargaining and reciprocity. *Psychological Bulletin, 74,* 297–308.

Nemeth, C. (1981). Jury trials: Psychology and law. In L. Berkowitz (Ed.), *Advances in experimental social psychology* (Vol. 14, pp. 309–367). New York: Academic Press.

Nemeth, C. (1986). Differential contributions of majority and minority influence. *Psychological Review, 93,* 23–32.

Nemeth, C. J. (1995). Dissent as driving cognition, attitudes, and judgments. *Social Cognition, 13,* 273-291.

Nemeth, C., & Chiles, C. (1988). Modelling courage: The role of dissent in fostering independence. *European Journal of Social Psychology, 18,* 275–280.

Nemeth, C., Swedlund, M., & Kanki, B. (1974). Patterning of the minority's response and their influence on the majority. *European Journal of Social Psychology, 4,* 53–64.

Nemeth, C., & Wachtler, J. (1983). Creative problem solving as a result of majority vs minority influence. *European Journal of Social Psychology, 13,* 45–55.

Nemeth, C., Wachtler, J., & Endicott, J. (1977). Increasing the size of the minority: Some gains and some losses. *European Journal of Social Psychology, 7,* 15–27.

Neuberg, S. L., & Fiske, S. T. (1987). Motivational influences on impression formation: Outcome dependency, accuracy-driven attention, and individuating processes. *Journal of Personality and Social Psychology, 53,* 431–444.

Neuberg, S. L., Kenrick, D. T., & Schaller, M. (2010). Evolutionary social psychology. In S. T. Fiske, D. T. Gilbert, & G. Lindzey (Eds.), *Handbook of social psychology* (5th ed., Vol. 2, pp. 761-796). New York: Wiley.

Newcomb, T. M. (1961). *The acquaintance process*. New York: Holt, Rinehart & Winston.

Newcomb, T. M. (1965). Attitude development as a function of reference groups: The Bennington study. In H. Proshansky & B. Seidenberg (Eds.), *Basic studies in social psychology* (pp. 215–225). New York: Holt, Rinehart & Winston.

Ng, B., Kumar, S., Ranclaud, M., & Robinson, E. (2001). Ward crowding and incidents of violence on an acute psychiatric inpatient unit. *Psychiatric Services, 52,* 521–525.

Ng, S. H. (1990). Androgenic coding of man and his memory by language users. *Journal of Experimental Social Psychology, 26,* 455–464.

Ng, S. H. (1996). Power: An essay in honour of Henri Tajfel. In W. P. Robinson (Ed.), *Social groups and identities: Developing the legacy of Henri Tajfel* (pp. 191–214). Oxford, UK: Butterworth-Heinemann.

Ng, S. H., & Bradac, J. J. (1993). *Power in language*. Thousand Oaks, CA: SAGE.

Ng, S. H., & Liu, J. H. (2000). Cultural revolution in psychology. *Asian Journal of Social Psychology, 3,* 289–293.

Ng, S. H., Bell, D., & Brooke, M. (1993). Gaining turns and achieving high influence in small conversational groups. *British Journal of Social Psychology, 32,* 265–275.

Nieburg, H. (1969). *Political violence: The behavioural process*. New York: St Martin's Press.

Niedenthal, P. M., & Beike, D. R. (1997). Interrelated and isolated self-concepts. *Personality and Social Psychology Review, 1,* 106–128.

Nisbett, R. E. (2003). *The geography of thought: How Asians and Westerners think differently . . . and why*. New York: Free Press.

Nisbett, R. E., & Cohen, D. (1996). *Culture of honor: The psychology of violence in the South*. Boulder, CO: Westview Press.

Nisbett, R. E., Krantz, D. H., Jepson, C., & Fong, G. T. (1982). Improving inductive inference. In D. Kahneman, P. Slovic & A. Tversky (Eds.), *Judgment under uncertainty: Heuristics and biases* (pp. 445–462). New York: Cambridge University Press.

Nisbett, R. E., Krantz, D. H., Jepson, C., & Kunda, Z. (1983). The use of statistical heuristics in everyday inductive reasoning. *Psychological Review, 90,* 339-363.

Nisbett, R. E., & Ross, L. (1980). *Human inference: Strategies and shortcomings of social judgment*. Englewood Cliffs, NJ: Prentice Hall.

Nisbett, R. E., & Wilson, T. D. (1977). Telling more than we can know: Verbal reports on mental behavior. *Psychological Review, 84,* 231–259.

Nisbett, R. E., Zukier, H., & Lemley, R. E. (1981). The dilution effect: Non-diagnostic information weakens the implications of diagnostic information. *Cognitive Psychology, 13,* 248–277.

Noels, K. A., Giles, H., & Le Poire, B. (2003). Language and communication processes. In M. A. Hogg & J. Cooper (Eds.), *The SAGE handbook of social psychology* (pp. 232–257). London: SAGE.

Noels, K. A., Pon, G., & Clément, R. (1996). Language and adjustment: The role of linguistic self-confidence in the acculturation process. *Journal of Language and Social Psychology, 15,* 246–264.

Nolen-Hoeksma, S., Girgus, J. S., & Seligman, M. E. P. (1992). Predictors and consequences of childhood depressive symptoms: Five-year longitudinal study. *Journal of Abnormal Psychology, 101,* 405–422.

Noller, P. (1984). *Nonverbal communication and marital interaction*. Oxford, UK: Pergamon Press.

Noller, P., & Fitzpatrick, M. A. (1990). Marital communication in the eighties. *Journal of Marriage and the Family, 52,* 832–843.

Noller, P., & Ruzzene, M. (1991). Communication in marriage: The influence of affect and cognition. In G. J. O. Fletcher & F. D. Fincham (Eds.), *Cognition and close relationships* (pp. 203–33). Hillsdale, NJ: Erlbaum.

Norman, P., & Conner, M. (2006). The theory of planned behaviour and binge drinking: Assessing the moderating role of past behaviour within the theory of planned behaviour. *British Journal of Health Psychology, 11,* 55–70.

Northhouse, P. (2004). *Leadership: Theory and practice* (3rd ed.). Thousand Oaks, CA: SAGE.

Norton, M. I., Monin, B., Cooper, J., & Hogg, M. A. (2003). Vicarious dissonance: Attitude change from the inconsistency of others. *Journal of Personality and Social Psychology, 85,* 47–62.

Nye, J. L., & Bower, A. M. (Eds.) (1996). *What's social about social cognition: Research on socially shared cognition in small groups.* Thousand Oaks, CA: SAGE.

Oaker, G., & Brown, R. J. (1986). Intergroup relations in a hospital setting: A further test of social identity theory. *Human Relations, 39,* 767–778.

Oakes, P. J. (1987). The salience of social categories. In J. C. Turner, M. A. Hogg, P. J. Oakes, S. D. Reicher, & M. S. Wetherell, *Rediscovering the social group: A self-categorization theory* (pp. 117–141). Oxford, UK: Blackwell.

Oakes, P. J., & Turner, J. C. (1990). Is limited information processing capacity the cause of social stereotyping? *European Review of Social Psychology, 1,* 111–135.

Oakes, P. J., Haslam, S. A., & Reynolds, K. J. (1999). Social categorization and social context: Is stereotype change a matter of information or of meaning? In D. Abrams & M. A. Hogg (Eds.), *Social identity and social cognition* (pp. 55–79). Oxford, UK: Blackwell.

Oakes, P. J., Haslam, S. A., & Turner, J. C. (1994). *Stereotyping and social reality.* Oxford, UK: Blackwell.

O'Barr, W. M., & Atkins, B. K. (1980). 'Women's language' or 'powerless language'? In S. McConnell-Ginet, R. Borker & N. Furman (Eds.), *Women and language in literature and society* (pp. 93–110). New York: Praeger.

Ochsner, K. N. (2007). Social cognitive neuroscience: Historical development, core principles, and future promise. In A. W. Kruglanski & E. T. Higgins (Eds.), *Social psychology: Handbook of basic principles* (2nd ed., pp. 39-66). New York: Guilford Press.

Ochsner, K. N., & Lieberman, M. (2001). The emergence of social cognitive neuroscience. *American Psychologist, 56,* 714–734.

O'Connor, J., Mumford, M. D., Clifton, T. C., Gessner, T. L., & Connelly, M. S. (1995). Charismatic leaders and destructiveness: A historiometric study. *The Leadership Quarterly, 6,* 529–558.

O'Connor, S., & Rosenblood, L. (1996). Affiliation motivation in everyday experience: A theoretical perspective. *Journal of Personality and Social Psychology, 70,* 513–522.

Oddone-Paolucci, E., Genuis, M., & Violato, C. (2000). A meta-analysis of the published research on the effects of pornography. In C. Violato, E. Oddone-Paolucci & M. Genuis (Eds.), *The changing family and child development* (pp. 48–59). Aldershot, UK: Ashgate.

O'Donnell, C. R. (1995). Firearm deaths among children and youth. *American Psychologist, 50,* 771–776.

Olson, J. M. (1988). Misattribution, preparatory information, and speech anxiety. *Journal of Personality and Social Psychology, 54,* 758–67.

Olson, J. M., & Zanna, M. P. (1993). Attitudes and attitude change. *Annual Review of Psychology, 44,* 117–54.

Omoto, A. M., & Snyder, M. (2002). Considerations of community: The context and process of volunteerism. *American Behavioral Scientist, 45,* 846–867.

Opotow, S. (1990). Moral exclusion and injustice: An introduction. *Journal of Social Issues, 46,* 1-20.

Oppenheim, A. N. (1992). *Questionnaire design, interviewing and attitude measurement* (2nd ed.). London: Pinter.

Orano, P. (1901). *Psicologia sociale.* Bari, Italy: Lacerta.

Orne, M. T. (1962). On the social psychology of the psychology experiment: With particular reference to demand characteristics and their implications. *American Psychologist, 17,* 776–783.

Ortony, A., & Turner, T. J. (1990). What's basic about basic emotions? *Psychological Review, 97,* 315–331.

Orvis, B. R., Kelley, H. H., & Butler, D. (1976). Attributional conflicts in young couples. In J. H. Harvey, W. J. Ickes & R. F. Kidd (Eds.), *New directions in attribution research* (Vol. 1, pp. 353–386). Hillsdale, NJ: Erlbaum.

Orwell, G. (1962). *The road to Wigan pier.* Harmondsworth, UK: Penguin.

Osborn, A. F. (1957). *Applied imagination* (rev. ed.). New York: Charles Scribner's Sons.

Osgood, C. E. (1962). *An alternative to war or surrender.* Urbana, IL: University of Illinois Press.

Osgood, C. E., Suci, G. J., & Tannenbaum, P. H. (1957). *The measurement of meaning.* Urbana, IL: University of Illinois Press.

Oskamp, S. (1977). *Attitudes and opinions.* Englewood Cliffs, NJ: Prentice Hall.

Oskamp, S. (1984). *Applied social psychology.* Englewood Cliffs, NJ: Prentice Hall.

Ostrom, T. M. (1968). The relationship between the affective, behavioural, and cognitive components of attitude. *Journal of Experimental Social Psychology, 5,* 12–30.

Ostrom, T. M. (1989b). Interdependence of attitude theory and measurement. In A. R. Pratkanis, S. J. Breckler & A. G. Greenwald (Eds.), *Attitude structure and function* (pp. 11–36). Hillsdale, NJ: Erlbaum.

Ostrom, T. M., & Sedikides, C. (1992). Outgroup homogeneity effects in natural and minimal groups. *Psychological Bulletin, 112,* 536–552.

Oswald, P. A. (1996). The effects of cognitive and affective perspective taking on empathic concern and altruistic helping. *Journal of Social Psychology, 136,* 613–623.

Otten, S., Mummendey, A., & Blanz, M. (1996). Intergroup discrimination in positive and negative outcome allocations: Impact of stimulus valence, relative group status, and relative group size. *Personality and Social Psychology Bulletin, 22,* 568–581.

Overall, N. C., Fletcher, G. J. O., & Simpson, J. A. (2006). Regulation processes in intimate relationships: The role of ideal standards. *Journal of Personality and Social Psychology, 91,* 662–685.

Oyserman, D. (2007). Social identity and self-regulation. In A. W. Kruglanski & E. T. Higgins (Eds.), *Social psychology: Handbook of basic principles* (2nd ed., pp. 432-453). New York: Guilford.

Oyserman, D., Coon, H. M., & Kemmelmeier, M. (2002). Rethinking individualism and collectivism: Evaluation of theoretical assumptions and meta-analyses. *Psychological Bulletin, 128,* 3–72.

Pagel, M. D., & Davidson, A. R. (1984). A comparison of three social-psychological models of attitude and behavioral plan: Prediction of contraceptive behavior. *Journal of Personality and Social Psychology, 47,* 517–533.

Paglia, A., & Room, R. (1999). Expectancies about the effects of alcohol on the self and on others as determinants of alcohol policy. *Journal of Applied Social Psychology, 29,* 2632–2651.

Paik, H., & Comstock, G. (1994). The effects of television violence on antisocial behaviour: A meta-analysis. *Communication Research, 21,* 516–546.

Pandey, J., Sinha, Y., Prakash, A., & Tripathi, R. C. (1982). Right–left political ideologies and attribution of the causes of poverty. *European Journal of Social Psychology, 12,* 327–331.

Pantin, H. M., & Carver, C. S. (1982). Induced competence and the bystander effect. *Journal of Applied Social Psychology, 12,* 100–111.

Papastamou, S. (1986). Psychologization and processes of minority and majority influence. *European Journal of Social Psychology, 16,* 165–180.

Parducci, A. (1968). The relativism of absolute judgments. *Scientific American, 219,* 84–90.

Park, B. (1986). A method for studying the development of impressions of real people. *Journal of Personality and Social Psychology, 51,* 907–917.

Park, B., & Hastie, R. (1987). Perception of variability in category development: Instance- versus abstraction-based stereotypes. *Journal of Personality and Social Psychology, 53,* 621–635.

Park, B., & Rothbart, M. (1982). Perception of outgroup homogeneity and levels of social categorization: Memory for the subordinate attributes of ingroup and outgroup members. *Journal of Personality and Social Psychology, 42,* 1051–1068.

Parker, D., Manstead, A. S. R., & Stradling, S. G. (1995). Extending the theory of planned behaviour: The role of personal norm. *British Journal of Social Psychology, 34,* 127–137.

Parkinson, B. (1985). Emotional effects of false autonomic feedback. *Psychological Bulletin, 98,* 471–494.

Parsons, J. E., Adler, T., & Meece, J. L. (1984). Sex differences in achievement: A test of alternate theories. *Journal of Personality and Social Psychology, 46,* 26–43.

Patch, M. E. (1986). The role of source legitimacy in sequential request strategies of compliance. *Personality and Social Psychology Bulletin, 12,* 199–205.

Patterson, F. (1978). Conversations with a gorilla. *National Geographic, 154,* 438–465.

Patterson, M. L. (1983). *Nonverbal behavior: A functional perspective.* New York: Springer.

Paulhus, D. L., & Levitt, K. (1987). Desirable responding triggered by affect: Automatic egotism. *Journal of Personality and Social Psychology, 52,* 245–259.

Paulus, P. B., Dzindolet, M. T., Poletes, G., & Camacho, L. M. (1993). Perception of performance in group brainstorming: The illusion of group productivity. *Personality and Social Psychology Bulletin, 19,* 78–89.

Pavelchak, M. A., Moreland, R. L., & Levine, J. M. (1986). Effects of prior group memberships on subsequent reconnaissance activities. *Journal of Personality and Social Psychology, 50,* 56–66.

Pawlik, K., & Rosenzweig, M. R. (Eds.) (2000). *International handbook of psychology.* London: SAGE.

Pechmann, C., & Esteban, G. (1994). Persuasion processes associated with direct comparative and noncomparative advertising and implications for advertising effectiveness. *Journal of Consumer Psychology, 2,* 403–432.

Pedersen, A., Walker, I., & Glass, C. (1999). Experimenter effects on ingroup preference and self-concept of urban Aboriginal children. *Australian Journal of Psychology, 51,* 82–89.

Pedersen, D. M. (1999). Models for types of privacy by privacy functions. *Journal of Environmental Psychology, 19,* 397–405.

Peeters, G., & Czapinski, J. (1990). Positive–negative asymmetry in evaluations: The distinction between affective and informational negativity effects. *European Review of Social Psychology, 1,* 33–60.

Pei, M. (1965). *The story of language* (2nd ed.). Philadelphia, PA: Lippincott.

Peng, K., & Nisbett, R. E. (1999). Culture, dialectics, and reasoning about contradiction. *American Psychologist, 54,* 741–754.

Pennebaker, J. W. (1997). Writing about emotional experiences as a therapeutic process. *Psychological Science, 8,* 162–166.

Penrod, S. (1983). *Social psychology.* Englewood Cliffs, NJ: Prentice Hall.

Penrod, S., & Hastie, R. (1980). A computer simulation of jury decision making. *Psychological Review, 87,* 133–159.

Pepitone, A. (1981). Lessons from the history of social psychology. *American Psychologist, 36,* 972–185.

Peplau, L. A., & Fingerhut, A. W. (2007). The close relationships of lebians and gay men. *Annual Review of Psychology, 58,* 400–424.

Peplau, L. A., & Perlman, D. (Eds.) (1982). *Loneliness: A sourcebook of current theory, research and therapy.* New York: Wiley.

Peretti-Watel, P., Obadia, Y., Dray-Spira, R., Lert, F., & Moatti, J.-P. (2005). Attitudes and behaviours of people living with HIV/AIDS and mass media prevention campaign: A French survey. *Psychology, Health and Medicine, 10,* 215–224.

Pérez, J. A., & Mugny, G. (1998). Categorization and social influence. In S. Worchel & J. M. Francisco (Eds.), *Social identity: International perspectives* (pp. 142–153). London: SAGE.

Perlman, D., & Oskamp, S. (1971). The effects of picture content and exposure frequency on evaluations of Negroes and Whites. *Journal of Experimental Social Psychology, 7,* 503–514.

Perlman, D., & Peplau, L. A. (1998). Loneliness. *Encyclopedia of mental health* (Vol. 2, pp. 571–581). New York: Academic Press.

Perry, D. G., Perry L., & Boldizar, J. P. (1990). Learning of aggression. In M. Lewis & S. Miller (Eds.), *Handbook of developmental psychopathology* (pp. 135–146). New York: Plenum.

Perry, D. G., Perry, L., Bussey, K., English, D., & Arnold, G. (1980). Processes of attribution and children's self-punishment following misbehaviour. *Child Development, 51,* 545–551.

Peters, L. H., Hartke, D. D., & Pohlmann, J. T. (1985). Fiedler's contingency theory of leadership: An application of the meta-analytic procedure of Schmidt and Hunter. *Psychological Bulletin, 97,* 274–285.

Peters, L. H., O'Connor, E. J., Weekley, J., Pooyan, A., Frank, B., & Erenkrantz, B. (1984). Sex bias and managerial evaluation: A replication and extension. *Journal of Applied Psychology, 69,* 349–352.

Peterson, C. (1980). Memory and the 'dispositional shift'. *Social Psychology Quarterly, 43,* 372–380.

Peterson, C., Semmel, A., von Baeyer, C., Abramson, L. Y., Metalsky, G. I., & Seligman, M. E. P. (1982). The attributional style questionnaire. *Cognitive Therapy and Research, 6,* 287–300.

Peterson, R., & Nemeth, C. (1996). Focus versus flexibility: Majority and minority influence can both improve performance. *Personality and Social Psychology Bulletin, 22,* 14–23.

Pettigrew, T. F. (1958). Personality and sociocultural factors in intergroup attitudes: A cross-national comparison. *Journal of Conflict Resolution, 2,* 29–42.

Pettigrew, T. F. (1971). *Racially separate or together.* New York: McGraw-Hill.

Pettigrew, T. F. (1979). The ultimate attribution error: Extending Allport's cognitive analysis of prejudice. *Personality and Social Psychology Bulletin, 5,* 461–476.

Pettigrew, T. F. (1981). Extending the stereotype concept. In D. L. Hamilton (Ed.), *Cognitive processes in stereotyping and intergroup behavior* (pp. 303–332). Hillsdale, NJ: Erlbaum.

Pettigrew, T. F. (1987). *Modern racism: American Black–White relations since the 1960s.* Cambridge, MA: Harvard University Press.

Pettigrew, T. F. (1998). Intergroup contact theory. *Annual Review of Psychology, 49,* 65–85.

Pettigrew, T. F., & Meertens, R. W. (1995). Subtle and blatant prejudice in Western Europe. *European Journal of Social Psychology, 25,* 57–75.

Pettigrew, T. F., & Tropp, L. R. (2006). A meta-analytic test of intergroup contact theory. *Journal of Personality and Social Psychology, 90,* 751–783.

Petty, R. E., & Cacioppo, J. T. (1979). Issue-involvement can increase or decrease persuasion by enhancing message-relevant cognitive responses. *Journal of Personality and Social Psychology, 37,* 1915–1926.

Petty, R. E., & Cacioppo, J. T. (1981). *Attitudes and persuasion: Classic and contemporary approaches.* Dubuque, IA: Brown.

Petty, R. E., & Cacioppo, J. T. (1986a). *Communication and persuasion: Central and peripheral routes to attitude change.* New York: Springer.

Petty, R. E., & Cacioppo, J. T. (1986b). The elaboration likelihood model of persuasion. In L. Berkowitz (Ed.), *Advances in experimental social psychology* (Vol. 19, pp. 123–205). New York: Academic Press.

Petty, R. E., Schuman, D. W., Richman, S. A., & Stratham, A. J. (1993). Positive mood and persuasion: Different roles for affect under high- and low-elaboration conditions. *Journal of Personality and Social Psychology, 64,* 5–20.

Petty, R. E., & Wegener, D. (1998) Attitude change: Multiple roles for persuasion variables. In D. T. Gilbert, S. T. Fiske & G. Lindzey (Eds.) *The handbook of social psychology* (4th ed., Vol. 2, pp. 323–390). New York: McGraw-Hill.

Pevers, B. H., & Secord, P. F. (1973). Developmental changes in attribution of descriptive concepts to persons. *Journal of Personality and Social Psychology, 27,* 120–128.

Pfau, M., Compton, J. A., Parker, K. A., Wittenberg, E. M., An, C., Ferguson, M., et al. (2004). The traditional explanation for resistance versus attitude accessibility: Do they trigger distinct or overlapping processes of resistance? *Human Communication Research, 30,* 329–260.

Pfau, M., Roskos-Ewoldsen, D., Wood, M., Yin, S., Cho, J., Lu, K. H., et al. (2003). Attitude accessibility as an alternative explanation for how inoculation confers resistance. *Communication Monographs, 70,* 39–51.

Pheterson, G. I., Kiesler, S. B. & Goldberg, P. A. (1971). Evaluation of the performance of women as a function of their success, achievements and personal history. *Journal of Personality and Social Psychology, 19,* 114–118.

Phillips, D. P. (1986). Natural experiments on the effects of mass media violence on fatal aggression: Strengths and weaknesses of a new approach. In L. Berkowitz (Ed.), *Advances in experimental social psychology* (Vol. 19, pp. 207–250). New York: Academic Press.

Phinney, J. S., & Rotheram, M. J. (Eds.) (1987). *Children's ethnic socialization: Pluralism and development.* Newbury Park, CA: SAGE.

Piaget, J. (1928). *The child's conception of the world.* London: Routledge & Kegan Paul.

Piaget, J. (1955). *The child's construction of reality.* London: Routledge & Kegan Paul.

Pilger, J. (1989). *A secret country.* London: Vantage.

Piliavin, J. A., & Charng, H.-W. (1990). Altruism: A review of recent theory and research. *Annual Review of Sociology, 16,* 27–65.

Piliavin, J. A., Piliavin, I. M., Dovidio, J. F., Gaertner, S. L., & Clark, R. D., III (1981). *Emergency intervention*. New York: Academic Press.

Pittam, J., & Gallois, C. (1996). The mediating role of narrative in intergroup processes: Talking about AIDS. *Journal of Language and Social Psychology, 15*, 312–334.

Pittinsky, T. (Ed.). (2009). *Crossing the divide: Intergroup leadership in a world of difference*. Cambridge, MA: Harvard Business Publishing.

Pittinsky, T. L., & Simon, S. (2007). Intergroup leadership. *The Leadership Quarterly, 18*, 586–605.

Platow, M. J., Reid, S. A., & Andrew, S. (1998). Leadership endorsement: The role of distributive and procedural behavior in interpersonal and intergroup contexts. *Group Processes and Intergroup Relations, 1*, 35–47.

Platow, M. J., & Van Knippenberg, D. (2001). A social identity analysis of leadership endorsement: The effects of leader ingroup prototypicality and distributive intergroup fairness. *Personality and Social Psychology Bulletin, 27*, 1508–1519.

Platz, S. J., & Hosch, H. M. (1988). Cross-racial/ethnic eyewitness identification: A field study. *Journal of Applied Social Psychology, 18*, 972–984.

Plous, S., & Williams, T. (1995). Racial stereotypes from the days of American slavery: A continuing legacy. *Journal of Applied Social Psychology, 25*, 795–817.

Pomazal, R. J., & Clore, G. L. (1973). Helping on the highway: The effects of dependency and sex. *Journal of Applied Social Psychology, 3*, 150–164.

Popp, D., Donovan, R. A., Crawford, M., Marsh, K. L., & Peele, M. (2003). Gender, race, and speech style stereotypes. *Sex Roles, 48*, 317-325.

Poppe, E., & Linssen, H. (1999). Ingroup favouritism and the reflection of realistic dimensions of difference between national states in Central and Eastern European nationality stereotypes. *British Journal of Social Psychology, 38*, 85–102.

Popper, K. (1969). *Conjectures and refutations* (3rd ed.). London: Routledge & Kegan Paul.

Postmes, T., & Spears, R. (1998). Deindividuation and antinormative behavior: A meta-analysis. *Psychological Bulletin, 123*, 238–259.

Postmes, T., Spears, R., & Lea, M. (1998). Breaching or building social boundaries? SIDE-effects of computer-mediated communication. *Communication Research, 25*, 689–715.

Postmes, T., Spears, R., Sakhel, K., & de Groot, D. (2001). Social influence in computer-mediated communication: The effects of anonymity on group behavior. *Personality and Social Psychology Bulletin, 27*, 1243–1254.

Potter, J. (1996). *Representing reality*. London: SAGE.

Potter, J., Stringer, P., & Wetherell, M. S. (1984). *Social texts and context: Literature and social psychology*. London: Routledge and Kegan Paul.

Potter, J., & Wetherell, M. S. (1987). *Discourse and social psychology: Beyond attitudes and behaviour*. London: SAGE.

Potter, J., Wetherell, M. S., Gill, R., & Edwards, D. (1990). Discourse: Noun, verb or social practice? *Philosophical Psychology, 3*, 205–217.

Powell, M. C., & Fazio, R. H. (1984). Attitude accessibility as a function of repeated attitudinal expression. *Personality and Social Psychology Bulletin, 10*, 139–148.

Pratkanis, A. R., & Greenwald, A. G. (1989). A sociocognitive model of attitude structure and function. In L. Berkowitz (Ed.), *Advances in experimental social psychology* (Vol. 22, pp. 245–285). New York: Academic Press.

Pratkanis, A. R., Greenwald, A. G., Leippe, M. R., & Baumgardner, M. H. (1988). In search of reliable persuasion effects: III. The sleeper effect is dead. Long live the sleeper effect. *Journal of Personality and Social Psychology, 54*, 203–218.

Pratto, F. (1999). The puzzle of continuing group inequality: Piecing together psychological, social and cultural forces in social dominance theory. In M. P. Zanna (Ed.), *Advances in experimental social psychology* (Vol. 31, pp. 191–263). New York: Academic Press.

Pratto, F., Sidanius, J., Stallworth, L. M., & Malle, B. F. (1994). Social dominance orientation: A personality variable predicting social and political attitudes. *Journal of Personality and Social Psychology, 67*, 741–763.

Prentice, D. A., & Eberhardt, J. (Eds.) (2008). *Social neuroscience and intergroup behavior*. (Special issue of *Group Processes and Intergroup Relations* – all Vol 11, Issue 2). London: SAGE.

Prentice, D. A., & Miller, D. T. (1993). Pluralistic ignorance and alcohol use on campus: Some consequences of misperceiving the social norm. *Journal of Personality and Social Psychology, 64*, 243–256.

Prentice, D. A., & Miller, D. T. (Eds.) (1999). *Cultural divides: Understanding and overcoming group conflict*. New York: Russell Sage Foundation.

Prentice, D. A., Miller, D., & Lightdale, J. R. (1994). Asymmetries in attachment to groups and to their members: Distinguishing between common-identity and common-bond groups. *Personality and Social Psychology Bulletin, 20*, 484–493.

Prentice-Dunn, S., & Rogers, R. W. (1982). Effects of public and private self-awareness on deindividuation and aggression. *Journal of Personality and Social Psychology, 43*, 503–513.

Price-Williams, D. (1976). Cross-cultural studies. In L. A. Samovar & R. E. Porter (Eds.), *Intercultural communication: A reader* (2nd ed., pp. 32–48). Belmont, CA: Wadsworth.

Prisbell, M. (1985). Assertiveness, shyness and nonverbal communication behaviors. *Communication Research Reports, 2*, 120–127.

Pruitt, D. G. (1981). *Negotiation behavior*. New York: Academic Press.

Pruitt, D. G. (1986). Achieving integrative agreements in negotiation. In R. K. White (Ed.), *Psychology and the prevention of nuclear war* (pp. 463–478). New York: New York University Press.

Pryor, J. B., & Ostrom, T. M. (1981). The cognitive organization of social information: A converging-operations approach. *Journal of Personality and Social Psychology, 41*, 628–641.

Przybyla, D. P. J. (1985). *The facilitating effects of exposure to erotica on male prosocial behavior*. Unpublished doctoral dissertation, State University of New York at Albany.

Purkhardt, S. C. (1995). *Transforming social representations*. London: Routledge.

Pyszczynski, T. A., & Greenberg, J. (1981). Role of disconfirmed expectancies in the instigation of attributional processing. *Journal of Personality and Social Psychology, 40*, 31–38.

Pyszczynski, T., Greenberg, J., & Solomon, S. (1999). A dual-process model of defense against conscious and unconscious death-related thoughts: An extension of terror management theory. *Psychological Review, 106*, 835–845.

Pyszczynski, T., Greenberg, J., & Solomon, S. (2004). Why do people need self-esteem? A theoretical and empirical review. *Psychological Bulletin, 130*, 435–468.

Quattrone, G. A. (1986). On the perception of a group's variability. In S. Worchel & W. Austin (Eds.), *The psychology of intergroup relations* (Vol. 2, pp. 25–48). New York: Nelson-Hall.

Quattrone, G. A., & Jones, E. E. (1980). The perception of variability within ingroups and outgroups: Implications for the law of small numbers. *Journal of Personality and Social Psychology, 38*, 141–152.

Quigley-Fernandez, B., & Tedeschi, J. T. (1978). The bogus pipeline as lie detector: Two validity studies. *Journal of Personality and Social Psychology, 36*, 247–256.

Rabbie, J. M., & Bekkers, F. (1978). Threatened leadership and intergroup competition. *European Journal of Social Psychology, 8*, 9–20.

Rabbie, J. M., & DeBrey, J. H. C. (1971). The anticipation of intergroup cooperation and competition under private and public conditions. *International Journal of Group Tensions, 1*, 230–251.

Rabbie, J. M., & Horwitz, M. (1969). Arousal of ingroup–outgroup bias by a chance win or loss. *Journal of Personality and Social Psychology, 13*, 269–277.

Rabbie, J. M., Schot, J. C., & Visser, L. (1989). Social identity theory: A conceptual and empirical critique from the perspective of a behavioural interaction model. *European Journal of Social Psychology, 19*, 171–202.

Rabbie, J. M., & Wilkens, G. (1971). Ingroup competition and its effect on intragroup relations. *European Journal of Social Psychology, 1*, 215–234.

Rafiq, U., Jobanuptra, N., & Muncer, S. (2006). Comparing the perceived causes of the second Iraq war: A network analysis approach. *Aggressive Behavior, 32*, 321–329.

Ramirez, J., Bryant, J., & Zillman, D. (1983). Effects of erotica on retaliatory behavior as a function of level of prior provocation. *Journal of Personality and Social Psychology, 43*, 971–978.

Rankin, R. E., & Campbell, D. T. (1955). Galvanic skin response to Negro and White experimenters. *Journal of Abnormal and Social Psychology, 51*, 30–33.

Rapley, M. (1998). 'Just an ordinary Australian': Self- categorization and the discursive construction of facticity in 'new racist' political rhetoric. *British Journal of Social Psychology, 37*, 325–344.

Rapoport, A. (1976). *Experimental games and their uses in psychology*. Morristown, NJ: General Learning Press.

Raven, B. H. (1965). Social influence and power. In I. D. Steiner & M. Fishbein (Eds.), *Current studies in social psychology* (pp. 371–382). New York: Holt, Rinehart and Winston.

Raven, B. H. (1993). The bases of power: Origins and recent developments. *Journal of Social Issues, 49*, 227–251.

Raven, B. H., & French, J. R. P. (1958). Legitimate power, coercive power and observability in social influence. *Sociometry, 21*, 83–97.

Ray, M. L. (1988). *Short-term evidence of advertising's long-term effect*. (Report no. 88–107). Cambridge, MA: Marketing Science Institute.

Reeder, G. D., & Brewer, M. B. (1979). A schematic model of dispositional attribution in interpersonal perception. *Psychological Review, 86*, 61–79.

Regan, D. T., & Fazio, R. H. (1977). On the consistency of attitudes and behavior: Look to the method of attitude formation. *Journal of Experimental Social Psychology, 13*, 38–45.

Regan, D. T., Williams, M., & Sparling, S. (1972). Voluntary expiation of guilt: A field experiment. *Journal of Personality and Social Psychology, 24*, 42–45.

Regan, J. (1971). Guilt, perceived injustice, and altruistic behaviour. *Journal of Personality and Social Psychology, 18*, 124–132.

Regan, P. C., & Berscheid, E. (1999). *Lust: What we know about human sexual desire*. Thousand Oaks, CA: SAGE.

Regoeczi, W. C. (2003). When context matters: A multilevel analysis of household and neighbourhood crowding on aggression and withdrawal. *Journal of Environmental Psychology, 23*, 457–470.

Reicher, S. D. (1982). The determination of collective behaviour. In H. Tajfel (Ed.), *Social identity and intergroup relations* (pp. 41–83). Cambridge, UK: Cambridge University Press.

Reicher, S. D. (1984). Social influence in the crowd: Attitudinal and behavioural effects of deindividuation in conditions of high and low group salience. *British Journal of Social Psychology, 23*, 341–350.

Reicher, S. D. (1987). Crowd behaviour as social action. In J. C. Turner, M. A. Hogg, P. J. Oakes, S. D. Reicher & M. S. Wetherell, *Rediscovering the social group: A self-categorization theory* (pp. 171–202). Oxford, UK: Blackwell.

Reicher, S. D. (1996). Social identity and social change: Rethinking the context of social psychology. In W. P. Robinson (Ed.), *Social groups and identities: Developing the legacy of Henri Tajfel* (pp. 317–336). Oxford, UK: Butterworth-Heinemann.

Reicher, S. D. (2001). The psychology of crowd dynamics. In M. A. Hogg & R. S. Tindale (Eds.), *Blackwell handbook of social psychology: Group processes* (pp. 182–207). Oxford, UK: Blackwell.

Reicher, S. D., & Emler, N. (1985). Delinquent behaviour and attitudes to formal authority. *British Journal of Social Psychology, 24*, 161–168.

Reicher, S. D., & Haslam, S. A. (2006). Rethinking the psychology of tyranny: The BBC prison study. *British Journal of Social Psychology, 45,* 1–40.

Reicher, S. D., & Hopkins, N. (1996a). Seeking influence through characterising self-categories: An analysis of anti-abortionist rhetoric. *British Journal of Social Psychology, 35,* 297–311.

Reicher, S. D., & Hopkins, N. (1996b). Self-category constructions in political rhetoric: An analysis of Thatcher's and Kinnock's speeches concerning the British miners' strike (1984–5). *European Journal of Social Psychology, 26,* 353–371.

Reicher, S. D., & Hopkins, N. (2001). *Self and nation.* London: SAGE.

Reicher, S.D., & Hopkins, N. (2003). On the science of the art of leadership. In D. van Knippenberg & M. A. Hogg (Eds.), *Leadership and power: Identity processes in groups and organizations* (pp. 197–209). London: SAGE.

Reicher, S. D., & Potter, J. (1985). Psychological theory as intergroup perspective: A comparative analysis of 'scientific' and 'lay' accounts of crowd events. *Human Relations, 38,* 167–189.

Reicher, S. D., Spears, R., & Postmes, T. (1995). A social identity model of deindividuation phenomena. *European Review of Social Psychology, 6,* 161–198.

Reid, S. A., & Ng, S. H. (1999). Language, power, and intergroup relations. *Journal of Social Issues, 55,* 119–139.

Reid, S. A., & Ng, S. H. (2000). Conversation as a resource for influence: Evidence for prototypical arguments and social identification processes. *European Journal of Social Psychology, 30,* 83–100.

Reis, H. T., & Sprecher, S (Eds.) (2009) *Encyclopedia of human relationships.* Thousand Oaks, CA: SAGE.

Reisenzein, R. (1983). The Schachter theory of emotion: Two decades later. *Psychological Bulletin, 94,* 239–264.

Rempel, J. K., Ross, M., & Holmes, J. G. (2001). Trust and communicated attributions in close relationships. *Journal of Personality and Social Psychology, 81,* 57–64.

Renzetti, C. M. (2006). Commentary on Swan and Snow's 'The development of a theory of women's use of violence in intimate relationships'. *Violence Against Women, 12,* 1046–1047.

Reynolds, K. J., Turner, J. C., Haslam, S. A., & Ryan, M. K. (2001). The role of personality and group factors in explaining prejudice. *Journal of Experimental Social Psychology, 37,* 427–434.

Rhodes, G. (2006). The evolutionary psychology of facial beauty. *Annual Review of Psychology, 57,* 199–226.

Rhodes, G., Hickford, C., & Jeffrey, L. (2000). Sex-typicality and attractiveness: Are supermale and superfemale faces super-attractive? *British Journal of Psychology, 91,* 125–140.

Rhodes, G., Sumich, A., & Byatt, G. (1999). Are average facial configurations attractive only because of their symmetry? *Psychological Science, 10,* 52–58.

Rhodes, G., & Tremewan, T. (1996). Averageness, exaggeration, and facial attractiveness. *Psychological Science, 2,* 105–110.

Rhodes, N., & Wood, W. (1992). Self-esteem and intelligence affect influenceability: The mediating role of message reception. *Psychological Bulletin, 111,* 156–171.

Rhodewalt, F., Madrian, J. C., & Cheney, S. (1998). Narcissism, self-knowledge, organization, and emotional reactivity: The effects of daily experiences on self-esteem and affect. *Personality and Social Psychology Bulletin, 24,* 75–86.

Rhodewalt, F., & Strube, M. J. (1985). A self-attribution reactance model for health outcomes. *Journal of Applied Social Psychology, 15,* 330–344.

Rholes, W. S., & Pryor, J. B. (1982). Cognitive accessibility and causal attributions. *Personality and Social Psychology Bulletin, 8,* 719–727.

Rholes, W. S., & Simpson, J. A. (2004). *Adult attachment: Theory, research, and clinical implications.* New York: Guilford Press.

Rholes, W. S., Simpson, J. A., & Blakely, B. S. (1995). Adult attachment styles and mothers' relationships with their young children. *Personal Relationships, 2,* 35–54.

Rholes, W. S., Simpson, J. A., & Friedman, M. (2006). Avoidant attachment and the experience of parenting. *Personality and Social Psychology Bulletin, 32,* 275–285.

Rice, M. E., & Grusec, J. E. (1975). Saying and doing: Effects on observer performance. *Journal of Personality and Social Psychology, 32,* 584–593.

Rice, R. W. (1978). Construct validity of the least preferred co-worker score. *Psychological Bulletin, 85,* 1199–1237.

Rice, R. W., Instone, D., & Adams, J. (1984). Leader sex, leader success, and leadership process: Two field studies. *Journal of Applied Psychology, 69,* 12–31.

Ridgeway, C. L. (2001). Social status and group structure. In M. A. Hogg & R. S. Tindale (Eds.), *Blackwell handbook of social psychology: Group processes* (pp. 352–375). Oxford, UK: Blackwell.

Ridgeway, C. L. (2003). Status characteristics and leadership. In D. van Knippenberg & M. A. Hogg (Eds.), *Leadership and power: Identity processes in groups and organizations* (pp. 65–78). London: SAGE.

Riess, M., Kalle, R. J., & Tedeschi, J. T. (1981). Bogus pipeline attitude assessment, impression management, and misattribution in induced compliance settings. *Journal of Social Psychology, 115,* 247–258.

Riess, M., Rosenfield, R., Melburg, V., & Tedeschi, J. T. (1981). Self-serving attributions: Biased private perceptions and distorted public descriptions. *Journal of Personality and Social Psychology, 41,* 224–231.

Riggio, H. R. (2004). Parental marital conflict and divorce, parent–child relationships, social support, and relationship anxiety in young adulthood. *Personal Relationships, 11,* 99–114.

Riggio, R. E., & Carney, D. R. (2003). *Social skills inventory manual* (2nd ed.). Redwood City, CA: MindGarden.

Riggio, R. E., Chaleff, I., & Lipman-Blumen, J. (Eds.). (2008). *The art of followership: How great followers create great leaders and organizations.* San Francisco: Jossey-Bass.

Ringelmann, M. (1913). Recherches sur les moteurs animés: Travail de l'homme. *Annales de l'Institut National Agronomique, 2(12),* 1–40.

Riopelle, A. J. (1987). Instinct. In R. J. Corsini (Ed.), *Concise encyclopedia of psychology* (pp. 599–600). New York: Wiley.

Robinson, J. P., Shaver, P. R., & Wrightsman, L. S. (Eds.) (1991). *Measures of personality and social psychological attitudes.* New York: Academic Press.

Robinson, R. J., Keltner, D., Ward, A., & Ross, L. (1995). Actual versus assumed differences in construal: Realism in intergroup perception and conflict. *Journal of Personality and Social Psychology, 68,* 404–417.

Robinson, W. P. (Ed.) (1996). *Social groups and identities: Developing the legacy of Henri Tajfel.* Oxford, UK: Butterworth-Heinemann.

Roccas, S., & Brewer, M. B. (2002). Social identity complexity. *Personality and Social Psychology Review, 6,* 88–109.

Roethlisberger, F., & Dickson, W. (1939). *Management and the worker.* Cambridge, MA: Harvard University Press.

Rogers, R. W., & Prentice-Dunn, S. (1981). Deindividuation and anger-mediated interracial aggression: Unmasking regressive racism. *Journal of Personality and Social Psychology, 41,* 63–73.

Rogers, W. S. (2003). *Social psychology: Experimental and critical approaches.* Maidenhead, UK: Open University Press.

Rohan, M. (2000). A rose by any name? The values construct. *Personality and Social Psychology Review, 4,* 255–277.

Rohrer, J. H., Baron, S. H., Hoffman, E. L., & Swander, D. V. (1954). The stability of autokinetic judgments. *Journal of Abnormal and Social Psychology, 49,* 595–597.

Rokeach, M. (1948). Generalized mental rigidity as a factor in ethnocentrism. *Journal of Abnormal and Social Psychology, 43,* 259–278.

Rokeach, M. (1973). *The nature of human values.* New York: Free Press.

Rokeach, M. (Ed.) (1960). *The open and closed mind.* New York: Basic Books.

Rokeach, M., & Mezei, L. (1966). Race and shared belief as factors in social choice. *Science, 151,* 167–172.

Rommetveit, R. (1974). *On message structure: A framework for the study of language and communication.* New York: Wiley.

Rosch, E. (1978). Principles of categorization. In E. Rosch & B. B. Lloyd (Eds.), *Cognition and categorization* (pp. 27–48). Hillsdale, NJ: Erlbaum.

Rose, H., & Rose, S. (Eds.) (2000). *Alas, poor Darwin: Arguments against evolutionary psychology.* London: Vintage.

Rosenberg, M. J. (1969). The conditions and consequences of evaluation apprehension. In R. Rosenthal & R. L. Rosnow (Eds.), *Artifact in behavioral research* (pp. 280–349). New York: Academic Press.

Rosenberg, M. J. (1979). *Conceiving the self.* New York: Basic Books.

Rosenberg, M. J., & Hovland, C. I. (1960). Cognitive, affective, and behavioral components of attitude. In M. J. Rosenberg, C. I. Hovland, W. J. McGuire, R. P. Abelson & J. W. Brehm (Eds.), *Attitude organization and change: An analysis of consistency among attitude components.* New Haven, CT: Yale University Press.

Rosenberg, S., Nelson, C., & Vivekanathan, P. S. (1968). A multidimensional approach to the structure of personality impressions. *Journal of Personality and Social Psychology, 39,* 283–294.

Rosenberg, S., & Sedlak, A. (1972). Structural representations of implicit personality theory. In L. Berkowitz (Ed.), *Advances in experimental social psychology* (Vol. 6, pp. 235–297). New York: Academic Press.

Rosenberg, S. W., & Wolfsfeld, G. (1977). International conflict and the problem of attribution. *Journal of Conflict Resolution, 21,* 75–103.

Rosenfeld, H. M. (1965). Effect of approval-seeking induction on interpersonal proximity. *Psychological Reports, 17,* 120–122.

Rosenfield, D., Greenberg, J., Folger, R., & Borys, R. (1982). Effect of an encounter with a Black panhandler on subsequent helping for Blacks: Tokenism or conforming to a negative stereotype? *Personality and Social Psychology Bulletin, 8,* 664–671.

Rosenfield, D., & Stephan, W. G. (1977). When discounting fails: An unexpected finding. *Memory and Cognition, 5,* 97–102.

Rosenkoetter, L. I. (1999). The television situation comedy and children's prosocial behavior. *Journal of Applied Social Psychology, 29,* 979–993.

Rosenthal, D. (1987). Ethnic identity development in adolescents. In J. S. Phinney & M. J. Rotheram (Eds.), *Children's ethnic socialisation: Pluralism and development* (pp. 156–179). Newbury Park, CA: SAGE.

Rosenthal, R. (1966). *Experimenter effects in behavioral research.* New York: Appleton-Century-Crofts.

Rosenthal, R., & Jacobson, L. F. (1968). *Pygmalion in the classroom.* New York: Holt, Rinehart & Winston.

Rosenthal, R., Hall, J. A., DiMatteo, M. R., Rogers, P. L., & Archer, D. (1979). *Sensitivity to nonverbal communication: The PONS test.* Baltimore, MD: Johns Hopkins University Press.

Rosenthal, R., & Rubin, D. B. (1978). Interpersonal expectancy effects: The first 345 studies. *Behavioral and Brain Sciences, 3,* 377–386.

Rosip, J. C., & Hall, J. A. (2004). Knowledge of nonverbal cues, gender, and nonverbal decoding accuracy. *Journal of Nonverbal Behavior, 28,* 267–286.

Roskos-Ewoldsen, D. R., & Fazio, R. H. (1992). On the orienting value of attitudes: Attitude accessibility as a determinant of an object's attraction of visual attention. *Journal of Personality and Social Psychology, 63,* 198–211.

Rosnow, R. L. (1980). Psychology of rumour reconsidered. *Psychological Bulletin, 87,* 578–591.

Rosnow, R. L. (1981). *Paradigms in transition: The methodology of social enquiry.* Oxford, UK: Oxford University Press.

Ross, E. A. (1908). *Social psychology.* New York: Macmillan.

Ross, L. (1977). The intuitive psychologist and his shortcomings. In L. Berkowitz (Ed.), *Advances in experimental social psychology* (Vol. 10, pp. 174–220). New York: Academic Press.

Ross, L., Greene, D., & House, P. (1977). The 'false consensus effect': An egocentric bias in social perception and attribution processes. *Journal of Experimental Social Psychology, 13,* 279–301.

Ross, L., Lepper, M. R., & Hubbard, M. (1975). Perseverance in self-perception and social perception: Biased attribution processes in the debriefing paradigm. *Journal of Personality and Social Psychology, 32,* 880–892.

Ross, L., & Nisbett, R. E. (1991). *The person and the situation: Perspectives of social psychology.* New York: McGraw-Hill.

Ross, L., & Ward, A. (1995). Psychological barriers to dispute resolution. *Advances in Experimental Social Psychology, 27,* 255–304.

Ross, L., Lepper, M., & Ward, A. (2010). History of social psychology: Insights, challenges, and contributions to theory and application. In S. T. Fiske, D. T. Gilbert, & G. Lindzey (Eds.), *Handbook of social psychology* (5th ed., Vol. 1, pp. 3-50). New York: Wiley.

Ross, M., & Fletcher, G. J. O. (1985). Attribution and social perception. In G. Lindzey & E. Aronson (Eds.), *Handbook of social psychology* (3rd ed., Vol. 2, pp. 73–122). New York: Random House.

Rothbart, M. (1981). Memory processes and social beliefs. In D. L. Hamilton (Ed.), *Cognitive processes in stereotyping and intergroup behavior* (pp. 145–182). Hillsdale, NJ: Erlbaum.

Rothbart, M., & John, O. P. (1985). Social categorization and behavioral episodes: A cognitive analysis of intergroup contact. *Journal of Social Issues, 41,* 81–104.

Rothbart, M., & Park, B. (1986). On the confirmability and disconfirmability of trait concepts. *Journal of Personality and Social Psychology, 50,* 131–142.

Rothman, A. J., & Salovey, P. (1997). Shaping perceptions to motivate healthy behaviour: The role of message framing. *Psychological Bulletin, 121,* 3–19.

Rothman, A. J., & Salovey, P (2007). The reciprocal relation between principles and practice: Social psychology and health behaviour. In A. W. Kruglanski & E. T. Higgins (Eds.), *Social psychology: A handbook of basic principles* (2nd ed., pp. 826-849). New York: Guilford Press.

Rotter, J. B. (1966). Generalized expectancies for internal versus external control of reinforcement. *Psychological Monographs, 80,* whole no. 609.

Rotter, J. B. (1980). Trust and gullibility. *Psychology Today, 14* (5), pp. 35–8, 40, 42, 102.

Ruback, R. B., & Pandey, J. (1992). Very hot and really crowded: Quasi-experimental investigations of Indian 'tempos'. *Environment and Behavior, 24,* 527–554.

Rubin, A. M. (1978). Child and adolescent television use and political socialization. *Journalism Quarterly, 55,* 125–129.

Rubin, J. (1976). How to tell when someone is saying no. *Topics in Culture Learning, 4,* 61–65.

Rubin, J. (1980). Experimental research on third-party intervention in conflict: Toward some generalizations. *Psychological Bulletin, 87,* 379–391.

Rubin, M., & Hewstone, M. (1998). Social identity theory's self-esteem hypothesis: A review and some suggestions for clarification. *Personality and Social Psychology Review, 2,* 40–62.

Rubin, Z. (1973). *Liking and loving: An invitation to social psychology.* New York: Holt, Rinehart and Winston.

Ruckmick, C. A. (1912). The history and status of psychology in the United States. *American Journal of Psychology, 23,* 517–531.

Rudman, L. A. (1998). Self-promotion as a risk factor for women: The costs and benefits of counter-stereotypical impression management. *Journal of Personality and Social Psychology, 74,* 629–645.

Rudman, L. A., & Glick, P. (1999). Feminized management and backlash toward agentic women: The hidden costs to women of a kinder, gentler image of middle managers. *Journal of Personality and Social Psychology, 75,* 1004–1010.

Rudman, L. A., & Glick, P. (2001). Prescriptive gender stereotypes and backlash against agentic women. *Journal of Social Issues, 57,* 743–762.

Ruggiero, K. M., & Taylor, D. M. (1995). Coping with discrimination: How disadvantaged group members perceive the discrimination that confronts them. *Journal of Personality and Social Psychology, 68,* 826–838.

Ruiz-Belda, M.-A., Fernández-Dols, J.-M., Carrera, P., & Barchard, K. (2003). Spontaneous facial expressions of happy bowlers and soccer fans. *Cognition and Emotion, 17,* 315–326.

Rumelhart, D. E., & Ortony, A. (1977). The representation of knowledge in memory. In C. R., Anderson, R. J. Spiro & W. E. Montague (Eds.), *Schooling and the acquisition of knowledge* (pp. 99–136). Hillsdale, NJ: Erlbaum.

Rummel, R. J. (1988). *Political systems, violence, and war.* Paper presented at the United States Institute of Peace Conference, Airlie, VA.

Runciman, W. G. (1966). *Relative deprivation and social justice.* London: Routledge and Kegan Paul.

Rusbult, C. E., Martz, J. M., & Agnew, C. R. (1998). The Investment Model Scale: Measuring commitment level, satisfaction level, quality of alternatives, and investment size. *Personal Relationships, 5,* 357–391.

Rusbult, C. E., & Zembrodt, I. M. (1983). Responses to dissatisfaction in romantic involvements: A multi- dimensional scaling analysis. *Journal of Experimental Social Psychology, 19,* 274–293.

Rushton, J. P. (1976). Socialization and the altruistic behavior of children. *Psychological Bulletin, 83,* 898–913.

Rushton, J. P. (1979). Effects of prosocial television and film material on the behavior of viewers. In L. Berkowitz (Ed.), *Advances in experimental social psychology* (Vol. 12, pp. 322–351). New York: Academic Press.

Rushton, J. P. & Teachman, G. (1978). The effects of positive reinforcement, attributions, and punishment on model induced altrusim in children. *Personality and Social Psychology Bulletin, 4,* 322–25.

Rushton, J. P. (1980). *Altruism, socialisation, and society.* Englewood Cliffs, NJ: Prentice Hall.

Russell, J. A. (1994). Is there universal recognition of emotion from facial expressions? A review of the cross-cultural studies. *Psychological Bulletin, 115,* 102–141.

Russell, J. A., Bachorowski, J.-A., & Fernandez-Dols, J.-M. (2003). Facial and vocal expressions of emotion. *Annual Review of Psychology, 54,* 329–349.

Russell, J. A., & Fernandez-Dols, J. M. (Eds.) (1997). *The psychology of facial expression: Studies in emotion and social interaction*. Cambridge, UK: Cambridge University Press.

Rutkowski, G. K., Gruder, C. L., & Romer, D. (1983). Group cohesiveness, social norms, and bystander intervention. *Journal of Personality and Social Psychology, 44*, 545–552.

Rutland, A. (1999). The development of national prejudice, ingroup favouritism and self-stereotypes in British children. *British Journal of Social Psychology, 38*, 55–70.

Rutland, A., & Cinnirella, M. (2000). Context effects on Scottish national and European self-categorizations: The importance of category accessibility, fragility and relations. *British Journal of Social Psychology, 39*, 495–519.

Rutte, C. G., & Wilke, H. A. M. (1984). Social dilemmas and leadership. *European Journal of Social Psychology, 14*, 105–121.

Ryan, E. R., Giles, H., Bartolucci, G., & Henwood, K. (1986). Psycholinguistic and social psychological components of communication by and with the elderly. *Language and Communication, 6*, 1–24.

Ryan, T. (1985). Human nature and the origins of war. *Hurupaa, 3*, 46–54.

Ryen, A. H., & Kahn, A. (1975). Effects of intergroup orientation on group attitudes and proxemic behavior. *Journal of Personality and Social Psychology, 31*, 302–310.

Sabini, J., & Silver, M. (1982). *The moralities of everyday life*. New York: Oxford University Press.

Sachdev, I., & Bourhis, R. Y. (1993). Ethnolinguistic vitality: Some motivational and cognitive considerations. In M. A. Hogg & D. Abrams (Eds.), *Group motivation: Social psychological perspectives* (pp. 33–51). Hemel Hempstead, UK: Harvester Wheatsheaf.

Sachdev, I., & Bourhis, R. Y. (2005). Multilingual communication and social identification. In J. Harwood & H. Giles (Eds.), *Intergroup communication: Multiple perspectives* (pp. 65-91). New York, NY, US: Peter Lang Publishing.

Sachdev, I., & Wright, A. (1996). Social influence and language learning: An experimental study. *Journal of Language and Social Psychology, 15*, 230–245.

Sagi, A., & Hoffman, M. (1976). Emphatic distress in the newborn. *Developmental Psychology, 12*, 175–176.

Saint-Blancat, C. (1985). The effect of minority group vitality upon its sociopsychological behaviour and strategies. *Journal of Multilingual and Multicultural Development, 6*, 31–44.

St Claire, L., & Turner, J. C. (1982). The role of demand characteristics in the social categorization paradigm. *European Journal of Social Psychology, 12*, 307–14.

Saks, M. J. (1978). Social psychological contributions to a legislative committee on organ and tissue transplants. *American Psychologist, 33*, 680–690.

Saks, M. J., & Marti, M. W. (1997). A meta-analysis of the effects of jury size. *Law and Human Behavior, 21*, 451–467.

Salovey, P., Rothman, A. J., & Rodin, J. (1998). Health behaviour. In D. T. Gilbert, S. T. Fiske, & G. Lindzey (Eds.), *The handbook of social psychology* (4th ed., Vol. 2, pp. 633–683). New York: McGraw-Hill.

Sampson, E. E. (1977). Psychology and the American ideal. *Journal of Personality and Social Psychology, 35*, 767–782.

San Antonio, P. M. (1987). Social mobility and language use in an American company in Japan. *Journal of Language and Social Psychology, 6*, 191–200.

Sanders, G. S. (1981). Driven by Distraction: An Integrative Review of Social Facilitation Theory and Research), *Journal of Experimental Social Psychology, 17*, 227–251.

Sanders, G. S. (1983). An attentional process model of social facilitation. In A. Hare, H. Blumberg, V. Kent & M. Davies (Eds.). *Small groups*. London: Wiley.

Sanders, G. S., & Baron, R. S. (1977). Is social comparison relevant for producing choice shift? *Journal of Experimental Social Psychology, 13*, 303–314.

Sanders, G. S., Baron, R. S., & Moore, D. L. (1978). Distraction and social comparison as mediators of social facilitation. *Journal of Experimental Social Psychology, 14*, 291–303.

Sanders, G. S., & Mullen, B. (1983). Accuracy in perceptions of consensus: Differential tendencies of people with majority and minority positions. *European Journal of Social Psychology, 13*, 57–70.

Sani, F., & Reicher, S. D. (1998). When consensus fails: An analysis of the schism within the Italian Communist Party (1991). *European Journal of Social Psychology, 28*, 623–45.

Sani, F., & Reicher, S. D. (2000). Contested identities and schisms in groups: Opposing the ordination of women as priests in the Church of England. *British Journal of Social Psychology, 39*, 95–112.

Sansone, C., Morf, C. C., & Panter, A. T. (Eds.) (2004). *The SAGE handbook of methods in social psychology*. Thousand Oaks, CA: SAGE.

Sargant, W. (1957). *Battle for the mind: A physiology of conversion and brainwashing*. Garden City, NY: Doubleday.

Saroja, K., & Surendra, H. S. (1991). A study of postgraduate students' endogamous preference in mate selection. *Indian Journal of Behaviour, 15*, 1–13.

Sassenberg, K. (2002). Common bond and common identity groups on the internet: Attachment and normative behavior in on-topic and off-topic chats. *Group Dynamics: Theory, Research, and Practice, 6*, 27–37.

Sassenberg, K. & Boos, M. (2003). Attitude change in computer-mediated communication: Effects of anonymity and category norms. *Group Processes and Intergroup Relations, 6*, 405–423.

Sato, K. (1987). Distribution of the cost of maintaining common resources. *Journal of Experimental Social Psychology, 23*, 19–31.

Sattler, D. N., & Kerr, N. L. (1991). Might versus morality explored: Motivational and cognitive bases for social motives. *Journal of Personality and Social Psychology, 60*, 756–765.

Saucier, G. (2000). Isms and the structure of social attitudes. *Journal of Personality and Social Psychology, 78*, 366–385.

Scandura, T. A. (1999). Rethinking leader–member exchange: An organizational justice perspective. *The Leadership Quarterly, 10*, 25–40.

Schachner, D. A., Shaver, P. R., & Mikulincer, M. (2005). Patterns of nonverbal behaviour and sensitivity in the context of attachment relationships. *Journal of Nonverbal Behaviour, 29*, 141–169.

Schachter, S. (1959). *The psychology of affiliation.* Stanford, CA: Stanford University Press.

Schachter, S. (1964). The interaction of cognitive and physiological determinants of emotional state. In L. Berkowitz (Ed.), *Advances in experimental social psychology* (Vol. 1, pp. 49–80). New York: Academic Press.

Schachter, S. (1971). *Emotion, obesity, and crime.* New York: Academic Press.

Schachter, S. & Burdeck, H. (1955). A field experiment on rumour transmission and distortion. *Journal of Abnormal and Social Psychology, 50*, 363–371.

Schachter, S., & Singer, J. E. (1962). Cognitive, social and physiological determinants of emotional state. *Psychological Review, 69*, 379–399.

Schaller, M., & Crandall, C. S. (Eds.). (2004). *The psychological foundations of culture.* Mahwah, NJ: Erlbaum.

Schaller, M., Simpson, J., & Kenrick, D. (2006). *Evolution and social psychology.* New York: Psychology Press.

Schank, R. C., & Abelson, R. P. (1977). *Scripts, plans, goals, and understanding: An inquiry into human knowledge structures.* Hillsdale, NJ: Erlbaum.

Scheier, M. F., & Carver, C. S. (1981). Private and public aspects of self. In L. Wheeler (Ed.), *Review of personality and social psychology* (Vol. 2, pp. 189–216). London: SAGE.

Scherer, K. R. (1974). Acoustic concomitants of emotional dimensions: Judging affect from synthesised tone sequences. In S. Weitz (Ed.), *Nonverbal communication* (pp. 249–253). New York: Oxford University Press.

Scherer, K. R. (1978). Personality inference from voice quality: The loud voice of extroversion. *European Journal of Social Psychology, 8*, 467–488.

Scherer, K. R. (1986). Vocal affect expression: A review and model for future research. *Psychological Bulletin, 99*, 143–165.

Scherer, K. R., Abeles, R. P., & Fischer, C. S. (1975). *Human aggression and conflict.* Englewood Cliffs, NJ: Prentice Hall.

Scherer, K. R., & Giles, H. (Eds.) (1979). *Social markers in speech.* Cambridge, UK: Cambridge University Press.

Schie, E. G. M., & Wiegman, O. (1997). Children and videogames: Leisure activities, aggression, social integration, and school performance. *Journal of Applied Social Psychology, 27*, 1175–1194.

Schiller, J. C. F. (1882). *Essays, esthetical and philosophical, including the dissertation on the 'Connexions between the animal and the spiritual in man'.* London: Bell.

Schimmack, U., Oishi, S., & Diener, E. (2005). Individualism: A valid and important dimension of cultural differences. *Personality and Social Psychology Review, 9*, 17–31.

Schlenker, B. R. (1980). *Impression management: The self-concept, social identity, and interpersonal relations.* Monterey, CA: Brooks/Cole.

Schlenker, B. R., Dlugolecki, D. W., & Doherty, K. (1994). The impact of self-presentation on self-appraisal and behavior: The roles of commitment and biased scanning. *Personality and Social Psychology Bulletin, 20*, 20–33.

Schlenker, B. R., Weingold, M. F., & Hallam, J. R. (1990). Self-serving attributions in social context: Effects of self-esteem and social pressure. *Journal of Personality and Social Psychology, 58*, 855–863.

Schmidt, C. F. (1972). Multidimensional scaling of the printed media's explanations of the riot of the summer of 1967. *Journal of Personality and Social Psychology, 24*, 59–67.

Schmitt, B. H., Gilovich, T., Goore, N., & Joseph, L. (1986). Mere presence and socio-facilitation: One more time. *Journal of Experimental Social Psychology, 22*, 242–248.

Schneider, D. J. (1973). Implicit personality theory: A review. *Psychological Bulletin, 79*, 294–309.

Schneider, D. J., Hastorf, A. H., & Ellsworth, P. C. (1979). *Person perception.* Reading, MA: Addison-Wesley.

Schofield, J. W. (1986). Black–White contact in desegregated schools. In M. Hewstone & R. J. Brown (Eds.), *Contact and conflict in intergroup encounters* (pp. 79–92). Oxford, UK: Blackwell.

Schofield, J. W. (1991). School desegregation and intergroup relations: A review of the literature. In G. Grant (Ed.), *Review of research in education* (Vol. 17, pp. 335–409). Washington, DC: American Education Research Association.

Schriesheim, C. A., Castro, S. L., & Cogliser, C. C. (1999). Leader–member exchange (LMX) research: A comprehensive review of theory, measurement, and data-analytic practices. *The Leadership Quarterly, 10*, 6–113.

Schriesheim, C. A., & Neider, L. L. (1996). Path–goal leadership theory: The long and winding road. *The Leadership Quarterly, 7*, 317–321.

Schriesheim, C. A., Tepper, B. J., & Tetrault, L. A. (1994). Least preferred co-worker score, situational control, and leadership effectiveness: A meta-analysis of contingency model performance predictions. *Journal of Applied Psychology, 79*, 561–573.

Schroeder, D. A., Penner, L. A., Dovidio, J. F., & Piliavin, J. A. (1995). *The psychology of helping and altruism.* New York: McGraw-Hill.

Schubert, T. W. (2004). The power in your hand: gender differences in bodily feedback from making a fist. *Personality and Social Psychology Bulletin, 30*, 757-769.

Schul, Y. (1983). Integration and abstraction in impression formation. *Journal of Personality and Social Psychology, 44*, 45–54.

Schul, Y., & Burnstein, E. (1985). The informational basis of social judgments: Using past impression rather than the trait description in forming new impression. *Journal of Experimental Social Psychology, 21*, 421–439.

Schullo, S. A., & Alperson, B. L. (1984). Interpersonal phenomenology as a function of sexual orientation, sex, sentiment, and trait categories in long-term dyadic relationships. *Journal of Personality and Social Psychology, 47*, 983–1002.

Schwab, D. P., & Grams, R. (1985). Sex-related errors in job evaluation: A 'real-world' test. *Journal of Applied Psychology, 70*, 533–539.

Shweder, R. A. (1991). *Thinking through culture: Expeditions in cultural psychology.* Cambridge, MA: Harvard University Press.

Schwartz, N., & Kurz, E. (1989). What's in a picture? The impact of face-ism on trait attribution. *European Journal of Social Psychology, 19,* 311–316.

Schwartz, S. H. (1977). Normative influences on altruism. In L. Berkowitz (Ed.), *Advances in experimental social psychology* (Vol. 10, pp. 222–279). New York: Academic Press.

Schwartz, S. H. (1992). Universals in the content and structure of values: Theoretical advances and empirical tests in 20 cultures. In M. P. Zanna (Ed.), *Advances in experimental social psychology* (Vol. 25, pp. 1–65). San Diego, CA: Academic Press.

Schwartz, S. H., & Bardi, A. (1997). Influences of adaptation to communist rule on value priorities in Eastern Europe. *Political Psychology, 18,* 385-410.

Schwartz, S. H., & David, T. B. (1976). Responsibility and helping in an emergency: Effects of blame, ability and denial of responsibility. *Sociometry, 39,* 406–415.

Schwarz, N. (2000). Social judgement and attitudes: Warmer, more social, and less conscious. *European Journal of Social Psychology, 30,* 149–176.

Schwarz, N., & Strack, F. (1991). Context effects in attitude surveys: Applying cognitive theory to social research. *European Review of Social Psychology, 2,* 30–50.

Schwerin, H. S., & Newell, H. H. (1981). *Persuasion in marketing.* New York: Wiley.

Scitovsky, T. (1980). Why do we seek more and more excitement? *Stanford Observer,* October, p. 13.

Searle, A. (1987). The effects of postnatal depression on mother–infant interaction. *Australian Journal of Sex, Marriage & Family, 8,* 79–88.

Searle, J. (1979). *Expression and meaning: Studies in the theory of speech acts.* Cambridge, UK: Cambridge University Press.

Sears, D. O. (1983). The person-positivity bias. *Journal of Personality and Social Psychology, 44,* 233–250.

Sears, D. O. (1986). College sophomores in the laboratory: Influences of a narrow data base on social psychology's view of human nature. *Journal of Personality and Social Psychology, 51,* 515–530.

Sears, D. O. (1988). Symbolic racism. In P. Katz & D. Taylor (Eds.), *Towards the elimination of racism: Profiles in controversy* (pp. 53–84). New York: Plenum.

Sears, D. O., Peplau, L. A., & Taylor, S. E. (1991). *Social psychology* (7th ed.). Englewood Cliffs, NJ: Prentice Hall.

Sedikides, C. (1993). Assessment, enhancement, and verification determinants of the self-evaluation process. *Journal of Personality and Social Psychology, 65,* 317–338.

Sedikides, C. (1995). Central and peripheral self-conceptions are differentially affected by mood: Tests of the differential sensitivity hypothesis. *Journal of Personality and Social Psychology, 69,* 759–777.

Sedikides, C., & Anderson, C. A. (1994). Casual perceptions of inter-trait relations: The glue that holds person types together. *Personality and Social Psychology Bulletin, 20,* 294–302.

Sedikides, C., & Brewer, M. B. (Eds.) (2001). *Individual self, relational self, and collective self.* Philadelphia, PA: Psychology Press.

Sedikides, C., & Gregg, A. P. (2007). Portraits of the self. In M. A. Hogg & J. Cooper (Eds.), *The SAGE handbook of social psychology: Concise student edition* (pp. 93-122). London: SAGE.

Sedikides, C., & Ostrom, T. M. (1988). Are person categories used when organizing information about unfamiliar sets of persons? *Social Cognition, 6,* 252–267.

Sedikides, C., & Strube, M. J. (1997). Self-evaluation: To thine own self be good, to thine own self be sure, to thine own self be true, and to thine own self be better. In M. P. Zanna (Ed.), *Advances in experimental social psychology* (Vol. 29, pp. 209–296). New York: Academic Press.

Seeley, E., Gardner, W., Pennington, G., & Gabriel, S. (2003). Circle of friends or members of a group? Sex differences in relational and collective attachment to groups. *Group Processes and Intergroup Relations, 6,* 251–263.

Segall, M. H. (1965). Anthropology and psychology. In O. Klineberg & R. Christie (Eds.), *Perspectives in social psychology* (pp. 53–74). New York: Holt, Rinehart & Winston.

Seligman, M. E. P., Abramson, L. Y., Semmel, A., & Von Baeyer, C. (1979). Depressive attributional style. *Journal of Abnormal Psychology, 88,* 242–247.

Semin, G. R. (1980). A gloss on attribution theory. *British Journal of Social Psychology, 19,* 291–300.

Semin, G. (2007). Grounding communication: Synchrony. In A. W. Kruglanski & E. T. Higgins (Eds.), *Social psychology: Handbook of basic principles* (2nd ed., pp. 630-649). New York: Guilford Press.

Semin, G. R., & Fiedler, K. (1991). The linguistic category model, its bases, applications and range. *European Review of Social Psychology, 2,* 1–30.

Semmler, T., & Brewer, N. (2002). Effects of mood and emotion on juror processing and judgments. *Behavioral Sciences and the Law, 20,* 423–436.

Senchak, M., & Leonard, K. E. (1993). The role of spouses' depression and anger in the attribution–marital satisfaction relation. *Cognitive Therapy and Research, 17,* 397–409.

Seto, M. C., Maric, A., & Barbaree, H. E. (2001). The role of pornography in the etiology of sexual aggression. *Aggression and Violent Behaviour, 6,* 35–53.

Shackelford, T. K. (2001). Cohabitation, marriage, and murder: Woman-killing by male romantic partners. *Aggressive Behavior, 274,* 284–291.

Shaffer, D. R., Rogel, M., & Hendrick, C. (1975). Intervention in the library: The effect of increased responsibility on bystanders' willingness to prevent a theft. *Journal of Applied Psychology, 5,* 303–319.

Shah, J., Higgins, E. T., & Friedman, R. S. (1998). Performance incentives and means: How regulatory focus influences goal attainment. *Journal of Personality and Social Psychology, 74,* 285–293.

Shamir, B., House, R., & Arthur, M. (1993). The motivational effects of charismatic leadership: A self-concept based theory. *Organization Science, 4,* 1–17.

Shamir, B., Pillai, R., Bligh, M. C., & Uhl-Bien, M. (Eds.). (2006). *Follower - centered perspectives on leadership: A tribute to the memory of James R. Meindl* . Greenwich, CT: Information Age Publishing.

Shapiro, P. N., & Penrod, S. (1986). Meta-analysis of facial identification studies. *Psychological Bulletin, 100,* 139–156.

Sharma, N. (1981). Some aspect of attitude and behaviour of mothers. *Indian Psychological Review, 20,* 35–42.

Sharpe, D., Adair, J. G., & Roese, N. J. (1992). Twenty years of deception research: A decline in subjects' trust? *Personality and Social Psychology Bulletin, 18,* 585–590.

Shartle, C. L. (1951). Studies in naval leadership. In H. Guetzkow (Ed.), *Groups, leadership, and men* (pp. 119–133). Pittsburgh, PA: Carnegie Press.

Shaver, P. R., & Mikulincer, M. (2007). Attachment theory and research: Core concepts, basic principles, conceptual bridges. In A. W. Kruglanski & E. T. Higgins (Eds.), *Social psychology: Handbook of basic principles* (2nd ed., pp. 650–677). New York: Guilford Press.

Shaver, P. R., Morgan, H. J., & Wu, S. (1996). Is love a 'basic' emotion? *Personal Relationships, 3,* 81–96.

Shaw, L. L., Batson, C. D., & Todd, R. M. (1994). Empathy avoidance: Forestalling feeling for another in order to escape the motivational consequences. *Journal of Personality and Social Psychology, 67,* 879–887.

Shaw, M. E. (1964). Communication networks. In L. Berkowitz (Ed.), *Advances in experimental social psychology* (Vol. 1, pp. 111–147). New York: Academic Press.

Shaw, M. E. (1976). *Group dynamics* (2nd ed.). New York: McGraw-Hill.

Shaw, M. E., Rothschild, G., & Strickland, J. (1957). Decision process in communication networks. *Journal of Abnormal and Social Psychology, 54,* 323–330.

Sheehan, P. W. (1983). Age trends and the correlates of children's television viewing. *Australian Journal of Psychology, 35,* 417–431.

Sheeran, P. (2002). Intention-behavior relations: A conceptual and empirical review. *European Review of Social Psychology, 12,* 1-36.

Sheeran, P., & Taylor, S. (1999). Predicting intentions to use condoms: A meta-analysis and comparison of the theories of reasoned action and planned behavior. *Journal of Applied Social Psychology, 29,* 1624–1675.

Sheeran, P., Trafimow, D., Finlay, K., & Norman, P. (2002). Evidence that the type of person affects the strength of the perceived behavioural control–intention relationship. *British Journal of Social Psychology, 41,* 253–270.

Sheppard, J. A. (1993). Productivity loss in performance groups: A motivational analysis. *Psychological Bulletin, 113,* 67–81.

Sherif, M. (1935). A study of some social factors in perception. *Archives of Psychology, 27,* 1–60.

Sherif, M. (1936). *The psychology of social norms.* New York: Harper.

Sherif, M. (Ed.) (1962). *Intergroup relations and leadership: Approaches and research in industrial, ethnic, cultural and political areas.* New York: Wiley.

Sherif, M. (1966). *In common predicament: Social psychology of intergroup conflict and cooperation.* Boston, MA: Houghton Mifflin.

Sherif, M., & Sherif, C. W. (1953). *Groups in harmony and tension: An integration of studies in intergroup relations.* New York: Harper & Row.

Sherif, M., & Sherif, C. W. (1964). *Reference groups.* New York: Harper & Row.

Sherif, M., & Sherif, C. W. (1967). Attitude as an individual's own categories: The social judgement–involvement approach to attitude and attitude change. In C. W. Sherif & M. Sherif (Eds.), *Attitude, ego-involvement, and change* (pp. 105–39). New York: Wiley.

Sherif, M., Harvey, O. J., White, B. J., Hood, W., & Sherif, C. (1961). *Intergroup conflict and cooperation: The robbers' cave experiment.* Norman, OK: University of Oklahoma Institute of Intergroup Relations.

Sherman, D. K., & Cohen, G. L. (2006). The psychology of self-defense: Self-affirmation theory. In M. P. Zanna (Ed.), *Advances in experimental social psychology* (Vol. 38, pp. 183–242). San Diego, CA: Academic Press.

Sherman, D. K., Hogg, M. A., & Maitner, A. T. (2009). Perceived polarization: Reconciling ingroup and intergroup perceptions under uncertainty. *Group Processes and Intergroup Relations, 12,* 95-109.

Sherman, S. J., Presson, C. C., & Chassin, L. (1984). Mechanisms underlying the false consensus effect: The special role of threats to the self. *Personality and Social Psychology Bulletin, 10,* 127–138.

Shibutani, T. (1966). *Improvised news: A sociological study of rumor.* Indianapolis, IN: Bobbs-Merrill.

Shore, T. H. (1992). Subtle gender bias in the assessment of managerial potential. *Sex Roles, 27,* 499–515.

Shotland, R. L., & Heinold, W. D. (1985). Bystander response to arterial bleeding: Helping skills, the decision-making process, and differentiating the helping response. *Journal of Personality and Social Psychology, 49,* 347–356.

Shotland, R. L., & Huston, T. L. (1979). Emergencies: What are they and do they influence bystanders to intervene? *Journal of Personality and Social Psychology, 37,* 1822–1834.

Shotter, J. (1984). *Social accountability and selfhood.* Oxford, UK: Blackwell.

Showers, C. (1992). Compartmentalization of positive and negative self-knowledge: Keeping bad apples out of the bunch. *Journal of Personality and Social Psychology, 62,* 1036–1049.

Showers, C., & Cantor, N. (1985). Social cognition: A look at motivated strategies. *Annual Review of Psychology, 36,* 275–305.

Shrauger, J. S., & Schoeneman, T. J. (1979). Symbolic interactionist view of self-concept: Through the looking glass darkly. *Psychological Bulletin, 86,* 549–573.

Shure, G. H., Meeker, R., & Hansford, E. A. (1965). The effectiveness of pacifist strategies in bargaining games. *Journal of Conflict Resolution, 9*, 106–117.

Shweder, R. A., & Bourne, E. J. (1982). Does the concept of the person vary cross-culturally? In A. J. Marsella & G. M. White (Eds.), *Cultural conceptions of mental health and therapy* (pp. 97–137). Dordrecht: Reidel.

Sidanius, J., Levin, S., Federico, C. M., & Pratto, F. (2001). Legitimizing ideologies: The social dominance approach. In J. T. Jost & B. Major (Eds.), *The psychology of legitimacy: Emerging perspectives on ideology, justice, and intergroup relations* (pp. 307–331). New York: Cambridge University Press.

Sidanius, J., & Pratto, F. (1999). *Social dominance: An intergroup theory of social hierarchy and oppression.* New York: Cambridge University Press.

Siegel, A. E., & Siegel, S. (1957). Reference groups, membership groups, and attitude change. *Journal of Abnormal and Social Psychology, 55*, 360–364.

Siegman, A. W., & Reynolds, M. A. (1983). Self-monitoring and speech in feigned and unfeigned lying. *Journal of Personality and Social Psychology, 45*, 1325–1333.

Sigall, H., & Ostrove, N. (1975). Beautiful but dangerous: Effects of offender attractiveness and the nature of the crime on juristic judgment. *Journal of Personality and Social Psychology, 31*, 410–414.

Sillars, A. L. (1981). Attributions and interpersonal conflict resolution. In J. H. Harvey, W. J. Ickes & R. F. Kidd (Eds.), *New directions in attribution research* (Vol. 3, pp. 281–305). Hillsdale, NJ: Erlbaum.

Simard, L., Taylor, D. M., & Giles, H. (1976). Attribution processes and interpersonal accommodation in a bilingual setting. *Language and Speech, 19*, 374–387.

Simmonds, D. B. (1985). The nature of the organizational grapevine. *Supervisory Management*, 39–42.

Simner, M. (1971). Newborn's response to the cry of another infant. *Developmental Psychology, 5*, 136–150.

Simon, B. (2003). *Identity in modern society: A social psychological perspective.* Oxford, UK: Blackwell.

Simon, B., & Brown, R. J. (1987). Perceived intragroup homogeneity in minority–majority contexts. *Journal of Personality and Social Psychology, 53*, 703–711.

Simonton, D. K. (1980). Land battles, generals and armies: Individual and situational determinants of victory and casualties. *Journal of Personality and Social Psychology, 38*, 110–119.

Simonton, D. K. (2003). Qualitative and quantitative analyses of historical data. *Annual Review of Psychology, 54*, 617–640.

Simpson, B., & Willer, R. 2008. Altruism and indirect reciprocity: The interaction of person and situation in prosocial behavior. *Social Psychology Quarterly, 71*, 37-52.

Simpson, J. A. (1987). The dissolution of romantic relationships: Factors involved in relationship stability and emotional distress. *Journal of personality and social psychology, 53*, 683–692.

Simpson, J. A., & Kenrick, D. (1997). *Evolutionary social psychology.* Mahwah, NJ: Erlbaum.

Simpson, J. A., Campbell, B., & Berscheid, E. (1986). The association between romantic love and marriage: Kephart (1967) twice revisited. *Personality and Social Psychology Bulletin, 12*, 363–372.

Sindic, D., & Reicher, S. D. (2008). The instrumental use of group prototypicality judgments. *Journal of Experimental Social Psychology, 44*, 1425–1435.

Singer, J., Brush, C., & Lublin, S. (1965). Some aspects of deindividuation: Identification and conformity. *Journal of Experimental Social Psychology, 1*, 356–378.

Singh, R., & Ho, S. Y. (2000). Attitudes and attraction: A new test of the attraction, repulsion and similarity–dissimilarity asymmetry hypotheses. *British Journal of Social Psychology, 39*, 197–211.

Singh, R., Bohra, K. A., & Dalal, A. K. (1979). Favourableness of leadership situations studies with information integration theory. *European Journal of Social Psychology, 9*, 253–264.

Sinha, D. (1997). Indigenising psychology. In J. W. Berry, Y. Poortinga & J. Pandey (Eds.), *Handbook of cross-cultural psychology.* Vol. 1: *Theory and method* (2nd ed., pp. 129–169). Boston. MA: Allyn & Bacon.

Sistrunk, F., & McDavid, J. W. (1971). Sex variable in conforming behavior. *Journal of Personality and Social Psychology, 17*, 200–207.

Skevington, S. (1981). Intergroup relations and nursing. *European Journal of Social Psychology, 11*, 43–59.

Skinner, B. F. (1963). Operant behavior. *American Psychologist, 18*, 503–515.

Skowronski, J. J., & Carlston, D. E. (1989). Negativity and extremity biases in impression formation: A review of explanations. *Psychological Bulletin, 105*, 131–142.

Slater, A., Von der Schulenburg, C., Brown, E., Badenoch, M., Butterworth, G., Parsons, S., & Samuels, C. (1998). Newborn infants prefer attractive faces. *Infant Behavior & Development, 21*, 345–354.

Slater, P. E. (1955). Role differentiation in small groups. *American Sociological Review, 20*, 300–310.

Smedley, J. W., & Bayton, J. A. (1978). Evaluative race–class stereotypes by race and perceived class of subjects. *Journal of Personality and Social Psychology, 3*, 530–535.

Smith, B. N., & Stasson, M. F. (2000). A comparison of health behaviour constructs: Social psychological predictors of AIDS-preventive behavioural intentions. *Journal of Applied Social Psychology, 30*, 443–462.

Smith, C. A., & Lazarus, R. S. (1990). Emotion and adaptation. In L. A. Pervin (ed.), *Handbook of personality: Theory and research* (pp. 609–637). New York: Guilford Press.

Smith, C. P. (1983). Ethical issues: Research on deception, informed consent, and debriefing. In L. Wheeler & P. Shaver (Eds.), *Review of personality and social psychology* (Vol. 4, pp. 297–328). Beverly Hills, CA: SAGE.

Smith, E. R., Fazio, R. H., & Cejka, M. A. (1996). Accessible attitudes influence categorization of multiply categorizable objects. *Journal of Personality and Social Psychology, 71*, 888–898.

Smith, E. R., & Zárate, M. A. (1992). Exemplar-based model of social judgment. *Psychological Review, 99*, 3–21.

Smith, M. B., Bruner, J. S., & White, R. W. (1956). *Opinions and personality*. New York: Wiley.

Smith, P. B., & Bond, M. H. (1998). *Social psychology across cultures* (2nd ed.). London: Prentice Hall Europe.

Smith, P. B., Bond, M. H., & Kağitçibaşi, Ç. (2006). *Understanding social psychology across cultures*. London: SAGE.

Smith, P. B., Dugan, S., & Trompenaars, F. (1996). National culture and the values of organisational employees. *Journal of Cross-Cultural Psychology, 27*, 231–264.

Smith, P. B., Misumi, J., Tayeb, M., Peterson, M., & Bond, M. (1989). On the generality of leadership style measures across cultures. *Journal of Occupational Psychology, 62*, 97–109.

Smith, P. M. (1985). *Language, the sexes and society*. Oxford, UK: Blackwell.

Smolicz, J. J. (1983). Modification and maintenance: Language among school children of Italian background in South Australia. *Journal of Multilingual and Multicultural Development, 4*, 313–337.

Sniderman, P. M., Hagen, M. G., Tetlock, P. E., & Brady, H. E. (1986). Reasoning chains: Causal models of policy reasoning in mass publics. *British Journal of Political Science, 16*, 405–430.

Snyder M. (1974). The self-monitoring of expressive behavior. *Journal of Personality and Social Psychology, 30*, 526–537.

Snyder, M. (1979). Self-monitoring processes. In L. Berkowitz (Ed.), *Advances in experimental social psychology* (Vol. 12, pp. 88–131). New York: Academic Press.

Snyder, M. (1981). On the self-perpetuating nature of social stereotypes. In D. L. Hamilton (Ed.), *Cognitive processes in stereotyping and intergroup behavior* (pp. 183–212). Hillsdale, NJ: Erlbaum.

Snyder, M. (1984). When belief creates reality. In L. Berkowitz (Ed.), *Advances in experimental social psychology* (Vol. 18, pp. 248–306). New York: Academic Press.

Snyder, M., & Cantor, N. (1998). Understanding personality and social behavior: A functionalist strategy. In D. T. Gilbert, S. T. Fiske & G. Lindzey (Eds.), *Handbook of social psychology* (4th ed., Vol. 1, pp. 635–679). New York: McGraw-Hill.

Snyder, M., & Gangestad, S. (1982). Choosing social situations: Two investigations of self-monitoring processes. *Journal of Personality and Social Psychology, 43*, 123–135.

Snyder, M., & Miene, P. K. (1994). On the functions of stereotypes and prejudice. In M. P. Zanna & J. M. Olson (Eds.), *The psychology of prejudice: The Ontario symposium* (pp. 33–54). Hillsdale, NJ: Erlbaum.

Snyder, M., & Omoto, A. M. (2007). Social action. In A. W. Kruglanski & E. T. Higgins (Eds.), *Social psychology: Handbook of basic principles* (2nd ed., pp. 940-961). New York: Guilford Press.

Snyder, M. L., Stephan, W. G., & Rosenfield, D. (1978). Attributional egotism. In J. H. Harvey, W. Ickes & R. F. Kidd (Eds.), *New directions in attribution research* (Vol. 2, pp. 91–120). Hillsdale, NJ: Erlbaum.

Solomon, S., Greenberg, J., & Pyszczynski, T. (1991). A terror management theory of social behavior: The psychological functions of self-esteem and cultural worldviews. In M. Zanna (Ed.), *Advances in experimental social psychology* (Vol. 24, pp. 93–159). San Diego, CA: Academic Press.

Solomon, S., Greenberg, J., Pyszczynski, T., & Pryzbylinski, J. (1995). The effects of mortality salience on personally-relevant persuasive appeals. *Social Behavior and Personality, 23*, 177-190.

Sommer, R. (1969). *Personal space: The behavioral basis of design*. Englewood Cliffs, NJ: Prentice Hall.

Sorrentino, R. M., & Field, N. (1986). Emergent leadership over time: The functional value of positive motivation. *Journal of Personality and Social Psychology, 50*, 1091–1099.

Sorrentino, R. M., King, G., & Leo, G. (1980). The influence of the minority on perception: A note on a possible alternative explanation. *Journal of Experimental Social Psychology, 16*, 293–301.

Sorrentino, R. M., & Roney, C. J. R. (1999). *The uncertain mind: Individual differences in facing the unknown*. Philadelphia, PA: Psychology Press.

Spacapan, S., & Oskamp, S. (Eds.) (1992). *Helping and being helped*. Newbury Park, CA: SAGE.

Sparrowe, R. T., & Liden, R. C. (1997). Process and structure in leader–member exchange. *Academy of Management Review, 22*, 522–552.

Spears, R., & Lea, M. (1994). Panacea or panopticon? The hidden power in computer-mediated communication. *Communication Research, 21*, 427–459.

Spence, J. T., Helmreich, R. L., & Stapp, J. (1974). The personal attributes questionnaire: A measure of sex role stereotypes and masculinity–femininity. *JSAS Catalog of Selected Documents in Psychology, 4*, 127.

Spitz, R. A. (1945). Hospitalism: An inquiry into the genesis of psychiatric conditions in early childhood. In A. Freud, H. Hartman & E. Kris (Eds.), *The psychoanalytic study of the child* (Vol. 1, pp. 53–74). New York: International University Press.

Sprecher, S. (1998). Insiders' perspectives on reasons for attraction to a close other. *Social Psychology Quarterly, 61*, 287–300.

Srull, T. K. (1983). Organizational and retrieval processes in person memory: An examination of processing objectives, presentation format, and the possible role of self-generated retrieval cues. *Journal of Personality and Social Psychology, 44*, 1157–1170.

Srull, T. K., & Wyer, R. S., Jr. (1986). The role of chronic and temporary goals in social information processing. In R. M. Sorrentino & E. T. Higgins (Eds.), *Handbook of motivation and cognition: Foundations of social behavior* (pp. 503–549). New York: Guilford Press.

Srull, T. K., & Wyer, R. S. Jr. (1989). Person memory and judgement. *Psychological Review, 96*, 58–83.

Stagner, R., & Congdon, C. S. (1955). Another failure to demonstrate displacement of aggression. *Journal of Abnormal and Social Psychology, 51,* 695–696.

Stang, D. J. (1972). Conformity, ability, and self-esteem. *Representative Research in Social Psychology, 3,* 97–103.

Stang, D. J. (1976). Group size effects on conformity. *Journal of Social Psychology, 98,* 175–181.

Stangor, C. (1988). Stereotype accessibility and information processing. *Personality and Social Psychology Bulletin, 14,* 694–708.

Stangor, C. (Ed.) (2000). *Stereotypes and prejudice: Essential readings.* Philadelphia, PA: Psychology Press.

Stangor, C. (2004). *Social groups in action and interaction.* New York: Psychology Press.

Stasser, G., & Davis, J. H. (1981). Group decision making and social influence: A social interaction sequence model. *Psychological Review, 88,* 523–851.

Stasser, G., & Dietz-Uhler, B. (2001). Collective choice, judgment, and problem solving. In M. A. Hogg & R. S. Tindale (Eds.), *Blackwell handbook of social psychology: Group processes* (pp. 31–55). Oxford, UK: Blackwell.

Stasser, G., Kerr, N. L., & Bray, R. M. (1982). The social psychology of jury deliberations: Structure, process, and product. In N. Kerr & R. Bray (Eds.), *The psychology of the courtroom* (pp. 221–256). New York: Academic Press.

Stasser, G., Kerr, N. L., & Davis, J. H. (1989). Influence processes and consensus models in decision-making groups. In P. B. Paulus (Ed.), *Psychology of group influence* (2nd ed., pp. 279–326). Hillsdale, NJ: Erlbaum.

Staub, E. (1974). Helping a distressed person: Social, personality and stimulus determinants. In L. Berkowitz (Ed.), *Advances in experimental social psychology* (Vol. 7, pp. 294–341). New York: Academic Press.

Staub, E. (1977). *Positive social behavior and morality: I. Social and personal influences.* New York: Academic Press.

Staub, E. (1989). *The roots of evil: The psychological and cultural origins of genocide and other forms of group violence.* New York: Cambridge University Press.

Staub, E. (1996). Cultural–societal roots of violence: The example of genocidal violence and contemporary youth violence in the United States. *American Psychologist, 51,* 117–132.

Staub, E. (2000). Genocide and mass killings: Origins, prevention, healing and reconciliation. *Political Psychology, 21,* 367–382.

Staub, E. (2010). *The panorama of mass violence: Origins, prevention, healing and reconciliation.* New York: Oxford University Press.

Steele, C. M. (1975). Name-calling and compliance. *Journal of Personality and Social Psychology, 31,* 361–369.

Steele, C. M. (1988). The psychology of self-affirmation: Sustaining the integrity of the self. In L. Berkowitz (Ed.), *Advances in experimental social psychology* (Vol. 21, pp. 261–302). New York: Academic Press.

Steele, C. M., & Aronson, J. (1995). Stereotype vulnerability and the intellectual test performance of African-Americans. *Journal of Personality and Social Psychology, 69,* 797–811.

Steele, C. M., Spencer, S. J., & Aronson, J. (2002). Contending with group image: The psychology of stereotype and social identity threat. In M. P. Zanna (Ed.), *Advances in experimental social psychology* (Vol. 34, pp. 379–440). San Diego, CA: Academic Press.

Steele, C. M., Spencer, S. J., & Lynch, M. (1993). Self-image resilience and dissonance: The role of affirmation resources. *Journal of Personality and Social Psychology, 64,* 885–896.

Steinberg, R., & Shapiro, S. (1982). Sex differences in personality traits of female and male master of business administration students. *Journal of Applied Psychology, 67,* 306–310.

Steiner, I. D. (1972). *Group process and productivity.* New York: Academic Press.

Steiner, I. D. (1976). Task-performing groups. In J. W. Thibaut & J. T. Spence (Eds.), *Contemporary topics in social psychology* (pp. 393–422). Morristown, NJ: General Learning Press.

Steir, C. (1978). *Blue jolts: True stories from the cuckoo's nest.* Washington, DC: New Republic Books.

Stephan, W. G. (1977). Cognitive differentiation in intergroup perception. *Sociometry, 40,* 50–58.

Stephan, W. G., & Rosenfield, D. (1978). Effects of desegregation on racial attitudes. *Journal of Personality and Social Psychology, 36,* 795–804.

Stephan, W. G., & Stephan, C. W. (1984). The role of ignorance in intergroup relations. In N. Miller & M. B. Brewer (Eds.), *Groups in contact: The psychology of desegregation* (pp. 229–255). New York: Academic Press.

Stephan, W. G., & Stephan, C. W. (1985). Intergroup anxiety. *Journal of Social Issues, 41,* 157–175.

Stephan, W. G., & Stephan, C. W. (2000). An integrated threat theory of prejudice. In S. Oskamp (Ed.), *Reducing prejudice and discrimination* (pp. 23–46). Mahwah, NJ: Erlbaum.

Stephan, W. G., & Stephan, C. W. (2001). *Improving intergroup relations.* Thousand Oaks, CA: SAGE.

Stephenson, G. M., Abrams, D., Wagner, W., & Wade, G. (1986). Partners in recall: Collaborative order in the recall of a police interrogation. *British Journal of Social Psychology, 25,* 341–343.

Stephenson, G. M., Clark, N. K., & Wade, G. (1986). Meetings make evidence: An experimental study of collaborative and individual recall of a simulated police interrogation. *Journal of Personality and Social Psychology, 50,* 1113–1122.

Sternberg, R. J. (1988). *The triangle of love.* New York: Basic Books.

Stern, P. C., Dietz, T., & Guagnano, G. A. (1995). The new ecological paradigm in social psychological context. *Environment and Behavior, 27,* 723–743.

Stevens, J. R., Cushman, F. A., & Hauser, M. D. (2005). Evolving the psychological mechanisms for cooperation. *Annual Review of Ecology, Evolution and Systematics, 36,* 499–518.

Stewart, J. E. (1980). Defendant's attractiveness as a factor in the outcome of criminal trials: An observational study. *Journal of Applied Social Psychology, 10,* 348–361.

Stiglitz, J. (2002). *Globalization and its discontents*. London: Penguin.

Stith, S. M., & Farley, S. C. (1993). A predictive model of male spousal violence. *Journal of Family Violence, 8*, 183–201.

Stogdill, R. M. (1948). Personal factors associated with leadership: A survey of the literature. *Journal of Psychology, 25*, 35–71.

Stogdill, R. M. (1974). *Handbook of leadership*. New York: Free Press.

Stone, J. (2003). Self-consistency for low self-esteem in dissonance processes: The role of self-standards. *Personality and Social Psychology Bulletin, 29*, 846-858.

Stone, J., & Cooper, J. (2001). A self-standards model of cognitive dissonance. *Journal of Experimental Social Psychology, 37*, 228–243.

Stone, J., Wiegand, A. W., Cooper, J., & Aronson, E. (1997). When exemplification fails: Hypocrisy and the motive for self-integrity. *Journal of Personality and Social Psychology, 72*, 54–65.

Stoner, J. A. F. (1961). *A comparison of individual and group decisions including risk*. Unpublished master's thesis, Massachusetts Institute of Technology, Boston.

Storms, M. D. (1973). Videotape and the attribution process: Reversing actor's and observer's points of view. *Journal of Personality and Social Psychology, 27*, 165–175.

Storms, M. D., & Nisbett, R. E. (1970). Insomnia and the attribution process. *Journal of Personality and Social Psychology, 16*, 319–328.

Stott, C. J., & Adang, O. M. J. (2004). 'Disorderly' conduct: social psychology and the control of football 'hooliganism' at 'Euro2004'. *The Psychologist, 17*, 318–319.

Stott, C. J., Hutchison, P., & Drury, J (2001). 'Hooligans' abroad? Intergroup dynamics, social identity and participation in collective disorder at the 1998 world cup finals. *British Journal of Social Psychology, 40*, 359–384.

Stouffer, S. A., Suchman, E. A., DeVinney, L. C., Star, S. A., & Williams, R. M., Jr (1949). *The American soldier. I: Adjustment during Army life*. Princeton, NJ: Princeton University Press.

Strauman, T. J., Lemieux, A. M., & Coe, C. L. (1993). Self-discrepancy and natural killer cell activity: Immunological consequences of negative self-evaluation. *Journal of Personality and Social Psychology, 64*, 1042–1052.

Straus, M. A., Gelles, R. J., & Steinmetz, S. K. (1980). *Behind closed doors: Violence in the American family*. Garden City, NY: Anchor Books.

Straus, S., & McGrath, J. E. (1994). Does the medium matter? The interaction of task type and technology on group performance and member reactions. *Journal of Applied Psychology, 79*, 87–97.

Straus, M. A. (2001). *Beating the devil out of them: Corporal punishment in American families and its effects on children*. New Brunswick, NJ: Transaction.

Straus, M. A., Sugarman, D. B., & Giles-Sims, J. (1997). Spanking by parents and subsequent antisocial behaviour of children. *Archives of Pediatrics and Adolescent Medicine, 151*, 761–767.

Strickland, L. H., Aboud, F. E., & Gergen, K. J. (Eds.) (1976). *Social psychology in transition*. New York: Plenum.

Strodtbeck, F. L., James, R., & Hawkins, C. (1957). Social status in jury deliberations. *American Sociological Review, 22*, 713–718.

Strodtbeck, F. L., & Lipinski, R. M. (1985). Becoming first among equals: Moral considerations in jury foreman selection. *Journal of Personality and Social Psychology, 49*, 927–936.

Stroebe, W., & Diehl, M. (1994). Why groups are less effective than their members: On productivity losses in idea-generating groups. *European Review of Social Psychology, 5*, 271–303.

Stroebe, W., Diehl, M., & Abakoumkin, G. (1992). The illusion of group effectivity. *Personality and Social Psychology Bulletin, 18*, 643–650.

Stroebe, W., & Frey, B. S. (1982). Self-interest and collective action: The economics and psychology of public goods. *British Journal of Social Psychology, 21*, 121–137.

Stroebe, W., Lenkert, A., & Jonas, K. (1988). Familiarity may breed contempt: The impact of student exchange on national stereotypes and attitudes. In E. W. Stroebe, A. Kruglanski, D. Bar-Tal, & M. Hewstone (Eds.), *The social psychology of intergroup conflict: Theory, research and applications* (pp. 167–187). New York: Springer.

Strube, M. J., & Garcia, J. E. (1981). A meta-analytic investigation of Fiedler's contingency model of leadership effectiveness. *Psychological Bulletin, 90*, 307–321.

Strube, M. J., Turner, C. W., Cerro, D., Stevens, J., & Hinchey, F. (1984). Interpersonal aggression and the type A coronary-prone behavior pattern: A theoretical distinction and practical implications. *Journal of Personality and Social Psychology, 47*, 839–847.

Struch, N., & Schwartz, S. H. (1989). Intergroup aggression: Its predictors and distinctiveness from ingroup bias. *Journal of Personality and Social Psychology, 56*, 364–373.

Stryker, S., & Statham, A. (1986). Symbolic interaction and role theory. In G. Lindzey & E. Aronson (Eds.), *The handbook of social psychology* (3rd ed., Vol. 1, pp. 311–378). New York: Random House.

Stürmer, S., & Simon, B. (2004). Collective action: Towards a dual-pathway model. *European Review of Social Psychology, 15*, 59–99.

Suls, J. M., & Miller, R. L. (Eds.) (1977). *Social comparison processes: Theoretical and empirical perspectives*. Washington, DC: Hemisphere Press.

Suls, J., & Wheeler, L. (Eds.) (2000). *Handbook of social comparison: Theory and research*. New York: Kluwer/Plenum.

Sumner, W. G. (1906). *Folkways*. Boston, MA: Ginn.

Sundberg, N. D. (1977). *Assessment of persons*. Englewood Cliffs, NJ: Prentice Hall.

Surowiecki, J. (2004). *The wisdom of crowds: Why the many are smarter than the few and how collective wisdom shapes business, economies, societies, and nations*. New York: Doubleday.

Swann, W. B. (1984). Quest for accuracy in person perception: A matter of pragmatics. *Psychological Review, 91*, 457–477.

Swann, W. B. (1987). Identity negotiation: Where two roads meet. *Journal of Personality and Social Psychology, 53,* 1038–1051.

Swann, W. B. Jr., & Bosson, J. K. (2010) Self and identity. In S. T. Fiske, D. T. Gilbert, & G. Lindzey (Eds.), *Handbook of social psychology* (5th ed., Vol. 1, pp. 589-628). New York: Wiley.

Swann, W. B., Hixon, J. G., & de la Ronde, C. (1992). Embracing the bitter 'truth': Negative self-concepts and marital commitment. *Psychological Science, 3,* 118–121.

Sweeney, P. D., Anderson, K., & Bailey, S. (1986). Attribution style in depression: A meta-analytic review. *Journal of Personality and Social Psychology, 50,* 974–991.

Swim, J. K. (1994). Perceived versus meta-analytic effect sizes: An assessment of the accuracy of gender stereotypes. *Journal of Personality and Social Psychology, 66,* 21–36.

Swim, J. T., Aikin, K., Hall, W., & Hunter, B. A. (1995). Sexism and racism: Old-fashioned and modern prejudices. *Journal of Personality and Social Psychology, 68,* 199–214.

Swim, J. K., Borgida, E., Maruyama, G., & Myers, D. G. (1989). Joan McKay vs John McKay: Do gender stereotypes bias evaluation? *Psychological Bulletin, 105,* 409–429.

Swim, J. T., & Stangor, C. (1998). *Prejudice from the target's perspective.* Santa Barbara, CA: Academic Press.

Szasz, T. (1970). *The manufacture of madness.* New York: Delta.

Szymanski, K., & Harkins, S. G. (1987). Social loafing and self-evaluation with a social standard. *Journal of Personality and Social Psychology, 53,* 891–897.

Tabachnik, B. G., & Fidell, L. S. (1989). *Using multivariate statistics* (2nd ed.). New York: HarperCollins.

Taft, R. (1973). Migration: Problems of adjustment and assimilation in immigrants. In P. Watson (Ed.), *Psychology and race* (pp. 224–239). Harmondsworth, UK: Penguin.

Tajfel, H. (1957). Value and the perceptual judgement of magnitude. *Psychological Review, 64,* 192–204.

Tajfel, H. (1959). Quantitative judgement in social perception. *British Journal of Psychology, 50,* 16–29.

Tajfel, H. (1969). Social and cultural factors in perception. In G. Lindzey & E. Aronson (Eds.), *Handbook of social psychology* (Vol. 3, pp. 315–394). Reading, MA: Addison-Wesley.

Tajfel, H. (1970). Experiments in intergroup discrimination. *Scientific American, 223,* 96–102.

Tajfel, H. (1972). Experiments in a vacuum. In J. Israel & H. Tajfel (Eds.), *The context of social psychology: A critical assessment.* London: Academic Press.

Tajfel, H. (1974). Social identity and intergroup behaviour. *Social Science Information, 13,* 65–93.

Tajfel, H. (1978). Intergroup behaviour: II. Group perspectives. In H. Tajfel & C. Fraser (Eds.), *Introducing social psychology* (pp. 423–445). Harmondsworth, UK: Penguin.

Tajfel, H. (1981a). Social stereotypes and social groups. In J. C. Turner & H. Giles (Eds.), *Intergroup behaviour* (pp. 144–167). Oxford, UK: Blackwell.

Tajfel, H. (1981b). *Human groups and social categories: Studies in social psychology.* Cambridge, UK: Cambridge University Press.

Tajfel, H. (1982). Social psychology of intergroup relations. *Annual Review of Social Psychology, 33,* 1–39.

Tajfel, H. (Ed.) (1984). *The social dimension: European developments in social psychology.* Cambridge, UK: Cambridge University Press.

Tajfel, H., & Billig, M. (1974). Familiarity and categorization in intergroup behaviour. *Journal of Experimental Social Psychology, 10,* 159–70.

Tajfel, H., Billig, M., Bundy, R. P., & Flament, C. (1971). Social categorization and intergroup behaviour. *European Journal of Social Psychology, 1,* 149–177.

Tajfel, H., & Fraser, C. (Eds.) (1978). *Introducing social psychology.* Harmondsworth, UK: Penguin.

Tajfel, H., & Turner, J. C. (1979). An integrative theory of intergroup conflict. In W. G. Austin & S. Worchel (Eds.), *The social psychology of intergroup relations* (pp. 33–47). Monterey, CA: Brooks/Cole.

Tajfel, H., & Wilkes, A. L. (1963). Classification and quantitative judgement. *British Journal of Psychology, 54,* 101–114.

Tanford, S., & Penrod, S. (1984). Social influence model: A formal integration of research on majority and minority influence processes. *Psychological Bulletin, 95,* 189–225.

Tanter, R. (1966). Dimension of conflict behavior within and between nations, 1958–1960. *Journal of Conflict Resolution, 10,* 41–64.

Tanter, R. (1969). International war and domestic turmoil: Some contemporary evidence. In H. D. Graham & T. R. Gurr (Eds.), *Violence in America* (pp. 550–569). New York: Bantam.

Tarde, G. (1890). *Les lois de l'imitation.* Paris: Libraire Felix Alcan.

Tarde, G. (1898). *Etudes de psychologie sociale.* Paris: V. Giard & E. Briére.

Tarde, G. (1901). *L'opinion et la foule.* Paris: Libraire Felix Alcan.

Taylor, A. J. W. (1987). *Antarctic psychology.* Wellington: Science Information Publishing Centre.

Taylor, D. M., & Brown, R. J. (1979). Towards a more social social psychology. *British Journal of Social and Clinical Psychology, 18,* 173–179.

Taylor, D. M., & Jaggi, V. (1974). Ethnocentrism and causal attribution in a S. Indian context. *Journal of Cross-cultural Psychology, 5,* 162–71.

Taylor, D. M., & McKirnan, D. J. (1984). A five-stage model of intergroup relations. *British Journal of Social Psychology, 23,* 291–300.

Taylor, D. M., Wright, S. C., & Porter, L. E. (1994). Dimensions of perceived discrimination: The personal/group discrimination discrepancy. In M. P. Zanna & J. M. Olson (Eds.), *The psychology of prejudice: The Ontario symposium* (Vol. 7, pp. 233–255). Hillsdale, NJ: Erlbaum.

Taylor, S. E. (1981). The interface of cognitive and social psychology. In J. Harvey (Ed.), *Cognition, social behavior, and the environment* (pp. 189–211). Hillsdale, NJ: Erlbaum.

Taylor, S. E. (1982). Social cognition and health. *Personality and Social Psychology Bulletin, 8,* 549–562.

Taylor, S. E. (1983). Adjustment to threatening events: A theory of cognitive adaptation. *American Psychologist, 38,* 1161–1173.

Taylor, S. E. (1998). The social being in social psychology. In D. T. Gilbert, S. T. Fiske & G. Lindzey (Eds.), *The handbook of social psychology* (4th ed., Vol. 1, pp. 58–95). New York: McGraw-Hill.

Taylor, S. E. (2003). *Health psychology* (5th ed.). Boston, MA: McGraw-Hill

Taylor, S. E., & Brown, J. D. (1988). Illusion and well-being: A social psychological perspective on mental health. *Psychological Bulletin, 103,* 193–210.

Taylor, S. E., & Fiske, S. T. (1975). Point-of-view and perceptions of causality. *Journal of Personality and Social Psychology, 32,* 439–445.

Taylor, S. E., & Fiske, S. T. (1978). Salience, attention, and attribution: Top of the head phenomena. In L. Berkowitz (Ed.), *Advances in experimental social psychology* (Vol. 11, pp. 249–288). New York: Academic Press.

Taylor, S. E., Fiske, S. T., Etcoff, N. L., & Ruderman, A. J. (1978). Categorical and contextual bases of person memory and stereotyping. *Journal of Personality and Social Psychology, 36,* 778–793.

Taylor, S. E., & Koivumaki, J. H. (1976). The perception of self and others: Acquaintanceship, affect, and actor–observer differences. *Journal of Personality and Social Psychology, 33,* 403–408.

Taylor, S. E., Peplau, L. A., & Sears, D. O. (2000). *Social psychology* (10th ed.). Upper Saddle River, NJ: Prentice Hall.

Taylor, S. E., & Thompson, S. C. (1982). Stalking the elusive 'vividness' effect. *Psychological Review, 89,* 155–181.

Taylor, S. P., & Sears, J. D. (1988). The effects of alcohol and persuasive social pressure on human physical aggression. *Aggressive Behavior, 14,* 237–243.

Taynor, J., & Deaux, K. (1973). Equity and perceived sex differences: Role behavior as defined by the task, the mode, and the actor. *Journal of Personality and Social Psychology, 32,* 381–390.

Teger, A. (1970). *Defining the socially responsible response.* Paper presented at the 78th annual meeting of the American Psychological Association.

Teger, A. I., & Pruitt, D. G. (1967). Components of group risk taking. *Journal of Experimental Social Psychology, 3,* 189–205.

Tellis, G. J. (1987). *Advertising exposure, loyalty, and brand purchase: A two-stage model of choice* (Report no. 87–105). Cambridge, MA: Marketing Science Institute.

Tennen, H., & Affleck, G. (1993). The puzzles of self-esteem: A clinical perspective. In R. F. Baumeister (Ed.), *Self-esteem: The puzzle of low self-esteem* (pp. 241–262). New York: Plenum.

Terry, D. J., Carey, C. J., & Callan, V. J. (2001). Employee adjustment to an organizational merger: An intergroup perspective. *Personality and Social Psychology Bulletin, 27,* 267–280.

Terry, D., Gallois, C., & McCamish, M. (1993). The theory of reasoned action and health care behaviour. In D. Terry, C. Gallois & M. McCamish (Eds.), *The theory of reasoned action: Its application to AIDS-preventive behaviour* (pp. 1–27). Oxford, UK: Pergamon Press.

Terry, D. J., & Hogg, M. A. (1996). Group norms and the attitude–behavior relationship: A role for group identification. *Personality and Social Psychology Bulletin, 22,* 776–793.

Terry, D. J., Hogg, M. A., & White, K. M. (1999). The theory of planned behaviour: Self-identity, social identity and group norms. *British Journal of Social Psychology, 38,* 225–244.

Terry, D. J., Hogg, M. A., & White, K. M. (2000). Attitude–behavior relations: Social identity and group membership. In D. J. Terry & M. A. Hogg (Eds.), *Attitudes, behavior, and social context: The role of norms and group membership* (pp. 67–93). Mahwah, NJ: Erlbaum.

Tesser, A. (1988). Toward a self-evaluation maintenance model of social behavior. In L. Berkowitz (Ed.), *Advances in experimental social psychology* (Vol. 21, pp. 181–227). San Diego, CA: Academic Press.

Tesser, A. (2000). On the confluence of self-esteem maintenance mechanisms. *Personality and Social Psychology Review, 4,* 290–299.

Tesser, A., Gatewood, R., & Driver, M. (1968). Some determinants of gratitude. *Journal of Personality and Social Psychology, 9,* 233–236.

Tesser, A., Martin, L., & Mendolia, M. (1995). The impact of thought on attitude extremity and attitude–behavior consistency. In R. E. Petty & J. A. Krosnick (Eds.), *Attitude strength: Antecedents and consequences* (pp. 73–92). Mahwah, NJ: Erlbaum.

Tesser, A., & Schwartz, N. (Eds.) (2001). *Blackwell handbook of social psychology: Intraindividual processes.* Oxford, UK: Blackwell.

Tesser, A., & Shaffer, D. R. (1990). Attitudes and attitude change. *Annual Review of Psychology, 41,* 479–523.

Tetlock, P. E. (1979). Identifying victims of groupthink from public statements of decision makers. *Journal of Personality and Social Psychology, 37,* 1314–1324.

Tetlock, P. E. (1983). Policymakers. Images of international conflict. *Journal of Social Issues, 39,* 67–86.

Tetlock, P. E. (1984). Cognitive style and political belief systems in the British House of Commons. *Journal of Personality and Social Psychology, 46,* 365–375.

Tetlock, P. E. (1988). Monitoring the integrative complexity of American and Soviet policy rhetoric: What can be learned? *Journal of Social Issues, 44,* 101–131.

Tetlock, P. E. (1989). The structural bases of consistency among political attitudes: Effects of political expertise and attitude importance. Structure and function in political belief systems. In A. R. Pratkanis, S. J. Breckler & A. G. Greenwald (Eds.), *Attitude structure and function* (pp. 129–151). Hillsdale, NJ: Erlbaum.

Tetlock, P. E. (2007). Psychology and politics: The challenges of integrating levels of analysis in social science. In A. W. Kruglanski & E. T. Higgins (Eds.), *Social psychology: A handbook of basic principles* (2nd ed., pp. 888-912). New York: Guilford Press.

Tetlock, P. E., & Boettger, R. (1989). Accountability: A social magnifier of the dilution effect. *Journal of Personality and Social Psychology, 57,* 388–398.

Tetlock, P. E., & Kim, J. I. (1987). Accountability and judgment processes in a personality prediction task. *Journal of Personality and Social Psychology, 52*, 700–709.

Tetlock, P. E., & Levi, A. (1982). Attribution bias: On the inconclusiveness of the cognition–motivation debate. *Journal of Experimental Social Psychology, 18*, 68–88.

Tetlock, P. E., & Manstead, A. S. R. (1985). Impression management versus intrapsychic explanations in social psychology: A useful dichotomy? *Psychological Review, 92*, 59–77.

Tetlock, P. E., Peterson, R. S., McGuire, C., Chang, S., & Feld, P. (1992). Assessing political group dynamics: A test of the groupthink model. *Journal of Personality and Social Psychology, 63*, 403–425.

Thakerar, J. N., Giles, H., & Cheshire, J. (1982). Psychological and linguistic parameters of speech accommodation theory. In C. Fraser & K. R. Scherer (Eds.), *Advances in the social psychology of language* (pp. 205–255). Cambridge, UK: Cambridge University Press.

Thatcher, M. (1993). *The Downing Street years.* London: HarperCollins.

Thayer, S. (1986). Touch: The frontier of intimacy. *Journal of Nonverbal Behaviour, 10*, 7-11.s

Thibaut, J. W., & Kelley, H. H. (1959). *The social psychology of groups.* New York: Wiley.

Thomas, W. I., & Znaniecki, F. (1918). *The Polish peasant in Europe and America* (Vol. 1). Boston, MA: Badger.

Thompson, J. B. (1990). *Ideology and modern culture: Critical social theory in the era of mass communication.* Stanford, CA: Stanford University Press.

Thompson, L. L. (2009). *The mind and heart of the negotiator* (4th ed.). Upper Saddle River, NJ: Prentice Hall.

Thompson, L. L., & Loewenstein, J. (2003). Mental models of negotiation: Descriptive, prescriptive, and paradigmatic implications. In M. A. Hogg & J. Cooper (Eds.), *The SAGE handbook of social psychology* (pp. 494–511). London: SAGE.

Thompson, L. L., Medvec, V. H., Seiden, V., & Kopelman, S. (2001). Poker face, smiley face, and rant 'n' rave: Myths and realities about emotion in negotiation. In M. A. Hogg & R. S. Tindale (Eds.), *Blackwell handbook of social psychology: Group processes* (pp. 139–163). Oxford, UK: Blackwell.

Thompson, L. L., & Pozner, J.-E. (2007). Organizational behavior. In A. W. Kruglanski & E. T. Higgins (Eds.), *Social psychology: A handbook of basic principles* (2nd ed., pp. 913-939). New York: Guilford Press.

Thompson, W. C., Fong, G. T., & Rosenhan, D. L. (1981). Inadmissible evidence and juror verdicts. *Journal of Personality and Social Psychology, 40*, 453–463.

Thompson, W. C., & Fuqua, J. (1998). 'The jury will disregard . . .': A brief guide to inadmissible evidence. In J. M. Golding & C. M. MacLeod (Eds.), *Intentional forgetting: Interdisciplinary approaches* (pp. 133–154). Mahwah, NJ: Erlbaum.

Thomson, R. (2006). The effect of topic of discussion on gendered language in computer-mediated communication discussion. *Journal of Language and Social Psychology, 25*, 167–178.

Thomson, R., & Murachver, T. (2001). Predicting gender from electronic discourse. *British Journal of Social Psychology, 40*, 193–208.

Thoreau, H. D. (1854/1997). *Walden.* Oxford, UK: Oxford University Press.

Thorndike, E. L. (1940). *Human nature and the social order.* New York: Macmillan.

Thurstone, L. L. (1928). Attitudes can be measured. *American Journal of Sociology, 33*, 529–554.

Thurstone, L. L. (1931). The measurement of social attitudes. *Journal of Abnormal and Social Psychology, 26*, 249–269.

Thurstone, L. L., & Chave, E. J. (1929). *The measurement of attitude: A psychophysical method and some experiments with a scale for measuring attitude toward the church.* Chicago, ILL: University of Chicago Press.

Tice, D. M. (1992). Self-presentation and self-concept change: The looking-glass self as magnifying glass. *Journal of Personality and Social Psychology, 63*, 435–451.

Tiedens, L. Z., & Fragale, A. R. (2003). Power moves: Complementarity in dominant and submissive nonverbal behavior. *Journal of Personality and Social Psychology, 84*, 558–568.

Tilker, H. (1970). Socially responsible behavior as a function of observer responsibility and victim feedback. *Journal of Personality and Social Psychology, 14*, 95–100.

Tindale, R. S., Davis, J. H., Vollrath, D. A., Nagao, D. H., & Hinsz, V. B. (1990). Asymmetrical social influence in freely interacting groups: A test of three models. *Journal of Personality and Social Psychology, 58*, 438–449.

Tindale, R. S., Kameda, T., & Hinsz, V. B. (2003). Group decision making. In M. A. Hogg & J. Cooper (Eds.), *The SAGE handbook of social psychology* (pp. 381–403). London: SAGE.

Tindale, R. S., Meisenhelder, H. M., Dykema-Engblade, A. A., & Hogg, M. A. (2001). Shared cognition in small groups. In M. A. Hogg & R. S. Tindale (Eds.), *Blackwell handbook of social psychology: Group processes* (pp. 1–30). Oxford, UK: Blackwell.

Tindale, R. S., Nadler, J., Krebel, A., & Davis, J. H. (2001). Procedural mechanisms and jury behavior. In M. A. Hogg & R. S. Tindale (Eds.), *Blackwell handbook of social psychology: Group processes* (pp. 574–602). Oxford, UK: Blackwell.

Titus, H. E., & Hollander, E. P. (1957). The California F-scale in psychological research (1950–1955). *Psychological Bulletin, 54*, 47–74.

Toch, H. (1969). *Violent men.* Chicago: Aldine.

Tolan, P., & Gorman-Smith, D. (2002). What violence prevention research can tell us about developmental psychopathology. *Development and Psychopathology, 14*, 713–729.

Tolan, P., Gorman-Smith, D., & Henry, D. (2006). Family violence. *Annual Review of Psychology, 57*, 557–583.

Tolstoy, L. (1869). *War and peace.* Harmondsworth, UK: Penguin.

Tomada, G., & Schneider, B. H. (1997). Relational aggression, gender, and peer acceptance: Invariance across culture, stability over time, and concordance among informants. *Developmental Psychology, 33,* 601–609.

Tönnies, F. (1955). *Community and association.* London: Routledge & Kegan Paul (originally published in German in 1887).

Tormala, Z. L., & Petty, R. E. (2002). What does not kill me makes me stronger: the effects of resisting persuasion on attitude certainty. *Journal of Personality and Social Psychology, 83,* 1298–1313.

Tormala, Z. L., & Petty, R. E. (2004a). Resistance to persuasion and attitude certainty: The moderating role of elaboration. *Personality and Social Psychology Bulletin, 30,* 1446–1457.

Tormala, Z. L., & Petty, R. E. (2004b). Source credibility and attitude certainty: a metacognitive analysis of resistance to persuasion. *Journal of Consumer Psychology, 14,* 427–442.

Tourangeau, R., Smith, T. W., & Rasinski, K. A. (1997). Motivation to report sensitive behaviours on surveys: Evidence from a bogus pipeline experiment. *Journal of Applied Social Psychology, 27,* 209–222.

Trafimow, D. (2000). Habit as both a direct cause of intention to use a condom and as a moderator of the attitude–intention and the subjective norm–intention relations. *Psychology and Health, 15,* 383–395.

Trager, G. L. (1958). Paralanguage: A first approximation. *Studies in Linguistics, 13,* 1–12.

Triandis, H. C. (1971). *Attitude and attitude change.* New York: Wiley.

Triandis, H. C. (1977). *Interpersonal behavior.* Monterey, CA: Brooks/Cole.

Triandis, H. C. (1980). Values, attitudes and interpersonal behavior. In H. H. Howe & M. M. Page (Eds.), *Nebraska symposium on motivation* (Vol. 27, pp. 195-259). Lincoln, NE: University of Nebraska Press.

Triandis, H. C. (1989). The self and social behavior in differing cultural contexts. *Psychological Review, 96,* 506–520.

Triandis, H. C. (1994a). *Culture and social behavior.* New York: McGraw-Hill.

Triandis, H. C. (1994b). Theoretical and methodological approaches to the study of collectivism and individualism. In U. Kim, H. C. Triandis, C. Kağitçibaşi, S. Choi & G. Yoon (Eds.), *Individualism and collectivism: Theory, methods, and applications* (pp. 41–51). Thousand Oaks, CA: SAGE.

Triandis, H. C., & Davis, E. G. (1965). Race and belief as shared determinants of behavior intentions. *Journal of Personality and Social Psychology, 2,* 715–725.

Triandis, H. C., Lambert, W., Berry, J., Lonner, W., Heron, A., Brislin, R., & Draguns, J. (Eds.) (1980). *Handbook of cross-cultural psychology* (Vol. 1–6). Boston, MA: Allyn & Bacon.

Triandis, H. C., Leung, K., Villareal, M. J., & Clack, F. L. (1985). Allocentric versus idiocentric tendencies: Convergent and discriminant validation. *Journal of Research in Personality, 19,* 395–415.

Triandis, H. C., & Suh, M. H. (2002). Cultural influences on personality. *Annual Review of Psychology, 53,* 133–160.

Tripathi, R. C., & Srivasta, R. (1981). Relative deprivation and intergroup attitudes. *European Journal of Social Psychology, 11,* 313–318.

Triplett, N. (1898). The dynamogenic factors in pacemaking and competition. *American Journal of Psychology, 9,* 507–533.

Trope, Y. (1986). Self-enhancement and self-assessment in achievement behavior. In R. Sorrentino & E. T. Higgins (Eds.), *Handbook of motivation and cognition* (Vol. 2, pp. 350–378). New York: Guilford Press.

Trope, Y., & Gaunt, R. (2007). Attribution and person perception. In M. A. Hogg & J. Cooper (Eds.), *The SAGE handbook of social psychology: Concise student edition* (pp. 176-194). London: SAGE.

Trotter, W. (1919). *Instincts of the herd in peace and war.* London: Oxford University Press.

Tucker, J. S., Friedman, H. S., Schwartz, J. E., Criqui, M. H., Tomlinson-Keasey, C., Wingard, D. L., et al. (1997). Parental divorce: Effects on individual behavior and longevity. *Journal of Personality and Social Psychology, 73,* 381–391.

Tuckman, B. W. (1965). Developmental sequence in small groups. *Psychological Bulletin, 63,* 384–399.

Tuffin, K. (2005). *Understanding critical social psychology.* Thousand Oaks, CA: SAGE.

Turner, D. D. (2005). Altruism – is it still an anomaly? [Review of *Kindness in a cruel world: The evolution of altruism* by N. Barber. Prometheus: Amherst, NY, 2004]. *Trends in Cognitive Sciences, 9,* 317–318.

Turner, J. C. (1975). Social comparison and social identity: Some prospects for intergroup behaviour. *European Journal of Social Psychology, 5,* 5–34.

Turner, J. C. (1978). Social categorization and social discrimination in the minimal group paradigm. In H. Tajfel (Ed.), *Differentiation between social groups* (pp. 101–140). London: Academic Press.

Turner, J. C. (1980). Fairness or discrimination in intergroup behaviour? A reply to Branthwaite, Doyle and Lightbown. *European Journal of Social Psychology, 10,* 131–147.

Turner, J. C. (1981a). Some considerations in generalizing experimental social psychology. In G. M. Stephenson & J. M. Davis (Eds.), *Progress in applied social psychology* (Vol. 1, pp. 3–34). Chichester, UK: Wiley.

Turner, J. C. (1981b). The experimental social psychology of intergroup behaviour. In J. C. Turner & H. Giles (Eds.), *Intergroup behaviour* (pp. 66–101). Oxford, UK: Blackwell.

Turner, J. C. (1982). Towards a cognitive redefinition of the social group. In H. Tajfel (Ed.), *Social identity and intergroup relations* (pp. 15–40). Cambridge, UK: Cambridge University Press.

Turner, J. C. (1983). Some comments on 'the measurement of social orientations in the minimal group paradigm'. *European Journal of Social Psychology, 13,* 351–368.

Turner, J. C. (1984). Social identification and psychological group formation. In H. Tajfel (Ed.), *The social dimension: European developments in social psychology* (Vol. 2, pp. 518–538). Cambridge, UK: Cambridge University Press.

Turner, J. C. (1985). Social categorization and the self-concept: A social cognitive theory of group behavior. In E. J. Lawler (Ed.), *Advances in group processes: Theory and research* (Vol. 22, pp. 77–122). Greenwich, CT: JAI Press.

Turner, J. C. (1991). *Social influence*. Buckingham, UK: Open University Press.

Turner, J. C. (1999). Some current issues in research on social identity and self-categorization theories. In N. Ellemers, R. Spears & B. Doosje (Eds.), *Social identity* (pp. 6–34). Oxford, UK: Blackwell.

Turner, J. C., & Bourhis, R. Y. (1996). Social identity, interdependence and the social group. A reply to Rabbie et al. In W. P. Robinson (Ed.), *Social groups and identities: Developing the legacy of Henri Tajfel* (pp. 25–63). Oxford, UK: Butterworth-Heinemann.

Turner, J. C., Hogg, M. A., Oakes, P. J., Reicher, S. D., & Wetherell, M. S. (1987). *Rediscovering the social group: A self-categorization theory*. Oxford, UK: Blackwell.

Turner, J. C., & Oakes, P. J. (1986). The significance of the social identity concept for social psychology with reference to individualism, interactionism and social influence. *British Journal of Social Psychology, 25*, 237–252.

Turner, J. C., & Oakes, P. J. (1989). Self-categorization and social influence. In P. B. Paulus (Ed.), *The psychology of group influence* (2nd ed., pp. 233–275). Hillsdale, NJ: Erlbaum.

Turner, J. C., Reynolds, K. J., Haslam, S. A., & Veenstra, K. E. (2006). Reconceptualizing personality: Producing individuality by defining the personal self. In T. Postmes & J. Jetten (Eds.), *Individuality and the group: Advances in social identity* (pp. 11–36). London: SAGE.

Turner, J. C., Wetherell, M. S., & Hogg, M. A. (1989). Referent informational influence and group polarization. *British Journal of Social Psychology, 28*, 135–147.

Turner, M. E., Pratkanis, A. R., Probasco, P., & Leve, C. (1992). Threat, cohesion, and group effectiveness: Testing a social identity maintenance perspective on groupthink. *Journal of Personality and Social Psychology, 63*, 781–796.

Turner, R. H. (1974). Collective behavior. In R. E. L. Faris (Ed.), *Handbook of modern sociology* (pp. 382–425). Chicago: Rand McNally.

Turner, R. H., & Killian, L. (1957). *Collective behavior*. Englewood Cliffs, NJ: Prentice Hall.

Turtle, A. M. (1994). Implications for Asian psychology of the adoption of a stance of theoretical indigenisation. In G. Davidson (Ed.), *Applying psychology: Lessons from Asia-Oceania* (pp. 9–13). Melbourne, Australia: Australian Psychological Society.

Tversky, A., & Kahneman, D. (1974). Judgment under uncertainty: Heuristics and biases. *Science, 185*, 1124–1131.

Tyerman, A., & Spencer, C. (1983). A critical test of the Sherifs' robbers' cave experiments: Intergroup competition and cooperation between groups of well acquainted individuals. *Small Group Behavior, 14*, 515–531.

Tyler, T.R., & Sears, D. O. (1977). Coming to like obnoxious people when we have to live with them. *Journal of Personality and Social Psychology, 35*, 200–211.

Tyler, T. R. (1997). The psychology of legitimacy: A relational perspective on voluntary deference to authorities. *Personality and Social Psychology Review, 1*, 323–345.

Tyler, T. R. (2003). Justice, identity, and leadership. In D. van Knippenberg & M. A. Hogg (Eds.) *Leadership and power: Identity processes in groups and organizations* (pp. 94–108). London: SAGE.

Tyler, T. R., & Jost, J. T. (2007). Psychology and the law: reconciling normative and descriptive accounts of social justice and system legitimacy. In A. W. Kruglanski & E. T. Higgins (Eds.), *Social psychology: A handbook of basic principles* (2nd ed., pp. 807–825). New York: Guilford Press.

Tyler, T. R., & Lind, E. A. (1992). A relational model of authority in groups. In M.P. Zanna (Ed.), *Advances in experimental social psychology* (Vol. 25, pp. 115–191). New York: Academic Press.

Tyler, T. R., & Schuller, R. A. (1991). Aging and attitude change. *Journal of Personality and Social Psychology, 61*, 689–697.

Tyler, T. R., & Smith, H. J. (1998). Social justice and social movements. In D. T. Gilbert, S. T. Fiske & G. Lindzey (Eds.), *The handbook of social psychology* (4th ed., Vol. 2, pp. 595–632). New York: McGraw-Hill.

Ulman, R. B., & Abse, D. W. (1983). The group psychology of mass madness: Jonestown. *Political Psychology, 4*, 637–661.

Umadevi, L., Venkataramaiah, P., & Srinivasulu, R. (1992). A comparative study on the concept of marriage by professional and non-professional degree students. *Indian Journal of Behaviour, 16*, 27–37.

Underwood, B., & Moore, B. (1982). Perspective-taking and altruism. *Psychological Bulletin, 91*, 143–173.

US Department of Justice (2001). Bureau of Justice Statistics: *Homicide trends in the United States*. Retrieved 2 January 2002, from http/www.ojp. usdoj.gov/bjs/homicide/homtrnd.htm.

US Department of Justice (2006). Office of juvenile justice and delinquency prevention: *Law enforcement and juvenile crime*. Retrieved 3 April, 2007 from http://ojjdp.ncjrs.org/ojstatbb/crime/JAR_Display.asp?ID=qa05235

Utz, S., & Sassenberg, K. (2002). Distributive justice in common-bond and common-identity groups. *Group Processes and Intergroup Relations, 5*, 151–162.

Valins, S. (1966). Cognitive effects of false heart-rate feedback. *Journal of Personality and Social Psychology, 4*, 400–408.

Valins, S., & Nisbett, R. E. (1972). Attribution processes in the development and treatment of emotional disorders. In E. E. Jones, D. E. Kanouse, H. H. Kelley, R. E. Nisbett, S. Valins & B. Weiner (Eds.), *Attribution: Perceiving the causes of behavior* (pp. 137–150). Morristown, NJ: General Learning Press.

Van den Bos, K. (in press). Making sense of life: The existential self-trying to deal with personal uncertainty. *Psychological Inquiry*.

Van der Pligt, J. (1984). Attributional false consensus, and valence: Two field studies. *Journal of Personality and Social Psychology, 46*, 57–68.

Van der Pligt, J., & De Vries, N. K. (2000). The importance of being selective: Weighing the role of attribute importance in attitudinal judgment. *Advances in Experimental Social Psychology, 32*, 135–191.

Van de Vliert, E., Huang, X., & Levine, R. V. (2004). National wealth and thermal climate as predictors of motives for volunteer work. *Journal of Cross-Cultural Psychology, 35*, 62–73.

Van Dijk, T. A. (1987). *Communicating racism: Ethnic prejudice in thought and talk*. Newbury Park, CA: SAGE.

Van Dijk, T. A. (1993). *Elite discourse and racism*. Newbury Park, CA: SAGE.

Van Dijk, T. A., & Wodak, R. (Eds.) (1988). *Discourse, racism and ideology* (special issues of Text, 8, nos 1 and 2). Amsterdam: Mouton de Gruyter.

Van Goozen, S. H. M., Cohen-Kettenis, P. T., Gooren, L. J. G., Frijda, N. H., & Van der Poll, N. E. (1995). Gender differences in behaviour: Activating effects of cross-sex hormones. *Psychoneuroendocrinology, 20*, 343–363.

Van Gyn, G. H., Wenger, H. A., & Gaul, C. A. (1990). Imagery as a method of enhancing transfer from training to performance. *Journal of Sport and Exercise Psychology, 12*, 366–375.

Van Knippenberg, A., & Van Oers, H. (1984). Social identity and equity concerns in intergroup perceptions. *British Journal of Social Psychology, 23*, 351–361.

Van Knippenberg, D., & Hogg, M. A. (2003). A social identity model of leadership in organizations. In R. M. Kramer & B. M. Staw (Eds.), *Research in organizational behavior* (Vol. 25, pp. 243–295). Greenwich, CT: JAI Press.

Van Knippenberg, D., Van Knippenberg, B., De Cremer, D., & Hogg, M. A. (2004). Leadership, self, and identity: A review and research agenda. *The Leadership Quarterly, 15*, 825–856.

Van Lange, P. A. M., Kruglanski, A. W., & Higgins, E. T. (Eds.) (2010). *Handbook of theories of social psychology*. Thousand Oaks, CA: SAGE.

Van Overwalle, F., & Siebler, F. (2005). A connectionist model of attitude formation and change. *Personality and Social Psychology Review, 9*, 231–274.

van Schie, E. G. M., & Wiegman, O. (1997). Children and videogames: Leisure activities, aggression, social integration, and school performance. *Journal of Applied Social Psychology, 27*, 1175-1194.

Van Vugt, M. (1997). When the privatization of public goods may fail: A social dilemma approach. *Social Psychology Quarterly, 60*, 355–367.

Van Vugt, M., & De Cremer, D. (1999). Leadership in social dilemmas: The effects of group identification on collective actions to provide public goods. *Journal of Personality and Social Psychology, 76*, 587–599.

Van Vugt, M., Hogan, R., & Kaiser, R. (2008). Leadership, followership, and evolution: Some lessons from the past. *American Psychologist, 63*, 182–196.

Van Vugt, M., & Hart, C. M. (2004). Social identity as social glue: The origins of group loyalty. *Journal of Personality and Social Psychology, 86*, 585–598.

Vandello, J. A., & Cohen, D. (2003). Male honor and female fidelity: Implicit cultural scripts that perpetuate domestic violence. *Journal of Personality and Social Psychology, 84*, 997–1010.

Vanneman, R. D., & Pettigrew, T. F. (1972). Race and relative deprivation in the urban United States. *Race, 13*, 461–486.

Vaughan, G. M. (1962). The social distance attitudes of New Zealand students towards Maoris and fifteen other national groups. *Journal of Social Psychology, 57*, 85–92.

Vaughan, G. M. (1964). The trans-situational aspect of conforming behavior. *Journal of Personality, 32*, 335–354.

Vaughan, G. M. (1977). Personality and small group behaviour. In R. B. Cattell & R. M. Dreger (Eds.), *Handbook of modern personality theory* (pp. 511–529). London: Academic Press.

Vaughan, G. M. (1978a). Social change and intergroup preferences in New Zealand. *European Journal of Social Psychology, 8*, 297–314.

Vaughan, G. M. (1978b). Social categorization and intergroup behaviour in children. In H. Tajfel (Ed.), *Differentiation between social groups: Studies in the social psychology of intergroup relations* (pp. 339–60). London: Academic Press.

Vaughan, G. M. (1986). Social change and racial identity: Issues in the use of picture and doll measures. *Australian Journal of Psychology, 38*, 359–370.

Vaughan, G. M. (1988). The psychology of intergroup discrimination. *New Zealand Journal of Psychology, 17*, 1–14.

Vaughan, G. M., & Guerin, B. (1997). A neglected innovator in sports psychology: Norman Triplett and the early history of competitive performance. *International Journal of the History of Sport, 14*, 82–99.

Vaughan, G. M. (2010a). Sherif, Muzafer. In John M. Levine, J. M. & and Hogg, M. A. (Eds.), *Encyclopedia of group processes and intergroup relations* (pp. 753–756). Thousand Oaks, CA: SAGE.

Vaughan, G. M. (2010b). Tajfel, Henri. In John M. Levine, J. M. & and Hogg, M. A. (Eds.), *Encyclopedia of group processes and intergroup relations* (pp. 897–899). Thousand Oaks, CA: SAGE.

Vaughan, G. M. (2010c). Territoriality. In John M. Levine, J. M. & and Hogg, M. A. (Eds.), *Encyclopedia of group processes and intergroup relations* (pp. 913–916). Thousand Oaks, CA: SAGE.

Vaughan, G. M. (2010d). Hate crimes. In John M. Levine, J. M. & and Hogg, M. A. (Eds.), *Encyclopedia of group processes and intergroup relations* (pp. 395–398). Thousand Oaks, CA: SAGE.

Vaughan, G. M., Tajfel, H., Williams, J. (1981). Bias in reward allocation in an intergroup and an interpersonal context. *Social Psychology Quarterly, 44*, 37-42.

Verkuyten, M. (2006). Multiculturalism and social psychology. *European Review of Social Psychology, 17*, 148–184.

Vermunt, R., Van Knippenberg, D., Van Knippenberg, B., & Blaauw, E. (2001). Self-esteem and outcome fairness: Differential importance of procedural and outcome considerations. *Journal of Applied Psychology, 86*, 621–628.

Verplanken, B., & Aarts, H. (1999). Habit, attitude, and planned behaviour: Is habit an empty construct or an interesting case of automaticity? *European Review of Social Psychology, 10*, 101–134.

Verplanken, B., & Holland, R. (2002). Motivated decision-making: Effects of activation and self-centrality of values on choices and behavior. *Journal of Personality and Social Psychology, 82,* 434–447.

Verplanken, B., Aarts, H, Van Knippenberg, A., & Moonen, A. (1998). Habit versus planned behavior: A field experiment. *British Journal of Social Psychology, 37,* 111–128.

Verplanken, B., Hofstee, G., & Janssen, H. J. W. (1998). Accessibility of affective versus cognitive components of attitudes. *European Journal of Social Psychology, 28,* 23–35.

Vescio, T. K., Hewstone, M., Crisp, R. J., & Rubin, J. M. (1999). Perceiving and responding to multiple categorizable individuals: Cognitive processes and affective intergroup bias. In D. Abrams & M. A. Hogg (Eds.) (1999). *Social identity and social cognition* (pp. 111–140). Oxford, UK: Blackwell.

Vescio, T. K., Sechrist, G. B., & Paolucci, M. P. (2003). Perspective taking and prejudice reduction: The mediational role of empathy arousal and situational attributions. *European Journal of Social Psychology, 33,* 455–472.

Vick, S.-J., Waller, B. M., Parr, L. A., Pasqualini, M. C. S., & Bard, K. A. (2007). A cross-species comparison of facial morphology and movement in humans and chimpanzees using the Facial Action Coding System (FACS). *Journal of Nonverbal Behavior, 31,* 1–20.

Vignoles, V. L., Chryssochoou, X., & Breakwell, G. M. (2000). The distinctiveness principle: Identity, meaning, and the bounds of cultural relativity. *Personality and Social Psychology Review, 4,* 337–354.

Vine, I. (1983). Sociobiology and social psychology – rivalry or symbiosis? The explanation of altruism. *British Journal of Social Psychology, 22,* 1–11.

Vinokur, A., & Burnstein, E. (1974). The effects of partially shared persuasive arguments on group-induced shifts: A problem-solving approach. *Journal of Personality and Social Psychology, 29,* 305–315.

Vinokur-Kaplan, D. (1978). To have – or not to have – another child: Family planning attitudes, intentions, and behavior. *Journal of Applied Social Psychology, 8,* 29–46.

Visser, P. S., & Cooper, J. (2003). Attitude change. In M. A. Hogg & J. Cooper (Eds.), *The SAGE handbook of social psychology* (pp. 211–231). London: SAGE.

Visser, P. S., & Cooper, J. (2007). Attitude change. In M. A. Hogg & J. Cooper (Eds.), *The SAGE handbook of social psychology: Concise student edition* (pp. 197-218). London: SAGE.

Visser, P. S., & Krosnick, J. A. (1998). Development of attitude strength over the life cycle: Surge and decline. *Journal of Personality and Social and Psychology, 75,* 1389–1410.

Vittengl, J. R., & Holt, C. S. (2000). Getting acquainted: The relationship of self-disclosure and social attraction to positive affect. *Journal of Social and Personal Relationships, 17,* 53–66.

Von Hippel, W., Sekaquaptewa, D., & Vargas, P. (1995). On the role of encoding processes in stereotype maintenance. *Advances in Experimental Social Psychology, 27,* 177–254.

Von Neumann, J., & Morgenstern, O. (1944). *Theory of games and economic behavior.* Princeton, NJ: Princeton University Press.

Vroom, V. H., & Jago, A. G. (1988). *The new leadership.* Englewood Cliffs, NJ: Prentice Hall.

Vygotsky, L. S. (1962). *Thought and language.* New York: Wiley.

Walker, I., & Mann, L. (1987). Unemployment, relative deprivation, and social protest. *Personality and Social Psychology Bulletin, 13,* 275–283.

Walker, I., & Pettigrew, T. F. (1984). Relative deprivation theory: An overview and conceptual critique. *British Journal of Social Psychology, 23,* 301–310.

Walker, I., & Smith, H. J. (Eds.) (2002). *Relative deprivation: Specification, development, and integration.* Cambridge, UK: Cambridge University Press.

Walker, L. E. (1993). The battered woman syndrome is a psychological consequence of abuse. In R. J. Gelles & D. R. Loseke (Eds.), *Current controversies on family violence* (pp. 133–153). Newbury Park, CA: SAGE.

Wallach, M. A., Kogan, N., & Bem, D. J. (1962). Group influence on individual risk taking. *Journal of Abnormal and Social Psychology, 65,* 75–86.

Walster, E. (1966). Assignment of responsibility for an accident. *Journal of Personality and Social Psychology, 3,* 73–79.

Walster, E., & Festinger, L. (1962). The effectiveness of 'overheard' persuasive communications. *Journal of Abnormal and Social Psychology, 65,* 395–402.

Walster, E., Walster, G. W., & Berscheid, E. (1978). *Equity theory and research.* Boston, MA: Allyn & Bacon.

Walther, E. (2002). Guilty by mere association: Evaluative conditioning and the spreading attitude effect. *Journal of Personality and Social Psychology, 82,* 919–934.

Walther, J. B., & Parks, M. R. (2002). Cues filtered out, cues filtered in: Computer-mediated communication and relationships. In M. L. Knapp & J. A. Daly (Eds.), *Handbook of interpersonal communication* (3rd ed., pp. 529-563). Thousand Oaks, CA: Sage.

Walther, J. B. (1996). Computer-mediated communication: Impersonal, interpersonal, and hyperpersonal interaction. *Communication Research, 23,* 23–43.

Walther, J. B., Loh, T., & Granka, L. (2005). Let me count the ways: The interchange of verbal and nonverbal cues in computer-mediated and face-to-face affinity. *Journal of Language and Social Psychology, 24,* 36–65.

Walton, D., & McKeown, P. C. (1991). Drivers' biased perceptions of speed and safety campaign messages. *Accident Analysis and Prevention, 33,* 629–640.

Walton, G. M., & Cohen, G. L. (2003). Stereotype lift. *Journal of Experimental Social Psychology, 39,* 456–467.

Wann, D. L., Carlson, J. D., Holland, L. C., Jacob, B. E., Owens, D. A., & Wells, D. D. (1999). Beliefs in symbolic catharsis: The importance of involvement with aggressive sports. *Social Behavior and Personality, 27,* 155–164.

Warren, P. E., & Walker, I. (1991). Empathy, effectiveness and donations to charity: Social psychology's contribution. *British Journal of Social Psychology, 30,* 325–337.

Watson, D. (1982). The actor and the observer: How are the perceptions of causality divergent? *Psychological Bulletin, 92,* 682–700.

Watson, J. B. (1913). Psychology as a behaviourist views it. *Psychological Review, 20,* 158–177.

Watson, J. B. (1930). *Behaviorism.* New York: Norton.

Waxman, C. (1977). *The stigma of poverty.* New York: Pergamon Press.

Weatherall, A. (1998). Re-visioning gender and language research. *Women and Language, 21,* 1–9.

Webb, E. J., Campbell, D. T., Schwartz, R. D., & Sechrest, L. (1969). *Unobtrusive measures: Nonreactive research in the social sciences.* Chicago: Rand McNally.

Weber, M. (1930). *The Protestant ethic and the spirit of capitalism.* London: Allen & Unwin.

Weber, R., & Crocker, J. (1983). Cognitive processes in the revision of stereotypic beliefs. *Journal of Personality and Social Psychology, 45,* 961–977.

Wegener, D. T., Petty, R. E., & Smith, S. M. (1995). Positive mood can increase or decrease message scrutiny: The hedonic contingency view of mood and message processing. *Journal of Personality and Social Psychology, 69,* 5–15.

Wegner, D. M. (1987). Transactive memory: A transactive analysis of the group mind. In B. Mullen & G. R. Goethals (Eds.), *Theories of group behavior* (pp. 185–208). New York: Springer.

Wegner, D. M. (1995). A computer network model of human transactive memory. *Social Cognition, 13,* 319–339.

Wegner, D. M., Erber, R., & Raymond, P. (1991). Transactive memory in close relationships. *Journal of Personality and Social Psychology, 61,* 923–929.

Weiner, B. (1979). A theory of motivation for some classroom experiences. *Journal of Educational Psychology, 71,* 3–25.

Weiner, B. (1985). 'Spontaneous' causal thinking. *Psychological Bulletin, 97,* 74–84.

Weiner, B. (1986). *An attributional theory of motivation and emotion.* New York: Springer.

Weiner, B. (1995). *Judgments of responsibility.* New York: Guilford Press.

Weiten, W. (1980). The attraction–leniency effect in jury research: An examination of external validity. *Journal of Applied Social Psychology, 10,* 340–347.

Weldon, E., & Weingart, L. (1993). Group goals and group performance. *British Journal of Social Psychology, 32,* 307–334.

Wells, G. L., & Turtle, J. W. (1988). What is the best way to encode faces? In M. Gruneberg, P. E. Morris & R. N. Sykes (Eds.), *Practical aspects of memory: Current research and issues* (Vol. 1, pp. 163–168). Chichester, UK: Wiley.

Wenzel, M., Mummendey, A., & Waldzus, S. (2007). Superordinate identities and intergroup conflict: The ingroup projection model. *European Review of Social Psychology, 18,* 331–372.

West, C. (1984). *Routine complications.* Bloomington, IN: Indiana University Press.

West, S. G., Whitney, G., & Schnedler, R. (1975). Helping a motorist in distress: The effects of sex, race and neighbourhood. *Journal of Personality and Social Psychology, 31,* 691–698.

Westie, F. R., & DeFleur, M. L. (1959). Automatic responses and their relationship to race attitudes. *Journal of Abnormal and Social Psychology, 58,* 340–347.

Wetherell, M. S. (1986). Linguistic repertoires and literary criticism: New directions for a social psychology of gender. In S. Wilkinson (Ed.), *Feminist social psychology* (pp. 77–95). Milton Keynes, UK: Open University Press.

Wetherell, M. S. (1987). Social identity and group polarization. In J. C. Turner, M. A. Hogg, P. J. Oakes, S. D. Reicher, & M. S. Wetherell, *Rediscovering the social group: A self-categorization theory* (pp. 142–170). Oxford, UK: Blackwell.

Wetherell, M. S., Taylor, S., & Yates, S. J. (2001). *Discourse as data: A guide for analysis.* London: SAGE.

Wetzel, C. G., & Walton, M. D. (1985). Developing biased social judgments: The false consensus effect. *Journal of Personality and Social Psychology, 49,* 1352–1359.

Weyant, J. (1978). The effect of mood states, costs and benefits on helping. *Journal of Personality and Social Psychology, 36,* 1169–1176.

Wheeler, L. (1991). A brief history of social comparison theory. In J. Suls & T. A. Wills (Eds.), *Social comparison: Contemporary theory and research* (pp. 3–21). Hillsdale, NJ: Erlbaum.

Wheeler, L., & Kim, Y. (1997). What is beautiful is culturally good: The physical attractiveness stereotype has different content in collectivist cultures. *Personality and Social Psychology Bulletin, 23,* 795–800.

Whitcher, S. J., & Fisher, J. D. (1979). Multidimensional reaction to therapeutic touch in a hospital setting. *Journal of Personality and Social Psychology, 37,* 87–96.

White, M. (2004). 30 worst atrocities of the 20th century [electronic version], http://users.erols.com/mwhite28/atrox.htm. Retrieved 25 October, 2006.

White, P. A. (1988). Causal processing: Origins and development. *Psychological Bulletin, 104,* 36–52.

White, P. A., & Younger, D. P. (1988). Differences in the ascription of transient internal states to self and other. *Journal of Experimental Social Psychology, 24,* 292–309.

Whittaker, J. O., & Meade, R. D. (1967). Social pressure in the modification and distortion of judgment: A cross-cultural study. *International Journal of Psychology, 2,* 109–113.

Whorf, B. L. (1956). *Language, thought and reality.* Cambridge, MA: MIT Press.

Whyte, W. F. (1943). *Street corner society* (2nd ed.). Chicago: University of Chicago Press.

Wicker, A. W. (1969). Attitudes versus actions: The relationship of verbal and overt behavioral responses to attitude objects. *Journal of Social Issues, 25,* 41–78.

Wicklund, R. A. (1975). Objective self-awareness. In L. Berkowitz (Ed.), *Advances in experimental social psychology* (Vol. 8, pp. 233–275). New York: Academic Press.

Widdicombe, S., & Wooffitt, R. (1990). 'Being' versus 'doing' punk: On achieving authenticity as a member. *Journal of Language and Social Psychology, 4,* 257–277.

Widdicombe, S., & Wooffitt, R. (1994). *The language of youth subcultures.* London: Harvester Wheatsheaf.

Widmeyer, W. N., Brawley, L. R., & Carron, A. V. (1985). *The measurement of cohesion in sports teams: The group environment questionnaire.* London, Ontario: Sports Dynamics.

Wiemann, J. M., & Giles, H. (1988). Interpersonal communications. In M. Hewstone, W. Stroebe, J.-P. Codol & G. M. Stephenson (Eds.), *Introduction to social psychology* (pp. 199–221). Oxford, UK: Blackwell.

Wieselquist, J., Rusbult, C. E., Foster, C. A., & Agnew, C. R. (1999). Commitment, prorelationship behavior, and trust in close relationships. *Journal of Personality and Social Psychology, 77,* 942–966.

Wilder, D. A. (1977). Perceptions of groups, size of opposition and social influence. *Journal of Experimental Social Psychology, 13,* 253–268.

Wilder, D. A. (1984). Predictions of belief homogeneity and similarity following social categorization. *British Journal of Social Psychology, 23,* 323–333.

Wilder, D. A. (1986). Social categorization: Implications for creation and reduction of intergroup bias. In L. Berkowitz (Ed.), *Advances in experimental social psychology* (Vol. 19, pp. 291–355). New York: Academic Press.

Wilder, D.A., & Simon, A. F. (1998). Categorical and dynamic groups: Implications for social perception and intergroup behavior. In C. Sedikides, J. Schopler & C. A. Insko (Eds.), *Intergroup cognition and intergroup behavior* (pp. 27–44). Mahwah, NJ: Erlbaum.

Wilder, D. A., & Shapiro, P. N. (1984). Role of out-group cues in determining social identity. *Journal of Personality and Social Psychology, 47,* 342–348.

Wilder, D. A., & Shapiro, P. N. (1989). Role of competition-induced anxiety in limiting the beneficial impact of positive behavior by an outgroup member. *Journal of Personality and Social Psychology, 56,* 60–69.

Wilkinson, S., & Kitzinger, C. (2006). Surprise as an interactional achievement: Reaction tokens in conversation. *Social Psychology Quarterly, 69,* 150–182.

Williams, A. (1996). Young people's evaluations of intergenerational versus peer under accommodation: Sometimes older is better. *Journal of Language and Social Psychology, 15,* 291–311.

Williams, A. & Nussbaum, J. F. (2001). *Intergenerational communication across the life span.* Mahwah, NJ: Erlbaum.

Williams, J. A. (1984). Gender and intergroup behaviour: Towards an integration. *British Journal of Social Psychology, 23,* 311–316.

Williams, J. E., & Best, D. L. (1982). *Measuring sex stereotypes: A thirty nation study.* Beverly Hills, CA: SAGE.

Williams, K. D. (2002). *Ostracism: The power of silence.* New York: Guilford Press.

Williams, K. D., Cheung, C. K. T., & Choi, W. (2000). Cyberostracism: Effects of being ignored over the internet. *Journal of Personality and Social Psychology, 79,* 748–762.

Williams, K. D., Harkins, S. G., & Karau, S. J. (2003). Social performance. In M. A. Hogg & J. Cooper (Eds.), *The SAGE handbook of social psychology* (pp. 327–346). London: SAGE.

Williams, K. D., Harkins, S. G., & Karau, S. J. (2007). Social performance. In M. A. Hogg & J. Cooper (Eds.), *The SAGE handbook of social psychology: Concise student edition* (pp. 291–311). London: SAGE.

Williams, K. D., Harkins, S. G., & Latané, B. (1981). Identifiability as a deterrent to social loafing: Two cheering experiments. *Journal of Personality and Social Psychology, 40,* 303–311.

Williams, K. D., & Karau, S. J. (1991). Social loafing and social compensation: The effects of expectations of co-worker performance. *Journal of Personality and Social Psychology, 61,* 570–581.

Williams, K. D., Karau, S. J., & Bourgeois, M. (1993). Working on collective tasks: Social loafing and social compensation. In M. A. Hogg & D. Abrams (Eds.), *Group motivation: Social psychological perspectives* (pp. 130–148). London: Harvester Wheatsheaf.

Williams, K. D., Shore, W. J., & Grahe, J. E. (1998). The silent treatment: Perceptions of its behaviors and associated feelings. *Group Processes and Intergroup Relations, 1,* 117–141.

Williams, K. D., & Sommer, K. L. (1997). Social ostracism by coworkers: Does rejection lead to loafing and compensation? *Personality and Social Psychology Bulletin, 23,* 693–706.

Williamson, G. M., & Clark, M. S. (1989). Providing help and relationship type as determinants of changes in moods and self-evaluations. *Journal of Personality and Social Psychology, 56,* 722–734.

Wills, T. A. (1981). Downward comparison principles in social psychology. *Psychological Bulletin, 90,* 245–271.

Wilpert, B. (1995). Organizational behavior. *Annual Review of Psychology, 46,* 59–90.

Wilson, E. O. (1975). *Sociobiology: The new synthesis.* Cambridge, MA: Harvard University Press.

Wilson, E. O. (1978). *On human nature.* Cambridge, MA: Harvard University Press.

Wilson, J. (2000). Volunteering. *Annual Review of Sociology, 26,* 215-240.

Wishner, J. (1960). Reanalysis of 'impressions of personality'. *Psychological Review, 67,* 96–112.

Wispé, L. G. (1972). Positive forms of social behavior: An overview. *Journal of Social Issues, 28,* 1–19.

Witte, K., Berkowitz, J. M., Cameron, K. A., & McKeon, J. K. (1998). Preventing the spread of genital warts: Using fear appeals to promote self-protective behaviours. *Health Education and Behavior, 25,* 571–585.

Wittenbrink, W., Judd, C. M., & Park, B. (1997). Evidence for racial prejudice at the implicit level and its relationship with questionnaire measures. *Journal of Personality and Social Psychology, 72,* 262–274.

Wittgenstein, L. (1953). *Philosophical investigations.* Oxford, UK: Blackwell.

Wood, G. S. (1982). Conspiracy and the paranoid style: Causality and deceit in the eighteenth century. *William and Mary Quarterly, 39,* 401–441.

Wood, J. V. (1989). Theory and research concerning social comparisons of personal attributes. *Psychological Bulletin, 106,* 231–248.

Wood, W. (2000). Attitude change: Persuasion and social influence. *Annual Review of Psychology, 51,* 539–570.

Wood, W., Lundgren, S., Ouellette, J. A., Busceme, S., & Blackstone, T. (1994). Minority influence: A meta-analytic review of social influence processes. *Psychological Bulletin, 115,* 323–345.

Worchel, S. (1979). Cooperation and the reduction of intergroup conflict: Some determining factors. In W. Austin & S. Worchel (Eds.), *The social psychology of intergroup relations* (pp. 262–273). Monterey, CA: Brooks/Cole.

Worchel, S. (1996). Emphasising the social nature of groups in a developmental framework. In J. L. Nye & A. M. Bower (Eds.), *What's social about social cognition: Research on socially shared cognition in small groups* (pp. 261–282). Thousand Oaks, CA: SAGE.

Worchel, S., Andreoli, V. A., & Folger, R. (1977). Intergroup cooperation and intergroup attraction: The effect of previous interaction and outcome of combined effort. *Journal of Experimental Social Psychology, 13,* 131–140.

Worchel, S., Cooper, J., & Goethals, G. R. (1988). *Understanding social psychology* (4th ed.). Chicago: Dorsey Press.

Worchel, S., & Novell, N. (1980). Effect of perceived environmental conditions during cooperation on intergroup attraction. *Journal of Personality and Social Psychology, 38,* 764–772.

Worchel, S., Rothgerber, H., Day, E. A., Hart, D., & Butemeyer, J. (1998). Social identity and individual productivity within groups. *British Journal of Social Psychology, 37,* 389–413.

Word, C., Zanna, M., & Cooper, J. (1974). The nonverbal mediation of self-fulfilling prophecies in interracial interaction. *Journal of Experimental Social Psychology, 10,* 109–120.

Wright, S. C. (2001). Restricted ingroup boundaries: Tokenism, ambiguity, and the tolerance of injustice. In J. T. Jost and B. Major (Eds.), *The psychology of legitimacy: Emerging perspectives on ideology, justice, and intergroup relations* (pp. 223-254). New York: Cambridge University Press.

Wright, S. C., Aron, A., McLaughlin-Volpe, T., & Ropp, S. A. (1997). The extended contact effect: Knowledge of crossgroup friendships and prejudice. *Journal of Personality and Social Psychology, 73,* 73–90.

Wright, S. C., Aron, A., & Tropp, L. R. (2002). Including others (and their groups) in the self: Self-expansion and intergroup relations. In J. P. Forgas & K. Williams (Eds.), *The social self: Cognitive, interpersonal and intergroup perspectives* (pp. 343–363). New York: Psychology Press.

Wright, S. C., & Taylor, D. M. (2003). The social psychology of cultural diversity: Social stereotyping, prejudice, and discrimination. In M. A. Hogg & J. Cooper (Eds.), *The SAGE handbook of social psychology* (pp. 432–457). London: SAGE.

Wrightsman, L. S. (1964). Measurement of philosophies of human nature. *Psychological Reports, 14,* 743–51.

Wundt, W. (1897). *Outlines of psychology.* New York: Stechert.

Wundt, W. (1916). *Elements of folk psychology: Outlines of a psychological history of the development of mankind.* London: Allen & Unwin (German original 1912).

Wyer, R. S., Jr. (1976). An investigation of relations among probability estimates. *Organizational Behavior and Human Performance, 15,* 1–18.

Wyer, R. S., Jr., & Carlston, D. E. (1994). The cognitive representation of persons and events. In R. S. Wyer Jr. & T. K. Srull (Eds.), *Handbook of social cognition* (2nd ed., pp. 41–98). Hillsdale, NJ: Erlbaum.

Wyer, R. S., Jr., & Gordon, S. E. (1982). The recall of information about persons and groups. *Journal of Experimental Social Psychology, 18,* 128–164.

Wyer, R. S., Jr., & Gordon, S. E. (1984). The cognitive representation of social information. In R. S. Wyer Jr. & T. K. Srull (Eds.), *Handbook of social cognition* (Vol. 2, pp. 73–150). Hillsdale, NJ: Erlbaum.

Wyer, R. S., Jr., & Gruenfeld, D. H. (1995). Information processing in social contexts: Implications for social memory and judgement. *Advances in Experimental Social Psychology, 27,* 49–91.

Wyer, R. S., Jr., & Martin, L. L. (1986). Person memory: The role of traits, group stereotypes, and specific behaviours in the cognitive representation of persons. *Journal of Personality and Social Psychology, 50,* 661–675.

Wyer, R. S., Jr., & Srull, T. K. (1981). Category accessibility: Some theoretical and empirical issues concerning the processing of social stimulus information. In E. T. Higgins, C. P. Herman & M. P. Zanna (Eds.), *Social cognition: The Ontario symposium* (Vol. 1, pp. 161–198). Hillsdale, NJ: Erlbaum.

Wyer, R. S., Jr., & Srull, T. K. (1986). Human cognition in its social context. *Psychological Review, 93,* 322–359.

Yamagishi, T., & Kiyonari, T. (2000). The group as the container of generalized reciprocity. *Social Psychology Quarterly, 63,* 116–132.

Yancey, G. (2007). Homogamy over the net: Using internet advertisements to discover who interracially dates. *Journal of Social and Personal Relationships, 24,* 913-930.

Yang, K. S. (2000). Monocultural and cross-cultural indigenous approaches: The royal road to the development of a balanced global psychology. *Asian Journal of Social Psychology, 3,* 241–263.

Yang, K. S., & Bond, M. H. (1990). Exploring implicit personality theories with indigenous or imported constructs: The Chinese case. *Journal of Personality and Social Psychology, 58,* 1087–1095.

Yarmouk, U. (2000). The effect of presentation modality on judgements of honesty and attractiveness. *Social Behavior and Personality, 28,* 269–278.

Yates, B. T., & Mischel, W. (1979). Young children's preferred attentional strategies for delaying gratification. *Journal of Personality and Social Psychology, 37,* 286–300.

Young, J. L., & James, E. H. (2001). Token majority: The work attitudes of male flight attendants. *Sex Roles, 45,* 299–219.

Younger, J. C., Walker, L., & Arrowood, A. J. (1977). Post-decision dissonance at the fair. *Personality and Social Psychology Bulletin, 3,* 247–287.

Yuki, M. (2003). Intergroup comparison versus intragroup relationships: A cross-cultural examination of social identity theory in North American and East Asian cultural contexts. *Social Psychology Quarterly, 66,* 166–183.

Yukl, G. (2010). *Leadership in organizations* (7th ed.). Upper Saddle River, NJ: Pearson Education.

Yzerbyt, V., & Demoulin, S. (2010). Intergroup relations. In S. T. Fiske, D. T. Gilbert, & G. Lindzey (Eds.), *Handbook of social psychology* (5th ed., Vol. 2, pp. 1024-1083). New York: Wiley.

Yzerbyt, V. Y., Leyens, J.-P., & Schadron, G. (1997). Social judgeability and the dilution of stereotypes: The impact of the nature and sequence of information. *Personality and Social Psychology Bulletin, 23,* 1312–1322.

Yzerbyt, V. Y., Schadron, G., Leyens, J.-P., & Rocher, S. (1994). Social judgeability: The impact of meta-informational rules on the use of stereotypes. *Journal of Personality and Social Psychology, 66,* 48–55.

Zaccaro, S. J. (1984). Social loafing: The role of task attractiveness. *Personality and Social Psychology Bulletin, 10,* 99–106.

Zahn-Waxler, C., Radke-Yarrow, M., Wagner, E., & Chapman, M. (1992). Development of concern for others. *Developmental Psychology, 28,* 126–136.

Zajonc, R. B. (1965). Social facilitation. *Science, 149,* 269–274.

Zajonc, R. B. (1968). Attitudinal effects of mere exposure. *Journal of Personality and Social Psychology, 9,* 1–27.

Zajonc, R. B. (1980). Cognition and social cognition: A historical perspective. In L. Festinger (Ed.), *Retrospections on social psychology* (pp. 180–204). New York: Oxford University Press.

Zajonc, R. B. (1989). Styles of explanation in social psychology. *European Journal of Social Psychology, 19,* 345–368.

Zanna, M. P. (1993). Message receptivity: A new look at the old problem of open- versus closed-mindedess. In A. A. Mitchell (Ed.), *Advertising exposure, memory and choice* (pp. 141–62). Hillsdale, NJ: Erlbaum.

Zanna, M. P., & Hamilton, D. L. (1972). Attribute dimensions and patterns of trait inferences. *Psychonomic Science, 27,* 353–4.

Zanna, M. P., Kiesler, C. A., & Pilkonis, D. A. (1970). Positive and negative affect established by classical conditioning. *Journal of Personality and Social Psychology, 14,* 321–328.

Zanna, M. P., & Rempel, J. K. (1988). Attitudes: A new look at an old concept. In D. Bar-Tal & A. W. Kruglanski (Eds.), *The social psychology of knowledge* (pp. 315–334). Cambridge, UK: Cambridge University Press.

Zebrowitz, L. A. (1996). Physical appearance as a basis of stereotyping. In C. N. Macrae, C. Stangor & M. Hewstone (Eds.), *Stereotypes and stereotyping* (pp. 79–120). New York: Guilford Press.

Zebrowitz, L. A., & Collins, M. A. (1997). Accurate social perception at zero acquaintance: The affordances of a Gibsonian approach. *Personality and Social Psychology Review, 1,* 204–223.

Zhang, S., & Hunt, J. S. (2008). The stereotype rebound effect: Universal or culturally bounded process? *Journal of Experimental Social Psychology, 44,* 489-500.

Zillmann, D. (1979). *Hostility and aggression.* Hillsdale, NJ: Erlbaum.

Zillmann, D. (1984). *Connections between sex and aggression.* Hillsdale, NJ: Erlbaum.

Zillmann, D. (1988). Cognition–excitation interdependencies in aggressive behavior. *Aggressive Behavior, 14,* 51–64.

Zillmann, D. (1996). Sequential dependencies in emotional experience and behavior. In R. D. Kavanaugh, B. Zimmerberg & S. Fein (Eds.), *Emotion: Interdisciplinary perspectives* (pp. 243–272). Mahwah, NJ: Erlbaum.

Zillmann, D., & Bryant, J. (1984). Effects of massive exposure to pornography. In N. M. Malamuth & E. Donnerstein (Eds.), *Pornography and sexual aggression* (pp. 115–138). New York: Academic Press.

Zimbardo, P. G. (1970). The human choice: Individuation, reason, and order versus deindividuation, impulse, and chaos. In W. J. Arnold & D. Levine (Eds.), *Nebraska symposium on motivation 1969* (Vol. 17, pp. 237–307). Lincoln, NE: University of Nebraska Press.

Zimbardo, P. G. (1971). *The Stanford prison experiment.* Script of the slide show.

Zimbardo, P. G., Ebbesen, E. E., & Maslach, C. (1977). *Influencing attitudes and changing behavior.* Reading, MA: Addison-Wesley.

Zimbardo, P. G., Haney, C., Banks, W. C., & Jaffe, D. (1982). The psychology of imprisonment. In J. C. Brigham & L. Wrightsman (Eds.), *Contemporary issues in social psychology* (4th ed., pp. 230–235). Monterey, CA: Brooks/Cole.

Zimbardo, P. G., & Leippe, M. R. (1991). *The psychology of attitude change and social influence.* New York: McGraw-Hill.

Zimbardo, P. G., Weisenberg, M., Firestone, I., & Levy, B. (1965). Communication effectiveness in producing public conformity and private attitude change. *Journal of Personality, 33,* 233–256.

Zimmerman, D. H., & West, C. (1975). Sex roles, interruptions, and silences in conversation. In B. Thorne & N. Henley (Eds.), *Language and sex: Differences and dominance* (pp. 105–29). Rowley, MA: Newbury House.

Zuckerman, M. (1979). Attribution of success and failure revisited, or: The motivational bias is alive and well in attribution theory. *Journal of Personality, 47,* 245–287.

Zuckerman, M., DePaulo, B. M., & Rosenthal, R. (1981). Verbal and non-verbal communication of deception. In L. Berkowitz (Ed.), *Advances in experimental social psychology* (Vol. 14, pp. 1–59). New York: Academic Press.

Zuckerman, M., Lazzaro, M. M., & Waldgeir, D. (1979). Undermining effects of the foot-in-the-door technique with extrinsic rewards. *Journal of Applied Social Psychology, 9,* 292–296.

Zuckerman, M., Miserandino, M., & Bernieri, F. (1983). Civil inattention exists – in elevators. *Personality and Social Psychology Bulletin, 9,* 578–586.

Zukier, H. (1986). The paradigmatic and narrative modes in goal-guided inference. In R. M. Sorrentino & E. T. Higgins (Eds.), *Handbook of motivation and cognition: Foundations of social behavior* (pp. 465–502). New York: Guilford Press.

Zuwerink, J. R., & Devine, P. G. (1996). Attitude importance and resistance to persuasion: It's not just the thought that counts. *Journal of Personality and Social Psychology, 70,* 931–944.

# Author index

# Subject index

# Other useful Psychology books from Pearson Education:

ISBN: 978-0-273-71556-6

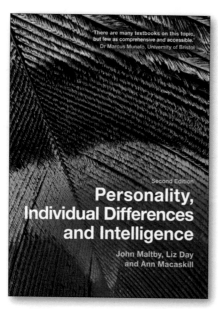

ISBN: 978-0-273-72290-8

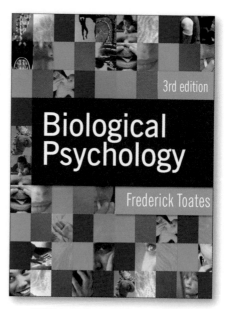

ISBN: 978-0-273-73499-4

Find out more about these great books and more at
## www.pearsoned.co.uk

- bystander effect
- bystander behaviour